6

Blackstone's

Student Police Officer Handbook

Blackstone's

Student Police Officer Handbook

Fourth Edition

Edited by

Dr Robin Bryant
and
Sarah Bryant

Contributors:
Dr Bryn Caless, Kevin Lawton-Barrett, Roy Murphy,
Robert Underwood, and Dr Dominic Wood

OXFORD
UNIVERSITY PRESS

OXFORD
UNIVERSITY PRESS

Great Clarendon Street, Oxford OX2 6DP

Oxford University Press is a department of the University of Oxford.
It furthers the University's objective of excellence in research, scholarship,
and education by publishing worldwide in

Oxford New York

Auckland Cape Town Dar es Salaam Hong Kong Karachi
Kuala Lumpur Madrid Melbourne Mexico City Nairobi
New Delhi Shanghai Taipei Toronto

With offices in

Argentina Austria Brazil Chile Czech Republic France Greece
Guatemala Hungary Italy Japan Poland Portugal Singapore
South Korea Switzerland Thailand Turkey Ukraine Vietnam

Oxford is a registered trade mark of Oxford University Press
in the UK and in certain other countries

Published in the United States
by Oxford University Press Inc., New York

© Oxford University Press 2009

The moral rights of the authors have been asserted
Database right Oxford University Press (maker)

Crown copyright material is reproduced under Class Licence
Number C01P0000148 with the permission of OPSI
and the Queen's Printer for Scotland

First published 2006
Fourth edition published 2009

British Library Cataloguing in Publication Data

Data available

Library of Congress Cataloging-in-Publication Data

Blackstone's student police officer handbook / edited by Robin Bryant and Sarah Bryant: contributors,
Bryn Caless ... [et al.]. --4th ed.
     p. cm.
  Includes bibliographical references and index.
  ISBN 978-0-19-957766-8 (pbk. : alk. paper)
1. Police--Great Britain--Handbooks, manuals, etc. 2. Police training--Great Britain. I. Bryant, Robin,
Dr. II. Bryant, Sarah.
  HV8196.A4B548 2009
  363.20941--dc22

                                                                                          2009039556

Typeset by MPS Limited, A Macmillan Company
Printed in Great Britain
on acid-free paper by
CPI William Clowes, Beccles

ISBN 978-0-19-957766-8

1 3 5 7 9 10 8 6 4 2

Acknowledgements

Robin Bryant

I would like to thank my colleagues Roy Murphy, Martin O'Neill, Leo Raznovich, and Ben Waters for reviewing parts of the Handbook and offering their professional advice; to my wife Sarah Bryant, for her ability to make sense out of convoluted prose and for her major contribution to the writing of this Handbook.

Sarah Bryant

I would like to thank the other contributors (especially Bob Underwood) for their advice, patience, effort, and resilience when explaining the finer points of the law and police procedures to me, and when reviewing the many draft versions of the text.

Bryn Caless

Clare because she lived with it for so long and read so much of it; Madryn for the computer (occasionally); Helen, Sally, and Kit (even if they thought fiction preferable) for their support.

Kevin Lawton-Barrett

My wife, Zoë, and my son, Jackson, deserve thanks for their patience. Nick Jordan for some photographs and all my colleagues at Crime Scene Training from 1990 onwards for the background material and unknowing guidance: all are simply known as 'Reg'. Thanks also to Andrew Turner at LGC Ltd for the images of drugs.

Roy Murphy

To Stephanie, in recognition of the tolerance and patience of a long suffering detective's wife, who was always promised that he would find more time for 'us'—but now finds me locked away, pounding a keyboard, and with my nose in a book.

Robert (Bob) Underwood

I would like to thank my family for their continued support and for remaining so incredibly patient whilst I prepared my contribution to this edition. My sincere gratitude also goes to Sarah Bryant for her meticulous editing of my original material, culminating in work of a much higher quality and a good deal easier to understand.

Dominic Wood

Thanks for the ongoing, patient support from my wife, Tanya.

Contents

Contents

Table of Cases

Tables of Legislation

Tables of Secondary Legislation

Circulars

Introduction

This is the fourth edition of *Blackstone's Student Police Officer Handbook*. All the material contained in the third edition has been reviewed and updated where necessary. New material has also been added, particularly in terms of legislation introduced since the third edition and as a result of recent developments in initial police training. Other changes have also been made after feedback from individual readers and police organizations, both in terms of structure and at the level of content. We are grateful for this feedback, and for the identification of the occasional error.

The authors of the Handbook have taken care to ensure the accuracy of the information contained within. However, neither the authors nor the publisher can accept any responsibility for any actions taken, or not taken, as a consequence of the information it contains.

Reader feedback on the fourth edition is welcome. Please email stupol.editor@OUP.com with your comments or queries.

References throughout the Handbook to IPLDP materials have not been reviewed or endorsed by the IPLDP Central Authority Executive Services.

Introduction to the First Edition

It is now more than 170 years since the formation of the 'new police' in London, arising from Robert Peel's notion of a civilian organization that would uphold the peace and only use coercion as a last resort. By the mid nineteenth century every county and every city and town had acquired a police 'presence' whose organization, approach, and even uniforms we would still easily recognize today as being drawn from the traditions of the British police. The so-called 'Golden Age' of policing (an indeterminate age, somewhere in the 1950s, of apparent public peace and tranquillity and unquestioning respect for the institutions of state) still resonates in the minds of many, if only as a symbolic representation of supposedly better times. Because of this, and because most of us have grown up with the police as a given in our society, there is a tendency to assume that the police are permanent. But they have not 'always been there' and there is no guarantee at all that they will continue to exist, at least as we know them now. There is also no guarantee that the public will continue to maintain its apparently high regard for the police. In a 2002 BBC poll, police officers were only tenth in a list of the most respected professions, behind doctors, nurses, teachers, fire fighters, paramedics, military personnel, scientists, and ambulance personnel (BBC, 2002). It must also be of some concern to the service that public confidence in the ability of the police to do a good job actually diminishes after an individual has been in contact with the police, in contrast to most other public services (Office of Public Services Reform, 2004). We note too, that even the definition of a police officer is losing clarity with the growth of the private security industry, police community support officers (PCSOs), wardens, both rural and parish, and other members of the extended police family. The warrant card may soon be the only meaningful distinction between the police officer and all the other agencies and groups who contribute to policing.

It is against this background of change that you will join the police, not at the outset as a confirmed police constable but as a student police officer. Police training, as with public policing itself, is in a phase of significant flux. Until recently, the initial training of police officers involved a co-operation between the national organization Centrex (previously National Police Training or NPT and now the NPIA) and local police forces. The programmes were often known as 'probationary', 'probationer', or 'foundation training'. This national model of police training typically consisted of an induction course (the responsibility of the local police force), 15 weeks' training at a regional Centrex police training centre alongside students from other police forces, followed by a series of further training courses within a two year probationary period. (The exception was the Metropolitan Police Service that delivered its own training at the Hendon Police College.) All this has now changed. One impetus for change was the HMIC 'Training Matters' thematic inspection report published in 2002. The inspection examined initial police training at both national (Centrex) and local (force) levels and made a total of 59 recommendations one of which was that 'A complete review of probation training is undertaken, as HMIC considers the present arrangements no longer fit for purpose' (HMIC, 2002). The reaction to the screening of *The Secret Policeman* programme on BBC television in October 2003, which uncovered racism at a regional police training centre, added urgency to these calls for change. The programme was followed by the HMIC 'Diversity Matters' report in 2003 and the 2005 Commission for Racial Equality report into the 'Police Service in England and Wales', both critical of the existing arrangements.

Subsequently, the Home Office determined that the responsibility for ensuring the delivery of probationary training should lie with police forces. Forces now have the option of contracting with Centrex (now incorporated within the NPIA), or working in partnership with education and training providers (such as further education colleges or universities), or using their own training facilities, or collaborating with each other, or combinations of these approaches, to deliver their own initial police training. The process of reform of police training is being implemented through the Initial Police Learning and Development Programme (IPLDP) linked in turn to the Wider Police Learning and Development Programme (WPLDP). Now the training of student police officers has become the responsibility of local forces which are delivering a new 'modernized' curriculum based on National Occupational Standards. There is a renewed emphasis on respect for diversity and for students to engage with their local communities, including 'hard to reach' groups. The gates to the 'secret garden' of police training are to be opened, and for the first time student police officers who successfully complete their training will gain a qualification. That, at least, is the vision.

For many police forces, the new era of the IPLDP began in April 2006. At the time of writing, only a small number of student police officers have completed the new form of training. Many aspects of the new approach are untested: the National Occupational Standards, the Student Officer Learning and Assessment Portfolio, and the Police Action Checklist to name a few. This Handbook is a response to these systemic changes to initial police training and to the advent of the IPLDP in particular. The chapters that follow reflect the new IPLDP curriculum. The onset of the IPLDP is one reason, amongst others, that you will not find yourself (unlike generations of 'probationers' before you) staying at a residential training centre separated from the rest of society (in an environment that some critics described as a 'boot camp'). Instead, you are likely to be 'trained in the community' which might even mean that you attend your local college or university alongside other students. Initial police training is at an interesting crossroads in other respects too. In some ways it retains its links with the 'military model' of policing (Bowling and Foster, 2002) in that 'probationers' are expected to know how to address police officers superior in rank (as Sir or Ma'am), wear a uniform, and carry a warrant card almost from the beginning of training (even though they have yet to gain the skills and knowledge to back this up), be subject to Police Regulations that know only the masculine personal pronoun ('he') and, most tellingly of all, soon after joining, be attested and immediately considered as part of the police 'complement', that is a person to be deployed during times of crisis if need dictates. You have joined a police force.

But in many other respects your training will be in keeping with a more liberal model of policing. You will probably be referred to as a 'student police officer' rather than 'probationer' (that is, until you undertake your first Supervised Patrol and encounter more seasoned colleagues), and the support staff you meet will no longer be referred to as 'civilians', and you will be encouraged to reflect on your own values and ideas and be expected to learn from, and to respect, the diverse communities that make up the UK population. You will probably attend college out of uniform. You will learn that reassurance is often as important as law enforcement. You have joined the police service.

No doubt you have already framed a number of questions in your mind, both about the police organization that you are joining, and the whole process of becoming a police officer. Amongst them may be: 'What am I joining? What do I have to do to pass my training? What do I have to know? What will it be like in ten or twenty years' time?'

Our powers of prediction are no more accurate or far-seeing than anyone else's, although we have all been in and around British policing for a long time. Our predictions may very well be wrong, and we have no monopoly on the truth. This Handbook paints a detailed picture of policing in the twenty-first century, and on occasions we discuss what perhaps the police aspire to be, rather than what they actually are. At times, we look ahead to where the police service is going—particularly in 'Developing as a Police Officer' in Chapter 14, and consider larger societal changes, such as the shifting demographics of our UK population. But let us take a moment now, right at the beginning of this Handbook, to talk about what being a police officer may mean to you, and to your family and friends, as you start your training.

At the outset it is obvious that you will not simply be performing one role and one role alone. The police undertake many jobs, and some of them are by no means obvious to the outside observer. However, to start with the obvious, there is the responsibility to tackle crime. However, what is meant by 'tackle' is far from obvious. Do we mean that you are to maintain order, so that crime does not occur, and people can undertake their 'lawful business'? Or do we mean that you are to investigate and detect crime, given that even the most optimistic of us acknowledges that a certain level of crime is inevitable? Or, most likely, do we mean both? If we mean both, which of these is more important: maintaining order or fighting crime?

We would not be the first to ask such questions. One answer was provided in 1829 by Sir Richard Mayne, one of the first two jointly-appointed Commissioners of the Metropolitan Police (Metropolitan Police, 2006):

> The primary object of an efficient police is the prevention of crime: the next that of detection and punishment of offenders if crime is committed. To these ends all the efforts of police must be directed. The protection of life and property, the preservation of public tranquillity, and the absence of crime, will alone prove whether those efforts have been successful and whether the objects for which the police were appointed have been attained.

So important was this definition of the role of the police that it was required reading for all new recruits to the Metropolitan Police Service from 1829 until the mid 1980s.

But the prevention and detection of crime is not all that you will be called on to do. Indeed, you will probably spend most of your time on tasks not related to crime (Waddington, 1999). You are also a key member of the emergency services; you will often be the first person to arrive at the scene of a road traffic collision or a critical incident. Finally, people will often turn to you for help on matters entirely unrelated to crime, because there is simply no one else left to turn to who might listen and do something.

All this means that policing today is probably more complex, and more demanding, than at any time since 1829. For example, there have been over a thousand new criminal offences created since 1997 alone (Miles, 2005), some of which feature in Chapter 9. The Government's Police Reform initiatives have led to a whole series of changes to the organization of policing and the responsibilities of police officers. How should the police respond? (We put aside at this point the debate about whether the police should be more of a 'profession'.) What is clear is that, as a student police officer, you will be required to learn more, to develop your skills more rapidly and in greater depth, and to demonstrate your knowledge and skills more thoroughly than any previous generation of new recruits. The job itself will also sometimes send you on a roller-coaster of emotions, from anger when watching a suspect walk free from the court on a technicality, to exhilaration when a missing child is found safe and well because of your actions. You will be expected keep a lid on your emotions; it is easy to say, 'Don't let your emotions affect the way you work', but it is much, much harder to achieve.

You probably already suspect that there will be more tedium than variety in the job, whatever the fictional portrayal. Policing is not about grumpy loners following hunches in grimy backstreets, nor is it a soap opera about sexual conflict in uniform. There is plenty of painstaking routine in police work of any kind, whether in road traffic policing or in serious crime investigation. The reality of police work is a constant attention to detail, the prosaic need to follow procedure and that, throughout your shift, there is the inescapable requirement to write up your pocket notebook.

You probably have not joined the police to become rich, or because you have a burning need to promote social justice, or because you like wearing uniforms, or because you are manically power-hungry (although all these reasons are possible). You have probably joined the police because you have concerns about society, about the way that people behave towards each other, about the vulnerability of the weak and the disadvantaged, and you want to do something about it. Yes, you could be naïve in your reasons for joining the police, but do not let an accumulated shell of cynicism and disillusionment so burden you that eventually you cannot remember why you are there. Your colleagues will also have doubts about what they are doing, they too will have crises of confidence in the police service, and have moments when they feel utterly defeated. Like you, they will bounce back, try again, wake refreshed, and do whatever it takes to get back to normal duty. Some of your colleagues will be ambitious, some selfish, some lazy; a very small number may be corrupt. But most will put themselves on the line for you, as they expect that you would for them. And if, as cynics will claim, that is not the case at all, how can we explain the fact that all those police officers came in off-duty and on rest days when a probationer police officer was shot dead in January 2006? No one ordered that; it was spontaneous action by people who cared for each other.

As you face the uncertainties of the future, of changes to the organization of policing, single issue politics, ambiguity about the essence of policing itself, evidence of growing violence in society, perhaps even a feeling that you are an anonymous cog in a large and impersonal machine, what can you hold on to? What could sustain you in your role? What could lead you, day after day, to face abuse, being spat on, being sworn at, being vilified, being criticized, and being alternately demonized and lauded in the media and finally being left to face a hard reality on your own?

Perhaps it is the fact that you are there to uphold the law, to support the vulnerable and to protect democratic values for the benefit of us all. Admittedly these commendable ambitions will not be at the forefront of your mind at the start of every late shift. But cumulatively, over the years to come, with occasional highs (and some lows), you will make a difference. All we would ask, as members of the society that has given you powers denied the ordinary citizen, is that you are worthy of our trust.

1 | Reference Material

1.1 Chapter Briefing

This chapter contains reference material likely to be of value to you during your initial training as a student police officer.

It is not necessary to memorize all of the information contained in this chapter—instead view it as a source of reference material that you may wish to return to from time to time during your training. For example, you may encounter more experienced police colleagues using an acronym or a form of jargon that you have not encountered. The glossary in this chapter (see 1.2 below) might well provide an answer.

1.1.1 Aim of the Chapter

The aim of this chapter of the Handbook is to provide you with some important background information as a reference point during your initial training. The chapter includes a glossary of terms used in policing, a brief chronology of police history, a summary of the IPLDP phases and modules, and a list of the National Occupational Standards (NOS) relevant to the student police officer.

This chapter will enable you to:

- refer to a glossary of terms used in policing when needed;
- assimilate some of the key dates and events in history of policing in England and Wales;
- gain an overview of the IPLDP phases and modules;
- refer to a summary of the NOS for initial police training.

1.1.2 National Occupational Standards

This chapter will provide you with the knowledge required to demonstrate aspects of the following NOS elements:

National Occupational Standard Elements

AB1.1   Develop and maintain communication with people
AE1.1   Maintain and develop your own knowledge, skills, and competence

---

You should refer to Chapter 3 for general information and advice concerning the NOS elements.

1.1.3 IPLDP Induction and Law, Policy, and Procedures Modules

This chapter will provide you with resources to support the Induction Module IND 4 to 'Develop effective relationships with colleagues' (and IND 4.1 in particular) and aspects of LPG 1 ('Police communication' in particular).

1.1.4 SOLAP

The contents of this chapter are relevant to the knowledge evidence requirements of CARs AB1 and AE1.

1.2 Glossary of Terms Used in Policing

You will meet many acronyms and forms of jargon during your training as a police officer. The following glossary of terms may assist you in understanding some of the often bewildering words and phrases used within policing. Note also that many police forces also publish their own glossary of terms.

5 × 5 × 5 A 'five by five by five' is an intelligence report. The numbers refer to a scale that is used to attempt to measure the reliability, access, and other factors about the source providing the intelligence.

16+1 Reference to the system used to record self-defined (as distinct from officer-defined) ethnicity: for example A1 is used for Indian. See IC1.

ABC (1) Acceptable Behaviour Contract. (2) Activity-Based Costing, a finance/budgeting methodology that enables costs of an activity to be calculated (as opposed to a value which can only be assessed).

ABE *Achieving Best Evidence*, Guidance on Interviewing Victims and Witnesses, and Using Special Measures.

ABH Assault resulting in actual bodily harm.

ACC Assistant Chief Constable; a command rank (see 6.3 and 6.4 below).

ACPO Association of Chief Police Officers. The term ACPO is also sometimes used as a vernacular proper noun for a chief officer (qv).

Active Defence A proactive approach to defence which involves a rigorous examination of police investigation procedures and the prosecution case; the title of an influential book by Roger Ede and Eric Shepherd.

ad hoc A Latin phrase meaning 'for this special purpose', but has come to mean 'off the cuff' or 'unrehearsed'.

ADVOKATE Mnemonic used in police training to assist the recollection of the so-called 'Turnbull' rules for witness recall where (usually) A is the Amount of time under observation, D is Distance, V is Visibility, O is Obstruction, K is Known, A is Any reason to recall, T is Time that has lapsed, and E is Error.

AFO Authorised Firearms Officer.

Airwave The digital national police radio communication system.

AirwaveSpeak A standardized form of communication when using Airwave (qv) expected to be in place by late 2009.

Alpha/Bravo/etc The phonetic alphabet used in police communication (see 6.5 below).

AMHP Approved mental health professional.

Analyst A professional police staff member whose role (usually) is to analyse and assess crime data and intelligence, and present research findings.

ANPR Automatic Number Plate Recognition system, see 'Nexus'.

APA Association of Police Authorities.

APACS Association of Payments and Clearing Services (the Financial Services' fraud group).

APL Accreditation of Prior Learning.

APEL Accreditation of Prior Experiential Learning.

ARU Armed Response Unit.

ARV Armed Response Vehicle.

ASBO Antisocial Behaviour Order.

ASP An informal term for an extendable metal baton (a reference to the US company Armament Systems and Procedures Inc).

ASU Air Support Unit.

Attestation The formal point at which the powers and responsibilities of the office of constable are assumed, accompanied by the swearing of an oath. The phasing of attestation is currently under discussion.

AVLS Automatic (or Automated) Vehicle Location System.

Awarding Bodies Organizations permitted to issue awards and qualifications such as NVQs (qv).

Baton A side-handled self-protection weapon carried by uniformed police officers.

Baton-round The formal term for a rubber or plastic bullet.

BAWP British Association for Women in Policing.

BCE Bad-character evidence.

BCU Basic Command Unit (Area, Division) or sometimes Borough Command Unit (particularly amongst MPS officers (qv)).

Biometrics The use of unique human physical characteristics (such as the iris of the eye) as identifiers.

Bolt-on ASBO An informal term for an ASBO (qv) ordered after a conviction (it is bolted on), usually by a magistrate.

BPA Black Police Association.

BTP British Transport Police.

Byford Report A review by Sir Lawrence Byford of the police investigation into the 'Yorkshire Ripper' (Peter Sutcliffe) murders between 1975 and 1981; the report was instrumental in the establishment of HOLMES (qv).

CAP Common Approach Path.

CAR Cumulative Assessment Record, used as part of assembling the SOLAP (qv).

Cat A/B/C murders Categories of homicide. 'A' is a serious or series of 'stranger' killing(s), 'B' a serious or cross-force murder where the offender is not known, and 'C' a local or domestic murder, where the offender is usually known.

CBRN Chemical, Biological, Radiological, or Nuclear

CCTV Closed-Circuit Television.

CCU Computer Crime Unit.

CDRP(s) Crime and Disorder Reduction Partnership(s).

Centrex Central Police Training and Development Authority, previously responsible for national police training, now subsumed within NPIA (qv).

CEOP Child Exploitation and Online Protection Centre (an affiliate of SOCA (qv)).

cf Latin for 'compare'.

Chief Officer A police officer with the rank of assistant chief constable and above; command rank.

CHIS Covert Human Intelligence Source (informant).

CI (1) Cognitive Interview. (2) Cell Intervention.

CID Criminal Investigation(s) Department, now replaced in many police forces by Specialist Crime Investigations, SCI, or similar.

CJPOA Criminal Justice and Public Order Act 1994.

CJ(S) A process or unit concerned with Criminal Justice (Systems).

CLDP Core Leadership Development Programme.

CLUE2 A case-tracking data system.

CNC Civil Nuclear Constabulary.

Collar To make an arrest (vernacular).

Compromise When a criminal target (a suspect) detects covert surveillance.

Confirmation The final stage of successful initial training, normally after a period of two years, when a student police officer is confirmed as a police constable.

Continuity Continuity (of evidence): an audited and continuous trail from crime scene or suspect to court, such that evidential items can be accounted for at all times, to prevent interference or contamination.

CPA (1) Crime Pattern Analysis. (2) Child Protection Agency.

CPIA Criminal Procedure and Investigations Act 1996.

CPS Crown Prosecution Service, the governmental body of qualified lawyers who prosecute criminal cases before the courts. CPS agreement to proceed is a mandatory factor in any criminal case. If the CPS believes that a conviction is unlikely, then a public prosecution will not proceed, unless more compelling evidence is discovered. Increasingly, the CPS is helping to determine the focus of police investigations and to decide criminal charges.

CRE Commission for Racial Equality.

CRFP Council for the Registration of Forensic Practitioners.

CRO (1) Criminal Records Office. (2) Criminal (vernacular).

CROPS Covert Rural Observation Posts (or Points).

CSI Crime Scene Investigator.

CSM Crime Scene Manager.

CSO Community Support Officer.

CSP Communications Service Provider.

CTM Contact Trace Material.

Cuff (1) Police vernacular for not doing something which one is supposed to do as a matter of duty or obligation. (2) To handcuff (vernacular).

Custody or custody suite A designated area in a police station (usually where the cells are located), where arrested persons are logged and processed by trained custody staff.

CW Cannabis Warning.

Dabs Colloquial term for fingerprints.

DC Detective Constable.

DCC Deputy Chief Constable.

DCI Detective Chief Inspector.

DCS Detective Chief Superintendent; command rank.

DDA Normally a reference to the Disability Discrimination Act 1995.

de minimis Latin for 'at the least risk', meaning the law is not concerned with trifles.

DI Detective Inspector.

DIC Drunk in charge.

Disclosure A reference to the requirement on the police and the prosecution to provide the defence with certain information and documents which may be pertinent evidence in a criminal case.

DNA Deoxyribonucleic Acid (genetic material used to obtain a 'genetic fingerprint').

Doctrine A body of knowledge and procedure concerned with police practice, notably criminal investigation—for example, as expressed in the MIM (qv) and Volume Crime Investigation Manuals of NCPE (qv).

DPP Director of Public Prosecutions.

DS Detective Sergeant.

DVLA Driver, Vehicle and Licensing Authority.

EAW European Arrest Warrant.

ECHR European Convention on Human Rights.

Element (of a Unit of an NOS) The Units of a NOS (qv) are usually divided into two or more elements which describe more precisely the skill or competence to be attained and measured.

ERO Evidence Review Officer.

ESDA Electrostatic Detection Apparatus.

ETA Estimated time of arrival.

et al Latin for 'and others'.

Europol The European Union Law Enforcement Organisation.

Extended Police Family A reference to the wider group of law enforcement and public order staff, beyond the traditional full-time police—for example, special constables and PCSOs (qv).

FA Forensic Alliance (an independent forensic science laboratory and service).

Family of forces Term once used by the HMIC (qv) to describe those police forces which were considered to be very similar in structure, size, budget, and so on. Now largely replaced by the Home Office's designation of 'Most Similar Forces' (MSF, (qv)).

FAO or FOAS First Attending Officer/First Officer Attending the Scene.

FBO Football Banning Order.

FCA Forensic computer analyst.

FCC Force Communications (or Control) Centre.

FCP Forward Control Point.

'Federation', The See Police Federation of England and Wales.

Fence Person who buys or exchanges stolen goods.

FIO Field Intelligence Officer.

Fishing Police vernacular for any speculative attempt, particularly where the intention is to try to recover evidence of potential value in a criminal case but the grounds for doing so (and the form of evidence to be seized) are uncertain.

FLINTS Forensic Linked Intelligence System; a database and comparative analysis system developed by West Midlands Police.

FLO Family Liaison Officer.

FOI Freedom of Information as in an FOI request.

Foundation degree/FD A qualification at higher education level. There are a number of foundation degrees in Policing, many incorporating the NOS (qv) for initial Policing.

FPN Fixed Penalty Notice.

FSS (1) Forensic Science Service. (2) Forensic Science Society.

FSU (1) Family Support Unit. (2) Firearms Support Unit.

FTS Forensic Telecommunications Services.

GBH Category of assault: Grievous Bodily Harm.

GMP Greater Manchester Police.

GPA Gay Police Association.

H2H House-to-house (as in conducting enquiries).

Handler Vernacular term for police officer responsible for liaising with and tasking a CHIS (qv).

Handling Taking illegal ownership of stolen or otherwise illegally obtained goods.

Hate Crime ACPO (qv) define a hate crime as any hate incident (qv), which constitutes a criminal offence, perceived by the victim, or any other person, as being motivated by prejudice or hate.

Hate Incident ACPO (qv) define a hate incident as any incident, which may or may not constitute a criminal offence, which is perceived by the victim, or any other person, as being motivated by prejudice or hate.

Hoarsay A reference to information which is not given directly (orally) to the court, but is somehow second hand. It is generally not usable in a court as evidence, although there are many notable common law and other exceptions to this general rule.

Hit A DNA sample which can be matched with an identified person (not always criminal).

HMCE Her Majesty's Customs and Excise, now HMRC (qv).

HMIC Her Majesty's Inspectorate of Constabulary (HMIC); an organization responsible for examining and improving the efficiency of the Police Service in England and Wales, now subsumed into the HMJI, an overall 'Justice' Inspectorate. HMIC inspects at BCU (qv) and force levels and also carries out thematic inspections (for example, into police training).

HMIS Her Majesty's Immigration Service, now IND (qv).

HMJI Her Majesty's Justice Inspectorate; see entry for HMIC above.

HMPS Her Majesty's Prison Service.

HMRC Her Majesty's Revenue and Customs (which has replaced 'Customs and Excise').

Home Office A government department responsible for policy relating to policing and crime. The Home Office is responsible for the Government's programme of police reform, including the IPLDP (qv). Home Office responsibilities were reorganized in late 2006; some law and law enforcement aspects were moved to a new Justice Ministry (qv).

HOLMES, HOLMES2 Home Office Large Major Enquiry System; an information system designed to support large-scale police investigations (for example, homicide).

HORTIES Police vernacular reference to driving document production records HO/RT/1 and HO/RT/2.

HOSDB Home Office Scientific Development Branch, now part of NPIA (qv).

Hot spot A geographical location where there is a high incidence (or a perceived high incidence) of current crime and criminality.

HPDS High Potential Development Scheme.

HQ Headquarters.

HRA Human Rights Act 1998.

HSE Health and Safety Executive.

ibid Latin for 'in the same place'.

IC1, IC2 to IC9 A reference to Identity Codes used by police officers to record ethnicity. IC1 is White European.

ICIDP Initial Crime Investigators' Development Programme.

ICF Integrated Competency Framework. This combines descriptions of behavioural requirements with the National Occupational Standards (NOS (qv)) and profiles for a number of policing roles such as patrol constable.

ICV Incident Command Vehicle used in situations where public order might be a problem.

IDENT1 (pronounced 'ident one'). The fingerprint database which replaced NAFIS (qv) in late 2004.

Idents Identifications (vernacular).

IED Improvised Explosive Device (a 'bomb').

ILP/ILPM Intelligence-Led Policing and hence Intelligence-Led Policing Model; sometimes referred to as Intelligence-Based Policing, and also related to Information-Based Policing or Information-Led Policing.

IMSC Initial Management of Serious Crime course.

IND Immigration and Nationality Directorate.

Independent Patrol The ability of a student police officer to conduct police patrol without the constant supervision of a qualified police officer. Usually achieved after successful completion of the PAC (qv).

Informant A person who passes intelligence to a source handler, see CHIS. Often a criminal, an informant is known in criminal argot by a variety of unflattering soubriquets, such as snout, grass, and nark.

Institutional racism A term used in 1999 during the Macpherson Inquiry (qv) which claims that institutions, through their policies and procedures (both written and unwritten) can unintentionally behave in a manner prejudicial to ethnic minorities. The suggestion was that the MPS (qv) was institutionally racist.

Inter-agency A term often employed in policing to describe approaches to crime investigation and reduction that involve partnership with non-police agencies: for example, collaboration with the probation service and social services. See also CDRP (qv).

inter alia Latin for 'among other things'.

Interpol International Criminal Police Organisation.

Intranet Often refers in police circles to a police internal electronic information system, with restricted access rights.

IO Investigating (police) Officer, usually a detective officer (for a crime), but can be a uniformed officer (for example, for traffic collisions).

IP Injured Person or Party (often literally the injured person in a crime involving personal violence).

IPCC Independent Police Complaints Commission; deals with serious complaints against the police and investigates instances where police officers have used firearms.

IPLDP Initial Police Learning and Development Programme; the programme of modernization of initial police training managed by the Home Office (qv). From April 2006 all new student police officers have been expected to undertake 'IPLDP-compliant' programmes of training in order to qualify as police officers.

IPLDP Central Authority Responsible for the implementation and policy direction of IPLDP (qv) and includes representation from the Home Office, Police Federation, Superintendents' Association, and NPIA (qv).

ISO Individual Support Order. An ISO may be imposed upon a young person between the ages of 10 and 17 as a form of positive inducement to stop committing antisocial behaviour.

JBB Joint Branch Board of the Police Federation of England and Wales (qv).

JRFT Job-Related Fitness Test.

Justice Ministry Created in 2007 (from part of the Home Office) and responsible for the courts, prisons, probation, criminal law, and sentencing.

KUSAB Knowledge, Understanding, Skills, Attitudes, and Behaviours as developed in the training of student police officers.

Latent prints Prints (such as fingerprints or even earprints) which are invisible to the naked eye but which can be revealed by dusting or other techniques.

Lawrence, Stephen /the Lawrence Inquiry/the Macpherson Inquiry references to the death of the black teenager Stephen Lawrence in 1993, the subsequent investigation conducted by the MPS (qv), and the reports that followed (for example, as conducted by Lord Macpherson, 1999).

LCN Low Copy Number; a minute DNA trace which can be recovered through advanced scientific processes.

LDR Learning Development Review. These are regular reviews (typically three in the course of training) as part of the IPLDP (qv) approach to monitoring achievement of a student police officer's skills and behaviour.

Learning Diary Under IPLDP (qv) student police officers are expected to keep a learning diary as part of the process of reflective learning. The learning diary may form part of the SOLAP (qv).

Learning Requirement A set of learning requirements that underpin the IPLDP (qv) curriculum designed by Professors John Elliott, Saville Kushner, and others (Elliott et al, 2003).

Level 1 Local crime signifier (used within NIM (qv)). Examples of level 1 crimes or criminals are crimes such as illegal possession of a controlled drug.

Level 2 Cross-BCU or cross-force crime signifier (used within NIM (qv)). Examples of level 2 crimes or criminals are crimes such as dealing in illegal drugs.

Level 3 National or international crime signifier (used within NIM (qv)). Examples of level 3 crimes or criminals are crimes such as organizing the importation or distribution of illegal drugs.

LGC Laboratory of Government Chemists (service provider for scientific analysis).

LIVESCAN Commercial computerized database for taking fingerprints digitally.

LOCARD Forensic database system.

loc cit Latin for 'at the place quoted'.

MAPPA Multi-Agency Public Protection Arrangements (part of the joint agency approach to managing violent and sex offenders).

Match An identified DNA (qv) sample.

MG 3 A form used to report to the CPS for an initial charging decision.

MG 11 Statement form.

MIM Murder Investigation Manual (sometimes called the 'Murder Manual'), distributed by ACPO (qv). The MIM was the first example of a comprehensive doctrine (qv) to assist in the investigation of serious crime. It sets out the various investigative strategies that may be employed (for example, the forensic strategy and the interview strategy). The MIM was written partly as a result of the enquiry into the death of Stephen Lawrence (qv Lawrence).

minutiae Latin for 'of small parts'; the individuality of a fingerprint through examination of its ridge characteristics (up to 150 characteristics in a single fingerprint).

Misper Missing person or missing person forms.

MO *Modus operandi* is Latin for a characteristic way of doing something. Often used to refer to a particular way of committing a crime.

MoDP Ministry of Defence Police.

modus vivendi Latin for 'a practical way to coexist' (between those who differ).

Morris Inquiry Reference to the inquiry conducted by Sir William (Bill) Morris in 2004 into professional standards and employment issues in the MPS (qv).

MOU Memorandum of Understanding.

MPS Metropolitan Police Service; London's police force.

MSF Most Similar Force (for comparison).

NACRO National Association for the Care and Resettlement of Offenders.

NAFIS National Automated Fingerprint Identification System, now replaced by IDENT1 (qv).

National Occupational Standards The National Occupational Standards (NOS) for policing were developed by Skills for Justice (qv). For student police officers there is currently a subset of 22 NOS which are required before confirmation (qv), but this may soon change to 9 or 10 NOS.

NB Latin for 'take especial note of'.

NBPA National Black Police Association.

NCALT National Centre for Applied Learning Technology. NCALT is a password-protected internet-based learning portal for the police service.

NCIS National Criminal Intelligence Service, now subsumed within SOCA (qv).

NCPE National Centre for Policing Excellence, part of the NPIA (qv).

NCS National Crime Squad, now subsumed within SOCA (qv).

NCSP National Community Safety Plan.

NDNAD National DNA (qv) Database.

Nexus A combined computer database system.

NFA (1) No Further (police or CPS) Action. (2) No Fixed Abode.

NFFID National Firearms Forensic Intelligence Database.

NFIB National Fraud Intelligence Bureau, expected to be introduced as a central access point for individuals and organizations who suspect cybercrime.

NFIU National Football Intelligence Unit.

NFLMS National Firearms Licensing Management System, a database containing details of all firearm or shotgun certificate holders (and those in the process of applying for certificates).

NFRC National Fraud Reporting Centre, currently under development, which will be responsible for collating all reports of fraud conducted through cybercrime (as well as 'conventional' fraud).

NHTCU National High Tech Crime Unit (part of SOCA).

Nick Vernacular for: (1) A police station. (2) To arrest a person.

NIE National Investigators' Examination.

NIM National Intelligence Model. All police forces are required to follow the NIM, which is sometimes described as a business model for policing. The focus is largely, but by no means exclusively, on crime and criminality. It describes both strategic approaches (for example, threat assessment) and tactical approaches (for example, the use of informants) to both police and inter-agency (qv) responses to crime and public disorder.

Nominals Vernacular police term for those perceived to be active and often recidivist and high-volume criminals.

Non-Home Office forces Somewhat misleading term that refers to police forces that are not one of the 43 county- or city-based forces. Examples of non-Home Office forces include BTP (qv).

NOS National Occupational Standards (qv).

NPB National Policing Board.

NPFF The National Police Promotion Framework (NPFF), a new system for promotion to Sergeant and Inspector ranks which is expected to replace the current arrangements.

NPIA National Police Improvement Agency, the umbrella term for organizations involved in police training, scientific developments, and other means to improve the professional quality of policing.

NPP National Policing Plan.

NPT Neighbourhood Policing Team.

NSLEC National Specialist Law Enforcement Centre; a consortium of representatives of national policing bodies which seeks excellence in policing, principally in covert operations (a part of NPIA (qv)).

NSY New Scotland Yard.

NTSU National Technical Services Unit.

NVQ National Vocational Qualification. There are NVQs at Levels 3 and 4 in Policing, incorporating the relevant NOS (qv).

OIC Officer in Charge.

OP Observation point for carrying out surveillance.

Op Operation. Usually taken as referring to a targeted police operation against a criminal problem and given names such as 'Op Damocles'. Note that the name of the operation is simply taken from a list and does not reflect the particular circumstances of that operation (indeed, police forces consider it better that the operational name has no connection with the operation it signifies).

op cit Latin for 'see the work cited'.

ORC Operational Response Commander.

OSPRE® Objective Structured Performance-Related Examination, from NPIA. The OSPRE examination process is undertaken by those who wish to become police sergeants or inspectors.

PAC Police Action Checklist. Satisfactory completion is one of the criteria for the right to undertake Independent Patrol (qv).

PACE Police and Criminal Evidence Act 1984.

PAS Police Advisers' (or Advisory) Service.

passim Latin for 'everywhere', but used in the sense of throughout.

PBE Pocket book entry.

PC or Pc Police constable.

PCeU Police Central e-Crime Unit, created in September 2008 and a national resource, though based at the MPS (qv).

PCSO Police Community Support Officer; a member of police staff in a police force whose role is nominally to support operational policing, but who usually patrols a small geographical area and deals with low-level civic nuisance.

PDP The Professional Development Portfolio is a tool to record an individual police officer's professional development. The PDP for student police officers is effectively the Student Officer Learning and Assessment Portfolio (SOLAP (qv)).

PDU A dedicated Professional Development Unit for the development of student police officers, police officers, and other police employees.

PEACE Acronym for an interviewing model, adopted by police forces in the UK. The letters represent the stages of an interview: *P*lanning and preparation; *E*ngage and explain; *A*ccount, clarification and challenge; *C*losure; and *E*valuation.

PI Performance Indicator; a type of quantitative measure which the Home Office often uses to assess the police service.

PIMS Performance Indicator Management System.

PIP (levels 1, 2, 3, and 4) 'Professionalising Investigation Programme' originally developed by NCPE (qv). Level 1 is embedded in the initial training of student police officers (through mapping to the NOS (qv) 2G2, 2H1, and 2H2).

PLO Prison Liaison Officer (a police officer).

PM Apart from its more common meaning (post meridian or afternoon), it means a post-mortem examination.

PNAC Police National Assessment Centre (sometimes 'Senior PNAC') for Superintendents and Chief Superintendents who aspire to Chief Officer (qv) ranks.

PNB (1) Pocket notebook. (2) Police Negotiation Board.

PNC Police National Computer.

PND Penalty Notice for Disorder.

PNLD Police National Legal Database.

POCA Proceeds of Crime Act 2002.

Police Federation of England and Wales The national staff association for the federated ranks of constable, sergeant, inspector, and chief inspector, resembling a trade union.

Police Staff Official designation of support (civilian) staff, some of whom are operational but who do not have warranted powers like police officers. Includes PCSOs (qv).

Police Superintendents' Association of England and Wales The national staff association for the ranks of superintendents and chief superintendents.

PolSA/POLSA Police Search Adviser.

POP/BritPOP Problem-Oriented Policing and its UK derivative.

PPU Prisoner Process Unit.

PRDLDP Police Race and Diversity Learning and Development Programme.

Probationer An informal term for a police officer in initial training in the first two years of service, and a reference to the probationary period. Now usually replaced by student police officer or student officer, but you may still hear the term used.

Profiling/Profilers An informal term often used in policing (as in 'offender profiling' and 'geographical profiling') but of uncertain meaning. Most often used to describe psychological profiling of an unknown offender (for example, when used to support the investigation into a linked serial rape case). However, the official ACPO (qv) term for those engaged in this latter form of activity is behavioural analyst or behavioural adviser.

PS or Ps Police sergeant.

PSD Professional Standards Department.

PSNI Police Service of Northern Ireland (previously called the RUC, Royal Ulster Constabulary).

QPM Queen's Police Medal.

qv Latin for 'for which see'—reference to another item or word.

R&D Research and Development Unit (usually for intelligence analysis and tasking at BCU (qv) level).

Redcap Vernacular term for an officer of the RMP (qv).

Re-coursing/Back-coursing An informal term for the process of student police officers repeating elements of initial training, normally as a result of failure or personal reasons.

Reflex Nationally funded project to deal with organized immigration crime.

Refs A vernacular reference to a refreshment break during a tour of duty.

Ridge and furrow Identifying features in fingerprints.

RIPA Regulation of Investigatory Powers Act 2000.

RMP Royal Military Police.

RTA (1) Road Traffic Act. (2) Road Traffic Accident—now largely replaced by RTI (qv) or RTC (qv).

RTC Road Traffic Collision. The term collision is preferred to 'accident' as it is more suggestive of the fact that most collisions on roads are due to human error, negligence, or a criminal act rather than a chance event. However, the term accident is still present in legislation.

RTI Road Traffic Incident.

RV(P) Rendez-vous (point) at a crime scene or major incident.

Sanitized Used to describe intelligence from which the identifying features and origins have been omitted.

SARA Scan, Analyse, Respond, and Assess.

SB Special Branch. A part of every police force that specializes in matters of national security and consisting of non-uniformed police officers.

Scarman Inquiry (Scarman Report) An official inquiry into the circumstances surrounding rioting in the Brixton area of London in 1981, concluding with a number of recommendations on reforming the law, changing police training and practice, and improving community relations.

SCAS Serious Crime Analysis Section. A database of homicides and stranger rapes housed at the Police College, Bramshill.

SDN Short Descriptive Note (part of a case file, such as a reference to a transcription of an interview with a suspect).

Secret Policeman Reference to the video documentary made in 2003 by an undercover reporter and subsequently aired by BBC television. The documentary produced evidence of racist behaviour by police recruits at a police regional training centre.

SFO Serious Fraud Office (now part of SOCA (qv)).

SGM Second Generation Multiplex; a DNA-profiling system using seven areas for discrimination between people (1 in 50 million). See STR.

SGM+ A similar DNA profiling system to SGM, using 11 areas for discrimination (1 in 1,000 million). See STR.

Sheehy A reference to the Sheehy Report of 1993 which made a number of recommendations on police conditions, pay, and rank, most of which were not implemented at the time.

Shoemarks Informal term for footwear prints which can match a suspect to a crime scene, in the same way as DNA and fingerprints can.

Show out A vernacular reference to a security problem on a surveillance operation when the suspect realizes that he/she is being observed.

SIA Security Industry Association.

sic Latin for 'as it is written'.

SIO Senior Investigating Officer (usually a detective officer) investigating a serious or major crime, such as a Category A or B murder (qv), or a rape or series of rapes.

SIODP Senior Investigating Officers' Development Programme.

SIU Special Investigation Unit (for child abuse and child protection investigations).

Skills for Justice/SfJ/S4J The Sector Skills Council (SSC) for Criminal Justice, including policing. Skills for Justice is also responsible for the National Occupational Standards (qv) for policing and other justice-related bodies and organizations (such as the Probation Service).

Skillsmark Quality-assurance scheme introduced by Skills for Justice (qv).

SLA Service Level Agreement.

SLDP Senior Leadership Development Programmes (SLDP1 and SLDP2) for those in chief inspector roles or above (including ACPO (qv) ranks in the case of SLDP2).

SMART(ER) Used in reference to objectives; *S*pecific, *M*easurable, *A*chievable, *R*ealistic, *T*imely (and *E*valuated and *R*eviewed).

SMT Senior Management Team (on a BCU (qv), it usually consists of the commander, a superintendent, (or a chief superintendent on large BCUs), together with one or more chief inspectors (Crime and Operations) and a Business Manager).

SO 19 Firearms unit in the MPS (qv).

SOCA Serious Organised Crime Agency; established by the government in 2005 to embrace the work of NCS, NCIS, SFO, and parts of HMCE (Investigation and Intelligence Divisions) and HM Immigration Service staff.

SOCO Scenes of Crime Officer; outmoded term replaced in many police forces by CSI (qv).

SOLAP Student Officer Learning Assessment Portfolio. In many forces this is replacing the PDP (qv) for student police officers.

SOLO Sex Offender Liaison Officer.

SOP Standard Operating Procedure.

SPoC/SPOC/spoc Single Point of Contact.

SPP Strategic Policing Priorities.

Stinger Device used to stop a speeding car by puncturing the tyres.

STR Short Tandem Repeat; a DNA profiling methodology which replaces the SGM and SGM+ terms (qv).

Superintendents' Association See Police Superintendents' Association of England and Wales.

Supervised Patrol Undertaken by student police officers under the supervision of a qualified police officer or officers.

T&CG Tasking and Coordinating Group.

Tac/TAC team (1) Tactical Support Team—for example, used to serve a warrant. (2) Terrorism and Crime Team (MPS (qv)).

TDA or TADA Taking and Driving Away; a reference to a form of vehicle crime. Also known as TWOC (qv).

Tenprint A fingerprinting process whereby all ten digits of a suspect or other individual are recorded.

Test Purchase The authorized purchase of drugs, alcohol, or other items (by an undercover police officer or another person) to provide evidence of illegal activity.

TFU Tactical Firearms Unit.

TIC Acronym for offences 'taken into consideration' by a court.

TIE Trace, Implicate, and/or Eliminate (in investigations).

TNA Training Needs Analysis.

TWOC Taken Without (or Without Owner's) Consent— normally used in reference to a motor vehicle; see TDA or TADA.

UKAEAC United Kingdom Atomic Energy Authority Constabulary, replaced in 2005 by the CNC (qv).

UKTA UK Threat Assessment (SOCA derived).

Unit (of an NOS) The NOS (qv) for initial policing consist of 22 Units: for example, Unit CK1 to 'Search Individuals'. Unit CK1 has just one element (qv).

UVP Ultra-Violet (Light) Photography.

VCSE Volume Crime Scene Examiner (forensic).

VEM Visible Ethnic Minority, refers to both the individuals and communities.

VIPER Video Identification Parade Electronic Recording.

ViSOR Violent and Sex Offender Register, a database of individuals considered a potential danger to the public because of their history of violence and/or sex offending.

Vol Volume.

VPS Victim Personal Statement.

WBA Work-based Assessment.

'Whorl' With 'loop' and 'delta' etc, names given to fingerprint characteristics.

TASK 1

There could well be terms, acronyms, and jargon particular to your own police organization and hence not on the list above. Your force might have a list on its intranet, or on a publicly-available website, or (more rarely) in a published form. Ask around to find out if such a list is available.

1.3   Chronology of Policing

An understanding of the past is an important precursor to understanding the present. There are no IPLDP learning outcomes that are explicitly concerned with the history of policing but there is an argument that, say, 'Understanding and being in the community' and 'Understanding social change' (both part of IND 11) benefit from placing what we currently do in an historical context.

We do not provide a comprehensive history of the police in the UK, nor do we offer much in the way of analysis, but we do provide you with some of the background that explains how we have arrived at the police service that you joined and a number of key dates that are milestones in that journey. It is surprising to note that the police (in the UK and elsewhere) are a relatively modern phenomenon and there have been a number of notable occasions when their very existence has been contested. Perhaps this is the key observation here: the police service as we would recognize it today is barely 180 years old and remains subject to continuing fundamental changes to its purpose and structure.

1.3.1   Background

If there is one key date in modern day policing it is probably 1829 when Sir Robert Peel, then Home Secretary, introduced a Bill in Parliament for the establishment of a 'Metropolitan Police Force' for London. The Bill was passed, became an Act, and the foundations of the modern police service were established. Initially, the police covered only the 'greater' part of London and not the capital's commercial centre, but ten years later the separate 'City of London Police Force' came into being (for just the square mile of the 'City of London').

Prior to 1829, the main official ways of keeping law and order rested, in serious instances, with the military and in less serious cases, with parish constables appointed by local Justices of the Peace. It is hard for us to imagine the way in which society was ordered in pre-industrial Britain. The fact that a genuine civil police force was only created after the end of the Napoleonic Wars (eight years before Queen Victoria came to the throne) suggests that there was probably no perceived official need for an integrated independent arm of criminal justice.

In fact, the origins of enforcing the law probably date back to the Saxons, or even earlier. The Saxons may well have brought with them the notion of dividing society into groups ('tythings' or 'tenths'), which would then assume some responsibility for social organization, acting under the control or oversight of a 'Shire Reeve'. Shire Reeves were responsible for law and order and controlled shires or large geographical districts (or towns, such as Nottingham—the word 'sheriff' may be derived from 'shire reeve'). They derived their authority from the King and could call upon able-bodied men in the community to hunt for fugitives or criminals by raising a 'hue and cry'.

After the Norman invasion in 1066 the Shire Reeves evolved to become Justices of the Peace, and rural communities came to have parish constables. 'Constable' is a Norman French word (derived from Latin) meaning 'count of the stable', an official who supervised the care of horses and who therefore had considerable social rank. However, the role of parish constable, though membership was originally drawn from members of the propertied classes, was often performed by the very poor (and very old) as substitutes, under the control of the magistrate. The office of constable was symbolized by the carrying of a painted or engraved 'stave' or 'truncheon', which in time developed into the wooden truncheon used during the first 150 years of official policing as a self-defence weapon.

In the eighteenth century the protection of law and order was largely performed by pressure of social opinion in the small rural communities together with harsh criminal penalties, including capital punishment and transportation. By the late eighteenth century the parish constable system had become widely acknowledged as inadequate, but survived despite its inefficiency, largely because there was apparently neither the will nor the imperative to change.

In the early 1800s the war with Napoleon and the increasing industrialization of Britain laid bare the inefficiencies of the old system. The use of military force was not a satisfactory way of dealing with the public. You may well have heard of the 'Peterloo Massacre' of 1819, in which local magistrates ordered the yeomanry to forcibly disperse a largely peaceable and unarmed crowd of 50,000 or more people gathered to hear a radical MP, Henry Hunt, speak on parliamentary reform, and arrest Hunt. The crowd was charged by the mounted militia with drawn swords. Several people were killed and over 400 were wounded; there was a major public outcry.

Allied to this was increasing lawlessness in the new towns and suburbs springing up throughout the UK, and the fear of mob rule. Large crowds formed in the towns and cities on slight pretexts, from the oratory of a radical to the perceived shortcomings of government. A crowd might stampede through a city for days, looting and killing, and the resultant disorder led to much criticism of the government. The conditions appeared (at least to some) to be ripe for anarchy, and the inadequacy of the military to deal with either mob rule or peaceable demonstration led the authorities to introduce a different kind of peace-keeping force.

There was a clear need for a non-military power acting on behalf of the Crown, though with its roots in the local community, so Peel's Police Force was established, at first only in London. Very soon, counties, cities, and towns followed suit and established their own police forces, using the Metropolitan Police Act as the basis for their authority (see below). Police officers were 'sworn officers' responsible to the Crown, as they are to this day. That responsibility, exercised on behalf of the Sovereign, stretches back to link with the notion of the Shire Reeve, some ten or more centuries earlier.

1.3.2 Chronology

Here we present a brief chronology (time-line) of the significant developments in the history of the police service of England and Wales, dominated (at least in the nineteenth century) by the Metropolitan Police in London.

1829 Sir Robert Peel established the first civilian police force in London. Sir Charles Rowan and Sir Richard Mayne were appointed as Justices of the Peace in charge of the force.

1831 Period of considerable unrest and mob violence, especially in the north of England and in London, where a crowd attacked the home of the Duke of Wellington and broke all the windows. The new police eventually imposed order.

1835 The Municipal Corporations Act 1835 established 'watch committees' to oversee policing of areas outside London. The term watch committee is derived from the old meaning of a watch as the provision of law and order at night (established by the Statute of Winchester in 1285).

1839/40 Various pieces of legislation allowed the setting up of provincial constabularies under a local police committee of magistrates, based on the Metropolitan Police model. An important difference was that the Metropolitan Police was answerable directly to the Home Secretary through its Commissioners (of which there were two at first), whereas provincial police forces were answerable to their local authorities through their magistrates' committees.

1842 Establishment of a detective force at Scotland Yard (Metropolitan Police HQ), but investigation was in its infancy and the numbers very small (it was only increased to ten staff in 1856). At first, formation of a detective branch was resisted at borough and county level because of a distaste for spies and informers.

1840s–50s A period of considerable hostility to the new police, particularly in the boroughs and counties. There was widespread resentment about the cost of supporting the police, a belief that a police force was illiberal, and that there was a lack of visibility of police officers when needed (this last is a remarkably modern complaint).

1856 The County and Borough Police Act 1856 made it mandatory for local government bodies to set up police forces. These were often shoe-string affairs organized on a parochial basis, but the introduction of inspections of constabularies improved the standards and helped ensure consistency in police force activities. Financial support (in the form of Exchequer Grants) was centrally awarded to forces which proved to be efficient and reliable, paving the way for the modern inspection regime by the HMIC (qv).

1860 A survey in this year established that there were more than 200 borough and county police forces in England and Wales, with similar arrangements being put in place in Scotland. Unrest and armed disaffection in Ireland (then a single colonial possession) led to the formation of the Royal Irish Constabulary, which was paramilitary from the outset.

The RIC served as a model for the establishment of colonial police forces in places like Kenya and South Africa in the later nineteenth century.

1872   Police officers went on strike for the first time.

1878   The Criminal Investigation Department (CID) was formed after a major corruption scandal (the 'Turf Fraud') among detectives in London in 1877. This pattern was followed with greater or lesser success across provincial forces during the next 30 years, but Scotland Yard detectives were still called in by county forces to lead criminal investigations well into the 1930s. By the 1940s most county forces had their own CIDs and no longer used Scotland Yard detectives.

1883   The Special Irish Branch was formed in the Metropolitan Police to deal with attacks by Irish republicans in London. This later became known simply as Special Branch and many of the larger police forces had their own branches by 1918, largely as a result of MI5's urging of the police to deal with German spies and saboteurs during the First World War.

1888   The oversight of local police was transferred from the committee of magistrates to a joint committee of magistrates and elected councillors—an important change. (This arrangement endured until around 2005, when Police Authorities became wholly elected.)

1890   The Police Act 1890 provided for the first time a police pension, payable after 25 years' service, together with other benefits such as one rest day off each week and regularized pay systems (see below). We tend now to think of pensions as perfectly normal (if expensive) adjuncts to employment, but in 1890 such notions were comparatively rare and a pension was a genuine inducement to join the police. The Act also brought in the concept in law of 'mutual aid' between police forces.

1900   Lord Belper headed a committee to ascertain the best system of identifying suspects as criminals. A year later, Scotland Yard's Fingerprint Bureau was formed and, by 1905, many of the larger provincial forces had their own fingerprint bureaux.

1910   Radio telegraphy was used to apprehend Dr Crippen who had fled from Britain by ship, after killing his wife.

1911   Police officers were armed for the first time, after assisting the military (overseen by the Home Secretary, Winston Churchill) to end a siege of armed anarchists in a house in Sidney Street in London.

1912   Establishment of Special Constables on a permanent basis, both in London and in the larger provincial forces.

1914   The first (unofficial) Police Union (NUPPO) was formed, following unrest and dissatisfaction about pay and conditions, but was not recognized by the authorities. The Women Police were founded (see below).

1914–18   The First World War put enormous pressure on the police. Not only were numbers of male officers severely depleted by enlistment in the armed forces, but recruitment into the police was suspended too. New tasks such as the pursuit of deserters, new roles such as the protection of vulnerable points, and new laws, such as the Defence of the Realm Act (DORA) of 1915, added considerably to police responsibilities. As a consequence, morale appeared to suffer, pay and conditions were comparatively poor, and the police became increasingly vocal in demands for reform and a pay rise.

1916   The Commissioner of the Metropolitan Police ruled that any officer joining a union rendered himself liable to dismissal.

1918–19   The police, particularly in Liverpool and London, embarked on a series of strikes for better pay and conditions and for recognition of police trades unions. This resulted in the Police Act 1919 which prohibited the formation of police trades unions and denied the police the right to strike, but allowed the formation of the Police Federation to represent the ranks from constable to chief inspector in negotiations over pay, conditions of service, and Police Regulations. Many of those who had been dismissed for having leading roles in the strike were never reinstated.

1918   Women had filled various police roles during the First World War, owing to the absence of many male officers in the armed forces. The regularizing of women police officers as equal members of the force is generally dated from 1916, though many would argue that women were not fully accepted in the police service until the Second World War, and even then, attitudes to female police officers were often negative. The Police Federation (qv), for example, took until 1948 to admit female officers as members.

1921   The first motorcycle patrols took place and the Police Pensions Act 1921 fixed an age limit for each police rank, on reaching which retirement was compulsory.

1922   After the creation of Eire in 1922, the RIC (created in 1860) became the Royal Ulster Constabulary (RUC).

1930s   The period between the Wars saw a major development of personal motor transport and for the first time brought the police into conflict with the middle class who could afford cars. The love/hate relationship between motorists and the law persists to this day.

1931   Lord Trenchard was appointed as Metropolitan Police Commissioner. Founder of the Royal Air Force in 1918 (previously the Royal Flying Corps), Trenchard believed in a two-tier entry system to the police, based on the officer/non-commissioned ranks recruitment in the armed forces. He established a Police College at Hendon in 1934 to train police officers, but his experiment with 'officer entry' was short-lived. The system remained that all police officers would enter the service as constables. It was only in the early twenty-first century that the possibility of multiple entry points into the police service was raised again as a serious proposition.

1935   The first police forensic laboratory was opened by the Metropolitan Police, paving the way for adoption of more scientific detection processes throughout the police service.

1937   The emergency telephone number 999 was introduced.

1946   The Police Act 1946 amalgamated police forces that served populations of fewer than 10,000. This reduced the number of forces to 125.

1950s   The so-called 'Golden Age' of policing in the UK (although less so in Northern Ireland) was characterized by apparent widespread acceptance of the legitimacy of the police, and relatively low levels of crime and disorder. However, the very existence of the Golden Age is the subject of some debate. Popular belief in its existence probably derives at least in part from a television series at the time called *Dixon of Dock Green* in which an elderly actor played an elderly police officer who appeared infinitely wise, able to talk to anyone, calm, inordinately knowledgeable, honest, and trusted (it seemed) by the entire nation.

1951   Police Cadets (aged 16–18) were introduced as a pathway to become police officers. They wore distinctive pale blue bands on their caps (much like today's PCSOs).

1964   Although the government abolished some small police forces during the Second World War, it was the Police Act of 1964 which brought about major amalgamations of police forces, reducing the overall number of separate and distinct forces from 117 to 49. In the same Act, the borough watch committees and county force joint committees were abolished and replaced with Police Authorities based on a county or city force.

1965   Police officers first had personal radios to maintain communication during their beat patrols.

1973   Women police officers were integrated directly into the police service.

1978   Lord Edmund-Davies headed an enquiry into police pay, which improved pay and allowances. Similar increases occurred for the armed forces.

1984–5 The National Union of Mineworkers (NUM) organized a strike in protest at pit closures and there were numerous clashes between picket lines and police, and allegations of heavy-handed behaviour by the police and political intervention by the Conservative government.

1984   The Police and Criminal Evidence Act 1984 (PACE) created the Police Complaints Authority (PCA), through which complaints about the police from members of the public were investigated. The PCA was formed in response to criticism of the police 'acting as judge and jury in their own cases' because police officers (although from another force) always investigated serious complaints. However, in the majority of cases, the PCA simply monitored investigations conducted by the police themselves.

1990 The Association of Chief Police Officers (ACPO) published its 'Statement of Common Purpose and Values', which emphasized that the police was more a service than a force.

1994 Creation of a centralized computer database for criminal records.

1997 NAFIS, the National Automated Fingerprint Identification System, was launched which allowed forces to access the national database for fingerprint records.

1999 The Macpherson Inquiry into the death of Stephen Lawrence (a black teenager murdered in London in 1993) criticized the whole police service as institutionally racist and major efforts were made, and continue to be made, both to communicate with diverse communities and to increase the proportions of ethnic minority communities within police ranks.

The RUC became the Police Service of Northern Ireland (PSNI), following the Patten Inquiry and Report.

2002 Introduction of Police Community Support Officers (PCSOs) under the provisions of the Police Reform Act 2002. PCSOs are not sworn officers, but are support staff and are the most visible part of an extending security industry, which some commentators argue runs the risk of marginalizing the police and usurping their functions. Others argue that society is becoming more complex and policing has to match a need for flexible responses; this results in policing also being undertaken by people other than the public police themselves.

2003 TV airing by the BBC of *The Secret Policeman* video uncovering racism at a regional police training centre. The Independent Police Complaints Commission (IPCC) was established to replace the Police Complaints Authority.

2005 Formation of the Serious Organised Crime Agency (SOCA) which brought together the National Crime Squad, the National Criminal Intelligence Service, parts of HM Immigration Department, the Serious Fraud Office, and the Investigation Branch of HM Customs and Excise into one body with federal powers to counter level 3 crime and criminality.

2006 Following a 2005 report by HMIC, a further amalgamation of police forces was proposed but then rescinded in 2006. The National Police Improvement Agency (NPIA) was formed, incorporating the old Centrex (police training) and other agencies such as Information Services.

2007 The Home Office was split into two parts: the 'justice' element was incorporated into a Ministry of Justice whilst the 'security' element (including the police) became part of a new Interior Ministry. Such a division did not take account of the fact that the police have as large a role to play in justice as they do in security, a point made explicit by Sir Richard Mayne at the founding of the 'new police' in London in 1830.

2008 Publication of the Flanagan Review of Policing containing recommendations on reducing unnecessary police bureaucracy and the implementation of Neighbourhood Policing.

TASK 2

What is the history of your own force? See if you can establish the dates of a few key events in the last 200 years or so.

1.4 IPLDP Phases and Modules

The Initial Police Learning and Development Programme (IPLDP) is the form of police probationary training used by all forces since April 2006. The following is presented as an overview
of the IPLDP Phases and Modules for reference purposes.

The IPLDP describes training for student police officers in terms of four phases, taking approximately 24 months to complete (when undertaken on a full-time basis):

Phase 1—Induction
Phase 2—Community Safety & Partnerships
Phase 3—Supervised Patrol
Phase 4—Independent Patrol

There are eleven Induction Modules, nine Operational Modules, and three Legislation, Policing,
and Guidelines Modules (although module LPG 0 is optional):

IPLDP Phases and Modules

Module	Title
IND 1	Underpinning ethics/values of the police service
IND 2	Foster people's equality, diversity, and rights
IND 3	Develop one's own knowledge and practice
IND 4	Develop effective relationships with colleagues
IND 5	Ensure your own actions reduce the risks to health and safety
IND 6	Assess the needs of individuals and provide advice and support
IND 7	Develop effective partnerships with members of the community and other agencies
IND 8	Operation of information technology systems
IND 9	Administer first aid
IND 10	Use police actions in a fair and justified way
IND 11	Social, community issues, and Neighbourhood Policing
OP 1	Deal with aggressive and abusive behaviour
OP 2	Obtain, evaluate, and submit information and intelligence to support local priorities
OP 3	Respond to incidents, conduct and evaluate investigations
OP 4	Participate in planned operations
OP 5	Search individuals and premises
OP 6	Prepare, conduct, and evaluate interviews
OP 7	Arrest and report suspects
OP 8	Escort suspects and present to custody
OP 9	Prepare and present case information, present evidence, and finalize investigations
LPG 0	Underpinning Legislation Policy and Guidelines (Phases 3 and 4)
LPG 1	Underpinning Legislation Policy and Guidelines (Phase 3)
LPG 2	Underpinning Legislation Policy and Guidelines (Phase 4)

Note however that forces:

- may decide to structure their own training (as long as they remain IPLDP compliant);
- may not use the same terminology as above. For example, instead of using the term 'modules' they may use 'courses' and they may not use 'phases' in the same way as the IPLDP.

The content of the IPLDP modules are underpinned by the **Learning Requirement** for initial
police training. The Learning Requirement was developed by Professors John Elliott, Saville
Kushner, and others.

1.5   The National Occupational Standards

There are a number of National Occupational Standards (NOS) for initial policing that underpin the training of student police officers, developed by Skills for Justice, a Sector Skills Council. Currently 22 NOS Units underpin initial police training. However, the number of Units is under review and it is likely that these will be reduced to 9 or 10 Units during 2010 (see below). The standards feature extensively throughout the Handbook and the following is a list of the headings of the 22 relevant Units.

Relevant NOS Units for Initial Policing	
Unit	**Unit Title**
AA1	Promote equality and value diversity
AB1	Communicate effectively with people
AE1	Maintain and develop your own knowledge, skills, and competence
AF1	Ensure your own actions reduce risks to health and safety
BE2	Provide initial support to victims, survivors, and witnesses and assess their needs for further support
CA1	Use law enforcement actions in a fair and justified way
CB1	Gather and submit information that has the potential to support law enforcement objectives
CD1	Provide an initial response to incidents
CD3	Prepare for, and participate in, planned law enforcement operations
CD5	Arrest, detain, or report individuals
CI101	Conduct priority and volume investigations
CJ101	Interview victims and witnesses in relation to priority and volume investigations
CJ201	Interview suspects in relation to priority and volume investigations
CK1	Search individuals
CK2	Search vehicles, premises, and open spaces
DA5	Present evidence in court and at other hearings
DA6	Prepare and submit case files
GC10	Manage conflict
2G4	Finalize investigations
2K1	Escort detained persons
2K2	Present detained persons to custody
4G4	Administer First Aid

Note that the Units for initial policing were the subject of review and change during 2008. For example, the Unit 1A1 was replaced by a new Unit, CA1. Throughout this Handbook we have used the new (2008) Units. However, your force may still be using the 2003 Units, particularly if it is also offering an NVQ. The table below shows both the 2003 and 2008 Units for purposes of mapping and comparison.

NOS Units for Initial Policing, 2003 and 2008			
2008 Unit	**Unit Title**	**2003 Unit**	**Unit Title**
AA1	Promote equality and value diversity	1A4	Fostering people's equality, diversity and rights
AB1	Communicate effectively with people	1A2	Communicate effectively with members of communities
AE1	Maintain and develop your own knowledge, skills, and competence	4C1	Develop one's own knowledge and practice
AF1	Ensure your own actions reduce risks to health and safety	4G2	Ensure your own actions reduce risks to health and safety

2008 Unit	Unit Title	2003 Unit	Unit Title
BE2	Provide initial support to victims, survivors, and witnesses and assess their needs for further support	1B9	Provide initial support to individuals affected by offending or antisocial behaviours and assess their needs for further support
CA1	Use law enforcement actions in a fair and justified way	1A1	Use police actions in a fair and justified way
CB1	Gather and submit information that has the potential to support law enforcement objectives	2A1	Gather and submit information that has the potential to support policing objectives
CD1	Provide an initial response to incidents	2C1	Provide an initial police response to incidents
CD3	Prepare for, and participate in, planned law enforcement operations	2C2	Prepare for, and participate in, planned policing operations
CD5	Arrest, detain, or report individuals	2C3	Arrest, detain, or report individuals
CI101	Conduct priority and volume investigations	2G2	Conduct priority and volume investigations
CJ101	Interview victims and witnesses in relation to priority and volume investigations	2H1	Interview victims and witnesses
CJ201	Interview suspects in relation to priority and volume investigations	2H2	Interview suspects
CK1	Search individuals	2I1	Search individuals
CK2	Search vehicles, premises, and open spaces	2I2	Search vehicles, premises, and land
DA5	Present evidence in court and at other hearings	2J2	Present evidence in court and at other hearings
DA6	Prepare and submit case files	2J1	Prepare and submit case files
GC10	Manage conflict	2C4	Minimize and deal with aggressive and abusive behaviour
2G4	Finalize investigations	2G4	Finalize investigations
2K1	Escort detained persons	2K1	Escort detained persons
2K2	Present detained persons to custody	2K2	Present detained persons to custody
4G4	Administer First Aid	4G4	Administer First Aid

In addition, you may be assessed against Unit 1D4 to 'Contribute to the protection of children and young people from abuse'.

Note that after an IPLDP 'stakeholder' consultation the number of NOS Units for initial policing may be reduced from 22 to 9 or 10 from 2010 onwards.

TASK 3

Why do you think the number of NOS Units may be reduced to nine or ten from 2010 onwards?

The NOS Units for initial policing to be introduced during 2010 are likely to be as follows:

Likely NOS Units for Initial Policing post 2009

Unit	Unit Title
BE2	Provide initial support to victims, survivors, and witnesses and assess their needs for further support
CB1	Gather and submit information that has the potential to support law enforcement objectives
CD1	Provide an initial response to incidents
CD5	Arrest, detain, or report individuals
CI101	Conduct priority and volume investigations
CJ101	Interview victims and witnesses in relation to priority and volume investigations
CJ201	Interview suspects in relation to priority and volume investigations
CK1	Search individuals*
CK2	Search vehicles, premises, and open spaces*
GC10	Manage conflict

*These two Units may be combined as a single Unit. Some existing Units such as AA1 are likely to be incorporated into the new Units.

1.6 Answers to Tasks

TASK 1

Police forces often publish a glossary of terms that they use in their documentation which they make available under the Freedom of Information Act 2000. An example of a glossary may be found at <http://www.devon-cornwall.police.uk/v3/help/glossary.htm>.

TASK 2

Police organizations sometimes describe their history on their websites (for example, the extensive MPS site at <http://www.met.police.uk/history/>). Many also have museums (for example, the Essex Police museum at Police HQ in Chelmsford) and some forces may also have a comprehensive and published written history (for example Ingleton, 2002).

TASK 3

A national 'stock-take' of IPLDP was conducted in late 2008 which concluded that the relatively large number of NOS Units created an excessive burden on both student officers and their forces. The review was undoubtedly influenced by the independent review of policing conducted by Sir Ronnie Flanagan, which reported in February 2008. The Flanagan review was critical of unnecessary bureaucracy in policing. However, note that although the proposed changes will reduce the number of NOS Units, some of the new Units are likely to be larger in size. For example, Unit AF1 'Health and safety' is not likely to disappear but instead feature within the content of other Units. The existing NVQs (levels 3 and 4) in initial policing are currently mapped to all 22 NOS Units; their relationship with the new reduced number of Units has yet to be determined.

2 | How to Use the Handbook

2.1   Chapter Briefing

In this chapter we provide advice about how to use the Handbook. We are familiar with the wide range of experiences that new entrants bring to the police service and the Handbook has been designed and written to be both accessible and of value to a wide range of readers.

2.1.1   Aim of the Chapter

This aim of this chapter is to provide you with guidance on how to use the Handbook, how it relates to your training, the NOS, the PAC and the Learning Requirement, and the importance of further reading.

This chapter will enable you to:

- understand how the Handbook has been set out;
- appreciate the reasons for including tasks for you to undertake;
- see the links between the Handbook, the IPLDP curriculum, the NOS, the PAC, and the Learning Requirement;
- understand the importance of referring to your own force policy when appropriate;
- follow our approach to referencing and how we quote from legislation, circulars, and codes;
- appreciate the necessity and benefits of undertaking further reading.

2.2   Survival First

When you joined the police service as a student police officer you probably did so with the intention of 'walking the walk' and not 'talking the talk'. Naturally you would prefer to be practising your profession rather than simply learning about it, particularly if you have spent the last two or three years studying at college or university or have waited some time to join the police. However, many would see it is as important that you first earn the right to exercise your powers and that you do so with professional judgement and with due respect for the rights and diversity of the citizens of the United Kingdom. Your training, and this Handbook, is designed to help you do just that.

The Handbook is designed as a form of survival guide to assist you in qualifying as a police officer. For example, in order to help you learn, we have omitted some of the more detailed aspects of the law and police procedure and instead provided a simplified version. Yet even this can look daunting in places. This is based upon our experience of teaching trainee police officers. Of course, this does not mean that the detail is not important; it is just that learning is usually easier when moving from the simple to the complex, so we start you off with the simple. In the case of the law, the full complexity will normally be introduced and explained to you by your police tutors and trainers using a variety of teaching and learning methods. However, you may be expected to learn new material for yourself, and if this is so then you are likely to find Chapter 4 particularly useful. You will also find the detail of legislation covered in other publications and sources including:

- the original legislation itself. (Most recent legislation is now available from the government website <http://www.opsi.gov.uk/legislation/whatsnew>.) However, note that attempting to understand original legislation can be confusing as it may have been subject to amendment and changed by subsequent legislation. This is not always obvious when reading the original. For example, the definition of a religiously aggravated offence (see 9.11 below) to be found in the Crime and Disorder Act 1998 was subsequently added to by the Anti-terrorism, Crime and Security Act of 2001. The 2001 legislation added a new subsection 28(5) to the four original subsections of the 1998 legislation. The new government website at <http://www.statutelaw.gov.uk/Home.aspx> provides 'updated' versions of original legislation, and you might also find the website <http://www.opsi.gov.uk/legislation/revised> useful;
- publications such as *Butterworth's Police Law* and the Blackstone's publications (notably the Police Operational Handbook and the annual Police Manuals);
- the NCALT learning portal for the police service at <http://www.ncalt.com>;
- the PNLD website at <http://www.pnld.co.uk/pnld/welcome.asp>;
- legal guidance from the CPS at <http://www.cps.gov.uk/legal/index.html>;
- the NPIA digests at <http://www.npia.police.uk/digest>;
- your own police force resources (for example, your force intranet).

TASK 1

Use the internet to identify the definition of 'designated area' in the law governing demonstrations in the vicinity of Parliament. It is defined within the Serious Organised Crime and Police Act 2005.

Finally, the style of the Handbook represents a judgement concerning the best ways of introducing and describing a subject area. For many aspects of the law (for example, as covered in Chapters 7 to 11 inclusive) we have adopted a bite-size approach with the legislation and police practice. We have simplified and condensed the topics into relatively short sections of text and diagrams dealing with that subject and that subject alone. This would seem to suit the subject matter and the need for you, on many occasions, to assimilate and be able to reproduce the facts. In other parts of the book we have adopted a more holistic approach—for example to interviewing, covered in Chapter 12. This reflects the reality that learning the skills of interviewing involves more than adherence to codes and legislation. You will also need, for example, to appreciate the structure an interview can take, the forms of communication used (particularly for questioning), and the role of the interview within a wider criminal investigation.

2.3 Tasks

In many chapters you are asked to undertake tasks, which occur within the body of each chapter rather than, more traditionally, at the end of the whole chapter. In some cases these tasks will also be useful to you as stimulus material for your SOLAP or Learning Diary. Answers are provided at the end of each chapter.

In many cases the tasks also provide further ideas for you to explore or point you in the direction of additional reading and study to undertake. For this reason it is helpful to read the answers to the tasks even though you may already be confident that you have a clear understanding of the answer to a question.

2.4 Links with the IPLDP

A typical pattern of training for student police officers in their probationary period is described in Chapter 3. Police forces have some flexibility and can vary these patterns in order to reflect local need and their own particular circumstances (for example, they may be in partnership with a local FE College or University and this might affect the pattern of delivery). However, in all cases, forces are required to be IPLDP-compliant—that is, to demonstrate how their curriculum delivers the learning outcomes of the modules of the IPLDP (Home Office, 2005a).

There are three clusters of modules in the IPLDP (Home Office, 2005e).

The **Induction modules** are referred to as the IND modules, and there are eleven of them. Induction would seem to suggest that these modules are all covered in the first few weeks of service. Although partly the case (for example, you are likely to undertake IND 9: 'Administer First Aid' early on), this is not wholly true. In some cases these modules are introduced during the induction process but then developed and revisited during the remainder of your training. An example of this is IND 10: 'Use police actions in a fair and justified way'.

This Handbook covers most, but not all, of the content of the IND modules. Some aspects of your training, such as First Aid, are more suited to specialist publications and others, such as IND 8: 'Operation of information technology systems', are very dependent on individual force policy and equipment. In these instances we provide an overview of the kind of training you are likely to receive rather than describing the detail. Similarly, a subject such as the multicultural nature of modern Britain and the diverse communities that you will police, is, we would wish to argue, better studied using textbooks or other learning material specifically devoted to this task rather than using this Handbook or even pages from your NPIA notes.

The **Operational Modules** are referred to as the OP modules, and there are nine of them. As you have probably guessed, these nine modules are concerned with the routine but vital operational tasks of the police officer, often (but not exclusively) those most closely associated with patrol. For example, OP 5 is concerned with your ability to 'search individuals and premises'. This Handbook covers, at an introductory level, the knowledge required for **most** of the OP modules.

The **Legislation, Policy, and Guidelines Modules** of the IPLDP are referred to as the LPG modules and there are three of them. These are the modules that are most closely linked with the acquisition of knowledge of the law, policy, and procedures that we often associate with initial policing. This Handbook provides you with much of the basic knowledge required for LPG 1

Curriculum areas of LPG 1 and 2 not covered	
LPG 1.2 (1) Standard operating procedures for dealing with cannabis	See local force policy
LPG 1.2 (1) Control measures and sources of assistance	See local force policy
LPG 1.3 (1) Their role in addressing anti-social behaviour within the community	See local force policy
LPG 1.3 (1) Individual Support Orders	Not covered
LPG 1.3 (1) Acceptable Behaviour Contracts	Not covered
LPG 1.3 (1) Parenting Contracts	Not covered
LPG 1.3 (1) Parenting Orders	Not covered
LPG 1.3 (1) Penalty Notice for night noise	Not covered

LPG 1.3 (1) Crack house closure powers	Not covered
LPG 1.3 (1) Anti-social behaviour and the TOGETHER campaign	Not covered
LPG 1.3 (2) Community safety units	See local force policy
LPG 1.3 (7) Meeting victims' needs	See local force policy
LPG 1.3 (11) Solvent abuse	Not covered
LPG 1.3 (12) Victim support	See local force policy
LPG 1.3 (13) Youth Offending Teams	See local force policy
LPG 1.3 (21) Welfare (eg positional asphyxia)	Part of force staff safety training
LPG1.3 (23) Firearms and support	See local force policy
LPG1.3 (23) Priorities in relation to spontaneous incidents	See local force policy
LPG1.3 (23) Responsibilities in relation to spontaneous incidents	See local force policy
LPG 1.4 (1) Transportation of detained persons	See local force policy
LPG 1.4 (3) Methods of briefing/debriefing	Not covered
LPG 1.4 (3) Crime reporting	See local force policy
LPG 1.4 (6) Stopping lost or stolen vehicles (Officer Safety Training (OST) issues)	Part of staff safety training
LPG 1.4 (7) Use of personal radios	See local force policy
LPG 1.4 (7) PNC source input documents	See local force policy
LPG 1.4 (9) Welfare matters (facilities and accountability)	See local force policy
LPG 1.4 (14) Police personnel procedures	See local force policy
LPG 1.5 (2) Police action at civil disputes	Not covered
LPG 1.5 (3) Civil trespass	See local force policy
LPG 1.5 (5) Illness in the street	Part of force First Aid training
LPG 1.5 (6) Lost and found property	See local force policy
LPG 1.5 (8) The social effects of alcohol	Not covered
LPG 1.7 (3) Explain the SARA model and its application	Not covered
LPG 1.7 (3) Explain the PAT model and its application	Not covered
LPG 1.7 (4) Completion of street ID procedures documentation	See local force policy
LPG 1.7 (15) Personal descriptions	Not covered
LPG 1.7(18) Reporting lost or stolen vehicles	See local force policy
LPG 1.8(1) Collision scene management	See local force policy
LPG 2.3 (1) Early Evidence Kits	See local force policy
LPG 2.3 (1) Rape Trauma Syndrome	Not covered
LPG 2.3 (1) Havens/safe houses	See local force policy

and LPG 2. Most of the aspects of LPG 1 and LPG 2 that we do not cover are related to local force policy and therefore inappropriate for a general textbook of this kind.

We do not cover all the content of the LPG 0 module; we cover only those areas we regard as essential for the student police officer, despite the fact that they are designated as optional under the IPLDP.

Note that the IPLDP curriculum is subject to regular review and change.

2.5   Links with the NOS, the PAC, and the Learning Requirement

The Handbook is linked throughout to the National Occupational Standards for initial policing (the NOS) and the Police Action Checklist (the PAC). You will find explicit reference to them at the beginning of many chapters and sometimes within the text itself. The underlying knowledge requirements of a number of headings of the PAC (a key requirement of Independent Patrol) are also covered. However, bear in mind that both the NOS and the PAC are concerned with performance and competence, and although an understanding of the theory is a necessary condition, it is not by itself sufficient for their attainment. The NOS and PAC are examined in more detail in Chapter 3.

The Learning Requirement for student police officers (as developed by Professors John Elliott, Saville Kushner, and others) is also referenced on a number of occasions. It is based around seven core learning goals (Elliott *et al.*, 2003):

1. Understanding and engaging with the community
2. Enforcing the law and following police procedures
3. Responding to human and social diversity
4. Positioning oneself in the role of a police officer inside the police organization
5. Professional standards and ethical conduct
6. Learning to learn and creating a base for career-long learning
7. Qualities of professional judgement and decision-making.

2.6   Local Force Policy

Each of the 43 Home Office police forces in England and Wales has its own local policies, often to be found on the organization's intranet, and usually expressed as 'Force Orders', 'Standard Operating Procedures (SOP)', 'Policies', and likewise. This Handbook should always be read in conjunction with local force policies, particularly when the Handbook describes procedures such as writing a statement or making a pocket notebook entry.

Your force may also wish you to learn verbatim definitions whilst you are a student police officer. These definitions are often concerned with the law, for example the definition of what constitutes theft. In this case we advise you to use the definitions given to you by your force rather than those reproduced in this Handbook or, indeed, in other textbooks. This is because there is sometimes a slight variation between forces in definitions of the same terms—for example, whether in the definition your force gives you to learn, 'he' in the original Act (a common occurrence) is replaced with 'he/she', 's/he', or 'they', or is left in its original form.

2.7   References and Further Reading

Referencing is a standard academic system for producing evidence for your arguments or for directing the reader towards further information. We have deliberately kept the volume of referencing in this Handbook to a minimum, and largely restricted referencing to where it is necessary to indicate to you the sources of our ideas and information. This is a common courtesy to those authors whose work we have utilized. It is also respect for the intellectual property rights of others. The main reason for minimizing the number of references is to try and make the Handbook more accessible to a wider range of readers; the flow is not disturbed by frequent references to other material. This is not to undermine the importance of referencing—far from it. In fact you may well be required to reference your own work, particularly if your training is linked with a higher education foundation degree.

We would also encourage you to undertake further reading (and on some occasions indicate so in the body of the Handbook or in the answers to tasks). As explained in 2.2 above, the Handbook is very much a survival guide and you will find more detail and further explanation in many other textbooks, in your NPIA (Centrex) or force notes, and via the NCALT and other websites. A small technical point—many internet sites will use the Adobe Acrobat portable document format for documents and written reports (particularly the Home Office), so ensure that you have the software available to view the .pdf formats (it is free and is also built in to later versions of MS Internet Explorer).

2.8 Extracts from Legislation, Circulars, and Codes

Throughout the Handbook there are numerous extracts from primary legislation or Codes—often from Acts of Parliament. These are quoted as the original but sometimes with minor changes. Often an explanation in everyday language is also given, normally in a text box to the right of the original legislation. Quotations are signified by the use of a different font (or quotation marks) while explanations and comments are in ordinary text, like this:

if when not at [his/her] place of abode.

The term place of abode means the place or site where someone lives. It normally includes the garage and garden of a house and should be given its normal meaning, but it will be a question of fact for the court to decide. If a homeless person sleeps in his or her car, the car counts as an abode while he/she is asleep. However, when the same car is being driven by the same person, it is not considered as a place of abode for the purposes of the offence of going equipped (see *R v Bundy* 1977).

When changes have been made, this is usually because legislation tends to use the personal pronoun 'he' to cover also 'he or she'. (There are some circumstances, however, particularly in legislation that covers sexual offences, when 'he' really does just mean 'he'.) We have changed 'he' to 'he/she' and 'him' to 'him/her', etc. A change of this kind can also have follow-on effects in the remainder of the sentence. We have also occasionally changed a word so that a sentence makes more sense when quoted alone. Minor changes to the wording of legislation or Codes in the Handbook are signified by the use of square brackets as in the following example. The original, from s 74 of the Sexual Offences Act 2003 states that:

For the purposes of this Part, a person consents if he agrees by choice, and has the freedom and capacity to make that choice.

Our revised version reads:

For the purposes of this [offence], a person consents if [he/she] agrees by choice, and has the freedom and capacity to make that choice.

As you can see in this example the changes made to the wording of the original legislation were as follows:

- 'Part' was changed to [offence];
- 'he' was changed to [he/she].

2.9 Answer to Task 1

The Serious Organised Crime and Police Act (SOCPA) 2005 can be located at <http://www.opsi. gov.uk/ACTS/acts2005/20050015.htm>. Demonstrations in the vicinity of Parliament are dealt with in Part 4 of the Act, 'Public Order and Conduct in Public Places etc' and in ss 132 to 138 inclusive. You should find a hypertext link to s 132. Section 132(7) explains that designated area means 'the area specified in an order under section 138'. Hence we now need to look at s 138 which states, in effect, that it is the responsibility of the Secretary of State to specify the area but that 'no point in the area so specified may be more than one kilometre in a straight line from the point nearest to it in Parliament Square'. This needs some thinking about. The SOCPA sets the limits to the maximum area that the Secretary of State can specify (essentially a buffer zone, 1 km wide, around the edge of Parliament Square) but allows some flexibility within this. Normally in these kinds of circumstances the Secretary of State will issue a Statutory Instrument which provides the detail of the decisions made. (The use of Statutory Instruments enables changes to be made on a frequent basis if required without having to make adjustments to the Act itself—see 5.11 below.) Sure enough, a little detective work locates Statutory Instrument 2005 No 1537, the Serious Organised Crime and Police Act 2005 (Designated Area) Order 2005 at <http://www.opsi.gov.uk/si/si2005/20051537.htm> which informs us that the designated area from 1 July 2005 was:

> the area bounded by an imaginary line starting at the point where Hungerford Bridge crosses Victoria Embankment, continuing along Hungerford Bridge to the point where it crosses Belvedere Road, right-wards along Belvedere Road as far as Chicheley Street

and so on.

Note that the Prime Minister, Gordon Brown, has declared his intention to re-examine ss 132 to 138 inclusive in the light of public criticism that the right to protest has been unduly restricted.

3 | Qualifying as a Police Officer

3.1   Chapter Briefing

This chapter examines the process of qualification as a police officer. We use the word 'qualification' in its wider sense of having the knowledge and skills to undertake professional responsibilities and to exercise judgement and discretion. Within this chapter we also examine the various ways in which your competence is measured and how other aspects of your attainment of skills, knowledge, and behavioural qualities are likely to be assessed. Note that some aspects of the assessment of initial policing are in the process of change, particularly the number of NOS Units to be assessed, the Student Officer Learning and Assessment Portfolio (SOLAP), the National Minimum Qualification, and aspects of the Integrated Competency Framework.

3.1.1   Aim of the Chapter

The aim of this chapter is to assist in your understanding of the route map from student police officer to full confirmation as a police officer, particularly in relation to assessment and the meaning of 'competence' in initial policing. We will consider how the qualification process and the notion of competence relate to the National Occupational Standards for initial policing, the process of assessment against these standards, and how your achievements and progress are recorded. Your confirmation will normally be at the end of two years' probationary service.

This chapter will enable you to:

- reflect on your reasons for joining the police service and why these reasons are important;
- observe a typical pattern of training in the first two years of service;
- appreciate the professional and legal context to training whilst on probation;
- understand the nature of competence and competencies in respect to initial policing and the place of the Integrated Competency Framework in your training;
- appreciate the importance of the National Occupational Standards (NOS) within the broader context of your training programme;
- identify the relationship between Units, Elements, and the Range within the NOS;
- know how to claim the achievement of elements and units of the NOS;
- understand how your achievements and plans for future development are identified and recorded;
- appreciate the links between the NOS, the PAC, Independent Patrol, and the stages of qualification;
- develop the underpinning knowledge required for a number of NOS elements, entries for your Learning Diary Phase 1, and a CAR of your SOLAP.

3.1.2 National Occupational Standards

This chapter will provide you with the knowledge required to demonstrate the following NOS elements, either within the first few months of service or during the remaining period of probation:

National Occupational Standard Element

AE1.1   Maintain and develop your own knowledge, skills, and competence

---

3.1.3 IPLDP Induction Modules

This chapter will provide you with resources to support the following induction modules of the IPLDP:

IND 1   Underpinning ethics/values of the police service
IND 3   Develop one's own knowledge and practice

3.1.4 SOLAP

The contents of this chapter are relevant to the 'knowledge' evidence requirements of CAR AE1.

3.1.5 Learning Diary Phases

The contents of this chapter may provide you with stimulus material for completion of your Learning Diary (Phase 1) and the following headings in particular:

- Introduction to the Organization;
- IPLDP.

3.2 Introduction

Before we look in more detail at the qualification process, let us first consider briefly how you are likely to develop and change during your training. So, starting at the beginning, why did you join the police? This may seem an obvious question but spend a few moments thinking about this as Task 1.

> **TASK 1**
>
> List your reasons for joining the police service. If possible, put these into some kind of order with the most important reason first.

You were obviously motivated to join the police. A common way of thinking about motivation is to subdivide it into **extrinsic** and **intrinsic** motivation (although the distinction is not always clear-cut). As the phrase suggests, extrinsic motivation comes from without and involves pull factors on our behaviour and actions. Examples of extrinsic motives for joining the police might include:

- a good wage (particularly in terms of the initial salary, one of the largest in the public sector);
- ample career opportunities, both in terms of rank and role;
- the prospect of early retirement (compared with most occupations) and a good pension.

Intrinsic factors on the other hand come from within and can be thought of as push factors. Examples of intrinsic motives for joining the police might include:

- the desire to do something to improve our society (for example, to protect the weak and the vulnerable);
- to have an interesting and exciting working life;
- to feel more important and to exercise power over others.

(We pass no value judgement on these.)

Extrinsic motivation, although a powerful factor, is probably not enough to guarantee your successful qualification as a police officer. Indeed, there is a debate in academic circles on whether tangible rewards that increase external motivation actually have a reverse effect of undermining intrinsic motivation.

> **TASK 2**
>
> Revisit your list in Task 1 and try to reclassify your reasons as either extrinsic or intrinsic (not always easy!).

Your intrinsic motivation for joining the police might help sustain you through the first difficult months of training until the extrinsic motivation reasons begin to deliver. Joining the police will mean many changes in your working and personal circumstances. You will find yourself juggling training with the rest of your life (such as family commitments), and travel can prove very demanding too. Remember, though it might seem obvious, you do not suddenly become a different person the moment you join the police.

Your ability to undertake the tasks and assume the responsibilities of a police officer will be judged against a number of criteria, including the occupational standards set down for initial policing. Occupational standards are a relatively new concept in policing. There are, however, existing National Occupational Standards (NOS) in many vocational areas, including homeopathy, early years care and education, and mechanical engineering. The NOS define what a person working in a certain occupation is expected to be able to do. These national standards apply across the whole country, so despite variations between forces in terms of training delivery or qualifications structure, the public can have reasonable confidence that a confirmed police officer, after achieving the NOS, has reached at least the same level of competence in Morecambe as in Maidstone.

If you have recently been assessed on academic courses at a college or university then the approach adopted for assessment of the NOS may be unfamiliar to you. Assessment for the NOS is much more like taking a driving test than sitting an examination in biology. First, the emphasis is on evidence of knowing **how to do something**. When you take a driving test, the examiner is not overly concerned with how you managed to gain the skills, but rather that you can actually drive—that you possess those skills. You could have been taught by the most expensive driving school in the country, or by your sister, or (most unlikely) have simply paid close attention to car-chase sequences in films. However, what matters is your ability to drive safely, competently, and to the agreed standards. Although the standards for initial policing do not work in quite the same way as they do for driving, nonetheless the emphasis is very much on the **assessment of the end product**. This is not to suggest that you will not be assessed and judged in other ways; for example, your attitudes and behaviour will come under close scrutiny against the core behavioural areas of the student police officer role profile (see 3.7 below) and you might well be expected to demonstrate that you have reached a certain level in your understanding of legislation and procedure. However, the main emphasis in your formal assessment is likely to be on the final 'threshold' standards that you will need to achieve before you can be confirmed as a constable.

3.3 Training, the Probationary Period, and Confirmation

In Chapter 4 we will look in more detail at how your personal and educational history can affect your learning as a student police officer. It is obvious that no student police officer is a blank canvas on which trainers and assessors are able to paint the idealized picture of a perfect modern-day police officer. For example, the average age of entry to a police force in the UK is around 25 years, and it is likely therefore that a student police officer has a significant personal and employment history, which is not abandoned the moment he/she joins.

It may be a cliché, but undoubtedly policing is not just any other job. When you become a student police officer profound changes occur which inevitably affect your relationships with family and friends. For example, studies have shown that, in Western Europe, about one-third of people have used cannabis on at least one occasion. Many people have also downloaded copyrighted music from the internet without the owners' permission, which is an offence in the UK. It is therefore highly likely that within any particular group of student police officers there will be people who have tried cannabis, illegally downloaded copyrighted music, or committed some other relatively minor offence which has not been detected or prosecuted. You may choose (like a number of politicians) not to reveal whether or not you have smoked cannabis or taken Ecstasy. However, if you have been involved in such activities then at least some of the people around you (including friends) are likely to know all about it. In these circumstances, a student police officer might:

- change his/her circle of friends;
- if questioned, diplomatically explain that his/her own personal behaviour and expectations of others have changed as a result of joining the police;
- continue the behaviour, even though it is against the law; or
- avoid thinking about the issue.

There are of course many other solutions. You will no doubt explore your own personal solution to this—after all, you enter the police service with approximately one-third of your life behind you, and all the baggage this brings.

However, it is still important that you establish and maintain a moral authority (see Chapter 5). This might sound a rather outmoded way of viewing police officers but it remains an important source of your legitimacy (see Chapter 5), particularly in relation to the exercise of powers not available to the rest of society. Establishing and maintaining your moral authority is not the same as claiming that you are better than the rest of society or that you have some special claim on judging what is right or wrong. Rather, it is an acknowledgement of the responsibility of the privileged position that you are placed in and is part, some would argue, of the social contract between the police and the communities they serve.

3.3.1 The Pattern of Training

The IPLDP approach consists of **four phases to the initial training of police officers**, with the following suggested content and activities (Home Office, 2004c):

Phase	Typical activities
Phase 1: Induction	• Introduction to your police force • Practical and organizational needs, eg uniform, Federation, etc • Learning about IPLDP, ethics, and diversity • Undertaking First Aid and Officer Safety Training (eg self-protection) • Introduction to the use of technology, eg radio, PNC, etc • Job-Related Fitness Test
Phase 2: Community Safety and Partnerships	• Receiving a crime and disorder 'package' • Community safety • Undertaking a community engagement
Phase 3: Supervised Patrol	• Learning legislation, policies, and guidelines • Operating the 'Crime Investigation Model' • Undertaking Supervised Patrol
Phase 4: Independent Patrol	• Learning legislation, policies, and guidelines • Developing police practice (particularly local practice) • Undertaking Independent Patrol

The exact pattern of training will vary from force to force but the following diagram describes a *typical* arrangement:

Time line	Stage	IPLDP Phases	Typical duration	Activities	Milestones
Weeks 1–2	Induction	1	2 weeks	Learning about the organization, Health & Safety, Personal Safety Training, First Aid, etc.	Undertaking the Job-Related Fitness Test. Completion of first Learning Diary entries. **Attestation**
Week 3	Community Engagement	2	1 week	Placement with a community group.	Completion of first SOLAP entry.
Week 4	Area familiarization	1	1 week	The work of a BCU.	Completion of more Learning Diary and SOLAP entries.
Weeks 5–10	Taught courses	1 and 3	6 weeks	Legislation, procedures, and other subjects.	Successful completion of assessments.
Weeks 11–12	Supervised Patrol	3	2 weeks	Coaching & assessment.	Beginning **Supervised Patrol.** Completion of some NOS.
Weeks 13–18	Taught courses	1 and 3	6 weeks	Legislation, procedures, and other subjects.	Successful completion of assessments.
Weeks 19–21	Supervised Patrol	3	3 weeks	Coaching & assessment.	Completion of some NOS.
Weeks 22–27	Taught courses	4	6 weeks	Legislation, procedures, and other subjects.	Successful completion of assessments.
Week 28	Supervised Investigation	3	1 week	Coaching & assessment.	Completion of some NOS.
Weeks 29–32	Taught courses	4	4 weeks	Legislation, procedures, and other subjects.	Successful completion of assessments. Completion of NOS units relevant to PAC. Satisfactory completion of PAC. Satisfactory Learning Development Review. **Independent Patrol status**

Time line	Stage	IPLDP Phases	Typical duration	Activities	Milestones
Weeks 33–35	Supervised Patrol and Supervised Investigation	3	3 weeks	Coaching & assessment.	**Beginning Independent Patrol.** Completion of some NOS.
Weeks 36–69	Independent Patrol	4	34 weeks	Patrol and or investigation, assessment against NOS units, taught courses.	Completion of some NOS.
Week 70	Independent Patrol	4	Part of 1 week	Meeting with supervisor.	Second Learning Development Review.
Weeks 71–104	Independent Patrol	4	34 weeks	Patrol and or investigation, assessment against NOS units.	Completion of remaining NOS units. Completion of SOLAP. Final Learning Development Review. **Confirmation**

For Supervised Patrol, Independent Patrol, and confirmation in particular, there are significant variations between forces. For example, in some forces Supervised Patrol occurs earlier than we suggest above, and may also occur more frequently and contain a greater coaching dimension. Similarly, Attestation and Independent Patrol may take place earlier or later than in this typical model. More profound differences include the decision by some forces to concentrate most of the taught elements of training in the first 52 weeks.

Forces often elect to organize their training in terms of a series of courses or modules designed to deliver the requirements of the IPLDP. For example, West Yorkshire Police structures its training in the following way:

A typical structure for training (West Yorkshire Police)

Phase 1 (3 Weeks)

The first two weeks are an induction into the organization at Bishopgarth, Wakefield. During this time recruits will be given more information about what the two years as a student officer will be like. They'll don the uniform for the first time and begin to see the responsibilities and obligations that come with it. A working knowledge of the Highway Code is an important part of everyday policing, so there's a Highway Code test to do during this first fortnight.

This isn't the same as the DSA Theory Test, but their website provides some useful study aids. We provide students with a copy of the Highway Code when they join, so there's no need to buy one. Also, there's an opportunity to resit for those who aren't successful first time.

On week 3 the uniform is set aside for a while and they change location to the University of Huddersfield where they begin to develop the knowledge and understanding required by the modern Police Officer by looking at wider social issues affecting policing.

Phase 2 (4 Weeks)

Students continue at the University for a further three weeks covering such areas as: Equality, Diversity & Rights; Professional Development and delving further into Social and Community Issues. The final week of this phase consists of a five-day community placement, based in the Division (area) to which they'll be posted. They are there to observe and learn about a section of the community that they're likely to encounter and be expected to engage with, when on patrol. This allows them the opportunity to interact with the communities outside the policing context. They don't wear uniform at all during Phase 2.

Phase 3 (24 Weeks)

This phase begins with 13 weeks of Legislation, Procedures and Guidelines training back at Bishopgarth. This is achieved through a combination of classroom-based training and practical exercises. It includes two weeks of detailed IT training in the key computer systems in general use within West Yorkshire Police. During this fortnight, one day is set aside for Public Order training at our dedicated training site. By the end of this part students look forward to a week of annual leave. On their return from leave they begin gaining practical experience with a tutor constable in a Professional Development Unit (PDU) at an Operational Division for at least ten weeks. This may be extended if necessary, to accommodate individual development needs.

Phase 4 (Up to the End of Year 2)

Once a student is judged as fit for independent patrol, which is measured against set criteria, they commence Phase 4 and head out on their own for the first time. This doesn't mean they are alone; they are part of a team. Students will be monitored and assisted by colleagues and supervisors throughout the rest of the two years and beyond. During the second year they also receive a further five weeks of formal training which is split between Bishopgarth and the University; with a further community placement week. These will be grouped into three fortnights, spaced through the second year.

Students actually spend 75 per cent of the first two years working at division, gaining practical experience.

(West Yorkshire Police, 2009, reproduced by kind permission of West Yorkshire Police.)

TASK 3

Find out about the pattern of training in your force and how it relates to IPLDP Phases 1 to 4.

3.3.2 The Probationary Period

The probationary period refers to the time that you are technically under or in probation. You are not a confirmed constable, you are still undertaking initial training, and you are subject to the regulations that apply to probationers (see 6.15 below). The normal probationary period for full-time student police officers is two years. Part-time student police officer training (now becoming increasingly available) will have an extended probationary period calculated according to Annex C of the Police Regulations 2003; training at half the full-time rate will take twice as long.

As with other aspects of initial training, the length of the probationary period may change in the future. It is expected that accredited prior learning (APL) or prior experiential learning (APEL) will shorten the length of training and the probationary period for some student police officers. This may be particularly important for PCSOs and special constables who subsequently join up as police officers. (This is already beginning to happen in some forces.) Foreshortened training through APL and APEL might also be open to trainees joining from other professions, or through 'approved' Foundation degree routes.

3.3.3 Independent Patrol

Attaining the right to undertake Independent Patrol is a key milestone in your development as a student police officer. It means that, although your training is far from over, you can undertake many police functions associated with fully qualified (confirmed) police officers without the need for constant supervision.

Independent Patrol normally occurs after about week 30 in training, although this does vary significantly from force to force. As with many aspects of initial police training, the timing of Independent Patrol remains under discussion. (The traditional approach was simply to say that it would, all other criteria being satisfied, happen on a certain week, but this makes less sense in an era of competence-based occupational standards.) A number of written reports have also highlighted problems in some forces in organizing and assessing the Independent Patrol phase of initial training. For example, a report for Skills for Justice noted that:

> [i]t is apparent that this phase of a Student Officer's development is still causing difficulties for some forces particularly where they are posted to small policing units without supervision and/or a dedicated assessor and as such officers are left without support or knowing how and when they will be assessed (Skills for Justice, 2007a, p 7).

Your suitability for Independent Patrol is assessed against various criteria, including the Police Action Checklist (the PAC, see 3.9 below) and normally takes place after a Learning Development Review (see 3.8.3 below). As you would expect, the main aim is to ensure that you are competent and safe to undertake Independent Patrol, including holding the appropriate values and behaviour (for example, in the seven core behavioural areas of respect for race and diversity, team working, community and customer focus, effective communication, problem solving, personal responsibility, and resilience: see 3.7 below). Although the PAC is a key component in this, it is important to realize that the PAC (according to the IPLDP) is only one trigger for Independent Patrol and does not automatically lead to it. The PAC is described in more detail in 3.9 below.

You will receive confirmation of competence from your Professional Development Unit (PDU) supervisor/assessor against the PAC during phases 1, 2, and 3 of your training (using the IPLDP terminology). In addition some forces may also expect the acquisition of advanced driving skills before you are granted Independent Patrol status. Finally, note that you will probably receive a pay rise when you achieve Independent Patrol status!

3.3.4 Confirmation

After two years (104 weeks) you should expect to be deemed 'fit for confirmation of appointment'—that is, you've made it! In our view, the criteria for confirmation under the IPLDP are currently less than clear and so you should look towards your own employer for a definitive statement of what is required. However, some or all of the following are likely to be involved:

- the attainment of all, or a subset of, the NOS for initial police training (see 3.6 below);
- the attainment of the seven core behavioural areas (see 3.7 below);
- the satisfactory completion of the SOLAP (see 3.8 below);
- the satisfactory completion of the PAC (see 3.9 below);
- a 'successful' final Learning Development Review (see 3.8.3);
- a minimum academic attainment;
- other requirements such as a level of fitness (the Job-Related Fitness Test), ability to administer First Aid, and being able to drive a car to a certain standard.

(Note that these requirements are not mutually exclusive but instead interrelate and overlap. For example, the SOLAP is likely to cross-reference with the PAC, and the Learning Development Review will involve the seven core behavioural areas. The list could also be summarized in IPLDP language as the successful completion of Phases 1 to 4 inclusive.)

This confirmation may also be linked to the attainment of a qualification, such as an NVQ Level 3 or 4 or a Foundation degree. The government has declared its intention to have a national minimum qualification (NMQ) for all successful student police officers who reach confirmation; the Home Office wrote to all Chief Police Officers in 2005 to explain that the NMQ would be a Policing NVQ Level 3 and a Policing NVQ Level 4. However, the situation is now less clear after the proposed reduction in the number of NOS Units required for successful completion of initial training (see 1.5 above and 3.6 below). There is likely to be a revised award replacing the existing NVQs, to be introduced during 2010 or 2011. The new award will use the new national Qualifications and Credit Framework (QCF) and hence will be credit-based and achievable by accumulating smaller units and in more flexible ways. The QCF embraces qualifications from Entry level (pre-GCSE) to Level 8 (PhD level).

3.4 Assessment

In our view, assessment can be one of the most confusing aspects of initial training. For this reason you are strongly advised to read carefully the information your force provides about assessment, and to ask about the assessment strategies and criteria if you are unclear. A key question might be 'How do I qualify for confirmation as a police officer?' Do not expect a simple answer.

In essence you may be assessed in the following ways:

Assessment focus	How likely?
Against the 22 NOS, or a subset of them.	Almost certain.
Against the PAC headings.	Almost certain.
Grading in your Learning Development Review (or your force equivalent) against skills and the core behavioural areas.	Likely; grades used may be 'exceptional', 'competent', or 'not yet displayed' (or similar grades used by your force).
Your practical skills such as Officer Safety and advanced driving and your physical fitness (a follow up to the Job-Related Fitness Test undertaken during induction).	Very likely, although the detail will vary.
Satisfactory completion of the SOLAP against certain criteria.	A completion requirement is very likely, but the standard of work required may vary.
Against some other criteria, linked with knowledge attainment.	Not certain—if you are tested in this way, the assessment instruments used are likely to include MCQs (multiple choice questions), unseen examinations, or assignments.

You also need to ask your trainers the following questions:

- Is there a pass mark?
- What is the pass mark?
- What happens if I don't pass?

Whatever the forms of assessment it is important that you are clear on **what** is being formally assessed. For example, there are over 250 learning outcomes in the IPLDP Induction Modules alone, and the LPG 1 module has over 75!

Your progression to full qualification as a police officer is inextricably linked with the gaining of the National Occupational Standards in initial policing. The standards set out the skills and abilities that you will need to demonstrate before being confirmed, although the detail of this is subject to local force policy.

Contrary to some impressions, achieving the NOS does not automatically lead to a National Vocational Qualification (NVQ), although some forces do provide access to NVQs at Levels 3 and/or 4 in Policing. Alternatively, your police force may have chosen to link the attainment of the NOS to the gaining of a Foundation degree, usually in association with a local university or college. Some other forces have decided, at least for the time being, against the need for any form of academic or vocational accreditation for their student police officers. The Home Office is, however, committed to requiring a minimum qualification for student police officers.

We therefore examine in some depth the National Occupational Standards for initial police training, as these standards are central to all the various forms of police training. The NOS are placed within the context of the Integrated Competency Framework (ICF). We will also examine in further detail other key aspects of the way your competence is measured and how you are assessed, including the Student Officer Learning and Assessment Portfolio (the SOLAP) and the Police Action Checklist (the PAC).

3.5 The Integrated Competency Framework and the National Occupational Standards

The **Integrated Competency Framework** (ICF) was developed by Skills for Justice. As with many of these things, it all may appear at first to be far more complicated than it is. It is important, however, to understand it because your future as a police officer will depend on your assessments against the NOS and the ICF during your probation. Failure to attain the overall standard required may mean that you have to repeat modules or even whole phases (in IPLDP speak) sometimes called re-coursing, or your probationary period may have to be extended (see 3.3 above and 3.12 below). Worst of all, you may have to leave policing altogether.

Putting aside these dire warnings, let us begin with an understanding of what the concepts **competence** and **competencies** mean, because you will be meeting them frequently.

> **TASK 4**
>
> Look **competence** and **competencies** up in a dictionary (such as the Shorter Oxford English Dictionary, or an internet site such as Wikipedia at <http://www.en.wikipedia.org>).

For **competence**, you should have found something which conveyed the sense of fitness, of 'sufficiency of qualification' (Shorter OED, 2002) or of capacity (meaning ability). But there is a much simpler sense in which the police use the term. By competence they mean generally your ability to do the job.

On the other hand, **competencies** are the individual assessed skills or assets you have for the job. When we refer to the Integrated Competency Framework, we mean all the skills you have learned, the qualities which you have, and your attitudes and behaviours, and how they all come together. The integrated part simply means that the competencies are bedded into the **requirements** (or NOS, see 3.6 below) for a particular role. The role we are going to examine in depth is obviously that of the **student police officer**.

You trainers may sometimes use the acronym **KUSAB** when discussing your learning, which is short for:

```
K Knowledge
U Understanding
S Skills
A Attitudes
B Behaviours
```

KUSAB (introduced to the police by the Police Training Council) is linked with competencies in the sense that your competence in any field (your ability to do the job) will be the product of how much you know, how much you understand, what skills you have, and your attitudes and behaviours.

KUSAB also relates to diversity (discussed further in 4.9 below). The assessment of KUSAB is very much geared to how you, as a trainee police officer, demonstrate your attitudes and what behaviours you show (see 3.7 below) when dealing with people who are different to you in some way. But before the attitudes and behaviours can be developed, the knowledge and understanding need to be in place, informed by the skills for the job. You cannot have one without the other, and it is only relatively recently that the police service accepted that all parts of KUSAB are interdependent; all aspects of KUSAB are needed if you are to demonstrate the required level of competence.

You are currently a student police officer and are developing the core responsibilities needed by a police officer (a confirmed constable). The Skills for Justice ICF defines your core responsibilities in the following way:

Core responsibilities for a student police officer

Core responsibilities	Activities
Community Safety	Conduct patrol.
Police Operations	Prepare for and participate in planned policing operations. Provide an initial response to incidents.
Investigation	Conduct investigation. Interview suspects. Interview victims and witnesses. Provide care for victims and witnesses. Search person(s) or personal property. Search vehicles, premises, and land.
Custody and Prosecution	Complete prosecution procedure. Conduct custody reception procedures (as arresting officer). Prepare and present case files. Present evidence in court and at other hearings.
Personal Responsibility	Comply with Health and Safety legislation. Maintain standards for security of information. Maintain standards of professional practice. Promote equality, diversity and human rights in working practices. Provide an effective response recognizing the needs of all communities.
Intelligence	Use intelligence to support policing objectives.
Health, Safety and Welfare	Provide first aid.

You will see from the various entries in the table above that KUSAB is woven through all activities that make up the core responsibilities. In practice, each of the entries has to be evidenced through a portfolio of work so that assessment may be made of your achievements. Correspondingly, areas for improvement can be identified as can areas requiring development (after all, if you have not yet assisted at, or managed, a road traffic collision (RTC), there will be an inevitable gap in your competence).

You will also have noticed that some of the entries represent **continuous themes** (the 'golden thread') that are relevant in many tasks; a good example is Health and Safety. Whether you are moving vehicles onto the hard shoulder after a RTC or searching premises, you have to know about the Health and Safety legal requirements as well as the safe practice. You need to be aware of potential risks such as the chance encounter of a needle hidden in a pocket when searching a drug addict, and you also need to know what to do in such a situation. Some elements seem to mask the depth of KUSAB which you have to demonstrate, such as 'interview suspects'; this is covered by a whole mass of legislation and also involves a complex battery of skills that you will be expected to deploy to a high standard. Look, for example, at 12.5 below for a detailed description and examination of what is involved in interviewing suspects.

In summary, the table above represents only the 'headlines' of the skills, understanding, knowledge, and attributes which you will be expected to demonstrate in full and detailed measure as a police officer. Many of the components of the core responsibilities are dealt with in detail in the pages which follow.

3.6   **The NOS Units for Initial Policing**

There are currently 22 Units of National Occupational Standards that underpin the initial training for student police officers (although the number of Units may change from 2010 onwards). The following is a list of all the relevant Units and their constituent elements:

Relevant NOS units for initial policing

Unit	Unit title	Elements
AA1	Promote equality and value diversity	AA1.1 Promote equality and value diversity
AB1	Communicate effectively with people	AB1.1 Develop and maintain communication with people AB1.2 Maintain the security of information
AE1	Maintain and develop your own knowledge, skills, and competence	AE1.1 Maintain and develop your own knowledge, skills, and competence
AF1	Ensure your own actions reduce risks to health and safety	AF1.1 Identify the hazards and evaluate the risks in the workplace AF1.2 Reduce the risks to health and safety in the workplace
BE2	Provide initial support to victims, survivors, and witnesses and assess their needs for further support	BE2.1 Provide initial support to victims, survivors, and witnesses BE2.2 Assess the needs and wishes of victims, survivors, and witnesses for further support
CA1	Use law enforcement actions in a fair and justified way	CA1.1 Apply principles of reasonable suspicion or belief CA1.2 Use law enforcement actions proportionately CA1.3 Use law enforcement actions fairly
CB1	Gather and submit information that has the potential to support law enforcement objectives	CB1.1 Gather and submit information that has the potential to support law enforcement objectives
CD1	Provide an initial law enforcement response to incidents	CD1.1 Gather information and plan a response CD1.2 Respond to incidents
CD3	Prepare for, and participate in, planned law enforcement operations	CD3.1 Prepare for, and participate in, planned law enforcement operations
CD5	Arrest, detain, or report individuals	CD5.1 Arrest, detain, or report individuals
CI101	Conduct priority and volume investigations	CI101.1 Conduct priority and volume investigations
CJ101	Interview victims and witnesses in relation to priority and volume investigations	CJ101.1 Plan and prepare interviews with victims and witnesses CJ101.2 Conduct interviews with victims and witnesses CJ101.3 Evaluate interviews with victims and witnesses and carry out post-interview processes
CJ201	Interview suspects in relation to priority and volume investigations	CJ201.1 Plan and prepare interviews with suspects CJ201.2 Conduct interviews with suspects CJ201.3 Evaluate interviews with suspects and carry out post-interview processes
CK1	Search individuals	CK1.1 Search individuals
CK2	Search vehicles, premises, and open spaces	CK2.1 Prepare to search vehicles, premises, and open spaces CK2.2 Conduct searches of vehicles, premises, and open spaces
DA5	Present evidence in court and at other hearings	DA5.1 Prepare for court or other hearings DA5.2 Present evidence to court or other hearings
DA6	Prepare and submit case files	DA6.1 Prepare case files DA6.2 Submit case files and progress enquiries

Unit	Unit title	Elements
GC10	Manage conflict	GC10.1 Apply conflict management skills and techniques GC10.2 Use personal safety skills and equipment
2G4	Finalize investigations	2G4.1 Finalize investigations
2K1	Escort detained persons	2K1.1 Escort detained persons
2K2	Present detained persons to custody	2K2.1 Present detained persons for custody process 2K2.2 Conduct initial custody reception actions
4G4	Administer First Aid	4G4.1 Respond to the needs of casualties with minor injuries 4G4.2 Respond to the needs of casualties with major injuries 4G4.3 Respond to the needs of unconscious casualties 4G4.4 Perform cardio-pulmonary resuscitation (CPR)

Note that an additional Unit 1D4, concerned with protecting children, may or may not feature in your assessment although you will certainly learn about the underlying knowledge and skills required for this Unit. You should be aware that the requirements for assessments relating to the NOS can change quite quickly, and you should check the current situation with your force, in terms of the number of Units and their content. There have been a number of agreed changes to the existing arrangements for the NOS Units, scheduled to be implemented in 2010. These changes include reducing the number of units to 9 or 10, from the current 22 (see 1.5 above for a list of the new Units). However, the reduction is not likely to be as dramatic as it may at first appear, as at least some of the new Units will be 'fatter' than the existing ones, incorporating aspects of the more 'generic' Units (such as AA1 and AF1), and some competencies within current Units (such as 4G4) will instead be assessed through other means. Throughout the remainder of this Handbook we use the existing (2009) arrangements—that is 22 NOS Units.

If your training includes attainment of an NVQ Level 3 and an NVQ Level 4 in Policing then you may find that you are working towards the 2003 NOS Units for initial Policing. In this case the numbering and some of the detail may differ from the list above (see 1.5 above).

Some of the Units are the same as those used by other occupational groups—for example, in Health and Safety and First Aid (which partly explains the unusual Unit numbering system). This makes sense as a number of tasks performed by a police officer will be similar to those performed by parallel occupational groups. Indeed there are likely to be many circumstances when you find yourself working alongside other professionals trained to the same occupational standard. You will also find that some other professional requirements on you, for example the CARs and PIP Level 1, are also linked closely with a subset of the NOS.

Each Unit is a self-contained and self-standing expression of a particular part of the role of police constable, together with a description of how competence for this part of the role can be assessed. The Units are not just concerned with 'can do' activities but (implicitly at least) also attempt to infer attitudes and behaviours. For example, Unit AA1 is concerned with your ability to 'promote equality and value diversity'. Without being unduly pedantic, we suggest that to 'promote and value' is a different type of skill from being able to 'apply handcuffs to a prisoner in a safe and secure manner'. So you need to be aware of the wide-ranging nature of the Units, particularly in terms of the evidence you must produce.

Unit AA1 is also an example of a holistic Unit which you will be assessed against during the whole period of training. These holistic Units link to the more technically-oriented Units and tend not to be assessed in isolation but alongside the other Units. For example, your force is likely to look for evidence against Unit AA1 whilst you are also engaged with Unit CD1.

Units are subdivided into a number of **elements**. For example, Unit CA1 is subdivided into three elements:

> **Unit CA1 Use law enforcement actions in a fair and justified way**
>
> CA1.1 Apply principles of reasonable suspicion or belief.
> CA1.2 Use law enforcement actions proportionately.
> CA1.3 Use law enforcement actions fairly.

To gain Unit CA1, it follows that you need to achieve each of the three elements. There are a total of 40 elements for initial policing, with between 1 and 4 elements to a Unit.

You are unlikely to achieve elements (or whole Units) early on in your training (although this is not impossible). Most forces appear to have structured their programmes to enable you to achieve elements and then whole Units after a few months, with the majority of Units being achieved in the second year of training.

3.6.1   How You Will Achieve a Unit

You achieve an element or Unit when you are competent to do so. Assessment of competence is not based on a pass mark system. Instead, you achieve the standard when it has been confirmed that you have provided reliable, valid, and sufficient evidence (in the correct format) to demonstrate your competence. Think of the analogy with the burden of proof in the courts—we are talking here of beyond reasonable doubt and **not** the balance of probabilities, but remember also that it is the quality of evidence that is important, not the volume.

Competence may be achieved at different times for different people. Indeed, you could be given credit if you can already meet a standard (perhaps through working as a special constable before joining as a full-time student police officer) through a process called the accreditation of prior learning (APL), or prior experiential learning (APEL), but to date this has been difficult to implement. However, your force will almost certainly have systems in place to encourage (and even require) you to plan the phasing of your assessment against the Units, according to a given schedule. This is relatively uncharted territory for the police service and the 'tying' of at least a subset of the NOS to confirmation (see 3.3 above) may well give rise to some adjustments to timescales. However, in some forces you may be expected, for example, to achieve 11 of the standards in the first year of training and the remainder in the second and final year.

3.6.2   Units and Elements

Here we look in detail at one particular Unit and its elements. We have chosen Unit CD1 (note that if you are working with the 2003 Units this will be listed as Unit 2C1):

> **Unit CD1 Provide an initial police response to incidents**
>
> CD1.1 Gather information and plan a response.
> CD1.2 Respond to incidents.

As you can see, this Unit has two elements, CD1.1 and CD1.2, and the attainment of these two elements will lead to the attainment of the Unit itself.

We have chosen CD1 for a number of reasons:

- You are likely to encounter it relatively early in your training (although not achieve it until sometime later).
- It has more than one element and so the interrelationship between elements is more easily illustrated.
- It demonstrates the links between the NOS and other aspects of your training, for example the PAC.
- It links with one of the holistic Units, AA1.

First, an overview of the Unit itself. Skills for Justice provide the following summary:

Unit CD1

This unit covers providing an initial response to incidents. The unit is not rank-specific and applies to all persons responding to incidents. The incidents covered by this unit include crime, non-crime, and traffic incidents. You must be able to deal with these types of incidents.

You will need to be able to gather information on the incident. Such information may include, for example, history, dangers, and witness information. Based on the information you have obtained you will need to be able to establish the nature of the incident, and plan your actions accordingly. This process will often happen fairly quickly en route to the incident.

You will need to take into account the health and safety of self and others during the incident. If it is a major or critical incident, and you are the first on the scene, you will need to take interim control until relieved by the appropriate person (Skills for Justice, 2008).

As you can see, it is a wide-ranging Unit and central to the work of a student police officer. The summary of a Unit usually contains the following information:

- a general description of the Unit, in terms of the kind of activities involved;
- any links with any other Units. In this case there are certainly implicit links with other Units in the suite for initial policing, but none are explicitly specified;
- the target group for the Unit—who is it for? The summary makes it clear that the 'Unit is not rank-specific and applies to all persons responding to incidents.' This obviously includes student police officers training to be confirmed constables.

You can see that plenty of learning is required (including practising skills and acquiring knowledge and understanding) before you will be able to demonstrate your attainment of Unit CD1, probably during Supervised or Independent Patrol. First, you will need adequate knowledge of legislation and police procedure concerning a whole range of incidents ('crime, non-crime and traffic incidents'). Hence you will need at least a working knowledge of the legislation surrounding public order offences (eg s 4 of the Public Order Act 1986), violent incidents (eg s 47 of the Offences Against the Person Act 1861—Actual Bodily Harm), and so on. You will also need to be familiar with:

- police procedure, such as the correct use of your pocket notebook and making police statements ('you will need to be able to gather information on the incident');
- health and safety ('take into account the health and safety of self and others');
- critical incident management ('take interim control' and 'establish the nature of the incident, and plan your actions accordingly');
- intelligence ('history'); and
- human rights and respect for diversity (as always).

This knowledge and understanding is likely to be incrementally achieved during your first year or so of training (and is covered throughout this Handbook).

In terms of skills, you will certainly need to know how to communicate with the control room and your fellow officers, and you might need your personal safety training too. You may also need to know how to support witnesses and victims, how to protect the scene (for forensic purposes), and possibly how to administer first aid.

It is now probably obvious to you that a Unit such as CD1 is not achieved overnight. It is a major milestone towards your confirmation as a competent police officer.

Unit CD1 has two elements:

NOS Elements of Unit CD1

CD1.1   Gather information and plan a response.
CD1.2   Respond to incidents.

These effectively subdivide CD1 into logical stages. Element CD1.1 is concerned with all those actions (mental as well as physical) that lead up to actual attendance at an incident—for example between the report of an incident being passed to you and your actual arrival at the scene. Element CD1.2 then takes over, and is concerned with your response to the incident itself. It makes sense to group these two elements together since the quality of your response is likely to partly depend on the quality of your planning. The Unit is quite realistic about when this planning is likely to occur: 'this process will often happen fairly quickly en route to the incident'. This is a reflection of the fact that much of the work of the student police officer, particularly whilst on Supervised Patrol, is involved with so-called 'reactive' policing.

TASK 5

Use the internet to locate and download the specifications for Unit 4G4 'Administer First Aid' (you might want to start at the site <http://www.skillsforjustice.com>). What are the knowledge and understanding requirements?

3.6.3   Evidence Towards an Element and Unit

The evidence for attainment of a Unit features at the level of the element. There are three important concepts to be grasped here: **performance criteria**, **range**, and **evidence requirements**.

3.6.3.1   Performance criteria

For each element, the performance criteria are the basic building blocks of the element and describe in more detail what actually has to be demonstrated. The performance criteria tend to be behavioural 'can do' descriptions, but are by no means always of this nature.

In terms of Unit CD1, element CD1.1 has the following performance criteria:

Performance Criteria of CD1.1—Gather information and plan a response

To meet the standard, you should:

1. identify and assess relevant information on the **incident**;
2. establish the nature of the **incident** based on the available information;
3. obtain any necessary additional information for the response to the **incident**;
4. prioritize and plan your actions according to the nature of the **incident**;
5. respond to the **incident** within the appropriate timescales and according to current policy;
6. provide the necessary information to **others** regarding the incident.

Notice the use of words such as identify, establish, obtain, prioritize, respond, and provide. These are more concrete in nature and hence considered more susceptible to direct observation and measurement. In this way, element CD1.1 has been opened up and made less abstract and more detailed. Notice also that certain words within the criteria are in bold; these relate to the 'range' (see 3.6.3.2 below).

In practice, each performance criterion is also put into context. For example, suppose you are undertaking Supervised Patrol and you and your supervisor are called to a road traffic collision. What does performance criterion 1 mean in this context? You would need to 'identify and assess relevant information on the incident'.

First, you need to 'identify... relevant information'. What do you need to know in advance of attending this RTC? Has all this information been given to you? Probably most of the relevant information has been provided already, for example, location, number of vehicles, and so on, but you need to identify precisely what is needed and to ensure that you have all this information (if possible). This might mean that you need to ask the control room or colleagues for more information (see 'others' in the description of the range below). For example, what are the weather conditions at the incident and how could thick fog be taken into account? Remember, you will not (or should not) be on your own during these circumstances; you will be under the supervision of more experienced colleagues.

Second, you need to 'assess relevant information' which means establishing its value. For example, you might decide that the information you have been given concerning the location of the incident is ambiguous and needs to be clarified. Of course, it is possible that exact locations are simply not known at this stage (because of the confusion surrounding the event). What is important however, in the context of element CD1.1, is that you have demonstrated that you have assessed the information and identified the problem.

3.6.3.2 Range

The range is a description of the kinds of circumstances in which you need to demonstrate each performance criterion.

For CD1.1 the range specified by Skills for Justice is as follows:

Range of CD1.1

1. **Incident**
   (a) crime
   (b) non-crime
   (c) traffic
2. **Others**
   (a) members of the public
   (b) control room
   (c) line management
   (d) other specialists, including external agencies
   (e) colleagues

Specifying the range in this way means that, in practice, it is rare that evidence from a single incident will be sufficient to prove CD1.1 so you will be expected to demonstrate competence in a number of different incidents, for example domestic violence, road traffic incidents, and public order incidents. You will also be required to show how this competence is employed when dealing with others, for example the control room and members of the public. In this way, it can be reasonably certain that your demonstration of competence is not down to chance or limited to just certain types of incident.

3.6.4 Evidence Requirements

A Unit also specifies the **evidence requirements**, setting out in detail how much evidence you will need and the sort of evidence required (for example from simulated incidents or role plays: see 3.6.4.2 below). Evidence requirements are particularly important if your training is linked to an NVQ. The evidence requirements for some Units (such as CD1) may be found in the 2003 or the 2008 list of Units on the Skills for Justice website.

For element CD1.1, Skills for Justice specify the following evidence requirements:

Evidence Requirements for CD1.1 (2C1 in the 2003 suite of Units)

For element CD1.1 Gather information and plan a response.
From the range ... you must show that you:

- have planned a response to five types of incident;*
- have provided the necessary information to all others.

*Items from the range not covered by performance evidence should be supported by knowledge evidence.

Note here the reference to the range that we described earlier. The evidence requirements state that you need to document (or otherwise evidence) your planning for **at least five** incidents, including at least one of each of the following types of incident:

(a) crime
(b) non-crime
(c) traffic.

(You may use more than five incidents to provide the evidence required.)

For the attainment of the overall unit CD1 (referred to as 2C1 in the 2003 suite of Units), Skills for Justice specify the following:

Evidence Requirements for Unit CD1

1. Where simulations are used for performance evidence, these should properly reflect the requirements of real working situations.
2. You must practically demonstrate in your work that you have met the standard for providing an initial police response to incidents on at least three separate occasions.

Hence you need to have both elements CD1.1 and CD1.2 signed off (as successfully achieved) on at least three separate occasions in order to be awarded Unit CD1. Further, the emphasis here is very much on real examples rather than the use of simulation, although the latter is permitted within limits.

3.6.4.1 Types of evidence

You will need to produce evidence that you have met the requirements of an element and Unit. This is regardless of whether your training is linked with an NVQ, a Foundation degree, or has no formal link with a qualification.

Producing evidence demonstrates that, as far as can be judged, you have attained the competence described. Unless properly organized, this can be a tedious process, particularly if it involves aspects of your work which would not normally need to be documented. Your more experienced colleagues will be making decisions in their heads and, in some cases at least, will not be asked to document and evidence the reasons for their actions. You may think that there is enough paperwork in policing as it is. However, during the period in which you are proving your competence, you need to document the evidence that supports your claims of 'knowing how to do the job' so that others can see how you are progressing. After all, they cannot read your mind.

You may be assisted in the process of identifying evidence for a Unit through the use of a Professional Discussion with your assessor in which you will look at a particular Unit or Units and discuss the evidence you have assembled.

The type and form of evidence depends in part on the particular element but is likely to include at least some of the following:

- direct observation;
- questioning by an assessor;
- testimony from witnesses;
- written evidence or 'work products';
- artefacts.

Further explanation of these is given below. (Note that the use of the terms 'witnesses', 'testimony', and 'evidence' is potentially confusing in the context of police training, but you are likely to hear these terms used).

Direct observation is a very common form of evidence. Put simply, a suitably qualified person, normally your assessor constable or PDU assessor (the terms vary from force to force), observes you carrying out a particular work-related task and confirms that your actions meet the standards. The assessor will use the criteria to help decide whether the evidence is appropriate and sufficient. Before and after the event the assessor will explain the process, and may also question you. However, during the actual observation the assessor should be unobtrusive (as your 'co-pilot'), although they are likely to intervene if your 'plane' is about to crash!

Questioning by an assessor is often used to check that you have the relevant underpinning knowledge for the element under consideration. On occasions an assessor may use written questions, although most assessors avoid referring to this as a test.

Testimony from witnesses can provide evidence to show that you have met the requirements of an element. The witnesses are most likely to be your more experienced and qualified police colleagues, but even fellow student police officers who have already achieved the relevant element are able to provide witness testimony. However, in all cases the witnesses need to be credible, and occupationally competent for the relevant Unit.

Written evidence or 'work products' come in a wide variety of forms. Common sources of written evidence include police statements you have written, your PNB entries, pro formae you have completed (for example FPNs), and reports. The assessor will obviously be interested in how far these products demonstrate the performance criteria of an element, but will also be checking on aspects such as authenticity (checking that it is your work and not 'borrowed' from elsewhere).

Artefacts are tangible objects such as photographs (for example of a cordon you established) or tape recordings (of an interaction with a member of the public for example). This evidence is indexed and cross-referenced in your SOLAP. Artefact evidence requires contextualization— you will be expected to provide a written description of the background and context for the artefact.

3.6.4.2 Simulation

In some circumstances your force may consider it more appropriate to test your competence by using a simulation or role play rather than by observing you in a real-life situation. This is not just because of safety considerations; it may also be difficult to arrange the necessary circumstances for you whilst on Supervised Patrol, and some situations are so complex it makes sense to use simulation for each separate element. Certain first-aid skills are more appropriately evidenced through simulation (using realistic mannequins) than for real.

However, according to the rules of Skills for Justice, the scope for simulation is very limited (only certain elements of Units BE2, CD1, CK1, CK2, GC10, and 4G4 allow for any kind of simulation). Many elements will not permit simulation to be used in lieu of the real thing (and in the case of NVQs these rules are mandatory).

If simulation is used to assess you against an element then you may need to think carefully; simulations, unless particularly carefully designed and organized, always run the risk of any hypothetical scenario (recollect those difficult interview questions that began with 'imagine the following')— that is, missing the rich detail of real-life contexts.

TASK 6

Is simulation allowed as evidence towards element 2K2.2, to 'conduct initial custody reception actions'?

3.6.5 Claiming Achievement of an Element or Unit

Finally, a few pointers on claiming achievement of an element or Unit:

- **Be proactive in claiming competence towards an element**: Familiarize yourself with the performance criteria—it is in your own interest. Do not slip into thinking that the standards are things that just happen to you; rather, think of the whole process as a series of opportunities to demonstrate your skills. Remember too that the elements of certain

Units may be demonstrated outside the context of traditional policing—for example, during a community placement in your second year of training. Although policy does differ from force to force, ask whether a suitably qualified person from outside your force is able to confirm competence.

- **Speak to one of your tutors** if you feel that you do not have sufficient opportunity (particularly on Supervised Patrol) to demonstrate attainment of an element, or if you feel that your assessor has it wrong. Forces are required to follow certain quality assurance procedures in terms of the NOS and these will almost certainly include the right to appeal against an assessment decision.

- **Be as efficient as possible**: A single incident that you have attended, or one simple task that you have completed could potentially be used as the basis of evidence for a whole range of elements and Units.

- **Do not leave it to the last minute**: If you leave it too long, you will discover that, like stamp collecting, you will have many 'doubles' for CD5.1 but you are still looking for the elusive 2G4.1!

- **Consider appealing** if you consider a decision to be unfair or unreasonable. All police forces will have a published policy concerning appeals against assessment decisions which set out the grounds for an appeal and the processes involved. Normally the appeal is made to the person responsible for the PDU where the decision was made rather than to the assessor who made the decision.

3.6.6 When Should I Achieve a Unit?

There is no simple answer to this question; when you achieve a Unit will depend on your own circumstances and the arrangements put into place by your force. However, the IPLDP suggests the following timetable (we have used IPLDP notation but your force might use other means of describing the phases of training and we have also updated the titles of Units):

NOS Units and IPLDP Phases

Phase 1 Induction

Evidence of the knowledge aspects (not the whole Unit) of Units AA1, AB1, AE1, AF1, and CD5 and the whole of Unit 4G4 (the First Aid Unit).

Phase 2 Community Safety and Partnerships

Evidence towards the knowledge, performance criteria, and range of Units AA1 and AB1.

Phase 3 Supervised Patrol

Evidence towards completion of all remaining Units.

Phase 4 Independent Patrol

The emphasis during this phase is towards completion of all required NOS Units.

The advice of your police force is likely to be more detailed.

3.7 The Student Police Officer Role Profile

In 3.5 above we glanced at the competencies and KUSAB that are used to assess your capability across a range of tasks, but principally in the role of patrol constable. Some of the core responsibilities relate to the knowledge, understanding, and skills (KUS) part of your learning. The remainder of the core responsibilities relate to attitudes and behaviours, the A and B of KUSAB. Finally, note that as a result of the 'stocktake' of IPLDP conducted in 2008, the assessment of behaviours is likely to be more closely linked with the assessment of competence from March 2010 onwards.

The attitudes (and some of the associated behaviours) required of a police officer are covered in many other places in this Handbook. We refer you to Chapter 14 which deals with your potential development as a police officer once your initial training is over, and to 4.9 and 5.18 below, about diversity and the attitudes and behaviours you will need when interacting with people who are different to you, or who may be vulnerable. You should also read 12.5 below about interviewing, which deals with how to approach and obtain responses from vulnerable victims and witnesses. As you can see, the principles embodied in KUSAB and the integrated competencies are woven tightly into this Handbook.

3.7.1 Behaviours Required of Police Officers

To follow our theme, we shall now look at the behavioural areas designated for the role of **patrol constable**. However, unlike specific job requirements which may change between roles, or have different emphases placed upon them (such as investigation for detectives, or driving competencies for traffic officers), the specified behaviours for patrol do not vary much between roles. This is because they are seen as **generic** and will require consistent application of the sorts of responses we have already discussed. The key behavioural areas are shown below:

Patrol constable—Key behaviour areas

Behaviour area	Behaviour	Minimum grade required
Achieving results	Problem solving	C
	Personal responsibility	B
	Resilience	A
Working with others	Respect for race and diversity	A
	Team working	C
	Community and customer focus	C
	Effective communication	B

It is important that we look behind the headlines at this point, and discuss what forms of behaviours are expected.

TASK 7

Look briefly at the discussion on diversity (in 5.18 below) which describes the structure for assessing behaviours, then write it down.

Each aspect of the behaviour (or behavioural area) is given **positive** and **negative indicators**. The list of indicators can be used to help structure the presentation of evidence of your competence in your SOLAP, and to identify precisely where the assessment of your performance will be focused.

3.7.1.1 Problem solving

This behaviour is part of 'Achieving results', and the detail looks like this:

Behaviour: Problem solving

1. Gathers information from a range of sources. Analyses information to identify problems and issues, and makes effective decisions.
2. Gathers enough relevant information to understand specific issues and events. Uses information to identify problems and draw logical conclusions. Makes good decisions.

What kind of evidence will help assessors in these areas? Both positive and negative indicators are used.

Positive indicators for problem-solving behaviours are:

- identifies sources of information and retrieves information;
- retrieves an appropriate quantity of information on all aspects of a problem;
- separates relevant information from irrelevant information, and important information from unimportant information;
- takes in information quickly and accurately;
- reviews all the information gathered to understand the situation and draw logical conclusions;
- identifies and links causes and effects;
- identifies what can and cannot be changed;
- takes a systematic approach to solving problems;
- remains impartial and avoids jumping to conclusions;
- refers to procedures and precedents as necessary before making decisions;
- makes good decisions that take account of all relevant factors.

(Adapted from Skills for Justice, 2003)

Negative indicators show where you will be marked down or assessed as less than adequate:

- does not deal with problems in detail and does not identify underlying issues;
- does not gather enough information before coming to conclusions;
- does not consult other people who may have extra information;
- does not research background;
- shows no interest in gathering or using intelligence;
- does not gather evidence;
- makes assumptions about the facts of a situation;
- does not notice problems until they have become significant issues;
- becomes enmeshed in the detail of complex situations and cannot see the main issues;
- reacts without considering all the angles;
- becomes distracted by minor issues;
- leaves others to solve problems and does not see it as part of the role.

(As before, adapted from Skills for Justice, 2003)

You can see from this that the negative indicators are not simply the opposite of the positive indicators, such as merely failing to take the actions that are on the positive indicator list. Rather it is about how well you understand what is required of you and how you respond to that expectation. Some of the negative indicators have to do with passivity too: the downside of sitting back and letting things happen around you, such as leaving it to others to solve problems, instead of attempting to take control of a situation and addressing matters.

It is not difficult to see why such emphasis is placed on problem-solving behaviour: very often, police arrive when a situation is chaotic, confused, or muddled. Much of the initial police response is concerned with bringing order to the situation and sorting out who did what to whom and who was involved. You will encounter this from your very first patrols at night, near pubs and clubs, where you will be expected to sort any problems out there and then, quickly and decisively, having regard for all the circumstances (or initially at least, observe more experienced colleagues doing so).

3.7.1.2 Teamworking

Let us look at another example which is considered of equal importance:

Behaviour: Teamworking

1. Develops strong working relationships inside and outside the team to achieve common goals. Breaks down barriers between groups and involves others in discussions and decisions.
2. Works effectively as a team member and helps [to] build relationships within [the team]. Actively helps and supports others to achieve team goals.

Again, these behaviours are underpinned by positive and negative indicators:

Positive indicators for team-working include:

- understands own role in a team;
- actively takes part in team tasks in the workplace;
- is open and approachable;
- makes time to get to know people;
- cooperates with and supports others;
- offers help to other people;
- asks for and accepts help when needed;
- develops mutual trust and confidence in others;
- willingly takes on unpopular or routine tasks;
- contributes to team objectives no matter what the direct personal benefit may be;
- acknowledges that there is often a need to be a member of more than one team.

(Adapted from Skills for Justice, 2003)

To the extent that these are ideal behaviours, we all should try to attain them, but they are especially important in the policing context. Much police work is repetitive, painstaking, and sometimes even boring. However, these tasks have to be done because otherwise some significant fact might be overlooked or some vital piece of evidence ignored. That is the reason why so much emphasis is placed on the behaviours which demonstrate that you can cope with complex and demanding tasks.

Negative indicators for teamworking include:

- does not volunteer to help team members;
- is only interested in taking part in high-profile and interesting activities;
- takes credit for successes without recognizing the contribution of others;
- works to own agenda rather than contributing to team performance;
- allows small exclusive groups of people to develop;
- plays one person off against another;
- does not let people say what they think;
- does not offer advice or get advice from others;
- restricts and controls what information is shared;
- shows little interest in working jointly with other groups to meet the goals of everyone involved;
- does not discourage conflict within the organization.

(Adapted from Skills for Justice, 2003)

We have all met people with some or all of these attributes. It is interesting and reassuring to note that these are precisely the behaviours which are **not** encouraged or rewarded in the police service, and it is especially reassuring to any person who may one day have to rely on members of the team pulling together. (In a very real sense, entering a conflict situation with a colleague who does not contribute appropriately can be positively dangerous.) Many police forces encourage individuality, the exercise of initiative, and independence of thought and attitude, but there is a fine dividing line between those attributes and selfish self-regard. Good policing involves cooperation and this does not mean that the individual is suppressed or diminished, but that each person has the right to be heard and to make a contribution.

We have examined two of the key behavioural areas for patrol constable, but there are others and you should read the rest yourself. Ask your training staff for the Skills for Justice CD–ROM or for hard copies which you can look at in your own time.

3.8   The SOLAP

The SOLAP is the Student Officer Learning and Assessment Portfolio, a record of achievement that you will probably keep during your initial training (not all forces use the SOLAP). The SOLAP was an innovation of IPLDP, although every police force used something similar before April 2006 (usually called a PDP, and not universally popular). Forces sometimes emphasize that it is **your** portfolio, although you are no doubt aware that this does not make the portfolio confidential to you, nor does this ownership necessarily offer you any kind of protection in the case of legal action.

The SOLAP is either a physical document or an electronic document (stored in a folder on the force intranet or housed on a Virtual Learning Environment such as Blackboard). Although the SOLAP has to follow certain national requirements, forces are permitted to customize it for their own purposes: from the relatively trivial act of adding their own logos to the more significant step of deciding to release the SOLAP requirements to you in parts, rather than as a whole at the outset.

The SOLAP is likely to be a key document for you as it charts your claim to be a professional and competent student police officer who is ready for confirmation as a constable. If your force offers an NVQ as part of its training, then the SOLAP also performs important functions in terms of accountability to an Awarding Body (see 3.13 below).

Much of the advice above concerning the assessment of the NOS Units applies to the completion of the SOLAP. So, for example, start your SOLAP as soon as possible and maximize the potential for evidence-gathering from each incident you attend or training you receive. Some forces might even provide you with (anonymized) SOLAPs from previous student police officers as examples to look at.

There has been some criticism of the SOLAP, notably in terms of the bureaucratic burden it places on the student officer and their assessors and a report by Sir Ronnie Flanagan (Flanagan, 2008) recommended that there should be a post-implementation review. This review was conducted in the summer of 2008 and a number of changes have already been introduced as a consequence (for example, to the arrangements for the Learning Development Reviews).

3.8.1   Components of the SOLAP

A typical SOLAP will be made up of the following (the format may vary from force to force):

The SOLAP

Chapter	Contents	Comments
1	Student Officer Personal Profile	You provide brief biographical details (name, DoB etc) together with a list of your previous educational and other achievements. You are expected to keep this up to date.
2	Student Officer Role Profile	Information concerning the Student Officer Role Profile including the ICF, the NOS, the PAC, assessment, and appeals.
3	Introduction to the Phases of Learning	A description of the four IPLDP phases.
4	The Learning Modules	A description of the three sets of IPLDP Learning Modules (the IND, OP, and LPG modules described in 2.4) and how the curriculum is structured.
5	Learner Development Framework	A description of Learning Diaries and Learning Development Reviews. You will be expected to keep a Learning Diary and take part in the Learning Development Reviews (or their equivalent in your own force).
6	Police Action Checklist	Information concerning the PAC. You need to achieve the PAC before Independent Patrol.

Chapter	Contents	Comments
7	National Occupational Standards	Detailed information concerning the NOS for initial policing at the level of the 22 Units and elements, and also how these will be assessed.
8	Assessment Process	Information concerning competence, collecting evidence, the assessment process (induction, planning etc), and a useful detailed example of an assessment activity.
9	Overview of Assessment Methods	Note that this chapter is concerned with the assessment of your competence.
10	Overview of Assessment	A description of the main forms of documentation involved in the assessment process. These include induction records, witness testimony forms, the evidence index, and the CARs.
11	Glossary of terms	A 'jargon-buster' of acronyms used in the IPLDP assessment process.

In addition there are a number of appendices which either contain additional information or templates to use in order to complete your SOLAP.

We examine some of the key components of the SOLAP in more detail below.

3.8.2 The Learning Diary

This is included in Chapter 5 of the SOLAP, and is a structured account of your learning during your probationary period. It is, however, unlikely to consist of entries beginning 'and then I did this'. Instead, most forces will expect you to write in a more reflective and evidenced manner and use the given subheadings. (Some forces emphasize the need for structure and criticality by renaming the Learning Diary a Reflective Diary or Reflective Journal.)

Under the IPLDP, the Learning Diary subheadings normally reflect your stage of training (Home Office, 2004c). For example, during the initial induction phase in the first few weeks you might well be required to address subheadings related to your introduction to the organization, and during your community placement you will be asked to reflect on what you learned during the placement, and so on. Under IPLDP, the Learning Diary is related to the first three phases of training (up to Independent Patrol) in the following way (Home Office, 2004c updated with Home Office, 2005d):

Learning diary and IPLDP phases

Phase	Learning diary activities
1. Induction	Critical reflections on, for example, the introduction to your police force and the IPLDP, the training you received on Health and Safety, OST, the PNC, etc. How you are going to balance work with the other demands on your time, your relationship with others in training, the ethics and values of policing.
2. Community Safety and Partnerships	Critical reflections on, for example, working with the community, your experiences and learning during the community placement, and how you will develop in the future.
3. Supervised Patrol	The entries may feature under seven headings that mirror the content of LPG 1: • Crime; • Stop and Search; • Protecting People; • Police Policies and Procedures; • Non-crime Incidents; • Investigation and Interview; • Road Policing. You may be asked to summarize the main learning points and reflect on how this learning will be put into practice.

In most cases the Learning Diaries also have a 'golden thread' running through them, about ethics, respect for diversity, relationships with colleagues, and health and safety. There is also normally a section for your trainers to complete. This is not only useful feedback but is also a way in which your force can monitor your completion of the diary. Although your Learning Diary is not formally assessed (in the way that a written examination would be) there is some scope for using the entries as partial evidence towards completion of some of the NOS elements. Chapter 4 of the Handbook (see 4.12 below) provides a (fictitious) example of a possible Learning Diary entry.

3.8.3 Learning Development Reviews

The **Learning Development Reviews** (LDRs) and other forms of self-assessment give rise to more formal documents than the Learning Diary. The documents are based on structured meetings with your tutors and assessors. The meetings consist of reviews and critical self-assessment which you then write up as a formal document, based on the behavioural requirements and role profile of student police officers. The LDRs are documented in Chapter 5 of the SOLAP, and you will probably have around ten during your training (it varies between forces). However, there are **three key reviews** during your training which are of particular note:

- the review for Independent Patrol, involving completion of the PAC;
- an interim review, for example after the first year of training;
- the final review for confirmation (see 3.3 above), probably involving completion of the NOS plus other professional requirements.

These LDRs are essentially a progress report and an agreement of what actions you may need to take within a specified timescale. The SMART model of objective setting may be used when agreeing targets for future development: that is, you are expected to make your targets Specific, Measurable, Relevant, Achievable, and Timed. Note also that you might be asked to link the objectives you set for yourself with the behavioural areas of the ICF that we discussed in 3.7.1 above. It has also been suggested that this part of the SOLAP could also contain a record of any disciplinary matters.

Note that forces are permitted to replace the National IPLDP Learning Development Reviews with their own local approach but only if the alternative meets criteria laid down by NPIA (2009a, p 4). The criteria include the necessity to link the LDR to the Student Officer Role Profile (see 3.7 above).

3.8.4 The Recording of Assessment

This is the final part of the SOLAP and usually consists of a large number of documents related to your assessment. Perhaps the most important documents are the Assessment Reports, the Evidence Index, and the Cumulative Assessment Records (CARs).

Assessment Reports are completed by your assessor and are likely to form the bulk of your evidence for competence. An assessment plan is agreed in advance between you and your assessor, and the assessment then undertaken. The plan is subsequently used and completed with feedback and action planning. Assessors will complete a report for each NOS Unit they assess and note which actions they directly observed (for example, how you may have treated a suspect when making an arrest). They will also make a note of the written evidence they examined (for example, your PNB), and what questions they asked (for example, to probe your knowledge or to discover your reasons for taking a certain action), and the responses you gave. You will be asked to countersign this record as a fair and accurate summary so you should make sure that you read it carefully.

The **Evidence Index** sets out clearly the location of evidence for each claim of competence. Each piece of evidence (for example, a PNB entry) may give rise to more than one claim for competence according to the performance criteria of the particular NOS Unit. Note, however, that the evidence itself is not normally kept in the SOLAP. You may be asked to reference where such evidence may be found, due to both the volume and confidentiality of the material.

CARs are records of the achievement of the NOS elements and Units for initial policing. They are usually annotated with reference to the parallel NOS Unit. For example, CAR CB1 relates to

NOS Unit CB1—'Gather and submit information that has the potential to support law enforcement objectives'—and hence will also be subdivided into the constituent elements of the Unit. The CAR describes where the evidence will be found for the performance criteria and the range for each element of the Unit.

3.9 The PAC

The Police Action Checklist (the PAC) is part of the system for checking whether you are ready to begin Independent Patrol (see 3.3.3 above).

The PAC is cross-referenced to a subset of the NOS. For example, the requirement that you are able to 'obtain a DNA sample' is linked to NOS Unit 2K2 that you are able to 'present detained persons for custody'. It follows that completing your PAC is a process that complements the achievement of the NOS and is not in competition or separate from this process.

The Police Action Checklist has ten main headings and each heading is broken into a number of specific requirements.

Police Action Checklist

Safety first

- First Aid
- Health and Safety—Dynamic assessment
- Health and Safety—Reporting
- Personal Safety Training (PST/OST etc)
- Fitness test—according to force policy

Information management

- Utilize the PNC
- Utilize force information management systems (eg intelligence/crime reporting/command and despatch)

Patrol

- Demonstrate patrol priorities in accordance with NIM. Demonstrate communication with control rooms

Search

- Conduct stops
- Demonstrate lawful search—persons
- Demonstrate lawful search—premises
- Demonstrate lawful search—vehicles

Investigation

- Use CCTV during an investigation
- Demonstrate initial crime scene management
- Conduct the initial investigation and report of missing persons
- Conduct the initial investigation and report of volume crime according to National Policing Plan
- Conduct the initial investigation and report of volume crime according to Local Policing Plan
- Conduct the initial investigation and report of a domestic incident.
- Conduct the initial investigation and report of racist and/or hate crime
- Conduct the initial investigation and report in relation to a child protection and/or vulnerable person incident
- Conduct the initial investigation and report of a sudden death
- Demonstrate initial RTC scene management
- Interview—conduct a witness interview using the PEACE model
- Interview—conduct a suspect interview using the PEACE model
- Demonstrate correct handling of exhibits
- Provide support and advice to victims and witnesses
- Respond to developments during an investigation

Disposal

- Report for summons
- Make lawful arrests
- Convey a suspect into custody

Custody office procedures

- Present suspect to custody in accordance with force procedures
- Obtain fingerprints
- Obtain photographs
- Obtain DNA sample
- Complete pre-charge procedures

Finalize investigations

- Complete case files (eg summons and post charge files)
- Prepare for court or other hearings
- Present evidence to court or other hearings

Road policing

- Check driving documents
- Demonstrate vehicle stops
- Complete traffic documents—including HO/RT1/FPN(E)/CLE2/VDRS
- Demonstrate correct administration of the appropriate tests for drink/drugs driving offences

Property

- Complete property register

The PAC is largely concerned with performance and, as the term 'checklist' suggests, it is not generally used as a tool for student officer development. The checklist is also usually contextualized—that is, your performance is also judged in the light of your behaviour, the role profile for a student police officer (see 3.7 above), and, in particular, your ability to communicate with others and your understanding of the needs of policing diverse communities.

Before you can be considered for Independent Patrol an assessor will confirm your competence against all 44 or so subheadings in the checklist. Note that successful completion of the PAC does not necessarily guarantee that you will be eligible for Independent Patrol. Some police forces will expect more from you—for example, to have reached a certain level in terms of driving skills. In many forces you will still attend formal training and in all forces you will certainly continue to collect evidence towards completion of the remaining NOS. Under the IPLDP for example, you should have at least 30 days of 'protected learning time' after being granted Independent Patrol, and before confirmation.

3.10 PIP Level 1

In 2004, the Home Office and ACPO commissioned the NCPE to devise a Professionalising Investigation Programme (PIP) in response to a widespread perceived need to improve the quality of police investigation of crime (Centrex, 2005). A total of four levels are envisaged:

Professionalising Investigation Programme

Investigative level	Example of role	Description of typical investigative activity
Level 1	**Patrol Constable**/Police Staff/Supervisors	Investigation of volume crime.
Level 2	Dedicated Investigator, eg CID officer	Substantive investigation into more serious and problem offences, including road traffic deaths.
Level 3	Senior Investigating Officer	Lead investigator in cases of murder, stranger rape, kidnap, or crimes of complexity—Category A–C.
Level 4	Principal Investigating Officer/Officer in Overall Command (OIOC)	Critical, complex, protracted, and/or linked serious crime—Category A +.

(Derived from Centrex, 2005, our emphasis)

It follows that during your training you will be assessed against PIP Level 1. In a sense this should be automatic as PIP Level 1 is integrated into the IPLDP curriculum and has also been mapped against a subset of the NOS (Units CI101 'Conduct priority and volume investigations', CJ101 'Interview victims and witnesses in relation to priority and volume investigations', and CJ201 'Interview suspects in relation to priority and volume investigations'). These standards feature within the operational modules of the IPLDP—for example, CJ101 and CJ201 have been mapped against OP6 'Prepare, conduct, and evaluate interviews'. It is therefore not likely that you will achieve PIP Level 1 until the end of your first year of training (at the earliest), and it is more likely it will be during your second year.

After you have successfully completed PIP Level 1 you will be 'signed off' as a Level 1 investigator and be registered with your force as having reached this standard. (Level 3 PIP investigators will be registered at the national level.) However, in order to remain registered it is likely that you will have to demonstrate on a regular basis that you have maintained your skills and knowledge. At the time of writing the system for this has not been agreed but may take the form of evidence in the PDP (which replaces your SOLAP after you have been confirmed).

3.11 Assessment in Practice

Fortunately you will find that your trainers are often able to combine different types of assessments and recording procedures, so you will not have to be assessed as many times as it might initially seem! In the example below we illustrate the links between the NOS (see 3.6 above) and the SOLAP (see 3.8 above).

Imagine that you are Sam Palmer, and whilst on Supervised Patrol you attend an incident of suspected shoplifting and make an arrest. You were accompanied by your assessor/tutor Pc Navarro. You complete a PNB entry concerning the circumstances of the incident, the arrest, and the other relevant details. This one event could in fact be used as evidence against a number of the NOS elements, within Units AA1, CD1, CD3, CD5, and CK1, for example.

In fact the PNB entry in particular provides evidence that Sam has met performance criterion 7 of element CA1.2, namely to 'record any **actions** correctly and within the required time' (note that performance criteria 1–6 have been omitted below):

NOS Element CA1.2 Use law enforcement actions proportionately

Performance Criteria

[1 to 6 omitted]
7. Record any **actions** correctly and within the required time.

The word 'actions' is in bold so Sam also needs to consider the range statement for law enforcement actions:

Element CA1.2 Use law enforcement actions proportionately

Range Statement

1. Actions

   (a) Law Enforcement Powers (statutory, non-statutory)
   (b) Procedures

In this case, the PNB entry is an example of range 1b 'Procedures' and so this too can be evidenced.

Sam then makes an entry in the Evidence Index (this is her 23rd entry):

Candidate: Sam Palmer
Assessor: Pc Navarro

Reference	Description of evidence
23	PNB entry made on 01/09/07

Note that Pc Navarro might complete a full assessment report concerning Sam's competence in responding to the incident and carrying out the arrest; this would have been agreed with Sam in advance in the assessment plan. Sam would keep a copy of the report, give it a reference and add it to her Evidence Index. Other suitably qualified officers who were involved with the incident could also produce Witness Testimony to be included in the Evidence Index.

It is important to note that simply referencing and recording evidence is not sufficient to prove competence. Sam's evidence from the PNB entry will require assessment and signing off by an assessor.

The CAR for element CA1.2 is then completed. Note that Sam's 23rd entry is her second piece of evidence for performance criterion 7 (her first piece of evidence came from her 9th entry in her PNB):

CAR for Element CA1.2

Performance Criteria	Ref 1	Ref 2	Ref 3
1. Consider options …			
2. Balance the …			
3. Use the …			
4. Deal with …			
5. Use legitimate …			
6. Ensure that …			
7. Record any actions correctly and within the required time	09	23	

(Unfortunately, in some police forces the word 'ref' is used in the CARs (see the column headings above), as well as in the context of a 'reference' in the Evidence Index, which can be confusing!)

Chapter 10 of the SOLAP usually also includes a number of summative documents largely concerned with the achievement of the NOS, including **Unit Assessment Summary Sheets** (for each of the NOS units) and a **Summative Assessment Record** (sometimes Summative Assessment **Report**). This summative document shows that the assessor, the internal verifier (a suitably qualified person who checks the decision-making of the assessor), and the external verifier all agree that all of the relevant NOS Units have been achieved.

3.12 What Can Go Wrong?

We have no wish to be negative, but, things **can** sometimes go wrong.

3.12.1 Could I Get Sacked?

At the outset it is important to note that most student police officers, as with qualified police officers, are not employees in the usual sense of the term. Technically they are 'holders of public office'(and for British Transport Police it is especially complicated). This means that the conditions of employment for student police officers are particularly complex. In terms of dismissal (officially called 'dispensing with your services') and resignation ('retirement'), the main source of definitive information is the Police Regulations 2003, Statutory Instrument No 527 (see 5.12 below for an explanation of Statutory Instrument, and the task in Chapter 2). The Regulations may be found at <http://www.opsi.gov.uk/si/si2003/20030527.htm>. Note that there are a number of Annexes to the Determinants which set out the important detail.

As with many aspects of police training, the position regarding probation, the regulations, and complaints may well be reviewed. The Morris Inquiry in particular highlighted the complexity of current arrangements (Morris, 2004).

Probably the most important paragraphs in the Police Regulations 2003 for the student police officer are Regulations 12 and 13 often known colloquially as Reg (pronounced with a hard 'g') 12 and Reg 13.

3.12.2 Extension of the Probationary Period

Regulation 12 provides for an extension to the usual probationary period of two years for full-time student police officers. Details are given in Annex C to the Regulations. Normally the probationary period is extended for the following reasons:

- training has been interrupted for some reason, for example illness or personal problems; or
- a student police officer has been 'back-coursed' (that is, required to retake a stage of training), perhaps because of failure.

Forces are unlikely to allow an indefinite extension to the probationary period and will usually provide you with detailed information concerning the implementation of 'Reg 12' on the local level.

3.12.3 Dispensing with Your Services

Regulation 13 allows for your dismissal. It is worth quoting in full:

Regulation 13

(1) Subject to the provisions of this regulation, during [his/her] period of probation in the force the services of a constable may be dispensed with at any time if the chief officer considers that [he/she] is not fitted, physically or mentally, to perform the duties of [his/her] office, or that [he/she] is not likely to become an efficient or well conducted constable.

(2) A constable whose services are dispensed with under this regulation shall be entitled to receive a month's notice or a month's pay in lieu thereof.

(3) A constable's services shall not be dispensed with in accordance with this regulation and any notice given for the purposes thereof shall cease to have effect if [he/she] gives written notice to the police authority of [his/her] intention to retire and retires in pursuance of the said notice on or before the date on which [his/her] services would otherwise be dispensed with; and such a notice taking effect on that date shall be accepted by the police authority notwithstanding that less than a month's notice is given.

(4) Where a constable has received a notice under this regulation that [his/her] services are to be dispensed with and [he/she] gives written notice of [his/her] intention to retire and retires under paragraph (3), [he/she] shall nevertheless be entitled to receive pay up to and until the date on which the month's notice [he/she] has received would have expired or where [he/she] has received or is due to receive a month's pay in lieu of notice [he/she] shall remain entitled to that pay notwithstanding the notice [he/she] has given under paragraph (3).

In practice Reg 13 dismissals are rare and are normally the end of a long process during which you would have been offered support and guidance. If you are issued with a Reg 13 notice then you are advised to contact your JBB (the Police Federation, see 6.17 below) representative if you are paying subscriptions to the Federation, or take other advice.

Note that the grounds for dismissal ('not fitted, physically or mentally, to perform the duties of [his/her] office, or that [he/she] is not likely to become an efficient or well-conducted constable') are quite broad. For example, persistent failure in assessments or examinations could be considered grounds to consider you not *mentally* fit to continue training. However, more common reasons for being dismissed or resigning are examples of inappropriate behaviour, an inability to maintain a certain level of fitness, and so on.

There are obvious reasons why you may wish to resign before being dismissed in terms of your future employment prospects. Further, note that although the regulation allows the possibility of 'retirement' (voluntary resignation) before 'dispensing' (dismissal), this does not mean that an individual would escape prosecution if the grounds for dismissal arose from a criminal act committed by the individual concerned.

3.13 Qualifications

Your force may link your initial training to an external qualification such as:

- a Foundation degree or other higher education (HE) award; or
- an NVQ Level 3 or possibly an NVQ Level 3 and 4.

These qualifications are not necessarily mutually exclusive. For example, some HE qualifications have NVQs embedded within them as confirmation of professional competence. Trainee probation officers, for example, are now required to achieve an NVQ Level 4 and a degree, and certain parts of your probationary period and training are linked with particular qualifications—for example, your First Aid training (part of IND 1). In some cases, confirmation (see 3.3 above) may depend on the minimum attainment of one of these qualifications, or a staged award within the qualification (for example, a Certificate in Higher Education as Level 1 of a Foundation degree).

The Home Office has declared its intention that there shall be a **single** national qualification for student police officers who successfully complete their probation (section 4.54 of the White Paper, *Building Communities, Beating Crime*). However, the IPLDP Central Authority (the body now responsible for probationary training) has stated that this will be a **minimum** level of qualification, and that forces may 'gold-plate' if they so wish (Home Office, 2005a, para 17). In 2006 the IPLDP Central Authority decided that this minimum level of qualification will be an NVQ Level 3 and an NVQ Level 4 in Policing, and in 2009 the NPIA began a consultation on introducing a new initial policing qualification based upon the national Qualifications and Credit Framework (QCF). In any case, it would appear reasonably obvious that whatever qualification your force offers, it should be, and in all likelihood will be, linked with the NOS for initial policing and be approved by Skills for Justice.

3.13.1 HE Awards

If a Foundation degree or other HE award (for example, a Cert HE, a Dip HE, or an HE Certificate) is part of your training then your force will be working in partnership with a university or a university college (higher education institution (HEI)), or a further education (FE) college with links to an HEI. This also probably means that you have a form of 'dual nationality' where you are both a student of the HEI or FE college and an employee of your police force. There are advantages and disadvantages to this. On the one hand you will gain a qualification still held in relatively high esteem around the world (useful for that second career after policing) and you will also be able to access the learning facilities (library, open learning centres, and so on) on the same basis as any other student of that HEI or FE college. Finally, in many cases, you will be able to study alongside students engaged in training in parallel occupations such as nursing and social work (both part of higher education). This is particularly important in terms of the inter-agency approaches to policing.

On the other hand there is no gain without pain; gaining HE qualifications will require you to demonstrate your knowledge and understanding in distinctive ways, and not just your professional competence in the field. You will almost certainly be required to undertake formal assessment, such as examinations and assignments with predetermined pass marks and strict rules concerning resubmission and missing deadlines. For example, depending on your force's policy, if you fail an examination and all resubmission possibilities have been exhausted, you may be re-coursed.

You should note however, that Foundation degrees in particular are not just another degree from a university. You are not undertaking, say, an undergraduate programme in History; Foundation degrees are **meant** to be different and to be linked inextricably with the practical skills needed for the occupation concerned, and for initial policing this means, at least in part, the NOS. It is unlikely therefore that you will be set essays asking you to 'Discuss the history of the use of police dogs' but instead your assignments will be professionally related and often linked with your Supervised and Independent Patrol experiences. However, they are higher education awards and may be used as credit towards an honours degree such as a BSc (Hons) in Policing (this is meant to be a design feature common to all Foundation degrees). This linkage to an honours degree could be important in terms of your subsequent professional development (see Chapter 14).

3.13.2 NVQs

National Vocational Qualifications (NVQs; SVQs in Scotland) are offered at Levels 1 to 5 and are available for a wide range of occupations including policing. For student police officers, NVQ Levels 3 and 4 in Policing are the most relevant. NVQs are approved by the Qualifications and Curriculum Authority (QCA), a national body that oversees a wide range of qualifications. The QCA does not issue awards—this is undertaken by the Awarding Bodies. NVQs in Policing are offered by a number of familiar Awarding Bodies, including City & Guilds, Edexcel, CMI, and OCR. Some Awarding Bodies, for example City & Guilds, suggest that the Level 4 NVQ is appropriate for 'those individuals undertaking Independent Patrol' (City & Guilds, 2005, p 1) but the rationale for this advice is unclear.

The following is the likely composition of the NVQ Level 3 in terms of the 11 mandatory NOS Units (Edexcel, 2005, updated by the authors with new Unit titles):

NVQ Level 3

Unit AA1	Promote equality and value diversity
Unit AE1	Maintain and develop your own knowledge, skills, and competence
Unit AF1	Ensure your own actions reduce risks to health and safety
Unit CA1	Use law enforcement actions in a fair and justified way
Unit CD1	Provide an initial response to incidents
Unit CD5	Arrest, detain, or report individuals
Unit CJ101	Interview victims and witnesses in relation to priority and volume investigations
Unit CK1	Search individuals
Unit GC10	Manage conflict
Unit 2K2	Present detained persons for custody
Unit 4G4	Administer First Aid

(Note that some Awarding Bodies may use instead the 2003 titles for NOS Units. For example Unit CA1 may instead be Unit 1A1 'Use police actions in a fair and justified way'.)

The following Units are required for the NVQ Level 4 in Policing (Edexcel, 2005, updated by the authors with new Unit titles):

NVQ Level 4	
Unit AB1	Communicate effectively with people
Unit BE2	Provide initial support to victims, survivors, and witnesses and assess their needs for further support
Unit CB1	Gather and submit information that has the potential to support law enforcement objectives
Unit CD3	Prepare for, and participate in, planned law enforcement operations
Unit CJ201	Interview suspects in relation to priority and volume investigations
Unit CK2	Search vehicles, premises, and open spaces
Unit DA6	Prepare and submit case files
Unit DA5	Present evidence in court and at other hearings
Unit 2G2	Conduct investigations
Unit 2G4	Finalize investigations
Unit 2K1	Escort detained persons

(Note that some Awarding Bodies may use instead the 2003 titles for NOS Units (see 1.5 above). For example, Unit AB1 may be Unit 1A2.

Your force will either be an approved centre of an Awarding Body (with the right to offer NVQs directly) or it will work in partnership with another education or training body (such as an FE college) that is an approved centre. However, if your force offers an NVQ at Levels 3 or 4, it must subscribe to the assessment strategy of Skills for Justice. For example, the force will need to have certain safeguards in place to ensure that its assessors are suitably skilled. You may hear about 'A1 assessors' which is a reference to a qualification that your assessors are undertaking or one that they have already gained. (Assessors for Foundation degrees linked to NOS are also required to have certain skills.)

As with Foundation degrees, there are advantages and disadvantages to linking initial police training with NVQs. In terms of advantages, the NVQ is now an established and widely recognized qualification. It also lends itself naturally to occupational standards (not surprisingly, as it is based upon them) and therefore has the potential to be seamlessly interwoven within your training. Finally, if other aspects of police training become linked with NVQs (this is certainly possible) then you will already be well versed in the philosophy and approach of NVQs. The disadvantages are that NVQs do not necessarily carry the same weight with other professional groups. Remember the Home Office IPLDP comment above about gold-plating? This is not, we think, just about some kind of educational snobbery but a realistic reflection of the historical development of professions in the UK. Ask the police surgeon, the defence solicitor, or even the custody nurse about their qualifications and you are unlikely to hear much at the moment about NVQs. The decision by the IPLDP Central Authority to make an NVQ Level 3 plus an NVQ Level 4 the minimum requirement for initial policing is, on the academic level at least, significantly lower than the academic demands made on trainees joining the Probation Service that we discussed earlier. It is interesting to note, for example, that the NPIA has linked the accreditation of the HPDS with a higher education Masters' programme rather than with an NVQ Level 5. At the time of writing the NPIA had begun a consultation on introducing a new qualification for initial police training, using the national Qualifications and Credit Framework (QCF). The QCF embraces credit-based qualifications at all academic levels, including higher education.

Finally, note that if the number of NOS Units required to achieve confirmation is reduced from 22 to 9 or 10 during 2010 (see 1.5 above) then this is likely to affect the structure of NVQs in initial Policing.

3.14   **Answers to Tasks**

TASK 1

Possible answers are discussed immediately after Task 1 in the text that follows.

Well, you have made it this far. On average for your one success there are six others who failed to even reach the first day of training. Statistically, you are likely to be male, aged in your mid-twenties, and white. There again, you are probably not (look up 'ecological fallacy' on <http://en.wikipedia.org/wiki/Main_Page>).

Disturbingly, if you are an ethnic minority recruit you are twice as likely to drop out of training as your white counterparts (Woolcock, 2006). The police service seems serious about tackling this issue.

TASK 2

This task is not easy because it is not always obvious whether a motivation is extrinsic or intrinsic in nature. On the surface they may appear one way or the other to us but it is evident that human motivation is highly complex (look at the number of psychology textbooks devoted to this subject alone). What is perhaps more important than classification is that you spend time thinking about your motivation for joining and how you might respond to the challenges presented by two years' training.

TASK 3

Well, how does it compare? Do not be surprised (or concerned) to find significant variation with the national template.

The internet will give you access to brief descriptions of a number of force approaches to structuring initial training, and it is surprising how varied these can be.

TASK 4

We give a variety of definitions in the text immediately after the task.

TASK 5

You should have found that the knowledge and understanding requirements of Unit 4G4 are:

1. Limitations and risks of applying first aid to others.
2. How to detect an obstructed airway and methods of clearing obstruction.
3. How to check for signs of life and for life-threatening conditions.
4. Methods of CPR and how to use this appropriately.
5. How to manage an unconscious casualty and the main causes of unconsciousness.
6. Precautions to be taken when performing CPR.
7. Different types of wound and their treatment.
8. Methods for controlling bleeding.
9. Signs and symptoms of shock.
10. Recognition and treatment of sprains, strains, and fractures.
11. Main safety considerations when dealing with burns or scalds.
12. How to recognize and assess the severity and extent of injuries.
13. Appropriate treatments for hypothermia, frostbite, heat-stroke, and heat exhaustion.
14. How to recognize and respond to local danger and risks when dealing with casualties.

TASK 6

No, simulation is not permitted for element 2K2.2.

TASK 7

You were asked to read a later part of the Handbook. You are likely to find that writing down information in different forms will help you memorize it more effectively.

4 | Learning as a Student Police Officer

4.1 Chapter Briefing

This chapter discusses how to build upon the ways you learn best in order to make learning easier for you. We suggest ways to help you to recall facts and how to apply reflective practice in your Learning Diary. Undertaking your community engagement and learning whilst with your Professional Development Unit are also examined and this is followed by a look at diversity training in the police.

Finally, the chapter examines forms of reasoning and argument that are relevant to learning for student police officers, together with the ways in which we can sometimes commit errors in reasoning—logical fallacies.

4.1.1 Aim of the Chapter

The aim of this chapter is to develop your understanding of learning as a student police officer and the forms of teaching you will receive, and to assist in the development of your skills for studying, reasoning, and argument.

This chapter will enable you to:

- understand the approaches to learning and teaching adopted by many police forces;
- appreciate the value of the experiential learning cycle;
- understand and, if appropriate, adopt the role of the reflective practitioner;
- place the community engagement stage of training into context;

- understand how a PDU supports your professional development;
- consider some of the questions and issues that surround diversity training in the police;
- develop skills of reasoning and argument;
- identify common logical errors.

4.1.2 National Occupational Standards

This chapter will provide you with some of the knowledge required to demonstrate the following NOS element:

> **National Occupational Standards Element**
>
> AE1.1   Maintain and develop your own knowledge, skills, and competence.

You should refer to Chapter 3 for general information and advice concerning the NOS elements.

4.1.3 IPLDP Phases and Modules

This chapter will provide you with resources to support the IPLDP Induction Module IND 3 'Develop one's own knowledge and practice'.

4.1.4 SOLAP

The contents of this chapter are relevant to the 'knowledge' evidence requirements of CAR AE1.

4.2 Introduction

In many respects a student police officer is just that: a student. You cannot be expected to know everything from the start although you will almost certainly encounter members of the public and even fellow police officers that believe that you should. Indeed, you will probably come to the conclusion that the end of your training is just the beginning of a career-long need to continue learning.

It is perhaps illuminating to compare the transition from student to qualified police officer with the parallel progression through nurse training: that is from **novice** nurse to **expert** nurse (Benner, 1984). In many of the models of nurse training in the UK there are five levels of proficiency, which we have adapted to police training:

> **Novice**—the new student police officer
> Decision-making is limited and based upon strict rules out of context—'just tell me what to **do**!'
> You are largely exposed to policing but play little active part.
> No occupational standards have been achieved.

> **Advanced beginner**—the student police officer on Supervised Patrol
> Enough competence has been demonstrated, in knowledge checks, real situations, and role play to allow limited autonomy although skills and knowledge are viewed as if in separate boxes (the Theft Act, diversity, forensic awareness, ABH)— 'let me have a go!'
> Some occupational standards have been achieved.

> **Competent**—the student police officer on Independent Patrol
> Mastery of many of the skills and competences of policing, although they are still compartmentalized and not yet joined up and they are still not second nature— 'I think I can do this'.
> The PAC has been achieved.

> **Proficient**—the student police officer at Confirmation
> Situations are viewed as a whole and patterns are discerned and analysed and subtleties recognized—
> 'I've been here before'.
> All required occupational standards have been achieved.

> **Expert**—the confirmed police officer after two or three years service
> An apparently intuitive grasp of situations, confident but now also questioning—
> 'Perhaps there is more to learn?'

When you start your training you are probably at the novice stage (unless you have joined after being a special constable or PCSO). All being well, in two years you will be proficient and perhaps even expert. Your training will have been designed to support your transition from novice to advanced beginner to competent and finally to proficient. This chapter will help you understand some of the processes involved.

Finally, note that there are a number of IPLDP requirements for police forces, in terms of the way they organize and deliver their teaching and assist in your learning. For example, the recommendation is that there is a maximum ratio of sixteen student police officers to one trainer for taught training-room activities but one to one for Supervised Patrol (Home Office, 2005b). This is not to say that you will not sometimes be taught in larger groups in a classroom (it could make sound pedagogical sense to do this) but rather the norm should be no more than sixteen to one. Although your trainers are expected to be 'occupationally competent' (Home Office, 2005b), bear in mind that police training is still often viewed as the remit of the 'generalist'. Your trainers, for example, might be expected to know and teach (or facilitate) everything from the detail of the Sexual Offences Act 2003 to theories concerning human communication.

4.3 Teaching and Learning Styles

To understand how you will learn in police training, you will need to understand **how you learn as an adult**. The educational backgrounds of those who read this Handbook are likely to be as varied as the people themselves. Some of you will have entered the police family earlier in another police-related role (eg as a PCSO), some of you will have become student police officers almost straight from school, some of you will have recently left full-time further or higher education (up to 30 per cent in recent years), whilst a number of you might not have undertaken training or study for a long time.

Whatever your previous educational background, police training should be innovative, diverse, and exciting. The IPLDP philosophy is to encourage police forces to adopt educational principles and practices that suit adults, whatever their personal educational backgrounds and learning style. It is worth noting that police training has existed in the UK for over 150 years, and hundreds of thousands of student police officers have been successfully trained before you. This does not mean, of course, that police training was perfect in the past nor, indeed, that it is now (HMIC, 2002); after all, we tend not to hear much from those who have been unsuccessful in their police training. What it does mean, however, is that many people like you have successfully trained to become police officers and moved on to rewarding careers in policing.

4.3.1 Safe Learning Environment

A phrase that you might well hear your trainers use (if not to you, then to each other) is 'safe learning environment'. The phrase is used in reference to Professional Development Units (see 4.10 below) as well as in the training room. There is no official definition of what 'safe learning environment' actually means but it probably contains elements of some or all of the following:

- **physical** safety—that is, the training room or the officer safety training facilities meet appropriate health and safety requirements (your trainers will often consider this as the first stage of 'Maslow's hierarchy of needs');

- **psychological** safety—that is, establishing a climate in the classroom where you feel free to express your ideas and feelings without fear of ridicule from others (bear in mind, however, that your trainers may also have a role in the requirement to assess your attitudes and behaviour);
- the existence of **well-defined parameters** that specify the boundaries of acceptable behaviour and actions in the classroom and other learning environments. These parameters sometimes form part of a learning agreement that you might even be asked to sign, signifying that you will demonstrate an awareness of the needs of others and so on.

4.3.2 Domains of Learning

Many of our day-to-day actions centre on three main areas of activity and so it follows that these three areas are the ones in which learning or education often take place. An understanding of these areas will help you to assess your own competencies and evaluate your own training needs. This will make it easier for you to learn and revise for exams and will provide you with a route map through any of your learning experiences.

These areas are referred to as the **learning domains** (eg. Bloom, 1964 and subsequent publications in this series), and you will no doubt hear your trainers refer to them from time to time.

1. The **cognitive domain** is associated with the ability to **reason**, and will include learning subject matter such as law, legislation, policy, and procedure, about which we have to **think**. We can therefore associate this domain with our **heads**.
2. The **affective domain** is associated with your feelings and emotions, for example, the way you react to situations (such as provocation), and what your values and prejudices are. A cliché in police training is that 'attitudes can be caught or taught', and therefore a great deal of your training will involve learning to adopt appropriate **attitudes** and behaviours towards the public and your colleagues, in areas such as respect, race and diversity, team working, community and customer focus, effective communication, problem solving, personal responsibility, and resilience. You can think of this domain as being associated with the **heart**.
3. The **psychomotor domain** is associated with **physical dexterity**, for example, personal safety training, first aid training, using a breath test machine, and traffic control. You can consider this domain as being associated with the use of your **hands**, but it could easily be associated with your legs, arms, or any part of your body you use to carry out an action.

Within these domains there are levels of complexity, beginning with the easiest and progressively becoming more difficult. In the table below these are read from left to right.

For the cognitive domain (the head):

Knowledge →	Comprehension →	Application
The ability to recall facts, words, or phrases, eg a definition of an Act or a section of law.	To understand and be able to explain component parts of policy, procedure, or legislation, eg the meanings of words within definitions, the variations and exceptions.	To use this knowledge and understanding to apply previous learning to a set task which is either simulated, paper-based, or in the work place.

For the affective domain (the heart):

Receives →	Responds →	Values
Listens to or sees demonstrated an attitude which is to be learned, eg 'We want you to be a non-discriminator, regardless of the prejudices you may actually have.'	Outwardly shows the learned attitude or behaviour, but does not necessarily believe in it, eg 'I have prejudices, but I will not discriminate because I've been told I must not.'	Adopts the learned attitude or behaviour and, without request and prompting, owns the feeling personally, eg 'Even though I have prejudices, I believe it is wrong to discriminate and therefore I will not do so.'

For the psychomotor domain (the hands):

Imitation →	Manipulation →	Precision
Performs the skill as a result of copying or repeating what has been observed, eg resuscitation techniques in first aid.	Executes the skill with some instruction or coaching.	Carries out the skill alone without copying instruction or the necessity for coaching.

It is almost an orthodoxy in police training that learning in one domain cannot easily be separated from learning in another. This is particularly the case in terms of cognitive and affective learning. Hence you will find your trainers often working simultaneously in these dimensions. For example, in a session on the police response to domestic violence, your trainer might well start with a group discussion on attitudes to domestic violence and through this encourage you to explore your own feelings and preconceptions. (Is it just 'a domestic' that the police should keep out of? Is it always male on female violence? What about elderly people as victims of their children?)

For a session involving the cognitive domain, you will probably be asked to assimilate at least some of the knowledge about the subjects involved before entering the training room, for example during the evening before. This will probably be referred to as 'organizing in advance' or an 'advanced organizer', and you may be tasked with learning an offence, Act, or section, perhaps in the form of a definition. The content could come from this Handbook, your NPIA (Centrex) or force notes, a virtual learning environment, or from a handout issued to you. This process is sometimes referred to in police training as a 'pre-read'; however you are required to learn material, and not just read it!

The next stage of the lesson will possibly involve a knowledge check to assess whether or not you have gained the appropriate level of understanding. A trainer or tutor will then probably be intent on moving you on to the next level in the cognitive domain (from knowledge to comprehension) by asking you to take part in one of the teaching and learning activities listed in 4.4 below, in order to check your understanding and clarify any misunderstandings.

Finally, you will be given an opportunity to develop your learning further, using one or more of the methods listed in 4.4 below. This will involve the third level of the domain—applying your learning.

Similar activities will be used in the other two domains for attitudinal and skills-based subjects, but each time you will probably start at the simplest level and move incrementally to the more complex. Then, whether it is through assimilation or work-based learning in your Professional Development Unit, you will be coached and mentored by your tutor to a level of competency in preparation for assessment against the National Occupational Standards (see 3.6 above).

4.3.3 Preferred Learning Styles

People prefer to learn in different ways (Kolb, 1984) and researchers have discerned the existence of four main families of learning styles which most people relate to in some way. To begin finding out about your own learning style work your way through the following four tasks. In each case, answer the questions 'yes' or 'no'. Of course, you probably wish to qualify your answers with 'sometimes' or 'mostly' but it will work better if you can just give a straight answer! (Note that answers are not provided to these four tasks at the end of the chapter, because there is no right or wrong here.)

TASK 1

- Do I like to be animated in my learning and do best when I am actively involved with a task?
- Do I prefer, for example, computer-based activities, compared with simply reading something?
- Do I normally like taking part in simulations or role-plays, but rarely like just to observe them?

If you answered mostly 'yes', you are using an **activist** learning style; here are some tips for you:

- Set yourself tasks, write your own questions or case studies involving the subject matter you are learning.
- Take part in computer-based learning, which is interactive and visual, for example through the NCALT portal at <http://www.ncalt.com>.
- Use pre-formed questions before sessions which will keep you active and enable you to continually check your learning.
- Do your learning in bite-sized chunks, and never stay too long without a break.
- At revision time, do not rely only on reading your notes, but engage yourself in activities that allow you to look back at the subject in more depth, such as setting yourself questions to answer.

TASK 2

- Do I like to have a logical outlook to my learning, with set outcomes for me to work towards?
- Do I like to produce a theory or attach an idea to the subject?
- Do I like reading about a subject and drawing my own conclusions as to its structure and adaptation?
- Do I like to challenge or question the underlying assumptions in subject matter presented to me?

If you answered mostly 'yes', you are using a **theorist** learning style; here are some tips for you:

- Establish the reasoning behind the subject matter. If there does not seem to be a clear theory which relates to the subject, research this for yourself. It might exist, even though you may not have been taught it in the training room.
- If you are learning a law-based subject, look for its origins in terms of the crimes or situations it is intended to prevent. Look for the period in time when it was written and introduced, and why.
- Whilst revising for an assessment process, design your own logical diagrams which summarize the subject matter as a sequence of points to be learned.

TASK 3

- Do I like to learn by thinking or dealing with the problem in a practical way, rather than using theory or abstract principles?
- Do I look at the learning requirements on me in a pragmatic way; for example, just how much of a new subject I need to learn, and why?
- When introduced to new subjects, do I almost immediately look for the practical applications and where I can use the learning in the work place?

If you answered mostly 'yes', you are using a **pragmatist** learning style; here are some tips for you:

- Adapt the material you are learning into a form with which you are more comfortable by making links with the practical applications.
- Produce examples to clarify your own understanding of the subject, construct flow-charts (like the ones to be found in Chapter 8 and elsewhere in this Handbook) or mind-maps on paper to make connections between the subject matter.
- Involve yourself in the assessment of others, so that you are learning at the same time.

TASK 4

- Do I like to learn in a slow, deliberate way, and would I rather take my time to reinforce what I have learned before moving on and risk possibly forgetting something?
- Do I like to take a step back and look at the subject from all angles before drawing a conclusion?
- Do I like to discuss issues, so that I fully understand what it is that I need to learn?
- Do I sometimes try to hide during simulations or role-plays and prefer to observe, but then fully participate in the debrief afterwards?

If you answered mostly 'yes', you are using a **reflective** learning style; here are some tips for you:

- Most of your learning will take place towards the end of a lesson or later on the same day. Organize your time so that you have the opportunity to look back over material you have learned earlier.
- Expose yourself to pre-formed questions, but allow yourself time to carry them out effectively.
- Use reinforcement tools, such as question and answer books, and try not to feel embarrassed if you want to do an exercise more than once.

So which group do you belong to, or perhaps (most likely) are your responses spread across two (or more) groups? The following task may provide you with a more precise measure of your preferred learning style.

TASK 5

You can find out more about your learning style(s) by taking part in an online question-naire; go to the Learning Styles interactive website at Canterbury Christ Church University: <http://www.canterbury.ac.uk/graduate-skills/preview/audits/learning-styles/index.html>.

4.4 Learning from Trainers and Others

If you are in a class of up to 16 people, there is every chance that each of you will have a differ-ent preferred learning style. Therefore, it is obviously a challenge to the training staff to accom-modate each student police officer with an appropriate learning activity. A popular approach in police training is that of 'facilitation' where trainers adopt styles and techniques to bring out (you may hear the phrase 'tease out') ideas and views from the group whilst at the same time reducing their own role as conventional didactic 'stand at the front and talk' teachers.

A number of activities commonly employed by trainers are described below. They are used to engage all members of the group at least once during a session.

The **'boardblast'** is a very popular teaching method used by police trainers. The tutor will invite responses from some or all of you which will be written down on a board or flip-chart and then discussed. The content of the boardblast will be assessed by the tutor and revisited at different stages of the lesson. This is often a very effective method but may be used to excess. Another occasional disadvantage to the boardblast approach is that most of the class will be at the level of novice or advanced beginner (see 4.2 above) and hence the suggestions from the class may not cover all the aspects of the topic required for that session.

Case studies involve a practical example of a police-related problem which will be given to you as an individual or a group activity. You will be invited to read the material and form con-clusions about its content to show your understanding of the subject. The NPIA has developed a number of case studies and extensive associated materials (including e-learning content) to support the delivery of the IPLDP curriculum. These include case studies concerned with rob-bery, theft, missing persons, burglary, terrorism, and so on.

Demonstration can be used if the subject matter involves the use of the body in the psycho-motor domain. The tutor will demonstrate how your body should move in order that you can repeat the activity afterwards.

Small-group work is a very common method in police training. You will be invited to work in small groups and share ideas between the group. For this approach to work well, it is impor-tant that each member of the group is actively involved in the task and that concentration is maintained (see 6.18.2 below which is concerned with listening skills). When the group reports back its findings, the trainer or trainers will probably be in facilitator mode and will tease out the learning.

Large-group work usually involves you being sent away in smaller numbers to research a subject using books, reference material, and computer-based learning. You will then be asked to come back as a large group and present all your small-group findings as one coherent piece. On the other hand, as a large group you may be presented with information on a large scale, perhaps from a specialist or guest speaker or by watching a video clip, for example.

Individual work provides an opportunity for you to work alone. You will be set work to do on your own, perhaps under exam conditions or, less informally, during lessons. This may take the format of knowledge checks, assignments, case building, or interviewing.

Electronic learning often uses computer-based learning (CBL) packages which are now available both nationally and locally. They provide you with an opportunity to interact with the resources available. CBL activity can be carried out individually or in small groups, both inside and outside the classroom environment. For example, CBL material supporting the IPLDP is to be found at <http://www.ncalt.com>. As a police officer, you should have access to the resources on the NCALT website through the use of a username and password.

Facilitated discussions are particularly useful for exploring attitudes and behaviour. The discussion may be initiated by watching a video or DVD, or by reflecting on the presentation of a guest speaker. Your trainers will encourage you to share your own thoughts with others (see 4.3.1 above on safe learning environments). You should be prepared to maintain confidentiality as you and your colleagues may disclose private and sensitive matters (you will certainly be reminded of this need on numerous occasions) but remember that confidentiality does not protect you from disciplinary action against inappropriate language, attitudes, or behaviour. From the discussion you will have the opportunity to draw your own conclusions.

Presentations are used for some topics. If the subject matter is appropriate for this form of delivery (for example, an introduction to the Theft Act 1968), or time is short, your trainers may well deliver a presentation, often using Microsoft PowerPoint software. Throughout the presentation, you will be given the opportunity to ask questions and make notes. Your trainer might well direct questions towards you. Different trainers will have different approaches to delivering presentations which may or may not coincide with your learning style. For example, some may use the technique of progressively revealing bullet points which, although it will keep your attention, can be irritating to some. Most trainers welcome feedback on matters such as this, possibly in the evaluation sheets you might be asked to complete and submit. Finally, if your organization uses Virtual Learning Environments (such as Blackboard) then you may well find copies of the presentations are available to you in an electronic format.

Role-plays are where you adopt or play given roles in a certain situation. For example, one of you may act the police officer and the other a member of the public in a simulated 'stop and account' scenario. Role-plays are normally used when you have gained sufficient knowledge and skills (particularly in terms of police procedure) to make them meaningful. Some police forces use semi-professional actors or volunteers from the local community to play roles. The latter approach may also have certain added advantages in terms of your diversity training. One underlying principle to the role-play approach is that adult learners are able to draw upon previous experiences to enhance their learning. Just as significant for your learning as the role-play itself is the debrief that normally happens later (you could even be videoed to assist with this). In all cases the brief for the role-play should be carefully explained to you at the outset. Note that, as we discuss in 3.6 above, role-plays and simulations cannot normally be used as evidence against achievement of the NOS. However, your experiences can certainly feature in your Learning Diary Phase 3.

Undertaking a **community engagement** is seen as an important way in which you will learn both about the diverse communities that you will police and your attitudes towards these communities (see 4.8 below). However, at this point note the importance that the IPLDP places on a self-critical approach to be adopted (Home Office, 2004c). This means an active self-questioning of your existing beliefs and attitudes. Your force will probably expect to see evidence of this self-criticality in your Learning Diary Phase 2 entries under headings such as 'What challenged you during the engagement, in what ways, and how did you respond?'

Syndicate exercises involve you working in small groups. You will first be divided into syndicates by your trainers. A syndicate is a group of people where each assumes a certain role. For example, in a syndicate exercise you might be a member of the public with a particular problem with anti-social behaviour in your neighbourhood. Other members of the syndicate may play the role of the local Pc, the police BCU commander, and so on. The exercise then takes place and you explore the various issues involved. Syndicate exercises can be useful learning devices but need to be carefully organized and managed by your trainers, with detailed instructions and briefing on the roles you will play. For example, if the syndicate group is quite large (six or more) then there is the danger that certain members of the group may dominate and that, because of time constraints, issues are examined in token and ineffective ways.

4.5   The Experiential Learning Cycle (ELC)

You have undoubtedly heard of the sayings 'if you don't succeed the first time, then try, try again' or 'we all learn by our mistakes'. Much of your learning will take place through your own experiences, and as adults we can actually teach ourselves, at least in part. How many times have you mentally said to yourself, 'I won't do that again!' or 'That didn't work! Is there another way?' or 'When I do that again, I'll do it better and safer!'?

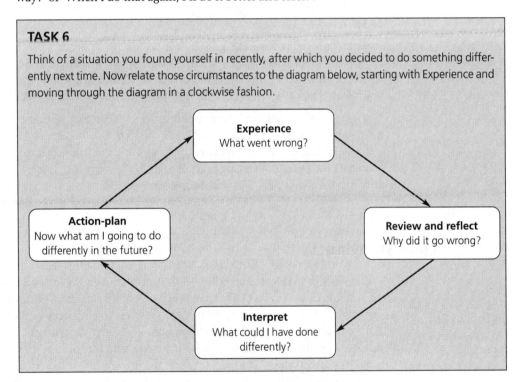

TASK 6

Think of a situation you found yourself in recently, after which you decided to do something differently next time. Now relate those circumstances to the diagram below, starting with Experience and moving through the diagram in a clockwise fashion.

Experience
What went wrong?

Review and reflect
Why did it go wrong?

Interpret
What could I have done differently?

Action-plan
Now what am I going to do differently in the future?

The diagram in Task 6 shows the **experiential learning cycle** (ELC) and has been adapted from the work of David Kolb (Kolb, 1984). It has been widely adopted (but is not without its critics) as an integral part of police learning and hence you will find it extensively used on an individual basis to inform your Learning Diary (all phases), and in the teaching environment, to help structure your taught sessions. The cycle can also be viewed as a dynamic (on-the-spot) assessment of how to carry out tasks in a manner that meets health and safety considerations, thereby informing safer working practices.

The four stages to the cycle are as follows:

• **Experience** (called 'Concrete Experience' in the Kolb original): This is **direct** experience, often through practical application. As a student police officer you will often want to know what the practical applications of the session will be. You may want to get 'hands on' as soon as possible. The trainer may prompt you—for example, by asking the question 'think of times in your own life when you have been subject to bullying or harassment'.

- **Review and reflect** ('Reflection'): What does the experience mean to me? This stage is the beginning of understanding through review and reflection. A task such as 'describe your feelings when you were bullied or harassed' may be given.
- **Interpret** ('Abstract Conceptualization'): This involves placing the experiences in some form of theoretical and more abstract framework such as 'how do victims feel about this?'
- **Action-plan** ('Active Experimentation'): The stage of action-planning is how we take this learning forward and test it against reality, such as 'how then do we act as a police service to support victims of harassment?'

The cycle is also used by trainers to evaluate the effectiveness of learning activities such as role-plays (see 4.4 above), and they may ask the participants: 'What did not go quite so well? How could we do it differently in the future?'

Many police trainers are taught to link the learning cycle with the styles of learning that we described in the latter part of 4.3 above—for example, by devising approaches for activist learners to help them through the 'interpret' stage of the ELC. This is part of the facilitation tradition in police training that we described earlier. However, if you feel uncomfortable with this way of learning (perhaps through unfamiliarity) then make your feelings known so your trainers will be more able to help you.

TASK 7

A student police officer, whilst undertaking Personal Safety Training, starts learning how to handcuff a suspect by taking part in supervised practice using a mannikin (dummy). The trainer, observing the student practise and testing the results, then asked: 'Were there any risks to you during the cuffing? How tight did that feel for the suspect? What might you have done differently?'

That night the student police officer reads up on how to handcuff suspects; the reasons for doing it in particular ways, force procedure, and the human rights of the suspect. The next day, presented with a fellow student officer to handcuff, the student thinks: 'Now what did I do wrong yesterday and what did it say in those notes I read? I'll try it like this today.'

Identify in the above, each of the four stages of Kolb's ELC.

4.6 Studying

We acknowledge that learning 'policing' is sometimes a confusing and disorientating experience. In some cases we even have to **unlearn** before we can learn. For example, if you do not know that there are major legal differences between the offences of robbery and theft, you will have to unlearn what you thought you knew already! We tend not to view differences in definition as being particularly important in everyday life, but they are when you are dealing with the law. Taylor (1986) suggests that the discomfort we experience is actually a necessary part of adult learning. In particular, she discerned four distinct phases of the learning experience:

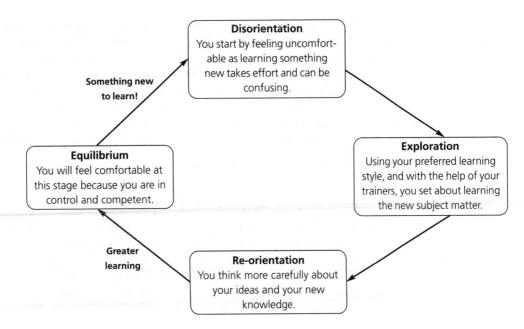

In summary, learning something new is often initially characterized by feelings of discomfort and anxiety. So, do not worry if you feel like this from time to time. Bear this in mind when studying and it will help you cope; it is quite normal to have some ups and downs as you learn.

4.6.1 Study Skills

There are numerous guides, books, and websites which can be used to help develop your ability to study. For example, if you are also undertaking a higher-education award as part of your training then you may find it useful to work through Stella Cottrell's *Study Skills Handbook* (Cottrell, 2003). If you are also based for part of your training at a college or university then you will almost certainly find that your host organization offers support for study skills. Broadly, the following skills are normally involved in studying as a student police officer:

- reading skills;
- note taking;
- memorizing;
- using libraries and learning centres;
- researching;
- writing skills;
- time management;
- revising for assessments.

Finally, note that you may have undiagnosed difficulties in learning which could affect your ability to study. If you are based in a college or university you may be offered screening for such problems at the outset of the programme.

TASK 8

Find out about the reading technique SQ3R, perhaps by using Google or another internet search engine. This will also prove useful to you if you undertake further training as an investigator over the next few years.

4.7 The Learning Requirement

When Her Majesty's Inspectorate of Constabulary (HMIC) published a report called **Training Matters** in 2002, it recommended 59 ways to improve the training of student police officers (HMIC, 2002).

As one response to the recommendations, the Home Office sponsored an independent review and the resulting 'Learning Requirement for Police Probationer Training in England and Wales' was described as 'society's validated expectation of what a police officer needs to know, to do and be disposed to do in the 21st century' (Elliott *et al*, 2003, p 2). The Learning Requirement has since played a major part in the design of the IPLDP curriculum, and has been used to produce a framework of principles upon which the KUSAB expectations (see 3.5 above) of a student police officer are based. It also helps inform your organization's approach to community engagement and PDUs (see 4.8 and 4.10 below respectively).

The Learning Requirement is divided into seven main headings:

1. Understanding and Engaging with the Local Community

Learning to position oneself appropriately as a police officer in the local community. In this context, local community includes temporary residential, Gypsy, and Traveller groups.

2. Enforcing the Law and Following Police Procedures

Learning to use the law appropriately in the context of professional judgement and learning to follow appropriate police procedures.

3. Responding to Human and Social Diversity

Learning to act appropriately in responding to human and social diversity including, but not exclusively, to race in (a) the community and (b) the police family.

4. Positioning oneself in the Role of a Police Officer Inside the Police Organization

Learning to position oneself appropriately as a police officer in relation to the organization and the occupational culture.

5. Professional Standards and Ethical Conduct

Learning to live up to one's service ideals and standards.

6. Learning to Learn and Creating a Basis for Career-Long Learning

Learning to learn about one's role as a police officer in the community and the police organization.

7. Qualities of Professional Judgement and Decision-Making

4.8   Learning from the Community

Under the IPLDP, all student police officers are expected to undertake at least 80 hours of community engagement in the first few months of their service, normally as part of Phase 2 or Phase 3 (if your force uses this terminology). These hours could be a continuous week of block placement or perhaps one or two days per week for a number of months. You will be based with a community group or a public, private, or voluntary organization such as a care home, a refugee support centre, or a youth-offending team. A particular emphasis is placed on the opportunities the placement provides for you to experience and explore issues around ethnicity and diversity (by 'issues around diversity' the police service normally means gender, disability, gay and lesbian groups, and age). However, the community engagement can also be used to give you an insight into the community's expectations of the police. Examples of these latter kinds of placement include being based in local supermarkets, hospitals, schools, and housing authority units.

You are not likely to be in uniform (or carrying personal safety equipment) whilst undertaking the community engagement. Your force and the community organization concerned may decide that it is best not to reveal to others involved that you are a student police officer in training. This is normally to allow you to interact as naturally as possible with the clients of the organization, particularly if some of these clients may be hostile to the police. If this is the case, bear the following in mind:

- Your force will have conducted a risk assessment concerning the placement but, if you feel uncomfortable in terms of your own personal safety, then you should make this known to your force. If the problem persists then you may wish to contact your Police Federation representative (see 6.17 below).
- There will be standard operating procedures (SOPs) in place to govern the relationships between your force and the organizations involved and also what you should do under certain circumstances—for example, in the case of questions concerning health and safety. Familiarize yourself with these SOPs.

> **TASK 9**
>
> You are on community engagement at a centre that provides support for young people who have been excluded from full-time secondary education. The young people at the day centre have been told that you are a student and that you are there to learn about their experiences and the work of the support group. However, they have not been told that you are a student police officer. During a break you observe one young person selling to another what appears to be Ecstasy, a class B drug (see 10.13 below). What do you do?

4.8.1 Achieving on Your Community Engagement

The following are some suggestions on making the most of your community engagement:

- **Find out about the organization** before you start your placement. For example, does it have a website setting out its aims and objectives? How is it funded? Is it inspected in some way? If so, you might find copies of inspection reports on the net.
- When on your placement, **engage** with people—for example, staff and clients of the organization. They will be as interested in you as you are in them and so you will probably find this quite easy.
- Keep in mind the **objectives** of the community placement. You are on placement to **learn** about community issues. Think also about how you could evidence the skills and knowledge you gained from the placement.
- Consider ways to demonstrate how your understanding of the **ethics and values** of the police service has been enhanced through engagement with the community.

You are sometimes required to present your findings to fellow student officers and perhaps even members of the BCU that you are based with for Supervised Patrol. Your community placement experiences will also form the basis for some of your Learning Diary entries in the SOLAP (see 3.8 above), or could be used in a professional assignment. It is also likely to be relevant to some of the NOS, in particular Unit AA1 to 'promote equality and value diversity'.

Your experience of learning from the community is unlikely to be restricted to the community engagement alone. As noted earlier, you will also receive inputs from guest speakers and community representatives during your training. It is perhaps important to realize that these speakers are not necessarily experienced or qualified as teachers. Instead they are normally invited to contribute to your programme as a form of professional witness. You should make a real effort as a learner to engage with the guest speakers and achieve as much as possible from the session.

4.9 Diversity Training in the Police

One of the reasons for undertaking a community engagement (see 4.8 above) is that it provides real and complex opportunities for you to witness and learn from the views and experiences of members of the diverse communities that make up the UK.

In general terms, diversity is about the range of features found in human life and culture including ethnicity, religion, gender, physical ability, age, sexual orientation, customs, and language. We ought perhaps to celebrate diversity as part of the richness of human cultures, but diversity is sometimes thought of as a form of 'otherness'—that is, qualities that make 'them' different from 'us'. We also examine diversity as a key theme in policing in Chapter 5.

As a student police officer, you will be asked to think carefully about your own experiences and attitudes, and how these might affect the way you relate to the diverse range of people you will encounter in your work. What skills do you need to work effectively in the community, and how can diversity training help you develop these skills? Diversity training is usually placed within IPLDP module IND 2, one of the Induction Modules. NOS element AA1.1 which requires you to 'promote equality and value diversity' is likely to be assessed through direct observation of your actions, the records you keep, and testimony from witnesses.

There is a tendency in some police environments to view diversity training as a form of inoculation. In fact, you sometimes hear police officers saying that they have 'had' their diversity training as if it were some form of one-off injection that would protect them for the rest of their careers. Perhaps it would be more appropriate to see diversity training as just the start of a process that will continue throughout your career.

4.9.1 Questions You Might Need to Consider

You might need to consider the following questions when undertaking your diversity training:

- What are my existing beliefs and attitudes about diversity?
- How will my beliefs and attitudes affect the way that I behave during my everyday and professional life?
- How will my behaviour affect other people around me?

But at the outset, why is it important to consider these questions? This is a crucial starting point because many (but not all) argue that our beliefs, attitudes, and values can spill over into our work whilst on duty as a police officer. Hence if you hold prejudices and bias towards certain groups of people (as most of us do), you are more likely to act upon your prejudices if you are not aware of them, and your conduct may fall short of the standards expected of police officers. There have been a number of reports in recent years about the policing of diverse communities, and in particular the relationship between the police and ethnic minorities. Most student police officers will have heard of the Macpherson Inquiry into the circumstances surrounding the death of the black teenager Stephen Lawrence. On close examination of your own beliefs, you may find that you feel that there are some parts of the community which seem less deserving of a good level of service, especially if they are antagonistic towards the police. You will need to think carefully about this.

Finally, respect for diversity makes good policing sense. You are more likely to gain the cooperation of others, to secure information and intelligence, and hence to progress an investigation, if you are aware of the pluralistic nature of the communities within the UK and know how best to work with them.

4.9.2 The Aim of Diversity Training within the Police Service

The aim of diversity training within the police service is usually to help you to meet the expectations of the public you serve and of your organization regarding your attitude and behaviour towards other people and members of diverse communities.

Perhaps your own personal objective should be that you also actually **believe** in the value of diversity and respectful behaviour. In other words, not only should you behave appropriately because you have been trained to do so, but you should also appreciate the value of such behaviour on a personal level.

4.9.3 Looking Inwards

As an individual, you will view the world in your own way, but you also need to remember that other individuals each have their own world-view that deserves respect. To consider these issues fully, you will need to genuinely engage with your trainers, your colleagues, and most of all, yourself. In particular you will need to examine what you know about yourself in relation to diversity and the following issues:

What I know about myself as an individual:

- how I currently behave;
- my current beliefs;
- my current values;
- my present attitudes;
- how my background has influenced me.

What I know about myself as a student police officer:

- my responsibilities;
- the duties I have to perform;
- my career history;
- the policies I have to follow;
- how the law affects me.

TASK 10

Take the time to think, then jot down your thoughts about the points above—you might find it quite hard to see yourself in these ways. Reflect upon your ideas—which parts have you found easy, and which parts have been more puzzling? Do you know why? Through asking yourself these questions, you will be preparing yourself for genuine engagement with police service diversity training.

TASK 11

Consider:

- your experiences in life so far and those you are likely to have in the near future;
- your prejudices and their influence on what you do;
- your assumptions and stereotypical views, and their consequences;
- your view of the world you live in and the people within it;
- your ability to mix well in a social environment with people from other backgrounds and cultures.

Again, take time to think about each point in turn. Make brief notes and reflect upon your answers.

4.9.4 Diversity and the Experiential Learning Cycle

We discussed the experiential learning cycle, and its use in police training and education, earlier in this chapter. A similar approach can be used to help you learn about your own attitudes and behaviour and how diversity can be valued. This is illustrated in the diagram below:

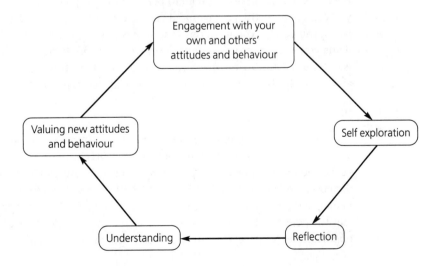

One starting point in the cycle could be **Engagement with Your Own and Others'
Attitudes and Behaviour**. You can observe diversity in a variety of locations:

• during your training in role-plays, simulations, and discussions;
• during your community engagement (see 4.8 above); and
• in the work place and off duty, with friends, colleagues, and relatives.

What differences do you see in how people behave and their attitudes and beliefs? Try to be
open to feedback and discussion; remember that other people probably feel as certain about
their beliefs and attitudes as you feel about yours!

The next stage of the cycle is **self-exploration**. Consider how you arrived at your existing
values, attitudes, and beliefs:

• What part of your history contributed towards how you behave now?
• Did you arrive at your existing beliefs as a result of influences in your background or from
self-teaching? In other words, were your attitudes 'caught' or 'taught'?

The **reflection** phase of the cycle might make you feel uncomfortable, frustrated, or even confused. After all, you may not have questioned your own values and beliefs before, and you might
be feeling some self-doubt. You might also feel uneasy about the other people's views. Remind
yourself why you are exploring the way you think and the future benefits of all your hard work.

After a period of disorientation, you will begin to have some **understanding** and feel more
comfortable. You will have recognized that your attitudes and behaviours are linked to the
environment you have been living in. You may well change some of your prejudices by facing
them head-on and seeing how self-defeating they can be.

With time, you may come to **value your new attitudes and behaviours**. Whatever happens
to you, as long as you have remained open minded, open to change, and taken part with enthusiasm and professionalism, you will have achieved greater understanding.

> **TASK 12**
>
> After completing the various suggested activities above, consider writing up your reflections as
> evidence towards the knowledge requirement of CAR AA1 in your SOLAP.

4.10 Professional Development Units (PDUs)

Earlier you read about the three learning domains (see 4.3.2 above) and that your learning
as a student police officer often (deliberately) begins with relatively simple tasks. This might
involve acquiring largely factual knowledge, and once this has been assimilated your learning
will be developed until you are able to **apply** your learning.

It will sometimes be appropriate to perform the simpler tasks in simulated situations, so that
you can easily rectify mistakes and clarify any misunderstandings. Eventually though, it will
be appropriate for you to go onto the streets of your town or city and begin the process of policing your community, first on Supervised Patrol and then later on Independent Patrol. As this
is initially a daunting prospect, you will be allocated a tutor, coach, or mentor to support you,
and probably also be attached to a Professional Development Unit (PDU).

4.10.1 PDUs

Professional Development Units (also known occasionally as Probationer Development Units)
are relatively new in policing. In some forces PDUs have only been established in the last few
years, and this might partly explain why some BCUs struggle to support a large number of student police officers (HMIC, 2005a, p 17). There has also been some criticism of the lack of police
management support of some force PDUs. A Skills for Justice report in 2007 noted that this
'has the potential to have a detrimental effect on the experience of Student Officers and their
opportunities for development and assessment' (Skills for Justice, 2007a, p 4).

PDUs are usually physically based within the BCU and they often carry out a large number of tasks. These include assisting police officers who have transferred from other forces, supporting police officers back into policing duties (for example, after a period of illness) as well as providing important aspects of initial police training—the training of student police officers. However, practice does vary significantly from force to force. In some forces there may be PDUs in every BCU whilst in others a single PDU serves the whole force. Staffing also varies, as does the management structure and the type of resources available, so it is difficult to describe a typical PDU. However, a BCU police officer of inspector rank or above is likely to carry responsibility for a PDU, line-managing sergeants and Pcs (sometimes referred to as training officers) based with the PDU itself.

The PDU is likely to work alongside the other departments in your organization and might be part of your training department (in fact you might receive all your training at the PDU, including classroom-based teaching). You can expect your tutor at the PDU (sometimes called a tutor constable or assessor constable) to be an experienced officer with skills in coaching and assessment. Whatever the particular arrangements, the PDU is likely to be of crucial importance to you during your training, an observation supported by the Home Office (2005b, p 22): 'The importance of the role of the Professional Development Unit in providing and supporting . . . learning experiences throughout the whole of the probationary period cannot be overstated.'

4.10.2 What Are the Advantages of the PDU?

PDUs provide you with the opportunity to apply your learning from the training room in a controlled environment. So, instead of being immersed straight away in a world of reactive policing, you can reinforce selected aspects of your learning in simulations of genuine policing tasks. These may be based around particular policing needs of your force, especially towards the end of your training.

The further advantages of this system include the opportunity for your tutor and you to carry out activities, usually on a one-to-one basis (Home Office, 2005b). You will be able to discuss what you intend to do and say at an incident (a **pre-brief**). You will then be able to deal with the incident itself in an effective, safe, and professional manner, albeit in a monitored or co-pilot fashion with your tutor/coach, and then discuss the incident afterwards in a safe environment (**debrief**). This will help you learn, and you will find yourself moving through the different stages of the learning cycle (the ELC, see 4.5 above). As further reinforcement, you will probably be asked to make entries in your Learning Diary (see 4.12 below), which will provide you with further opportunities for self-assessment and reflection.

Within the PDU, staff members (possibly including your tutor) will assess your competence against the NOS and PAC. In turn, the Home Office expects the assessors to be competent to perform this task, perhaps demonstrated through undertaking an assessor's award (Home Office, 2005b). Both your tutor and your line manager will take responsibility for your development and you will be advised by your force to use every opportunity to prove your competency by collecting evidence in your SOLAP (see 3.8 above).

You may find yourself wondering if you could learn everything you need by being out on the streets. There are one or two police forces that may believe this too, but most subscribe to the view that you will succeed best through a combination of learning in the training room (and through reading and study) and learning in practice.

4.11 Coaching

In police training, coaching is normally carried out one-to-one, and will be one of the responsibilities of your tutor or mentor, particularly when you are based with a PDU (see 4.10 above).

As soon as you have been given details of your tutor(s), try to arrange a meeting at the earliest opportunity. When you meet, you may find yourself talking about your background, how you came to join the police, and what you are aiming for. Do not say too much if it makes you feel uncomfortable, and remember to tell your tutor the name by which you wish to be referred to.

Take your SOLAP with you if it contains any feedback from your training staff at university or training centre, so that your tutor can start to get to know you.

Be prepared to explain your own preferred learning style having completed the first five tasks of this chapter. Show them entries from your Learning Diary (see 4.12 below) to help illustrate your strengths and weaknesses, so that together you can create a development plan for the future. Make a list of subjects that you have already learned in theory, so that together you can plan how to apply your learning in the work place.

4.11.1 The Coaching Process

Your tutor will use a variety of techniques to help you learn.

Questioning is a valuable technique and can involve closed questions (with a yes or no answer), open questions which need fuller answers, and reflective questions to check your understanding. If your tutor uses multiple questions you need to answer one question at a time to avoid confusion. Watch out for 'leading' questions which might also confuse you or lead you to agree, even though you might have a different opinion. (Remember, this could equally well apply to your own use of questions, so you should be aware of what style of questions to ask your tutor.)

Coaching often takes place before and after you attend an incident as part of Supervised Patrol. These incidents may have been carefully selected by the PDU, that is they wait for a particular incident to be reported (such as a suspected shoplifting incident) and then accompany you to that incident. In some cases, for practical or other reasons, you may attend any incident that day, regardless of its nature. Your response to incidents (but not necessarily on the first occasion) will be important in terms of your subsequent assessment against the NOS (see 3.6 above).

Pre-briefs are a good way of preparing for attending an incident. Your tutor will question you about the theory you have learned in the training room and then ask you how you intend to deal with the incident.

Debriefs take place after an incident. Your tutor will choose a suitable environment in which to debrief you. You will probably be asked to reflect on the incident and make notes (which you can use later for your Learning Diary) of what went well for you at the incident, and what did not go quite so well for you. Using these points, your tutor may employ the ELC we described in 4.5 above to develop greater learning by asking questions such as 'What happened at the incident? What are you going to do differently (or better) in the future?'

The **feedback** your tutor offers you serves two main purposes: first to reassure you that your contribution has been recognized and noted, and second to help you develop the skills and abilities required. When giving feedback your tutor might well use the following guidelines:

- giving feedback only on things that can be changed;
- only describing what they have observed;
- being specific;
- resisting the temptation to make judgements;
- choosing the most appropriate time to give the feedback;
- giving the feedback as soon as possible after making the observation;
- accepting that tutors cannot force an individual to change.

A common technique employed is to structure the feedback as a kind of sandwich, by first making an observation on something you did well, then discussing a developmental point, and then returning to something else you did well.

Identifying your learning needs helps you and your tutor plan for the future. As a result of the pre-brief, your performance during the incident, and the debrief, both you and your tutor will be able to identify your learning needs and these can be entered in your Learning Diary. You may need to revise the theory once more, or take part in a simulated exercise, or it may be that you simply need more practice.

After time you may come to the conclusion that some aspects of policing are largely based upon using a 'reference library' of previous experiences that you can call upon. Eventually, incidents, calls, and circumstances will begin to look familiar and you will feel more confident in dealing with situations—the stage of proficiency that we described in 4.2 above.

4.12 The Learning Diary

The place of the Learning Diary in the SOLAP and its function within Learning Development Reviews are described in Chapter 3. You will be asked to keep a Learning Diary throughout your training, but the format of the diary is likely to reflect the particular phase of training (for example, the style used for community engagement will not be the same as that used for Supervised Patrol). This should be explained to you during the induction phase of your training. Your Learning Diary is for writing down personal reflections, so that you will be able to make judgements on your progress, evidence competency for assessment purposes, and plan future development. Consider structuring your diary entries to follow the four stages of the ELC; in each entry you should try and answer the following questions:

- What happened?
- How did you, and the others around you, respond?
- What was the outcome of the events?
- What could you do differently, or better, in the future?

During the first two phases of training you will probably be asked to make weekly entries in your Learning Diary and then on a monthly basis.

The following is an example of a number of (fictitious) Learning Diary entries.

Student Police Officer: PC Phillips

Crime

Whilst on night duty on mobile patrol, my tutor and I were sent along with other patrols to an audible alarm activation at a newsagents on a housing estate where suspects had been seen to make off on foot with cigarettes and alcohol.

Key learning points:
Choosing the right search parameters when called to incidents.

What surprised me?
My tutor did not drive us straight to the newsagents but began an area search for the suspects some distance away having judged how long it took for the alarm to be notified to control, how long it took for us to be sent to the call, and how far the suspects could have travelled on foot in that time.

How will I put this learning into practice?
In the future, if appropriate I will also notify control of my intention not to go straight to the scene, but to judge how long it has been since the incident took place, taking into consideration direction of travel of the suspect(s) and begin my search some distance away from the scene. I will also consider sitting in a static location with the engine of the car switched off, waiting and listening, as well as requesting a dog patrol to attend to track the suspect.

Intelligence

Today in our briefing we were given intelligence about a known criminal who is suspected of committing burglaries in our area during the daytime. The MO of the suspect is to gain entry via insecure windows at the back of terraced houses, make an untidy search, take high-value electronic equipment in pillow cases from the house, and leave via the front door.

Key learning points:

The importance of intelligence to police operations.

What surprised me?

Whilst on foot patrol today, my tutor and I saw the same suspect from the briefing on a housing estate, apparently trying to hide from us in the back garden of a house. We confirmed with the homeowner that the suspect did not have permission to be in the garden. His behaviour, the existence of information, time of day, and location were our grounds to look for stolen property and we carried out a s 1 PACE search. In a pillow case just a few feet from the suspect we found an iPod, another make of MP3 player, and a DVD recorder. I arrested the suspect as his arrest was necessary for one of the reasons we learnt about during training.

How will I put this learning into practice?

This incident reinforced the importance of intelligence. I will pay more attention to briefings as the information in them helps my patrol skills and gives me the opportunity to pay attention to specific areas and to specific people. I see now that intelligence-led policing can really work and help me to add to my reasonable suspicion to carry out s 1 PACE searches. I will also go to the Intel unit by myself from time to time to get current information on disqual drivers and their cars.

Investigation and interview

While observing my tutor constable interviewing a shoplifter I had arrested in the shopping centre, I saw how to prove the offence by interview.

Key learning points:

Questioning techniques for interviewing.

What surprised me?

I was expecting my tutor to use words like 'Did you dishonestly appropriate the property from the shop with the intention of keeping it?' What actually happened was that my tutor used open questions and everyday language and kind of managed the conversation. Questions were used such as 'Why did you go into the shop?', 'What were you thinking about when you picked up the bottle of scotch?', 'How much money did you take to go shopping today?', 'What did you want to do with the scotch?'

How will I put this learning into practice?

In my interviews I will attempt to establish the truth not by using the words in the legislation so much as general conversation which will get a better response from the suspect for the points we may need to prove. I will attempt to use open questions when appropriate to get as much information from the suspect and begin my questions with 'Tell me about. . .' This appeared to me to be a better way of interviewing a suspect.

Non-crime incidents

Today my tutor and I were requested to attend a misper call which involved a 10-year-old child who had gone missing from the parental home.

Key learning points:

An appropriate initial response to child mispers.

What surprised me?

Before we started to complete the misper form my tutor asked the parents if they had looked for the child themselves. They said they had searched the whole house but even so, my tutor said that another search would have to be done. I observed my tutor searching the house and gardens of the misper looking for anywhere that a child of that age could hide. We looked for any voids or spaces which could contain a child. After a little while, we went to an old shed at the bottom of the garden and found the child hiding. My tutor then asked some questions of the parents and the child about why he might have chosen to hide in the way he did.

How will I put this learning into practice?

When I receive the report of a misper, especially a child, I will normally consider starting the enquiry by making a thorough search of the home address, even if the family have said they have already done one. This might save a lot of time in the long run and might prevent a large-scale search involving lots of time and people. I will look for any spaces which would contain a child and concentrate my efforts to locate these spaces in the first place.

Police policies and procedures

Today we attended the scene of a road traffic collision between two cars. Neither of the drivers were accompanied nor injured. The vehicles themselves had very slight damage and the collision took place at a T-junction at very slow speed.

Key learning points:

The importance of following force policy.

What surprised me?

I did not have any suspicion that either of the drivers had been drinking, but even so, my tutor reminded me of our force policy to give a breath test to every driver involved in a road traffic collision using the powers under the Road Traffic Act. I was surprised to discover that, even though it was only 8.30 am, one of the drivers proved positive and I arrested him.

How will I put this learning into practice?

In the future I will take care to implement force policy and breathalyse every driver involved in a crash whether I suspect them of having been drinking or not. This will be the case in whatever circumstances the crash takes place and whether or not any other driving offences are suspected or not.

Protecting people

Whilst on foot patrol in the shopping centre today, my tutor asked me to imagine I was a thief, to look around at the shoppers, and to consider who is most likely to become a victim of a crime whilst out shopping.

Key learning points:

Crime prevention is just as important as crime detection.

What surprised me?

When I looked around I saw people paying very little attention to their valuable property. I saw people of all ages carrying mobile telephones very insecurely in their hands, giving a thief the opportunity to snatch them out of their hands. This was a similar thing for others with their iPods, it was as if they didn't see the dangers. There were also a number of people holding large amounts of money in their hands and a great number of older and more vulnerable women carrying their purses very high up in handbags which could easily be snatched. Together with my tutor we began advising some of these people about the possible consequences of their actions.

How will I put this learning into practice?

Whenever it is appropriate to offer crime-prevention advice I will do so. For example, if I observe a vulnerable person keeping their purse near the top of their bag I will take the opportunity to tell them that it could be snatched and that they should think about fixing a chain onto the purse at one end and attaching the other end to their bag.

Stops and searches

While out with my tutor today I saw a number of searches being carried out by other officers. Some of the searches did not go quite as well as the others and in some of them the suspects were clearly not as compliant.

Key learning points:

The importance of following a professional 'stop, account, and search' routine.

What surprised me?

Most of the searches in which the suspects had been more compliant were the ones where the searching officers gave the suspect the PACE Codes of Practice requirements for searching. What I saw was the searching officers going through the requirements using the mnemonic GOWISELY. The effect of this seemed to be that the suspects thought the searching officers really knew their powers and so they did not try to obstruct or interfere in the process.

How will I put this learning into practice?

When I carry out my searches I will do exactly the same thing and use the mnemonic GOWISELY to remind me of what to say. Before today, I have to say that I thought I was taught it only to help me remember what was in the code for my exam, but now I realize how important it is and the effect it has on people that are being searched.

Traffic

Today on mobile patrol, we must have stopped about 15 vehicles at various times of the day. Each time we stopped a vehicle it was to give some advice to the driver.

Key learning points:

The need to address driver and passenger safety.

What surprised me?

The reasons why we stopped the vehicles did not appear to be major issues as far as I was concerned. The stops were for no seat belts, children that were too short to be in the front seat of a car, parking near crossings, and minor speeding. Then, after speaking to my tutor, I realized that we have a responsibility towards road safety and that it is part of our job to prevent injury to drivers, passengers, or pedestrians, not just to 'catch criminals'. After all, if we can prevent someone's head hitting the windscreen or the head of another passenger when the vehicle is involved in a crash by reminding them to wear their seat belt or wearing it properly, then we might have saved a lot of pain and misery. Equally, parking near crossings cannot take place as it endangers the lives of pedestrians using the crossings. Finally, we learnt recently in class that 30 mph areas are there for a purpose and exceeding the speed limit by even a small amount may mean the difference between life and death for a pedestrian.

How will I put this learning into practice?

Even when I am over-worked with calls to attend, I will try to take the time to give advice to road users as there are thousands of deaths and injuries on the road each year as a result of bad driving, not wearing seatbelts, bad parking, and insecure children. I will point out that the problem lies in the unexpected situations that can arise within split seconds that cannot be avoided. It will be difficult for me sometimes to be motivated to give advice to a road user when I am tired and hungry, but I must remember that one day I might not take up the opportunity to say something and a moment or two later that same road user is involved in a crash and is injured or possibly dies. I would find that very hard to cope with.

TASK 13

Use the theories we have discussed in this chapter to plan a number of entries in your Learning Diary related to your experiences when being coached or taught, using the following suggestions:

- Make reference to your preferred learning style.
- Determine which learning domain(s) you have been working within for any particular incident and what level of that domain you reached.
- Assess what level of the domain you need to return to if you were not competent to carry out the task, and produce a plan in your diary to develop greater learning.
- Use the diagnosis of your preferred learning style to create a learning method that suits you.

- Describe how you will employ memory tools to improve your ability to recall facts.
- Use the outcomes of your pre-briefs and debriefs to make diary entries which include using the ELC process to make an action plan for learning.
- During the 'classroom' part of your training, reflect on the legislation, policy, and procedure you have learned and how you will put the theory into practice, and follow this up in later diary entries.
- During your placements in the community and within the extended police family, reflect on the benefit of interacting with these groups and how you might be able to use that learning in the future.
- Reflect on your ability to satisfy the performance criteria of the NOS, and assess yourself against the PAC and make diary entries accordingly (see Chapter 3).

4.13 Forms of Reasoning and Argument

An important aspect of learning, either as a student police officer undertaking training, or as an experienced police officer, is a **logical and structured** approach to problem solving. This is not to deny the use of intuition as a problem-solving approach; many cases of intuition in fact rest on rational thought processes, but the person is unaware of this because the reasoning is not part of their conscious thought. Of course we should not all behave like the Star Trek character Mr Spock with his absolute adherence to purely logical argument; we must always leave room for creativity. Many people would also probably claim to be naturally logical, and hence not require any particular training (or to have any particular need to read this part of the Handbook). However, logical ways of thinking are skills that need to be nurtured and developed, and cannot simply be assumed to already exist at the appropriate level.

Logic underpins the development of sound arguments which we use to express ourselves, sometimes in a formal context (such as in court), or on other occasions, probably less formally, in a Learning Diary entry. Perhaps just as important in the policing context, is the ability to identify **fallacious** (incorrect) lines of argument. On occasions these have contributed to miscarriages of justice and to innocent people enduring long prison sentences.

Reasoning is also an important skill to develop within investigation and you will find references to investigative reasoning in the IPLDP Crime Investigation Model during your training (see Chapter 12).

4.13.1 Inductive Reasoning

Inductive reasoning involves generalizing from a number of previous examples to establish a rule or theory. This form of reasoning is very common in everyday life and, indeed, was the basis for much scientific discovery in the past. (There are some suggestions that this form of reasoning is hardwired into our brains, as most people appear able to use this reasoning without any training.) For example, early humans undoubtedly realized that there is a cycle consisting of day–night–day–night and generalized from this pattern to conclude that, in all future events, night would follow day. On a certain intellectual level most of us are probably content that induction is sufficient grounds for us to retain our acceptance of the day–night–day cycle. We do not necessarily require convincing with the use of astronomical arguments concerning the motions of the Earth, Sun, and the energy in the Solar System. The more this confidence is reinforced by subsequent events, the more we are persuaded by the truth of the generalization. This is known as the **rule of inductive generalization**.

However, despite being a widespread technique for reasoning, induction has an inherent weakness. As Bertrand Russell, Karl Popper, and others have demonstrated (Popper, 1990), there is no **logical reason** why the generalization should follow from the observations. A famous example concerns swans. If every swan we have ever seen so far is white, then we (not unnaturally) conclude that **all** swans are white. This is all very well until we observe our first black swan. (They occur in the southern hemisphere.)

This is not to say that inductive reasoning has no value, but simply that we should be cautious in its application. The danger for student police officers (and indeed, for all of us) of using inductive methods resides in the problem of generalizing from observation, particularly if these observations are limited in number or unrepresentative. For example, consider the white detective investigating gun crime within inner London. In all likelihood, given the social demography of the area (there are significant numbers of ethnic minority people living in inner London), these crimes are likely to involve members of ethnic minorities to an extent that might appear disproportionate to a detective new to the area. However, these parts of Britain also tend to feature amongst some of the poorest (as do parts of Manchester and Birmingham). A false generalization here would be for our detective to conclude, using induction, that gun crime is somehow endemically black in nature rather than symptomatic of some other social factors that have independent links with gun crime and being black. There is no evidence to show that ethnicity can cause gun crime. In some senses the incorrect reasoning of the detective is a natural response; hence the need for an understanding of the nature and limitations of inductive reasoning. The detective's error in judgement is not helped by some parts of the media referring to gun crime in London as a 'black on black' phenomenon. In summary, the mistake made here by our detective is to mistake association for causality, through the incorrect application of inductive reasoning.

Similarly, unless unchecked, we all have a tendency to look for evidence which supports our generalized inductive theories and to ignore other evidence. This is particularly problematic in investigations. (The proper scientific approach is to look for evidence which might contradict our theories.)

It helps, particularly if you move on later to more advanced training in investigation, to be aware that there are a number of forms of inductive reasoning. A very common form of inductive reasoning used within criminal investigation is the so-called 'argument from analogy'. A number of terms are used to explain these ideas; note that in the following example about A,B,C and D:

- **premises** are starting points for an argument (here, premises are not buildings);
- the letters A, B, C, and so on are shorthand for observations or other known facts;
- **has the property of** is a technical term meaning that the two listed items share a quality in common.

Argument from Analogy

- A has the property of C.
- B has the property of C.
- B has the property of D.
(Together, these statements are called the **premises**).

Therefore (and this is the **argument** part):
- A has the property of D (the **conclusion**).

In fact, there are usually more than three premises, as illustrated below (adapted from an example devised by Thomas R. O'Connor, Associate Professor of Justice Studies):

- Tuesday's burglary was committed during the night (T has the property of N).
- Wednesday's burglary was committed during the night (W has the property of N).
- Tuesday's burglary took place in Acacia Gardens (T has the property of A).
- Wednesday's burglary took place in Acacia Gardens (W has the property of A).
- Tuesday's burglary involved forcing a window (T has the property of F).
- Wednesday's burglary involved forcing a window (W has the property of F).
- Tuesday's burglary involved a careful search for property (T has the property of C).
- Wednesday's burglary involved a careful search for property (W has the property of C).

Suppose we now know that:

- Tuesday's burglary was committed by Bill (T has the property of B).

Therefore our conclusion is that:

- Wednesday's burglary was probably also committed by Bill (W has the property of B).

Note that we cannot be **certain** that Bill committed the burglary on Wednesday, as this is inductive reasoning. It is also true that we could probably work out that Bill is a suspect (due to the similarities in circumstances) without knowing about 'arguments from analogy'. However, formalizing the reasoning used in this way has two main advantages:

- we know where this reasoning comes from;
- we know its strengths and limitations.

TASK 14

You are given the numbers 2, 4, 8, and 16.
What is the next number in the pattern?
(Check the answer—it is not 32!).

4.13.2 Deductive Reasoning

In contrast with inductive reasoning, deductive approaches start with assumptions (or a general rule) and **deduce** other conclusions from these starting points. For example, we may assume that all human beings have DNA. If we arrest John, a human being, then we can deduce that John has DNA. Deductive reasoning forms part of a wider set of concepts and methods known as logic. In fact there are two main schools of logic:

- formal logic or sometimes symbolic logic which is mathematically derived (using, for example, set theory); and
- informal logic which uses everyday language.

We will examine informal logic in this Handbook. We can use deductive logic to draw conclusions from initial assumptions. For example, in terms of John and DNA we can describe our logical process in the following ways:

> - All humans have DNA.
> - John is a human.
> - Therefore John has DNA.

This is known as an **argument** (see 4.13.4 below).

Deductive reasoning also has its drawbacks. In essence, it helps us to extend what we already know by demonstrating the consequences of our assumptions rather than adding directly to the pool of new knowledge. Further, although the logic is impeccable the value of our conclusions is entirely dependent on the truth of our assumptions (see 4.13.5 below).

4.13.3 Inductive and Deductive Reasoning: The Debate

In conclusion, inductive reasoning is a useful means of adding to our knowledge, but is inherently untrustworthy. On the other hand, deductive reasoning is logically watertight but only extends what we already know. The two approaches are not in competition or contradiction (as some writers claim) but perhaps should be viewed as complementary ways of reasoning. A good example is falling from a building. We can observe that on every occasion somebody jumps or is pushed from a building then they fall a distance before they are stopped (usually by the ground). Inductive reasoning tells us that this will always be the case. Deductive reasoning would use Newton's Laws, with the added advantage of being able to predict, say, the velocity on impact. The two approaches are not contradictory. Indeed, the starting points for deductive reasoning are often determined inductively.

TASK 15

Classify the following statements as examples of inductive or deductive reasoning or a combination of the two (use only the statements given to you—make no other assumptions).

(a) Every person's fingerprint is unique to him/her, as no two fingerprints have ever been found to match.

(b) If anything made up largely of water boils at approximately 100°C, and blood is mostly water, then it must boil at roughly 100°C.

(c) You need to take care when searching the clothes of a suspect as many criminals are drug addicts and they may have syringe needles hidden somewhere.

(d) Defence barristers cannot have a conscience, because they are prepared to defend somebody like Myra Hindley (a notorious child killer).

> (e) Anyone who works long and difficult hours in their job should be paid well. Police officers work long and difficult hours, so they should be paid well.
>
> (f) If DNA is entirely inherited and two people are found with identical DNA then they must be identical twins.

4.13.4 Arguments

Technically speaking, an **argument** is a group of propositions of which one is claimed to follow from the others—the process known as **inference**.

Consider the following simple example of an argument:

> - All humans have DNA.
> - John is human.
>
> (We now draw the inference)
> - Therefore John has DNA (the conclusion).

Of course, in everyday policing, arguments are not usually expressed in this way. Instead they are incorporated into sentences, sometimes with information extraneous to the argument, and often with the conclusion presented first. Written arguments often contain hidden premises (see 4.13.1 above for a description of premises) which are not immediately obvious to the untrained eye. It requires skill (derived from practice) to identify the premises, forms of argument, and the conclusions and, most importantly, to decide whether these arguments are logically justified or not.

There are however, various key words which give clues to the structure of the argument, in terms of the premises and the conclusions: (see opposite)

TASK 16

Just for fun, try the following Critical Thinkers' Questionnaire (some questions are adapted from Facione (1998), most are original). Answer each question with an Agree or a Disagree. Then calculate your critical thinker index by turning to the answer to Task 16 at the end of this chapter.

(a) I dislike those parts of talk shows where people just state their opinions but never give any reasons at all.

(b) I'm entitled to my opinions.

(c) If a person's DNA is found at the scene of a crime then they must have been there.

(d) No matter how complex the problem there is probably a simple solution.

(e) God either exists or doesn't exist. Therefore the chances that he exists are 50:50.

(f) Rather than relying on someone else's notes, I prefer to read the material myself.

(g) Working out what people really mean by what they say is important to me.

(h) If somebody is really sincere in their arguments then the case they are making is more likely to be correct.

(i) I prefer not to make decisions until I've thought through my options.

(j) I try to see merit in other people's opinions even if I disagree with them.

(k) The reason why the US has such a high murder rate is because of the widespread availability of guns.

(l) The validity of an idea is enhanced by effective communication skills.

(m) A theory is always false if it is incorrectly argued.

(n) I dislike it when tutors discuss problems rather than just giving the answers.

(o) You can't disprove the existence of leprechauns.

4.13.5 Forms of Argument and Proof

As you have seen, an argument is the process of drawing inferences from premises. As well as logic, arguments also tend to take certain assumptions as being inherently true. For example, the 'law of the excluded middle' which states that it is not possible for something to be and not be at the same time. So a person committed arson or they did not. Similarly we have the 'law of identity': if A is the same as B, and B is the same as A, then A and B are the same. So if a substance is tested by a forensic laboratory and has the same chemical composition as diamorphine then it is diamorphine.

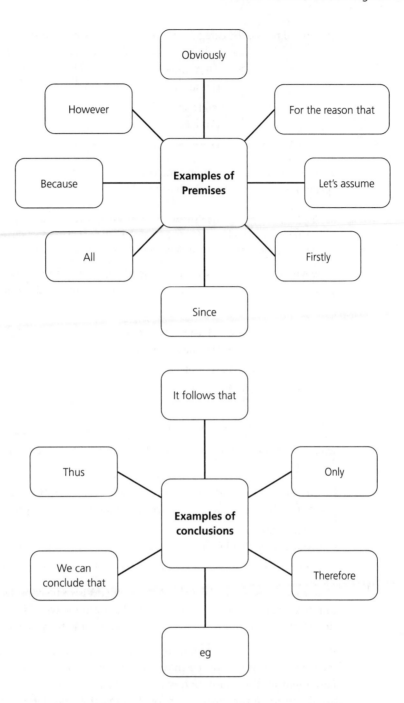

There are many forms of argument which are logically justifiable and we will examine those most relevant to both learning as a student police officer and more widely in policing itself. Likewise, there are some forms of argument which are not valid arguments at all and, unfortunately, these are very common and are referred to as **fallacies** (see 4.13.7 below). In order to learn, it is important that we avoid fallacies and so we need to be able to spot them.

The most famous forms of deductive argument are drawn from a family of arguments referred to as **syllogisms** (eg categorical, disjunctive, and hypothetical syllogisms). For example, the categorical syllogism is an argument consisting of two premises and a conclusion; usually employing the concepts of 'all', 'some', and 'none'. Probably the most famous example is as follows:

> **A famous syllogism**
> - All men are mortal (called the major premise).
> - Socrates was a man (called minor premise).
>
> Therefore (as before, this is the inference)
> - Socrates was mortal (conclusion).

In general terms, the categorical syllogism goes something like this:

> - All As are Bs.
> - C is an A.
>
> Therefore:
> - C is a B.

As another example of a syllogism, consider the famous logic of Conan-Doyle's Sherlock Holmes (paraphrased as 'the dog that didn't bark'):

> The Simpson incident had shown me that a dog was kept in the stables, and yet, though someone had been in and had fetched out a horse, he had not barked enough to arouse the two lads in the loft. Obviously the midnight visitor was someone whom the dog knew well (Conan-Doyle, 1894, p 9).

However, there are many other forms of argument beyond the syllogisms (some of which are potentially probably more useful to you). An example is the **modus tollens** form of argument:

> - If P then Q (a premise).
> - Q is false (a premise).
>
> We conclude:
> - P is false (the conclusion).

An everyday example of *modus tollens* might occur during an investigation into homicide (adapted from an example written by Thomas R. O'Connor, Associate Professor of Justice Studies):

> - If Mary's boyfriend is to be considered as a suspect, he must have a motive (a premise).
> - Mary's boyfriend does not have an apparent motive (a premise).
>
> We then have a conclusion:
> - Mary's boyfriend is probably not the offender (the conclusion).

Note that the first premise ('If Mary's boyfriend is to be considered as a suspect, he must have a motive') might well have been established using inductive reasoning (see 4.13.1 above) as most victims of murder are murdered by those they know, and there is normally a motive for the murder.

It is important to note that, if we begin our arguments with correct premises and then argue logically, we can be assured that our conclusions are also correct. However, if we start with false premises then, although we may use a logical and deductive argument, **we cannot say anything** about the truth of our conclusions: they may be true or untrue. This is an important observation in the context of policing.

For example, consider the following argument:

> - All humans are self-centred (a premise).
> - Criminals are humans (a premise).
>
> Therefore:
> - Criminals are self-centred (the conclusion).

This is a perfectly valid **argument** but the validity of the **conclusion** depends entirely upon the truth of the premise. The premise that 'all humans are self-centred' might not be correct.

The relationship between premises, arguments, and conclusions is summarized in the table below:

Premises	Argument	Conclusion
Valid	Valid	Valid
Invalid	Valid	Valid or invalid (we do not know)
Valid	Invalid	Valid or invalid (we do not know)
Invalid	Invalid	Valid or invalid (we do not know)

As an example, consider the following written argument taken from a report in the late 1990s:

Human rights training in the RUC also lags behind other police organizations we have spoken to. In the new curriculum (introduced only this year), of 700 sessions of training there are only 2 sessions dedicated to human rights, compared with 40 of drill and 63 of firearms training (Patten Commission, 1999, para 4.5).

We can summarize this argument as follows:

> - The proportion of time taken in training a skill or subject reflects its relative importance (a premise).
> - A new curriculum provided an opportunity for the RUC to reassess the relative importance of these skills and subjects (a premise).
> - The RUC spends proportionally more time training drill than human rights compared with others (a premise).
> - The RUC spends proportionally more time training firearms than human rights compared with others (a premise).
>
> Therefore
> - Human rights training in the RUC lags behind other police forces (the conclusion).

How valid is the conclusion based upon the premises?

Well, we can probably take issue with a number of the premises. For example, the first—that the time taken is proportional to the relative importance. What else could it be proportional to? Drill is an example of a psychomotor skill (see 4.3.2 above). Psychomotor skills quite often take longer to perfect than others. (For example, a joiner could explain to you the theory of how to plane a door to fit its frame relatively easily, but in practice, fitting the door neatly is an entirely different matter.) Taking longer to perfect a skill does not, by itself, prove that we attach more importance to it. So, even though the argument is a valid one, if we have serious doubts concerning the premises then we must also have doubts concerning the validity of the conclusion.

(Remember, we are not saying that Patten's conclusion concerning human rights in the RUC was **wrong**, rather that it is not justified on the grounds that were given. The Commission could well have been correct on this point, but perhaps should have used a different set of premises.)

Understanding the reasoning used (or sometimes the lack of it!) is an important tool in learning. As a trainee police officer you will be presented with many arguments: on the streets, in the training room, and by fellow student officers. Without making yourself too unpopular, you may wish to subject some of these arguments to scrutiny in terms of the validity of their premises and arguments and hence the validity of the conclusions.

TASK 17

Which of the following are arguments?

(a) The registration numbers of all cars can be found on the Police National Computer (PNC). Hence if I stop a car I should be able to check its details on the PNC.

(b) Forensic investigators have a particularly stressful occupation. They are an important part of the criminal justice system. Some work for police forces, whilst others work in the private sector.

(c) I'm tall, so the sight of blood doesn't worry me.

4.13.6 Proof

Within logic, **proof** is the means by which we demonstrate that a deductive argument is valid. In mathematics there are many such proofs, but in everyday life, and criminal investigation in particular, it is very rare.

Indeed, within criminal investigation and policing in general the word proof may also assume other meanings beyond a strictly formal meaning, and is often related to the level of certainty. After all, we speak of proving a person's guilt beyond reasonable doubt. Osterburg and Ward (2004) have provided a useful summary of the levels of certainty that may be involved within criminal investigation:

Levels of Certainty and Levels of Proof

Level of Proof	Intuition	Probable cause	Preponderance of evidence	Clear and convincing	Beyond reasonable doubt	Scientific certainty
Evidence	Hunch, guess, or gut feeling	Facts a reasonable person would accept	Corroborated facts, eyewitness testimony, physical evidence, or evidence interpreted by an expert			Precise facts with known accuracy
Quantity	Articulable suspicion about possible facts	Prima facie, presumptive but rebuttable facts	Over 50% of facts are in support	Slightly less facts than beyond reasonable doubt	Sufficient facts to preclude every reasonable alternative hypothesis	Overwhelming facts
Certainty	Apparent	Possible	Basis for hypothesis formulation		Basis for theory construction	Seldom achieved
Law	Suppressed	Basis for binding over to next stage	Civil law standard of proof	International law standard of proof	Criminal law standard of proof	Seldom used
Investigation	Useful during early stages	Basis for arrest or search warrant	Basis for confession and informant law		Basis for conviction	Seldom used

(Reprinted from Criminal Investigation, 4th edition, with permission. Copyright 2004 Matthew Bender and Company Inc, a member of the Lexis Nexis Group. All rights reserved).

4.13.7 Fallacies

Fallacies (the full technical term is 'informal logical fallacies') are incorrect forms of argument. At the risk of stating the obvious, fallacies are a bad thing and should be avoided. There are dozens of fallacies, some of which are so infamous that they have been given Latin names. Indeed, it is quite a long list; here are just a few:

- affirmation of the consequent;
- anecdotal evidence;
- *argumentum ad antiquitatem*;
- *argumentum ad baculum*.

There are many websites and books which will explain the meaning of these terms. We will concentrate here on some of the more common fallacies. These fallacies are not necessarily mutually exclusive: it is perfectly possible, for example, that a single statement may contain more than one logical fallacy. Bear in mind that in what follows, the conclusions may or may not be valid (most are not); what we are interested in here is the **validity of the argument** not the conclusions. We have used everyday language as the name for each fallacy but have also included their more traditional Latin names where appropriate. If nothing else, this may impress your family and friends.

Anecdotal evidence. One of the most common fallacies is to use personal experience or hearsay as a form of argument. There are a number of problems with this, not least of which is the fact that each of our experiences is unique to us. An example of the anecdotal evidence fallacy is:

Miscarriages of justice are more common today as evidenced by increased coverage in the media.

Appeal to force (*'argumentum ad baculum'*). Appealing to force is the fallacy of using force (or more usually simply the threat of force) in order to try and win an argument. An example of the appeal to force fallacy is:

> If you are innocent you shouldn't be concerned about having your fingerprints taken. However, your consent is really irrelevant as the authorities can force you to give your fingerprints anyway. So, the most sensible policy is cooperation.

Attacking the person (*'argumentum ad hominem'*). This is a particularly common form of fallacy. In fact it divides into two distinct forms: **abusive** and **circumstantial**. The abusive form is the fallacious argument that seeks to undermine the position of an opposing view by attacking the person or people that hold that view. An example of the abusive form is:

> It is the policy of the British National Party that we should reintroduce corporal punishment for petty criminals (BNP, 2005) and this demonstrates how wrong the policy is.

The circumstantial form is an attempt to undermine a particular conclusion by drawing attention to the (irrelevant) personal circumstances of the person constructing the argument. An example would be:

> Naturally you are against speed cameras as you drive a fast car.

Argument from ignorance (*'argumentum ad ignorantiam'*). This fallacy takes two forms: arguing that since something has not been proven false, it must be true and the converse (the argument that since something has not been proven true, it is therefore false). An example of an argument from ignorance is:

> Of course taking an intimate forensic sample from a victim is psychologically damaging. Nobody has proved otherwise.

Appeal to pity (*'argumentum ad misericordiam'*). With this fallacy we try to persuade somebody of our argument by appealing to their pity, often the dire consequences that will follow if the argument is not accepted. An example of an appeal to pity is:

> The government must accept the recommendations of the HMIC report on the FSS. The report took many months and thousands of pounds to produce and this will all be wasted if the recommendations are not accepted.

Appealing to the people (*'argumentum ad populum'*). This is the fallacy of claiming that a proposition is true because it is subscribed to by popular opinion. An example would be:

> The most appropriate penalty for child murder committed by paedophiles is the death sentence. Opinion poll after opinion poll demonstrates that the British people believe this to be the case.

Appeal to authority (*'argumentum ad verecundiam'*). This fallacy needs to be carefully distinguished from the acceptable argument of referring to an authority in a particular field of study as evidence to support an argument **within** that field. The fallacy occurs when an authority is invoked in an irrelevant context. This is sometimes quite subtle. An example of an appeal to authority would be:

> Sir Alec Jeffries invented the DNA profile. His support in 2001 for a National DNA database for all UK citizens lends credibility to the idea.

(Sir Alec is an undoubted expert on DNA genetic fingerprinting, but is he an expert on the implications of a national DNA database?)

Accident (*'dicto simpliciter'*). This fallacy occurs when a generalized rule is applied in circumstances for which it was not intended or designed. An example would be:

> The law states that we are not allowed to 'jump' the red lights at a set of traffic lights. It is therefore wrong for the police to be allowed to do so, even in an emergency.

Converse accident. Needless to say, this is the converse of the fallacy of accident. It occurs when a generalization is based upon an exceptional case. An example is:

> The government is being asked to consider allowing patients with MS to use cannabis for pain relief. If this happens it is only right that they should legalize cannabis for everyone's use.

False cause and effect ('*non causa pro causa*'). This fallacy often occurs when we assume association (often measured as mathematical correlation) is the same as causation. Just because two events occur together does not automatically mean that one caused the other. To assume so is a fallacy. An example of an argument that assumes association and causation are the same would be:

> The widespread availability of guns is a major contributory factor to the murder rate of a country. This is demonstrated by the fact that the countries with the highest gun ownership (such as the US) also have the highest rates of homicide.

There is also the fallacy of assuming an event to be the cause of another event simply because it happened before that event. An example would be:

> Since the availability of hard-core gay pornography on the internet we have witnessed a significant increase in the incidence of anal rape of men.

Begging the question ('*petitio principii*'). This fallacy may take various forms, some of which are quite difficult to spot. In its simplest form a begging-the-question fallacy starts with a questionable premise before making a deduction or sometimes repeating the premise in different words. In more subtle cases the premises are actually a consequence of the conclusion rather than the converse (as it should be). The fallacy often takes the form of circular argument. An example of begging the question would be:

> Freedom of speech is an essential right in a police service, since every police employee should have the right to express him- or herself with complete freedom.

An even more subtle example would be:

> Gays should not be encouraged to join the police. The reason is that any police officer who is 'outed' as gay would find it very difficult to remain in the police after it was revealed that he kept this secret from his fellow officers. Therefore gay police officers will do anything to keep their sexuality secret and will thus be open to blackmail. Therefore gays should not be allowed to join the police.

Irrelevant conclusion ('*ignoratio elenchi*'). This is a fallacious argument which sets out to prove a certain conclusion but instead proves a somewhat different conclusion. An example would be:

> Hundreds of rare bird's eggs are stolen each year, even though we have the Wildlife and Countryside Act. Clearly, we should repeal the Act.

Non sequitur. This is a particularly infamous fallacy, which probably accounts for why there is no common equivalent English phrase. A *non sequitur* is an argument where the conclusion is derived from a set of premises which are not logically connected with the conclusion. The *non sequitur* fallacy happens more often in spoken arguments than in a written form. An example would be:

> We should return to 'bobbies on the beat' in this country. If the police need additional powers then they should receive them.

TASK 18

Identify the fallacies in the following statements (remember, this is not an exercise on the validity of the statement, but on identifying errors in argument):

(a) We must introduce a 'Sarah's Law' against paedophiles in this country in memory of the young girl who was tragically killed.

(b) The police use of test purchasing is wrong. The law states that 'impersonating another for gain' is unlawful and this is exactly what test purchasing involves.

(c) The Intelligence-led Policing model was a mistake. The vast majority of people prefer 'bobbies on the beat' instead of the emphasis on intelligence.

(d) Since the recent increase in asylum-seeker numbers in the UK we have witnessed a big increase in the prostitution problems in Maidbury.

(e) The police reform process is self-evidently moving us in the right direction as evidenced by the support of the Home Office, ACPO, and the 'rank and file' police officers themselves.

(f) Fingerprints are one the most trusted forms of forensic evidence. DNA is sometimes difficult to collect.

(g) When investigating child-abuse allegations if we must err, then we must err on the side of the child.

(h) It is well known that the prime minister, Tony Blair, is a practising Christian. So there must be something in Christianity.

(i) Dr Shipman was able to kill his patients because he was permitted to prescribe diamorphine. We should therefore legislate to stop GPs having this power.

(j) Capital punishment deters crime because it ensures criminals do not recommit murder.

4.14 Answers to Tasks

TASKS 1–4 INCLUSIVE

Possible responses and interpretations are given immediately after these tasks.

TASK 5

You will find that the site will describe each of the categories that we explored in Tasks 1, 2, 3, and 4 as 'activist', 'theorist', 'pragmatist', and 'reflector' and undertaking the online questionnaire would have placed your preferred learning style into a grid:

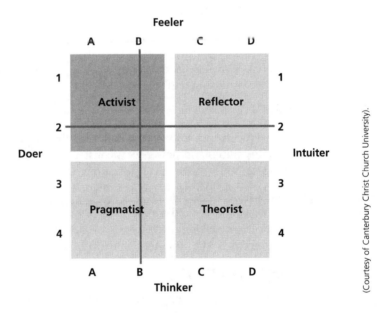

(Courtesy of Canterbury Christ Church University).

Where the two lines intersect gives you some measure of your preferred learning style. It shows that I am a predominantly activist learner, which the site then explains means that I seek hidden possibilities; I learn by talking with others; I get totally involved; I take risks; I am enthusiastic, working quickly and involving others and my favourite question is 'what if'?

The site is not the only way of exploring your preferred learning styles. A popular method in police training is to use Honey and Mumford's Learning Styles Questionnaire. Further details may be found at <http://www.peterhoney.com/>.

TASK 6

Not everybody finds that the Kolb process works for them. Indeed, there are a number of more general critiques of the theory underlying ELC. Rogers, for example, has argued that 'learning includes goals, purposes, intentions, choice and decision-making, and it is not at all clear where these elements fit into the learning cycle' (Rogers, 1996, p 108).

TASK 7

A student police officer, whilst undertaking Personal Safety Training, starts learning how to handcuff a suspect by taking part in supervised practice with a dummy—this is the **experience** stage.

The trainer, observing the practice of the student and testing the results, then asked, 'Were there any risks to you during the cuffing? How tight did that feel for the suspect? What might you have done differently?'—this is the **review and reflect** stage.

That night the student police officer consults his/her notes on how to handcuff suspects and reads about the reasons for doing it in particular ways, including force procedure and the human rights of the suspect—this is the **interpret** stage.

Next day, presented with a fellow student officer to handcuff, the student thinks, 'As a result of what happened yesterday, and because of what I read last night I ought to do it like this'—this is the **action-planning** stage.

TASK 8

SQ3R stands for:

- **S**urvey/Skim the material you need to read
- formulate **Q**uestions that you expect the material to answer
- do the **R**eading
- **R**ecall what you have read and
- **R**eview.

In terms of investigation (particularly preparing for interview), you may wish to read Eric Shepherd's book *SE3R A Resource Book* (Shepherd, 2001), where SE3R stands for 'Survey, Extract, Read, Review, and Respond'.

TASK 9

This is a difficult issue for you. You have probably been attested, and hence have assumed the full responsibilities and powers of a constable and yet you are barely trained and even less experienced. You are with the organization to learn, not to disrupt their usual ways of working. However, dealing in drugs is a serious offence.

Your force will have standing operating procedures to help you decide what to do and these often involve you taking advice from your supervisor and referring to the policies of the organization concerned. The important point is not to keep this to yourself.

TASKS 10, 11, AND 12

Your answers will reflect your own particular experiences and thoughts.

As background reading you might wish to consider looking at the 2003 HMIC thematic inspection 'Diversity Matters' which examined training on matters of race and diversity in the police service. This report should be available from your police force. The 2005 CRE (now part of the Equality and Human Rights Commission) report on the 'Police Service of England and Wales' is also available from <http://83.137.212.42/sitearchive/cre/downloads/PoliceFI_final-2.pdf>. You will find (in Chapter 5 of the report) that the CRE were quite critical of the early versions of the proposed IPLDP curriculum. Finally, you might wish to read the Equality and Human Rights Commission document 'Police and racism: What has been achieved 10 years after the Stephen Lawrence Inquiry report?' available at <http://www.equalityhumanrights.com/ uploaded_files/ raceinbritain/policeandracism.pdf>.

TASK 13

Your responses should have provided some stimulus material to help with Learning Diary entries.

TASK 14

We gave you 2, 4, 8, and 16 to look at and asked you the next number. You would probably have given the answer as 32, if we had not ruled this out. The answer we were thinking of is 31. This is not a trick question!

To explain this, consider the following ways of dividing up a circle:

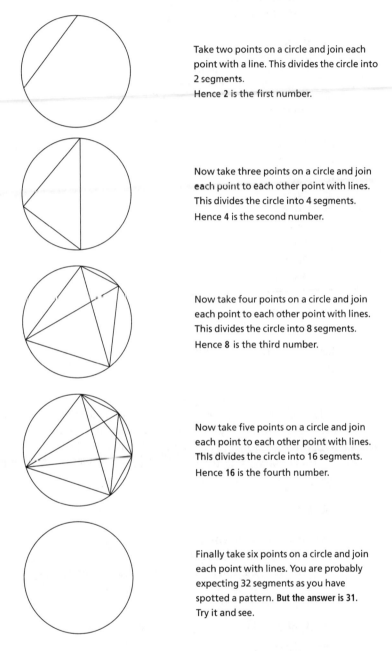

Take two points on a circle and join each point with a line. This divides the circle into 2 segments.
Hence **2** is the first number.

Now take three points on a circle and join each point to each other point with lines. This divides the circle into 4 segments. Hence **4** is the second number.

Now take four points on a circle and join each point to each other point with lines. This divides the circle into 8 segments. Hence **8** is the third number.

Now take five points on a circle and join each point to each other point with lines. This divides the circle into 16 segments. Hence **16** is the fourth number.

Finally take six points on a circle and join each point with lines. You are probably expecting 32 segments as you have spotted a pattern. **But the answer is 31.** Try it and see.

(If you want to know the next numbers in the list then look up 'Moser's circle').

By this stage you might well be thinking, 'What has all this got to do with training as a student police officer?' There are a couple of points here:

• Guessing '32' is a form of inductive reasoning—we are generalizing from past events and making predictions about the future. As explained in this chapter, there are inherent dangers in this that we should be aware of—for example, the likelihood of being wrong. This is easy to spot with 2, 4, 8, 16, and 31 but less easy to identify when we encounter our third example in a week of arresting a member of a minority community for theft.

• When establishing a hypothesis it is tempting to look for evidence which supports the hypothesis rather than refutes it. Remember that, when investigating and interviewing, your main objective is to establish the truth, not to prove a point.

TASK 15

(a)   Inductive reasoning
(b)   Deductive reasoning
(c)   Inductive reasoning
(d)   Deductive reasoning
(e)   Deductive reasoning
(f)   Deductive reasoning

TASK 16

Score 1 for each of the following answers, otherwise score 0. Total your score.

(a)   Agree
(b)   Disagree
(c)   Disagree
(d)   Disagree
(e)   Disagree
(f)   Agree
(g)   Agree
(h)   Disagree
(i)   Agree
(j)   Agree
(k)   Disagree
(l)   Disagree
(m)   Disagree
(n)   Disagree
(o)   Disagree

Remember, this is just for fun.

If you scored:

12–15   You are already a critical thinker.
6–11   You are close to being a critical thinker, but there is room to develop your skills.
0–5   Consider developing your critical thinking skills.
Whatever you scored, you might find it useful to look at Stella Cottrell's *Critical Thinking Skills* (Cottrell, 2005). A 'taster' sample chapter can be located at <http://www.palgrave.com/products/title.aspx?PID=274013>.

TASK 17

(a)   This is an argument.
(b)   This is not an argument.
(c)   This is the basis of an argument, but as it stands, is not really an argument.

TASK 18

(a)   Appeal to pity.
(b)   Accident.
(c)   Appealing to the people.
(d)   False cause and effect.
(e)   To some extent appeal to authority but also begging the question (the Home Office are the originators of the formal police reform process).
(f)   Non sequitur.
(g)   To some extent appeal to pity but also some element of begging the question.
(h)   Appeal to authority.
(i)   Converse accident.
(j)   Begging the question.

5 Key Themes in Policing

5.1 Chapter Briefing

This chapter brings together a number of the underpinning concepts and theories that are important to initial police training.

5.1.1 Aim of the Chapter

The aim of this chapter is to explore a number of key themes in policing that are relevant to the student police officer, through both an analysis of the underlying theory and an examination of the application of those theories.

This chapter will enable you to:

- understand a number of key themes important to policing as a profession, in particular ethics and policing, the nature of personal authority, legitimacy, and discretion;
- comprehend the nature of different models of policing and criminal justice systems;

- place crime reduction, Policing Plans, and the Neighbourhood Policing Programme within the context of contemporary policing;
- discern the basic building blocks of the law and the relationship of the police with the CJS;
- appreciate how an understanding of crime, criminality, and criminology can support your development towards becoming a qualified police officer;
- appreciate the importance of the Police and Criminal Evidence Act 1984 (PACE) in governing your powers as a constable;
- understand how respect for and understanding of human rights is a central requirement of modern-day policing;
- understand how a respect for diversity and the needs of all communities in the UK is central to your professional role;
- understand the particular challenge of domestic violence;
- appreciate the importance of the extended policing family to your role, but also the issues that arise with this extension of private and public policing;
- develop the underpinning knowledge required for a number of NOS elements, entries for your Learning Diary (Phase 3) and a number of CARs of your SOLAP.

5.1.2   National Occupational Standards

This chapter will provide you with the knowledge required to demonstrate aspects of the following NOS elements:

National Occupational Standards Elements

AE1.1   Maintain and develop your own knowledge, skills, and competence

CA1.1   Apply principles of reasonable suspicion or belief

CA1.2   Use law enforcement actions proportionately

CA1.3   Use law enforcement actions fairly

5.1.3   IPLDP Phases and Modules

This chapter will provide you with resources to support the following Induction Modules of the IPLDP:

IND 1   Underpinning ethics/values of the police service (particularly IND 1.2, Applying police ethics)

IND 2   Foster people's equality, diversity, and rights

IND 4   Assess the needs of individuals and provide advice and support (particularly IND 4.5, Challenging inappropriate behaviour)

IND 10   Use police actions in a fair and justified way (particularly IND 10.2, Use police actions fairly)

IND 11   Social, community issues, and neighbourhood policing (particularly IND 11.6, Crime reduction)

It also provides support for the following topic areas of LPG 1:

- Discretion (LPG 1.7);
- Domestic Violence (LPG 1.3).

5.1.4   SOLAP

The contents of this chapter are relevant to the 'knowledge' evidence requirements of CARs AE1 and CA1.

5.1.5 Learning Diary Phases

The contents of this chapter may provide you with stimulus material for completion of your Learning Diary (Phase 3) and the following headings in particular:

- Police policies and procedures;
- Protecting people.

5.2 Introduction

Some parts of this chapter may appear abstract and even unrelated to the day-to-day work of a student police officer. However, much of what follows could form the basis of any claim that policing is a profession. As we shall discuss in 5.3 below, one hallmark of a profession is the existence of a *corpus* of knowledge that influences the actions and decisions of the members of that profession. The principles of law would naturally feature within any such *corpus* of knowledge, but we would also argue for the inclusion of authority, legitimacy, and discretion. Crime and criminality must also surely feature, as should their ancillary concerns of how we model, plan, and implement our policing. Domestic violence, as one of the major contributors to the statistics for volume crime, is also worthy of special consideration. All these matters are considered alongside more recent developments such as the need for our police forces to better represent our pluralisms of communities and the continuing growth of the extended policing family.

5.3 Policing as a Profession

You will often hear references during training to 'adopting a professional attitude' or the need for student police officers to 'behave in a professional manner'. But what does this actually mean? Here we consider the extent to which policing can be considered a profession and what this means for the student police officer.

Before we examine the idea that policing is a profession, we need to consider what we might generally mean by the term 'profession'.

TASK 1

Make a list of professions. What features do you look for in an occupation that makes it a profession? Are there any common features that are found in all the professions you have listed?

5.3.1 What is a Profession?

We encounter the word profession in many different contexts and applied to numerous occupational groups. You might have already suspected that there is not a universally accepted definition of the meaning of profession, though there is a general agreement that not all occupations qualify as professions. It is also potentially confusing that the word 'professional' is often appended to an activity simply to acknowledge that its practitioners receive some form of payment or that it is undertaken more seriously. For example, we know that a reference to a 'professional singer' means that the singer probably earns a living this way. However, there is likely to be more to a profession than this.

Traditionally, there were just four professions: law, medicine, the church, and the military. Later, accountancy became a profession, and now there are many more occupations commonly regarded as professions.

There is a broad consensus in the academic world that at least some of the following are required for an occupation to also be a profession:

- an accepted *corpus* of knowledge and theory underpinning the practice of the profession;
- controls on entry to the profession, normally through qualification, coupled with a need to maintain the currency of qualification;

- autonomy, discretion, and a degree of self-regulation;
- its practitioners have a form of vocational calling;
- a code of ethics.

For most professions, many of the control and regulatory functions are carried out by a professional body.

To illustrate these ideas and to explore them further, we now consider medical practice as an example of a profession and measure it against our list above.

Requirements of a profession	The medical profession
Corpus of knowledge and theory	The scientific basis to medical practice (eg physiology and biochemistry), knowledge of clinical practice (eg conducting physical examinations), aspects of the behavioural and social sciences.
Controls on entry to the profession and continuing professional development	Completing a recognized medical degree, followed by a period of supervised practice (eg foundation training followed by postgraduate training). There is a need to demonstrate regular Continuous Professional Development under seven headings in order to maintain a place on the professional register.
Autonomy, discretion, and self-regulation	Medical doctors have significant autonomy and discretion. Their conduct is regulated by the General Medical Council (GMC). Their representative body is the British Medical Association (BMA). Their authority is largely epistemic in nature (see 5.5 below).
Vocational calling	Difficult to prove, as no clear definitions of a vocation exist. However, interviews for entry to medical degrees often attempt to test applicants for this.
Code of ethics	A code is published by the GMC. It includes the need for doctors to 'make the care of your patient their first concern', to 'respect patients' dignity and privacy', and 'to give patients information in a way they can understand'.

We can see that medicine matches our working definition of a profession very closely.

5.3.2 Is Policing a Profession?

First attempt the following task.

TASK 2

Complete the following table for the occupation of policing:

Requirements of a profession	The policing profession
Corpus of knowledge and theory	?
Controls on entry to the profession and maintenance of position	?
Autonomy, discretion, and self-regulation	?
Vocational calling	?
Code of ethics	?

You probably found that policing in the UK meets some of our criteria for being a profession. Some of the 'missing' elements (such as the need to maintain skills and knowledge) are currently being developed by the NPIA and others. For example, in 2008 the NPIA introduced a new 'Professional Register' for senior investigating officers (SIOs). It is envisaged that the Register will contain the details of all investigators accredited through the Senior Investigating Officer Development Programme (SIODP), or through other means of demonstrating competence. In order to remain 'live' on the register an SIO will be required to provide details of the CPD activity they have undertaken in order to maintain their expertise (NPIA, 2008e). This is similar to the new requirements on medical practitioners who, after 2009, will be required to show evidence that they have kept up to date and are fit to practise in order to retain their place on a professional register (GMC, 2008).

5.3.3 Does It Matter If Policing Is Not Yet a Profession?

As a student police officer, the debate concerning policing as a profession is probably not at the forefront of your thinking. However, some would argue that establishing and maintaining policing as a profession is important for the following reasons:

- to develop the body of knowledge (for example, doctrine) and skills required for modern-day policing. Professions usually take the lead in determining what research and development best suit the needs of the clients;
- to protect the right of the police, in certain key respects, to regulate themselves;
- to improve public confidence in the work of the police. For example, a professional register would almost certainly imply the need for its members to regularly demonstrate that they have met the requirement to maintain their skills and knowledge;
- to distinguish the work and the professional standing of the police officer from other members of the extended police family (see 5.19 below) and other law enforcers (you might not agree that this is a good reason, but it is certainly behind some thinking).

There are alternative arguments. For example, many of the traditional professions such as law are not noted for their inclusivity, and striving for a professional status may reduce the representative nature of the policing family.

5.4 Ethics and Policing

Here we consider some of the qualities required of individual officers, and the practical impact of ethics on everyday policing. We saw in 5.3 above that a code of ethics is often a hallmark of a profession.

5.4.1 Introduction

Ethics is concerned with analysing the moral principles that govern human conduct. We can think of individuals as operating according to moral principles that may be derived from two main sources:

- their own assumptions, ideas, and principles;
- external sources, such as cultural norms, religion, or other rules imposed by society.

Ethics are important for the student police officer for two important reasons. First, the function of a police service is much more than upholding the law. The police also play an important role in maintaining an ordered society and in providing peaceful resolutions to conflicts that are not necessarily dealt with through law. A police officer is often required to make decisions, based upon what is in the public interest and what is the right thing to do, and this requires ethical reasoning above and beyond a good understanding of the law.

A second reason for the student police officer to be concerned with ethics is that police are partly judged by the way they carry out their work. If the police are deemed to be unethical in how they conduct an investigation the results will be discarded even if justice, in the sense of the correct identification of the offender, has been served.

If police methods and procedures do **not** meet high ethical standards then the authority of the police will be undermined, and the public may well have less trust in the police and the law. The police in the UK have prided themselves on the support gained from the general populace in a way that has not been achieved in other jurisdictions. (For example, many East Germans feared and distrusted their secretive and repressive police force, the STASI, before the reunification of Germany in the 1990s.) A police force that shows respect for human rights will encourage ordinary citizens to support the police. This has been demonstrated in the UK, for example by:

- public assistance with hate crime investigations;
- significant public support for the MPS in the aftermath of terrorist bombings in London in July 2005.

Such conduct by the police is closely bound up with ethical standards and what is morally right. For the student police officer, the standards of behaviour expected are clearly defined in existing documents—you are expected to act according to these externally imposed rules. You will be introduced to some of the key principles in the course of this chapter. We will also consider how ethics are linked with notions of moral authority. But ethics is also about your own ideas, and if your actions as a police officer are to ring true, your own rules of moral behaviour (your personal ethics) need to correspond with the formal requirements of the police force you work for. Diversity training (see 4.9 above) will provide you with further opportunities to consider your own views and feelings about your role in society, both as an individual and as a student police officer

---

TASK 3

All student police officers attest their responsibility to uphold the law and keep the peace (the twin aspects of the office of constable) at an early point in their first year (see Chapter 6). But is there more to the moral role of a police officer than this? Does the public expect more? Isn't it enough just to tell student police officers to be honest? Should we really concern ourselves about notions like proportion, trust, and the duty of care?

5.4.2   Documents Providing Guidance about Police Ethics and Behaviour

There are a number of official documents that set out guidance (in varying degrees of detail and levels of official standing) concerning police ethics and behaviour. These documents include the Police (Conduct) Regulations 2008, the Police (Performance) Regulations 2008, and the European Code of Police Ethics.

The **Police (Conduct) Regulations 2008** contain the 'Standards of Professional Behaviour' which refer to:

- honesty and integrity;
- authority, respect, and courtesy;
- equality and diversity;
- use of force;
- orders and instructions;
- duties and responsibilities;
- confidentiality;
- fitness for duty;
- discreditable conduct;
- challenging and reporting improper conduct.

Guidance is also offered on how police officers should behave when off duty. In essence, off-duty activities should not impact adversely on their ability to discharge public office without fear or favour. The Standards are discussed more fully in 6.14 below.

The Police (Conduct) Regulations 2008 also contain the misconduct procedures you will be subject to, should you fail to meet the expectations placed upon you (see 6.16 below).

The **Police (Performance) Regulations 2008** oblige police officers to maintain an appropriate level of performance and attendance. These regulations do not apply to student police officers. However, you are being constantly monitored during the first two years of your career, for example against the seven core behavioural areas for student police officers within the IPLDP. These are described in 3.7 above.

The **European Code of Police Ethics** was published in 2001, and noted that:

- the police help to safeguard the law;
- the police depend upon the public for support (consensual policing);

- public confidence in the police, in any country, is tightly bound up with how the police treat the public, especially over fundamental rights, such as those set out in the Human Rights Act 1998.

Finally, force mission statements and policy guidelines often relate to ethical aspects of police work. For example, in 2007 the then Home Secretary John Reid sent a letter to all police services in England and Wales outlining what he felt summed up 'the mission, values, goals and aspirations essential to successful policing' (Reid, 2007). The values he expected to see were:

- fairness and impartiality;
- integrity;
- freedom from corruption;
- respect for liberty and compassion;
- freedom from racism;
- equality of service to all communities;
- a commitment to the protection and well-being of all individuals.

5.4.3 Ethics and Policing in a Changing World

It would seem misguided to suppose that ethical standards never change. As society and technologies change, people develop new activities and our attitudes may change too. Some of these changes provide new opportunities for crime and present new challenges for policing.

5.4.4 Changes in Society and New Crimes

The interrelationships between new technologies and changing social attitudes might look like this:

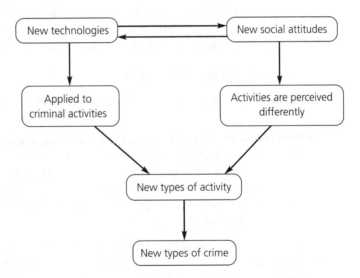

5.4.4.1 New technologies and new social attitudes

We can all list many forms of new technology and suggest some examples of new social attitudes. What is more interesting, however, is the interaction between the two. For example, how might new technologies affect social attitudes? It is more straightforward to see how social attitudes affect technology—after all, if people want a certain product or service, a company will usually try and provide it for them—a feature of business.

TASK 4

1. Make a list of six new technologies (new during the past 30 years).
2. Make a list of changes in social attitudes (limit yourself to no more than ten!).
3. Try and find links between the new technologies and social attitudes—you might find it helpful to discuss this with your colleagues, friends, or family.

5.4.4.2 New activities and new crimes

The availability of new technologies and changes in social attitudes have led to the development of new activities such as downloading mp3 file-format music from the internet. At least some of this music is copyright protected. This particular example illustrates a number of interesting points; the activity was only made possible by easy access to computers and the internet, and (when it involves copyrighted music) has only recently been classified as a crime.

It takes time for some new activities to be classified in law as crimes. Some new activities are clearly existing crimes carried out in a new way, for example using computers to illegally transfer money out of your employer's bank account into your own bank account (the so-called 'retooling' of a crime for the electronic age). This is theft, and it does not require much thought to see it as such. But other processes, such as 'phishing', are new types of activity, and it is difficult to find a precedent for this in existing law. So, new laws have to be made, laws which classify some of the new activities as new types of crime.

A hundred years ago, police actions at the operational level were almost entirely parish- or county-based, or limited to the boroughs of a large city. Now, the policing horizon is much wider, partly because at least some crime has become internationalized. For example, until about twenty years ago, the majority of fraud crimes were local, committed locally and investigated locally, and only occasionally did such frauds or embezzlements reach beyond national boundaries. However, with the advent of the internet, the electronic transfer of money, and the widespread use of bank accounts in different countries, fraud has rapidly become global. A recent case of international fraud began with the arrest of an individual who had drawn out large sums of cash from an account (the presumption being that this was to pay off an illegal drugs shipment). The bank became suspicious when large sums were deposited in the account just before the large withdrawal took place, and informed the police. Within hours enquiries relating to the investigation were being made in the USA, Switzerland, Liechtenstein, Thailand, and Oman. The essence of the crime had not changed, but the size, range, and complexity of the financial transactions certainly had changed the scope of the investigation.

5.4.5 Ethics and Changes in Policing

Just as new technologies and changing social attitudes influence crime, these changes also influence the police methods and attitudes. These changes are due to different types of influence:

- New crimes and behaviours present new challenges, and the police react to these particular challenges, in order to facilitate the fight against crime. These changes are **demand-led**: the changes are in direct response to changing patterns of crime.
- The police are part of society so they are directly affected by any changes, in the same way that other organizations and people are affected. These changes do not occur in response to any particular demand.

Demand-led responses to the challenge of coping with new crimes and changing behaviours occur on a number of different levels. They occur informally, at the level of the individual (for example, officers may find themselves modifying the way they speak to certain aggressive individuals in order to facilitate communication during an arrest). The police also respond as an organization; new approaches will be imposed formally within the organization through new procedures, laws, codes, and conduct. This inevitably takes time, as formal changes have to be carefully planned and implemented. These demand-led changes in police practice are part of a pragmatic response.

The police are also directly affected by more general changes in attitudes and society, as are other organizations. For example, in today's society, great emphasis is placed on accountability, so even if crime and criminals remained unchanged, and therefore presented no new challenges to policing, police practice is still likely to change in response to this new emphasis.

TASK 5

Suggest some ways in which new methods of communication have affected police practice.

You may be able to see what some of these factors have to do with policing, but what have they to do with ethics? One answer could be that it may be considered as ethical for policing practice to respond to changing patterns of crime in order that laws (which are ethical themselves) are upheld. We have observed that, as part of society, the police are exposed to changes in society and those changes include changes in ethical values.

5.4.5.1 Ethics and Demand-led Changes in Policing Practice

We have noted that it can be argued that it is inherently ethical that the police seek to solve and prevent crime. However, new police methods and procedures adopted in order to further this aim may also present ethical dilemmas. For example, there are concerns about the large amount of information stored about individuals on police computers. Is it right for information to be held about innocent individuals, and does the storage of information about criminals and suspects need further regulation? This is a new problem; the technology to store and retrieve information simply did not exist until recently, so although there are undoubtedly huge benefits in terms of solving and preventing crime, there is a danger of abusing the rights of individuals and invading their privacy. Questions arise about the ethics of holding information about individuals, and about who should vet its contents for accuracy, probity, and the way it is recorded. There are safeguards in place, but these need to be interpreted with care. A current example is the extensive debate in 2009 about routinely recording the DNA of every person who is arrested—even if no charge results (the debate has been given impetus by the European Court of Human Rights ruling that retaining the DNA details of innocent people on the national DNA database (NDNAD) breaches Article 8 of the European Convention on Human Rights). In separate cases, two murderers were identified in 2007 through DNA taken for other purposes and sent for trial. They were sentenced to heavy prison terms in early 2008, leading some commentators to argue that the DNA record of every person who is arrested should be retained indefinitely, although others argue that the police should not retain records of those against whom no charges have been brought. It has also been proposed that a record should be made of everyone's DNA; the argument in favour of such universal recording from birth is that if you are innocent you have nothing to fear. Conversely, civil libertarians point to the lapses in government confidentiality and the safe-keeping of personal data, as well as what is seen as unethical conduct in keeping data on people who have committed no crime. This debate and the ethical values involved continue to generate considerable discussion, so you should note that ethical and moral discussions about the police or about police methods are very current.

Round-the-clock criminal activity is now commonplace, in line with the 24/7 society, and the police have to keep up with these changes, leading to an expansion of the policing role and a blurring of the boundaries between **sworn officers** (those in the office of constable: see 6.12 below) and those who have some limited powers (acting in support of sworn officers) such as community support officers, rural or parish wardens, crime scene investigators, detention officers, and many other civilian roles within a police force. These police support staff must also have ethical codes, standards of behaviour and action, honesty, and probity, to the same extent as police officers. Yet there is no agreed national standard, such as those in the Police Regulations, no ratified code of behaviour, no national guidance to 'morality in public office' with which all such support staff must comply. This is despite the deliberations of Lord Nolan and his report on *Standards in Public Life* (Nolan, 1995).

Consider international peace keeping. Alongside the military presence, there may be a host of supporting agencies, including the police. If the peace keepers are to have moral (rather than imposed or forced) authority (see 5.5 below), there must be an ethical consistency in their behaviours—all the more so if they are police officers. If there is no code of conduct and no consistent guidance is provided, should we be surprised that problems sometimes occur? Partly as a consequence of round-the-clock crime, the British police and police staff cooperate with other police forces around the world, perhaps with people who do not share common behavioural boundaries or shared cultural identities with those commonly associated with British people. In other countries there may be:

- widespread corruption;
- routine bribery of public officials;

- governments using their police as a political arm;
- very low rates of pay for police officers;
- very low status for police officers;
- paramilitary-style force employed by the police.

TASK 6

Consider the bullet points listed above. Draw a flow diagram showing how these factors might interact. Use arrows to show how one factor causes another. (An example of this particular use of arrows is shown in the diagram below; the arrow shows that poor pay leads to low status.)

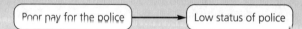

Poor pay for the police ⟶ Low status of police

Note that there are no certain answers to this exercise; you might argue that it is the low status that is causing the low pay.

5.4.5.2 Ethics and Non-demand-led Changes in Police Practice

Along with the changes in society and societal norms, there is renewed debate about policing methods. There is even some ambiguity about what the police are for. This may be seen, for example, in organizational name changes; some counties now have Police Service titles, others have retained the original Police Force in their title. Is the use of force a fundamental part of policing? Some commentators argue that, increasingly, the use of force by the police, particularly deadly force in the use of firearms, is not tolerable in modern society. Others assert that, as society seems to be becoming more violent, especially with gun crime, police officers should be routinely armed, as in Continental Europe or the USA. Clearly the more frequent use of firearms by the police is to some extent a demand-led response stimulated by the increasing level of gun crime in Britain.

The debate can be widened to include changes in the public perception of the police. Some of the questions raised are very general, and others are more specific, such as:

- Are the police still the repositories of authority? If so, on whose authority?
- Is the use of force sanctioned by law (and therefore at the mercy of political changes and amendments) or is the use of force sanctioned by society as necessary for public protection?
- Should the police target teenage vandals and graffiti artists rather than fraudsters?
- Should car thieves or burglars be made a higher priority for police action than catching speeding drivers on the basis that theft and burglary have a bigger negative impact than speeding on the lives of ordinary citizens?
- What does society fear most, and should the police be responsive to that fear?

The public perception of the police is clearly an issue here. Can the public trust the police to know best, and may the police therefore set their own priorities, such as tackling invisible crimes like fraud or drug smuggling? Or are the police morally obliged to focus on issues of immediate public concern, such as minor vandalism and dispersing groups of young people hanging about on street corners? Despite the fact that public anxiety is not fully justified by available data, the public perception of the level of crime is widely regarded as one of the many factors police need to take into account when considering their priorities.

5.4.6 Managerialism, Ethics, and the Police

The police have faced a dilemma in recent years between the official structuring of its responses to crime and criminality (the government's target-setting approach) and the impatience within its ranks concerning measurement systems (the internalized approach). This has led to accusations of managerialism, and the suggestion that the police are more concerned with reaching targets set by the government than they are with maintaining order, protecting the vulnerable, and catching criminals. It has also been argued that 'what gets measured gets done' and this leads the police into mechanistic and target-driven responses to society's problems, avoiding consideration of wider and more complex general issues. Others argue that the police, like any other public service, should be seen to be providing value for money and that the best way to ascertain that is to set targets for the reduction of specific crimes.

The targets and tick-boxes of managerialism are probably unavoidable. Some would argue that accountability is a central part of any programme for change in all public services, not just the police, and that it is the best way to improve standards. However, critics of such changes assert that the drive for accountability disrupts effective practice within most organizations. It has been claimed that increased managerialism in police forces has fundamentally changed the nature of policing, including its ethical position. Consider, for example, the Home Office measure of the speed of response by police to 999 calls. How quickly the police respond is measured quantitatively, but what officers do at the scene when they arrive is not directly measured, nor assessed qualitatively. Which is the more important: getting there quickly, or doing the right thing once at the scene?

Performance and delivery of outcomes with measurable targets are increasingly used to determine whether or not a police force is effective, efficient, and economic. In 2002, the link between police performance and police budgets was made explicit by the Home Office. The controversy over the rights and wrongs of managerialism is not within the scope of this Handbook, but the issue presents forces with a real dilemma and is the subject of active debate. A decision to concentrate on meeting targets, rather than providing an effective police service per se is likely to impact on individual moral behaviour as much as it impacts on community or societal behaviour.

We do not offer solutions to these complex issues, but they are important parts of the context in which we can discuss ethics and police codes of conduct. It follows that you should know a little about these issues and be prepared to think about what is involved. The ethical dilemmas are likely to increase rather than recede during your service as a police officer.

5.4.7 Ethics and Your Everyday Work

You may feel that the principles underpinning the documents referred to at the start of 5.4 are sound, but you might also be wondering how the rather abstract principles might actually apply in day-to-day situations. Even in these short summaries, you may have noted that there are some words used without qualification, such as integrity and diligence. There appears to be a subjective flavour to the guidance and an assumption of shared understanding about particular concepts, and how they relate to conduct. Do you know what all the words mean? Does everyone else know what these terms mean?

> **TASK 7**
>
> Take a moment to think about the meaning of the terms **should**, **must**, and **will** in the context of police ethics. Write down your reflections and consider making a Learning Diary Phase 1 entry under the 'Ethics and values of the police' heading.

5.4.8 Ethics and Police Discretion

One of the key skills you will be required to develop whilst training as a student police officer is the ability to apply **discretion** (see 5.7 below). You might imagine that the language used in our laws is pretty cut and dried and that your subsequent role as a qualified police officer will involve merely deciding which laws and offences apply to whatever activity you are investigating. However, you may know already that it is not that simple! If an offence has been committed, you will need to decide if enforcing the law is the most appropriate response in those particular circumstances. Further, in making these choices, you need to be prepared to justify the reasons for your decision.

The Standards of Professional Behaviour contained within Police (Conduct) Regulations 2008 (see 6.14 below) do not try to restrict the discretion of police officers, but they do define the parameters of conduct within which a police officer can exercise discretion. Police officers, once sworn, have powers not granted to the ordinary citizen and therefore it is expected that police officers will exercise judgement whether to use those powers or not as circumstances, common sense, or experience dictate.

A practical example may be drawn from a recent skills exercise, in which student police officers on Supervised Patrol were called to deal with a theft at a supermarket, with instructions to investigate the matter and decide upon a course of action. The student police officers attended the scene of the alleged crime; the offender was a confused, 94-year-old man who had apparently picked up a bag of sweets and wandered out of the store, pursued by store detectives. What would you do in these circumstances?

The exercise brings home to the police officers that their powers need to be tempered with a mixture of good sense and humanity. Yes, the elderly person had technically committed a crime, but there were **mitigating circumstances**; his age and frailty must be taken into account, and proving 'intention permanently to deprive' (the basis of the Theft Act 1968: see 10.3 below) would be somewhat difficult.

Discretion is not simply the exercise of good sense; it is a matter of making **judgements**, some of which can only come with experience. Two important situations requiring the use of discretion are:

- **Making an arrest**—no other police officer, not even a chief constable, can command another officer to make an arrest. This is because the responsibility for an arrest is that of the arresting officer alone, who may have to answer for his or her actions in court (see 8.7 below).
- **Opening fire**—no police officer can order another police officer to open fire with a weapon (a gun, baton-round, or Taser). The personal responsibility to open fire is a judgement exercised by the individual officer. (However, a police officer receiving a lawful order **not** to open fire **must** obey since a commander at a firearms incident may be in possession of knowledge not possessed by other officers at the scene.)

From the beginnings of policing in Britain more than 170 years ago, great emphasis has been placed on the individual officer's responsibility for behaviour and conduct, with regard to what actions should be refrained from as well as what actions should be taken. The Police Regulations, in effect, set out this key responsibility of the 'office of constable' in detail.

You should note that such ethical difficulties accompany many specialist roles in policing, not just firearms, and in your career as a police officer you could be called to account for your actions (or lack of action), and asked to justify your decisions at any time. This leads us to state an important principle: you should be able to defend any action which you take as a police officer on the basis that it was:

- **proportional** (the action was justified in the circumstances);
- **legal** (having a basis in the law);
- **appropriate** (it was fitting and right to act in that way); and
- **necessary** (action was required there and then).

There are many variations on this basic theme, and you are certain to encounter one of them in your initial training. This one is often called **PLAN**.

However, we should not assume that the daily life of a police officer is constantly beset with moral ambiguity and that there is a need to make fundamental ethical judgements all the time. In fact, most of the complexity of policing lies in the technical or legal requirements for evidence, which are dealt with extensively throughout this Handbook.

5.4.9   Police Corruption

In October 2006, two police officers from Nottingham were sentenced to a total of eight years' imprisonment for passing information about police investigations to suspected criminals. The major offender, a police constable who had joined the force in 1999, passed details of the investigation into the murder of Marian Bates, a jeweller shot dead in 2003, to the owner of a fashion shop. The officer was rewarded with discounts on clothes from the store. Evidence was produced which showed that the officer also carried out intelligence checks at the behest of suspected criminals.

A subsequent case almost exactly a year later in London involved six men, five of whom were former police officers, who were sentenced to varying terms of imprisonment for conspiracy to intercept communications and with 'aiding and abetting misconduct in a public office'. The offences were committed over a period from 1999 to 2004 and were investigated by the Metropolitan Police's Anti-Corruption Command. The men had set up an illegal company offering private investigation services, and were paid by clients to hack into computers or bug telephone lines.

Almost every year, there is a headline case of this kind which involves a corrupt police officer working alone or with others. Any investigation into criminality or corruption by the police is more difficult when insiders are involved; there is a danger that the details of the investigation will become known, and that the criminal officers involved will be tipped off. This did not happen in either of the cases described above, but it has been known to happen elsewhere. It is clear that the police forces involved in the two cases described above are not unique. Research has shown that corruption can occur in any part of the police service, and therefore we need to understand how widespread corruption is likely to be, and how we might prevent it. But we must start at the beginning.

TASK 8

Consider the following questions:

- What is corruption?
- What are the theories about corruption?
- Why does corruption happen?
- What makes a police officer or police staff member act corruptly?
- Can we predict who is likely to act corruptly?
- Can theories help tackle corruption?

5.4.9.1 The Definition of Corruption

Consider the following definition of corruption:

> Corruption exists when a member of a police force illegally puts personal interests, or the interests of others, above those of the people he or she is pledged to serve (adapted from Klitgaard, 1988).

No doubt there are some problems with this definition, but we will take it as a working definition for the purposes of our discussion here. You need also to be aware of technical and legal definitions of some aspects of corruption in a public office. These are:

Definitions of corruption

- Non-feasance (not doing what you should)
- Misfeasance   (doing what you should not do)
- Malfeasance   (the commission of indictable crimes)

Misfeasance occurs in the examples given above; some of the officers involved were charged with 'aiding and abetting misconduct in a public office'. In the Nottingham Police case, this involved the improper use of a police computer. Misfeasance includes all aspects of doing something contrary to your duty and it is implicit that the act is knowingly done; in other words, it is presumed that an offender knew the difference between what he/she **should** do and the actions he/she actually carried out. This should not be confused with the exercise of initiative and discretion, which we looked at in the discussion about ethics.

In **non-feasance**, the reverse applies (and it is, to some extent, a lesser charge) because an individual has failed to do something which is part of his/her duty. Examples of this might include not reporting someone for a traffic offence or, more seriously, not intervening when there is a fight in a pub. There is frequently some ambiguity about some aspects of non-feasance. For instance, the decision whether or not to charge a suspect (with an offence) requires the use of discretion. In general terms though, police officers and staff should know what they are supposed to do in the proper discharge of their duties, and it is a matter of **making a judgement** and being able to **justify your decision**. Most student police officers could justify not charging the elderly man in the supermarket but few could justify not intervening to stop a fight.

If we take Klitgaard's definition of corruption and the legal descriptions of offences as our starting point, we should now turn to the question: what makes a police officer act corruptly?

5.4.9.2 The Causes of Corruption

We all have the potential for corruption, even if we generally behave ethically. We have all been tempted at some time or other to do something we know is wrong. Many people use a formal belief system such as a religion to help guide their actions, though in some cultures it is more common for people to use their own personal code of ethics. Others rely on what the law proscribes and will refrain from certain acts for fear of being caught. It is likely that the majority of people are influenced by a combination of external and internal factors. Whatever the reasons, we need to find out what tempts an individual to ignore religious, cultural, social, or legal restraints.

It does not seem that officers begin their careers with a conscious disposition to be corrupt. Indeed, Sir John Woodcock (cited in Morton, 1993), then HM Inspector of Constabulary, said in 1992, when looking at people who join the police:

> I see young men and women who join the police service. Invariably, they join out of a sense of idealism, to serve their society. I find it very unlikely that many individuals join so that they can give perjured evidence against fellow citizens and send them to prison.

Sir John Woodcock was referring to a genuine concern of his time, that police officers had falsified evidence or invented confessions in order that known criminals would receive a prison term. This form of behaviour was given the title 'noble cause corruption', the 'noble cause' of convicting a known criminal. What thought processes or experiences could lead officers to act this way?

We suggest the following could be potentially corrupting factors, which any new police officer might encounter in the first five years of service. It is not exhaustive and only partly based upon empirical research (there is very little to draw upon in this field):

- corrupt police officers providing a role model;
- the pressure for results;
- abuse or assault from members of the public;
- the difficulties in securing convictions;
- belief that sentencing was not adequate for the crime committed;
- the first arrival at the scene of a crime, when cash or goods may be lying about;
- personal financial pressures;
- handling and storing drugs from police investigations;
- the 'long hours, low reward' culture, leading to envy of others more fortunately placed;
- lack of effective supervision;
- the excessive exercise of discretion without challenge;
- feelings of bitterness or resentment at not receiving expected promotion;
- animosity towards their police force as the result of other disciplinary offences;
- managing informants without adequate supervision or scrutiny.

So far we have considered factors that might result in the **predisposition** to act corruptly. Any or all of the experiences outlined above could be enough to make someone think about acting corruptly, but an **opportunity** is also required.

TASK 9

Look at the list of factors above that might contribute to an officer's decision to act corruptly. Most of them are about predisposition—motivations for an officer to act corruptly. But as well as predisposition, an opportunity is also required. List the five factors from the list above which are opportunities to act corruptly.

There are a number of theories about the causes of corruption. In some cases these theories are largely descriptive in nature: that is, they set out a typical sequence of events leading to corruption but do not really provide much in the way of explanation. One such theory is that the metaphorical (in some cases, actual) **free cup of coffee** is enough to start a police officer on the **slippery slope** to corruption. The suggestion is that, once a police officer accepts a free cup of coffee, it is but a short step to a free meal, then free entry to a club, then preferential treatment, then provision of goods and inducements, and finally the offer to engage in joint criminal exploits. By accepting the free cup of coffee the officer signals his or her willingness to be corrupted. One commentator noted that:

> a free cup of coffee may not in itself constitute a bribe, but the taking of it might condition a police officer to accept other larger gratuities which were indeed intended as bribes (Feldberg, 1985, p 267).

TASK 10

How convinced are you by the 'free cup of coffee' theory? Can you see any flaws in it? Can you think of examples that might challenge the theory? Jot down three scenarios (these may be real or imaginary) that illustrate any problems with this theory.

As with most complex issues, there are other theories to consider. One of these is the **bad apple theory**, often put forward by those who appear to have a vested interest in hushing matters up or in trying to make things look better, at least on the surface. The argument here is that a corrupt police officer or staff member is an isolated instance, different from the norm and by no means typical. Keeping the bad apple could infect the whole barrel, so you have to remove the individual officer; the problem and threat are simultaneously solved.

How convincing do you find this theory? What does it presume or imply? Who is likely to put forward such an explanation of corruption? Why should he or she do so?

TASK 11

Try to put yourself in the shoes of the bad apple officer. What sort of events or feelings would make you, the bad apple, more likely to act corruptly? Why might other officers not succumb to the same pressures or temptations?

The **bent for the job** theory is a third explanation for corruption. According to this account, the law does not give the police sufficient powers, so the police themselves have to invent ways to circumvent the criminal justice system. A former Commissioner of the Metropolitan Police, Sir David McNee, said:

> Many police officers have, early in their careers, learned to use methods bordering on trickery or stealth in their investigations because they were deprived of proper powers by the legislature (McNee, 1983, p 180).

This may have been a quite widespread perception in 1983 when McNee wrote his book; it was argued that the law was so inadequately structured that substantial numbers of the guilty went unpunished and that officers were forced to be devious and underhand because that was the only way in which they could achieve results.

> **TASK 12**
>
> How convinced are you by this theory? Do you accept that the end is more important than the means, and, if so, does that mean that inexperienced officers have to be taught trickery or stealth?

You can see from these three theories that there is a wide range of ideas about corruption and why it happens, but we hope that you have some scepticism concerning their adequacy as explanations. We now examine some of the problems encountered when applying these theories to reality.

5.4.9.3 Testing the theories against reality

The free cup of coffee/slippery slope theory depicts a gradual and inevitable decline into full-blown criminality and is favoured by moral absolutists and those who believe that people (including police officers) are infinitely corruptible. But if that is true, why are the vast majority of police officers patently **not** corrupt? If all corruption starts small and grows big, then we should all be wary of accepting anything from anyone, ever. The main flaw in this theory is the premise that the first step entails the second, the second the third, and so on. This is probably not the case; people can (and do) say no at any point. One step does not **necessarily** lead to another.

The bad apple theory is in some respects the opposite of the free cup of coffee theory. Whereas the slippery slope is open to all, and anyone could be corrupted on the slightest pretext, the bad apple theory only applies to the select few. It begins and ends with one bad person being caught and punished. However, there is evidence to suggest that corruption breeds corruption and that corrupt officers often act together, as we saw in the two examples described above. Another corruption case, also from the Metropolitan Police, but dating from the mid-1990s, involved a series of successful prosecutions of police officers who were acting together for corrupt purposes. One of the principal cases involved a serving police detective and an ex-officer conspiring to steal and resell drugs, and another involved a police officer in the Flying Squad who was prosecuted for theft (and sentenced to a substantial prison term). He claimed that the pressures of joining an elite squad and wanting to fit in had corrupted him; other corrupt officers effectively tested him by providing opportunities for him to demonstrate his corruptibility and, when he succumbed, he was 'in'. This demonstrates the inadequacy of the bad apple theory, at least in the UK context.

What of the 'bent for the job' theory of corruption? There is plenty of evidence to suggest that these were widespread practices in the 1970s and 1980s. However, it is still not clear whether the corrupt police officers used falsified evidence or corrupt testimony in order to get around a poor law, or whether poor law occasioned the corrupt officers' actions. Miscarriages of justice still happen today, but there appear now to be fewer opportunities for police officers to 'fit up' criminals. There is closer scrutiny of the evidence-gathering process; detailed procedures are specified in a series of laws, such as the Police and Criminal Evidence Act 1984. Internal police procedures have changed; it is now recognized that elite squads, unchanged over time, unsupervised and free to do more or less what they want, are conducive to corrupt practices. Limited tenure, obtrusive supervision, and stronger countermeasures have all blunted the power of such elites, and there are very few forces, if any, where secretive squads function without oversight and appropriate challenge.

Is there then a persuasive theory of police corruption to which we might all sign up? We know that corruption flourishes when **predisposition** coincides with **opportunity**, and the individual or group succumbs to the temptation. However, it could be argued that there are as many variants of corruption as there are variants of human character. You might try discussing with your colleagues and friends whether any theory (or theories) can account for the specific nature of corruption in the police and, if such a theory or theories do exist, whether they can be used predictively. For information about corruption cases in the last ten years, see Caless (2008b).

5.4.9.4   **Classifying Corruption**

We could classify episodes of corruption in terms of two factors:

- the seriousness of the offence;
- the context of the offence.

The table below gives examples of corrupt acts. The seriousness increases as you move down the table.

Examples of Corrupt Acts

Seriousness	Descriptor
Corruption of authority	This can range from the relatively minor, such as not being assertive enough to take charge of a situation, or allowing undue familiarity, through to turning a blind eye to the relatively minor misdemeanours of friends or colleagues. It might entail a free dinner or free entry to an event. It gives a handle to the unscrupulous to exploit any predisposition to corruption. Blackmailable behaviour, especially of a sexual kind, comes into this category.
Favours	A wide spectrum of activities, from letting someone know that a lucrative maintenance contract is in the offing, through to using a particular crash recovery service for motorway accidents and taking a percentage of the resulting business.
Bribery	This includes accepting cash not to book a motorist for speeding or having defective tyres, taking money to lose a file or a report, or taking a holiday paid for by someone to whom the corrupt officer has given valuable information.
Protection of criminals	Overlapping with bribery (because it inevitably involves payment of some sort) but even more serious: informing criminals about police investigations into their activities, warnings about raids, seizures, sting operations or intelligence information, perverting the course of justice to ensure that the criminal is not convicted.
Direct criminal activities	Pimping for prostitutes, theft, embezzlement, violence, resale of stolen drugs, intimidation of witnesses. All entail the commission of indictable offences for which the penalty at law would be a sentence of not less than two years' imprisonment.

The context in which an officer works is also relevant;

- **Peer groups** are a powerful influence, particularly in the workplace. If an individual felt that his or her peer group would thoroughly disapprove of a corrupt action, that disapproval might act as an inhibitor. If, on the other hand, a peer group approved of a corrupt action and deliberately inveigled an individual into joining in, then resistance to corruption would be much harder.
- **Supervisors**, the sergeant or inspector who wants to know what is going on and has a thorough understanding of the tricks and misdemeanours that people can get up to, can obviously reduce the chances of corruption. Where supervision is tight and vigilant, any signs (for example) of an informant 'turning' a handler (see 12.4.1 below) can be quickly noted and acted on so that a professional relationship could be re-established or the handler moved away. This proper use of supervising authority goes all the way up the chain of command in a police force.
- A **conspiracy** is when two or more police officers or police staff act together in corruption. The corrupt officers can look out for each other, providing further protection against discovery or suspicion. We noted above that this was a characteristic of the old-style remote, secretive, and elite squads, but it need only involve two officers to be effective and recent cases, such as the examples we gave above, illustrate how corruption can breed corruption.
- The **consequences** of the corruption being discovered are also an influence: clearly if it is likely to be discovered the corruption will be more difficult to accomplish. In addition, if the tempted officers know that the likely outcome of discovery is a mere warning or a ponderous, inconclusive investigation, then corruption may be encouraged. There have been instances when juries have found it hard to credit that police officers could act corruptly.

> **TASK 13**
>
> Based on what you have read and discussed in these analyses of ethics and corruption, attempt short responses to the following:
>
> - Bent coppers are so rare that it is hardly worth all the machinery to inhibit or catch them. Do you agree?
> - Do you accept that anyone defaulting, even in a minor way, from expected ethical standards should be dismissed from the police?
> - Consider a published corruption case in terms of the seriousness and context of the acts.

5.5 Personal Authority

Authority may seem a somewhat old-fashioned concept in the era of supposed late modernity. It conjures up images of strict Victorian fathers and the arbitrary exercise of power by officials (civil servants, teachers, and the like) and may even seem to run contrary to the desire of a modern police force to serve the community. However, we would argue that authority is a key concept for the police and of particular interest and concern to the student police officer. The exercise of authority is often viewed as a mark of a professional although it is often expressed or described instead as autonomy or credibility and related concepts.

5.5.1 Introduction

As a student police officer your authority will no doubt be challenged on occasions and you will find yourself thinking deeply about where your authority comes from, and maybe about how to increase it! There are a number of behaviours that you need to exhibit before completing training (see 3.5 above) and some of these are clearly related to your personal authority.

In the 1960s and 70s, the educational philosopher Richard Peters (often referred to as 'RS Peters', who usually wrote and worked in collaboration with Paul Hirst) argued that there are different forms of personal authority which nonetheless interrelate (Peters, 1973). Although Peters's focus was authority in education we have adapted his work here to apply to policing.

5.5.2 The Main Forms of Personal Authority

The main forms of personal authority are considered to be:

- **epistemic**: authority from knowledge (knowing more than the next person);
- **natural** (sometimes called 'charismatic authority'): derived from personality, demeanour (non-verbal communication);
- ***de facto*** (from fact): authority that exists through convention rather than as a matter of right;
- ***de jure*** (from right): authority as a matter of right;
- **moral**: authority that arises from a moral high ground.

Note that these categories are not intended to be mutually exclusive. As we shall note below, *de facto* and moral authorities, for example, are often linked. It is also important to note that authority here can relate to two distinct concepts. There is the general authority of the police service, often thought about in terms of legitimacy and which is discussed in 5.6 below. The second is the authority of the individual police officer, which may and will vary from individual to individual and which concerns us here.

5.5.2.1 What do these mean in policing terms?

As a student police officer your **epistemic** authority stems from knowledge of the law and procedure. The public expect you to know the rudiments of the law. Although members of the public may know that an offence has occurred (by applying their common sense), they will expect you to know which particular law or laws have been broken. In part, this expectation is fed by media portrayals of the police which often feature a police officer using the words 'I arrest you for [specifics of the offence]'. (Indeed, you may find that your friends and family will expect you to become an expert on the law overnight, even though they know you have only just commenced training!) Therefore, if in certain situations your grasp of the law or proper procedure seems uncertain, then your epistemic authority declines in the opinion of those around you. The law, policy, and guidelines that you study as a student police officer (for example, the IPLDP LPG modules: see 1.4 above) are the basis for establishing your epistemic authority. This form of authority needs to be worked on throughout your subsequent career and in some respects the proposal for a professional register (see 5.3 above) is a response to this need.

Some people appear to have more **natural** authority, through sheer presence (charisma), than others and hence seem more able to take control when required, to direct others, and so on. This is a form of authority that comes from within and it would appear that it is more natural to some than it is to others. Note that natural authority is not necessarily related to physical size or appearance. Being over six feet tall with a powerful physique may go some way to enhancing your natural authority but is certainly no guarantee, and there are plenty of authoritative people without these physical advantages. The word 'natural' is possibly misleading in this context and implies somehow that this form of authority resembles other aspects of our being, such as the shape of our ears which we can do little about. However, natural authority **can** be developed and you will receive training on your demeanour, on your use of language, on your non-verbal communication (body language), and other more subtle ways in which your natural authority can be enhanced. Other aspects of your appearance, such as your clothing, can also either enhance or undermine your natural authority. Being smartly dressed (polished shoes, clean and tidy uniform, etc) may seem a strangely old-fashioned topic for a Handbook of this kind but, as we shall discuss in 12.10 below, they are important aspects of your authority when, for example, giving evidence in court.

Police officers are seen to have *de facto* authority in certain circumstances, for example, in the aftermath of a road traffic collision. This authority comes, not just from the law, but through custom. A more controversial example (in some eyes) is the common practice of other road users moving out of the way of police patrol cars using their sirens and lights. Police cars also frequently pass red lights at junctions in order to respond to emergency calls. All this is common knowledge and accepted by most of the public as a *de facto* right of the police. However, this form of authority is easily lost if abused or even if simply perceived as being abused. Your friends and family will no doubt carry on making wry comments about the police using their sirens and lights to get back to the station more quickly for their cup of cocoa and a biscuit!

It is a simple fact that police officers have powers that other members of society do not, and many of those powers feature in this Handbook. These powers are the main source of your *de jure* authority. The wearing of a uniform symbolizes this form of authority, to separate you from the rest of society, as does the possession of a warrant card.

Police officers are expected to subscribe to a code of ethics and behaviour which is of a higher standard than the rest of society, and this gives them a **moral** authority. Some may dispute this claim; however, there are certainly greater moral obligations on the police when compared to many other occupational or professional groups, for example, in terms of honesty, integrity, fairness, impartiality, politeness, and general conduct. Gross examples of inappropriate police behaviour (such as the ill-treatment of prisoners) undermine the moral authority of the police service as a whole, but there are other less dramatic examples that happen at the level of the individual. Put simply, members of the public do not expect to witness police officers swearing in public, smoking on duty, or acting other than seriously in the role. More challengingly, these restrictions on the personal behaviour of police officers, and the effect on moral authority, also extend to life off duty. Where is the moral authority of a police officer who arrests an acquaintance for possession of cocaine during a raid on Saturday, having smoked cannabis with the same person the previous evening? How is your moral authority affected if you use your police warrant card to gain free entry to a nightclub? Retaining moral authority also requires police officers to take the moral high ground when dealing with the public. It is not appropriate, for example, to judge a member of the public by the same high standards that a police officer must follow and it is for this reason (amongst others) that the 'attitude test' (see 5.7.5 below) is an unacceptable means of deciding whether to arrest a person.

5.5.3 Development of Personal Authority

It is likely that there will be opportunities for you to develop your personal authority during your initial training. These may include:

- preparing and delivering presentations to others, including groups of students and training staff;
- increasing your knowledge and recall of the law and procedure;
- observing your own behaviour, including your demeanour and use of language, for example, by analysing video of your performance whilst undertaking a particular task;
- feedback from others including your trainers, assessors, fellow student police officers, representatives of community groups (for example, whilst undertaking your community attachment).

TASK 14

You have arrested a woman on suspicion of assault and theft in a shopping centre. The victim has identified the suspect, who cannot explain her possession of the victim's mobile phone. Give examples of how the five forms of personal authority would feature in this particular scenario.

5.6 Legitimacy

The issue of legitimacy is central to debates about the police role in democratic societies. The existence of police authority requires individuals to willingly sacrifice a degree of personal freedom and liberty in order to secure a greater degree of collective freedom and liberty. The logic behind this way of thinking is made explicit in the writings of the seventeenth-century English philosopher Thomas Hobbes: without authority in society there would exist 'a war of all against all'. For Hobbes, therefore, the existence of any authority is preferable to none at all. This is an important point to note because, as Nozick (1974) and Simmons (2001) argued, the necessity for authority must be considered before questioning the legitimacy of authority. The difficulty in justifying police authority is illustrated by the fact that it took six attempts (from 1785 onwards) to pass a Police Bill through the Houses of Parliament, finally leading to the creation of the 'new' police in 1829. Clearly there was opposition at the time to the very existence of a professional standing body of police in England and Wales. Today, we largely take the existence of the police for granted and few in society seriously question whether we would be better without any police.

Nonetheless, in terms of civil liberties, it is important to be able to justify a police presence, especially given the extent to which we could argue that such a presence may be expensive (for example at football matches) or disproportionate (such as in shopping malls). We may even go beyond justifying the existence of the police to consider a more pressing and ongoing 'libertarian' concern: the legitimacy of the police. Here it is worth noting two distinct ways in which the police obtain legitimacy: consensual and moral.

5.6.1 Consensual Legitimacy of the Police

The police are quite rightly governed by the law but the issue of legitimacy is central to debates about the police role in democratic societies in other ways too. Consensual legitimacy is gained through the support of those who are being policed. It is reflected in the notion of 'policing by consent' (Reiner, 2000). Discussion about legitimacy in the early years of the police was almost exclusively concerned with this aspect. The Home Office's (2004a) focus on Neighbourhood Policing has also stressed the importance of this issue.

From the perspective of those advocating consensual legitimacy, the police are legitimate to the extent that they are consented to by the public. Of course there are differing degrees to which we might say the public consents to the police. One view is to say that the public consents **passively** by not opposing what the police do. On the other hand we might insist on the public having an ongoing engagement with the police in order for consent to be given **actively**. In practice, the kind of consent gained will be dependent upon the type of police response and the particular problem addressed. For example, if the police are required to deal with a serious threat of terrorism then the consent will have to be passive in order to allow the police to be effective. The more the public know about how the police intend to counter the terrorists, the more the terrorists will also know and the police intervention might fail as a consequence. Conversely, when the police are required to resolve low-level but persistent offending, there is a greater need for the police to communicate adequately with the local community to establish and agree the most appropriate means of addressing the problem. In this latter case, the consent must be active and ongoing. The police need to negotiate their response to the problem and ensure that the community supports, as much as is possible, any police interventions. In this respect, the process for ensuring the consensual legitimacy of the police involves making sure that the public involvement in negotiating police responses is appropriate and that the response deals effectively with the problem at hand. An appeal for witnesses to an event is a common form of this nexus between police and public.

5.6.1.1 The limits of consensual legitimacy

Consensual legitimacy is important but it is possible for the police to be **too** responsive to the views of the communities being policed. As Waddington (1999a) has noted, the police are required to deal with conflicts in society and in the exercise of this function they may have to police 'against' sections of the community. A real concern exists that the police might be overly responsive to one section of the community against another. This could lead to the exclusion and/or targeting of groups of individuals who are seen to be on the periphery of a community. Put another way, the popularity of the police, which is effectively what consent measures, is no guarantee that the police are acting in a legitimate way. Equally, people's fears or concerns may not necessarily match the prevailing crime patterns, and may not help the police to focus effort appropriately.

There are various ways of establishing the legitimacy of police authority; approval from citizens is just one. As Simmons (2001) observes, this particular way of establishing legitimacy focuses on how an authority is perceived rather than what it does. In other words it measures the attitudes of the recipients of the authority rather than the authority itself.

5.6.2 The Moral Legitimacy of the Police

It is also becoming increasingly important for the police to 'do the right thing' from a moral perspective. The popular police option is not always the correct one. Conversely the police will not always be able to gain consensual support when called upon, for example, to protect a known paedophile living within a residential area or to allow a racist organization to march through the town centre. However, the reason why the police do what they do is often a matter of moral legitimacy rather than consensual legitimacy. As far as possible, the police will try to achieve both moral and consensual legitimacy, but this is not always possible. The former Chief Constable of Devon and Cornwall, John Alderson, has been an advocate of what he refers to as 'principled policing' for a number of years (see Alderson, 1998). He has argued that policing should be more firmly founded upon moral principles rather than pragmatic concerns. The Human Rights Act 1998 has given legislative support to this point of view. Increasingly, police officers must take into account a number of (often different or contradictory) moral considerations in order to make professional judgements. Policing by consent remains an important part of police legitimacy, but the police must operate primarily within both legal and moral boundaries if they are to be truly legitimate.

> **TASK 15**
>
> What judgements would you make if you had to control a march by the British National Party through your town, knowing that the Anti-Nazi League was planning to turn up in large numbers to oppose the march? (Note that our interest here is in judgements based on police legitimacy rather than the detail of operational orders.)

5.7 Discretion

Here we extend the discussion of discretion. We have already looked briefly at discretion (in 5.4 above) and considered its fundamental place in modern policing in relation to ethics and corruption.

Police officers are not robots, programmed to respond to every crime they encounter (however trivial) by arrest and charging. There are a number of reasons for this:

- It is not practically feasible (the police officer would have no time to respond to more serious offences or to undertake more important work).
- It is not fair (it would undermine the relationship between police and public).
- It is not effective (it is not likely to have any significant impact on levels of crime, although see Zero-Tolerance Policing models and also the association between offences and criminality).

Thus the exercise of discretion may be seen as an important, even fundamental policing skill. Indeed, Lord Scarman stated:

> the exercise of discretion lies at the heart of the policing function. It is undeniable that there is only one law for all: and it is right that this should be so. But it is equally well recognised that successful policing depends on the exercise of discretion on how the law is enforced. ... Discretion is the art of suiting action to particular circumstances (Scarman, 1981, para 4.58).

Chan (2003) has noted that in the early stages of initial police training, officers are hungry for basic technical knowledge, a statement you might agree with. This is understandable; police officers require the basic know-how skills in order to feel confident enough to perform duties (under the supervision of a tutor) in operational settings such as Supervised Patrol. Police discretion is a subject that does not fit easily under the umbrella of basic technical knowledge and in this respect it differs from much of the other initial learning of student police officers. Nonetheless, it is important that student police officers understand what police discretion is and what it is not, because discretion informs much of what a police officer does. Discretion is the vital ingredient which justifies police work as a profession, or in Neyroud and Beckley's (2001, p 86) words, is 'the essence of informed professionalism in policing'. We noted this earlier in 5.3 above.

5.7.1 Defining Discretion

Police discretion does not apply only to front-line officers but also to the kinds of decision that police managers and chief officers must make. These were described by Neyroud and Beckley (2001) as 'prioritizing decisions' and 'tactical decisions'. The former relates primarily to the allocation of limited resources and the latter relates to the balancing of liberty and order in a democratic society.

In a similar vein, Delattre (2002) discusses the need for senior investigative officers to make anticipatory and planning decisions about, for example, when to identify and release information concerning a serial killer. These are all good examples of police discretionary decisions and it is important for new police officers to be aware of why and how these kinds of decision are made. However, the focus here will be on the discretion of front-line officers; in other words, the kind of decisions that patrol constables (and therefore student police officers) are expected to make on a daily basis.

It is also important to note that discretion often involves choosing between different law enforcement options. For example, officers are regularly confronted with minor offences that present a choice of issuing fixed penalty tickets or making an arrest and taking the suspect to the police station. 'Under-enforcement as opposed to choosing how to enforce the law, has led to concerns because it is seen by some to occur as a consequence of either an officer's "misappropriation of judicial power" or an officer's "discrimination"' (Neyroud and Beckley, 2001, pp 85–6). Clearly those people that do not have the law enforced against them but are instead given a verbal warning or reprimand, are unlikely to complain about it. At the same time, what defence can the perpetrator of an offence have when subjected to law enforcement? It could be argued that the perpetrator has no defence; he/she has committed an offence and therefore merits the law's full weight of sanction. But, if one person deserves to be punished for committing an offence, why do not all persons (committing identical offences) also deserve to be punished in the same way? The unfairness of this situation is not so much that some are having the law enforced against them, but rather that others are not. Critics of under-enforcement therefore point to the inconsistency in applying the law which may result. As a consequence, the fundamental right of the police to employ discretionary powers is called into question.

One simple answer (proposed by the critics of police discretion) is to remove police discretion altogether or at least to reduce the extent to which officers can draw upon it. There are practical problems that prevent this from happening completely. For instance, the Criminal Justice System (CJS) already struggles to cope with the existing load presented to it; how would it cope if the police enforced the law without discretion? Another example is that police work is extremely difficult to manage (Reiner, 2000, Chapter 2). Most officers operate alone or with a partner and as Crawshaw *et al*. (1998, p 24) note, police supervision tends to occur after the event. These examples illustrate the amount of discretion police officers have, but they are not arguments for keeping it.

Governments have periodically introduced legislation and guidelines to restrict the amount of discretion a police officer has. This may be reflected in force policies as well, for example in relation to the policing of domestic violence. Positive action policies (which would include an arrest when attending a domestic incident) have been applied across the UK. If police discretion is to be maintained, it is important that we make a positive case for it. As part of the argument for discretion we need to identify a number of ways in which police discretion is often misrepresented. We begin by considering the view that police discretion is nothing more than applying common sense.

5.7.2 Discretion and Common Sense

The view that police discretion is a matter of applying common sense to policing situations would appear to have some merit. It helps police officers understand how real operational experiences complement the necessarily theoretical and abstract learning which takes place during the initial period of police training. Importantly, officers learn in this way to use the law as a means to an end rather than as an end in itself. However, the problem with viewing police discretion as the application of common sense is that it is too simplistic. It suggests that discretionary decisions are straightforward and could be applied by anyone. This view also fails to distinguish between decisions that are just simple common-sense decisions and decisions that genuinely require the use of discretion. As Davis (1996) notes, not all choices are discretionary. This is an important point. Police discretion cannot be reduced simply to being a matter of making choices or decisions.

5.7.3 Police Discretion and Subjectivity

Another way of understanding discretion is to consider the view that every police officer has a unique subjectivity that produces different approaches to how the law is interpreted and enforced. Within this perspective, police discretion is understood as the means by which individual subjectivity can be realized. It is undoubtedly true to say that the individual subjectivities of officers play an important role in how they police, but this should not be confused with police discretion. Indeed, police discretion is necessary precisely because it provides a way of curbing the influence of individual subjectivity.

To illustrate what this point means, consider the following question: should we expect all police officers to make the same decision in identical circumstances? Student police officers answer this question in different ways; some answer that there will be as many different decisions as there are officers making them, but others assert that every officer should make the same decision. So what is the correct answer? We should note that the question is not entirely fair because different contexts would probably produce different answers (in reality no two sets of circumstances are ever identical). Nonetheless, the existence of police discretion implies that we should not accept either of the extreme answers presented above. If we expect every officer to make the same decision then why are we considering discretion at all? Alternatively, if every officer makes a different decision, in what sense are these decisions connected? That is, in what sense are these decisions related to policing principles and practice?

The answer is that we should expect officers' decisions to differ, but that there will be a finite number of decision categories, normally two or three. Ideally, each of these categories would represent good police decisions that could be justified and explained. (More realistically, we might expect a few officers to make decisions that fall into another separate category, one that represents bad police decisions.) In other words, police discretion assumes that there is more than one way to deal with most situations, but at the same time, there is only a limited number of valid options open for consideration. So what is it that limits the options and thereby the individual subjectivity of each officer?

The answer is that decisions are discretionary but only to the extent that they relate to professional standards, integrity, the law, and force policy. The legal philosopher Ronald Dworkin has explained this point by referring to discretion as the 'hole in the doughnut' (see Neyroud and Beckley, 2001, p 83). The doughnut analogy suggests that discretion is given meaning by the professionalism surrounding it in the same way that the hole in a ring doughnut is given meaning by the dough surrounding it. If we eat the ring, the hole disappears; likewise, without professional standards, discretion becomes meaningless; discretion has to exist and has to be applied within a policing context.

Just as professional standards limit the number of options available to officers, the same standards also allow for different responses. We can say that subjectivity is not an adequate answer because it would mean that law enforcement is too arbitrary. It is not acceptable that an individual is arrested only because he/she encountered officer A rather than officer B or officer C. All police responses are only valid to the extent that they can be explained and justified, and this has to be related to professional standards, and not just a product of a subjective perspective. To reiterate and emphasize the point, discretion curbs subjectivity by providing an objective, professional guide.

5.7.4 Discretion and Judicial Misappropriation

It was noted earlier that, for some critics, police discretion is seen as nothing more than an individual officer's misappropriation of judicial power. The reasoning behind this is that when officers decide not to enforce the law against an individual who has clearly committed an offence, they are effectively acting as judge and jury. This view is based upon a misconception of the police officer's role, that the police are merely law enforcers. This view is summarized by Waddington (1999b) with reference to the surprise expressed by researchers (into policing) in the 1960s. He says:

> the prevailing assumption had been that policing was little more than the application of the law ... Criminals committed crimes and the police captured the criminals who were tried and convicted by the courts (Waddington, 1999b, p 31).

Indeed, such was the surprise of these early researchers that Waddington refers to the discretionary powers of the police as being 'discovered' in the 1960s. Of course police officers had been exercising discretion since at least the creation of the modern police in 1829 but it was not an aspect of police work that had received much attention. As more research was conducted, it was found that the police would consistently enforce the law against certain sections of society and not others (see 5.7.5 below). There can be no defence for the police discriminating against certain sections of society but that does not mean in turn that the police should therefore have their discretion removed. Instead, what needs to be learnt from these experiences is that the police officers are not so much law enforcers as peace officers (Banton, 1964). Waddington (1999b) has argued that the police use the law as and when appropriate in order to bring about a greater sense of peace and order in society. He refers also to Lord Scarman's warning following the Brixton riots in 1981 'that the maintenance of "public tranquillity" was a higher priority than "law enforcement" ' (Waddington, 1999b, p 42).

The police make law-enforcement decisions based upon their interpretation of what is in the public interest. It is this balancing act between law enforcement and the needs of society that gives rise to police discretion. The police are expected to use the law to maintain order, and therefore they need discretionary powers in order to use the law as effectively as possible. This does not mean that the police can operate outside the law; they must work within legal boundaries. But they should not be required to enforce the law mechanically in every circumstance. In this respect the police are not only accountable to the law but also to the people they police.

5.7.5 Discretion and Discrimination

The view that discretion is the means by which certain sections of society are discriminated against has arisen from research conducted since the 1960s. Why are some sections of society more likely than others to have the law enforced against them? In their defence, police officers have argued that they do not discriminate against any sections of society but respond to each individual they encounter according to how that individual responds to them. This is referred to in police circles as the **attitude test**. (You will no doubt hear more experienced police officers using this phrase, or more colloquial versions.) Quite simply, if an individual is polite and repentant, they are less likely to have the law enforced against them. The reason for this is that the individual appears to have learnt a lesson and is judged to be unlikely to reoffend. An intervention by a police officer is in itself an effective form of remonstration and can help to prevent repeat offending. It may not be in the public interest to pursue certain cases further, as it would contribute nothing towards achieving a more ordered society (and apart from the wasted expense, it could have a negative effect on the individual stopped). On the other hand, if the individual stopped by the police officer is rude, abusive, and unrepentant then it is assumed that further action needs to be taken against the individual in order to make sure he/she feels sufficiently reprimanded.

The problem with this defence is that it perpetuates problems that exist in society. It is likely that those who regularly come into contact with the police will be immune to police warnings and will feel more confident in challenging the police officer's authority. They are more likely to be abusive and to have an existing antagonistic relationship with the police. Historically, individuals from certain ethnic minority groupings have had a disproportionately high interaction with the police and so the attitude test does nothing to break this cycle; indeed, it helps to perpetuate it. It is for this reason that police officers are obliged to take the moral high ground in such confrontations.

Efforts have been made to promote the absorption of this kind of information into police culture, and to rectify any resulting adverse or confrontational attitudes. There have undoubtedly been some low points (see Macpherson, 1999 and *The Secret Policeman* programme, 2003), but police officers today are in a better position to understand the cycle and to respond accordingly. The important difference between discriminatory decisions and discretionary decisions is that discrimination is based upon prejudice, whereas discretion is premised upon professional judgement (which incorporates many different factors, including the prevalence of discrimination in previous times). This requires officers to go beyond simply providing a common standard by which every individual encounter is measured. Officers are required to respond to each encounter individually, taking into account the specifics of each situation. As Rowe (2002) has noted, since the Macpherson Report (1999) policing no longer treats everyone equally but rather pursues specific policies aimed at reducing discrimination, for example by actively promoting an anti-racist agenda. It is now part of the police officer's role to break the cycle of discrimination.

TASK 16

In the following task you are given two scenarios to consider. The first is taken from the National Police Training notes issued to student police officers in 1995 and the second is our own invention.

1. You see a woman, who appears to be slightly drunk, pick up a street sign that has fallen from a wall, conceal it under her raincoat and walk off. When stopped, she readily admits that she intends to keep it as a trophy. She is a medical student who is celebrating passing her final exam (NPT, 1995, p 4).
2. You are on duty outside a football ground when you observe a young man, clutching a can of super-strength lager, pick up an 'Away Supporters' sign that has fallen from a wall, conceal it under his hoodie and walk off. When stopped, he readily admits that he intends to keep it to start a collection. He is a football fan who is celebrating his club's victory in an important match.

In each case consider what discretion, if any, you would exercise.

5.8 Systems of Justice and Models of Policing

We all tend to think that systems which are familiar are the norm, and that all good systems will be just about the same as ours. It can therefore come as a surprise to find that other countries have systems that are very different to our own. In some countries guilt is presumed and innocence has to be proven, whereas in the UK, we presume innocence and expect the prosecution to prove guilt. Partly as a consequence of the system of justice used by a particular country, the organization of policing and police forces varies too.

TASK 17

What is the system of justice used in the last overseas country that you visited on holiday or business?

5.8.1 Systems of Justice

The system used in England and Wales is **adversarial**, whereas elsewhere in Europe (in France or The Netherlands, for example) the system used is **inquisitorial**.

The adversarial model requires that a person, the defendant, is accused of an offence and is tried by a court (usually in open session), and that the defendant's guilt must be proved beyond reasonable doubt. The prosecution is conducted on behalf of the Crown, often referred to in written case law as 'R', meaning 'Regina' or 'Rex' (the Queen or King respectively, depending whether a King or a Queen is on the throne when the case is heard). The Crown Prosecutor is a lawyer employed (or, rarely, retained) by the Crown Prosecution Service. The defendant is normally represented by a lawyer, usually a barrister, who is also called 'defence counsel', or generically 'the defence'.

In an inquisitorial system the questioning of the accused may be undertaken, not by a prosecuting counsel but by an investigating judge; correspondingly, the role taken by defence counsel is of much lower profile (and of lesser significance) than it is here.

At the time of writing (2009), imports from the USA (such as increased use of litigation, the dominance of the defence, and televising of trials) may be influencing our view of what policing and criminal justice systems are best suited to the UK. But let us make a confident assertion: in matters such as jury trial and continuity of evidence, the early signs are that England and Wales may well incline more to the European Continental models than to North American ones. Although unthinkable ten years ago, trial without a jury for complex fraud cases is now being widely considered. The increasingly interventionist role of the Crown Prosecution Service (CPS) in criminal investigations is actually closer to the European model (the *juge d'instruction* or 'investigating magistrate') than it is to any US model.

5.8.2   Models of Policing in England and Wales

We have already noted above that systems of justice vary widely across Europe. Here we will consider some of the models of policing used in England and Wales.

> **TASK 18**
>
> What do you think characterizes our approach to policing? What can you point to that is essentially British about it?

Some key features are given below and in the answer to the task, but if you want to read further, we refer you to the bibliography at the end of the Handbook.

Beyond this generalized 'consensus' approach to policing we are able to discern more distinctive **operational** models. These include intelligence-led policing, problem-oriented policing, community-based policing (or neighbourhood-policing models), and zero-tolerance policing.

In England and Wales each chief constable can decide (to some extent) which operational model of policing best suits his/her force. In practice, a force is likely to adopt a combination of models. You may be able to identify several forces which have tried to do all of them simultaneously, and where the police officers themselves are confused about what particular model is operating at any one moment. We also know of forces which have implemented intelligence-led (or intelligence-based) policing alongside community-based policing and have done so very efficiently and effectively. Much depends on the conceptual planning of the individual chief constable and his or her Police Authority.

An excellent starting point to find out more concerning these operational models is Nick Tilley's chapter in Newburn's *Handbook of Policing* (Newburn, 2003). It is perhaps misleading to suggest that these models are somehow in competition or are mutually exclusive although there are significant points of departure between them. Rather, they focus on different things. Intelligence-led policing tends to be seen as a response to the inevitable and unavoidable existence of criminals in society and the existence of high-volume repeat criminals at that. On the other hand problem-oriented policing, as the label suggests, attempts to model crime or disorder in terms of problems that we analyse and attempt to solve. Finally, community-based policing suggests that crime and disorder must always be viewed in the wider context of the community or communities from which it originates.

> **TASK 19**
>
> How would intelligence-led policing, problem-oriented policing, and community based policing, adopted in their purest form (that is, to the exclusion of all other approaches), each deal with the phenomenon of anti-social behaviour?

> **TASK 20**
>
> We have considered models of policing in England and Wales, but elsewhere in Europe other models are used. What differences have you noticed when you have travelled abroad?

5.9   National Priorities for Policing

In this part of Chapter 5 we consider how the national priorities for policing affect the local Policing Plans that forces are expected to construct and deliver, together with the new Policing Pledge and the Neighbourhood Policing Programme.

5.9.1 Introduction

Every police force in England and Wales has a Policing Plan which outlines its commitments and what it expects to be able to deliver during the forthcoming three or so years. These Plans detail the specific targets for a force expressed in 'Smart' objectives (such as 'by 2011 to increase by 5 per cent the number of drug users referred to the Drug Interventions Programme and assessed by that team'). Scotland and Northern Ireland have very similar policing plans to those for the police forces of England and Wales. However, there are important regional differences too and individual priorities which a blanket plan cannot cover. A police force's Policing Plan is likely to be based in part on the national Strategic Policing Priorities (SPP) which in turn reference the national Public Service Agreements (PSAs) and cross-refer to the national Analysis of Policing and Community Safety (APACS) measures.

> **TASK 21**
>
> What do you think the value of a Policing Plan may be? Write down a few bullet points.

5.9.2 Strategic Policing Priorities

The national SPP are part of the government's **National Community Safety Plan** (NCSP) which incorporates strategies for the work of a number of departments of state, including the Department of Health and the Department for Employment and Learning. The SPP in its current form covers the year 2009–10, and sets out the Home Secretary's strategic priorities and the key performance indicators for that period.

The Home Secretary has set four key priorities for the police service of England and Wales for 2009–2010 (Home Office 2008b):

- increase public confidence in the police, reducing crime in line with a number of the PSAs;
- tackle serious and organized crime;
- tackle terrorism and violent extremism in line with the counter-terrorism strategy;
- ensure the best use of resources to deliver significant 'cashable' improvements, more effective deployment of the workforce, and to realize the benefits of new technology.

In its SPP, the government emphasizes that the delivery of these key priorities is critical at all levels; from the neighbourhood teams, to the BCUs, at force level, and thence to national and international levels through the SOCA and other agencies.

Your force is likely to have incorporated into its own local plan the provisions of the SPP and the need for partnership working outlined in the NCSP. Recent developments have tied local planning into the same business cycle as the national plan. Most force Policing Plans will be based on a three-year cycle (updated and refreshed annually), to reflect the provisions in the NCSP from 2010 onwards.

We cannot predict what your force will do because there are too many variations between forces and too many local considerations to take into account. However, some recurrent themes will no doubt figure in the planning for all forces. These in turn will influence the way that you do your job.

> **TASK 22**
>
> Can you suggest what some of those themes or subjects will be?

5.9.3 The Policing Pledge

The Flanagan Report (Flanagan, 2004) and other reports indicated that there was some uncertainty amongst the public concerning the standards of service that they should receive from their local police force, and a desire to learn more about police actions in response to local problems of crime and anti-social behaviour. As a result the Home Office have introduced a 'Policing Pledge' which describes the expectations the public should have of its local police force. Most of the ten 'pledges' are very general in nature but a number have specific targets such as to 'aim to answer 999 calls within ten seconds'.

In practice, the introduction of the Policing Pledge has meant the following:

* local priorities are set for action at the ward or borough level (eg dealing with anti-social behaviour at the local park) together with the action taken in response;
* the dissemination of information about the neighbourhood policing team for the area (see 5.9.4 below), including photographs and the means of contact (by email or voicemail, for example);
* greater publicly available information on crime rates and specific criminal activities;
* monthly public meetings, meetings between the neighbourhood policing team and local residents, and the provision of drop-in surgeries.

You may find that at least some of your Supervised or Independent Patrol is undertaken with a neighbourhood policing team (see 5.9.4 below), and part of their work will be dedicated to fulfilling the Policing Pledge.

5.9.4   The Neighbourhood Policing Programme

The Home Office have made it clear that 'neighbourhood policing' is now one of their main priorities for policing. Undoubtedly one reason for this emphasis has been a perceived desire by the public for more 'visible' forms of policing, and it is linked with the so-called 'reassurance' agenda. Despite official figures indicating falling levels of most crimes, comparatively high proportions of people continue to believe crime has risen across the country as a whole and in their local area (see 5.15.2 below).

The fear of crime may be linked to a number of local and national factors, one of which is 'signal crime' (see 5.15.4.2 below). For example, relatively minor acts of vandalism or anti-social behaviour can produce a sense of insecurity and even fear within individuals—that such crimes are a 'signal' of more serious underlying crime and disorder problems within a community. Neighbourhood policing is a response to these anxieties as well as being part of a more general government drive for a more locally responsive police service.

The Neighbourhood Policing Programme is, in effect, an NPIA initiative designed to support the introduction and development of neighbourhood policing in all police forces in England and Wales. As a result, neighbourhood policing teams have been created (whose objectives are determined in part by the Policing Pledge: see 5.9.3 above) consisting (typically) of a mixture of PCSOs, Special Constables, local authority Wardens, and police constables.

Neighbourhood policing initiatives in England and Wales have yet to be evaluated. However, they would appear to draw at least some of their guiding principles from community-based and problem-orientated policing models. This is not to say that the National Intelligence Model (see 12.3 below) has no place in neighbourhood policing—the Home Office and ACPO, for example, both suggest that the NIM is a valuable way to support building up knowledge of a community and in devising successful 'interventions'.

The Home Office, however, expects that neighbourhood policing teams will spend at least 80 per cent of their time 'visibly working on behalf of the public' (Home Office, 2008d) in their neighbourhood. This means that you might find that part of your time on Supervised Patrol is spent with a neighbourhood policing team.

5.10 Principles of Law

Although policing involves more than upholding the law (and criminal law in particular), we saw in 5.5 above how an understanding of the law is an important factor of a police officer's personal authority. Here we will examine some of the basic principles of the law that are relevant to the work of the student police officer, and these principles will be built upon in subsequent chapters.

5.10.1 Criminal Liability

Student police officers will find themselves thinking about more than just the laws relevant to crime—for example, you may become involved in policing a picket line established during a strike, and this is not a criminal matter. However, most of the law relevant to your first few years of service undoubtedly is of the criminal rather than the civil form. Indeed, if you look at the list of subjects in the IPLDP LPG modules you will find the list dominated by criminal law.

We begin with the notion of 'criminal liability'—how do we know and then prove that a person has broken the law? There is a cardinal rule in the criminal law of England and Wales born out of a Latin proverb or short saying which is '*actus non facit reus, nisi sit mens rea*'. For those of you (like some of the authors) who did not take Latin at school, this means 'an act does not make a person criminally liable unless it is accompanied by a guilty mindset'. There are therefore two elements of criminal liability:

1. The **action** that the defendant undertook, which must always be proved beyond reasonable doubt (see 5.10.2 below)—commonly known as *actus reus*.
2. The **guilty mindset** that the defendant had at the time the action was taken which also must be proved, that is they intended to commit the crime—commonly known as *mens rea*.

Although the use of Latin can seem off-putting and exclusionary to some people, these terms are still used quite extensively in policing and so are worth remembering. (See also the discussion about interviewing in 12.5 below.) We will now look at these two building blocks of criminal liability in more detail.

5.10.1.1 *Actus reus*

If a person is to be found guilty of a criminal offence, then it must be proved that he/she either:

- acted criminally in some way: for example, committed murder;
- omitted to do an act which brought about a criminal outcome: for example, knowing that someone was going to commit a crime but doing nothing to stop it or report it;
- caused a state of affairs to happen: for example, being found drunk and incapable at the wheel of a car; or
- failed to do an act which brought about a criminal outcome: for example, by failing to ensure that a vehicle was roadworthy when offering it for hire.

5.10.1.2 *Mens rea*

Although the Latin term appears to be very narrow in its meaning, in reality there are a number of thought processes that satisfy the requirements of many offences other than just having guilty knowledge. You will find these states of mind listed under different terms in a number of offences. The most common words are:

- dishonestly: such as theft;
- wilfully: such as in neglect of children;
- recklessly: as in causing criminal damage;
- with intent: as in burglary with intent to steal.

The level of *mens rea* in criminal offences can generally be grouped in three main levels of intent. These are described below, starting with the lowest level.

1. Offences requiring an element of negligence

The defendant's negligence is usually measured against the standards of a reasonable person (usually a hypothetical person in the mind of a jury member or magistrate). An example of an offence that uses such a test is careless or inconsiderate driving.

2. Offences requiring a low level of intent

A defendant's low-level intention is only that required to achieve their objective in carrying out a criminal offence. When some offences are committed, therefore, it is relatively straightforward to prove that the defendant had a low level of intent, such as when they are caught outside a building with stolen property from a burglary. Such offences include theft, and driving with excess breath/blood alcohol.

3. Offences requiring a particular mens rea

There are two groups of offence requiring a particular *mens rea*:

- The first group of offences involves **specific** intent. This is where the defendant is proved to have a specific aim to achieve a specific objective. Offences involving specific intention include murder and 'wounding or inflicting grievous bodily harm with intent'.
- The second group of offences involves **ulterior** intent. This is where the defendant is proved to have a second or hidden intention other than the main criminal act. An example of this would be when a defendant is charged with burglary with intent. Under these circumstances it must be proved that the defendant not only intended to enter a building as a trespasser, but also to inflict grievous bodily harm, cause damage, or steal.

5.10.2 Burden of Proof

How do we prove that a person is guilty of a criminal offence? The law tells us that:

> throughout the web of the English criminal law one golden thread is always to be seen: that it is the duty of the prosecution to prove the prisoner's guilt (*Woolmington v DPP* [1935] AC 462).

Therefore, in criminal proceedings:

1. The onus is on the prosecution to prove the guilt of the defendant, not for the defendant to prove his or her innocence.
2. Further, the degree of proof (in criminal cases) is that of **beyond reasonable doubt**. This was famously expressed by Geoffrey Lawrence (cited in Johnston and Hutton, 2005, p 133) in the following way:

> The possibility of guilt is not enough, suspicion is not enough, probability is not enough, likelihood is not. A criminal matter is not a question of balancing probabilities and deciding in favour of probability.

5.11 The Law in England and Wales

An understanding of the law in England and Wales, if only at the level required to exercise your day-to-day responsibilities as a student police officer, is an important aspect of the **epistemic authority** that you will exercise as a confirmed police officer (see 5.5 above).

In 5.10 above, we examined the basic principles that underpin the law in England and Wales. Although we have noted on a number of occasions that policing is much more than simply enforcing the law, here we examine in more detail the basic aspects of the criminal law that are particularly relevant to police work. This understanding is a necessary condition for you to be able to demonstrate the achievement of a large number of the NOS elements. Law also features extensively during most Operational Modules and in LPG 1 and LPG 2.

5.11.1 The Law

There are several different forms of law: common law, statute law, case law, Acts of Parliament, Statutory Instruments, and by-laws. These all interrelate in a number of ways, but first we consider each one in turn.

5.11.1.1 Common law

In the past, when laws were not written down, courts made decisions that were then passed by word of mouth to other courts. These were known as **precedents** or decisions. An example would be where a court decided that for one human being to kill another is unlawful. This decision was then accepted by other courts throughout the country and, from that point onwards, such a killing would be contrary to common law. No new common law offences are created now since, apart from the setting of precedents by the courts, the making of new laws is undertaken by Parliament through the enactment of statutes.

Examples of common law offences which remain today are:

- murder;
- manslaughter;
- perverting the course of justice;
- escape from lawful custody.

5.11.1.2 Statute law

Statute law is written law and it is the foundation of the current legal system in England and Wales. It is made up of **Acts of Parliament** (see below) which start off as documents called **Bills** or **draft law**.

The Bill is written by ministry officials as a proposal and then submitted to the Houses of Parliament for a decision. If it is accepted, it is given Royal Assent before becoming an Act of Parliament. For student police officers, commonly encountered Acts of Parliament in criminal law include:

- The Theft Act 1968 (principal offences of dishonesty);
- The Criminal Damage Act 1971 (some offences of damage);
- The Misuse of Drugs Act 1971 (the principal drug-related offences);
- The Public Order Act 1986 (the main offences of public disorder).

5.11.1.3 Case law

Case law helps establish the precise meaning of legislation. Decisions made by a particular court about legislation are then accepted by the judicial system throughout the country. An example of this would be a decision that was made about identification evidence in the case *R v Turnbull* [1976] 3 All ER 549. (Note the system for referencing cases: 'R' is an abbreviation for Regina (the Crown as prosecutor), 'v' for versus, and 'Turnbull' is the name of the defendant. This case can be found in Volume 3 of the 1976 All England Law Reports on p 549.)

5.11.1.4 Acts of Parliament

Acts of Parliament are divided into sections that may contain definitions, offences, powers of arrest, exemptions, and interpretations of words and expressions used. An Act is a complex document that often includes technical details, such as fines and penalties, which may need frequent revision and updating. Sorting out these details is often left to government ministers in order to reduce the pressure on parliamentary time. These details are provided in the form of Orders, Regulations, and Rules, known as Statutory Instruments.

5.11.1.5 Statutory Instruments

Statutory Instruments (SIs) make it possible for details of an Act to be revised without having to be subjected to parliamentary procedures every time. Importantly, SIs are as much part of the law of England and Wales as is the main body of the Act of Parliament. An example is the Road Vehicles (Construction and Use) (Amendment) (No 2) Regulations 2001. The Home Secretary, using powers given to him by s 41 of the Road Traffic Act 1988, introduced a number of detailed provisions regarding seat belts in road vehicles. As with Acts of Parliament, SIs are given a number as well as a title, so the number of these Regulations is SI 2001 No 1043.

5.11.1.6 By-laws

By-laws are local laws which have been made by a local authority and approved by a Secretary of State of the government. These are passed by a local authority and normally deal with local matters, for example dogs on leads in recreational areas.

TASK 23

Under s 41 of the Road Traffic Act 1988, the Statutory Instrument called Road Vehicle Lighting Regulations 1989 (SI 1989 No 1796) was introduced. Use *Blackstone's Police Manual: Volume 3 Road Policing*, the internet, or other publications to determine what regs 11–22 inclusive cover in relation to motor vehicles.

5.12 Human Rights

The concept of human rights and the responsibilities of police officers in the preservation and maintenance of those rights runs throughout this Handbook. However, it is perhaps worth noting that recent legislation concerning human rights marked a significant mood change towards an emphasis on rights ('you shall') rather than the usual focus of the law on prohibition ('you shall not'). By this we mean that most laws, until recently, defined what constitutes wrong-doing and how law enforcers and the criminal justice system should respond to these crimes. Human rights legislation on the other hand stresses an individual's **entitlement** to expect certain fundamental rights as part of their social contract with the state and other forms of authority. The Human Rights Act 1998 is the prime example. It falls to public authorities such as the police (and by extension, to student police officers as members of that police service) to maintain the fundamental rights of all individuals who come into contact with that authority.

So important is this emphasis on the proactive protection of human rights that some police forces, notably the Police Service of Northern Ireland, may even be described as 'human rights-based'.

There are a number of NOS elements relevant to human rights and the student police officer, most notably the element:

National Occupational Standards Element

AA1.1   Promote equality and value diversity

Here, we provide background information relevant to performance criterion 1 of element AA1.1 (to 'act in accordance with relevant legislation, employment regulations and policies, and Codes of practice related to promoting equality and valuing diversity'). As with the majority of NOS elements, direct observation by your assessor or other qualified witnesses is likely to form the main method of assessing this element.

The roots of the Human Rights Act 1998 are to be found in a set of articles containing rights agreed by the European Convention on the Protection of Human Rights and Fundamental Freedoms (or in short often referred to as 'the Convention' or ECHR), which came into force in 1953 as part of the reconstruction of Europe after the Second World War.

There are two main features of human rights legislation. First, all new statute law must be compatible with the rights. Second, an individual may take a public authority to a UK court if the authority has not acted in a manner compatible with the rights.

5.12.1   What Are the Rights?

These are normally described in terms of the Article number:

Article number	Article title
2	Right to life
3	Prohibition of torture
4	Prohibition of slavery and forced labour
5	Right to liberty and security
6	Right to a fair trial
7	No punishment without law
8	Right to respect for private and family life
9	Freedom of thought, conscience, and religion
10	Freedom of expression
11	Freedom of assembly and association
12	Right to marry
14	Prohibition of discrimination
16	Restriction on the political activities of aliens
17	Prohibition of the abuse of rights
18	Limitation on use of restrictions on rights

(You may be wondering what has happened to Article 1. As far as student police officers need be concerned, there is no Article 1. This is a technical aspect of the adoption of the European Convention. Articles 13 and 15 are not included above as they are unlikely to be relevant to policing.)

5.12.2   The Three Types of Convention Rights within the Act

There are three types of convention right within the Human Rights Act 1998: absolute, limited, and qualified rights. We examine each in turn.

5.12.2.1   Absolute rights

Within these rights, the interests of the community as a whole cannot restrict the rights of the individual in any way. They are absolute.

Article number	Article title
2	Right to life
3	Prohibition of torture
4	Prohibition of slavery and forced labour
7	No punishment without law

5.12.2.2   Limited rights

These rights are not absolute because the articles are limited.

Article number	Article title
5	Right to liberty and security
6	Right to a fair trial

An example of a limitation is in Article 5: the right to liberty does not apply if the detention is lawful as a result of six listed arrest situations. One of these circumstances is when the arrest is made to ensure attendance in court if there is a reasonable suspicion that a crime has been committed, or to prevent crimes being committed. (However, although the right to liberty may be limited by these circumstances, there is still the right to security, conflated with liberty in Article 5.)

A further example occurs within Article 6, where there is a right for both the public and the press to have access to any court hearing. However, this right is subject to certain restrictions in the interests of morality, public order, national security, or where the interests of those under 18, or the privacy of the parties require the exclusion of the press and public.

5.12.2.3 Qualified rights

These rights relate to matters where interference by the public authority is permissible if it is in the public interest and can be qualified, for example to prevent disorder or crime, for public safety, or for national security.

Article number	Article title
8	Right to respect for private and family life
9	Freedom of thought, conscience, and religion
10	Freedom of expression
11	Freedom of assembly and association

However, a public authority (such as the police) may only interfere with one of these qualified rights under one of three circumstances:

- The interference is lawful and must form part of existing common or statue law (see 5.11 above) such as the power to stop and search.
- The interference is made for one of the specifically listed permissible acts in the interests of the public, in order to prevent disorder or crime for public safety.
- The interference is necessary in a democratic society because the wider interests of the community as a whole often have to be balanced against the rights of an individual; but it must be proportionate, not excessive or heavy-handed.

5.12.3 Applying the Human Rights Act to Everyday Policing

You may need to ask yourself the following questions in relation to an individual or group before you interfere with their qualified rights:

1. Are my actions **lawful**? Is there a common or statute law to support my interference with a person's rights?
2. Are my actions **permissible**? Am I permitted to interfere with a person's rights because it is in support of a duty such as the preventing of crime?
3. Are my actions **necessary**? Do the needs of the many outweigh the needs of the few; in other words, must I take into account the interests of the community and balance one individual's rights against another's?
4. Are my actions **proportionate**? Having considered everything, will my actions be excessive or could I do something less intrusive and more in proportion to the outcome I need to achieve?

During training you may be given a mnemonic to use to help remember the questions you should ask yourself about any action you might take that affects human rights. These mnemonics vary from force to force, from JAPAN (Justifiable, Accountable, Proportionate, and Necessary) to PLAN (Proportionality, Legality, Accountability, and Necessity) but in essence all refer to the criteria described above.

A standard that you will need to achieve in order to qualify as a police officer is NOS element AA1.1: to 'promote equality and value diversity' of people. (Note that Skills for Justice defines people to include a 'child, adult, group, community or agency that [you] come into contact with, either directly or indirectly. It includes members of the public, individuals who are clients of the justice sector, and colleagues in the workplace.') The NOS and their component elements are covered in 3.6 above.

This element has the following **performance criteria** (see 3.6.3.1 above) which expect you to:

1. act in accordance with relevant legislation, employment regulations and policies, and Codes of practice related to promoting equality and valuing diversity
2. act in ways that:

   - acknowledge and recognize individuals' background and beliefs;
   - respect diversity;
   - value people as individuals;
   - do not discriminate against people

3. provide individuals with the information they need to make informed decisions about exercising their rights
4. provide information in a format appropriate to the individual
5. take account of how your behaviour affects individuals and their experience of your organization's culture and approach
6. seek feedback from individuals on your behaviour and use this to improve what you do in the future
7. challenge people when they are not promoting equality and valuing diversity
8. actively help others to promote equality and value diversity
9. seek support from appropriate sources when you are having difficulty understanding how to promote equality and value diversity.

(Skills for Justice, 2007c).

TASK 24

How would you seek to meet the first bullet point of criterion 2, that is to 'acknowledge and recognize individuals' background and beliefs'? What evidence would satisfy the performance criteria for this?

5.13 The Police and Criminal Evidence Act 1984

We consider later in this Handbook (Chapters 7 and 8) the powers which you have as an attested student police officer that enable you to arrest individuals, to search people and property, to enter buildings, and to seize objects whilst on Supervised or Independent Patrol. Many of these powers (and restrictions on their use) are to be found in the Police and Criminal Evidence Act 1984 (known as the PACE Act 1984). Here, we examine the PACE Act 1984 in more detail. It is important that you become familiar with this Act, and it is very likely that your police tutors will provide you with many opportunities to check your understanding. It also worth noting that there have been significant changes to the PACE Act 1984 as a result of the Serious Organised Crime and Police Act 2005. Note also that aspects of the PACE Act 1984 and its associated Codes of Practice may be subject to change as part of the Home Office's 'Modernizing Police Powers' programme. For further information view the Home Office website <http://www.police.home-office.gov.uk/operational-policing/powers-pace-codes/PACE-Review/>.

A good understanding of a number of sections of the PACE Act 1984 (and particularly, the associated Codes of Practice) is an essential prerequisite of meeting the whole of NOS Unit CA1 and the NOS element CD5.1:

National Occupational Standards

CA1   Use police actions in a fair and justified way
CD5.1   Arrest, detain, or report individuals

The demonstration of a knowledge of the PACE Act 1984 in practical policing contexts is also an important milestone of the PAC—for example, the parts of the checklist concerned with your ability to search. You are likely to encounter this subject matter when undertaking Phase 3 of the IPLDP and within LPG 1 under the heading 'Police Policies and Procedures' and, specifically, parts of LPG 1.4(1) and LPG 1.4(8).

5.13.1 Key Features of the PACE Act 1984

Some key features of the PACE Act 1984 are shown in the diagram below:

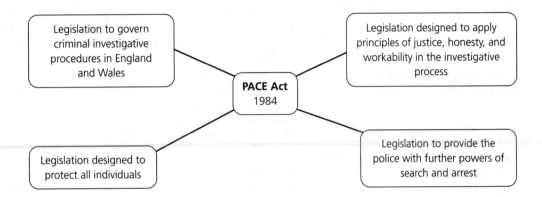

5.13.2 PACE Codes of Practice

The Codes are guidelines that regulate the investigative process. They are divided into seven main sections, and refer to contacts between the police and the public in the exercise of the following police powers, which include searching, detaining, and questioning suspects:

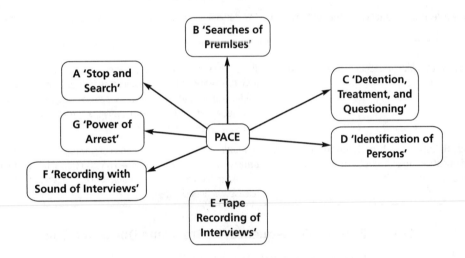

The Codes can be downloaded in full via the website <http://police.homeoffice.gov.uk/operational-policing/powers-pace-codes/pace-code-intro>

Note that the subsections of each Code are numbered, for example 'Code C 10.1'. We use the same notation throughout this Handbook.

A brief summary of each code is provided here.

The PACE Act 1984 Codes of Practice

Code of Practice	Summary
Code A deals with the exercise by police officers of statutory powers of **stop and search**, and the requirements for police officers and police staff to record public encounters.	This provides guidelines on searching people who are not under arrest. It provides guiding principles for the justification needed to use a power of search, the circumstances in which the search can take place, and the responsibility of those making the search towards the individual. The code outlines considerations and recommendations for the protection of an individual's rights and leaves very little doubt about the extent of the search and where it can take place. In addition, the code outlines what documentation must be completed at the end of such a search or encounter.

Code of Practice	Summary
Code B deals with **searches of premises** by police officers and the seizure of property found by police officers on persons or premises.	This provides guidelines as to how a person's rights can be protected prior to a search of premises being made by police officers, in relation to the conduct of the search itself and the recording of such a search on its completion. It includes searches which are pre-planned (and therefore use warrants issued by magistrates) as well as powers of search which police officers are given for the purposes of making an arrest or to search in order to find stolen or unlawfully possessed property in premises and on persons.
Code C deals with the **detention, treatment, and questioning** of persons by police officers.	This outlines the procedure for protecting a person's rights whilst in detention having been arrested and the care he/she must be given while in custody at a police station. It underlines the rights that detained people have whilst in police detention to communicate with other people, including legal representation, and sets out the process to protect those rights when being questioned, whether under arrest or not.
Code D deals with the **identification of persons** by police officers.	This protects the rights of the suspect regarding identification before he/she can be named and arrested, as well as the identification of any person who has been arrested and is going to be identified by a witness. Such processes therefore include identification parade procedures and identification by body samples and fingerprints, as well as showing witnesses photographs of suspects.
Code E deals with **tape-recording interviews** with suspects.	This safeguards the rights of an individual while being interviewed and recorded on tape. It considers the necessity for the tapes to be handled in confidence and securely and allows for the process of taking breaks during the interview in order to further consider the rights of the individual. The code requires that the person is informed of the process through which they are being taken at every stage.
Code F deals with **visual recording with sound of interviews** with suspects.	This outlines procedures that should take place while the interview of a person is being recorded both with sound and vision. At the time of writing there is no statutory requirement on the police to visually record interviews.
Code G deals with the statutory **power of arrest** by police officers.	This outlines procedures that you should adopt when arresting a person in order that his/her right to liberty is considered at all times. It defines what a lawful arrest is and that an arrest is made up of two parts. The first is the person's involvement in the commission of the offence and the second is a list of reasons why the arrest is necessary. It also describes the information to be given on arrest.
Code H deals only with the **detention**, treatment, and **questioning** of suspects arrested under s 41 of the Terrorism Act 2000.	This outlines the procedure for protecting a suspect's rights whilst they are in detention, but **only** when they have been arrested on suspicion of being a terrorist under s 41 of the Terrorism Act 2000 and at no other time. Once the suspect has been charged with an offence, released without charge, or transferred to a prison, the Code no longer applies.

5.13.3 Possible Consequences of Breaching One of the Codes

If a Code is breached there is a possibility of:

- disciplinary action, depending on the circumstances;
- a court deciding that your evidence is inadmissible;
- a court deciding that your evidence poses a threat to fairness;
- liability for civil or criminal proceedings.

TASK 25

Study the summaries of the Codes and for each one write down a brief description of a situation you have witnessed (for example, on Supervised Patrol) when the Code has been applied. The descriptions may provide you with knowledge evidence for Unit CA1 in the CAR of your SOLAP.

5.14 The Criminal Justice System

The **Criminal Justice System**, or **CJS**, is defined by the government as the police, the courts, the Prison Service, the Crown Prosecution Service (CPS), and the National Probation Service. Here, we will concentrate on the police, the courts, and the CPS.

Inevitably the focus of the CJS is on crime, the consequences of crime, and punishment. How we define crime (or perhaps, more accurately, criminal offences) is discussed elsewhere, most notably in 5.15 below. For the purpose of the explanations here, we presuppose that a crime has been committed and reported to the police.

As a student police officer, you will soon come into contact with the CJS. Indeed, in many forces a criminal justice placement forms part of IPLDP Phase 2 of training, and this provides an opportunity for you to meet other professionals working within the CJS. Many of these professionals are also undertaking programmes of education and training linked to NOS elements determined by Skills for Justice. There are likely to be numerous opportunities for you to demonstrate achievement of NOS when involved in such collaborative activities. Remember that some of these fellow professionals may also be A1 assessors (see Chapter 3) and hence capable of signing off elements of standards relevant to their areas of expertise.

5.14.1 Investigation and Prosecution

Once an alleged crime has been reported, the police undertake most of the tasks involved in an investigation. Any subsequent prosecution is formally undertaken on behalf of the Crown (the state) and is handled by the CPS. A decision to prosecute means that the courts are likely to be involved. Depending on their seriousness, the cases are dealt with at different courts (see 5.14.3 below). The defendant may represent his/her own case, though he/she is usually represented by a solicitor or barrister. The courts may be assisted by Social Services and the Probation Service.

A number of the NOS elements relate to carrying out investigations, preparing cases, and appearing in court (covered in more detail in 12.10 below), for example:

> **National Occupational Standards Elements**
>
> DA5.1 Prepare for court or other hearings
> DA5.2 Present evidence to court or other hearings
> DA6.1 Prepare case files
> DA6.2 Submit case files and progress enquiries

The PAC heading 'Finalize investigations' also requires you to demonstrate your ability to 'adhere to court procedures' and 'give evidence at court' before you are declared fit to undertake Independent Patrol.

5.14.2 Criminal Offences

Offences are classified according to their seriousness and at which court they can be tried. Note that the term arrestable offence is no longer used as offences are no longer classified in this way. This can be confusing if you are already familiar with the term (through, for example, undertaking special constable training). Offences are now classified as either 'summary' offences, 'indictment-only' offences, or 'either-way' offences. There is a further term of 'indictable' offence which is a collective name for both 'indictment-only' and 'either-way' offences.

5.14.2.1 Summary offences

Summary offences can only be tried in the magistrates' court. Examples are: common assault, assaulting a police officer in the execution of his/her duty, and most motoring offences.

5.14.2.2   Indictment-only offences

Indictment-only offences can only be dealt with at the Crown Court and are the most serious cases. Examples are: murder, manslaughter, causing death by dangerous driving, rape, robbery, aggravated burglary, and wounding with intent.

5.14.2.3   Either-way offences

Either-way offences may be tried either in the magistrates' court or at the Crown Court. The magistrate decides initially where the case is most suitably tried. Examples are: theft, obtaining by deception, assault occasioning actual bodily harm, and indecent assault.

5.14.2.4   Indictable offences

This is a collective term for both 'indictment-only' and 'either-way' offences. The term 'indictable offences' is used extensively in the legislation and codes surrounding stop and search (see 7.5 below).

Two questions may occur at this stage:

- Where will I find the classification for each criminal offence?
- Where will I find the mode of trial and penalty for each of these offences?

The answers will be found either by reference to the legal texts themselves (for example, through the Home Office website) or secondary sources such as Blackstone's Police Manuals. For example, for the offence of theft, the following will be found:

- the relevant legislation is in s 1 of the Theft Act 1968;
- the offence of theft is triable either way;
- the maximum penalty for a person found guilty is seven years' imprisonment on indictment (Crown Court) or six months' imprisonment and/or a fine summarily (magistrates' court).

TASK 26

Use an appropriate textbook, or the internet, with the offence of robbery to determine:

- the relevant Act, including section;
- the mode of trial;
- the maximum penalty for a person found guilty.

5.14.3   The Courts

As you probably guessed from 5.14.2 above, the structure of the courts in England and Wales tends to be arranged according to the subject matter and seriousness of the cases brought before them.

Below is a simplified diagram of the court system in England and Wales:

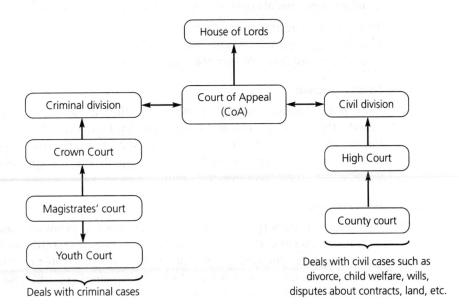

For student police officers, the courts dealing with criminal offences are the most important as there are only rare occasions when a police officer would be giving evidence at a court dealing with civil cases.

5.14.3.1 Youth court

Young people aged 10 to 17 years would normally have their cases dealt with at the youth court (unless they are being charged jointly with an adult or they are charged for murder or manslaughter). Procedures in the youth court are very similar to those in the magistrates' court; indeed, within the magistrates' courts, certain courts are formally designated as youth courts. Their procedures are adapted to take account of the age of the defendant, and they are not open to the public.

5.14.3.2 Magistrates' court

Less serious criminal cases (which comprise over 90 per cent of criminal cases) are sent for summary trial in one of over 400 magistrates' courts. A summary trial means there is no committal (that is, no transfer is necessary to the Crown Court) and no jury. The trial is before a bench of magistrates. In most cases there are three magistrates, who are lay people—in other words they are not professional judges nor lawyers but are people drawn from the local community. However, there are now an increasing number of stipendiary magistrates—paid magistrates who are qualified lawyers.

Because of the nature of the criminal cases dealt with by the magistrates' court, they cannot order sentences that exceed six months for a single offence, twelve months for consecutive sentences, or fines exceeding £5,000 (at the time of writing). If an offence is triable either way (see 5.14.2 above), and the magistrates believe that a more severe sentence is necessary, the magistrates' court can commit the offender to the Crown Court for sentence. If a defendant is dissatisfied with the verdict from the magistrates' courts, he or she may appeal to the Crown Court.

5.14.3.3 Crown Court

The Crown Court deals with more serious criminal cases such as murder, rape, or robbery. Other cases in the Crown Court may be on appeal or may have been referred from magistrates' courts. These cases are tried on the basis of a document called an **indictment** (see 5.14.2 above). The trial takes place before a judge and a 12-person jury. Members of the public are selected for jury service. Other members of the public may have to attend court as witnesses.

In summary, the Crown Courts deal with the relatively small proportion of offences triable only on indictment. They also deal with:

- cases transferred from the magistrates' courts;
- cases sent for sentence from the magistrates' courts;
- appeals against decisions from the magistrates' courts.

5.14.3.4 Court of Appeal

The Court of Appeal is the highest court within the Supreme Court of Judicature, which also includes the High Court and the Crown Court. It normally sits in up to 12 courts in the Royal Courts of Justice in London. On matters of fact and law, it is possible to appeal from the Crown Court to the criminal division of the Court of Appeal. Similarly, appeals from the High Court would go to the civil division of this Court.

5.14.3.5 House of Lords

The House of Lords is the final Court of Appeal on points of law and important legal dispute for criminal cases in England, Wales, and Northern Ireland, and civil cases for the whole of the United Kingdom. This work is carried out by the Law Lords. Note that a 'UK Supreme Court' is expected to take effect from 1 October 2009. The Supreme Court will replace the House of Lords as the final court of appeal in the United Kingdom.

5.14.3.6 Summary of the Courts

Courts	Type of offences	Features	Appeals go to
Youth courts	Offences involving persons aged 10 to 17.	Usually not open to public.	Crown Court
Magistrates' courts	Offences triable summarily only. Offences triable either way.	Bench of magistrates. Local, over 400 across the UK. Usually open to public. Over 95% of cases dealt with here. Sentence cannot exceed 6 months (or 12 months for consecutive sentences), or £5,000 in fines. More serious offences committed to Crown Courts.	Crown Court
Crown Courts	Offences triable only on indictment. Offences triable either way (cases referred from magistrates' court for trial or sentence). Appeals from magistrates' court.	Judge and jury. Regional. About 90 across the UK.	Court of Appeal
Court of Appeal	Appeals from Crown Court.	Criminal and civil division.	House of Lords
House of Lords*	Appeals from Court of Appeal.	Law Lords.	Final point of appeal

* Expected to be replaced by a UK Supreme Court after October 2009.

TASK 27

Find out the exact location of your nearest magistrates' and Crown Courts. Use as many resources as necessary including the web and local telephone directories. (Cross-check the results, identifying any inconsistencies in spelling, postcodes, and so on, if they are present.) When off duty, consider visiting one of the courts and sitting in the public gallery to observe proceedings.

5.15 Crime and Criminality

Here, we will take a brief look at the nature of crime and criminality in the UK and try to synthesize some modern thinking about crime. Every day, the contents of news bulletins on TV and radio and the pages of newspapers are dominated by crime, ranging from fraud investigations in the City through to muggings on housing estates, and from the sadistic torture of young children through to the murder of a solicitor for her watch and mobile phone. Many articles and research papers are devoted to trying to understand criminal motivations, why people commit crimes, and why certain crimes are more prevalent than others. You will read some of these criminological texts and papers in the course of your own work as a student police officer or through your participation in a higher education programme.

We have deliberately simplified these issues because this is not a Handbook of crime or criminology, and the issues are very complex, drawing on psychological, philosophical, sociological, and political perspectives. In a very real sense, they are issues which you will be grappling with for the whole of your time in the police and certainly include matters on which you will have to reflect during your time as a student police officer.

TASK 28

- What makes a crime sensational?
- What makes a crime of little apparent interest?
- What makes a crime impact on a community?

Increasingly over the past 40 years, criminologists have become interested in studying the police. This has produced numerous publications concerning the organization, administration, and general understanding of police work. However, beyond this, criminology has also provided the police with a number of important theories about the nature of crime and criminal behaviour that can be of great assistance to the police in different ways. For example, the move towards proactive policing has been assisted by developments in criminological theories concerning crime prevention, the study of victims, and the spatial movements of criminals. The scope of criminological studies is too vast to cover here but by providing a selection of important ways in which criminology informs contemporary policing, it is hoped that you will be encouraged to consult the growing body of criminological research concerning many different policing matters. But first we will consider some more basic questions, some possible definitions of crime, and some possible causes of crime.

5.15.1 Definitions of Crime

What is crime? We tend to think we know the answer until we begin to think through the details and test out our general ideas on some specific examples. We might say that crime is what is forbidden, that crime is activity which society wants to stop happening, or that crime is a measure of society's health: the more unbalanced the society, the more the crimes on the statute book. Technically, an activity is a crime because the law defines it as such. But remember that laws are made by people so, in the end, we are back to where we started: people (albeit only certain categories of people such as judges and MPs) decide which activities are crimes. Without reference to existing concepts of crime and laws there is nothing about an activity in itself that marks it out as a crime. Consider, for example, how some forms of sexual activity between consenting adult men were treated as crimes in the recent past but are no longer treated as such. There are a very few acts that have been consistently considered crimes throughout modern history (try Task 29). Other types and definitions of crime are mutable (they change as society changes). Think about our attitudes to the environment in which we live: how activities like collecting birds' eggs or hunting foxes with dogs are now seen by many as unacceptable and how laws have followed suit.

In this part of the Handbook we look first at defining crime narrowly by what it is not—that is, in terms of those acts sanctioned by the law. This provides us with a definitive statement but does not really explain why particular acts and behaviours are treated as criminal whilst others are not. However, if we look beyond the law as part of the definition of crime, we then find that the task becomes no easier. Finally, we consider the thoughts of J. S. Mill, a nineteenth-century philosopher who proposed that deviant behaviour might have a role in promoting beneficial changes in society, though some deviant behaviours would be classed as crime if they caused harm to other people (see 5.15.1.3 below).

5.15.1.1 Crimes are defined by law

Originally, the word crime actually meant judgement or accusation (from Latin *crimen*, a judgement), later coming to be associated with the act of offence or wrong-doing. By the Middle Ages, crime was something against the law, and thus a crime was an action punishable by law. On one level, we now simply define crime as action which is against the law, and clearly the act needs to be against a specific criminal law. Critics of this definition of crime point to an obvious tautology we are essentially saying the same thing twice but in a different form. Using such a circular argument, that crime is defined by law, takes us no further forward in our understanding.

5.15.1.2 Crimes are defined by society

Others have argued conversely that crime is a social construction. By this they mean that no act or behaviour is in itself wrong but rather that different societies will identify different activities as crimes, according to the specific needs of a given society at particular points in history. This challenges the notion that there are fixed laws that classify certain acts as crimes and argues instead that laws are created by humans in social situations in order to bring greater cohesion and order to those situations.

> **TASK 29**
> - List three crimes that would appear to be universal.
> - List three offences that are considered criminal in the UK today but were not 100 years ago.
> - List three offences that are considered criminal in other parts of the world but not in the UK.

On the other hand, crime is defined more broadly by some as **all social wrong-doings and anti-social behaviour**. This sociological approach to understanding crime addresses the question from the perspective of **why** certain acts are criminalized, but the clarity of legal definitions of particular crimes may be compromised. A current example of this kind of dispute occurs in debates about how we deal with anti-social behaviour. Some have argued that the use of Anti-social Behaviour Orders (ASBOs) is a way of criminalizing behaviour through the back door. This is because ASBOs are a civil procedure at the outset but the breaking of the terms of an order may invoke criminal proceedings. Others have argued that ASBOs represent a civil procedure against criminal activities that are not readily and effectively dealt with by existing criminal proceedings.

5.15.1.3 Mill's principle of 'harm to others'

John Stuart Mill was an English philosopher writing in the nineteenth century. For Mill it was important for the development of a healthy society to allow individuals as much freedom as possible, primarily because a society needs individuals to deviate from the norm if it is to advance. The problem confronting any authority is establishing when a deviation from the norm might be beneficial and when it is not. In other words, it is not always possible to decide whether an individual acting differently is being innovative or criminal.

There are numerous examples throughout history of individuals (some of whom we now celebrate as heroes) who were considered a threat to society at an earlier time. Think, for example, about the suppression of scientific thinkers, such as Galileo, who were considered to be heretics, or (more recently) civil-rights protesters, like Martin Luther King in the USA. In the UK today there are many examples of people willing to break the law for causes that they see as being a future morality, ranging from animal-rights activists, Fathers for Justice, anti-abortionists, to environmentalists. What these different groups have in common is a belief that they represent values that are not normal today but will become so in the future, in the same way that those fighting at previous times in history for equal rights for women or the abolition of the slave trade eventually came to be recognized as heroic figures.

For Mill, the way to permit individuals or groups to deviate from existing norms, and indeed to challenge them, is to allow people to make mistakes and act immorally, providing these acts do not harm others. This is Mill's famous 'harm to others' principle. It is largely from this perspective that we have established a separation between the law and morality; it is argued that the law pertains to public matters and morality to private individual concerns. This view was supported in the 1957 Wolfenden Report into homosexuality and prostitution in which it was argued that private acts between consenting adults should not be the concern of law enforcement (Wolfenden Report, 1957). Campaigners for gay rights have criticized this finding for putting too much emphasis on the word private as they feel this suggests that public expressions of homosexuality should be regulated and controlled.

However, other critics have challenged the view that law and morality can be so neatly separated. They argue that there is a significant grey area which we might characterize as social morality, that it is simply not possible to insulate our private activities completely, that there will always be leakage, and our actions will always have consequences in ways that we could not have predicted. This challenges Mill's 'harm to others' principle because it suggests that others are harmed by our actions even if this was not our intention. Perhaps a good example of this, to illustrate the point, is passive smoking. For many years it has been argued that smokers are harming themselves and campaigns have encouraged smokers to stop for their own sake. However, until recently, little was done to prohibit smoking. Increasingly though, smoking has come to be regulated on grounds of others' health and safety. In many parts of the world smoking is banned in public places, including bars and restaurants, and the bans are justified in terms of the health of employees working in these public places. Since 2007 it has been unlawful in England and Wales to smoke in 'an enclosed public space' (see 9.12.5 below).

This also illustrates that harm is more widely defined today than when Mill was writing. We have become more sophisticated in identifying different forms of harm. For example, consider the extent to which we have broadened our understanding of domestic violence to include psychological, emotional, and financial harm in addition to physical damage.

5.15.2 The Causes of Crime

When examining the causes of crime an important starting point is to acknowledge some fundamental differences in how we might understand crime and how these differences in turn can inform police work. Blackburn (1995) makes a distinction between crimes and criminality. Crimes are seen to be a rational response to the environment in which people find themselves. Criminality, on the other hand, is a characteristic of an individual and emphasizes the propensity of an individual to commit crimes.

5.15.2.1 Crimes—a rational response?

Some crimes are apparently easily explained as a product of the social situation in which they occur. For example, an unemployed single mother shoplifting nappies for her baby is certainly committing a crime, but it could be said that a more serious problem is that she should be in such a difficult position in the first place. Others will point out that not all mothers in the same situation would resort to shoplifting but would find a legal solution to the problem. Irrespective of which moral position is adopted, from a policing perspective this particular crime can be understood better as a social response rather than an individual failing. This view is associated with what is referred to as classical criminology, which emerged in the late eighteenth century and informed the thinking of law reformers at this time (eg Bentham, Howard, Beccaria). This view of crime suggests that anyone could become a criminal given the right circumstances, and that punishment is required to act as a deterrent to crime.

5.15.2.2 Criminals—a breed apart?

Conversely, it is difficult to understand the actions of a violent serial murderer as the consequence of injustices in society. No matter how bad society is, it is hard to view such brutality as a reasonable response in any sense. A contrasting explanation for the causes of crime is the concept of **criminality**. This view developed from what is referred to as the positivist school of criminology, associated with Cesare Lombroso's *L'Uomo Delinquente* (The Criminal Man) published in 1876. Positivists differed from the classical approach to criminology by arguing that:

- Criminality is determined by factors beyond the immediate control of an individual and is not a product of his or her free will.
- Criminals are a certain type of individual distinct from non-criminal individuals.
- Criminals are pathological (see Jones and Newburn, 1998, pp 101–2).

5.15.2.3 Nature and nurture

We have debated these kinds of question for centuries. It is often referred to as the nature/nurture debate. Nature refers to what we are born with or, in recent terms, our genetic make-up, and nurture relates to the environmental contexts in which we develop. This includes everything from our schooling, how our parents raised us, whom we chose to associate with, and every arbitrary experience that has good, bad, or indifferent outcomes. However, the nature/nurture dichotomy can often be misleading. The debates have frequently been polemical and exclusionary; that is, those favouring nature explanations would dismiss nurture as an influence and those supporting nurture explanations would exclude completely the view that nature has any part to play. Increasingly today we recognize that both nature **and** nurture form part of the explanation and, indeed, that it is not always easy to distinguish one from the other. Modern biology continues to uncover examples of genetic predispositions being either masked or revealed by environmental factors. We cannot hope for simple answers; both nature and nurture have to be taken into account.

5.15.3 Hate Crime

A consideration of hate crime raises issues around the definition of crime and the causes of crime. Interestingly, hate crime (including homophobic or racist crimes) can be defined as such by the victim(s) or any other person, irrespective of the views of the police officer dealing with it. This amendment arose from the enquiry into the death of the black London teenager Stephen Lawrence and a subsequent report into the police investigation chaired by Sir William Macpherson. (This report famously branded the police service as 'institutionally racist'.) The following question then arises: 'If any person present can define a crime as a "hate crime", why cannot *any* individual define *any* incident in which they feel disadvantaged, wronged, or frightened, as a "crime"?' The law provides the answer. There must have been an identifiable criminal offence (such as assault) before the qualification of whether or not it is homophobic or racist can be considered. It is the hate which is defined by the individual and not the crime. Once again, the close interrelationship between the law, society, and individuals is a key factor in understanding crime. The law surrounding hate crime and harassment is covered in 9.7.5 and 9.9 below.

5.15.4 Measuring Crime

There are various means of measuring crime, through the police and criminal justice statistical records, large-scale, mostly government-sponsored surveys, and small-scale academic studies. However, we know that the problems of under-reporting, under-recording, political interest, intellectual bias, and/or perspective all contribute to distortions in actually determining the levels of crime at any given time. This is particularly so if we wish to make comparisons with the past. The problems of under-reporting and under-recording are particularly problematic for the police and are factors that have been given much attention in recent years.

Discovering a truer picture of the extent of crime and ensuring that it is recorded properly are important aspects of modern policing. However, what exactly needs to be reported and recorded?

5.15.4.1 Reported and recorded

An important distinction is between reported crime-related incidents and recorded crime. It is obvious that not all crimes that occur will be reported to the police. Given our discussion earlier concerning the definition of crime it is not difficult to appreciate the major methodological issues that surround this subject. Often the police prefer to start instead with the idea of an **incident**. Imagine that I have witnessed a heated argument in the street, perhaps with some pushing, shoving, and screaming. I phone the police and report this; the police will register the contents of my call. This registration is what most commentators mean when they refer to **reported**. However, the police then have to decide whether this reported incident should be **recorded** as a crime (a so-called 'notifiable offence'). They are required to use the Home Office criterion which states that if, on the balance of probability, the circumstances as reported amount to a crime defined by law, and there is no credible evidence to the contrary, then it should be recorded as a crime (Home Office, 2008a).

As our incident described above illustrates, the decision is far from simple. In response to my call the police are required to make all reasonable enquiries to identify specific victims and secure any supporting evidence. Although pushing and shoving could technically be an offence of assault or battery (see 10.15 below) or a public order offence (see 9.7 below) this would depend on the circumstances, and these would probably not be clear from my account over the phone. More importantly, a victim is unlikely to be identified and the basic recording rule of 'no victim, no crime' would be applied. (Note, however, that there are exceptions to this rule.) Hence in my example, it is highly unlikely that the pushing and shoving that I witnessed, although registered as an incident ('reported'), would actually result in the police recording a notifiable offence.

Crime recording and counting methods have in recent times been made more consistent across police organizations and are audited for accuracy and reliability. The three main group headings for classifying the status of a recorded crime are:

- detected (or 'cleared up'—that is a crime has been recorded and a suspect has been identified);
- undetected (a crime has been recorded but no suspect has been identified);
- no crime (of which there are a number of possibilities, including that the crime as reported is already part of another recorded crime).

The processes of reporting and recording crime are complex and you will find the full detail at <http://www.homeoffice.gov.uk/rds/pdfs09/countgeneral09.pdf>.

In terms of statistics, the police service as a whole claimed to clear up 28 per cent of all recorded crime in 2007/2008 (Home Office, 2009), which appeared to be an impressive record. However, it was estimated in 1991 that recorded crime represented only 7 per cent of all crime committed, and data from 2002 suggests that, for all crimes that take place, 47 per cent are reported, 27 per cent are recorded, 5 per cent are cleared up, and 2 per cent result in conviction (Wright, 2002). In 1771, the clear-up rate for crime was estimated at 24.6 per cent (Emsley, 1996).

5.15.4.2   The perception of crime

There is a general acceptance that the fear of crime and disorder has increased in the last decade or so, despite the fact that most forms of recorded crime have shown a decrease in the same period (although see Farrall and Gadd, 2004, for a critique). As Walker *et al* (2006, p 34) note, 'despite the total number of crimes estimated by the BCS [British Crime Survey] falling over recent years, comparatively high proportions of people continue to believe crime has risen across the country as a whole and in their local area'. It would also appear that particular communities are more likely to believe that crime has risen significantly when compared to others and also to worry more about crime. For example, the British Crime Survey for 2007/2008 suggests the following demographic factors are significant (Kershaw *et al* (2008) p 126 and table 5/06) in terms of perceptions and worry about crime:

- **gender**: women are more likely than men to feel that burglary and violent crime has risen;
- **age**: young people worry more about violence and car crime (although men and women in the 65 to 74 age group are most likely to perceive that there has been a significant increase in crime overall);

- **ethnicity**: people from non-white ethnic groups are more likely to be concerned about crime than those from white groups;
- **location**: those living in urban areas are more likely to worry about crime than those who live in rural areas;
- **newspapers**: readers of the 'red top' (tabloid) newspapers are more likely to worry about crime than those who read the 'broadsheets' or 'quality press'.

However, it is important to note that, according to official statistics, those who feel most worried about crime or who perceive crime to be increasing are not necessarily those who are actually the most likely to become victims of recorded crime. Having said this, it could be argued that fear of crime alone is a form of harm to an individual, regardless of the statistical reality. For some people who are very anxious and fearful about crime, the lifestyle implications can be profound; an elderly person's statistically 'irrational' fears about crime are in fact quite rational if the effect of crime on this person is factored in. Think of this as some kind of calculation: the risk may be low but the negative consequences are very high (eg in terms of recovery from an injury) and so overall the product is one of significant size for the individual concerned.

One possible reason for this apparently irrational overestimation of the volume of crime and disorder is that many of us may make our judgements concerning the level of insecurity of our communities based not only on those 'invisible' but often very serious crimes (such as domestic violence, burglary, sexual crimes etc) but also on the more obvious and usually less serious local examples of incivility such as repeated vandalism and graffiti, groups of young people that shout abuse at passers-by, and so on. These latter forms of incivility are examples of 'signal crimes' (Innes, 2004) or 'signal disorders' which are, in effect, warning signals to people about the level of insecurity in their neighbourhoods. As Innes (2005, p 192) notes, 'major crimes such as homicides can and do function as signals, but (for most people, most of the time) the signals that they attend to and that assume particular salience for them are what have tended to be treated by the criminal justice agencies as less serious'. The signals may arise from other people's behaviour (eg 'rowdy' groups of people) and physical signs such as damage to public amenities. Possible examples of signal crimes and disorder, particularly when a number of these examples coincide in a local community, include:

- public drinking, swearing, rowdy and uncivil behaviour by groups of individuals;
- graffiti and other forms of damage and vandalism, litter;
- evidence of drug taking and dealing, prostitution;
- speeding;
- rubbish dumped in the street or outside houses, burnt-out cars, and other vehicles.

Once spotted, these signals can give rise to a heightened sense of awareness amongst individuals of other similar examples—a form of non-virtuous feedback loop.

5.15.5 Modelling Crime and Criminality

In 5.15.2 above we provided an overview of some of the theories that attempt to explain the existence of crime and criminality. We now move on from these general theories (often concerned with human nature and society) to more detailed models that seek to explain the existence of crime or criminality and also suggest some possible responses for the police and others.

5.15.5.1 Opportunities for crime

Pease (2002) notes three different ways in which crime has been understood, and he defines these in terms of structure, human psyche, and circumstance. Structure can be characterized in terms of the major social issues that are seen to be linked to crime, eg poverty and inequality. Human psyche concerns the attributes of the criminal, in other words the reasons why he/she has a propensity to commit offences. However, Pease proposes that it is the circumstance dimension of crime, or the opportunity for crime to occur, that is the key factor for causing crime.

Rational-choice theory assumes that when criminals decide to commit offences they go through the same kind of thought process as is used by non-criminals when making everyday, non-criminal decisions:

> It is not the case (except for a tiny handful of pathological personalities) that criminals are so unlike the rest of us as to be indifferent to the costs and benefits of the opportunities open to them (Wilson, 1996, p 312).

This suggests that crimes occur if and when they are easy to commit, and the results are sufficiently rewarding.

Routine-activity theory is also predicated upon an understanding of the relationship between an individual's everyday experiences and his or her criminal behaviour. Importantly, it defines criminal opportunities in terms of three interrelated and necessary components:

- a motivated offender;
- a suitable target;
- the absence of a guardian.

Criminal opportunities arise when these three components coincide. We may observe that the number of offences might increase even if there is no increase in the number of motivated offenders. This occurs if a small number of motivated offenders are in situations where there are few guardians and plenty of suitable targets. Schools are a prime example of this kind of scenario: there are significant numbers of vulnerable children with mobile phones, computer games, and mp3 players largely unsupervised, and there are other children who are keen to take these items.

5.15.5.2 The 'hot' model

One way to consider the phenomenon of crime in society is to think about some of its constituent elements as being hot: that is, both frequently occurring and worthy of attention. (The following owes much to Clarke, 1999, although terms such as 'hot offender' are ours.)

Hot spots are places that are particularly prone to crime, such as railway-station concourses, shopping malls, town centres, particular shops, houses, post offices, or flats. This may be related to the easy pickings for the criminal intent on theft, shoplifting, mugging, or similar. In addition, it may also be related to opportunity, because these are places where people may be carrying large quantities of cash (railway stations close to race courses for example, or streets leading away from ATMs or cash machines). This leads to an unevenness of crime distribution; across a city in which some particular and precise geographical areas can be pinpointed as always or nearly always productive of crime (of all types), other areas will be virtually crime free. Until some preventive action is taken, these hot spots will persist. The hot spots may even return some time after action is taken (see 5.16.1.2 below).

Hot offenders are defined as the relatively small number of people that are responsible for the majority of crime. However, opinion and research continue to differ concerning just how small a minority of criminals is responsible for just how large a majority of crime. For example, the 1993 Audit Commission report (Audit Commission, 1993) cited Home Office research, which claimed that '7 per cent of males who had been convicted of 6 or more offences accounted for 65 per cent of all convictions' (Home Office, 1989, p2). Heaton argued instead that a more 'realistic' ratio is 3 per cent of offenders being responsible for 24 per cent of offences (Heaton, 2000). Given that there was probably some exaggeration in early claims (particularly as the oft-repeated '7 per cent responsible for 65 per cent' began to lose the connection with the original and more detailed context) there is nonetheless clear evidence for a skew in offending. For example, in a 2004 study in Brighton and Hove the 'top' 40 of the 400 identified high-volume offenders were responsible for 691 convictions out of the 3,453 total (Center for Problem Oriented Policing, 2009). Further, research (eg Everson and Pease, 2001) on repeat victimization (see 'Hot victims' below) suggests that prolific offenders may be responsible for the bulk of these repeated crimes against the same person or target.

The typical hot offender is a volume-crime offender who either steals or burgles to feed a drug habit, or because he/she is a lifestyle or career criminal. Many high-volume offenders start committing crimes at a relatively young age; they make what is called an 'early debut' into crime. Initial offences may be stealing from cars, shoplifting, or theft (for example, Svensson, 2002—although this is Scandinavian research and may not be applicable to the UK).

Hot products are the items we know are more attractive to thieves, burglars, or muggers (street robbers) than others and there is a form of logic to what is stolen or snatched. Currently, car Sat-Navs, mobile phones, jewellery, and small electronic products like DVD players, iPods, laptops, and minidisc players are popular, but these things go in fashions. Once it was televisions (which were heavy, bulky, and difficult to steal without a car or van for transport). Indeed, plasma screen TVs are still objects of desire for housebreakers and burglars but the average, small-time, drug-abusing, volume criminal will go for small items of value which are easily transportable and not easily traced. This is why cash (pre-eminently) and jewellery are popular targets for thieves. Cash, of course, is easily disposed of and generally untraceable. Jewellery is somewhat harder to fence, and some items can be so individual as to be easily traced, but the bulk of rings and watches are easily converted into money.

As you might suppose with police training, there is a mnemonic (Clarke, 1999) used to estimate the hotness of products; it is **CRAVED**, which stands for:

```
C   Concealable
R   Removable
A   Available
V   Valuable
E   Enjoyable
D   Disposable
```

The CRAVED model may be used as a means of judging just how attractive an object will be in terms of its stealability. Imagine assigning a score to each heading in turn and totalling these scores. Those objects with high CRAVED scores are more likely to be stolen. (Granted, it is not as simple as this, but the scoring system gives a relatively easy way of using the checklist.)

Above all, thieves prefer things which they can get rid of quickly and without fuss to a trusted fence, or receiver of stolen goods, in all probability taking only a tenth or a fifth of the actual value of the item from the fence. In the original work by Clarke (1999) disposability was considered to be one of the most important factors in determining the stealability of items.

TASK 30

Estimate how CRAVED the following articles might be:

- an iPod;
- a Blackberry or equivalent hand-held computer;
- a laptop;
- £642.89p in coins;
- a computer with separate screen and keyboard;
- a CRT (conventional) television;
- a mobile phone;
- £350 in £50 notes;
- a manuscript copy of The Lindisfarne Gospels;
- 12 Japanese ivory netsuke dating from the late sixteenth century;
- a Rolex watch, engraved and dated;
- an unframed oil painting by Rubens, measuring 23 × 19 cm.

(Readers may find this list somewhat reminiscent of the Generation Game.)

Hot victims are perhaps the least studied and least understood part of the equation. Intuitively, it could be expected that old age, frailty, and naivety would make a person more vulnerable than the average person, but there is little empirical evidence to support this other than for distraction burglary (sometimes called 'burglary artifice') that we mention in 10.5 below. However, studies have shown that once someone has been a victim of certain types of crime (the classic example is burglary) on one occasion, they are more likely than other people to be a victim again even if all other variables have been taken into account. If repeat victimization is planned or contemplated, we know it will happen again pretty quickly and that often high crime rates and hot spots exist precisely because of repeat victimization (if not the same person, then the same address or the same street).

Why some people, or some premises, or some organizations should be repeat victims of crime is not always clear. There is some evidence (although not conclusive) that it is the same offenders that tend to return to the same places and reoffend. Some of it may have to do with the notion that, from a thief's perspective, 'it worked once and will work again'. Some of it could be a clever thieves' strategy: give a houseowner time to claim on insurance for a valuable item, and return when the house is restocked to steal the replacement. (See for example Bowers *et al*, 1998.) Whatever the explanation, we should emphasize that people who do not take elementary precautions after having been victims of crime on one occasion should not be surprised if they are targeted again. This is particularly the case with domestic burglary—it is simply not the case that if it has happened once, then it is unlikely to happen again. The reverse is true.

Finally, we know that those who repeatedly victimize the same target tend to be more established as lifestyle or career criminals than those who do not. All this should suggest that intelligence about the nature of a crime, why it is repeated in the same spot with the same victim, should enable police forces to predict with a limited degree of accuracy where, when, and by whom the next attempt will be made (see for example Bowers *et al*, 2004). In terms of operational practice however, this would appear to be a long way off.

TASK 31

Following what we have said about hot victims, what operational strategies do you think that the police should employ to help reduce repeat victimization?

Clearly, there are many possible **interactions** between hot spots, hot offenders, hot products, and hot victims. Hot offenders are more likely to want hot products. Hot victims are more likely to be in hot spots, and this is certainly the case for domestic burglary. Hot offenders are likely to target hot spots because, as we noted above, there are relatively easy opportunities for crime and relatively little chance of being caught. And, as mentioned above, the same offenders may return to burgle the same house again. It is hard to disentangle cause and effect, but the unevenness of the distribution of crime cannot be ignored.

TASK 32

What are the practical policing implications that can be derived from the following quotation, assuming that the argument being made is valid?

Becoming criminal can be explained in much the same way we explain becoming a midwife or buying a car (Wilson, 1996, p 307).

5.16 Crime Reduction

We often hear the terms 'crime prevention', 'crime reduction', and 'community safety' used both within policing and more widely. Ekblom (2001) draws subtle distinctions between these concepts whereas Pease (2002) suggests they are different expressions of the same thing, and that the use of different terms is an indication of different political perspectives. We will follow Pease and use the terms interchangeably.

The focus within police work is increasingly oriented towards reducing crime. This can be achieved to some extent through detecting crimes and imprisoning the offenders, with the result that fewer prospective offenders have the opportunity to commit crime. However, it is also acknowledged that preventing crimes from happening in the first place represents a far more rational approach. Of course it is hard to imagine a situation where the police are not required to investigate crimes that have occurred. Nonetheless, reducing crime through earlier prevention techniques provides clear benefits to society. In other words, it can be assumed that prevention is better than cure.

A crime reduction agenda has also been bolstered by the move towards partnership approaches in policing, and in this respect the increasing emphasis on crime prevention entails a relative decline in the role of the police:

> One of the key messages put out by the government and the police … was that the police could not be expected to carry responsibility for the prevention of crime unaided (Morgan and Newburn, 1997, p 58).

The partnership approach towards tackling crime had already been strengthened in the Crime and Disorder Act 1998 and reflects the current government's commitment to a joined-up approach to tackling crime and disorder.

5.16.1 Crime Reduction in Practice

In order to prevent and reduce crime we need to understand as much as possible about why and how crime occurs. Pease (2002) focuses on the circumstance dimension of crime or the opportunity for crime to occur (see 5.15.5.1 above).

5.16.1.1 Reducing the opportunities for crime

Routine-activity theory and rational-choice theory are also used to explain the causes of crime (see 5.15.5.1 above). Using these different factors we can suggest that preventative techniques could be organized under three headings:

- increasing the effort (eg target hardening);
- increasing the risks (eg CCTV);
- reducing the rewards (eg marking property).

Pease (2002) also adds a fourth heading of 'reducing the excuses'. The relative significance of each of these strategies depends upon the particular crime in question; which strategy is most likely to have the greatest deterrent impact on the potential criminal? These ideas are illustrated in Task 33.

TASK 33

Consider the following scenarios and identify whether increasing the effort, increasing the risk, or reducing the reward would be the most effective preventative measure. (We acknowledge that, to some extent, all three would be appropriate but try to identify the one that you think addresses the problem most directly.)

1. There have been a number of thefts from vehicles in a supermarket car park. The cars targeted have had valuable items stolen from them.
2. A shop is being repeatedly targeted at night by a group of known drug addicts.
3. Small amounts of money are being stolen by a member of staff from within a bank.

A consideration of routine-activity theory suggests some other approaches that may be used in crime reduction: for example, ensuring that motivated offenders are not left unobserved where there are easy criminal targets. From this perspective, we do not have to reduce the number of motivated offenders in order to reduce crime; we simply need to ensure that they are monitored more closely or that we design goods in a way that makes them less attractive as criminal targets.

5.16.1.2 The prevention of hot spots

A persistent police presence would undoubtedly have a deterrent effect, but that cannot be sustained over the long or even the medium term. Equally, the use of PCSOs or Wardens as a visible deterrent is costly, intermittent at best, and dubious as other than a temporary solution. CCTV cameras are a possible short-term solution, especially if coordinated with police action on the ground such as 'blitzes' on pickpockets, for example. But if the CCTV is to be effective it needs 24-hour live monitoring—which is expensive and is only really cost effective in town centres.

A longer-term (but potentially very effective) solution is to 'design out' crime through the use of features such as more carefully designed walkways and better street lighting. Allied to CCTV and unpredictable police presence, this could be an effective combination. The use of intelligence (see Chapter 12) is likely to be an important part of any approach to dealing with hot spots. The kinds of crime, the times when the crimes take place, the sorts of people who commit those crimes, the seasonal impact, if any, upon the nature of the crime, and the likelihood of achieving a result will all be important considerations for the intelligence analyst. It is this intensity of knowledge, allied to detailed understanding about the hot spot and other contributory factors, which may bring a hot spot down several degrees in temperature.

5.16.2 Displacement

One problem that has been identified with crime prevention is that it leads to crime displacement; crimes are not prevented but merely displaced to other places or other times. New types of crime may also occur through criminal innovation (see below). Displacement is often explained as a consequence of criminality: those with a disposition to commit crimes will adapt and find different ways in which to realize their criminal disposition. The following types of displacement have been identified:

Temporal displacement: The crime takes place at a later time. As an example consider the depot that introduces a security guard overnight to counter a number of burglaries that have occurred during the night-time hours. However, there is a one-hour gap between the security guard finishing and the day staff arriving so criminals adapt and choose this time to commit the offence.

Spatial displacement: The crime happens somewhere else. In this case imagine that in police force Area 1, a high police presence is introduced to curb the incidents of anti-social behaviour from a group of teenagers. The teenagers move to force Area 2 to avoid the police presence.

Displacement by type of crime: The criminals turn to different crimes. Suppose that the local council introduces better street lighting on an estate that has seen a high number of street robberies. This reduces the number of these offences but there is an increase in the number of burglaries in the area.

Displacement by innovation: The criminals become better at what they do. An example is credit cards which allow people to spend relatively large sums of money without having to carry large amounts of cash with them, thus reducing the reward for potential muggers. Criminals develop ways of using credit cards fraudulently, thereby gaining access to even larger sums of money.

5.16.2.1 The consequences of displacement

Displacement is clearly a problem that needs to be considered within crime-prevention strategies. However, Pease (1997) has suggested that the extent to which displacement is a problem is often exaggerated. He suggests that there are ideological rather than empirical grounds for raising the issue of displacement and in this respect it is used as an excuse for doing nothing.

Furthermore, Pease argues that displacement is never likely to be 100 per cent and he also illustrates ways in which it can be benevolent. For example, it might be beneficial to move a crime from one area to another to reduce its overall impact on society or to change the type of crimes that offenders are committing. Take for example a scenario in which prostitutes are operating in a residential area where many children live. We could assume that a high police presence in the area would move the prostitutes on to another area. The question would then be to establish whether this movement is beneficial or not. If the prostitutes move to a non-residential area it would clearly reduce the concern that children would be affected, although this might need to be balanced against a separate concern for the safety of the prostitutes. We might also consider that some of the prostitutes would potentially turn to other forms of crime, for example, shoplifting, whilst others would innovate and use more discreet means of operating as a prostitute, for example, by using cards in telephone boxes to advertise their services. We might also assume that some of the prostitutes will desist from any kind of criminal activity. The important point is that an assessment can be made as to what are the likely consequences following from anticipated displacement, which can then also be tested empirically in order to establish what the effect actually was. As Pease puts it, displacement is positive as long as 'the deflected crime causes less harm and misery than the original crime' (Pease, 1997, p 978).

5.16.3 The Advantages and Disadvantages of Crime Reduction Strategies

A final consideration follows from the recognition that the consequences of crime-prevention strategies can be to varying degrees either benevolent or malevolent. This raises a fundamental question and challenges our initial premise that prevention is necessarily better than cure.

By seeking to reduce crime we are intending to make society better in some way. However, intervening in the lives of individuals will not always make things better and there are occasions when we have to accept that doing nothing is actually preferable to taking action. This may be hard to accept because we do not want to feel as though we are ignoring problems in society and just standing by, letting bad things happen. Police officers (especially) have a duty of care and they respond to problems. Nonetheless, it is important that any intervention is properly evaluated. To this end, policing in general (and crime reduction in particular) is increasingly subjected to research and evaluation, and the results of this research will help ensure that any claims used to justify preventative strategies are based on firm evidence (see for example Smith and Tilley, 2005).

The view that crimes are informed by rational considerations has been an important feature of situational crime-prevention programmes. There are many examples of how this understanding has led to reductions in crime through architectural design and other measures aimed at making it more difficult for criminals to operate, and more likely that they will be identified, caught, and prosecuted if they commit an offence. Other measures have been introduced to reduce the potential rewards of committing offences: for example, the introduction of phone cards in place of the old coin-operated public telephone boxes.

However, critics of the rational view of crime argue that all crime-prevention measures result in displacement. As we noted earlier, this criticism has been widely acknowledged but is countered by evidence that suggests displacement is never complete. In other words we might expect some individuals to stop committing crime altogether as a consequence of crime-prevention measures because the extra effort and risk makes the proposition less attractive. In this respect we begin to see a distinction between criminals who are driven by favourable opportunities and more prolific offenders who are driven by a desire to commit an offence. This can allow the police to concentrate resources against those offenders least affected by general crime-prevention strategies.

5.17 Policing Domestic Violence

At the outset, you should note that there is no legal definition of domestic violence nor is it a legally separate and distinct category of crime (although it involves criminal activity, such as unlawful violence). The term domestic violence relates to the **context** within which various crimes and acts of violence occur.

The boundaries of what constitutes domestic violence are continually refined and reconsidered in terms of the meanings we attribute to both 'domestic' and 'violence'. These boundaries have varied historically from force to force. Some have adopted narrower definitions, for example, emphasizing married heterosexual couples where there is evidence of physical violence. Others have broadened the definition to include same-sex and cohabiting couples outside marriage. Violence could also include emotional and psychological abuse. Likewise, the term domestic could be restricted to activities within the home or include violence between partners wherever it happens, in public as well as in private. A definition provided by the Home Office Violent Crime Unit in 2004 demonstrates the extent to which a broad understanding of domestic violence is favoured:

> Any incident of threatening behaviour, violence or abuse (psychological, physical, sexual, financial or emotional) between adults who are or have been intimate partners or family members, regardless of gender or sexuality (Home Office, 2004e, p 12).

It has been noted by a number of commentators that in the past domestic violence had been seen by police officers as 'messy, unproductive, and not "real" police work' (Reiner, 1997, p 1012). This attitude is not officially accepted today and the Crime and Disorder Act 1998 established in legislation the need for the police and local authorities to work through partnerships with appropriate local bodies to address the problem of domestic violence locally.

5.17.1 The Police Response to Domestic Violence

Despite the political commitment to deal with domestic violence it remains a difficult area in practical terms for the police. This is partly because of the relationship of the offender to the victim. By definition, the offender and victim within a domestic context are part of a more complex relationship than is the case in most non-domestic crimes. There will be, or at least will have been, a loving and caring aspect of the relationship and there will be many shared memories, friends, family, and possibly children involved.

This partly explains the difficulty of establishing the true prevalence of domestic violence in our society. The problem of under-reporting is particularly acute for domestic violence: research suggests that women are abused up to 35 times before reporting the abuse to the police. Additionally, in the past the police were guilty of under-recording because their experience suggested victims of domestic abuse would withdraw complaints and drop the charges against their spouse offender.

However, despite not having precise figures on domestic violence (varying accounts estimate that domestic violence comprises 16–25 per cent of all violent offences), we do know that an average of **two women die every week** in domestic violence incidents (Home Office, 2003, p 6). It is not always an easy crime to identify, yet the consequences are potentially fatal; policing domestic violence is clearly one of the most serious and pressing aspects of police work.

5.17.2 Factors Involved in Domestic Violence

The violence that occurs in domestic settings will often be triggered by the same factors as in other violent offences, such as alcohol and jealousy. However, in domestic contexts, the stresses and strains of everyday life can become exaggerated. As with other crimes, the circumstances in which the crime occurs can provide a better explanation for why it occurred than the characteristics of the offender or, more controversially, the characteristics of the victim. In this respect we might make a distinction between one-off acts of violence that occur in the heat of the moment during exceptionally bad family circumstances and persistent acts of abuse that occur regularly and in which offenders actively seek opportunities to inflict violence upon their partners.

In cases where the violence is persistent, domestic violence is often seen as part of a cycle of abuse: some victims of domestic violence and/or children who witness domestic violence may become domestic violence victims and/or offenders at a later date. Knowledge of this cycle of abuse links domestic violence to child protection. The cycle is not simply historical. There is also evidence to suggest that where a man is beating his spouse, he may also be beating his children. Alternatively, where a man is beating his wife, his wife may in turn be beating the children. This raises questions as to how the policing of domestic violence should be organized. The benefits of linking it to child protection units is that duplication of work can be avoided and risk factors can be identified and responded to earlier.

5.17.3   Domestic Violence and the Position of Women in Society

Another key factor identified in domestic violence is that general discrimination against women leads to abuse. Gelles and Cornell (1990) refer to Blackstone's codification of English common law in 1768 which asserted that a husband has the right to 'physically chastise' his wife provided that the stick was no thicker than his thumb. This piece of common law was not abolished until 1891. Zedner (2002) notes the influence of the women's movement in the late 1960s and 1970s in raising the profile of domestic violence as a serious issue that required immediate attention. In particular, Erin Pizzey's campaigning resulted in the establishment of the first refuge for battered women in the UK in Chiswick, London in 1972.

5.17.4   The Government Response

The late 1980s and early 1990s also witnessed a significant change in the attitude of the Home Office and police towards domestic violence. The Home Office Circular 60/1990 (revised in HO Circular 19/2000) is seen as an important influence upon the development of a proactive policing policy towards domestic violence (see Grace, 1995; Plotnikoff and Woolfson, 1998). There were three main recommendations of Circular 60/90:

1. The police should take a more interventionist approach to domestic violence cases, with a presumption in favour of arrest

All forces have adopted positive action policies to ensure that officers attending the scene of a domestic incident treat it with the utmost seriousness. Although there is an assumption of arrest in all cases and the officer's discretion would appear (on the surface at least) to have been completely removed, it should be stressed that positive action, not arrest, is required. Indeed, always making an arrest could be counterproductive. Levi (1997) suggests that, far from reducing the violence, arrests can lead to an increase in the rate of recidivism amongst certain social groupings. Likewise, Waddington (1999a) refers to studies in the USA that show a difference in this deterrent's effectiveness depending upon the social class of those involved. Elsewhere, Waddington (1999b) supports this with reference to Hoyle's (1998) research which suggests women tend to want nothing more than an immediate break from the violence and a warning given to their partners. A fear is that making arrests could stop women from calling the police because they feel that the action they take goes too far.

2. Domestic violence crimes are recorded in the same way as other violent crimes

The problem of under-recording has already been mentioned but this recommendation suggests that not only should all incidents of domestic violence be recorded but also that they should be recorded in a way that clearly identifies the level of seriousness of the alleged offence. A good example of research that looked at how the recording of domestic violence could be improved, is provided in the Killinbeck Project (Hanmer *et al*, 1999), which focused on reducing repeat victimization in domestic violence by establishing appropriate responses to domestic incidents according to the severity of each case and the extent to which repeat victimization could be established.

3. The police adopt a more sympathetic and understanding attitude towards victims of domestic violence

As far as victims of domestic abuse are concerned, the circular emphasized the need for the police to adopt a duty of care. In this respect the policing of domestic violence should be less concerned with instrumental goals and more concerned with doing the right thing (see 5.4 above and Neyroud and Beckley, 2001, for a discussion of different ethical approaches in policing).

However, this presents us with an important question: should the police give greater priority to tackling domestic violence (and treat it as a core mandate of police work) or should other agencies become more involved? Likewise, what happens when there is a clash between supporting the wishes of a victim who decides not to press charges and responding to a perceived social need to punish domestic offenders? The answer to this question is largely dependent on the varying roles and status of the domestic violence unit (DVU) and domestic violence officer (DVO) within the force, eg whether the DVU/DVO is part of the criminal investigation department or not.

In addition to those works cited in the text above, there are many documents dealing with different aspects of policing domestic violence available online at the Home Office 'Violence against Women' section at <http://www.homeoffice.gov.uk/rds/violencewomen.html>.

5.18 Diversity and the Police

It would be advisable to read the following in conjunction with 4.9 above, where we discuss diversity training for the police.

We have noted throughout this Handbook that one of the characteristics of policing in this country is that it is undertaken by **consent**. You and I (as citizens) accept, or consent, that some of our individual freedoms will be curtailed or limited for the common good. We allow some of our citizens greater powers than the rest of us in order that they may police our society. We expect in exchange to be protected and that our society will be ordered and peaceful under the law. When that security or law and order is disturbed, we expect the 'citizen police' to find the likely perpetrators and the criminal justice system to determine guilt or innocence on the basis of fair process. In essence, this is the social contract view of the relationship between the police and society.

If you accept the social contract model, it follows that, if the police service needs to have the consent of the populace in order to do its work effectively then, in turn, the police should represent that populace in all its variety and permutations. This is where the issue of **diversity**, and what it means to the police, becomes important.

5.18.1 What is Important about Diversity?

A whole book could be written on this subject alone, but the essential point is that, as a student police officer, you will come into contact with all kinds of people in the course of your job. Some will be vulnerable because they are very young or very old; some will be vulnerable because they come from a minority group in the community and may have been targeted because of the colour of their skin, or because they are female, or because they are gay; some may be vulnerable and confused because of impaired hearing or failing vision; some may have been harassed because they have different beliefs from the majority and some may have mental illnesses which isolate them from normal relationships.

All such people are vulnerable in one way or another, and one of your roles as a police officer is to protect them. Society looks to the police to protect the weak or vulnerable wherever they may be found. In other words, as a police officer and as a member of society, it is considered your duty to recognize and embrace diversity and to sustain it wherever possible.

5.18.2 What is Diversity?

Put simply, **diversity is recognizing and understanding difference**. The fact that someone (compared with you) has a different coloured skin, or a different belief system, or different sexual orientation, or is older or younger, or is disabled in a way that you are not, does not make that person worse, better, weird, mad, or scary; only different. It is the mark of a truly benevolent society that difference between its members is a cause for celebration rather than a cause for anxiety or hatred. Of course, we do not have a truly benevolent society but perhaps we ought to, just as we ought to be stimulated by difference rather than feeling threatened by it. You may recollect the controversy about *The Secret Policeman* programme from the BBC in 2003. We have made reference to this on previous occasions in the Handbook. The attitudes to black people and others exhibited by some of the student police officers in that film have no place anywhere in modern policing. It not only does a disservice to the training system for the police, and to the police service as a whole, but it does a disservice to society as it reinforces the stereotypes on which our prejudices are based. Remember: diversity is about **difference**, not about better or worse.

TASK 34

As we have already suggested in the examples used above, there are perhaps six strands to diversity. Can you suggest what they are?

Several of the strands of diversity are subject to law. It is unlawful to discriminate on the ground of race, disability, age, sexual orientation, and gender. The government has tried to introduce legislation to outlaw discrimination on the grounds of belief (that is, hatred against someone based on religion; see 9.7.5 below) but the subject is fraught with difficulty and it may be some time before a law is comprehensively framed which can allow criticism of belief but which prohibits actions that discriminate against belief systems. We now have legislation (since 2006) which makes discrimination on the grounds of age unlawful, but this is also a complex area since age discrimination applies to the young as well as to the old (or indeed any age). In practical terms, trying to prevent discrimination on the grounds of age has much to do with the laws of employment and a progressively 'greying' population, and is more likely to be an issue about employing people who are past the conventional retirement age than about discriminating against people because they are young. (However, note in the context of discrimination against the young, the decisions by some shopping malls, notably Bluewater in Kent, to ban the wearing of baseball caps and hoodies, which are currently the dress preferences for some young people, because they are perceived by some to be associated with theft and violence.)

Let us look at what the integrated competency framework (ICF) says about 'respect for race and diversity' behaviours. You are expected to:

- consider and show respect for the opinions, circumstances, and feelings of colleagues and members of the public, no matter what their race, religion, position, background, circumstances, status, or appearance;
- understand other people's views and take them into account;
- [be] tactful and diplomatic when dealing with people, treating them with dignity and respect at all times;
- understand and [be] sensitive to social, cultural, and racial differences.

The behavioural competency standard goes on to note that there are positive indicators about how you deal with diversity and negative indicators.

TASK 35

Without referring to the competency standard, what do you think would be some of the positive and what would be some of the negative behaviours? (The answers are provided below rather than at the end of the chapter, so no peeking.)

You might have referred to all or any of these **negative** indicators:

- not considering other people's feelings;
- not encouraging people to talk about personal issues;
- criticizing people without considering their feelings and motivation;
- making situations worse with inappropriate remarks, language, or behaviour;
- being thoughtless and tactless when dealing with people;
- being dismissive and impatient with people;
- not respecting confidentiality;
- unnecessarily emphasizing power and control in situations where this is not appropriate;

- intimidating others in an aggressive and overpowering way;
- using humour inappropriately;
- showing bias and prejudice when dealing with people.

You might have included all or any of these in the **positive** indicators:

- seeing issues from other people's viewpoints;
- being polite, tolerant, and patient when dealing with people, treating them with respect and dignity;
- respecting the needs of everyone involved when sorting out disagreements;
- showing understanding and sensitivity to people's problems, vulnerabilities, and needs;
- dealing with diversity issues and giving positive, practical support to staff who may feel vulnerable;
- making people feel valued by listening to and supporting their needs and interests;
- using language in an appropriate way and [being] sensitive to the way that your use of language may affect people;
- identifying and respecting other people's values *within the law*;
- acknowledging and respecting a broad range of social and cultural customs and beliefs;
- respecting confidentiality, wherever appropriate;
- delivering difficult messages;
- challenging attitudes and behaviour(s) which are abusive, aggressive, and (or) discriminatory.

You can see from these specific indicators that your assessors will be looking at your negative behaviours as much as at your positive behaviours. In other words, you can actively fail this competency rather than simply not reach the required standard.

There is one other thing you should know: If your behaviour is proven to show racial, sexual, gender, or other kinds of discrimination and brings the police service into disrepute, you might be disciplined and dismissed. Worse, you could be charged with a criminal offence. Your force will be serious about the standards it expects from you.

5.18.3   Diversity and Being 'Politically Correct'

You might well hear the claim during your training that diversity is just about being politically correct. Recognizing diversity is more about being tolerant of those who are different from yourself and about trying to understand them. For example, when questioning, police officers should ask for a given name or first name instead of a Christian name; this has nothing to do with politics or appearing to be conventionally correct, and everything to do with being professional and sensitive to others.

Sensitivity towards gay people and understanding that many still feel vulnerable in a society which is often aggressively heterosexual can pay dividends in terms of police work, as well as building bridges between the police and minority communities. We know of several forces where gay or lesbian officers have linked into the gay and lesbian communities and that, subsequently, police investigators have been helped by the gay community when homophobic and other crimes have occurred. It takes time to build up trust of this kind, and it can be undone in one unthinking moment. That is why the police service as a whole deplored *The Secret Policeman* and why it welcomed the dismissal of the officers who expressed racist opinions in the film.

However, we have to accept that if the police service is to be broadly representative of society as a whole, there will be some officers who are prejudiced against black people and other officers who dislike gays, lesbians, or transsexuals, or who resent dealing with people who are mentally ill. But what really matters here is what such discriminators actually **do**.

Your police force will not (and indeed, cannot) dictate to you what you should believe or think about in the private recesses of your mind, and nor can anyone else. But these beliefs and feelings must stay inside your mind and must not become translated into action or behaviour. As we discussed in 4.9 above, this is often difficult to do. If, in your dealings with the public, including people from ethnic minorities and gay communities, you act fairly, honestly, and impartially you will have fulfilled your duty.

A parallel issue is how the police deal with the arrest and detention of a paedophile. Most would deplore what paedophiles do (or try to do) to vulnerable children, but you know that detained suspects have to be treated with the same courtesy and consideration as anyone else, and that extends to paedophiles as well as to those who commit rape or domestic violence, or any of the other myriad crimes of violence in which others are exploited or hurt.

If we sound passionate about this aspect of your work as a police officer, it is because we are. Professional tolerance can be important in defusing rows, calming situations, understanding motivations, and communicating with members of the public who might be frightened and feel abused. Private intolerance, once expressed publicly, damages the police service in ways far beyond the merely individual. If you police with society's consent, you cannot afford to break trust with those whom you police. Once the trust goes, so does the legitimacy of what you do as a police officer (see 5.5 and 5.6 above). There is little enough trust about, and precious little in the way of consent, but you need all the trust and consent you can get if you are to be an effective officer. That is why there is such emphasis upon the proper, proportionate, and fair treatment of people, without abusing those powers entrusted to you.

5.19 The Extended Police Family

This Handbook is aimed primarily at the student police officer, but it is worth taking a moment now to look at the wider police family, especially as there are many people engaged in law enforcement and what could loosely be called policing in addition to sworn officers.

5.19.1 Special Constables

You will probably be familiar already with special constables (known in-force as 'specials') who are volunteers, but sworn officers with powers, who undertake police duties on a part-time basis. Most have day jobs; the specials function very much in the same way as the Territorial Army, or RAF or Naval volunteer reserve forces, applying themselves to the reserve task with whatever hours each week that they can afford. Some use the specials as a route into the regular police force. The days have gone when specials only turned out at weekends to marshal car parking at village fetes. Now, in most forces, they work alongside regular officers, go out on patrol and deal with the range of activities which a patrol constable would encounter during an ordinary shift. The number of specials in England and Wales has been in decline in recent years (from approximately 20,000 in 1997 to 11,000 in 2004, although there have been slight increases since). At the time of writing, it seems likely that during their training, specials will be assessed using a subset of the NOS that are also used to assess you during your training.

5.19.2 Police Support Staff

Another part of the immediate police family and which you will encounter from your first day in the job is the police support staff member. These used to be termed 'civilian' and the word was often associated with administration or work which was 'non-police'. Those days are long gone in most police forces. Indeed, in many forces, support staff can make up to a third of total numbers, and they undertake a wide range of tasks which used to be performed by police officers (more or less amateurishly) or which never existed before about 1980.

TASK 36

Can you think of examples of the types of work which the (58,000 in England and Wales) police support staff do?

You might have included the following (which vary from force to force, of course, but which most forces have most support staff engaged in):

- **Crime Scene Investigators**: (CSIs, who used to be called 'scenes of crime officers' or SOCOs): an operational role which used to be undertaken exclusively by police officers, modern CSIs are often well qualified in forensic investigation (see 13.5 below).
- **Statement takers**: Many of the statements taken from witnesses and victims of crime, particularly volume crime, are taken, not by police officers but by support staff. The reason is that such statements do not have to be taken under caution (unlike statements by suspects) and therefore do not have to be taken by sworn officers. This can free up a great deal of time for police officers to pursue the investigation, and there can be a marked increase in the professionalism with which victims and witnesses are interviewed because the support staff involved are undertaking these tasks all the time.
- **Volume Crime Scene Examiners (VCSEs)**: This role may not exist in all forces, but VCSEs are employed to undertake specialist forensic examination of extended areas of crime on a large scale. They are particularly used in vehicle crimes.
- **Detention officers (jailers)**: These are support staff trained in custody and holding prisoners.
- **Human resources (HR)**: HR can include the whole range of specialist people management from recruitment, through promotions and postings, training, assessment and appraisal, to retirement, secondment, dismissal, or capability issues. HR also deal with all matters to do with police support staff, including negotiations with staff associations and the like.
- **Information technology**: This embraces everything from AIRWAVE communications to laptops, databases to PCs; these specialists are almost exclusively support staff, though some forces retain police officers in areas like the force communication centres or control rooms where there is direct interface with police officers on patrol. IT often includes telephony and wireless communications (including personal radios) within its remit.
- **Lawyers**: Force legal advice (civil and/or criminal) is now seen as an important resource particularly for the chief officer team and the Police Authority, and in dealing with complaints from the public, or litigation by employees (for example employment tribunals).
- **Estates**: Police forces occupy considerable numbers of buildings and possess vast stocks of property which need specialist handling, particularly in negotiations with planning authorities.
- **Finance**: With police budgets in the hundreds of millions of pounds annually, there is a need for specialist financial and budget management. In most forces, 80 per cent or more of the budget goes on salaries or pensions, leaving a relatively small operational revenue budget to which is added the capital budget for aspects such as the estate and buildings, the vehicle fleet or projects.
- **Administration**: From paper files to computerized records, from sickness certificates to awards ceremonies, from shotgun certificates to booking training courses, the administrative tasks in a police force are complex and numerous. The bureaucratic nature of policing (meaning that things have to be formalized in a process) lends itself to a large administrative tail. We have left the days when police officers had to type reports with two fingers and forces now employ trained inputters and clerks who can do the work. Nonetheless, the modern police force, however computerized, relies heavily on a corps of administrators who assume responsibility for the burden of recording and processing.

You may be able to think of other police support staff roles (such as training) which exist in your force, but the above are the principal functions which are now carried out in support of the operational policing side of the work. The original intention was to free up all police officers to return to front-line duties (though this was always somewhat tenuous), but the situation now is that no police force can do without its specialist support staff—from HR to estates manager—because of the complexity of the work, the fact that police officers could not master the breadth of knowledge entailed, and because litigation is at such a pitch generally that punitive awards against a force for the amateur handling of a specialist process might cost it dear. There are still some areas in policing itself where it may be more appropriate to employ specialist support staff (high-tech crime and fraud being two obvious examples) than relying on 'omnicompetent' officers, but this is part of a wider debate about what the purpose of sworn officers is, where police powers are needed, and where they are not. We continue this debate in looking at other roles below.

5.19.3   Other Police Forces

There are police forces apart from the Home Office forces of England and Wales, such as the British Transport Police and military police forces. You will come across some of them during your career in the police (you may even be a member of one) and it is worth noting why they exist separately from your own force.

British Transport Police are responsible for policing the railway network in the UK over- and underground rather than other forms of transport such as roads, sea, or air. With its headquarters in London, BTP has officers in uniform and in plain clothes travelling on the railways and performing police functions in upholding law and order, preventing and detecting crime, and so on. BTP figured very prominently in cooperation with the MPS in the wake of the tube train bombings in London on 7 July 2005.

The **Ministry of Defence Police** guard MoD establishments such as naval dockyards, airfields, and army regimental depots. It operates across the UK (that is, including Scotland). Other police forces within the armed forces are the **Royal Military Police** (RMP) and the RAF's **Provost and Security Services** (P&SS). These have jurisdiction only within their force establishments and then only for crimes which are not classified as major crimes. Murders and serious assaults are usually investigated by the local police force. You have no doubt read about the civil police investigations into allegations of bullying at Deepcut Barracks in Surrey which emerged after several young soldiers died. The official verdict was that the soldiers had killed themselves but some of the families of the soldiers believed that a bullying culture may have resulted in their sons or daughters being murdered or driven to kill themselves. Repeated investigations have failed to support the parents' contentions but have served to underline the sometimes rather difficult relationships between a local police force and the military or air force equivalent.

Finally, there is one police force with an unusual function: the **Civil Nuclear Constabulary** (the CNC), under the Energy Act 2004, protects civil nuclear installations and fuels in shipment and storage. Unusually, all of its officers are firearms trained.

5.19.4   Other Law Enforcement Agencies

There are other agencies with investigative powers which can also prosecute their own cases, and agencies which investigate and then turn their findings over to the police to take to court. Prior to the formation of the **Serious Organised Crimes Agency** (SOCA) in 2005, **HM Revenue and Customs** had its own Investigation Division which looked at smuggling, especially of contraband and drugs. It mounted its own operations sometimes independently and sometimes in conjunction with the **National Crime Squad.** Some aspects of the work of the Investigation division now reside with SOCA, but HM Revenue and Customs still has powers to investigate other crimes such as evasion of VAT or other taxes, improper importing, and other matters.

The **Immigration and Nationality Directorate** has a component which investigates illegal entry to the UK, and this includes the crime of people trafficking. Again, parts of the Immigration and Nationality Directorate's investigation capability have been absorbed into SOCA, and the remainder were incorporated into the United Kingdom Border Agency (UKBA) in 2008.

HM Prison Service has powers in dealing with convicted criminals who have been sent to prison, as well as those on remand awaiting their trials. Other state departments, such as **Social Services** and the **Department of Health** have small teams which investigate matters such as fraud, false documents, and fraudulent claims.

5.19.5   Regulatory Bodies

These are bodies which have a particular interest in a specialized matter such as public health or environmental crime. They can prosecute offenders. This category includes bodies which regulate, such as:

* the Health and Safety Executive (HSE);
* Trading Standards Authorities;
* the National Society for the Prevention of Cruelty to Children (NSPCC);

- the Royal Society for the Prevention of Cruelty to Animals (RSPCA);
- the Royal Society for the Protection of Birds (RSPB).

In a sense, most of these bodies focus on niche crime, such as maltreatment of animals and stealing birds' eggs. It is only the HSE and the NSPCC which impact on police work substantially, in terms of sanctions for safe working and the prevention or detection of child abuse. It also seems likely that environmental crime may have a higher profile in the future.

5.19.6   Police Community Support Officers (PCSOs)

The concept of a visible, non-police patrol function originated with Sir Ian Blair, among others, when he was Deputy Commissioner of the Metropolitan Police in 2001–02. PCSOs were introduced partly in response to public pressure to have 'bobbies on the beat', a desire particularly echoed by politicians and harking back to the (probably mythical) Golden Age of policing (see 1.3 above).

Sir Ian's concept was an achievable and imaginative one and it immediately found favour with the government of the day, especially when sufficient numbers of volunteers were found who wanted to become PCSOs or Wardens (the latter on rural beats particularly). The Community Support Officer soon acquired the prefix 'Police' to show that the officer was part of the extended police family, though the PCSO is without any special police powers and initially did not have a police function other than the supposed prevention of crime by the deterrent effect of visible presence.

However, the PCSO, despite some initial hostility from quarters within the police themselves, appears popular with the public, particularly in London. PCSOs are encouraged to engage with the public, to walk or travel on a limited beat where they can be seen and spoken to, and there is an emphasis on their meeting and talking to young people.

We noted above that PCSOs do not receive anything like the same kind of training which a police officer would receive. They are assessed, however, against half (11) of the same NOS used for initial police training, in a similar way to the training and assessment of special constables, and the consequence has been that some PCSOs are using the scheme as a route into regular policing. Most of the behavioural competences for PCSOs are identical with those for police officers.

TASK 37

Think about what you know about PCSOs and the work they do. What form do you imagine PCSO training takes, and how long does it last?

Police forces have remained uneasy about the precise long-term role of PCSOs and their cousins, the local and rural Wardens (and indeed some forces have proved remarkably reluctant to embrace the concept at all). This does not simply reflect the professional unease of police officers (or the complaint from the Police Federation that this may represent a form of 'policing on the cheap'). It is also to do with how the PCSO as a concept can be sustained over a period, especially since the government has withdrawn separate PCSO funding after 2008.

5.19.7   Agencies and Partnerships

The extended police family has developed in recent years to include a number of agencies and service providers on a local basis. You will look at some of these in more detail during your initial training because such partnerships vary from force to force. This variation is because of differences in emphasis placed on them by your chief constable and your police authority. In general terms, your force is likely to have the following:

- **Crime Reduction Partnerships**: these are sometimes called Crime and Disorder Reduction Partnerships (CDRPs) and are based within local, municipal, or unitary authorities. They include representatives from housing, social services, education as well as the police, the Probation Service, and others.

- **Multi-Agency Public Protection Arrangements**: MAPPA are much concerned with the control of violent and sexual offenders, especially their reintegration into society on release from prison. MAPPA work on plans for assimilation and control of such offenders.
- **Partnerships with local councils or authorities over fixed-penalty notices**: fixed-penalty notices are often issued for parking infringements or driving offences (such as those recorded by speed cameras). This partnership is likely to include close cooperation with local authority CCTV monitoring, especially of city centres and popular club or pub venues.

5.19.8 The Private Sector

The private security industry is expanding rapidly.

> **TASK 38**
>
> What do you think is meant by the 'private security industry' and can you think of some examples?

You may have thought straight away about bouncers at clubs, or, to give them one of their more official titles, door stewards. Other examples include security guards who control access to buildings or who patrol areas frequented by the public. But there are many others who are engaged in the business of giving security reassurance to the private and propertied sectors. There has been a growth in the last few years of the 'gated community' (following a US model) in which access to a group of private and exclusive dwellings is controlled by uniformed guards, 24 hours a day. This not only reassures the householder that his or her privacy is guaranteed, but it also increases physical security, making burglaries, robberies, and assaults more difficult to attempt.

Security extends outwards to the community through people like bailiffs, who recover property that has not been fully paid for, or seize goods in lieu of debt. Bailiffs can work on behalf of private companies seeking to recover debts or can work on their own behalf as a debt collection agency. On some occasions, particularly with evictions, or where there is concern about public order, bailiffs work with the police.

Our high streets and shopping malls are monitored through a network of CCTV cameras. There is little current regulation of the operation of CCTV cameras, though licensing was introduced for CCTV cameras in public spaces from March 2006. The use of CCTV in police surveillance work is discussed in 12.4.3.1 below, and the police have become used to routine seizure of CCTV footage in the initial investigations of nearly any kind of crime (see 13.5.13 below). We may conclude that the extension of the police family includes the large surveillance system which now cobwebs the whole of the urban geography of the UK. The movement of vehicles in rural areas and on motorways can also be monitored through automated number plate readers (ANPR) linked to cameras mounted on bridges and gantries.

When considering the steady growth of private security, we should not ignore the successful security companies, such as Group4 and Securitas AB. They are involved in all aspects of private security, such as cash collection from businesses, 'cash in transit' arrangements, the provision of physical security and guarding, and latterly, prison management and the transportation of prisoners. Thus, even the public sector is not immune to contracting security tasks out to the private sector. Indeed, there is a blurring of roles between public policing and private policing when such companies are used to provide security for organizations which engage in live animal research and which, consequently, find themselves the target of animal rights' protesters. At places like Huntingdon Life Sciences, for example, external security seems to be run by the police whilst internal security seems to be managed by a private company. The degree of cooperation that exists between the two is not clear, but there must be some and therefore the distinctions between 'accountable police activity' and 'unaccountable police activity' remain blurred.

Finally (though we have by no means exhausted the examples of the private security industry), we may look at private investigators. These are small-scale enquiry companies, usually staffed by ex-police officers, which seldom exceed half a dozen employees. They are principally engaged in matters such as gathering evidence for presentation in divorce cases or tracking down missing persons. They present little in the way of conflict with the regular police, except when attempts are made to access official records or data (such as vehicle number plates). The world of the private investigator has always been one where small budgets rather than large profits operate, and that is probably the reason why they remain small-scale and somewhat under-developed. They do not operate in the UK on anything like the scale of the USA, nor do they conform to the exciting image beloved of pulp fiction. It remains a fact that the private detective is seldom likely to detect public crime.

5.19.8.1 Unregulated private security activities

Commentators have not been slow to look at the extension of the police family. Professor Adam Crawford (cited in Newburn, 2003, p 148) asserts that:

> a pluralized, fragmented and differentiated patchwork has replaced the idea of the police as monopolistic guardians of public order.

Crawford argues that, in the past, the police provided the only form of public order, but now this has multiplied into many different providers. He goes on to ask what regulation there is of the private security industry; this is a good question which the government appears to have been slow to answer. Professor Crawford (p 149) also shows us the size of this industry by quoting some figures compiled by the British Security Industry Association (BSIA, now the SIA) for 2001:

- the commercial security industry employs 350,000 people;
- there are estimated to be 8,000 security companies in the UK market;
- the industry turnover in staffed security services (excluding in-house security) was estimated at £1.68 billion in 2001.

This is growth on a serious scale. Employees in security exceed police officers by nearly three to one, and such employees are not answerable in the same way that police officers are. After all, such employees would probably detain you, hold you, or eject you if you caused any kind of disturbance on premises which they were guarding. They have no more rights of detention, or arrest, or use of physical force than any other citizen, but when did you last see a prosecution of such a guard (or his/her company) for such an action?

The SIA is introducing codes of practice, but there are many companies (most of which operate on a small scale) that are not members and there is no compulsion on anyone setting up or managing a security company to register it or to join the Association. These companies are therefore unregulated and it is this which worries commentators like Professor Crawford and others. If the security industry is unregulated and not subject to mandatory government control of standards, how can it be trusted? It gains more and more power over private space and has functions of prevention and deterrence, but no obligation to investigate. Indeed, its interests are largely with its stakeholders and these interests do not necessarily coincide with the greater public good.

5.19.9 Policing Cyberspace

Cybercrime is an example of a digital crime that has now taken on a more defined meaning as a reference to crimes occurring in a networked environment (such as the internet), but more than simply facilitated by that environment. The term cybercrime therefore usually embraces the following criminal activities (Bryant, 2008, p. 18):

- computer hacking and cracking;
- developing and/or spreading malicious code (eg viruses, Trojans);
- spamming;

- network intrusion;
- software piracy;
- network-based or network-enabled crimes such as phishing, identity theft (see below), IPR crimes (eg illegal file-sharing) and distribution of child pornography.

Police forces in the UK have their own locally-based resources to investigate cybercrime. The centre of responsibility however may vary, although typically it will involve variously either a 'High-Tech Crime Unit' (eg Lincolnshire Police), a 'Computer Crime Unit' (eg Strathclyde Police), 'Digital Forensics Unit' (eg Kent Police), or even be part of an 'Economic Crime Unit'. These units, often evolved from earlier force 'Fraud Squads', tend to be small (according to Young (2007), the majority have fewer than five investigators), and most of their work appears to be taken up with child abuse investigations.

Until 2006 the main national police organization responsible for investigating cybercrime was the National High Tech Crime Unit (NHTCU) which was subsequently incorporated into SOCA to form an e-Crime Unit. The Unit works closely with the Child Exploitation and Online Protection (CEOP) Centre. A National Fraud Intelligence Bureau (NFIB) is planned as a central access point for individuals and organizations who suspect cybercrime. A National Fraud Reporting Centre (NFRC) is also under development, which will be responsible for collating all reports of fraud conducted through cybercrime (as well as 'conventional' fraud).

The Police Central e-Crime Unit (PCeU) was created in September 2008 and is a national resource, though based at the MPS. Within the PCeU, the Computer Crime Team (CCT) has the remit to investigate and prosecute, *inter alia*, 'Electronic attacks upon the Critical National Infrastructure, Significant Intrusions (Hacks), Denial of Service attacks (DDoS/BotNet attacks), Significant False Identity websites and large-scale successful Phishing' (PCeU, 2009).

Thus responsibility for cybercrime investigation is not restricted to the police service, nor do they have the resources to investigate all reported cybercrimes. For example, it is widely acknowledged in the UK that the police are unable to investigate all reported plastic (credit and debit) card offences that result from phishing and pharming (eg through a 'botnet'), or more traditional methods (eg City of London Police, 2005). In effect, these crimes are 'screened' and a decision made concerning whether to conduct further investigations. Level 1 and Level 2 (see 12.3 below) plastic-card crimes, if investigated, are likely to be tackled by a force-based unit. Any Level 3 plastic-card related crime is likely to be passed to SOCA for investigation. There has recently been some suggestion (and even criticism) that in future, screening for further investigation might be carried out by the banks and other financial institutions themselves, rather than by the police (Caulfield, 2007). The industry itself already supplements the police resources available to investigate plastic-card crime: for example, the industry body APACS sponsors the work of the Dedicated Cheque and Plastic Crime Unit (DCPCU).

Although the investigation of cybercrime will invariably involve the collection of 'traditional' forms of evidence (eg in written form) it might also involve, because of its nature, digitally-based evidence such as a deleted file recovered from a PC's hard drive, or the address book from a mobile phone SIM card. The forensic techniques required from recovery to analysis (often known as digital forensics), are a specialist field within investigation. ACPO has published good practice guidelines for the handling of digital evidence and recommends that digital evidence strategies should form part of the wider investigative process (ACPO, 2007a). Police forces may choose to 'outsource' some digital forensic analysis to non-police contractors, but these contractors are also expected to meet the good practice guidelines.

5.20 Answers to Tasks

TASK 1

It is highly likely that you included some of the following under the list of professions:

- medicine (eg a doctor);
- law (eg a barrister);

- Church (eg a vicar);
- teaching (eg a school teacher).

It is less likely, but still possible, that you listed the following:

- military (eg a General);
- nursing;
- accountancy.

Did you include policing?

Professions are occupations that normally have the following qualities:

- They provide an income which is normally referred to as a salary. Interestingly, in many respects police officers are paid a wage rather than a salary—for example, below certain ranks they qualify for overtime payments calculated at an hourly rate.
- Entry to the profession is regulated and controlled. Quite often a higher education degree in an approved area of study is required. Members of the profession are then licensed to practise but there are also procedures for the removal of this licence (which in some professions is referred to as being struck off). Others are prohibited from practising the profession unless they are licensed. (The title may even be legally controlled, as in the case of the medical profession.)
- There is a code of ethics and behaviour that members of the profession subscribe to.

TASK 2

Some possible answers are:

Requirements of a profession	The policing profession
Corpus of knowledge and theory	There is underpinning knowledge and theory for some aspects of policing, for example the law. There is also doctrinal development undertaken by the NCPE. However, there is no universally accepted corpus of knowledge which is unique to policing.
Controls on entry to the profession and maintenance of position	Entry is controlled through the national selection process. However, there are no formal academic requirements to enter the profession, beyond relatively simple tests of English and numeracy. There is currently little formal requirement to maintain skills.
Autonomy, discretion, and self-regulation	Police officers enjoy relatively high levels of autonomy and discretion. The title of police constable is controlled so that only those that qualify are entitled to use it. Self-regulation of policing exists in a restricted form but is increasingly under challenge.
Vocational calling	Policing is more than just a job and affects many aspects of an individual's life.
Code of ethics	There is an established code of ethics.

TASK 3

There are two major problems with simply telling student police officers to be honest:

- Telling people is no guarantee that they will internalize the values that underpin the police service.
- Honesty is too vague a term. As we have discussed, in certain forms of police corruption, the officers themselves probably feel that they are being honest, at a deeper level.

The relationship between our values, attitudes, beliefs, and actions is obviously a complex one. (See, for example, just about any textbook in social psychology.) The concepts themselves are also particularly slippery and hence difficult to pin down. The following is an overview of the usual meaning of the terms:

Concept	Meaning
Values	Concerned with the relative worth or importance of people, groups, objects. Those things that we value most we put first in our priorities. Our values can be drawn, inter alia, from: • ourselves; • those around us; • social norms and expectations; • religious and cultural belief systems.
Attitudes	An overall tendency to view matters in certain ways, either positively or negatively—for example to like or dislike something or somebody. We are not always aware of our attitudes.
Beliefs	Convictions about the truth of assumptions that we hold. Belief, however, does not have to be blind. We can base our beliefs on inductive reasoning (see 4.13 above) or sound evidence. Belief in a religious context often refers to faith.

The relationship between values, attitudes, beliefs, and actions is a fraught one in police training. Some may argue that our actions do not by necessity follow from our values, attitudes, and beliefs. In an earlier chapter we discussed *The Secret Policeman* documentary of 2003. In that case a police recruit was heard to claim that he exercised his discretion in a racist manner against members of ethnic minorities. However, there was no clear evidence that this had actually occurred. In his case there did not appear to be a clear link between his beliefs and his actions.

TASK 4

No doubt you found it easy to answer parts 1 and 2 of Task 4, but part 3 is less easy. Here we provide some suggested responses to Task 4. Many of these changes are very rapid, even though it may seem to us that society changes imperceptibly. By way of illustration, we can point to a few things which have developed enormously quickly in the last couple of decades and which impact on policing.

The 24-hour economy Clubs, pubs, bars, and places of entertainment are now open for much longer, stretching the commercial world across 24 hours. Additionally, people expect to be able to access services such as shops, supermarkets, banking, cash machines, and insurance at any time.

Disposable income Most people earn more and therefore feel at ease about spending more.

Profits from crime Some of the profits from drug taking, contraband, and criminal businesses are immense and criminals reinvest such sums in legitimate business ventures where dirty money can be laundered with clean (legitimate) money. Paradoxically, the illegal money helps to fuel economic growth, thus creating greater criminal opportunity.

Variety of social conventions Conventional marriages no longer dominate social structures. More older people are living alone and for longer; partners live together rather than marrying; divorce is higher than ever before (which has contributed to the rise of single-parent families); social groupings are more flexible and smaller, so that the nuclear family is more common than an extended family. This, combined with earlier economic independence enjoyed by some young people, has changed many social conventions. Some commentators have suggested that changing social conventions have led to lack of respect for authority (including the police) and to the abandoning of parental controls. Others think that more emphasis on freedom has encouraged society to question authority more freely and that the police, among others, should rethink its role in controlling and perhaps emphasize more its capacity for enabling.

Single-issue politics: Some people who had previously confined their political activities to voting are becoming active in single issues, such as live animal exports, ecological issues, animal experimentation, abortion, and so on. The mass spectrum of party politics does not appear to interest them, nor do they necessarily support a single party. At one end of the scale, this may involve well-planned, peaceful demonstrations with strong media coverage. At the other end of the scale it can entail violence and threatening behaviour (such as with some animal rights' groups).

Travel and personal mobility: There has been a major increase in travel over the past 20 years. People regularly travel hundreds of miles in the course of their work, and more leisure time is spent travelling than ever before. The number of cars and drivers on our roads has increased dramatically.

Credit-based consumerism: There is more debt now than there has ever been, and calculations by economists have indicated that the average personal debt in the UK is in excess of £4,000 (not including mortgages on property). It is not necessarily just the fault of the individual that we all owe more, because credit is often easy to obtain. This has fuelled a buoyant market for goods: more people own things than ever before (and, as a corollary, have more that is worth stealing). Correspondingly, there are more insolvencies, bankruptcies, and defaulting on debts than at any time since the Great Depression of 1926–9.

TASK 5

From the internet to the mobile phone, from computer to Blackberry, the communications revolution is perhaps the most profound change in modern society. Put simply, more information on more subjects is available to more people more quickly than ever before. We do not need to labour this point, but information technology of all kinds has changed our lives. It has also changed policing irrevocably. A couple of simple examples: a few years ago, people had to find a static phone (landline) to report a crime or an accident. The emergency services could cope (just) with responses to 999 calls. Now, when there is a road traffic accident or a street brawl, as many as fifty 999 mobile phone calls may be made virtually simultaneously to the police concerning one event. Even computer-based force communication centres find it difficult to cope at such times. Correspondingly, the police can access more information about individuals than previously, through centralized databanks such as the IDENT1 (for fingerprints) and the Police National Computer (PNC) for vehicle registration plates, or a central criminal records bureau to trace criminal histories. The overall result is that the police have more information about people than ever before.

TASK 6

As we suggested, there are no certain answers to this task.

There are interesting examples of attempts by a number of countries to tackle, for example, corruption amongst their police officers through using the kind of analysis that you have just undertaken. For example, in Kenya, police wages in 2004 were almost doubled and corruption subsequently fell. (However, proving that the two events are cause and effect is somewhat more difficult.)

TASK 7

No doubt you have your own impressions of the meanings of these terms in the context of police ethics. You may have noted that the word **should** can mean either that you 'must' do something or that 'it is best if you do it, but not essential'; this is an ambiguity you are likely to encounter frequently.

TASK 8

We discuss the meanings of these terms in the text that follows.

Drugs policing, in particular, gives rise to a number of opportunities for corruption both in type and frequency (Lee, 2003). These include:

- theft (stealing from arrested drug dealers);
- planting drugs (to imply guilt);
- illegally protecting drug dealers (eg by classifying them as a CHIS);
- participation in dealing.

TASK 9

The five opportunities from the list are:

- first arrival at the scene of a crime, when cash or goods are lying about;
- handling and storing drugs from police investigations;
- the excessive exercise of discretion without challenge;
- managing informants without adequate supervision or scrutiny;
- lack of effective supervision.

TASK 10

The free cup of coffee theory may seem to you to be an unlikely explanation. However, think about those circumstances in the past where police officers (including student police officers) used their warrant cards to secure financial advantage—for example, to gain free entry to a club. No doubt most of the officers justified this to themselves on the grounds that their (non-uniformed) presence would somehow be to the benefit of the club concerned. But did this not lead to at least a small sense of obligation on the side of the police officer and a potential compromise of their position? As they say in the USA, 'nobody ever gave a cop something for nothing'. The situation is made even more complex when a police officer has a second job (with the approval of his/her force). For example, the *Observer* newspaper reported in February 2006 that almost 80 police officers in Norfolk held second jobs, including at least one as a car salesman (*Observer*, 5 February 2006).

This is not to say that accepting gratuities is always wrong. The circumstances will be a guide, as will force policy. For example, you may well be offered cups of tea (or coffee!) by well-meaning members of the public if you are engaged in long and tiring public order duties. There would appear to be little to be lost and much to be gained by accepting the offer on those occasions.

TASK 11

Remember that this theory assumes that you have a predisposition towards corruption or deviant behaviour. If you have this predisposition, you are likely to find many reasons that will justify undertaking corrupt acts.

TASK 12

For a comprehensive discussion of this and other aspects of police corruption you might want to read Caless (2008a and 2008b), as well as Newburn (1999) and Miller (2003). Both the latter, now slightly out of date, are downloadable from the Home Office website.

TASK 13

When thinking about these questions you might like to read at least parts of the 1999 HMIC report into police integrity (HMIC, 1999). The report gave rise to the introduction of integrity tests. These are situations designed to test the integrity of police officers. Note, however, that they are not usually directed at police officers in general (blanket testing) but are targeted at an individual or individuals as a result of information or intelligence. However, consult your force policy on this.

In terms of assessing the seriousness and context of corrupt acts, you might like to examine the 1998 case of DCI Elmore Davies, Merseyside Police, jailed for five years for corruption and perverting the course of justice. You should be able to find the details on the internet.

TASK 14

The following are examples of how the five forms of authority might feature in the scenario:

Form of authority	Examples
Epistemic	You have a clear understanding of the definition of the possible offences involved in this incident. You have knowledge of the appropriate procedures to be followed and this is conveyed in speech to those present, including the victim and the offender.
Natural	You use your demeanour and language to take control of the situation, including indicating when you wish a person to answer a question and in which order.
De facto	Your right to question those involved is probably accepted without challenge (but not necessarily with cooperation!).
De jure	You have the authority to arrest if the circumstances require this.
Moral	You demonstrate, through your behaviour and attitudes, that you do not immediately jump to conclusions concerning the sequence of events and attributing guilt or otherwise.

TASK 15

You would have had to arbitrate between the right to freedom of expression (however extreme such views may be) and the need to sustain law and order. The legitimacy of your presence may not be consensual, but it may be both legitimized in law and necessary for preservation of the peace. The police would endeavour to control the marchers by determining the safest route for the parade to follow whilst also ensuring that direct clashes with the protesters were avoided. Someone, somewhere, would have individual freedoms circumscribed (even if only the rights of Saturday shoppers to go about their lawful business) however you managed the event, and thus the police are using moral as well as legal legitimacy in the policing of the march.

TASK 16

You have probably spotted our intentions with this task; the two situations are very similar. The first scenario is the more serious in policing terms as you are told that the woman appears to be slightly drunk whereas the young man is simply clutching a can of lager. In the first case the fact that she is a medical student who will soon (presumably) join the medical profession may well have influenced your thinking towards exercising discretion. However, you were **not** appointed to be a moral guardian of society; the place that a person holds in society should not feature in your decision whether or not to exercise discretion.

In terms of your answer you might well have considered other aspects such as the intent of each person concerned, the precise nature of the apparent offence, and so on. The problem with presenting these scenarios in a written form (or as simulations in training) is the lack of this context; this is so important when making decisions.

When exercising discretion it is important that you are able to justify your actions to an outsider looking in—that is, to show how discretion is the result of rational decision making rather than instinct or some other gut reaction. Doing so will also help you meet the evidence requirements of the NOS elements. During your training and assessment you must **evidence** your decision making; your assessor cannot read your mind!

Taylor (1999) has produced a useful checklist for the exercise of discretion. You are asked to consider issues such as:

- fairness;
- justice;
- accountability;
- consistency;
- wider community interests and expectations.

TASK 17

The last overseas country visited by the author (on business) was Estonia. Here (since independence from the Soviet Union in 1994) the adversarial system of justice is employed for criminal cases.

TASK 18

You might have included things like:

- it is **decentralized**: public policing is still largely local, autonomous, and non-political (with shades of grey, viz the Miners' Strike in 1982–3);
- policing is **consensual**: it cannot operate without the active support of the public;
- approaches to policing are characterized by provisions in the Human Rights Act 1998 and the Police and Criminal Evidence Act 1984, which **respect human dignity and ensure fairness of process**;
- police officers, for the most part and on most occasions, are **unarmed**;
- police officers have **independence** in conducting investigations; they may still exercise initiative in whether to investigate or not;
- we have an adversarial criminal justice system, which requires the prosecution to **disclose evidence**;
- there is a **presumption of innocence** until proven guilty; the burden of proof lies with the prosecution.

TASK 19

In terms of anti-social behaviour (and with our *caveat* about not treating the models as being in some form of competition) you might have suggested the following:

- **Intelligence-led policing** Target the most active and serious contributors to the anti-social behaviour. This might require the use of informants and surveillance. When these individuals have been identified then examine all appropriate means, within the law, of removing them from exercising leadership and direction over the rest. For example, consider what offences they may have committed, whether ASBOs might be suitable, what other agencies may be engaged to bring pressure to bear (for example, do we have information that they are illegally claiming benefits?), what evidence we will need, and so on. If we cannot detect the crime, then disrupt it.
- **Problem-oriented policing** What is the fundamental problem here? The anti-social behaviour may simply be the visible manifestation of a less obvious problem or change. For example, has the removal of fences between the gardens of publicly-owned houses meant that spaces are no longer as defensible for those living in the area? This might mean involving other agencies in an agreed and concerted strategy to address the underlying problem.
- **Community-based policing** First we need to talk to those that can really help us: members and representatives of the local community, and the patrol officers who work with them. If young people are involved then how can we mobilize their parents and others in the community to address both the anti-social behaviour and its underlying causes? What support can be offered? In summary, do not simply view this as a question of law enforcement but more as a wider question concerning the stability and cohesion of the local community.

TASK 20

You might have noticed that:

- uniformed police officers routinely and openly carry **arms** (so do detectives, but concealed);
- **stop and search** can be more widespread than in the UK; also, European citizens routinely carry an **identification card** or identifying papers;
- there are often **several types of police officer** (*gendarmes, carabinieri, guardia civil, police municipale*, city police as well as national police) in the same country;

- most European police forces are **nationally organized**, even when they have variations in police types (such as the paramilitary *gendarmes*, as against the *agents de police* in France);
- particularly in Eastern Europe and Russia, as well as further afield, you may have detected a **hostility** to the police or even a fear of them, especially at border controls. This is a legacy and, in some cases, a continuation of the role of the **police as an arm of the state** (in the case of the ex-USSR, as an arm of the Communist Party) and is associated with repression and denial of freedom. Citizens in countries which have suffered under occupation or tight state control may show contempt and loathing of the police to a degree you seldom find in the UK.

There are other differences which you will find only by close comparative study or by investigation into the individual country's criminal justice system. Did you know, for example, that the Dutch abolished the jury system in 1804 and never reinstated it? Or that Italy has provision for a jury trial system but has never used it?

TASK 21

Remember that a major theme in policing is that you police by consent, that is, through the active cooperation and tolerance of the majority of the populace. It is important that your force shows, in its Policing Plan, how it intends to respond to local concerns and how it will meet criticisms of its actions (such as faster responses to 999 calls or more neighbourhood police action to counter criminal damage). It is also a communication exercise which shows how the budget is allocated, sets out what the priorities are, and also shows that some aspects of policing are not determined locally but nationally. Finally, it is a document, revised and rewritten approximately annually, which is potentially a good promotional tool for the force and for the Police Authority. Most force Policing Plans are quite glossy, expensively produced publications or web-page designs which, naturally enough, put a positive spin on what the force does. You might consult your own Policing Plan for detail specific to your force.

TASK 22

You might include the provisions of the Strategic Policing Priorities, which we summarized above, as modified or amended to fit local conditions. However, you could also have included themes such as:

- citizen focus, including engagement with the public and responsiveness to public fears about crime, anti-social behaviour, criminal damage, and alcohol-initiated violence or disorder;
- developing witness and victim care programmes (see also 'providing assistance' below);
- building and sustaining good relationships with the communities which you police;
- reducing crimes, with especial focus on reducing those crimes which adversely affect local communities such as domestic burglary, vehicle crime, drugs misuse, and street robberies;
- partnership working, especially in the fields of combating illegal drugs and domestic violence;
- crime investigation, particularly in improving the 'brought to justice' statistics, identifying and dealing with persistent and prolific offenders, and in seizing criminals' assets;
- reducing the incidence of violent crime, especially the abuse of children, crimes involving guns and knives, sexually-motivated crimes, and hate crime;
- promoting public safety, such as reducing anti-social behaviour, dealing with abandoned, unlicensed, and nuisance vehicles, crime prevention strategies, Crimestoppers and Neighbourhood Watch initiatives, and roads policing;
- providing assistance through effective call-handling, case investigations, liaison with partner agencies, 'visible policing', witness protection, and victim support;
- effective use of resources, especially those of the force itself through effective budgeting, financial management and accountability, managing people from recruitment to retirement, healthy workforce initiatives, race and diversity equality issues, training and skills acquisition, the retention and development of a representative work force, and the effective use of information technology.

If you managed to include all these points in your answer, you may very well be asked to help with the force Policing Plan in future years! The essential point for you is that, although the SPP and the aspirations of the government (or even the closer-to-home joint planning by your force and your Police Authority) may seem somewhat remote, these things constantly affect you and the way that you do your job.

TASK 23

You should have found that these regulations cover the fitting of lights, reflectors, and rear markings on vehicles.

TASK 24

You may have considered a number of possible scenarios that might take place on Supervised Patrol. Remember that these rights extend to suspects as well as victims and witnesses. For example, you may be involved in the arrest of an individual whose grasp of spoken English is poor or non-existent, and subsequently involved in the procedures used when suspects have difficulty communicating in English. Skills for Justice indicate that, for this element, evidence must come from real-life situations. Your assessor may well be able to observe directly your actions in this case but you would also need to provide evidence of your knowledge and understanding—for example, through evidence in your SOLAP cross-referenced to your Learning Diary or pocket notebook.

TASK 25

Your answers may include the following:

Code A You may have seen searches of people being conducted under a number of powers. Bear in mind that s 1 of the PACE Act 1984 is one power amongst others and the remainder are listed in Annex A of the PACE Act 1984 Code A. You may therefore have seen searches taken place under s 23 of the Misuse of Drugs Act, s 47 of the Firearms Act, and s 1 of the PACE Act 1984.

Code B You may have seen searches of premises take place in order to arrest a person using s 17 of the PACE Act 1984. You may also have observed searches of premises at the time of an arrest under s 32 of the PACE Act 1984 and after arrest you may have witnessed searches of premises taking place under s 18 of the PACE Act 1984. You may also have seen a warrant executed and all these searches would have been carried out under the guidance of Code B.

Code C You may have observed people suspected of committing road traffic offences interviewed at the roadside and the interview recorded in an officer's pocket notebook. You may also have seen suspects interviewed contemporaneously, perhaps as a result of their involvement in a road traffic collision.

Code D You may have seen the identification by a witness or victim of a suspect take place in the local neighbourhood of an offence soon after it takes place. You may also have observed an identification parade in which a witness was requested to make a choice concerning the identity of a suspect in an offence.

Code E You may have seen suspects being interviewed at the police station which were recorded on tape, and the steps taken to respect their rights—for example, offering a service to give the suspect the opportunity to have a copy made of the tape.

Code F You may not have seen suspects' interviews visually recorded with sound as there is no statutory requirement to record interviews this way; however your force may be doing so and you may have seen this take place.

Code G You may have seen suspects arrested (see 8.7 below). You will also have seen them cautioned at the time of arrest.

TASK 26

For the offence of robbery, you should have found:

- the Theft Act 1968, s 8(1);
- mode of trial: triable on indictment only;
- maximum penalty for a person found guilty: life imprisonment.

TASK 27

You will find the website <http://www.hmcourts-service.gov.uk/HMCSCourtFinder> a useful resource. **Note**, however, that postcodes are given in some cases but not in others (you may need to use your investigative skills).

TASK 28

There are many different explanations for what registers as a crime, or series of crimes, in public imagination through the media. A sensational crime is often one which has something out of the ordinary, something different, even a little outrageous, to make it stand out.

Some violent crimes involving children may feature highly in media and thus public consciousness (possibly because many of us are expected to identify with the parents of the victim, or because the vulnerability of a child evokes sympathy and pity in us), as may crimes in which single young women are involved. (There is some suggestion of an ethnic bias in reporting crimes of this type, with victims of ethnic minorities less likely to receive extensive media coverage than their white counterparts. However, this discussion is beyond the scope of this Handbook.)

Crimes which tend not to make the headlines, unless really bizarre or huge, are the so-called victimless crimes such as defrauding a large company or embezzling insurance money. There are victims, of course, with any crime (because that helps to define the nature of a crime), but what frightens a community or spreads anxiety is the thought that some sort of terror or dread is stalking the streets. A series of rapes can do this, especially in a small community like a town or at a college, and the abduction of a child also causes widespread concern.

TASK 29

There are a large number of possible answers, and we provide some examples below. The answer for 'universal crimes' is somewhat speculative.

Crimes	Examples
Universal	Theft, murder, and rape.
In the UK now, but not 100 years ago	Stalking, computer crimes (eg hacking), and some categories of outdoor music and dancing events at night.
In other parts of the world, but not in the UK	Adultery (Nigeria), consuming alcohol (Saudi Arabia), keeping African Pygmy Hedgehogs (some states of the USA).

TASK 30

There is a difference between intrinsic value and 'CRAVED'. The thieves would probably leave the coins behind because they are bulky and very heavy, but they would pocket the £350 in notes immediately. The PC would probably be left; again it is bulky and heavy and could even be secured by steel straps to its desk or to the wall. Thieves would not want to waste valuable time cutting the cables. The laptop would be easily picked up and sold on, as would the iPod, Blackberry, mobile phone, and the Rolex. Beware though—traffic in electronic goods is transient and short-lived. It is often the next generation white goods that the fences demand. Steal a mobile phone which is out of date and you could get nothing. (This does not include those thieves who use stolen mobiles to set up other crimes or who want them to use abroad.) The Rolex might later cause problems because of the engraving (which potentially makes it traceable), but in snatching or mugging for it the thieves would not stop to check. Only when the fence jibbed at the engraving and date, and knocked pounds off the price, would the thieves realize that they had lost out. They would get something though; the fence could always file the engraving out.

As to the rest, well, they are small but would be very difficult to sell on. The Gospel and the Rubens' painting would be worth several million pounds and enormously hard to fence on any art market. (For all that, we know that organized drugs importers and traffickers have used valuable art such as paintings or sculptures as 'cash' for their theft transactions—the more so since the Proceeds of Crime Act 2002 made depositing large amounts of cash in a bank account subject to scrutiny and investigation.)

The *netsuke*, which are small carved figures, would be worth several thousand pounds each but only through an expert dealer. It is doubtful that the average fence would know what they were. That said, some thieves steal to order and might target such items specifically, but these are not likely to be volume criminals working on hot spots.

TASK 31

In this task you were asked to consider police strategies to combat repeat victimization. A useful starting point is the government's crime reduction website concerned with 'RV' at <http://www.crimereduction.gov.uk/repeatvictimisation02.htm>. There is a popular phrase, 'once bitten, twice shy', which suggests that we become more vigilant after an unpleasant incident such as being the victim of a crime. Whilst it might be true that we become more wary, it is certainly not the case that we become less vulnerable. As we suggested in terms of burglary, by far the best predictor of future victimization is whether we have been a victim in the recent past. Put another way, if you knew the following about a person:

(a) age
(b) sex
(c) ethnicity
(d) income
(e) the football club, if any, that he supports
(f) whether he had been the victim of a burglary in the previous month
(g) height
(h) annual investment in household security devices
(i) whether he has previous convictions or not

then by far the best way of predicting whether he/she is more or less likely than average to be burgled in the next month would be (f), that is, whether he/she has been the victim of burglary in the last month.

TASK 32

The quotation assumes that criminal behaviour will follow a rational pattern thus allowing the police to anticipate appropriate points at which to intervene. We can anticipate hot products that will be targeted in hot spots; markets will exist for the products of crime.

TASK 33

1. Reducing the reward. The fact that the cars targeted have valuables on show suggests that the offenders are looking for easy rewards. Increasing the risk by introducing better lighting, CCTV cameras, or security guards would also be beneficial but the most cost-effective measure is likely to be encouraging people not to leave valuables in the car.

2. Increasing the effort. We can assume that these particular offenders are desperate and therefore unlikely to be overly concerned at being caught (increasing the risk) and will be prepared to take risks for small rewards (reducing the reward). Therefore making it physically difficult to break in by installing metal bars and stronger locks is likely to be the most effective measure.

3. Increasing the risk. The rewards are already limited and making it more difficult to take the money is impractical because of the need for employees to handle money. Therefore increasing the risk, for example by installing CCTV, is likely to have a deterrent effect because the employees have much to lose if they are caught.

TASK 34

You would probably have picked up on race and gender, but did you get sexual orientation, age, or belief? And, mindful of the references throughout this Handbook to the Disability Discrimination Act (the DDA), did you get disability?

TASK 35

The negative behaviours are discussed in the paragraphs that follow the task.

TASK 36

We provide a comprehensive list immediately after the task. Force websites often provide descriptions of the roles undertaken by police staff. A good example is Essex Police and its website <http://www.essex.police.uk/recruitment/r_sta_07.php>.

TASK 37

The volume and exact nature of the training is very much determined by the chief constable in your force, or the local BCU Commander in terms of any specific training. There is still debate about the outline of a training package which all PCSOs should receive. In most forces it would look something like this:

Training for PCSOs

Training lasts for at least five weeks; in some forces it is seven and there have been calls for much longer and more specific PCSO training systems to be set up as a form of continuous development.

Week 1 is an induction course, which contains health and safety instruction, learning about diversity, and some introduction to the general nature of being a community support officer.

Weeks 2–4 include attitude and behaviour development, combined with knowledge of outside agencies and other tools for successful community problem solving.

Week 5 is the 'Powers' week where PCSOs are provided with knowledge of their existing powers and their practical effectiveness. This would also include some rudimentary safety training and training in how to defuse potentially dangerous situations and how to calm angry people.

Finally, there will be BCU or beat training and familiarization until independent patrol.

TASK 38

We provide some examples of the work of the private security industry in the paragraphs that follow the task. We also discuss the regulation of the industry. Licensing is being introduced to a raft of security occupations such as door supervision (door stewards, bouncers), vehicle immobilizers (clampers), and so on. You can find a complete list of licensed activities and timetables for introduction of licences at the SIA website at <http://www.the-sia.org.uk/home>. You could well find that the law and regulation surrounding private security features more extensively in your work as a police officer in the years to come.Nullaorerci blamcon erciduisim

6 | Induction into a Police Organization

6.1   Chapter Briefing

This chapter will assist you during your induction and involves an understanding of your position within the organization together with an appreciation of your own responsibilities and the responsibilities of those around you. Normally the formal stage of induction occupies the first three to five weeks of your training (IPLDP Phase 1) although a number of aspects are likely to be revisited at later stages during your (probable) two-year probationary period.

6.1.1   Aims of the Chapter

This chapter will enable you to:

- understand the basic configuration of the rank structure in policing;
- gain an overview of a typical police force organizational structure;
- learn the phonetic alphabet when required by your trainers;
- understand the fundamentals of safe police practice;
- learn something of the background to the use of Information Technology systems by police organizations, particularly the PNC;

- appreciate the need to respect confidentiality but also acknowledge the need to make information available;
- understand the milestone of attestation, whilst appreciating that the staging of attestation has proved problematic for the service;
- understand the role of the attested student police officer as a constable in terms of the codes, rules, and regulations governing conduct;
- further develop understanding of interpersonal skills such as communication and listening;
- develop the underpinning knowledge required for a number of NOS elements, several of the PAC headings, and entries for your Learning Diary Phase 1 and the CARs of your SOLAP.

6.1.2 Police Action Checklist

This chapter will provide you with some of the underlying knowledge and theory to meet aspects of the following requirements of the Police Action Checklist:

6.1.2.1 Safety first

- first aid;
- health and safety—dynamic assessment;
- Personal Safety Training (PST/OST etc).

6.1.2.2 Information management

Utilize the PNC.

6.1.3 National Occupational Standards

This chapter will provide you with some of the knowledge required to demonstrate the following NOS elements.

National Occupational Standard Units and Elements

AB1.2 Maintain the security of information.
AE1 Maintain and develop your own knowledge, skills, and competence.
AF1.1 Identify the hazards and evaluate the risks in the workplace.
GC10.1 Apply conflict management skills and techniques.
GC10.2 Use personal safety skills and equipment.
4G4 Administer first aid.

You should refer to Chapter 3 for general information and advice concerning the NOS elements. There is a possibility that you might be able to gain the whole of Unit 4G4 during the induction period of training.

6.1.4 IPLDP Phases and Modules

This chapter will provide you with resources to support the following Induction Modules of the IPLDP.

IND 1 Underpinning ethics/values of the police service (particularly IND 1.2 Applying police ethics).
IND 2 Foster people's equality, diversity, and rights (particularly IND 2.4 Provide information about the complaints system; IND 2.8 Demonstrate confidentiality of information; and IND 2.9 Disclosing information to others).
IND 5 Ensure your own actions reduce the risk to health and safety.
IND 8 Operation of information technology systems.
IND 9 Administer first aid.

Much of the content of this chapter relates to IPLDP Phase 1 Induction.

6.1.5 SOLAP

The contents of this chapter are relevant to the 'knowledge' evidence requirements of CARs AA1, AF1, GC10, and 4G4.

6.1.6 Learning Diary Phases

The contents of this chapter may provide you with stimulus material for completion of your Learning Diary (Phase 1) and the following headings in particular:

- Introduction to the Organization;
- Information and Communication Technology;
- Health and Safety;
- Ethics and values of the police;
- Rights and responsibilities.

6.2 Introduction

Induction is the process of 'bringing in' or initiation. In some senses it also refers to a kind of transformation—in this case from being a member of the public to becoming both a member of the public and a police constable. Normally, this transformation will take a significant length of time. Although it is suggested that the induction phase of IPLDP should take between three and five weeks (Home Office, 2004c), the actual process of induction can be measured in months. This is because it is more than simply learning the rules of the organization: it involves more fundamental shifts in the way that you organize both your personal and professional life, and the ways in which you think about those individuals and communities around you.

You will discover that there are certain symbolic aspects to this induction, such as the ceremony that surrounds attestation. In many cases, though, induction takes more tangible forms, such as learning your way around the organization in terms of its structures, locations, and people. Perhaps another way of explaining what induction really means is to describe it as an assimilation into an organizational culture or cultures. In policing, the process of 'buying into' the existing organizational culture has not been without controversy. For some observers, the prevailing cultures within the police have often been characterized as male-dominated and exclusionary. Allied to this view is the suggestion that initial police training moves you from being an individual to being part of a group, and into a group where it is 'dangerous to be different'. (This is the so-called police 'canteen culture' that you may hear or read about.) The police service is aware of these criticisms and one of the driving forces behind recent changes to initial police training is to create a learning environment which is more inclusive.

In this chapter, you will learn some of the small but important details which make up the organization you are joining, namely the police service. It may be that you are familiar with the police already, perhaps by working as a special constable, or as a member of the police support staff, or as a PCSO, or through undertaking a pre-entry Foundation degree. You may have received some of the material which we are about to look at, in briefing packs when you applied to join, and some elements, especially police rank structures, may have been part of the student police officer package when you received your acceptance letter.

However, we are going to work on the assumption that you know little about this police organization that you are joining. We begin your induction by examining the rank structure, where badges denoting rank for uniformed officers are shown on epaulettes and cap peak-decorations denoting rank more generally (the more silver braid on show, the higher the rank, as a general rule). From looking at the rank structure, we move on to examine how a typical police force is structured and organized. Your own force will probably vary in detail from the general picture we present here, but most forces will have most of what we describe. Then we look at the phonetic alphabet, which assigns words to letters of the alphabet. This is used so that letters—for example, registration plates or the spelling of a surname—may be accurately communicated when using a radio or mobile phone. Understanding the role of health and safety is an important part of a police officer's ability to make risk assessments, both for you and for others, and this is often covered in conjunction with first aid, a vital skill for patrol constables. Your own safety and that of others will be covered in Personal Safety Training (the title varies between forces), where you will learn self-defence, how to manage angry and tense situations, and the appropriate use of rigid-pattern handcuffs, the ASP baton, and incapacitant spray.

From these tools we move to look at operating IT systems (an increasingly important part of information management) and what is done with information, including matters covering confidentiality as well as the implications of the Freedom of Information Act 2000. Finally, we look at your attestation and role as a constable. We examine the Code of Conduct (and refer you again to the discussions about ethics and corruption which we covered in 5.4 above) and Police Regulations, and we discuss conduct, misconduct, discipline, and complaints. We then introduce your staff association, the Police Federation, as well as looking at specialist support groups such as the British Association of Women Police Officers, the National Black Police Association, and the Gay Police Association. Finally we look at the importance of effective communication and your engagement with the community that you will police.

6.3 Police Ranks

You may sometimes hear your police force referred to as a 'disciplined organization'. This refers not only to the need for self-discipline and restraint but also to the fact that at least parts of the organization (those parts concerned with police officers) are organized into ranks in a hierarchical fashion, involving the issuing and receiving of orders. Apart from the MPS and one or two other forces, the rank structure (and the associated badges on the epaulettes of uniforms) are as follows:

> **Rank Structure**
>
> In order of decreasing superiority:
> - Chief Constable
> - Deputy Chief Constable
> - Assistant Chief Constable
> - Chief Superintendent
> - Superintendent
> - Chief Inspector
> - Inspector
> - Sergeant
> - Constable

In the non-uniformed equivalents 'Detective' often precedes the rank, eg Detective Chief Inspector.

The insignia of the ranks are as follows (as before, this may vary from force to force, as, for example, in the case of the PSNI):

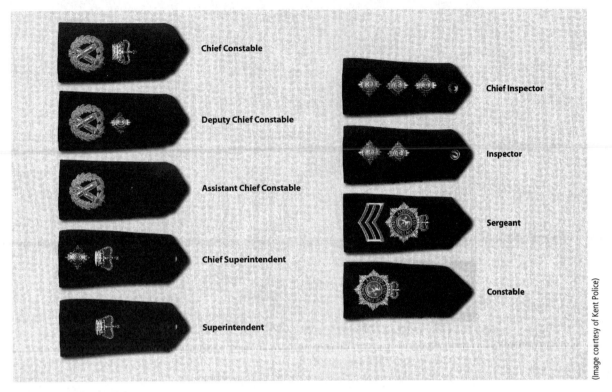

Insignia of police ranks

(Image courtesy of Kent Police)

In the MPS the rank structure is different above the chief superintendent rank; the three highest ranks are commissioners rather than chief constables, and there are two additional ranks marked with asterisks below:

MPS Rank Structure

- Commissioner
- Deputy Commissioner
- Assistant Commissioner
- Deputy Assistant Commissioner*
- Commander*
- Chief Superintendent
- Superintendent
- Chief Inspector
- Inspector
- Sergeant
- Constable

The City of London Police is a little different again.

You should also take the time to familiarize yourself with the insignia of uniformed members of the extended police family (see 5.19 above), such as special constables and PCSOs.

TASK 1

Construct a set of memory cards to help you learn the police ranks and their associated insignia. Memory cards are best made from thick paper or cardboard (you may have used them as a child!). On one side of card put the rank, the other side the associated insignia, like so:

Superintendent

(Image courtesy of Kent Police)

Now take cards at random from your collection. If the name of the rank is given then describe the insignia. Reverse the card and check your answer. If the insignia is given, then you need to name the rank. As before, turn over to check your answer.

Keep playing (alone or in a group) until you have memorized all the ranks and insignia.

6.4 Typical Police Organizational Structure

The following is a typical police force structure for organizations with 6,000-plus staff (although remember that variations on this basic structure are probable):

Typical police force structure

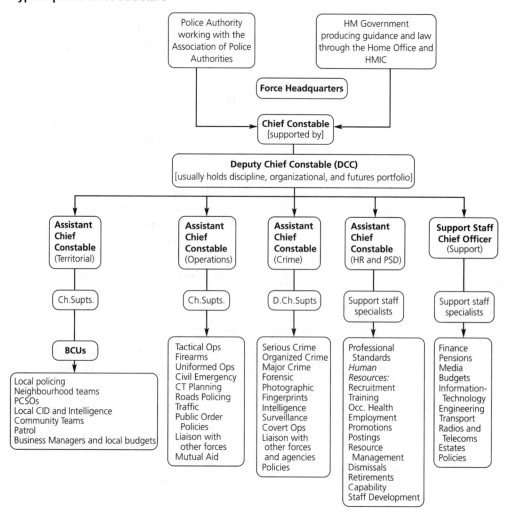

6.5 The Phonetic Alphabet

If you have ever attempted to spell out a word on the phone to another person you have probably experienced the difficulty of clarifying the difference between 'm' and 'n', 's' and 'f', and so on. Mistakes made in the context of ordinary phone calls are seldom life-threatening, but if these same mistakes were made during a police communication it could prove costly, both in time and in terms of your safety and the safety of others. For this reason the 'phonetic alphabet' (sometimes referred to as the 'radio alphabet') was developed and subsequently adopted by police forces throughout the UK. The purpose of giving each letter a different name is to avoid confusion over letters which sound the same, such as 'p', 'b', and 'd'; instead of using the letters themselves, you use the phonetic equivalent. So instead of saying 'a' you say 'alpha'. (There are similar problems when using numbers—for example, five and nine. These are sometimes replaced by 'fyfe' and 'niner' respectively.)

The following is a list of the phonetic alphabet as normally employed by police forces in the UK (and beyond). You may well be asked to memorize and use it.

The phonetic alphabet

a Alpha	j Juliet	s Sierra
b Bravo	k Kilo	t Tango
c Charlie	l Lima	u Uniform
d Delta	m Mike	v Victor
e Echo	n November	w Whisky, Whiskie or Whiskey
f Foxtrot	o Oscar	(but same pronunciation)
g Golf	p Papa	x X-ray
h Hotel	q Quebec	y Yankee
i India	r Romeo	z Zulu

(For a time 'Indigo' was used instead of 'India' but this practice is now very uncommon in police circles.)

6.6 Fitness Training

In order to join the police you will have undertaken the Police Initial Recruitment Test. As part of the test, your level of fitness will have been assessed in two main areas, namely endurance and dynamic strength ('push and pull'). The process of fitness testing is known as the Job-Related Fitness Test (JRFT). As a student police officer, your force will expect you to maintain a minimum standard of fitness that will probably be based upon the JRFT. (If, after confirmation, you subsequently join specialist departments such as Firearms then there may be an ongoing fitness requirement.)

Soon after joining you may be required to take a new fitness test, using the JRFT. This typically happens after about week three of training. At this time you will be tested again for endurance and dynamic strength.

6.6.1 Endurance

If your new endurance assessment is based upon the JRFT, then you will be required to run a 'bleep test' between two fifteen-metre points in time with a series of bleeps played to you while you carry out the exercise. The amount of time between the bleeps will decrease successively through a series of five levels and therefore you will need to run faster as the exercise progresses.

6.6.2 Dynamic Strength

You may need to pass another test in dynamic strength which will involve using the Dyno ergometer ('push and pull') machine. In the pushing exercise you will be required to perform three warm-up pushes, and then the test will consist of five pushes at maximum effort with a three-second break in between each one. You will need an average of 34 kg to pass.

The pulling exercise will take place at the other end of the machine where you will be required to warm up with three pulls and then give maximum effort to five further pulls reaching an average of 35 kg to pass. The machine will calculate the average for you.

If you fail the fitness test then you will be given an opportunity to retake the test, probably at about week nine. Obviously, if this happens then you will be well advised to attempt to improve your fitness in the intervening weeks. Forces are normally supportive in this matter (they appreciate that there may have been a long period between you undertaking the JRFT as part of the recruitment process and then starting). They may suggest a programme of activities such as swimming, road running, gymnasium circuits, rowing, or cycling, together with aerobic exercise.

If you fail a second time, you will probably be given a final attempt. Failure at the third and final attempt may lead to you being 'Reg thirteened' and dismissed from the force (see 3.12 above). However, policy can vary and you should consult your force on this and perhaps also your Police Federation representative (see 6.17 below).

6.7 Health and Safety

By its very nature, policing has always been and will continue to be a potentially hazardous occupation. Whilst risks are present in all work activities, operational staff are more frequently exposed to risks, whether dealing with environmental incidents or disorderly behaviour. Therefore, health and safety is not just another bureaucratic burden, but an issue you must consider and have in mind at all times during your day-to-day work to prevent people getting injured or becoming ill. After all, ill health or an accident could reduce the quality of your life and adversely affect the lives of those around you. Health and safety duties are covered by sections 2–7 of the Health and Safety at Work etc. Act 1974, becoming applicable to police officers, special constabulary officers, and cadets by virtue of the Police (Health and Safety) Act 1997. Home Office publications from 1996 provide guidance for police managers. Your force will also have its own published health and safety policy.

All employers have a duty to ensure (as far as is reasonably practicable) the health, safety, and welfare of their employees. Each employee has a duty to take reasonable care for his or her own health and safety and that of other persons who might be affected by his or her acts or omissions. In other words, you are expected to look after yourself and the people around you.

Here we provide some of the knowledge required to attain the following NOS elements:

> **National Occupational Standard Elements**
>
> AF1.1   Identify the hazards and evaluate the risks in the workplace
> AF1.2   Reduce the risks to health and safety in the workplace

The topics covered here are also linked with PAC heading 'Safety First' and in particular the subheadings:

- Health and Safety—Legislation;
- Health and Safety—Dynamic assessment.

You will also find health and safety addressed during the IPLDP Induction Module IND 5 'Ensure your own actions reduce the risks to health and safety'.

6.7.1   The Employer's Role in Health and Safety

Section 2(2) of the Health and Safety at Work etc Act (HSWA) 1974 sets out the role of employers in relation to the health and safety of their employees, and states that employers are responsible for:

- providing and maintaining plant and systems of work that are, so far as is reasonably practicable, safe, and without risks to health;
- making safe arrangements for the use, handling, storage, and transport of articles and substances;
- providing necessary information, instruction, training, and supervision for ensuring, so far as is reasonably practicable, the health and safety at work of employees;
- maintaining places of work under the employer's control in a condition which is safe and free from health risks, with safe means of entry and exit;
- providing and maintaining a working environment for employees that is, so far as is reasonably practicable, safe, without risks to health, and has adequate facilities for their welfare at work.

(Adapted from the Home Office publication *A Guide for Police Managers*, 1997)

6.7.2   The Employee's Role in Health and Safety

Health and safety legislation places general duties on employees while they are at work. It requires an employee:

- to take reasonable care for their own health and safety and that of other persons who might be affected by his or her acts or omissions (s 7(a));
- to cooperate with his or her employer to enable the employer to comply with statutory duties for health and safety (s 7(b));
- to use correctly all work items provided by his or her employer, in accordance with his or her training and instructions received (Reg 14(1) Management of Health and Safety etc Work Regulations 1999);
- to inform their employer, or the person responsible for health and safety, of any work situation which might present a serious and imminent danger and any shortcoming in the health and safety arrangements (Reg 14(2) Management of Health and Safety etc Work Regulations 1999).

(Adapted from the Home Office publication *A Guide for Police Managers*, 1997)

6.7.3   Hazards, Risks, and Threat Level

Consider the potential threats to the health and safety of a student police officer on foot patrol. You have probably thought of several scenarios in which the student police officer could be harmed. But how much harm, and how likely is it to happen? This is a matter of judgement for each different situation, but it makes it easier to judge if you think of each type of harm in terms of the **hazard**, the **risk**, and the **threat level**.

A **hazard** is something with a potential to cause harm, for example:

- Slipping over on a wet surface;
- Being hit by moving traffic;
- Seizing drugs and used needles;
- Falling from a height;
- Being hit by a meteorite;
- Being in proximity to a person with an infectious disease.

The **risk** is the likelihood of such an event actually happening. You might have already thought that some hazards are more likely to happen than others and that the likelihood of such events needs to be taken into account when assessing the overall threat of an activity.

The **threat level** (sometimes referred to as overall risk) is a combination of the hazard and the risk. (Note the possibility of confusing risk and overall risk. You will find the word risk may be used in these two different ways, and you will need to seek clarification from someone using the term risk if the context does not make their meaning clear.)

Some examples will help you see the interaction between hazard, risk, and threat level.

1. Death by meteorite—the hazard is very high as meteorites are heavy and fall from the sky at high speeds. But the risk is low as this event is very unlikely to occur. So the threat level is low.
2. Bruising from arresting a drunken suspect—the hazard is minor. However, the risk is high as this is quite likely to occur. But the threat level is low as the consequences are unlikely to be serious.
3. Gunshot wounds when pursuing armed suspects—the hazard is serious, and there is quite a high risk of shots being fired. In this situation the threat level is high (and special precautions should be taken).

So there are varying levels of hazard and risk; each may be formally rated as high, medium, or low. The combined effect of the hazard and risk is the threat level.

6.7.4 Hazard Criteria

Remember, the hazard level is about how serious the consequences would be if the event occurs. The formal levels of hazard level classification are:

- High   Death, major injury, or serious illness may result;
- Medium   Serious injuries or ill health; off work for more than three days;
- Low   Less serious illness or injury; off work for less than three days.

6.7.5 Risk Criteria

The risk level is about how likely it is to occur, and the levels are described as follows:

- High   It is very likely or near certain to occur;
- Medium   It is likely to occur;
- Low   It is very unlikely to occur.

6.7.6 Threat-Level Grid

The level of hazard and risk both need to be taken into account when assessing the threat level. The grid below shows different combinations of hazard and risk, and the resulting threat levels.

THREAT LEVEL		HAZARD		
		High	Medium	Low
RISK	High	INTOLERABLE **high** threat level	SUBSTANTIAL **high** threat level	MODERATE **medium** threat level
	Medium	SUBSTANTIAL **high** threat level	MODERATE **medium** threat level	ACCEPTABLE **low** threat level
	Low	MODERATE **medium** threat level	ACCEPTABLE **low** threat level	TRIVIAL **low** threat level

(Adapted from the Home Office, 1997)

Another way of looking at assessing the threat level is to multiply the hazard and risk in an equation: **hazard × risk = threat level**.

(For those of you who are more mathematically minded, this is not the conventional kind of formula—after all there are no numbers to put into the formula—it is just a way of helping you to remember the relationship.)

This shows clearly that it is the **combination** of hazard and risk that determines the threat level.

Consider another example. You are on duty at the scene of a road traffic collision. Your colleague is dealing with an injured person in one of the vehicles and you are directing the traffic.

Hazards	You could be struck by a motor vehicle and your colleague could also be hit whilst attending to the injured person, therefore the hazard level is high, as death or major injury is likely to occur if another vehicle collides with you or your colleague.
Risk	Take into account day or night time, volume of traffic, weather conditions, and location. The risk level is medium as it is likely or possible that you might be struck by a vehicle.
Threat level	The threat level is therefore assessed as substantial.

6.7.7 Control Measures

Control measures are steps that you can take to lower the risk and therefore reduce the threat level. You could use a five-step approach to assess the threat level and the control measures required.

Threat level assessment

Step 1   Identify the hazards.
Step 2   Who may be harmed and how?
Step 3   Evaluate the risks.
Step 4   Record your findings.
Step 5   Review your assessment from time to time and revise it if necessary.

Let us consider foot patrol in further detail and make an assessment of the risks involved so that we can put control measures into place to lower the threat level.

Threat-level assessment example

Step 1

Identify the hazards

Whilst you use the road network as a pedestrian you are exposed to danger from moving vehicles.
Whilst moving about on foot you face unpredictable confrontation with members of the public.

Step 2

Who may be harmed and how?

You, a colleague, or a member of the public.
A moving vehicle or a weapon used by a member of the public could cause death or major injury.
Therefore the hazard level would be **high**.

Step 3

Evaluate the risks

Your up-to-the minute location is not always known and you are sometimes alone, as a result of which harm is possible/likely to occur.
You are always at risk of walking into an unexpected situation in which harm is possible/likely to occur.
You may face radio communication, reception, and transmission difficulties, or faulty systems as a result of which harm is possible/likely to occur.
Therefore the risk potential is **medium** as there is a likely or possible risk that harm would occur.

Step 4

Record your findings

Using the threat level grid, the threat level is assessed as **substantial** and therefore you should use control measures to lower the threat level.

Step 5

Review your assessment from time to time, and revise it if necessary.

What control measures could be used to lower the threat level?

You may have considered the following:

- in relation to the road network, adopting the correct procedures that you have been trained in, wearing the correct personal protective equipment (fluorescent), and using your first aid training if required;
- applying what you have learnt: control and restraint techniques, firearms training and knife awareness, and using personal protection equipment;
- keeping the Control Room updated with your location;
- using your local knowledge and requesting all available information to assess situations;
- being aware of the limitations of communications equipment.

TASK 4

We are not always good at judging risk. As an exercise, arrange the following risks in order of likelihood, putting the most likely first. They are given to you in a random order.

The likelihood of death in the next year for the average person in the UK:
- by falling down stairs;
- through being struck by lightning;
- in an aircraft crash;
- in a train crash;
- in a cycling accident;
- as the victim of homicide;
- by drowning in a bath;
- as a consequence of lung cancer.

(Adapted from Haigh, 2006)

TASK 5

You are carrying out a search of a person (under s 1 of the PACE Act 1984: see 7.5 below). What are your considerations in relation to your own and your colleagues' safety whilst carrying out this search? What is your estimation of the threat level and what may be required to lower this level?

Completion of Task 5 will assist you in preparing to meet NOS standard AF1.1 'Identify the hazards and evaluate the risks in the workplace'. In turn, this links with PAC heading 'Safety First' and the checklist sub-headings 'Health and Safety—Legislation' and 'Health and Safety—Dynamic assessment'.

6.8 First Aid Training

It is the duty of every police officer to 'protect life' (see 6.13 below). Inevitably you will find yourself attending accidents or scenes of crimes where there are seriously injured people. You may also be called upon by members of the public to assist in helping family members, friends, or strangers who are suffering medical conditions ranging from a sprained ankle or scalding by hot water through to heart attacks or epileptic seizures. The public will expect you to know what to do. Although you can expect specialized medical personnel to be present (or on their way) on most occasions, you will almost certainly encounter situations where not only are you the 'first officer on the scene' but also the first person on the scene with any kind of training for dealing with emergencies.

It is for this reason that, during the induction phase of your training, you will receive instruction in how to administer basic first aid. Your training is likely to be based around the NPIA programme 'First Aid Skills for Policing (FASP) Module 2—First Aid Skills'. It is also likely that you will be assessed against NOS Unit 4G4 ('Administer First Aid') which has four elements:

Elements of Unit 4G4—Administer First Aid

4G4.1   Respond to the needs of casualties with minor injuries
4G4.2   Respond to the needs of casualties with major injuries
4G4.3   Respond to the needs of unconscious casualties
4G4.4   Perform cardio-pulmonary resuscitation (CPR)

Skills for Justice inform us that that the unit has been 'imported' from the Royal Marines Public Services NOS (Unit 4) and was developed by the British Red Cross in consultation with the St John Ambulance Service.

Note however, that after 2010 (as part of the reform of the NOS Units—see 1.5 and 3.6 above) it is likely that Unit 4G4 will no longer be used to assess your ability to administer first aid.

First Aid is also one of the headings in the Police Action Checklist and hence the successful completion of first aid training is likely to be a necessary condition of achieving Independent Patrol (see 3.3 above). Your first aid training is likely to contain some or all of the following:

- **managing scenes and casualties:** for example, assessing the extent of casualties, communicating with others;
- **Basic Life Support (BLS) for Adults:** an algorithm of actions to administer immediate life support including the need first to ensure the safety of yourself and others, to check for a response from the injured person, the actions required in the event of a response or no response, the checking of airways and breathing, and actions in the event of breathing (eg recovery position) and no breathing (eg chest compression, rescue breaths), performing cardio-pulmonary resuscitation (CPR);
- **Basic Life Support (BLS) for Infants and Children:** variations on the system used for adults;

- **specific critical medical conditions:** this may include shock, bleeding, spinal injuries, heart attacks, and epilepsy;
- **choking:** techniques employed to counter choking;
- **sprains, strains, and fractures:** dealing with broken bones and similar injuries;
- **scalds and burns:** methods of dealing with possibly life-threatening injuries in the short term before more specialist medical treatment can be obtained;
- **hypothermia, frostbite, heatstroke, and heat exhaustion:** ways to treat potentially difficult medical conditions, especially when the individuals concerned are vulnerable.

Most police forces also expect their student police officers to maintain their level of first aid training after the completion of the initial probationary period. Typically, this involves a 'refresher course' every three years or so. If after confirmation you assume a specialist role, you may be required to undertake more specialist first aid training, such as Kent Police's Tactical Emergency Aid Medical Support (TEAMS) First Aid Skills.

> **TASK 6**
>
> Read and reflect on the contents of Chapter 10 ('First Aid') of the 1999 Macpherson Inquiry into the death of Stephen Lawrence. It is freely available on the internet at:
> <http://www.archive.official-documents.co.uk/document/cm42/4262/sli-10.htm>.

Undertaking this task may provide you with stimulus material for completing an entry in your Learning Diary, Phase 1 under the 'Health and Safety' heading.

6.9 Personal Safety Training

Police officers are permitted to use reasonable force if necessary to prevent crime or to arrest a person. This right exists under common law and s 3 of the Criminal Law Act 1967. Section 117 of the PACE Act 1984 also allows a police officer to use reasonable force to exercise powers granted by that Act. You may also use reasonable force in your own self-defence (see *R v McInnes* [1971] 1 WLR 1600 (CA)). However, in all cases the force used must be **proportionate** and exercised with due regard to the human rights of the individuals concerned.

You will receive practical training in both protecting yourself and others from attack and also how to use reasonable force against others. In most police forces this is referred to as Personal Safety Training (PST) or the Personal Safety Programme although you might also hear reference to Officer Safety Training (OST). (One reason why PST is now preferred as a title is that the training, or at least parts of it, is also undertaken by some members of the extended police family: see 5.19 above.) Alternatively, your force may have contracted with NPIA to enable it to deliver the 'Personal Safety—Basic Course' (PSMB). In all cases, the relevant NOS element is GC10.2, to 'use personal safety skills and equipment'. The training you receive will take place in specialist facilities and will probably last for five to ten days.

As further reading, you might like to consult the ACPO Centrex 'Personal Safety Manual' and the ACPO 'Guidelines on the use of Handcuffs and Incapacitant Spray' available from your force.

These are the typical components of PST:

- **conflict management:** for example, typical signs of potential conflict;
- **searching people and places:** for example, health and safety when searching people with hidden weapons;
- **protective equipment:** for example, body armour, baton, and 'less lethal weaponry' such as the Tazer;
- **use of handcuffs and limb restraints:** for example, the use of the 'Speedcuff' rigid handcuffs and leg restraints;
- **'unarmed' skills of self-protection:** for example, 'distraction strikes';
- **particular considerations when attending scenes:** for example, possible actions to be taken in the event of trying to help someone experiencing problems in water;

- **edged weapon skills:** for example, the appropriate responses to those carrying edged weapons such as knives;
- **incapacitant sprays:** for example, the use of PAVA (Captor spray);
- **use of batons and ASPs:** for example, the use of the 21-inch expandable baton (the ASP) and the Arnold baton.

Successful completion of PST is a target within the PAC (under the 'Safety First' heading) and hence has to be achieved before Independent Patrol. Indeed, your force will probably expect you successfully to complete your PST before your first Supervised Patrol and, in many cases, before your community engagement.

TASK 7

Your police force will have officers trained in the use of equipment used to protect against a CBRN (Chemical, Biological, Radiological, or Nuclear) incident. What is the standard CBRN personal protective equipment used by police officers in the UK?

6.10 Operating IT Systems

Throughout your training you will be expected to operate IT systems on both a general level (such as basic word-processing tasks and sending emails) and in specific police-related ways such as communicating with the Police National Computer (PNC) and using your own force information systems. Some police forces encourage their staff to take advantage of schemes such as the European Computer Driving Licence (ECDL). It is likely that you already have many generic IT skills, gained before joining the police service. You should certainly consider having a PC with internet connection at home; it is likely to be a good investment in terms of your future training and career development.

Check that you know how to do at least the following with your own preferred operating system (Windows XP or Vista, Mac OS X, Linux, or other):

- search the internet;
- create folders;
- manage files (eg naming, saving, and retrieving files);
- word-process documents;
- print documents;
- use presentational software (such as MS Powerpoint);
- send and receive emails.

We put 'search the internet' first because once you are able to do this you will find numerous internet sites that will help you with the other basic IT skills.

The ability to use 'force information management systems' is one of the requirements of the PAC under the 'Information Management' heading.

6.10.1 The PNC

You are likely to be given training on the use of the Police National Computer (PNC) at a relatively early stage in your training. In IPLDP language, use of the PNC is part of LPG 1. The ability to utilize PNC is also listed under the 'Information Management' heading of the PAC. Hence you will need to demonstrate this ability before you can undertake Independent Patrol.

The PNC is a large database containing information on, amongst other things, people (for example, those with criminal records), vehicles, and property. The police service is not the only agency to access the PNC—it is also used by other agencies such as the Crown Courts (for checking potential jurors) and the Forensic Science Service. You will normally use the PNC to establish important information, such as checking that a driver is not disqualified from driving or assessing the potential for the behaviour of a particular suspect to be problematic. However, the PNC can do more than perform these relatively simple checks. You can also use the PNC to search for more 'fuzzy' information such as nicknames used by offenders, tattoos, scars, hair colour, and similar distinguishing features (try Task 8).

During your training you will be instructed in how to use the PNC. You will normally access the PNC by contacting an operator based at the Force Control Room using your radio. You will need to master the routine; this involves following a particular sequence of requests made to the operator. For example, you will probably be taught that you first specify your request (eg a vehicle check) then give your name and force number, and then the reason for the check, and so on. You will often need to use the phonetic alphabet to spell out words to ensure there is no mistake in transmitting the information (see 6.3 above). Always make a note in your pocket notebook of the details of the checks you have carried out so that your work is auditable (see 8.3 below).

What is sure to be emphasized during your training is the requirement to access the PNC in a responsible and professional manner. Inappropriate use of the PNC is viewed by police forces as a serious matter and could well lead to the dismissal of a student police officer found to be abusing the system. (Not only is it a contravention of the PNC code of practice; it is also against the law.) Unfortunately, examples of inappropriate use are only too easy to find. In the past these have included:

- checking on a daughter's new boyfriend (Wadham, 2004);
- accessing information about 'soap stars' to sell to the red-top press (*Guardian*, 2005);
- selling information to private investigators (Wadham, 2004).

Alleged misuse of the PNC can be the subject of an IPCC inquiry (see 6.16 below).

TASK 8

1. What are VODS and QUEST? (You may need to use the internet or ask more experienced colleagues to answer this question.)
2. The HMIC is carrying out PNC-compliance inspections of police forces. These may be viewed via the HMIC <http://inspectorates.homeoffice.gov.uk/hmic> internet site. Check whether your force has yet been inspected. If so, read the report. If not, read one from your Most Similar Force (MSF) comparator.

6.11 Confidentiality, Management of Police Information, and Freedom of Information

Here we examine the need both to protect the confidentiality of information or data, and to share some information under the requirements of the Freedom of Information Act 2000.

6.11.1 Confidentiality

During your training and in your subsequent career as a police officer, you will frequently encounter information of a sensitive and confidential nature. It is probably obvious but you are expected to maintain the confidentiality of the information you access. Individual force policies may also make reference to the Data Protection Act 1998 and perhaps to the Human Rights Act 1998 (particularly those sections relevant to the right to privacy). Confidentiality is one of the Standards of Professional Behaviour (as described in the Police (Conduct) Regulations 2008: see 6.14 below). You are expected to 'treat information with respect and access or disclose it only in the proper course of police duties'.

Your respect for confidentiality can be evidenced through achievement of NOS element AB1.2 'to maintain the security of information'. To meet this element of the standard, you need to:

1. Comply with relevant legislation, policies, and procedures related to the security of information.

2. Disclose information only to those who have the right and need to know it.
3. Take the appropriate precautions when communicating confidential or sensitive information.
4. Maintain the security of records when handling and storing them.
5. Alert the appropriate person when you think the security of information is not being maintained or information is being misused.

(Skills for Justice, 2007d)

Your main source of evidence for meeting element AB1.2 is likely to come from your Supervised Patrol in the workplace. The evidence could take the form of artefacts such as records, or direct observation by your assessor (normally your tutor constable) or witness statements. It is very unlikely that simulations in a classroom environment would meet the requirements for element AB1.2.

6.11.2 Management of Police Information (MoPI)

How the police collect, record, share, and retain information has been the subject of some controversy in recent years, most notably as a result of the inquiry into the circumstances surrounding the murders at Soham and the subsequent police investigations (see Bichard, 2004). As a result a new Police National Database (PND) is expected to begin deployment in 2010 which will enable police forces to share intelligence better. The PND will enable one police force to check on what information or intelligence is held on an individual (a 'nominal') by another police force.

A statutory Code of Practice on the Management of Police Information was published in 2005 (followed by Guidance in 2006) and sets out the basic principles that police organizations should adopt for the collection, recording, sharing, and retaining of information that is relevant to their usual work. At the level of the individual police officer, this information may take the form of intelligence and evidence gathering, details concerning domestic crime, search form completion, and pocket note book entries.

Further, the Human Rights Act 1998 (see 5.12 above) requires all UK legislation to be matched with the European Convention on Human Rights. Any act by a public authority, such as the police, that contravenes the rights of the Convention will be unlawful. An individual's rights to privacy and family life (Article 8) can be 'interfered' with by the collection of personal information, and this interference is only permitted under certain circumstances (see 5.12.2.3 above).

Further constraints are placed upon holding personal data by the Data Protection Act 1998. The Act defines personal data as any information which can identify a living person from the data. However, when data is used for the prevention or detection of crime, or the apprehension or prosecution of offenders, exemptions are permitted.

Finally, ACPO have also published their own Manual of Guidance on Data Protection (2006) with a greater level of detail than provided by the Code.

The Code, the Human Rights Act 1998, the Data Protection Act 1998, and ACPO's Manual all mean that there is an obligation to manage police information in ways that are both effective and which meet certain ethical and professional standards. Many of these obligations are at the level of the organization rather than the individual and manifest themselves in the form of standing orders, policies, strategies (the force 'Information Management Strategy'), and similar instruments. However, the principles involved also apply at all levels of police staff, regardless of rank or role and are likely to feature in your training. For example, there is the need to ensure that the information that you record is necessary (it is for policing purposes), accurate (check your facts), adequate (you do not omit important information), relevant (address the facts, record opinions only if necessary, and clearly mark as such), and timely (make the entry as soon as possible).

6.11.3 Freedom of Information

The Freedom of Information Act 2000 (FoI) gives a general right of access to all types of recorded information held by public authorities. Police forces are included under the definition of public authorities. (By contrast, ACPO, as a private company, is not.) Your force will publish, normally on the internet, details concerning the public's right under the FoI to access recorded information kept by the force, and the process that needs to be followed to receive that information. The force will also have a publication scheme that, amongst other details, describes what information is available as a matter of routine. This avoids the need for repeated requests to be made for the same information. Not all requests for information will be successful—there are obvious exceptions, for example, requests that relate to matters such as the identity of a CHIS. However, it is important to note that the right to information is the **norm** rather than the exception. Requests can be made, and are made, on all kinds of subjects. For example, we learn from a FoI request to Sussex Police the rather unremarkable fact that the Chief Constable's expenses included £4.99 for a car wash on 6 December 2004 (Sussex Police, 2006).

There are two main ways that the FoI might directly affect you. Firstly, you may personally receive a request for information under the FoI, perhaps in the form of a letter addressed to you or by email. (Many people will know, for example, that your work email is likely to be of the form x.y@force.pnn.police.uk where x is your first name, y is your surname and 'force' is a shortened version of the name of your force, for example btp.) In this case you should not respond yourself but should promptly pass the request to the person designated as responsible for FoI requests in your force.

Secondly, and put simply, you should be aware at all times that if you are recording information as a police officer then somebody, some day, may apply under the FoI to view the record you have made. Unless there are very good reasons not to, this will be permitted, so choose your words accurately and carefully.

6.12 Attestation

Attestation is the stage at which a student police officer is formally given the powers of a police constable—for example, he or she is able to arrest somebody according to the law and Codes of practice. The legal detail is set out in Sch 4 to the Police Act 1996, as substituted by s 83 of the Police Reform Act 2002. Attestation often coincides with the issuing of a warrant card, although practice may vary from force to force (some forces instead issue a form of 'trainee police officer identity card' at attestation). In many police organizations, attestation happens early on in a student officer's career—sometimes on initial appointment and certainly within the first few weeks.

Compared to other professional groups, this is an unusual and perhaps anomalous position. It is as if a trainee doctor were given a right to treat patients after a few weeks' training even though they still had almost five years of study and practice to complete. The position and timing of attestation remains under review, partly as a result of the HMIC thematic inspection report 'Training Matters', the recommendations of the Morris Inquiry, and the Commission for Racial Equality report into police training (Morris, 2004).

You also begin your training on one of the highest initial wages for an unqualified public sector professional. For example, nurses start their training on a bursary of about £6,530 per annum, less than a third of your starting wage. (They also have to pass their training **before** they can undertake full-time work.) Again, it seems inevitable, at a time when police forces have assumed greater responsibility for their own training, that the employment status and pay of student police officers is likely to be reviewed.

At attestation you will make a formal declaration. This is described in 6.15.1 below.

6.13 The Role of the Constable

After attestation (see 6.12 above) you will hold the office of probationary **constable**, with your position being confirmed after about two calendar years. The origins of the office of constable within law enforcement in the UK can be traced back hundreds of years, although many commentators consider the most significant starting point for the modern-day police service as the year 1829 (see 1.3 above).

In recent years, constables have become just one of many members of the extended police family; they no longer have a monopoly on certain traditional policing powers. They nonetheless continue to hold a special position within a police organization, as you will discover when working through this chapter and those that follow. This privilege brings additional responsibilities to the role of constable, particularly in terms of attitudes, values, and professional knowledge. Many of the NOS elements for initial policing are concerned with the need for you to demonstrate the appropriate attitudes and values, and, by extension, to have gained the appropriate underpinning skills and knowledge.

For example, you are likely to be required to achieve the following NOS elements before confirmation as a constable:

National Occupational Standard Unit and Elements

AA1.1   Promote equality and value diversity
AB1.2   Maintain the security of information
AE1.1   Maintain and develop your own knowledge, skills, and competence
CA1.3   Use law enforcement actions fairly

Similarly, one of the Induction Modules of the IPLDP is concerned with the 'Underpinning Ethics/Values of the Police Service' (IND 1).

There has been much discussion about the possible effects of an individual's personal beliefs and values, and the manner in which these are expressed in their day-to-day actions and decisions. Student police officers may sometimes say (somewhat defensively) that they are 'entitled to their opinions' with the implication that their attitudes have no bearing on their actions, even if their personal opinions were to be at odds with their actual behaviour. This is obviously an important question for those engaged in police training and education, and is addressed on occasions in other parts of this Handbook. However, here we are concerned with how your own professional development as a student police officer (and your progress to confirmation as constable) links up with the wider common purpose and values of the police service.

We noted in 5.3 above that the existence of a code of professional conduct was a common feature of the professions. The Police Service Statement of Common Purpose and Values was first issued by ACPO in 1990 and is reflected today, almost word for word, in most police forces' own statements. It is a relatively consistent declaration of the guiding principles of the police service, and all police officers, including student police officers, are required to work towards the achievement of this statement.

According to this statement, the purpose of the police service is to:

… *uphold the law firmly and fairly* …	neither too weak or too aggressive, and with no bias
… *prevent crime* …	not to let it happen if it can be stopped first
… *pursue and bring to justice those who break the law* …	and hence we need to understand the requirements of the criminal justice system
… *keep the Queen's peace* …	not to allow public disorder and criminality to occur unchallenged
… *protect, help and reassure the community* …	that is, all our communities and not just those that appear to support the police or those that we *belong to*

We have already referred to *The Secret Policeman* documentary, first screened on BBC television in October 2003. An undercover journalist, Mark Daly, joined Greater Manchester Police as a student police officer and then spent 15 weeks in training at the Bruche Centrex regional Police Training Centre, near Warrington. During his time at Bruche, Daly secretly filmed some of the behaviour of his fellow students and the trainers delivering the course. He uncovered evidence of racist language and attitudes amongst some of his fellow student police officers and inappropriate behaviour by some of his trainers. However, as Daly himself noted in 2003:

> The majority of the officers I met will undoubtedly turn out to be good, non-prejudiced ones intent on doing the job properly. But the next generation of officers from one of Britain's top police colleges contains a significant minority of people who are holding the progress of the police service back (Daly, 2003).

Examples of inappropriate behaviour by some student police officers at Bruche included:

- use of offensive racist terms to describe members of ethnic minorities, including unsubstantiated slurs on the character of the family of murdered black teenager Stephen Lawrence;
- donning an imitation Ku Klux Klan hood and threatening to knock on the door of a fellow student police officer of British Asian heritage;
- claims that they used police powers in a discriminating way against ethnic minorities.

One NPIA (at the time, Centrex) police trainer was also secretly filmed expressing his happiness to his group of students that the single British Asian heritage police recruit had been re-coursed (required to retake certain aspects of his training), although there was no suggestion that this was as a result of racism.

TASK 9

Now take a moment to consider why the Police Service Statement of Common Purpose and Values is important to you as a student police officer.

Write up your reflections so that they can be used as evidence for your SOLAP—for example, as evidence cross-referring to the knowledge requirement of your Cumulative Assessment Record (CAR) for element AE1.1. Your reflections could also feature in your Learning Diary, under the heading 'Police Policies & Procedures'.

6.14 Standards of Professional Behaviour

Much of your time as a student police officer will involve direct contact with both the public and fellow members of the extended policing family (for example, police community support officers). Many of the NOS elements for initial policing are concerned with the nature and quality of these interactions.

Attested police officers are not employees in the conventional meaning of the term; instead they are **holders of public office**. One consequence is that the activities of student police officers, both on and off duty, are regulated by law and contained in Statutory Instruments (see 5.11.1.5 above). For this reason, references to complaints, and misconduct, as well as a number of restrictions and expectations are contained in Police Acts and the Police Regulations.

Whether the person you encounter is a victim, suspect, work colleague, partner, relative, friend, or any other member of the community, they all have expectations of you in terms of your conduct and integrity. If these expectations are reasonable but are not met then the consequences can be damaging for both the individuals concerned and for the reputation and standing of the police service as a whole. There may be accusations of double standards and a breakdown in the ability to police by consent. This is discussed in further detail in Chapter 5.

For this reason, all police officers have Standards of Professional Behaviour or ethics that they must work towards, and these are outlined below in 6.14.1. We noted in 5.5 above that the Standards of Professional Behaviour form an integral part of your personal moral authority as a trainee police officer, and also relate directly to the following NOS elements:

National Occupational Standard Elements

AA1.1   Promote equality and value diversity
AB1.2   Maintain the security of information
AE1.1   Maintain and develop your own knowledge, skills, and competence
CA1.1   Apply principles of reasonable suspicion or belief
CA1.2   Use law enforcement actions proportionately
CA1.3   Use law enforcement actions fairly

The material covered here is likely to be relevant to Phase 3 of the IPLDP and the Induction Module IND 1: 'Underpinning Ethics/Values of the Police Service'.

The legal standing of the Standards is complex and links in turn with other Police Regulations. A number of texts, including *Blackstone's Police Manual: Volume 4 General Police Duties* consider this in more detail. Note that there is also a European Code of Police Ethics (see 5.4 above).

TASK 10

Write down examples of the kinds of conduct the public should expect from police officers. Compare your answers to the standards outlined in 6.14.1 below.

6.14.1   Standards of Professional Behaviour

The Standards of Professional Behaviour are the minimum standards you must maintain both as a student police officer and as a confirmed police officer. They are contained within the Police (Conduct) Regulations 2008 (see 5.4.2 above). The ten Standards of Professional Behaviour are as follows:

1. Honesty and Integrity

Police officers are honest, act with integrity and do not compromise or abuse their position.

You must never for example:

- knowingly write down anything which is false in your pocket note book, duty statement, or during any declaration whilst off duty;
- accept any gift from a member of the public in acknowledgement for your services. It may be that you are offered light refreshment whilst on duty in which case consider whether your impartiality remains intact;
- use your position to obtain discount or free entry to paid events or premises. However, your organization may well have a recreation association, and as a member you may well receive offers which have been approved.

2. Authority, Respect, and Courtesy

Police officers act with self-control and tolerance, treating members of the public and colleagues with respect and courtesy. Police Officers do not abuse their power or authority and respect the rights of all individuals.

You must never for example:

- use degrading or offensive language to members of the public or your colleagues;
- use your position to abuse, threaten, or cause harassment, alarm, or distress to anyone unless you are empowered by the law in England and Wales;
- mistreat or disrespect individual rights thereby disregarding the PACE Codes of Practice and The Human Rights Act.

3. Equality and Diversity

Police officers act with fairness and impartiality. They do not discriminate unlawfully or unfairly.

You must never for example:

- discriminate against a person or group of people on the grounds of their race, disability, background, ethnicity, or sexual orientation whether on or off duty;
- show favouritism towards a particular group.

4. Use of Force

Police officers only use force to the extent that it is necessary, proportionate, and reasonable in all the circumstances.

You must never for example:

- exceed the use of reasonable force in the prevention or detection of crime or for your own self-defence;
- use any force whilst off duty unless you are lawfully empowered to do so by common law or the Criminal Law Act 1976.

5. Orders and Instructions

Police officers only give and carry out lawful orders and instructions. Police officers abide by police regulations, force policies, and lawful orders.

You must never for example:

- disobey a lawful order given to you by one of your supervisors or managers;
- disregard your own organizational policies;
- ignore the Standards of Professional Behaviour.

6. Duties and Responsibilities

Police officers are diligent in the exercise of their duties and responsibilities.

You must never for example:

- overlook the investigation of criminal offences you have identified;
- fail to get involved in any matter which requires the intervention of a police officer;
- submit case files late or incomplete.

7. Confidentiality

Police officers treat information with respect and access or disclose it only in the proper course of police duties.

You must never for example:

- disclose information to anybody unless they are authorized to receive it;
- allow restricted information to be revealed as a result of leaving it insecure;
- use information that you have discovered during your duties for personal benefit.

8. Fitness for Duty

Police officers when on duty or presenting themselves for duty are fit to carry out their responsibilities.

You must never for example:

- purposefully make yourself so drunk before going to work that you cannot perform your duty;
- neglect your own health by disregarding the advice of medical practitioners;
- leave an injury or an illness without seeking medical attention;
- take part in activities likely to retard your return to duty if absent through sickness or injury.

9. Discreditable Conduct

Police officers will behave in a manner which does not discredit the police service or undermine public confidence, whether on or off duty. Police officers report any action taken against them for a criminal offence, any conditions imposed on them by a court, or the receipt of any penalty notice.

You must never for example:

- fail to disclose a criminal conviction;
- consume alcohol whilst on duty unless authorized to do so;
- wear your uniform in such a way that it brings discredit to your organization;
- intentionally leave personal safety equipment or any other articles belonging to your organization to get lost.

10. Challenging and Reporting Improper Conduct

Police officers report, challenge, or take action against the conduct of colleagues which has fallen below the Standards of Professional Behaviour.

You must never for example:

- disregard the actions of your colleagues if they are being discriminatory;
- endorse harassing or victimizing behaviour without making a challenge.

Note that the Police Service of Northern Ireland (PSNI) has its own Standards of Professional Behaviour.

TASK 11

Ask yourself why the public has the right to expect police officers to behave in an ethical way and what the consequences are if their expectations are not met.

TASK 12

In January 2005, an off-duty police officer from South Wales Police was suspended from duty after allegedly taking a police car without permission, subsequently crashing the car, and then testing positive for alcohol.

Take a moment to consider and then list which Standards of Professional Behaviour may have been breached during the alleged incidents. What are the consequences of this neglect for both the individual concerned and the police service as a whole?

Your written reflections may be relevant to the knowledge requirements of the 'Underpinning Ethics/Values of the Police Service' sections of your SOLAP.

Adherence to the code can also be evidenced, at least in part, through the achievement of the appropriate NOS. For example, the need to ensure fairness and impartiality can be evidenced through achievement of Unit CA1 'Use law enforcement actions in a fair and justified way' and the three elements CA1.1 'Apply principles of reasonable suspicion or belief', CA1.2 'Use law enforcement actions proportionately', and CA1.3 'Use law enforcement actions fairly'.

TASK 13

Consider standards 2, 3, 4, and 7 of the Standards of Professional Behaviour (see above), and list the element of the NOS Unit that is most relevant. Give some thought to how you are likely to able to produce evidence that you have met these elements. Bear in mind that evidence usually takes the form of tangible objects such as written documents to which you cross-refer in the relevant CAR of your SOLAP and by direct observation and questioning by your assessor (see Chapter 3).

6.15 The Police Regulations and Conditions of Service

In addition to maintaining Standards of Professional Behaviour, your conditions of service are also regulated by law under various Police Regulations contained in Statutory Instruments. Because of their length and complexity these will not be dealt with in their entirety here, but they are presented below in a summarized and simplified form. Full details may be found in other textbooks such as *Blackstone's Police Manual: Volume 4 General Police Duties* and on the internet.

As a student police officer in your probationary period you are not bound by The Police (Performance) Regulations 2008. However, your performance during this time is constantly monitored and any under-achievement may be dealt with under reg 13 (see 6.15.4 below).

At the moment of attestation you become subject to other Police Regulations.

6.15.1   Declaration at Attestation

We described attestation in 6.12 above. The declaration (sometimes referred to as an 'Oath') is as follows:

> I ... of ... do solemnly and sincerely declare and affirm that I will well and truly serve the Queen in the office of constable, with fairness, integrity, diligence, and impartiality, upholding fundamental human rights and according equal respect to all people; and that I will, to the best of my power, cause the peace to be kept and preserved and prevent all offences against people and property; and that while I continue to hold the said office I will, to the best of my skill and knowledge, discharge all the duties thereof faithfully according to law.

There is an alternative Welsh-language version which may be used by student police officers in Dyfed-Powys, Gwent, North Wales, or South Wales. There are also alternatives for police officers in Scotland, Northern Ireland, and for student police officers of BTP.

At attestation, and comparatively early in your training, you will be asked to read out one of the declarations. The making of a declaration may seem somewhat old fashioned. However, it is worth bearing in mind that the declaration you make has a statutory basis in law and its symbolic importance remains strong, both within police culture and in the wider political and social world.

TASK 14

Learn the declaration for your attestation word for word! Note that you will probably be given an *aide mémoire* to read from at actual attestation, or be asked to follow another's lead. However, you are likely to be required to memorize information on a number of occasions during training (for example, definitions) and this task is good practice.

We have added extra explanations to the extracts from the Police Regulations 2003 below.

6.15.2   Restrictions on the Private Life of Members of Police Forces

These are set out in Sch 1 to the Police Regulations 2003 which state that:

> The restrictions on private life ... shall apply to all members of a police force (reg 6(1)).

> A member of a police force shall at all times abstain from any activity which is likely to interfere with the impartial discharge of [his/her] duties or which is likely to give rise to the impression amongst members of the public that it may so interfere; and in particular a member of a police force shall not take any active part in politics (Sch 1, para 1).

In other words, a police officer must not pursue a course of conduct which members of the public will perceive as favouritism and especially must not be active in politics.

> A member of a police force shall not wilfully refuse or neglect to discharge any lawful debt (Sch 1, para 4).

This does not mean to say you cannot have a mortgage or a car loan, but any other debt which could place you in danger of being coerced is unacceptable.

6.15.3   Business Interests Incompatible with Membership of a Police Force

Regulation 7 of the Police Regulations 2003 states that:

> If a member of a police force or a relative included in [his/her] family proposes to have, or has, a business interest within the meaning of this regulation, the member shall forthwith give written notice of that interest to the chief officer unless that business interest was disclosed at the time of [his/her] appointment as a member of the force.

For the purposes of their integrity and credibility, police officers must disclose business interests in order that they may be checked for compatibility with the role of a constable.

> **TASK 15**
>
> What is the procedure used in your force for declaring business interests?

6.15.4   Discharge of a Student Police Officer

The procedure for discharge is set out in reg 13 of the Police Regulations 2003 which states that:

> [s]ubject to the provisions of this regulation, during [his/her] period of probation in the force the services of a constable may be dispensed with at any time if the chief officer considers that [he/she] is not fitted, physically or mentally, to perform the duties of [his/her] office, or that [he/she] is not likely to become an efficient or well-conducted constable.

The first two years of your service are crucial to your confirmation of appointment at the end of that period. However, under the same regulation, before being discharged, you can give notice of retirement (in other words, resign (see also 3.12 above)).

6.15.5   Contents of Personal Records

Regulation 15 of the Police Regulations 2003 states that:

> [t]he chief officer of a police force shall cause a personal record of each member of the police force to be kept.

Throughout your service a personal record will be maintained, containing details of you and your relatives, as well as a history of courses that you have attended, expertise that you have gained, and promotions that you have achieved. It will also contain outcomes of any disciplinary investigations.

6.15.6   Fingerprints

Regulation 18 of the Police Regulations 2003 states that:

> [e]very member of a police force shall in accordance with the directions of the chief officer have [his/her] fingerprints taken.

For the purposes of eliminating you from any forensic investigation, a record of your fingerprints will be kept. Quite often this takes place early on in your training and sometimes as part of your training on forensic awareness.

6.15.7   Samples

Regulation 19 of the Police Regulations 2003 states that:

> [e]very member of a police force, except those members appointed following their transfer from another police force, shall on appointment and in accordance with the directions of the chief officer have a sample taken.

Once again, for the purposes of elimination, each officer will supply a sample, such as a mouth swab for DNA.

6.15.8   Duty to Carry out Lawful Orders

Regulation 20 of the Police Regulations 2003 states that:

> [e]very member of a police force shall carry out all lawful orders and shall at all times punctually and promptly perform all appointed duties and attend to all matters within the scope of [his/her] office as a constable.

The police service has a rank structure in which supervisors and managers may require certain actions to be carried out. It is an expectation that you will carry out these orders, but only if they are lawful.

> **TASK 16**
>
> Take the opportunity to reflect upon these regulations and how you are going to work within them. Which areas do you think are going to be easy for you to satisfy, and which areas do you need to consider at greater length?
>
> The PSNI Code of Ethics, article 1.5 states that:
>
> > [a] police officer should carry out orders properly issued by [his/her] superior, but [he/she] shall refrain from carrying out any order [he/she] knows, or ought to know, is unlawful.
>
> How would you know that an order was unlawful?
>
> This task will support you in preparing to demonstrate NOS element AE1.1 'Maintain and develop your own knowledge, skills, and competence', and particularly the performance criterion that asks you to 'identify your own values, interests, and priorities in relation to the work you are undertaking'.

6.16   Misconduct and Complaints Procedures

Allegations concerning the conduct of a police officer fall into one of two categories: 'complaints' and 'conduct matters'. A complaint about the conduct of a police officer refers to an allegation made by a member of the public. Allegations of misconduct made against a police officer by a colleague (not a member of the public, and not currently or previously the subject of a 'complaint'), are called 'conduct matters'.

Before we look at the details, who is involved in decisions and disciplinary action when complaints and conduct matters are considered? Depending on the severity of the matter, the following may be involved:

- your line manager;
- an 'appropriate authority' which is a police officer of at least the rank of chief inspector, or another police staff member of at least a similar level of seniority to a chief inspector, or the Independent Police Complaints Commission (IPCC): see 6.16.4 below.

There is likely to be an investigation into the allegations. Investigations may involve the IPCC, but there are also local investigations conducted by senior officers (the appropriate authority—see above).

6.16.1   Conduct Matters

Both you and your colleagues are required to abide by the Standards of Professional Behaviour. Failure to do so may make you liable to allegations of misconduct which include:

- committing a criminal offence; or
- behaving in a manner which would justify the bringing of disciplinary proceedings.

In addition, the tenth Standard of Professional Behaviour requires you and your colleagues to report, challenge, or take action against the conduct of any colleague whose behaviour has fallen below any of the other Standards of Professional Behaviour. Failure to do so will render you liable for consideration of misconduct, in addition to those who have breached the standards in the first place. There may be occasions when you witness possible wrongdoings by a colleague. Normally you would report this to your supervisor or your force's Professional Standards Department. However, you can also raise concerns confidentially with the IPCC (see 6.16.4 below) as it is designated as an official body for the purposes of public interest disclosure.

The flowchart summarizes the procedures for handling an allegation relating to 'conduct matters'.

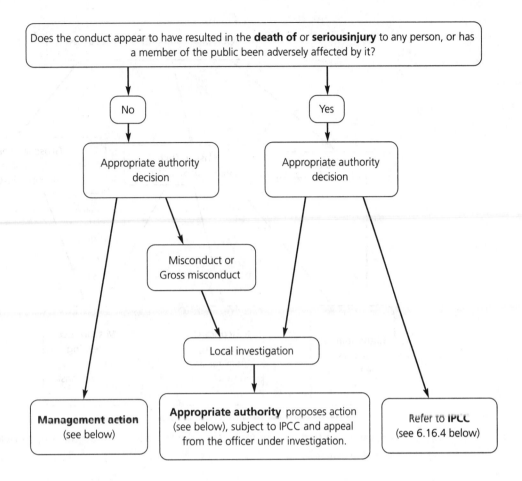

Management action would involve:

- pointing out how the behaviour fell short of the the Standards of Professional Behaviour;
- identifying expectations for future conduct;
- establishing an improvement plan;
- addressing any underlying causes of misconduct.

The appropriate authority may propose action after a local investigation. An investigator will be appointed and the officer under investigation will be notified (reg 15: see 6.16.4.1 below). The investigation will involve interviews and case-file building, and may result in either the case being discontinued or the appropriate authority proposing actions to be taken, subject to IPPC recommendation or direction. The actions that may be proposed by the appropriate authority are shown in the flow chart below.

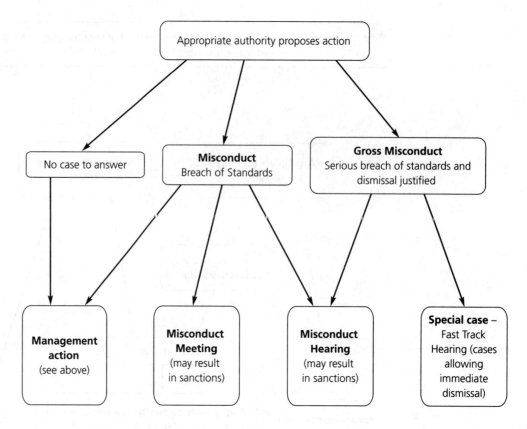

The sanctions that may be applied as a result of a Misconduct Meeting or Hearing are described in 6.16.3 below.

6.16.2   Complaints

External allegations that are made by members of the public concerning the conduct or behaviour of a police officer (student or confirmed) are called complaints. Examples include allegations of rudeness or the use of excessive force and unjustified arrest. When a complaint is made, or a police officer is suspected of misconduct, the process used to deal with the matter is known as the Police Complaints System.

Allegations can only be made by a member of the public who:

(a) claims to be the victim of the conduct
(b) is not the victim but claims to have been adversely affected by the conduct
(c) claims to have witnessed the conduct
(d) is a person who is representing any of the above.

The course of action will be decided by an 'appropriate authority' (defined in 6.16 above). If it appears to the investigator that the police officer subject of the complaint has committed a criminal offence or behaved in such a way that disciplinary proceedings will be required, the investigation will be certified as one subject to 'Special Requirements'. The flowchart below summarizes the process for managing complaints:

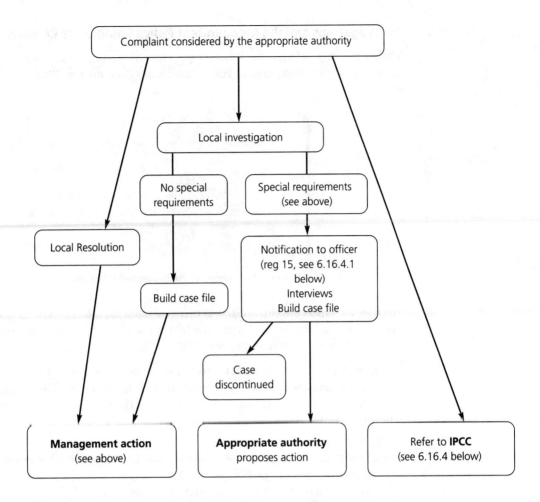

The actions that may be taken by management or the appropriate authority as a result of a complaint are the same as for investigations into conduct matters (see 6.16.1 above), except that the complainant may appeal against any action proposed by the appropriate authority.

6.16.3 Sanctions

There are a variety of sanctions if found guilty after an investigation into 'conduct matters' or complaints.

For less serious breaches at the first level of the Standards of Professional Behaviour, or under-performing, the possible sanctions are:

1. no further action
2. management action
3. written warning
4. final written warning.

For more serious breaches at the second level or when the officer has an existing final written warning the possible sanctions are:

1. 1–4 above
2. dismissal with notice
3. dismissal without notice.

Remember that in addition to the above sanctions your services can be dispensed with at any time as a student police officer under reg 13 of the Police Regulations 2003 (see 6.15.4 above).

6.16.4 Investigations and the Independent Police Complaints Commission

The diagram below shows the different ways in which complaints and matters of misconduct are handled by the Independent Police Complaints Commission (IPCC).

IPCC stands for **Independent Police Complaints Commission**

The diagram tapers towards the top as there are fewer high-level investigations. As you might expect, the more serious the matter, the higher the level of the investigation, and the greater the level of direct involvement by the IPCC.

Beginning with the lowest level, to **dispense or withdraw** means that a police organization is unable to bring about a successful conclusion to the matter, or it is no longer practicable to continue with an investigation. The permission of the IPCC is sought to discontinue for the following reasons:

1. the complainant is uncooperative
2. the complaint or allegation of misconduct is brought about with the intention of annoying, is harsh, or an abuse of procedure
3. the complaint or allegation of misconduct is repetitious
4. a local resolution is agreed.

A **local investigation** is carried out if the complaint or matter is assessed to be of a relatively minor nature, and so a supervisor or manager can investigate it locally. Local informal resolution may be possible; of the many ways of dealing with complaints or allegations, this is often the best outcome for all those involved. Regulation 15 notices (see below) are not required, and there is no blame attached or need to involve disciplinary procedures. The process will not affect a student police officer's personal development plan (usually the SOLAP, then the PDR), staff appraisal, or any subsequent misconduct hearing. Note that a police force cannot make an apology to the complainant unless the officer concerned (the officer against whom the complaint was made) authorizes such an apology.

6.16.4.1 Local police investigation and the regulation 15 notice

If an investigation is necessary, it will be in proportion to the seriousness of the complaint or allegation of misconduct. The investigation is usually carried out by personnel from the Professional Standards Department within your organization, and the complainant has the right of appeal against the decision to the **Independent Police Complaints Commission**.

Regulation 15 of the Police (Conduct) Regulations 2008 outlines the requirement for a notice to be issued to the officer concerned, to safeguard his/her rights and inform him/her that he/she is under investigation. You will hear the notice being referred to in police circles as a 'reg 15' (with a hard 'g'). The notice will be issued as soon as practicable after the investigation begins in order that the officer is better able to recall the incident.

If an officer receives a reg 15 notice, the Police Federation advises him/her not to say anything at that stage and to seek the advice of a Federation representative. If the officer is to be interviewed, once again the advice is to contact a Federation representative who will arrange to attend the interview or, in some circumstances, arrange for legal representation.

6.16.4.2   **Investigations with direct IPCC involvement**

An **IPCC-supervised** investigation is used for complaints or allegations of misconduct which are of considerable significance and probable public concern. The investigation is supervised by an IPCC commissioner but is still conducted, directed, and controlled by the police. The complainant has the right of appeal to the IPCC.

An **IPCC-managed** investigation is used when the alleged incident is more serious and likely to cause higher levels of public concern, and therefore the subsequent investigation must have an independent element. The IPCC direct and control the process, whilst the police conduct the investigation.

An **independent investigation** is used for incidents that cause the greatest level of public concern, or have the greatest potential to impact on communities, or have serious implications for the reputation of the police service. These require a wholly independent investigation conducted in its entirety by IPCC staff. Examples of such incidents include deaths in custody.

There is no right of appeal against an IPCC-managed or independent investigation except through judicial review. This is a form of court proceedings which checks that the correct procedures have been used.

6.17   The Police Federation, the BAWP, the NBPA, and the GPA

When you join the police service as a student police officer you also join the Police Federation. This is automatic. You may decide, additionally, to join one or more of the following organizations: the British Association for Women in Policing (BAWP), the National Black Police Association UK (NBPA), and/or the Gay Police Association (GPA). There are links between the Federation and these other organizations. For example, the BAWP is represented on the Equality Subcommittee of the Police Federation.

6.17.1   The Police Federation

England and Wales have a single Police Federation (s 64(1) of the Police Act 1996, Membership of Trades Unions), as do each of Northern Ireland and Scotland. This part of the Handbook describes the Police Federation of England and Wales, but many of the observations also apply to Scotland and Northern Ireland.

It is important to realize that the Federation is not a trades union in the usual sense of the term. Indeed, as a student police officer (and also when you become a Confirmed constable) you are forbidden to join a trades union:

> Subject to the following provisions of this section, a member of a police force shall not be a member of any trades union, or of any association having for its objects, or one of its objects, to control or influence the pay, pensions or conditions of service of any police force (s 64(1) of the Police Act 1996, Membership of Trades Unions).

The Federation therefore does not have the right to call for any kind of industrial action such as a strike and cannot affiliate itself to the Labour Party or any other political organization.

However, in many other respects the Federation has been established to represent the views of its members (police officers below the rank of superintendent) on local, regional, and national levels in much the same way as any other staff association.

6.17.1.1   Structure of the Police Federation

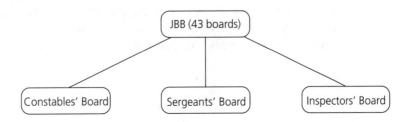

Each of the police forces in England and Wales has a Joint Branch Board (JBB). Within the JBB there are separate boards, representing the interests of constables, sergeants, and inspectors. These are known as, naturally enough, the Constables' Branch Board, the Sergeants' Branch Board, and the Inspectors' Branch Board. These boards each have separate agendas and meetings but also combine to form the force JBB. The JBB represents the views of police officers to the chief constable or commissioner, others in positions of responsibility, and members of the police authority.

The Federation of England and Wales has eight regions, with each region electing representatives to form the national Joint Central Committee. For example, Region No 2 of the Federation consists of the police forces of Cleveland, Durham, Humberside, Northumbria, North Yorkshire, South Yorkshire, and West Yorkshire. The Joint Central Committee is responsible for the national policy of the Federation.

6.17.1.2 Pay, pensions, and allowances

On behalf of its members, the Police Federation negotiates aspects of pay, pensions, and allowances through a National Police Negotiating Board. The board consists of representatives from the Police Federations (England and Wales, Scotland, and Northern Ireland), the Superintendents' Association, and ACPO. These meet with representatives of the government ministers responsible for the police: the Home Secretary, the Scottish Secretary, the Northern Ireland Secretary, and representatives of the local authorities and magistrates.

The Police Negotiating Board has an independent chairperson (appointed by the Prime Minister).

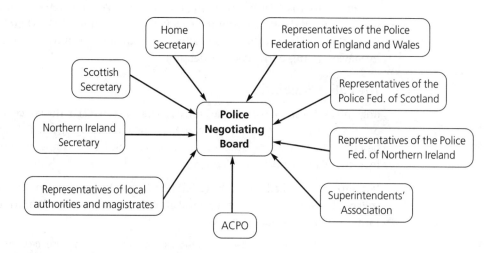

6.17.1.3 Training, promotion, and discipline

Under the chairmanship of the Home Secretary, the Federation is represented on the Police Advisory Board which meets to discuss professional subjects such as training, promotion, and discipline. After taking these discussions into account, the Home Secretary may then make proposals to amend Police Regulations.

6.17.1.4 Student officer personal discipline

One of the primary functions of the Federation is to give advice and assistance to its members when they are the subject of a formal complaint or internal investigation. If you are the subject of a complaint (see 6.16 above), the Federation advises you to remain calm and, if you are unsure of the procedure or what to do next, to contact your local Federation representative. The Federation has produced a leaflet concerning complaints which is downloadable from <http://www.ipcc.gov.uk/ipcc_policestaff_lr.pdf>.

6.17.1.5 Personal injury

The Federation offers advice and assistance to police officers (including student police officers) who sustain injuries while on duty and who wish to claim compensation from the Criminal Injuries Compensation Authority (CICA).

6.17.1.6 Personal conditions of service

The Federation also offers advice and assistance to police officers (including student police officers) on matters arising from the conditions of service set out in the various Acts and regulations governing the police service.

TASK 17

- Which Federation Region does your force belong to?
- Who is the Chair and Secretary of your force JBB?
- How are your concerns addressed and your views canvassed?

6.17.2 The BAWP

The British Association for Women in Policing seeks to address women's issues in policing and not simply to represent women; membership is open to both men and women. Further information is to be found at <http://www.bawp.org>.

6.17.3 The NBPA

The National Black Police Association UK is an independent charitable organization. The NBPA seeks to further the position of all police officers of 'African, African-Caribbean, Middle-Eastern, Asian or Asian sub-continent origin'. You join the NBPA through membership of your local Black Police Association or BPA. There are approximately 40 BPAs throughout the UK. Further information concerning the NBPA is to be found at <http://www.nbpa.co.uk>.

TASK 18

Does your force have a BPA? If it doesn't, can you find out why there is no BPA or equivalent?

6.17.4 The GPA

The Gay Police Association seeks to represent the interests of gay and lesbian police staff in the UK. Membership is on an individual basis and you join by contacting the national GPA. The GPA has a website to be found at <http://www.gay.police.uk>.

6.18 Effective Communication

As a student police officer you will need to be aware of how you speak to everybody you come into contact with, so that you can adjust accordingly what you say and how you say it.

This links with the NOS element:

National Occupational Standards Element

AB1.1 to 'develop and maintain communication with people' and in particular, performance criteria 2, 3 and 4 (see 6.18.4 below).

Performance criterion 2—to communicate with people in a form and manner and using language that:
- is open and respectful of them as individuals;
- is consistent with their level of understanding, culture, background, and preferred ways of communicating;
- is appropriate to the context in which the communication is taking place;
- promotes equality and values diversity.

Performance criterion 3—to give people opportunities to check their understanding of the information you have given to them and ask questions.

Performance criterion 4—to take the appropriate action to reduce any barriers to effective communication (Skills for Justice, 2007d).

The chapter also supports the Learning Requirements of the IPLDP and is typically introduced during module IND 4 of IDLDP.

The ideas presented here should help you become more aware of the way you speak, and the effect it has on other people. In turn, this will help you develop strategies to help you communicate more clearly in the future, and to choose the most appropriate way to speak to another person. This is obviously of critical importance both during the induction period and during the rest of your subsequent career as a police officer. In 6.18.3 below we will also examine the other side of the communication equation—listening skills.

It is important to note that the ideas presented here are based on **only one particular theory** concerning human communication. This theory is known as transactional analysis, and originated from the psychodynamic tradition in psychology. This does not mean that other theories concerning human communication are not equally valid for the student police officer; indeed, you may encounter quite different approaches during your training—for example, Shannon and Weaver's Information Theory. We are not asking you to buy into transactional analysis to the exclusion of other theories; instead we use it in this part of the Handbook as an example of the benefits that may flow from a careful and structured analysis of patterns of communication.

We also refer to non-verbal communication (NVC) in 6.18.2 below as this is an important means of communication that can easily affect exchanges between all individuals, including police officers.

6.18.1   Transactional Analysis

Transactional analysis was originally developed by Eric Berne, (for an introduction see Berne, 1968) and is based upon the assumption that people tend to adopt the characteristics or ego states of a **parent** (critical or nurturing), **adult**, or **child** (adapted or free). This affects their attitudes and the way they speak to each other.

The typical attitudes, behaviour, and words or phrases that people use when adopting one of these ego states can be roughly categorized as follows:

Ego state	Typical words/phrases	Typical behaviour	Typical attitudes
Critical parent	'That's disgraceful!'	Furrowed brow, pointed finger.	Condescending, judgemental.
	'You ought to … !'		
	'Always do it!'		
Nurturing parent	'Well done, that's clever!'	Benevolent smile, pat on back.	Caring, permissive.
Adult	'How … '?	Relaxed, logical, attentive.	Open-minded, clear-thinking, interested.
	'When … '?		
	'Where … '?		
	'What … '?		
Adapted child	'Please can I?'	Vigorous, nodding head, downcast eyes, whiny voice.	Compliant, defiant, complaining.
	'I'll try harder.'		
Free child	'I want.'	Laughing with someone, uninhibited.	Curious, fun-loving, spontaneous.
	'I feel great.'		

Note that no one operates in one or other of these states on a permanent basis. Instead, once you become more aware of it, you may find yourself switching between states, even within the course of a single conversation.

TASK 19

If this Handbook were a person, which of the ego states would fit best and most often?

6.18.1.1 Types of transaction

According to this theory, the response of the person you are speaking to will vary, partly due to the way you spoke to him/her and the ego state you were in. As a student police officer, you need to be able to analyse (to some extent) the way that **you** speak and respond and the way that **others** speak and respond, and to be able to identify the most appropriate way to manage the conversation. Having identified the ego states, the next task is to recognize the category of conversation or transaction, ie whether it is **complementary**, **crossed**, or **ulterior**.

6.18.1.2 Complementary transactions

Complementary transactions occur when the ego state of each side of the conversation makes a pair with the other. Here is an example of a complementary transaction. For the purpose of this example, let us call the student police officer 'SPO' and the member of public 'M'.

> The SPO stops a car to give advice to the driver.
>
> **M** I don't know why you've stopped me. Haven't you got anything better to do?
>
> **SPO** Is this your car? I've stopped you because I've got the right, and what's your problem anyway?
>
> **M** Get lost.
>
> **SPO** You can't say that; any more lip and I'll report you.

How could you try and make sure that unsatisfactory exchanges like the one above do not happen to you? To start with, you need to analyse the way it happened, then you will be able to see more easily how it could be done differently.

In the above example, the opening transaction is from M in the child ego state: 'I don't know why you've stopped me. Haven't you got anything better to do?' The SPO responds in parent mode: 'Is this your car? I've stopped you because I've got the right, and what's your problem anyway?' The response of the SPO is in the ego state of parent and is directed at M's child ego state. The transaction therefore forms a complementary transaction sequence of:

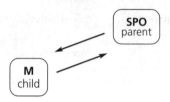

The exchange will continue in this way as long as the transactions are complementary. In the next part you will see how to interrupt and change the flow of the conversation by changing **your** ego state.

6.18.1.3   Crossed transactions

The last example showed how transactions can flow back and forth when they are complementary. They are likely to continue in the same style, with each person rather unproductively locked into their ego state. To interrupt this flow, and to change the style of the transaction, either SPO or M could employ a crossed transaction.

> Let us begin the conversation again, but with a subtle difference.
>
> **M**   I don't know why you've stopped me. Haven't you got anything better to do?
>
> **SPO** Hello, let me introduce myself, I'm PC Williams from Lewes police station and I've stopped you because I need to give you some advice about your car. Did you know that one of your brake lights isn't working? This could affect your safety as well as the safety of others.
>
> **M**   Oh right, I didn't realize about my lights—thanks for telling me—I'll get them fixed straight away.
>
> **PC** Thanks for your cooperation. Good afternoon.

In this case M is still in the child ego state but the reply by SPO is different; it is now from the adult ego state. It is a reply that has reasoning in its content, which has an effect on M, who may not have expected this type of response. M responds accordingly in the adult ego state which brings about a satisfactory conclusion. This is referred to as a crossed transaction, as the SPO's response has broken the adult–child–adult pattern, and the transaction has crossed over into a different style.

6.18.1.4   Ulterior transactions

In an ulterior transaction there are actually two different messages, an open message and a hidden message. Frequently with ulterior transactions, the open message is adult–adult, but the **hidden message** is parent–child or child–parent.

> For example, M begins the transaction sarcastically, and emphasizes the word 'such'.
>
> **M**   It's nice to see the local police making **such** good use of their time.
>
> **SPO** Yeah, it's all part of the service to **you**.

In this transaction it is not just about words; it is also about body language and the tone of voice. The opening transaction has a hidden meaning; M dislikes the police (or at least SPO); M feels the police (or SPO in particular) waste his or her time rather than catching real criminals; and hence the sarcastic emphasis on the word 'such'. SPO's response also has a hidden meaning: hence it is said with a smirk and an emphasis on the word 'you'. Each component is complementary. So, unless one of the participants crosses a transaction, the dialogue will continue in this manner. Your skill, therefore, is to be aware of what is happening, respond accordingly to break the transaction, and thereby change the ego state of the other person.

Try using these ideas to help you understand your own and other people's styles of communication, and then choose the most appropriate way of saying what it is that you want to say.

TASK 20

Over the next two days, listen carefully to conversations around you. What ego states are operating and what type of transactions are taking place? Write down three brief extracts and explain what is happening in terms of transactional analysis.

6.18.2   Non-verbal Communication

People may communicate anxiety, confidence, despair, or any other emotion through body language. These behavioural signs or 'leakages' are usually described as **non-verbal communication** (NVC). You should not ascribe depths of insight to NVC; the leakage is an indicator, no more, and it is difficult to separate signs of stress from those caused by lying. Beware of suggestions that hand gestures are 'windows on the soul'; they are not. (Unfortunately, these kinds of scientifically unjustified 'tips and tricks' used to feature in police training in the past.) In particular, the use of 'body language' in an attempt to identify deception or lying is problematic (see Vrij, 2000, for a comprehensive consideration of this). You must be alert to 'ethnocentrism' in your interpretations of NVC, such as a refusal to make eye contact—for some ethnic groups this is related to cultural attitudes to authority, and does not necessarily indicate guilt or remorse.

6.18.3   Listening Skills

Of all the skills that we develop during our lives, the ability to **listen** is probably the most difficult of all. We hear, but we do not always listen; this ability has to be learned and practised. (Interestingly, we teach children how to speak and write but we place less emphasis on how to listen.) Most of us will learn just enough to function successfully as social beings. However, as a student police officer, the ability to listen has to be developed more fully. What people tell us may be of critical importance when dealing with a public order situation or when investigating a crime.

Here we shall simply offer some basic advice on listening. During the two years of your training you will no doubt receive more detailed advice on listening skills.

- Pay full attention to the person you are listening to. Do not look away when the person is talking to you (think what it feels like for **you**, if the person you are speaking to keeps glancing away). You should give verbal and non-verbal feedback (for example nodding) to the speaker that says, in effect, 'I'm listening'.
- Train yourself to let the speaker finish before you ask another question or make a comment—don't interrupt. Most of us think we already do this but research shows that this is normally not the case! (However, there may be occasions when there are sound operational reasons which mean you **must** interrupt.) A good way of training yourself to let someone finish is to mentally count a few seconds after he/she has finished talking before you respond. You may also notice that he/she then fills this silence, and carries on speaking, almost as an afterthought. Sometimes, this extra information is of critical importance. Family doctors have long known this; often the most important part of the surgery consultation is when the patient stands to leave and then remarks, 'Oh yes doctor, there is one more thing ... '.
- Try echoing back if you need to clarify something being said, for example by using a phrase already used by the speaker—'You said, "He asked me for a cigarette," ... '

6.18.4   NOS Element AB1.1

The NOS element AB1.1, to 'develop and maintain communication with people', requires that you:

1. communicate in a manner that is consistent with relevant legislation, policies and procedures
2. communicate with people in a form and manner and using language that:
   - is open and respectful of them as individuals;
   - is consistent with their level of understanding, culture, background, and preferred ways of communicating;

- is appropriate to the context in which the communication is taking place;
- promotes equality and values diversity

3. give people opportunities to check their understanding of the information you have given to them and ask questions
4. take the appropriate action to reduce any barriers to effective communication
5. make records that:

- are accurate, legible, and complete;
- contain only the information necessary for the record's purpose;
- are free from labelling and discrimination

6. seek support when you are having difficulty communicating effectively.

(Skills for Justice, 2007d)

TASK 21

List some examples of questions that you might ask people with reference to performance criterion 2.

6.19 Answers to Tasks

TASK 1

It might seem childish to use memory cards but they work!

TASK 2

Many police websites have a 'Who's Who' section (although not always up to date), particularly for their Senior Management Team. Kent Police SMT for example is described at this site: <http://www.kent.police.uk/About Kent Police/How We Are Structured/How we are structured. html>.

TASK 3

You might like to test yourself by trying the NASA online phonetic alphabet tester available at <http://www.virtualskies.arc.nasa.gov/alphabet/alphabetIntro.htm>.

TASK 4

The correct order (from most likely to least), based upon statistics for 2004, is:

1. as a consequence of lung cancer
2. as the victim of homicide
3. by falling down stairs
4. in a cycling accident
5. by drowning in a bath
6. in a train crash
7. in an aircraft crash
8. through being struck by lightning.

TASK 5

What hazards would you identify? The person you are searching could cause you injury as a result of using:

- physical force;
- weapon he/she is carrying;
- weapon he/she picks up;

- an object that he/she takes from you such as your own personal safety equipment;
- infection such as hepatitis C, tuberculosis (TB), or influenza (flu);
- infestation such as scabies;
- needle injury.

Therefore the hazard level is medium, as you could receive serious injuries or ill health and as a result could be absent from work for more than three days if the person does attack you.

What are the risks involved? Take into account the:

- person's level of agitation;
- length of time it takes you to carry out the search;
- level of aggression shown by the person towards you;
- opportunity you give to the person to use force against you.

Also take into consideration:

- the locality of the search in terms of its proximity to other members of the public;
- how well lit the area is if it is carried out in the dark;
- whether or not you are alone when you carry out the search.

The risk level is medium as it is likely or possible that you may be injured. What therefore is the threat level? The threat level is calculated to be moderate.

What control measures can you take? There are many more but, for example, request a cover officer if you are alone. Carry out personal safety techniques such as searching from the side of the person; be aware of the movements of the person you are searching at all times; keep him or her in conversation (because it is difficult to think of answers to questions and do other things at the same time); wear gloves to reduce the risk of injury, consider your own personal hygiene, and wash exposed body parts such as your hands; consider carrying out the search in the sight line of a town CCTV camera; and remain alert at all times.

TASK 6

Naturally, much media attention at the time of the Macpherson Inquiry report centred on the charge of institutional racism. Unfortunately, this inadvertently diverted national attention from the very serious issue of the training of police officers in first aid and the need for them to maintain their skills, throughout their careers and at all ranks. Although the Report is clear that Stephen Lawrence's death from his injuries was probably unavoidable, Chapter 10 remains a shocking catalogue of incompetence and ineptitude.

The Report concludes Chapter 10 with the observation that:

> This evidence reinforced the Inquiry's views as to the lack of satisfactory and proper training in First Aid for officers of all ranks. Not only should officers be properly trained and be given proper refresher training at regular intervals, but it must be made plain that more senior officers need instruction just as much as junior officers. An officer in the position of [name] must be able to ensure that what is being done by his juniors is proper and satisfactory and in accordance with well co-ordinated and directed training. The notion that it may be good enough simply to wait for the ambulance and the paramedics must be exploded (Macpherson, 1999, s 10.6).

TASK 7

The new standard CBRN personal protection equipment issued to trained police officers in the event of an incident is the CR1 (CR stands for Civil Responder; the military are issued with their own version). The CR1 is identical to that used by the fire service in similar circumstances.

You should be able to find the CBRN procedures 'Aide Mémoire' on your force intranet, and, in 9.28.4.1 below we briefly describe your role when attending CBRN incidents.

TASK 8

1. VODS and QUEST are both functionalities of the PNC. VODS is a Vehicle Online Descriptive Search application that assists in identifying vehicles. Combinations of details such as

make and model, colour, and VIN (see 11.7 below) can be searched. QUEST is a Query Using Extended Search Techniques facility within PNC. This is the fuzzy capability we referred to earlier. The operator can input partial descriptions of people and produce a list of names that match the characteristics. HMIC have reported the following example of a successful outcome when using QUEST:

In the West Midlands, counterfeit currency was used in a public house. A search was carried out on the description of a white male, 6' tall, thin build with a skinhead haircut, brown hair, aged 20–22 years. The offender had a tattoo of a swallow on his left hand. Enquiries at the scene suggested he lived in Solihull and may have been called 'Barry'. A QUEST search produced one suspect who was dealt with for the offence (HMIC, 2005b, p 36).

You might like to conduct further research on the use of Boolean search techniques that use AND, OR, and NOT. These are also useful for conducting internet searches.

There is some evidence that knowledge of these aspects of PNC is not widespread amongst police officers in some forces (HMIC, 2006, p 9). However, you can find out more by visiting the NPIA website at <http://www.npia.police.uk/en/10508.htm>.

2. HMIC is interested in many aspects of a force's use of PNC including:

- accuracy;
- timeliness;
- completeness;
- relevancy.

The overall security of the system will also be of interest to HMIC.

TASK 9

The circumstances surrounding the documentary and the political fallout are well documented on the internet and elsewhere. Many commentators have argued that the documentary gave added impetus to the reforms contained within the IPLDP, and particularly those aspects concerned with the values and attitudes of police officers.

The reasons you gave in response to the task may well have been centred on one or more of the following:

- **Ethical or moral reasons:** You subscribe to the values of the Statement as they coincide (more or less) with your own values. Indeed, the reason you joined the police was perhaps in order to 'protect, help and reassure the community'.
- **Professional reasons:** You have chosen to join a profession of your own free will and so should abide by the rules of that profession.
- **Instrumental reasons:** For example, in order to do my job properly (or indeed, to keep my job) I need to subscribe to, and implement, the requirements of the Statement.

TASK 10

You will see how closely your own guesses coincided with the Police (Conduct) Regulations 2008, Standards of Professional Behaviour. You may like to reflect on any differences between your list and the Standards, and use these as a basis for an entry in your Learning Diary.

TASK 11

On one level, the public should expect a certain level of service from police officers as they pay their wages! More fundamentally (as we have discussed in 5.6 above) the police represent the most obvious forms of State legitimacy and still retain a monopoly of certain forms of power and the use of force. In simplistic terms there is always a delicate balance between a police service and a police force. If standards of service are undermined then there is a danger that the public will start to question your legitimacy.

TASK 12

Although the police officer concerned was off duty when the alleged incidents took place you have probably noted that the Standards surrounding general conduct apply whether you are on or off duty. There may also have been an abuse of authority in gaining access to the police car.

TASK 13

The most appropriate elements of the NOS would appear to be:

Standard	Relevant NOS elements
2. Authority, Respect and Courtesy	AB1.1 and CA1.3
3. Equality and Diversity	AA1.1
4. Use of Force	GC10.1 and GC10.2
7. Confidentiality	AB1.2

(However, some alternative answers are entirely possible.)

TASK 14

There are many techniques for memorizing information (the author Tony Buzan, for example, has written extensively on the subject).

One technique for memorizing the declaration is as follows:

(a) First gather ample supplies of blank paper!
(b) Now write out (or word-process) the declaration on a blank piece of paper by copying the original. Check and double-check that you have the words **exactly** as they should be.
(c) Now read the first sentence several times (not the whole paragraph) and try to commit this to memory.
(d) Now turn the page and write down (or word-process), from memory, the first sentence on another piece of paper.
(e) Check your recollected version against the original, correct, version word for word.
(f) Repeat stages (c) to (e) above until you have the sentence completely correct.
(g) Now attempt to memorize the first two sentences (not just the second sentence, but the first two together in order).
(h) Repeat the process above until you have the first two sentences completely correct.
(i) Now add the third sentence and so on.
(j) Continue until you have committed the complete declaration to memory.

This may take you some hours to achieve. The same technique can be used for memorizing other information—for example your 'definitions' if your force request so.

TASK 15

In many police forces, such as West Midlands Police, you will need to gain the permission of at least your BCU commander:

> The chief constable has delegated responsibility for the approval of Business Interests to Operational Command Unit (OCU) Commanders/Heads of Department, who will decide whether a business interest is compatible with an individual's position as a West Midlands officer, taking into account the requirement for officers to discharge and be seen to discharge their duties impartially (<http://www.west-midlands.police.uk/foi/publication-scheme/policies-procedures/policy-BI.asp?id=82>).

In many forces, the person with delegated responsibility over monitoring of police officers and police staff having 'secondary business interests' is the professional Head of HR.

TASK 16

You will have your own response to the first part of the task.

You are not likely to receive an unlawful order. The part of the PSNI Code of Ethics referred to in the task was inspired by the Council of Europe Declaration on the police, paras A(4) and A(7). This Declaration makes the case that obeying a superior's orders to undertake unlawful actions such as the ill-treatment of an individual, or to carry out an unlawful killing, would be no defence for the individual concerned. Similarly, the Basic Principles on the Use of Force and Firearms by Law Enforcement Officials as adapted by the Eighth Crime Congress of the UNCJIN (the United Nations Criminal Justice Information Network) in 1990 make it clear that:

[o]bedience to superior orders shall be no defence if law enforcement officials knew that an order to use force and firearms resulting in the death or serious injury of a person was manifestly unlawful **and** had a reasonable opportunity to refuse to follow it. (Our emphasis.)

TASK 17

The National Police Federation has a website as do a number of branch boards. For example, the Kent Police Federation may be found at <http://www.kentpolfed.org.uk/>. These may well provide you with the information that you need.

TASK 18

You can establish whether your local force has a branch of the BPA by searching the database at <http://www.nationalbpa.com/>.

TASK 19

Agreed, this task requires a gross oversimplification of the theory. However, on most occasions the Handbook would appear to be in adult mode—but there are certainly also aspects of the critical and nurturing parent.

TASK 20

We obviously provide a simplified version of transactional analysis (TA). You might want to read further. A good starting point is Berne's very readable and popular 1968 book *Games People Play* (reissued in the late 1990s) which you are likely to be able pick up second-hand on eBay or at boot fairs for very little. The games that Berne refers to are transactions that lead inevitably to predictable outcomes.

Note that TA is not without its critics and some of its academic standing has been damaged by popularized and over-simplified accounts. Another frequent approach (in police training) to analysing the interactions between individuals (or groups) is the use of the so-called 'Johari' window. The unusual name Johari originates from its two inventors, **Joseph Luft** and **Harry Ingham** (Luft, 1970). This proposes that one way of analysing aspects of human interaction is to identify areas of personal awareness and ignorance:

	Known to self	Not known to self
Known to others	**Open area**	**Blind area**
Not known to others	**Hidden area**	**Unknown area**

For example, the blind area includes aspects which are unknown by the person about him/herself but which others know. This can range from straightforward information (such as a medical complaint like halitosis) to more developed personality features, such as feelings of inadequacy, which are barely discerned by the individuals concerned and yet can be seen by others.

TASK 21

The kind of questions you might ask are with reference to your actions such as entering a person's home, touching them when conducting a search, and religious requirements for the treatment of the dead.

7 | Stop, Search, and Entry

7.1 Chapter Briefing

This chapter describes police procedures and duties in relation to stopping people and vehicles, searching people, vehicles, and premises, and your powers of entry into premises. You will certainly be involved in stop and search procedures whilst on Supervised and Independent Patrol, and are likely to use your various powers of entry too.

Much of the content of this chapter concerns legislation. As we explained in Chapter 2, we often provide a simplified and abbreviated version of the law, and use flow charts to explain points when appropriate. If you require further details you should consult the original legislation, other textbooks, your IPLDP notes, or w ebsites.

7.1.1 Aims of the Chapter

This chapter will enable you to:

- understand your rights and responsibilities when stopping a person, asking him/her for an account, and searching him/her;
- search premises with or without a warrant;
- appreciate your right to enter buildings for the purposes of arrest or to save life;
- develop the underpinning knowledge required for a number of NOS elements, several of the PAC headings, and entries for your Learning Diary Phases 3 and 4 and the CARs of your SOLAP.

7.1.2 Police Action Checklist

This chapter will provide you with the underlying knowledge and theory to meet the following requirements of the Police Action Checklist:

7.1.2.1 Search

Conduct stops
Demonstrate lawful search—persons
Demonstrate lawful search—premises
Demonstrate lawful search—vehicles

7.1.3 National Occupational Standards

This chapter will provide you with some of the knowledge required to demonstrate aspects of the following NOS elements:

National Occupational Standard Elements

AA1.1 Promote equality and value diversity
BE2.1 Provide initial support to victims, survivors, and witnesses
CA1.1 Apply principles of reasonable suspicion or belief
CA1.2 Use law enforcement actions proportionately
CA1.3 Use law enforcement actions fairly
CK1.1 Search individuals
CK2.1 Prepare to search vehicles, premises, and open spaces
CK2.2 Conduct searches of vehicles, premises, and open spaces.

You should refer to Chapter 3 for general information and advice concerning the NOS elements.

7.1.4 IPLDP Phases and Modules

This chapter will provide you with resources to support the following Operational Modules of the IPLDP:

OP 3 Respond to incidents, conduct and evaluate investigations.
OP 5 Search individuals and premises.

It will also cover aspects of the following topic areas of Legislation, Policy and Guidelines of the IPLDP:

- Crime (LPG 1.1);
- Stop and Search (LPG 1.2);
- Protecting People (LPG 1.3);
- Police Policies and Procedures (LPG 1.4);
- Non-Crime Incidents (LPG 1.5).

Much of the content of this chapter relates to IPLDP Phase 3 'Supervised Patrol' and Phase 4 'Independent Patrol'.

7.1.5 SOLAP

The contents of this chapter are relevant to the 'knowledge' evidence requirements of CARs AA1, BE1, CA1, CK1, and CK2.

7.1.6 Learning Diary Phases

The contents of this chapter may provide you with stimulus material for completion of your Learning Diary Phase 3, particularly for the following headings:

- Crime;
- Non-crime incidents;

- Police policies and procedures;
- Protecting people;
- Stop and searches.

7.2 Introduction

We should perhaps have a general word about **Stop and Account** and **Stop and Search** to put both in context and highlight their distinguishing features. Firstly, 'stop and account' is not a power. It is a requirement by the PACE Codes of Practice to record encounters with the public which are **not** governed by statutory powers. 'Stop and search' on the other hand is an umbrella term given to a number of powers in various pieces of legislation which provide powers to detain people for the purposes of search. The most widely used of these powers is s 1 of the PACE Act 1984.

However, you are probably already aware of the considerable sensitivities around the exercise of these powers. Stop and search has been particularly associated with racial harassment; it is claimed that ethnic-minority members of the public have been stopped and searched disproportionately, compared with their proportion in the general population. There are, however, arguments concerning the statistical basis for this claim, which highlight the difference between the 'resident' and 'available' populations that you police (for example, see Waddington *et al.*, 2004). Problems arise when there are no justifiable grounds for the stop and search and this has led to charges that the police are racist. As a rule, you should ask yourself whether you have a justification (within the context of the powers of search that you employ) to stop and search someone. In other words, are you sure of your grounds? Are you stopping this person for a reason that will withstand scrutiny?

The record of all stops and searches and stops and accounts is a conventional quantitative measurement of police performance, and you may find that your own force has very clear policy guidelines on when you may and when you may not exercise these powers. You should not be concerned if such policies are not available; just remember that whatever search power you use, it must conform to the guidelines of the PACE Act 1984 Codes of Practice relating to searches.

The police are also provided with various separate powers of entry for a number of purposes. One of these powers is for the purposes of entering premises, by force if necessary, to make an arrest, for example under s 17 of the PACE Act 1984. Another is to search a person or property directly after an arrest for dangerous articles or property relating to a criminal offence, for example under s 32 of the PACE Act 1984. There is a further power to search premises which are occupied or controlled by a person under arrest for an indictable offence, for example under s 18 of the PACE Act 1984. The precise circumstances are considered, together with the procedures that must be followed .

7.2.1 Definitions of Places and Other Locations

Appropriate locations for stop and account and searches are referred to in the legislation. You may also find the definitions of locations and places useful for other aspects of police work and its associated legislation. The table below clarifies the meaning of some of these terms.

Location	Definition
Public place	This will be a question of fact for the court to decide as it is not defined by statute. The court will consider: • whether the general public gain ready access to the place in question. This must apply to **all** members of the public (and not just some, such as people who belong to a club). For example, the grounds of a hospital would undoubtedly be privately owned by a health trust, but would be a public place because the general public would have ready access to the grounds when using the hospital to obtain treatment. • whether a landowner has given permission for the public to use a privately owned place. For example, motorway service areas are usually private property, but the owners encourage people to use their services (see also 7.5.2 below). A further example is a farmer's field being used for a boot fair; the general public has access, and the field becomes a public place for the duration of the fair.

Location	Definition
Private place	Land or premises which are privately owned to which the general public does NOT have ready access, for example a private residence or a private office block. It includes privately owned land or premises to which the general public have general access during opening hours, but when access is denied during closing times, it once gain reverts to being a private place.
Premises	'Includes any place and in particular, includes (a) any vehicle, vessel, aircraft or hovercraft; (b) any offshore installation; (ba) any renewable energy installation; and (c) a tent or movable structure' (s 23, PACE Act 1984)
Dwelling	This is any place where a person or people live and is defined in two pieces of legislation. A dwelling is: • '[a]ny structure or part of a structure occupied as a person's home or as other living accommodation (whether the occupation is separate or shared with others) but does not include any part not so occupied, and for this purpose 'structure' includes a tent, caravan, vehicle, vessel or other temporary or moveable structure' (s 8, Public Order Act 1986); • '[a]n inhabited building, or a vehicle or vessel which is, at the time of the offence, inhabited (irrespective of whether or not the person who occupies the vehicle/vessel is present at the time of the burglary)' (s 9(4) Theft Act 1968)
Place of residence	This will be a question of fact for the court to decide as it is not defined by statute, but clarification can be sought from the definition of dwelling above.

7.3 Stop and Account

There are a large number of statutes that provide you with the power to stop a person or vehicle, including such diverse legislation as s 43 of the Terrorism Act 2000 (see 9.28.5.3 below), s 6 of the Public Stores Act 1875, and s 4 of the Crossbows Act 1987.

Here we are concerned with recording of encounters with the public that are **not** governed by statutory powers, and the more general circumstances when you interact with members of the public. One such interaction is 'Stop and Account', where members of the public are stopped and asked to account for their behaviour, actions, or presence in a public place, or for their possession of a particular item. It does not involve searching. 'Stop and Account' is covered in the Police and Criminal Evidence (PACE) Act 1984, Code A, paras 3.1 and 4.12–4.19 inclusive. As we noted in the introduction, there is some controversy surrounding the use of stop, account, and search powers by the police, and in particular the claims made that these interactions disproportionately involve people from ethnic minorities. The debate is beyond the scope of this Handbook; however if you wish to read further on this, see Waddington *et al.* (2004) as a starting point. The PACE Act 1984 Codes of Practice state that, when carrying out your duties:

> all stops and searches should be carried out with courtesy, consideration and respect for the person concerned. This has a significant impact on public confidence in the police (Code A, para 3.1).

To help you achieve this, the Codes regulate chance meetings with the public. These situations include any conversation with a member of the public when you ask him/her to account for him/herself. In some circumstances you are required to record information on the ethnicity of the person and make a receipt available to him/her (see Code A, paras 4.12–4.19).

7.3.1 Recording of Encounters Not Governed by Statutory Powers

This is covered in the PACE Act 1984, Code A, para 4.12 which states that:

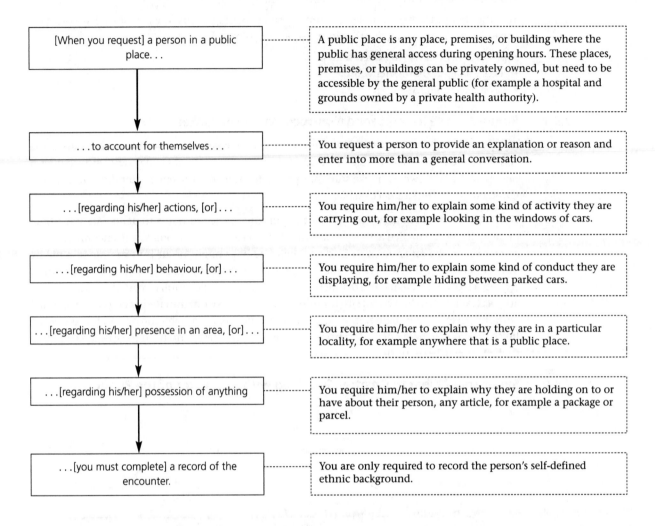

[When you request] a person in a public place. . .

A public place is any place, premises, or building where the public has general access during opening hours. These places, premises, or buildings can be privately owned, but need to be accessible by the general public (for example a hospital and grounds owned by a private health authority).

. . .to account for themselves . . .

You request a person to provide an explanation or reason and enter into more than a general conversation.

. . .[regarding his/her] actions, [or] . . .

You require him/her to explain some kind of activity they are carrying out, for example looking in the windows of cars.

. . .[regarding his/her] behaviour, [or] . . .

You require him/her to explain some kind of conduct they are displaying, for example hiding between parked cars.

. . .[regarding his/her] presence in an area, [or] . . .

You require him/her to explain why they are in a particular locality, for example anywhere that is a public place.

. . .[regarding his/her] possession of anything

You require him/her to explain why they are holding on to or have about their person, any article, for example a package or parcel.

. . .[you must complete] a record of the encounter.

You are only required to record the person's self-defined ethnic background.

You must both

- inform the person of their entitlement to a receipt for the encounter (para 4.15); and
- make a record of the person's self-defined ethnic background (paras 4.12A and 4.17).

If you provide the person with a receipt, it must include your name (para 4.12); however, you are not empowered to require the person to provide his/her own personal details.

If he/she refuses to give his/her self-defined ethnic background, you should instead record your own observed description of his/her ethnic background (para 4.18). If he/she gives you what appears to be an obviously incorrect self-defined ethnic background, you should record both his/her original response and your own perception of the ethnic background (note 18).

You must make a record at the time of the encounter unless it is completely out of the question to do so (for example in serious public order situations or when you have to leave urgently). If you do not make a record at the time, you must do so as soon as practicable afterwards (Code A para 4.1).

7.3.2 Exceptions

These are listed in paras 4.13 and 4.14 of Code A, so for example you do not have to complete a form if you are:

- in general conversation;
- giving directions;
- looking for witnesses;
- seeking general information;

- questioning people in order to establish the background to incidents which have required you to become involved, for example in order to resolve a dispute or to restore order; or
- requiring a specimen of breath for a breath test.

You also do not have to complete a form if you are issuing a person with a Penalty Notice for Disorder (PND) or issuing another form requesting him/her to:

- produce his/her driving documents;
- rectify a defect on his/her vehicle;
- pay a fixed penalty.

7.3.3 Requests for a Receipt for a Non-recordable Encounter

If a person requests a receipt but the encounter or chance meeting does not satisfy the conditions to make it recordable (see Code A, para 4.12) you should still provide him/her with one (para 4.19). However, make sure that you state on it that the encounter did not meet the criteria to make the stop recordable.

However, if you reasonably believe that the purpose of the request is to deliberately frustrate or delay legitimate police activity, you can refuse to issue one (as long as the encounter is not recordable). Such an attempt to frustrate police activity might occur for example in a public order situation such as a large demonstration—people might engage you (or shout at you) to request a receipt, just to try and distract you from the lawful execution of your duty. You need to keep a clear head in this type of situation; as long as you have not initiated or engaged in contact with the person about his/her individual circumstances (such as why the person is there, what he/she is doing, where he/she has been or is going) then there is no need to issue a receipt (see Code A, para 4.19, note 20).

7.3.4 Summary of What to Do after Speaking with a Member of the Public

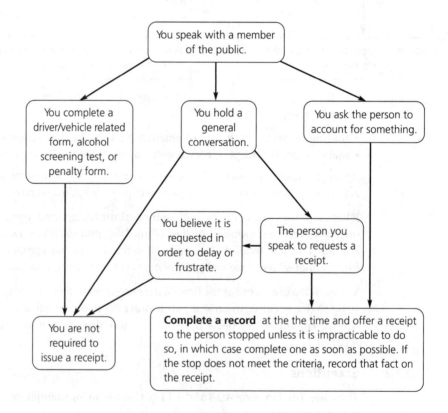

7.4 Road Checks (Section 4 of the PACE Act 1984)

In Chapter 11 you will read that you have the power, under s 163 of the Road Traffic Act 1988 to stop a 'mechanically propelled vehicle' on a road (see 11.3 below, and 11.2 for definitions of vehicles and roads). In addition, s 4 of the PACE Act 1984 provides a senior officer with the power to authorize a 'road check' for the specific purpose of determining whether a vehicle is carrying people connected with indictable offences (other than road traffic or vehicle excise offences), or people who are unlawfully at large. The authorization of a senior officer for a 's 4 road check' is necessary because every vehicle will be stopped in a certain area for the purposes of locating a specific person, and the rights of all the individuals stopped must be considered. Section 4 of the PACE Act 1984 sets out the circumstances under which a road check can take place for the purposes of selecting vehicles to be stopped (using s 163 of the Road Traffic Act 1988), in a specified locality, during a specified time, for a specific reason.

So, to summarize, you **set up road checks** under s 4 of the PACE Act 1984 and **stop the vehicles** under s 163 of the RTA 1988. Section 4 does not affect your power to stop vehicles at any other time using s 163 of the Road Traffic Act 1988.

7.4.1 Purpose of a Road Check

Section 4 of the PACE Act 1984 states that the purpose of the road check must be to find a person who:

- has committed an indictable offence other than a road traffic offence or a vehicle excise offence; or
- is intending to commit such an offence; or
- is a witness to such an offence; or
- is unlawfully at large.

There must be reasonable grounds for suspecting that the person is, or is about to be, in the locality selected for the road check.

7.4.2 Authorization for a Road Check

A police officer of the rank of superintendent or above must authorize a s 4 road check in writing. If such a police officer is not available, a road check may be authorized by an officer below the rank of superintendent (see s 4(5) of PACE 1984). Any use of the power to impose a road check must be conducted in accordance with Code of Practice A, PACE Act 1984, which is concerned with stop and search.

> **TASK 1**
>
> Consider the health and safety implications of holding a road check. What are the considerations in terms of you, your colleagues, and the general public?

7.5 Stop and Search (Section 1 of the PACE Act 1984)

Sections 1 and 2 of the PACE Act 1984 give you the power to stop, search, and detain individuals and vehicles under the circumstances described below. Whatever the power, the Codes of Practice safeguard the rights of an individual while you carry out a search.

(Powers to stop and search that arise from other legislation are covered elsewhere in this Handbook where appropriate: for example, see 7.6 below in relation to incidents with serious violence, 9.28.5 below in relation to terrorism, 10.14.7 in relation to searching for controlled drugs, and 9.20.3 in relation to firearms).

This part of the Handbook provides information about 'Stop and Search' (or, more precisely, 'Stop, Search and Detain') under s 1 of the PACE Act 1984. Note that you do not have to be in uniform to carry out such a search.

The ability to 'conduct stops' and to 'demonstrate lawful search of persons, premises, and vehicles' are requirements within the Police Action Checklist 'Search' heading and can contribute evidence for the attainment of NOS element CK1.1:

National Occupational Standard Element

CK1.1 Search individuals.

Note that element CK1.1 requires that you conduct the search on the appropriate 'grounds and legal authority' and that you also identify and deal with any potential risks. These risks may include offensive weapons, assault, sharps (eg hypodermic needles), or hazardous substances (see 6.7 above). As with most NOS elements, you will achieve CK1.1 largely through your assessor's direct observations of when you carry out a search for real. The requirement is that you successfully complete a minimum of five searches in a variety of circumstances.

7.5.1   Grounds for 'Stop, Search and Detain'

Under s 1(3) of the PACE Act 1984, you do not have the power to search unless you have **reasonable grounds** for suspecting that you will find stolen or prohibited articles. Reasonable grounds for suspicion depend on the circumstances in each case (see Code A, para 2.2), but the following factors can all be considered:

- a suspect's behaviour, for example trying to hide something;
- accurate and current intelligence or information; and/or
- reliable information that members of a particular group habitually carry prohibited articles.

Reasonable grounds do **not** include personal factors, such as ethnicity, age, appearance, or previous convictions (either alone, or in combination with each other or with any other factor). You must never generalize or stereotype groups of people as being more likely to take part in criminal activity, nor should a person's religion contribute to forming grounds for reasonable suspicion.

If you discover an article which you have reasonable grounds to suspect to be stolen or prohibited, you can seize it (s 1(6), PACE Act 1984).

7.5.2   Appropriate Locations for 'Stop, Search and Detain'

Section 1(1) of the PACE Act 1984 states that you may search:

    (a) in any place to which … the public or any section of the public has access, on payment or otherwise, as of right, or by virtue of express or implied permission;

    (b) in any other place to which people have ready access at the time when [you propose] to exercise the power but which is not a dwelling.

The public have a **right** to use roads and footpaths, and other public areas during opening hours. They have **express permission** to enter cinemas, theatres, or football grounds having paid an entrance fee and they can remain there until that particular entertainment is over, when permission to be there ends. There is an **implied permission** for persons to enter buildings to carry out business transactions with the owners, and even to use a footpath to a dwelling-house for the purposes of paying a lawful call upon the householder. That implied permission remains until withdrawn by the householder or the owner of the business premises. Places to which the public has **ready access** include places such as a private field if that field is regularly used by trespassers, or a garden if it is accessible by jumping over a low wall.

This power cannot be used to search inside a place of residence (a dwelling). If the search is to be carried out on land attached to a dwelling (including a garden or yard), you cannot search any person who lives in the dwelling, or any other person who has the resident's permission to be on the attached land. The same principles apply to searching vehicles; you cannot search a vehicle located on land attached to a dwelling if the person who lives in the dwelling has permitted the vehicle to be on that land.

You must carry out the search at the place where the person or vehicle was first detained, or 'nearby'. Code A, para 3.4, note 6 defines 'nearby' as 'within a reasonable travelling distance', but gives no indication of actual distance. Without any further guidance from case law, the term should be interpreted relatively cautiously. For example, consider an officer in a police van in a busy street drawing up next to a pedestrian whom he/she detains for the purposes of a search. If the suspect was taken out of the public eye to the waiting police van, it would be nearby. Similarly, if a vehicle and occupants are stopped on a busy main road for the purposes of a search, and are then taken to the very next side road to ease traffic congestion and maintain the health and safety of all concerned, the search would be nearby.

7.5.3 Who or What Can Be 'Stopped, Searched and Detained'?

Having made sure that you first of all satisfy the above requirements concerning the location, under s 1(2)(a) of the PACE Act 1984 you can search:

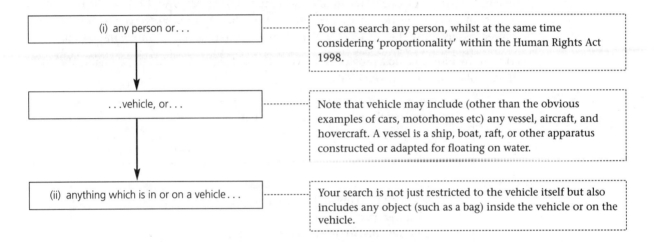

7.5.4 Items You May Search for under 'Stop, Search and Detain'

Section 1 of the PACE Act 1984 can **only** be used for searching for stolen or prohibited articles. Stolen articles include any article which you have reasonable grounds for suspecting to be stolen. The table below provides further details about prohibited articles.

Prohibited article	Description
Offensive weapons	Includes any article made, intended, or adapted for causing injury to a person (see 9.19.1.1 below), for use either by the person having it with him/her or by someone else. A firearm, as defined by s 57 of the Firearms Act 1968 (see 9.20.1 below). See: • s 1(9), PACE Act 1984; • Note 22 Code A, Codes of Practice, PACE Act 1984.
Bladed or sharply pointed articles	Includes any article which is bladed or sharply pointed, but excludes a small folding pocket knife (see 9.19.2 below).
Any articles used in the course of or in connection with certain criminal offences	Includes any article made, intended, or adapted for use (by either the person having it with him/her or by someone else) in the course of or in connection with any: • burglary (see 10.5 below) eg screwdriver, gloves; • theft (see 10.3 below) eg pliers, large bag; • taking a conveyance (see 10.7 below) eg master keys; • fraud (see 10.12 below) eg false identity documents; • criminal damage (see 10.21 below) eg spray cans.
Fireworks	Only includes fireworks possessed in contravention of a prohibition imposed by any of the firework regulations (see 9.18 below).

Note that some items (such as drugs) do not fall within this definition of prohibited articles, and therefore other statutory powers of search must be used to search for such items (see Code A, Annex A). Searches for drugs are covered in 10.14 be low.

7.5.5 Requirements Regarding the Search of Persons and Vehicles

These requirements are explained in s 2 of the PACE Act 1984. Briefly, you must take reasonable steps to provide certain information to the person to be searched (or to the person in charge of the vehicle to be searched).

This obligation relates not only to a search carried out under s 1 of the PACE Act 1984 but also to any other power to search a person or vehicle which takes place outside the circumstances of an arrest. In the case of *O (a juvenile) v DPP* (1999) 163 JP 725, it was decided that a breach of s 2 of the PACE Act 1984 would render a search (and probably any later arrest and detention) unlawful. This decision was confirmed in a case (*R v Christopher Bristol* (2007) EWCA Crim 3214) that involved a search carried out under s 23 of the Misuse of Drugs Act 1971 (see 10.14.7 below) and resulted in a conviction for obstructing a police officer. On appeal, the conviction was over-turned because s 2 of the PACE Act 1984 had not been complied with during the search.

The information you must provide is shown in the table below and can be best remembered by the use of the mnemonic GO WISELY:

G	Grounds of the suspicion for the search
O	Object/purpose of search
W	Warrant card (if you are in plain clothes or if requested by the person)
I	Identity of the officer performing the search
S	Station to which the officer is attached
E	Entitlement to a copy of the search record
L	Legal power used
Y	You are detained for the purposes of a search

After searching an **unattended vehicle**, or anything in or on it, you must leave a record of the search inside the vehicle. However, if the vehicle has not been opened (see Code A, para 4.8), or it is not reasonable or practical to leave the record inside without causing damage (see s 2(7), PACE Act 1984), the record should be attached to the outside of the vehicle.

The Metropolitan Police Authority has produced a DVD called 'Go Wisely—everything you need to know about Stop and Search'. It explores the controversy surrounding the legislation and will help you to put the application of the power into context. The DVD can be watched online at <http://www.mpa.gov.uk/scrutinies/stop-search/dvd-large/> (lower resolution versions of the DVD are also available from the same website).

7.5.5.1 Conducting the search

When searching persons:

- You must seek the **cooperation** of the person to be searched. Reasonable force under s 117 PACE 1984 (see also 7.9.4 and 8.9.2 below), may be used as a last resort, but only after your attempts to search have been met with resistance (see Code A, para 3.2).
- You must keep the search **relevant**: the extent of the search must relate to the object you are searching for, and if the suspicion relates to a certain pocket, then only that pocket can be searched (see Code A, para 3.3).
- You cannot search a member of the **opposite sex** if it involves removal of more than outer coat, jacket, gloves, headgear, or footwear, and you cannot be present at such a search, unless the person being searched specifically requests it (see Code A, para 3.6).
- You cannot require any person to remove any **clothing** in public other than an outer coat, jacket, and gloves.
- You can place your hands inside the **pockets** of outer clothing and feel round the inside of collars, socks, and shoes (see Code A, para 3.5).
- You can search a person's **hair** as well, but only if this does not require the removal of headgear (see Code A, para 3.5).

- You can carry out a **more thorough search**, for example requiring the removal of a T-shirt, but it must be undertaken out of public view, for example in a police van or police station if it is nearby (see Code A, para 3.6).

You may detain a person or vehicle for the purpose of such a search, but the length of time the person or vehicle is detained must be reasonable and kept to a minimum (Code A, para 3.3).

7.5.5.2 Recording a stop or a search

You must make a record of the stop or search at the time unless it is completely out of the question to do so, for example in serious public order situations or when you have to leave urgently (see Code A, paras 4.1 and 4.2). In such cases you should make a record as soon as possible afterwards.

7.5.5.3 Documents to be provided to the person

You must give either a full copy of the record or an 'electronic receipt' (printed) to the person you have searched unless it is impracticable to do so.

The copy of the record can be either:

- an 'electronic' copy (printed from an electronic record) if you have a portable printer available (see Code A, para 4.10A); or
- a paper copy of the form completed by hand (see Code A, para 4.10B).

If you instead provide an electronic receipt you must inform the person that it is an alternative to a copy of the full record, and that a full record is available, and explain how it can be accessed (see Code A, para 4.2A).

If it is not possible to provide either a full copy of the record or an electronic receipt for technical reasons (for example you have no access to either a printer or a paper-based version of the form), or you have to leave urgently, you must still provide some form of receipt. This 'receipt' (a business card for example) must include your name, a unique reference number, the power used, and information on how to obtain a full copy of the search record (see Code A, para 4.10 B and note 21).

7.5.6 Searches in Practice

We have covered a large amount of information in this part of the Handbook on searches, when, where, and how to search, and what to do afterwards. We now consider some examples to illustrate how this might all apply in practice.

7.5.6.1 Searching a suspected burglar

One evening, at the start of a night duty, you are provided with an electronic briefing containing information that a number of burglaries have taken place on the local housing estate. The MO of the suspect (see 13.5.5 below) is to enter the rear of dwellings through insecure doors or windows during the early hours of the morning, and take small electrical items.

Later on, at 02.00 hours the next day, you are on mobile patrol when you are called to several reports from members of the public regarding a prowler in the rear gardens of a number of houses within the housing estate. You make a search of the area on foot and locate a suspect hiding in the back garden of a house carrying a small rucksack which obviously contains several items. You carry out a PNC check of the suspect on the details he provides, and there is a record of an individual with the same details who has previous convictions for burglary. A colleague speaks to the occupant of the house and asks if the suspect lives there and whether the suspect has permission to be in the garden. The occupant categorically replies 'no' to both questions.

Under these circumstances you can justify your 'reasonable grounds' to carry out a s 1 PACE search; you have the intelligence you gained from the earlier briefing regarding the burglaries in the area, the behaviour of the suspect and the fact that he is a trespasser, and your suspicion that the rucksack carried by the individual may contain stolen articles. Having established your reasonable grounds for suspecting that you will find stolen or prohibited articles on the person, and after you have complied with the Codes of Practice (see 7.5.5 above) you go ahead and detain the suspect for the purposes of a s 1 PACE search.

7.5.6.2   Searching a vehicle in relation to a suspected street robbery

A street robbery takes place within your area in which a suspect jumps out of a car and steals a mobile phone from a pedestrian at knifepoint. The registration number of the car is taken by a witness. Some minutes later a member of the public informs you that a car fitting the description of the one used in the robbery has been left abandoned in the driveway of a nearby house. You go to the house and see a car with the same registration number as the one used in the robbery. You locate the owner of the house who informs you that nobody in the house has any connection to the car, and that he/she has not given permission for it to be there. These observations and information justify your 'reasonable grounds' for suspecting that you will find stolen or prohibited articles in the vehicle as a result of the robbery and therefore you go ahead and search the vehicle. At the end of the search you remember to comply with the Codes of Practice (see 7.5.5 above).

TASK 2

As you have seen, there are a number of requirements that you must meet when making a search under s 1 of the PACE Act 1984. Some of these relate to what you must tell the person you are searching. In order for this to become second nature, write down the list of things you have to say, in a way that will help you remember them (for example, make a mind-map or your own mnemonic). Completion of this task will help you towards meeting the knowledge requirements of CAR CK1 in your SOLAP under the headings 'Legal and organizational requirements' and 'Searching individuals'.

7.6   Stop and Search Powers for Incidents with Serious Violence

If you find yourself in a situation where it seems likely that a serious breakdown in public order might occur or has occurred, s 60 of the Criminal Justice and Public Order Act 1994 empowers a senior police officer to authorize you to stop and search people for offensive weapons or other dangerous instruments. Under s 60(5), you have this power even if you do **not** have reasonable grounds for suspecting that the person or vehicle is carrying weapons or dangerous articles.

Section 60(1) of the Criminal Justice and Public Order Act 1994 states that:

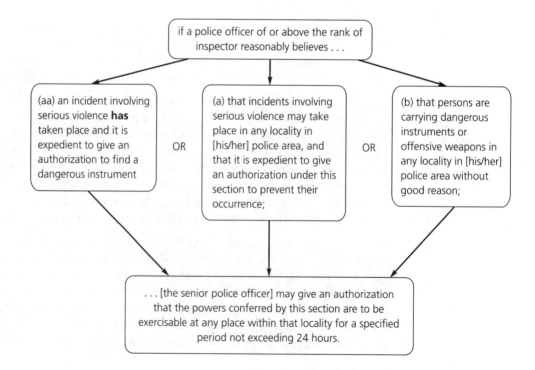

The table below explains the meaning of key terms used in the flow chart.

Term	Explanation
Dangerous instruments	This means bladed or sharply pointed articles (see 9.19.2.1 below).
Offensive weapon	This means the same as in s 1(9) PACE Act (see 7.5.4 above and 9.19.1.1 below). For the purposes of s 60(1)(aa), an offensive weapon also includes 'any article used in the incident to cause or threaten injury to any person, or otherwise to cause intimidation'.
Carrying	Carrying a dangerous instrument or an offensive weapon means having it in his/her actual possession.
Vehicle	Includes a caravan.

7.6.1 Authorization

The authorization giving you these additional powers can only be given by a police officer of or above the rank of inspector, and it:

- must be written and signed (unless it is made under s 60(1)(aa) **and** it is impracticable to do so in which case it must be recorded in writing as soon as practicable);
- may be extended for a further 24 hours (s 60(3)).

If an inspector gives an authorization he/she must inform an officer of or above the rank of a superintendent as soon as it is practicable to do so (s 60(3A)).

7.6.2 Implementation

The authorization provides you with the power to search for offensive weapons or dangerous instruments (s 60(4) of the Criminal Justice and Public Order Act 1994). The search must still comply with s 2 of the PACE Act 1984 (see 7.5.5 above). You may stop and search:

(a) any pedestrian and anything he/she is carrying

(b) any vehicle and its driver and passenger(s).

If you discover a dangerous instrument or an article which you have reasonable grounds for suspecting to be an offensive weapon, you may seize it (s 60(6)). A person who fails to stop (including his/her vehicle) when required to do so by you (under this legislation) commits an offence (s 60(8)).

This offence is triable summarily and the penalty is one month's imprisonment and/or a fine.

7.6.3 Searches Involving the Removal of Clothing

You can only ask someone to remove clothing if it seems to you that the clothing is being used in an attempt to conceal his/her identity (s 60 of the Criminal Justice and Public Order Act 1994). You have the power under s 60AA(2) to seize any item which you reasonably believe a person is intending to use for that same purpose.

A person who fails to remove an item of clothing when required to do so by a constable (under this legislation) commits an offence (s 60AA(7)).

This offence is triable summarily and the penalty is six months' imprisonment and/or a fine.

TASK 3

A town has recently experienced several outbreaks of serious public disorder between two rival gangs. The disorder has mainly occurred in the local park. Subsequently, an order is in force under s 60 of the Criminal Justice and Public Order Act 1984.

You are on patrol in the local park when you see a person wearing a full-face ski mask which is concealing his/her face. Under what circumstances can you ask the person to remove the mask? Choose one of the following:

1. You reasonably believe that the person was carrying a dangerous instrument or an offensive weapon.
2. You reasonably believe that the person was attempting to conceal his/her identity.
3. No further circumstances are required as a s 60 order is in force.
4. You reasonably believe that the person was likely to be involved in violence.

7.7 Search of Premises after Arrest

It is reasonable to suppose that few suspects are ever caught the first time they break the law. Equally, when suspects are arrested, there are few occasions when they are still in possession of the evidence connected with the crime for which they have been arrested. The PACE Act 1984 allows you to search the premises of suspects who have been arrested for indictable offences for evidence relating to that offence (or a similar one).

The information provided here will help you develop the underpinning knowledge to achieve the PAC checklist heading 'Search' and in particular the ability to 'demonstrate a lawful s 18 PACE search'. The relevant NOS element is CK2.2:

National Occupational Standard Element

CK2.2   Conduct searches of vehicles, premises, and open spaces

---

Skills for Justice requires that evidence be provided from a minimum of two real searches for each type of search, ie two searches of vehicles, two searches of premises, and two searches of land. These searches must be real and not simulated.

7.7.1 Searching Premises under section 18(1) of the PACE Act 1984

Section 18(1) of the PACE Act 1984 states that:

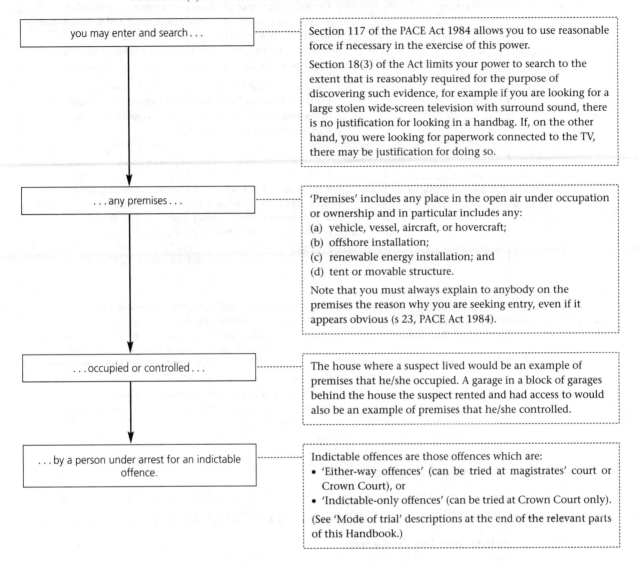

you may enter and search . . .	Section 117 of the PACE Act 1984 allows you to use reasonable force if necessary in the exercise of this power. Section 18(3) of the Act limits your power to search to the extent that is reasonably required for the purpose of discovering such evidence, for example if you are looking for a large stolen wide-screen television with surround sound, there is no justification for looking in a handbag. If, on the other hand, you were looking for paperwork connected to the TV, there may be justification for doing so.
. . . any premises . . .	'Premises' includes any place in the open air under occupation or ownership and in particular includes any: (a) vehicle, vessel, aircraft, or hovercraft; (b) offshore installation; (c) renewable energy installation; and (d) tent or movable structure. Note that you must always explain to anybody on the premises the reason why you are seeking entry, even if it appears obvious (s 23, PACE Act 1984).
. . . occupied or controlled . . .	The house where a suspect lived would be an example of premises that he/she occupied. A garage in a block of garages behind the house the suspect rented and had access to would also be an example of premises that he/she controlled.
. . . by a person under arrest for an indictable offence.	Indictable offences are those offences which are: • 'Either-way offences' (can be tried at magistrates' court or Crown Court), or • 'Indictable-only offences' (can be tried at Crown Court only). (See 'Mode of trial' descriptions at the end of the relevant parts of this Handbook.)

7.7.2 Evidence Requirements

Section 18 of the PACE Act 1984 states that you must have reasonable grounds to suspect that there is evidence on the premises that relates to that offence or to some other indictable offence connected with or similar to that offence. For example, if you arrest a suspect who was in the process of stealing a camera from a store, you may want to search his/her car for other stolen property. He/she could well have received other items and be in the process of selling them on; this would constitute the offence of handling stolen goods, a similar offence to theft.

You may:

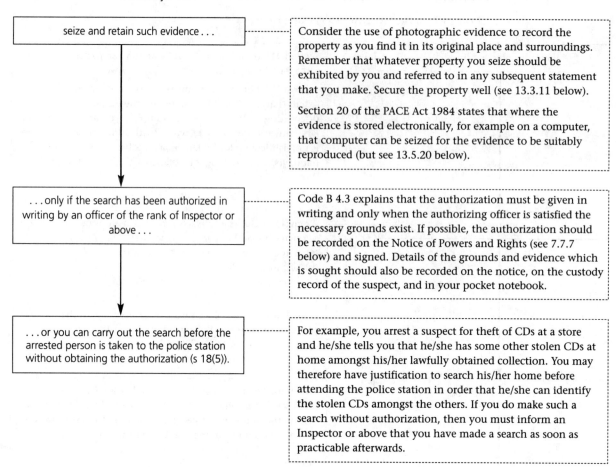

seize and retain such evidence . . .	Consider the use of photographic evidence to record the property as you find it in its original place and surroundings. Remember that whatever property you seize should be exhibited by you and referred to in any subsequent statement that you make. Secure the property well (see 13.3.11 below).

Section 20 of the PACE Act 1984 states that where the evidence is stored electronically, for example on a computer, that computer can be seized for the evidence to be suitably reproduced (but see 13.5.20 below). |
| . . . only if the search has been authorized in writing by an officer of the rank of Inspector or above . . . | Code B 4.3 explains that the authorization must be given in writing and only when the authorizing officer is satisfied the necessary grounds exist. If possible, the authorization should be recorded on the Notice of Powers and Rights (see 7.7.7 below) and signed. Details of the grounds and evidence which is sought should also be recorded on the notice, on the custody record of the suspect, and in your pocket notebook. |
| . . . or you can carry out the search before the arrested person is taken to the police station without obtaining the authorization (s 18(5)). | For example, you arrest a suspect for theft of CDs at a store and he/she tells you that he/she has some other stolen CDs at home amongst his/her lawfully obtained collection. You may therefore have justification to search his/her home before attending the police station in order that he/she can identify the stolen CDs amongst the others. If you do make such a search without authorization, then you must inform an Inspector or above that you have made a search as soon as practicable afterwards. |

7.7.3 The Timing of Searches

Searches should be made at a reasonable hour. However, searches may be carried out at any time if the results of the search might otherwise be prejudiced (Code B 6.2).

7.7.4 Before Starting the Search

If the premises are occupied before the search begins (Code B 6.5) you should:

- identify yourself and state the purpose and grounds of the search;
- identify and introduce anybody with you.

7.7.5 Using Force to Enter

Reasonable and proportionate force may be used if necessary (Code B 6.6):

- if the occupier has refused entry;
- if it is impossible to communicate with the occupier.

7.7.6 Communication with People on the Premises during a Search

If you are in charge of the search, you should communicate with people on the premises (Code B 6.4) unless there are reasonable grounds for believing that alerting the occupier would frustrate the object of the search or put you in danger.

7.7.7 Documentation to be Left on the Premises after a Search

A copy of the Notice of Powers and Rights should be given to the occupier or left on the premises if they are empty (Code B 6.7). You will probably be given specimen copies of a notice to examine whilst training.

TASK 4

You are called to your custody area where your inspector is waiting to give you a signed 's 18' authority to search the premises of a person in custody for burglary of an electrical store which sells small electrical goods. The burglary took place yesterday and the person in custody was not in possession of any stolen property at the time of arrest.
- What are your considerations before leaving the custody area?
- What are you going to do on arrival at the premises to be searched?
- How will you conduct the search?
- What will you do before leaving the premises?

7.8 Search Warrants for Evidence of Indictable Offences

Section 8 of the PACE Act 1984 (extended by the Serious Organised Crime and Police Act 2005) provides the grounds and procedure to be followed when applying for a warrant to search premises in connection with an investigation into an indictable offence. It also provides a power to seize certain evidence.

Section 8 states that a justice of the peace may issue a warrant authorizing you to enter and search premises if there are reasonable grounds for believing:

(a) that an indictable offence has been committed; and
(b) that there is material on the premises mentioned … below which is likely to be of substantial value (whether by itself or together with other material) to the investigation of the offence; and
(c) that the material is likely to be relevant evidence; and
(d) that it does not consist of or include items subject to legal privilege, excluded material or special procedure material.

However in relation to each set of premises specified in the application, at least **one** of the following conditions must apply:

Condition 1
It is not practicable to communicate with any person entitled to grant entry to the premises.
or
Condition 2
It is not practicable to communicate with a person entitled to grant access to the evidence (even if it is practicable to communicate with a person entitled to grant entry to the premises).
or
Condition 3
Entry to the premises will not be granted unless a warrant is produced.
or
Condition 4
The purpose of a search may be frustrated or seriously prejudiced unless a constable arriving at the premises can secure immediate entry.

Premises may be entered and searched on more than one occasion under the same application, although the second and any other subsequent entries must be authorized by an officer of the rank of inspector or above.

There are two different types of search warrant:
- **Specific Premises Warrants**, which apply only to the premises specified in the application and
- **All Premises Warrants**, which apply to any premises occupied or controlled by the person specified in the application (and can include specified premises if this is required).

For an 'All Premises Warrant' the justice of the peace must be satisfied that this type of warrant is necessary, either because of the particulars of the offence, or because it is not reasonably practicable to specify every single premises which might need to be searched.

7.9 Entry for Purposes of Arrest and to Save Life

The PACE Act 1984 gives you a power of entry to premises where you believe a person you are seeking to arrest is located. The list of offences for which you can enter to arrest has been extended under Sch 7 of the Serious Organised Crime and Police Act 2005. You can also enter premises in order to save life.

7.9.1 Power of Entry to Arrest

There are a number of situations in which you have the power of entry to premises in order to arrest a person, such as having a relevant warrant, or in order to arrest for certain offences.

In relation to the extent of such an entry and search, s 17 of the PACE Act 1984 states that:

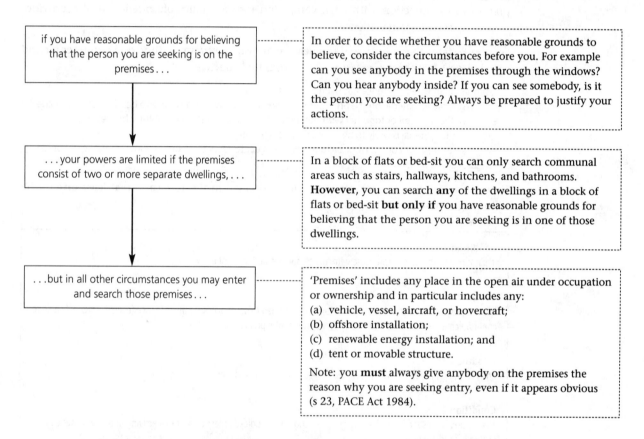

if you have reasonable grounds for believing that the person you are seeking is on the premises . . .

In order to decide whether you have reasonable grounds to believe, consider the circumstances before you. For example can you see anybody in the premises through the windows? Can you hear anybody inside? If you can see somebody, is it the person you are seeking? Always be prepared to justify your actions.

. . .your powers are limited if the premises consist of two or more separate dwellings, . . .

In a block of flats or bed-sit you can only search communal areas such as stairs, hallways, kitchens, and bathrooms. **However,** you can search **any** of the dwellings in a block of flats or bed-sit **but only if** you have reasonable grounds for believing that the person you are seeking is in one of those dwellings.

. . .but in all other circumstances you may enter and search those premises . . .

'Premises' includes any place in the open air under occupation or ownership and in particular includes any:
(a) vehicle, vessel, aircraft, or hovercraft;
(b) offshore installation;
(c) renewable energy installation; and
(d) tent or movable structure.

Note: you **must** always give anybody on the premises the reason why you are seeking entry, even if it appears obvious (s 23, PACE Act 1984).

7.9.1.1 Power of entry to arrest on warrant

You may search and enter those premises to arrest a person under the execution of the following warrants:

- An **arrest warrant** issued in connection with or arising out of criminal proceedings: Home Office Circular 88/1985, para 8 stated that this section 'is deliberately widely drawn and the words "in connection with" enable a constable to enter and search premises for the purpose among other things of executing a warrant for the arrest of a person for non-payment of a fine'.
- A **warrant of commitment** (i.e. a commitment warrant to prison): this goes further than a default warrant (which orders an offender to appear before a court to explain the reasons for

non-payment of a fine). A warrant of commitment requires the offender to be taken straight to prison unless the monies are paid, and is issued under s 76 of the Magistrates' Courts Act 1980 (for failure to pay fines).

7.9.1.2 Power of entry to arrest for specified offences

You may also search and enter premises in order to arrest a person for any indictable offence (this includes either-way offences, see 5.14.2 above), and also for certain non-indictable offences shown below:

Non-indictable offence with a power of entry to arrest	Explanation
s 163 of the Road Traffic Act 1988	This legislation requires a person driving a mechanically propelled vehicle or riding a cycle on a road to stop if you require him/her to do so. Failing to stop is an offence. Note that you can only use this power when you are in uniform.
s 4 of the Road Traffic Act 1988	This is an offence of driving or being in charge of a mechanically propelled vehicle on a road or other public place when unfit through drink or drugs (see 11.16.2 below).
s 27 of the Transport and Works Act 1992	This offence may be committed by certain staff operating the railways and other guided transport systems when they are under the influence of drink or drugs.
ss 6, 7, 8, or 10 of the Criminal Law Act 1977	These offences include using violence to secure entry (s 6), trespassing with a weapon of offence (s 8), and entering and remaining on premises (s 7), also known as 'squatting' (see 9.8 below). Note that you can only use this power when you are in uniform.
s 4 of the Public Order Act 1986	The result of the suspect's conduct in this offence is to bring about a feeling of fear or provoke a reaction of violence in the victim or recipient (see 9.7.3 below, and note that this power of entry does not extend to s 4A of the same Act).
s 61 of the Animal Health Act 1981	This offence relates to the control of rabies and sets out a power for you to arrest any person you have reasonable cause to suspect to be committing (or to have committed) an offence in relation to bringing animals into the UK.
s 1 of the Public Order Act 1936	This offence (not very common) involves wearing a political uniform in a public place or at a public meeting if it signifies association with any political organization or with the promotion of any political object. The offence originates from the existence of extreme political organizations in the years before the Second World War.
ss 4, 5, 6(1) and (2), 7, 8(1) and (2) of the Animal Welfare Act 2006	These are offences relating to the prevention of harm to animals.

7.9.1.3 Power of entry to arrest for other specified circumstances

You also have a power of entry to arrest anyone whom you are immediately **pursuing**. This could include a person who had escaped from you or a colleague having just been arrested, as well as a patient who has escaped from involuntary custody at a psychiatric unit. Note, however, that the chase must be under circumstances of hot pursuit, for example the person must have only just escaped from lawful custody or a hospital; it cannot be used after a period of days or weeks.

You also have the power of entry to arrest anyone who is liable to be **detained** in a prison, remand centre, young offenders' institution, or secure training centre. Circumstances could include perhaps an escape from the prison itself or whilst being transported in a vehicle between establishments. A person can also be detained at other places, and if he/she was to escape from such detention, then you can use this power of entry to recapture him/her (s 92 of the Powers of Criminal Courts Sentencing Act 2000). Note that under s 92 it is mandatory that any young person (aged 18 years or under) found guilty of an offence for which the penalty has been fixed by law as life imprisonment shall be detained at Her Majesty's prisons.

Section 32(1A) of the Children and Young Persons Act 1969 gives you a power of arrest to arrest a **child** who is absent from care, but only if the child is in care after having been remanded or committed to local authority accommodation (s 23(1) of the Children and Young Persons Act 1969).

7.9.1.4 Searching premises for a suspect

The power of entry to arrest under s 17 of the PACE Act 1984 permits you to search premises in order to find the person to be arrested, but does not allow you to search for anything else unless you have other justifications for searching. For example, if you have entered premises by force in order to search for and to arrest an adult, there is no justification for looking in a teapot.

7.9.2 Power of Entry and Breach of the Peace

Nothing in s 17(6) of the PACE Act 1984 affects any power of entry to deal with or prevent a breach of the peace. You are entitled to enter either private or public premises in order to make an arrest for a breach of the peace or to prevent a breach of the peace. However, you should **always** make sure that the circumstance you are faced with really constitutes a breach of the peace as shown in *R v Howell* [1982] QB 416 (see 9.6 below).

Once the breach has finished you should not remain on private premises (unless there is another reason to do so) and should be given a reasonable time in which to leave. If you are assaulted (by a resident of the property for example) during that reasonable time, this could be regarded as an assault on a police officer in the lawful execution of his/her duty. However, if you do not vacate the premises after a reasonable time, you may not be acting lawfully and therefore might not be protected under criminal law (*Robson v Hallett* [1967] 2 QB 939).

7.9.3 Power of Entry to Save Life and Property

Subsection 17(1)(e) of the PACE Act 1984 gives you the power to enter premises to save human life and limb and also to prevent serious damage to property. Under part (e) you can enter and search:

- even if you do not have reasonable grounds for believing any person is on the premises;
- all the flats within a block of flats and not just one of them.

(Note that s 17(1)(e) does not give you power of entry in order to arrest a person.)

In the case of *Mandy Baker v Crown Prosecution Service* (2009) EWHC 299 (Admin), it was further decided that you can enter and search under part (e):

- without seeking the permission of the occupant (otherwise this might be self-defeating);
- to save someone from him/herself as well as from a third party;
- without having to give an occupant a reason for using the power of entry if it is impossible, impracticable, or undesirable to do so;
- only to the extent that was reasonably required to satisfy the objective for using the power of entry. For example, if the reason was the danger to life or limb posed by a knife, then the powers available would relate only to a search for that knife (s 17(4) PACE 1984).

7.9.4 The Use of Reasonable Force to Secure Entry

Section 117 of the PACE Act 1984 states that:

> where any part of the PACE Act 1984 grants [you] a power … [you] may use reasonable force, if necessary, in the exercise of the power.

In a similar way to s 3 of the Criminal Law Act 1967, a court must decide that you honestly believed that the force you used was reasonable and whether the circumstances surrounding the use of that force were proportionate to the amount of force you used. In other words, if you are met with force, you may have to equal that force to negate it, and then use even more force in order to take control. You will receive training on this subject as part of your personal safety training.

7.9.5   Health and Safety when Entering Premises

Health and safety issues were examined in 6.7 above. You should always consider the potential risks involved when you search in unplanned situations, as you do not know who or what you will encounter. Note that it might not be necessary to enter premises immediately—it might be better to stay outside, watch the front and back, and secure the area until colleagues with appropriate equipment and resources arrive.

> **TASK 5**
>
> You and a colleague are required to arrest a person on suspicion of theft. You have followed the suspect to her house which has a front and rear entrance, but you lose sight of her at the last moment. How are you going to carry out the arrest (in relation to the premises) and what are your considerations at this time?

7.10   Answers to Tasks

TASK 1

Considerations at road checks:

1. Wear your personal safety equipment including high-visibility clothing.
2. Carry out the road check in an area which is well lit by street lamps.
3. Use signs to reduce the speed of vehicles entering the checking area.
4. Remain alert to the presence of vehicles at all times.
5. Reduce the risk to the general public by asking them to stay in or near their vehicles.
6. Bear in mind the possibility that a vehicle might fail to stop at the road check.
7. Only use the techniques for which you have trained to bring to a halt a vehicle which has failed to stop.
8. Give clear indications to drivers of what you want them to do.
9. Communicate with your colleagues and do not become detached from the main group involved in the check.
10. Select a location with clear views of oncoming traffic.
11. Select a location which is suitable to stop vehicles (particularly large vehicles) such as a lay-by.
12. Provide the opportunity for vehicles to return to the traffic flow safely.
13. Consider the classification of the road and the speed of oncoming traffic if it is part of the 'fast road network' such as a dual carriageway.
14. Make allowances for the safe stopping distances of moving traffic during periods of adverse weather conditions.
15. Avoid certain locations if practicable, such as road junctions, bends, the brow of a hill and crossings.

TASK 2

You are likely to find that making a mind-map and working on your own mnemonic or other way of remembering will really help fix the key points in your mind. Of course, you have GOWISELY to use too.

TASK 3

The power is not absolute and cannot be exercised unless you reasonably believe that the person is wearing the item to conceal his or her identity, so response 3 is incorrect.

There is no reason to believe the person was carrying a dangerous instrument or an offensive weapon, or that the person was likely to be involved in violence, so numbers 1 and 4 are incorrect.

Therefore, the answer is 2. You reasonably believe that the person was attempting to conceal his or her identity.

TASK 4

You probably considered the following:

(a) Is there a door key in the prisoner's property that you can take in case there is no one at the premises to allow you entry?

(b) Is the 's 18' authorization signed and is it in your possession?

(c) At the premises follow the PACE Act 1984 Code of Practice in relation to the searching of premises:
- identify yourself and state the purpose and grounds of the search;
- identify and introduce anybody with you.

(d) Limit your search to the extent that is reasonably required for the purpose of discovering evidence from an electrical store.

(e) A copy of the 'Notice of Powers and Rights' should be given to the occupier or left on the premises if they are empty.

TASK 5

You probably considered the following:

(a) How can you secure all entrances so she does not escape (for example, through the back door)?

(b) Should and can you obtain further support from your colleagues to achieve this?

(c) With the back door secured, knock on the door or ring the bell to locate the suspect.

(d) If there is no response consider what reasonable grounds you have for believing that she is on the premises—for example, can you see her through the window, or have you had the entrances and exits under continuous observation since you saw her enter the premises?

(e) Is this now taking the form of a pre-planned event for which you should consider calling for further assistance? For example, by requesting colleagues with appropriate equipment to order to enter the premises by force, and maintaining your and others' health and safety?

Investigation, Arrest, Detention, and Disposal

8.1   Chapter Briefing

This chapter describes the legislation and police procedure surrounding the detention and arrest of people and the collecting of evidence. You are likely to undertake many of the tasks described in this chapter whilst on Supervised and Independent Patrol.

8.1.1   Aims of the Chapter

This chapter will enable you to:

- understand how to deal with a number of aspects of handling suspects, including their identification by others;
- comprehend the powers to detain and arrest individuals;

- perform some of the regular duties of a police officer, such as the correct completion of your Pocket Notebook and the making of duty statements;
- develop the underpinning knowledge required for a number of NOS elements, several of the PAC headings, and entries for your Learning Diary Phases 3 and 4, and the CARs of your SOLAP.

8.1.2 Police Action Checklist

This chapter will provide you with the underlying knowledge and theory to meet the following requirements of the Police Action Checklist:

8.1.2.1 Disposal

Reporting a suspect for an offence

Make lawful arrests

Convey a suspect into custody

8.1.2.2 Custody office procedures

Present suspect to custody in accordance with force procedures

8.1.3 National Occupational Standards

This chapter will provide you with some of the knowledge required to demonstrate aspects of the following NOS elements:

National Occupational Standard Unit Elements

AA1.1   Promote equality and value diversity
CA1.1   Apply principles of reasonable suspicion or belief
CA1.2   Use police actions proportionately
CA1.3   Use police actions fairly
CD5.1   Arrest, detain, or report individuals
CI101   Conduct priority and volume investigations
CK2.1   Prepare to search vehicles, premises, and open spaces
CK2.2   Conduct searches of vehicles, premises, and open spaces
2K1.1   Escort detained persons
2K2.1   Present detained persons for custody process

8.1.4 IPLDP Phases and Modules

This chapter will provide you with resources to support the following Induction and Operational Modules of the IPLDP.

8.1.4.1 Induction modules

IND 2   Foster people's equality, diversity, and rights (particularly IND 2.1 Identify people's rights and their responsibilities)

IND 10   Use police actions in a fair and justified way (particularly IND 10.3 Use police actions proportionately)

8.1.4.2 **Operational modules**

> OP 3   Respond to incidents, conduct and evaluate investigations
> OP 5   Search individuals and premises
> OP 7   Arrest and report suspects
> OP 8   Escort suspects and present to custody

8.1.4.3 **Legislation, policy, and guidelines**

Aspects of the following topic areas of LPG 1:

- Crime (LPG 1.1);
- Protecting People (LPG 1.3);
- Police Policies and Procedures (LPG 1.4);
- Non-Crime incidents (LPG 1.5).

Much of the content of this chapter relates to IPLDP Phase 3 'Supervised Patrol' and Phase 4 'Independent Patrol'.

8.1.5 **SOLAP**

The contents of this chapter are relevant to the 'knowledge' evidence requirements of CARs CA1, CD5, CK2, CI101, 2K1, and 2K2.

8.1.6 **Learning Diary Phases**

The contents of this chapter may provide you with stimulus material for completion of your Learning Diary (Phase 3) and the following headings in particular:

- Crime;
- Police policies and procedures;
- Stops and searches;
- Ethics and values of the police;
- Rights and responsibilities.

You may also find some content of this chapter relevant to your Learning Diary (Phase 1) under the heading 'Rights and responsibilities'.

8.2 Introduction

In this chapter, we look in detail at the law surrounding detention and arrest, and collecting evidence—both from a crime scene and from people who were victims, witnesses, or perpetrators of a crime. Again, as we have commented throughout this Handbook, you will need to know the law and how to apply it, in relation to detaining a person, arresting someone, and so on, because only with a thorough knowledge of the law allied to a proper understanding of police procedure can you be sure that you are doing the right thing. The forensic procedures are covered in detail in Chapter 13.

Before we go into the detail of the relevant legislation, let us have a quick knowledge check.

If your answer to all or any of these questions was 'No', then this is a chapter you need to study well. We have referred to the general need for the use of your powers to be **proportionate** and this certainly applies to procedures involving detention.

The exercise of your powers should be consistent with the Human Rights Act 1998 and the provisions of the Police and Criminal Evidence (PACE) Act 1984. You have to be able to show that your use of your powers to detain, arrest, and gather evidence was justified and proportionate to what had taken place.

Over the years of your service, you will become very familiar with the layout of a police station, the location of the cells, the role of the custody officer, the procedures for taping and/or video-recording an interview using PEACE principles, the use of the caution, the making of statements, and the use of legal jargon. You will become so used to it in fact that much of it will become automatic to you. That is part of the nature of professionalism. However, do not assume that just because you are so familiar with the criminal justice system that other people will be too. Some of your witnesses and victims might be anxious when first visiting a police station. Your suspects, some of whom will not be hardened criminals, may be anxious too, or confused, or disorientated, so you should remember to explain processes and to anticipate people's unease or discomfort.

All this is part of being a professional and part of your response to safeguard every person's right to dignity and respect. It is all too easy to forget that people can be overwhelmed by the experience of being caught up in the ponderous machinery of criminal justice, and that they may often rely on you to be the centre of reassuring normality, to help them through it. An individual is more likely to respond to you if you show the acceptable, professional, and impartial face of policing. A suspect may start to talk, a victim may feel able to describe what happened, a witness may tell you what he/she saw, felt, smelt, touched, or tasted—all without being forced, intimidated, or humiliated.

Whilst you will learn specialist interview techniques and procedures (we cover some of them in Chapter 12) as your training unfolds, you can offer such reassurance as we have described above from your first day in the police service. A professsional approach to your work as a police officer is nowhere more important than when you are processing a person's arrest and detention. You are taking away a fundamental liberty, and you must be entirely conversant with your powers to do so.

You must also understand the risk assessments which must be made when a person is detained, especially when there is a risk of self-harm. 'Death in custody' is a devastating occurrence to all concerned and treated very seriously by the IPCC investigators.

You do not want your actions to be the pretext or reason for any criticism of police procedure. Any errors or mistakes in process can be a gift to defence counsel; you do not want to lose a case because you had the details wrong. Worse, you do not want someone who is guilty to walk free, and possibly offend again, because of a procedural or technical lapse on your part.

8.3 The Pocket Notebook

Very soon after joining your police force as a student police officer you will be issued with a pocket notebook (commonly referred to as a 'PNB'). No doubt at the same time you will be given instructions on force policy concerning the keeping and use of the PNB, its surrender, the issuing of new PNBs, and so on. However, there are a number of fundamental aspects of the PNB common to virtually all police forces:

- it notes the start and finish time of each period of duty;
- it is used to keep a contemporaneous account (unless impossible) of information collected during an incident: for example, a statement made by a suspect or a description given by a witness;
- it should note clearly where you have consulted with another police officer (for example your assessor whilst on Supervised Patrol) in the writing of an entry;
- it may be used to increase the extent and accuracy of recall in court (see 8.3.4 below and 12.10);
- there is a need to ensure that the language you employ in writing the notebook is clear, factually based, and does not employ exclusionary language.

8.3.1 How to Use the Pocket Notebook

Although it may appear on the surface rather trivial, the importance of your PNB cannot be overemphasized. Your force places obligations upon you to record matters within it and, if you use it to give evidence, the courts have the opportunity to examine it. Therefore, rules have been established in relation to its completion and if these rules are not followed then the correctness or even the authenticity of the entries will be questioned.

We have already seen how a number of NOS elements are concerned with the need to keep accurate, legible, and complete records

> **Top ten hints for using a PNB:**
> 1. Carry it at all times on duty.
> 2. Use it to record evidence (not your opinion, except in the case of drunkenness!).
> 3. Remember that it is a supervisor's responsibility to issue you with a new one when needed.
> 4. Always apply the general rules (see below).
> 5. It often contains other useful information.
> 6. You may refer to it while giving evidence (but see 8.3.4 below).
> 7. Remember, it is police property.
> 8. Use it for drawing diagrams as well as writing.
> 9. On duty, do not use additional pieces of paper either to supplement your PNB, or as an alternative.
> 10. Don't lose it!

The following depicts some pages from a PNB outlining the **general rules** that you should apply for making PNB entries:

01

<u>Write the day, date and year at the beginning of entries for each day and underline them</u>

DO   NOT   LEAVE   SPACES

If you do leave a space, then ——— draw ——— a ——— line to ———

indicate nothing further can be added. ————————————————

Always make the pocket book entries in black ink. ———————————

Make all entries legible. —————————————————————

WRITE	Write in the pocket book at the same time as the event happens. If the ———
THE	circumstances make it impossible to do so at the time, then do it as soon as —
TIME	practicable after the event, in which case always give a reason for not doing so,
IN THIS	e.g.: 'Whilst using officer safety techniques, I was unable to make any entries'.
COLUMN	Each entry should include the time and name the location where the notes ———
USING	were made. ——————————————————————————
THE	Write your entries in a single line of writing on the lines of the pages of the —
24 HR	book ONLY, not anywhere else in the book (except when you make drawings, in
CLOCK	which case, draw across the page). ———————————————————

Use every line and page of the pocket note book. ————————————

Do NOT overwrite errors. ——————————————————

Do NOT erase or obliterate errors. ——————————————————

If you do make a mistake, cross it out with a single line, ~~so it can be still~~ —

~~read~~, then put your initials beside the deletion, and then write down —

the words(s) you wish to use straight after the ~~mistake~~ I.N.I.T.I.A.L.S. —

If you accidentally turn over two pages by mistake and leave some blank pages,

draw a diagonal line across the blank pages and write 'omitted in error' across

the page.————————————————————————

Do NOT tear out or remove any of the pages or parts of the pages. ————

Write all SURNAMES in BLOCK CAPITALS. ——————————————

Write down the names and addresses of victims, suspects and witnesses.———

Write down all identifying features such as serial numbers of property, ———

including vehicles or documents, e.g. the registration numbers of vehicles.——

If you write down what a person says to you 'Then do so in direct speech!' and

make sure that you record the conversation verbatim or word for word. ———

8.3.2 Example of a PNB Entry

The following is an example of a typical PNB entry:

01

<u>Wednesday 16th January (0000)</u>

	Duty 0600–1600 ———— Patrol ZZ 10 ——————
	Refreshment time 0900 and 1400 —————
0545	Briefing at ZZ ———————————
0550	Collected keys for ZZ 10 patrol vehicle index number ZZ 00 ZZZ ———
0600	Checked vehicle seats and feet areas for property—no trace of any property —
0605	Commenced patrol ———————————
0610	At the time stated on the date above, I was alone on mobile patrol in uniform travelling in an easterly direction along Sheerbury Road, Ramstone , ———— approximately 50 metres east of the junction with Applebreaux Road, when I saw a Fordover motor vehicle, index number YY 00 ZZZ being driven in the — same direction approximately 20 metres in front of me. There was a clear —— unobstructed view of this vehicle. I caused the vehicle to stop in Sheerbury — Road, 20 metres west of the junction with Applebreaux Road and spoke to the driver who was the sole occupant of the car. The driver identified him/herself to me as First Middle <u>LASTNAME</u>, born 00/00/00 address 101 Hernegate —— Road,Ramstone, Kentshire. ———————
Q	'May I see your driving Licence and insurance for this vehicle please?' ———
R	'Haven't got my insurance with me, but here is my driving licence.' ———— Driving licence details LASTN0000FM9ZZZ —————
Q	'As a result of what you have just told me, I suspect you of failing to produce or not having a certificate of insurance for this vehicle.' I cautioned Mr(s) —— <u>LASTNAME</u> and said s/he was not under arrest and free to leave at any time.
Q	'Where is your insurance certificate right now?' —————
R	'It's at home, I think. It's been a while since I last saw it.' ————
Q	'What is the name of your insurance company?' —————
R	'I can't remember that either.' ———————
Q	'How much did you pay for the insurance?' —————
R	'Again, sorry, can't remember.' ———————
Q	'How long have you owned this vehicle?' —————
R	'About a month.' ————————
	PNC CRO check no trace <u>LASTNAME</u>. PNC vehicle check <u>LASTNAME</u> RO at —— address given. Voter's register check confirmed <u>LASTNAME</u> living at address — I completed an HO/RT/1 form . —————

	Q	'As you haven't been able to produce your insurance to me now, please produce your certificate of insurance and this form at a police station within 7 days — Have you got any questions for me, and do you understand what you have to — do?' LASTNAME made no reply.
	Q	'I have been making a record of our conversation, would you please read these notes I have made, and if you agree they are a true record of what we have — said, would you please sign my notes to that effect?' ————— This is a true record. FM Lastname
	Q	'As you have been unable to produce your certificate of insurance to me here, I am going to report you for the offence of failing to produce or not having a — certificate of insurance for this vehicle.' I cautioned LASTNAME and there was no reply. These notes were made at the time between 0610 and 0630. ———— CL Underwood PC 118118
0630		Resumed patrol.
0900		Refs ZZ
0945		Resumed patrol.

8.3.3 Summary of the Rules

PNB rules can be summarized by the mnemonic 'no ELBOWS(S)', commonly used in police training.

E	no Erasures
L	no Leaves torn out/Lines missed
B	no Blank spaces
O	no Overwriting
W	no Writing between lines
S	no Spare pages
(S)	but Statements should be recorded in 'direct speech'

8.3.4 Effective Use of the PNB in Court

Courtroom skills, protocols, and behaviour are considered in detail in 12.10 below. However, it is worth noting at this point that you may have to refer to your PNB when giving evidence in court, and if given permission to do so (although technically your notes themselves do not constitute evidence). There is a certain art to this. In a Police Research Series publication by Stockdale and Gresham in 1995 it was noted that:

> [w]hile it was recognised that reference to notes was often essential, for a variety of very good reasons, many officers were criticised for being over dependent and for reading rather than referring to their notes. Such behaviour was judged to reduce the credibility of the police evidence and was held to be damaging to the prosecution case. (Stockdale, 1995, p 25).

TASK 1

Write down the reason why we should not refer in a PNB to the 'Christian name' of a witness.

TASK 2

Formulate your own system for remembering the general rules concerning PNB entries—for example, a mind-map or mnemonic.

8.4 Cautions

From the moment you start dealing with anybody you suspect of committing an offence, you must remember that he/she has the right to certain information. Code C 10 of the PACE Act 1984 Codes of Practice outlines the necessity to give a suspect a warning or caution at certain points during the investigative process.

The type of caution given depends on the stage of the investigation. The caution may be given:

(a) at the very beginning of an investigation, when he/she is first arrested and interviewed, or interviewed without having been arrested. In this case use the **when questioned** caution

(b) right at the end of the investigation, just before he/she goes to court (whether arrested or not), as a result of charge or reporting the suspect. In this case use the so-called **now** caution. This caution is his/her last chance to have what he/she says put on record before going to court.

To summarize therefore, there are **two** different kinds of caution with an apparently very small difference between them. The difference is the words 'when questioned' and the word 'now'. In both cases you are warning the suspect about how his/her words can be used as evidence. The difference is about the precise stage in the investigative process when the caution is given. The 'when questioned' caution is before the interview of the suspect, and the 'now' caution is right at the end of the investigative process. In both cases, whatever they say can be used in evidence.

8.4.1 The Three Parts to a Caution

There are three parts to a caution which we describe below (Code C 10.5):

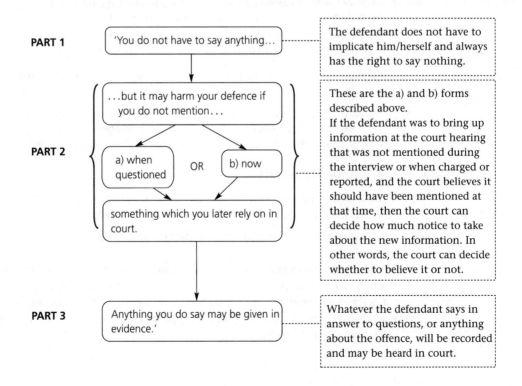

PART 1 'You do not have to say anything... — The defendant does not have to implicate him/herself and always has the right to say nothing.

PART 2 ...but it may harm your defence if you do not mention... a) when questioned OR b) now something which you later rely on in court. — These are the a) and b) forms described above. If the defendant was to bring up information at the court hearing that was not mentioned during the interview or when charged or reported, and the court believes it should have been mentioned at that time, then the court can decide how much notice to take about the new information. In other words, the court can decide whether to believe it or not.

PART 3 Anything you do say may be given in evidence.' — Whatever the defendant says in answer to questions, or anything about the offence, will be recorded and may be heard in court.

8.4.2 When to Caution a Suspect

The following describes the circumstances in which to caution a suspect (Code C 10.1):

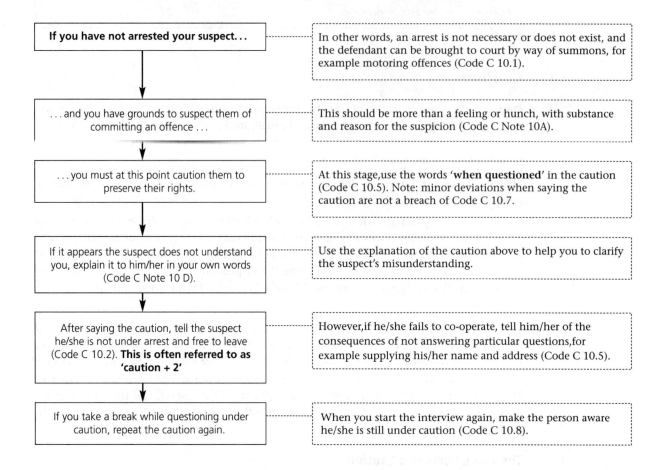

If you have arrested your suspect, you must caution him/her at the time of the arrest unless:

- it is impossible for you to do so because of his/her condition or behaviour: for example, he/she may be unconscious or fighting (Code C 10.4 and Code G 3.4);
- the suspect has already been cautioned before he/she was arrested, because he/she was suspected of committing an offence (Code C 10.4 and Code G 3.4).

The correct time to give a caution was explained succinctly in *R v Nelson and Rose* [1998] 2 Crim App R 399:

> The appropriate time to administer the caution ... is when, on an objective test, there are grounds for suspicion, falling short of evidence which would support a *prima facie* case of guilt, not simply that an offence has been committed, but committed by the person who is being questioned.

8.4.3 Is a Caution Required?

If you have not arrested your suspect, and your questions are for other purposes (Code C 10.1), you do not need to use a caution. Examples of such situations are:

- when you ask for a driver's name and date of birth under the Road Traffic Act 1988 (see Code C 10.9);
- when you ask for a person's identity or the identity of the owner of a vehicle;
- when you ask a suspect to read and sign records of interviews and other comments (see Code C para 11 and Note 11E, and 'unsolicited comments' in 8.5.1 below);
- whilst you carry out a search using an appropriate power and at the same time following the PACE Codes of Practice.

8.4.4 Other Times when a Caution is Needed

You need to use a caution when informing someone that he/she may be prosecuted, for example:

- when you charge (a charge is a written accusation) a detained person with an offence or inform a person that he/she may be prosecuted (reported for an offence). At this stage, use the word 'now' in part 2 of the caution in 8.4.1 above (see Code C 16.2);
- when you inform a person not under arrest that he/she may be prosecuted for an offence. At this stage, use the word 'now' in the caution (see Code C 16.2). This is not a requirement within the Codes of Practice, but if the 'now' caution is not given at this time, the court cannot draw its own conclusions if the defendant then enters new information at the hearing; the court might be more likely to believe the new information (see Code C Note 10 G). The advice is therefore to use the 'now' caution after informing a person that they may be prosecuted.

8.4.5 Recording a Caution

Always write down in your PNB (or on a record of the interview) when you give a caution. You must also record whether it was the 'when questioned' or the 'now' version (See Code C 10.13).

8.4.6 Caution after Charge

Having been charged with, or informed he/she may be prosecuted for an offence, a detained person may not be interviewed further unless the interview is necessary for the following reasons (listed in Code C, para 16.5):

- to prevent or minimize harm or loss to some other person, or the public;
- to clear up an ambiguity in a previous answer or statement;
- in the interests of justice for the detainee to have put to him/her, and have an opportunity to comment on, information concerning the offence which has come to light since he/she was charged or informed he/she might be prosecuted.

The caution that is given to a detainee before an interview takes place is often referred to as the 'restricted' caution as it is much shorter in length when compared to the 'when questioned' or 'now' cautions described in 8.4.1 above. Before any interview, the interviewer should:

(a) caution the detainee, using the words 'you do not have to say anything unless you wish to do so, but anything you do say may be given in evidence'
(b) remind the detainee about his/her right to legal advice.

8.4.7 Understanding the Caution Properly

The caution is a necessary warning that must be given to a person to protect his/her rights and keep him/her informed of the consequences of what he/she says during an investigation. This can only be done if you have a thorough understanding of the 'when questioned', 'now', and 'restricted' variations of the caution so that you can pass the meaning on to the suspect. The suspect can be made more aware of the importance of a caution if you are aware of its significance yourself.

Some people, particularly those who do not have English as their first language, may not understand the caution when formally made. You have an obligation under PACE (Code C 10.7 and Note 10D) to ensure that the detained person comprehends the caution. However, this may not be appropriate at the time of arrest and a full explanation of the caution may only be possible at the time of interview. When in doubt, try to get an interpreter fluent in the suspect's own first language (you may need an interpreter in the interview process as well: see 12.5 for further details on interviewing).

8.4.8   Cautions in Scotland and Wales

The Scottish caution is:

> You are not obliged to say anything but anything you do say will be noted and may be used in evidence.

However, if a suspect was arrested having committed an offence in Scotland, then either he/she would be escorted back to Scotland for interview or a member of the Scottish police force would travel to interview the suspect.

You may provide the caution directly in Welsh where the use of the Welsh language is appropriate.

TASK 3

You will of course learn the cautions and when to use them. However, you will often have to explain a caution to an individual in your own words. Imagine you have arrested somebody. Firstly, decide which caution you will use at this stage. Secondly, after you have cautioned your suspect, she tells you that she did not understand what it meant. Write down how you would explain the caution to her.

8.5   Unsolicited Comments by Suspects

Following a decision to arrest a suspect, he/she must not be interviewed about the relevant offences except at a police station (Code C 11.1). Bear in mind that an interview is defined as the 'questioning of a person regarding his/her involvement in a criminal offence', which must be carried out under caution (Code C 11.1A).

So what do you do when a suspect who has been arrested suddenly says something that applies to the offence in question, or to another offence? After all, the comments may contain information that could be used in evidence.

Such utterances are referred to as 'unsolicited' or voluntary comments. The procedures for recording unsolicited comments (and their possible subsequent use in a court hearing) are provided in the Codes of Practice. Unsolicited (or voluntary) comments by suspects are of two types; relevant comments and significant statements.

A relevant comment can be made by a suspect at any time, and includes anything which might be **relevant to the offence** (Code C 11.13 and Note 11E), for example:

> That other person you've arrested, it was them that did it, you'll see, just ask the witness you've been talking to, they'll back me up, you'll see!

A **significant statement** includes anything which appears capable of being used in **evidence against the suspect**, and in particular an admission of guilt (Code C 11.4A). The term derives from Part III of the Criminal Justice and Public Order Act 1994:

> A significant statement or silence is one which appears capable of being used in evidence against the suspect, in particular a direct admission of guilt, or a failure or refusal to answer a question or to answer it satisfactorily which may give rise to an inference.

It may be part of a relevant comment and must be made by a suspect at any time in the presence and hearing of a police officer (or other police staff member), for example:

> I wish I hadn't done it now, but I lost my temper, the knife was on the table and I just kept stabbing and stabbing and stabbing!

8.5.1   Recording Unsolicited Comments

Write down any such comment made by the suspect in your PNB, noting when the comment was made, and then sign the entry. When practicable, ask the suspect to read it and to check whether it is a true record of what was said. If the suspect agrees that it is a true record, ask him/her to endorse the record with the words 'I agree that this is a correct record of what was said' and to sign (Code C Note 11E).

If the suspect does not agree with the record, you should record the details of any disagreement in your PNB, and then ask the suspect to read your record and to sign that it accurately reflects his/her disagreement. You should also record any refusal to sign (Code C Note 11E).

8.6 Identification of Suspects whose Identity is Unknown

A significant number of the incidents you will deal with on the street whilst undertaking Supervised or Independent Patrol will involve criminal offences which have been witnessed by other members of the public. In many cases the witness is able to remember something about what the suspect(s) looked like, but the identity of the suspect is probably not known. The Codes of Practice outline a process to safeguard the rights of a possible suspect. The Codes specify that a record must be made of the **first description** of the suspect that is given by a witness, and describe the procedures for taking a witness to a particular neighbourhood or place to identify the suspect. Finally, if the witness is successful in pointing out the suspect to you, the circumstances under which the identification was made must be recorded in line with the precedent set in the case of *R v Turnbull* [1976] 63 Cr App R 132. The following subsections provide more detail of the procedures involved.

8.6.1 Circumstances for Identifying a Suspect

The only circumstance under which you can carry out such an identification is when the identity of the suspect is **not known**, ie you do not have reasonable grounds to suspect a particular person or group of people of committing that offence (Code D 3.2)).

Do not take a witness to identify a suspect who has already been arrested. In such circumstances the suspect's identity is regarded as being known (Code D 3.4). Other identification procedures are used once a suspect has been arrested—for example identification parades, video identification, and group identification.

8.6.2 The First Description

Where it is practicable, a record should be made of the witness's description before asking him/her to make any kind of identification (Code D 3.2a). This first description must be clearly recorded in a visible and legible form which can be given to the suspect or the suspect's solicitor. Ideally, it should be recorded in your PNB, and a copy made for the suspect or the solicitor.

8.6.3 Support for the Witness During the Identification

Care must be taken not to direct the witness's attention to any individual, unless, taking into account all the circumstances, it cannot be avoided (Code D 3.2b). However, this does not prevent a witness being asked to look carefully at the people around or to look towards a group, or in a particular direction. This might be necessary to ensure that the witness does not overlook a possible suspect or to enable the witness to make comparisons between any suspect and others who are in the area.

The identification may be compromised if you specifically draw the witness's attention to the suspect (see Note 3F), or the suspect's identity becomes known before the procedure. Therefore do not point at the suspect or ask the witness to verify your choice.

8.6.4 More than One Witness

Witnesses should be taken **separately** to see whether they can identify the particular person independently. This may mean that you will have to call for other patrols to help you with the identification process (Code D 3.2c).

8.6.5 Recording an Identification

The student police officer or police support employee accompanying the witness must record as soon as possible in his/her PNB full details of the action taken (Code D 3.2e).

The record should include:

1. the date, time, and place of the relevant occasion the witness claims to have previously seen the suspect;
2. where any identification was made;
3. how it was made;
4. the conditions at the time (for example the distance the witness was from the suspect, the weather, and light);
5. if the witness's attention was drawn to the suspect;
6. the reason for his/her attention being drawn;
7. anything said by the witness or the suspect about the identification or the conduct of the procedure.

8.6.6 Evidence to be Gathered from the Witness

The witness has had two opportunities to see the suspect. First, around the time the offence was committed, and second, when taken to the neighbourhood of the incident. Always consider that the visual evidence from the first sighting may be disputed in court. You should try to minimize that possibility by applying the guidelines set by case law in *R v Turnbull* [1976] 63 Cr App R 132. A helpful way to remember the component parts of *Turnbull* (as it is commonly referred to in police circles), is to use the mnemonic ADVOKATE, an approach common within police training:

A Amount of time the suspect was under observation

D Distance between the witness and the suspect

V Visibility (for example what was the lighting like, what were the weather conditions?)

O Obstructions to his/her view of the suspect

K Known or seen before (does he/she know the suspect and, if so, how?)

A Any reason for remembering the suspect (this would apply if the witness has seen the suspect before and could include a distinguishing feature or peculiarity of the person, or the very nature of the incident itself that made the person memorable; this can relate to previous or present sightings)

T Time lapse between the first and any subsequent identification to the police (this is not the time between first seeing the suspect and the writing of the statement)

E Errors between the first recorded description of the suspect and his/her actual appearance

---

8.6.7 ADVOKATE in detail

In essence, the circumstances of an observation will alter from moment to moment and this needs to be recorded in detail.

In terms of the **Amount** of time the suspect was under observation, consider the following:

- During the time that the witness saw the suspect carrying out the criminal act, for how long was he/she looking at the suspect?
- Record the total time but also identify how long the witness observed the suspect at specific moments throughout the entire period; it is highly unlikely that a suspect stood in exactly the same position for the whole observation period.
- Was there a break (however brief) in his/her observation?
- What were the various distances involved (see below) and how long was the suspect observed for at that particular distance?
- Was it a frontal view, rear view, profile view?

In terms of the **Distance** between the witness and the suspect consider the following:

- How far away was the witness from the suspect when the incident took place?
- If in the street, count kerbstones as a guide: they are usually one metre long.

- Record the distance between the suspect and the witness. The distance is likely to vary during the course of the observation and will rarely be one measurement.
- Record furthest distance, shortest distance, and timings involved at each level.
- Where was the witness in relation to the suspect?

In terms of the **Visibility**, consider the following:

- Was it day or night?
- Were the street lamps on?
- Was the witness wearing glasses or contact lenses?

Weather conditions must be included in detail, for example it is not sufficient to say 'It was raining':

- Was it heavy rain, drizzle, etc?
- Was sunlight a factor?
- Where was the sun in relation to the suspect and the witness?
- Were there shadows cast?
- Include, if possible, the distance of available visibility.

In terms of **Obstructions** to his/her view of the suspect, consider the following:

- Any obstruction between the witness and the suspect should be described in detail. It is insufficient to say, for example, that the view was obstructed by a hedge. How tall, how wide, how dense was it?
- Obstructions include glass and the glass would need to be described as well: its size, was it clean or dirty, frosted, open, closed, double-glazed, was there glare from the sun, etc?
- How did the obstruction actually obstruct the view of the witness and to what extent?
- Record the distance between the witness and any obstructions.

In terms of whether the suspect is **Known** or has been seen before, consider whether there is an association between the witness and the suspect, for example a relationship, friendship, or do they work together? If there is an association then:

- How long has the witness known the suspect?
- How does he/she know the suspect?
- In what context and how well?
- When did he/she last see the suspect?
- Has his/her description changed in the interim period?

In terms of the existence of **Any** reason why the witness should remember the suspect consider the following:

- This could be a distinguishing feature or peculiarity of the person, or the very nature of the incident itself that made the person memorable. This can relate to previous or present sightings.
- Was there anything unusual about the suspect's appearance (for example distinguishing features) or the prevailing circumstances?
- What, if anything, attracted the witness's attention?
- What has stuck in his/her mind?

In terms of the **Time** lapse between the first and any subsequent identification to the police consider the following (note that this is not the time between first seeing the suspect and the writing of the statement):

- How much time elapsed between recording or obtaining a description and the sighting of the suspect?
- How much time elapsed between recording or obtaining a description and the subsequent identification?

In terms of **Errors** between the first recorded description of the suspect and his/her actual appearance consider the following:

- Remember, you must have recorded a first description.
- Once the victim identified the suspect later on, what was the similarity between the first description and what the suspect actually looked like?
- Record any errors, or differences between the first description, and the actual appearance of the suspect when he/she was identified (for example a suspect is identified while wearing a black sweatshirt when the original description recorded a hooded top).
- You must record the difference to show integrity of the evidence.

One of the most important issues to consider when using this process of identification is the question whether or not you had sufficient evidence upon which to justify an arrest prior to taking the witness to make an identification. If you had such evidence, then the courts may consider that an identification method relating to known identity of the suspect might be more appropriate.

Remember also that, although you can ask a witness to look carefully at the people around at the time or to look towards a group or in a particular direction, you must **not** draw the witness's attention to the suspect.

TASK 4

You attend an incident involving criminal damage of property belonging to a householder. The victim tells you the incident happened five minutes ago and that he/she can definitely identify the suspect. What are your actions going to be at this point and what will you say to the victim?

8.7 Arrest Without Warrant

It is no surprise that the right to liberty is an important principle within the Human Rights Act 1998 (see 5.12 above) and your power to arrest and take away a person's liberty clearly challenges that right. It is therefore obvious that the proper use of your power to arrest a person for the right reason and at the right time is paramount.

The information provided here will assist you in providing evidence to meet NOS element CD5.1:

National Occupational Standard Element

CD5.1 Arrest, detain, or report individuals

---

and in particular the following performance criteria:

- to 'check that there are the grounds and legal authority for your actions';
- to 'identify the individual subject to your actions in accordance with legislation and current policy'.

The information provided here is also relevant to the PAC heading 'Disposal' and in particular 'make lawful arrests', and also contains material likely to be relevant to Phase 3 of the IPLDP LPG 1 under the 'Police Policies and Procedures' heading, particularly LPG 1.4(1).

The term 'arrest without warrant' may need explaining. You may have heard the phrase 'the judge ordered a warrant for his arrest' used by the media when reporting, for example, the failure of somebody to attend court. In these circumstances a **warrant** (in the form of a document) is issued and it is the responsibility of the police, or in some cases a civilian enforcement officer, to serve the warrant on the person concerned (see 8.8 below). However, the police also have powers to arrest without the need for a warrant, for example, in response to a public order crime. These powers are referred to as 'arrest without a warrant' and are the most common forms of street-level arrest that you are likely to use.

In the course of your duties whilst on Supervised or Independent Patrol, you may need to arrest without a warrant someone who you suspect of committing a criminal offence. Apart from the power to arrest for a breach of the peace (see 9.6 below), and specific powers of arrest from other legislation, you also have a 'general' power of arrest without a warrant that stems from s 24 of the PACE Act 1984 (as amended by s 110 of the Serious Organised Crime and Police Act 2005). Using these powers, you may arrest a person whether you are in uniform or not; however, you may arrest a person **only if** certain criteria are met. These criteria are discussed below.

8.7.1 The Two Conditions for an Arrest to be Lawful

The two conditions for an arrest to be lawful are:

1. that a person is about to commit an offence, or is in the act of committing an offence, or that there are reasonable grounds to suspect that a person is involved, or has attempted to be involved in the commission of an offence and
2. that there are reasonable grounds for believing that the person's arrest is necessary.

So you must not arrest a person only because of his/her involvement, or suspicion of involvement in a criminal offence. You must make an arrest **only if it is necessary**. The reasons for which an arrest may be necessary are specified in s 24(5) of the PACE Act 1984 and its Code G, para 2.9 (see 8.7.4 below).

Before we look further at the power of arrest, it is important that you understand the term 'reasonable grounds to suspect', as it is a central component part of the power.

8.7.2 Reasonable Grounds to Suspect

It is important to bear in mind that although words such as 'suspicion', 'grounds', and 'belief' are in common usage they have particular meanings within the context of policing and the law. You may need to relearn some of the concepts in order that you can exercise your powers within the law—do not assume that these terms necessarily mean what you think they mean.

- Whether or not something is **reasonable** is a conclusion that one or more people reach in agreement as a result of personal experience or understanding. It is a practical, level-headed, and logical result.
- **Grounds** for something include a reason or argument for a thought to exist.
- To **suspect** something is to think that it is probably true, although you are not certain.
- To **believe** something is a stronger and more concrete conclusion.

Therefore, in order to decide whether you have reasonable grounds to suspect, consider the offence you are investigating. Then consider the component parts of that offence, and whether or not a like-minded person would draw the same conclusion as you about the suspect and the offence. For example, did the person have the opportunity, the motive, the presence of mind, and the incentive to commit the offence? And did he/she have the means? Alternatively, the person could have the same employment as the suspect, have previous convictions for similar offences, live near the crime, wear similar clothing, have a similar name, make visits to similar localities, or fit the description of the suspect (see *Chief Constable of West Yorkshire v Armstrong* (2008) EWCA Civ 1582).

Note however, that an arrest can never be justified simply on the basis of obeying the orders of one of your supervisors or managers (*O'Hara (AP) v CC of the RUC* (1997) 1 CrAppR 447). Equally, it is insufficient for you to infer that your supervisors or managers had reasonable grounds for suspicion (see *Commissioner of Police of the Metropolis v Mohamed Raissi* (2008)

EWCA Civ 1237). To justify such an arrest, you must have been given sufficient information by a supervisor or manager to generate your own reasonable grounds to suspect the person to be arrested, (see *(1) Sonia Raissi (2) Mohamed Raissi v Commissioner of Police of the Metropolis* (2007) EWHC 2842 (QB)). If the information is insufficient (for whatever reason: for example, it may be too sensitive to be passed to you), then the supervisor or manager must make the arrest him- or herself.

8.7.3   Involvement in the Commission of a Criminal Offence

The first condition for an arrest to be lawful is that you know, or have reasonable grounds to suspect, that a criminal offence is in the process of being committed (or is about to be committed). This is shown in the table below:

You may also arrest someone on suspicion of committing an offence on an earlier occasion.

Level of involvement	Example
A person is **about to commit** an offence.	You are on duty, in non-uniform clothing, in an electrical store when you see a woman, who is obviously not a member of the shop staff, walk up to a display of mp3 players, select one, and put it under her coat. You see her walk towards the entry/exit of the shop, making no attempt to pay for the item. You stop her as she is about to leave the shop, as she is about to commit an offence. If it is **necessary**, you may arrest her (see 8.7.4 below).
A person is **in the act of committing** an offence.	You are on duty, in non-uniform clothing, in an electrical store when you see a man walk up to a display of DAB radios, cut a security link, pick up a radio, and walk towards the door of the shop past the check-outs, without paying for the radio. The store alarm is activated and the man continues to walk out of the shop. You decide the man is stealing the radio and stop him just outside the shop as he is in the act of committing the theft of the radio. If it is **necessary**, you may arrest him (see 8.7.4 below).
You have **reasonable grounds** for **suspecting** a person to be **about to commit** an offence.	You are on duty, in non-uniform clothing, in an electrical store when you see a man walk up to a display of mobile phones. He appears to be extremely nervous. You see him take a metal cutter out of his pocket. He then reaches out with the tool in his hand towards the security chain of the mobile and appears to be about to cut the chain when he is disturbed and puts the tool back in his pocket and walks away. A few seconds later the same man returns to the display of mobiles, takes out the same tool, places the tool around the security chain, and sets off the alarm. At this moment you walk up to the man having decided you have reasonable grounds for suspecting he is about to commit an offence. If it is **necessary**, you may arrest him (see 8.7.4 below).
You have **reasonable grounds** for **suspecting** a person **to be** committing an offence.	You are standing outside a store that sells electrical goods when you see a person standing just inside the store near the doorway. The person is carrying an unpacked, brand new DVD player underneath his arm with the lead and plug dragging behind. He also has a rucksack on his back and appears nervous. You see him use a tool to cut away the security tag from the DVD player which he throws in a bin by the door, and then starts to place the player in the rucksack. The person then walks towards the door as if to leave the store. You note the obvious facts: • the player should be boxed or at least in a bag supplied by the shop; • the person carrying it should not be so anxious to leave the shop quickly, especially with the lead dragging along the ground; • the person should not have cut the security tag; • he should not be placing the DVD player inside a rucksack. You therefore form reasonable grounds for suspecting that he has been found to be in the process of committing an offence of theft of a DVD player. If it is **necessary**, you may arrest him (see 8.7.4 below).

Note that you **do not have to be certain** that:

- the offence actually took place. As an example, imagine that you are standing outside the shop mentioned above when a man runs out of the shop carrying an unpacked, brand new DVD player underneath his arm with the lead dragging behind. The store alarm is activated. You therefore suspect that an offence has recently been committed, but you cannot be certain.
- the suspect is the actual person who carried out the suspected offence. You run after the person but lose sight of him in a crowd. A short while later you are still without confirmation that a DVD player has been stolen from the store, but you see a person fitting the description of the person you ran after earlier. You decide you have reasonable grounds for suspecting he is the same person that you saw earlier, and reasonable grounds for suspecting the player has been stolen.

Remember, however, you must be certain that it is **necessary** to arrest the suspect, and have clear **reasons** in mind (see 8.7.4 below).

In other situations, it will be clearer that an offence has definitely been committed. For example, a shop owner who deals with **every** sale in their shop sees a woman walk up to a display of cameras, pick one up, and walk towards the door of the shop without paying for it. The store alarm is activated. The shop owner decides that she has stolen the camera, runs after the suspect, stops her, and then calls the police and you attend to investigate the offence of theft.

In these circumstances, you may arrest (if it is **necessary**):

- **anyone who is guilty of the offence**. For example, when you arrive at the shop, the shop owner tells you the circumstances in the presence and hearing of the suspect, and you therefore have information that an offence has been committed. The shop owner confirms an offence of theft has occurred.
- **anyone who you have reasonable grounds for suspecting to be guilty**. Assume that, in the above example, the shop owner runs after her, but is unable to catch up. He calls the police and supplies a first description of the woman. The description is passed to you and later during the day, several miles away from the shop, you see a woman fitting the description given by the shop owner earlier. You decide therefore that you have reasonable grounds for suspecting her of the theft.

8.7.4 Reasons that Make an Arrest Necessary

Note at the outset that an arrest is not always necessary, and as a student police officer you will need to make decisions for each particular situation, such as:

- what action to take when you first come into contact with the suspect—for example, when to caution, search, use personal safety equipment or techniques;
- whether to arrest, report for summons, grant street bail, issue a fixed penalty notice, or take any other action.

In 8.7.1 above, we explained that there are two conditions which need to be satisfied before an arrest should be made. The first concerns the existence of an offence, and we discussed this in 8.7.3 above. The second condition is that one or more of a number of **reasons** make the arrest **necessary**. The possible reasons are set out in the PACE Act 1984, Code G 2.9 (Code G is available at <http://www.police.homeoffice.gov.uk/news-and-publications/publication/operational-policing/PACE_Chapter_G.pdf>).

An arrest is deemed to be necessary if one or more of the following reasons apply:

(a) to obtain someone's name

(b) to obtain someone's address

(c) to prevent injury, damage, indecency, or obstruction

(d) to protect a vulnerable person

(e) to ensure prompt investigation

(f) to prevent a suspect disappearing.

These reasons are explained below in more detail.

8.7.4.1 To obtain someone's name or address

You must always explain the consequences if the person refuses to provide his/her name or address, ie that it may lead to his/her arrest. Remember, this is not a power to arrest a person who simply refuses to give you his/her name or address. Instead, this is just one of several reasons that make a person's arrest necessary in particular circumstances. You may arrest someone in a situation where:

1. You do not know and cannot readily ascertain the person's name or address

Do not just ask him/her for his/her name and address once, or in a manner that lacks confidence. Make it clear to him/her that you need his/her name and address, and explain that you suspect that he/she has committed an offence, and that you require his/her name and address in order that the process of investigation can be followed.

2. You have reasonable grounds for doubting whether a name or address given by the person is real

You must have a logical reason for not believing that the name or address he/she gave you is correct, for example:

- he/she cannot give you anything which identifies him/her with the name or address (for example a driving licence with a photograph);
- you suspect he/she is using the name or address of a close relative with the same details (which are therefore false);
- there is no record of the name or address he/she provided in the voters' register or telephone directory;
- you suspect his/her name or address is fictitious because it is the name or address of a famous person or character.

Code D of the PACE Act 1984 Codes of Practice provides more detailed information about the definition of a satisfactory address.

Examples of **unsatisfactory** addresses include:

- that of a person who is working in the UK and leaving very soon, never to return;
- that of a person of 'no fixed abode' who cannot supply any other permanent addresses;
- the address the person supplies does not exist;
- the existence of a person with a different name registered as a voter at the address he/she has given.

However, an address will be satisfactory if some other person (for example employer or relative) at that address will accept service of the summons on his/her behalf. This could be used by a person whose home address is not in the UK.

8.7.4.2 To prevent injury, damage, indecency, or obstruction

A reason for arresting someone could be to prevent the person:

- **causing physical injury to any other person:** for example, if you were investigating an offence of throwing fireworks in a street or public place under s 80 of the Explosives Act 1875, you might reach the conclusion that the suspect may harm him/herself or somebody else;
- **suffering physical injury:** for example, if you were investigating a person for an offence of

being a pedestrian on the carriageway of a motorway under s 17(4) of the Road Traffic Regulation Act 1984, you might reach the conclusion that the suspect may suffer physical injury him/herself from a passing vehicle veering off the main carriageway;

- **causing loss of or damage to property:** for example, if you were investigating a person for an offence of interference with a motor vehicle or trailer under s 9 of the Criminal Attempts Act 1981, you might reach the conclusion that the suspect might cause damage to a vehicle during the interference;
- **committing an offence against public decency:** for example, if you were investigating a person for an offence of using profane or obscene language under the Town Police Clauses Act 1847, you might reach the conclusion that the suspect was committing an offence against public decency (however, this legislation can only be used when the acts are committed in the presence of members of the public who cannot avoid the suspect);
- **causing unlawful obstruction of the highway:** for example, if you were investigating a person for an offence of wilful obstruction of the highway under s 137 of the Highways Act 1980 and the suspect was stopping or slowing vehicular traffic on the highway, you might reach the conclusion that the person would need to be removed.

At this stage, do not lose sight of the need for reasonable grounds for believing that the arrest is necessary to prevent the person from causing one of these outcomes. Remember, this is not a power of arrest for a person who just carries out one of these actions. Instead, they are reasons that make a person's arrest **necessary**.

8.7.4.3 To protect a child or other vulnerable person

A reason for arresting someone could be if you were investigating a person for any offence and you suspected that the suspect was putting the health and safety of a vulnerable person or child at risk as a result of his/her conduct. An example would be that he/she was standing on the hard shoulder of a motorway with an elderly relative, and refused to move away from the traffic.

8.7.4.4 To allow the prompt and effective investigation of the offence or of the conduct

There may be many reasons why you may feel that an investigation might be jeopardized if you do not arrest the suspect, such as where it is necessary to obtain evidence by questioning or where there are grounds to believe that the person:

- has made false statements (for example, dates of birth, denials of disqualification from driving);
- has made statements which cannot readily be verified (for example, ownership of property for which he/she has no records, such as vehicle registration documents);
- has presented false evidence (for example, forged driving licences or MOT certificates);
- may steal or destroy evidence (for example, disposing of stolen property from a burglary);
- may make contact with co-suspects or conspirators (for example, a warning through the use of mobile telephones which would make the co-suspects more difficult to locate);
- may intimidate, threaten, or make contact with witnesses (for example in cases where the identities of the suspect and victim are known to each other).

This may include cases such as when you are considering an arrest in connection with an **indictable** offence (see 5.11 and 5.14 above) and there is an operational need to:

- enter and search any premises occupied or controlled by the person being considered for arrest: if you do not arrest him/her, you will not be able to use s 18 of the PACE Act 1984 to search his/her premises;
- search the person: if you do not arrest him/her, you will not be able to use s 32 of the PACE Act 1984 to search and seize property;
- prevent contact with others: if you do not arrest him/her, you will not be able to seek the authority to delay the right of the detained person to have someone informed of his/her detention;
- take fingerprints, footwear impressions, samples, or photographs of the suspect: if you do not

arrest him/her, you will not be able to obtain forensic evidence from the suspect;

- test him/her for drugs, thereby ensuring compliance with statutory drug-testing requirements: if you do not arrest the person, you will not be able to use s 63B of the PACE Act 1984 to obtain samples from the suspect to ascertain whether he/she has taken a Class A drug.

8.7.4.5 To prevent the disappearance of the person in question

This may arise if there are reasonable grounds for believing that:

- if the person is not arrested, he/she will fail to attend court: for example, there is currently a warrant for the arrest of the person for failing to appear at court and he/she has now committed another offence;
- street bail after arrest would be sufficient to deter the suspect from trying to evade prosecution: for example, the arrest and subsequent use of street bail would be beneficial and would make the suspect more inclined to answer to bail at the appropriate time and place.

The reasons that make an arrest necessary may be remembered by the mnemonic **ID COP PLAN**.

I	Investigation	To allow the prompt and effective **investigation** of the offence or of the conduct of the person in question.
D	Disappearance	To prevent any prosecution for the offence from being hindered by the **disappearance** of the person in question.
C	Child	To protect a **child** or other vulnerable person from the relevant person.
O	Obstruction	To prevent the relevant person causing an unlawful **obstruction** of the highway.
P	Physical Injury	To prevent the relevant person causing **physical injury** to him/herself or any other person.
P	Public Decency	To prevent the relevant person committing an offence against **public decency.**
L	Loss or damage	To prevent the relevant person causing **loss** of, or damage to, property.
A	Address	To enable the **address** of the relevant person to be ascertained.
N	Name	To enable the **name** of the relevant person to be ascertained.

8.7.5 Arrest Without Warrant by Other Persons

We have described the reasons why you, as an attested student police officer (a constable), may arrest a person. However, other persons (other than a constable) may arrest someone but only if a constable is not present to carry out the arrest (s 24A(3)(b) of the PACE Act 1984) and the offence concerned is an indictable offence, and only if it is necessary in order to prevent:

- injury to the suspect;
- injury to another person;
- damage to property;
- the suspect escaping before a constable can arrest him/her.

A person (other than a constable) may also arrest without a warrant, if he/she sees:

- anyone in the act of committing an indictable offence (s 24A(1)), for example shoplifting or burgling a house;
- anyone whom a person has reasonable grounds for suspecting to be committing an indictable offence (s 24A(1)), such as a member of the public who sees a person climbing through a window into his/her neighbours' house and suspects this person to be committing burglary (without actually knowing if the person has the neighbours' permission to enter the premises);
- where an indictable offence has been committed (s 24A(2)), such as when a store detective

observes a person taking property from a display and leave the shop without paying. The next day, the same person returns to the shop and the store detective is positive it is the same person and decides to arrest him/her.

8.7.6 Summary

The power of arrest without warrant is governed by Code G of the PACE Act 1984 Codes of Practice. Remember that the arrest of a suspect is not mandatory in every case where an offence has been committed. There are other ways of processing a suspect who has committed an offence, such as reporting for summons, granting street bail, or issuing a fixed penalty notice. These are covered later in this chapter. The power to arrest without warrant is no different from any other power that you have been given as a police officer, and if you fail to observe the rights of an individual, your investigation will be discredited at best and at worst discontinued. Finally, remember, you can only use the power of arrest if it meets **both** of the criteria in 8.7.1 above and is **necessary** (see 8.7.4 above).

TASK 5

Think of a practical example for each of the offences of unlawful possession of drugs (see 10.13 below), criminal damage (see 10.21 below), theft (see 10.3 below), and a s 5 Public Order Act offence (see 9.7 below). Consider the circumstances under which you would arrest for these offences and what possible reasons you would have for believing that arrest to be necessary.

8.8 Warrants of Arrest

In 8.7 above, we discussed your general power to arrest without a warrant. Occasionally however, whilst on Supervised or Independent Patrol you may be required to arrest a person on the basis of a warrant.

A warrant is a formal written document of authority issued by a magistrate or judge, which directs the person to whom it is addressed to carry out an action on behalf of the court. A warrant is normally, but not exclusively, addressed to the police, and may be directed towards a group as well as to an individual. A warrant of arrest therefore authorizes the arrest of a named individual to take place.

The following warrants of arrest and committal may be executed by you even though the warrant might not be physically in your possession at the time, under s 125 of the Magistrates Courts Act 1980. The most common warrants that you are likely to be involved with are for failure to answer bail, non-payment of fines, non-appearance at court, and warrants associated with witnesses giving evidence at court.

8.8.1 Non-Payment of Fines

Section 76(1) of the Magistrates Courts Act 1980 states that:

> [w]here default is made in paying a sum adjudged to be paid by a conviction or order of a magistrates' court, the court may issue a warrant of distress for the purpose of levying the sum or issue a warrant committing the defaulter to prison.

8.8.2 Non-Appearance at Court

Section 55(2) of the Magistrates Courts Act 1980 states that:

> [w]here the court, instead of proceeding in the absence of the defendant, adjourns or further adjourns the hearing, the court may, if the complaint has been substantiated on oath, issue a warrant for [his/her] arrest.

8.8.3 Witness Warrant for Arrest

Section 97(2) of the Magistrates Courts Act 1980 states that:

> [i]f a justice of the peace is satisfied by evidence on oath that it is probable that a summons would not procure the attendance of the person in question, the justice may, instead of issuing a summons, issue a warrant to arrest that person and bring [him/her] before such a court, at a time and place specified in the warrant.

8.8.4 Warrant of Arrest for Material Witness in Committal Proceedings

Section 97A(5) of the Magistrates Courts Act 1980 states that if:

(a) a person fails to attend before a justice in answer to a summons under this section,

(b) the justice is satisfied by evidence on oath that [he/she] is likely to be able to make a statement or produce a document or other exhibit,

(c) it is proved on oath, or in such other manner as may be prescribed, that [he/she has] been duly served with the summons and that a reasonable sum has been paid or tendered to [him/her] for costs and expenses, and

(d) it appears to the justice that there is no just excuse for the failure, the justice may issue a warrant to arrest [him/her] and bring [him/her] before justice at a time and place specified in the warrant.

TASK 6

Find out about and then describe in your own words the process for executing a warrant.

TASK 7

What is the 'European Arrest Warrant'? How does it work?

8.9 Making an Arrest

Here, we deal with the process of making an arrest and your responsibility towards the suspect in relation to protecting his/her rights.

It will therefore cover:

- what information should be given to the suspect on arrest;
- how much force you can use when making an arrest;
- under what circumstances you can release the suspect before arriving at the police station;
- what you can and cannot ask the suspect before arrival at the police station;
- how long that journey should take;
- under what circumstances you can search the arrested person;
- when you should inform him/her that he/she is under arrest for a further offence.

Making an arrest is an important milestone to achieve with your Police Action Checklist. In particular the 'Disposal' heading of the PAC is relevant here and particularly the confirmation that you can make lawful arrests.

The relevant NOS element is:

National Occupational Standard Elements

CD5.1 Arrest, detain, or report individuals

The information given here will help you develop some of the knowledge and understanding required for CD5.1 and in particular:

> **Legal and organizational requirements**
>
> 1. Current, relevant legislation, policies, procedures, codes of practice and guidelines for conducting arrests, detentions, and reporting procedures.
> 4. The legal rights of individuals who have been arrested, detained, and reported.
>
> **Conducting arrests, detentions, and reporting procedures**
>
> 5. How to check there is sufficient evidence or legal authority for arrest, detention, and reporting procedures
> 10. When and how interviews may be conducted with a detained person to obtain urgent information.
> 11. The need to release individuals without delay where information is obtained which negates the need for arrest or detention.

The evidence for the achievement of this element will come from successfully conducting arrests whilst under supervision on at least five different occasions.

Finally, ensure that you read about your general powers of arrest (see 8.7 above) before you consider the more detailed information on arrest provided below.

8.9.1 Information to be Given on Arrest

Section 28 of the PACE Act 1984 states that:

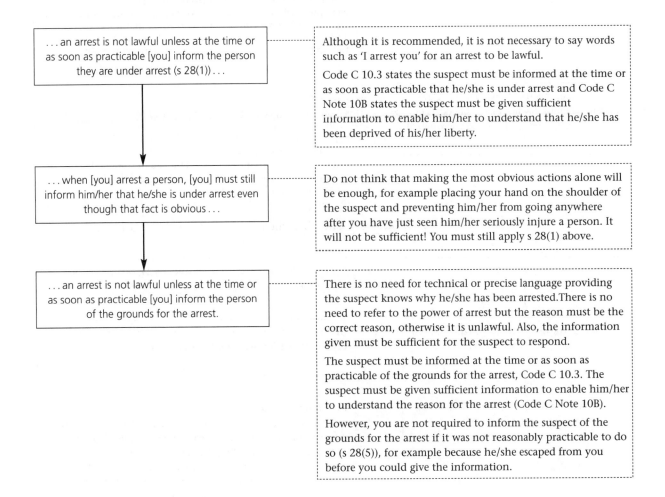

...an arrest is not lawful unless at the time or as soon as practicable [you] inform the person they are under arrest (s 28(1))...	Although it is recommended, it is not necessary to say words such as 'I arrest you' for an arrest to be lawful. Code C 10.3 states the suspect must be informed at the time or as soon as practicable that he/she is under arrest and Code C Note 10B states the suspect must be given sufficient information to enable him/her to understand that he/she has been deprived of his/her liberty.
...when [you] arrest a person, [you] must still inform him/her that he/she is under arrest even though that fact is obvious...	Do not think that making the most obvious actions alone will be enough, for example placing your hand on the shoulder of the suspect and preventing him/her from going anywhere after you have just seen him/her seriously injure a person. It will not be sufficient! You must still apply s 28(1) above.
...an arrest is not lawful unless at the time or as soon as practicable [you] inform the person of the grounds for the arrest.	There is no need for technical or precise language providing the suspect knows why he/she has been arrested. There is no need to refer to the power of arrest but the reason must be the correct reason, otherwise it is unlawful. Also, the information given must be sufficient for the suspect to respond. The suspect must be informed at the time or as soon as practicable of the grounds for the arrest, Code C 10.3. The suspect must be given sufficient information to enable him/her to understand the reason for the arrest (Code C Note 10B). However, you are not required to inform the suspect of the grounds for the arrest if it was not reasonably practicable to do so (s 28(5)), for example because he/she escaped from you before you could give the information.

According to Code G2 of the PACE Act 1984 Codes of Practice you are required to inform the arrested person of the relevant circumstances of the arrest in relation to both elements of s 24 of the PACE Act 1984. That is, you are required to tell him/her:

- the circumstances surrounding his/her involvement, or suspected involvement, or attempted involvement in the commission of a criminal offence;
- and the reason(s) why the arrest is necessary (see 8.7 above).

For example:

> I have just seen you run out of the store with a brand new digital radio under your arm. I heard the store alarm sound at the same time and I therefore suspect that you have stolen the radio. I am arresting you on suspicion of theft of that radio as the arrest is necessary to allow the prompt and effective investigation of the offence by interviewing you on tape at the police station and through the search of any premises occupied or controlled by you for evidence relating to similar offences of theft.

8.9.2 The Use of Force to Arrest a Person

You may need to use force to arrest a person, but the amount of force you use must be reasonable. Two pieces of legislation will help you here: s 3 of the Criminal Law Act 1967 and s 117 of the PACE Act 1984.

Section 3(1) of the Criminal Law Act 1967 states that:

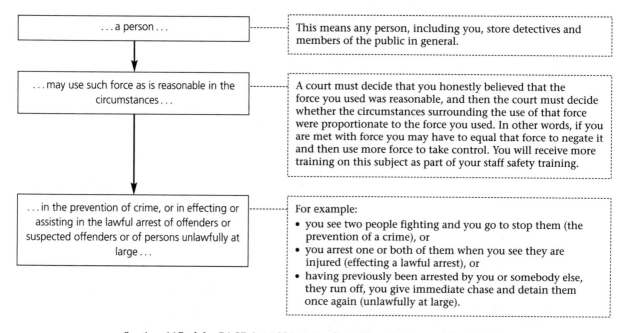

Section 117 of the PACE Act 1984 states that where any part of the PACE Act 1984:

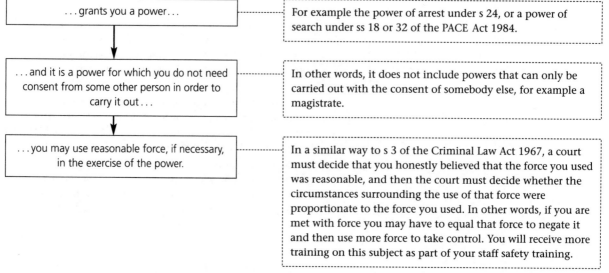

8.9.3 What to Do Immediately after an Arrest

First, do not forget to caution the suspect! (see 8.4 above and the PACE Act 1984, Code G 3.4) Second, unless it is impracticable to do so, record in your PNB:

- the nature and circumstances of the offence leading to the arrest;
- the reason or reasons why the arrest was necessary;
- the fact that you gave a caution;
- anything said by the person at the time of arrest.

8.9.4 Searching a Suspect after Arrest

Section 32(1) of the PACE Act 1984 states that you can search any person who has been arrested elsewhere than at a police station if you have reasonable grounds for believing that the arrested person may present a danger to himself or others. This is not a power to search everybody after arrest; you must have reasonable grounds for believing that the person to be searched may have concealed on his/her person anything that could be used to escape or provide evidence of an offence.

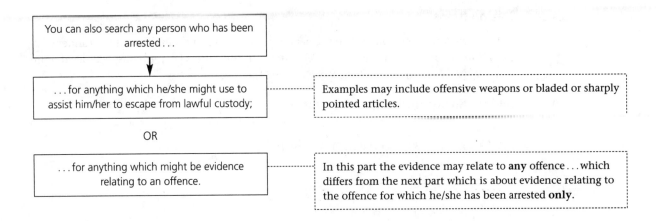

When using these powers to search a person, you only have a power to search to the extent required to find the item you are seeking—for example if you are looking for a plasma TV, there is no reason to be looking in a trouser pocket. You cannot require him/her to remove any clothing in public other than an outer coat, jacket, or gloves, but you may search a person's mouth.

8.9.5 Searching Premises after an Arrest

Under s 32(2)(b) of the PACE Act 1984 you may search premises, but only if the offence for which the person has been arrested is an indictable offence. However, you must have reasonable grounds

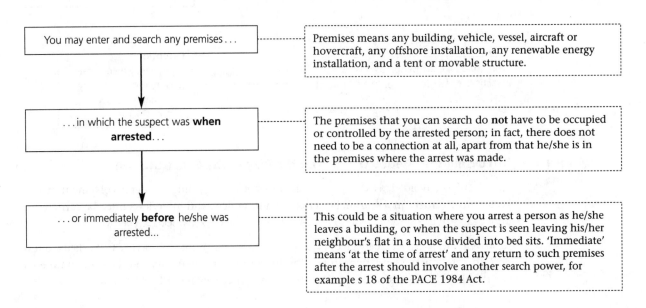

for believing that there is evidence relating to that offence on the premises. You may **only** search for evidence relating to the offence for which the person has been arrested; it is **not** a 'fishing trip'.

When using these powers to search such premises, you only have a power to search to the depth required to find the item you are looking for. For example, if you are searching for a petrol generator taken from a building site, there is no justification for looking in a toilet cistern.

This also means that when, for example, using these powers to search a block of flats or a bed sit you must limit the power to search to:

- a dwelling where the arrest took place or the arrested person was immediately before the arrest; or
- communal areas, for example stairs, hallway, etc.

If permission is not given to search then you may enter a premises by reasonable force, under s 117 of the PACE Act 1984. This section applies to any other part of the Act, including s 32 (PACE Act 1984) searches of premises, referred to immediately above.

Further details on searching premises after an arrest are given in 7.7 above.

8.9.6 Seizing Items

You can seize anything you find on the person or premises as a result of searching (under s 32), apart from items to do with legal privilege—for example letters from the suspect's legal representative (ss 19, 32(8), 32(9) of the PACE Act 1984).

8.9.7 Taking the Suspect to a Police Station

If someone is arrested (but not in a police station), he/she must be taken to a police station as soon as possible (s 30(1) of the PACE Act 1984).

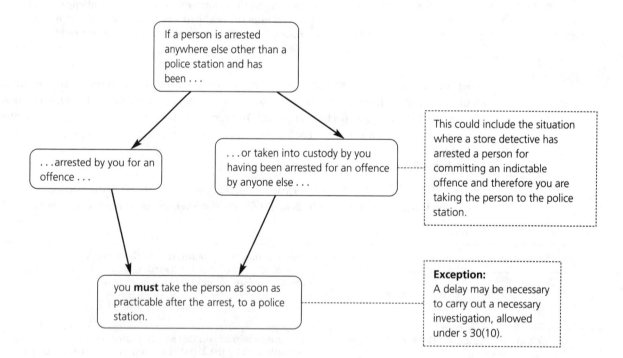

8.9.8 Discussing the Alleged Offence on the Way to the Police Station

This should be avoided, as any questioning of a person regarding his/her involvement or suspected involvement in a criminal offence is an interview, and interviews must be carried out under caution in a suitable place (PACE Act 1984, Code C 11.1A: see 12.5 below).

However, if the suspect freely gives information to you without you having first asked a question, then follow the guidelines in relation to significant statements and relevant comments (see 8.5 above, and see also how we use this during interviewing in 12.5.5 below).

8.9.9 Location for an Interview

After an arrest it is likely that you will conduct an interview with the suspect. Any interview should take place at a police station (PACE Act 1984, Code C 11.1A), but there might be reasons for conducting the interview elsewhere. This would apply if taking the suspect to a police station would cause a delay that could:

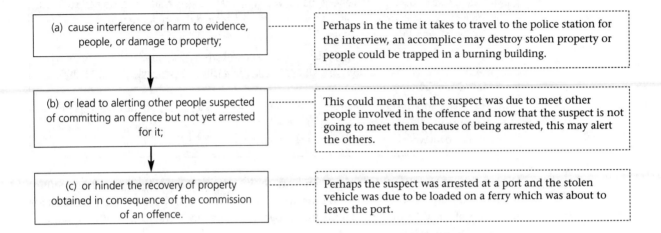

If any of these risks cease to apply, the interview should be stopped and moved to a police station. If the risks no longer exist and you continue the interview without moving to a police station, you may be jeopardizing the whole investigation.

8.9.10 'De-arresting' a Suspect

Any person you arrest in a place other than at a police station must be released if you are satisfied that there are no longer any grounds for keeping him or her under arrest (s 30(7), PACE Act 1984): for example, if you initially decided that an arrest was necessary because the suspect did not give you his/her name but on the way to the police station the person supplied his/her name. As a result, the reason for the arrest would no longer exist, there would be no need to go to the police station, and the person would have to be released. Under these circumstances you are required to make a record of the release. Make a record in your PNB explaining why the circumstances for keeping him/her under arrest no longer exist.

8.9.11 The Suspect has Committed Further Offences

Section 31 of the PACE Act 1984 states that:

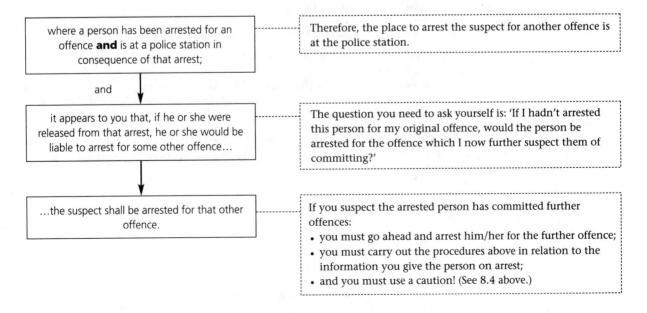

TASK 8

Consider the following scenario:

You are standing outside a tool shop when you see a man run out of the shop carrying an unpacked, brand-new drill with a label still attached. The shop alarm is activated. During your briefing at your police station before commencing patrol you were made aware that this shop had suffered a number of walk-in thefts over the last few days. You therefore decide to arrest him.

You say (on a bad day):

> Hey ... you're not going anywhere, you've got to come with me, I'll tell you why later ... for now just do as I say ... have you got a problem with that? Got anything to say, well it doesn't matter. Come on, give me that drill'.

Take a moment to write down what is wrong as far as the PACE Act 1984 and the Codes of Practice are concerned.

Next write down what you should have said to the person.

Undertaking this task will help you demonstrate the knowledge and understanding requirement of NOS Unit CD5. It could also form the basis of evidence of the knowledge required for Unit CD5 of the CAR in your SOLAP and in particular the 'legal and organizational requirements' evidence sections.

8.10   Power to Retain Property from a Detained Person

There will be occasions when it is necessary to seize and retain a suspect's property. This normally occurs when the property is potentially to be used as evidence against the suspect.

The main guidance is found in s 22 of the PACE Act 1984 although you will also be given detailed guidance by your police force when undertaking training. Note that s 22(4) states that 'nothing may be retained if a photograph or copy would be sufficient for that purpose', so you must ensure that the property itself is required and that a photograph or copy would not be sufficient.

Section 22 of the PACE Act 1984 also explains that the property 'may be retained so long as is necessary in all the circumstances' but does not elaborate further on the meanings of 'necessary' and 'circumstances'. However, common respect for the property rights of others (as described, for example, in the Human Rights Act 1998) would suggest that property that is no longer relevant to an investigation should be returned to its owner as soon as possible. Your force is likely to have a 'Property Management Policy' that sets out the protocols for return (see, for example, that of Leicestershire Constabulary at <http://www.leics.police.uk/files/library/documents/property_policy20060103.pdf>).

The legislation describes two main reasons for seizing and retaining property:

(a) anything seized for the purposes of a criminal investigation may be retained ...
   • for use as evidence at a trial for an offence, or
   • for forensic examination or for investigation in connection with an offence ...
(b) anything may be retained in order to establish its lawful owner ... where there are reasonable grounds for believing that it has been obtained in consequence of the commission of an offence.

When seizing and retaining property bear in mind the need to minimize contamination and to maintain a continuity record (see 13.5 below) and also the rules concerning 'Retaining, Recording, and Revealing' (see 12.6 below).

TASK 9

Familiarize yourself with the forms used by your force that are used to record 'special' property (property relating to a crime) which you seize from a suspect, or 'special' property which you take possession of, having been abandoned or recovered from a criminal activity.

Once you have seized such property, where is it initially stored and, if required, where is it stored for longer periods of time? What are your organizational procedures for retrieving exhibits in order to take them to court, for example, evidential recordings of interviews?

8.11 Presentation of Detained Persons to Custody Officers

The experience of being arrested can be a highly charged emotional event, and as a police constable you are required to maintain your professionalism throughout. An arrest is the start of a long process for the suspect, and you have a responsibility to preserve his/her rights throughout the whole detention process. Having deprived him/her of his/her liberty, you have to prioritize your activities surrounding the detention, so that the suspect and the incident you are investigating receive the appropriate attention.

The information given here is relevant to the custody office procedures checklist in the PAC, in particular the requirement to 'provide grounds of arrest to custody officer' and 'search suspect and place in cell where appropriate', and the 'disposal' checklist, in so far as it requires you to 'convey a suspect into custody'.

It is also relevant to the following NOS elements:

National Occupational Standard Elements

2K1.1   Escort detained persons
2K2.1   Present detained persons for custody process
2K2.2   Conduct initial custody reception actions

8.11.1 Arrival at the Police Station with an Arrested Person

When an arrested person reaches the boundary of a police station, he/she should be taken before a **custody officer** as soon as practicable after arrival (Code C 2.1A).

The time that the arrested person arrived at the police station is relevant because he/she can only be kept in custody for 24 hours after arrival. The arrival time is referred to as the **relevant time**. Therefore, make a note of this time in your PNB.

8.11.2 The Custody Officer

A custody officer is a police officer of at least the rank of sergeant, or a police support employee designated as a staff custody officer (although the latter arrangement is unusual). His/her main duty is to ensure that all persons in police detention are treated according to the PACE Act 1984 and the Codes of Practice, and that such treatment is recorded on a custody record.

You are required to inform the custody officer of the relevant circumstances of the arrest in relation to both criteria of s 24 of the PACE Act 1984, ie the suspect's **involvement in the commission of a criminal offence** and the **reason(s)** why the arrest was necessary (Code G 2.2, see 8.7 above).

Here is an example of what you might say to the custody officer:

> At 1100 hours today I was on duty outside an electrical store in the High Street when I saw this person run out of the store with a brand new digital radio under his arm. I heard the store alarm sound at the same time and I therefore suspected that he had stolen the radio. I arrested him on suspicion of theft of

the radio to allow the prompt and effective investigation of the offence by interviewing him on tape here at the police station, and also to obtain authority from an Inspector to search any premises occupied or controlled by him for evidence relating to similar offences of theft.

You should then remain with your arrested person during this initial custody process.

8.11.3 The Decision to Charge a Suspect

The custody officer must decide if there is enough evidence to charge your arrested person at this point (s 37(2), PACE Act 1984). If the custody officer decides there is not enough evidence to charge the suspect, he/she can still detain the arrested person if they have reasonable grounds for believing that detention without being charged is necessary to:

* secure or preserve evidence relating to an offence for which he/she is under arrest, for example to carry out searches for evidence; or
* obtain such evidence by questioning the suspect, such as by using a tape recording.

The time that the custody officer authorizes the detention of the arrested person is important, as it is from this moment that the **review times** of the detention are calculated. The reviews are carried out by an inspector not more than:

* six hours from the time of authorized detention; then
* nine hours after the first review; then
* at nine-hour intervals after that.

8.11.4 The Detainee's Rights After the Arrest

If the custody officer decides to detain your arrested person he/she must inform the detainee of the following rights, which continue throughout his/her detention (PACE Act 1984, Code C 3.1):

1. the right to have someone informed of his/her arrest
2. the right to consult privately with a solicitor and receive free legal advice, and
3. the right to consult the PACE Act 1984 Codes of Practice.

The detainee must be given two written notices (Code C 3.2). The **first notice** sets out:

* the three rights noted above;
* the arrangements for obtaining legal advice;
* the right to a copy of the custody record; and
* an explanation of the caution, for example what it means to him/her (see 8.4 above).

The **second notice** sets out the detainee's entitlements while in custody: for example the provision of food and drink, access to toilets, and so on.

The detainee will be requested to sign the custody record to confirm his/her decision about legal advice and informing someone of his/her arrest (Code C 3.5). The custody officer will also determine whether the detainee requires:

* medical attention, for example as a result of an injury or lack of medication;
* an appropriate adult, for example, the parent or guardian for a juvenile, or a relative or guardian for a mentally vulnerable person;
* help to check documentation, for example clarification of any of the rights; or
* an interpreter, for example for non-English-speaking detainees or those with speech or hearing impairments.

The custody officer will record his/her decision about the requirements on the custody record and will also carry out an assessment of the detainee to determine whether he/she will be a risk to him/herself or others. Such assessment will include a check of the PNC, and consultation with you as the arresting officer and appropriate healthcare professionals, for example custody nurses (Code C 3.6).

8.11.5 The Detainee's Right to Inform Someone of the Arrest

The detainee may have one friend, relative, or interested person informed of his/her whereabouts as soon as practicable (s 56, PACE Act 1984 and Code C 5.1). If the attempt fails, the detainee can suggest two other people to be contacted, to try and ensure that one person knows the detainee's whereabouts. At the discretion of the custody officer or the officer in charge of the investigation, further attempts can be made to contact other people until the information has been conveyed to one person. In the case of a juvenile, the person responsible for his/her welfare **must** be informed of his/her detention.

The detainee shall be given writing materials on request, and be allowed to telephone one person (in addition to the person informed above) for a reasonable time.

The right to have someone informed of the arrest can be delayed, but only if the offence is an **indictable** offence (see 5.11 and 5.14 above) or if there are reasonable grounds for believing that to allow the communication will lead to:

- interference with or harm to evidence or other people;
- alerting other people suspected of committing an indictable offence, but not yet arrested;
- hindrance relating to the recovery of property.

The delay can only be authorized by an officer of at least the rank of inspector, and the delay must not be for more than 36 hours (s 56, PACE Act 1984 and Code C, Annex B).

A detainee's right to legal advice can be delayed (Code C, Annex B) but this is very rare. The decision must be taken by an officer of the rank of superintendent or above, who must have reasonable grounds to believe the solicitor for the detainee will pass on a message or act in some way which will lead to:

- interference with or harm to evidence or other people;
- the alerting of other people suspected of committing an indictable offence but not yet arrested;
- hindrance relating to the recovery of property.

8.11.6 Searching the Detainee

The custody officer has the power to search detainees, though he/she may ask you to carry out the search. The custody officer will decide the extent to which the search will be made (s 54(6), PACE Act 1984), but the search must not be intimate (it must not involve the physical examination of orifices other than the mouth), and it must be carried out by a constable of the same sex as the detainee (s 54(7)).

A **strip search** can be authorized, but only if it is necessary to remove an article which the detainee would not be allowed to keep (Code C, Annex A 10), and if it is reasonably considered that the detainee has concealed such an article. A strip search must be carried out:

- by an officer of the same sex;
- in an area away from other people;
- in a safe place with at least two other people present;
- with regard to sensitivity.

The following should also be noted:

- to assist with the search, the detainee can be required to lift his/her arms and stand with his/her legs apart;
- if anything is found the detainee should be asked to hand it over;
- the strip search should be carried out as quickly as possible.

8.11.6.1   Items found during a search

All or any of the items found during a search may be recorded on the custody record. Clothes and effects can only be seized (s 54(3)) if the custody officer believes the detainee would use them to:

- harm him/herself;
- damage property;
- interfere with evidence;
- assist in escape; or
- there are reasonable grounds for believing they may be evidence relating to an offence.

The custody officer is responsible for the detainee's possessions after the arrest (Code C 4.1) and must arrange the safekeeping of property which is taken from the detainee.

TASK 10

Earlier you were standing outside a tool shop when you saw a person run out of the shop carrying an unpacked, brand new drill (see Task 8 above). The shop alarm was activated. During your briefing at your police station before commencing Independent Patrol, you were made aware that this shop had suffered a number of walk-in thefts over the last few days. You therefore arrested this person and followed the PACE Act 1984 Codes of Practice accordingly. Having arrived at the police station, you are about to present the arrested person to the custody officer. Consider what you are going to say.

Completion of this task will help you towards achieving the knowledge requirements of CAR 2K2 in your SOLAP.

As you can see, making the arrest and bringing your suspect to the police station is just the beginning of an extended process, at the end of which the detainee may or may not be presented to the court. Whether this happens or not, each detained individual must have his/her rights protected and as the arresting officer you will be partly responsible for this.

8.12   Code D of the PACE Act 1984 and Examinations of Suspects

The Police and Criminal Evidence (PACE) Act 1984, and its associated Codes, are the main sources of legislation that define the way the police should behave toward suspects or volunteers assisting the police. Sections 4–6 of **Code D** of the PACE Act 1984 are concerned with establishing identity through the use of the forensic intelligence and evidence taken or recorded from a person following a search and examination of that person and his/her clothing. Detailed descriptions of the sampling procedures from a forensic perspective are given in 13.5.17; here we concentrate on more general procedures in relation to the rights of the individual detainee.

There are two main reasons why we may wish to collect material from a person for forensic examination: to identify an individual and to provide material for comparison to that found at a crime scene. Normally DNA and fingerprint samples are subsequently retained in databases for 'speculative' (untargeted) searches, but other samples are destroyed.

Some of the key points from ss 4–6 are:

- samples should be **relevant** and should be proportional to the offence (unless they are for speculative searching and are covered by blanket policies, such as DNA and fingerprints);
- **appropriate adults** are required in many circumstances, including where juveniles, the mentally disordered, or the visually impaired are concerned;
- a number of **records** are to be kept concerning consent, authority, and warnings to the detained person. It is vital that these procedures are followed.

Note that when PACE refers to somebody attending a police station voluntarily (s 5.19 of the Code), this is not just referring to a 'volunteer' who is a victim of crime. CSIs, in particular, may use the term volunteer for an entirely innocent person who is attending to supply an elimination sample, or set of fingerprints.

8.12.1   Intimate and Non-Intimate Samples

Samples under Code D fall into several categories, but two are particularly important: intimate and non-intimate samples.

A **non-intimate** sample is:

- a sample of hair, other than pubic hair, which includes hair plucked with the root;
- a sample taken from a nail or from under a nail;
- a swab taken from the mouth or any part of the body apart from other body orifices or the genitals;
- saliva;
- skin impressions from non-intimate areas.

An **intimate** sample is:

- a dental impression;
- a sample of blood, semen, or any other tissue fluid;
- urine;
- pubic hair;
- a swab taken from any part of a person's genitals or from a person's body orifices other than the mouth.

A police officer may take a non-intimate sample from a detained person but must call for the assistance of a **registered** medical practitioner (a doctor, dentist, nurse, or paramedic) for intimate samples.

8.12.2   Fingerprints and Footwear Impressions

These procedures are covered in section 4 of Code D.

Section	Contents	
4	**Identification by fingerprints and footwear impressions**	
	A Taking fingerprints in connection with a criminal investigation	4.1–4.9
	B Taking fingerprints in connection with immigration enquiries	4.10–4.15
	C Taking footwear impressions in connection with a criminal investigation	4.16–4.21
	Notes for guidance	4A–4B

Fingerprints means any record of the fingers or palms taken by any means, such as using traditional ink and paper, or electronically by a device such as Livescan. (This digitized method has been installed in most main police stations. Smaller police stations, and those with limited opening hours, might not have this and may rely on inked impressions.) Importantly, fingerprint and digital technology has moved on since the PACE Act 1984 was first enacted. It is now possible to scan a fingerprint on portable equipment and transmit this to a Fingerprint Bureau direct from a hand-held unit. You can require people to provide their fingerprints when those taken previously have proved unsatisfactory for analytical use. The advent of Livescan makes this less likely, but for the police it is an important right that directly affects the performance of the IDENT1 database.

Impressions taken of footwear are important intelligence tools since they may be compared to a database or file of marks recovered from crime scenes. This might lead to a full shoe: shoe-mark comparison. Hence, one arrest might lead to other crimes also being considered. In essence, the data recovered provide an indication that the detained person may be involved in other offences. This is particularly relevant where property crime is considered, but a well-populated database can also be valuable as an intelligence tool in the investigation of major crimes.

Taking footwear impressions was previously an ill-defined area, since many forces wished to take images or prints of a suspect's shoes covertly, particularly after a number of observations made by the HMIC about using forensic intelligence. A change was brought about by s 118(3) of the SOCPA 2005, which amended s 63A of the PACE Act 1984 by including references to 'impressions of footwear' as well as fingerprints.

8.12.3 Examinations to Establish Identity and Taking Photographs

These procedures are covered in section 5 of Code D.

Section	Contents	
5	**Examinations to establish identity and the taking of photographs**	
	A Detainees at police stations	5.1–5.18
	B Persons at police stations not detained	5.19–5.24
	Notes for guidance	5A–5F

Certain features, such as tattoos and scars, provide valuable identification evidence, and a recent injury may indicate a suspect's involvement in an offence. The Code is not explicit regarding injuries; however, it is common, especially in major crimes, for suspects to be examined by a doctor (or nurse) and to be photographed by a suitable person in connection with injury evidence. Such injuries can include burns from arson attacks, and bruises or lacerations caused by one or both or more parties defending themselves.

8.12.4 Taking Body Samples and Impressions

Parts of s 6 of Code D are relevant to the taking of both intimate and non-intimate body samples and impressions, and also include regulations concerning DNA swabs and pulled hair for use by the National DNA Database (NDNAD).

Intimate samples are essential when the investigator is attempting to prove a sexual assault or rape and other serious offences against the person. It is especially important in these offences to

Section	Contents	
6	**Identification by body samples and impressions**	
	A General	6.1
	B Action	6.2–6.12
	Notes for guidance	6A–6F

attempt to establish the existence, or otherwise, of a 'two-way transfer' to and from both parties (see 13.5.2.2 below). You should attempt to recover intimate samples as quickly as possible after the incident. Failure to secure these samples can hamper an investigation. However, even if intimate samples are not available, your CSI may be able to assist in some circumstances since DNA and other trace evidence can be sourced from a variety of non-intimate sampling procedures.

Non-intimate samples typically yield DNA and trace material from the hair, nails, and skin in addition to prints taken of, say, the bare feet and ears. Code D covers these more unusual body impressions and other forms of evidence comprehensively, but this section of the Code does not permit the taking of impressions from an intimate area.

Finally, note that, although s 6.7 of the Code refers to the use of 'reasonable' force to take a buccal swab, you should not do so since the undue use of force in the mouth areas could be dangerous and swabs can fall apart if force is used.

8.13 Statements from Witnesses and Victims

As a student police officer you will increasingly become involved, under supervision, in incidents involving the investigation of criminal offences, subsequent arrests, and the presentation of suspects to the custody officer. One important part of this is to support witnesses (including victims) and help them make a witness statement. The form used for this is MG 11 and this will form part of the case file for the incident (see 12.7 for more details on MG forms and case files). Victim personal statements are also recorded on the MG 11 form, either following an evidential witness statement or as a separate statement.

The MG 11 form has a front sheet and continuation sheets if required. The back of the MG 11 (once completed) is for police and prosecution use only, in order to protect witnesses. Two different versions of the MG forms are available; one for completing by hand (always use black ink for MG forms), and an electronic version which is completed on a computer and then printed out.

Some of the following guidance is adapted from the unpublished document 'A Guide to Form MG 11, General Completion' by Kent Police.

8.13.1 Witness Statements

Witness statements are generally written by the interviewing officer after he/she has interviewed the witness (see 12.5 below) and they have together agreed the facts that are to be recorded. After the officer has written the statement the witness reads it through and must not sign unless he/she agrees with what has been written. The officer should outline to the witness the consequences of stating anything which is false or that he/she does not believe to be true, and draw the witness's attention to the need to sign a declaration to that effect at the end of the process.

When completing MG 11 forms (or any other MG form):

- do not use abbreviations;
- do not use jargon;
- do not staple the pages together (use a paperclip instead);
- do not use correction fluid or overwrite a mistake.

Any mistakes should be crossed out with a single line and initialled in the margin by the witness.

The witness's name should be written out in full at the top of the form, but only use capitals for the family name. (If you write entirely in capitals, then underline the family name.) In the actual statement, where a witness statement refers to a person, the name the witness gives that person should be used.

For all descriptions of a person, object, or incident, ADVOKATE must be adhered to in full (see 8.6.7 above). Descriptions should be recorded in detail, and any uncertainties should also be fully recorded.

Witness statements must record only what he/she has experienced directly through his/her senses. Opinion should not be recorded apart from:

- a relevant expert providing an expert opinion; or
- a competent witness on whether another person is drunk (see 9.3.1 below).

Exhibits are items that could be used as evidence in court. The exhibit must be given a reference number that includes that person's initials. So for example, the bag of shopping Alice Stoner gave to PC Hoddim will have the reference number AMS/1. PC Hoddim will refer to the exhibit as AMS/1 in his/her statement having taken possession of it from Alice Stoner. The other bag (the orange bag held by the man on the pavement) will have the reference number CU/1 because it was the first item of evidence collected by PC Underwood in this incident. (In 13.5.8 below we give further guidance for officers with respect to the numbering of exhibits.)

8.13.2 Victim Personal Statements

A witness may also be a victim. A victim personal statement (VPS) consists of a further statement by the victim in addition to the evidential witness statement. A VPS provides extra information on how the crime has affected the victim and what support he/she may need. A VPS can also be made by the relatives or partners of homicide victims, or the parents (or carers) of children or of adults with learning difficulties.

MG 11 (T)

RESTRICTED (when complete)

WITNESS STATEMENT

(CJ Act 1967, s.9; MC Act 1980, ss.5A(3) (a) and SB; MC Rules 1981, r.70)

URN

Statement of: *Alice Marion STONER*

Age if under 18: *over 18* (if over 18 insert 'over 18')   Occupation: *Customer service assistant*

This statement (consisting of *one* page(s) each signed by me) is true to the best of my knowledge and belief and I make it knowing that, if it is tendered in evidence, I shall be liable to prosecution if I have wilfully stated anything in it, which I know to be false, or do not believe to be true.

Signature: *AMStoner*   Date: *01.03.08*

Tick if witness evidence is visually recorded ☐ *(supply witness details on rear)*

At 4.00 p.m. on Wednesday 1st March 2008, I was in Kerrie's corner shop which is situated on the north pavement of the High Street at its junction with Hythewell Road, Maidbury. I was standing by the fruit which is located inside the shop approximately 10 metres from the front door but my view of the front door was obscured by upright shelving. The shop sells groceries and is approximately 15 metres by 15 metres with one door for customers in and out. There is shelving fixed to the walls and three lines of upright shelving along the entire length of the shop which is approximately 2 metres high. I could not see any other customers inside the shop at the time, but I could see the shop assistant but only when she leant over to the shelf. She was unpacking ~~some bacon out of a box~~. I would describe the assistant as ... [ADVOKATE]. I will refer to her as Assistant one.

I then heard some sort of a struggle approximately 10 metres away from me towards the back of the shop. I didn't see anything because there was shelving in between me and the scuffle. I heard a man's voice say in a cross way 'what's it to you if some of us ain't got nothing to eat' or something like that and then I heard a long bang like a box falling over or a door slamming. Then I heard a thump and a shout outside. I picked up my bag and went over to the door and Assistant one was standing there rubbing her head like it was hurting. I could see a man in a dark blue or black jacket half lying on the ground outside, holding onto something orange, but I didn't have my glasses on so I couldn't see what it was quite. I would describe the man as... [ADVOKATE]. He was rubbing his leg like it was hurting him a lot.

From the back of the shop, another assistant and a customer came walking towards me. I would describe the assistant as ... [ADVOKATE] and will refer to her as Assistant two. Assistant two had a telephone in her hand. I would describe the customer as ... [ADVOKATE].This customer and Assistant two went out of the front door and held on to the man, but he didn't look like he was struggling much. At 4.10 p.m.. the same day two police officers arrived at the shop, one male and one femle. One of them (PC Hoddim) came into the shop and spoke with Assistant one. I found a bag with some shopping in it by the cold cabinet, which I gave to PC Hoddim (exhibit labelled and marked AMS/1). Then I went out and spoke to the lady officer. AMStoner

This statement was taken by me at 13.26 hours on Saturday 28th March 2009 at Maidbury Police Station. At the end I read it over to Alice Stoner and she read and signed it in my presence. C.Underwood PC 118118, 01.03.08

Signature: *AMStoner*   Signature witnessed by: *C Underwood PC 118118*

PTO

Marginal notes (left column):

The unique reference number will be generated by the unit or department that deals with case file.

Complete the number of pages **after** the statement is finished.

Always begin with the time, day, date, and location. Use the words used by the witnesses (for example 4 p.m. rather than the 24 hour clock).

All descriptions must follow ADVOKATE (see 8.6.7 above).

Any uncertainties must be included.

For starting a new paragraph, do not leave any whole blank lines. There is no need to rule off the space at the end of a line.

Utterances must be recorded in direct speech. Hearsay evidence (she said that he said) should be recorded in direct speech (see 12.9).

The officer who wrote the statement on behalf of the witness must write this declaration at the end of the statement.

The officer must sign and date (including his/her rank and number) immediately after the last word of the declaration and at the end of each page.

The witness should sign at the foot of every page, and after the last word of the statement.

MG 11

RESTRICTED—FOR POLICE AND PROSECUTION ONLY
(when complete)

Witness contact details

Home address: *31 JENNER ROAD, MAIDBURY, KENT*

.... Postcode: *MA99 1XX*

Home telephone No: *1234567* .... Work telephone No: *123456789*

Mobile/Pager No: *1234567* .... E-mail address: *N/A*

Preferred means of contact: *HOME PHONE*

~~Male~~/Female (delete as applicable)   Date and place of birth: *12.00.65 BIG CITY*

Former Name: *N/A* .... Height: *163cm* Ethnicity Code: *W1*

Dates of witness non-availability: *see MG 10*

....

Witness care

(a) Is the witness willing and likely to attend court? ~~Yes~~/No. If 'No', include reason(s) on form MG6. What can be done to ensure attendance?

....

(b) Does the witness require 'special measures' as a vulnerable or intimidated witness? ~~Yes~~/No. If 'Yes' submit MG2 with file.

(c) Does the witness have any specific care needs? ~~Yes~~/No. If 'Yes' what are they? (Healthcare, childcare, transport, disability, language difficulties, visually impaired, restricted mobility or other concerns?)

....

....

....

Witness Consent (for witness completion)

a) The criminal justice process and Victim Personal Statement scheme (victims only) has been explained to me: Yes/~~No~~

b) I have been given the leaflet 'Giving a witness statement to to the police—what happens next?   Yes/~~No~~

c) I consent to police having access to my medical record(s) in relation to this matter: Yes☐ No☐ N/A☑

d) I consent to my medical record in relation to this matter being disclosed to the defence: Yes☐ No☐ N/A☑

e) I consent to the statement being disclosed for the purposes of civil proceedings e.g. child care proceedings (if applicable):   Yes☐ No☐ N/A☑

f) The information recorded above will be disclosed to the Witness Service so that they can offer help and support, unless you ask them not to. Tick this box to decline their services: ☑

Signature of witness: *AMStoner*

Statement taken by (print name): *PC 118118 UNDERWOOD* Station: *Maidbury Police Station*

Time and place statement taken: *17.50 01.03.08 MAIDBURY POLICE STATION*

Sidebar notes:

Use capital letters for all this part.

For example, if previously married.

If no MG 10 form is available then record the relevant information here.

Remember to get the witness to sign here.

The time and date the statement was made should be recorded in your PNB.

A VPS is normally made immediately after a witness statement and using the same MG 11 form. This is known as a Stage 1 VPS. There should be a clear separation between the evidential part of the statement and the VPS, and a caption (see below) should be inserted between the two to emphasize this separation. However, victims may choose instead to make a VPS (or make an additional VPS) at a later stage, which is known as a Stage 2 VPS. A caption should also be used at the start to emphasize that it is a VPS and not an evidential witness statement.

The caption should read as follows (you will need to amend it according to whether it is a Stage 1 or Stage 2 VPS):

> I have been given the Victim Personal Statement leaflet and the VPS scheme has been explained to me. What follows is what I wish to say in connection with this matter. [In addition to what I said in my previous victim personal statement] I understand that what I say may be used in various ways and that it may be disclosed to the defence.

Although he/she can write anything he/she sees fit, you can explain that the statement can express one or more of the following:

- if he/she wants to be told about the progress of the case;
- if he/she would like extra support (particularly if appearing as a witness at a trial);
- if he/she feels vulnerable or intimidated;
- if he/she is worried about the offender being given bail (for example, if the offender knows him/her);
- how the crime has affected him/her, if racial hostility is felt to be part of the crime, or if he/she feels victimized because of his/her faith, cultural background, or disability;
- if he/she is considering trying to claim compensation from the offender for any injury, loss, or damage suffered;
- if the crime has caused, or made worse, any medical or social problems (such as marital problems);
- anything else he/she thinks might be helpful or relevant.

(adapted from Home Office, 2006).

8.14 Duty Statements

A duty statement is a witness statement made by a police officer as a **witness to events.** The general guidance for completing MG 11 forms (8.13.1 above) still applies but there are additional aspects for completing an MG 11 form as a duty statement, and these are shown below.

On the back of the MG 11, for the 'home' contact details sections (at the top) you should use your work address, email, and telephone number. NEVER include your home address or any other personal contact details on the back of the MG 11—consider the potential consequences if a defendant obtained this information. Note that the lower sections on the back (Witness care and Witness Consent) do not need to be filled in for a duty statement; simply put 'N/A' where appropriate.

8.14.1 How to Write Names in Duty Statements

When referring to other police officers, the first time the officer is mentioned in the statement you should write his/her family name in capitals, and include his/her rank and number. If the officer is mentioned again later in the statement, only the rank and name need be used. Witnesses should be referred to using either both names or Mr/Mrs (etc) and the family name in capitals. For suspects, the first time a suspect is named in a duty statement you should give his/her full name with the family name in capitals, but after that use only his/her family name.

MG 11 (T)

RESTRICTED (when complete)

WITNESS STATEMENT

(CJ Act 1967, s.9; MC Act 1980, ss.5A(3) (a) and SB; MC Rules 1981, r.70)

URN

Statement of: *Charlotte UNDERWOOD*

Age if under 18: *over 18* (if over 18 insert 'over 18')   Occupation: *Police Constable 118118*

This statement (consisting of *one* page(s) each signed by me) is true to the best of my knowledge and belief and I make it knowing that, if it is tendered in evidence, I shall be liable to prosecution if I have wilfully stated anything in it, which I know to be false, or do not believe to be true.

Signature: *C. Underwood PC 118118*   Date: *01.03.08*

Tick if witness evidence is visually recorded ☐ *(supply witness details on rear)*

At 1600 hours on Wednesday 1st March 2008 I was on uniformed patrol in a marked police vehicle with PC 69900 HODDIM. At this time we attended Kerrie's Corner shop, 98 High Street, Maidbury, Kentshire. As we arrived I saw a man who I now know to be Nathan JONAH born 09.09.1970 sitting on the pavement holding a plastic carrier bag approximately 1 metre from the front door of the shop on the pavement outside. I got out of the car and walked towards JONAH. I would describe JONAH as... The plastic carrier bag JONAH was holding looked as if it contained something lumpy. I heard JONAH shout 'That's it, you're all for it now!' and he tried to stand up, but stumbled and fell. As I approached him I could smell intoxicating liquor on his breath, his speech was slurred, and his eyes were glazed. He tried to stand up again but could not. He was drunk or otherwise intoxicated. He was groaning and looking downwards with his eyes shut sometimes.

A woman came up to me and introduced herself as Mrs STONER. She said in the presence and hearing of the suspect 'I heard him say "what's it to you if some of us 'ain't got nothing to eat" and then I heard a long bang—I think he pushed the shop assistant against the wall behind the door and ran out'. PC HODDIM came over with a shop assistant from the store, a person I now know to be Janis DEE. In the presence and hearing of the suspect I said to Mrs DEE 'Can you please tell me what happened?' Mrs DEE replied 'I was filling the refrigerator with packets of bacon when this bloke here took a pack from out of the box on the floor. He walked around the store for a little while, well staggered really. I tried to stop him and then he just walked out without paying for it.' At 1635 hours the same day I said to the suspect JONAH 'As a result of what this person has told me I am arresting you on suspicion of theft of a pack of meat from the shop. Your arrest is necessary for the prompt and effective investigation of the offence and because you are drunk you may suffer physical injury to yourself'. I then cautioned him to which he replied 'It wasn't me, you've got the wrong person ... why me?' ... As JONAH was drunk I believed that he may present a danger to himself or others if he had possession of a weapon. I also believed he may have other articles from the store which he had not paid for. Therefore I searched him before placing him into the police vehicle. I looked inside the bag he was carrying and it contained a large packet of meat which I seized (exhibit labelled and marked CU/1). JONAH was placed in a police vehicle and conveyed to Maidbury Police Station arriving at 1645 hours the same day where he was introduced to the custody officer PS BENN.

C. Underwood PC 118118, 01.03.08

Signature: *C. Underwood PC 118118*   Signature witnessed by: *n/a*

PTO

Enter your rank and force number.

Sign with your rank and number.

Use the 24 hour clock and use 'at' not 'at approximately'.

Always begin with the time, day, date, location, and other persons present. Do not include your name, title, number, or station in the main body of the text.

This is hearsay evidence (she said that he said), and should be recorded in direct speech; see 12.9 below.

Arrests must be recorded in direct speech, but the caution does not have to be. Any response from the suspect must be accurately recorded.

Sign and date after the last word of the statement, and include your rank and number.

For a duty statement, the signature does not need to be witnessed.

Sign at the foot of every page, and include your rank and number.

8.15   Methods of Disposal of Criminal Suspects

Here we describe the various methods of 'disposing' of a criminal suspect, including directing him/her to court or by imposing penalties without going to court.

The methods of disposal described below are:

1. written charge and requisition by a public prosecutor
2. penalty notices (PNDs and FPNs)
3. juvenile warnings and reprimands
4. bail from elsewhere than a police station: 'street bail'
5. charge
6. bail from a police station
7. police caution
8. conditional caution, and
9. refused charge.

8.15.1   Written Charge and Postal Requisition by a Public Prosecutor

When a suspect is suspected of committing an offence, criminal proceedings can be instituted by way of a written charge and issue of a postal requisition. An example of such criminal proceedings would be when you report a suspect at the roadside for a road traffic offence, or a suspect attends a police station voluntarily at your request.

Once you have gathered your evidence in relation to the suspect, you will submit your case file. If a decision is reached to prosecute the suspect, a person authorized by your organization to institute criminal proceedings (a public prosecutor) will issue a written charge to the suspect. This will describe the offence for which the suspect is being prosecuted, including the title of the Act under which the offence was created. At the same time, the public prosecutor will issue a requisition which requires the suspect to appear before a magistrates' court to answer the written charge. The written charge and requisition will be served on the person concerned by post, and a copy of both will be served on the court named in the requisition.

To report a person for the purposes of issuing a written charge, you will always need to go through the following process:

1. identify the offence(s) involved
2. gather evidence in the usual way, that is using your senses, what you saw, felt, smelt, and so on)
3. point out the offence(s) to the suspect
4. caution the suspect using 'when questioned' form of caution and ensure you meet the PACE Act 1984, Code C 10.2 (explaining to the suspect, in a situation where an arrest has not been made, that he/she is not under arrest and does not have to remain with you, sometimes referred to as 'caution + 2' (see the flow chart in 8.4.2 above))
5. write down questions and answers about the offences in your PNB, including points to prove and negating any defences available
6. offer your PNB to the suspect to read and sign that the notes were a true record of the interview (see PACE Act 1984, Code C 11.11)
7. tell the suspect 'I am reporting you for the offence(s) of ...'
8. caution the suspect (using the 'now' caution, see 8.4 above).

8.15.2   Penalty Notices

These provide offenders with an opportunity to pay a fine for an offence without going to court. Initially, penalty notices were introduced for motoring and road traffic offences as Fixed Penalty Notices (FPNs: see 11.11.2 below). Following their success, the Penalty Notice for Disorder (PND) scheme was introduced (ss 1 to 11 of the Criminal Justice and Police Act 2001).

The key aims and objectives of penalty notice schemes are:

- to reduce the amount of time that police officers spend completing paperwork and attending court, while simultaneously reducing the burden on the courts;
- to increase the amount of time officers spend on the street and dealing with more serious crime;
- to deliver swift, simple, and effective justice that carries a deterrent effect.

Under the Criminal Justice and Police Act 2001 the following procedures are adopted:

1. If you have reason to believe that a person has committed a penalty offence, you may give that person a penalty notice for that offence (see your local policy for the minimum age of the recipient).
2. The notice may be issued either:
   - on the spot by an officer in uniform; or
   - at a police station by an authorized officer (in the majority of cases, this takes place in the custody area of a police station, by the custody officer, after the person has been investigated).
3. The issue of a penalty notice gives the recipient the opportunity to pay the penalty, in order to discharge liability to conviction for the offence.
4. Once the notice has been issued, the recipient may elect to either:
   - pay the penalty; or
   - request a court hearing.

He/she must do one or the other within 21 days of the date of issue.

5. Failure to undertake either option may result in:
   - the registration of a fine of one-and-a-half times the penalty amount as a fine against the recipient; or
   - court proceedings against him/her.

The following should also be noted in order to avoid confusion; first, the PND scheme involves fixed penalties and second, the Anti-Social Behaviour Act 2003 also provides for local authority personnel and PCSOs to issue penalty notices for graffiti, littering, and other more minor disorder offences. The term FPN is normally reserved for use in relation to motoring offences, though it is also used for the second type listed above,

8.15.2.1   **Offences included in the PND scheme for which the penalty is £80**

Offence	Legislation
Wasting police time/giving false report	Criminal Law Act 1967, s 5(2)
Using public electronic communications network in order to cause annoyance, inconvenience, or needless anxiety	Communications Act 2003, s 127(2)
Knowingly giving a false alarm to a person acting on behalf of a fire and rescue authority	Fire and Rescue Services Act 2004, s 49 (England only) Fire Services Act 1947, s 31 (Wales only)
Causing harassment, alarm, or distress	Public Order Act 1986, s 5
Throwing fireworks	Explosives Act 1875, s 80
Drunk and disorderly	Criminal Justice Act 1967, s 91
Selling alcohol to person under 18 (anywhere)	Licensing Act 2003, s 146(1)
Supply of alcohol by or on behalf of a club to a person aged under 18	Licensing Act 2003, s 146(3)
Selling alcohol to a drunken person	Licensing Act 2003, s 141
Purchasing or attempting to purchase alcohol on behalf of a person under 18 (includes licensed premises and off-licences)	Licensing Act 2003, s 149(3)
Purchase of alcohol for consumption in licensed premises by person under 18	Licensing Act 2003, s 149(4)
Delivery of alcohol to person under 18 or allowing such delivery	Licensing Act 2003, s 151
Destroying or damaging property worth £500 or under	Criminal Damage Act 1971, s 1(1)
Unlawful possession of cannabis and its derivatives	Misuse of Drugs Act 1971, s 5(2)
Theft (retail) of property worth £200 or under	Theft Act 1968, s 1

Offence	Legislation
Breach of fireworks curfew (2300–0700hrs)	Reg 7 of the Firework Regulations 2004 (Fireworks Act 2003, s 11)
Possession of a category 4 firework	Reg 5 of the Firework Regulations 2004 (Fireworks Act 2003, s 11)
Possession by a person under 18 of an adult firework in public	Reg 4 of the Firework Regulations 2004 (Fireworks Act 2003, s 11)

The table below summarizes which offences may be dealt with under the PND scheme by an £80 fine for offenders 16 years old and over. For the same offence committed by a 10–15-year-old, the fine is £40.

8.15.2.2 Offences included in the PND scheme for which the penalty is £50

Offence	Legislation
Trespassing on a railway	British Transport Commission Act 1949, s 55
Throwing stones at a train	British Transport Commission Act 1949, s 56
Drunk in the highway	Licensing Act 1872, s 12
Consumption of alcohol in designated public place, contrary to a requirement by constable not to do so	Criminal Justice and Police Act 2001, s 12
Depositing and leaving litter	Environmental Protection Act 1990, ss 87(1) and 87(5)
Consumption of alcohol by a person under 18 in a bar	Licensing Act 2003, s 150(1)
Allowing consumption of alcohol by a young person (aged under 18) in a bar	Licensing Act 2003, s 150(2)
Buying or attempting to buy alcohol for a young person (aged under 18)	Licensing Act 2003, s 149(1)

The table below summarizes the offences that may be dealt with under the PND scheme by a £50 fine for offenders aged 16 years old and over. For the same offence committed by a 10–15-year-old, the fine is £30.

8.15.3 Power to Photograph Persons Away from a Police Station

Section 64A (1A) of the PACE Act 1984 states that a person may be photographed elsewhere than at a police station (for example, on the street) with the consent of the person concerned, or without consent (either withheld or if it is not practicable to obtain it), but only if the person in question has been:

- arrested by you for an offence;
- taken into custody by you after being arrested for an offence by a person other than another police officer;
- made subject to a requirement to wait with a community support officer;
- given a penalty notice for disorder, or a penalty notice for truancy or a road policing offence by you whilst in uniform;
- given a fixed penalty notice by a community support officer;
- given a fixed penalty notice by an accredited person (a person outside the extended police family).

Section 64A(2) of the PACE Act 1984 states that, when you are proposing to take such a photograph, you may:

(a) for the purpose of doing so, require the removal of any item or substance worn on or over the whole or any part of the head or face of the person to be photographed; and
(b) remove the item or substance if the requirement is not complied with.

However, if a person declines to remove in public religious garments covering part of the head then you should consider taking the person out of public view so that a photograph can be made in private.

8.15.4 Juvenile Warnings and Reprimands

This is a new system of pre-court actions aimed at diverting children and young people (aged 10–17 years) away from their offending behaviour, and providing progressive and effective interventions to help prevent reoffending (ss 65–66 of the Crime and Disorder Act 1998). The court system and repeat police cautions will therefore be avoided.

A reprimand is a formal verbal warning given by a police officer to a young person who admits guilt for a minor first offence. The young person may also be referred to the Youth Offending Team (YOT) to take part in a voluntary programme to help him/her address the offending behaviour.

A final warning is a formal verbal warning given by a police officer to a young person who admits guilt for a first or second offence. The final warning triggers an automatic referral to the YOT, where the young person is assessed to determine the causes of the offending behaviour, and a programme of activities is identified in an attempt to address them.

Both the reprimand and the final warning are designed to divert young people from the criminal justice system. If they do go to court for a further offence, the court will take the reprimand and final warning into account when deciding on the appropriate sentence for the offence. If a final warning has been given within the last two years, the court cannot give a conditional discharge unless there are exceptional circumstances.

8.15.5 Bail Elsewhere than at a Police Station—'Street Bail'

Under s 30A–D of the PACE Act 1984, street bail is a discretionary power which allows police officers to release an offender on bail (without taking them to a police station), on the condition that the offender must attend a specified police station at a later specified date.

Benefits for the police include:

- a reduction in the amount of time travelling to and from the police station;
- less time waiting at the police station to progress the investigation;
- better opportunities for planning the investigation and work caseload;
- better opportunities for appropriate representation on answering bail.

Benefits for the suspect include:

- less need to travel to a police station;
- no need to spend time in detention whilst awaiting representation;
- it is more likely that any time spent in detention is focused on the investigation and not awaiting representation.

For legal representatives, parents, and appropriate adults, there are improved opportunities to plan and prepare for attendance.

Street bail enables 'front-line' officers to apply their discretion at the point of arrest. There are four key considerations for you:

- the **nature** of the offence;
- the ability to progress the investigation at the station;
- your confidence in the suspect's answering bail;
- the level of awareness and understanding of the procedure by the suspect.

Your decision to grant street bail should follow the normal arrest procedures in s 24 of the PACE Act 1984 (see 8.7 above). Statements concerning guilt are not relevant to the decision to grant bail—interview and examination of evidence will take place in more detail when the person answers bail.

Whilst on the street ask yourself the following questions when deciding whether to grant street bail:

1. **What type of offence has been committed and how serious is the offence?** There is no definitive list of offences to which street bail can be granted; it is a matter for a police officer's discretion. However, it is unlikely that street bail would be granted in relation to a serious offence.

2. **What has been the impact of the offence?** The impact on the victim, the offender, and other persons should all be considered.

3. **Would a delay in dealing with the offender result in loss of vital evidence?** It might be necessary to take an arrested person to a police station to preserve and examine forensic evidence which could be lost if the suspect is released.

4. **Is the arrested person fit to be released back onto the streets?** A drunk driver or a person with mental health problems, for example, may not be in a fit state to be returned to the streets. In the case of a juvenile, consideration must be given to the welfare of the child.

5. **Does the arrested person understand what is happening?** This particularly applies to vulnerable people who would normally require the assistance of an appropriate adult. Vulnerable people include not only mentally disordered people and juveniles, but may also include people suspected to be under the influence of drink and/or drugs.

6. **If released on bail, is the arrested person likely to commit a further offence?** You should not grant street bail if there are reasonable grounds to believe that the arrested person might continue to commit that or another offence if released, for example where fighting is involved.

7. **Am I satisfied that the arrested person has provided a correct name and address?** You must not grant bail if you are not satisfied that the identification and address details provided are correct.

If you are satisfied that street bail is appropriate you should explain the decision to the offender, and issue him/her with a street bail notice. The offender should be released as soon as possible. It is important that the arrested person understands that:

- he/she is not being legally discharged;
- court proceedings or other disposal action may be taken against him/her;
- he/she is required to attend a police station at a later, specified date.

A verbal explanation of the points above should be given to the person granted street bail, even though it is also clearly stated on the notice to be handed to the arrested person. No requirement other than attendance can be imposed as a condition of bail.

8.15.5.1   Length of time for street bail

The length of time for street bail is partly determined by the time it takes for you to carry out investigations, but you should also be guided by your force policy (maximum periods may be specified).

8.15.5.2   Failure to attend the police station to answer street bail

You have the power to rearrest without warrant those who fail to answer bail at the specified time (s 30A of the PACE Act 1984).

8.15.5.3   Attaching conditions to street bail

You may impose conditions on the bail (s 30A (3A) of the PACE Act 1984) in order to ensure that the person:

- surrenders to custody;
- does not commit an offence while on bail;
- does not interfere with witnesses or otherwise obstruct the course of justice (whether in relation to him/herself or any other person).

Section 30B (4A) states that, if conditions are attached to the bail, the notice given to the suspect must specify the requirements of the conditions, the opportunities to vary the conditions, and the police station at which the conditions can be varied. However, the following conditions **cannot** be imposed on a person as a provision for his/her surrender to custody:

1. a recognizance (a declaration by the bailed person which is 'recognized' as an obligation, such as a recorded promise of appearance)
2. a security (a declaration by the bailed person or anyone on his/her behalf, to forfeit property such as cash, for non-appearance)
3. a provision of surety or sureties (the bailed person providing details of a person or persons who would be responsible for his/her appearance), or
4. a requirement to be a resident of a bail hostel (an establishment provided by the National Probation Service for prisoners who will soon complete a prison sentence).

You have the power to arrest without warrant if you have reasonable grounds for suspecting that the person has broken any of the conditions of bail (s 30D of the PACE Act 1984).

8.15.6 Charge

A charge is a formal accusation that a person has carried out an illegal act and will be required to stand trial in a court of law. A person will be notified of such an allegation by way of a written notice.

Code C, paras 16.1–16.3 of the PACE Act 1984 states that:

> [w]hen the officer in charge of the investigation reasonably believes there is sufficient evidence to charge a person with an offence, [he/she] shall without delay … inform the custody officer who will be responsible for considering whether the detainee should be charged.
> When a person is detained in respect of more than one offence, it is permissible to delay informing the custody officer until the above conditions are satisfied in respect of all the offences.

As soon as there is sufficient evidence for a prosecution to succeed, the custody officer will decide whether or not the person should be charged with the offence or released, with or without bail. If the person is classified as a 'person at risk', then any action taken should be taken in the presence of an appropriate adult. When charged, he/she (or the appropriate adult) should be given a written notice which shows:

1. the particulars of the offence (that is, the precise offence)
2. the name of the police officer in the case
3. the reference number of the case.

The notice should also begin with the following words which include the 'now' caution (see 8.4 above):

> You are charged with the offence(s) shown below. You do not have to say anything. But it may harm your defence if you do not mention now something which you later rely on in court. Anything you say may be given in evidence.

A person who is to be charged or informed that he/she may be prosecuted for an offence, should always be cautioned using the 'now' caution as outlined above.

8.15.7 Bail from a Police Station

Bail is a process of attempting to ensure that a person appears at a specified time at a specified place, such as a police station or court, and is used in a variety of situations. For example, there may be further evidence to collect before a person can be charged with an offence, and the custody officer can bail a person to return to the police station at a later date to be charged. Alternatively, once a person has been charged with an offence, the custody officer must release the person on bail (unless the person comes within the terms of the Bail Act 1976; in these circumstances, the person will be kept in custody and be brought before a magistrates' court).

There are four main reasons for bail that you will encounter on a regular basis:

1. Continued detention in police custody cannot be justified; the offender may be bailed under s 34(5) of the PACE Act 1984 to return to the police station. Conditions cannot be attached to the bail under this section.
2. Insufficient evidence to support a charge; the offender may be bailed under s 37(2) of the PACE Act 1984 to return to the police station. Conditions (for example, not to return to a crime scene) can be attached.
3. Consultation with the CPS is required to agree charges; the offender may be bailed under s 37(7) of the PACE Act 1984 to return to the police station. Conditions can be attached to the bail under this section, for example not to communicate with a co-suspect.

Section 46(1) of the PACE Act 1984 states you may:

> arrest without a warrant any person who, having been released on bail ... subject to a duty to attend at a police station, fails to attend at that police station at the time appointed for [him/her] to do so.

In addition, s 46A (1A) of the PACE Act 1984 states that any person:

> who has been released on bail under section 37[(2) or (7)] ... may be arrested without warrant ... if [you have] reasonable grounds for suspecting that the person has broken any of the conditions of bail.

4. Once a person has been charged with an offence, he/she may be bailed to court under s 38(1) of the PACE Act 1984. Conditions can be attached to the bail under this section, for example not to communicate with a co-suspect.

Bail after charge may also be refused by the custody officer, after taking into account factors such as the seriousness of the offence. When bail is refused, the suspect will be taken before the next available court.

8.15.8 Police Caution

A police caution is a formal warning given by a senior police officer or by another police officer on the instructions of a senior police officer (and must not be confused with the other forms of caution that we discussed in 8.4 above). A police caution can be only given to an adult who has admitted guilt, and for a minor or less serious offence. The police caution is recorded on the PNC and can be taken into consideration by the court if that person is convicted and sentenced for a further offence.

8.15.9 Conditional Caution

One of the changes following the Criminal Justice Act 2003 was to introduce a new statutory system of cautioning, to be called conditional cautions.

As the term suggests, conditional cautions are cautions with attached conditions for the offender. They do not replace the non-statutory police cautions described above, but can be used where they might be an appropriate and effective way of addressing the offender's behaviour, or making reparation for the effects of the offence on the victim and others. Failing to comply with the conditions attached to the caution will result in criminal proceedings and the caution being cancelled. Such cautions can only be used for adults (people aged 18 years or over).

Conditional cautions can be given by a police constable, an investigating officer, or a person authorized by the prosecutor. Five requirements must be met:

1. The officer has evidence that the person has committed an offence.
2. The relevant prosecutor decides that:
   (a) there is sufficient evidence to charge the person with the offence and
   (b) a conditional caution should be given.
3. The offender admits the offence to the authorized person.
4. An explanation of the effect of a caution and the warnings about the consequences of failure to observe the conditions has been given to the offender.

5. The offender signs:
   - a document that sets out details of the offence;
   - an admission;
   - consent to the caution; and
   - consent to the attached conditions.

Note that s 24A of the Criminal Justice Act 2003 states that if you 'have reasonable grounds for believing that the offender has failed, without reasonable excuse, to comply with any of the conditions attached to the conditional caution, [you] may arrest [him/her] without warrant'.

8.15.10 Refused Charge

If there is insufficient evidence to charge a detainee, the custody officer will release the person without charge. If this is done without bail, the process is called 'refused charge'.

> **TASK 11**
>
> Research what offence, if any, a person commits if he/she does not return on bail to a police station, or fails to surrender to custody at a court after having been bailed.

Remember you will also need to know your force's policy in relation to:

1. written charge and requisition by a public prosecutor
2. penalty notices for disorder
3. juvenile warnings and reprimands
4. bail from elsewhere than a police station—street bail
5. charge
6. bail from a police station
7. police caution
8. conditional cautions
9. refused charge.

8.16 Handover Procedures

After your initial enquiries into a suspected crime (eg taking statements, collecting potential evidence, the arrest of a suspect) your force may expect you to 'hand over' responsibility for the subsequent investigation to another colleague, for example a volume-crime investigator. Alternatively you may be required to hand the case files over to a 'Criminal Justice Unit' or 'Criminal Justice Department' where 'case builders' will assume responsibility for obtaining further statements and evidence, and (where appropriate) preparing files for submission to the CPS (using the 'MG' forms: see 12.7 below). Note, however, that practice does vary from force to force. In some cases, and with some crimes, you may be expected to see the process through to a more advanced stage.

8.16.1 Handover Packages

A fundamental principle underpinning the process of handover is that the information you provide will enable the colleague or Department to whom you pass responsibility to become as familiar with the circumstances of the alleged offence as you are. In practice this means providing a 'handover package' consisting of a collection of documents (both in written and electronic forms) and references to artefacts (eg forensic evidence) together with an overarching checklist (sometimes called a 'Single Source Document'). The checklist will be likely to include the following:

Checklist entry	Examples/Notes
Names of the alleged offender(s)	Provide names, DoB, and custody numbers
Your account of the circumstances leading up to arrest	Remember to avoid offering opinion in this section.
Investigation checklist	A series of tickbox lists addressing: • the arrest (including a copy of your PNB entries); • searches; • exhibits; • scene and forensic evidence; • prisoner and custody considerations; • PNC/force intelligence database checks.
Witness details and statements	You should include • names, addresses, and contact numbers of witnesses; • a summary of witness statements.
Other officers involved	You should include: • details of those who also attended; • copies of their PNB entries and statements.

Note that the checklist itself is potentially 'relevant material' (see 12.6) and thus it has to be included on the MG 6C form.

8.17 Answers to Tasks

TASK 1

The 'first' or 'given' name is the term to use, rather than 'Christian' name. The latter is a reflection of a time when the assumption was made that all UK residents subscribed (at least notionally) to Christianity as a religion.

TASK 2

The use of mind-maps as tools for learning and analysis was pioneered by Tony Buzan and others. The website <http://www.mindtools.com/pages/article/newISS_01.htm> has some useful advice on the application of Buzan's ideas. Of course, we have provided you with the ELBOWS(S) mnemonic already, but developing your own mnemonic is good practice and will help fix the ideas in your long-term memory.

TASK 3

There are many examples but you might have considered the following:

> The caution means that you have the right to silence and you do not have to say anything or give any reply to any question put to you. However, if you choose not to say anything during the investigation and then you decide to say something during the court proceedings instead, the court has the opportunity to deal with this fresh evidence as they choose. Having said all that, anything that you do say during the investigation can also be given to the court for consideration.

TASK 4

You probably considered the following:

1. obtaining a first description from the alleged victim and recording this description
2. asking if the victim would consider accompanying you to other locations in order to attempt an identification
3. explaining to the victim that during that process you cannot direct the victim's attention to any individual
4. explaining to the victim that during the process he/she should look carefully at the people in the vicinity.

TASK 5

Whatever examples you chose, each should have clearly addressed:

- a person's involvement, or suspected involvement, or attempted involvement in the commission of a criminal offence; **and**
- the reasonable grounds for believing that the person's arrest is necessary.

TASK 6

- Locate the person who is subject of the warrant through the use of intelligence, a stop check, the PNC, or your local force database.
- Identify yourself, then confirm the identity of the person, and then arrest and caution the person.
- When you arrest a person on warrant and you are not in possession of that warrant, you must show him/her the warrant as soon as is practicable on the demand of the person arrested.
- Endorse the back of the warrant (also known as 'backing up').
- Record the event in your PNB.
- Send the 'backed-up' warrant to the appropriate court as per your local procedures.

TASK 7

The European Arrest Warrant (EAW) is an EU-wide arrest warrant which allows for the extradition of a person suspected of a serious crime from a participating EU country.

The important and relevant feature of the EAW is that application for a person to be 'surrendered to answer a warrant' is made from a judge in one country to a judge in another (where the suspect is). The process is therefore within the criminal justice systems of both countries. Previously, 'extradition' was highly politicized and people or cases were subject to long delay, political processes, appeals, and so on. The aim of the EAW is to speed things up. It is debatable whether this is yet the case. Further details may be found at <http://www.eurowarrant.net/>.

TASK 8

You probably considered the following:

(a) When you arrest a person, you must inform him/her that he/she is under arrest (s 28(2) and Code G 2.2).
(b) An arrest is not lawful unless at the time or as soon as is practicable you inform the person of the ground for the arrest (s 28(3)).
(c) You are required to inform the arrested person of the relevant circumstances of the arrest in relation to both elements of s 24 of the PACE Act 1984 (Code G 2).
(d) You are required to caution a person you arrest (Code G, para 3.4).

In the second half of the task your answer was probably along the following lines:

> I have just seen you run out of the shop with a brand new drill under your arm. I heard the store alarm sound at the same time and I suspect that you have stolen the drill. I am therefore arresting you on suspicion of theft of the drill as your arrest is necessary to allow the prompt and effective investigation of the offence, and also, because you were running away, to prevent any prosecution for the offence from being hindered by you leaving the area. You do not have to say anything, but it may harm your defence if you do not mention when questioned something which you later rely on in court. Anything you do say may be given in evidence.

TASK 9

'Suspect's special property' (also known as 'prisoner's special property') is property that you seize directly from the suspect after his/her arrest. The item(s) may either be directly linked to the crime (such as objects you suspect to have been stolen), or be other items which are to be sent for forensic examination, such as a weapon, a suspected illegal substance, or clothing.

There is a second category of special property (known simply as 'special property') which is not seized directly from the suspect, but may be relevant to the offence in question. This would include items you suspect to have been abandoned by him/her after committing the crime, such as a TV which has been taken from a house and then left in a front drive because it is too heavy to carry. Such items are likely to require forensic examination in order to establish a link between the suspect and the offence.

It will be necessary to record both categories of 'special property' on a form which may be contained in the same 'book' of forms or separately. The form in each case will require similar information to be entered:

- sequential number (to be attached to the property for the purposes of recognition);
- name of the person from whom it was taken;
- address of the person from whom it was taken;
- place where taken;
- details of the police officer who took possession;
- exhibit reference (if known);
- description of article(s);
- reasons for taking into police possession;
- proposed method of disposal;
- current location of the property (see 'transit store' below).

Once the appropriate special property form has been completed and a copy attached to the property for the purposes of recognition, your force will have its own procedure for the storage of property. In the majority of cases, if you do not have access to the main property store because it is closed (at night for example), the property will have to be placed in a 'transit store' (a secure cupboard) before it is transferred by the property officer to the main store.

TASK 10

You probably considered the following:

> I have just seen this person run out of a store with a brand new drill under his arm. I heard the store alarm sound at the same time and I suspected he had stolen the drill. I therefore arrested him on suspicion of theft of the drill and the arrest was necessary to allow the prompt and effective investigation of the offence through a taped interview, and also, because he was running away, to prevent any prosecution for the offence from being hindered by him leaving the area.

TASK 11

Bail to a police station: Section 46A of the PACE Act 1984 states that 'where a person is bailed to return to a police station [you] may arrest without warrant a person who fails to attend at the appointed time'.

Bail to a court: Section 7(3) of the Bail Act 1976 states that 'where a person has been bailed to a court [you] may arrest without warrant if [you] have reasonable grounds to believe the person is not likely to surrender to bail, likely to break his/her conditions or has broken their conditions'.

9 | Managing People and Incidents in the Community

9.1 Chapter Briefing

This chapter describes police procedures and duties relevant to policing of your local communities. It covers a wide range of topics, from managing drunk and anti-social behaviour to policing emergencies, major or critical incidents. You will probably be expected to meet many of the responsibilities described in this chapter whilst on Supervised and Independent Patrol.

Much of the content of this chapter concerns legislation. As we explained in Chapter 2, we often provide a simplified and abbreviated version of the law, and use flow charts to explain points when appropriate. If you require further details you should consult the original legislation, other textbooks, or websites.

9.1.1 Aims of the Chapter

This chapter will enable you to:

- implement, when appropriate, the law concerned with the use and purchase of alcohol;
- understand how an aggravating feature of some offences can be a racially or religiously motivated intention;
- exercise the powers concerning 'breach of the peace' and deliver the policing of public order in a professional manner;
- learn how the police may support those experiencing harassment from others;
- comprehend the particular legislative and procedural issues surrounding the behaviour of those with 'mental disorders';
- understand the range of legislation and powers available to counter anti-social behaviour;
- note the law surrounding the ownership and use of firearms, shotguns, and air weapons;
- contribute effectively to the management of missing persons investigations;
- understand procedures and policies in respect to emergencies, major incidents, and critical incidents (including terrorism);
- develop the underpinning knowledge required for a number of NOS elements, several of the PAC headings, and entries for your Learning Diary Phases 3 and 4 and the CARs of your SOLAP.

9.1.2 Police Action Checklist

This chapter will provide you with the underlying knowledge and theory to meet some of the requirements of the 'Investigation' heading of the Police Action Checklist.

9.1.3 National Occupational Standards

This chapter will provide you with some of the knowledge required to demonstrate aspects of the following NOS elements:

National Occupational Standard Elements

AA1.1 Promote equality and value diversity
BE2.1 Provide initial support to victims, survivors, and witnesses
CA1.1 Apply principles of reasonable suspicion or belief
CA1.2 Use law enforcement actions proportionately
CA1.3 Use law enforcement actions fairly
CD1.2 Respond to incidents

You should refer to Chapter 3 for general information and advice concerning the NOS elements.

9.1.4 IPLDP Phases and Modules

This chapter will provide you with resources to support the following Operational Module of the IPLDP:

OP 3   Respond to incidents, conduct and evaluate investigations

---

It will also cover aspects of the following topic areas of Legislation, Policy and Guidelines of the IPLDP.

- Crime (LPG 1.1);
- Protecting People (LPG 1.3);
- Police Policies and Procedures (LPG 1.4);
- Non-Crime Incidents (LPG 1.5).

Much of the content of this chapter relates to IPLDP Phase 3 'Supervised Patrol' and Phase 4 'Independent Patrol'.

9.1.5 SOLAP

The contents of this chapter are relevant to the 'knowledge' evidence requirements of CARs AA1, BE1, CA1, CD1, and AF1.

9.1.6 Learning Diary Phases

The contents of this chapter may provide you with stimulus material for completion of your Learning Diary Phase 3, particularly for the following headings:

- Crime;
- Non-crime incidents;
- Police policies and procedures;
- Protecting people.

9.2 Introduction

In this chapter, we shall be looking at what you do, more or less routinely, as part of your general police duties. As usual, we have to generalize somewhat because we are discussing a typical police force, and yours may possibly vary in details from the average force described in this chapter. This might apply particularly to the applications of force policies, though the essence of what we talk about will hold for all forces. Not all the police procedures and duties expected of you are covered in this chapter, but you will find most of the remainder elsewhere in the Handbook. It is a long chapter too, and you may not want to read it all through in one sitting. You are more likely to dip into it to cover what you need, but we think, all the same, that there is a coherence to what is being described and discussed here.

We are considering your powers and responsibilities **other** than in the investigation of a crime (though there is some overlap). This chapter covers offences and the actions you can take to address these offences. This is not to say that offences described and analysed in this chapter would not lead on to a criminal investigation, nor that some things (for example, possession of a bladed knife) might not result in arrest. They may well. But these will be ancillary offences, arising from original offences.

Consider, for example, the power to confiscate alcohol. If, on patrol, you decide that it would be appropriate to take alcohol away from a young person in a town centre, the individual (if intoxicated) may try to hit you for depriving him or her of the bottle or can. This assault would be an ancillary offence (criminally grave enough in its own right) which followed from your intervention.

Public order offences are considered in some detail, and these will apply whether you are policing a large rally in a town centre or an individual breach of the peace. You will study your powers under the Public Order Act 1986, and even more importantly, the exercise of discretion (which we discussed extensively in Chapter 5). It is as important to you as a student police officer to know when **not** to make an issue of something as when you should. There are plenty of examples where the intelligent use of police discretion can defuse situations which might otherwise get out of hand. Take, for example, a demonstration with placards demanding the death of a particular individual because of his/her activities or beliefs (this is not restricted to recent matters of race and religion; there was a well-known vigilante case in Hampshire in the 1990s where an alleged paedophile was subject to such public death threats). Technically, the placards are incitements to kill and therefore a criminal offence. But what might happen if you go in forcibly and wrest the placards from people's hands? Might it not make an inflamed situation even worse? Might you not provoke some really serious rioting or criminal damage by intervening so publicly and aggressively?

Certainly, some commentators (and some senior police officers) believe that such actions will only make things worse. The priority for the police at a heated demonstration of this kind is to keep the peace and prevent serious disorder. The intelligent thing to do would be to monitor such events carefully and take action, if justified, after the event when temperatures have cooled.

That is not to say that the police should not intervene decisively and in force if serious rioting seems likely. Most of the time, in most situations of public order, arresting people for criminal intent can be carried out once the event itself is controlled or has ended. Such judgements come with experience, and even now not all senior officers get the tactics right every time, so you should not expect to be infallible.

Further on in the chapter we consider **offensive weapons** and, in particular, knives and firearms. Socially, and in terms of media attention, the illegal possession of such items is a source of considerable (and understandable) anxiety for the public. Many parents are concerned with the perception that, particularly in schools, knives and bladed articles are almost commonplace. Unlicensed and replica guns are also matters of concern in society. Hardly a year goes by when a police force in England and Wales is not being investigated for a fatal shooting of a person who was subsequently found to be carrying a replica weapon. You should be aware of this context when you are looking into matters concerning such weaponry, and aware too of your powers. The use of a firearm in the commission of a crime carries a substantially heavier sentence and criminals may be ruthless in their attempts to avoid arrest or detection. Police officers are obviously at risk from such criminals, and the importance of preventive action is self-evident. Your own force will have clear policies on licensed and unlicensed weapons.

The final part of the chapter examines the complex subject of emergencies, major and critical incidents. Major incidents include events such as multiple road traffic collisions, the evacuation of people because of floodwater, and terrorist bombings. However, there are also other forms of incident which may be critical in some respect, either because of their potential to become major incidents or because the effectiveness of the police response may have an effect on the confidence of the community (Newburn and Neyroud, 2008, p. 70).

Lastly, when using the powers which are described in this chapter remember the provisions of the **Human Rights Act 1998** (see 5.12 above). When you exercise your powers, you must be able to justify what you do as proportionate and necessary. You must know what your powers are and under what authority you operate. Above all, ask yourself if you would be able to defend your actions in court or in an enquiry.

9.3   Alcohol-related Offences

It is likely that many of the incidents you will investigate whilst on Supervised and Independent Patrol will be alcohol-related, particularly on late shifts. Remember, you must consider your own health and safety and the health and safety of everybody around you when dealing with incidents fuelled by alcohol; the potential for injury can be very high. Drunken people are sometimes subject to rapid mood swings, happy one minute and then violent the next, and people who are normally quite reserved may lose some of their normal social inhibitions and behave unpredictably. During your training you will be helped to develop skills to defuse potentially dangerous situations involving people under the influence of alcohol. For example in *McMillan v Crown Prosecution Service* (2008) EWHC 1457 (Admin), police officers had warned a woman about her drunken behaviour in the street. Later the same day she was found shouting and swearing at the front door of her daughter's house, still drunk. One of the officers advised the woman to leave but she continued to shout and swear. As a result the officer took the woman by the arm and escorted her down the garden steps and onto the public footpath. It was held that the officer had not assaulted the woman and had been acting within generally accepted parameters.

Alcohol-related offences are dealt with under the following legislation:

- s 12 of the Licensing Act 1872;
- s 2 of the Licensing Act 1902;
- s 91(1) of the Criminal Justice Act 1967.

9.3.1 The Definition of 'Being Drunk'

The terms 'drunk' and 'drunkenness' are not defined in law. As a precedent, the case of *R v Tagg* [2002] 1 Cr App R 2 determined that the everyday meaning of 'drunk' should be used. The OED defines drunk as 'having drunk intoxicating liquor to an extent which affects steady self-control' (*Shorter Oxford English Dictionary*, 1933). The Court of Appeal also accepted that the *Collins Dictionary* definition (used by the Judge in the original case under appeal) and the *Shorter Oxford English Dictionary* definitions were essentially the same, and were helpful in determining the existence of a state of drunkenness.

The court itself must decide whether or not a suspect was drunk. The general rule that the opinion of a witness is inadmissible does not apply in this particular context; a competent witness may give evidence that, in his/her opinion, a person was drunk (*R v Davies* [1962] 1 WLR 1111). A competent witness is a person who understands questions put to them and gives answers that can be understood. As a police officer, you can therefore state your opinion (as a competent witness) on whether a particular person was drunk. You should also be able to give the facts on which your opinion is based, such as:

- he was unsteady on his feet;
- her eyes were glazed;
- his speech was slurred; or
- you could smell intoxicating liquor on her breath.

9.3.2 Drunkenness as an Offence

Section 12 of the Licensing Act 1872 states that it is an offence for a person to be:

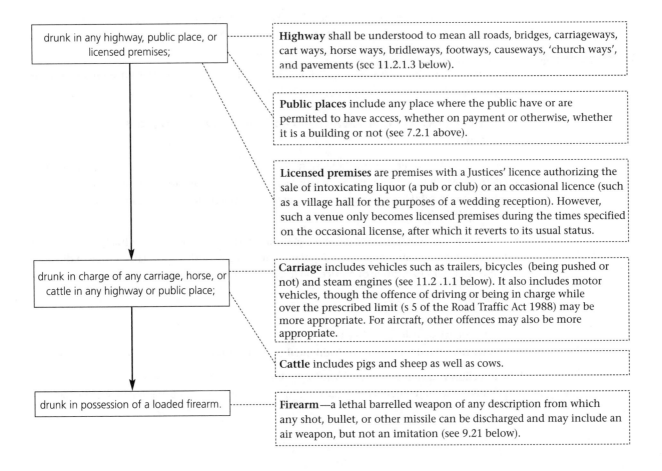

| drunk in any highway, public place, or licensed premises; | **Highway** shall be understood to mean all roads, bridges, carriageways, cart ways, horse ways, bridleways, footways, causeways, 'church ways', and pavements (see 11.2.1.3 below). |

Public places include any place where the public have or are permitted to have access, whether on payment or otherwise, whether it is a building or not (see 7.2.1 above).

Licensed premises are premises with a Justices' licence authorizing the sale of intoxicating liquor (a pub or club) or an occasional licence (such as a village hall for the purposes of a wedding reception). However, such a venue only becomes licensed premises during the times specified on the occasional license, after which it reverts to its usual status.

drunk in charge of any carriage, horse, or cattle in any highway or public place;

Carriage includes vehicles such as trailers, bicycles (being pushed or not) and steam engines (see 11.2.1.1 below). It also includes motor vehicles, though the offence of driving or being in charge while over the prescribed limit (s 5 of the Road Traffic Act 1988) may be more appropriate. For aircraft, other offences may also be more appropriate.

Cattle includes pigs and sheep as well as cows.

drunk in possession of a loaded firearm.

Firearm—a lethal barrelled weapon of any description from which any shot, bullet, or other missile can be discharged and may include an air weapon, but not an imitation (see 9.21 below).

This offence is triable summarily and the penalty is one month's imprisonment or a fine. It is also a penalty offence for the purposes of s 1 of the Criminal Justice and Police Act 2001 (see 8.15.2 above).

9.3.3 Drunk and Disorderly Behaviour

The precise meaning of the term 'disorderly behaviour' is not defined by statute but its everyday meaning is 'unruly or offensive behaviour'. Under s 91(1) of the Criminal Justice Act 1967, it is an offence for any drunk person to display such behaviour in any highway, public place, or licensed premises.

This offence is triable summarily and the penalty is one month's imprisonment or a fine. It is also a penalty offence for the purposes of s 1 of the Criminal Justice and Police Act 2001 (see 8.15.2 above).

9.3.4 Drunk in Charge of Children

Under s 2 of the Licensing Act 1902, it is an offence for a person to be drunk while 'having charge' of a child under the age of seven years, in any highway, public place, or licensed premises.

The precise meaning of 'having charge' is not defined by statute, but probably means some sort of care or control over the child(ren); for this offence the suspect must be the only person with the child, or alternatively everyone in the group with the child must be drunk.

This offence is triable summarily and the penalty is one month's imprisonment or a fine.

9.3.5 Drinking Alcohol in Designated Public Places

If you reasonably believe that a person is consuming alcohol (or has been consuming or intends to consume alcohol) in a designated public place (designated by a local authority), you may require the person 'not to consume in that place anything which is, or which [you] reasonably believe to be intoxicating liquor' (s 12(2) of the Criminal Justice and Police Act 2001).

You must inform the person that under s 12(4) of the Criminal Justice and Police Act 2001, it is an offence to fail to comply (without reasonable excuse) with your requirement. You may also confiscate the alcohol; this is covered in 9.4 below.

This offence is triable summarily and the penalty is a fine. It is also a penalty offence for the purposes of s 1 of the Criminal Justice and Police Act 2001 (see 8.15.2 above).

9.3.6 Power to Direct a Person Away from an Area of Alcohol-related Crime and Disorder

Under s 27 of the Violent Crime Reduction Act 2006, you may give a direction to an individual aged 16 or over who is in a public place (which includes on a means of transport) to leave the locality, and prohibit him/her from returning to that locality for a certain specified period (not exceeding 48 hours).

You may give the direction if the presence of the individual in that locality is likely to cause or to contribute to the occurrence (or repetition or continuance) of alcohol-related crime or disorder and it is necessary to remove or reduce the likelihood of such an occurrence.

The direction you give **must**:

- be given in writing;
- clearly identify the locality to which it relates;
- specify the period for which the individual is prohibited from returning to that locality.

The direction you give may require the individual to leave the locality either immediately or by a specified time, and it may also specify the manner in which the individual leaves the locality, including his/her route. You can subsequently vary the direction (but it cannot be extended to more than 48 hours), and you may withdraw the direction completely.

Any direction you give must **not** prevent the person from having access to a place where he/she resides or from attending any place which he/she is:

- required to attend for the purposes of employment, or by a court or tribunal;
- expected to attend for education or training, or for receiving medical treatment.

Having given the direction, you must make a record of:

- the terms of the direction and the locality to which it relates;
- the individual to whom it is given;
- the time at which it is given; and
- the period during which that individual is required not to return to the locality.

Under s 27(6) of the Violent Crime Reduction Act 2006 it is an offence for a person to fail to comply with such a direction.

This offence is triable summarily and the penalty is a fine.

9.3.7 Banning Orders

Under s 1 of the Violent Crime Reduction Act 2006 a court may order a person aged 16 or over to be excluded from pubs and clubs in a defined geographic area for a given length of time. An interim order may be used while a court considers an application for a full banning order.

It is an offence under s 11 of the Violent Crime Reduction Act 2006 for the subject of a drinking banning order (or interim order) to carry out any action prohibited by the order (without reasonable excuse).

This offence is triable summarily and the penalty is a fine.

> **TASK 1**
>
> In your area you often see a habitual drunk who often drinks large quantities of strong lager and then becomes very abusive to members of the public passing by. You are requested to deal with this. How will you approach her and what long-term solution will you consider to resolve the situation? Look at s 34(1) of the Criminal Justice Act 1972 to help determine a suitable course of action.

9.4 Alcohol and Young People

Concern about young people drinking alcohol has increased considerably over the past few years. Section 1 of the Confiscation of Alcohol (Young Persons) Act 1997 does not make it illegal for young people to consume alcohol, but its intention is to prevent the consumption of alcohol in a 'relevant place', ie in public (except in licensed premises where other legislation applies). Alcohol can also be confiscated from young people in private places to which they have unlawfully gained access.

A relevant place includes:

- any public place, eg streets, parks, and shopping centres (but not licensed premises such as pubs or clubs);
- any place (other than a public place) to which the person has unlawfully gained access, such as gate-crashing a party at a private house where the trespasser did not have the consent of the homeowner to gain entry.

Section 1(1) of the Confiscation of Alcohol (Young Persons) Act 1997 states that:

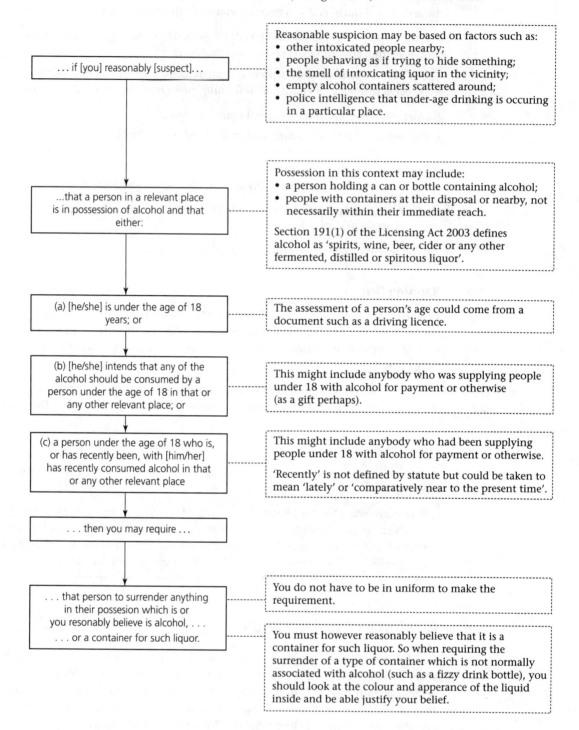

... if [you] reasonably [suspect]...

Reasonable suspicion may be based on factors such as:
• other intoxicated people nearby;
• people behaving as if trying to hide something;
• the smell of intoxicating iquor in the vicinity;
• empty alcohol containers scattered around;
• police intelligence that under-age drinking is occuring in a particular place.

...that a person in a relevant place is in possession of alcohol and that either:

Possession in this context may include:
• a person holding a can or bottle containing alcohol;
• people with containers at their disposal or nearby, not necessarily within their immediate reach.

Section 191(1) of the Licensing Act 2003 defines alcohol as 'spirits, wine, beer, cider or any other fermented, distilled or spiritous liquor'.

(a) [he/she] is under the age of 18 years; or

The assessment of a person's age could come from a document such as a driving licence.

(b) [he/she] intends that any of the alcohol should be consumed by a person under the age of 18 in that or any other relevant place; or

This might include anybody who was supplying people under 18 with alcohol for payment or otherwise (as a gift perhaps).

(c) a person under the age of 18 who is, or has recently been, with [him/her] has recently consumed alcohol in that or any other relevant place

This might include anybody who had been supplying people under 18 with alcohol for payment or otherwise.

'Recently' is not defined by statute but could be taken to mean 'lately' or 'comparatively near to the present time'.

... then you may require ...

... that person to surrender anything in their possesion which is or you resonably believe is alcohol, ...
... or a container for such liquor.

You do not have to be in uniform to make the requirement.

You must however reasonably believe that it is a container for such liquor. So when requiring the surrender of a type of container which is not normally associated with alcohol (such as a fizzy drink bottle), you should look at the colour and apperance of the liquid inside and be able justify your belief.

If you impose the above requirements set out in s 1(1) on a person, ss 1AA and 1AB state that you:

• must require that person to state his/her name and address (1AA):
• may remove the person to his/her place of residence or a place of safety (1AB) (see 9.12.4.2 below for case law regarding the definition of 'remove' and 9.13.2.1 below in relation to 'a place of safety'.

Under s 1(4) of the Confiscation of Alcohol (Young Persons) Act 1997, you must inform the person of your suspicion under s 1(1) and that it is an offence to fail to comply (without reasonable excuse) with one of your requirements in ss 1(1) or 1AA above.

You may dispose of anything surrendered to you under s 1(1) in such manner as you consider appropriate (s 1(2)). Your own force policies will be very clear about what you should do under these circumstances, therefore refer to these in order to establish a suitable course of action.

Under the Police Reform Act 2002, a suitably designated PCSO also has the power to impose all the requirements described above.

9.4.1 Failing to Comply with a Requirement

It is an offence under s 1(3) of the Confiscation of Alcohol (Young Persons) Act 1997 for a person to fail (without reasonable excuse) to comply with a requirement imposed on him/her under ss 1(1) or 1AA. But remember, for the person to commit this offence you must have **informed** the person that failure to comply with your requirement (without reasonable excuse) is an offence (s 1(4)).

This offence is triable summarily and the penalty is a fine.

9.4.2 Persistently Possessing Alcohol in a Public Place

Section 29 of the Police and Crime Act 2009 states that it is an offence for a person under the age of 18 years to be in possession of alcohol without reasonable excuse:

* in any relevant place (see 9.4 above); and
* on three or more occasions within a year.

This offence is triable summarily and the penalty is a fine.

9.4.3 Wider Considerations

This legislation will be a useful addition to your toolbox of policing skills. If you find a child carrying unopened cans of alcohol and you do not have grounds to reasonably believe that he/she has been consuming alcohol (or is about to consume it) at a relevant place, then at least consider where he/she bought the cans and the welfare of the child, and then take action accordingly.

> **TASK 2**
>
> You have identified a group of young people drinking alcohol in a 'relevant place'. What requirements will you make of them? Write down a list of things you would say in order to make your requirements lawful.

9.5 Offences and Powers Relating to Licensed Premises

The Licensing Act 2003 includes legislation to address drunkenness in 'relevant premises'. **Relevant premises** within this legislation are:

* licensed premises, eg a pub;
* club premises with a **club premises certificate**, eg a working men's club;
* premises with **permitted temporary activity** such as village halls used for a wedding reception.

Staff managing or working in places where alcohol is served have a legal responsibility to try to prevent drunkenness and disorder. People with these responsibilities are listed in s 140(1) of the Licensing Act 2003, and are referred to here as responsible staff (a term of our own invention, not a legal term).

Responsible staff include:

- the holder of a premises licence;
- the designated supervisor of a licensed premises;
- any person who works at the premises in a capacity which authorizes him/her to prevent disorderly conduct;
- any member or officer of a club (with a club premises certificate) who has the capacity to prevent disorderly behaviour;
- the user of a premises with permitted temporary activity, at the permitted time.

9.5.1 Allowing Disorderly Conduct

An offence is committed by responsible staff who knowingly allow disorderly conduct on licensed premises. This offence is triable summarily and the penalty is a fine.

9.5.2 Selling Intoxicating Liquor to a Drunk Person

An offence is committed under s 141(1) of the Licensing Act 2003 by responsible staff who knowingly sell (or attempt to sell) alcohol to a person who is drunk on relevant premises.

This offence is triable summarily and the penalty is a fine. It is also a penalty offence for the purposes of s 1 of the Criminal Justice and Police Act 2001.

9.5.3 Obtaining Alcohol for a Drunk Person

An offence is committed under s 142(1) of the Licensing Act 2003 by a person who knowingly obtains (or attempts to obtain) alcohol for consumption on relevant premises by a person who is drunk.

This offence is triable summarily and the penalty is a fine. It is also a penalty offence for the purposes of s 1 of the Criminal Justice and Police Act 2001.

9.5.4 Entering or Leaving Premises when Drunk or Disorderly

If a person is drunk or disorderly and fails to leave relevant premises when requested to do so, he/she has committed an offence under s 143(1) of the Licensing Act 2003. Such a person may be requested to leave by a constable or responsible staff. This offence is triable summarily and the penalty is a fine.

As a police officer, you have a responsibility to respond to requests for help from responsible staff to help expel or refuse entry to a drunk person, (s 143(4) of the Licensing Act 2003).

9.5.5 Powers of Entry into Licensed Premises

Under s 180(1) of the Licensing Act 2003 you can use reasonable force to gain entry to premises for the purposes of detecting an offence under other sections of the Licensing Act 2003.

You also have the power to enter a club with a club premises certificate if you have reasonable cause to believe that an offence relating to supplying a controlled drug has been committed there, or is about to be, or is being committed at that moment (s 97(1) of the Licensing Act 2003). The same section allows you to enter if you believe that there is likely to be a breach of the peace in the club. Whilst exercising this power you may use reasonable force (s 97(2)). See 10.13 below for a discussion of 'controlled drugs'.

For premises with **permitted temporary activities**, under s 108(1) of the Licensing Act 2003 you may enter the premises at any reasonable time to assess the effect of the event in terms of:

- the prevention of crime and disorder;
- public safety;

- the prevention of public nuisance;
- the protection of children from harm.

There is no specific offence of obstructing a police officer under this section, so if this occurs, you should consider the offence of obstruction in the lawful execution of your duties under the Police Act 1996.

9.5.6 Selling Alcohol to Children and Young People

Children (any person under the age of 18 years) may not purchase alcohol.

An offence is committed by a person who:

- sells alcohol to a person under 18 in any place (s 146(1) of the Licensing Act 2003). This is also a penalty offence under s 1 of the Criminal Justice and Police Act 2001 (see 8.15.2 above);
- knowingly allows the sale of alcohol on relevant premises to an individual aged under 18 (s 147(1) of the Licensing Act 2003).

A further more serious offence is committed if on two or more different occasions (within a period of three consecutive months) alcohol is unlawfully sold on the same licensed premises to an individual aged under 18 (s 147A of the Licensing Act 2003).

These offences are triable summarily and the penalty is a fine.

TASK 3

In the course of your investigations into offences concerning public disorder, public indecency, criminal damage, and theft, you may discover that many of these offences are committed by people who have consumed large amounts of intoxicating liquor on relevant premises. This intake of alcohol may have contributed towards these offences being committed.

Look up your force policy to establish how you will inform the licensing authority of the premises about such activities.

9.6 Breach of the Peace

You have no doubt heard of the phrase 'breach of the peace'. However, there is some considerable debate concerning both its meaning and whether it should still be dealt with by the police. Part of the reason for this debate is that the law surrounding a breach of the peace is somewhat unusual as it is not a criminal offence or part of statute law (see 5.11 above). It is however part of common law, and case law has set a precedent in defining its meaning (see 9.6.1 below).

Any person committing a breach of the peace can be arrested by any other person, and this includes you as a student police officer. Having been arrested, individuals can be detained until there is no likelihood of a breach of the peace happening again. Alternatively, a police officer can 'lay a complaint upon' a person and place him/her before a criminal court. (A complaint is similar to the process of charge.) The court can 'bind over' the person for a sum of money, which he/she will have to pay to the court if he/she causes a breach of the peace in the future.

9.6.1 Definition of Breach of the Peace

The case of *R v Howell* [1981] 3 All ER 383 provides a definition of the meaning of breach of the peace:

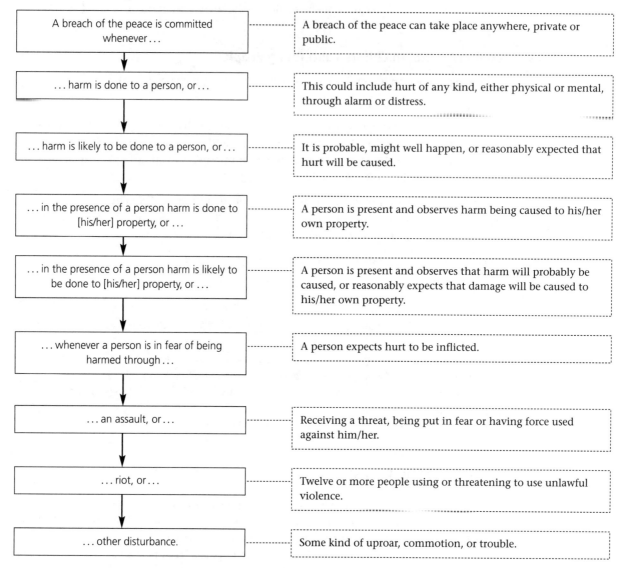

A breach of the peace is committed whenever . . .	A breach of the peace can take place anywhere, private or public.
. . . harm is done to a person, or . . .	This could include hurt of any kind, either physical or mental, through alarm or distress.
. . . harm is likely to be done to a person, or . . .	It is probable, might well happen, or reasonably expected that hurt will be caused.
. . . in the presence of a person harm is done to [his/her] property, or . . .	A person is present and observes harm being caused to his/her own property.
. . . in the presence of a person harm is likely to be done to [his/her] property, or . . .	A person is present and observes that harm will probably be caused, or reasonably expects that damage will be caused to his/her own property.
. . . whenever a person is in fear of being harmed through . . .	A person expects hurt to be inflicted.
. . . an assault, or . . .	Receiving a threat, being put in fear or having force used against him/her.
. . . riot, or . . .	Twelve or more people using or threatening to use unlawful violence.
. . . other disturbance.	Some kind of uproar, commotion, or trouble.

9.6.2 Powers of Arrest for Breach of the Peace

R v Howell also provides guidance on your powers of arrest in the case of a breach of the peace:

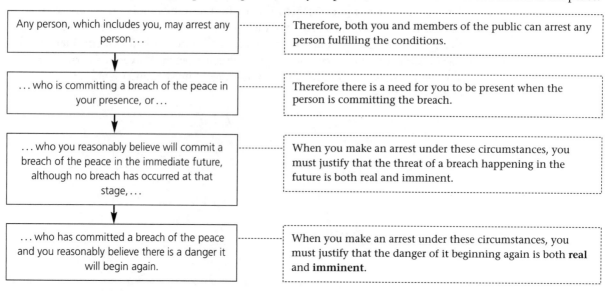

Any person, which includes you, may arrest any person . . .	Therefore, both you and members of the public can arrest any person fulfilling the conditions.
. . . who is committing a breach of the peace in your presence, or . . .	Therefore there is a need for you to be present when the person is committing the breach.
. . . who you reasonably believe will commit a breach of the peace in the immediate future, although no breach has occurred at that stage, . . .	When you make an arrest under these circumstances, you must justify that the threat of a breach happening in the future is both real and imminent.
. . . who has committed a breach of the peace and you reasonably believe there is a danger it will begin again.	When you make an arrest under these circumstances, you must justify that the danger of it beginning again is both **real** and **imminent**.

Breach of the peace is unique. You can use it in all manner of circumstances but you must apply the precedent set by the case *R v Howell* and satisfy its elements rigorously. Before making an arrest, always identify the all-important ingredients of **harm** and compare the actual circumstances with the definition. Then check that the breach took place in your presence, or that the threat or its renewal is both real and imminent.

TASK 4

In November 2003, a 61-year-old woman climbed the gates of Buckingham Palace to protest at the visit of US President George Bush. She then unfurled the Stars and Stripes flag on top of the gates with the words 'ELIZABETH WINDSOR AND CO … HE'S NOT WELCOME' written on the flag. After about two hours she voluntarily climbed down from the gates and was reported as being arrested by the police on suspicion of criminal damage and breach of the peace.

Explain whether or not a breach of the peace occurred at this incident.

9.7 The Public Order Act 1986

Sections 1–5 of the Public Order Act 1986 deal with a wide range of behaviours and offences. The diagram below shows these clearly, with the more serious and rare offence of riot (s 1) at the top of the triangle, and the less serious but more common offences of causing harassment, alarm, or distress (ss 4A and 5) at the base of the triangle.

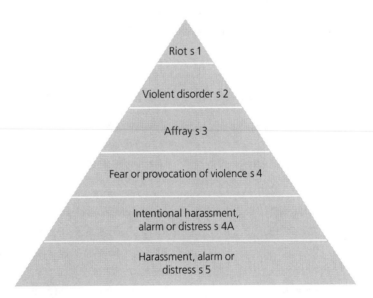

9.7.1 Intoxication Is Not a Defence

Some people accused of Public Order Act 1986 offences may claim in their defence that they were very drunk at the time that they committed public order offences. However, s 6(5) of the Public Order Act 1986 specifically states that in these circumstances a person will be taken by the court to have the same level of awareness had he/she not been intoxicated, unless it can be proved that either the intoxication:

- was not self-induced (eg 'spiked' drinks); or
- was caused solely by the taking or administration of a substance in the course of medical treatment (eg prescribed medicine).

Note that s 6(5) does not apply to s 4A of the Act, as s 4A was introduced at a later date.

9.7.2   Locations for Public Order Offences

The more serious public order offences (riot, violent disorder, and affray) can take place in private, as well as in public places.

Offences under ss 4, 4A, and 5 of the Public Order Act 1986 can occur in a public or private place, but if the conduct takes place inside a dwelling (a private place of residence excluding communal parts) then the person who is harassed, alarmed, or distressed must be outside in a public place. For example, if a neighbour attaches an offensive poster to the inside of a window, which is then seen by a person from the street outside, the offence has been committed. However, if the poster is seen by the same person but from inside their own house next door (perhaps through a side window), then the offence has not been committed. The reason for this is simply that the offence is part of the **Public** Order Act 1986. (Other legislation is available for circumstances which are completely private, for example the Protection of Harassment Act 1997 (see 9.9 below)).

9.7.3   Offences under ss 5, 4A, and 4

Members of the public usually prefer to be able to walk along the street without being intimidated, frightened, or stressed by other people's actions. Sections 5 and 4A of the Public Order Act 1986 offer safeguards against relatively minor forms of public disorder, such as persistent swearing, shouting, and other anti-social behaviour. Section 4, on the other hand, deals with a more serious type of public disorder, involving fear or provocation of violence.

Before looking at the sections in detail, you might find it useful to consider the following terms and definitions used in the legislation. The distinctions between offences under ss 5, 4A, and 4 require careful consideration and still cause some debate in legal and police circles. The offences will be described individually, and then compared in order to highlight important differences between them.

Definitions

Threatening	A physical or verbal act which indicates harm will be inflicted. It can also include violent conduct.
Abusive	Using or containing insulting or degrading language.
Insulting	Disrespectful, especially if done in a way that is offensive, or suggesting that a person is beneath consideration, but in a way that is more than annoyance or causing bitterness.
Harassment	A feeling of annoyance, persecution, irritation, and aggravation.
Alarm	A state of surprise, fright, fear, terror, and panic.
Distress	A feeling of suffering, anguish, and misery.
Words	Spoken or shouted.
Behaviour	Display of conduct involving the treatment of others.
Disorderly behaviour	Rowdy, unruly, boisterous, loud, raucous, or unrestrained conduct.
To display	To show or exhibit for all to see, such as placing a sign or poster in a window.
Distribute	To hand out, share out, give out, or issue to a particular person or people, not just simply left 'lying about'.
Writing, sign, or other visual representation	A notice containing lettering or other visible form of copied picture, text, or image, leaflet, pamphlet, or fly poster.

9.7.3.1 Section 5 of the Public Order Act 1986

The offence is also referred to as **non-intentional** harassment, alarm, or distress. Section 5 of the Public Order Act 1986 states that a person is guilty of this offence if he/she:

(a) uses threatening, abusive or insulting words or behaviour, or disorderly behaviour, or

(b) displays any writing sign or other visible representation which is threatening, abusive or insulting, within the hearing or sight of a person likely to be caused harassment, alarm or distress thereby.

The key features of s 5 offences are that:

- the conduct does not have to be aimed towards a specific person;
- the conduct must take place within the presence of a person who can see or hear the conduct, but that person does not need to be identifiable;
- the type of conduct must be likely to cause harassment, alarm, or distress;
- any material used (such as a poster) is not distributed;
- the suspect must intend or be aware that their conduct is threatening, abusive, or insulting in general terms;
- however, there is no need to prove he/she actually intended to cause any person to be harassed, alarmed, or distressed.

You may feel that the last two bullet points appear contradictory, but consider the example below and the precise nature of a s 5 offence will become clear.

In an interview with the suspect (S), you (SPO) might have the following exchange:

> **SPO** Why did you behave the way you did back there in the street?
>
> **S** I was trying to be hard in front of my mates.
>
> **SPO** Didn't you think about the effect it might have on other people?
>
> **S** Not really, it didn't even cross my mind they'd take any notice—I was only messing about.
>
> **SPO** What was the point of it all then?
>
> **S** Not a lot—I was showing off, I'd had a couple of drinks, but I wasn't drunk. I knew what I was doing and I wanted to be as loud and proud as I could, just to show my mates I could do it. In the end they just laughed and made out I was acting stupid.
>
> **SPO** Yes, and you might have upset a few elderly people passing by; how do you think they felt hearing that lot?
>
> **S** I just didn't think—yeah, I knew they were there . . . But if I did, I didn't mean to upset them . . .

It might now be clear from this example how a suspect might intend his/her conduct to be threatening, abusive, or insulting but still have no intention to make any person harassed, alarmed, or distressed.

There are three defences to this offence (listed in s 5(3)):

- that he/she had no reason to believe, whilst **in public**, that anybody could hear or see his/her conduct and had become harassed, alarmed, or distressed as a result. In other words, the suspect believed that his/her poster or behaviour could not be seen or his/her voice could not be heard by anybody else;
- that he/she had no reason to believe, whilst **inside a dwelling** (place of residence), that his/her words, behaviour, or conduct could be seen or heard by a person outside that same or another dwelling. For example a poster was positioned on a wall inside the front room, and could not be clearly seen from the road outside;
- that his/her conduct was **reasonable** and did not cause anybody to be harassed, alarmed, or distressed. For example he/she shouted at a group of people who were carrying out an unlawful act outside his/her home.

This offence is triable summarily and the penalty is a fine. This offence can be racially or religiously aggravated (see s 31(1)(c) of the Crime and Disorder Act 1998 and 9.11.4 below).

> **TASK 5**
>
> Take a moment now to consider what evidence you would need to obtain before making a decision whether to consider a person for a s 5 Public Order Act 1986 offence.
>
> 1. Who would you collect evidence from?
> 2. What evidence would they be able to provide?
> 3. What evidence would you be able to provide?

9.7.3.2 **Section 4A of the Public Order Act 1986**

A s 4A offence is often referred to as causing **intentional** harassment, alarm, or distress.

Section 4A(1) of the Public Order Act 1986 states that a person is guilty of this offence if he/she:

with intent to cause a person harassment, alarm or distress ...

(a) uses threatening, abusive or insulting words or behaviour, or disorderly behaviour, or

(b) displays any writing, sign or other visible representation which is threatening, abusive or insulting, thereby causing that or another person harassment, alarm or distress.

The key features of S 4A offences are that:

- the suspect **intends** the conduct to be threatening, abusive, or insulting and to cause a person harassment, alarm, or distress;
- the conduct does **not** have to be aimed towards a specific person;
- at least one **identifiable person** must be harassed, alarmed, or distressed;
- material (if used) cannot be distributed.

This piece of legislation is aimed at supporting the most vulnerable members of the community, who may be specifically targeted because of their inability to respond appropriately to intentionally directed acts which cause them harassment, alarm, or distress. These victims may feel particularly uncomfortable as witnesses, so you should take every opportunity to support them throughout any police or legal process.

As a possible defence, a suspect could demonstrate that:

- he/she had no reason to believe his/her words, behaviour, or conduct inside a dwelling (a place of residence) could be seen or heard by a person anywhere outside, eg a poster hanging on an inside wall within a house was not able to be seen from the road outside (s 4A(3)(a));
- his/her conduct was reasonable, eg if a person shouted at a group of people who were carrying out an unlawful act outside his/her home (s 4A(3)(b)).

This offence is triable summarily and the penalty is six months' imprisonment and/or a fine. This offence can be racially or religiously aggravated (see s 31(1)(b) of the Crime and Disorder Act 1998 and 9.11.4 below) .

9.7.3.3 **Section 4 of the Public Order Act 1986**

A s 4 offence is also referred to as **fear or provocation of violence**.

Section 4 of the Public Order Act states that a person is guilty of this offence if he/she:

(a) uses towards another person threatening, abusive or insulting words or behaviour, or

(b) distributes or displays to another person any writing, sign or other visible representation which is threatening, abusive or insulting,

with intent to cause that person to believe that immediate unlawful violence will be used against [him/her] or another by any person, or to provoke the immediate use of unlawful violence by that person or another, or whereby that person is likely to believe that such violence will be used or it is likely that such violence will be provoked.

For this offence, the **intentions** of the suspect are the key issue; the actual effect of the behaviour on other people is not relevant. Their intention must be to make the person (or persons) to whom the conduct is addressed (the recipient(s)) feel fear, or to provoke anyone to be violent. Despite the fact that the actual effect of the conduct is not relevant for this offence, for the intentions of the suspect to be held to be genuine, his/her conduct must be directed towards a recipient who must be present at the time when the words or behaviour are used. The recipient must be able to see or hear the conduct; alternatively, the suspect must believe that the recipient is able to see or hear the conduct (see *Atkin v DPP* [1989] Crim LR 581).

The suspect's intentions may be to cause **fear of violence**. If so, the suspect must intend the recipient to fear that violence will be used (or is likely to be used). The violent acts could be threatened by the suspect against the recipient. Or the suspect can intend to put the recipient in fear that violence will be used against another person instead. Also the suspect can intend to cause fear in the recipient that violent acts will be carried out by another person, rather than by the suspect, and that those violent acts could be against anyone at all. The key point is that if the suspect is intent on causing fear, the fear must be experienced by the recipient. The violent acts threatened by the suspect may or may not involve the suspect or the recipient directly, but it must be the intention of the suspect that the recipient should feel the fear.

Alternatively, there is a need to prove that the suspect had an intention (a determined state of mind) to **provoke violence**. The intention can be to provoke any person to use violence. For example, an extremist shouts at an animal research worker at a demonstration, 'A dog is for life, not just for you to torture and experiment on, you sadist! You'll get the same, I promise you that!' If the intention is to provoke immediate violence on the part of a group of animal rights activists who are nearby, the offence is committed.

The key features of s 4 offences are that:

- the conduct must be **directed** towards a person or persons present at the scene;
- any material used is **distributed** and not just displayed;
- the suspect must **intend or be aware** that his/her conduct is potentially threatening, abusive, or insulting (but it does not matter if the recipient does not actually feel threatened, abused, or insulted);
- the suspect may intend to cause fear or provoke a reaction of violence (but it **does not matter** if the conduct does not actually have either of these effects);
- if the suspect intends to cause fear (that violence will be or is likely to be used), the intention to cause fear **need only concern the recipient**;
- if the suspect intends to provoke violence, the intention can be to **provoke any person** present and not just the recipient.

You may enter any premises to arrest any person you reasonably suspect is committing an offence under s 4 of the Public Order Act 1986 (s 17, PACE Act: see 7.9 above).

This offence is triable summarily and the penalty is six months' imprisonment and/or a fine. This offence can be racially aggravated (see s 31(2)(b) of the Crime and Disorder Act 1998).

9.7.3.4 Comparing sections 4, 4A, and 5 of the Public Order Act 1986

The diagram below enables the precise wording for each of the sections of the Public Order Act 1986 to be easily compared:

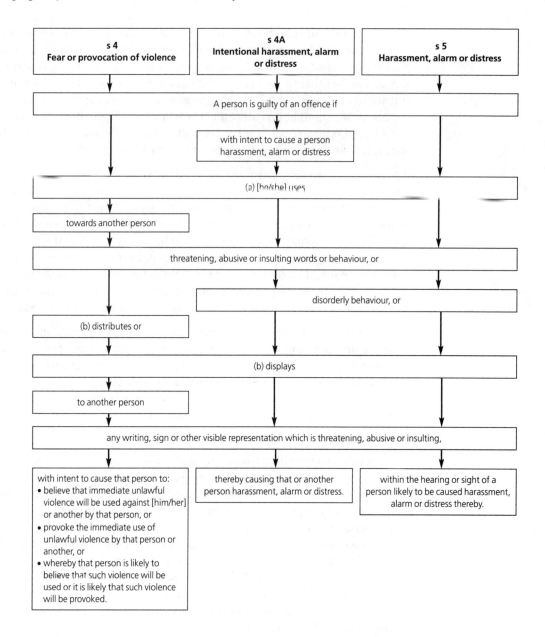

The table below identifies some important differences between ss 4, 4A, and 5:

	s 4	s 4A	s 5
Intentions of the suspect	Intends or is aware that the conduct is threatening, abusive, or insulting.	Intends the conduct to be threatening, abusive, or insulting.	Intends or is aware that the conduct is threatening, abusive, or insulting.
Recipient of the conduct	Conduct aimed towards a specific person.	Conduct does not have to be aimed towards a specific person.	Conduct does not have to be aimed towards a specific person (but has to be carried out in the hearing or sight of a person likely to be caused harassment, alarm, or distress).
Includes disorderly behaviour?	Does not include disorderly behaviour.	Includes disorderly behaviour.	
Distribution of material?	Includes distribution of material.	Does not include distribution of material.	
Outcome of the behaviour	Intends to cause fear or provocation of immediate unlawful violence. No requirement that someone experiences that fear, or that violence is provoked.	Evidence required that an identifiable person has been harassed, alarmed, or distressed.	Evidence is **not** required that an identifiable person has been harassed, alarmed, or distressed.

TASK 6

Often whilst on Independent Patrol, you may well be within the sight or hearing of a person whom you suspect by his or her behaviour to be causing harassment, alarm, or distress. Consider how you will deal with a situation such as this if there is nobody else in the area at the time to whom this conduct is aimed and hence it appears to be directed at you.

While drawing your conclusions, refer to *DPP v Orum* [1988] Crim LR 848.

TASK 7

You are on Independent Patrol when you see a man walk up to the door of a club and adopt an aggressive posture towards the door supervisor. You are about two metres away. The aggressor has clenched fists, bulging eyes, and has taken up a 'boxing' position. The suspect then pushes his shoulder into the door supervisor's chest causing the door supervisor to move back. You hear the suspect say 'You're a dead man'. You believe that the door supervisor is about to be attacked and so you arrest the suspect under s 4 of the Public Order Act 1986.

When you return to the club to obtain a statement from the door supervisor, you are informed that he is not willing to make a statement. In your opinion could a successful prosecution be brought against the suspect under these circumstances?

When drawing a conclusion, consider *Swanston v DPP* [1997] 161 JP 203.

9.7.4 Serious Public Order Offences

These offences under the Public Order Act 1986 are, in increasing order of seriousness:

- affray (s 3);
- violent disorder (s 2);
- riot (s 1).

Remember, these more serious public order offences can be committed in private as well as in public. Offences under ss 1–3 all involve **unlawful violence**.

Briefly, **violence** is aggressive or hostile conduct towards property or persons, and includes acts capable of causing injury, even if no injury or damage is caused.

Section 8 of the Public Order Act offers guidance on the meaning of **unlawful** violence:

    (a) except in the context of affray, it includes violent conduct towards property as well as violent conduct towards persons; and

    (b) it is not restricted to conduct causing or intended to cause injury or damage but includes any other violent conduct (for example, throwing at or towards a person a missile of a kind capable of causing injury which does not hit or falls short).

The legislation describing offences under ss 1–3 also uses the term a 'person of reasonable firmness' (sometimes referred to as the 'hypothetical bystander'). This is not defined under law but can be taken to mean an average person in terms of their reaction to violent incidents around them (that is, not somebody who is unduly frightened by the most minor of incidents, nor somebody who is completely hardened to acts of violent behaviour).

9.7.4.1 Affray

For an affray (s 3 of the Public Order Act 1986) the threat of violence needs to be capable of affecting others. The primary objective of the law is to protect the general public around the affray, not the participants themselves. For an affray, the level of the threat of violence needs to be capable of affecting others and the court will consider how a hypothetical person of reasonable firmness (see above) witnessing the incident would feel (*R v Sanchez*, The Times, 6 March 1996). (If an individual is threatening another person in a relatively un-alarming manner, such that no one else would be likely to be worried by the incident or is involved, then other offences such as common assault are available to deal with the situation.)

Therefore, there are in effect three parties involved in an affray:

1. the individual making the threats
2. the person subject to the threats
3. any bystander(s).

Section 3(1) of the Public Order Act 1986 states:

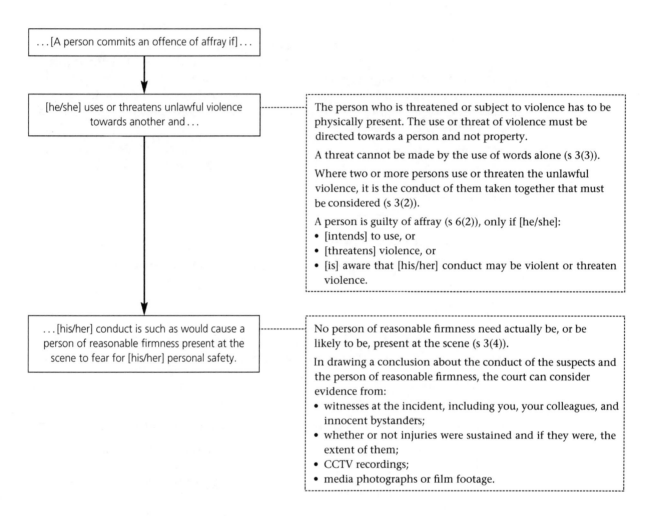

...[A person commits an offence of affray if]...

[he/she] uses or threatens unlawful violence towards another and...

The person who is threatened or subject to violence has to be physically present. The use or threat of violence must be directed towards a person and not property.

A threat cannot be made by the use of words alone (s 3(3)).

Where two or more persons use or threaten the unlawful violence, it is the conduct of them taken together that must be considered (s 3(2)).

A person is guilty of affray (s 6(2)), only if [he/she]:
• [intends] to use, or
• [threatens] violence, or
• [is] aware that [his/her] conduct may be violent or threaten violence.

...[his/her] conduct is such as would cause a person of reasonable firmness present at the scene to fear for [his/her] personal safety.

No person of reasonable firmness need actually be, or be likely to be, present at the scene (s 3(4)).

In drawing a conclusion about the conduct of the suspects and the person of reasonable firmness, the court can consider evidence from:
• witnesses at the incident, including you, your colleagues, and innocent bystanders;
• whether or not injuries were sustained and if they were, the extent of them;
• CCTV recordings;
• media photographs or film footage.

This offence is triable either way:

• summarily: six months' imprisonment, and/or a fine;
• on indictment: three years' imprisonment.

9.7.4.2 Violent disorder

For this offence under s 2 of the Public Order Act 1986, three or more persons must be present together and use (or threaten to use) unlawful violence. If it was only possible to arrest and investigate one person out of such a group, then that person can still be charged with this offence. However, it must still be proved that at least two other people using or threatening violence were present, and they must also be mentioned in the charge.

Section 6(2) states that a person is guilty of violent disorder only if he/she:

• intends to use;
• threatens violence; or
• is aware that his/her conduct may be violent or may threaten violence.

Section 2(1) of the Public Order Act 1986 states an offence of violent disorder is committed:

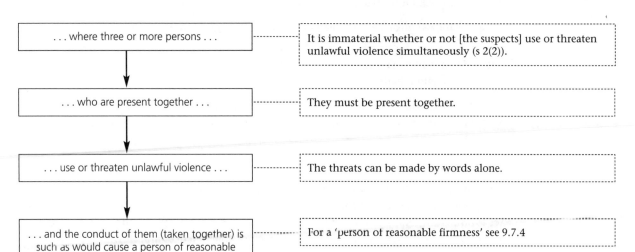

. . . where three or more persons . . .	It is immaterial whether or not [the suspects] use or threaten unlawful violence simultaneously (s 2(2)).
. . . who are present together . . .	They must be present together.
. . . use or threaten unlawful violence . . .	The threats can be made by words alone.
. . . and the conduct of them (taken together) is such as would cause a person of reasonable firmness present at the scene to fear for [his or her] personal safety.	For a 'person of reasonable firmness' see 9.7.4

This offence is triable either way:

- summarily: six months' imprisonment and/or a fine;
- on indictment: five years' imprisonment.

9.7.4.3 Riot

A person who takes part in a riot using unlawful violence commits an offence under s 1(1) of the Public Order Act 1986. The offence of riot is similar to that of violent disorder, but twelve or more people must be present. Charges of riot are very rare. This offence is triable on indictment only and the penalty is ten years' imprisonment.

TASK 8

Whilst on Independent Patrol you respond to a call from a customer of a local nightclub alleging that a member of the door staff has pushed a female customer out of the door and that she fell over as a result of the push. There are no other witnesses to the incident and no CCTV footage. Disregarding the investigation of the assault, could an investigation into an affray be sustained? Refer to *R v Plavecz* [2002] Crim LR 837 for your answer.

9.7.5 Hatred on the Grounds of Race, Religion, and Sexual Orientation

The Public Order Act 1986 has recently been modified to address the 'stirring up' (the phrase used in the legislation) or the inciting of hatred against a group of people on the grounds of race, religion, or sexual orientation. The table below shows some of the relevant offences and the section numbers in the Public Order Act 1986. The boxes outlined in bold relate to the more commonly encountered versions of these offences.

Activity \ Grounds	Racial	Religious or sexual orientation
Using threatening words or behaviour, or displaying written material.	s 18	s 29B
Publishing or distributing written material.	s 19	s 29C
Distributing, showing, or playing a recording.	s 21	s 29E
Possessing racially inflammatory material.	s 23	s 29G

Racial hatred means 'hatred against a group of persons defined by reference to colour, race, nationality (including citizenship) or ethnic or national origins'.

Religious hatred means hatred against a group of persons defined by reference to:

- religious belief, for example Christianity, Islam, Hinduism, Judaism, Buddhism, Sikhism, Rastafarianism, Baha'ism, Zoroastrianism, and Jainism; or
- a lack of religious belief, for example atheists and humanists.

Hatred on the grounds of sexual orientation means 'hatred against a group of persons defined by reference to sexual orientation (whether towards persons of the same sex, the opposite sex or both)'.

9.7.5.1 Possible defences

In practice, the offences you are most likely to encounter are those involving the use of threatening words or behaviour or the display of written material (ss 18 and 29B of the Public Order Act 1986). The offences can be committed in a public or a private place, although the effects of the actions must be felt in a public place. Some possible defences are shown in the flowchart below.

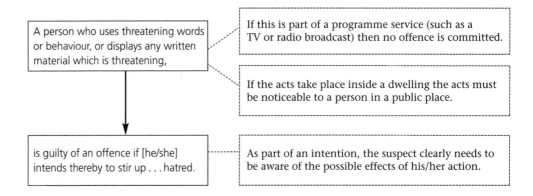

These offences are triable either way:

- summarily: six months' imprisonment and/or a fine;
- on indictment: seven years' imprisonment and/or a fine.

9.8 Using Violence to Enter Premises

It is an offence, under s 6 of the Criminal Law Act 1977 to use violence to gain entry into premises which are being occupied by any person opposing the entry. Under the law, it makes no difference that the person using the violence has a right or interest in the property. For example, a person trying to force his way into his own flat is committing an offence if his live-in partner is inside the flat and she does not want him to come in. (Originally, forced entry was identified as an offence in order to prevent the owners, tenants, or occupiers of premises from using violence to gain entry into those premises while they were being occupied by squatters.)

Under s 6 of the Criminal Law Act 1977 it is an offence:

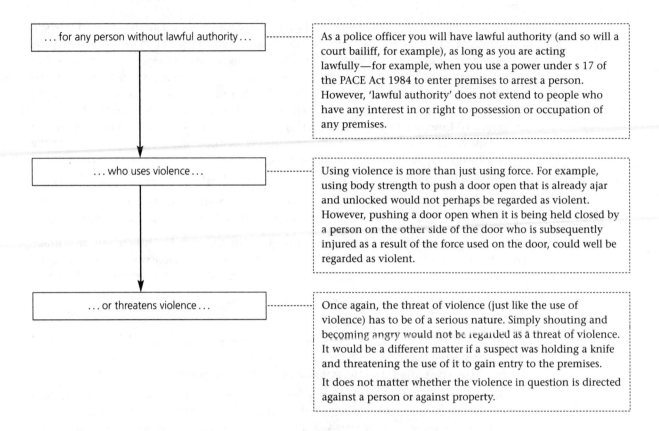

... for any person without lawful authority ...

As a police officer you will have lawful authority (and so will a court bailiff, for example), as long as you are acting lawfully—for example, when you use a power under s 17 of the PACE Act 1984 to enter premises to arrest a person. However, 'lawful authority' does not extend to people who have any interest in or right to possession or occupation of any premises.

... who uses violence ...

Using violence is more than just using force. For example, using body strength to push a door open that is already ajar and unlocked would not perhaps be regarded as violent. However, pushing a door open when it is being held closed by a person on the other side of the door who is subsequently injured as a result of the force used on the door, could well be regarded as violent.

... or threatens violence ...

Once again, the threat of violence (just like the use of violence) has to be of a serious nature. Simply shouting and becoming angry would not be regarded as a threat of violence. It would be a different matter if a suspect was holding a knife and threatening the use of it to gain entry to the premises.

It does not matter whether the violence in question is directed against a person or against property.

So for this offence, the suspect must not have lawful authority, and must either use violence or threaten to use violence:

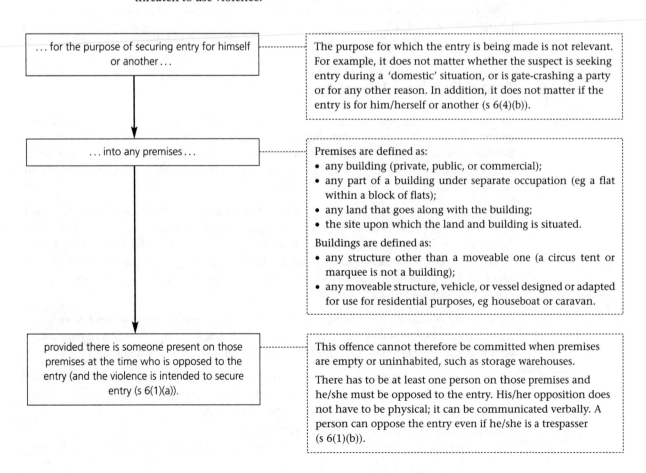

... for the purpose of securing entry for himself or another ...

The purpose for which the entry is being made is not relevant. For example, it does not matter whether the suspect is seeking entry during a 'domestic' situation, or is gate-crashing a party or for any other reason. In addition, it does not matter if the entry is for him/herself or another (s 6(4)(b)).

... into any premises ...

Premises are defined as:
• any building (private, public, or commercial);
• any part of a building under separate occupation (eg a flat within a block of flats);
• any land that goes along with the building;
• the site upon which the land and building is situated.

Buildings are defined as:
• any structure other than a moveable one (a circus tent or marquee is not a building);
• any moveable structure, vehicle, or vessel designed or adapted for use for residential purposes, eg houseboat or caravan.

provided there is someone present on those premises at the time who is opposed to the entry (and the violence is intended to secure entry (s 6(1)(a)).

This offence cannot therefore be committed when premises are empty or uninhabited, such as storage warehouses.

There has to be at least one person on those premises and he/she must be opposed to the entry. His/her opposition does not have to be physical; it can be communicated verbally. A person can oppose the entry even if he/she is a trespasser (s 6(1)(b)).

A home owner may enter by force if there are trespassers inside but only if the home owners are:

* **Displaced Residential Occupiers** (defined in s 12 of the Criminal Law Act 1977): this would include people who leave the home they live in for a short while, and during the time they are away, a person or persons enter the premises as trespassers to take up residence themselves. This does not give the owners the right to carry out unlawful acts (such as assault) in relation to the trespassers; it only means they do not commit the particular offence of violence to secure entry (under s 6 of the Criminal Law Act 1977) if they use violence to enter their own home.
* **Protected Intended Occupiers** (defined in s 12A of the Criminal Law Act 1977): this would include people who do not live in their homes yet, because they have only just bought the premises or only just agreed to rent them. Therefore they are intending to take up occupancy. However, they must have completed a legal process to reach this stage.

This offence is triable summarily and the penalty is six months' imprisonment and/or a fine. There is a power of entry to arrest someone for this offence under s 17 of the PACE Act 1984.

This offence occurs frequently, in a wide range of situations. If you suspect that such an offence may have been committed you need to run through a mental checklist before you act. Check that the events you are considering match all the requirements of the legislation describing this offence.

TASK 9

Charlie and partner Sam have been facing up to the fact that their three-year relationship is drawing to an end. Recently there have been several episodes where they shouted angrily at each other, and both of them have taken to going out separately and getting very drunk.

They share a house which is owned jointly. One evening Charlie stays at home while Sam goes to a club nearby. Sam arrives home in the early hours of the following morning, very drunk, to find the front door will not open with the key. Sam begins to hammer on the door, and the awakened neighbours hear Charlie shouting (from inside the house) telling Sam to stop banging on the door and to go away. One of the neighbours calls the police and you attend the scene to find Sam still hammering on the door. In relation to s 6(1) of the Criminal Law Act 1977, has Sam committed an offence?

9.9 Protection from Harassment

Sections 1–5 of the Protection from Harassment Act 1997 can be applied in a wide range of situations, including the investigation of disputes between partners in a relationship and disputes between neighbours. More recently, the government has made additions to the Act to protect people from extremist campaigns, and it is now an offence to harass two or more people on separate occasions.

The definition of harassment is in terms of the effect it has on the victim rather than the actual events that took place. The victim must be distressed and the perpetrator must know that his/her actions are likely to cause distress. However, the behaviour must be consistent with the behaviour that a **reasonable person** would see as harassing (s 1(2), Protection from Harassment Act 1997). The final decision of whether or not particular behaviour led to a person being alarmed or distressed is taken by the court.

Only individuals can suffer harassment under the Act. Companies or corporate bodies cannot be harassed, but their employees can, and so references to 'a person' in the context of harassment refer to a person or persons as **individuals** (s 7(5), Protection from Harassment Act 1997).

The harassment must consist of a **course of conduct** (s 7(3)(a)(b), Protection from Harassment Act 1997). Harassment is not just a one-off event; it must occur on more than one occasion. A course of conduct exists when conduct is directed towards:

* an individual on at least two occasions (s 7(3)(a)); or
* two or more people, and on at least one occasion in relation to **each** of those persons (s 7(3)(b)).

By precedent it has been decided that it is not just the number of incidents that are important, but whether those incidents are connected (*Lau v DPP* [2000] All ER (D) 224). However, it is less likely that the court will accept that behaviour constitutes a course of conduct if there is a long period of time between the events under consideration. The course of conduct does not have to comprise similar types of conduct; indeed it is often not obvious that separate incidents are connected, so be aware of this during any investigation. However, even if the conduct appears (to you) to be one continuous course of conduct from start to finish, the court may decide that there was a sequence of separate incidents instead (see *(1) Sylvia Buckley (2) Lisa Smith v Director of Public Prosecutions* (2008) EWHC 136 (Admin)).

Conduct includes speech, letters, and e-mails so you will need to gather evidence from a wide range of sources such as diary entries, emails, letters, photographs, and interviews with witnesses. What might begin as a bona fide enquiry to a company, for example, could become harassing if it is followed up in a manner that is persistent (see *DPP v Hardy* (2008) All ER (D) 315 (Oct)). The conduct can involve a third person. For example, if person A asks person B to give a threatening letter to the victim, person C, then both A and B are guilty of the offence if B has guilty knowledge of the harassment.

Harassment can also be caused by a person (as well a group of people) who on two or more occasions take part in the planning of (or otherwise assisting with) a course of conduct, but not actually carrying it out. An example of where a group of people could be guilty of harassment would involve three people, X, Y, and Z, who stand along the route which A takes to and from work, in order to give A some threatening letters. They give the letters to A, and later Z makes a threatening phone call to A. Provided A feels alarmed or distressed, and X, Y, and Z knew (or ought to know) that their actions were likely to be alarming or distressing, X, Y, and Z would all be committing an offence (s 7(3A), Protection from Harassment Act 1997).

Two offences described in the Protection from Harassment Act 1997 are:

- harassment (without violence) (ss 1 and 2);
- putting people in fear of violence (s 4).

9.9.1 Harassment

It is an offence under ss 1 and 2 of the Protection from Harassment Act 1997 for a person:

- to pursue a course of conduct (s 1(1)); or
- to aid, abet, counsel, or procure the pursuance of a course of conduct (s 7(3A))

which involves harassment of one or more persons (s 1(1) and (1A)) which they know (or ought to know) amounts to harassment of the other(s) (s 1(1A)(b)).

It will be up to the court or jury to decide whether they believe a reasonable person would have considered the conduct was alarming or distressing in the particular circumstances. Otherwise, it would be relatively simple for the suspect(s) to claim a defence that they did not know their actions amounted to harassment (s1(2)) (see also s 1(3)(c) of the Act which we describe below).

In addition to the harassment of two or more persons in s 1(1A)(a), an offence can also be committed when the course of conduct is intended to persuade any person to change his/her current routine (s 1(1A)(c)(i) and (ii)). Such attempts to persuade may form part of a wider campaign about political or social issues. The attempt to persuade any person must:

- be directed towards two or more person(s) in the first instance; and
- must occur on at least one occasion in relation to **each** of those persons.

The offender might try to persuade any person (not only the two or more persons to whom the contact is directed) **to do something** that he/she is **not** under any obligation to do (s 1(1A)(c)(ii)). For example, an animal rights' extremist may pressurize employees to supply information by:

- making a threatening phone call to an individual who works for a company using animals for scientific research;
- verbally abusing another individual working for the same company.

If the intention is to persuade both individuals that they should supply information about other employees, suppliers, or clients, then the extremist has committed an offence.

This offence can be also be committed when there is an intention to persuade any person (not only the two or more persons to whom it is directed) to **not** do something that he/she is **entitled or required to do** (s 1(1A)(c)(i)). For example, an animal rights' extremist may pressurize employees to stop working for a company that uses animals for research by:

- sending a threatening email to an individual who works for that company;
- sending a threatening email to an individual who works for another similar company.

If the extremist intends to persuade both individuals to resign because they both work for companies that supply animals for scientific research, the extremist would have committed an offence.

9.9.1.1 Possible defences

As a possible defence, the suspect could try and show on the balance of probabilities that his/her course of conduct was pursued either:

(a) 'for the purpose of preventing or detecting crime' (eg police officers working in the lawful execution of their duties), (s 1(3)(a));

(b) 'under any enactment or rule of law' (eg court officers seeking a person for the purposes of serving a warrant), (s 1(3)(b));

(c) 'in reasonable circumstances': this will be for the court to decide and will probably be undertaken in a similar way to the 'reasonable person' test in s 1(2): '. . . if a reasonable person . . . would think the course of conduct amounted to . . . harassment', (s 1(3)(c)); or

(d) 'on certain government business', (s 1(3)(b)) (the police, customs, and the security services).

These offences are triable summarily and the penalty is six months' imprisonment and/or a fine. This offence can be racially or religiously aggravated (see 9.11 below).

9.9.2 Isolated Events Causing Distress

If distress is only caused on one occasion then, under the Protection from Harassment Act 1997, this does not constitute a course of conduct. Instead an actual or apprehended harassment may be the subject of a claim in **civil proceedings** by the distressed or alarmed person under s 3(1) of the same Act.

The main points of this option are:

- a 'course of conduct' is not necessary;
- the result of such a civil claim can be damages (a court order to pay money) and/or an injunction (a court order to impose sanctions on a person) against the offender;
- a company can apply for an injunction (rather than individuals).

If such an injunction is breached, the offence is triable either way:

- on indictment: five years' imprisonment and/or a fine;
- summarily: six months' imprisonment and/or a fine.

Within the Crime and Disorder Act 1998, there are no racially or religiously aggravated versions of the civil proceedings under s 3 of the Protection from Harassment Act 1997.

9.9.3 Putting People in Fear of Violence

This offence is described under s 4 of the Protection of Harassment Act 1997 and involves more than sending threatening letters or emails. The victim must experience a real fear of violence, and they must believe that whatever they are frightened of will really happen (as opposed to the possibility that it might happen).

There are several key differences from the harassment (s 2) offence we described earlier. In s 4 offences:

- the victim must believe the violence will happen as opposed to believing it might happen;
- the victim must fear the violence personally, not on behalf of somebody else, such as a family member (*Mohammed Ali Caurti v DPP* [2002] Crime LR 131);

- the fear of violence cannot be achieved through a third party. In other words, an individual cannot be put in fear of violence via an intermediary.

In most other ways, the conditions for this offence are similar to those for the offence of harassment (s 2) described in detail above; it is an offence to pursue or assist the conduct, there must be a course of conduct, and the court decides what is reasonable.

The defences to this offence are similar to the defences for s 2 but with one major addition: the course of conduct was pursued reasonably for the protection of themselves (or another), or for the protection of their (or another's) property. For example, a group of people threaten to damage person G's house. Person G threatens retributions should they do so but, as the intention is to protect property, he/she is not guilty of the offence of putting people in fear of violence.

This offence is triable either way:

- summarily: six months' imprisonment and/or a fine;
- on indictment: five years' imprisonment and/or a fine.

This offence can be racially or religiously aggravated (see 9.11 below).

9.9.4 Restraining Orders

A court may make a restraining order under s 5 of the Protection from Harassment Act 1997 against a person convicted of the offences described above. A restraining order will place restrictions on a defendant's future behaviour and in particular attempt to inhibit any further harassment of the victim. The order may last indefinitely or for a period stated by the court. You can use the PNC to find out if a person is subject to a restraining order.

If such a restraining order is breached an offence is committed, and is triable either way:

- summarily: six months' imprisonment an/or a fine;
- on indictment: five years' imprisonment and/or a fine.

Clearly, the Protection from Harassment Act 1997 is a potentially valuable piece of legislation which offers a number of options for providing support to victims of harassment. Victims will want to see results, or be given advice on how to put an end to current problems they are facing. However, note the considerable amount of evidence required to secure a successful prosecution within this Act, and be very clear about what can constitute a course of conduct and what proof is required. You may need to seek advice from the CPS at an early stage.

TASK 10

You are requested to attend an address in your area where a complaint of harassment has been made. Write brief answers to the following questions:

1. If appropriate, what evidence will you need to collect to prove an offence under either s 2 or s 4 of the Protection from Harassment Act 1997?
2. What other methods could be used to stop the conduct?
3. How can future evidence be recorded?
4. What reason(s) would make an arrest necessary in these circumstances?

9.9.5 Harassment of Persons in their Homes

Harassing or intimidating behaviour by individuals towards a person in his/her home is an offence under ss 42 and 42A of the Criminal Justice and Police Act 2001. The Act also enables you to give directions to a person to leave a particular area, and can be used, if appropriate, with protesters. You can subsequently arrest a person if they knowingly contravene a direction.

The following section outlines the offence and the power to direct a person to leave who is harassing someone in his/her home.

(a) ... they are present outside or in the vicinity of any premises that are used ... as a dwelling ...	There is no legal definition of 'vicinity'. It is for the courts to decide what is meant by it as a matter of fact and degree in the particular circumstances of each case. Vicinity is not simply determined by distance, it can also be measured by the impact on the householder. For example, someone protesting at the end of a quarter-mile long drive which is the only access road for the inhabitants may be out of sight and hearing, but they could still have the ability to cause harassment, alarm, or distress to the residents.
(b) ... [they are] there for the purpose of representing to the resident or another individual or persuading the resident or another individual (i) [that he/she] should not do something they are entitled ... to do; [or] (ii) [that he/she] should do something they are not under any obligation to do;	For example to try and persuade a person to resign from an animal research company or not to take up employment with such a company.
(c) ... the person intends [his/her] presence to amount to the harassment of, or to cause alarm or distress to the resident; [or knows or ought to know that their presence is likely to do so; and]	This could mean climbing onto the roof of a dwelling belonging to a person who is the employee of an animal research organization, thereby intending harassment, alarm, or distress. Courts will use the 'reasonable person' test to decide whether a person would find the presence so disturbing.
(d) ... [their] presence amounts to the harassment of, or causes alarm or distress to the resident, [or is likely to result in the harassment of, or cause alarm or distress of any such person.]	This could mean aggressive or abusive conduct such as shouting, heckling, or shouting abusive slogans (such as 'animal killer!') or continuous loud chanting at persons coming into or out of a dwelling, or any visitors to that dwelling. Such conduct could also be accompanied by the aggressive use of banners or placards. For example, they could be used to block or impede vehicular or pedestrian access to another dwelling which shares a drive.

As well as causing distress to the resident, other categories of people can also be affected, such as other people in the resident's dwelling or a person living nearby.

Courts will use the reasonable person test to decide whether a person would find the presence and activities significantly disturbing. Behaviour that may cause harassment, alarm, or distress includes:

- persistent, sustained, and aggressive hammering on doors;
- ringing doorbells or shouting through letter boxes;
- climbing onto the roof of a dwelling;
- shouting abusive slogans;
- continuous loud chanting;
- aggressive use of banners or placards used to block or impede access.

You do not have to be present when the behaviour occurs. If the resident has CCTV evidence of particular individuals on the roof of his/her house and had been harassed, alarmed, or distressed by the presence of the protesters, you could arrest the suspects for the offence.

This offence is triable summarily and the penalty is six months' imprisonment and/or a fine.

9.9.5.1 Giving Directions in Order to Prevent Harassment, Alarm, or Distress

You have powers under s 42(1) of the Criminal Justice and Police 2001 Act to give 'directions' to people in order to prevent them from causing harassment, alarm, or distress to residents (or other people in the vicinity), but only when a senior officer is not present to give the direction.

The wording of a direction might be 'you have caused harassment and distress to people living in this area. I therefore require you to leave immediately.' However, your ability to give directions to protesters (and to arrest them if they knowingly contravene a direction) is only effective if you are present at the scene of a protest. It does not cover a situation where, for example, a resident makes a complaint about the presence of protesters outside his/her home, but the protesters leave the scene before you arrive. Nor does it cover a person exercising the right to picket peacefully at a workplace.

A direction under s 42(2) may require the person to whom it is given:

> to do all such things as the constable giving it may specify as the things [he/she] considers necessary to prevent one or both of the following:
>
> (a) the harassment of the resident; or
> (b) the causing of any alarm or distress to the resident.

The direction can be given orally, and it can be given to a group as individuals, or to the group as a whole. It will instruct the person(s) to leave the vicinity and for any period not exceeding three months, and other conditions may be attached.

Note that giving directions will not serve any purpose if you do not have the resources to enforce the instructions at the scene.

9.9.5.2 Failure to Comply with a Direction

An offence is committed under s 42(7) and (7A) of the Criminal Justice and Police Act 2001 by any person:

- who knowingly fails to comply with a direction (other than to leave and not return for a period not exceeding three months) (s 42(7));
- who, having received a direction to leave, then returns (within the specified period to the vicinity of the premises in question) for the purpose of attempting to persuade a resident to follow a particular course of action.

This offence is triable summarily and the penalty is six months' imprisonment and/or a fine.

These sections of the Act should not be seen as a way of stopping people carrying out their lawful rights to protest peacefully or express strong opinions. Nor are they intended to prevent a fan from standing outside the home of his/her favourite television celebrity, or to stop media commentators from trying to record first-hand comments from people in the news. Rather, this legislation aims to provide a balance between the right to carry out such activities and the right of individuals to be protected from harassment, alarm, or distress in their own homes.

These sections of the Criminal Justice and Police Act 2001 provide you with more than one tool to deal with this type of situation. The direction to leave is useful, but of course it does not prevent the same protesters from returning time after time to increase the harassment, alarm, or distress of the residents. The offence (causing harassment, distress, or alarm), however, is more final, and therefore you will need to consider carefully which of the powers to use. This will depend on various issues such as the number of people in the vicinity of the person's home, the behaviour of those individuals, the purpose for which they have gathered there, and the impact of their presence on the resident, on anyone living with them, and on people in the surrounding area.

> ### TASK 11
>
> Whilst on Supervised Patrol you have been asked to attend the address of a person who reports being harassed by people in the street outside his house. What factors are you going to consider in order to decide:
> - whether or not to direct anybody away from the house;
> - whether you will investigate the offence in relation to the harassment?

9.10   Intimidation of Witnesses, Jurors, and Others

Witnesses often feel vulnerable and concerned about the consequences of their actions, and some become victims of intimidation by the suspect(s) in the case. The 'No witness, No justice' project is a joint initiative between the CPS, ACPO, the Home Office, and the Cabinet Office's Office of Public Service Reform. It highlights the importance of providing support to people who are crucial in the successful prosecution of offenders.

To successfully investigate and prosecute people suspected of intimidation relating to current or past proceedings, a total of four offences are available and these are to be found in the Criminal Justice and Police Act 2001 (for civil proceedings) and the Criminal Justice and Public Order Act 1994 (for criminal proceedings).

Under the Criminal Justice and Public Order Act 1994 (CJPOA 1994), the following definitions apply:

- an 'investigation' is a process carried out by the police or other person charged with the duty of investigating offences or charging offenders;
- an 'offence' can be either alleged or suspected;
- a 'potential juror' is a person who has been summoned for jury service at the court at which the offence will be tried (s 51(9)).

The person making the threat in the first place commits an offence if, instead, a third party is used to convey those threats (s 51(3)). The harm or intimidatory act that may be done or threatened can be financial as well as physical, either to the person or the person's property (s 51(4)). During the relevant periods there is a presumption of an intention to intimidate unless the suspect can prove otherwise (s 51(7) and (8)).

9.10.1   Intimidation Relating to Current Proceedings

The person suspected of intimidation must have carried out an act which intimidates and is intended to intimidate another person (the victim). The suspect must intend that the result of his/her actions will either obstruct, pervert, or otherwise interfere with the course of justice, and the act must occur between the start of the investigation and the end of the proceedings, for example at the conclusion of a court hearing.

Intimidation relating to current civil proceedings is covered under s 39(1) of the Criminal Justice and Police Act 2001, and the victim of the intimidation can be a witness in any relevant proceedings (not necessarily related to an offence) in the Court of Appeal, the High Court, the Crown Court, a county court, or a magistrates' court.

Intimidation relating to current criminal proceedings is covered under s 51(1) of the Criminal Justice and Public Order Act 1994. The victim of the intimidation must be either:

- assisting in the investigation of an offence;
- a witness or potential witness; or
- a juror or potential juror in proceedings for an offence.

9.10.2   Intimidation Relating to Proceedings in the Past

The person suspected of intimidation must have carried out an act (or acts) which either:

- caused harm to, and was intended to harm, another person; or
- threatened to harm another person, and was intended to cause the other person to fear harm.

Intimidation in relation to civil proceedings in the past is covered under s 40(1) of the Criminal Justice and Police Act 2001. The person suspected of intimidation must know (or believe) that his/her victim had been a witness in the relevant proceedings (as above), and the intimidation must take place within the period from the start of the proceedings until twelve months after the end of the proceedings.

Intimidation in relation to criminal proceedings in the past is covered under s 51(2) of the Criminal Justice and Public Order Act 1994. The person suspected of intimidation must know (or believe) whilst carrying out the relevant acts that the victim has either:

- assisted in an investigation into an offence;
- has acted as a juror; or
- concurred in a particular verdict in proceedings for an offence.

In addition, the intimidatory acts must take place within a certain time frame as shown in the table below.

Role of the intimidated victim in criminal proceedings	Period in which the intimidation must take place	
	Starts	Ends
A witness or juror	The start of the proceedings.	Twelve months after the end of the trial or appeal.
A person who assisted in an investigation into an offence, but was not a witness	The start of any assistance in the investigation (or the start date as believed by the suspect).	Twelve months after any assistance was given.
A person who assisted in the investigation into an offence and was a witness in proceedings for the offence	The first act of assistance in the investigation (or the start date as believed by the suspect).	Twelve months after the end of the trial or appeal.

The offences of intimidation are triable either way and the penalties are:

- summarily: six months' imprisonment and/or a fine;
- on indictment: five years imprisonment and/or a fine.

9.11 Racially or Religiously Aggravated Offences

The term 'racially or religiously aggravated' is defined by s 28 of the Crime and Disorder Act 1998. In everyday language certain offences, such as a s 29 assault, can be aggravated (regarded as more serious, and hence carrying a heavier sentence on conviction) by being motivated, at least in part, by racial or religious factors.

The following categories of offence can be racially or religiously aggravated:

- assaults (s 29);
- criminal damage (s 30);
- public order offences (s 31);
- harassment (s 32).

Such an offence without racial or religious aggravation is sometimes referred to as a 'basic offence' in order to distinguish it from the aggravated form of the offence.

9.11.1 The Definition of Racially or Religiously Aggravated

The definition is provided in s 28(1) of the Crime and Disorder Act 1998. An offence becomes racially or religiously aggravated for the purposes of ss 29 to 32 if the offender:

(a) . . . **demonstrates** . . . hostility (on racial or religious grounds); or
(b) . . . is **motivated** . . . by hostility (on racial or religious grounds).

Clearly, it is easier to prove that an aggravated offence has been committed if the hostility has actually been demonstrated through the suspect's behaviour.

For s 28(1)(a), the offender demonstrates hostility if:

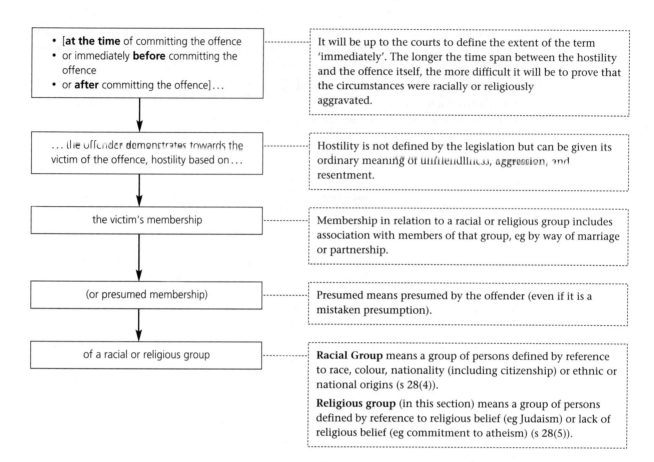

• [at the time of committing the offence • or immediately before committing the offence • or after committing the offence]...	It will be up to the courts to define the extent of the term 'immediately'. The longer the time span between the hostility and the offence itself, the more difficult it will be to prove that the circumstances were racially or religiously aggravated.
...the offender demonstrates towards the victim of the offence, hostility based on...	Hostility is not defined by the legislation but can be given its ordinary meaning of unfriendliness, aggression, and resentment.
the victim's membership	Membership in relation to a racial or religious group includes association with members of that group, eg by way of marriage or partnership.
(or presumed membership)	Presumed means presumed by the offender (even if it is a mistaken presumption).
of a racial or religious group	**Racial Group** means a group of persons defined by reference to race, colour, nationality (including citizenship) or ethnic or national origins (s 28(4)). **Religious group** (in this section) means a group of persons defined by reference to religious belief (eg Judaism) or lack of religious belief (eg commitment to atheism) (s 28(5)).

The person's behaviour might be partly motivated by other factors with no racial or religious basis. However, it is immaterial for this offence whether or not the person's hostility is partly related to any other non-racial or non-religious factor (s 28(3) Crime and Disorder Act) and this is a question of fact for the court to decide. For example in the case of *Johnson v DPP* (2008) EWHC 509 (Admin), two car park attendants were the victims of hostility, partly based upon their job status and partly upon their membership of a racial group. It was subsequently held that a racially aggravated s 5 Public Order Act 1986 offence had been committed against them. The accused had made reference to the skin colour of the attendants ('white'), and told them to leave the black community in which they were working and to go instead to a predominantly white area.

As a police officer you are as entitled as anyone else to protection from any racial or religious aggravation.

9.11.2 Racially or Religiously Aggravated Assaults

Under s 29(1) of the Crime and Disorder Act 1998, the following types of assault as a basic offence can be racially or religiously aggravated.

Basic offence	Notes
Any offence under s 20 of the Offences Against the Person Act 1861	Includes malicious wounding or grievous bodily harm, but excludes s 18 'with intent' (see 10.16 below).
Any offence under s 47 of the Offences Against the Person Act 1861	See 10.15 below on occasioning actual bodily harm.
Common assault	See 10.15 below on unlawful personal violence.

The motivation for the basic offence must be taken into account—it must be racially motivated or based on racial hostility. For example, in the case of *DPP v Roshan Kumar Pal* (unreported, 3 February 2000) the charge of racially aggravated common assault was not proved. Even though the assault on an Asian-heritage caretaker was accompanied by abuse, the assault was held to be motivated by the perceived low status of the victim's job, and not by racism.

If the racial or religious aggravation aspect of the offence charged is not proved, the basic offence may be substituted by the court in most cases.

Aggravated s 20 and s 47 offences from the Offences against the Person Act 1861 (offences are committed under s 29(1) of the Crime and Disorder Act 1998) are triable either way:

- summarily: six months' imprisonment and/or a fine;
- on indictment: seven years' imprisonment and/or a fine.

Aggravated common assault offences are triable either way:

- summarily: six months' imprisonment and/or a fine;
- on indictment: two years' imprisonment and/or a fine.

9.11.3 Racially or Religiously Aggravated Criminal Damage

These offences are covered in s 30 of the Crime and Disorder Act 1998.

A person is guilty of an offence if he/she:

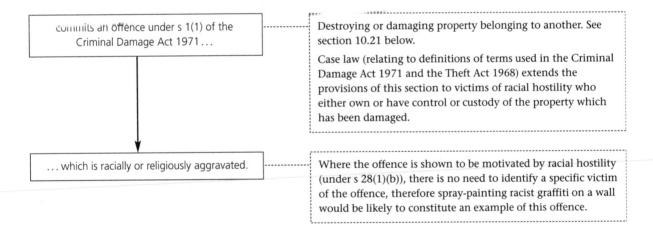

Unlike the basic offence under s 1(1) of the 1971 Criminal Damage Act, the racially aggravated offence is triable either way, regardless of the value of the property damaged:

- summarily: six months' imprisonment and/or a fine;
- on indictment: imprisonment (not exceeding 14 years) and/or a fine.

9.11.4 Racially or Religiously Aggravated Public Order Offences

Section 31 of the Crime and Disorder Act 1998 covers offences that are aggravated forms of basic public order offences. The table below shows the basic public order offences (see 9.7 above) that may be racially or religiously aggravated, and also identifies the corresponding subsections of the Crime and Disorder Act 1998 for the aggravated forms of the offences:

Basic offence	Aggravated offence
Fear or provocation of violence: s 4 (Public Order Act 1986)	s 31(1)(a) (Crime and Disorder Act 1998)
Intentional harassment, alarm, or distress: s 4A (Public Order Act 1986)	s 31(1)(b) (Crime and Disorder Act 1998)
Causing harassment, alarm, or distress (see *Norwood v DPP* [2003] EWHC 1564): s 5 (Public Order Act 1986)	s 31(1)(c) (Crime and Disorder Act 1998)

Where the offence is motivated towards the individual victim (and not towards members of his/her racial group) it is not racially aggravated. For example in the case *Director of Public Prosecutions v Howard* (2008) EWHC 608 (Admin), an off-duty police officer heard his neighbour shouting 'I'd rather be a paki than a cop'. It was held that the only motivation for the neighbour's shouting was his intense dislike and hostility towards the police officer (and as a consequence an offence under s 5 of the Public Order Act 1986), and that the comments had not been racially aggravated.

The penalty for a s 31(1)(a) or (b) offence (triable either way):

• summarily: six months' imprisonment and/or a fine;
• on indictment: two years' imprisonment and/or a fine.

An offence under s 31(1)(c) of the Crime and Disorder Act 1998 is triable only summarily as it relates to a summary-only basic offence (s 5 of the Public Order Act), and therefore has no alternative verdict. The penalty is a fine.

For trials on indictment of a person charged with a racially aggravated s 4 or s 4A public order offence, if the jury find him/her not guilty, s 31(6) of the Crime and Disorder Act 1998 states that the jury may still find him/her guilty of the basic public order offence.

9.11.5 Racially or Religiously Aggravated Harassment

This is covered in s 32 of the Crime and Disorder Act 1998. The offences are racially and religiously aggravated forms of basic offences from the Protection from Harassment Act 1997, s 2 (harassment) and s 4 (putting people in fear of violence) (see 9.9 above).

Offences under s 32(1)(a) of the Crime and Disorder Act 1998 (aggravated harassment) are triable either way:

• summarily: six months' imprisonment and/or a fine;
• on indictment: two years' imprisonment and/or a fine.

Offences under s 32(1)(b) of the Crime and Disorder Act 1998 (aggravated putting people in fear of violence) are also triable either way:

• summarily: six months' imprisonment and/or a fine;
• on indictment: seven years' imprisonment and/or a fine.

For trials on indictment of a person charged with a racially aggravated form of these offences, if the jury finds the person not guilty, the Crime and Disorder Act 1998 (s 32(5) and (6)) states that the jury may still find the person guilty of the basic offence under the Protection from Harassment Act 1997.

TASK 12

Consider the following groups of people. In relation to racially or religiously aggravated offences, decide whether they constitute a racial or a religious group, or neither or both:

1. Jews (see *Seide v Gillette Industries* [1980] IRLR 427)
2. Rastafarians (see *Dawkins v Crown Suppliers (Property Services Agency)*, The Times, 4 February 1993; [1993] ICR 517)
3. Muslims (see *J H Walker v Hussain* [1996] ICR 291)
4. Gypsies (see *Commissioner for Racial Equality v Dutton* [1989] QB 783).

9.12 Management of Difficult People in the Community

Here we examine some relatively new approaches to countering anti-social behaviour. Areas with particular problems can be targeted by the police, who can provide support for communities seeking to improve their lives by reducing intimidation and other forms of anti-social behaviour. The target area can be as small as a parking area or as large as a whole housing estate.

9.12.1 Power to Require Name and Address of a Person Acting in an Anti-social Manner

Section 50(1) of the Police Reform Act 2002 states that if you have reason to believe that a person has been acting (or is acting) in an 'anti-social manner' you may require that person to give his/her name and address. An anti-social manner is one that 'caused or was likely to cause harassment, alarm or distress to one or more persons not of the same household as [him/herself]' (s 1, Crime and Disorder Act 1998).

Section 50(2) Police Reform Act 2002 states that it is an offence if any person under s 50(1):

(a) fails to give his/her name and address when required to do so or

(b) gives a false or inaccurate name or address.

This offence is triable summarily and the penalty is a fine.

9.12.2 Anti-social Behaviour Orders

Anti-social behaviour orders (or ASBOs as they are commonly known) may be used for individuals over ten years of age who continually behave in such a way as to cause harassment, alarm, or distress to members of the local community. Section 1 of the Crime and Disorder Act 1998 enables a magistrates' court to make an ASBO against such an individual. An ASBO is intended to prevent problem behaviour in the future rather than punishing behaviour that has already occurred; if the individual breaches an ASBO, he/she commits a criminal offence. This is intended to act as a deterrent.

An ASBO is made following a complaint about behaviour that occurred in the preceding six months and:

- lists the types of behaviour that are prohibited for that particular individual;
- lasts at least two years;
- can be discharged (discontinued) if both parties agree;
- may be varied (changed) if new and different complaints are made.

In some situations, a banned behaviour might not be in breach of the ASBO if it can be proved that the behaviour was reasonable under those particular circumstances. A breach of such an order is an offence under s 1(1) of the Crime and Disorder Act 1998.

This offence is triable either way:

- summarily: six months' imprisonment and/or a fine;
- on indictment: five years' imprisonment and/or a fine.

9.12.3 Local Child Curfews

Local child curfews ban children under 16 from being in a specified area of a public place between 9 pm and 6 am unless they are under the effective control of a parent or a responsible person aged 18 or over. This legislation is covered in s 14 of the Crime and Disorder Act 1998. A local authority or a chief officer of police may introduce a local child-curfew scheme for a specified period not exceeding 90 days.

Before making a local child-curfew scheme, the applicant will consult with the chief officer of police in the area and with appropriate bodies such as the local authority. A local child-curfew scheme will not come into effect until it is confirmed by the Secretary of State. The notice will be given by displaying it in the area or by any other suitable method.

Section 15 of the Crime and Disorder Act 1998 describes the action you should take if you find a child contravening a local child curfew. If you have reasonable cause to believe that a child is in contravention of a ban imposed by a curfew notice you must inform the local authority (s 15(1)). You may take the child back to his or her home unless you have reasonable cause to believe that the child would be likely to suffer significant harm (s 15(3)).

9.12.4   Dispersal and Removal Powers for Anti-social Behaviour

Section 30 of the Anti-Social Behaviour Act 2003 describes police powers that may be used if a senior police officer of, or above the rank of, superintendent has reasonable grounds for believing:

(a)   that any members of the public have been intimidated, harassed, alarmed, or distressed as a result of the presence or behaviour of groups of two or more persons in public places within the relevant locality; and

(b)   that anti-social behaviour is a significant and persistent problem in the relevant locality.

The senior police officer can make an authorization under s 30(2) that provides you with the power (should the need arise) in the relevant locality to:

- give directions to groups of people (any age); and
- remove a person under 16 years of age to his/her place of residence.

The authorization is for a period not exceeding six months. You must be in uniform to give such directions, and a direction may be given to either a group or an individual.

9.12.4.1   Dispersal of groups

The term 'group' is not defined in the legislation but has been held to include protesters (see *R (on the application of Singh and another) v CC of West Midlands Police* [2006] EWCA Civ 1118) and must be two or more persons. Once the authorization has been made (see above), and if the circumstances recur (as detailed above), you have the power (s 30(4)) to give a direction requiring the people in a group to disperse (either immediately or within in a certain time limit). You can also direct any person in the group whose place of residence is not within the relevant locality to leave (either immediately or within in a certain time limit) and not to return within a specified period (not exceeding 24 hours).

Section 32 of the Anti-Social Behaviour Act 2003 provides more guidance on how to give a direction for the purposes of s 30(4) above. Under s 32(1) a direction may be:

(a)   given orally

(b)   given to any person individually or to two or more persons together, and

(c)   withdrawn or varied by the person who gave it.

Section 32(2) states that it is an offence to knowingly contravene a direction.

This offence is triable summarily and the penalty is three months' imprisonment and/or a fine.

9.12.4.2   Removal of Young People Under 16

The authorization will have been made in response to a group of people, but it empowers you to remove particular individuals too. This applies to a young person found:

- in any public place within the relevant locality; and
- only between the hours of 9 pm and 6 am.

Therefore, under s 30(6), if you find such a young person and you have reasonable grounds for believing he/she is is both:

- under the age of 16; and
- not under the effective control of a parent or a responsible person aged 18 or over;

you may remove the person to his/her place of residence (unless you have reasonable grounds for believing that he/she would be likely to suffer significant harm once at the residence). If he/she is unwilling to go voluntarily, the word 'remove' has been held to mean 'take away using reasonable force if necessary' (*R (W) v Commissioner of Police for the Metropolis and another, Secretary of State for the Home Department, interested party* [2004] EWCA Civ 458).

9.12.5 Smoking in a Smoke-Free Place

Under s 7 of the Health Act 2006, a person commits an offence if he/she smokes in a 'smoke-free' place. Smoking includes the smoking of cigarettes (hand-rolled and manufactured), pipes, cigars, herbal cigarettes, and the use of waterpipes (for example, 'hubble-bubble' pipes).

Smoke-free places include 'enclosed or substantially enclosed premises which are open to the public, and shared workplaces'. The Smoke-free (Premises and Enforcement) Regulations 2006 define enclosed and substantially enclosed premises as follows:

- enclosed premises have a ceiling or roof and, except for doors, windows, or passageways, are wholly enclosed, whether on a permanent or temporary basis;
- substantially enclosed premises have a ceiling or roof, but the permanent openings in the walls are **less than half** of the total areas of walls, including other structures which serve the purpose of walls and constitute the perimeter of premises (known as the '50% rule').

(A roof includes any fixed or moveable structure or device which is capable of covering all or part of the premises as a roof, including, for example, a canvas awning.)

Therefore premises (with a ceiling or roof) that have permanent openings in the wall of **more than half** of the total wall area are not subject to this legislation.

This offence is triable summarily and the penalty is a fine.

9.12.6 Nuisance or Disturbance on Hospital Premises

This is covered by s 146 of the Criminal Justice and Immigration Act 2008 which states that an offence is committed by a person:

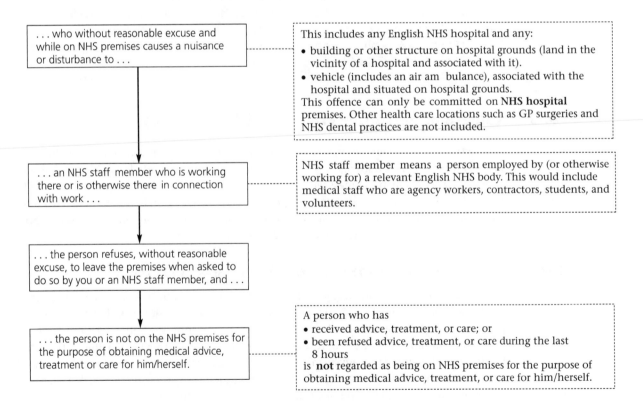

The offence is triable summarily and the penalty is a fine.

9.12.6.1 Power to remove person causing nuisance or disturbance

Section 147 states that if you reasonably suspect that a person is committing or has committed an offence under s 146, you may remove the person from the NHS premises concerned, using reasonable force if necessary.

You might consider using s 147 under the following circumstances:

1. A group of protesters block the doors to the accident and emergency department of a local hospital and cause nuisance and disturbance to NHS staff who are walking in and out of the entrance. The protesters are asked to leave but refuse to comply.
2. Whilst visiting a sick relative in hospital, several members of a large family make a nuisance of themselves to hospital staff including some of the doctors and nurses caring for their relative. To prevent a nuisance situation from deteriorating further into violence, the family members are asked to leave but they take no notice.

9.12.6.2 Nuisance or disturbance on Health and Social Services premises

An almost identical offence and power to remove people is available to deal with nuisances and disturbances in Health and Social Services hospitals under s 149 of the Criminal Justice and Immigration Act 2008.

TASK 13

What power is available to you to help identify a person who you believe has been acting, or is acting, in an anti-social manner?

TASK 14

You are on Supervised Patrol in a part of a city which has a recognized significant and persistent problem with anti-social behaviour, and is therefore subject to an order under s 30 of the Anti-Social Behaviour Act 2003. The order enables you to disperse people from the locality if you believe this is required. During your patrol, you see a group of about a dozen or so young people who appear to be local residents. A member of the group appears to intimidate a passer-by. What precise powers do you have to deal with the young people involved?

9.13 Vulnerable Persons in Private and Public Places

During the course of your duties, you will frequently find yourself in situations involving people who are behaving in a strange way, or who seem not be able to think clearly. They may either be suffering from a mental illness with distorted thoughts and feelings, or just find it hard to take in basic facts and make decisions. There is often an association between mental disorder and an impaired decision-making capacity. This incapacity may be transient during severe periods of illness, or longer during periods of enduring mental illness.

9.13.1 The Mental Health Act 1983 and the Mental Capacity Act 2005

The two Acts that you are most likely to employ are the Mental Health Act 1983 (for mental illness) and the Mental Capacity Act 2005 (for impaired ability to make decisions). Both Acts are directed primarily towards the provision of healthcare in the UK. Currently, the National Health Service is responsible for providing care and treatment for people suffering from mental illness. Therefore health professionals may already be in attendance at some incidents you attend involving a person with a severe mental illness, but if no health professionals are present and you suspect a person may have mental health problems that require urgent attention, you should contact your control room and request the attendance of an ambulance crew, a doctor, or an approved mental health professional to help you choose the right course of action for the individual.

The location of the person in need of help can influence which Act you might use. If a person is in a public place and you decide they are in need of immediate psychiatric care, then the Mental Health Act 1983 is available to you. If the person is elsewhere, in their own home for example, then the Mental Health Act 1983 is only available to health professionals. If the person is incapable of making a decision and requires care for any other reason, such as a medical condition, the Mental Capacity Act 2005 is the more appropriate piece of legislation for you to use. The scenario in 9.13.4 below illustrates this further.

A common misconception is that many people who suffer from mental disorders are also violent, but this is not the case; most pose no physical threat to others, but may be confused or unable to cope. You need to learn how to recognize the symptoms of mental disorder and you will receive information and advice on this during your training. Here we will examine the relevant legislation and parts of the Mental Health Act 1983 Code of Practice. The Code of Practice can be viewed in full at <www.dh.gov.uk/en/Publicationsandstatistics/Publications/PublicationsPolicyAndGuidance/DH_084597>.

9.13.2 Mentally Disordered Persons in Public Places

It is not an offence to be mentally disordered in a place to which the public have access (see 7.2.1 above for further information on the definition of a public place). However, you have the power to remove such a person and take him or her to a place of safety. Section 136 of the Mental Health Act 1983 states that if you find:

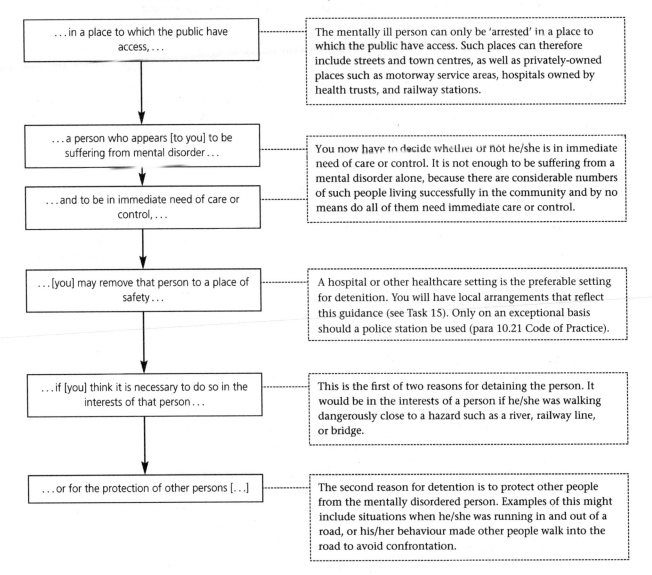

Your powers of arrest under s 24 of the PACE Act 1984 cannot be used because no offence has been committed. However the Code of Practice (para 10.45) states that a person who is removed under s 136 of the Mental Health Act 1983 is deemed to be 'arrested' for the purposes of the PACE Act 1984, and as such you have the power to search them under s 32 of the PACE Act 1984 (see 8.9.4 above).

Hospital or ambulance transport will be used if a person needs to be transported to a place of safety (as set out in agreed local policies). Only exceptionally, such as in cases of extreme urgency or where there is a risk of violence, should police transport be used (Code of Practice, para 10.17).

9.13.2.1   Detention in a Place of Safety

A person removed from a public place to a place of safety may be detained there for the purposes of:

- examination and assessment by a registered medical practitioner;
- being interviewed by an approved social worker; and
- making any necessary arrangements for his/her treatment or care.

The detention period must not exceed 72 hours.

9.13.3   Mentally Disordered Persons in Private Places

You might need to help or restrain a mentally disordered person in his/her home. You do not have the same removal and detention powers in a private place as you do in a public place. If a disturbed person in a private place will not accept the need for treatment and might be a danger to him/herself or to others you should contact your control room and request the attendance of an AMHP (approved mental health professional), and remain at the scene until he/she arrives.

Once an AMPH begins to assess a patient for possible detention he/she assumes overall responsibility for coordinating the process of assessment (Code of Practice, para 4.40), and for arranging for transport to take the patient to hospital, should this be required (see 9.13.3.2 below). You may leave once you have provided the relevant information to the AMHP, unless he/she requests your further assistance, for example, if the patient is violent or dangerous (Code of Practice, para 11.18). You may be asked by the AMPH to assist during the transportation of the patient to hospital, but see 9.13.3.2 below.

If you feel an AMHP is not required you can detain the person in order to prevent a breach of the peace, but remember the particular conditions relating to the use of force which must be met (see 9.6 above on 'breach of the peace'). There may be reasons to arrest the person if he/she is suspected of committing an offence, but arrest will not necessarily be the most appropriate way of dealing with a mentally disordered person. If you do arrest a person for a criminal offence who appears to be suffering from a mental disorder, a police medical practitioner will examine the suspect and decide on his/her fitness to be interviewed.

9.13.3.1   Using force to enter

If he/she refuses to let you in and there is nobody else present to grant you entry, you can use force, but only if:

- you have a magistrate's warrant (granted to an AMPH under s 135 of the Mental Health Act 1983) authorizing you to search for and remove persons believed to be suffering from mental disorder;
- there is a breach of the peace (see 9.6 above);
- it is to save life or limb (s 17(1)(e) of the PACE Act 1984) (see 7.9 above); or
- it is to prevent serious damage to property (s 17(1)(e) of the PACE Act 1984) (see 7.9 above).

9.13.3.2   Removing the Person to a Place of Safety from His or Her Home

If there is no breach of the peace and no offences have been committed, there is no power available under the Mental Health Act 1983 to detain or convey a person from a private place to a hospital (or other place of safety) **unless** at least one of the following conditions is met:

- the person consents;
- the person is 'sectioned' for admission to hospital (see 9.13.3.3 below); or
- a magistrate's warrant (see 9.13.3.1 above) already exists for that private place.

If an AMHP arranges for the detention of a person and his/her removal to hospital, the police may be involved in transportation, but only for more challenging patients. The extent of such police involvement will be set out in locally agreed policies (Code of Practice, para 1.19).

9.13.3.3   'Sectioning'

This is an unofficial term normally associated with the process carried out by an AMPH and medical practitioner(s) in a person's home or other private place. If a person clearly requires urgent psychiatric hospital treatment, but will not seek it voluntarily and is a danger to him/

herself or to others, he/she can be 'sectioned' (under one of the sections of the Mental Health Act 1983). The application is made by an AMHP or the nearest relative and is considered by two medical health practitioners (or just one in an emergency). If the application is agreed, you **may** be asked to help remove the person to hospital (but see 9.13.3.2 above), by force if necessary (s 6, Mental Health Act 1983), but it is essential that a Section Application form is completed and signed as recommended prior to any police action of this sort.

9.13.4 Acting in the Best Interests of a Person Who Lacks Capacity

The Mental Capacity Act 2005 constitutes a far-reaching legal framework which aims to protect vulnerable people who do not have the capacity (are not able) to make their own decisions, such as people with a learning disability. It also empowers and offers protection to carers and others (such as police officers) who find themselves involved in the protection of vulnerable people. Of particular interest is s 5 which provides the power to carry out acts related to the care or treatment (including restraint) of a person who lacks capacity (and aged 16 years or over).

As you read on below to find out more about the meaning of the term 'capacity' and making decisions you might find it useful to consider how the Act might apply in practice; one such scenario is presented here and you can also probably bring to mind other vulnerable people you have encountered whilst undertaking Supervised or Independent Patrol.

You have been asked by a paramedic team to attend a bed sit in town. An extremely thin and naked man is lying in bed with several open wounds on his body, which look as if they could have been caused by hypodermic needles. He appears heavily intoxicated, and you suspect the use of controlled drugs. Blood-filled syringes are strewn all around the bed and the floor of the room and the man appears to be bleeding from body orifices. You consider the health and safety of the people around you as a priority, so you and the paramedics don protective clothing and remove dangerous and contagious items to a toxic chemical receptacle and a 'sharps box'. The paramedics have tried to persuade the man to go to hospital but every time they have got close to him he has mumbled and moved away violently. You also try to communicate with him, but without success. You must now decide how to help him, and under which legislation.

You would probably not use the Mental Health Act 1983, partly because the person is not in a place to which the public have access and therefore s 136 would not apply, but also because the man is in need of immediate medical and not psychiatric care. Although he might be suffering from a temporary mental disorder, it is his inability to make a decision and gain medical attention that is the immediate concern. The use of the Mental Capacity Act in these circumstances would seem logical, so that he can be transported to hospital for medical treatment.

9.13.4.1 General principles underlying the Mental Capacity Act 2005

Section 1 of the Act sets out some underlying principles to be followed whenever you are involved with a person whom you suspect has reduced capacity. These principles include for example that a person:

- must be treated as if he/she has capacity (see below) unless you establish otherwise; and
- must not be treated as if he/she is unable to make a decision just because he/she has made an unwise decision previously.

The Act also specifies that any decision or action you take must be in the person's best interests and must avoid (as far as possible) interfering with his/her rights and freedom.

9.13.4.2 Mental capacity

Capacity is the ability to take in information and use that information to make decisions. A lack of capacity could be caused by an impairment or disturbance in the functioning of the mind or brain, for example (s 2) through:

- a learning disability;
- dementia;

- brain damage; or
- toxic confusion.

Of course, you can only judge on the balance of probabilities whether a person has such a condition. However, when judging a person's capacity, no reference can be made to the person's age or appearance, and you must make sure you don't make unjustified assumptions based solely on the person's condition or behaviour. Instead you need to concentrate on the person's ability to make decisions.

9.13.4.3 Judging a person's ability to make decisions

Section 3 of the Act provides specific guidance on how to judge a person's ability to make a decision. You need to apply a functional test to check if he/she is able to:

- understand and retain any information relevant to the decision,
- use the information to help make a decision; or
- inform you of that decision.

The means of communication used (by you or the person) is not important; it could be talking, writing or typed text, a sign language, or other gestures.

9.13.4.4 Making decisions and acting on behalf of a person who lacks capacity

If you conclude that a person cannot make decisions and therefore lacks capacity, you might need to make a decision on his/her behalf. Under s 4 of the Act both your decision and the action you take must be made in the person's **best interests**. You must consider the likelihood of the person having the capacity at some point in the future; if there is no immediate need to make a particular decision and the person is likely to regain the capacity to make the decision, then it should be delayed until he/she has recovered sufficiently.

If the person seems to have a reduced capacity you should take into account the views of:

- his/her carer;
- anyone else he/she would like to be consulted;
- anyone with power of attorney; and/or
- a deputy appointed by a court.

You should consider as far as possible the person's wishes and feelings, and especially his/her beliefs and values from the past (when he/she might have had a greater capacity than at the present time). If a decision relates to life-sustaining treatment you must guard against considering that you should maybe allow a person to die.

The person must be encouraged to participate as fully as possible in any act or decision affecting him/her, and you should take all reasonably practicable steps to achieve this.

You do not incur any liability (s 5) for acts you carry out in connection with care or treatment if (before you act) you have taken reasonable steps to establish that the person lacks capacity, and you reasonably believe your actions are in the person's best interests.

9.13.4.5 The use of restraint

If the person is resisting your actions (despite your efforts to communicate and to encourage participation) you may need to use restraint. Under s 6 of the Act you can only use restraint in your care or treatment of a person if:

- you reasonably believe it is **necessary** in order to prevent harm to him/her; and
- the restraint is **proportional** to the likelihood and seriousness of that harm.

Actions defined as restraint under s 6 include:

- using **force** (or threatening to use it) in order to apply care or treatment which is resisted by him/her; and
- **restricting** a person's liberty of movement, whether or not he/she resists.

However, such restraint does not include depriving a person of his/her liberty within the meaning of Article 5 of the ECHR, or contravening a decision made by a court or a person with a relevant power of attorney.

Applying the Mental Capacity Act

In the scenario above, all practicable steps to help the man have been unsuccessful. You believe he needs medical treatment in a hospital if he is not to become more seriously ill or even die. On the balance of probabilities he is suffering from toxic confusion which has caused an impairment or disturbance of his mind or brain. He is therefore unlikely to have the capacity to make the decision to go to hospital and appears to be incapable of understanding the information relevant to the decision—that he is seriously ill and needs treatment. You have tried to communicate with him and to encourage him to participate in making the decision to go to hospital but your efforts have failed. You have no information pertaining to any of his family, friends, or carers (or indeed if he has any), and there is no indication of how he might have wished to be treated (when he had capacity).

Through your actions you have taken all reasonable steps to establish that he does in fact lack capacity, and cannot make the relevant decision. You therefore need to make a decision on his behalf. The least restrictive action or decision to avoid interfering with his rights and freedom is to ensure he receives hospital treatment. You judge that the least restraint required under the circumstances is to help him onto a stretcher for transportation to hospital.

9.13.5 Ill-treatment or Neglect of a Person who Lacks Capacity

Some people have particular caring or legal responsibilities for particular individuals who lack capacity. Such a caring or responsible person may have the care of, or have been given power of attorney for, an individual who lacks capacity.

It is an offence under s 44 of the Mental Capacity Act 2005 for any such carer or responsible person to ill-treat or wilfully neglect the relevant individual.

The offence is triable either way:

- summarily: 12 months' imprisonment and/or fine;
- on indictment: five years' imprisonment.

TASK 15

1. What is your force policy in terms of the use of s 136 powers?
2. You are requested to attend the home of the parents of a 20-year-old person who seems to be suffering from a mental disorder. On arrival the parents inform you that their son is in his bedroom holding on to the door handle so that nobody can come in. Using the minimum force necessary (and limiting your answers to the Mental Health Act 1983):
   (a) how are you going to gain entrance for the parents, and
   (b) what options are available to you should you decide the person is in need of medical attention in relation to his or her apparent mental disorder?

9.14 Trespassing on Land

Travelling people with no fixed abode sometimes find a temporary place to live on land that is privately owned by others. This may cause anxiety and distress for the owners of the land or for local residents. A senior police officer attending the scene has the power under the Criminal Justice and Public Order Act 1994 to order two or more trespassers to leave (with their vehicles) as soon as reasonably practicable, if that officer believes the trespassers are there for the common purpose of residing on the land.

If the intention of the trespassers is not to reside, gather, or disrupt lawful activity, or if only one trespasser is involved, then the situation might be a civil matter and it will be for the landowners themselves to find a solution.

9.14.1   Trespass or Nuisance on Land

This offence is described under s 61(1) of the Criminal Justice and Public Order Act 1994. A senior police officer must believe that:

- at least two suspects are involved;
- the suspects have the common purpose of living on the land for a period of time; and
- the suspects have been asked to leave by the owner or legal occupier of the land.

In addition, the senior police officer must believe that the suspects have either:

- caused damage to the land or to property on the land, or used threatening, abusive, or insulting words or behaviour towards the occupier, a member of his/her family, or an employee or agent of his/hers; or
- have six or more vehicles with them on the land (a vehicle includes caravans and unroadworthy vehicles).

A senior police officer present at the scene must reasonably believe that the above conditions have been fulfilled. He/she may then direct those persons to leave the land, and to remove any of their vehicles or other property from the land.

It is an offence (s 61(4)) for a person to:

- fail to leave the land as soon as reasonably practicable; or
- enter again within the period of three months.

These offences are triable summarily and the penalty is three months' imprisonment and/or a fine.

9.14.2   Seizing and Removing Vehicles

If the trespassers will not leave (having been given an order to do so), s 62 of the Criminal Justice and Public Order Act 1994 gives you the power to seize and remove vehicles. Under s 62(1), if a person fails to remove any vehicle on the land or again enters the land as a trespasser within the period of three months, you may seize and remove the vehicle.

9.15   Open-air Gatherings with Music

Although complaints about excessive noise from gatherings in residential properties are often dealt with by staff from local authorities, complaints about larger gatherings in the open air may sometimes require police action. You may need to use ss 63, 64, and 65 of the Criminal Justice and Public Order Act 1994 to deal with such situations.

The type of gathering (also referred to as an 'open-air rave') is defined in s 63; the gathering must be in the open air and at night, and must:

- involve 20 or more people;
- involve amplified music with repetitive beats;
- involve music that is either loud or goes on for a long time;
- be likely to cause serious distress to local residents.

The Act includes the power for you to give directions to people present at such gatherings (and to people travelling to the locality). There are some predictable exemptions; the following categories of people cannot be given directions under ss 63–65:

- the occupier of the land;
- any member of his/her family;
- any employee or agent of his or hers; and
- any person whose home is situated on the land.

The occupier (in England and Wales) is 'the person entitled to possession of the land by virtue of an estate or interest held by him [or her]' (s 61(9)).

9.15.1 Powers of Entry and Seizure

Section 63 of the Criminal Justice and Public Order Act 1994 gives you powers of entry and seizure for open-air musical gatherings at night. Under s 63, the gathering does not have to involve trespass and, therefore, if you wanted to hold such a gathering on your own land, this legislation would still apply.

9.15.2 Powers to Disperse Persons at a Gathering in the Open Air

This power (under s 63(2)), applies to people preparing for such a gathering as well as to people attending.

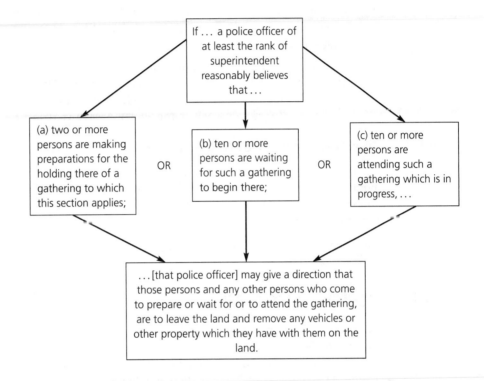

Such a direction, if not communicated by the police officer giving the direction, may be communicated by any constable at the scene (s 63(3)).

A person shall be treated as having had the direction communicated to him/her if reasonable steps have been taken to bring it to his/her attention (s 63(4)). It is an offence (s 63(6)) if a person (knowing that a direction has been given which applies to him/her) then:

(a) fails to leave the land as soon as reasonably practicable or
(b) having left, again enters the land within the period of seven days...

If the suspect can show that he/she had a reasonable excuse for failing to leave the land as soon as reasonably practicable (or for entering the land again) he/she has not committed an offence (s 63(7)).

9.15.3 Moving on to Another Gathering

A person who has been directed to leave a gathering who then moves on to another similar gathering within 24 hours commits an offence under s 63(7A). A person commits an offence if he/she:

(a) knows that a direction under subsection (2) above has been given which applies to [him/her], and
(b) makes preparations for, or [attends] a gathering to which this section applies within the period of 24 hours starting when the direction was given.

These offences are triable summarily and the penalty is three months' imprisonment and/or a fine.

9.15.4 Powers of Entry and Seizure for Outdoor Musical Gatherings at Night

Section 64 of the Criminal Justice and Public Order Act 1994 gives powers of entry to the police when dealing with night-time open-air musical gatherings; police officers may need to be deployed to find out what is happening at such gatherings. A warrant is not required (s 64(3)). Under s 64(1) if a police officer of at least the rank of superintendent reasonably believes:

> that circumstances exist in relation to any land which would justify the giving of a direction under s 63 in relation to a gathering to which that section applies, [he/she] may authorise any constable to enter the land

to ascertain whether such circumstances exist and to give directions under s 63.

Vehicles and sound equipment may be seized if a direction has been given under s 63 and a constable reasonably suspects that any person to whom the direction applies has, without reasonable excuse:

(a) failed to remove from the land any vehicle or sound equipment which appears to the constable to belong to that person (or to be in his/her possession or under his/her control) or
(b) entered the land as a trespasser with a vehicle or sound equipment within seven days (beginning with the day on which the direction was given).

9.15.5 Directing People Away from a Gathering

Section 65 of the Criminal Justice and Public Order Act 1994 gives you powers to direct persons **not to proceed** towards a gathering to which s 63 applies (see 9.15 above). You must be in uniform and within five miles of the gathering. It is an offence (s 65(1)) for a person not to comply with such a direction.

This offence is triable summarily and the penalty is a fine.

9.16 Aggravated Trespass

This offence and the police powers to deal with it are covered in ss 68 and 69 of the Criminal Justice and Public Order Act 1994. The legislation is intended to deal with trespassers who disrupt or obstruct any lawful activity taking place on land or adjoining land (hence the 'aggravated' nature of the trespass), such as protesters at military bases.

9.16.1 Disrupting Lawful Activity

A person commits the offence of aggravated trespass under s 68(1) of the Criminal Justice and Public Order Act 1994 if:

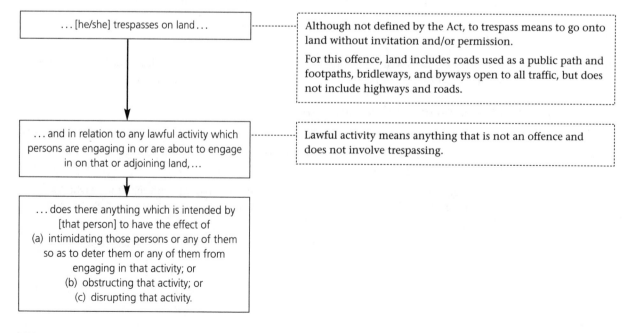

This offence is triable summarily and the penalty is three months' imprisonment and/or a fine.

9.16.2 Powers to Direct Trespassers to Leave

Section 69 of the Criminal Justice and Public Order Act 1994 provides the senior police officer at the scene of an aggravated trespass with the power to direct a person to leave the land. The senior police officer must reasonably believe that the person is committing (or has committed or intends to commit) the offence of aggravated trespass.

Under s 69(1) of the Criminal Justice and Public Order Act 1994:

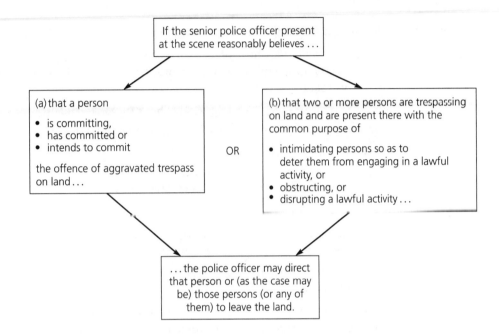

Under s 69(3), it is an offence for a person who has been directed to leave if he or she:

(a) fails to leave the land as soon as practicable, or

(b) having left, again enters the land as a trespasser within a period of three months (beginning with the day on which the direction was given).

It is a defence if the accused can show that he/she:

• was not trespassing on the land, or
• had a reasonable excuse for failing to leave the land as soon as practicable or for re-entering the land as a trespasser.

This offence is triable summarily and the penalty is three months' imprisonment (maximum) and/or a fine.

9.17 Football-related Offences

Football-related offences do not feature within the compulsory LPG modules of the IPLDP. We cover them here since the policing of football matches often features as part of the training of student police officers whilst on Supervised or Independent Patrol. Hence, although the policing of football matches is not a common occurrence for every police officer in England and Wales, you might well be involved in it during your training, particularly if you are a student police officer within a force responsible for the policing of large towns and cities.

The offences described in this section are covered under two Acts:

• Sporting Events (Control of Alcohol etc) Act 1985;
• Football (Offences) Act 1991.

The Sporting Events (Control of Alcohol etc) Act 1985 applies only to sports grounds, certain sporting events, and designated periods relating to those sporting events. Currently the only sport which it is considered necessary to control is football, and therefore no restrictions have been placed upon the people attending other sporting events such as rugby or cricket matches.

Many football clubs will take steps to inform their supporters of the main points of the law and the regulations governing behaviour. A good example is Ipswich Town Football Club: <http://www.itfc.premiumtv.co.uk/page/TicketNews/0,,10272~1024967,00.html>.

The two Acts above specify certain offences associated with the behaviour of supporters at particular types of football match. Offences involving alcohol only apply to so-called 'designated' matches.

9.17.1 The Sports Grounds and Sporting Events (Designation) Order 2005

The Sporting Events (Control of Alcohol etc) Act 1985 only applies if **both** the sports ground (for football) **and** the sporting event (football match) have been **designated** as such by the Secretary of State.

Schedule 1, Art 2(1) of Statutory Instrument 2005 No 3204 states that designated sports grounds (football grounds) will include **any sports ground in England or Wales**.

The same Statutory Instrument includes the following as **designated sporting events**:

1. Association football matches in which one or both of the participating teams represent a country (or territory) or a club which is a member (for the time being, and whether a full or associate member) of:
   - the Football League, [or]
   - the Football Association Premier League, [or]
   - the Football Conference National Division, [or]
   - the Scottish Football League or Welsh Premier League.

2. Association football matches in competition for the Football Association Cup (other than in a preliminary or qualifying round).

Note that the list may vary from year to year to reflect changes in the organization of football leagues. The 2005 Statutory Instrument may be found at <http://www.homeoffice.gov.uk/documents/Guidance-NL-alcohol-final.pdf>.

The following events are examples of matches which would be likely to be **designated** for the purposes of the Sporting Events (Control of Alcohol etc) Act 1985, as they meet both the ground and the match (teams) criteria:

- A football match played between Bristol City and Scunthorpe United at Bristol City's ground, Ashton Gate. This is because Ashton Gate is a designated sports ground and both teams are currently members of the Football League.
- A match played between Dover Athletic and Manchester United at Dover, because the Crabble is a designated sports ground and Manchester United is currently a member of the Football Association Premier League (although Dover Athletic is not).

So, in these cases the Sporting Events (Control of Alcohol etc) Act 1985 would apply for a certain period of time (see 9.17.2 below).

The following events are examples of matches which are **not designated** for the purposes of the Sporting Events (Control of Alcohol etc) Act 1985:

- An international hockey match being played at the Millennium Stadium in Cardiff, because although the stadium is a sports ground and will therefore be designated, it is not hosting one of the categories of football match listed above.
- A football match played between Croydon Athletic and the Metropolitan Police FC at Croydon because although the Keith Tuckey Stadium at Croydon is a sports ground and therefore designated, both teams are currently in the Ryman Football League Division One South which is not designated.

Further, the Statutory Instrument explains that the Act does not apply to any sporting event in which players are not paid, nor if spectators are admitted free of charge, such as amateur weekend football matches which take place on school sports fields or recreation grounds.

9.17.2 Period of a Designated Sporting Event (Football Match)

Offences under the Sporting Events (Control of Alcohol etc) Act 1985 can only be considered if they occur during the period commencing two hours before the start of a football match and ending one hour after the end of the match. For example, if a football match is scheduled to start at 7.45 pm and the match ends at approximately 9.30 pm, the period of this match would be from 5.45 pm to 10.30 pm. (We ignore here the added complexity of added time being played to compensate for stoppages, or extra time to decide a match, or the match starting late.)

We now consider a number of offences covered by the Act.

9.17.3 Vehicles Transporting Passengers to Sports Events

Drivers, owners, and passengers of some types of vehicle which are used to transport fans to sports events are subject to legislation under s 1 of the Sporting Events (Control of Alcohol etc) Act 1985.

9.17.3.1 Public service vehicles

Only certain types of vehicles used for the principal purpose of carrying passengers for the whole or part of a journey to or from a designated sporting event are covered by this legislation (s 1 of the Sporting Events (Control of Alcohol etc Act 1985)). They include buses and coaches, passenger trains, and mini-buses.

It is an offence under s 1(2) for the following persons to knowingly cause or permit intoxicating liquor to be carried on such a vehicle:

- the operator of a public service vehicle (or the servant or agent of the operator);
- a person who has hired such a vehicle (or the servant or agent of that person).

It is also an offence for such a person to have intoxicating liquor in their possession while on a specified vehicle (s 1(3)) or to be drunk on a vehicle to which this section applies (s 1(4)).

This offence is triable summarily only and the penalty depends on the subsection:

- subsection 1(2)—a fine;
- subsection 1(3) (possession)—three months' imprisonment and/or a fine;
- subsection 1(4) (drunk)—a fine.

9.17.3.2 Vehicles other than public service vehicles

Section 1A of the Sporting Events (Control of Alcohol etc) Act 1985 refers to a motor vehicle (see 11.2 below) which is not a public service vehicle but:

- is adapted to carry more than eight passengers;
- is being used for the principal purpose of carrying two or more passengers for the whole or part of a journey to or from a designated sporting event.

Under s 1A(2), it is an offence for the following persons to knowingly cause or permit intoxicating liquor to be carried on such a motor vehicle:

- the driver;
- the vehicle's keeper;
- the servant or agent of the vehicle's keeper;
- any person to whom it is made available (by hire, loan, or otherwise) by its keeper (or the keeper's servant or agent), or the servant or agent of the person to whom the vehicle is so made available.

It is an offence for such a person to have intoxicating liquor in his or her possession while on such a vehicle (s 1A(3)) or to be drunk on a vehicle to which this section applies (s 1A(4)).

This offence is triable summarily only and the penalty depends on the subsection:

- subsection 1A(2)—a fine;
- subsection 1A(3) (possession)—three months' imprisonment and/or a fine;
- subsection 1A(4) (drunk) —a fine.

9.17.4 Alcohol and Drinks Containers at a Designated Sporting Event

Section 2(1) of the Sporting Events (Control of Alcohol etc) Act 1985 is generally imposed for football matches where there is a potential for disorder. Under this legislation it is an offence to possess alcohol or drinks containers likely to contain alcohol.

The containers covered by this legislation are defined in s 2(3) as:

> any article capable of causing injury to a person struck by it, being:—
> (a) a bottle, can or other portable container (including such an article when crushed or broken) which:—
> (i) is for holding any drink, and
> (ii) is of a kind which, when empty, is normally discarded or returned to, or left to be recovered by the supplier, or
> (b) part of an article falling within paragraph (a) above,
> but does not apply to anything that is for holding any medicinal product (within the meaning of the Medicines Act 1968).

Section 2(1) applies at any time during the period of a designated sporting event when the person is:

- in any area of the sports ground from which the event may be directly viewed; or
- entering (or trying to enter) the sports ground.

This offence is triable summarily and the penalty is three months' imprisonment and/or a fine.

It is also an offence for a person to be drunk inside the ground, or to be drunk while entering or trying to enter such a ground at any time during the period of a designated sporting event at that ground (s 2(2) of the same Act).

This offence is triable summarily and the penalty is a fine.

9.17.5 Fireworks, Flares, and Similar Articles during a Designated Sporting Event

Section 2A of the Sporting Events (Control of Alcohol etc) Act 1985 covers the possession of fireworks and similar objects at designated sporting events. The prohibited objects (s 2A(3) and (4)) include fireworks, rockets, distress flares, fog signals, pellets and capsules intended to be used as fumigators or for testing pipes, and any other item which is for 'the emission of a flare for purposes of illuminating or signalling, or the emission of smoke or a visible gas'. It does not include matches, cigarette lighters, or heaters.

The times and places to which this legislation applies are the same as for the possession of alcohol at a sports ground. Therefore a person is guilty of a s 2A offence if he/she has a firework or similar object (see above) at any time during the period of a designated sporting event when the person is:

- in any area of the sports ground from which the event may be directly viewed; or
- entering (or trying to enter) the sports ground.

This offence is triable summarily and the penalty is three months' imprisonment and/or a fine.

9.17.6 Powers of Entry for Sports Grounds

Section 7 of the Sporting Events (Control of Alcohol etc) Act 1985 allows you to enter and search any part of the ground if you have reasonable grounds to suspect that an offence under the same

Act is being committed (or is about to be committed), or to enforce the provisions of the Act. This relates to the possession of alcohol, fireworks, and similar articles and applies during the period of a designated sporting event at any designated sports ground (see 9.17.1 and 9.17.2 above).

Section 7 of the Act states that you may search a person (s 7(2)) or a vehicle (s 7(3)) if you have reasonable grounds to suspect that an offence under this Act has been committed (or is about to be committed). However, remember that you must carry out any searches in line with the PACE Codes of Practice and s 2 of the PACE Act 1984 (see 7.5 above).

9.17.7 Designated Football Matches and the Throwing of Objects

The Football (Offences) Act 1991 also deals with forms of misbehaviour at football matches and defines a designated match as a match in which one or both of the participating teams either represent a country (or territory) or are members (full or associate) of:

* the Football League;
* the Football Association Premier League;
* the Football Conference; or
* the League of Wales.

Here, the notion of a designated match is similar to that described earlier in 9.17.1 and 9.17.2 above, but with a number of quite subtle differences. Subsequent Statutory Instruments and Orders have made it clear that the Football Conference includes the two feeder leagues (Conference North and Conference South) as well as the Conference National Division. The League of Wales is taken to refer to the Welsh Premier League.

The time period is also relevant to the Football (Offences) Act 1991. Section 1(2) states that:

references in this Act to things done at a designated football match include anything done at the ground:—
(a) within the period beginning two hours before the start of the match or (if earlier) two hours before the time at which it is advertised to start, and ending one hour after the end of the match; or
(b) where the match is advertised to start at a particular time on a particular day, but does not take place on that day, within the period beginning two hours before and ending one hour after the advertised starting time.

This is very similar to the definition of the time period in the Sporting Events (Control of Alcohol etc) Act 1985.

9.17.8 Indecent or Racist Chanting at a Designated Football Match

Section 3(1) of the Football (Offences) Act 1991 states that it is an offence to engage in chanting of an indecent or racialist nature at a designated football match. Section 3(2) goes on to clarify that:

(a) **chanting** means the repeated uttering of any words or sounds (whether alone or in concert with one or more others); and
(b) of **racialist nature** means consisting of or including matter which is threatening, abusive or insulting to a person by reason of [his/her] colour, race, nationality (including citizenship) or ethnic or national origins.

This offence is triable summarily and the penalty is a fine.

9.17.9 Spectators on the Playing Area at a Designated Football Match

Section 4 of the Football (Offences) Act 1991 states that it is an offence for a person at a designated football match:

to go onto the playing area, or any area adjacent to the playing area to which spectators are not generally admitted, without lawful authority or lawful excuse (which shall be for [the suspect] to prove).

This offence is triable summarily and the penalty is a fine.

TASK 16

As a student police officer you are deployed whilst on Supervised Patrol to a football match. The club concerned plays within the Football Conference National Division, so you can therefore assume that both the ground and the matches played in the ground are designated under both the Sporting Events (Control of Alcohol etc) Act 1985 and the Football (Offences) Act 1991. Consider each of the following offences and match them against the situations given below by putting the appropriate letter(s) in the right-hand column. The first answer has been given to you. You may need to consult the original legislation for the detail.

(a) s 2(1) of the Sporting Events (Control of Alcohol etc) Act 1985
(b) s 2(2) of the Sporting Events (Control of Alcohol etc) Act 1985
(c) s 2 of the Football (Offences) Act 1991
(d) s 3 of the Football (Offences) Act 1991
(e) s 4 of the Football (Offences) Act 1991
(f) s 1(2) of the Sporting Events (Control of Alcohol etc) Act 1985
(g) s 1(3) of the Sporting Events (Control of Alcohol etc) Act 1985
(h) s 1(4) of the Sporting Events (Control of Alcohol etc) Act 1985
(i) s 2A of the Sporting Events (Control of Alcohol etc) Act 1985

1.	You see a fan fumbling for money to pay for a cup of tea from the refreshment stand. When you approach, he is hardly able to stand and his breath smells of intoxicating liquor, his eyes are glazed, and his speech is slurred.	b
2.	You are on duty at the edge of the pitch near the entrance to the players' tunnel as the teams enter after half time. Whilst observing the crowd, you see a dark metal object hit the ground near your feet and see one of the players stop in his stride and grab his head in pain. You look up and see a youth in the crowd with his right hand raised as if he has just thrown an object.	
3.	One of the mid-field players is black. Every time he receives the ball you hear opposition supporters make 'monkey' sounds and shout racist abuse.	
4.	Whilst on duty outside the ground you see a fan waiting to get a ticket and enter. Under his arm you clearly see a four-pack of lager cans.	
5.	Before the start of a match you see a supporter waiting to purchase a ticket to enter the ground. He finishes drinking from a can, drops it to the ground, and stands on it to crush it. He is now at the front of the queue to get in, looks around, picks up the crushed tin, and puts it in a coat pocket out of view.	
6.	One of your responsibilities is to monitor the away supporters arriving by coaches and minibuses hired for the occasion. On one of the minibuses you observe a person drinking from a bottle of cider. As the vehicle stops, the door of the mini-bus is opened by the driver; at that moment you see one of the other passengers offer the driver a can of lager. Just then a third passenger gets up from a seat and falls down the steps of the minibus, apparently drunk.	
7.	At the end of one of the matches when the final whistle is blown, the two teams leave the pitch and a group of fans go onto the pitch to follow the players and congratulate them.	
8.	At the end of a match in early November, you see a youth reach into his pocket as the crowd is leaving the ground. As he withdraws his hand from his pocket, a firework falls to the ground.	

9.18 Firework Offences

Under the law, a firework is any device which:

• burns and/or explodes to produce a visual and/or audible effect; and
• is intended for use as a form of entertainment.

Some offences relating to fireworks are about misuse, some relate to the time of year, and some relate to the age of the person buying fireworks. Of particular concern in recent years has been the use of powerful fireworks which distress others because of their force and loudness. These include 'aerial shells, aerial maroons, shells-in-mortar and maroons-in-mortar' which can register sound levels above 120 dB—about the noise level of a jet aircraft from 100 metres away. The sale of these products to the public is now banned but people can still purchase these products abroad (where the law is different) and bring them back to the UK. Concern has also been expressed about the use of fireworks to damage or even destroy objects such as phone boxes or cars.

It is for these reasons that we include fireworks as a subject for the Handbook. Relevant legislation includes the Explosives Act 1875, the Fireworks Act 2003, the Fireworks Regulations 2004, and the Fireworks (Safety) Regulations 1997.

It is an offence for any person:

- to throw, cast, or fire any firework in or into any highway, street, thoroughfare, or public place (s 80, Explosives Act 1875);
- to wantonly (deliberately) throw or set fire to a firework in the street to the obstruction, annoyance, or danger of residents or passengers (s 28, Town Police Clauses Act 1847);
- under the age of 18 years to possess fireworks in a public place, except for indoor fireworks (see below) (reg 4, Fireworks Regulations 2004).

A **public place** includes 'any place to which at the material time the public have or are permitted access, whether on payment or otherwise' (reg 4(2), Fireworks Regulations 2004).

Indoor fireworks include: a cap, cracker snap, novelty match, party popper, serpent, sparkler, or 'throwdown'. (A throwdown is a firework containing impact-sensitive explosive and grains of inert material (wrapped in paper or foil) which produces a sound when thrown onto the ground.)

These offences are triable summarily.

Offences (except for the s 28 of the Town Police Clauses Act 1847 offence) can be dealt with by way of a Penalty Notice for Disorder (upper tier, see 8.15.2.1 above).

9.18.1 Period of Sale

Fireworks may only be sold by traders to members of the public during the following periods:

- first day of Chinese New Year and three days prior to this;
- Diwali and three days prior to this;
- between 15 October and 10 November;
- between 26 and 31 December.

However, a trader may have a special licence to sell outside these periods.

9.18.2 Fireworks in Public Displays

Public displays frequently use large fireworks, known as category 4 fireworks. They may only be used by a professionally qualified, trained person (reg 5, Fireworks Regulations 2004). Members of the general public are prohibited from possessing such fireworks, except for any person who is employed by a local authority, or who is involved in public or commercial firework displays. A breach of reg 4 or 5 is a criminal offence, under s 11 of the Fireworks Act 2003.

This offence is triable summarily, and the penalty is a fine.

9.18.3 Supplying Fireworks to Persons under 18

Under s 12(1) of the Consumer Protection Act 1987 it is an offence to supply fireworks (including sparklers but excluding all other indoor fireworks) to persons under the age of 18 years.

This offence is triable summarily, and the penalty is a fine.

9.18.4 Firework Curfews

A 'firework curfew' is a period of time where the general use of fireworks is not permitted. Under reg 7(1) of the Fireworks Regulations 2004 it is an offence for a person to use an 'adult firework' (essentially all fireworks other than indoor fireworks) between 2300 and 0700 hrs the next day except during the following periods:

Date or Event	Finish
First day of the Chinese New Year	0100 hrs the following day
5 November	Midnight
Diwali	0100 hrs the following day
31 December	0100 hrs the following day

There are exemptions for people employed by a local authority using a firework during a local authority display or national commemorative event.

This offence is triable summarily and the penalty is six months' imprisonment and/or a fine.

The breaking of a firework curfew can be addressed through a Penalty Notice for Disorder (upper tier, see 8.15.2.1).

9.19 Offensive Weapons, Bladed, and Sharply Pointed Articles

Serious wounding and possibly death can result from the use of these items, but you will hear numerous excuses from people found in possession of such articles. In some cases, the individuals concerned may genuinely be vulnerable to attack by others. However, whatever the circumstances, it is your responsibility to attempt to prevent crimes involving the use of these weapons and, if at all possible, to detect the presence of such items before they are used.

The legislation covered here concerns offensive weapons, bladed, and sharply pointed articles in public places and on school premises, and is to be found in:

- s 1 of the Prevention of Crime Act 1953;
- s 139 of the Criminal Justice Act 1988.

You have the power to search for offensive weapons, or bladed, or sharply pointed articles under s 1 of the PACE Act 1984 (see 7.6 above).

9.19.1 Offensive Weapons in a Public Place

Section 1 of the Prevention of Crime Act 1953 is an important piece of legislation relating to the discovery of an offensive weapon in the possession of a member of the public.

When searching for offensive weapons always consider health and safety implications—the PAC Safety First checklist is relevant as is NOS element AF1.1—'to identify the hazards and evaluate the risks in the workplace' (see 6.7 above).

Section 1(1) of the Prevention of Crime Act 1953 states that it is an offence for:

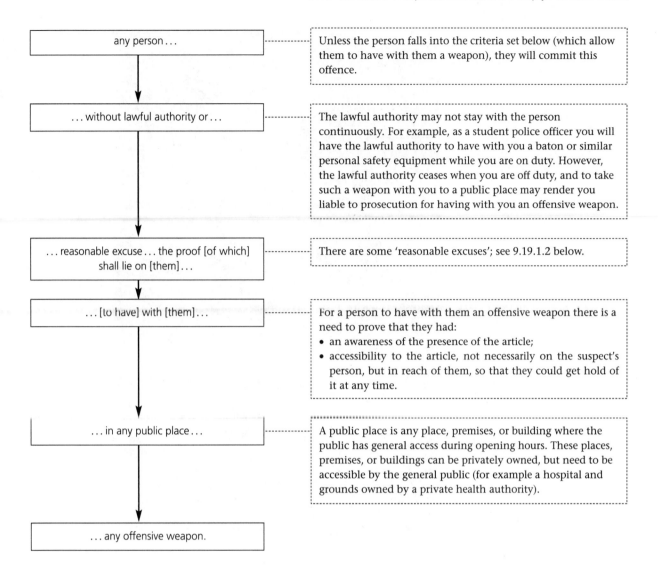

any person…	Unless the person falls into the criteria set below (which allow them to have with them a weapon), they will commit this offence.
…without lawful authority or…	The lawful authority may not stay with the person continuously. For example, as a student police officer you will have the lawful authority to have with you a baton or similar personal safety equipment while you are on duty. However, the lawful authority ceases when you are off duty, and to take such a weapon with you to a public place may render you liable to prosecution for having with you an offensive weapon.
…reasonable excuse…the proof [of which] shall lie on [them]…	There are some 'reasonable excuses'; see 9.19.1.2 below.
…[to have] with [them]…	For a person to have with them an offensive weapon there is a need to prove that they had: • an awareness of the presence of the article; • accessibility to the article, not necessarily on the suspect's person, but in reach of them, so that they could get hold of it at any time.
…in any public place…	A public place is any place, premises, or building where the public has general access during opening hours. These places, premises, or buildings can be privately owned, but need to be accessible by the general public (for example a hospital and grounds owned by a private health authority).
…any offensive weapon.	

9.19.1.1 Definition of an offensive weapon

An offensive weapon (s 1(4)) is any article made, adapted, or intended for causing injury:

- A **made** article includes any article which has been made or manufactured with the intention of causing injury to people, for example a flick knife or telescopic baton. These are offensive weapons per se; the courts need no proof of their intended use, but do require proof that the defendant had no reasonable excuse for possessing such an item.
- An **adapted** article includes any article which has been modified in some way, with the intention of causing injury, for example a broken bottle with sharp edges, or a potato embedded with protruding razor blades. A jury can decide whether or not articles have been specifically **adapted** to be offensive weapons. For example in the stated case of *Prosecution right of appeal (No. 23 of 2007) sub nom R v R (2007) EWCA Crim 3312* it was decided that gloves filled with sand were offensive weapons as the prosecution had produced evidence that similar gloves had been advertised for sale on a website as 'self-defence gloves'.
- An **intended** article includes any article in the suspect's possession, with which he/she intends to cause injury. The precise nature of the article is not important: it is what the suspect intends to do with it. A pillow could become an offensive weapon if it can be proved that the suspect intended to use it to cause injury to an elderly relative. Once again, gathering evidence through interview is important here.

Of course some items that may be classed as an offensive weapon may have innocent uses, and the person would therefore have a reasonable excuse for carrying such an item.

(Photo by Kevin Lawton-Barrett)

Example of intended article

The articles shown in the photograph above were unlikely to have been manufactured as offensive weapons, but may be owned by a person who intends to use them as offensive weapons.

9.19.1.2 Reasonable and unreasonable excuses

A person **may** have a reasonable excuse if he/she fears for his/her safety: for example a security guard who fears attack while picking up or dropping off money at a bank, or a person who feels he/she is about to be assaulted (and cannot escape) and picks up a chair to defend him- or herself. Other reasonable excuses include having an **innocent reason**, such as a chef carrying knives.

Unreasonable excuses include:

- **Forgetfulness**—a person may not have a reasonable excuse if he/she has forgotten he/she has an offensive weapon with him/her (for example forgetting that there is a machete under the seat in his/her car) see *R v McCalla* (1988) 87 Cr App R 372. However, when the forgetfulness is combined with other circumstances (such as 'relating to the original acquisition of the article') it will be for the court to decide if there was a reasonable excuse (see *R v Vasil Tsap* (2008) EWCA Crim 2679). An example might be when a weapon is left by a passenger in a taxi and the driver moves it to the front of the vehicle for the purposes of disposing of it. If the taxi is subsequently stopped by the police the driver may claim to have forgotten that the weapon was there (see *R v Raymond Glidewell* LTL 19/5/99, The Times, May 14, 1999).
- **Ignorance**—a person may not have a reasonable excuse just because he/she does not know the true identity of the item, for example believing that a truncheon is a telescope.
- **General self-defence**—a person does **not** have reasonable excuse to have an offensive weapon with him/her generally for self-defence, 'just in case' he/she is attacked.

In any prosecution the burden of proving a reasonable excuse for possession of an offensive weapon lies with the defendant; if the defendant can persuade the court to consider the likelihood that he/she had a reasonable excuse, that could be enough for a not-guilty verdict. Therefore, when you investigate a person for this offence, be prepared to counteract later defences by gathering together as much evidence as possible—before, during, and after interview under caution.

This offence is triable either way:

- summarily: six months' imprisonment and/or a fine;
- on indictment: four years' imprisonment and/or a fine.

9.19.2 Bladed or Sharply Pointed Articles in a Public Place

Historically, under the Prevention of Crimes Act 1953, if the defendant was able to persuade the court on the balance of probabilities that he/she had reasonable excuse for having an offensive weapon, such as a kitchen knife, pair of scissors, or large pocket knife, he/she would not be found guilty (see above).

The offence of having a bladed or sharply pointed article (s 139(1), Criminal Justice Act 1988) was created in an attempt to prevent serious crimes involving the use of everyday items. An offence is committed by any person who possesses a bladed and sharply pointed article in a public place.

9.19.2.1 The definition of bladed and sharply pointed articles

The definition of '**bladed**' includes any kind of bladed article, for example a kitchen knife, scissors, a craft knife, a pocket knife, a dagger, or any other article which has been given a cutting edge or blade. Pocket knives with a blade less than 7.62 cm long which cannot be locked in the open position are not classed as bladed under this legislation.

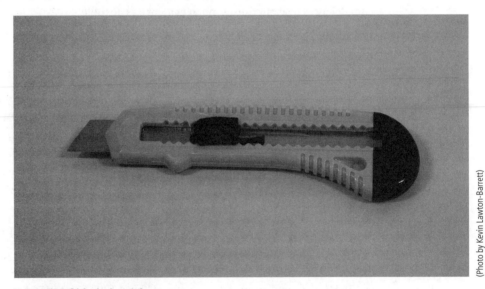

(Photo by Kevin Lawton-Barrett)

Example of bladed article

The definition of '**sharply pointed**' includes any kind of sharply pointed article, for example a needle, geometry compasses, or any other article which has been given a sharp point. This is in contrast to the Prevention of Crimes Act 1953, which is more concerned with objects that are more obviously weapons than everyday articles. A court must decide whether or not an article has a blade or is sharply pointed, so the prosecution must be able to prove that the article fits this description. In *R v Davis* [1998] Crim LR 564 the suspect was carrying a screwdriver which the court was asked to consider was a bladed article capable of causing injury. The court decided that that it was more important to decide whether the screwdriver had a cutting edge or point than to consider whether it was capable of causing injury. Therefore, unless a screwdriver has a pointed end or has been sharpened to make a blade, it is still not an article for the purposes of this Act.

9.19.2.2 Defences for having bladed or sharply pointed articles

There may be a good reason for a person having a bladed or sharply pointed article in their possession, such as a carpet layer carrying a specialist knife for cutting carpet at work. But neither general self-defence, ignorance, nor forgetfulness is a suitable defence; see the description of reasonable excuses for carrying an offensive weapon in 9.19.1.2 above.

Other grounds for defence (s 139 of the Criminal Justice Act 1988)

Defence	Example
Lawful authority	The lawful authority may not stay with the person continuously. For example, as a student police officer you will have the lawful authority to have with you a bladed or sharply pointed article after seizure and before placing it into a special property store. Members of the armed services will also have lawful authority to carry articles such as bayonets whilst on duty, but if such an article was carried off duty they may be liable for prosecution.
For use at work	A joiner uses wood chisels with very sharp cutting edges during the course of his/her work and may need to carry them in a bag in the street while moving between jobs. He/she, however, would not be able to use this claim if he/she had a chisel in a nightclub whilst socializing.
Religious reasons	Genuine followers of the Sikh religion carry *kirpans* (a small rigid knife) for religious reasons.
Part of any national costume	Whilst wearing national costume, some Scots carry a *skean dhu* (a small dagger, tucked in the top of the socks). However, this defence could not be used if the person was carrying the knife and was not wearing national costume.

As mentioned earlier, when you investigate a person for this offence, be prepared to counteract later defences by gathering as much evidence as possible.

This offence is triable either way:

- summarily: six months' imprisonment and/or a fine;
- on indictment: four years' imprisonment and/or a fine.

TASK 17

Whilst on duty during Supervised and Independent Patrol there will be many occasions when you have the opportunity to see inside vehicles. If you see items such as scissors and craft knives on the floor of the vehicle, what do you need to consider and what action might you need to take?

9.19.3 School Premises and Offensive Weapons, Bladed, or Sharply Pointed Articles

The Criminal Justice Act 1988 states that it is an offence for any person to have with them on school premises an offensive weapon (s 139 A(2)) or a bladed or sharply pointed article (s 139A(1)). School premises are defined (by s 139A(6)) as land used for the purposes of a 'school' including open land, such as playing fields or playgrounds. 'School' is further defined (by s 14(5) of the Further and Higher Education Act 1992) as educational institutions providing primary and secondary education. Further and higher educational establishments (for example FE colleges or universities) are not covered by this Act.

The classification of these offences and powers of search are the same as for s 1(1) of the Prevention of Crime Act 1953 above (see 9.19.1 above). You do not have to be in uniform to enter such premises if you suspect an offence under this section is being committed (or has been committed), and you may use reasonable force to secure an entry. If you find offensive weapons, or bladed, or sharply pointed articles on school premises, you may seize them (s 139B of the Criminal Justice Act 1988).

9.19.4   Arranging the Minding of a Weapon

Under s 28 of the Violent Crime Reduction Act 2006, a person commits an offence if he/she:

(a) uses another to look after, hide, or transport a dangerous weapon for [him/her]; and
(b) does so under arrangements or in circumstances that facilitate, or are intended to facilitate, the weapon's being available to [him/her] for an unlawful purpose.

A dangerous weapon is regarded as 'available to a person for an unlawful purpose' if the weapon is available for him/her at a particular time and place and its possession either constitutes an offence or is likely to lead to the commission of an offence.

This offence is triable either way.

The table below lists those items which are classified as dangerous weapons for the purposes of s 28 of the Violent Crime Reduction Act 2006. Some descriptions (in quotes) are taken from the relevant Acts and Statutory Instruments.

Item	Comments
Bladed or sharply pointed article	'Any article which has a blade or which is sharply pointed and which is made or adapted for use for causing injury to [a] person.'
Firearm	'Other than an air weapon or a component part of, or accessory to, an air weapon' (see 9.20 below).
Axe	The usual meaning of the term.
Knife	With the exception of a 'folding pocket-knife if the cutting edge of its blade does not exceed 7.62 centimetres (3 inches)'.
Disguised knife	'Any knife which has a concealed blade or concealed sharp point and is designed to appear to be an everyday object of a kind commonly carried on the person or in a handbag, briefcase, or other hand luggage (such as a comb, brush, writing instrument, cigarette lighter, key, lipstick or telephone).'
Stealth knife	'A knife or spike, which has a blade, or sharp point, made from a material that is not readily detectable by apparatus used for detecting metal and which is not designed for domestic use or for use in the processing, preparation or consumption of food or as a toy.'
Razor blades	With the exception of 'razor blades permanently enclosed in a cartridge or housing where less than 2 millimetres of any blade is exposed beyond the plane which intersects the highest point of the surfaces preceding and following such blades'.
Knuckleduster	'Band of metal or other hard material worn on one or more fingers, and designed to cause injury.'
Telescopic truncheon	'A truncheon which extends automatically by hand pressure applied to a button, spring or other device in or attached to its handle.'
Baton	'A straight, side-handled or friction-lock truncheon.'
Shuriken, *Shaken* or Death Star	'A hard non-flexible plate having three or more sharp radiating points and designed to be thrown.'
Push dagger	'A knife the handle of which fits within a clenched fist and the blade of which protrudes from between two fingers.'
Belt-buckle knife	'A buckle which incorporates or conceals a knife.'
Swordstick	'A hollow walking-stick or cane containing a blade which may be used as a sword.'
Handclaw	'A band of metal or other hard material from which a number of sharp spikes protrude, and worn around the hand.'
Hollow *kubotan*	'A cylindrical container containing a number of sharp spikes.'

Item	Comments
Footclaw	'A bar of metal or other hard material from which a number of sharp spikes protrude, and worn strapped to the foot.'
Balisong or Butterfly knife	'A blade enclosed by its handle, which is designed to split down the middle, without the operation of a spring or other mechanical means, to reveal the blade.'
Blowpipe or blow gun	'A hollow tube out of which hard pellets or darts are shot by the use of breath.'
Kusari gama	'A length of rope, cord, wire or chain fastened at one end to a sickle.'
Kyoketsu shoge	'A length of rope, cord, wire or chain fastened at one end to a hooked knife.'
Manrikigusari or *kusari*	'A length of rope, cord, wire or chain fastened at each end to a hard weight or hand grip.'
Samurai sword	'A sword with a curved blade of 50 cms or over in length which is measured in a straight line from the top of the handle to the tip of the blade.'

Your ability to search for and discover offensive weapons may prevent further and perhaps more serious offences taking place. Many offensive weapons have been cleverly disguised; what you initially recognize as an everyday item might possibly be concealing a weapon. The law regarding weapons is different in some other countries, and therefore certain weapons are easily obtainable elsewhere and then brought into the UK.

TASK 18

Ahmed, a 17-year-old at a local FE College, is under genuine threat from others at the college and has good grounds to fear for his safety. He carries a knife for his own personal protection. Put aside any discussion whether Ahmed has a reasonable excuse; what factors do you need to take into account when deciding what action (if any) to take?

Note that your reflections may be relevant to the knowledge requirement of NOS element BE2.1 'Provide initial support to victims, survivors and witnesses'.

9.20 Introduction to Firearms

Your safety and the safety of others around you is **paramount**. Your force will have specially trained and equipped personnel to deal with all firearms incidents, and your control room will consider the deployment of firearms officers to all firearms incidents. However, there always remains the possibility that you could find yourself unexpectedly at the scene of a firearms incident. You may also come across firearms during a search of a premises, or you may be deployed to investigate people using air weapons, or required to investigate whether a firearm is legally owned or not.

The forensic aspects of firearms are covered in 13.5.16 below.

9.20.1 What is a Firearm?

A firearm is any 'lethal barrelled weapon of any description from which any shot, bullet or other missile can be discharged'. The legislation (s 57(1) of the Firearms Act 1968) states that a firearm is:

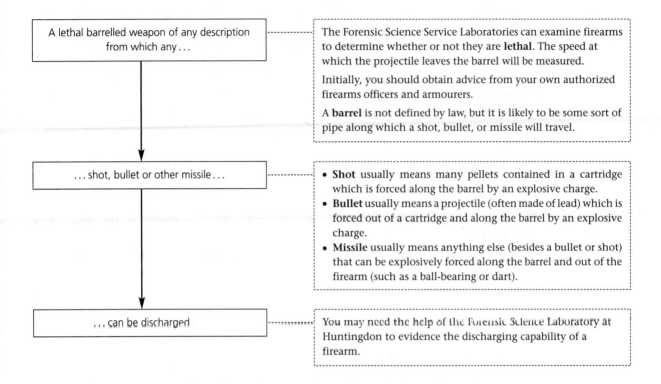

A lethal barrelled weapon of any description from which any...

> The Forensic Science Service Laboratories can examine firearms to determine whether or not they are **lethal**. The speed at which the projectile leaves the barrel will be measured.
>
> Initially, you should obtain advice from your own authorized firearms officers and armourers.
>
> A **barrel** is not defined by law, but it is likely to be some sort of pipe along which a shot, bullet, or missile will travel.

...shot, bullet or other missile...

> - **Shot** usually means many pellets contained in a cartridge which is forced along the barrel by an explosive charge.
> - **Bullet** usually means a projectile (often made of lead) which is forced out of a cartridge and along the barrel by an explosive charge.
> - **Missile** usually means anything else (besides a bullet or shot) that can be explosively forced along the barrel and out of the firearm (such as a ball-bearing or dart).

...can be discharged

> You may need the help of the Forensic Science Laboratory at Huntingdon to evidence the discharging capability of a firearm.

Smooth-bore weapons have a barrel which is smooth inside to enable the easy passage of shot. Although normally associated with lead shot, as used in sport shooting, these weapons can also fire a single or several larger lead 'slugs'. Generally, smooth-bore weapons have a limited range, but find popular use in crime because accuracy is not required due to the spread of shot. For **rifled-bore** weapons the inside of the barrel is rifled or grooved in a spiral pattern to impart a spin to the bullet. This gives the bullet stability that increases accuracy and range. The number of grooves in a barrel is normally between 2 and 16 and they can twist clockwise or anti-clockwise.

Calibre is the measurement of the diameter of the barrel. In rifled weapons this figure is normally expressed in metric or imperial figures (eg 7.62 mm, 9 mm, .38 inch, .357 inch). The units are readily convertible between the two measuring systems. In Britain and the USA, calibre is measured differently for smooth-bore weapons owing to the inability of engineers in the past to be accurate to hundredths of one inch. The calibre denotes the number of lead spheres, each exactly fitting the barrel, which would together weigh one imperial pound. So, a twelve-bore (UK) or twelve gauge (US) is a barrel diameter that would fit 12 balls of lead each weighing approximately 1.33 ounces.

In a typical **bulleted cartridge** the bullet, made of lead, is at the front of the assembly, whilst behind it is a quantity of powder stored in a brass cartridge. At the closed end of the cartridge (the head) is a quantity of primer, a sensitive powder which is ignited by the action of the trigger and, hence, the firing pin. This causes the burning of the main powder charge and the resultant forcing of the bullet through the barrel.

Firearms are loosely grouped into four categories under the Act:

1. Section 1 firearms (s 1 of the Firearms Act 1968)
2. Shotguns
3. Air weapons
4. Prohibited weapons.

Items referred to as imitation firearms may or may not be firearms in a legal sense (see 9.25 below). Details concerning each of these categories of firearm are provided in 9.21–9.24 below.

Some components and accessories for firearms also fall within the definition of a firearm.

Item	Notes
Any component part of such a lethal or prohibited weapon; and	This includes all the working parts of the firearm (the trigger mechanism, the firing pin, and so on) but does not include the additions such as the trigger guard.
Any accessory to any such weapon designed or adapted to diminish the noise or flash caused by firing the weapon.	A court will decide whether the silencer or flash eliminator could be used with the firearm in question, and whether the suspect had the accessory for that purpose.

9.20.2 Requesting a Person to Hand Over a Firearm or Ammunition

Remember your health and safety!

Section 47(1) of the Act authorizes you to require any person whom you have reasonable cause to suspect :

- of having a firearm (with or without ammunition) with him/her in a public place; or
- to be committing (or about to commit), elsewhere than in a public place, an offence relevant for the purposes of this section (see below)

to hand over the firearm (and/or ammunition) for you to examine.

(A public place includes any highway and any other premises or place to which, at the relevant time, the public have access.)

Relevant offences for the purposes of this legislation include other offences from the Firearms Act 1968:

- carrying a firearm with criminal intent (s 18);
- trespassing in a building with a firearm (s 20(1));
- trespassing on land with a firearm (s 20(2)).

It is an offence for a person in possession of a firearm or ammunition to fail to hand it over when required to do so (s 47(2)).

This offence is triable summarily and the penalty is three months' imprisonment and/or a fine.

9.20.3 Stop and Search for Firearms

You can stop and search a person (s 47(3) of the Firearms Act 1968) or a vehicle (s 47(4)) if you suspect that a firearms offence has been committed or is about to be committed, but, as ever, first and foremost remember your own and others' health and safety.

In order to carry out such a search, you must follow s 2 of the PACE Act and its Codes of Practice and provide the following information to the person you are searching:

G   Grounds of the suspicion for the search
O   Object/purpose of search
W   Warrant card (if in plain clothes or requested)
I   Identity as a police officer
S   Station to which you are attached
E   Entitlement to a copy of the search record
L   Legal power used
Y   'You are detained for the purposes of a search'

GO WISELY is covered in more detail in 7.5.5 above. You also have power of entry (s 47(5)) to search for firearms.

9.20.4 Firearms Certificates

A certificate is needed for s 1 firearms and for shotguns. Other categories of firearms such as air weapons and some imitation firearms (see 9.25 below) do not require certificates.

Under s 48(1) of the Firearms Act 1968 you may demand the production of a firearm certificate from any person whom you believe to be in possession of any firearm(s) or ammunition requiring a firearms certificate.

You will need to check your force's interpretation of the term 'demand'. In some forces it could mean that the certificate should be produced on the spot, while in others it would mean the certificate could be produced at some specified time in the future.

Section 48(2) states that if a person upon whom a demand is made fails to:

- produce the certificate/document; or
- permit you to read it; or
- show that he/she is entitled to have the firearm or ammunition in his/her possession without holding a certificate

you may seize and retain the firearm or ammunition and require the person to give his/her name and address.

9.20.5 Possessing a Firearm in a Public Place

Section 19 of the Firearms Act 1968 states that it is an offence for a person to have in a public place (without lawful authority or reasonable excuse):

(a) a loaded shotgun or
(b) an air weapon (whether loaded or not) or
(c) any other firearm (whether loaded or not) together with ammunition suitable for use in that firearm or
(d) an imitation firearm.

The offence of possessing an air weapon ((b) above) in a public place is triable summarily and the penalty is six months' imprisonment and/or a fine.

The offence of possessing (a), (c), or (d) above is triable either way:

- summarily: six months' imprisonment and/or a fine;
- on indictment in the case of (a) or (c) above: seven years' imprisonment and/or a fine;
- on indictment in the case of (d) above: twelve months' imprisonment and/or a fine.

> **TASK 19**
>
> Find out about the firearms incident in Hungerford, Berkshire in 1987 (there are numerous websites that will provide the details). Consider also the subsequent White Paper, *Firearms Act 1968: Proposals for Reform* (Cm 261, 1987) and the amendment to the 1968 Act which was effected by s 1 of the Firearms (Amendment) Act 1988. Why was a change in the list of prohibited weapons thought to be necessary at this time?

9.21 Section 1 Firearms

Section 1 firearms include a broad range of firearms. They are defined in s 1 of the Firearms Act 1968 as any firearm **except** for shotguns, legal air weapons, prohibited weapons, and imitation firearms.

9.21.1 Certificate for a s 1 Firearm

Under s 1 of the Firearms Act 1968 a certificate is required for all s 1 firearms; it is an offence for a person:

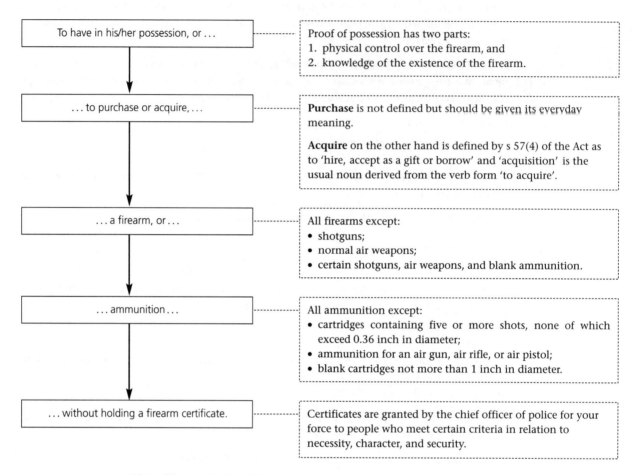

| To have in his/her possession, or ... | Proof of possession has two parts:
1. physical control over the firearm, and
2. knowledge of the existence of the firearm. |

| ... to purchase or acquire, ... | **Purchase** is not defined but should be given its everyday meaning.

Acquire on the other hand is defined by s 57(4) of the Act as to 'hire, accept as a gift or borrow' and 'acquisition' is the usual noun derived from the verb form 'to acquire'. |

| ... a firearm, or ... | All firearms except:
• shotguns;
• normal air weapons;
• certain shotguns, air weapons, and blank ammunition. |

| ... ammunition ... | All ammunition except:
• cartridges containing five or more shots, none of which exceed 0.36 inch in diameter;
• ammunition for an air gun, air rifle, or air pistol;
• blank cartridges not more than 1 inch in diameter. |

| ... without holding a firearm certificate. | Certificates are granted by the chief officer of police for your force to people who meet certain criteria in relation to necessity, character, and security. |

This offence is triable either way:

- summarily: imprisonment for six months and/or a fine;
- on indictment: imprisonment for five years and/or a fine (seven years for a sawn-off shotgun; once the barrel length of a shotgun has been reduced it can no longer be classified as a shotgun and the owner will require a s 1 firearms certificate).

There are special arrangements which might mean that a s 1 firearm certificate is not required. This is a complex area, but special arrangements are in place for certain types of firearm including antique firearms and handguns used for killing animals which negate the necessity for an owner to possess a certificate. Members of rifle and pistol clubs, visiting overseas forces, and theatrical performers in a show are also excluded from the requirement to hold a firearms certificate.

9.21.2 Age Restrictions and s 1 Firearms

The table below shows the age restrictions for s 1 firearms. An empty box in the table means the activity is not permitted. As noted earlier, the age restrictions for shotguns are slightly different (see 9.22 below).

Age restrictions for s 1 firearms

	Under 14	Age 14+	Age 15+	Age 17+
Hold a firearm certificate		✓	✓	✓
Receive a s 1 firearm as a gift		✓	✓	✓
Purchase or hire a s 1 firearm				✓

9.22   **Shotguns**

Subsection 1(3)(a) of the Firearms Act 1968 describes shotguns as a separate group of firearms and states that:

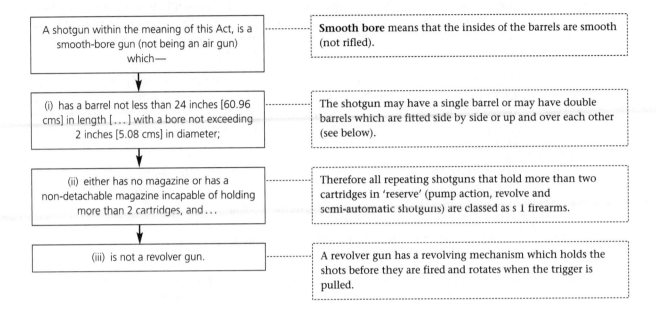

A shotgun within the meaning of this Act, is a smooth-bore gun (not being an air gun) which—	**Smooth bore** means that the insides of the barrels are smooth (not rifled).
(i) has a barrel not less than 24 inches [60.96 cms] in length [. . .] with a bore not exceeding 2 inches [5.08 cms] in diameter;	The shotgun may have a single barrel or may have double barrels which are fitted side by side or up and over each other (see below).
(ii) either has no magazine or has a non-detachable magazine incapable of holding more than 2 cartridges, and . . .	Therefore all repeating shotguns that hold more than two cartridges in 'reserve' (pump action, revolve and semi-automatic shotguns) are classed as s 1 firearms.
(iii) is not a revolver gun.	A revolver gun has a revolving mechanism which holds the shots before they are fired and rotates when the trigger is pulled.

Note that a sawn-off shotgun cannot be classed as a shotgun as its barrel length is too short, it therefore becomes a s 1 firearm for which the owner must possess a s 1 firearms certificate.

Shotguns may have one or two barrels; the main types of barrel configuration for shotguns are shown below.

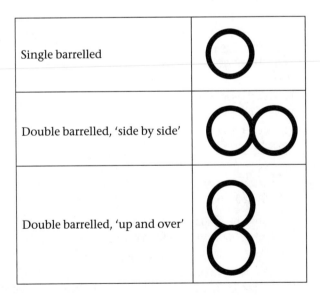

Single barrelled	
Double barrelled, 'side by side'	
Double barrelled, 'up and over'	

A typical **shot cartridge** contains primer, charge, shot, wadding, and the outer case. The primer and propellant are stored in a battery cup at the base, which is made of brass, and the rest of the assembly is stored in a tube made up of plastic or compressed card. The controlled explosion forces all the shot and wadding through the barrel. Different manufacturers place different types of wad in various positions within the cartridge depending upon the function of the shot, but the main function of wadding is to act as a shock absorber to prevent the spherical shot being deformed since a non-spherical shot would tend to stray from the intended path.

9.22.1 Shotgun Certificates

Individuals possessing, purchasing, or acquiring a shotgun without holding a relevant certificate commit an offence under s 2(1) of the Firearms Act 1968. In certain circumstances however, a person may 'have' a shotgun without a shotgun certificate, such as when he/she borrows it from a person who holds a certificate and uses it on that person's premises (including land) and in his/her presence. Neither is a certificate required in order to possess shotgun ammunition that contains five or more shot pellets in a cartridge, none of which pellets is larger than 0.36 inch in diameter.

A shotgun certificate (also referred to as a 'licence') is granted by the chief police officer of the force in which the applicant lives. Shotguns are frequently used for sporting purposes (eg clay pigeon shooting) and for shooting game. Therefore, unless there is a specific reason to refuse the application it will normally be granted, in marked contrast to the issue of s 1 firearms certificates.

The offence (of not holding the relevant certificate) is triable either way:

- summarily: six months' imprisonment and/or a fine;
- on indictment: five years' imprisonment and/or a fine.

9.22.2 Conditions Placed upon the Holder of a Shotgun Certificate

A number of conditions are placed upon the holder of a shotgun certificate. An important requirement is that shotguns will be kept secure when not in use, for example in a specially designed steel gun cabinet. It is an offence for a person to fail to comply with a condition relating to a shotgun certificate (s 2(2)).

This offence is triable summarily and the penalty is six months' imprisonment and/or a fine.

9.22.3 Age Restrictions for Shotguns

The following table summarizes the age limits for shotguns. An empty box in the table means the activity is not permitted.

The person may	Under 14	Age 14+	Age 15+	Age 17+
Hold a shotgun certificate	✓	✓	✓	✓
Possess a shotgun (received as a gift)			✓	✓
Purchase or hire a shotgun				✓

TASK 20

1. Describe the general characteristics of a firearm.
2. What are your powers to demand production of certificates?
3. Under what circumstances may you require a person to hand over a firearm or ammunition for examination?
4. What firearms are covered by s 1 and so require a s 1 certificate?
5. What ammunition is covered by s 1 and therefore requires a s 1 certificate?
6. What shotguns need a certificate?

9.23   Air Weapons

An air weapon is usually less dangerous to other people than many other firearms because the pellets are discharged from the barrel relatively slowly and have less mass than, for example, a handgun bullet. (Remember from your science lessons at school or college that kinetic energy is related to both the square of the speed and the mass.) The velocity is relatively low because the pellets are propelled by air pressure only, rather than by an explosive charge. However, air weapons are capable of producing serious injury including causing blindness. Indeed, air weapon offences make up more than half of all recorded firearms offences. Fatalities are also not unknown, particularly with children. It is clear that air-weapon offences should be taken very seriously and no doubt this message will be reinforced during your training.

Air weapons include air pistols, air guns, and air rifles which are different in shape and size.

(Photo by Kevin Lawton-Barrett)

Air rifle

9.23.1   Definition of Lawful Air Weapons

The missiles from this category of weapon are pellets propelled by air. The kinetic energy rate (the energy used to fire the pellet) must not exceed 6 ft lb (for air pistols), or 12 ft lb (for air weapons other than air pistols).

A lawful air weapon does not require a certificate under s 1 of the Firearms Act 1968. However, if the air weapon exceeds the authorized kinetic energy, it becomes a s 1 firearm and must be certified as such. A forensic laboratory will be able to measure the kinetic energy of the pellets produced by an air weapon. A weapon with a self-contained gas cartridge system (containing both a charge of compressed air or other gas as well as the pellet) is not classified as a lawful air weapon, and is a prohibited weapon under s 5 of the Firearms Act (see 9.24 below).

9.23.2 Age Limits and Firing Restrictions for Air Weapons

For a person under the age of 17 it is an offence to possess an air weapon or ammunition for an air weapon (s 22(4), Firearms Act 1968), unless (s 23) the child or young person:

- is accompanied by someone over 21 years of age in which case he/she can be allowed to fire the air weapon on premises, but the missiles must not go beyond the premises (otherwise both the firer and the supervisor commit an offence); or
- is aged 14 years or over, in which case he/she may possess the weapon on premises with the permission of the occupier, and can fire the air weapon, but the missiles must not go beyond the premises; or
- is a member of an approved club for target shooting; or
- is at a shooting gallery with only air weapons or miniature rifles not exceeding .23 calibre.

Firing an air weapon (or allowing it to be fired) beyond the premises from where it is fired is also an offence (s 21A of the Firearms Act 1968). However it will be a defence (for the firer or the supervisor) to show that the occupier of the premises into or across which the missile was fired, had consented to the firing of the missile (whether specifically or by way of a general consent).

'Premises' is not defined in this Act but examples will include houses and gardens and other private places which are enclosed.

These offences are triable summarily and the penalty is a fine.

9.23.3 Selling and Purchasing Air Weapons

The buying and selling of air weapons is an offence for any person who is not a registered firearms dealer or an air weapon-only registered firearms dealer (s 3(1), Firearms Act 1968). It is also an offence to possess or expose such items for sale or transfer.

This offence is triable either way:

- summarily: six months' imprisonment and/or a fine;
- on indictment: five years' imprisonment.

For a person under the age of 18 it is an offence to purchase or hire an air weapon or ammunition for an air weapon (s 22(1) of the Firearms Act 1968). The seller or hirer would also have committed an offence under s 24(1) of the same Act.

These offences are triable summarily and the penalty is six months' imprisonment and/or a fine.

9.23.4 Air Weapons as Gifts to Young People

It is an offence under s 24(4) of the Firearms Act 1968 to make a gift of an air weapon (or ammunition for an air weapon) to a person under the age of 18. It is also an offence to lend (or otherwise part with the possession of) such items to a person under the age of 18 except in the circumstances listed in s 23 of the Act (see 9.23.2 above).

This offence is triable summarily and the penalty is a fine.

9.24 Prohibited Weapons

Parliament decided that the general public have no reasonable need to possess certain types of potentially highly dangerous weapons such as machine guns, PAVA (an incapacitating pepper spray), or CS spray. Under s 5 of the Firearms Act 1968, no one may possess or make such items without special authority.

Prohibited weapons with exceptions

Prohibited type of weapon	Exceptions to the prohibition
The barrel is less than 30 cm long	• None
The weapon is less than 60 cm long overall	• an air weapon; • a muzzle-loading gun; or • a firearm designed as signalling apparatus
Two or more missiles can be successively discharged without repeated pressure on the trigger	• None
Self-loading or pump-action rifled gun	• chambered for .22 inch rim-fire cartridges
Any self-loading or pump-action smooth-bore gun which • has a barrel less than 60.96 cm (24 inches) long, or • overall is less than 101.6 cm (40 inches) long	• chambered for .22 inch rim-fire cartridges • air weapon
Smooth-bore revolver gun	• chambered for 9 mm rim-fire cartridges • muzzle-loading gun
Rocket launcher or any mortar for projecting a stabilized missile	For the following purposes: • line throwing or • pyrotechnics or • as signalling

There are other categories of weapon which are prohibited with no exceptions. Some of these are listed below:

• any weapon or ammunition of whatever description designed or adapted for the discharge of any **noxious** liquid, gas, or other matter;
• any cartridge with a **bullet designed to explode** on or immediately before impact;
• any **explosive object** such as grenades, bombs, rockets, or shells, if capable of being used with a firearm of any description;
• any air weapon that uses, or is designed or adapted for use with, a self-contained **gas cartridge** system (this may be similar in appearance to a bullet and its casing);
• any firearm which is **disguised** as another object.

Any person who has in his/her possession, purchases, acquires, manufactures, sells, or transfers a prohibited weapon or ammunition commits an offence under s 5(1) of the Firearms Act 1968. However it is not an offence if the person has the written authority of the Defence Council (the Secretary of State for Defence, other MoD Ministers, the Chiefs of Staff, and senior civil servants).

This offence is triable either way:

• summarily: six months' imprisonment and/or a fine;
• on indictment: ten years' imprisonment and/or a fine.

(Images courtesy of Kent Police)

The two canisters on the left are examples of CS Spray and those on the right, pepper spray. All are examples of s 5 prohibited weapons.

9.25 Imitation Firearms

The definition of an imitation firearm provided in s 57(4) of the Firearms Act 1968 is

> anything which has the appearance of being a firearm whether or not it is capable of discharging any shot, bullet or other missile.

This does not include replicas of prohibited weapons. Imitation or replica firearms will generally fall into two categories:

- imitations that **can be readily converted** into a firearm of a type requiring a firearm certificate under s 1 of the Firearms Act 1968;
- imitations that **cannot** be readily converted into a firearm to which s 1 of the 1968 Act applies. These are not required to be licensed or certified and are therefore not subject to most of the regulations regarding firearms. To all intents and purposes, they are treated as toys or collectibles.

As you may know, it is often difficult to distinguish an imitation firearm from the 'real thing'.

(Images courtesy of Kent Police)

On the left a real Mauser, on the right the imitation

9.25.1 The Meaning of 'Readily Convertible'

The meaning of 'readily convertible' is explained in s 1(6) of the Firearms Act 1982. An imitation firearm is regarded as readily convertible if it can be converted **without** special skills or special tools. Special tools are defined as tools that would not generally be used by people for construction and maintenance in their homes. Therefore if the conversion only required the simple use of a normal screwdriver, the imitation firearm could be described as readily convertible.

9.25.2 Control of Readily Converted Imitation Firearms

A readily convertible imitation firearm requires a firearms certificate, whether it is in its converted or unconverted form. Any such firearm would normally need to be submitted for testing at a forensic laboratory before any lawful proceedings were undertaken. Ultimately, only a court can decide whether or not a particular imitation firearm requires a firearms certificate.

If a certificate is required but none is held, an offence will have been committed. It may be a defence if the accused can show that he/she did not know (and had no reason to suspect) that the imitation firearm was constructed or adapted to be readily convertible (s 1(5) of the Firearms Act 1982).

9.25.3 Other Offences Relating to Imitation Firearms

It is an offence to buy or sell an imitation firearm if the buyer is under the age of 18 (s 24A of the Firearms Act 1968). This offence is triable summarily and the penalty is 12 months' imprisonment and/or a fine.

It is also an offence to have an imitation firearm in a public place without lawful authority or reasonable excuse (see 9.20.5 above).

9.25.4 Ball Bearing ('BB') Guns

These are guns that fire ball bearings (small round objects made of plastic or aluminum) powered by a spring, batteries, or gas (eg carbon dioxide) from an external aerosol canister. They are low-powered and do not require a licence. A typical BB gun will not be classified as a firearm as it is not lethal; the power generated by the spring or other means will not propel the projectile out of the gun with sufficient force to kill. However, you should consider the following:

- If the gun appears more powerful than a typical BB gun or has large projectiles, the power level may need to be assessed by the Forensic Science Service. Such a gun might be sufficiently powerful to be classified as a firearm, either as an air weapon or a 's 1 firearm' (see 9.21 above).
- If the projectile of the BB gun is forced out of the weapon by a self-contained gas cartridge (similar in appearance to a bullet and casing) but not an external aerosol cartridge, then the BB gun is a prohibited weapon (see 9.24 above).

Finally, note that BB guns can easily resemble lethal firearms and carrying an imitation gun in public is an offence (see 9.25.3 above). In 2006 over 80 per cent of all firearms incidents dealt with by Derbyshire police involved BB guns.

TASK 21

1. You attend an incident where a 16-year-old boy has been firing an air rifle from his parents' bedroom window at baked-bean cans on top of their garden wall. The pellets have clearly gone into the next door neighbour's garden. What offence has the boy committed?
2. You see a boy carrying an air rifle along the High Street (the rifle is not in a gun cover). After questioning you establish that he is 17 years old. What offence, if any, has he committed?

TASK 22

Whilst on Independent Patrol you are tasked with attending the local park where an adult has detained a young person who is apparently carrying an imitation firearm. What offence are you going to consider?

9.26 The Prevention of Harm to Animals

The use of legislation to protect animals in the UK began in 1822 with an Act to Prevent the Cruel and Improper Treatment of Cattle. Indeed, this was the first animal welfare legislation passed by a parliament anywhere in the world. More recently, research findings summarized by the organization People for the Ethical Treatment of Animals (PETA) have indicated that there may be links between animal abuse and human abuse (see <http://www.peta.org.uk/factsheet/files/FactsheetDisplay.asp?ID=172>).

The legislation we cover here is from:

- the Wildlife and Countryside Act 1981 (for all types of wild animals, including invertebrates);
- the Wild Mammals (Protection) Act 1996 (for wild mammals only);
- the Animal Welfare Act 2006 (for animals that are not wild animals).

Note that the definition of 'animal' and 'wild animal' varies slightly between the Acts.

9.26.1 The Animal Welfare Act 2006

This Act applies only to animals that are vertebrates (ie have a backbone) and therefore excludes insects, snails, worms, and any other invertebrates (animals without a backbone). It also refers to 'protected animals' which are defined as a type of animal that is either:

- normally domesticated in the UK (such as a cat);
- under the control of a person (such as fish kept in a garden pond); or
- not living wild (a lion that has escaped from a zoo is not truly living wild).

The Animal Welfare Act 2006 places a 'duty of care' on animal owners (including farmers and owners of pets) in an attempt to ensure the basic needs of animals are met, as well as outlawing certain forms of suffering. Offences which can be committed under the Animal Welfare Act 2006 include:

- causing or permitting unnecessary suffering (s 4);
- mutilation (s 5);
- docking of dogs' tails (s 6);
- administration of poisons (s 7);
- arranging animal fighting (s 8);
- failure of person responsible for animal to ensure welfare (s 9);
- transfer of animals by way of sale or prize to persons under 16 (s 11).

Other parties involved in investigating possible animal welfare offences include local authorities and the state veterinary service.

All the offences listed below under the Animal Welfare Act 2006 are triable summarily and the penalty is imprisonment not exceeding 51 weeks and/or a fine.

9.26.1.1 Causing unnecessary suffering to an animal

Section 4(1) of the Animal Welfare Act 2006 concerns protected animals only and states that a person commits an offence if:

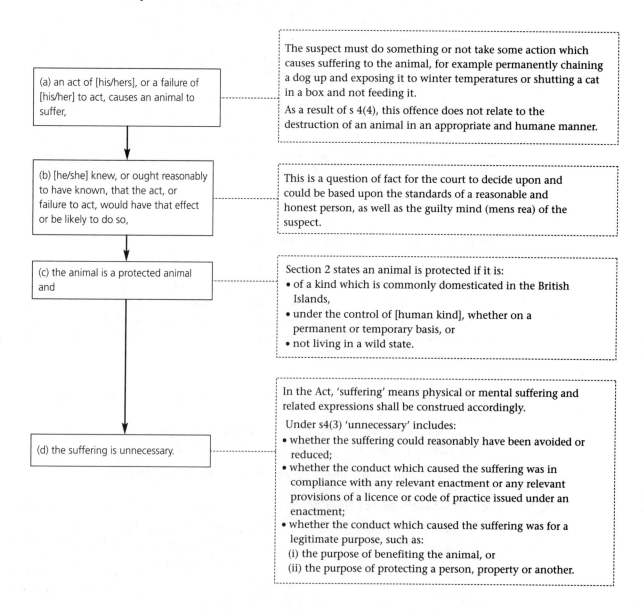

(a) an act of [his/hers], or a failure of [his/her] to act, causes an animal to suffer,

The suspect must do something or not take some action which causes suffering to the animal, for example permanently chaining a dog up and exposing it to winter temperatures or shutting a cat in a box and not feeding it.

As a result of s 4(4), this offence does not relate to the destruction of an animal in an appropriate and humane manner.

(b) [he/she] knew, or ought reasonably to have known, that the act, or failure to act, would have that effect or be likely to do so,

This is a question of fact for the court to decide upon and could be based upon the standards of a reasonable and honest person, as well as the guilty mind (mens rea) of the suspect.

(c) the animal is a protected animal and

Section 2 states an animal is protected if it is:
- of a kind which is commonly domesticated in the British Islands,
- under the control of [human kind], whether on a permanent or temporary basis, or
- not living in a wild state.

(d) the suffering is unnecessary.

In the Act, 'suffering' means physical or mental suffering and related expressions shall be construed accordingly.

Under s4(3) 'unnecessary' includes:
- whether the suffering could reasonably have been avoided or reduced;
- whether the conduct which caused the suffering was in compliance with any relevant enactment or any relevant provisions of a licence or code of practice issued under an enactment;
- whether the conduct which caused the suffering was for a legitimate purpose, such as:
  (i) the purpose of benefiting the animal, or
  (ii) the purpose of protecting a person, property or another.

Section 4(2) Animal Welfare Act 2006 refers to animals in general and states that a person commits an offence through the actions of another if:

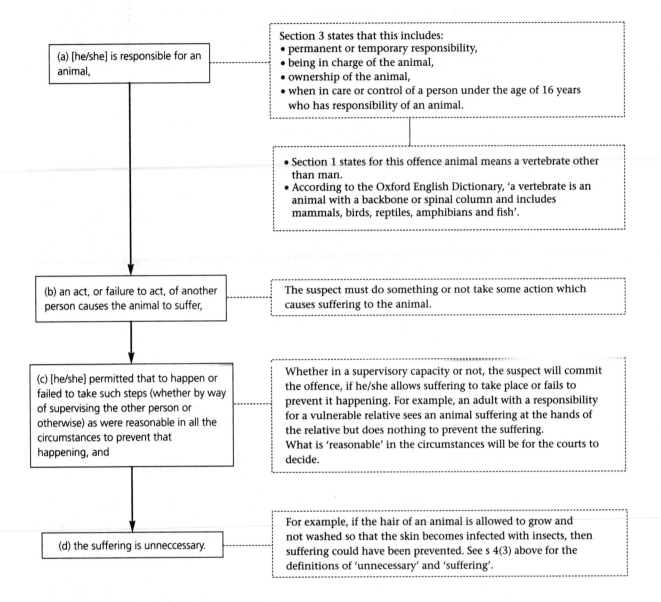

(a) [he/she] is responsible for an animal,

Section 3 states that this includes:
• permanent or temporary responsibility,
• being in charge of the animal,
• ownership of the animal,
• when in care or control of a person under the age of 16 years who has responsibility of an animal.

• Section 1 states for this offence animal means a vertebrate other than man.
• According to the Oxford English Dictionary, 'a vertebrate is an animal with a backbone or spinal column and includes mammals, birds, reptiles, amphibians and fish'.

(b) an act, or failure to act, of another person causes the animal to suffer,

The suspect must do something or not take some action which causes suffering to the animal.

(c) [he/she] permitted that to happen or failed to take such steps (whether by way of supervising the other person or otherwise) as were reasonable in all the circumstances to prevent that happening, and

Whether in a supervisory capacity or not, the suspect will commit the offence, if he/she allows suffering to take place or fails to prevent it happening. For example, an adult with a responsibility for a vulnerable relative sees an animal suffering at the hands of the relative but does nothing to prevent the suffering.
What is 'reasonable' in the circumstances will be for the courts to decide.

(d) the suffering is unneccessary.

For example, if the hair of an animal is allowed to grow and not washed so that the skin becomes infected with insects, then suffering could have been prevented. See s 4(3) above for the definitions of 'unnecessary' and 'suffering'.

9.26.1.2 The duty to ensure welfare

A person who is responsible for an animal has a duty to ensure its welfare. Section 9(1) of the Animal Welfare Act 2006 states that a person commits an offence if he/she does not meet an animal's needs, which under s 9(2) include:

(a) its need for a suitable environment
(b) its need for a suitable diet
(c) its need to be able to exhibit normal behaviour patterns
(d) any need it has to be housed with, or apart from, other animals, and
(e) its need to be protected from pain, suffering, injury, and disease.

9.26.1.3 Mutilation of a protected animal

This relates to interference with the sensitive tissues or bone structure of an animal (except for veterinary procedures). Section 5(1) of the Animal Welfare Act 2006 states that a person commits an offence if he/she mutilates a protected animal. It is also an offence for a person who is responsible for an animal to permit another person to mutilate, or to fail to prevent him/her from mutilating a protected animal (s 5(2)). This legislation does not apply to the removal of a dog's tail (see below), or in certain circumstances specified by the regulations of an appropriate national authority (for example the armed services).

9.26.1.4 Docking a dog's tail

The docking of a dog's tail is covered in s 6 of the Animal Welfare Act 2006. It is an offence to remove (or cause to be removed) a dog's tail (or part of it), other than for medical treatment. The legislation is mainly intended to prevent the removal of dogs' tails for purely cosmetic reasons. It does not apply if the dog is a 'certified working dog' that is less than six days old. A dog is a certified working dog if:

- evidence has been given to a vet;
- a national authority has proved the dog will be used for work (eg pest control or emergency rescue); or
- the dog is of a specified working type.

9.26.1.5 Administration of poisons

Section 7(1) of the Animal Welfare Act 2006 states that a person commits an offence if without lawful authority or reasonable excuse he/she administers (or causes to be administered) any poisonous or injurious drug or substance to a protected animal, knowing it to be poisonous or injurious. This includes any drug or substance which, due to the quantity or manner in which it is administered or taken, has a harmful effect (such as large amounts of salt).

A person responsible for any animal also commits an offence by permitting or failing to stop someone else allowing the animal to take poisonous substances (s 7(2) of the Animal Welfare Act 2006). This only applies if the person responsible for the animal:

- knew that the substance was poisonous; and
- 'failed to take such steps (whether by way of supervising the other person or otherwise) as were reasonable in all the circumstances to prevent that happening'.

9.26.1.6 Transfer of animals by way of sale or prize to persons under 16

Section 11(1) of the Animal Welfare Act 2006 states that it is an offence to sell an animal to a person who the seller has reasonable cause to believe to be under the age of 16 years. Here, selling an animal includes 'transferring, or agreeing to transfer, ownership of the animal in consideration of entry by the transferee into another transaction' (s 11(2)).

Section 11(3) of the Animal Welfare Act 2006 explains what this means for a person offering an animal as a prize (for example a goldfish at a funfair) to a person aged under 16 years. The person offering the prize does not commit the offence if the arrangement takes place:

- face to face, but the young person is accompanied by another person who is aged 16 years or over;
- not face to face (for example by telephone) but with the consent of the relevant carer; or
- in a family context.

9.26.1.7 Animal fighting

An animal fight involves placing a 'protected animal' with any animal (including a human) for 'fighting, wrestling, or baiting'. Section 8(1) of the Animal Welfare Act 2006 states that a person commits an offence if he/she either:

- causes an animal fight to take place, or attempts to do so;
- knowingly receives money for admission to an animal fight;
- provides information about an animal fight to another with the intention of enabling or encouraging attendance at the fight, or knowingly publicizes a proposed animal fight;
- makes or accepts a bet on the outcome of an animal fight or the occurrence of a particular event during an animal fight;
- takes part in an animal fight;
- has in his/her possession any item designed or adapted for an animal fight, with the intention of the item being used in a such a fight;
- keeps or trains an animal for animal fights; or
- keeps any premises for animal fighting.

It is also an offence to:

- be present at an animal fight, without lawful authority or reasonable excuse (s 8 (2));
- knowingly supply, publish, show, or possess with intent to supply a video-recording of an animal fight (s 8(3)).

Section 22(1) of the Animal Welfare Act 2006 states you may seize an animal if it appears to you that it has been involved in an offence under s 8(1) or (2). Under s 22(2) you may enter and search premises (but not a private dwelling) for the purpose of exercising the power under s 8(1) if you reasonably believe:

(a) that there is an animal on the premises, and
(b) that the animal is one in relation to which the power under subsection 8(1) is exercisable.

9.26.1.8 Protected animals in distress

Animals in distress may need to be taken into your possession, and some might need to be destroyed. You should refer to your own force policy in relation to the use of the following powers.

Section 18(1) of the Animal Welfare Act 2006 states that, if you reasonably believe that a protected animal is suffering, you may 'take, or arrange for the taking of, such steps as appear to [you] to be immediately necessary to alleviate the animal's suffering'. Note that this in itself does not authorize destruction of an animal (s18(2)).

A protected animal may be destroyed if a veterinary surgeon certifies that its condition is so poor that it should be destroyed in its own interest (s 18(3) of the Animal Welfare Act 2006). You may destroy it yourself or arrange for another person to destroy it, either at the site or at another location.

Section 18(4) states you may act under s 18(3) without the certificate of a veterinary surgeon if it appears to you:

(a) that the condition of the animal is such that there is no reasonable alternative to destroying it; and
(b) that the need for action is so urgent that it is not reasonably practicable to wait for a veterinary surgeon.

You may take a protected animal into possession if a veterinary surgeon certifies that it is suffering, or is likely to suffer if its circumstances do not change (s 18(5)). If you believe that action is needed urgently (and it is not reasonably practicable to wait for a vet) then you may act under s 18(5) without the certificate of a veterinary surgeon (s 18(6)). Any dependent offspring of an animal taken into possession under s 18(5) may also be taken into possession (s 18(7)).

Section 18(8) states that where an animal is taken into possession under s 18(5) you may take the following actions yourself or arrange for another person to:

(a) remove it to a place of safety;
(b) care for it (either on the premises where it was being kept or at another suitable place);
(c) mark it for identification purposes.

You have the power of entry (s 19(1)) to premises for the purpose of searching for a protected animal and of exercising any power under s 18 if you reasonably believe that there is a protected animal on the premises and that it is suffering (or if the circumstances of the animal do not change, it is likely to suffer).

You may use reasonable force (if necessary), but only if it appears that entry is required before a warrant under s 19(4) can be obtained and executed. Section 19(1) does not authorize entry to any part of premises which is used as a private dwelling; under these circumstances a s 19(4) warrant will be required.

It is an offence to intentionally obstruct a person acting under s 18 of the Animal Welfare Act 2006 (s 18(12)).

9.26.1.9 Other powers under the Animal Welfare Act 2006

You may enter and search any premises to arrest any person you reasonably suspect of committing an offence under ss 4, 5, 6(1), 6(2), 7, 8(1), and 8(2) of the Animal Welfare Act (s 17 of the PACE Act 1984: see 7.9 above).

You may stop and detain a vehicle under s 54(1) of the Animal Welfare Act 2006 in order to:

- search it to prevent animal suffering (s 19(1)); or
- to seize an animal that you suspect may be involved in animal fighting (s 22(2)).

You must be in uniform to exercise this power. The vehicle may be detained for as long as is reasonably required (s 54(4)) for a search or inspection to be carried out (including the exercise of any related power under this Act). You may search the vehicle either at the place where it was first detained or nearby.

9.26.2 Cruelty to Wild Animals

The law concerning cruelty to wild animals is to be found largely in:

- the Wildlife and Countryside Act 1981(for most types of wild animal); and
- the Wild Mammals (Protection) Act 1996 (for wild mammals only).

Here, 'wild animals' includes all types of animals—mammals, birds, frogs, toads, fish, insects, and snakes, but there are some particular exclusions (see below). A mammal is an animal whose female produces milk for the nourishment of its young, such as rabbits, foxes, squirrels, hedgehogs, bats, and dolphins.

The offences of cruelty to wild animals listed here are all triable summarily only, and the penalty is six months' imprisonment and/or a fine.

9.26.2.1 The Wildlife and Countryside Act 1981

Wild birds are covered under s 1 of the Wildlife and Countryside Act 1981. A 'wild bird' is any bird of a species that is resident in (or is a visitor to) the European Territory of any member state, and living wild. Game birds (such as pheasants) are not considered as wild birds for the purposes of this Act, and there are also other current exceptions (as determined by the Secretary of State for the Environment), such as wood pigeons and herring gulls.

Under s 1 of the Wildlife and Countryside Act 1981 it is an offence to intentionally:

    (a) kill, injure or take any wild bird;
    (b) take, damage or destroy the nest of any wild bird while that nest is in use or being built; or
    (c) take or destroy an egg of any wild bird.

Other types of wild animal are protected under s 9 of the Wildlife and Countryside Act 1981, under which it is an offence to intentionally kill, injure, or take 'any' wild animal. However there are some exclusions, and some of these are shown in the table below. (You are likely to be able to find examples of animals that are hard to place within these definitions, and it will be for a court to decide whether a particular animal is covered under this section of the legislation.)

Included	Excluded
Named mammals, such as dormice, hedgehogs, bats, otters, and red squirrels	Rats and rabbits
Other mammals and certain named reptiles, fish, amphibians, insects, molluscs, and other types of animal	Birds (covered in s 1 instead)
Animals living wild	Animals bred and held in captivity

Section 19 of the Wildlife and Countryside Act states that if you suspect with reasonable cause that any person has committed an offence under this Act you may:

- stop and search that person;
- search and examine anything the person has in his/her possession;
- seize and detain evidence;
- enter premises (other than a dwelling) to arrest a person.

Section 2 PACE Act 1984 (see 7.5 above) and Code A of the PACE Codes of Practice apply to these searches.

9.26.2.2 The Wild Mammals (Protection) Act 1996

Under this Act a mammal is wild if it is:

- not of a kind which is commonly domesticated in the British Islands; or
- not under the control of human kind, whether on a permanent or temporary basis.

It is an offence to mutilate, kick, beat, nail or otherwise impale, stab, burn, stone, crush, drown, drag, or asphyxiate any wild mammal with intent to inflict unnecessary suffering (s 1 of the Wild Mammals (Protection) Act 1996).

The following are **not** offences under the Wild Mammals (Protection) Act 1996:

- mercy- and attempted mercy-killing, for example the action of putting an injured wild animal 'out of its misery';
- actions under authorization, for example by a vet;
- lawful killing by traps, dogs, birds, or poisons.

If you have reasonable grounds for suspecting that a person has committed an offence under the Wild Mammals (Protection) Act 1996 and you believe that evidence relating to the offence may be found on the person, or in (or on) his/her vehicle you may:

(a) stop and search the person, and any vehicle or article that is with him/her; and
(b) seize and detain anything which may be evidence of the commission of the offence.

Code A of the PACE Act 1984 Codes of Practice applies to this search, for example GOWISELY (see 7.5.5 above).

TASK 23

1. In the Animal Welfare Act 2006 an animal can only 'suffer' physically. True or false?
2. What are the three different ways a 'protected animal' may be defined under the Animal Welfare Act 2006?
3. You are resourced by Control to a flat about which it has been anonymously reported that the pet cat and dog have been suffering from long periods of starvation and physical maltreatment by their owners. Restricting your answer to s 19 of the Animal Welfare Act 2006 (entering for the purpose of searching for a protected animal and of exercising any power under s 18 in relation to it), could you enter the premises under this section?
4. You attend an incident where a cat has been found with a discharged firework taped to its body which had been recently ignited. The cat is still alive but badly injured. The suspects were seen running into a nearby house. Restricting your answer to the Animal Welfare Act 2006, what power of entry, if any, could you use if required to enter and arrest the suspects?

9.27 Missing Persons

Every year, in England and Wales, about 200,000 people are reported missing. Many are found very quickly, a few are found dead after many weeks, and some are never found. Searching for missing persons is part of the **police emergency response** for civic and societal purposes, rather than law enforcement. You are likely to be involved in a search for a missing person during your initial training as a student police officer, and almost certainly a number of times during your police career. Not all disappearances attract media attention, but missing children or young women often spark intense media interest.

Missing persons incidents frequently become critical incidents, requiring the support of services other than your own force. The police become involved when a report is made of a missing person. This can entail a considerable expenditure of resources and time, including rural and urban searches, dragging of waterways, and exhaustive enquiries, particularly if the missing person is in some way **vulnerable**, such as a child or a mentally ill adult.

Some missing person investigations reveal a criminal aspect to the disappearance. The missing person may have been abducted, the victim could have been murdered and the body concealed, or the missing person might have been targeted for some other reason, such as a forced marriage. A small proportion of missing persons are found dead, and this can involve the force's major crime unit (or equivalent) extensively, especially if the circumstances suggest a suspicious death.

The national policy on the police response to 'misper' incidents was extensively redrafted in the light of the Soham murders in 2002. That case highlighted how smaller police forces were reliant on 'mutual aid' for large-scale searches, and is cited as part of the argument for more radical amalgamations of police forces into larger organizations which are capable of mounting such searches independently. Where criminal aspects (such as abduction, kidnap, and murder) are involved or suspected, there are distinct impacts on the force's investigative capability.

9.27.1 Missing person enquiries

The requirements of each case are specific to the individual who has gone missing, but there are standard considerations (some of which we have indicated above). One of the first things to be done in a **'misper'** (missing person) enquiry is to conduct a risk assessment. The disappearance of a child can never be a low risk; it must always be medium or high. Information is required about the missing person and their circumstances prior to their disappearance, particularly any factors which indicate the vulnerability of the subject. (Some of what follows is drawn from ACPO, 2005.)

Personal factors include:

- Age (under 18 is technically and legally a child).
- Is he/she on the Child Protection Register?
- Any drugs or alcohol dependency?
- Essential medication (for example, diabetes, epilepsy).
- Is there any known or suspected physical, mental, or psychological impairment (such as amnesia, dementia, visual impairment) which might increase the risk of harm to him/herself or others?

The **circumstances** of the disappearance are also important. Enquiries should consider:

- Did the person leave intentionally (items have been taken)?
- Has the person been involved in crime?
- Employment or financial problems (are credit cards or money missing)?
- Conflict, abuse, self-harm, or emotional problems in relationships.
- Abduction (for example of a child by an estranged parent).
- Evidence of violence or struggle at any scene of the disappearance.
- Usual place/country of residence.
- Weather conditions (may also have a bearing on the subsequent search).

Remember too to think about the person giving you the information. Sadly, there have been a number of occasions when information about a disappearance is provided by the person who actually caused the disappearance. Consider the Soham murders as an example: Ian Huntley, a caretaker at a school in Soham, had murdered two young girls. The first alarm that was raised was the disappearance of the two girls. Imagine that you were the first police officer to respond to the alert. What triggers or signatures would you expect?

Your notes might include questions about what you were told. How long had the girls been missing? Was it normal for them to wander off without telling anyone? Were they going anywhere specific, such as to a shop or to visit a relative or friend? Had there been any difficulty at home, such as a row or a quarrel because one of them had been forbidden to do something? Had anyone seen anything suspicious? Did the girls have a favourite 'bolt hole' to which they might go if they thought they were in trouble? Did either have a special or particular friend? Did they have mobile phones? Where did they like to go for a walk or hang about? What were they wearing? Are there any recent photographs? Remember that, in instances like this, parents, guardians, or carers might well be distraught with anxiety and worry, and that it is not unusual for anxiety to turn to anger.

Finally, in a misper operation, there are **practical considerations** about the nature and extent of the police operation:

- Make a thorough search of the person's house, garden, and any adjoining premises. Remember that children can hide themselves in very small spaces.
- Look at personal papers belonging to the individual who has gone missing, especially diaries, work schedules, planners, and financial information. You may need to retain these as evidence.
- Check with the work place or school for absence records.
- Try to establish recent movements and behaviour.
- Check on police databases, locally and nationally.
- List relatives, friends, contacts, and work colleagues/fellow students.
- Obtain recent photographs that are a good likeness.
- Prepare a search of the surrounding area, concentrating first on the person's 'habitual haunts' and then hazardous places such as pools, streams, caves, empty buildings, and so on.
- Prepare to widen the search systematically, including making house-to-house enquiries.
- Prepare publicity and contact with the media (see 9.28.3 below for more details).

If, for any reason, the circumstances of the disappearance are suspicious, the police will work on the assumption that a crime has been committed and therefore the scene of the disappearance must be preserved for evidential and investigative purposes.

9.27.1.1 The Belgian indicator system

It is interesting to note the Belgian experience in this field. The Belgian Federal Police have a missing persons department ('Chiffres Disparitions'), which was set up in 1995 in the wake of the disappearance of six children. It coordinates the work of the 189 Belgian police districts (broadly equivalent to our BCUs, if a little smaller) when a person is reported missing. The Belgian Federal Police note that they have about 1,200 reports of missing persons each year, and that over 90 per cent of these turn up in due course. However, the Belgians use a sophisticated checklist and risk assessment system which, they claim, is a reliable indicator as to whether the police should launch a full-scale search or not.

Briefly, the Belgian assessment requires detailed answers to three questions:

1. **Who is missing?**
The profile of the missing person, their behaviour patterns, family knowledge, and movements.

2. **Is it worrying?**
Factors to consider include:

- age—under 12 years old?
- mental or physical disabilities?
- dependent on essential medication or other medical treatment?

- circumstances of the disappearance that may suggest life-threatening danger;
- victim of a possible crime?
- behaviour appears completely out of character?

3. **What happened?**
Accident, crime, suicide, prepared departure, quarrels, family tensions? How? When? Where?

Much of the Belgian work is straightforward and common sense, but it can serve as a helpful risk assessment model in conjunction with your individual force policy.

TASK 24

Consider the following scenario:

A 16-year-old boy has been reported missing by his mother. Checks with his school showed that he did not arrive at school that morning, despite having left his house at the normal time and in school uniform. His whereabouts are unknown and he may have been missing for as much as ten hours before his absence was reported. There are indications that the boy has recently become moody and depressed, and that he may have been subject to some bullying at school. He is asthmatic and needs regular medication. He is a keen shot and has his own shotgun, properly licensed, for use on the farm where he lives. He had a quarrel with his father the night before; his father had refused to allow him to attend a party. There is a history of the boy acting rebelliously and his father only reluctantly granting limited freedom.

1. You might note that there are a number of vulnerabilities, or potential areas for concern, in this case. What further information would you need to pursue the enquiry?
2. If the missing person enquiry becomes prolonged, what national guidance can you obtain in order effectively to process the investigation?

9.28 Emergencies, Major Incidents, and Critical Incidents

During your initial training you are likely to receive tuition and instruction on the police role in handling **emergencies**, **major incidents**, and **critical incidents**. You might even find yourself an initial responder at the scene of an emergency.

Useful background documents for this part of Chapter 9 include the 2009 NPIA publication *Guidance on Emergency Procedures* (available from <www.acpo.police.uk/asp/policies/Data/Emergency Procedures 202009.pdf>) and the 2007 NPIA document *Practice Advice on Critical Incident Management* (available from <www.acpo.police.uk/asp/policies/Data/critical_incident_management_17x08x07.pdf>).

An **emergency** is defined by s 1 of the Civil Contingencies Act 2004 as 'an event or situation which threatens serious damage to human welfare in a place in the United Kingdom' including one or more of the following:

- human illness or injury, or loss of life;
- homelessness;
- damage to property;
- disruption of a supply of money, food, water, energy, or fuel;
- disruption of a system of communication;
- disruption of facilities for transport;
- disruption of services relating to health;
- serious environmental damage (eg radioactive contamination);
- war or terrorism which threatens serious damage to the security of the United Kingdom.

(You can find a full copy of the Act at <http://www.opsi.gov.uk/acts/acts2004/20040036.htm> and a guide via the PNLD website.)

A **major incident** is an emergency that requires the implementation of special arrangements, by one or all of the emergency services, for:

- the rescue and transport of a large number of casualties; and/or
- the involvement, either directly or indirectly, of large numbers of people; and/or
- the handling of a large number of enquiries likely to be generated both from the public and the news media, usually to the police; and/or
- any incident that requires the large-scale combined resources of the three emergency services and supporting organizations—eg local authority.

(South Yorkshire Police, 2007)

A **critical incident** is any incident or event which has the potential to escalate beyond your control and become a major incident. However, more recent thinking suggests that part of the definition of a critical incident may be that it creates a strong public perception of community **vulnerability**, and hence the definition is not simply limited to major incidents (ACPO, 2007b). Definitions of both 'major incident' and 'critical incident' vary from force to force although they do all tend to refer to either the size of the incident or its potential to escalate in some way, and often correspond closely with ACPO definitions given in the NPIA publications referred to above. It is for this reason that we have grouped together emergency, major incidents, and critical incidents in this part of Chapter 9.

As a student police officer, much of your Supervised Patrol will be spent dealing with incidents ranging from minor disputes to the complexities of a homicide. It is likely that as you gain experience and specialist skills (see Chapter 14) you will attend incidents which are increasingly complex. However, you could be caught up in, and be expected to control effectively, almost **any** incident from the moment you go out on the streets wearing a police uniform. The public see the uniform and expect you to take charge and resolve the problem effectively and immediately. This is why, throughout your student officer training, great emphasis is laid upon your use of common sense, 'life skills', or 'nous'; it can be described in many ways.

You will practise and rehearse many times the effective ways in which you can intervene to resolve a problem before it gets out of hand, such as a domestic dispute, dealing with a shoplifter, or calming people down who have been involved in a minor road collision. You will learn to defuse, control, restrain, or manage any of a great variety of incidents. But what about an incident which has the potential to 'go major' and get really out of hand?

TASK 25

What would your first responses be, for example, if you were the first police officer to arrive at:

- a serious road collision;
- the scene of a brawl in which someone had been knifed;
- an accident on a railway line;
- a burning house where people are trapped on upper floors;
- a situation where a person has taken a child hostage?

What would your **responsibilities** be, as opposed to your instincts? What would you be expected to do? Is there an order in which you should do things? What are the priorities at the scene? What should be your priorities at the scene? What communication is needed and with whom?

The incidents listed above are all emergencies, major or critical incidents; your actions as the first police officer on the scene are crucial to the proper and managed outcome of the incident, and relying on your instincts is not sufficient in such situations. For example, at an incident involving a large brawl in a club, control of the scene is not best effected by wading into the middle of the fracas and grabbing the first brawler you can get hold of. You are likely to provoke more violence and get hurt yourself (and you will not be much use lying on the ground trying to cover your kidneys as the brawl carries on around you). House-fire incidents may also tempt you to act heroically, and to plunge straight in to save the occupants from death by burning. However, without the proper apparatus or an understanding of the 'seat' of the fire and the risk of structural collapse of the building, you may become a victim yourself, rather than a rescuer.

You may find it difficult to control your reactions and adjust. However the rule is: only try to rescue someone from a life-threatening situation if you do **not** endanger yourself or others. For example, at a brawl where people have been injured, you can (and must) intervene if you have sufficient support from colleagues. But you cannot intervene and stop a brawl on your own.

On occasions you have to be **counter-intuitive**, that is, you have to go against your instincts and allow your training to rule and control your emotions. You need to think and act calmly and rationally. You need to:

* assess the situation and work out what is going on;
* communicate as quickly as possible;
* prioritize your (and others') actions.

At some incidents there may be bystanders, and they may be a help or a hindrance. When interacting with bystanders you need to be calm, think, act rationally, and retain control as panic is sometimes infectious and can spread quickly through a large group of people. Consider crowd control at a football match or at an open-air concert; panic can turn a lively gathering into an uncontrollable mass and people can fall and be trampled. You must retain control of people's movements, even at a relatively limited incident.

You may be overwhelmed by offers of help from well-intentioned people (though probably not when a large-scale fight is in progress). Use any volunteers to direct and contain people, to direct traffic and conduct evacuation until more help arrives. In one incident, a messy road traffic collision involving pedestrians outside a school, a single police officer was assisted immeasurably by a passing bus-load of rugby players. They helped to shepherd people to safe exits, keep back crowds of sightseers, and direct traffic until police reinforcements and ambulances arrived.

Bystanders may not always be so helpful; police and other emergency service support can be delayed because of passers-by who want to look at what is going on. This is often an impediment to effective scene management, and you should always be prepared to move such onlookers away from the incident.

There is another and very important reason why the area itself must be controlled. It could be a crime scene, and your role in controlling access and the preservation of evidence is of absolutely vital importance, otherwise crucial evidence could be lost, overlooked, or damaged. We look at this in detail in 13.5 below.

We have discussed your first actions when attending an incident; indeed, a professional, calm, and authoritative police presence is often enough to prevent an incident becoming major or critical, but not always. You will certainly need to prioritize your actions.

TASK 26

Consider an incident in which a man with a hostage appears to have barricaded himself into a semi-detached house in a cul-de-sac. About a dozen people are milling about, and the event has been described to you by two very excited and incoherent witnesses. You have one other police officer to assist you. Assuming that police back-up will arrive within 10 minutes and other emergency services (fire and rescue service, ambulance) are also on their way (with an estimated time of arrival of 15 minutes), what would be your list of things to do in priority order at such an incident? Remember that you need to manage the incident, protect life, and contain the scene, as well as preparing for the arrival of your supporting police officers.

What you will need to keep in your mind throughout is that **you** are in control of the incident (as 'Silver', the forward Commander: see 9.28.2 below) until you are relieved by someone of superior rank. Remember too that you may be at a crime scene, so preservation of evidence and keeping the scene clear and untouched is very important. (That is why any rendezvous point

(RV) for vehicles bringing support or assistance needs to be kept well back from the scene.) In an emergency involving firearms or the risk of violence, you would not let other emergency services go forward into the 'line of fire' either (see 13.3 below).

All this sounds complicated and difficult to remember in the urgency of dealing with an incident which is critical and which could become a major incident or crime. However, there are ways in which you can keep priorities and procedures firmly in your mind, always assuming that you act calmly, positively, purposefully, and promptly.

9.28.1 CHALETS

We noted above that any incident has the potential to 'go major'. Procedures for major or critical incidents are well defined; after all, the police have plenty of experience in dealing with such incidents. The mnemonic **CHALETS** will help you remember the standard procedure for major incidents, including the order of priorities and what actions need to be taken first.

In more detail, you will need to consider:

C	Casualties	How many, their location and type of injuries.
H	Hazards	• Immediate (fire, exposed electrical wires, flood water, chemicals, or hazardous substances) • potential (gas cylinders near heat sources, spilled fuel, overhead power lines, firearms).
A	Access/Egress	How to enter and leave the site, selecting RV points, setting up priority routes.
L	Location	Where is the incident? (Are precise map references needed?)
E	Emergency services	• Are people hurt? • Is there a fire? • Are the services already on the scene or do they need to be called? • Is there a bomb or other explosive substance?
T	Type of incident	For example, vehicles in an accident, buildings in danger of collapse, affray in progress, underground tunnel collapse, public order, civil emergency, armed siege.
S	Safety/Start a Log	Conduct a health and safety assessment, start an incident log in your PNB.

(Note that 'SAD CHALETS' is also sometimes used as a mnemonic. In this case the 'SAD' part normally stands for 'Survey, Assess, and Disseminate'.)

Every force and every emergency service will have **contingency plans** to deal with a wide range of emergencies and incidents. Some of these plans will be legal requirements under the Civil Contingencies Act 2004.

All forces (and emergency services) will have **generic plans** for the following types of emergency, major or critical incident:

• aircraft crash;
• bomb or suspect device;
• casualty bureau for major emergency;
• contamination of food products;
• disaster, including civil emergency;
• evacuation;
• gas emergency;
• hazardous substances;
• hostage or siege incident;

- hostage involving kidnap;
- influenza pandemic;
- maritime incident;
- major fire or conflagration (including evacuation);
- rail incident;
- transportation of irradiated fuel.

Out of all the services that may attend such an incident, only the police will be constantly alert to the possibility that a crime has been committed, in which case the emergency, major or critical incident will also be a crime scene (see Chapter 13). For example, after a road traffic collision, you need to consider whether the driver was under the influence of drink or drugs. After a fall from height, did the woman fall or was she pushed; is this a natural or a suspicious death? You should be suspicious and be alert to any signatures or characteristic signs that there is something wrong. For example, a witness may remark 'funny thing—that man hanging round all morning', or you may spot an article at the scene (or nearby) such as an empty wallet or purse. This might suggest that all is not what it seems.

The critical factor in any incident is that you **take charge**, demonstrating **leadership** and capability in a crisis. Much of your training will seek to develop your skills as a leader and will focus upon what you are expected to do in any given situation.

TASK 27

Describe a problem-solving and decision-making model used in your police force.

The first period of any incident at a major crime scene or at a critical incident is often described as 'the golden hour'. It is actually unlikely that you will be on your own for that long, unless the incident is in a really remote and inaccessible place, or there are corollary problems (such as a natural disaster of some kind) and access roads are blocked. You may be relieved by a senior officer quite quickly, but you might not. If you are not, the golden hour is your responsibility (and that of your colleagues, if present). Chapter 13 covers the Golden Hour in more detail (see 13.3.4 below).

9.28.2 Control and Responsibility

Coordination of control of the incident is important. Throughout all stages of an incident, force control must be kept fully informed about the development or progress of events. There are many good reasons why a central focus is sustained in such incidents, and it is organized along national guidelines.

9.28.2.1 The Command Sequence

There is a standard command sequence in use in all police forces across the UK. The levels refer to the function of the command level and not necessarily to the rank of the officers concerned.

Levels of command

Gold	Strategic command of the incident, usually at police headquarters or at a designated strategic police command centre.
Silver	Tactical police command at a forward point closer to the scene of immediate crisis.
Bronze	Operational local response at the crisis point itself (for example cordons or firearms), often carried out by a number of people (Operational Response Commanders or ORC), rather than one designated commander.

When a more senior officer becomes available the command level will transfer to the officer with the higher rank. Therefore whilst on Independent or Supervised Patrol you as a student police officer may be 'Silver' for a short period of time before a more senior or more experienced officer arrives on the scene. This tiered structure is considered by many in the police service to work effectively (and has been exhaustively tested) at local or force level and also at national level, as you will see when we come to look at a terrorist incident (9.28.5 below).

9.28.2.2 **Resources and Risk Assessment**

Resources should not be committed too early, unless there is a clear picture of what is happening on the ground, because over-resourcing is wasteful and inefficient. Police officers attending an incident are clearly not available for deployment elsewhere, and swamping a site with armed officers, dog teams, underwater search teams, and the Royal Engineers (for example), is not necessary if the incident turns out to be trivial.

In the case of missing persons (especially when there may be other factors, possibly criminal) there are many components to the response: search teams are called out, assessments of transport needs are made, command and control, strategic, and tactical responses are all being set up, and the control room will alert other emergency services.

For larger incidents the invoking of 'military aid to the civil power' (MACP) might be required. Specialists such as explosives ordnance (bomb disposal), helicopters, search and rescue, engineers, nuclear, chemical and radiological detection and containment units, and a host of others may be called upon. Note that deployment of armed officers is usually a top-level command decision ('Gold'), made by a chief superintendent or chief officer.

To determine the level of resources required, a risk assessment must be carried out as this relates to both resources and coordination of control of the incident. When in possession of all the known facts, a senior officer (from a duty inspector up to chief officer rank) can carry out a risk assessment of the situation. He/she will ask the person who is 'Silver' at the time about the situation—and this may be you if you have not been relieved.

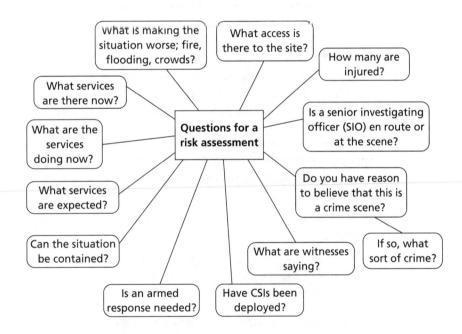

The purpose of a risk assessment is to facilitate a propotionate response in the right sequence. The assessment is about allocation of resources and the intensity of the required response, in addition to deciding what other services are required at the scene.

9.28.2.3 **Command, resources, and risk assessment in practice**

In 2002 extensive flooding occurred in some southern counties of England following a prolonged period of very heavy autumnal rain. River levels were dangerously high, many flood plains were already inundated and there was a risk that widespread evacuation from premises in the path of further flooding would be required. The strategic command of the incident was coordinated by the police, as is usual in the UK in civil emergency, supported by other services. Several south-eastern forces were in contact with each other in readiness for the provision of mutual aid: one police force might be required to go to the aid of another police force. At each Gold Command, chaired by a chief police officer, a number of senior representatives from a range of services were present, each with the power to deploy resources. In this instance, there were senior officers from Fire and Rescue, the Ambulance Service, health, housing, and the county council or unitary authority. In addition representatives from the regional water company, specialist surveyors, power companies (power lines were being brought down by high winds) were also present at some meetings, and various parts of the armed forces, including the Royal Engineers, signallers, and the Royal Air Force (aircraft were deployed).

This structure was replicated, on a smaller scale and at tactical level in Silver Command. The equipment, machinery, crews, vehicles, and those engaged in the actual operations on the ground were located at Bronze or the ORC 'forward control point' (FCP).

TASK 28

What problems might potentially arise within command structures? Make a list of what could go wrong and what would avoid problems.

You may feel that you are only a small and insignificant cog in this machinery; however everyone has an important part to play, and what matters is the professional execution of each of those roles, from the chief constable at Gold through to the Pc on the ground at the unfolding incident. Whatever the incident, command is exercised in the same way, and therefore coordination is properly structured. So, when you are at your first incident and all around you seems chaotic and purposeless, remember that control is being put in place, with the correct risk assessment and the proportionate deployment of resources. As we have discussed, **your role is to contain and control the incident, on the spot, there and then**. Let others worry about resources and deployments.

9.28.3   Media Interest

At any major (and often critical) incident, there is one common factor which we have not yet considered: media interest. Newspapers, radio, and television have apparently inexhaustible appetites for crime stories; sometimes critically, sometimes supportively, always dramatically (it is their job). This quest for the news story has produced an edgy, sometimes fraught, relationship between the media and the police; on the one hand the media are helpful distributors of appeals for information to help solve complex crimes, but on the other the media can be irritatingly vacuous and superficial in an endless desire for headlines. Leishman and Mason (2003) consider the complex relationship between police and the media in more detail.

TASK 29

The media have a huge appetite for dramatic stories. How long might it take for the media to respond to a major incident such as a train crash?

You should never be tempted to stop what you are doing to give press or broadcast interviews; your headquarters will have a media services unit trained for these functions (and some BCUs have media relations staff too). It is not that you should be 'muzzled', but what you say may inadvertently be misleading because you do not have the full picture and it is unlikely that you have much experience in communicating through the media. The short and simple guide is: do not talk to the media and refer them always to media services. In major cases the police will convene and preferably manage a press conference to brief the press with information and to report progress.

9.28.4   Disasters

In larger and more serious emergencies and incidents the principles of incident management are no different; only the scale has changed. When the Pan Am 103 aircraft exploded in December 1988 over Lockerbie in Scotland, debris was scattered over several miles of countryside as well as within the village of Lockerbie itself. The whole area was declared a crime scene and was treated in the same way as any other crime scene. Unsurprisingly, the incident required the provision of mutual aid.

The UK seldom has large-scale natural disasters, although some isolated or freak weather conditions do occur (the long, hot, dry summer of 1976, the prolonged February freeze in 1987, and flooding in the West Country in 2007) but we do not anticipate such conditions as in any way likely. This can cause unpreparedness, and consequently the country can experience greater disruption than if the weather conditions or natural disaster were more frequent or predictable.

However, whatever the weather, policing must be maintained, and you may well be involved in civil emergencies as a result. People may die if they are ill-equipped to deal with severe conditions such as extreme cold or heavy snow. In addition, in the aftermath of an immediate crisis there may be a rapid degeneration of law and order, such as in New Orleans in the wake of Hurricane Katrina. If such a natural disaster were to happen in the UK, we should anticipate at least some of the same sort of chaos; there is no reason to believe that this is a specifically American phenomenon.

Let us look at **a man-made disaster** such as a train crash. This usually involves derailment, injury, fire, and sometimes fatalities. Train crashes often happen in inaccessible places, which can pose logistical problems in gaining access, escorting uninjured passengers to safety, and bringing out the injured for treatment. A train crash will engage all emergency services as well as specialists from the railway companies, involving heavy lifting equipment and metal cutting tools.

All incidents which happen on railway property (including homicide) are the responsibility of British Transport Police (BTP) and the ACPO guidelines detailing the relevant protocols should be available from your force. However, it is likely that you and your more junior colleagues will be first on the scene and you will have to take charge until relieved by BTP officers or senior officers from your own force.

The procedure for a train crash would be to:

- control access;
- clear, or arrange to be cleared, a reception area for emergency services;
- preserve the scene (there may be evidence of a crime, for example, an obstruction placed on the line which caused the crash);
- secure an inner cordon around the site until the arrival of BTP officers;
- once relieved, continue to secure an outer cordon;
- once you have been assured that the power is switched off in that section of railway line and that oncoming trains have been halted, you may approach the crash site.

You should be wearing high-visibility clothing. Note the weather conditions, as you may need a torch and hazard lights (indeed, getting lighting to the crash site should be an early priority). You should not go anywhere near the live rail or overhead power cables unless absolutely necessary, even though you know that the power has been switched off. Then you can go to the carriages to help rescue the injured and escort passengers to safety, but remember that the carriages themselves may be unstable or dangerous. When in doubt wait for assistance, particularly the specialist assistance of the Fire and Emergency Service and the railway company.

9.28.4.1 CBRN incidents

A chemical, biological, radiological, or nuclear (CBRN) incident has the potential to cause extreme devastation and very widespread loss of life, and fortunately this type of incident is rare. When dealing with a CBRN incident, the considerations and procedures are the same as for dealing with any other type of suspect device (see 9.28.5.5 below).

You might be wondering how to recognize a chemical, biological, radiological, or nuclear attack. If you receive reports of groups of people suddenly collapsing or suddenly feeling unwell, or a strong or noxious smell is reported, or people suddenly experience skin blisters, you could be in the presence of a chemical attack, or chemicals may have been released from another source, such as a tanker carrying cleaning materials that has been involved in a road traffic collision.

In a suspected CRBN incident the **Steps** procedure must be followed for your safety.

For a Step 3 incident, you should provide a CHALETS assessment if you can, but the rule is never to compromise your own or colleagues' safety.

Step	Number of casualties	Actions required
Step 1	One	Approach the site using the usual procedures.
Step 2	Two	Approach with caution and do not discount any possibility. Report your arrival and be careful that you do not touch any object. Update your report continually.
Step 3	Three or more	Do not enter the scene. Create an RV point outside the area and await instructions.

9.28.5 Counter-Terrorism

Terrorist incidents can be regarded as those incidents that involve the use or threat of violence (often extreme violence) to further or to publicize a political or extremist belief. The definitions of terrorism and extreme violence are considered further by Matassa (Newburn, 2003).

The Terrorism Act 2000 provides particular powers for situations which might involve terrorism. Similar powers (eg to stop, search, and arrest people) are available under other primary legislation or procedure, but in suspected terrorist cases additional powers may need to be used. For example, the Terrorism Act 2000 provides you with wider powers to stop and search than under other legislation (see below).

9.28.5.1 Powers of arrest

Section 41(1) of the Terrorism Act 2000 states that you may arrest without warrant any person whom you reasonably suspect to be a terrorist. However, you must still comply with s 28 of PACE 1984 (see 8.9.1 above) and tell the arrested person that he/she is under arrest, and the grounds for the arrest.

Once a person has been arrested under s 41 of the Terrorism Act 2000, you have the power to search him/her for anything which may constitute evidence that he/she is a terrorist (s 43 of the Terrorism Act 2000: see 9.28.5.3 below).

9.28.5.2 Powers in designated cordoned areas

The cordoned area must be 'designated' under s 34(2) of the Terrorism Act 2000 by a police officer holding the rank of superintendent or above (or any other constable if he/she considers it urgent).

Under s 34(1) of the Terrorism Act 2000 you have certain additional powers in a designated cordoned area. The powers are listed in s 36(1) and state that you may:

1. Order a person to immediately:
   (a) leave a cordoned area;
   (b) leave any premises which are wholly or partly in or adjacent to a cordoned area; and/or
   (c) move a vehicle from a cordoned area if he/she is the driver or in charge of the vehicle.

2. Arrange for the:
   (a) removal of a vehicle from a cordoned area; or
   (b) movement of a vehicle within a cordoned area.

3. Prohibit or restrict pedestrian or vehicular access to a cordoned area.

If a person fails to comply with any of the above restrictions, prohibitions, or orders he/she commits an offence (s 36(2) of the Terrorism Act 2000). However, a defence is available to the accused if he/she can prove reasonable excuse for the non-compliance (s 36(3)).

This offence is triable summarily only and the penalty is three months' imprisonment and/or a fine.

9.28.5.3 Section 43 stop and search powers

You may stop and search any person whom you reasonably suspect of being a terrorist for any item(s) which may constitute evidence that he/she is a terrorist (s 43(1) of the Terrorism Act 2000). No authorization is required to use this power.

(For the purposes of this power, 'a terrorist' means a person who has committed an offence under the Terrorism Act 2000, or is or has been concerned in the commission, preparation, or instigation of acts of terrorism (s 40 of the Terrorism Act 2000)).

The search can be carried out in any place but you must;

- be of the same sex as the person you are searching (s 43(3) Terrorism Act 2000);
- satisfy the requirements of s 2 of the PACE Act 1984 and Code A PACE Codes of Practice (see 7.5.5 above); and
- seek the cooperation of the person to be searched, but if your attempts to search are met with resistance then reasonable force may be used (s 114(2) of the Terrorism Act 2000).

Section 43(4) of the Terrorism Act 2000 provides you with the power to seize and retain any such article.

9.28.5.4 Section 44 stop and search powers

This power (s 44 of the Terrorism Act 2000) relates to searching (a vehicle or a person) for articles that are linked to terrorism, but it is not necessary to have any grounds for suspecting the presence of such articles. However, the s 44 power to search must be authorized by an assistant chief constable/commander or a higher rank, and relates only to the places specified in the authorization.

Section 44(1) of the Terrorism Act 2000 states you can stop and search:

- a vehicle;
- any person in the vehicle;
- any item in or on the vehicle, or carried by the driver or a passenger.

Section 44(2) of the same Act states you can stop and search:

- a pedestrian; and/or
- anything carried by him/her.

Under s 45(1) of the Terrorism Act 2000, the power may be exercised only for the purpose of searching for articles (including a substance and any other thing (s 121 of the Terrorism Act 2000)) which could be used in connection with terrorism. You do not have to have grounds for suspecting the presence of such articles (in complete contrast to s 1 of PACE Act 1984, for example). You may seize and retain any relevant article (s 45(2) of the Terrorism Act 2000).

In searches under s 44 you:

- may detain the person or vehicle at or near where they are stopped and for a reasonable time in order to carry out the search (s 45(4));
- must seek the cooperation of the person to be searched, but reasonable force may be used if your attempts to search have been met with resistance (s 114(2));
- cannot require a person being searched to remove any clothing in public, except for a jacket, outer coat, gloves, headgear, or footwear (s 45(3));
- must provide a record of the search if a request is made (by the person who has been searched or the driver of the vehicle that has been searched) within 12 months of the incident (ss 45(5) and (6)).

If a pedestrian or the driver of a vehicle fails to stop when you require him/her to do so, or intentionally obstructs you during the course of a search, he/she commits an offence whether or not any articles which could be used in connection with terrorism are found (s 47(1) of the Terrorism Act 2000).

This offence is triable summarily only and the penalty is six months' imprisonment and/or a fine.

ACPO advice on stop and search in relation to terrorism is available at <http://www.npia.police.uk/en/docs/Stop_and_Search_in_Relation_to_Terrorism_-_2008.pdf>.

9.28.5.5   Attending a scene where there is a suspect device

Suspect devices include bombs; incendiary devices (designed to start or sustain a fire); and CBRN devices, with or without explosive triggers. Any incident involving a suspect device is most certainly an extreme case of a major or critical incident. Incidents involving CBRN devices are still rare, but they have been known. In 1995, a small and secretive Japanese sect, called AUM released small quantities of diluted Sarin (a nerve gas) inside a crowded Tokyo subway in the morning rush hour. Twelve people died and around 5,000 people required hospital treatment for their injuries. Had the gas been in concentrated form, the Japanese authorities believe that thousands could have died because of Sarin's extreme toxicity.

If any suspect device is encountered, its precise nature cannot be determined by visual means alone, and even if you could see the internal mechanism or contents you are unlikely to know what you are dealing with. The cardinal rule is: **do not touch it**. Your role (as the first police officer on the scene) in managing this ultra-critical incident is to create a very wide space around the suspect device (as wide as is practicable), and to get people out of the area. **Public safety** is your highest concern. Whilst the requirement to preserve evidence is high, this is secondary to public safety at all times. Your response will involve all the things we have looked at above, from clearing the scene to ensuring that you remain in constant communication with the force control centre. Until your force knows more about the device, it cannot determine what resources are required, and what specialist help to call in.

Bomb alerts can represent major commitments for police and other emergency service resources, and terrorists know full well that hoaxes can be just as disruptive (in the initial stages at least) as the real thing. Nonetheless, your duty is preservation of life, which means that you have to assume that every suspect device has the potential to kill and injure: you cannot afford to take chances.

BOMB ALERT is a useful mnemonic to help remind you what to do:

B	Buildings: evacuate
O	Occupants: get them out and away
M	Move people right away from the scene
B	Back off: there could be secondary devices or other targets
A	Accurate information relayed back to control
L	Locate witnesses
E	Evacuate the neighbourhood of the device
R	Rendezvous (RV) points for arriving support
T	Tape off a cordon at the most practicable distance.

As a general rule, cordons for small objects (up to briefcase size), should be a minimum of 100 metres. For larger items (up to and including cars), the cordon should be a minimum of 200 metres, and for very large objects (such as vans or heavy goods vehicles), the cordon should be a minimum of 400 metres. There are rules about the colour of cordon tapes, but do not concern yourself with this in the initial stages.

Be aware that streets crowded with buildings provide a blast with a corridor which channels its energy: personnel are safer behind 'hard cover' (such as concrete buildings) than in view of the suspected device. Do not place the public or colleagues behind or beneath windows or other glass panels, however far away from the device they might be.

To expand a little on what you should do at the scene of a suspect device (after installing the cordon and moving people away) it may be expedient to establish why the object itself is suspicious. What size and shape is it, are there visible electrical components, does it smell, and are there stains or other marks on it? Did anyone see it being installed or placed? Are there descriptions of the person(s) who placed it? What alerted people to the suspect device? Witnesses are likely to provide information relating to some of these points.

Hand-held radios or mobile phones must not be used within 10 metres of the object, while vehicle-based radios must not be used to transmit within 50 metres of the object. You must (of course) make sure that the device is not touched, handled, or lifted.

You should mark out the CAP to the object, consistent with your overriding priority of public safety. Control will also want to know the precise location of the device, especially if there is a wider evacuation going on outside your immediate cordon. You must pass as much information as possible about the object (and the whole situation) so that specialists can determine if the device is viable or not. If you carry out the above procedures correctly, you will make it much easier for the specialist support coming in after you. Lives have been saved in the past through prompt and effective action by the first officers to arrive at the scene.

9.28.5.6 Attending the scene of a bomb explosion

If you are first to arrive at a scene after a device has exploded, you should expect the kinds of chaos you associate with the disaster scenes we discussed above. There will possibly be devastation, wreckage, smoke, flames, badly injured people, dead bodies (and parts of bodies), panic, noise, and confusion. Your role is the same, in principle, as for a train crash or major road traffic accident: take charge, clear those who can walk out of the area, close off the area with a cordon, attend to the injured if you can, and remember that you are dealing with a crime scene. In addition to the CHALETS principles we discussed earlier in 9.28.1, the mnemonic ICICLE may help you to keep cool and in control:

I	Identify the source of threat or suspicion
C	Communicate all available details to force control
I	Investigate the circumstances
C	Contain the threat to people where possible
L	Lead and reassure people at the scene
E	Ensure that major incident procedures are put in hand

You will remember (probably from the newspapers and television) the disturbing scenes which follow terrorist attacks such as the destruction of the Twin Towers in New York and the July 2005 explosions in London (particularly after the explosion on the bus). Nothing prepares you for the emotional impact of witnessing such scenes; indeed, many police officer first-responders report experiencing an initial sense of helplessness at a major disaster. It all looks so chaotic, so awful—how can any action be of the slightest use? Where do you start with helping the injured (and what do you do with the bodies)? How can you clear a path through the debris, and how many people may be trapped under that collapsed building? It has been said (and in our view rightly) that what distinguishes a police officer from the general public is not his/her exercise of powers, or uniform, or knowledge of the law, but **knowing what to do in an emergency**. That professional response is what marks you out and gives you the authority and ability to take appropriate action in chaotic and dangerous situations. It does not matter whether the appropriate action is as small as giving first aid at a road traffic collision or as significant as coping with the aftermath of a terrorist bomb; what matters is that you can make a difference by bringing calmness to chaos, order to disorder, method to mayhem. Ultimately, that is your professional role and the role of your many police colleagues, in managing a major or critical incident.

TASK 30

Note your priority actions now in response to (a) a suspect CRBN device and (b) a subsequent detonation. What should you do initially and thereafter?

9.29 Answers to Tasks

TASK 1

Look at s 34(1) of the Criminal Justice Act 1972 to help with the answer.

- The health and safety of the individual is paramount—is she injured in any way?
- How drunk is she?
- What offence has she committed? Is she just drunk or drunk and disorderly?
- Is arrest necessary to prevent her from causing physical injury (to herself or others)?
- Can the matter be dealt with by another process?
- What other agencies should you involve?
- Does your force have a local agreement whereby she could be taken to an approved treatment centre for alcoholism? If so you can treat her as being in lawful custody for the purposes of the journey under s 34(1) Criminal Justice Act 1972.

TASK 2

- Introduce yourself and the station you are from.
- Explain to the person that you suspect he/she is under 18 years of age.
- Depending on the location, state to the person that he/she is in a public place or a place to which he/she has gained unlawful access.
- Make clear to the person that you wish him/her to surrender anything in his/her possession which is intoxicating liquor, and to state his/her name and address, and that failure without reasonable excuse to comply with your requirement is an offence.

TASK 3

Your own force may have staff whose responsibility it is to represent the police at applications for premises licences or renewals. If this is the case, then notify the relevant person of incidents where suspects have been drinking excessively. This will enable the licensing authority to have sufficient information in order to make an informed decision about the granting of the licence (or its renewal), or otherwise.

TASK 4

You probably considered the following:

1. There was no evidence in the description given of harm being done to a person.
2. There was no evidence in the description given of harm likely to be done to a person.
3. There was no evidence in the description given that, in the presence of a person, harm was done to their property.
4. There was no evidence in the description given of a person fearing being harmed through assault, riot, or other disturbance.

It would therefore be very difficult from the information in the description alone to prove a breach of the peace.

TASK 5

You probably considered the following:

1. You would collect evidence from the suspect and other people in the area.
2. That the suspect was aware that:
   - while he/she was in public anybody could hear or see his/her conduct or (if the behaviour took place inside a dwelling) it could be heard outside that same or another dwelling;
   - the suspect was aware that his/her conduct was unreasonable and was likely to cause harassment, alarm, or distress.

Evidence could be gathered from people in the public area at the time confirming that they felt alarmed or distressed.

3. You could provide evidence of what you saw and heard in relation to the suspect's conduct and that there were other people in the public area at the time.

TASK 6

As a police officer you can also be harassed, alarmed, or distressed, but remember that this is a question of fact to be decided in each case by the magistrates. In determining this, the magistrates may take into account the familiarity that police officers have with the words and conduct typically seen in incidents of disorderly conduct. The evidence of other people in the area is an important factor.

TASK 7

In the case of *Swanston v DPP* [1997] 161 JP 203, the incident had occurred in a very small area and the officer was within 5 feet (about 1.5 m) of the suspect. Unless the door supervisor had impaired hearing or sight, he could not have failed to understand what was said and the actions committed by the suspect. In the *Swanston* case, the prosecution proved that the suspect had the intention of causing the door supervisor to fear that violence was going to be used against him. Those facts were proved by the admissible evidence including evidence of the police officer who was a witness to the incident.

TASK 8

In *R v Plavecz* [2002] Crim LR 837, having been found guilty of affray, the defendant appealed and the court decided that affray was a public order offence and was inappropriate where the incident was essentially 'one on one'. The conviction was therefore quashed. It is doubtful therefore, given these circumstances, that an investigation for affray could be sustained, but always seek guidance from the CPS in such matters.

TASK 9

Section 6(1) of the Criminal Law Act 1977 states that any person who, without lawful authority, uses or threatens violence for the purpose of securing entry into any premises for [him/her] self or for any other person is guilty of an offence provided:

- 'that there is someone present on those premises at the time who is opposed to the entry which the violence is intended to secure'; and
- 'the person using violence or threatening the violence knows that that is the case'.

In the circumstances it appears that Sam is only hammering on the door and therefore the actions of Sam fall short of the 'violence' that is required for this offence. If Sam's actions escalate to the likelihood of damage being caused, or threats or use of violence, then the offence would be committed provided that Sam knew Charlie was on the premises and opposed the entry.

TASK 10

1. For either of these two offences to be proven, you must investigate what evidence exists to prove a course of conduct; for example, are there any letters, photographs, or eye-witness accounts?
   - If the harassment involves phone calls, you should seek the assistance of your own department to liaise with the service provider in order to obtain evidence of the calls.
   - Clarify with the victim whether there have been any previous instances of harassment or being put in fear of violence, and whether the police were informed or any civil remedy taken under s 3 of the Act.
   - Collect statements from colleagues who have seen the victim on previous occasions.
   - Collect evidence from any other witnesses and paperwork, letters, and photographs from the victim and exhibit them in a statement (see 13.3.11 below).

- Consider discussing the case with a CPS Evidence Review representative or anyone involved in the investigation in an advisory capacity.

2. If the suspect is known and a course of conduct cannot be proved but the victim has been harassed or put in fear of violence, then consider warning the suspect and recording the warning in your pocket book in the way that your force prescribes, and make sure it is recorded on your force database for future reference. This may be evidence towards proving a course of conduct in the future. Advise the victim to:

   - seek legal advice, if pursuing a civil remedy under s 3 of the Act is appropriate;
   - contact Victim Support representatives in your area;
   - contact the victim's service provider if the phone is being used to harass or put him/her in fear of violence, in order that a block can be placed on incoming 'number withheld' calls.

3. Future events can be recorded by advising the victim to keep a diary of events, to retain physical evidence (such as letters), and take photographs of any visible evidence.

4. If a course of conduct can be proved or suspected, then consideration must be given to the most appropriate course of action. If an arrest is considered, a reason for the arrest being necessary is required. The reason could be to protect a child, or to allow the prompt and effective investigation of the conduct of the person in question, or to prevent any prosecution for the offence being hindered by the disappearance of the person in question.

TASK 11

The following are factors for consideration:

- How many times has the victim been harassed by people congregating outside his own home?
- Has he asked the people to leave the area?
- What is the severity of the harassment?
- How many people are in the vicinity?
- What is their behaviour?
- What is the purpose of their gathering?
- What is the impact on the person in his home?
- Have the people causing the harassment been told on a previous occasion to leave and then subsequently returned?
- Is there sufficient evidence to investigate the offence, or can the situation be better resolved in its early stages by directing the people to leave the area?

TASK 12

The answers are:

1. Racial group and religious group
2. Not a racial group but a religious one
3. Not a racial group but a religious one
4. Racial group but not a religious one.

TASK 13

A constable in uniform may require a person to give his or her name and address if the constable has reason to believe that a person has been acting (or is acting) in an anti-social manner (within the meaning of s 1 of the Crime and Disorder Act 1998 (which deals with anti-social behaviour orders)). This power is given under s 50(1) of the Police Reform Act 2002.

Further, s 50(2) states that an offence is committed by any person who:

   (a) fails to give [his or her] name and address when required to do so under subsection (1), or
   (b) gives a false or inaccurate name or address in response to a requirement under that subsection.

TASK 14

Since the young people in the group appear to be local residents, you will only be able to require the people in the group to disperse immediately or by a time as you may specify. As they are all local residents, you will not be able to prohibit them from returning within 24 hours. Even though only one of the group was actually apparently intimidating a member of the public, you have the power to disperse the whole group as two or more persons were present.

TASK 15

1. There are likely to be policy agreements with local Social Services and the Healthcare Trusts.
2. (a) A dynamic risk assessment of the situation should be made first. Can you safely enter the room or should you seek the assistance of other officers with appropriate personal safety equipment? Entrance can be gained by seeking the permission of the parents/owners of the property to unscrew the door handle, withdrawing the bar sufficiently to enable you to turn the handle from your side of the door and using the element of surprise to enter the room safely.
   (b) Does the person want to go voluntarily to hospital or do you need to call an approved social worker to begin the process of determining if the person can be taken into hospital under one of the sections within the Mental Health Act 1983?

TASK 16

The answers are as follows:

1b, 2c, 3d, 4a, 5a, 6fgh, 7e, 8i.

TASK 17

You probably considered the following:

1. Do the occupants have a reasonable excuse for the presence of the items?
2. Who do the items belong to?
3. Will you be preventing a crime from taking place if you investigate the matter further?
4. How will you progress this matter further? Do the circumstances (and a reason to make an arrest) exist?
5. Can you deal with the matter by reporting the suspect?

TASK 18

You probably considered the following:

1. Is Ahmed above the age of criminal responsibility?
2. How is Ahmed carrying the knife?
3. What type of knife is Ahmed in possession of?
4. Has it been made, adapted, or intended to cause injury?
5. How long has Ahmed carried the knife?
6. Will Ahmed give you the knife or do you need to use a power of search?

TASK 19

As a result of the shootings at Hungerford on 12 August 1987, it was considered that certain firearms were so dangerous that they should be classified as prohibited weapons. These include self-loading and pump-action rifles (other than those chambered for .22 rim-fire), and certain self-loading and pump-action shotguns (see the White Paper *Firearms Act 1968: Proposals for Reform* (Cm 261, 1987) and the amendment to the 1968 Act which was effected by s 1 of the Firearms (Amendment) Act 1988). Similarly the 1968 Act was also amended so as to extend the level of control on certain shotguns so that a firearm certificate was required.

TASK 20

1. Any lethal barrelled weapon of any description from which any shot, bullet, or other missile can be discharged. This includes a prohibited weapon (whether it is a lethal weapon or not), any component part of such a lethal or prohibited weapon, and any accessory designed or adapted to diminish the noise or flash caused by firing any such weapon.
2. You may demand the production of the relevant s 1 firearm or shotgun certificate from any person whom you believe to be in possession of a s 1 firearm (or ammunition) or a shotgun.
3. When you have reasonable cause to suspect a person of having a firearm in a public place (with or without ammunition), or to be committing (or be about to commit) an offence relevant to the Firearms Act 1968, anywhere other than in a public place.
4. All firearms except shotguns, prohibited weapons, air weapons (unless 'specially dangerous'), or imitation firearms (unless converted).
5. Any ammunition for a firearm except:

   - cartridges containing five or more shot, none of which exceeds .36 inch in diameter;
   - ammunition for an air gun, air rifle, or air pistol;
   - blank cartridges not more than 1 inch in diameter.
6. A smooth-bore gun which:

   - has a barrel not less than 60.96 cm long;
   - has a barrel bore not exceeding 5.08 cm;
   - has either no magazine or a non-detachable magazine incapable of holding more than two cartridges;
   - is not a revolver gun.

TASK 21

1. It is an offence for a person under the age of 17 to have an air weapon (or ammunition for an air weapon) with him or her. There are exceptions. For example, it is not an offence for the person 14 years or over to possess the air weapon on private premises with the consent of the occupier, and he/she does not have to be supervised.

However, under s 21A of the Firearms Act 1968 a person commits an offence if he/she:

   (a) has an air weapon on any premises and
   (b) uses it for firing a missile beyond those premises.

2. A person commits an offence if, without lawful authority or reasonable excuse, he/she has with him/her in a public place any loaded or unloaded air weapon (s 19, Firearms Act 1968).

TASK 22

Section 19 of the Firearms Act 1968 states that a person commits an offence if, without lawful authority or reasonable excuse (the proof whereof lies on him/her), he/she has with him/her, in a public place, an imitation firearm.

TASK 23

1. False. In the Act, 'suffering' means physical or mental suffering and related expressions shall be construed accordingly.
2. Section 2 states an animal is protected if it is:

   - of a kind which is commonly domesticated in the British Islands;
   - under control of humankind whether on a permanent or temporary basis; or
   - not living in a wild state.

3. Section 19 does not authorize entry to any part of premises which is used as a private dwelling. Under these circumstances a warrant will need to be obtained under section 19(4).

4. You may enter and search any premises to arrest any person you reasonably suspect of committing an offence under s 4 Animal Welfare Act 2006 using s 17 of the PACE Act 1984 (see 7.9 above). Always follow your force policy in relation to using force to gain entry in such circumstances.

TASK 24

1. The boy needs regular medication; has he taken that medication with him? Are there factors which will make his medical condition worse (such as dust allergies or stress-induced attacks of asthma)? Can the condition be life-threatening in any way? Is his shotgun (and any other weapons on the farm) accounted for? If not, what is missing? Can an estimate be made of how much ammunition may have gone missing? How was the boy able to leave the house apparently normally for school without anyone noticing that he might be carrying a gun? Has the boy mentioned any particular individuals in connection with the apparent bullying at school? Has the boy said anything about revenge? What about the quarrel with the father? Was it more violent or tense than the usual family falling-out? Had the boy said anything to indicate that he contemplated any further action (such as saying 'I'll get even, you wait!' or 'I'll make you sorry for this')? What occasioned his depression and anxiety? Was he struggling with his school work? Are exams imminent or results due? Has he a close companion with whom he has had a quarrel? Has he ever talked about suicide or mentioned that, for example, life was not worth living? Does he have a religious belief or strong ethical principles? Has he taken drugs? Has he ever been in trouble with the police?

2. ACPO guidance can be found at
<www.acpo.police.uk/asp/policies/Data/missing_persons_2005_24x02x05.pdf >.

TASK 25

Your answers could well have been 'I do not know' which would have been entirely understandable. (In fact your trainers might be more worried if you claim already to know the answers to these questions.) We aim to go on to provide you with some general principles and some possible answers.

TASK 26

Your list could read something like this:

- clear the immediate scene;
- note any injuries to anyone;
- ensure that the area around the house (the 'stronghold') is evacuated and 'sterile';
- move people as far from the scene as possible;
- continue to ask for information on what has happened;
- calm the hysterical or over-excited;
- create one way into the incident and one way out;
- clear a wide area to receive the support which is coming (keep arriving vehicles away from the scene itself);
- keep in constant communication with your control centre, making sure that they know what is happening and what you are doing;
- use your colleague proactively to control the immediate area, to talk to witnesses, to communicate with the incoming support;
- find out all you can about the alleged hostage-taker, including name and any relationship with anyone likely to be inside the house with him;
- make notes: keep a careful log of what has taken place to the best of your knowledge, recording names and addresses of witnesses (see 12.6 below);

- if it is safe to do so, try to open a dialogue with the hostage-taker, making sure that he understands that you are a police officer;
- emphasize that your aim is to end this incident peacefully and without anyone getting hurt.

Compare this list to the one you will be probably be given during your training. No doubt there will be many points in common.

TASK 27

The usual model taught during police training adopts a six-stage process, starting with defining the problem:

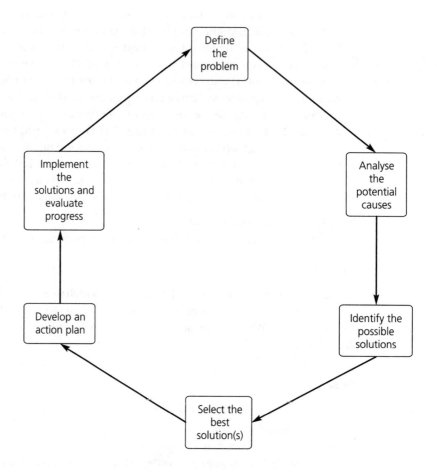

TASK 28

The 'Gold, Silver, Bronze' system has come under critical scrutiny in recent years. In his report into the investigation of the Soham murders, Sir Ronnie Flanagan made the following observation:

> Ironically, the overlaying of the Gold, Silver and Bronze command structure on this operation contributed to a lack of clarity of command of the incident, particularly in relation to the role of the SIO and was subject to comment in the internal review (Flanagan, 2004, p 13).

The report also contained a recommendation that the system when applied to homicide should be clarified.

We list possible problems below the task.

TASK 29

We were not exaggerating when we discussed the extent of media interest earlier. In the case of the Watford train crash in 1996, Hertfordshire police reported that media interest in the incident commenced within five minutes of the crash happening (Moses, 1997).

TASK 30

(a) You should remember from the discussion earlier that your role does not include identifying the type of device. Your role is to contain the scene, evacuate anyone within the cordon, and manage the site until help arrives. You should be communicating to the force control centre all that you see and learn, including location of the device and its description.

(b) Think about secondary devices, containment, and the ICICLE principles.

Further advice from the UK Government concerning CBRN and 'aimed at those responsible for the safety of others in businesses and other public/private sector organisations' may be found in the 2009 NPIA document *Guidance on Emergency Procedures* (available at: <www.acpo.police.uk/asp/policies/Data/Emergency Procedures 202009.pdf>).

10 | Criminal Law and Procedure

10.1   Chapter Briefing

This chapter examines the law and procedure concerned with a number of criminal offences. We present the basic knowledge of the criminal law required by student police officers whilst undertaking initial training.

10.1.1   Aim of the Chapter

The aim of this chapter is to introduce you to the legislation and police practice associated with the application of the criminal law and the investigation of crime. You are likely to encounter this aspect of policing whilst undertaking Supervised and Independent Patrol and whilst studying the IPLDP LPG modules.

This chapter will enable you to:

- understand the legislation surrounding theft, acts of violence and cruelty, and fraud;
- identify a number of sexual offences;
- understand some of the law surrounding criminal damage and criminal attempts;
- develop the underpinning knowledge required for a number of NOS elements, entries for your Learning Diary Phase 3, and a CAR of your SOLAP.

10.1.2 Police Action Checklist

This chapter will assist in meeting the following requirements of the Police Action Checklist under the Investigation heading: namely, that you are able to:

- conduct the initial investigation and report of volume crime according to Local/National Policing Plans;
- conduct the initial investigation and report in relation to a child protection and/or vulnerable person incident.

10.1.3 National Occupational Standards

This chapter will provide you with some of the knowledge required to demonstrate aspects of the following NOS elements:

National Occupational Standards Elements

CD1.1   Gather information and plan a response
CD1.2   Respond to incidents
CI101.1 Conduct priority and volume investigations

10.1.4 IPLDP Phases and Modules

This chapter will provide you with resources to support the following Operational Modules, LPGs, and Phases of the IPLDP:

OP 3   Respond to incidents, conduct and evaluate investigations
LPG 1.1 Crime
Phase 3 Supervised Patrol

As we noted in Chapter 2, we cover in this Handbook the material which we believe is of critical importance to you at this stage of your policing career. This means that the Handbook does not correspond exactly with the current IPLDP syllabus. For example, a compulsory IPLDP subject is the law contained within s 70 of the Sexual Offences Act 2003 concerned with the offence of 'sexual penetration of a corpse'. We judge that you are unlikely to require knowledge of this kind of detail at this stage of your training. On the other hand, 'aggravated burglary' is an optional subject within IPLDP but we include it in this Handbook because we think it important to understand the difference between the basic offence of burglary and its aggravated form. Note, however, that the IPLDP curriculum is subject to periodic 'maintenance' and hence you should check with your force what aspects of the criminal law and police procedure you need to know and be familiar with.

10.1.5 SOLAP

The contents of this chapter are relevant to the 'knowledge' evidence requirement of CAR CD1.

Learning Diary Phases

The contents of this chapter may provide you with stimulus material for completion of your Learning Diary (Phase 3) and the 'Crime' heading in particular.

10.2 Introduction

In this chapter, we look at your role as a student police officer in the application of the criminal law. We must repeat that, although this Handbook will provide you with the essence of the individual law and some interpretations (both academic and from case law or precedent), there is no substitute for reading and understanding the law itself.

The professionalism of your police force tends to be judged on the effectiveness of its investigation and detection of crimes such as theft, robbery, vehicle crime, other types of volume crime, drugs crimes, violent crime, and sexual crime. The data show a decrease in the numbers of most types of reported crime over the past decade, and the total number of crimes has fallen over recent years. The British Crime Survey (2008, p 21) reports that:

> Since peaking in 1995, BCS [British Crime Survey] crime has fallen by 48 per cent, representing over nine million fewer crimes. Both BCS overall crime and the risk of victimisation are now at their lowest ever levels since the first BCS results in 1981.

Unfortunately, although your force's performance ought perhaps to have a direct impact on public confidence in the police and on the public's fear of crime, repeated surveys show that this is not the case. We considered some of the reasons for this in 5.15.4.2 above. Recently, this disparity between perception and actual risks from crime has featured within a more general debate over the role the police should play in reassuring the public concerning their personal safety and that of their communities. For example, the Home Office's National Community Safety Plan describes a specific objective to increase community confidence as well as a greater emphasis on countering serious crime.

10.3 Theft

Theft is a so-called 'volume crime'. Of all the dishonest criminal offences you will deal with, theft will probably be the most common. The primary source of legislation relating to theft is to be found in ss 1–6 of the Theft Act 1968. The information here is therefore relevant to the PAC requirement that you conduct the Initial Investigation and Report of Volume Crime according to National/Local Policing Plans.

You are likely to encounter theft early on in your career as a student police officer. Offences of theft include shoplifting and stealing from an employer, as well as a number of other similar crimes. There are many legal complexities surrounding theft and we will simply examine the basic principles involved. However, it is worth clarifying at this point two particular examples of theft that occur commonly but are examined separately in this Handbook. These are robbery (theft from a person, accompanied by violence or the threat of violence) and burglary (theft or the intention of theft from a building); these are covered in 10.4 and 10.5 below.

10.3.1 The Definition of Theft

Section 1 of the Theft Act 1968 states that a person is guilty of theft if he/she 'dishonestly [appropriates] property'. We examine each of the concepts of dishonesty, appropriation, and property in turn.

10.3.1.1 Dishonesty

Dishonesty is not defined by the Act, but s 2(1) of the Theft Act 1968 defines where a person will **not** be treated as dishonest. The person is not acting dishonestly if he/she believes:

- that he/she had the lawful right to take the item (for example a person mistakenly taking the wrong coat in a changing room believing it was his or her own);
- that he/she would have had the owner's consent if the owner had known the circumstances (for example a person's lawnmower breaks down and, whilst looking after the property of the neighbour who is on holiday, he/she takes the neighbour's);
- that the owner cannot be discovered by taking reasonable steps (for example a person finds cash in the street).

But s 2(2) of the Theft Act 1968 states that a person may be treated as dishonest even though he/she was willing to pay for the property (for example a person wants to buy a particular garden ornament, but the shopkeeper cannot be found, so the person takes the ornament and leaves behind what he/she thinks it is worth in money). In the end, a court must decide if a person acted dishonestly or not.

10.3.1.2 Appropriation

With reference to theft, the term **appropriate** is given the following meaning in the Theft Act 1968, s 3(1):

- assuming the rights of an owner of property by stealing it (for example, by shoplifting); or
- obtaining property innocently and later keeping it and using it as his or her own (for example hiring a piece of machinery and not returning it).

However, when an innocent purchaser pays the right price to a person who is selling some kind of property which later turns out to be stolen, the innocent purchaser will not have committed theft. For example, if a person buys a second-hand bicycle in good faith and then discovers it is stolen, the innocent purchaser will not have committed theft. This will be a matter for the civil court to decide (s 3(2), Theft Act 1968).

10.3.1.3 Property

The definition of **property** (s 4, Theft Act 1968) is not straightforward. Property is:

- money;
- personal property, for example personal effects and pets;
- real property, for example land and things forming part of the land, such as plants and buildings. However, land can only be stolen:
    - (a) by a trustee (someone who has the legal control over the land) for example during its transfer in some kind of a legal process
    - (b) by persons who do not own the land, for example by removing turf, top soil, or digging up cultivated trees and shrubs
    - (c) by tenants, for example by removing fixtures and fittings;
- things in action, for example patents, copyrights, and trademarks;
- plants or fungi growing wild, but only if they are picked for sale, reward, or a commercial purpose (but always consider other legislation that might prohibit such activities such as the Wildlife and Countryside Act 1981);
- wild creatures, but only if they are tamed and have not been lost or abandoned since they were kept in captivity;
- tangible property, for example gas.

(Note that electricity is not legally property, so it cannot be stolen: see 10.10 below.)

10.3.2   Summary of Theft

So, a person is guilty of theft if he/she **dishonestly appropriates property:**

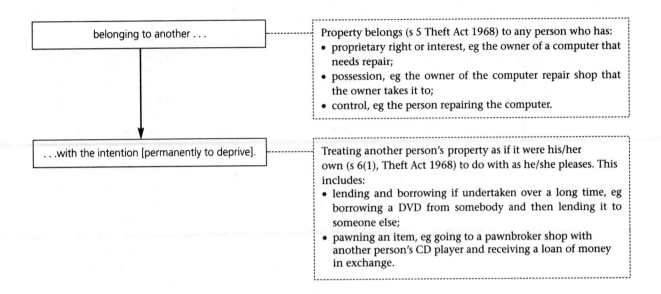

The offence of theft is triable either way and the penalty is:

- summarily: six months' imprisonment and/or a fine;
- on indictment: seven years' imprisonment.

TASK 1

Now that you know what constitutes a theft, think of three incidents of theft that you are aware of, either through the media or other means, and try and identify the elements of theft within each of those incidents.

10.4   Robbery

Robbery is the act of stealing from a person whilst using (or threatening the use of) force or violence. It is an aggravated form of the primary offence of theft and therefore, for robbery to be proved, theft has to be proved first. Robbery is covered in s 8 of the Theft Act 1968.

First, note that a robbery must involve at least one of the following elements:

- force or a threat of force is used on any person, immediately before, at the time of the theft, or in order to carry out the theft; or
- any person is 'put in fear' that force will be used to carry out a theft.

There are two main ways of establishing the 'put in fear' element of the offence:

- Actually to put in fear: this can be proved from the victim's statement. The fear of being subjected to force must be genuine. The fear could be evidenced by what he/she saw the suspect do and the way that made the victim feel as a result.
- To seek to put in fear: the state of mind of the offender is what is important, and this could be evidenced from the suspect's statement. The suspect must seek to put some person in fear of force. However, it is not necessary to prove that any person was actually put in fear; if the victim is not intimidated by the suspect, it is enough that the suspect tried to frighten the victim. This might be proved by either the evidence of other witnesses or circumstantial evidence, such as the suspect wielding an offensive weapon.

The offence of robbery is defined by s 8(1) of the Theft Act 1968 which states that a person is guilty of robbery if:

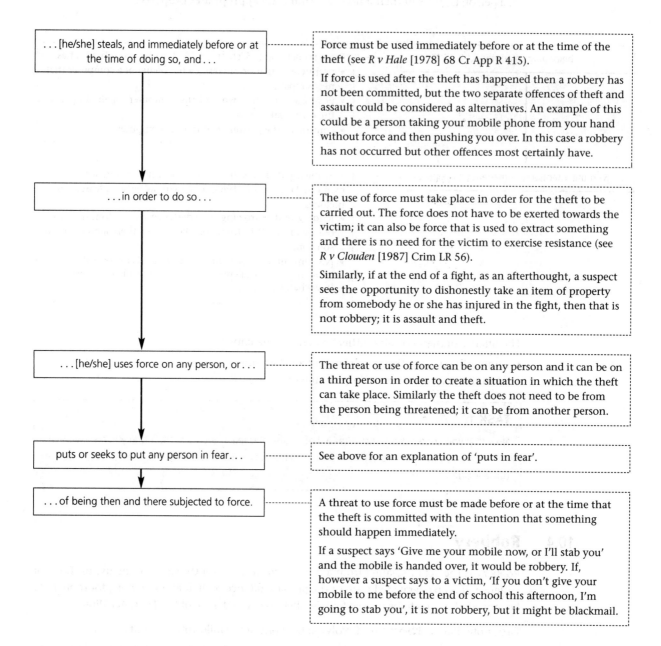

... [he/she] steals, and immediately before or at the time of doing so, and ...

Force must be used immediately before or at the time of the theft (see *R v Hale* [1978] 68 Cr App R 415).

If force is used after the theft has happened then a robbery has not been committed, but the two separate offences of theft and assault could be considered as alternatives. An example of this could be a person taking your mobile phone from your hand without force and then pushing you over. In this case a robbery has not occurred but other offences most certainly have.

... in order to do so ...

The use of force must take place in order for the theft to be carried out. The force does not have to be exerted towards the victim; it can also be force that is used to extract something and there is no need for the victim to exercise resistance (see *R v Clouden* [1987] Crim LR 56).

Similarly, if at the end of a fight, as an afterthought, a suspect sees the opportunity to dishonestly take an item of property from somebody he or she has injured in the fight, then that is not robbery; it is assault and theft.

... [he/she] uses force on any person, or ...

The threat or use of force can be on any person and it can be on a third person in order to create a situation in which the theft can take place. Similarly the theft does not need to be from the person being threatened; it can be from another person.

puts or seeks to put any person in fear ...

See above for an explanation of 'puts in fear'.

... of being then and there subjected to force.

A threat to use force must be made before or at the time that the theft is committed with the intention that something should happen immediately.

If a suspect says 'Give me your mobile now, or I'll stab you' and the mobile is handed over, it would be robbery. If, however a suspect says to a victim, 'If you don't give your mobile to me before the end of school this afternoon, I'm going to stab you', it is not robbery, but it might be blackmail.

The offence of robbery is triable by indictment only and the maximum penalty is life imprisonment.

TASK 2

Chris is walking in her local shopping centre when she accidentally drops a bag full of shopping. Jo, who is nearby, grabs the dropped bag and makes off, but the bag breaks, spilling all its contents onto the floor of the shopping centre. Throwing down the empty bag, Jo picks up one of the items from the dropped bag which is on the ground, changes direction quickly and runs into Chris causing her to fall over heavily and break her arm. Has Jo committed the offence of robbery?

10.5 Burglary and Trespassing

Burglary is a so-called 'volume crime' and you will undoubtedly encounter crimes of burglary whilst on Supervised and Independent Patrol. Indeed, burglary may feature as one of your case studies during Phase 3 of the IPLDP (if your force uses that approach).

Despite being a volume crime, burglary is a serious offence; aggravated burglary (see 10.5.4 below), for example, carries a maximum sentence of life imprisonment. There is also the phenomenon of distraction burglary (in some forces called 'burglary by artifice') where entry is gained to the home of a person (usually an elderly person) by an offender pretending to be an official such as the gasman.

The legislation concerning burglary is to be found in ss 9–10 of the Theft Act 1968. We look separately at the basic offence of burglary, then at aggravated burglary, and finally at various aspects of trespass associated with this type of crime.

10.5.1 The Basic Offence of Burglary

The basic offence of burglary is set out in s 9 of the Theft Act 1968 which states that a person is guilty of burglary if:

(a) [he/she] enters any building or part of a building as a trespasser and with intent to commit any such offence as is mentioned in subsection 2 below; or
(b) having entered into any building or part of a building as a trespasser [he/she] steals or attempts to steal anything in the building or that part of it or inflicts or attempts to inflict on any person therein any grievous bodily harm.

The subsection 2 offences (referred to in the quoted law above) are listed in s 9(2) of the Theft Act 1968. They are:

- 'stealing anything in the building or part of a building in question' or
- 'inflicting on any person therein any grievous bodily harm' (the entry has to be with intent to inflict GBH and thus enough evidence to satisfy a charge under s 18 of the Offences Against the Person Act 1861 is required (see 10.15 and 10.16 below)) or
- 'doing unlawful damage to the building or anything therein' (see 10.21 below and s 9(2) of the Theft Act 1968).

Note that part (a) offences involve a person entering a building with the **intent** to steal or cause injury or damage (but these actions do not actually need to be carried out). For part (b) offences, the theft or injury must be **carried out** or at least attempted.

10.5.2 Part (a) Burglary

Certain terms, such as 'entry', 'building', and 'intent' need to be carefully defined in order to fully appreciate the range of activities that might count as burglary under s 9(1)(a) of the Theft Act 1968.

10.5.2.1 Entry as a trespasser

Trespass means entering without the consent of the owner. **Entry** can be gained in a number of clearly defined ways:

- **In person**, by walking or climbing into a building, either completely or by inserting a body part (such as an arm or a leg) through a window or letter box. However, there must be more than minimal insertion; sliding a hand between a window and frame from the outside of a building in order to release the catch would be insufficient.
- **Using a tool or article** as an extension of the human body to carry out one of the relevant offences. In these circumstances no part of the body needs to be inserted, only the article that is being used. However, the article must be used for more than just gaining entry. Using a crowbar just to prise open a door would not qualify as the full offence, but a length of garden

cane pushed through the letter box of a shop to hook a scarf from a display would qualify as the full offence.

- **Using a blameless accomplice** in a similar way to using an article as an extension of the suspect's body. Here, for example, a child below the age of criminal responsibility (ten years of age) could be lifted through a small window to obtain property from inside. On the other hand, if the child is used for the purposes of preparing an entry point for the burglar only and nothing is stolen, then the full offence is not committed; it has only been attempted.

Trespass involves a person entering a building or part of a building (for the purpose of committing one of the relevant offences) in one of the following ways:

- **Entering a building** for a purpose other than the intended purpose of that building, for example going into a shop with the intention to steal (rather than an intent to browse or buy).
- **Entering by some kind of deception**, for example pretending to represent a utility company for the purpose of reading a meter and being invited into the building ('burglary by artifice', referred to earlier).
- **Crossing over a demarcation line** of some kind, unlawfully and without invitation or permission, whether or not the owner knows he/she is trespassing.

The person must have guilty knowledge (*mens rea*: see 5.10 above) that what he/she is doing amounts to trespass, or alternatively, not care about whether they are trespassing or not.

(Image © Zoe Lawton-Barrett)

Burglary involves entering a building as a trespasser

10.5.2.2 Building or part of a building

The term 'building' is used within the Theft Act, but is not defined. Details on the definitions of other places and locations are provided in 7.2.1 above.

The meaning of 'a building' is reasonably well established through case law:

- building is an ordinary word, which is a matter of fact (*Brutus v Cozens* [1973] AC 854, 861);
- 'a structure of considerable size and intended to be permanent or at least to endure for a considerable time' (*Stevens v Gourley* (1859) 7 CBNS 99);

- an unfinished building becomes a building when it reaches a point at which it has all its walls and a roof, because 'a building need not necessarily be a completed structure; it is sufficient that it should be a connected and entire structure' (Judge Lush in *R v Manning & Rogers* (1871) CA).

Examples of buildings other than houses include garages and garden sheds, but see your force policy or procedure for an interpretation of burglary from different types of buildings.

A **dwelling** is defined within the Theft Act as an inhabited building or a vehicle or vessel which, at the time of the offence, is inhabited (irrespective of whether or not the person who occupies the vehicle/vessel is present at the time of the burglary). For example, a houseboat which is moored alongside a river bank, and is inhabited by its owners, is regarded as a building for the purposes of the Theft Act 1968. Similarly, a motor home or caravan, if inhabited during a holiday, is a building (though it is not regarded as a building when parked and empty during the winter). However, even during the holiday season and inhabited, a tent would not be included, since it is not a semi-permanent structure.

This legislation also covers the circumstances where a person is in a building lawfully but enters a part of it that he/she is not meant to enter. For example:

- a customer who leaves the front of a shop where purchases take place and walks through to the back, past a sign clearly stating 'Staff Only—No Unauthorized Entry' and into a storeroom;
- a customer in a pub who hides behind the bar at closing time;
- a student at evening classes in an adult education centre who, during a break in lessons, goes into the administrative offices of the centre which are only staffed during the day.

10.5.2.3 Intent

The suspect must intend to commit certain specified offences. The intent can be proved in a number of ways or in combination:

- during the interview of the suspect when he/she admits to having guilty knowledge or criminal intent to commit the offence;
- during the interview of other suspects involved in committing the offence, who name their accomplices and the part they played in its commission;
- circumstantial evidence.

Circumstantial evidence may include:

- witness statements;
- observations of the arresting officer(s) in relation to the suspect's proximity to the crime scene when he/she was arrested;
- the retrieval of stolen property from the crime scene, subsequently found in the possession of the suspect when arrested;
- the results of forensic examination of the suspect's clothes indicating he/she was present at the crime scene, or the retrieval of fingerprint evidence demonstrating the same (see 8.12 above and 13.5 below).

In summary, for a part (a) burglary, the suspect does not actually need to have committed any of the acts described below.

10.5.3 Part (b) Burglary

Under s 9(1)(b) of the Theft Act 1968, burglary involves acts (or attempted acts) of theft or injury committed by a trespasser:

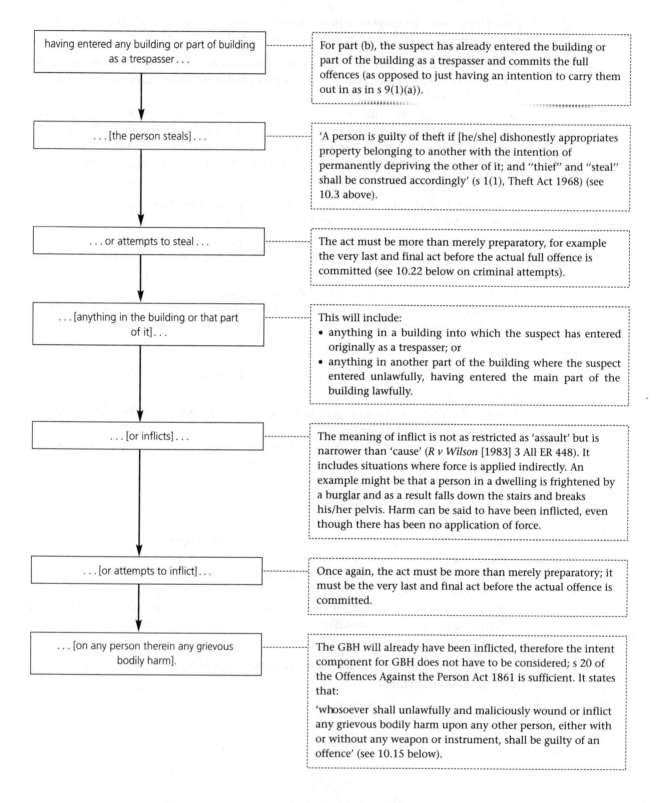

having entered any building or part of building as a trespasser . . .

For part (b), the suspect has already entered the building or part of the building as a trespasser and commits the full offences (as opposed to just having an intention to carry them out in as in s 9(1)(a)).

. . . [the person steals] . . .

'A person is guilty of theft if [he/she] dishonestly appropriates property belonging to another with the intention of permanently depriving the other of it; and "thief" and "steal" shall be construed accordingly' (s 1(1), Theft Act 1968) (see 10.3 above).

. . . or attempts to steal . . .

The act must be more than merely preparatory, for example the very last and final act before the actual full offence is committed (see 10.22 below on criminal attempts).

. . . [anything in the building or that part of it] . . .

This will include:
• anything in a building into which the suspect has entered originally as a trespasser; or
• anything in another part of the building where the suspect entered unlawfully, having entered the main part of the building lawfully.

. . . [or inflicts] . . .

The meaning of inflict is not as restricted as 'assault' but is narrower than 'cause' (*R v Wilson* [1983] 3 All ER 448). It includes situations where force is applied indirectly. An example might be that a person in a dwelling is frightened by a burglar and as a result falls down the stairs and breaks his/her pelvis. Harm can be said to have been inflicted, even though there has been no application of force.

. . . [or attempts to inflict] . . .

Once again, the act must be more than merely preparatory; it must be the very last and final act before the actual offence is committed.

. . . [on any person therein any grievous bodily harm].

The GBH will already have been inflicted, therefore the intent component for GBH does not have to be considered; s 20 of the Offences Against the Person Act 1861 is sufficient. It states that:

'whosoever shall unlawfully and maliciously wound or inflict any grievous bodily harm upon any other person, either with or without any weapon or instrument, shall be guilty of an offence' (see 10.15 below).

This offence is triable either way and the penalty is:

• summarily: six months' imprisonment and/or a fine;
• on indictment: 10 years' imprisonment (14 years' imprisonment if the building or part of the building was a dwelling) and 3 years' minimum imprisonment on conviction for a third domestic burglary.

10.5.4 Aggravated Burglary

Aggravated burglary (s 10, Theft Act 1968) is a more serious offence than burglary, and may involve the use of weapons or explosives. The types of weapon or explosive (articles) covered by this legislation are shown in the table below.

Articles within the definition of aggravated burglary

Article	Details	Theft Act 1968
Firearm	Includes an airgun or air pistol (see 9.23 above).	s 10(1)(a)
Imitation firearm	Anything which has the appearance of being a firearm, whether capable of being discharged or not (see 9.25 above).	s 10(1)(a)
Weapon of offence	Any article made or adapted for use for causing injury to or incapacitating a person, or intended by the person having it with him for such use (see 9.19 above).	s 10(1)(b)
Explosive	Any article manufactured for the purpose of producing a practical effect by explosion, or intended by the person having it with [him/her] for that purpose.	s 10(1)(c)

A person commits an offence of aggravated burglary if he/she:

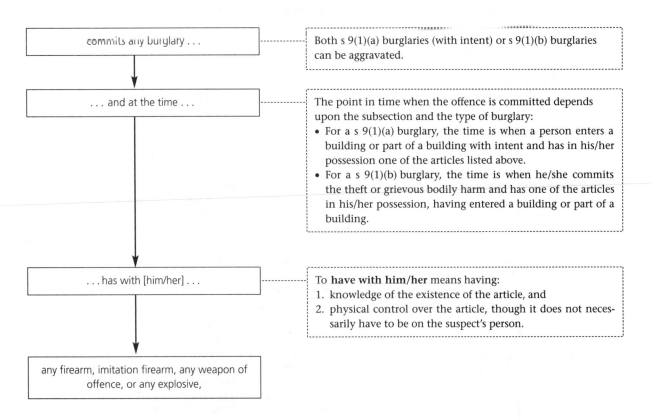

This offence is triable by indictment only and the penalty is life imprisonment.

10.5.4.1 Trespassing with a weapon of offence

If the suspect has no criminal intention other than trespassing with a weapon, he/she still commits an offence. To commit this offence, the entry must have been as a trespasser. Therefore a person will not commit this offence having innocently entered but then subsequently been asked to leave, even if he/she possesses the weapon of offence. Section 8 of the Criminal Law Act 1977 states:

> A person who is on any premises as a trespasser, after having entered as such, is guilty of an offence if, without lawful authority or reasonable excuse, [he/she] has with [him/her] on the premises any weapon of offence.

This offence is triable summarily and the penalty is three months' imprisonment and/or a fine.

10.5.5 Trespassing with an Intent to Commit a Sexual Offence

This offence is covered under s 63 of the Sexual Offences Act 2003. The offender must:

- be on premises or land without the owner's or the occupier's consent (ie trespassing);
- know that he/she is trespassing (or be reckless as to whether he/she is trespassing);
- intend to commit a sexual offence.

It is immaterial whether any sexual offence is actually committed. Proof of the intent might include statements from the offender or intended victim, or items seized from the offender at the scene (such as a knife). The intention to commit the sexual offence can be formed at any time the suspect is trespassing, for example before entering the premises, or while on the premises (having entered without any intention to commit a sexual offence).

This offence is triable either way and the penalty is:

- summarily: six months' imprisonment and/or a fine not exceeding the statutory maximum;
- on indictment: ten years' imprisonment.

10.5.6 Vagrancy and Trespassing

Where a suspect is found on enclosed premises or land, perhaps preparing to commit a burglary or theft, he/she can be investigated for offences under the Vagrancy Act 1824. It may also be useful at this point to read 9.14 above about trespass.

Section 4 of the Vagrancy Act 1824 states it is an offence for every person found:

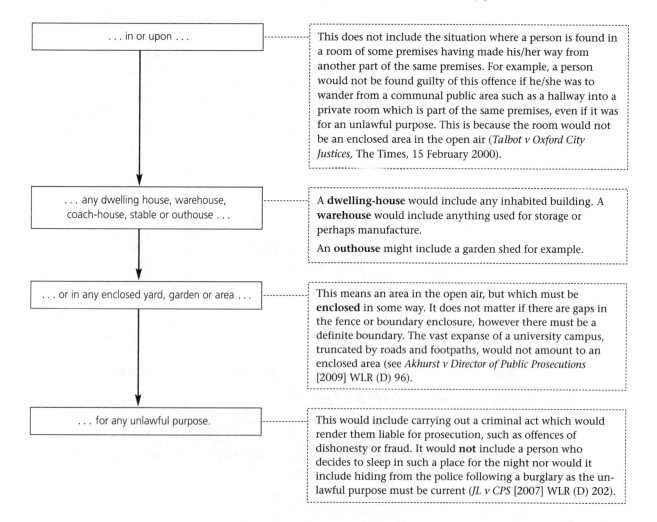

This offence is triable summarily and the penalty is three months' imprisonment and/or a fine.

TASK 3

In which of the cases set out below has burglary been committed? Give reasons for your answers.

(a) On the way home from a nightclub in the early hours of the morning, Jo walks through an industrial estate where there are a number of storage warehouses. She decides to go into one of the warehouses without permission, through an open door, with the intention of finding somewhere to sleep for the night. Having entered the warehouse, she forces open a door to another room and in so doing damages the lock. Once inside the room, she switches on an electric fire to keep warm and falls asleep until awoken by a security guard patrolling the industrial estate.

(b) Terry enters a house as a trespasser with intent to steal small items of electrical equipment for which there is a demand at local car boot sales. While he is on the premises, and as a precaution against capture, he takes a screwdriver from a drawer underneath the stairs where some tools are kept and continues the search for electrical goods, still with the screwdriver. Twenty minutes later, the occupier returns and Terry stabs her, causing serious injury. (Consider only the offences relating to burglary here.)

10.6 Vehicle Crime

Every year thousands of cars are stolen in England and Wales. Where do they go and why are they stolen? How do we identify stolen vehicles? Here we examine some of the legal aspects and police procedures surrounding a number of vehicle crimes.

10.6.1 Why are Cars Stolen?

There are a number of possible reasons why cars are stolen:

Reasons for Car Theft

Joyriding	Cars are stolen to be used for a usually brief period of excitement and as a means of transport. However, joyriders often abandon and set alight cars they have stolen, possibly in order to destroy forensic evidence.
Parts	After it reaches a certain age, the overall value of a vehicle is often much higher if it is broken down into parts.
Insurance claims	The cost of repairing or maintaining a vehicle leads some people to fraudulently claim that their vehicle has been stolen (or they actually get somebody to 'steal' it), so that the owner can claim on the insurance.
Export	For some vehicles there is a ready market in other countries, so these vehicles are either driven or shipped out through UK ports.

10.6.2 Innocent Purchase of a Stolen Vehicle

There are a number of ways in which an innocent purchaser could take possession of a stolen vehicle. The most common method is:

1. The thief obtains the identifying features of a vehicle (see below) that has been declared uneconomical to repair (see below regarding DVLA V23 form).
2. The thief steals a similar vehicle.
3. The thief removes the identifying features from the stolen vehicle and replaces them with those from the badly damaged vehicle.
4. The stolen vehicle (with its new identity) is then sold to an innocent purchaser.

A **V23 form** is used either by insurance companies to notify the DVLA about a vehicle when the company makes a total loss payment on a vehicle, or by a police officer to make a report on a vehicle written off in an accident. These vehicles, however, may subsequently be repaired and used on the roads.

10.6.3   The Identifying Features of a Vehicle

Vehicles normally have a number of identifying features unique to each vehicle. Consider using the police mnemonic VICE to help you recall the identifying features of a vehicle:

V **V**ehicle Identification Number (VIN)	The 17-character VIN unique to that vehicle is on a metal plate attached to a part of the vehicle not normally subject to replacement, and in a conspicuous and readily accessible position. All vehicles used on or after 1 April 1980 have such a plate.
I **I**ndex number or registration plate	All mechanically propelled vehicles used on public roads require a registration mark (number).
C **C**hassis number (same as VIN)	All vehicles used on or after 1 April 1980 will have their 17-character VIN (see above) stamped into the chassis or frame of the car.
E **E**ngine number	Not always as easy to find as the VIN since engine numbers are often tucked away in locations most easily seen when (or if) the engine is taken out of the vehicle. Engines are also sometimes replaced, so the fact that you cannot see an engine number should not in itself be a cause for suspicion.

If you have difficulty finding the identifying features on a vehicle, contact your control room with details of the make and model of the car you want to check. Control-room staff have access to databases listing the positions of the stamped-in VIN, the VIN plate, and the engine number, for each make and model of vehicle.

Example of a VIN on the chassis of a VW camper van

(Image © Kevin Lawton-Barrett)

10.6.4   Detection of Stolen Vehicles

You might need to consider the following points to help you decide if a particular vehicle is a stolen vehicle:

- Is the car reported lost or stolen? You can identify a stolen vehicle relatively easily by undertaking a PNC check on the registration number or, if the car is without registration plates, finding the VIN plate or stamped-in number and doing a PNC check on the VIN.
- Does it belong to a group of vehicles more likely to be stolen? (You can increase your chances of finding a stolen car by undertaking Task 5 in this chapter and researching police intelligence, noting which cars are stolen most often in your area.)
- Does the PNC show that a DVLA form V23 has been submitted on the car? If someone nonetheless has gone ahead with repairs, those repairs will be extensive and may be easy to see, for example, welding. If there are no indications of major repairs, the vehicle displaying the VICE details may not be the original, but a stolen one.
- Is the vehicle displaying the correct registration plates? Do the plates look as though they have been replaced or have new plates been stuck over the old plates? Do the plates have

a completely different character from the rest of the car—for example, is the car clean and the plates old and dirty, or the other way round; or are the plates plain, with no reference to the dealership that sold the car?

In other situations it will be less obvious that the vehicle has been stolen. You might need to check whether there are any differences between the identifying marks of the car (VICE) and the details of the identifying features which appear on PNC. In training, you may be asked to follow the procedure outlined below.

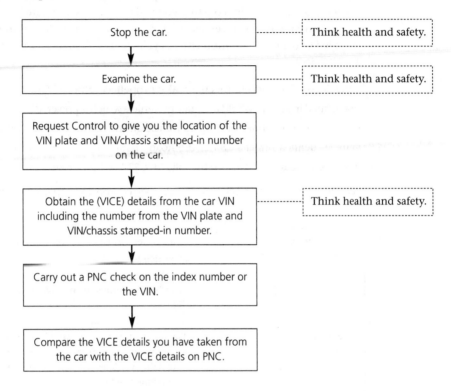

Are there any differences in the:

- colour;
- model;
- make;
- VICE identifying features?

If there are any differences, then you may have detected a stolen vehicle. If you need the vehicle examined still further, you may need to request attendance from a force vehicle examiner.

TASK 4

In the above flow chart, references are made to:
- stopping the car;
- examining the car;
- locating the VIN and VIN/chassis number.

Find out:
1. What powers or regulations allow you to stop and examine a car?
2. What regulations require the car to be equipped with a VIN or chassis number?

10.7 Taking a Conveyance without the Owner's Consent or Authority (TWOC)

This offence (TWOC) is described within s 12 of the Theft Act 1968. Taking a conveyance is a very common offence in England and Wales and unfortunately, modern technology has so far failed to deter criminals from this activity. The offence is often referred to as joyriding, especially in the media. It was created as a separate offence (from theft itself) in the Theft Act 1968, because although the suspects take the vehicle, they do not have the intention permanently to deprive the owner of it, so they cannot be committing the offence of s 1 theft. The offence may also result in damage and injury, so we also describe a second offence of 'aggravated vehicle taking'.

Some of the relevant legislation refers to 'conveyances'. A **conveyance** is any equipment constructed or adapted for the carriage of a person or persons whether by land, water, or air. It does not include a conveyance constructed or adapted for carrying items other than people, such as the pedestrian-controlled vehicle used by postal workers to transport mail. Pedal cycles are not included under this legislation either; cycle theft is covered by separate legislation described in 10.7.2 below.

Other legislation refers to **mechanically propelled vehicles**. A mechanically propelled vehicle is not defined in law but would include any vehicle which is powered by a mechanical means, but does **not** have to be intended or adapted for use on the roads. It should not be confused with a **motor vehicle**, defined under s 185 of the Road Traffic Act 1968 as 'a mechanically propelled vehicle intended or adapted for use on the road' (see 11.2.1.1 for more details on various types of vehicles).

Section 12 of the Theft Act 1968 states a person commits an offence if:

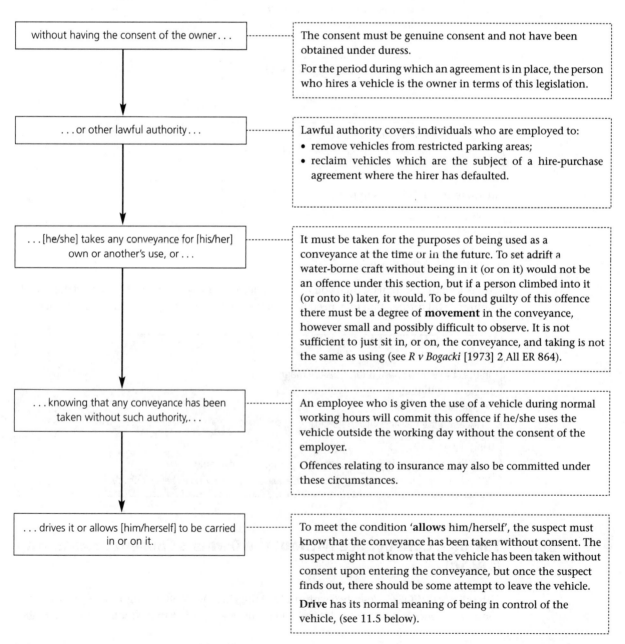

without having the consent of the owner . . .	The consent must be genuine consent and not have been obtained under duress. For the period during which an agreement is in place, the person who hires a vehicle is the owner in terms of this legislation.
. . . or other lawful authority . . .	Lawful authority covers individuals who are employed to: • remove vehicles from restricted parking areas; • reclaim vehicles which are the subject of a hire-purchase agreement where the hirer has defaulted.
. . . [he/she] takes any conveyance for [his/her] own or another's use, or . . .	It must be taken for the purposes of being used as a conveyance at the time or in the future. To set adrift a water-borne craft without being in it (or on it) would not be an offence under this section, but if a person climbed into it (or onto it) later, it would. To be found guilty of this offence there must be a degree of **movement** in the conveyance, however small and possibly difficult to observe. It is not sufficient to just sit in, or on, the conveyance, and taking is not the same as using (see *R v Bogacki* [1973] 2 All ER 864).
. . . knowing that any conveyance has been taken without such authority, . . .	An employee who is given the use of a vehicle during normal working hours will commit this offence if he/she uses the vehicle outside the working day without the consent of the employer. Offences relating to insurance may also be committed under these circumstances.
. . . drives it or allows [him/herself] to be carried in or on it.	To meet the condition '**allows** him/herself', the suspect must know that the conveyance has been taken without consent. The suspect might not know that the vehicle has been taken without consent upon entering the conveyance, but once the suspect finds out, there should be some attempt to leave the vehicle. **Drive** has its normal meaning of being in control of the vehicle, (see 11.5 below).

There is no definition of **driving** or **driven** within the legislation but there are precedents which provide guidelines. The decision finally rests with the court and is a question of fact. The court will consider:

- the degree to which the person had control over the direction and movement of the vehicle;
- the period of time during which the person had control; and
- the point at which the person stopped the driving.

As a possible defence, s 12(6) of the Theft Act 1968 states that a person does not commit this offence if he/she:

1. believes that he/she has the consent of:
   - the owner, or
   - other lawful authority to do it

or

2. has a mistaken belief of such lawful authority or consent of the owner.

This offence is triable summarily and the penalty is six months' imprisonment and/or a fine.

The basic offence of taking a conveyance cannot be attempted (see 10.22 below on criminal attempts), as the offence is not indictable; more appropriate offences might include vehicle interference or tampering with a motor vehicle (see 10.8 below). Note that theft is an indictable offence, so the offence of theft could also be considered if some form of attempt has taken place.

10.7.1 Aggravated Vehicle-Taking

A further offence may have been committed under s 12A(1) of the Theft Act 1968 if damage or injury is caused when a vehicle is taken without consent. Injuries may also include shock. Damage includes any damage caused during the whole incident and does not have to be deliberately inflicted damage; it could be accidental damage. Note that the damage can be caused to any property including the vehicle itself.

Section 12(A)(1) of the Theft Act 1968 states that a person commits the offence of aggravated vehicle-taking if he/she first of all commits:

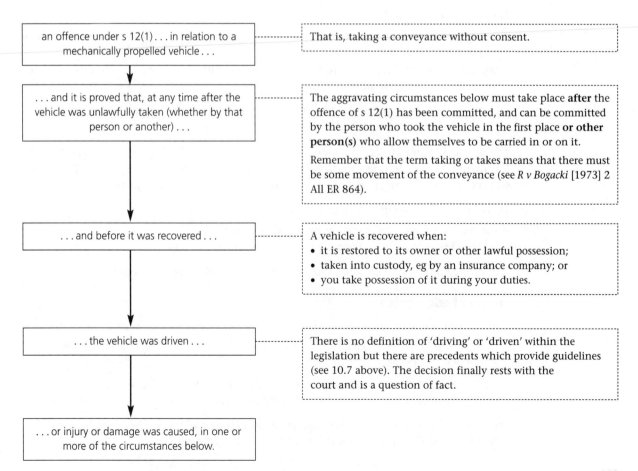

an offence under s 12(1)...in relation to a mechanically propelled vehicle...	That is, taking a conveyance without consent.

| ...and it is proved that, at any time after the vehicle was unlawfully taken (whether by that person or another)... | The aggravating circumstances below must take place **after** the offence of s 12(1) has been committed, and can be committed by the person who took the vehicle in the first place **or other person(s)** who allow themselves to be carried in or on it. Remember that the term taking or takes means that there must be some movement of the conveyance (see *R v Bogacki* [1973] 2 All ER 864). |

| ...and before it was recovered... | A vehicle is recovered when:
• it is restored to its owner or other lawful possession;
• taken into custody, eg by an insurance company; or
• you take possession of it during your duties. |

| ...the vehicle was driven... | There is no definition of 'driving' or 'driven' within the legislation but there are precedents which provide guidelines (see 10.7 above). The decision finally rests with the court and is a question of fact. |

| ...or injury or damage was caused, in one or more of the circumstances below. | |

The aggravating circumstances for this offence are that:

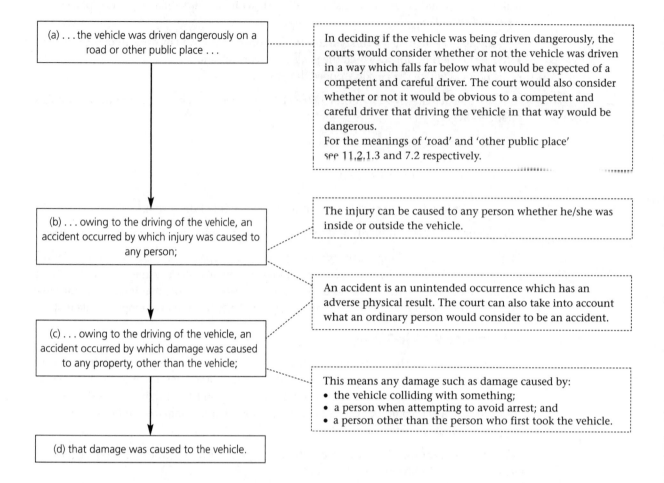

(a) . . . the vehicle was driven dangerously on a road or other public place . . .	In deciding if the vehicle was being driven dangerously, the courts would consider whether or not the vehicle was driven in a way which falls far below what would be expected of a competent and careful driver. The court would also consider whether or not it would be obvious to a competent and careful driver that driving the vehicle in that way would be dangerous. For the meanings of 'road' and 'other public place' see 11.2.1.3 and 7.2 respectively.
(b) . . . owing to the driving of the vehicle, an accident occurred by which injury was caused to any person;	The injury can be caused to any person whether he/she was inside or outside the vehicle.
	An accident is an unintended occurrence which has an adverse physical result. The court can also take into account what an ordinary person would consider to be an accident.
(c) . . . owing to the driving of the vehicle, an accident occurred by which damage was caused to any property, other than the vehicle;	This means any damage such as damage caused by: • the vehicle colliding with something; • a person when attempting to avoid arrest; and • a person other than the person who first took the vehicle.
(d) that damage was caused to the vehicle.	

Possible defences include:

- the aggravating circumstances occurred before the suspect committed the basic offence of taking the vehicle;
- the suspect was not in, on, or in the immediate vicinity of the vehicle when that driving, accident, or damage occurred.

Immediate vicinity is not defined by the legislation and therefore it will be for the court to determine in each case.

The suspect will need to demonstrate on the balance of probabilities that the aggravating factors occurred before he/she committed the basic offence of 'taking a conveyance'. Even if the suspect can disprove aggravating factors, he/she can still be found guilty of the basic offence.

This offence is triable either way and the penalty is:

- summarily: six months' imprisonment and/or a fine;
- on indictment: two years' imprisonment and/or a fine.

If the accident (under s 12A(2)(b)) caused death, the penalty is 14 years' imprisonment.

10.7.2 Theft of Pedal Cycles

A pedal cycle is not a conveyance for the purposes of s 12(1) of the Theft Act 1968, so the theft of cycles cannot be covered by s 12(1) (TWOC). However, s 12(5) of the Theft Act 1968 states it is an offence for a person:

> without having the consent of the owner or other lawful authority [to take] a pedal cycle for [his/her] own or another's use, or to ride a pedal cycle knowing it to have been taken without such authority.

The defence for this offence is the same as for ss 12(1) and 12A(1) of the Theft Act 1968. The penalty for this offence is six months' imprisonment and/or a fine.

TASK 5

Approximately 1,000 vehicles are taken without the owner's consent in the UK every day. Find out the answers to the following questions from your area to assist you to trace stolen vehicles:

- What type of vehicle is most often taken in your area?
- What time of the day are these vehicles taken?
- Where are they taken from?
- Where are they abandoned?

10.8   Interference and Tampering with Motor Vehicles

When a suspect takes a conveyance without the consent of the owner, in many cases he/she will go through a process of selecting a vehicle, gaining entry either forcibly or by trying door handles, overcoming anti-theft devices such as alarms and steering locks, and then applying a technique such as hot wiring to start the engine. This process inevitably takes time, and sometimes the suspect can be apprehended before the vehicle is taken. However, TWOC is a summary offence (and therefore cannot be attempted under s 1(1) of the Criminal Attempts Act 1981, see 10.22 below). Therefore, the Criminal Attempts Act 1981 Act includes a specific offence of 'interference and tampering with motor vehicles'.

10.8.1   Interference

In everyday language, a person is interfering with a motor vehicle when it is apparent that he/she is attempting to commit a crime such as stealing the car. However, actually proving intent is tricky. In 5.10 above, we discussed the two main building blocks to a criminal act: *actus reus* (the act itself), and *mens rea*, an intention to commit an act. In this case, the act cannot simply be preparation but needs to go further than this. Unfortunately, case law provides us with little guidance on what interference actually means in practice.

Nonetheless, s 9(1) of the Criminal Attempts Act 1981 states that it is an offence for a person to interfere with a motor vehicle or trailer, or with anything carried in or on a motor vehicle or trailer with the intention of committing:

- 'theft of the motor vehicle or part of it';
- 'theft of anything carried in or on the motor vehicle or trailer'; or
- the offence of taking a conveyance.

You need to prove that the suspect had at least one of the three intentions, but you do not need to prove which particular one.

This is a summary offence and the penalty is three months' imprisonment and/or a fine.

10.8.2   Tampering

The act of tampering is more readily understood than interference. Section 25(1) of the Road Traffic Act 1988 states it is an offence for a person without lawful authority or reasonable cause to:

- tamper with the brake or any other part of its mechanism; or
- get on or into

a motor vehicle which is on a road or a parking place provided by a local authority.

This is a summary offence and the penalty is a fine.

10.8.3 Holding or Getting onto a Motor Vehicle

This offence concerns 'holding or getting onto a vehicle in order to be towed or carried'. Section 26(1) of the Road Traffic Act 1988 states it is an offence for a person who:

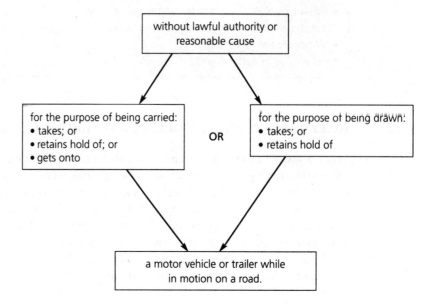

This is a summary offence and the penalty is a fine.

TASK 6

Which of the following would constitute an offence of interfering with a motor vehicle?
1. Trying to removing a horse box from the tow bar of a vehicle in order to steal the horse box.
2. Attempting to remove a go-kart from the garden of a house in order to steal it.
3. Opening the unlocked front driver's door of a car to steal a CD player in the dashboard.
4. Putting super glue in a car door lock to prevent the owner from opening the door.

10.9 Handling Stolen Goods

Section 22 of the Theft Act 1968 states that:

> a person [handles stolen goods] if otherwise than in the course of stealing knowing or believing them to be stolen goods [he/she]
>
> (i) dishonestly receives the goods, or
> (ii) dishonestly undertakes their retention, removal, disposal or realisation by or for the benefit of another person, or
> (iii) dishonestly assists in their retention, removal, disposal or realisation by or for the benefit of another person, or

arranges to do (i), (ii) or (iii) above.

There are three types of offence for which goods are considered to be stolen with respect to the offence of handling stolen goods. These are:

1. blackmail (s 21, Theft Act 1968)
2. fraud (s1, Fraud Act 2006)
3. theft (s 1, Theft Act 1968).

Let us first consider the meaning of the terms 'handling', 'stolen', and 'goods'. The meanings of some other terms used in the Act are shown later.

10.9.1 The Distinction between 'Handling' and 'Theft'

It is important to distinguish clearly between 'handling' and 'theft'. To help you decide whether or not the goods were handled (other than in the course of stealing), you have to decide whether or not the actions of the suspect followed on from the theft continuously (ie without a break), and consider whether:

- the theft was complete; and
- there was a break in the proceedings; and
- the suspect became involved only after the theft had occurred.

For example, Ellis goes to a large out-of-town electrical store. She steals two digital radios from the store, goes outside, and hides them in a rubbish bin to evade detection. Sal then takes the radios. The table below presents a number of different scenarios and shows whether the activity amounts to handling or theft.

Offences committed by Sal the accomplice

Sal's actions ...	Offence committed by Sal	Other factors to be taken into account
Sal is waiting by pre-arrangement and takes the radios away.	Theft	
Sal arrives half an hour later by pre-arrangement, and takes the radios away.	Theft	Particularly if the proceeds are to be shared out between Ellis and Sal.
	Handling	May be considered if Sal subsequently pays Ellis for the goods.
Sal is told where the radios are, but only **after** they have been stolen. Sal then collects the radios.	Handling	

A thief can become a handler of the property that he/she originally stole, but only if he/she loses control of the property and later decides (whilst the goods can still be referred to as stolen goods) to have dealings with the property once again.

10.9.2 Knowing or Believing that Goods are 'Stolen Goods'

Another key issue for this offence is that the person handling the stolen goods must know or believe that the goods are stolen. In the legislation, if someone knows or believes that the goods are stolen, he/she is said to be handling the goods dishonestly. The court has to decide what is dishonest by everyday standards, and whether the suspect was aware he/she was dishonest by those standards. Dishonesty in relation to handling goods would **not** include:

- believing he/she has a right to the property in law;
- believing he/she would have the owner's consent;
- believing that the owner cannot be traced.

The difference between knowing and believing is not clear cut; the following points could be considered:

- **knowing** them to be stolen goods means having actually been told that the goods are stolen by the thief or burglar or someone with first-hand knowledge;
- **believing** them to be stolen goods means being uncertain as to whether or not the goods are stolen, but then thinking there is no other likely explanation in those particular circumstances (see *R v Hall* [1985] 1 QB 496).

Knowledge or belief could be proved by:

- direct evidence from the thief;
- admission by the handler; or
- circumstantial evidence, such as non-standard packaging or where they were being sold.

10.9.3 The Definition of Goods

The Theft Act (s 34(2)(b)) extends the definition of goods to include:

money and every other description of property, except land, and includes things severed from the land by stealing.

Under s 24(2) of the Theft Act 1968, the meaning of 'goods' also includes the proceeds of the disposal of the original stolen items. The proceeds could be money or other items which have been received in exchange for the items that were originally stolen. After the original theft there is often a whole chain of events, and each of the handlers in this process commits the offence of handling stolen goods, so long as each has guilty knowledge (*mens rea*) that the goods he/she is handling represent the original stolen goods. The chain will only be broken when a person is **unaware** that the goods he/she receives represent the original stolen goods. If, for example, a person who is unaware of the origin of the goods sells or exchanges those goods, whatever he/she receives cannot be considered stolen goods because without the person having guilty knowledge, the proceeds can no longer represent the original stolen goods.

Section 22 of the Theft Act 1968 states:

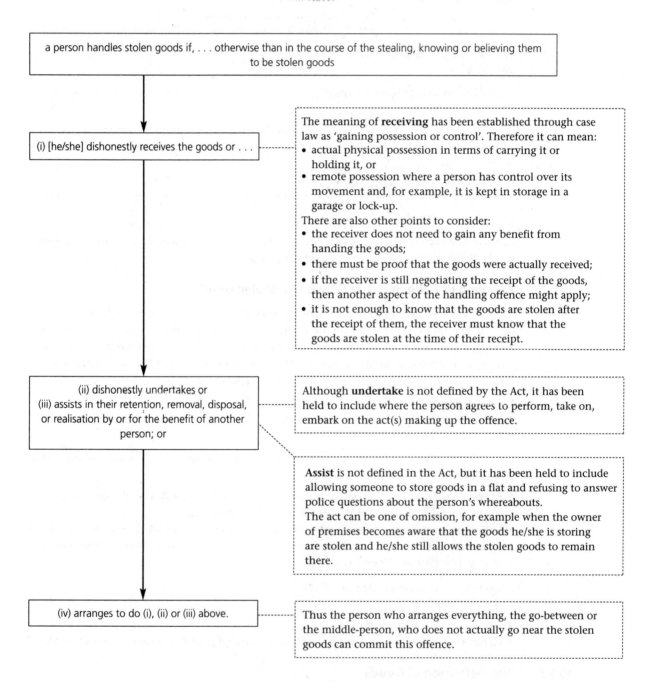

a person handles stolen goods if, . . . otherwise than in the course of the stealing, knowing or believing them to be stolen goods

(i) [he/she] dishonestly receives the goods or . . .

The meaning of **receiving** has been established through case law as 'gaining possession or control'. Therefore it can mean:
- actual physical possession in terms of carrying it or holding it, or
- remote possession where a person has control over its movement and, for example, it is kept in storage in a garage or lock-up.

There are also other points to consider:
- the receiver does not need to gain any benefit from handing the goods;
- there must be proof that the goods were actually received;
- if the receiver is still negotiating the receipt of the goods, then another aspect of the handling offence might apply;
- it is not enough to know that the goods are stolen after the receipt of them, the receiver must know that the goods are stolen at the time of their receipt.

(ii) dishonestly undertakes or
(iii) assists in their retention, removal, disposal, or realisation by or for the benefit of another person; or

Although **undertake** is not defined by the Act, it has been held to include where the person agrees to perform, take on, embark on the act(s) making up the offence.

Assist is not defined in the Act, but it has been held to include allowing someone to store goods in a flat and refusing to answer police questions about the person's whereabouts.
The act can be one of omission, for example when the owner of premises becomes aware that the goods he/she is storing are stolen and he/she still allows the stolen goods to remain there.

(iv) arranges to do (i), (ii) or (iii) above.

Thus the person who arranges everything, the go-between or the middle-person, who does not actually go near the stolen goods can commit this offence.

The following is an explanation of the various key terms used within the Act:

Term	Explanation or definition
Benefit	Some kind of an advantage, although the person does not have to be aware of it at the time, nor does it have to be financial.
Another	The term 'another' must refer to someone who is not the defendant or one of the co-accused.
Retention	Continuing to possess something (especially when someone else wants it).
Removal	Take something away from the place where it was.
Disposal	Passing on, getting rid of, giving away.
Realization	To obtain an amount of money or profit by selling something.

To prove 'undertaking' or 'assisting' (or arranging to undertake or assist), you must prove that the actions taken were for the benefit of another person. This does not have to be proved for a charge of **receiving** stolen goods. This offence is triable either way and the penalty is:

- summarily: six months' imprisonment and/or a fine;
- on indictment: 14 years' imprisonment.

10.9.4 Proceeds of Crime

It is not always possible for a criminal to benefit from a crime if the proceeds of the felony remain in their original state. In the majority of cases, the profits have to be realized, exchanged, or hidden to be of any worth. One way in which the proceeds of crime are converted into assets in order to make their origin appear legitimate is known as money laundering. However, the Proceeds of Crime Act 2002 (POCA) makes it an offence to benefit from any kind of proceeds, not just money. These proceeds are known as 'criminal property'. There are three main offences which cover most eventualities in benefiting from the proceeds of crime and these are described below.

10.9.4.1 The definition of criminal property

For the purposes of ss 327, 328, and 329 of the POCA 2002, criminal property is any property which the suspect knows or suspects to be or represent, the benefit from any criminal conduct (s 340(3)). Criminal conduct is conduct which constitutes (or would constitute) an offence in the UK (s 340(2)). Criminal property (s 340(9)) includes

- money;
- property (real, personal, inherited, and moveable);
- things in action such as patents, copyrights and trademarks;
- other intangible or incorporeal property such as property rights, leases or mortgages.

(Real property is land and things forming part of the land, such as plants and buildings, and moveable property is not attached to the land (eg furniture, art, books, or household goods).

10.9.4.2 Concealing, converting, or transferring criminal property

Under s 327(1) of the POCA 2002, a person commits an offence if he/she carries out one of the following acts in relation to criminal property:

- concealment;
- disguise;
- conversion;
- transference; or
- removal from the UK.

> Shona knows that her husband brings back large quantities of alcohol from cross-Channel ferry-trips to sell on to local youths under 18 years old. Their 'business' is thriving, but Shona does not want to raise suspicions by depositing the money in their bank account so she hides the money from the sales in a secure cash box, which she places behind the panel of the bath in their house. She is guilty of concealment of criminal property.

10.9.4.3   Involvement in arrangements for criminal property

It is an offence to be involved with arrangements for someone else to deal with criminal property. Under s 328(1) of the POCA 2002, a person commits an offence if he/she enters into (or becomes concerned in) an arrangement which he/she knows (or suspects) will help with the:

- acquisition;
- retention;
- use; or
- control

of criminal property, by (or on behalf of) another person.

> Drew works in a large DIY store and supplies the local under-16-year-olds with spray cans of paint to use when 'tagging' around the town. To avoid being seen meeting up with them, Drew leaves the cans in a secret location known only to him and the youths. Drew tells his brother Wayne about the 'scam' and arranges that Wayne will collect the payment for the cans from the youths, as Wayne used to go to school with them. For his 'trouble', Wayne receives a proportion of the payment from the sale of the spray cans. He is guilty of an offence as he has taken part in arrangements to acquire criminal property on behalf of someone else.

10.9.4.4   Acquisition, Use, and Possession of Criminal Property

Under s 329(1) of the POCA 2002 a person commits an offence if he/she acquires, uses, or possesses criminal property.

> Warren is a small-time drug supplier and, in order to evade detection, gives some of his profits from selling drugs to the mother of his new-born baby. She knows very well where the money comes from as Warren discusses it freely with her (and they met as a result of Warren supplying drugs to her in the past). She uses the money to buy food and clothes for their child; she has 'used' criminal property.

10.9.4.5   Defences

There are three shared defences available for ss 327(1), 328(1), and 329(1) of the POCA 2002:

- the suspect makes or intends to make (with reasonable excuse) an 'authorized disclosure' to a police, customs, or nominated officer, informing them of his/her actions:
- law enforcement authorities (such as the police) have a defence should they convert or transfer seized criminal property and place it for example in an interest-earning account;
- the suspect knows (or reasonably believes) that the criminal conduct took place outside the UK and that it was not unlawful in that other country (s 327(2) and (2)A).

There is an additional defence available for s 329(1) where a person acquires, uses, or has possession of the criminal property for 'adequate consideration', such as goods (or services) bought at their proper market price with the money from crime. For example, a shopkeeper could claim this defence if the consumable goods and services she sells to a customer at an appropriate retail price are paid for in money that comes from crime. Similarly, solicitors or accountants who receive money for or on account of costs, also have this defence.

These offences under ss 327, 328, and 329 are all triable either way and the penalty is:

- summarily: six months' imprisonment and/or a fine;
- on indictment: 14 years' imprisonment and/or a fine.

TASK 7

1. With regard to handling stolen goods, which, if either, of the following statements is true?

   (a) For the purposes of committing an offence of handling, 'stolen goods' includes money and every other description of property, except land, but includes things severed from the land by stealing.

   (b) Property obtained as a result of a fraud under s 1 of the Fraud Act 2006 is considered to be 'stolen goods' for the purposes of the offence of handling.

2. You carry out a lawful s 1 PACE Act 1984 stop and search on Terri and comply with the PACE Codes of Practice throughout the process. Terri is an 18-year-old persistent offender and prolific shoplifter. His MO is to steal items such as chocolate and clothes from shops, to sell on quickly and cheaply. Local intelligence has indicated that Terri has also become a courier for local drug suppliers, and that he has an extremely modest lifestyle; he does not own any vehicles, lives alone in a one-room bed sit, doesn't drink, but occasionally smokes cannabis. He is registered unemployed, receives state benefits, and has no close family. During the search, you find £100,000 in used £50 notes in various locations about his clothing. Terri cannot account for this money and there is no evidence of its origin. Considering what you know about Terri, you suspect that the money is the proceeds of crime, and therefore criminal property. In this case, what would be the likelihood of a successful prosecution for acquiring, retaining, using, or controlling the criminal property under s 328(1) of the POCA 2002? Refer to the cases of *R v NW, SW, RC & CC* (2008) EWCA Crim 2 and the conjoined cases of *R v Sylvia Allpress; R v Deborah Symeou; R v Miguel Casal; R v Paul Winter Morris; R v Stephen Martin* (2009) EWCA Crim 8 for your answer.

10.10 Abstracting Electricity

Electricity does not fall within the definition of property in the Theft Act 1968, and therefore, in legal terms, it cannot be stolen. Instead, 'abstracting' is the legal term used for the offence of illegally taking and using electricity, and it is covered under s 13 of the Theft Act 1968. As electricity is not property within the Theft Act 1968, an entry into premises with the sole intention of abstracting electricity will not amount to burglary.

Section 13 of the Theft Act 1968 states that a person commits an offence:

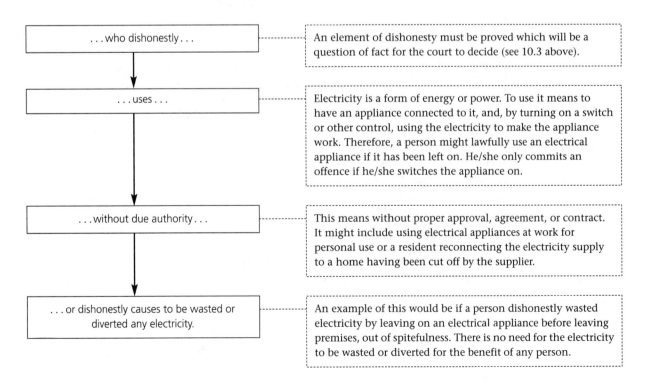

. . . who dishonestly . . .	An element of dishonesty must be proved which will be a question of fact for the court to decide (see 10.3 above).
. . . uses . . .	Electricity is a form of energy or power. To use it means to have an appliance connected to it, and, by turning on a switch or other control, using the electricity to make the appliance work. Therefore, a person might lawfully use an electrical appliance if it has been left on. He/she only commits an offence if he/she switches the appliance on.
. . . without due authority . . .	This means without proper approval, agreement, or contract. It might include using electrical appliances at work for personal use or a resident reconnecting the electricity supply to a home having been cut off by the supplier.
. . . or dishonestly causes to be wasted or diverted any electricity.	An example of this would be if a person dishonestly wasted electricity by leaving on an electrical appliance before leaving premises, out of spitefulness. There is no need for the electricity to be wasted or diverted for the benefit of any person.

The electricity does not have to be mains electricity to be abstracted. It can be electricity from a battery in a caravan, for example.

This offence is triable either way and the penalty is:

- summarily: six months' imprisonment and/or a fine;
- on indictment: five years' imprisonment.

10.11 Going Equipped

This offence is described in s 25 of the Theft Act 1968. A wide range of articles are used to carry out burglary, or theft, such as:

- equipment for removing security tags, eg from clothing;
- instruments used for gaining entry to vehicles, including keys;
- tools used to gain entry to buildings or vehicles.

The offence is not committed simply by the suspect being in possession of the articles. In order to commit the offence of going equipped, the suspect must have possession of the articles **and** be on his/her way to carry out a theft or burglary (see *R v Ellames* [1974] 3 All ER 130). The offence cannot be committed when coming away from the crime. A direct connection to a specific burglary or theft does not need to be established, but it must be possible to prove that the article is intended to be used to commit crime by the suspect (or another person).

Section 25(1) of the Theft Act 1968 states it is an offence for a person:

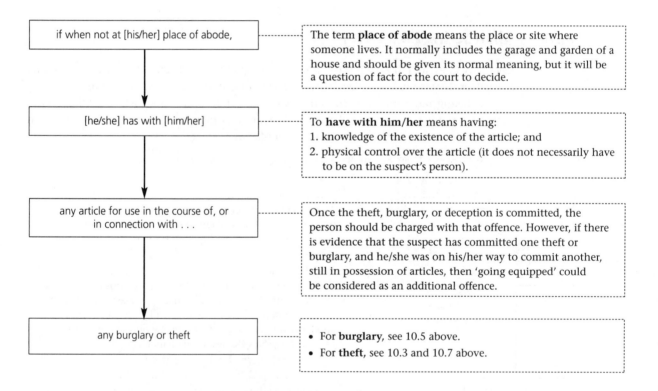

This offence is triable either way and the penalty is:

- summarily: six months' imprisonment and/or a fine;
- on indictment: three years' imprisonment.

10.12 Fraud Offences

As we discussed in 10.3 above, theft involves the dishonest appropriation of property belonging to another. In addition to theft itself, the various Theft Acts (1968, 1978, and 1996) also contained sections addressing aspects of what we tend to call fraud and deception. This proved confusing and much of the law surrounding the crime of fraud is now encapsulated instead in the Fraud Act 2006, which came into effect in January 2007. (Given its recency, there are as yet few precedents to help with a deeper understanding of some parts of the new fraud legislation. For example, it might well be that an intention to carry out a 'phishing' crime could be prosecuted as a s 2 offence but this has not yet been tested.)

Section 1 of the Fraud Act 2006 states that the offence of fraud can be committed in one or more of three distinctive ways:

1. by **false representation**, eg returning stolen goods to a shop to try to obtain a refund (s 2, Fraud Act 2006);
2. by **failing to disclose information**, eg omitting important information when applying for a job or health insurance (s 3, Fraud Act 2006);
3. through **abuse of position**, eg whilst driving a local authority mini-bus, demanding fares from local residents when the service is actually free (s 4, Fraud Act 2006).

10.12.1   False Representation

Section 2, Fraud Act 2006 states that a person commits an offence if he/she:

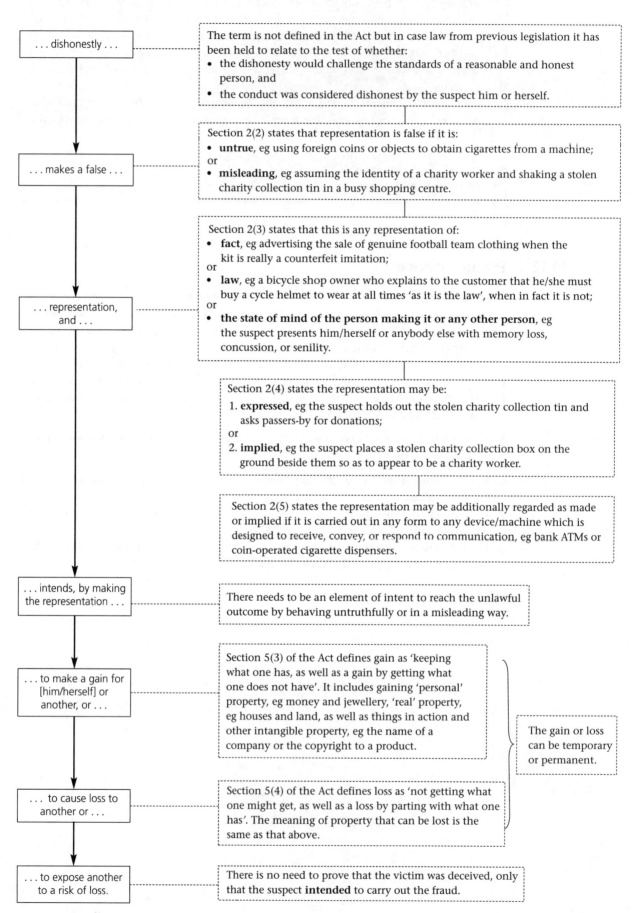

... dishonestly ...

The term is not defined in the Act but in case law from previous legislation it has been held to relate to the test of whether:
- the dishonesty would challenge the standards of a reasonable and honest person, and
- the conduct was considered dishonest by the suspect him or herself.

... makes a false ...

Section 2(2) states that representation is false if it is:
- **untrue**, eg using foreign coins or objects to obtain cigarettes from a machine; or
- **misleading**, eg assuming the identity of a charity worker and shaking a stolen charity collection tin in a busy shopping centre.

... representation, and ...

Section 2(3) states that this is any representation of:
- **fact**, eg advertising the sale of genuine football team clothing when the kit is really a counterfeit imitation; or
- **law**, eg a bicycle shop owner who explains to the customer that he/she must buy a cycle helmet to wear at all times 'as it is the law', when in fact it is not; or
- **the state of mind of the person making it or any other person**, eg the suspect presents him/herself or anybody else with memory loss, concussion, or senility.

Section 2(4) states the representation may be:
1. **expressed**, eg the suspect holds out the stolen charity collection tin and asks passers-by for donations; or
2. **implied**, eg the suspect places a stolen charity collection box on the ground beside them so as to appear to be a charity worker.

Section 2(5) states the representation may be additionally regarded as made or implied if it is carried out in any form to any device/machine which is designed to receive, convey, or respond to communication, eg bank ATMs or coin-operated cigarette dispensers.

... intends, by making the representation ...

There needs to be an element of intent to reach the unlawful outcome by behaving untruthfully or in a misleading way.

... to make a gain for [him/herself] or another, or ...

Section 5(3) of the Act defines gain as 'keeping what one has, as well as a gain by getting what one does not have'. It includes gaining 'personal' property, eg money and jewellery, 'real' property, eg houses and land, as well as things in action and other intangible property, eg the name of a company or the copyright to a product.

The gain or loss can be temporary or permanent.

... to cause loss to another or ...

Section 5(4) of the Act defines loss as 'not getting what one might get, as well as a loss by parting with what one has'. The meaning of property that can be lost is the same as that above.

... to expose another to a risk of loss.

There is no need to prove that the victim was deceived, only that the suspect **intended** to carry out the fraud.

10.12.2 Failure to Disclose Information

Section 3 of the Fraud Act 2006 states that a person commits an offence if he/she:

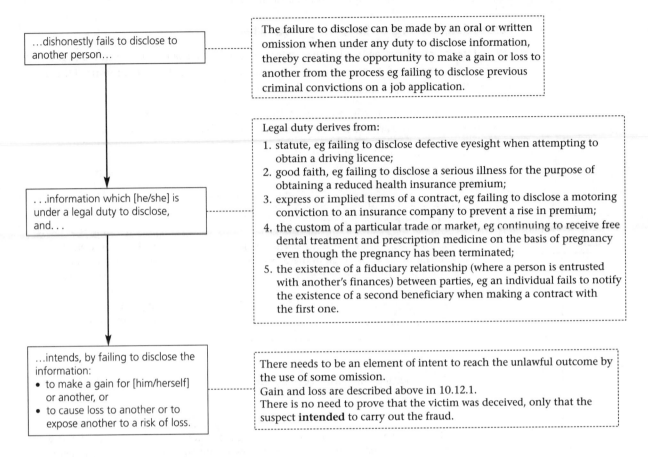

...dishonestly fails to disclose to another person...

The failure to disclose can be made by an oral or written omission when under any duty to disclose information, thereby creating the opportunity to make a gain or loss to another from the process eg failing to disclose previous criminal convictions on a job application.

...information which [he/she] is under a legal duty to disclose, and...

Legal duty derives from:

1. statute, eg failing to disclose defective eyesight when attempting to obtain a driving licence;
2. good faith, eg failing to disclose a serious illness for the purpose of obtaining a reduced health insurance premium;
3. express or implied terms of a contract, eg failing to disclose a motoring conviction to an insurance company to prevent a rise in premium;
4. the custom of a particular trade or market, eg continuing to receive free dental treatment and prescription medicine on the basis of pregnancy even though the pregnancy has been terminated;
5. the existence of a fiduciary relationship (where a person is entrusted with another's finances) between parties, eg an individual fails to notify the existence of a second beneficiary when making a contract with the first one.

...intends, by failing to disclose the information:
- to make a gain for [him/herself] or another, or
- to cause loss to another or to expose another to a risk of loss.

There needs to be an element of intent to reach the unlawful outcome by the use of some omission.
Gain and loss are described above in 10.12.1.
There is no need to prove that the victim was deceived, only that the suspect **intended** to carry out the fraud.

10.12.3 Abuse of Position

Section 4 of the Fraud Act 2006 states that a person commits an offence if he/she occupies a position in which he/she:

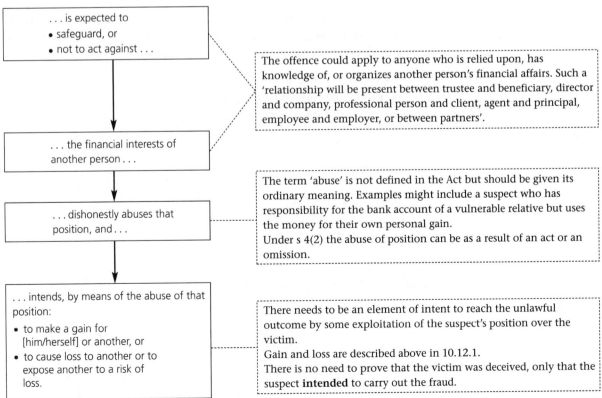

... is expected to
- safeguard, or
- not to act against ...

The offence could apply to anyone who is relied upon, has knowledge of, or organizes another person's financial affairs. Such a 'relationship will be present between trustee and beneficiary, director and company, professional person and client, agent and principal, employee and employer, or between partners'.

... the financial interests of another person ...

... dishonestly abuses that position, and...

The term 'abuse' is not defined in the Act but should be given its ordinary meaning. Examples might include a suspect who has responsibility for the bank account of a vulnerable relative but uses the money for their own personal gain.
Under s 4(2) the abuse of position can be as a result of an act or an omission.

... intends, by means of the abuse of that position:
- to make a gain for [him/herself] or another, or
- to cause loss to another or to expose another to a risk of loss.

There needs to be an element of intent to reach the unlawful outcome by some exploitation of the suspect's position over the victim.
Gain and loss are described above in 10.12.1.
There is no need to prove that the victim was deceived, only that the suspect **intended** to carry out the fraud.

425

This offence is triable either way and the penalty is:

- summarily: 12 months imprisonment and/or a fine;
- on indictment: ten years imprisonment and/or a fine.

10.12.4 Possession, Making, or Supplying of Articles

Just as it is with burglary (see 10.11 above), it is also possible for a person to commit an offence if they are 'going equipped' to carry out a fraud, rather than actually having committed the fraud itself. In this context, going equipped means either:

1. possession or control of articles for use in frauds (s 6 of the Fraud Act 2006)
2. making or supplying articles for use in frauds (s 7 of the Fraud Act 2006).

Section 6 of the Fraud Act 2006 states that a person commits an offence if he/she:

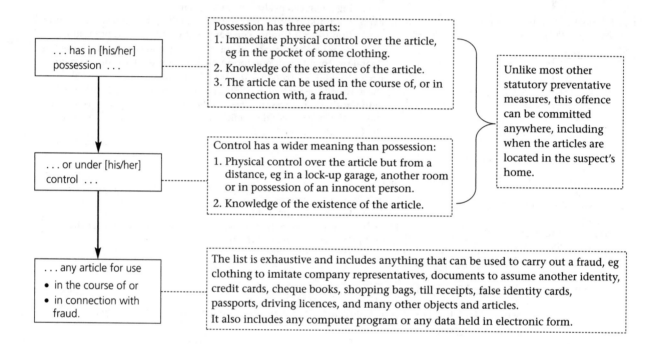

(Statutory preventative measures (mentioned in the flowchart above) are pieces of legislation designed to prevent criminal offences from taking place, for example 'going equipped' to steal (see 10.11 above) and 'carrying offensive weapons' (see 9.19 above).)

This offence is triable either way and the penalty is:

- summarily: 12 months' imprisonment and/or a fine;
- on indictment: five years' imprisonment and/or a fine.

Section 7 of the Fraud Act 2006 states that a person commits an offence if he/she:

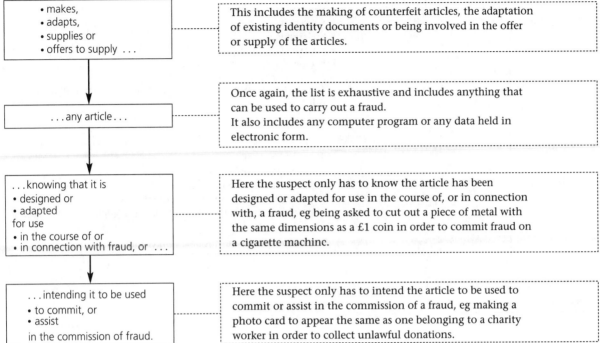

Under s 1 of the PACE Act 1984, you have the power to search for articles made or adapted for use in fraud (see 7.5.4 above).

This offence is triable either way and the penalty is:

- summarily: 12 months' imprisonment and/or a fine;
- on indictment: 10 years' imprisonment and/or a fine.

10.12.5 Fraudulent Obtaining of Services

In the previous fraud offences of false representation, failing to disclose information, and abuse of position, the gain or loss related to tangible and intangible property. However, in circumstances where a service has been provided, eg a taxi ride or a stay in a hotel room, there is no gain or loss of property, only the provision of a facility or service. For this reason, an additional offence is provided for by the Fraud Act 2006 when a service is obtained by dishonest means.

Section 11 of the Fraud Act 2006 states that a person commits an offence if he/she:

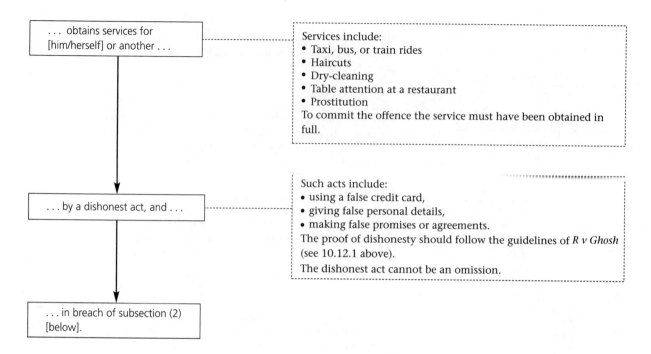

Section 11(2) of the Fraud Act 2006 states that a person obtains services in breach of this subsection if:

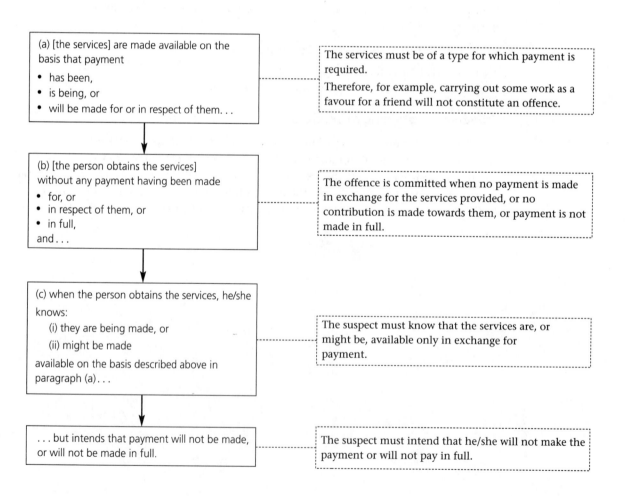

This offence is triable either way and the penalty is:

- summarily: 12 months' imprisonment and/or a fine;
- on indictment: 5 years' imprisonment and/or a fine.

10.12.6 Making Off Without Payment ('Bilking')

If no fraud is practised but goods are still obtained dishonestly and without payment, it is an offence under s 3 of the Theft Act 1978 rather than fraud under s 1 of the Fraud Act 2006. This particular offence is often referred to as 'bilking'. For example, a person might fill up with petrol on the forecourt of a filling station with every intention of paying for the petrol, but on seeing the staff otherwise engaged and no other customers around, decide to drive off without paying.

Note that this offence only applies if 'payment on the spot' is the norm in that particular situation, such as collecting goods on which work has been done (for example, shoe repairs) or paying for a service which has been provided (for example, a haircut). This offence does not cover circumstances in which a customer has a credit arrangement or a 'tab' with the service provider.

Section 3 of the Theft Act 1978, states that it is an offence for a person:

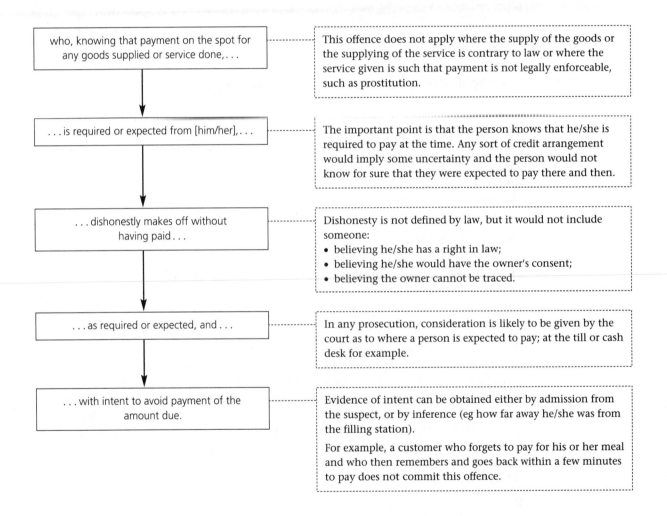

who, knowing that payment on the spot for any goods supplied or service done, . . .	This offence does not apply where the supply of the goods or the supplying of the service is contrary to law or where the service given is such that payment is not legally enforceable, such as prostitution.
. . . is required or expected from [him/her], . . .	The important point is that the person knows that he/she is required to pay at the time. Any sort of credit arrangement would imply some uncertainty and the person would not know for sure that they were expected to pay there and then.
. . . dishonestly makes off without having paid . . .	Dishonesty is not defined by law, but it would not include someone: • believing he/she has a right in law; • believing he/she would have the owner's consent; • believing the owner cannot be traced.
. . . as required or expected, and . . .	In any prosecution, consideration is likely to be given by the court as to where a person is expected to pay; at the till or cash desk for example.
. . . with intent to avoid payment of the amount due.	Evidence of intent can be obtained either by admission from the suspect, or by inference (eg how far away he/she was from the filling station). For example, a customer who forgets to pay for his or her meal and who then remembers and goes back within a few minutes to pay does not commit this offence.

This offence is triable either way and the penalty is:

- summarily: six months' imprisonment and/or a fine;
- on indictment: two years' imprisonment and/or a fine.

TASK 9

At what stage of a visit to a restaurant are the following offences potentially committed by people who fail to pay for a meal:

- s 1 Fraud Act 2006;
- s 3 of the Theft Act 1978;
- s 11 Fraud Act 2006?

To answer the question, complete the table below by describing in the right-hand column the likely actions and thought processes of the customers at each stage of the visit to the restaurant, linking these to ss 1 and 11 of the Fraud Act 2006 and s 3 of the Theft Act 1978. The case of *DPP v Ray* [1974] AC 370 may assist.

People enter the restaurant and order a meal.	
Having ordered the meal, they wait at the table for it to be served.	
The meal is served to the table.	
Having consumed the meal, they are expected to pay.	
They leave the restaurant.	

10.13 Unlawful Possession of a Controlled Drug

In this part of Chapter 10, we examine the most important piece of legislation available to the police and the CJS in countering the street-level use and distribution of illegal drugs. The legislation for the offence of 'unlawful possession of a controlled drug' is covered in s 5(2) of the Misuse of Drugs Act 1971. Drugs that are subject to legal control are referred to as **controlled drugs.** Some controlled drugs are addictive and/or dangerous, and the results of their misuse are obvious to us all. The Misuse of Drugs Act 1971 was enacted to curb the use of controlled drugs and to outlaw various actions by those people who are unlawfully in possession of them.

Unless you have a great deal of experience in relation to controlled drugs, you will initially find recognizing them very difficult as there are so many different forms, shapes, colours, and sizes including pills, tablets, liquids, powders, and resins. Therefore, your first thought when finding such substances without pharmaceutical company packaging, should not be to try and work out exactly what drug it is, but to suspect that the person may be in possession of controlled drugs.

A great number of criminal procedures are linked to drug-related activities, so you will frequently be faced with such situations. Remember, you must assess risk and hazard levels carefully when dealing with people who have been taking drugs as they may behave unpredictably. Always be prepared to use your personal safety equipment; remember the possible consequences of contamination from bodily fluids or equipment used by a drug addict. The merest micro-cut from a sharp article contaminated by a transferable virus could infect you and cause a serious illness. Demonstration of appropriate health and safety measures will also help you meet the Safety First requirements of the PAC and NOS elements in Unit AF1.

10.13.1 What Is a Controlled Drug?

Drugs are controlled because of their effect on the human body, and are divided into classes A, B, and C (Misuse of Drugs Act 1971) according to the potential for harm they are thought to present to individuals and to society at large:

Class A	eg Ecstasy, heroin, cocaine, crack cocaine, 'magic mushrooms' (containing psilocin) and LSD.
Class B	eg cannabis leaves, cannabis resin, amphetamines, and barbiturates.
Class C	eg tranquilizers (such as Temazepan), and some painkillers.

You will find a full list of controlled drugs via the website <http://www.drugs.gov.uk>.

A block of cannabis resin is normally the size of a glasses case and weighs about 9 ounces. Cannabis users normally buy an eighth (1/8) of an ounce at a time, with a street cost of approximately £7.

A wrap of coke (cocaine) with a street cost of about £45.

Crack cocaine is a form of cocaine. The street price is about £10 per 'rock'. A crack rock is about the size of a raisin.

(Photographs copyright LGC Limited 2007. Reproduced with permission)

10.13.2 Unlawful Possession

As a police officer in training, the most common offence that you will deal with in relation to the misuse of drugs is that of **unlawful possession**.

It is an offence under s 5(2) Misuse of Drugs Act for a person unlawfully to:

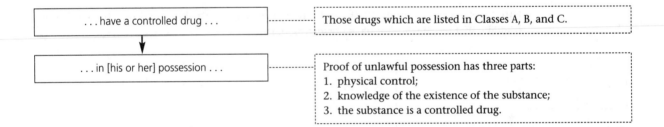

| . . . have a controlled drug . . . | Those drugs which are listed in Classes A, B, and C. |
| . . . in [his or her] possession . . . | Proof of unlawful possession has three parts: 1. physical control; 2. knowledge of the existence of the substance; 3. the substance is a controlled drug. |

The Misuse of Drugs Regulations 2001 exempt some workers from the main offence of possession of a controlled drug. Regulation 5 provides a licence for some categories of worker that allows them to have drugs in their possession, for example a drug supplier to the pharmaceutical trade. Regulation 6 allows the following categories of worker to possess drugs whilst acting in the course of their duties:

- police officers;
- police support employees;
- customs officers;
- postal workers.

The remainder of the regulations give exemptions to members of the medical profession and state the necessity to keep records in relation to drugs and to patients who have been lawfully prescribed drugs by a medical practitioner. Any other person (other than those listed in the regulations) is therefore acting unlawfully if they possess a controlled drug.

10.13.3 The Three Parts of the Proof for Unlawful Possession

The following are the three parts required for proof of unlawful possession of a controlled drug. (The term 'part' is our own notation, not that of the law.)

Part 1—Physical control	The drug must be in the physical control of the suspect and the suspect must know where the drug is, though it does not have to be on his or her person. For example, if a suspect keeps drugs in a lock-up garage and gives the keys to an innocent person, the drugs remain in the suspect's control and possession, but in the custody of the innocent person. However, if two people use a car and they both use drugs from the glove compartment, they both possess the drugs.
Part 2—Knowledge of the existence of the substance	What is important is that the suspect knows of, or suspects the existence of, the substance in question. If the substance was in a small tin for example, you must show that the suspect knew the tin contained a substance. It does not matter whether or not the suspect knows if the substance is a controlled drug.
Part 3—The substance is a controlled drug	The drug must be a controlled drug in Class A, B, or C.

As an example, imagine that whilst on Supervised Patrol you carry out a search of a man and a woman under the powers within the Misuse of Drugs Act 1971, and you find a cigarette lighter and aluminium foil with traces of brown powder on it in the man's pocket. After examination of the substance it is found to be heroin. To prove the offence of possession you must therefore show:

- that the foil was in his pocket;
- that he knew there was powder on the foil (it does not matter whether or not he knew the substance was a controlled drug); and
- that the powder was heroin.

10.13.4 Defences to Unlawful Possession of a Controlled Drug

Section 28 of the Misuse of Drugs Act 1971 provides a suspect with a potential defence in terms of satisfying Part 1 together with either Part 2 or Part 3 as described earlier. The flow charts below provide more explanation of the ways each part could be used in defence.

Part 1, remember, is about the suspect having **physical control** of the drug. His/her defence could be that he/she did not have possession of it.

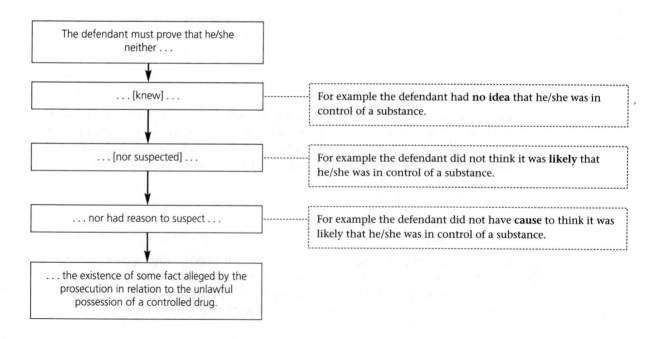

If the woman from our example above had slipped the aluminium foil into the man's pocket (before they were both searched) and the man **did not know** the woman had put it there, he could claim this defence. Similarly, if a package containing controlled drugs is mistakenly delivered to a person's home, so long as the package has not been requested by the homeowner, they can claim they do not possess the drugs.

In addition to Part 1, **either** Part 2 or Part 3 must be satisfied as part of the defence.

Part 2 is about the defendant's **knowledge about the substance**. A defence could be that he/she did not **believe**, **suspect**, or have **reason to suspect** that the substance was a controlled drug.

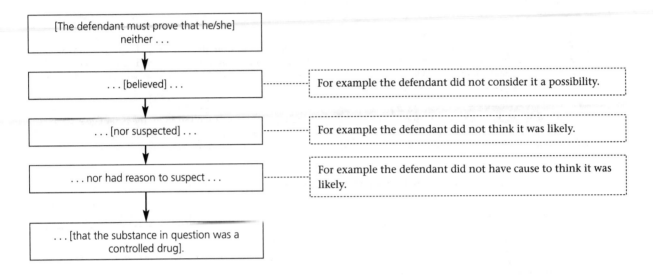

The man in our example who was subsequently found with the aluminium foil package in his pocket claimed that he did not know what the substance was, had never seen anything like it before, and would not be able to have a guess at what it was—he could claim this as a defence to unlawful possession.

Part 3 is about the substance being a **controlled drug**. A defence could be that the defendant believed it was a drug he/she was lawfully entitled to possess:

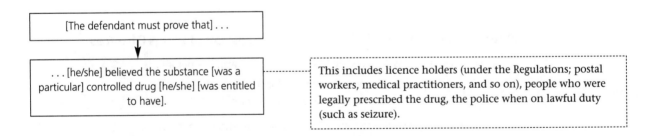

If the man (with the aluminium foil containing heroin in his pocket) was a cocaine addict and had been prescribed heroin instead, and if he neither knew, nor suspected, nor had reason to suspect the substance was actually heroin (and not cocaine), he will have a defence, unless the prosecution can prove otherwise.

10.13.4.1 Further Defences to Unlawful Possession of a Controlled Drug

There are other circumstances which can also provide a defence (s 5(4), the Misuse of Drugs Act 1971), for example:

- parents temporarily possess drugs they have taken from their child (to prevent the child having unlawful possession);
- a member of the public finds a package of drugs and takes it to a police station.

The flowcharts below provide more details about these particular circumstances and the conditions that must be satisfied.

Preventing unlawful possession under s 5 of the Misuse of Drugs Act 1971 means:

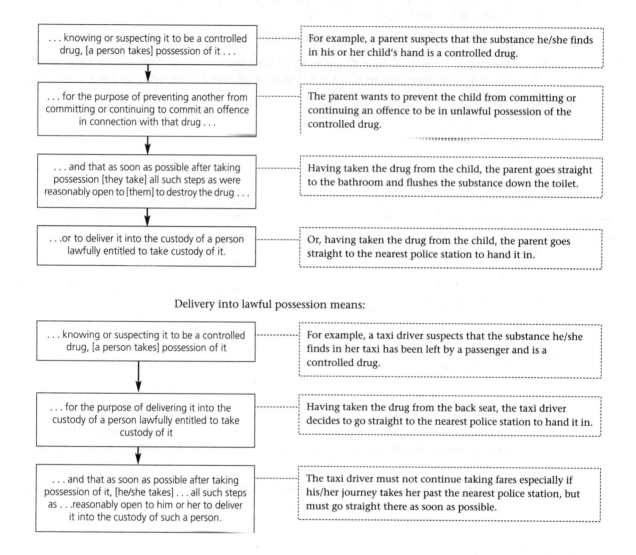

. . . knowing or suspecting it to be a controlled drug, [a person takes] possession of it . . .	For example, a parent suspects that the substance he/she finds in his or her child's hand is a controlled drug.
. . . for the purpose of preventing another from committing or continuing to commit an offence in connection with that drug . . .	The parent wants to prevent the child from committing or continuing an offence to be in unlawful possession of the controlled drug.
. . . and that as soon as possible after taking possession [they take] all such steps as were reasonably open to [them] to destroy the drug . . .	Having taken the drug from the child, the parent goes straight to the bathroom and flushes the substance down the toilet.
. . .or to deliver it into the custody of a person lawfully entitled to take custody of it.	Or, having taken the drug from the child, the parent goes straight to the nearest police station to hand it in.

Delivery into lawful possession means:

. . . knowing or suspecting it to be a controlled drug, [a person takes] possession of it	For example, a taxi driver suspects that the substance he/she finds in her taxi has been left by a passenger and is a controlled drug.
. . . for the purpose of delivering it into the custody of a person lawfully entitled to take custody of it	Having taken the drug from the back seat, the taxi driver decides to go straight to the nearest police station to hand it in.
. . . and that as soon as possible after taking possession of it, [he/she takes] . . . all such steps as . . .reasonably open to him or her to deliver it into the custody of such a person.	The taxi driver must not continue taking fares especially if his/her journey takes her past the nearest police station, but must go straight there as soon as possible.

10.13.5   Mode of Trial and Penalty for Unlawful Possession of Drugs Offences

Offences involving class A drugs are triable either way and the penalty is:

- summarily: six months' imprisonment and/or prescribed fine;
- on indictment: seven years' imprisonment and/or fine.

Offences involving class B drugs are triable either way and the penalty is:

- summarily: three months' imprisonment and/or fine;
- on indictment: five years' imprisonment and/or fine.

Under the Criminal Justice and Police Act 2001, unlawful possession of cannabis can also be dealt with by way of a PND for £80 (see 8.15 above and 10.13.6 below).

Offences involving class C drugs are triable either way and the penalty is:

- summarily: three months' imprisonment and/or fine;
- on indictment: two years' imprisonment and/or fine.

10.13.6   Unlawful Possession of Cannabis

During the last decade, cannabis was initially reclassified to class C but more recently has been returned to class B. With the aim of providing a consistent national approach during these periods of change, ACPO has produced guidance including various models of intervention for unlawful possession of cannabis. The current model only applies to adults (18 years or over) who are found in unlawful possession of cannabis for personal use.

ACPO recommend that the term 'Cannabis Warning' is used (rather than 'Street Warning') and a typical format for the warning is given in 10.13.6.1 below.

10.13.6.1 **Intervention model for the unlawful possession of cannabis**

The guidance provides you with an opportunity to give a justifiable and proportionate response, and aims to send out a message that cannabis remains harmful and illegal. Three levels of escalating intervention are provided for, but the ACPO guidance emphasizes that although your discretion can be used at all times (see 5.7 above), arrest remains your first presumption.

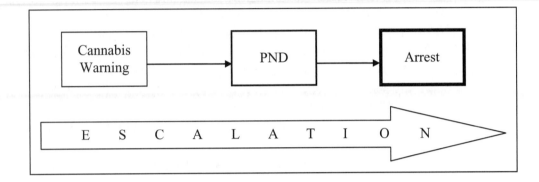

The model only applies to a person who:

- is aged 18 years or over;
- is not vulnerable;
- is competent enough to grasp the meaning of your questions and his/her replies;
- is not under the influence of alcohol or drugs at the time a warning or PND is issued;
- possesses an amount of cannabis suitable for personal use only;
- has verifiable personal details eg name, date of birth, and address.

For a 'Cannabis Warning' he/she must also be willing to admit the offence.

Suspects aged 17 years and under cannot be issued with a Cannabis Warning or a PND for unlawful possession of cannabis. They will have to be given a reprimand, a final warning (see 8.15.4 above), or prosecuted.

Aggravating factors must be taken into consideration when deciding which option to take in the intervention model. If, for example, there are no aggravating factors then a Cannabis Warning is the likely outcome; however, if one or more aggravating factors are present you should use your discretion to decide whether to issue a PND or make an arrest.

Aggravating factors include a suspect who:

- was smoking cannabis in a public place or in the view of the public, eg at a sports ground, on a bus, near a pub, or on educational premises;
- is a repeat offender (other criminal offences) or someone who continually engages in anti-social behaviour; or
- appears not to recognize the seriousness of possessing cannabis.

The location where the person is found to be in possession of cannabis may also be an aggravating factor, for example:

- previously identified 'hot spots' for anti-social behaviour due to cannabis use, eg shopping centres, street corners, parks, and shops; or
- schools, playgrounds, or youth clubs: places where young people may come into contact with cannabis users.

Cannabis Warnings can only be issued when there are no aggravating factors (see above), and only to a person who is compliant with the procedure and:

- has no previous records of Cannabis Warnings, PNDs, or convictions; and
- is not listed on police intelligence records as a persistent offender.

The general principle stated in the current guidance is that no more than one Cannabis Warning should be issued to an individual; however, the previous guidance was slightly different and considered two warnings to be a cut-off point. Therefore, Cannabis Warnings issued after 26 January 2009 must be taken into account when deciding a level of intervention, whereas those issued before this date should be considered only as part of any previous offending history.

There is no formal group of words that make up a Cannabis Warning; however, you might want to say to the person that it will:

- be recorded by you and will be added to local police databases for future reference;
- produce a record of a detected crime for the purposes of statistics as a recordable crime;
- not amount to a criminal record or conviction against them;
- lead to the issuing of a PND or maybe arrest if he/she is found in unlawful possession of cannabis in the future.

A Penalty Notice for Disorder (see 8.15.2) or arrest must be used if the suspect has previously received either:

- a Cannabis Warning after 26 January 2009 (you can either issue a PND or arrest the suspect); or
- a PND—your only option is to arrest (even if he/she has never previously received a Cannabis Warning).

You can use your discretion to escalate to a PND or arrest even if the suspect has never received a Cannabis Warning, if the circumstances dictate such action. Similarly, you can escalate directly to the arrest option for suspects who have never been issued a PND.

If the suspect does not admit the unlawful possession of cannabis you can only issue a PND if you have sufficient evidence (see 10.13.3 above) to prove the offence. For further information on the issue of PNDs, see 8.15.2 above.

The flowchart below shows the main factors to take into account when dealing with suspects in possession of cannabis. Individual circumstances and your use of discretion mean that the diagram can only provide an indication of the more usual outcomes, and does not cover every eventuality. The shaded boxes relate only to the intervention model.

10.13.6.2 Unlawful possession of small amounts of cannabis: practical aspects

The ACPO guidance described in 10.13.6.1 above relates to dealing with some categories of suspects in possession of small amounts of cannabis. The list below concerns some of the more practical aspects of managing such encounters, and also refers you to other relevant parts of this Handbook.

For suspects unlawfully in possession of small amounts of cannabis you should:

1. Investigate the suspected unlawful possession, remembering your obligations under the PACE Codes of Practice to protect the rights of the individual (see 8.4 above), and determine if there is:
   (a) any lawful excuse (see 10.13.2 –10.13.4.1 above); or
   (b) evidence of a further offence such as intent to supply (see 10.14.2. below).
2. Seize the cannabis (see 13.5.8 below) and secure it according to your local policy.
3. Record the incident contemporaneously in your pocket note book (see 8.3.2 and 8.15.1 above).
4. Manage the recorded information effectively (see 6.11 above), remembering to complete stop and search forms (see 7.5.5 above), intelligence reports (see 12.4.5.2 below) and crime reports (see 5.15.4 above).

Any arrest you make must be necessary (see 8.7.4 above).

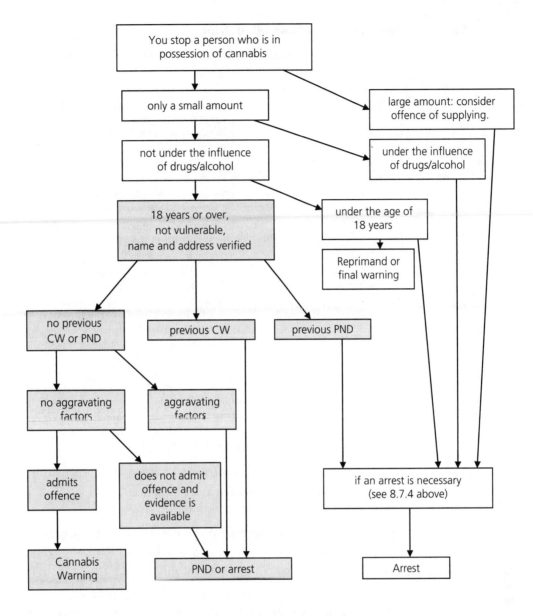

Part of this section has been adapted from the ACPO 'Guidance on Cannabis Possession for Personal Use: Revised Intervention Framework'. The full document which includes a useful list of frequently asked questions can be viewed at: <http://www.acpo.police.uk/asp/policies/Data/ACPO_Cannabis_Guidance_-_28_Jan_09.doc>.

TASK 10

Identify the common street names for the most common Class A, B, and C drugs in your policing area.

10.14 Production, Supply, and Search for Controlled Drugs

Drugs legislation has been carefully worded so that it is not only the illegal end user of controlled drugs who is subject to prosecution, but also (and perhaps more importantly) those people involved in the supply of the drugs.

The offences of production and supply will be dealt with here; the legislation involved is from ss 4(2), 4(3), 5(3), 6(2), 8, and 28 of the Misuse of Drugs Act 1971.

10.14.1   Production of a Controlled Drug

Section 4(2) of the Misuse of Drugs Act 1971 states that it is an offence for a person to:

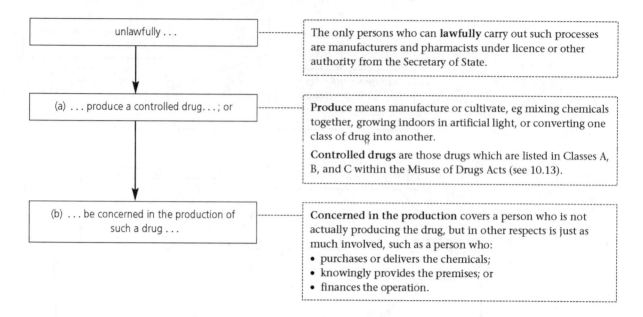

Offences involving class A drugs are triable either way and the penalty is:

- summarily: six months' imprisonment and/or prescribed fine;
- on indictment: life imprisonment and/or fine.

Offences involving class B drugs are triable either way and the penalty is:

- summarily: six months' imprisonment and/or fine;
- on indictment: fourteen years' imprisonment and/or fine.

Offences involving class C drugs are triable either way and the penalty is:

- summarily: three months' imprisonment and/or fine;
- on indictment: five years' imprisonment and/or fine.

This is a 'trigger' offence under s 63B of the PACE Act 1984; you can demand a sample from a person in police custody (see 8.12 above on taking samples from people).

10.14.2   Supplying a controlled drug

Section 4(3) of the Misuse of Drugs Act 1971 states it is an offence for a person to:

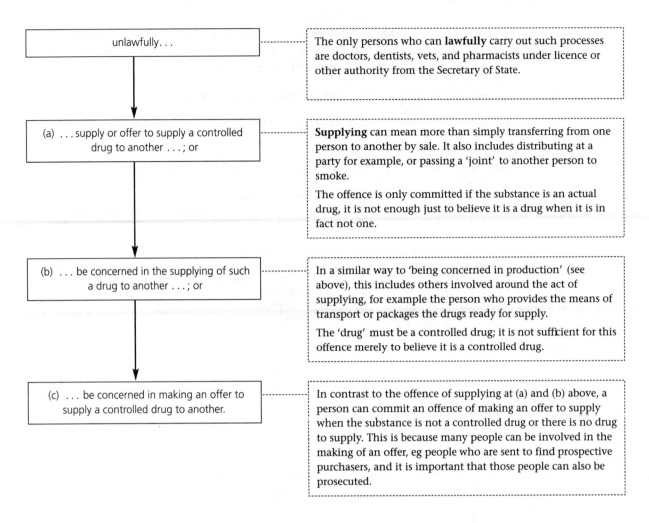

| unlawfully... | The only persons who can **lawfully** carry out such processes are doctors, dentists, vets, and pharmacists under licence or other authority from the Secretary of State. |

(a) ...supply or offer to supply a controlled drug to another ...; or

Supplying can mean more than simply transferring from one person to another by sale. It also includes distributing at a party for example, or passing a 'joint' to another person to smoke.

The offence is only committed if the substance is an actual drug, it is not enough just to believe it is a drug when it is in fact not one.

(b) ...be concerned in the supplying of such a drug to another ...; or

In a similar way to 'being concerned in production' (see above), this includes others involved around the act of supplying, for example the person who provides the means of transport or packages the drugs ready for supply.

The 'drug' must be a controlled drug; it is not sufficient for this offence merely to believe it is a controlled drug.

(c) ...be concerned in making an offer to supply a controlled drug to another.

In contrast to the offence of supplying at (a) and (b) above, a person can commit an offence of making an offer to supply when the substance is not a controlled drug or there is no drug to supply. This is because many people can be involved in the making of an offer, eg people who are sent to find prospective purchasers, and it is important that those people can also be prosecuted.

Under s 4A of the Misuse of Drugs Act 1971, a court must treat this offence more seriously if it was committed on or in the vicinity of a school, or the suspect used a courier who was under the age of 18 years.

The penalties are the same as for the production or supply of a controlled drug (see 10.14.1 above), and the offence is a trigger offence; you can demand a sample from a suspect in custody (see 8.12 above on taking samples from people).

10.14.3 Possession with Intent to Supply a Controlled Drug

Section 5(3) of the Misuse of Drugs Act 1971 states it is an offence for a person to:

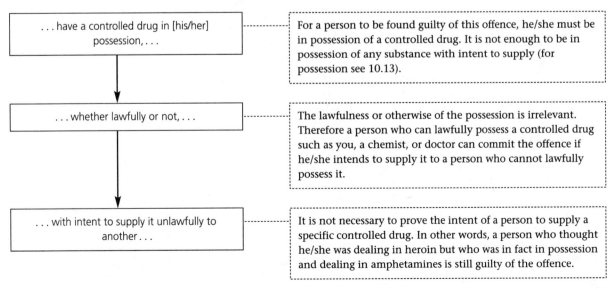

...have a controlled drug in [his/her] possession,...

For a person to be found guilty of this offence, he/she must be in possession of a controlled drug. It is not enough to be in possession of any substance with intent to supply (for possession see 10.13).

...whether lawfully or not,...

The lawfulness or otherwise of the possession is irrelevant. Therefore a person who can lawfully possess a controlled drug such as you, a chemist, or doctor can commit the offence if he/she intends to supply it to a person who cannot lawfully possess it.

...with intent to supply it unlawfully to another...

It is not necessary to prove the intent of a person to supply a specific controlled drug. In other words, a person who thought he/she was dealing in heroin but who was in fact in possession and dealing in amphetamines is still guilty of the offence.

The penalties are the same as for the production of, supply, or intent to supply a controlled drug (see 10.14.1 above), and the offence is a trigger offence; you can demand a sample from a suspect in custody (see 8.12 above on taking samples from people).

10.14.4   Occupier or Manager of Premises Permitting Drug Abuse

Section 8 of the Misuse of Drugs Act 1971 states it is an offence for a person:

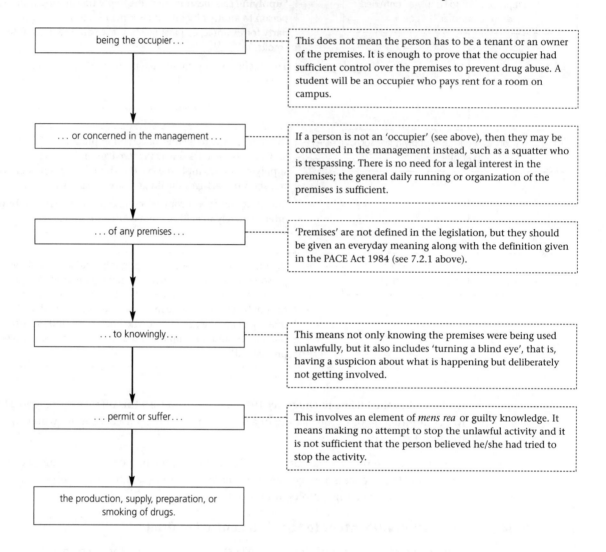

being the occupier... — This does not mean the person has to be a tenant or an owner of the premises. It is enough to prove that the occupier had sufficient control over the premises to prevent drug abuse. A student will be an occupier who pays rent for a room on campus.

...or concerned in the management... — If a person is not an 'occupier' (see above), then they may be concerned in the management instead, such as a squatter who is trespassing. There is no need for a legal interest in the premises; the general daily running or organization of the premises is sufficient.

...of any premises... — 'Premises' are not defined in the legislation, but they should be given an everyday meaning along with the definition given in the PACE Act 1984 (see 7.2.1 above).

...to knowingly... — This means not only knowing the premises were being used unlawfully, but it also includes 'turning a blind eye', that is, having a suspicion about what is happening but deliberately not getting involved.

...permit or suffer... — This involves an element of *mens rea* or guilty knowledge. It means making no attempt to stop the unlawful activity and it is not sufficient that the person believed he/she had tried to stop the activity.

the production, supply, preparation, or smoking of drugs.

More details of the type of drug-related activities and the possible role of the occupier of the premises are given in the table below.

Drug-related activity	Role of the occupier of the premises
s 8(a) production or attempted production of a controlled drug	Here the occupier or manager would need to know or 'look the other way' in relation to the production of a controlled drug, or perhaps conspiring with the producer.
s 8(b) supply or attempt to supply a controlled drug to another	It is not necessary to prove that the occupier knew exactly which type of drug was being supplied, only that the substance was a controlled drug.
s 8(c) preparation of opium for smoking	The occupier would be guilty of an offence if he/she permitted an activity such as raw opium (obtained from the unripe seed pods of the opium poppy) being 'cooked' to make it suitable for smoking. At the time this was drafted, the legislators were particularly keen to outlaw this practice.
s 8(d) smoking of cannabis, cannabis resin, or prepared opium	The action of smoking must actually occur for the offence to be committed; it is not enough for the occupier or manager just to give permission for these activities to take place. The cleaner of premises which he/she knows to exist primarily for the smoking of cannabis would not be guilty of this offence because he/she is not occupying or managing the premises.

Offences involving class A, B, and C drugs are triable either way and the penalty is:

- summarily: a prescribed fine and/or imprisonment (six months for classes A and B, and three months for class C) ;
- on indictment: 14 years' imprisonment and/or fine.

10.14.5 The Offence of Growing Cannabis

Section 6(2) of the Misuse of Drugs Act 1971 states it is an offence 'for a person to cultivate any plant of the genus Cannabis'. 'Cultivate' is not defined but would involve some sort of attention such as watering the plants. There is no need to prove that the defendant knew it was a cannabis plant.

This offence is triable either way and the penalty is:

- summarily: six months' imprisonment and/or fine;
- on indictment: 14 years' imprisonment and/or fine.

10.14.6 Defences to Drugs Offences

Section 28 of the Misuse of Drugs Act 1971 provides a defence to the following drugs offences:

- s 4(2) production of a controlled drug;
- s 4(3) supplying a controlled drug;
- s 5(3) possession with intent to supply a controlled drug;
- s 6(2) unlawful cultivation of cannabis.

The defences relate to physical possession and knowledge of the possession by the suspect, and whether the substance in question actually is a controlled drug; see 10.13.4 above for full details of these defences.

10.14.7 Stop and Search for Controlled Drugs

Drugs are **not** prohibited articles under s 1 of the PACE Act 1984, but s 23(2) of the Misuse of Drugs Act 1971 has its own power of search (for persons and vehicles) which states that:

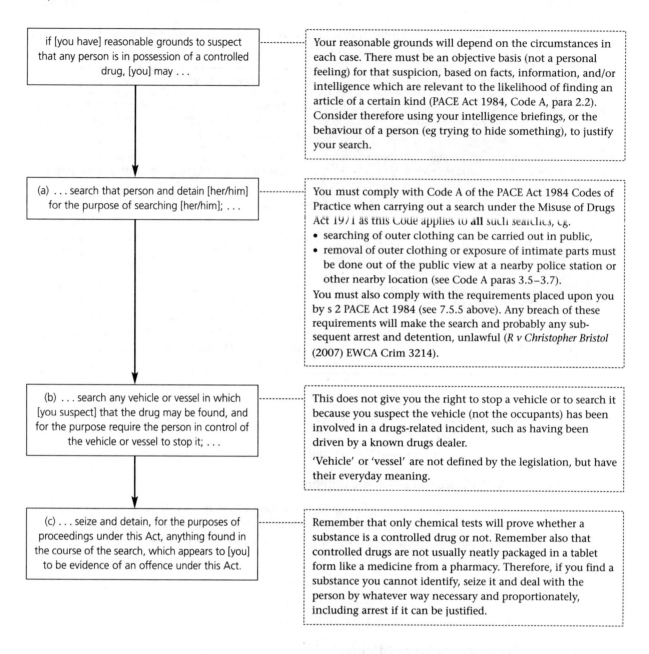

if [you have] reasonable grounds to suspect that any person is in possession of a controlled drug, [you] may . . .	Your reasonable grounds will depend on the circumstances in each case. There must be an objective basis (not a personal feeling) for that suspicion, based on facts, information, and/or intelligence which are relevant to the likelihood of finding an article of a certain kind (PACE Act 1984, Code A, para 2.2). Consider therefore using your intelligence briefings, or the behaviour of a person (eg trying to hide something), to justify your search.
(a) . . . search that person and detain [her/him] for the purpose of searching [her/him]; . . .	You must comply with Code A of the PACE Act 1984 Codes of Practice when carrying out a search under the Misuse of Drugs Act 1971 as this Code applies to **all** such searches, eg. • searching of outer clothing can be carried out in public, • removal of outer clothing or exposure of intimate parts must be done out of the public view at a nearby police station or other nearby location (see Code A paras 3.5–3.7). You must also comply with the requirements placed upon you by s 2 PACE Act 1984 (see 7.5.5 above). Any breach of these requirements will make the search and probably any subsequent arrest and detention, unlawful (*R v Christopher Bristol* (2007) EWCA Crim 3214).
(b) . . . search any vehicle or vessel in which [you suspect] that the drug may be found, and for the purpose require the person in control of the vehicle or vessel to stop it; . . .	This does not give you the right to stop a vehicle or to search it because you suspect the vehicle (not the occupants) has been involved in a drugs-related incident, such as having been driven by a known drugs dealer. 'Vehicle' or 'vessel' are not defined by the legislation, but have their everyday meaning.
(c) . . . seize and detain, for the purposes of proceedings under this Act, anything found in the course of the search, which appears to [you] to be evidence of an offence under this Act.	Remember that only chemical tests will prove whether a substance is a controlled drug or not. Remember also that controlled drugs are not usually neatly packaged in a tablet form like a medicine from a pharmacy. Therefore, if you find a substance you cannot identify, seize it and deal with the person by whatever way necessary and proportionately, including arrest if it can be justified.

If a person intentionally obstructs you during the course of a search under this section, he/she commits an offence under s 23(4) of the Misuse of Drugs Act 1971, incidental to whether or not any drugs are found.

This offence is triable either way and the penalty is:

• summarily: six months' imprisonment and/or prescribed fine;
• on indictment: two years' imprisonment and/or fine.

TASK 11

• Make a list of factors and circumstances that would provide reasonable grounds for suspecting a person is in unlawful possession of drugs with intent to supply.
• Consider what you would say to a person before carrying out a search under s 23 of the Misuse of Drugs Act 1971.
• Having found an unidentifiable substance, what are some of the reasons that would make it necessary to arrest the person?

10.15   Unlawful Personal Violence

Here we cover several different types of offence:

* **common assault** under s 39 of the Criminal Justice Act 1988;
* **common assault by beating (battery)** under s 39 of the Criminal Justice Act 1988;
* **assault occasioning actual bodily harm** under s 47 of the Offences Against the Person Act 1861.

You are likely to find the information given here relevant to Phase 3 of the IPLDP and LPG 1 under the 'Crime' heading. The law regarding unlawful personal violence concerns two groups of offences, assaults and batteries, which each has a separate legal meaning. In law an **assault** does not actually mean physical attack; instead it is any act, such as a threat made by an assailant, which makes a victim understand they are going to be immediately subjected to some personal violence. An example of this would be: 'I'm going to smash your head in!' A **battery**, on the other hand, is the actual use of force by an assailant on a victim such as a kick or a punch.

10.15.1   Common Assault

Common assault is an offence under s 39 of the Criminal Justice Act 1988. Common assault consists of either an assault **or** a battery (for more details on the distinction between these two, see below). If there is a serious outcome, then the injuries may constitute **actual bodily harm** (ABH) and the offender will receive a greater penalty if found guilty at court. If the outcome is even more serious, then the injuries may constitute **grievous bodily harm** (GBH).

First, we should look at the distinction between assault and battery. The case of *Fagan v MP Commissioner* [1969] 1 QB 439 has set a precedent for the definition of an assault.

10.15.2 Assault

An assault (s 39, Criminal Justice Act 1988) is:

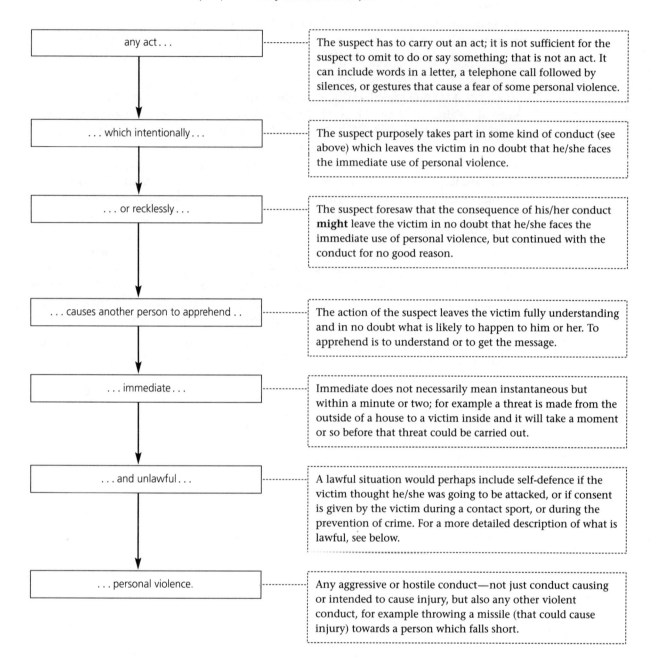

10.15.3   Battery

A person commits a battery (s 39, Criminal Justice Act 1988) if they:

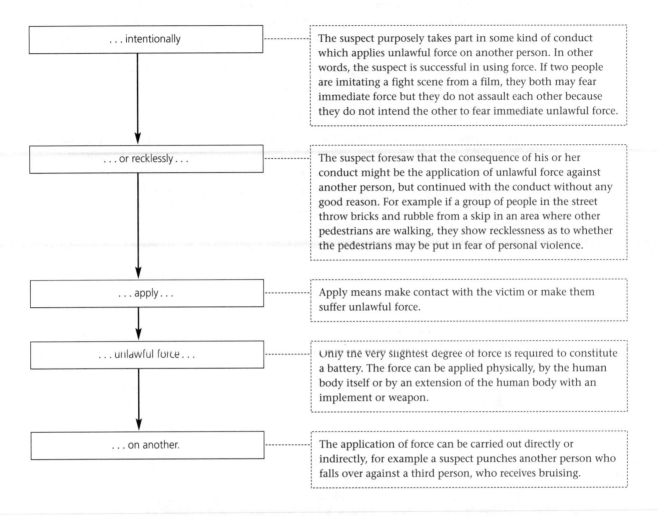

...intentionally	The suspect purposely takes part in some kind of conduct which applies unlawful force on another person. In other words, the suspect is successful in using force. If two people are imitating a fight scene from a film, they both may fear immediate force but they do not assault each other because they do not intend the other to fear immediate unlawful force.
...or recklessly...	The suspect foresaw that the consequence of his or her conduct might be the application of unlawful force against another person, but continued with the conduct without any good reason. For example if a group of people in the street throw bricks and rubble from a skip in an area where other pedestrians are walking, they show recklessness as to whether the pedestrians may be put in fear of personal violence.
...apply...	Apply means make contact with the victim or make them suffer unlawful force.
...unlawful force...	Only the very slightest degree of force is required to constitute a battery. The force can be applied physically, by the human body itself or by an extension of the human body with an implement or weapon.
...on another.	The application of force can be carried out directly or indirectly, for example a suspect punches another person who falls over against a third person, who receives bruising.

By now, you will probably have realized that most batteries are preceded by an assault, but not all of them. For example if a person is punched to the ground in the dark without anything being said there has definitely been a battery, but because of the lack of light, it is unlikely there has been an assault as the victim could not have been aware that immediate unlawful violence was about to be used against him/her.

10.15.4   Defences

There are several defences for the offence of battery, such as consent or the lawful application of force. A fuller list is provided below.

Consent could be given for being tattooed, having a piercing, or being operated on for a medical condition. Consent does not include:

- being reckless as to whether consent was or was not actually given, for example knowing an injury might occur and still taking a risk of causing it;
- submitting to an assault, for example by giving in; nor
- duress, which means giving in as a result of pressure or a threat.

Lawful sports such as boxing and rugby involve the participants in contact, and they consent to the injuries they may receive while playing within the rules of that sport. (If the rules are broken and the injuries are caused as a consequence, then this defence no longer applies.)

Self-defence may also be used as a legal defence: the court must decide if the actions of the person defending him or herself were reasonable under the circumstances and not excessive.

Prevention of crime or lawful arrest can also be used as a defence: s 3(1) of the Criminal Law Act 1967 allows a person to use such force as is reasonable in the prevention of crime, or in effecting or assisting in the lawful arrest of offenders (see 8.9.2 above). However, if a police officer restrains a person without making a declaration (or intending) to arrest him/her, the officer commits an assault, even if an arrest could have been justified (see *Fraser Wood v Director of Public Prosecutions* (2008) EWHC 1056 (Admin)).

10.15.4.1 The meaning of 'reasonable force' in crime prevention

The Criminal Justice and Immigration Act 2008 provides guidance about the meaning of 'reasonable force' in the context of self-defence or prevention of crime as a legal defence. The question whether the degree of force is reasonable is based upon consideration of:

- the belief of the person using the force that it was reasonable (it is immaterial if the belief is mistaken, unless this is attributable to voluntarily induced intoxication);
- the proportionality of the force used;
- any possible inability of the person using the force to judge (in the heat of the moment) the exact degree of force required; or
- evidence that the person using the force did what he/she honestly and instinctively thought was necessary for self-defence, prevention of crime, or to assist in the lawful arrest of persons.

Note, however, that as a result of s 58 of the Children Act 2004, a parent no longer has the legal right to apply moderate and reasonable physical chastisement to their children. In other words, if any injury is inflicted on the child, there is no defence at all.

TASK 12

Consider the following incidents in relation to s 39, Criminal Justice Act 1988, and state for each which offence has been committed:

1. You are called to investigate an incident in the street. Two men have been arguing and one man has pushed and shoved the other, but very little force has been used upon the victim, who is therefore uninjured. What offence has been committed, battery or common assault?
2. You are called upon to investigate an incident where no force has been used upon the victim, but the victim was left in no doubt that he/she was about to face unlawful personal violence. What offence has been committed?

The offence of common assault is triable summarily only and the penalty is six months' imprisonment. Note that this offence can be racially or religiously aggravated (see 9.11 above).

10.15.5 Actual Bodily Harm (ABH)

The offence of Assault Occasioning Actual Bodily Harm (s 47 of the Offences Against the Person Act 1861) has been committed if there is a more serious outcome and the injuries of the victim (owing to the assault or battery) result in actual bodily harm. The aspects of intention or recklessness are the same for actual bodily harm as they are for common assault.

In this offence, the assault can be either an assault or a battery, so long as actual bodily harm has been caused. Actual bodily harm means any injury which interferes with the health or comfort of person in more than a trivial way. The injury must be real and it should be capable of being seen or felt by the victim (or by witnesses such as yourself). This includes psychiatric injury caused by an assault such as a threat which has put a victim in fear of immediate, unlawful violence. Similarly, a battery can be committed if the victim suffers some unlawful force such as a punch which causes the loss of a tooth.

In terms of intent, there is only a need to prove that the assault or battery was intended or that it was carried out recklessly. There is no need to prove that the accused intended to cause injuries amounting to actual bodily harm (or was reckless as to whether the injuries amounting to actual bodily harm would be caused).

This offence is triable either way and the penalty is:

- summarily: six months' imprisonment and/or fine;
- on indictment: five years' imprisonment.

Note that this offence can be racially or religiously aggravated (see 9.11 above).

Unlawful personal violence is a very common occurrence and you will be called upon to investigate such incidents with alarming frequency. The incidents may or may not be drink- or drug-related. The health and safety of you and the general public is paramount, therefore always consider whether you need to use your personal protective equipment.

TASK 13

You attend a domestic crime incident involving two partners in a relationship. One of the partners complains that she has been punched by the other. How will you identify what type of assault has been committed?

10.16 Serious Offences of Personal Violence

Here we cover the following serious offences of personal violence:

- unlawful and malicious wounding, or inflicting grievous bodily harm (inflicting GBH);
- wounding or causing grievous bodily harm **with intent** to do grievous bodily harm, or to resist or prevent arrest (referred to as 'GBH with Intent');
- assaults on the police;
- assault with intent to resist arrest;
- obstructing a police officer.

10.16.1 Unlawful and Malicious Wounding or Inflicting GBH

Section 20 of the Offences Against the Person Act 1861 states that it is an offence 'unlawfully and maliciously' to either:

- 'wound another person'; or
- 'inflict grievous bodily harm [(GBH) upon another person]'.

The suspect must know that the actions would result in some kind of injury, but not necessarily foresee the degree of the injury. The injuries can be caused either with or without a weapon.

To understand this offence, careful consideration needs to be given first to the meaning of the words 'unlawfully' and 'maliciously'. **Unlawfully** means 'without lawful justification', (as opposed to cases of lawfully inflicted injury, for example some instances of self-defence.

Maliciously means:

- an actual intention to do that particular kind of harm; or
- recklessness (unreasonably persisting in taking that risk) as to whether such harmful consequences would occur as a result of the actions taken. For example, in the reckless passing-on of a sexually transmitted infection, the suspect would foresee that the victim might contract the infection through sexual activity but would still go on to take that risk.

Note that, although malice (ill-will or a malevolent motive) must be present, it is not limited to, nor does it require, any ill-will towards the injured person him or herself.

10.16.1.1 The extent of the injury

The injury must amount to either wounding or grievous ('really serious') bodily harm.

Wounding is defined as breaking of **all** the layers of the skin. It is not necessary to cause the wound with a weapon (though of course this is often the case, for example using a deliberately smashed glass for the attack).

Grievous bodily harm is not defined in the Act but in the case of *DPP v Smith* [1960] 3 All ER 161 it was agreed that it should be given its ordinary meaning which is 'really serious bodily harm'. The bodily harm must be serious, but not necessarily dangerous or permanent.

Examples of GBH include:

- injury resulting in some permanent disability, loss of function;
- visible disfigurement;
- broken or displaced limbs or bones, fractured skull;
- injuries with substantial blood loss, usually requiring blood transfusion;
- injuries resulting in lengthy treatment or incapacity;
- psychiatric injury (expert evidence is required).

(The list above is adapted from CPS, 2006b.)

GBH does not have to include an assault or a battery (see 10.15 above). For example, a person infecting his/her partner knowingly with the HIV AIDS virus while concealing the infection from the partner is committing the offence of grievous bodily harm. In England and Wales, there have been ten convictions for GBH based on the reckless transmission of HIV (up until March 2008 (CPS, 2008)). Telephone calls that would result in serious psychiatric injury to the victim can also amount to grievous bodily harm.

This offence is triable either way and the penalty is:

- summarily: six months' imprisonment and/or a fine;
- on indictment: five years' imprisonment.

This offence can be racially or religiously aggravated (see 9.11 above).

10.16.2 GBH with Intent

The full name for this offence is 'wounding or causing grievous bodily harm with intent to do grievous bodily harm or to resist or prevent arrest'.

Section 18 of the Offences Against the Person Act 1861 states it is an offence to:

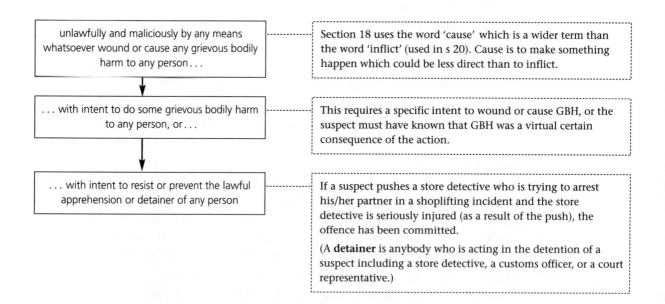

The main difference between ss 18 and 20 offences is that s 18 offences have the element of intent (whilst s 20 refers to the concept of 'malicious'). Of course intent is sometimes difficult to prove, although there will be some obvious examples, for instance if a weapon is used.

This offence is triable on indictment only and the penalty is life imprisonment.

There was no perceived need to create a racially or religiously aggravated offence for this offence as the maximum sentence is already life imprisonment.

10.16.3　Assaults on Police Officers and Persons Supporting a Police Officer

Section 89(1) of the Police Act 1996 states it is an offence:

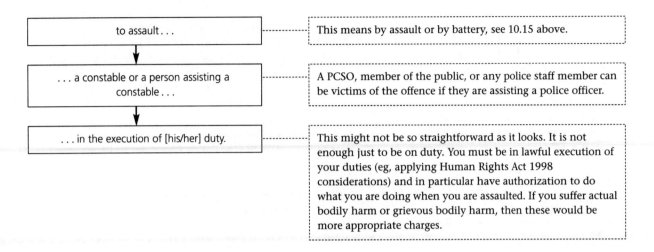

to assault . . .	This means by assault or by battery, see 10.15 above.
. . . a constable or a person assisting a constable . . .	A PCSO, member of the public, or any police staff member can be victims of the offence if they are assisting a police officer.
. . . in the execution of [his/her] duty.	This might not be so straightforward as it looks. It is not enough just to be on duty. You must be in lawful execution of your duties (eg, applying Human Rights Act 1998 considerations) and in particular have authorization to do what you are doing when you are assaulted. If you suffer actual bodily harm or grievous bodily harm, then these would be more appropriate charges.

This offence is triable summarily and the penalty is six months' imprisonment and/or a fine.

10.16.4　Assault with Intent to Resist Arrest

Section 38 of the Offences Against the Person Act 1861 states it is an offence to:

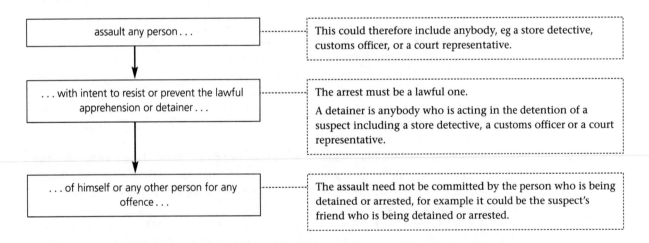

assault any person . . .	This could therefore include anybody, eg a store detective, customs officer, or a court representative.
. . . with intent to resist or prevent the lawful apprehension or detainer . . .	The arrest must be a lawful one. A detainer is anybody who is acting in the detention of a suspect including a store detective, a customs officer or a court representative.
. . . of himself or any other person for any offence . . .	The assault need not be committed by the person who is being detained or arrested, for example it could be the suspect's friend who is being detained or arrested.

Even if the suspect believes the person making the arrest had no lawful power to make the arrest, or the suspect believes he/she is innocent, this makes no difference to whether the offence has been committed.

This offence is triable summarily and the penalty is two years' imprisonment.

10.16.5 Obstructing a Police Officer

Section 89 of the Police Act 1996 states it is an offence for any person:

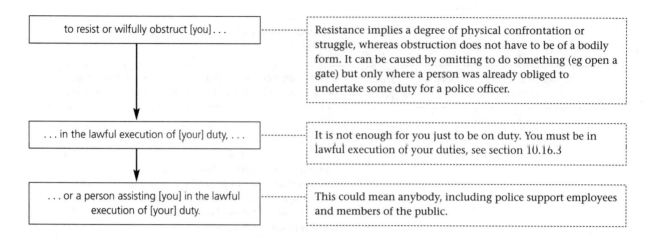

to resist or wilfully obstruct [you] . . .	Resistance implies a degree of physical confrontation or struggle, whereas obstruction does not have to be of a bodily form. It can be caused by omitting to do something (eg open a gate) but only where a person was already obliged to undertake some duty for a police officer.
. . . in the lawful execution of [your] duty, . . .	It is not enough for you just to be on duty. You must be in lawful execution of your duties, see section 10.16.3
. . . or a person assisting [you] in the lawful execution of [your] duty.	This could mean anybody, including police support employees and members of the public.

This offence is triable summarily and the penalty is one month's imprisonment and/or a fine.

TASK 14

You are deployed by your control room to each of the following incidents. Using the information you are given (and no more), decide what offence or offences may have been committed in relation to the injuries sustained by the victims. In some cases you may wish to give more than a single answer.

1. Two people are arguing in the street. The dispute reaches a point where one of the couple head-butts the other, who then has a severe nose bleed.
2. An apparently drunken man throws a glass bottle from a moving car in the direction of a woman waiting at a bus stop. The bottle hits the shelter and breaks. A large fragment of glass hits the woman on her head, causing a deep wound which bleeds profusely. The woman's skull can be easily seen through the wound. Subsequently, the victim attended accident and emergency at a local hospital and had several stitches inserted.
3. CCTV images show a woman taking goods from a clothes store and hiding them under her jacket. A store detective follows her out and into the street, stops her, explains who he is, and why he is detaining her. She makes a sudden move, pushes the store detective backwards, and he falls over and grazes his hand.
4. After months of alleged harassment by local youths in the street outside her house, the occupant loses her temper, goes out to one of the youths, and slaps him round the face, leaving a large red slap mark on his cheek.

10.17 Protecting Children from Harm

Children are sometimes exposed to significant harm by their parents, relatives, and other people involved in their care and supervision. 'Harm' is not specifically defined in the Children Act 1989, but s 31 provides some guidance on the meaning of the term. The diagram below summarizes the different types of harm, and shows the many ways in which children can suffer harm.

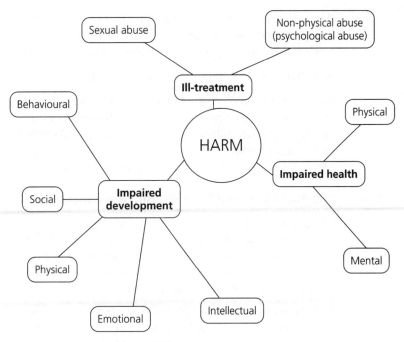

Different types of harm to children

Some of the legislation relating to children's safety and well-being is considered below, and this is followed by an account of the procedures to be followed by the police, to help protect children from harm.

Section 1(1) of the Children and Young Persons Act 1933 states that an offence is committed by any person over the age of 16 years (with responsibility for a child or young person under 16) who:

- wilfully 'assaults, ill-treats, neglects, abandons or exposes' the young person; or
- causes or procures him/her to be treated in such a way;

if this is likely to cause the child or young person unnecessary suffering or injury to health including:

- physical injury or loss of 'sight, hearing, limb or organ of the body';
- psychological problems such as 'mental derangement'.

This offence is triable either way and the penalty is:

- summarily: six months' imprisonment and/or a fine;
- on indictment: ten years' imprisonment and/or a fine.

10.17.1 Cigarettes and Young People

As a police officer you have a responsibility to help prevent young people from smoking and gaining access to cigarettes (and rolling tobacco). Section 7(3) of the Children and Young Persons Act 1933 (CYPA) states that it is your duty as a constable in uniform to seize any tobacco or cigarette papers in the possession of a person apparently under the age of 16 years whom you find smoking in any street or public place. You should dispose of any seized items following your force's policy and procedures.

10.17.1.1 Selling tobacco to young people

It is an offence to sell cigarettes to young people under the age of 18 years. Section 7(1) of the CYPA 1933 states:

> A person who sells to a person under the age of eighteen years any tobacco or cigarette papers, whether for [his/her] own use or not, commits an offence.

However, shopkeepers may be relieved to know that under s 7(1A) of the CYPA 1933 it is a defence for a person charged with such an offence if he/she can prove that he/she 'took all reasonable precautions and exercised all due diligence to avoid the commission of the offence'.

This offence is triable summarily and the penalty is a fine.

Should a person be convicted of an offence under s 7(1) or 7(2) of the CYPA 1933 on at least two occasions within two years, a magistrates' court can apply restriction orders. These orders (under s 12) ban the offender from selling tobacco-related products or managing a premises for selling such products. It is an offence for a person to knowingly contravene such a restriction order; this offence is triable summarily and the penalty is a fine.

10.17.2 Injuries to Children from Heating Appliances

Carers have a responsibility to ensure that children are kept safe when heating appliances are in use. The legislation applies to people over the age of 16 who are caring for children under the age of 12. Section 11 of the YPA 1933 states that a person commits an offence if a child is killed or suffers serious injury because he/she allowed 'the child to be in a room containing an open fire grate or any heating appliance' and the appliance was:

- 'liable to cause injury to a person by contact with it'; and
- 'not sufficiently protected to guard against the risk of being burnt or scalded without taking reasonable precautions against that risk'.

This offence is triable summarily and the penalty is a fine.

10.17.3 Police Protection

The police can act to prevent further harm to a child. Whether or not a child would otherwise be likely to suffer significant **harm** will be a matter for you (as a police officer) to decide. The Children Act 1989 provides you with the powers to take children (under 18 years of age who are at risk of significant harm) into police protection. However, Home Office Circular 17/2008 states that:

> [p]olice protection is an emergency power and should only be used when necessary, the principle being that wherever possible the decision to remove a child/children from a parent or carer should be made by a court (para 15).

Apart from in exceptional circumstances (for example, an imminent threat to a child's welfare), no child is to be taken into police protection until the **initiating officer** (see below) has seen the child and assessed his or her circumstances.

10.17.3.1 Procedure for police protection

Section 46(1) of the Children Act 1989 states that:

> where [you have] reasonable cause to believe that a child would otherwise be likely to suffer significant harm, [you] may …
> (a) remove [the child] to suitable accommodation and keep [him/her] there; or
> (b) take all reasonable steps to ensure that [his/her] removal from a hospital, or other place, in which [he/she] is accommodated, is prevented.

There are two separate and distinct roles for the police in relation to police protection: the **initiating** officer and the **designated** officer (Home Office Circular 17/2008). The initiating officer takes the child into police protection, undertakes the initial enquiries, and completes a Police Protection Form as soon as possible. The designated officer's role is to have an independent overview of the circumstances in which the child was taken into police protection. The designated officer will have at least the rank of inspector and cannot be the initiating officer in the same case.

10.17.3.2   The role of the initiating officer

Under s 46(3) of the Children Act 1989, having taken a child into police protection the initiating officer must as soon as is reasonably practicable:

    (a) inform the local authority where the child was found of the police protection steps that have been taken (and are proposed to be taken) concerning the child , and the reasons for taking these actions;

    (b) tell the authority in which the child usually lives ('the appropriate authority') where he/she is now being accommodated;

    (c) inform the child (if he/she appears capable of understanding) about:

        (i)   the steps taken with respect to him/her and the reasons; and

        (ii) any further steps that may be taken with respect to him/her under police protection;

    (d) try and establish the wishes and feelings of the child;

    (e) ensure that a designated officer has been assigned for the case; and

    (f) arrange for the child to be moved to local authority-provided accommodation ('suitable accommodation', [see below] if the child is not already in such a place.

In addition, as soon as is reasonably practicable, the initiating officer must contact the adults who have been caring for the child (s 46(4)). As well as the child's parents, this would include every person who has parental responsibility (see below) for the child and any other person with whom the child was living immediately before being taken into police protection.

The adults who have most recently been caring for the child must be informed of:

- the police protection steps you have taken concerning the child;
- the reasons for taking these steps;
- any further steps that may be taken.

A child can be in police protection for up to 72 hours (s 46(6), Children Act 1989).

10.17.3.3   The meaning of 'parental responsibility'

In s 3(1) of the Children Act 1989 parental responsibility means 'all the rights, duties, powers, responsibilities and authority which by law a parent of a child has in relation to that child and [his/her] property'. It can be held by the parents, the step-parents, and in certain circumstances, by other people or bodies. The question of who has parental responsibility is dealt with in ss 2 and 3 of the Children Act 1989 and the key points are:

- If the father and mother were **married** to each other when the child was born, they will each have parental responsibility (s 2(1)). The rule of law that a father is the natural guardian of his legitimate child has been abolished (s 2(4)).
- If the father and mother were **not married** to each other when the child was born, the mother will have parental responsibility, but the father will not automatically have this, unless it has been assigned to him (s 2(2)).
- More than one person may have parental responsibility for the same child at the same time (s 2(5)) and each may act alone to meet that responsibility (s 2(7)).
- A person who has parental responsibility for a child at any time does not cease to have that responsibility simply because another person acquires such responsibility for that child (s 2(6)).

The spirit of the legislation is that all the parties including the parents, the child, and the local authority must be kept informed and given reasons for any actions. The child's wishes must be listened to but do not necessarily have to be acted upon.

10.17.3.4   Suitable accommodation

A definition of suitable accommodation is given in the Home Office Circular 44/2003 as local authority accommodation, a registered children's home, or foster care. Alternatively, if the designated officer and social services consider it appropriate, the child may also be placed with relatives or other appropriate carers. The child may also be taken to hospital if he/she requires medical attention.

The circular also emphasizes that a child under police protection should not be brought to a police station unless there is absolutely no alternative, and under no circumstances should he/she be taken into the custody suite or cell area.

TASK 15

Jo is a single parent struggling to care for a four-year-old called Sam whilst employed part-time. Recently Sam has been ill, and although Jo's employer has been very understanding, Jo does not want to take any more time off work. Jo's parents often care for Sam while Jo is at work.

However, on one occasion the grandparents are unavailable to supervise Sam. Jo realizes that there is no food in the house and, when Sam falls asleep, Jo decides to go to buy some food at the supermarket. During the journey, Jo's car breaks down.

Sam awakes and is distraught. Having heard the child screaming hysterically, the neighbours call the police and you attend. Although you can clearly hear Sam inside, all the doors and windows are shut and Sam refuses to open the door.

1. What power of entry, if any, is available to you?
2. What offence might you consider investigating Jo for?

10.18 Exposure, Voyeurism, Pornography, and Prostitution

Here, we will begin with the offences related to sexual activity in public places, which may or may not be related to exposure and voyeurism. We will then consider the more extreme forms of pornography, which are illegal. Finally, we look at prostitution; some of the related activities (but by no means all) are offences under the Sexual Offences Act 2003.

10.18.1 Sexual Activity and Public Places

Members of the public may have very different attitudes about what is acceptable sexual behaviour in a public place. Here we cover the offences of 'outraging public decency' and sexual activity in a public lavatory.

10.18.1.1 Outraging public decency

The common law offence of outraging public decency states that it is an offence:

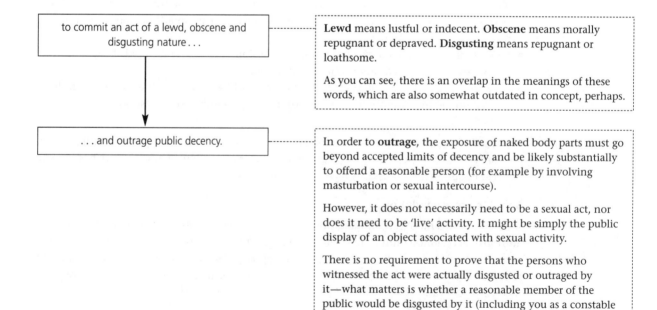

to commit an act of a lewd, obscene and disgusting nature . . .

Lewd means lustful or indecent. **Obscene** means morally repugnant or depraved. **Disgusting** means repugnant or loathsome.

As you can see, there is an overlap in the meanings of these words, which are also somewhat outdated in concept, perhaps.

. . . and outrage public decency.

In order to **outrage**, the exposure of naked body parts must go beyond accepted limits of decency and be likely substantially to offend a reasonable person (for example by involving masturbation or sexual intercourse).

However, it does not necessarily need to be a sexual act, nor does it need to be 'live' activity. It might be simply the public display of an object associated with sexual activity.

There is no requirement to prove that the persons who witnessed the act were actually disgusted or outraged by it—what matters is whether a reasonable member of the public would be disgusted by it (including you as a constable for the purpose of this offence).

For this offence:

- the public must have access to (whether they have a right to such access or not), or be able to see the relevant location, such as a private balcony in public view (*R v Walker* [1996] 1 Cr App R 111; *Smith v Hughes* [1960] 1 WLR 830);
- more than one person must have been able to witness the act.

This offence is triable either way and the penalty is:

- summarily: six months' imprisonment and/or a fine;
- on indictment: unlimited powers of sentence.

10.18.1.2 Sexual activity in a public lavatory

For this criminal offence (under s 71 of the Sexual Offences Act 2003) there is no need for any person to witness the activity, and if there are witnesses they do not have to be in any way outraged or distressed. The activity must be such that a reasonable person would regard it as sexual in nature.

This offence is triable summarily only and the penalty is six months' imprisonment and/or a fine.

10.18.2 Exposure

This offence (s 66(1), Sexual Offences Act 2003) is commonly referred to as 'flashing'. A person commits an offence if he/she:

(a) intentionally exposes his/her genitals, and
(b) intends that someone will see this and be caused alarm or distress.

It is not necessary for a person to actually have seen the exposed genitals or to have been distressed as a result; the offence is still committed.

However, a 'streaker' intending 'merely' to create amusement does not commit this offence, nor does a nudist who, on a site specifically set aside for naturism, does not conceal his or her genitals, but whose purpose is not for onlookers to become alarmed or distressed.

This offence is triable either way and the penalty is:

- summarily: six months' imprisonment;
- on indictment: two years' imprisonment.

10.18.3 Voyeurism

People who commit this offence (s 67(1), Sexual Offences Act 2003) are commonly known as Peeping Toms. In this category, there is a variety of offences, but most commonly you will come across the situation where a suspect secretly observes another undressing or having sexual intercourse (a 'private act') for the purposes of the suspect's own sexual gratification.

Section 68(1) of the Sexual Offences Act 2003 explains that, for the purposes of s 67, a person does a **private act** if he/she is in a place which would reasonably be expected to provide privacy, such as in a home or hotel (but not on a beach or in an open-plan changing room) **and** at least one of the following conditions is met:

- his/her genitals or buttocks, or her breasts are exposed or covered only with underwear (see *R v Kevin Bassett* (2008) EWCA Crim 1174);
- he/she is using a lavatory;
- he/she is 'doing a sexual act that is not of a kind ordinarily done in public'.

A private act would not include kissing or cuddling, but would include sexual intercourse or oral sex.

Under s 67(1) of the Sexual Offences Act 2003 a person commits an offence if:

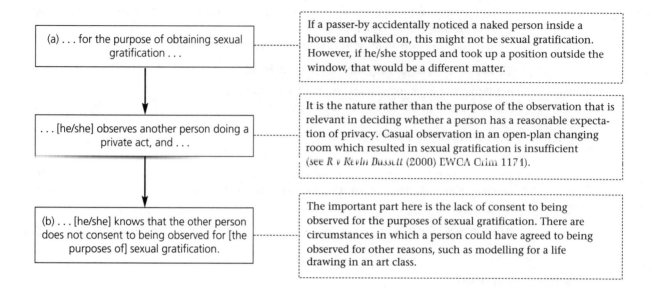

| (a) . . . for the purpose of obtaining sexual gratification . . . | If a passer-by accidentally noticed a naked person inside a house and walked on, this might not be sexual gratification. However, if he/she stopped and took up a position outside the window, that would be a different matter. |

| . . . [he/she] observes another person doing a private act, and . . . | It is the nature rather than the purpose of the observation that is relevant in deciding whether a person has a reasonable expectation of privacy. Casual observation in an open-plan changing room which resulted in sexual gratification is insufficient (see *R v Kevin Bassett* (2000) EWCA Crim 1174). |

| (b) . . . [he/she] knows that the other person does not consent to being observed for [the purposes of] sexual gratification. | The important part here is the lack of consent to being observed for the purposes of sexual gratification. There are circumstances in which a person could have agreed to being observed for other reasons, such as modelling for a life drawing in an art class. |

There is a form of voyeurism linked to 'dogging' (outdoor sexual activities); however, if the 'doggers' encourage people to watch, the offence of voyeurism is not committed because consent has been given. Other offences, however, may have been committed, depending on the particular circumstances.

10.18.3.1 Voyeurism using live link equipment

Under s 67(2) of the Sexual Offences Act 2003 a person (A) commits an offence if he/she operates equipment with the intention of enabling another person (B) to observe, for the purpose of obtaining sexual gratification, a third person (C) doing a private act, and A knows that C does not consent to the operation of equipment with that intention.

For example, a landlord commits an offence if he operates a webcam so that people on the internet can gain sexual gratification from viewing his tenant having sexual intercourse. The landlord must know that the tenant did not agree to this. Also, there is no need to prove that the landlord personally gained sexual gratification.

10.18.3.2 Voyeurism and making recorded images

Under s 67(3) of the Sexual Offences Act 2003 a person (A) commits an offence if:

• he/she records another person (C) doing a private act, with the intention that he/she (A) or a third person (B) will obtain sexual gratification looking at an image of C doing the act; and
• knowing that C does not consent to the recording of the act with that intention.

For example, an offence is committed by a person who secretly photographs another person masturbating in a bedroom and intends to show the photos to others for their sexual gratification. The photographer must know that the subject of the photos does not consent to the photos being taken with that intention. Proof that the intention was sexual gratification could be that the image was posted on a pornographic website or that it was offered for sale to an adult (pornographic) magazine.

10.18.3.3   Voyeurism and installing equipment

Under s 67(4) of the Sexual Offences Act 2003 a person commits an offence if:

- he/she instals equipment; or
- constructs or adapts a structure or part of a structure

with the intention of committing an offence (or enabling himself or another person to commit an offence) of simple voyeurism (s 67(1)).

For example, an offence is committed by a person who drills a spy-hole in a wall for the purposes of spying on someone for sexual gratification. The offence is committed even if the peephole is discovered before it is used. Note that a 'structure' (a site where the equipment is installed) can include a tent, vehicle, vessel, or some other temporary or movable structure.

Offences relating to voyeurism are triable either way and the penalty is:

- summarily: six months' imprisonment;
- on indictment: two years' imprisonment.

> **TASK 16**
>
> On the drive back to their home ground, some members of a rugby club team have taken to celebrating their wins by exposing their naked buttocks ('mooning') out of the rear window of the team bus. You have been tasked to deal with the most recent incident in the busy main high street, and are now considering what offence might have been committed. What is your conclusion?

10.18.4   Possession of extreme pornographic images

Section 63(1) of the Criminal Justice and Immigration Act 2008 states that it is an offence to be in possession of an extreme pornographic image (defined quite literally as an image which is both pornographic and extreme (s63(2))).

An image is said to be pornographic if it appears to have been produced solely or principally for the purpose of sexual arousal (s 63(3)). An image includes moving images such as those on film. It also includes electronic data capable of conversion into an image; this may be stored on mobile phones, computers, and other storage devices (s 63(8)).

An **extreme** image is any image of an act which depicts (or appears to depict) activities which:

- threaten a person's life;
- result in (or are likely to result in) serious injury to a person's anus, breasts, or genitals (including parts of the body surgically constructed particularly through gender reassignment surgery);
- involve sexual interference with a human corpse (necrophilia); or
- involve a person performing an act of intercourse or oral sex with an animal (bestiality), where any such act, person, or animal depicted in the image is or appears to be real (s 63(7)).

This offence does not apply for **excluded images** (s 64(2)). An excluded image is an image which forms part of a series of images contained in a recording of either a part of or the whole of a classified work (classified for showing to the public in cinemas by the British Board of Film Classification for example). However, to be an excluded image, a recording of an extract from a classified work must **not** have been made solely or principally for the purpose of sexual arousal (s 64(3)).

This legislation has been introduced following a campaign led by Liz Longhurst whose daughter Jane, a Brighton schoolteacher, was strangled by Graham Coutts in 2003. At the trial the jurors were told that Coutts had an obsession with strangulation and that he used internet sites connected with the fetish. The Internet Watch Foundation (IWF) now operates an internet hotline for the public and IT professionals to report potentially illegal websites.

10.18.4.1 Defences for possessing extreme images

It is a defence (under s 65 of the of the Criminal Justice and Immigration Act 2008) for a person found in possession of such images to prove that he/she:

- had a legitimate reason for possessing the image (s 65(1));
- had not seen the image and did not know (nor had any cause to suspect) it was an extreme pornographic image (s 65(1)); or
- had received the image without any previous request having been made, and did not keep it for an unreasonable time (s 65(2).

The offence cannot be prosecuted without the consent of the Director of Public Prosecutions and is triable either way.

For images which are life-threatening acts, or involve serious injury the penalty is:

- summarily: 12 months' imprisonment and/or fine;
- on indictment: 3 years' imprisonment.

For images which involve necrophilia or bestiality the penalty is:

- summarily: 12 months' imprisonment and/or fine;
- on indictment: 2 years' imprisonment.

The Ministry of Justice has issued guidance for dealing with the offence of possession of extreme pornographic images. Circular 2009/01 can be found at <http://www.justice.gov.uk/docs/circular-criminal-justice-01-2009.pdf>.

10.18.5 Indecent Photographs of Children

Section 1 of the Protection of Children Act 1978 states that it is an offence for a person:

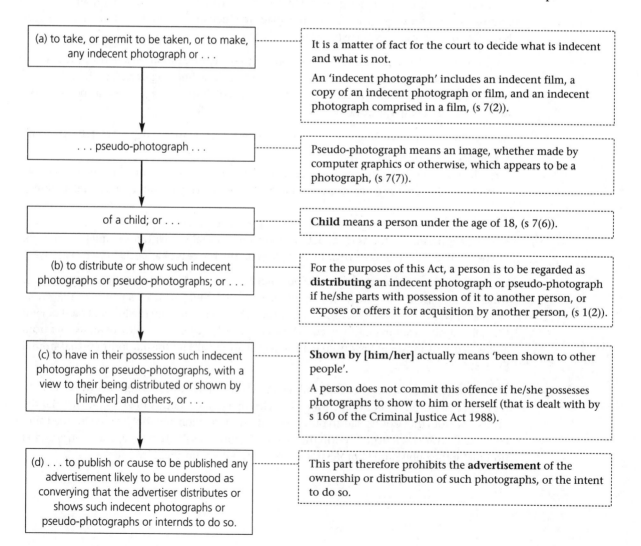

(a) to take, or permit to be taken, or to make, any indecent photograph or . . .

It is a matter of fact for the court to decide what is indecent and what is not.

An 'indecent photograph' includes an indecent film, a copy of an indecent photograph or film, and an indecent photograph comprised in a film, (s 7(2)).

. . . pseudo-photograph . . .

Pseudo-photograph means an image, whether made by computer graphics or otherwise, which appears to be a photograph, (s 7(7)).

of a child; or . . .

Child means a person under the age of 18, (s 7(6)).

(b) to distribute or show such indecent photographs or pseudo-photographs; or . . .

For the purposes of this Act, a person is to be regarded as **distributing** an indecent photograph or pseudo-photograph if he/she parts with possession of it to another person, or exposes or offers it for acquisition by another person, (s 1(2)).

(c) to have in their possession such indecent photographs or pseudo-photographs, with a view to their being distributed or shown by [him/her] and others, or . . .

Shown by [him/her] actually means 'been shown to other people'.

A person does not commit this offence if he/she possesses photographs to show to him or herself (that is dealt with by s 160 of the Criminal Justice Act 1988).

(d) . . . to publish or cause to be published any advertisement likely to be understood as converying that the advertiser distributes or shows such indecent photographs or pseudo-photographs or internds to do so.

This part therefore prohibits the **advertisement** of the ownership or distribution of such photographs, or the intent to do so.

This offence is triable either way and the penalty is:

- summarily: six months' imprisonment and/or a fine;
- on indictment: ten years' imprisonment.

Two defences to this offence are listed in s 1(4) of the Protection of Children Act 1978:

- the defendant had a legitimate reason for distributing, showing, or having possession of the photographs or pseudo-photographs;
- the defendant saw the photographs or pseudo-photographs and did not know, nor had any cause to suspect them to be indecent.

10.18.5.1 Indecent photograph exceptions

It may be that a particular photograph is not indecent in terms of the legislation, and the situations where this may be so are listed as exceptions in s 1 of the Protection of Children Act 1978.

Exception 1A applies if the suspect can prove that the photograph was of a person aged 16 or over, and that, at the time of the alleged offence, the person and the suspect:

(a) were married or
(b) lived together as partners in an enduring family relationship.

Exception 1B applies if the suspect proves it was necessary to make the photograph or pseudo-photograph for the purposes of the prevention, detection, or investigation of crime, or for the purposes of criminal proceedings in any part of the world.

10.18.5.2 Possession of a prohibited image of a child

Section 49(1) of the Coroners and Justice Bill 2009 proposes that it will be an offence to be in possession of a prohibited image of a child (person under 18). Under the Bill, an image (moving, still, or in data form) is said to be prohibited if it is pornographic (assumed to have been produced solely or principally for the purpose of sexual arousal) or 'grossly offensive, disgusting or otherwise of an obscene character'.

In addition, the image must either focus solely or principally on a child's genitals or anal region, or portray a child in association with at least one of the following activities:

- sexual intercourse or oral sex with a person or an animal (the animal can be dead, alive, or imaginary);
- masturbation;
- penetration of the anus or vagina (with a part of the body or anything else).

A child must be portrayed in the image, and this can be as either:

- a participant in the activities; or
- a witness to the activities (with no physical involvement).

For the purposes of this legislation an image does not include an indecent photograph or pseudo-photograph (s 52(3)) as these are dealt with by other legislation (see 10.18.5 above), nor does this offence apply to excluded images (see 10.18.4 above).

Where an image forms a part of a series, in order to determine if it is pornographic reference will be made to both the image itself and the context in which it appears in the series of images (similar to the way in which excluded images are considered in 10.18.4 above). For example, if the image appears as part of a series in a full-length mainstream or documentary film, it will not be considered as pornographic.

Defences for the offence of possession of a prohibited image of a child (s 51) include:

- having a legitimate reason for possessing the image;
- having not seen the image, nor having cause to suspect what it was;
- receiving the image without requesting it and not keeping it for an unreasonable time.

The offence cannot be prosecuted without the consent of the Director of Public Prosecutions and is triable either way and the penalty is:

- summarily: 12 months' imprisonment and/or a fine;
- on indictment: 3 years' imprisonment and/or a fine.

10.18.6   Prostitution

Almost all public manifestation of prostitution is illegal. So, for example, it is an offence for a prostitute to be clearly waiting for potential customers in a public place, or for a person to be seen to actively seek the services of a prostitute in a public place.

A prostitute is defined as 'a person ... who, on at least one occasion and whether or not compelled to do so, offers or provides sexual services to another person in return for payment or a promise of payment to [him/her] or a third person' (s 51(2), Sexual Offences Act 2003).

Some of the activities of a prostitute are described in s 1(1) of the Street Offences Act 1959 which states that it is an offence for a person (whether male or female) to:

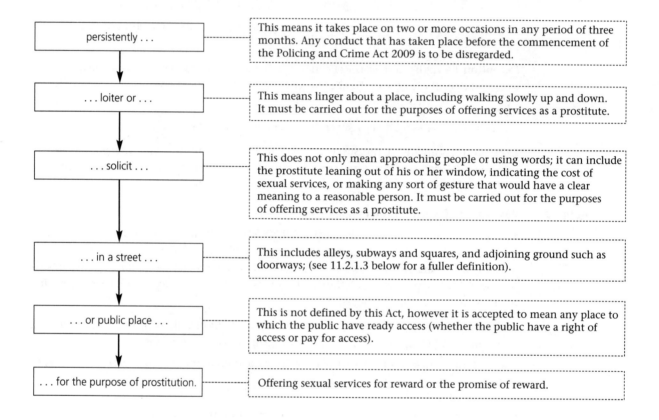

persistently ...	This means it takes place on two or more occasions in any period of three months. Any conduct that has taken place before the commencement of the Policing and Crime Act 2009 is to be disregarded.
... loiter or ...	This means linger about a place, including walking slowly up and down. It must be carried out for the purposes of offering services as a prostitute.
... solicit ...	This does not only mean approaching people or using words; it can include the prostitute leaning out of his or her window, indicating the cost of sexual services, or making any sort of gesture that would have a clear meaning to a reasonable person. It must be carried out for the purposes of offering services as a prostitute.
... in a street ...	This includes alleys, subways and squares, and adjoining ground such as doorways; (see 11.2.1.3 below for a fuller definition).
... or public place ...	This is not defined by this Act, however it is accepted to mean any place to which the public have ready access (whether the public have a right of access or pay for access).
... for the purpose of prostitution.	Offering sexual services for reward or the promise of reward.

This offence is triable summarily and the penalty is a fine or a court order requiring the offender to attend three meetings with a 'suitable person' who will be specified in the order.

10.18.6.1 Procuring the services of a prostitute

It is an offence for the potential clients (on foot or in a vehicle) to 'solicit' the services of a prostitute in a public place. This offence is known as 'kerb-crawling' when it is carried out from a vehicle. Section 51A of the Sexual Offences Act 2003 states that an offence is committed by:

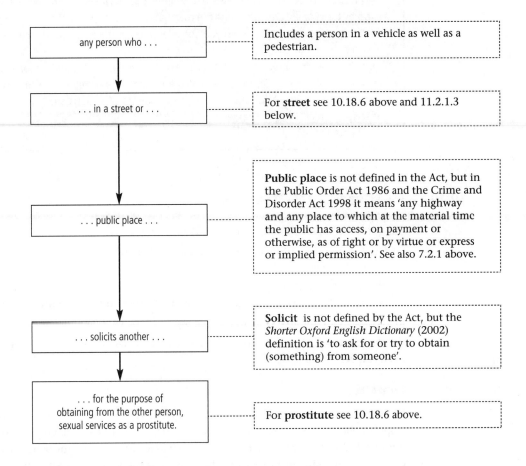

any person who . . .	Includes a person in a vehicle as well as a pedestrian.
. . . in a street or . . .	For **street** see 10.18.6 above and 11.2.1.3 below.
. . . public place . . .	**Public place** is not defined in the Act, but in the Public Order Act 1986 and the Crime and Disorder Act 1998 it means 'any highway and any place to which at the material time the public has access, on payment or otherwise, as of right or by virtue or express or implied permission'. See also 7.2.1 above.
. . . solicits another . . .	**Solicit** is not defined by the Act, but the *Shorter Oxford English Dictionary* (2002) definition is 'to ask for or try to obtain (something) from someone'.
. . . for the purpose of obtaining from the other person, sexual services as a prostitute.	For **prostitute** see 10.18.6 above.

This offence is triable summarily and the penalty is a fine.

10.18.6.2 Paying for Sexual Services of Controlled Prostitutes

A controlled prostitute is a prostitute whose activities (sexual services) are intentionally controlled for gain (or in the expectation of gain) by another person, commonly known as a 'pimp'. (The gain can be for the pimp him/herself, or for another party.)

Section 53A of the Sexual Offences Act 2003 states that it is an offence to pay (or promise payment) for the sexual services of a controlled prostitute. It is irrelevant:

• whether the 'customer' knows (or ought to know or be aware) that the prostitute is controlled for gain. Because the offence is one of strict liability, the suspect does not have to form an intent;

• where in the world the sexual services are to be provided, though the 'controlling' must take place in the UK; or

• whether the sexual services are in fact provided or not.

This offence is triable summarily and the penalty is a fine.

> **TASK 17**
>
> 1. You are on uniform patrol near a railway station and you notice a woman standing in the car park, for no apparent reason. As you approach the woman she walks away towards the town centre, but is back in the same place a few minutes later. Later on in the evening you see two cars stop by the woman and each time the male drivers or occupants of the cars talk to the woman and then drive off. What would you consider doing in these circumstances, in relation to the woman?
> 2. A person offering a professional body-piercing service passes round a mobile phone amongst a group of strangers. On the screen of the phone can be clearly seen the images of female breasts and genitals into which sharp metal objects of various shapes and sizes have been inserted. In relation to the possession of extreme pornographic images, have any offences been committed?

10.19 Further Sexual Offences

This part of Chapter 10 covers the following offences:

- sexual assault (touching) (s 3, Sexual Offences Act 2003);
- assault by penetration (s 2);
- rape (s 1);
- causing another person to engage in sexual activity without consent (s 4).

In law, for these offences the offender and victim can be of any age. Remember that the question of consent is of paramount importance when considering whether a sexual act amounts to an offence.

10.19.1 Consent

In many sexual offence cases, the defence will focus on the issue of consent. It is a defence if the suspect believes that consent was given, and he/she would also have to prove that this belief was reasonable. In any prosecution the court will decide whether the belief was reasonable after considering the circumstances and the steps that the suspect took to obtain consent (s 1(2), Sexual Offences Act 2003).

In general terms, the court will seek to establish whether the suspect made a conscious effort to:

- establish consent; and
- monitor the consent—the other person might change his/her mind and withdraw consent, indicated by a change of physical expression or voice tone, for example.

Section 74 of the Sexual Offences Act 2003 states that a person consents if he/she agrees by choice, and has the freedom and capacity to make that choice. **Freedom to make the choice** means that the choice is not made under duress or through being put in fear of violence. **Capacity to agree** means the ability to decide either way, and to be able to communicate the decision. If a person is 'unable to refuse', through mental disorder or intoxication for example, he/she does not have the capacity to make the choice.

Under s 75 of the Sexual Offences Act 2003 the court will make the presumption that the victim did **not** consent if evidence presented in court proves that the circumstances involved:

- use of and fear of violence;
- unlawful detention;
- unconsciousness;
- inability to communicate from physical disability; and/or
- substances (such as drugs) non-consensually administered, that are capable of stupefying or overpowering.

It also has to be proved that the defendant knew of these circumstances and that the defendant carried out the act in question.

In order to increase the conviction rate for those guilty of sexual assault, the Sexual Offences Act 2003 introduced two sets of presumptions which courts can make in relation to the guilty knowledge of the defendant: evidential and conclusive presumptions about consent.

10.19.1.1 Evidential presumptions about consent

Under s 75 of the Sexual Offences Act 2003, the defence can provide evidence that the victim did in fact consent (to contradict the presumption that consent was not given: see 10.19.1 above). The defence will need to convince the judge (through the use of evidence) that there is a definite issue about consent, and then produce relevant evidence from the defendant, a witness, or the victim under cross-examination. If the judge is not convinced, the jury will be directed to find that the victim did not consent to the sexual assault, and that the defendant could not have reasonably believed that consent was given.

10.19.1.2 Conclusive presumptions about consent

Section 76 of the Sexual Offences Act 2003 covers circumstances in which the victim has been deceived. The presumption about consent (ie the lack of consent) is conclusive and final; if the victim has been deceived, no amount of evidence can prove that consent had been given. The court will make the presumption that the victim did **not** legally consent if it is proved in court that the defendant intentionally:

- deceived the complainant about the nature or purpose of the relevant act (for example telling the victim it was a necessary medical procedure); or
- impersonated an individual personally known to the victim, with whom the victim would have consented to such activity (for example, the defendant pretends to be the victim's current sexual partner and engages in sexual activity during complete darkness).

(Of course it also has to be proved that the defendant carried out the relevant act.)

These are important considerations if you are gathering evidence in relation to a prosecution for many of the sexual offences that are covered here.

10.19.2 Rape

Section 1 of the Sexual Offences Act 2003 makes it an offence for a person intentionally to penetrate with his penis the vagina, anus, or mouth of another person without that person's consent, and when he does not reasonably believe that the other person consents. This offence can only be committed by a man.

Section 1 of the Sexual Offences Act 2003 states that 'a person (A) commits an offence if he':

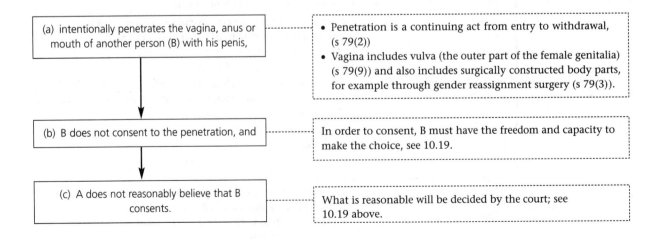

The offence of rape is triable on indictment only and the maximum penalty is life imprisonment.

10.19.3 Assault by Penetration

Section 2 of the Sexual Offences Act 2003 covers the situation where a person intentionally (and not just recklessly) penetrates the vagina or anus of another person. It can be committed by a man or a woman. This offence is very similar to rape in terms of the guilty knowledge of the suspect, and evidential and conclusive presumptions must be considered (see 10.19.1 above).

Section 2 of the Sexual Offences Act 2003 states that a person (A) commits an offence if:

- he/she intentionally penetrates the vagina or anus of another person (B) with a part of his/her (A's) body or anything else;
- the penetration is sexual;
- B does not consent to the penetration;
- A does not reasonably believe that B consents.

Therefore, the points to prove in this offence are that the suspect intentionally penetrated the vagina or anus of another person, and the guilty knowledge that penetration occurred (outlined in evidential presumptions under s 75 and conclusive presumptions under s 76 (see 10.19.1 above)).

Note that as for rape:

- penetration is a continuing act from entry to withdrawal (s 79(2));
- references to a part of the body also include parts that may have been surgically constructed (in particular through gender reassignment surgery) (s 79(3)).

This offence is triable by indictment only and the maximum penalty is life imprisonment.

10.19.4 Sexual Assault (Touching)

Section 3 of the Sexual Offences Act 2003 states a person (A) commits an offence if he/she:

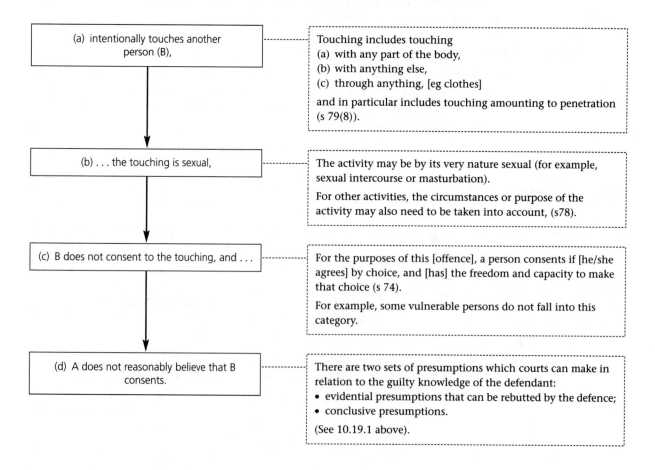

(a) intentionally touches another person (B),	Touching includes touching (a) with any part of the body, (b) with anything else, (c) through anything, [eg clothes] and in particular includes touching amounting to penetration (s 79(8)).
(b) . . . the touching is sexual,	The activity may be by its very nature sexual (for example, sexual intercourse or masturbation). For other activities, the circumstances or purpose of the activity may also need to be taken into account, (s78).
(c) B does not consent to the touching, and . . .	For the purposes of this [offence], a person consents if [he/she agrees] by choice, and [has] the freedom and capacity to make that choice (s 74). For example, some vulnerable persons do not fall into this category.
(d) A does not reasonably believe that B consents.	There are two sets of presumptions which courts can make in relation to the guilty knowledge of the defendant: • evidential presumptions that can be rebutted by the defence; • conclusive presumptions. (See 10.19.1 above).

This offence is triable either way and the penalty is:

- summarily: six months' imprisonment and/or a fine;
- on indictment: ten years' imprisonment.

10.19.5 Causing Another Person to Engage in Sexual Activity without Consent

Section 4(1) of the Sexual Offences Act 2003 states that a person (A) commits an offence if:

(a) he/she intentionally causes another person (B) to engage in an activity;
(b) the activity is sexual;
(c) B does not consent, and
(d) A does not reasonably believe that B consents.

This offence is triable either way and the penalty is:

- summarily: six months' imprisonment and/or a fine;
- on indictment: ten years' imprisonment.

10.19.5.1 Causing another person to engage in penetration without consent

If the s 4(1) offence described in 10.19.5 above involves:

(a) penetration of B's anus or vagina
(b) penetration of B's mouth with a person's penis
(c) penetration of a person's anus or vagina with a part of B's body or by B with anything else
(d) penetration of a person's mouth with B's penis

then the offence (s 4(4)) is triable on indictment only, and the penalty is life imprisonment.

TASK 18

Many victims of rape will be concerned about their identity becoming known during the investigation and any subsequent court case. What legislation is available to provide anonymity in relation to complaints of rape and restrictions on evidence at trials for rape?

10.19.6 Sexual Activity with an Animal or a Human Corpse.

These are rare offences.

10.19.6.1 Sexual intercourse with an animal

This is covered under s 69 of the Sexual Offences Act 2003 and covers penile penetration of animals by humans, and of humans by animals. The animals and the human participants must be alive and the penetration can be of the vagina or the anus. This activity is also known as bestiality.

The offence can be committed by allowing or causing such an act, as well as by direct physical involvement in the penetration. (Note that penetration of an animal's sexual organs with an object does not come under this legislation and would be pursued through legislation for prevention of cruelty to animals—see 9. 26 above).

This offence is triable either way and the penalty is:

- summarily: six months' imprisonment and/or a fine not exceeding the statutory maximum;
- on indictment: two years' imprisonment.

10.19.6.2 Sexual penetration of a human corpse

This is covered under s 70 of the Sexual Offences Act 2003 and can be committed by men or women. Any part of the body or any object can be used to perform the penetration, and any part of the corpse may be penetrated. The offender must have some kind of sexual motivation, and must know or be reckless about whether he/she is penetrating a corpse.

This offence is triable either way and the penalty is:

- summarily: six months' imprisonment and/or a fine not exceeding the statutory maximum;
- on indictment: two years' imprisonment.

10.20 Children, Young People, and Sexual Offences

Here we cover some of the sexual offences legislation that applies specifically to offences involving younger victims. (The offences listed in 10.19 above can of course also be considered for younger victims.) Any sexual activity with a child under the age of 16 is unlawful, but there may be a defence if the suspect believes that the young person was more than 16 years old (see 10.20.2 below).

Consent cannot be given until a person reaches the age of 16 years. (The issue of consent does not apply if the child is under 13 years of age; such a young person cannot legally give consent.) However the law considers that there is a possibility that children aged 13 to 15 might have 'voluntarily agreed' to sexual activities with other children or young people, provided there was no use of coercion or corruption. In these circumstances a prosecution is not always considered in the public interest. Further information concerning this complex and sensitive area of the law may be found via the CPS website <http://www.cps.gov.uk/legal/s_to_u/sexual_offences_act/>.

The offences fall into two main groups, relating to the age of the victim:

- offences where the victim is under 13 and the offender is over the age of 10 years (see 10.20.1 below); and
- offences where the victim is under 16 (see 10.20.2 below) and the offender is over the age of 18 years (however s 13 of the Sexual Offences Act 2003 does make exceptions to this rule).

10.20.1 Sexual Offences where the victim is under the age of 13

The legislation relating only to victims under 13 is important as it applies to younger suspects (10 years of age and over) as well as to adult suspects over the age of 18. Proof that the victim was under the age of 13 must be provided. Whether the victim appears to consent to the activity is of absolutely no relevance.

10.20.1.1 Rape of a child under the age of 13

This offence (under s 5 of the Sexual Offences Act 2003) can only be committed by a man, but the victim can be male or female. The victim's anus, vagina, or mouth must be penetrated by the offender's penis. The sexual organs involved can include those constructed through surgery (as with s 1 rape: see 10.19.2 above).

This offence is triable on indictment only and the maximum penalty is life imprisonment.

10.20.1.2 Sexual assault on a child under the age of 13 by penetration

This offence (under s 6 of the Sexual Offences Act 2003) can be committed by a man or a woman as the penetration (of the anus, vagina, or mouth) can be carried out using any part of the body (such as a finger) or a separate object. The child does not need to be aware of the nature of the penetrating object.

This offence is triable on indictment only and the maximum penalty is life imprisonment (as for s 5 rape).

10.20.1.3 Sexual assault on a child under the age of 13

Under s 7(1) of the Sexual Offences Act 2003 it is an offence for a person (male or female) to intentionally touch a child under the age of 13, if the touching is sexual. For further explanation of the terms 'touching' and 'sexual', see 10.19.4 above.

This offence (s 7) is triable either way and the penalty is:

- summarily: six months' imprisonment and/or a fine not exceeding the statutory maximum;
- on indictment: 14 years' imprisonment.

10.20.1.4 Inciting a child under the age of 13 to engage in sexual activity

This offence is covered under s 8 of the Sexual Offences Act 2003, and can be committed by a man or a woman. The sexual activity caused or incited will involve touching and/or penetration and might involve the child acting alone or with another person. The offender might not be physically involved and no sexual activity actually has to occur; here the incitement is the offence.

Section 8(1) offences (no penetration) are triable either way and the penalty is:

- summarily: 6 months' imprisonment and/or a fine not exceeding the statutory maximum;
- on indictment: 14 years' imprisonment.

Section 8(2) offences (these involve penetration) are triable on indictment only and the maximum penalty is life imprisonment.

10.20.2 Sexual Offences committed by Adults in relation to Children

For all the offences listed here the suspect must be over 18 years of age.

If the victim is aged 13 to 15, there is a defence available if the suspect reasonably believed that the victim was over 16 and the victim appeared to consent, but there is no defence available if the victim is under 13. Proof that the victim is under 16 must be entered as evidence (eg birth certificate).

10.20.2.1 Non-penetrative sexual activity with a child

Section 9 of the Sexual Offences Act 2003 states that it is an offence for an adult (male or female, and over the age of 18) to intentionally touch a child, when the touching is sexual in nature. For further explanation of the terms 'touching' and 'sexual', see 10.19.4 above. This offence is very similar to the s 7 offence (see 10.20.1.3) except that the child does not have to be under 13.

This offence is triable either way and the penalty is:

- summarily: 6 months' imprisonment and/or a fine not exceeding the statutory maximum;
- on indictment: 14 years' imprisonment.

10.20.2.2 Touching a child and penetration

Section 9(2) of the Sexual Offences Act 2003 states that person A commits an offence if the touching (see 10.20.2.1 above) involved the:

(a) penetration of B's anus or vagina with a part of A's body or anything else;
(b) penetration of B's mouth with A's penis;
(c) penetration of A's anus or vagina with a part of B's body; or
(d) penetration of A's mouth with B's penis.

Note that penetration is a continuous act from entry to withdrawal (s 79(2)) and that references to a part of the body also include parts that may have been surgically constructed (in particular through gender reassignment surgery) (s 79(3)).

This offence is triable by indictment only, and the penalty is up to 14 years' imprisonment.

10.20.2.3 Inciting a child to engage in sexual activity

The offence of causing or inciting a child to engage in sexual activity (s 10 of the Sexual Offences Act 2003) is very similar to the s 8 offence (see 10.20.1.4 above) except the child does not have to be under the age of 13.

For inciting non-penetrative sexual activity (s 10(1)) the offence is triable either way and the penalty is:

- summarily: six months' imprisonment and/or a fine;
- on indictment: 14 years' imprisonment.

For inciting penetrative sexual activity (s 10(2)), the offence is triable on indictment only and the penalty is up to 14 years' imprisonment.

10.20.2.4   Adult involvement in children witnessing sexual acts

There are two offences here under the Sexual Offences Act 2003: one where the offender him/herself commits the sexual acts and the other where the offender arranges for the child to witness other people committing sexual acts.

For the offence of **engaging in sexual activity in the presence of a child** (s 11) the offender commits some sexual act with the intention that a child will be aware of the activity in some way (such as seeing the activity live or on a webcam or hearing the activity). The offender has to gain some sexual gratification from his/her knowledge or belief that the child is aware of the activity. However, the victim does not actually have to be aware of it (for example if he/she does not notice or falls asleep without the offender noticing).

For the s 12 offence of **causing a child to watch a sexual act** the offender must gain sexual gratification from causing a child to watch a third party involved in sexual activity. The activity could take place live in front of the child, or a recording could be shown, for instance pornographic films on a TV screen. The child need not be coerced to watch, and may even agree to watch; this is irrelevant to whether the offence has been committed.

These offences are both triable either way and the penalty is:

- summarily: six months' imprisonment and/or a fine;
- on indictment: ten years' imprisonment.

TASK 19

You are asked to attend the home of a 15-year-old girl. In discussion with you and her mother, the girl alleges that a family friend has been visiting the house on a regular basis, and on each occasion the family friend massages the girl's genitals (but no penetration takes place). Could the family friend have a defence to any possible charge, if the allegations are substantiated? Would it make a difference if the victim was 12 years old?

10.21   Damage to Property

The Criminal Damage Act 1971 lists several different offences and the following are covered here:

- criminal damage (s 1(1));
- criminal damage life endangered (s 1(2));
- arson (s 1(3));
- threats to damage (s 2);
- possession with intent to damage (s 3).

Other offences covered here are causing damage to ancient monuments (s 28 of the Ancient Monuments and Archaeological Areas Act 1979) and graffiti (s 54(1) of the Anti-Social Behaviour Act 2003).

The kind of criminal damage that you will meet as a student police officer is usually graffiti and minor damage to fences, cars, and bus shelters. Occasionally, the damage can be much more serious, when, for example, the damage has been caused by fire.

An understanding of the law surrounding damage to property will assist your achievement of the police action required to 'Conduct the Initial Investigation and Report of Volume Crime According to National Policing Plan' under the 'Investigation' PAC heading.

10.21.1 Criminal Damage

Section 1(1) of the Criminal Damage Act 1971 states that an offence is committed by:

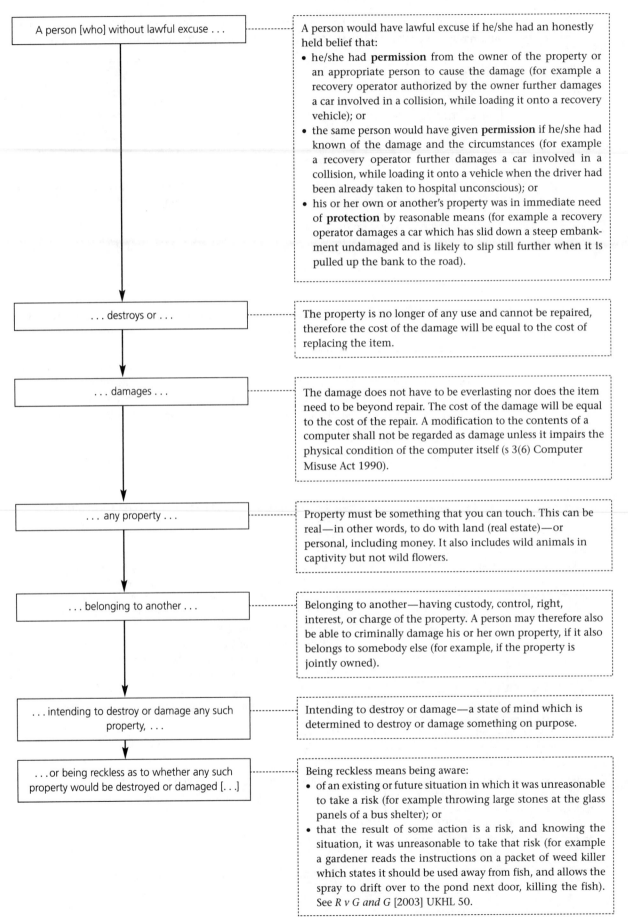

| A person [who] without lawful excuse . . . | A person would have lawful excuse if he/she had an honestly held belief that:
• he/she had **permission** from the owner of the property or an appropriate person to cause the damage (for example a recovery operator authorized by the owner further damages a car involved in a collision, while loading it onto a recovery vehicle); or
• the same person would have given **permission** if he/she had known of the damage and the circumstances (for example a recovery operator further damages a car involved in a collision, while loading it onto a vehicle when the driver had been already taken to hospital unconscious); or
• his or her own or another's property was in immediate need of **protection** by reasonable means (for example a recovery operator damages a car which has slid down a steep embankment undamaged and is likely to slip still further when it is pulled up the bank to the road). |

| . . . destroys or . . . | The property is no longer of any use and cannot be repaired, therefore the cost of the damage will be equal to the cost of replacing the item. |

| . . . damages . . . | The damage does not have to be everlasting nor does the item need to be beyond repair. The cost of the damage will be equal to the cost of the repair. A modification to the contents of a computer shall not be regarded as damage unless it impairs the physical condition of the computer itself (s 3(6) Computer Misuse Act 1990). |

| . . . any property . . . | Property must be something that you can touch. This can be real—in other words, to do with land (real estate)—or personal, including money. It also includes wild animals in captivity but not wild flowers. |

| . . . belonging to another . . . | Belonging to another—having custody, control, right, interest, or charge of the property. A person may therefore also be able to criminally damage his or her own property, if it also belongs to somebody else (for example, if the property is jointly owned). |

| . . . intending to destroy or damage any such property, . . . | Intending to destroy or damage—a state of mind which is determined to destroy or damage something on purpose. |

| . . . or being reckless as to whether any such property would be destroyed or damaged [. . .] | Being reckless means being aware:
• of an existing or future situation in which it was unreasonable to take a risk (for example throwing large stones at the glass panels of a bus shelter); or
• that the result of some action is a risk, and knowing the situation, it was unreasonable to take that risk (for example a gardener reads the instructions on a packet of weed killer which states it should be used away from fish, and allows the spray to drift over to the pond next door, killing the fish). See *R v G and G* [2003] UKHL 50. |

This offence is triable either way and the penalty is:

- summarily: six months' imprisonment and/or a fine;
- on indictment: ten years' imprisonment.

Note that if the value of the property damaged or destroyed is less than £5,000, the offence is tried summarily only (s 22, Magistrates' Courts Act 1980) but it still remains an 'either way' offence.

TASK 20

Robyn, after her arrest for being drunk and disorderly, smears her own excrement on the walls of the police station cell. Discuss whether this constitutes criminal damage.

10.21.2 Criminal Damage Life Endangered

The offence of 'criminal damage life endangered' is committed by a person who destroys or damages property intending (or being reckless as) to endanger life.

The following points explain the meaning of the term to 'endanger life':

- There is no requirement for the person to try and kill someone; murder or manslaughter would be the more appropriate charge in such cases.
- There is no requirement for any actual injury to occur. For instance, the ex-employee of a garage owner damages the brake system on one of the vintage motorcycles owned by his ex-boss. By chance, the ex-boss decides to put it on display (and therefore not ride it for the foreseeable future) so, although no harm may actually come to the intended victim, the potential for harm exists.
- The actual damage caused must also be the cause of the danger; for example shooting at someone in a room through a window both endangers life and damages the window, but it is the shot, bullet, or missile that endangers the life, not the damage from the window. Therefore the offence here would not be criminal damage (however, another offence such as attempted murder may have been committed).

Section 1(2) of the Criminal Damage Act 1971 states that it is an offence if a person:

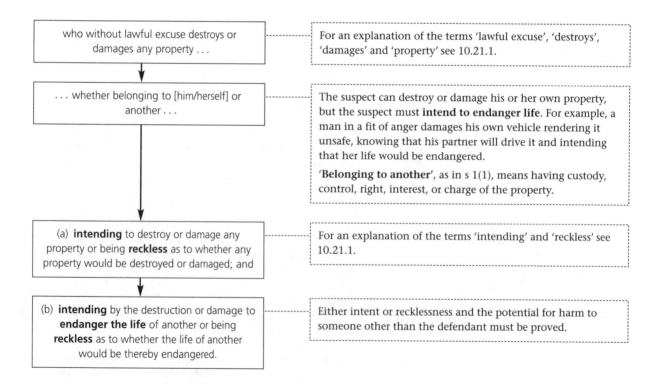

This offence is triable by indictment only and the penalty is life imprisonment.

10.21.3 Arson

Arson is destroying or damaging property by fire and is covered under s 1(3) of the Criminal Damage Act 1971. For a person to be found guilty of this offence at least some of the damage must have been caused by fire, but this does not include smoke damage. For the offence to be proved there must be an intent or an element of recklessness in relation to the use of fire.

This offence is triable either way and the penalty is:

- summarily: six months' imprisonment and/or a fine;
- on indictment: life imprisonment.

10.21.4 Threats to Damage

This offence is covered in s 2 of the Criminal Damage Act 1971 and there are two points to prove in relation to such a threat;

- the conduct that is threatened must refer to damage;
- the extent of the threatened damage must constitute an offence under s 1 of the Criminal Damage Act 1971. This can include acts of simple damage under s 1(1) as well as criminal damage where life is endangered under s 1(2).

However, the offence of making threats to damage cannot be committed if the threat involves an element of recklessness as to whether the property would actually be destroyed or damaged (see the final box in the flowchart in 10.21.1 above in relation to the meaning of 'reckless'). An example of such recklessness might include an angry person who shouts to a neighbour 'if your kid keeps throwing stones over the wall near my windows, I'll throw them straight back'; there is no threat to actually break anything, so this cannot amount to a threat to damage.

A stated intention to destroy or damage the property can be communicated in any way—for example email, text message, fax, letter, or phone call—and it could be an idle threat; there need be no intention to actually carry it out. The recipient does not have to believe the threat will be carried out immediately (if at all), nor does the recipient need to be put in fear. In any prosecution it will be for the court to decide whether what was communicated had enough substance and immediacy to constitute a threat.

Note that in some circumstances considering an offence under s 4 of the Public Order Act 1986 (see 9.7 above) might be more appropriate.

Section 2 of the Criminal Damage Act 1971 states it is an offence for a person:

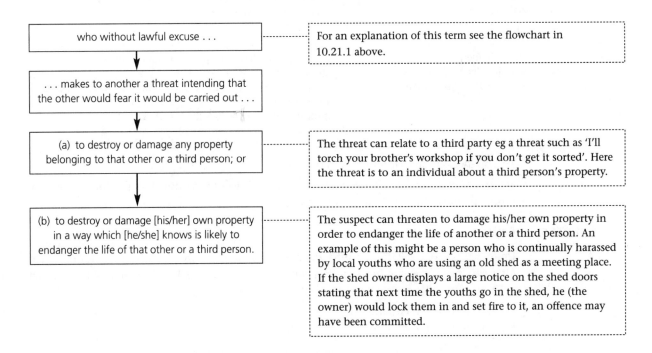

This offence is triable either way and the penalty is:

- summarily: six months' imprisonment and/or a fine;
- on indictment: ten years' imprisonment.

10.21.5   Possessing an Article with Intent to Cause Criminal Damage

This offence is covered in s 3 of the Criminal Damage Act 1971. The type of article involved here can be literally anything. The Law Commission, who advised on the Act, explained that:

> [t]he essential feature of the proposed offence is to be found, not so much in the nature of the thing, as in the intention with which it is held (Law Commission No 29, para 59).

Section 3 of the Criminal Damage Act 1971 states it is an offence for a person who has anything:

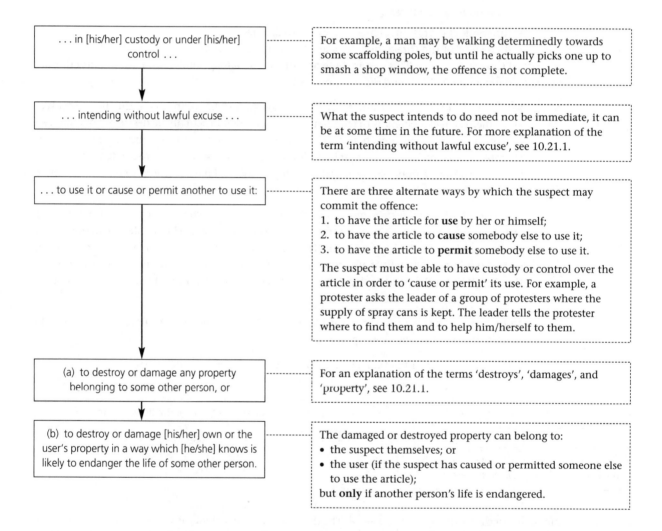

This offence is triable either way and the penalty is:

- summarily: six months' imprisonment and/or a fine not exceeding the statutory maximum;
- on indictment: ten years' imprisonment.

10.21.6   Powers to Search

Under s 1(2)(a) of the PACE Act 1984 you have the power to search for articles made or adapted for use in the course of or in connection with an offence under s 1 of the Criminal Damage Act 1971. It states that you may search:

- any person or vehicle; and
- anything which is in or on a vehicle for stolen or prohibited articles.

You may also detain a person or vehicle for the purpose of such a search.

Prohibited articles include articles which are used to destroy or damage property, used in the course of or in connection with offences under s 1 of the Criminal Damage Act 1971.

Remember that you must follow s 2 of the PACE Act 1984 and its Codes of Practice when conducting a search, and supply the person searched with the information contained in para 3.8 of Code A.

10.21.7 Damaging Ancient Monuments

It is an offence under s 28 of the Ancient Monuments and Archaeological Areas Act 1979 to damage or destroy (without lawful excuse) certain monuments, but the person must also:

- know that it is a protected monument; and
- intend to destroy or damage the monument or be reckless as to whether the monument would be destroyed or damaged.

This offence is triable either way and the penalty is:

- summarily: six months' imprisonment and/or a fine;
- on indictment: two years' imprisonment and/or a fine.

10.21.8 Graffiti

As graffiti is among the commonest forms of criminal damage, it is an offence to sell aerosol paint to children. Section 54(1) of the Anti-Social Behaviour Act 2003 states that it is an offence for a person to sell an aerosol paint container to a person under the age of 16. Section 54(2) states that an 'aerosol paint container' is a device which:

(a) contains paint stored under pressure, and
(b) is designed to permit the release of the paint as a spray.

This offence is triable summarily and the penalty is a fine.

10.22 Criminal Attempts

A person planning a criminal offence might not actually commit the full offence. This could be because the suspect lost his/her nerve, or was disturbed, or simply found that his/her plans were impracticable. The offence of criminal attempts (s 1 of the Criminal Attempts Act 1981) enables courts to penalize a criminal for carrying out an act just short of committing the full offence, even if he/she did not commit the full offence. The attempted offence must be an indictable offence. (Indictable offences are those offences which can be tried on indictment in a Crown Court or either way at a magistrates' court or a Crown Court (see 5.14 above).) Summary offences cannot be attempted in terms of this legislation.

This offence is described under s 1(1) of the Criminal Attempts Act 1981:

> If with intent to commit the offence to which this section applies, a person does an act which is more than merely preparatory to the commission of the offence, [he/she] is guilty of attempting to commit the offence.

10.22.1 Criminal Intent

The suspect must have formed criminal intent (*mens rea*) in all three of the following areas:

The suspect must have the intent to:	Example
Commit the full offence.	The suspect intended to steal a car or intended to rob a person.
Take part in a series of events which will lead to a final outcome of committing the full offence.	The suspect made a point of collecting the tools together, going to a house, and forcing a window in order to break in.
Fulfil **all** the elements of the offence.	In order to attempt a theft, the suspect must have acted dishonestly with the intention **both** of appropriating the property belonging to another **and** of permanently depriving the other of it.

For a person to be found guilty of an attempt to commit an offence, the suspect must have more than an intention to do it. In this context, merely thinking about committing an offence, such as deciding upon what article to use and what time to carry it out, is not enough: the suspect must demonstrate his or her guilty intent by carrying out acts which are more than just preparing to commit the full offence. Therefore, it would not be enough if the suspect simply thought about setting fire to a rival's house and only considered the location of the required articles. Similarly, if the suspect carried some cloth and a container of petrol in a bag, and transported them to the rival's house, his/her actions might still be considered as preparatory. If, on the other hand, the suspect went to the front door of his/her rival's house with cloth soaked in petrol, put it in the letterbox, and then used a lighter to attempt to light the cloth, this would show a clear intent to carry out the offence of arson (even if the cloth would not light). These acts would probably be considered as more than merely preparatory and therefore constitute an attempt under the Criminal Attempts Act 1981.

10.22.2 Thorough Planning and Practical Preparation

Section 1(2) of the Criminal Attempts Act 1981 states that there must be evidence that the person actually planned to carry out the act him- or herself rather than just planning it (in which case someone else could have carried it out):

> the person does an act which is more than merely preparatory to the commission of the offence.

Therefore, if there is something else to be done before the completion of the offence, it does not amount to an attempt. Similarly, the final act carried out by the accused must be in combination with all the other preparatory acts, and have no other aim than to complete the full offence. For example, a group of people might be seen getting out of a car and then standing close to a fenced enclosure that contains scrap copper and other metals. They cut a hole in the fence that would big enough for someone to climb through. On seeing a security guard, the group drives away from the scene and is stopped some miles away. One of the group still has some wire clippers in his pocket and another throws a pair of bolt croppers out of the van. They have done more than merely prepare to steal the metal; they have committed an attempt under s 1(1) of the Criminal Attempts Act 1981 (see *Davey v Lee* [1967] 51 Cr App R 303).

It does not matter (for the offence of criminal attempt) if the attempted offence would actually be impossible to carry out:

> A person may be guilty of attempting to commit an offence (to which this section applies), even though the facts are such that the commission of the offence is impossible (s 1(2)).

In addition, s 1(3)(b)) states that, if the person **believes** that he/she is committing an offence, he/she will still be regarded as having attempted it, even if it is proved later that it would not have been possible to commit the full offence. For example, a woman is paid money to travel from another country to the UK with a suitcase that she believes contains heroin. On arrival at the UK port her suitcase is searched and she admits to importing heroin into the UK. However, tests on the substance in the suitcase reveal it to be harmless vegetable matter, and not drugs. The offence of importing controlled drugs has therefore not been committed, but the person has still attempted to commit the crime.

10.22.3 Offences which Cannot Be Criminally Attempted

Section 1(4) of the Criminal Attempts Act 1981 lists several categories of offence that cannot be 'attempted'. Summary-only offences cannot generally be attempted unless specifically stated in the legislation, such as attempting to drive whilst unfit through drink or drugs. 'Taking a conveyance without the owner's consent' is a summary-only offence and therefore cannot be attempted, which is why the offence of 'Interfering with vehicles' (itself a summary offence) was created in the Criminal Attempts Act 1981.

However, there are a number of ways in which indictable offences **cannot** be attempted. These include:

- **conspiracy** to commit an indictable offence: that is, an agreement between people to commit an offence;
- **aiding, abetting, counselling, procuring, or suborning** the commission of an indictable offence: for example, a person knew all the circumstances surrounding a person's murder by the suspect and did everything apart from deliver the fatal kick to the head;
- **assisting** offenders: for example, knowingly helping offenders avoid arrest or concealing information, perhaps by paying money to a witness to stop him/her giving testimony in any trial.

The mode of trial is the same as for the main offence and the penalty is:

- for either-way offences; the same maximum penalty as the substantive offence when tried summarily;
- for an indictment-only offence; the same maximum penalty as the substantive offence.

TASK 21

Look at the following case relating to an attempt. The case subsequently went to appeal. Predict the result of the appeal and explain your reasoning.

A suspect was seen by a teacher in the lavatory block at a school. A cider can carrying the suspect's fingerprints was in one of the cubicles. The suspect's rucksack, containing a large kitchen knife, some rope, and a roll of masking tape, was found in some nearby bushes. The suspect was charged and convicted of attempted child abduction, the prosecution putting forward the argument that the suspect had been hiding in the lavatories to abduct a child. The suspect appealed on the grounds that he had not attempted to commit the offence (*R v Geddes* [1996] Crim LR 894)

10.23 Encouraging or Assisting Crime

Quite commonly, criminal offences involve two or more accomplices. However, more often than not, only some of the accomplices are the actual perpetrators of the offence and the role of others at the scene is to offer encouragement. Yet others may assist in the commission of a crime from a distance, providing information, transport, or finances. A person who encourages or assists in a crime (but does not perpetrate the main offence) may believe or claim that he/she was not a true accomplice. However, under the Serious Crime Act 2007 there are three criminal offences (see below) in which a person becomes criminally liable for encouraging or assisting another person to commit an offence. Together they replace the common law offence of incitement (now abolished), and also provide additional scope for prosecution in cases where the crime has not yet taken place; previously there was no criminal liability for assisting the commission of an offence unless the offence had been committed or attempted.

10.23.1 Intentionally Encouraging or Assisting an Offence

This is covered by s 44 of the Serious Crime Act 2007, which states that an offence is committed by a person who:

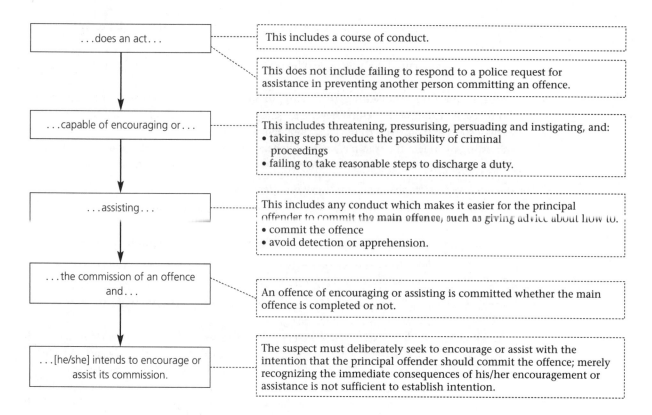

It may seem that some of this is rather complicated, so we provide a few examples below to illustrate some key points:

1. At a noisy and angry street demo, a police officer speaks to Dodie (a protestor) to try and help him calm down, but Dodie becomes increasingly irate and aggressive. Due to the loud noise, the officer is unable to summon assistance from a colleague. Instead the officer requests Neil, another protestor, to help restrain Dodie, but Neil refuses. Neil's failure to respond to the officer's request for assistance in preventing the breach of the peace would probably **not** be regarded as encouraging or assisting a person to commit a criminal act.

2. Frankie lends a baseball bat to a neighbour who is scared that someone might possibly break into his house to steal some antiques. Frankie knows that a baseball bat is sometimes used as a weapon to injure people, but gives it to her neighbour with the sole purpose of helping him feel more confident. Subsequently an intruder is seriously injured by the neighbour using the baseball bat. For Frankie, this would probably **not** amount to assistance or encouragement to cause grievous bodily harm.

3. Kristoff is married to Shazia but is having an affair with Bella, one of Shazia's work mates. Kristoff intends to murder Shazia and dispose of the body and make it seem that she has moved away. Bella knows all about Kristoff's plan and agrees to provide him with up-to-date information on Shazia's whereabouts during the day to give Kristoff a better opportunity to murder Shazia and hide the body without being caught. In the meantime, another work colleague overhears Bella on her mobile talking to Kristoff about the plan to kill Shazia. The work colleague alerts Shazia who flees the country to live abroad. However, Bella **has** still committed the offence of intentionally assisting in the commission of murder.

4. Brown works for a double-glazing firm and in return for payment gives his friend Mal a spare key from a recently installed door, knowing that Mal will use the key to burgle a particular house. One night Mal enters the house, takes the keys of an expensive car, and drives off in it with the intention of selling it abroad (he is not 'joy riding'). Brown has committed the offence of intentionally assisting in the commission of burglary (for burglary, see 10.5 above).

10.23.2   Encouraging or Assisting an Offence and Believing it Will Be Committed

This relates to belief rather than intent, and is covered by s 45 of the Serious Crime Act 2007, which states that an offence is committed by a person 'who does an act capable of encouraging or assisting the commission of an offence' and he/she believes that:

- the offence will be committed; and
- his/her act will encourage or assist its commission.

This differs from the s 44 offence above in that the person A offering the encouragement and assistance to person B must believe that person B will definitely commit the main offence and that A's encouragement and assistance is crucial to the commission of the main offence. It is immaterial whether the main offence is completed or not.

Again, some of these concepts are quite difficult to follow, so we have provided an example as an illustration. The following is likely to constitute a s 45 offence.

> Black is a car salesman who makes a copy of a key to the most expensive car on his forecourt. During an evening out, he gives the spare key to his friend Steve (a car thief), knowing full well it is very likely that Steve will steal the car in the near future. However, Black hopes that Steve will change his mind about stealing the car. Steve does not steal the car but is arrested during a burglary and is found in possession of the spare key. During his interview, Steve outlines his reasons for possessing the spare key, including Black's involvement. In this example, Black has committed the s 45 offence because, although he did not **intend** that Steve should commit theft, Black still **believed** that Steve would commit the offence.

10.23.3   Encouraging or Assisting Offences and Believing One or More Will Be Committed

This offence (s 46 of the Serious Crime Act 2007) is very similar to the s 45 offence described above, but applies in circumstances where there are a number of possible main offences planned by person B (rather than just one), and person A (who has provided encouragement or assistance) does not know which offence(s) person B is going to commit.

It is immaterial:

- whether the person has any belief as to **which** offence will be encouraged or assisted; or
- whether the main offence is completed.

> As an example of a possible s 46 offence, consider the actions of Jas in helping her friend Tilly. Tilly has been disqualified from driving and is now concerned that the local police will recognize her if she drives. Late one night she pays Jas to drive her to the next town. From what Tilly has said recently, Jas believes Tilly plans to carry out three offences; a serious assault in one house and two burglaries at a house and a flat. Scared of getting caught, Jas drops Tilly off around the corner from the first house and drives off. However Tilly suspects that she is under surveillance and so decides to delay her plans for another time. Here, Jas believed that all three offences were going to be committed, and therefore she can be prosecuted and convicted for encouraging or assisting the commission of offences that she believed were to be committed.

10.23.4 Possible Defences to Encouraging or Assisting Offences

If the defendant can prove that it was **reasonable** for him/her to act the way he/she did (in the circumstances he/she was aware of or believed existed) this may be a defence to an offence under ss 44, 45, or 46. When determining if it was reasonable, the following will be considered:

- **The seriousness of the anticipated main offence:** it might be reasonable to encourage or assist in the commission of a minor offence in order to prevent a more serious offence being committed. For example, Peta infiltrates a gang who are conspiring to commit an armed robbery. He tells one of the other members of the gang to steal a car for the gang to use when making off from the robbery. Peta's intention is to look credible in front of the other gang members so he can achieve his main objective of preventing the robbery from taking place. Therefore he may have a 'reasonable' defence.
- **The purpose of the act of encouragement or assistance:** it might be reasonable to encourage or assist in the commission of a minor offence in order to prevent more serious harm from being inflicted. For example Manny and Sam are members of a teenage gang on a housing estate. Sam meets with other members of the gang and together they plan to attack a rival gang and stab the leader, Taz. However, Manny does not want Taz to be injured and succeeds in persuading Sam and the others to smash the windows of Taz's house instead. Manny is charged with encouraging Sam to commit criminal damage but may have a 'reasonable' defence that his actions were to prevent a more serious offence.
- **The authority under which he/she was acting:** it might be reasonable to encourage or assist in the commission of an offence if it was done for the benefit of collecting evidence during an investigation by law enforcement agencies. For example, Boris, a 15-year-old, is tasked by a local authority trading standards department with going into a local shop and purchasing a lottery ticket.

The maximum penalties for an offence under ss 44, 45, or 46 of the Serious Crime Act 2007 will be the same as the maximum available on conviction for the relevant main offence.

10.24 Answers to Tasks

TASK 1

You probably considered the following:

1. Was the person dishonest?
2. Did he/she take the property?
3. Whom did the property belong to?
4. Did the person show an intention never to give the property back to its owner?

TASK 2

The circumstances do not amount to an offence of robbery because violence was not used in order to steal. This is because Jo picked up the bag and attempted to run off with it; she did not use force to steal it. Jo then picked up an item from the floor of the shopping centre and ran into Chris, causing her to fall over and break her arm, and it is only now that force is used. However, this force is used after the theft has taken place. Force was not used immediately before, at the time, nor in order to steal the bag and the goods, and therefore robbery has not been committed.

TASK 3

(a) No burglary has been committed. Although Jo entered the storage warehouse as a trespasser, her intention was to sleep, and not to commit any of the offences specified in s 9(1)(a) of the Theft Act 1968. Once inside the warehouse, she damaged the door (which is property), and also abstracted electricity by using the fire, but neither damage to property nor abstraction of electricity are included in the acts listed under s 9(1)(b) of the Theft Act 1968 (which is confined to theft and grievous bodily harm).

(b) The following offences are likely to have been committed:

- burglary with intent to steal (s 9(1)(a), of the Theft Act 1968), since Terry entered as a trespasser with the necessary intent;
- burglary (s 9(1)(b), Theft Act 1968) has also taken place since Terry, having entered as a trespasser, inflicts grievous bodily harm on the occupier;
- aggravated burglary (s 10, Theft Act 1968) has taken place because, whilst committing the s 9(1)(b) burglary, Terry was armed with a weapon of offence at the time of the search for something to steal.

TASK 4

1. Section 163 of the Road Traffic Act 1988 states that 'a person driving a mechanically propelled vehicle on a road must stop on being required to do so by a constable in uniform' (see 11.3 below). You will be authorized as an examiner by your chief officer. This is covered under s 67 of the Road Traffic Act 1988. You will have the authority to test a vehicle (and a drawn trailer) on a road, for the purposes of ascertaining compliance with:

- the construction and use requirements including lighting and
- the requirement that the condition of the vehicle is not such that its use on the road would involve a danger of injury to any person.

2. All wheeled vehicles after 1 April 1980 should be equipped with a plate in a conspicuous and readily accessible location on a part not normally subject to replacement which clearly shows the:

- vehicle identification number;
- name of manufacturer;
- type approval number (possibly on a separate plate).

This is described under reg 67 of the Road Vehicles (Construction and Use) Regulations 1986. The VIN should also be stamped on the chassis or frame and together these identifying features can be matched against details on PNC to enable identification of stolen vehicles.

TASK 5

National research in the late 1990s showed that the risk of theft of cars was greatest for older cars, common makes of car (for example, Fords), and performance models. The same survey showed that the type of car least likely to be stolen was a 'people carrier', such as the Ford Galaxy or Renault Espace.

The cars that are reported most often as stolen are listed by the Home Office (but their current list is based on data from 2005). In order, the cars most likely to be stolen are:

1. Vauxhall Belmont
2. Vauxhall Astra Mk2
3. Ford Escort Mk3
4. Austin/Morris Metro
5. Vauxhall Nova.

The Home Office report (with the full top ten of the most stolen cars) is available at <http://www.homeoffice.gov.uk/about-us/news/car-theft-2006> and more general information on vehicle crime is available at <http://www.crimereduction.homeoffice.gov.uk/toolkits/vc00.htm> .

TASK 6

1. Yes; a horse box is a trailer.
2. No, a go-kart is not a motor vehicle adapted or intended for use on the road.
3. Yes, there is an intention to commit theft of the CD player which is 'anything carried in or on the motor vehicle'.
4. No, there is no intention to steal the vehicle, anything in or on it, or take it without the owner's consent.

TASK 7

1. Both statements are true.
2. Without identifying the specific criminal conduct (or at least recognizing the type of criminal conduct which produced the money in the first place), there is unlikely to be a successful prosecution. The case of *R v NW, SW, RC & CC* (2008) EWCA Crim 2 was important with respect to the interpretation of the POCA 2002. The Court of Appeal ruled that the CPS could not just focus on inexplicable affluence, make the assumption that there was no lawful reason for its presence, and then presuppose that the affluence must result from the proceeds of crime. Unless there is evidence that Terri had the necessary knowledge or suspicion that the property represented a benefit from criminal conduct there could not be a successful prosecution under s 328(1) of the POCA 2002. Even if it could have been proved that the money was from the unlawful supply of controlled drugs, it was decided in *R v Sylvia Allpress; R v Deborah Symeou; R v Miguel Casal; R v Paul Winter Morris; R v Stephen Martin* (2009) EWCA Crim 8 that, if a suspects's only role in relation to the drug money was to act as a courier on behalf of another, such property did not amount to property for which the court could have ordered confiscation from him under the POCA 2002. Therefore, only if it could have been proved that Terri had benefited (for example, by receiving payments for passing on the money), could he have been successfully prosecuted under s 328(1) of the POCA 2002.

TASK 8

1. In response to this task you may have asked yourself a series of questions:
   - **Is he at his place of abode?** If the answer is no, it is possible that you are talking to the prolific car thief; it is not that likely that he will be sitting outside his own house. You might need to ask further questions to clarify the reasons for his presence in the car at the location in question.
   - **Has he 'control' over a pair of gloves, a large bunch of approximately 40 car keys, and a short length of scaffold pole?** Yes, they are on the passenger's seat and therefore he has control over them.
   - **Are the gloves, a large bunch of approximately 40 car keys, and a short length of scaffold pole 'any article'?** Yes, they are.
   - **Are the articles for use in the course of or in connection with any 'burglary, theft or cheat'?** Clearly, these are articles which are often used for breaking into cars. (The short length of scaffold pole for example, can be used to break a steering lock.) However, it is not clear at this point whether or not the person has used the articles for any burglary, theft, or cheat, or whether he was going to use them for such in the future. In order to be found guilty of going equipped the suspect must have some future intention to carry out a burglary, theft, or cheat, and therefore this particular case would need further investigation.

2. (c) only, abstracting electricity.

TASK 9

People enter the restaurant and order a meal

There is an expectation that people who enter a restaurant will pay for food which is prepared for them and served accordingly. By entering a restaurant, therefore, people imply that they have the means by which to pay for goods which are ordered and the intention to do so unless there is a special credit agreement whereby payment can be delayed until a later date. If people enter the restaurant with the appearance of paying customers (the false representation), but with an express intention not to pay for the meal they are about to order and consume (the property), or knowing they do not have the means to pay for it, they will commit a s 1 Fraud Act 2006 offence of 'fraud by false representation'. This is because the 'dishonest representation' took place before the property was obtained.

Having ordered the meal, they wait at the table for it to be served

When people enter a restaurant and order the meal, initially intending to pay but then change their mind about paying before it is obtained, then the offence is again one of s 1 'dishonest representation' as once more they assume the role of paying customers (the false represenation) before the meal is obtained (the property).

The meal is served to the table

When obtaining a meal at a restaurant, some of the charge is for the service that the customer receives. If the customer implies that he/she is an ordinary customer but intends not to pay for the service of the meal, then a s 11 Fraud Act offence of 'obtaining services dishonestly' may be committed.

Having consumed the meal, they are expected to pay

If people who enter a restaurant intend at the start to pay for their meal, but change their minds after their meal is obtained, then the dishonesty has occurred after obtaining the property, so a s 1 Fraud Act offence has not been committed. However, because the meal was served to the table, a s 11 Fraud Act offence of 'obtaining services dishonestly' may be committed.

They leave the restaurant

If the people continue to make out that they are ordinary customers, intending to pay (waiting for the bill for example), and then make off out of the restaurant at a convenient moment without paying, there is dishonesty but it takes place after obtaining the property and the offence is more likely to be s 3 Theft Act 1978, that is, 'bilking'. Seek the advice of a CPS representative in such cases for the most appropriate charge.

TASK 10

Some common street names are:

- **amphetamines**—speed, crystal, crank, meth, black beauties, bennies, uppers, dexies, 357 magnums;
- **cocaine**—crack, coke, booth, blow, railers, snow, ringer, divits, toot, cola, rocks, blast, white dust, ivory flakes, nose candy, mobbeles;
- **heroin**—china white, fix, horse, smack, whack, mother pearl, H, junk;
- **cannabis**—dope buds, bhang, goof butt, grass, hash, hay, hemp, herb, jive, pot, rope, stinkweed, stuff, tea, weed, wacky backy, whack.

TASK 11

Factors and circumstances that would provide reasonable grounds for suspecting a person is in unlawful possession of drugs with intent to supply might include:

- intelligence that drugs are being supplied or used in that particular area;
- information on the descriptions of people supplying or using drugs in that area;
- behaviour of the person (for example, is he/she trying to hide something? Or preparing to throw away something small, seemingly with the intention that you will not notice?);
- behaviour of people who approach the person (for example, do a number of individuals walk up to the person from different directions, exchange small items, and walk away again? Note that these may well be very open acts, in order to discourage attention.)

What to think about and what to say before carrying out the search:

- purpose of the search;
- entitlement to a copy of the record of search;
- grounds for the search;
- warrant card if you are not in uniform;
- explain to the person that he/she is being detained for a search;
- legal search power title you are using (s 23 of the Misuse of Drugs Act);
- police station name;
- your name.

Any of the following might be reasons for making an arrest:

- to enable the name or address of the person in question to be ascertained;
- to prevent him/her from causing physical injury to him/herself;
- to prevent him/her from suffering physical injury;
- to allow the prompt and effective investigation of the offence or of the conduct of the person in question;
- to prevent any prosecution for the offence from being hindered by the disappearance of the person in question.

TASK 12

1. Common assault by beating (battery): only the very slightest degree of force is required to constitute a battery and little or no visible injury is necessary to prove the offence.
2. Common assault: if a person is threatened with immediate unlawful personal violence of a minor nature, he/she is the victim of common assault (remember that assault is the **threat** of violence or harm, not the harm itself). The suspect can only be charged or reported for the offence of common assault, or common assault by beating (battery), not both.

TASK 13

You probably considered the following:

(a) Through questioning you will be able to determine if the injury affects the health or comfort of the victim in more than a trivial way.
(b) Through questioning and observation you will be able to collect and collate evidence concerning the injury and whether it can seen or felt by the victim or witnesses (which include you).
(c) If there is no evidence of the offence of **actual bodily harm** then consider **common assault** as an alternative.

TASK 14

The problem with these kinds of scenarios is that you lack all the other information that would actually be potentially available to you in a real incident. However, based entirely on the limited information available to you in the questions, the following are the possible offences that could be considered:

- s 47, Offences Against the Person Act 1861;
- ss 18 or 20, Offences Against the Person Act 1861 (until evidence is gathered from witnesses and an interview with the suspect is held, the offence could be either s 18 or s 20, depending on what the suspect intended);
- assault with intent to resist lawful arrest;
- common assault;
- s 38, Offences Against the Person Act 1861;
- s 39, Criminal Justice Act 1988;
- common assault and s 39, Criminal Justice Act 1988.

TASK 15

1. Under s 17(e) of the PACE Act 1984 you 'may enter and search any premises for the purposes of saving life or limb or preventing serious damage to property'. The witness evidence of hysterical screaming and the suspicion that the child is alone and does not open the door together justify the use of s 17 to save the life and limb of the child.
2. It would appear that Jo has committed an offence under s 1 of the Children and Young Persons Act 1933. This is committed by any person who is 16 years old or over who has responsibility for a child under the age of 16 years and who 'wilfully assaults, ill-treats, neglects, abandons or exposes the child in a manner likely to cause unnecessary suffering or injury to health'. In these circumstances Jo has 'abandoned' Sam in a manner likely to cause unnecessary suffering or injury to health. It appears that, although an offence has been committed,

the child is no longer in immediate danger and arrangements could be made perhaps with the neighbours or the grandparents for the child's safety while Jo is absent. If you had any reason to believe the child was in immediate danger you could consider taking Sam into police protection and arresting the mother. However, you must be guided by prosecution guidelines and you should seek the guidance of a CPS representative in relation to this matter. Whatever action you take, it must be proportionate.

TASK 16

Section 66 of the Sexual Offences Act only applies to exposure of a person's genitals, not the buttocks (although it is possible that 'mooning' may also result in exposure of the genitals, even though this was not intended). However, in any case the suspects might excuse themselves by stating that their intention was to entertain or amuse, not to alarm or distress.

In the common law offence of Outraging Public Decency, there must be a deliberate act that is lewd, obscene, or disgusting. In *R v Rowley* [1991] 4 All ER 649, Lord Simon decided that outraging public decency goes considerably beyond offending the sensibilities of 'reasonable' people.

Therefore you should seek advice from your local evidence-review representative or CPS representative as to whether the common law offence might be committed by members of the rugby team, and also consider public order offences as well, eg s 5 of the Public Order Act—non-intentional harassment, alarm, or distress.

TASK 17

1. You may consider investigating the woman under s 1(1) of the Street Offences Act 1959 as 'persistently loitering or soliciting in a street or public place for the purposes of prostitution'. However, in order to prove 'persistently' there must be evidence of the behaviour on two or more occasions in any period of three months. You may therefore consider speaking to the woman and, having found out her name, address, and date of birth, check whether there is a record on your organization's database of previous incidents of soliciting in the last three months. If it was apparent that she is a persistent offender you may need to consider further action. Otherwise you might consider warning her about the possible consequences of continuing her behaviour, ensuring of course that the warning is recorded in the appropriate place according to local procedures. This will provide evidence that she has already been acting in this way to any police officer who may need to check in the future. Record the incident in your PNB.
2. It depends; this offence can certainly be committed by the possession of extreme images stored on a mobile telephone. However, body piercing carried out hygienically and with consent is unlikely to result in serious injury to a person's breasts or genitals. Also, if the owner of the mobile was a professional piercer trying to get business he/she could claim the images were for advertising and not for sexual arousal; this may be a legitimate reason for possessing the images. Therefore he/she is likely to have a defence.

TASK 18

Section 7 of the Sexual Offences (Amendment) Act 1976 provides anonymity for victims of rape, attempted rape, aiding, abetting, counselling and procuring rape or attempted rape, incitement to rape, and conspiracy to rape.

TASK 19

In the case of sexual activity with a child under s 9(1) of the Sexual Offences Act 2003, there is a defence available if the family friend reasonably believed that the girl was over 16. If the girl was 12 years old or younger the defendant would have no defence.

TASK 20

The excrement will not have destroyed the walls of the police cell, but the walls will need to be cleaned, therefore they have been damaged. The cost of the damage will be equal to the cost of the cleaning operation. The suspect will need to be interviewed to prove or disprove whether she intended to damage the walls or was reckless as to whether or not the damage was caused. If the drunken state was self-induced, it will not be a defence.

TASK 21

The suspect had never had communication with any children nor made any other contact with a child. As a result, the Court of Appeal concluded that the acts of the suspect were merely preparatory and that the suspect had not attempted to abduct any children.

11 | Road and Traffic Policing

11.1   Chapter Briefing

This chapter describes police procedures and duties relevant to road and traffic policing. You will probably be expected to demonstrate competence in many of the areas described in this chapter whilst on Supervised and Independent Patrol.

Much of the content of this chapter concerns legislation. As we explained in Chapter 2, we often provide a simplified and abbreviated version of the law, and use flow charts to explain points when appropriate. If you require more detail then you may need to consult the original legislation, other textbooks, or websites.

11.1.1   Aim of the Chapter

The aim of this chapter is to introduce you to the legislation and police practice when involved with road and traffic policing.

This chapter will enable you to:

- understand the legislation surrounding the use of vehicles;
- identify a number of common offences related to vehicles and to driving, and how to take the appropriate action according to the powers legally granted to you;
- develop the underpinning knowledge required for a number of NOS elements, one of the PAC headings, and entries for your Learning Diary Phase 3 and a CAR of your SOLAP.

11.1.2 Police Action Checklist

This chapter will assist in meeting the following requirements of the Police Action Checklist under the Road Policing heading:

- check driving documents;
- complete traffic documents—including HO/RT1, FPN(E), CLE2, and VDRS;
- demonstrate correct administration of the appropriate tests for drink/drugs-driving offences.

11.1.3 National Occupational Standards

This chapter will provide you with some of the knowledge required to demonstrate aspects of the following NOS elements:

National Occupational Standard Elements

CD1.1 Gather information and plan a response
CD1.2 Respond to incidents

11.1.4 IPLDP Phases and Modules

This chapter will provide you with resources to support the following Operational Module of the IPLDP:

OP 3   Respond to incidents, conduct and evaluate investigations

---

It will also cover aspects of the following topic areas of Legislation, Policy and Guidelines of the IPLDP:

- Police Policies and Procedures (LPG 1.4);
- Road Policing (LPG 1.8).

Much of the content of this chapter relates to IPLDP Phase 3 Supervised Patrol and Phase 4 Independent Patrol.

11.1.5 SOLAP

The contents of this chapter are relevant to the 'knowledge' evidence requirement of CAR CD1.

11.1.6 Learning Diary Phases

The contents of this chapter may provide you with stimulus material for completion of your Learning Diary (Phase 3) and the Traffic heading in particular.

11.2 Introduction

It is perhaps apocryphal to remark that the first time the middle classes encountered the police was in the introduction of traffic law in the first decades of the last century (see 1.3 above). However, if we substitute the phrase 'otherwise law-abiding' for 'middle' in the sentence above, it may still be the case.

Most of us are law-abiding most of the time. We do not attack our neighbour as he or she passes in the morning, nor do we steal from, rob, knife, bludgeon, or attack our work colleagues. We do not routinely murder passers-by or set light to public buildings. We may sometimes get drunk and fall over, or make inappropriate comments, or have an irrational hatred of garden gnomes but, generally speaking, most of us observe most laws, most of the time. Except, that is, when we are driving.

What happens when we get behind the wheel of a car? For a start, a significant number of us routinely **drive too fast** for the legal speed limit. The following table gives the proportion of vehicles observed to be moving either at or over the speed limit in surveys conducted in Great Britain in 2007.

Vehicles exceeding (or at) the speed limit (%)

	Motorways	Non-urban dual carriageways	Urban 40 mph	Urban 30 mph
Cars	54	45	23	48
HGVs	no data	79	25	49
Coaches/ buses	50	37	13	28

(Adapted by the authors from data to be found in Department of Transport, 2008)

Of particular concern must be the one in seven of HGVs that travel at speeds of more than 35 mph in 30-mph urban speed limit areas (ibid), where, of course, there are more people on foot, particularly children.

The majority of urban accidents are caused by excessive speed, whilst other factors, including driver inattention, driving too close to the vehicle in front, not allowing for adverse weather conditions, and mechanical defect, often dominate motorway and rural collision statistics. Very few of us who drive keep to the legal limit all the time, and those who do are often abused by those who do not. These are daily occurrences on any of our roads.

In the pages which follow you will be learning the law about highways, driving, road traffic collisions (the preferred term for accidents), insurance, offences, driving standards, drink-driving, drug-taking and driving, and arcane subjects such as 'fireworks and highways'. Whilst all of this law and procedure is relevant to your function as a police officer, what is not quite so explicit is that:

- there are a great many vehicles on the roads, particularly in urban areas;
- drivers are increasingly litigious towards you and towards each other (especially as a result of 'no win, no fee' practice);
- 'road rage' is widely reported;
- many privately owned (and some publicly owned) vehicles are poorly maintained and consequently, drivers are less aware of vehicle defects and safety rules.

Bear in mind, as you read and learn from the following, and as you go out on Supervised Patrol, that for British drivers it is often a case of 'love me, love my car'. You may encounter more hostility and aggression among the nation's drivers than among its drunks. Sometimes, of course, they are one and the same.

Finally, we should perhaps note the link between road and traffic offences and other forms of criminality. Research by Rose (2000) demonstrated that 79 per cent of disqualified drivers had a criminal record (four times the average). Approximately 50 per cent of dangerous drivers had a previous conviction and approximately 25 per cent were reconvicted within a year (three times the average). Drink-drivers had less extensive criminal records than other groups of serious traffic offenders—40 per cent had a criminal record, the average time since their last court appearance was eight years, and 12 per cent were subsequently convicted within a year. However, these figures are still twice the average. Similarly Junger et al. (2001) identified links between 'risky' traffic behaviour and more general violent crime. All of this leads us to the notion of 'self-selecting' road and traffic behaviour that you might usefully consider as indicators of perhaps more serious criminal predisposition. For example, in a famous study, Chenery *et al* (1999) demonstrated the links between the relatively minor offence of illegal parking in disabled bays, active criminals, and illegal vehicles.

11.2.1 Definitions of Vehicles, Driving, and Roads

Numerous terms for vehicles and roads are used in the various Acts that relate to the policing of roads. Some of the Acts were written over a hundred years ago; technological progress is just one of the reasons the terminology in everyday use has changed over the years. The term 'public place' is also widely used within legislation relating to roads and driving; the term is defined (along with other definitions relating to locations) in 7.2.1 above.

11.2.1.1 Definitions of vehicles

Within the legislation, there are named references to different types of vehicle and to other wheeled objects such as carriages, conveyances and cycles. The table below provides some useful definitions, but is by no means comprehensive.

Named vehicle type	Definition	Examples
'Vehicle'	According to the Vehicle Excise and Registration Act 1994, a vehicle is: • a mechanically propelled vehicle or • anything (whether or not it is a vehicle) that has been, but has ceased to be, a mechanically propelled vehicle. The ordinary dictionary meaning can also be used.	Milk float, ride-on grass cutter
'Mechanically propelled vehicle'	'Mechanically propelled' means that the vehicle is powered by a motor (driven by electricity, petrol, diesel, or other fuels). The meaning is not defined by any Act of Parliament, and it is therefore not a question of law but a question of fact for the court to decide whether or not a particular vehicle is a mechanically propelled vehicle.	Car, van, lorry, go-ped, quad bike, speedway motorcycles, Formula One racing cars, invalid carriages such as powered wheelchairs and scooters, for footway use only
'Motor vehicle'	This is a mechanically propelled vehicle that is intended or adapted for use on roads (s 185, Road Traffic Act 1988).	Car, van, lorry
'Motor bicycle'	This means a motor vehicle which: • has two wheels • has a maximum design speed exceeding 45 kph • if powered by an internal combustion engine, has a cylinder capacity exceeding 50cc and • includes a combination of such a motor vehicle and a side-car. (s 108, Road Traffic Act 1988)	Motorcycle with two wheels
'Pedal cycle'	This is either: (a) propelled only by pedals and not propelled by mechanical power or (b) an electrically assisted pedal cycle (see 11.4.6.4 below). (Reg 3 of the Pedal Cycles (Construction and Use) Regs 1983)	Mountain bike, racing bike, BMX bike
'Bicycle'	This includes a motorbike for the purposes of vehicle excise duty.	
'Moped'	Moped means a motor vehicle which has fewer than four wheels and: (a) if first used before 1st August 1977, has a cylinder capacity not exceeding 50cc and is equipped with pedals by means of which the vehicle is capable of being propelled and (b) in any other case, has a maximum design speed not exceeding 50 kph and, if propelled by an internal combustion engine, has a cylinder capacity not exceeding 50cc. (s 108, Road Traffic Act 1988)	

Named vehicle type	Definition	Examples
'carriage'	This means a motor vehicle or trailer (s 191, Road Traffic Act 1988). The ordinary dictionary meaning also applies.	Any motor vehicle described above, and caravans
'conveyance'	This is a vehicle for transporting person(s). A conveyance is 'constructed or adapted for the carriage of a person or persons whether by land, water or air, except that it does not include a conveyance constructed or adapted for use only under the control of a person not carried in or on it' (s 12(7), Theft Act 1968).	Motorcycle, bus, boat and plane

(Images courtesy of Kent Police)

This adapted bicycle would be classified as a moped under s 108 of the Road Traffic Act 1988, as it has a small engine but can also be propelled by its pedals.

11.2.1.2 Definitions relating to driving

Legislation relating to road and traffic policing often refers to 'driving' and 'attempting to drive', and these are defined and explained below.

Driving is not defined within any act pertaining to roads policing, but there are precedents to give guidelines. The decision finally rests with the court and is therefore a question of fact. The court will consider:

- the degree to which the person had control over the direction and movement of the vehicle;
- the length of time the person had control;
- the point at which the person stopped the driving;
- the use of the vehicle's controls by the person in order to direct its movement.

Attempting to drive is not defined by statute, but the general principles of attempting should be applied and these are that an attempt is:

- the last action before the full offence is committed;
- more than merely preparatory to the act (see 10.22 above).

For example, trying to drive a vehicle which has a fault and therefore will not start could be considered as attempting to drive.

11.2.1.3 Definitions of roads and highways and related terms

Legislation relating to road and traffic policing often includes the words 'road' and 'highway'. Each term is used in different pieces of legislation, though the term 'road' is used far more frequently, particularly since the introduction of the Road Traffic Act 1988.

- A **road** is defined as any (length of) highway **to which the public has access**, and includes bridges over which a road passes (s 192, Road Traffic Act 1988). The limits of a road are the hedgerows on either side, so a public footpath alongside a road is part of the road.
- A **highway** (s 5, Highways Act 1835) is defined as a road, bridge, carriageway, cart way, horseway, bridleway, footway, causeway, church way, or pavement, so highway has a broader and more general meaning than the term road.
- A **public road** is a road maintained at the public's expense (for the purposes of vehicle excise duty legislation) as defined in s 62 of the Vehicle Excise and Registration Act 1994.

Note the potentially confusing overlap between a road and a highway; in practice this does not matter as each relates to individual pieces of legislation.

There are also are number of other terms used in legislation:

- A **carriageway** is a way marked or arranged in a highway over which the public have a right of way for the passage of **vehicles**, but does not include cycle tracks (s 329, Highways Act 1980).
- A **bridleway** is a highway over which the public have a right of way on foot, on horseback, or leading a horse (s 329, Highways Act 1980).
- A **footpath** is a highway **not** adjacent to a road, over which the public have a right of way on foot only (s 329, Highways Act 1980).
- A **footway** (such as a pavement) is a highway adjacent to a road over which the public have a right of way on foot only (s 329(1), Highways Act 1980).
- A **street** includes roads, lanes, alleys, subways, squares, and any other similar places open to the public. It also includes doorways, entrances to premises, and any ground adjoining a street (*Smith v Hughes* [1960] 2 All ER 859).

The maintenance of a private road is usually the responsibility of the landowner; this one is in a good state of repair. Private roads may or may not be subject to public rights of way.

(Photo by Kevin Lawton-Barrett)

11.3 Powers to Stop a Vehicle and 'Using, Causing, and Permitting'

Whilst on foot or mobile patrol it will be necessary for you to investigate offences connected with the use of a variety of vehicles on roads. These offences may relate to the way in which a vehicle has been driven (you might suspect that a driver's ability has been impaired through drink or drugs), or the condition of a vehicle. You may suspect that the occupants of a vehicle have been involved in committing other offences using the vehicle, or you may wish to speak to them about other matters. For whatever reason, if a vehicle is in motion on a road, you will need to stop it safely in order to speak to the people inside. To do this you must be on duty in full uniform, and give a clear direction (whether from a police vehicle or while you are on foot patrol).

The power to stop a mechanically propelled vehicle on a road is to be found in s 163 of the Road Traffic Act 1988, which states that:

- A person driving a mechanically propelled vehicle on a road must stop the vehicle on being required to do so by a constable in uniform.
- If a person fails to comply with this section, [he/she] is guilty of an offence.

This offence is triable summarily and the penalty is a fine.

The power of entry to premises in order to arrest a person for this offence is in s 17 of the Police and Criminal Evidence (PACE) Act 1984 (see 7.9 above).

11.3.1 Using, Causing, and Permitting

Many road traffic offences relating to vehicles can be committed not only by people who **use** the vehicle (such as the driver), but also by people associated with the vehicle who may **cause** or **permit** its use (such as owners and people who hold supervisory responsibilities). You need to have a clear understanding about the meanings of these terms. We illustrate the principles below using an employer and employee as an example, but 'using', 'causing', and 'permitting' also occur in other circumstances, for example within families or between friends.

11.3.1.1 Using

In road traffic law, the user of a vehicle is not always the driver of a vehicle, and in addition a vehicle can be 'in use' while parked, or while being towed.

The user of a vehicle can be:

- the **driver** of a vehicle, including an employee driving a company vehicle for business purposes. (The employee is likely to be held responsible if the vehicle was being used for purposes other than company business);
- the **employer** of the driver if the vehicle is a company vehicle used on company business. (The employer can be held responsible for committing an offence relating to a vehicle defect even if he/she is unaware of the defect. In some circumstances, both the employer and the driver (an employee) can be held responsible);
- the **owner** of a vehicle driven by another person, but with the owner present and for the benefit of the owner;
- a person **steering** the vehicle, for example when it is being towed.

11.3.1.2 Causing

There are two elements required in causing a vehicle to be used:

1. The 'causer' must have the **authority** to make a subordinate carry out a particular action (for example, the line manager of a transport company orders one of the company's drivers to make an urgent delivery using a particular company vehicle).
2. The causer must also have **knowledge** about the unroadworthy state of that vehicle.

If one of these elements cannot be proved, 'causing' cannot be considered as an offence. However, the use of the vehicle might be considered as an alternative offence. In some cases, the company can be held responsible for causing the use of an unroadworthy vehicle if the company director knows the vehicle is defective. Also, note that, if a person tows a vehicle, then this person is causing that vehicle to be used on a road.

11.3.1.3 Permitting

There are two elements in permitting a vehicle to be used. The 'permitter' must:

1. be in a position to either **allow** or forbid its use. Such permission can be given verbally or it can be written down, or merely implied, and
2. have **knowledge of** (or 'turn a blind eye' to) the unroadworthy state of the vehicle or its lack of documentation. Therefore an offence is committed by an employer who allows an employee to use a defective company vehicle for business purposes, but only if the employer knows about the defect.

However, many companies give a general permission to their employees to use company vehicles, for private as well as company purposes. In these cases it is unlikely that the employer can be held responsible for permitting the vehicle to be used (depending on the circumstances).

If one of these elements cannot be proved, then the 'use' of the vehicle is an alternative to 'permitting the use' because there will be no requirement to prove the existence of a permission or knowledge of the defect. It is also important to note that it will be for the courts to decide as a question of fact whether any of these offences has been committed in particular circumstances; the descriptions above are general guidelines.

TASK 1

You see a car being towed by a van and there is no one in the car. You stop both vehicles and examine the car briefly. It appears to have many defects; one wheel is not turning, the steering appears defective, the brakes are seized and the engine will not start.

What offence is the van driver committing in relation to the presence of an unroadworthy vehicle on a road and what evidence will you need to prove the offence?

11.4 Driving Licences

Over the years, the government has introduced new policies and procedures (such as updated driving tests and compulsory basic training for motorcyclists) with the aim of improving driving standards. There will obviously be members of the public who disregard these requirements or standards, and in the course of your Supervised and Independent Patrol it is inevitable that you will investigate and detect a number of offences relating to driving licences. This is an introduction to those offences.

The table below shows the age requirements for driving particular categories of vehicle.

	Vehicle category	Minimum age requirement
A	Motorcycles	17
B	Cars and light vans	17
C	Large goods vehicles	21
D	Passenger-carrying vehicles with 9 to 16 passenger seats	21
E	Trailers	18
F to K	Other vehicles	16
P	Mopeds	16

11.4.1 Information Shown on Driving Licences

Driving licences are made up of two parts: the photocard and the counterpart. Photocard full licences (see below) are pink, but provisional licences are green. The driver number contains information about the driver.

How to interpret the driver number

The Driver Number is:	**GARDN 605109C99LY**
The first five characters are the first five letters of the surname.	**GARDN**
The first and last digits are derived from the year of birth.	605**1**09 shows the year of birth is 19**69**
The second and third digits represent the month of birth and the gender of the licence holder.	6**05**109 shows that the person was born in May and is male. For women, 5 is added to the second digit so for a female born in May the number would be 6**55**109, and for a female born in December, it would be 6**62**109
The fourth and fifth digits show the day of birth.	605**10**9 shows that the date of birth was the 10th of the month.
The first two characters of the final cluster represent the initials	**C** (if there is only one initial, **9** is used in place of a second initial)
The middle number of the final cluster is computer-generated, in order to avoid duplicate records.	**9** (can be any digit between 0 and 9)
The final two letters are also computer-generated.	**LY** in this case

Full details concerning the driving licence, including the meaning of the various symbols and codes, may be found at the DVLA website <http://www.dvla.gov.uk>.

11.4.1.1 The photocard

The following describes the main features of the front of the photocard.

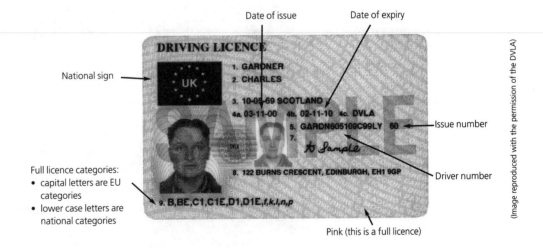

(Image reproduced with the permission of the DVLA)

The reverse of the photocard contains the following information.

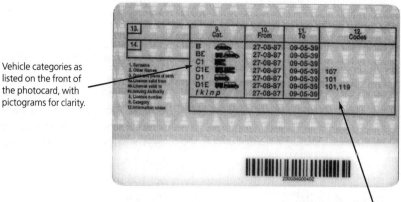

Vehicle categories as listed on the front of the photocard, with pictograms for clarity.

Information codes showing restrictions applying to the adjoining category. For example, 101 means that the licence holder cannot drive that category of vehicle for hire or reward.

(Image reproduced with the permission of the DVLA)

11.4.1.2   The counterpart

The counterpart is a paper document (see below) showing additional information, such as the vehicle categories the holder is entitled to drive provisionally, the entitlement history (superseded categories), and any endorsements. It is green and pink for both full and provisional licences.

The issue number on the counterpart will be followed by a letter

List of categories for which the holder is entitled to drive provisionally

Superseded categories of vehicles

List of endorsement with dates and codes

(Image reproduced with the permission of the DVLA)

11.4.2 Requesting to See a Driver's Licence

Under s 164(1) of the Road Traffic Act 1988 you may require a person to produce his/her driving licence. This applies to any person:

(a) **driving** a motor vehicle on a road;

(b) who you have reasonable cause to believe to have been driving a motor vehicle involved in an **accident** on a road;

(c) who you have reasonable cause to believe to have **committed an offence** in relation to the use of a motor vehicle on a road; or

(d) supervising a provisional-licence holder in any of the above three circumstances.

A failure to produce the licence is an offence unless the driver produces it within specified time limits (see 11.4.2.2 below).

11.4.2.1 Requiring a person to state his/her date of birth

Under s 164(2) of the Road Traffic Act 1988 you may require a person to state his/her date of birth if he/she:

- has failed to produce his/her licence;
- has produced a licence that is unsatisfactory (for example it seems to have been altered or if it contains information you suspect to be incorrect);
- is the supervisor of a learner driver at the time of an accident or an offence, and you have reason to suspect that he/she (the supervisor) is under 21 years of age.

11.4.2.2 Offences relating to failing to produce a licence

Under s 164 of the Road Traffic Act 1988 it is an offence for a person to fail to:

- produce his/her licence and its counterpart; or
- produce his/her certificate of completion of a motorcyclist's training course (CBT; Compulsory Basic Training); or
- state his/her date of birth.

Under s 164(8) of the Road Traffic Act 1988 it will be a defence for that person to produce the relevant licence either:

- within **seven days** in person at a police station (specified by her/him at the time of the request);
- as soon as **reasonably practicable**; or
- at a **later time** if he/she can prove it was not reasonably practicable to do so before the day on which written charge proceedings were commenced).

'As soon as is reasonably practicable' will be a question of fact for the court to decide, given the circumstances of the case.

11.4.2.3 Failure to update a change of address on a driving licence

This is an offence under s 99(5) of the Road Traffic Act 1988 and the penalty is a fine.

11.4.2.4 Driving a vehicle otherwise than in accordance with a licence

Breaches of licence conditions or no-licence driving are covered in s 87 of the Road Traffic Act 1988. It is an offence for a person:

- to drive a motor vehicle on a road if he/she does not have a licence authorizing him/her to drive a motor vehicle of that class (s 87(1));
- to cause or permit another person to drive on a road if that other person does not have a licence authorizing him/her to drive a motor vehicle of that class (s 87(2)).

This offence includes circumstances where the offender is **driving under age.**

11.4.3 Seizing a Vehicle

Under s 165A of the Road Traffic Act 1988, you have the power to seize a vehicle if you have reasonable grounds for believing that the driver does not have a suitable licence or that the vehicle is not adequately insured. To seize a vehicle you must be in uniform and you must have:

- requested to see the driver's licence and counterpart or evidence of insurance, but the appropriate document has not been produced;
- warned the driver that you will seize the vehicle unless he/she produces the required documentation immediately (it might not be practical to warn the driver; if so, this stage may be omitted) (s 165A(6)).

You can also seize a vehicle if you have required a vehicle to stop (you must be in uniform to require a vehicle to stop: see 11.3 above), but it has not stopped, or has not stopped long enough for appropriate enquiries, **and** you have reasonable grounds for believing that the driver does not have a suitable licence or that the vehicle is not adequately insured. If you are unable to seize the vehicle immediately because the person driving it has failed to stop or has driven off, you may seize the vehicle at any time within 24 hours from the incident. In order to seize a vehicle you may enter premises (other than a private dwelling house) if you have reasonable grounds for believing the vehicle to be present, using reasonable force if necessary. Note that a private dwelling-house does not include any outbuildings or adjacent land, so you may seize a vehicle from areas such as driveways and garages.

11.4.4 Provisional-Licence Holders

A provisional driving-licence holder must not drive a vehicle unless he/she is accompanied and supervised by a qualified driver (see 11.4.4.1 below). Details are provided in reg 16(2)(a) of the Motor Vehicles (Driving Licences) Regulations 1999.

There are exceptions; supervision is not required when:

- driving a motor vehicle of certain categories: for example three-wheeled vehicles;
- riding a moped or motor bicycle (with or without a side-car);
- driving a motor vehicle on an exempted island (except large goods vehicles and passenger-carrying vehicles);
- driving a motor vehicle having just passed a test (having been given a certificate authorizing the person to drive the res'pective class of vehicle).

11.4.4.1 Meaning of qualified driver

The meaning of qualified driver is given in reg 17(1) and (2) of the Motor Vehicles (Driving Licences) Regulations 1999.

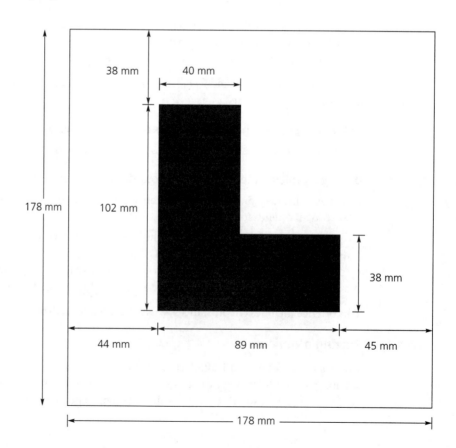

A qualified driver (for the purposes of reg 16):

- is 21 years of age or over;
- holds a relevant licence for the relevant category of the vehicle (a full British (including Northern Ireland) or a Community (EC) licence);
- has the relevant driving experience;
- has held the relevant licence for a continuous period of not less than three years.

11.4.4.2 Displaying learner driver plates correctly

A provisional driving-licence holder must not drive a vehicle unless 'L' plates are displayed on the vehicle in such manner as to be clearly visible to other road users from within a reasonable distance from the front and back of the vehicle. Details are provided in reg 16(2)(b) of the Motor Vehicles (Driving Licences) Regulations 1999.

'D' plates can be displayed in Wales, but if such a vehicle is driven in England these must be replaced with 'L' plates. The appropriate sizes and measurements of an 'L' plate are shown in the diagram. The corners can be rounded, but the dimensions of the 'L' plate must be as shown.

11.4.4.3 Provisional-licence holders and towing

A provisional driving-licence holder must not drive a vehicle while it is being used to draw a trailer. Details are provided in reg 16(2)(c) of the Motor Vehicles (Driving Licences) Regulations 1999. There are exceptions, such as for holders of provisional licences for certain vehicle categories such as articulated lorries.

11.4.5 Provisional Licences for Mopeds or Motorcycles

As you might expect, a motorcycle rider with only a provisional licence is subject to certain restrictions. No passengers may be carried on a moped or a motor bicycle (with or without a side-car) if the driver has only a provisional driving licence. Details are provided in reg 16(2)(b) of the Motor Vehicles (Driving Licences) Regulations 1999.

A Certificate of **Compulsory Basic Training** (CBT) is required by all motorcycle and moped provisional-licence holders before they ride on a road (except during the training itself). The CBT lasts for two years and then has to be renewed. This legislation is described in s 97(3)(e) of the Road Traffic Act 1988.

For a provisional-licence holder a breach of these conditions amounts to an offence of driving otherwise than in accordance with a licence under s 87(1) of the Road Traffic Act 1988.

These offences are triable summarily.

11.4.6 Motorcycle Training and Licensing Arrangements

These arrangements are complicated and are summarized in 11.4.6.1 to 11.4.6.3 below. The power of the motorcycle engine is an important factor for the type of licence required.

11.4.6.1 Category P licence

A category P licence is for riding a moped only. The following conditions must be met:

- rider age: minimum 16 years;
- engine size: maximum 50 cc capacity/50 kph speed.

New riders and drivers need a provisional licence and CBT before riding on the road (apart from riding on the road during training). The CBT certificate is valid for two years.

Other conditions apply for moped riders who already have a licence that allows them to ride a moped:

- **Full Cat P holders** who took the Cat P test after 1 December 1990 need to complete CBT. The Certificate is valid for two years.
- **Car drivers** with a full Car Cat B licence automatically have a full Cat P licence, but if the Cat B test was passed on or after 1 February 2001, CBT is still required. (The CBT Certificate does not have to be periodically renewed.)

11.4.6.2   Category A motorcycle licence

There are different types of Category A motorcycle, and the licence requirements also depend on the rider's age.

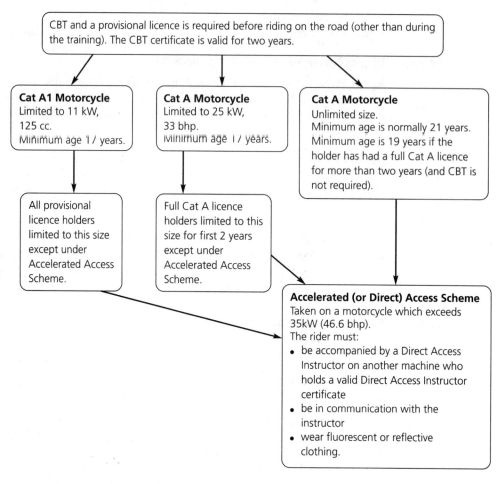

CBT and a provisional licence is required before riding on the road (other than during the training). The CBT certificate is valid for two years.

Cat A1 Motorcycle
Limited to 11 kW,
125 cc.
Minimum age 17 years.

Cat A Motorcycle
Limited to 25 kW,
33 bhp.
Minimum age 17 years.

Cat A Motorcycle
Unlimited size.
Minimum age is normally 21 years.
Minimum age is 19 years if the holder has had a full Cat A licence for more than two years (and CBT is not required).

All provisional licence holders limited to this size except under Accelerated Access Scheme.

Full Cat A licence holders limited to this size for first 2 years except under Accelerated Access Scheme.

Accelerated (or Direct) Access Scheme
Taken on a motorcycle which exceeds 35kW (46.6 bhp).
The rider must:
- be accompanied by a Direct Access Instructor on another machine who holds a valid Direct Access Instructor certificate
- be in communication with the instructor
- wear fluorescent or reflective clothing.

11.4.6.3   Motorcycles with sidecars

Provisional-licence holders and full-licence holders are restricted to a power/weight ratio of 0.16W/kg for two years after passing a test. The power of the vehicle (the brake horse power (bhp), engine size, or power output (kW)) is stated on a metal plate attached to the vehicle, and the same information is also given on the registration document of the vehicle.

11.4.6.4   'Mini-motos', 'go-peds', and electrically assisted pedal cycles

The use of miniature motorbikes (mini-motos) and petrol-driven scooters (go-peds) may pose potential risks to the health and safety of other road and pavement users, and is considered by many members of the public as an example of anti-social behaviour. There have been a number of fatalities and serious injuries as the result of the use of mini-motos.

The Department of Transport have clarified that mini-motos and go-peds are in fact 'light-weight powered motor vehicles' and must therefore comply with the usual road traffic and vehicle excise licence laws. So, for example, it is illegal to use a mini-moto or go-ped on the pavement under s 72 of the Highways Act 1835. Further information can be found in a government publication at the Department for Transport website < http://www.dft.gov.uk/pgr/roads/vehicles/vssafety/factsheetminimotos.pdf>. For case law on go-peds, refer to *DPP v Saddington* [2000] The Times, November 1 QBD and *Burns v Currell* [1963] 2 QB 433, 440.

An electrically assisted pedal cycle is classified as a pedal cycle (see 11.2.1.1 above) as long as:
- it is no heavier than 40 kg;
- it can be propelled by its pedals as well as by its electric motor;
- the electric motor does not exceed 0.2 kW and the maximum speed (due to the motor alone) is less than 15 mph.

Similar exemptions are made for powered wheelchairs and powered scooters designed for people with disabilities.

TASK 2

1. Familiarize yourself with the form you would need to use to request a person to produce his/her driving licence within seven days.
2. What problems might there be in establishing the person's true identity?
3. What extra checks will you undertake to make sure you have obtained the person's real name and address?

11.5 Insurance

All users of cars, motorcycles, and other vehicles are required by law to have third-party insurance as a minimum level of cover. Additions such as cover for fire and theft of the insured's vehicle are made at the discretion of the insured person. Fully comprehensive insurance goes further: it covers damage to the insured and his/her vehicle as well as cover for third parties, fire, and theft.

11.5.1 Third-Party Motor Vehicle Insurance

Third-party motor insurance is the minimum level of insurance allowed and guarantees that injuries or damage to third parties can be compensated. Third parties include passengers in the user's car and other people's property (damaged due to an accident caused by the insured person).

Sections 143(1) and (2) of the Road Traffic Act 1988 state it is an offence for a person:

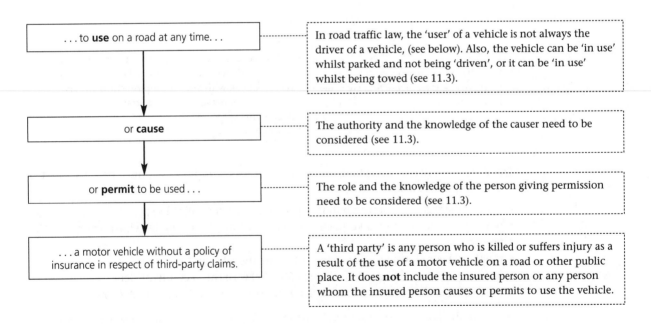

... to **use** on a road at any time. . .

> In road traffic law, the 'user' of a vehicle is not always the driver of a vehicle, (see below). Also, the vehicle can be 'in use' whilst parked and not being 'driven', or it can be 'in use' whilst being towed (see 11.3).

or **cause**

> The authority and the knowledge of the causer need to be considered (see 11.3).

or **permit** to be used . . .

> The role and the knowledge of the person giving permission need to be considered (see 11.3).

. . . a motor vehicle without a policy of insurance in respect of third-party claims.

> A 'third party' is any person who is killed or suffers injury as a result of the use of a motor vehicle on a road or other public place. It does **not** include the insured person or any person whom the insured person causes or permits to use the vehicle.

(An explanation of using, causing, and permitting is given in 11.3.1 above).

It is a defence (s 143(3), Road Traffic Act 1988) if it can be proved that:

- the vehicle did not belong to the user, nor was it hired by him/her;
- the user was using the vehicle in the course of her/his employment and had no reason to believe that the vehicle was not properly insured (an employee is unlikely to know about his/her employer's insurance arrangements).

11.5.1.1 Keeping a vehicle which does not meet insurance requirements

This may be an offence in some circumstances. Section 144A of the Road Traffic Act 1988 states that:

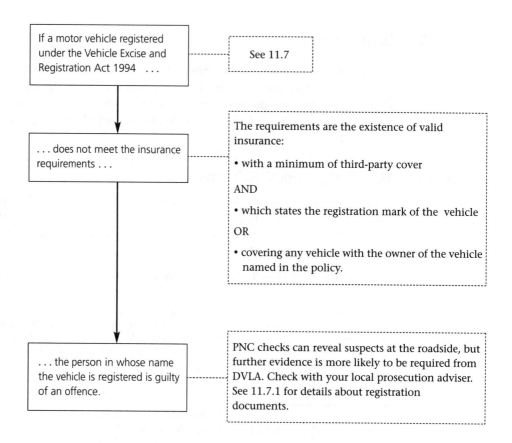

If a motor vehicle registered under the Vehicle Excise and Registration Act 1994 . . .

See 11.7

. . . does not meet the insurance requirements . . .

The requirements are the existence of valid insurance:

- with a minimum of third-party cover

AND

- which states the registration mark of the vehicle

OR

- covering any vehicle with the owner of the vehicle named in the policy.

. . . the person in whose name the vehicle is registered is guilty of an offence.

PNC checks can reveal suspects at the roadside, but further evidence is more likely to be required from DVLA. Check with your local prosecution adviser. See 11.7.1 for details about registration documents.

There are a number of exceptions to this offence which, if produced, must be substantiated. These exceptions include vehicles:

- kept by the registered keeper, but not on a road or other public place;
- not kept by the registered keeper at the relevant time, for example, whilst lent to another person;
- that have been stolen and not recovered before the relevant time;
- driven by an owner who has deposited £500,000 with the Accountant General; or
- owned, for example, by councils, police authorities, the NHS, Army, or Air Force.

You have the power to seize a vehicle without adequate insurance under s 165A of the Road Traffic Act 1988. Details of the procedure are described in 11.4.3 above.

11.5.2 Key Features on a Certificate of Insurance

There are in excess of 50 companies in the UK offering insurance to drivers. An insured driver will receive a certificate of insurance from such a company which will include at least the following features:

	Insurance Company Name and Address:
	AAA Insurance Ltd.
	The High Street
	Maidbury MB1 1AB
Certificate number: 000/999/123	**Registration Number:** AA 00 AAA
Policyholder's name: Orlando SMITH	**Expiry date:** Noon 16th April 2008

Permitted Drivers: (Those specified including the policyholder must have a licence to drive the vehicle and must not be disqualified from driving it.)

Limitations as to use: Use for social, domestic, and pleasure purposes including travel between the driver's home and place of work.

11.5.3   Requesting to See a Motor Insurance Certificate

You may require any of the following persons to produce their insurance certificate (s 165(1), Road Traffic Act 1988):

(a) a person driving a motor vehicle ... on a road; or

(b) a person whom [you have] reasonable cause to believe to have been the driver ... at a time when an accident occurred owing to [the vehicles's] presence on a road or other public place;

(c) a person whom [you have] reasonable cause to believe to have committed an offence in relation to the use on a road of a motor vehicle.

You may also request him/her to provide his/her name and address and, if different, the name and address of the owner of the vehicle.

It is an offence under s 165(3) of the Road Traffic Act 1988 to fail to produce a certificate of insurance when required.

Under s 165(4) of the Road Traffic Act 1988 it will be a defence for that person to show that:

* he/she produced the documents in person within seven days at a police station that was specified at the time of the request or as soon as reasonably practicable; or
* it was not reasonably practicable for him/her to produce the documents before the day on which the written charge proceedings were commenced.

('As soon as is reasonably practicable' will be a question of fact for the court to decide given the circumstances of the case.)

This offence is triable summarily only.

TASK 3

You stop a vehicle using your powers under the Road Traffic Act. The driver is very young. You establish from the Police National Computer that the vehicle he is driving has a large engine capacity.

* What questions would you put to him about his insurance policy?
* How would you check that the insurance company has been notified of the large engine capacity, and that the insurance cover is adequate?

11.6   Test Certificates

Certain categories of vehicle must have an MOT test certificate if they are to be used on the road. The type and age of vehicles concerned are given in s 47 of the Road Traffic Act 1988 which states that it is an offence for a person:

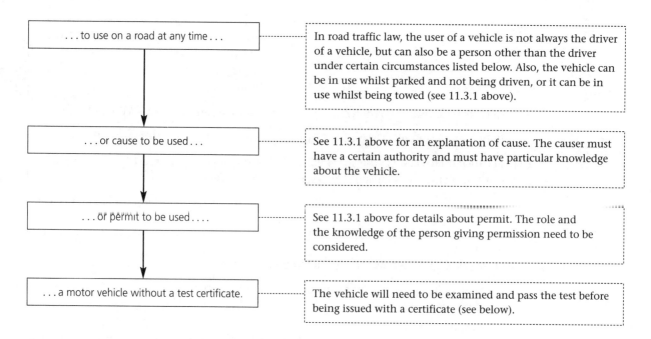

The following vehicles must be submitted for annual tests with effect from the third anniversary of their registration (s 47(2)):

- passenger vehicles with not more than eight seats (excluding the driver's seat), for example family cars;
- rigid goods motor cars (unladen weight not exceeding 1,525 kg), for example small commercial vans which are not articulated;
- dual-purpose vehicles, for example pick-up trucks;
- motorcycles (including three-wheelers and mopeds);
- motor caravans.

However, other categories of vehicle must be submitted for annual testing from the **first** anniversary of their registration (s 47(3)):

- passenger vehicles with more than eight seats exclusive of the driver's seat (mainly public-service vehicles, but also, for example, 11-seat school mini vans);
- taxis licensed to ply for hire; and
- ambulances.

11.6.1 Exemptions from Having a Valid Test Certificate

There are the following exemptions under the Motor Vehicles (Tests) Regulations 1981:
- vehicles travelling to a pre-arranged MOT test;
- where the vehicle has failed the MOT test and whilst being driven from the test for the purpose of delivering it by previous arrangement to a place for work to be carried out or being broken up for scrap.

11.6.2 Date of Registration and Date of Manufacture

Under s 47(2) of the Road Traffic Act 1988 a test certificate must be obtained three years from the date of registration of the vehicle.

When the vehicle is used on a road in the UK or elsewhere **before** it is registered, then a test certificate must be obtained three years from the date of manufacture. The date of manufacture of a vehicle shall be taken to be the last day of the year during which its final assembly was completed. This situation would include those people who live and work abroad and return to the UK with a vehicle.

11.6.3   Key Features of an MOT Test Certificate

The following diagram illustrates the key features of the MOT certificate.

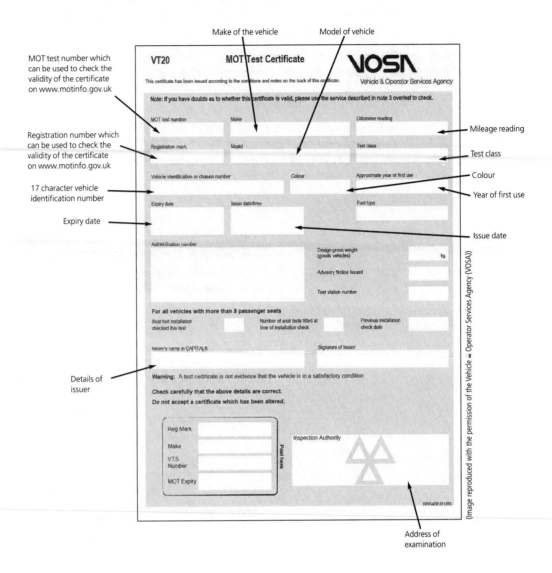

11.6.4   Requiring to See a Test Certificate

The procedures concerning such a requirement are the same as those for requiring to see a a motor insurance certificate. You may require any of the persons listed in 11.5.3 above (eg the driver or a person you believe to have been driving when involved in an accident) to produce his/her test certificate, under s 165(1) of the Road Traffic Act 1988. You may also request him/her to provide his/her name and address and, if different, the name and address of the owner of the vehicle. If the person fails to produce the test certificate, the offence and penalty are the same as for failing to produce a certificate of motor insurance.

TASK 4

Whilst on Independent Patrol you have stopped a vehicle using your powers under the Road Traffic Act 1988 and have asked the driver to produce a valid test certificate.

- How will you establish the date of first registration of a UK registered vehicle?
- If the driver does not have a valid test certificate, what questions will you put to the driver to negate any defences?

11.7   Vehicle Registration and Licensing

When a vehicle is first registered, the Secretary of State issues a Registration Certificate, formally known as a Registration Document and assigns a registration mark (also known as a registration number or an index number) to the vehicle.

Most vehicles used on a road are also subject to vehicle excise duty, otherwise known as road tax. The licence disc shows that road tax has been paid.

11.7.1   Registration Documents

The annotations below draw attention to just some of the information on the new style Registration Certificate; further details (other than those identified here) are available from the document. All the information can be useful in the investigation of a variety of offences.

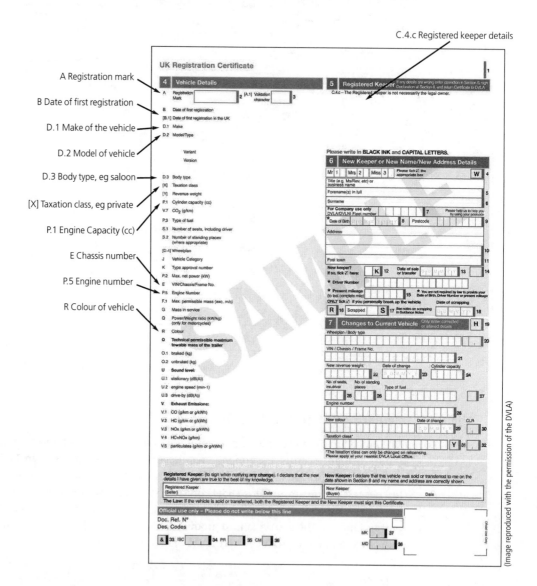

(Image reproduced with the permission of the DVLA)

11.7.2   The Layout of Registration Marks on Number Plates

You are no doubt familiar with number plates used on vehicles in the UK. The following system has been in use for several years.

AB5I DVL

Local memory tag denoting where a vehicle is first registered. AB refers to Peterborough.

Age identifier which changes twice yearly in March and September. The number 51 refers to September 2001.

Random letters which will never include I or Q and which uniquely define the vehicle.

The number plate should use a standard font, and the font should not be customized in any way.

These and further details on number plates may be found at the DVLA website <www.dvla.gov.uk/forms/~/media/pdf/leaflets/V796.ashx >.

11.7.3 Offences Relating to Vehicle Registration and Number Plates

If a vehicle is not properly **registered**, it is an offence to use it on a road or in a public place (s 43C(1) of the Vehicle Excise and Registration Act 1994). This applies to vehicles to which vehicle excise duty is chargeable and also to vehicles that are exempt from duty; such vehicles should appear on the vehicle licensing register (exempt vehicles are issued with a 'nil licence'). A vehicle is not properly registered if:

(a) the name and address of the keeper are not recorded in the register; or

(b) any of the particulars recorded in the register are incorrect.

Defences for using a vehicle that is not properly registered include:

- no reasonable opportunity was given to supply the name and address of the keeper (for example if the purchaser had only just bought the vehicle); or
- reasonable grounds for believing that the recorded particulars were correct.

It is also an offence to fail to produce a registration document when required to do so by a constable (s 28A(1), Vehicle Excise and Registration Act 1994). There are exceptions:

- the person produces the registration document at a police station (specified by him/her at the time of the request) within seven days after the date on which the request was made or as soon as is reasonably practicable; or
- the vehicle is subject to a lease or hire agreement.

Other offences related to registration documents include the failure to notify the DVLA about the disposal of a vehicle, a change of registered keeper's address, or a change of vehicle details. Most of these offences will be committed under the Road Vehicles (Display of Registration Marks) Regulations 2001 and the Vehicle Excise and Registration Act 1994.

For **number plates**, the following are all offences, mostly under the Road Vehicles (Display of Registration †Marks) Regulations 2001:

- no number plate or an obscured number plate;
- forgery of a number plate;
- incorrect fitting, number, or position of plates;
- incorrect style, size, and spacing of characters (see 11.7.2 above for the correct font).

These offences are all triable summarily.

11.7.4   Vehicle Excise Duty

Vehicle excise duty is the administrative name for what is colloquially known as road tax, and is covered under s 1 of the Vehicle Excise and Registration Act 1994. Not all vehicles are subject to this duty but it does apply to every mechanically propelled vehicle used or kept on any public road (see 11.2.1.2 above). The excise duty is paid in the form of a licence taken out by the person keeping the vehicle. (A **keeper** means a person who causes a vehicle to be on a public road for any period.)

11.7.4.1   Exemptions from vehicle excise duty

There are approximately 20 categories of exempted vehicle (s 5(2), Vehicle Excise and Registration Act 1994), including:

- goods and passenger vehicles being used for current commercial purposes;
- fire engines and ambulances; and
- vehicles for disabled people.

For a full list visit <www.opsi.gov.uk/acts/acts1994/Ukpga_19940022_en_8.htm#sdiv2>.

11.7.4.2   Key features of a vehicle excise duty licence

The vehicle excise duty licence is commonly known as a tax disc. It displays information about the vehicle and the vehicle excise duty paid.

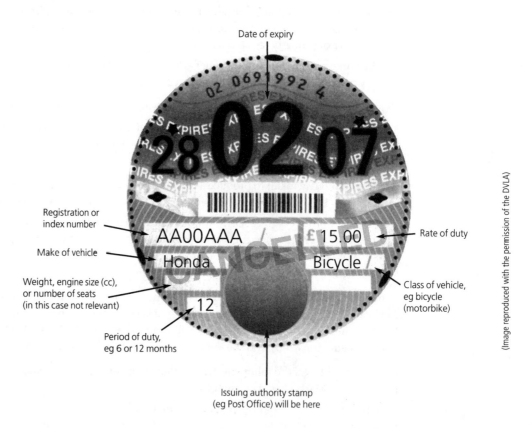

(Image reproduced with the permission of the DVLA)

There are a number of taxation classes. The example here denotes that this tax disc is for a two-wheeled motorcycle. Other classes include private/light goods vehicles (PLG) such as family cars, buses, and heavy goods vehicles.

11.7.4.3   Correct display of the vehicle excise duty licence

The licence (tax disc) must be displayed in the vehicle, exhibited so that it is clearly visible in daylight from the nearside of the road (reg 16, Road Vehicle (Registration and Licensing) Regulations 1971), and protected from the weather.

Required position of tax disc

Type of vehicle	Position for licence disc
Cars and most common vehicles	On or adjacent to the nearside.
Other vehicles	On the nearside in front of the driver or, if no driver's seat, towards the front between 2'6" and 6' from the ground.
Solo motorcycles, motor tricycles, and invalid vehicles	On the nearside in front of the driving seat.
Motorcycle and side-car	On the nearside of the handlebars of the motorcycle or on the nearside of the side-car in front of the driving seat.

11.7.5 Offences Relating to Vehicle Excise Duty

It is an offence under the Vehicle Excise and Registration Act 1994:

- to use or keep on a public road an **unlicensed** vehicle (s 29);
- to **forge** or fraudulently use, alter, lend a vehicle licence, or allow it to be used by another person (s 44(1));
- to use or keep a vehicle on a public road without a vehicle licence on display in the manner prescribed above (s 33).

TASK 5

When you are on Supervised Patrol in your BCU area and you see a vehicle not displaying a licence.
- How could you report the user (or keeper) of the vehicle?
- What would you do if the driver or keeper of the vehicle is not present?
Find out what forms you can use for these processes at your police station.

11.8 Construction and Use of Vehicles

Your responsibility to prevent crime does not apply only to preventing those crimes associated with theft or violence; criminal acts can also be committed by people driving motor vehicles on the road, and the potential to cause danger to other road users is very high. You also have the responsibility to 'pursue and bring to justice those who break the law', and 'protect, help and reassure the community'. You will therefore be required to investigate offences in relation to the use of vehicles and to contribute to road-safety campaigns in order to help reduce the death toll on roads in the UK.

11.8.1 Authority to Examine a Vehicle Being Used on the Road

Under s 67 of the Road Traffic Act 1988 you will be designated as an authorized examiner by your chief officer of police. An examiner is authorized to test a vehicle (and drawn trailer) on a road for the purposes of ascertaining compliance with:

- the construction and use requirements (including lighting);
- the requirement that the condition of the vehicle (if used on the road) is not a danger to any person.

11.8.2 Tyres

The component parts of a tyre profile are shown in the diagram below.

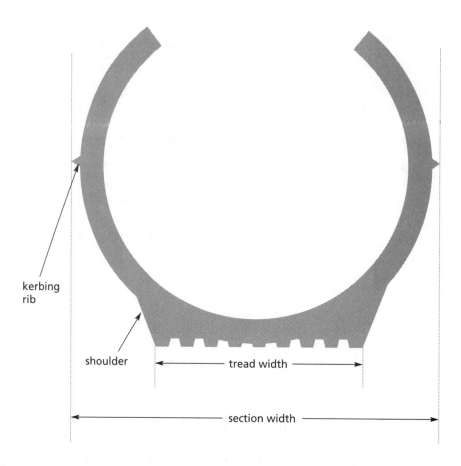

kerbing
rib

shoulder

tread width

section width

For the purposes of evidence gathering, you should make a note of **all** the identifying codes and features on the wall of a tyre, including serial numbers and characters relating to type of tyre. The photograph below shows a typical location for the numbers.

(Image © Kevin Lawton-Barrett)

In our example above we would note:

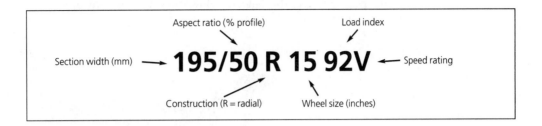

(You will find the full details of what each letter and number refers to at <http://www.blackcircles.com/general/sidewall>.)

11.8.2.1 Offences relating to the condition and maintenance of tyres

Regulation 27 of the Road Vehicle Construction and Use Regulations 1986 describes a range of tyre problems relating to their condition and the circumstances in which they are being used. These regulations only apply to vehicles and trailers used on roads with pneumatic (inflatable) tyres. Some types of vehicle or circumstances are not subject to the regulations. A summary of the regulations and the exemptions is shown in the table below.

Regulations relation to the condition and maintenance of tyres

Regulations	Exemptions
The **type** of tyre must be: • the correct type for the vehicle, including taking into account the type of tyres fitted to the other wheels • the correct type for the road conditions or purpose.	• Agricultural motor vehicles which have a maximum speed of 20 mph</TBBL
The tyre must not be **damaged** in the following ways: • cuts in excess of 25 mm or 10% of the section width of the tyre (whichever is the greater), measured in any direction on the outside of the tyre, and deep enough to reach the ply or cord • lumps, bulges, or tears caused by separation or partial failure of its structure • exposed ply or cord.	• Agricultural trailers • Agricultural trailed appliances • Broken-down vehicles or vehicle en-route for breaking up or being towed at a maximum speed of 20 mph
The tyre must be inflated to the correct **pressure** for the purpose.	
The tyre must not be so **worn** that the base of any groove which showed in the original tread pattern of the tyre is not clearly visible.	• Cars (and other passenger vehicles carrying no more than eight passengers), but see below • Light goods vehicles and trailers
The tyre must be correctly **maintained** so it is fit for the use to which the vehicle or trailer is being put, and must not have defects which might cause damage to the road surface or persons in the vehicle or road.	• No exemptions

11.8.2.2 Offences relating to bald tyres

A tyre is said to be 'bald' if part of the original tread is no longer visible on the tread width (reg 27). The position of bald patches is significant. Bald patches on the central three-quarters of the tread width **do** matter, but bald patches on the outer eighth of each side of the tread width do **not** matter unless they are associated with cuts or deeper wear. (Furthermore, the tyres for some vehicles, such as motorcycles, are manufactured with no grooves or tread on the outer eighths of the tread width.) Clearly, you need to be able to accurately identify the central three-quarters and the outer eighths of the tread width for any tyre you examine.

Note that the tread width (the surface in contact with the road) is always less than the maximum width of the tyre (the section width). To calculate the width of the central three-quarters of the tread width, see the diagram below showing a new unworn tyre.

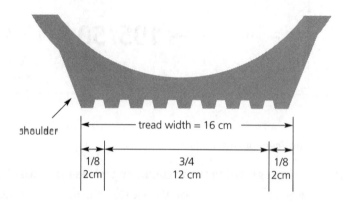

To calculate the central three-quarters of the tread width, using the tyre in the diagram above:

1. Measure the breadth of the tyre in contact with the road (total width = 16cms).
2. Obtain the width of the central three-quarters of the tyre by dividing the total width by 4, then multiplying by 3 (16cm/4 = 4cm, and then 4cm + 3 = 12cm).
3. Obtain the width of each of the two outer eighths of the tyre by dividing the total width by 8 (16cm/8 = 2cm).
4. Check that your calculations are correct by adding the value for the central three-quarters to twice the value for the outer eighth (12cm + 2cm + 2cm = 16cm, hence correct).

For **cars, light goods vehicles, and trailers**, if any groove or tread is less than 1.6 mm deep in the central three-quarters anywhere round the tyre, an offence is committed. Note therefore, that if the depth of any grooves is less than 1.6 mm in the outer eighths of the tread, no offence is committed. These outer areas can therefore be bald (see the diagram below, showing a tyre that is worn on the outer eighths, but which still has 1.6 mm of tread over the central three-quarters of its tread width).

This 1.6 mm rule does not apply to agricultural vehicles or any vehicle which is:

• broken down;
• en route for breaking up; or
• being towed at a maximum speed of 20 mph.

For **other types of vehicle**, such as motorcycles, larger passenger vehicles, and larger goods vehicles, the groove depth over the central three-quarters of the tread must be at least 1.0 mm. Note that some tyres are manufactured with no grooves in the outer eighths of the tread width (see the diagram below).

11.8.3 Danger of Injury from the Use of Vehicles or Trailers

A person is guilty of an offence under s 40A of the Road Traffic Act 1988 if they use, cause, or permit another person to use a motor vehicle or trailer on a road when the use of the motor vehicle or trailer involves a danger of injury to any person because of:

- the condition of the motor vehicle or trailer (or of its accessories or equipment);
- the purpose for which it is used;
- the number of passengers carried by it or the manner in which they are carried; or
- the weight, position, or distribution of its load or the manner in which it is secured.

See 11.3 above for an explanation of 'use, cause, or permit'. Details of the types of situation that could lead to injury or the danger of injury are listed below.

11.8.3.1 Poor maintenance of a vehicle and some associated offences

When you consider the condition of a vehicle, a general rule is to consider how it was first constructed; this will be a guide to how the vehicle should be maintained throughout its life. If you examine a vehicle and a component part of it is missing or is not working, an offence is likely to have been committed. The examples below relate to just some of the offences which can be committed in relation to poor maintenance of a vehicle. The list is by no means exhaustive:

- The **wipers** and **washers** (those that are required to be fitted) must be maintained in efficient working order and be properly adjusted (reg 34).
- An audible warning instrument (**horn**) must be fitted to any motor vehicle with a maximum speed of more than 20 mph (reg 37).
- The **braking** systems must be maintained in good and efficient working order and be properly adjusted, including the handbrake (reg 18(1)).
- **Exhaust** systems and silencers must be maintained in good and efficient working order, and must not be altered to increase the noise made by the escape of the exhaust gases (reg 54).
- **Motorcycle exhausts** must be the correct type (this applies only to a moped or motorbike first used after 1 January 1985) (reg 579A (1) or (4)). The silencer should be either the original fitted by the manufacturer or a replacement marked with an approved British Standard marking. (A motorcycle should not be used on a road if the exhaust fitted is marked 'not for road use' or similar.)
- Vehicle **emissions** must not contain any smoke, visible vapour, grit, sparks, ashes, cinders, or oily substance that causes (or is likely to cause) damage to property, or injury or danger to other road users (reg 61). Your force may have instruments to test vehicle emissions.

Using a vehicle in a dangerous condition such as having **jagged edges to bodywork** (reg 100(1)) may lead to disqualification (obligatory if the offence is committed within three years of a previous conviction under s 40A, Road Traffic Offenders Act 1988).

11.8.3.2 Incorrect use of a vehicle and some associated offences

There are many ways in which a vehicle can be used incorrectly, and only a few of the more commonly encountered means are listed here:

- **Loads** carried by a vehicle must not be a danger or nuisance to any person or property. The weight, packing, distribution, and adjustment of a load must be taken into account (reg 100(1)). The load carried by a motor vehicle or trailer must be secured if necessary, by physical restraint other than its own weight, for example the luggage on the roof bars of a car must be tied down (reg 100(2)).

- **Passenger** numbers must not exceed the number that seats allow (reg 100(1) and (3)). For example, passengers must not be carried in the rear of a small van with no fixed seating.
- The **horn** (reg 99) must not be used when the vehicle is stationary (other than an emergency involving another vehicle, or when using a reversing alarm or boarding aid alarm). In addition, the horn must not be used by vehicles in motion on restricted roads between 2330 hours and 0700 hours.
- **Excessive noise** from motor vehicles on roads must be avoided by the exercise of reasonable care on the part of the driver (reg 97).

11.8.4   Offences in Relation to Parking and Braking

The following practices must be observed, though exemptions apply to emergency services vehicles and to vehicles that need to keep the engine running, for example to power machinery (such as a crane) or to charge the battery.

- The **engine** must be turned off when the vehicle is stationary for any length of time (reg 98) in order to prevent noise or exhaust emissions. It is an offence to leave the engine running whilst stationary in a confined space with other vehicles.
- When leaving an **unattended motor vehicle** (quitting) the engine must be turned off and the parking brake applied, unless there is another person in the vehicle who is licensed to drive it (reg 107 and s 42 of the Road Traffic Act 1988). This would apply to a driver who parks outside a shop and runs inside to buy something, leaving the engine running.

11.8.5   Driver and Passenger Safety and Associated Offences

There are a number of considerations concerning the personal safety of drivers and passengers of vehicles.

11.8.5.1   Helmets

It is an offence under s 16 of the Road Traffic Act 1988 to drive or ride on a motor bicycle (see 11.2.1.1 above) on a road without suitable protective headgear. Helmets must:

- be securely fastened to the head of the wearer by means of straps or other fastening provided for that purpose (if it has a chin cup there must be an additional strap to go under the jaw);
- bear a mark indication in compliance with the British Standard/equivalent EU standard (or be of a type which, due to its shape, material, and construction could reasonably be expected to afford protection similar to, or greater than a helmet which conforms to the latest British Standard 6658:1985 (or equivalent EU standard)).

There are some people who do not have to wear a helmet in some circumstances, such as:

- drivers of ride-on motor mowers;
- turban-wearing followers of the Sikh religion, whilst on a two-wheeled motorcycle;
- passengers in a sidecar;
- any person pushing the two-wheeled motorcycle on foot.

In addition, riders or drivers of **three-wheeled vehicles** will not require a helmet, if the vehicle's unladen weight does not exceed 550kg and the distance between the centre of contact of the rear wheels exceeds 460mm.

11.8.5.2   Motorcycle eye protection

There is no legal requirement that a visor or goggles be used at all. However, if eye protection is used and it does not meet the British Standards (BS EN 1938:1999), an offence has been committed under s 18(3) of the Road Traffic Act 1988.

11.8.5.3   Seatbelts

The requirements for the use of seatbelts depend on the age of the person and where he/she is sitting (s 14(3), Road Traffic Act 1988). Details are shown in the table below (based on extracts from the Highway Code, 2004 and *Child Car Seats—The New Law 2006* available from <http://www.childcarseats.org.uk/law/documents/newlaw06v2.pdf>). Note that there are a few very limited exceptions for children in taxis or the rear seats of family cars. In addition, some older cars such as classic cars may not have seatbelts fitted.

Seat Belts requirements

	Front seat	Rear seat	Who is responsible?
Driver	Must be worn if fitted.	Not applicable.	Driver
Babies and children up to 135 cms tall (or 12th birthday whichever comes first)	Correct child restraint must be used; this might employ an adult seatbelt as part of the restraining mechanism.		Driver
Child aged 12 or 13 or younger child who is 135 cms or taller	Adult seat belt must be worn if fitted.		Driver
Passenger aged 14 years or over	Adult seat belt must be worn if fitted.		Passenger

Child restraints consist of four types as described in the table below:

	Child weight and age	Notes
Baby seats	Less than 13kg (approx birth to 9–12 months)	Rear-facing
Child seats	Between 9–18kg (approx 9 months to 4 years)	Forward-facing
Booster seats	Over 15kg (approx 4 years and up)	May or may not have a back
Booster cushions	Over 22kg (approx 6 years and up)	Do not normally have backs

In some situations a seat belt does not have to be worn, such as:

- a driver engaged in deliveries (for example, delivering post or newspapers) or collections;
- a driver reversing a vehicle, or supervising provisional-licence holders who are reversing a vehicle (or conducting a manoeuvre which includes reversing);
- an examiner conducting a driving test, if wearing the belt would be dangerous;
- people in vehicles being used for police purposes (but consider your force policy in relation to people under arrest) and people in vehicles being used for fire brigade purposes;
- taxi drivers while 'plying for hire', answering calls for hire, or carrying passengers and private-hire drivers while carrying passengers;
- people taking part in processions organized by, or on behalf of, the Crown;
- people holding a medical certificate exempting them from wearing a seat belt (provided the certificate is produced at the time or within seven days) and disabled people wearing a disabled person's belt;
- the vehicle is driven under a trade licence for the purposes of investigating or remedying mechanical fault;
- where the seat belt is an inertia type which is locked as a result of being, or having been, on a steep incline.

11.8.6 Vehicle Identification Regulations for the Detection and Prevention of Crime

Under reg 67 all wheeled vehicles registered after 1 April 1980 should be equipped with a plate in a conspicuous and readily accessible location (on a part not normally subject to replacement) which clearly shows the:

- Vehicle Identification Number (the 'VIN' which is also stamped on the chassis or frame);
- name of manufacturer; and
- type approval number, possibly on a separate plate (providing confirmation that the specifications of the vehicle, eg brakes, lights etc, meet UK performance standards).

These identifying features can be matched against details on PNC to enable identification of stolen vehicles (see 10.6 above).

TASK 6

You stop a car using your powers under the Road Traffic Act 1988 as you suspect the vehicle may have a number of serious defects.

1. What will you to say to the driver?
2. What process are you going to go through if you find a defect?

11.9 Lights on Vehicles

The following information relates in part to the Road Vehicles Lighting Regulations 1989.

There is a possibility of underestimating the importance of lights on vehicles when placed alongside other demands on your time, particularly when compared with incidents involving violent criminal activity. However, the position, style, maintenance, and colour of vehicle lights are all very important for road safety. Your many responsibilities include identifying vehicles with lights that are not working properly, testing and inspecting lights, and bringing the faults to the attention of the owner and/or driver.

Drivers are also expected to employ their lights with consideration towards other road users; you can offer advice to drivers about how they use their vehicles' lights: for example, lights should not be used in a way that causes undue dazzle or discomfort to other persons using the road.

To help you understand the extensive lighting regulations, a family saloon has been chosen as an example to illustrate the two main categories of lights on vehicles:

* **obligatory lights** that **must** be fitted and maintained; and
* **optional lights**.

TASK 7

List all the types of light that you think are **obligatory** for a car. Then compare your list with the list in the below (no peeping!).

11.9.1 Obligatory Lights

On the front of a car, the following lights are obligatory:

* front-position lights ('side lights');
* dipped-beam headlights;
* main-beam headlights;
* direction indicators.

On the back of the car, the following are obligatory:

* rear-position lights;
* direction indicators;
* rear stop-lights (brake);
* rear fog-light;
* rear registration-plate lamp;
* rear reflector (not strictly a light, but obligatory).

A 'hazard warning-signal device' to operate the direction indicator lights on the front and back of the car is also obligatory.

These obligatory lights may be clustered as a group of lights underneath a plastic or glass cover; some **typical** arrangements are shown in the diagrams below:

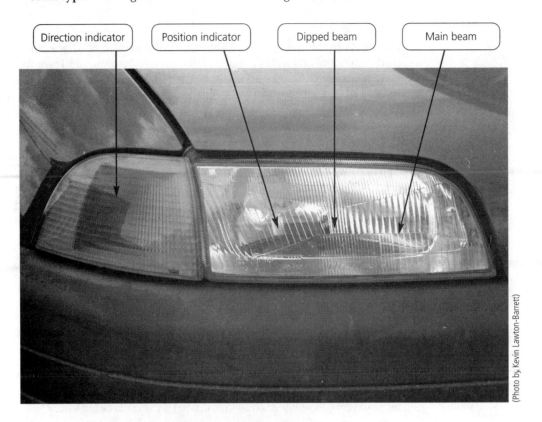

Direction indicator · Position indicator · Dipped beam · Main beam

(Photo by Kevin Lawton-Barrett)

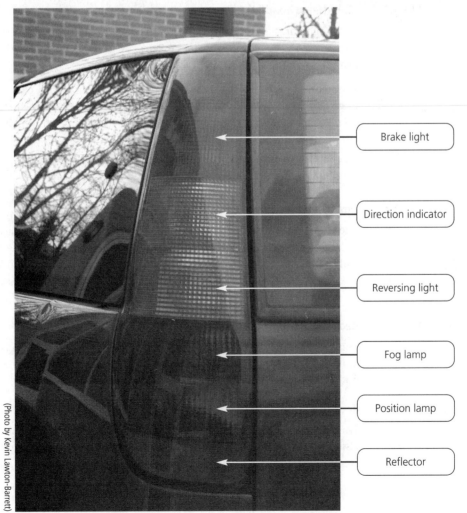

Brake light · Direction indicator · Reversing light · Fog lamp · Position lamp · Reflector

(Photo by Kevin Lawton-Barrett)

515

Remember, these are typical arrangements, but there is significant variation between makes and models of cars.

11.9.1.1   Position lights

These lights must be present on all four corners of a vehicle, and their purpose is to indicate the vehicle's presence and width to other road users. On the front of the car they are also known as side lights. They are white and not particularly bright, and they are often switched on by the first click of the switch near the steering wheel. On the back of the vehicle, the position lights are also known as tail lights. They are red, but not as bright as brake lights, and are operated by the same switch as the front position lights.

The position lights must be lit when the vehicle is moving at night (between sunset and sunrise) and when the vehicle is moving during the day if visibility is reduced. When the vehicle is parked at night on a road, the position lights must be illuminated, unless the vehicle is parked with its nearside against the nearside kerb on a 30-mph road with street lighting (and see 11.9.4 below).

11.9.1.2   Dipped-beam headlamps

These are powerful white lights at the front of the car, and are also known as headlights. They illuminate the road ahead but they should shine downward and to the left of the vehicle to prevent oncoming vehicles being dazzled. They are often switched on with two clicks of the lights switch.

These lights must be lit when the car is being driven during hours of darkness, except when:

- driving on a 30-mph road with street lighting;
- the fog lights are illuminated.

They should also be used when the car is driven during the day in seriously reduced visibility. The headlights do not need to be illuminated if the car is being towed.

11.9.1.3   Main-beam headlights

These lights are very bright white lights at the front of the car which shine straight ahead to illuminate the road over a long distance. They are usually operated with a pull or push of a switch near the steering wheel when headlamps are already on.

The main-beam headlight switch must be wired so that they can be 'deflected' by the driver in order to avoid dazzling oncoming traffic. The deflection-switching mechanism does not involve any movement in the headlamp unit; it switches on the dipped beam headlights and switches off the main beam headlights.

If the front fog-lamps are switched on (in seriously reduced visibility), there is usually no need to use the main-beam headlights.

11.9.1.4   Direction indicators

These are found at each corner of the car (and sometimes at the sides) and are used to indicate to other road users that the driver is intending to move the car to the right or left. They must be amber and must flash on and off between 60 and 120 times a minute. They are usually operated by pushing a switch near the steering column upwards or downwards. There must be an indicator near the driver to show that the direction indicators are in use.

11.9.1.5   Rear registration-plate lamp

This is a small white light at the rear shining on to the registration plate, and it automatically illuminates when the position indicator lights are switched on. The registration lamp should not shine directly into the eyes of the driver of the vehicle behind.

11.9.1.6   Rear fog-lamps

These lamps are very bright red to help other drivers see the vehicle in conditions of reduced visibility. They are operated by an independent switch that will only work when the headlights are illuminated. They do not need to be used when the car is towing a trailer.

11.9.1.7   Rear stop-lamps

These are also known as brake lights and are very bright red. They are positioned at the rear corners of the car and must operate when the braking system (eg foot brakes) of the car is applied. They warn other road users that the vehicle is slowing down or stopping.

11.9.1.8   Hazard warning-signal device

This is not a lamp or set of lamps, but a switching device to enable all the direction indicators to flash at the same time. It is only to be used:

- when the vehicle is stationary to alert other road users of the obstruction; or
- on a motorway or dual carriageway to warn drivers behind of an obstruction ahead; or
- by the driver of a bus to summon help; or
- by the driver of a bus when children under 16 are getting on or off.

The switch of this device must be in reach of the driver. The switch button surface often has a small triangle which will be illuminated when the hazard warning lights are switched on.

11.9.2   Optional Lamps

Some optional lamps are fitted to a vehicle which are **extra** or additional to those already fitted, but perform the same function as obligatory lights: for example, extra front-position lights (sidelights), extra stop-lamps, extra direction indicators, and extra dim/dipping and hazard-warning devices. As these optional extra lamps have the same functions as obligatory lights, they must be maintained and in full working order, just like obligatory lights.

Other optional lamps include lamps such as reversing lights and front fog-lights. They are not obligatory in type, and are put on the vehicle by the manufacturer or the owner to help the driver. There is no need for these lamps to be maintained and working, as they do not fall into any of the categories of obligatory lights. However, they must not be used in such a way that they cause undue dazzle or discomfort to other persons using the road.

11.9.3   Sunrise, Sunset, Lighting-Up Times, and Hours of Darkness

To establish when position lamps or sidelights must be illuminated, published sunrise and sunset times may be consulted. Times can be found in diaries, the internet, or local publications such as newspapers, and databases accessible by your control room.

> Remember: Sunset and Sunrise for Sidelights

To find out when dipped headlights must be illuminated, hours of darkness can be calculated by adding 30 minutes to sunset time and taking 30 minutes away from sunrise time, in other words half an hour after sunset and half an hour before sunrise.

> Remember: Hours of Darkness for Dipped headlights

11.9.4   Parking without Lights between Sunset and Sunrise

In certain situations, some categories of vehicle may park between sunset and sunrise without lights.

These categories of vehicle are:

- passenger vehicles which do not exceed 8 passenger seats and the driver, such as most family **cars**;
- light goods vehicles, for example **vans**;
- motorcycles and invalid carriages.

The categories of vehicle listed above may park without lights between sunset and sunrise on a road with a speed limit of 30 mph or less, but only:

- in a designated parking area or lay-by; or
- parked facing the right way on that road and no less than ten metres from a junction; or
- parked on a one-way street, facing' the right way (on either side of the road).

11.9.5 Legitimate Use of a Vehicle with Defective Lights

Vehicles with defective lights may be driven in some circumstances without an offence being committed. A vehicle may be used on the road with defective lights but only:

- during the day between sunrise and sunset; **and**
- if the lights became defective during that journey, or if arrangements have been made to repair the fault.

Remember: the examples above relate to a family car only and therefore there are a number of other regulations regarding other forms of transport which you may have to identify in the future.

TASK 8

Consider each of the following statements in turn, and decide if each statement is true or false:

1. The term 'hours of darkness' refers to a period in time which is half an hour after sunset to half an hour before sunrise.
2. The legislation that covers the use of lights on vehicles is the Road Vehicles (Construction and Use) Regulations 1986.
3. The permitted flash rate of an indicator lamp fitted to a vehicle is between 80 and 100 pulses per minute.
4. Hazard-warning signals on a vehicle may be used lawfully when the vehicle is being towed by another vehicle.
5. A defect occurring during a journey during daylight hours is a defence to a defective light fitted to a vehicle.
6. A reversing light is an optional lamp.
7. The term 'obligatory light' means a light that is required by the legislation to be fitted to a vehicle.

11.10 Pedestrian Crossings and Road Signs

Over the years, the number of road signs and regulations in England and Wales has increased greatly in an attempt to keep the road environment as safe as possible for all road users. These signs and regulations, however, are only of value if road users take notice of them. When you are considering enforcement of these regulations in the future, do not restrict your intentions only to detecting offences; remember, you are in a position to help the public develop their road-safety awareness.

11.10.1 Pedestrian Crossings

The table below shows the key characteristics of the three main types of pedestrian crossing described in the Zebra, Pelican, and Puffin Pedestrian Crossings Regulations 1997.

Pelican	• Pedestrians can push a button to operate traffic lights to bring vehicles to a stop.
	• The traffic light sequence is the usual one except that, after the red light, the amber light flashes to indicate that vehicles may proceed, but only if the crossing is clear.
Puffin	• Sensors detect anyone waiting to cross and change the traffic lights accordingly for vehicles to stop.
	• The traffic light signal is the same as regular traffic lights.
Zebra	• Not supported by traffic lights.
	• Pedestrians walk across a section of road indicated by alternate white and black stripes.
	• Drivers and riders of vehicles are warned of the presence of a crossing by two black and white striped poles with yellow flashing beacons on top, on each pavement.

11.10.1.1 Layout of crossings

The **limits** of crossings are by marked out by two parallel lines of studs across the carriageway.

The **stop line** for a Pelican or Puffin crossing is a solid white line across the road, just before the first line of studs. Drivers and riders must not cross the stop line if the traffic lights are red or there are pedestrians on the crossing.

The **give-way line** at the start of a zebra crossing is indicated by a broken white line across the road, just before the first line of studs. Drivers and riders must not cross the give-way line if pedestrians are on the crossing.

The **controlled area** of a crossing is a certain length of road before and after a crossing. It is indicated by white zigzag lines painted along the edge and the middle of the road (between 2 and 18 zigzags, depending on the road layout in the immediate vicinity). It is an offence to park anywhere in the controlled area of a crossing. Overtaking in a controlled area when approaching a crossing is also an offence (but overtaking in the controlled area after a crossing is not).

Where there is a refuge for pedestrians or a central reservation on a zebra crossing, each part of the crossing is treated as a separate crossing.

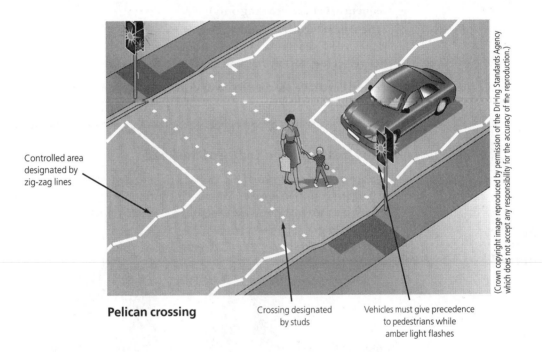

Controlled area designated by zig-zag lines

Pelican crossing

Crossing designated by studs

Vehicles must give precedence to pedestrians while amber light flashes

(Crown copyright image reproduced by permission of the Driving Standards Agency which does not accept any responsibility for the accuracy of the reproduction.)

11.10.1.2 The correct use of crossings

The regulations for the use of crossings are given in the Zebra, Pelican and Puffin Pedestrian Crossings Regulations 1997. The regulations give rise to several offences which can be committed by the drivers of vehicles or by pedestrians on pedestrian crossings. The offences listed below are committed under the Zebra, Pelican and Puffin Pedestrian Crossings Regulations 1997, s 25(5) of the Road Traffic Regulation Act 1984, and Sch 2 to the Road Traffic Offenders Act 1988. Many of the offences apply to all types of crossing, so these offences are listed first.

1. Vehicles must not stop on crossings (all crossings)

Drivers must not stop their vehicles within the limits of a crossing, unless the way is blocked or it is nec'essary for them to stop to avoid injury or damage to persons or property (reg 18).

2. Pedestrians must not delay on crossings (all crossings)

No pedestrian shall remain on the carriageway within the limits of a crossing longer than is necessary for that pedestrian to pass over the crossing [in a reasonable time] (reg 19).

3. Vehicles must not stop in controlled areas (all crossings)

The driver of a vehicle shall not cause it or any part of it to stop in a controlled area (reg 20).

This does not apply to pedal cycles or public service vehicles, nor if the vehicle is beyond the driver's control. There are some other exceptions; a driver may stop in the controlled area in order to:

- allow pedestrians to cross or to prevent injury or damage;
- carry out building work;
- remove obstructions from the road;
- carry out maintenance of the road or crossing;
- make a right or left turn (regs 21–22).

4. Vehicles must not overtake approaching a crossing (all crossings)

Whilst any motor vehicle (or any part of it) is within the limits of a controlled area and is proceeding **towards** the crossing, it must not overtake any stationary vehicles or vehicle approaching the crossing (reg 24).

5. Vehicles must stop at red/steady amber lights (Pelican or Puffin crossings only)

When vehicular traffic-light signals at a Pelican or Puffin crossing are displaying the red light or a non-flashing amber light, the driver must stop (reg 23).

6. Pedestrians have precedence over vehicles at crossings during a flashing amber light sequence (Pelican crossing only)

When the vehicular traffic light signals at a pelican crossing are showing the flashing amber signal, every pedestrian on the crossing has precedence over approaching vehicles that are not yet on the crossing (reg 26).

7. Pedestrians have precedence over vehicles at crossings (zebra crossings only)

A pedestrian on a zebra crossing (not controlled by a constable in uniform or traffic warden) has precedence 'over approaching vehicles that are not yet on the crossing (reg 25).

11.10.2 White Lines along the Centre of the Road

These are covered in reg 26 of the Traffic Signs Regulations and General Directions 2002. The lines may be continuous on both sides, or continuous on one side and broken on the other. The lines are used to indicate parts of the road where vehicles may not be permitted to stop or to cross the lines:

Double white lines both continuous

Double white lines one continuous, one broken

(Crown copyright images reproduced by permission of the Department for Transport)

11.10.2.1 No stopping if there is a continuous white line

No vehicle is permitted to stop on any length of road with a continuous white line marked in the centre of the road. This applies to roads with a broken line on one side, and applies to vehicles on either side of the road (reg 26(2)(a)).

This regulation does not apply to dual carriageways, nor to vehicles used for fire brigade, ambulance, or police purposes. Exceptions also apply for vehicles that have stopped in order to:

- allow passengers to board/alight from a vehicle;
- allow goods to be loaded or unloaded from the vehicle;
- facilitate building or demolition work;

- enable the removal of any obstruction to traffic, road works, or public utility work; or
- avoid an accident.

Exceptions also apply for vehicles that are prevented from proceeding by circumstances outside the driver's control, or are required to stop by law or with the permission or direction of a constable in uniform or a traffic warden.

11.10.2.2 No crossing or straddling a continuous white line

It is an offence for a vehicle to cross or straddle a continuous line when the line is to the **left** of the broken line or another continuous line (reg 26(2)(b)).

There are exceptions:

- when a vehicle is turning right, or to pass a stationary vehicle;
- to enable a vehicle to overtake a pedal cycle, horse, or road-maintenance vehicle moving at a speed not exceeding 10 mph;
- when the action is unavoidable, or to avoid an accident;
- to comply with the directions of a police officer or a traffic warden in uniform.

The above offences relating to crossing white lines are committed under s 36(1) of the Road Traffic Act 1988, reg 10 of the Traffic Signs Regulations 2002, and Sch 2 to the Road Traffic Offenders Act 1988.

11.10.3 Disobeying a Traffic Sign

This is an offence only in relation to signs of the prescribed type (listed under reg 10 of the Traffic Signs Regulations and General Directions 2002) that have been lawfully placed on or near a road (s 36 of the Road Traffic Act 1988). Drivers are therefore under no obligation to heed informal signs erected by members of the public.

Regulation 10 of the Traffic Signs Regulations and General Directions 2002 creates two lists of relevance to s 36 of the Road Traffic Act 1988:

List 1: contravention of a List 1 sign is an offence under s 36 of the Road Traffic Act 1988.
List 2: contravention of a List 2 sign may lead to disqualification or endorsement of the driver's licence.

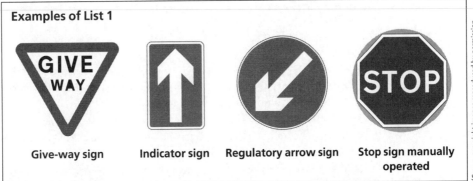

Examples of List 1

Give-way sign | Indicator sign | Regulatory arrow sign | Stop sign manually operated

(Crown copyright images reproduced by permission of the Department for Transport)

Examples of List 2

Stop sign | No-entry sign | Red light of permanent or portable traffic signal

(Crown copyright images reproduced by permission of the Department for Transport)

TASK 9

1. The following is a list of some of the main contributory factors leading to a fatal road accident or collision in 2005 (not all factors are listed here; we have omitted the 18 per cent of fatal accidents that were attributed to the involvement of pedestrians). Put them in order, with the most frequently occurring first.

    (a) road environment (eg road layout, slippery road)
    (b) vehicle defects (eg defectivev tyres, defective brakes)
    (c) injudicious action (eg exceeding speed limit, going too fast for conditions)
    (d) driver/rider error or reaction (eg loss of control, failed to look properly)
    (e) impairment or distraction (eg impaired by alcohol, illness, or disability)
    (f) behaviour or inexperience (eg careless, reckless, or in a hurry; aggressive driving)
    (g) vision affected (eg by road layout, dazzling sun).
    (Adapted from data provided in Robinson & Campbell, 2006).

2. List three ways that you and your colleagues might be able to help reduce the number of deaths in subsequent years.

TASK 10

For each of the following road traffic signs, find an image to show either the symbol for the sign or the sign as marked on the road surface itself.

1. Vehicular traffic entering the junction must give priority to vehicles from the right: for example, a mini-roundabout.
2. Priority is to be given to vehicles from the opposite direction.
3. Warning of a weak bridge.
4. Prohibition of vehicles exceeding a stated height.
5. Drivers of large or slow vehicles to stop and phone for permission to cross a level crossing.
6. Route for use by buses and pedal cycles only.
7. Route for tramcars only.
8. Stop sign, manually operated.
9. Convoy vehicle, no overtaking.
10. Stop for road works.
11. Vehicles to stay to the right of a vehicle involved with mobile road works.
12. Zigzag lines for an equestrian (horse) crossing (also called 'Pegasus') or Toucan crossing (crossing for pedestrian and cyclists to use together).
13. Line markings across a junction at which a vehicle must give way.
14. Variations of double white-line markings including the use of hatched areas.
15. Variations of yellow bus-stop markings.
16. White lines and hatched areas dividing lanes or a main carriageway from a slip road (on motorways or dual carriageways).
17. Yellow grid markings within a box junction preventing entry without a clear exit.
18. Red-light signal of permanent/portable traffic signals and green filter arrows.
19. Tramcar not to proceed further.
20. Intermittent red-light signals at railway level crossings, swing bridges, etc.
21. Matrix prohibition.

11.11 Methods of Disposal for Motoring Offences

When investigating the kind of road traffic offences we have described so far, there are potentially several ways in which you can deal with the suspect. Your decision will be based upon a number of issues, including your own force's policy and your own discretion (see 5.7 above). The methods of disposal for such offences include:

- a verbal warning;
- the Vehicle Defect Rectification Scheme;
- a fixed-penalty notice;
- reporting a suspect for the purposes of issuing a written charge;
- notice of intended prosecution.

11.11.1 Vehicle Defect Rectification Scheme

Drivers in possession of a vehicle found to be in an unsuitable condition can be given the opportunity to join the **Vehicle Defect Rectification Scheme**, or VDRS. This will depend upon both the circumstances of the offence and your discretion. The VDRS is a way of dealing with certain minor vehicle defects without the need to prosecute or issue a fixed-penalty notice.

The advantages of this scheme include:

- the defects are rectified, which contributes to road safety;
- the offender does not have to go to court;
- better police and public relations: the only time many people will come into contact with you is during the investigation of road traffic matters and VDRS is partly supportive rather than wholly punitive.

When you consider using the VDRS you must:

- point out the offence to the person responsible for the vehicle;
- inform him/her that no further action will be taken if he/she agrees to participate in the scheme;
- inform the driver that he/she does not have to participate, as VDRS is voluntary.

If the driver declines to participate in the VDRS, you should then proceed with a fixed-penalty notice, or report the driver for the offence.

11.11.1.1 The VDRS timescale

To avoid the possibility of prosecution, the driver must complete the following within 14 days of the ticket being issued:

1. Repair the defect or renew the faulty body part.
2. Submit the vehicle for examination at a Department of Transport approved testing station (an MOT testing station).
3. Have the VDRS form endorsed at the MOT testing station to confirm that the fault is rectified.
4. Forward the completed VDRS form to the Central Ticket Office within the time specified on the ticket.

If the driver fails to return the form within the time specified on the form, he/she may be considered for prosecution by way of written charge, as if the driver had never been entered on the VDRS in the first place. The copy of the form will be returned to you after 21 days, to enable you to expedite the reporting process. You will then need to write a duty statement (see 8.14 above) to include evidence relating to the offence, in the same way that you would when reporting a suspect for the purposes of issuing a written charge (see 11.11.3 below).

You will then be required to submit a case file including a report requesting a written charge to be issued. The charge will outline the offences for which the driver was reported.

11.11.2 The Fixed-Penalty System

The fixed-penalty system for motoring offences (Pt III, Road Traffic Offenders Act 1988) provides offenders with the opportunity to pay a fixed fine instead of going to court. The system is similar to the Penalty Notice for Disorder (PND) system for anti-social behaviour offences (see 8.15.2 above).

A fixed-penalty notice (FPN) can only be issued to the person actually committing the offence or driving the vehicle involved; a FPN cannot be used for people who cause or permit an offence (see 11.3 above for 'cause' or 'permit'). In some circumstances a FPN can be issued by leaving the documents on the vehicle without the need for the driver to be present, such as a parking ticket affixed to a car's windscreen.

If the FPN is not accepted by the driver, there is no further action to be taken on the street, and the driver will have to be reported and prosecuted. A fine for a FPN must be paid within 28 days (to the Central Ticket Office in the area). If the fine is not paid within this time, it will be increased by 50 per cent and be recovered by the courts.

There are two kinds of FPN:

1. **Non-endorsable fixed-penalty notices (NEFPN),** for offences which do not add penalty points to an offender's driving licence, such as offences relating to:
   - parking;
   - seatbelts; and
   - vehicle lighting.
2. **Endorsable fixed-penalty notices (EFPN),** for offences which add penalty points to an offender's driving licence. Such offences include:
   - contravening a red traffic light;
   - failing to conform to a stop sign; and
   - driving a vehicle with defective tyres.

11.11.2.1 Issuing a non-endorsable fixed-penalty notice

When you are in uniform and you have reasonable grounds to believe that a person is committing or has committed a fixed-penalty offence, you may issue that person with a FPN in respect of that offence (s 54, Road Traffic Offenders Act 1988). If the driver is present you should:

1. Point out the offence.
2. Caution the driver using 'when questioned' and satisfy Code C10.2 (explaining to the suspect that they are not under arrest and do not have to remain with you, sometimes referred to as 'caution + 2'—see 8.4 above).
3. Question the driver and allow the driver to ask questions (in relation to the offence(s)).
4. Check that the driver wishes to proceed with a FPN.
5. Complete and issue the NEFPN.
6. Report the driver or owner for the offence.
7. Use the 'now' caution (again, see 8.4 above).

If the driver is not present and the offence relates only to the vehicle you may attach a NEFPN to a stationary vehicle (s 62(1)). Note that it is an offence to remove or interfere with any FPN fixed to a vehicle.

The flow chart below summarizes the process.

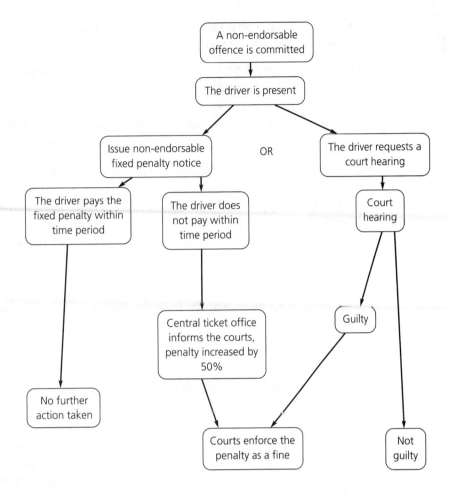

11.11.2.2 Endorsable fixed-penalty notice

Where the penalty for the offence is obligatory endorsement, s 54 of the Road Traffic Offenders Act 1988 states that you may only issue an EFPN if:

- the driver produces a licence and its counterpart for inspection and surrender;
- you are satisfied on inspecting the licence and its counterpart that the driver would not be liable to disqualification; and
- the driver accepts an EFPN.

The procedure for issuing an EFPN is the same as that for a NEFPN, except for checking and retaining the driving licence. You must provide a receipt to the driver for the surrendered licence.

11.11.2.3 The significance of the driver's licence

If the driving licence contains less than 12 points and the driver accepts an EFPN then:

- ask the driver to surrender the licence and pr.ovide a receipt to the driver;
- issue a fixed-penalty notice and explain to the driver that he/she needs to pay within the specified time or face an increased fine (as for NEFPN; see 11.11.2.1 above).

If the licence contains more than 12 points a EFPN cannot be used; you must report the driver for prosecution.

If the driver does not have a driving licence available, you should issue a provisional EFPN and instruct him/her to produce the licence for inspection at a police station (of his/her choice) within seven days.

11.11.3 Reporting for the Purposes of Issuing a Written Charge

You may choose to report a person for the purposes of issuing a written charge (see 8.15.1 above) as the method of disposal. And remember that you will still need to report a driver for the offence even if he/she has elected for the VDRS scheme or a FPN, as he/she might not comply with the VDRS or FPN requirements.

To report a person for the purposes of issuing a written charge, you will always need to go through the following process:

1. Examine the vehicle or see the offence being committed
2. Decide what offence(s) was (were) detected (having gathered evidence in the usual way, that is using your senses, what you saw, felt, smelt, and so on)
3. Point out the offence(s) to the driver
4. Caution the driver using the 'when questioned' form of caution and ensure you meet the PACE Act 1984, Code C10.2 (explaining to the suspect that he/she is not under arrest and does not have to remain with you, sometimes referred to as 'caution + 2'—see 8.4 above)
5. Write down questions and answers about the offences in your PNB (eg when the person last inspected the vehicle, how long ago he/she began his/her journey, was he/she already aware of the defect?)
6. Offer your PNB to the driver to read and sign that the notes were a true record of the interview
7. Offer the driver (if appropriate) the opportunity to have his/her vehicle rectified or pay the penalty notice
8. Tell the driver 'I am reporting you for the offence(s) of ...'
9. Caution the driver (using the 'now' caution—see 8.4 above).

11.11.4 Notice of Intended Prosecution (NIP)

You must give notice to a suspect if he/she is to be prosecuted for certain categories of motoring offence. This is known as a Notice of Intended Prosecution (NIP). If you do not issue such a notice, the prosecution cannot proceed. A NIP specifies the nature of the offence and the time and place where it is alleged to have been committed. It must be given to the offender (the driver or the registered keeper of the vehicle), at the time of the offence (or sent within 14 days of the offence). A NIP is not required when the vehicle concerned has been involved in an accident or if a FPN (see 11.11.2 above) has been issued.

The following offences require a NIP (s 1, Road Traffic Offenders Act 1988):

- dangerous driving;
- careless and inconsiderate driving;
- dangerous cycling;
- careless and inconsiderate cycling;
- failing to conform with the indication of a police officer when directing traffic;
- failing to comply with a traffic sign;
- speeding offences.

A person cannot be prosecuted for any of the offences listed above unless he/she has been:

- **warned** at the time of the offence of the possibility of prosecution (s 1(1)(a));
- **given a notice** setting out the possibility of prosecution (Notice of Intended Prosecution) (s 1(1)(c)), specifying the nature of the offence, and the time and place where it is alleged to have been committed;
- **served with a written charge** within 14 days of commission of the offence (s 1(1)(b)). It is advisable to provide a NIP as a document. Legally, you can give the suspect just a verbal NIP when you first speak with him/her after the offence, but he/she may later claim not to have fully understood what was said (see *Gibson v Dalton* [1980] RTR 410), and in any court case it would be the responsibility of the prosecution to prove that the defendant understood the verbal notice.

11.11.5 Flowchart of the Investigative Process for Dealing with Motoring Offences

The following flowchart summarizes the investigative process for dealing with motoring offences.

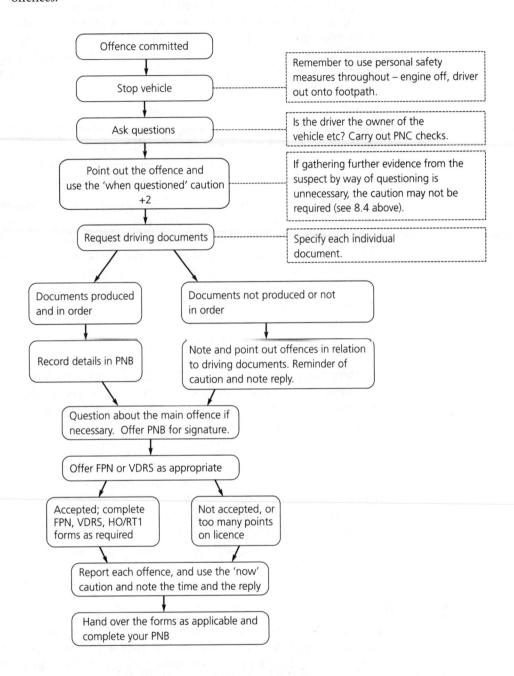

TASK 11

1. Write down the sequence of what you need to say and do when dealing with a driver in each of the following three situations:

   (a) driver unable to produce driving documents

   (b) an offence for which you can use a fixed-penalty notice

   (c) an offence for which you can use the Vehicle Defect Rectification Scheme.

2. Find out about and list the road traffic offences for which you can issue a non-endorsable fixed-penalty notice.

11.12 Road Traffic Collisions (Section 170 of the Road Traffic Act 1988)

We often refer to collisions between vehicles (of various degrees of seriousness) as 'accidents' and the older police term RTA (for Road Traffic Accident) has even entered the popular language. However, it is more common now in police circles to refer to road traffic **collisions** rather than accidents, partly to reflect that incidents of this kind are often due to driver error rather than simply a random accident. However, you are still likely to find 'accident' used frequently during training by other police officers and members of the public, and the term is used in much of the relevant legislation.

Regardless of whether we refer to the incident as an accident or a collision, incidents of this sort are very common and result in a large number of injuries. In 2006, there were 33 million vehicles in Britain and 189,000 injury accidents (Department of Transport, 2007). It is difficult to overstate just how dramatic these numbers are. It is as if the whole population of a town the size of Milton Keynes were to be injured every year, year after year.

The Road Traffic Act 1988 takes a common-sense approach to collisions (referred to as accidents in this Act) and dictates that the driver of a vehicle involved in a collision must stop and be prepared to provide details to anybody who reasonably requires information. This information might be needed for compensation claims for repairs, injuries, or deaths. During your training you are likely to be tested on your detailed understanding about what information must be exchanged after a collision, and what offences can be committed by a person who fails to meet his/her obligations in this regard.

11.12.1 Reportable Accidents

A road collision requiring police involvement is usually a 'reportable accident'. The meaning of 'accident' has not been defined by statute and remains a question of fact for the courts to decide. However, in *R v Morris* [1972] RTR 201 'accident' was held to be 'an unintended occurrence which has an adverse physical result'. However, the meaning of the term 'reportable accident' is clearly defined in s 170(1) of the Road Traffic Act 1988. For a collision to be a reportable accident **all** of the following crite'ria must be met; further details about each criterion are provided further below:

> A reportable accident must:
> * take place on a road or other public place;
> * involve a mechanically propelled vehicle;
> * result in damage to property or injury to a person **other** than the driver or his/her vehicle.

11.12.1.1 Location

Reportable accidents must take place on a road or other public place such as hospital grounds, household garage blocks, private roads, or motorway service areas (see 7.2.1 for further discussion on the definition of a public place). If the collision takes place in any location other than a road maintained at public expense, then you will have to gather evidence concerning the location in relation to its use (that is, the frequency of use, used by whom, and under what circumstances) in order to prove it is a public place.

11.12.1.2 Type of vehicle

A reportable accident must be due to the presence of a mechanically propelled vehicle (see 11.2.1.2 above). This includes vehicles intended or adapted for use on roads (motor vehicles, see 11.2.1.2 above), as well as other vehicles intended or adapted for use off-road (for example dumper trucks and off-road motorbikes).

11.12.1.3 Damage or injury

The **damage** must be to another vehicle or object, such as a bicycle, road sign, or a garden wall. The damage can be to private property, but the accident itself must take place on a road or other public place. So if the vehicle leaves the road or other public place during the accident and ends up in a private dwelling, or grounds adjacent to the road or public place, a reportable accident has still occurred. Damage does not have to be permanent or beyond repair, but the physical appearance must have been altered in some way.

The **injury** must be to another person, and injury includes shock as well as actual bodily harm. Any harm caused to farm animals or dogs during a reportable accident is classified as damage within the Act, but harm caused to cats or wild animals is not.

Note that if the only injury or damage caused is to the driver or his/her vehicle itself (or an animal in or on it), the incident is not a reportable accident in terms of the Road Traffic Act 1988.

11.12.2 Providing Information after a Reportable Accident

After an accident, the driver must **stop**, which includes remaining at the scene for as long as necessary to provide information to others (s 172(2), Road Traffic Act 1988). Failing to stop at an accident is a serious offence and is committed even if the person reports the accident to the police at a later time. At the scene, the driver must provide particulars to anyone who has reasonable grounds for needing the information, such as the driver or rider of any other vehicle involved, the passengers in any of the vehicles, property owners, pedestrians, or their representatives. The driver must provide:

- his/her name and address;
- the name and address of the vehicle's owner;
- the identification marks of the vehicle (for example, the vehicle registration number).

Failing to stop or report an accident is an offence under s 170(4) of the Road Traffic Act 1988. This offence is triable summarily, the penalty is six months' imprisonment and/or a fine, and the offender may also be disqualified.

11.12.2.1 Reporting a reportable accident

Under ss 170(3) and (6) of the Road Traffic Act 1988, if the driver of the mechanically propelled vehicle does not provide the appropriate information (see above), then the accident must be reported as soon as reasonably practicable but not later than 24 hours later (it is a matter for a court to decide what is 'reasonably practicable' for the particular circumstances). The driver must report in person to a constable or police station; it is not sufficient to telephone or send a fax or email, nor should the driver just wait for the police to make contact.

11.12.2.2 Providing a certificate of insurance

Where personal injury is caused to a person (other than the driver) and the driver does not produce a certificate of insurance at the time, the driver has a further seven days to produce the relevant documents (at a police station specified by him/her at the time of the accident).

Failing to produce proof of insurance after an injury accident is an offence under s 170(7) of the Road Traffic Act 1988. This offence is triable summarily and the penalty is a fine.

TASK 12

Your force policy may include the administration of a preliminary breath test to every driver involved in a road traffic collision. What legislation gives you the power to carry out such a test?
What computer checks would you carry out on the drivers involved?

(Photo by Kevin Lawton-Barrett)

11.13   Offences Involving Standards of Driving

When investigating the consequences of a road traffic collision or the anti-social behaviour caused by a driver's careless or inconsiderate driving, you may need to consider the offences described here. Standards of driving are assessed as sufficient when a driver passes his/her driving test, but this minimum standard should be maintained. Careless and inconsiderate driving can result in damage to property or injury to a person, but poor driving can also be alarming, distressing, or annoying to members of the public. You have a power to stop, seize, and remove the vehicle in such situations.

Here we cover the following offences:

- dangerous driving (s 2 of the Road Traffic Act 1988);
- careless and inconsiderate driving (s 3 of the Road Traffic Act 1988);
- wanton and furious driving (s 35 of the Offences against the Person Act 1861);
- careless and inconsiderate cycling (s 29 of the Road Traffic Act 1988);
- causing death by dangerous driving (s 1 of the Road Traffic Act 1988);
- causing death by careless or inconsiderate driving (s 2B of the Road Traffic Act 1988);
- causing death by driving whilst unlicensed, disqualified, or uninsured (s 3ZB of the Road Traffic Act 1988);
- causing the death of another person whilst under the influence of drink or drugs (s 3A of the Road Traffic Act 1988);
- unauthorized off-road driving (s 34 of the Road Traffic Act 1988).

11.13.1   Dangerous Driving

There are two main causes of dangerous driving defined in s 2 of the Road Traffic Act 1988:

- 'bad driving' due to the driver's style of driving;
- driving a vehicle that is in a dangerous condition.

11.13.1.1 Bad driving

Section 2A(1) of the Road Traffic Act 1988 states that 'a person is to be regarded as driving dangerously if :

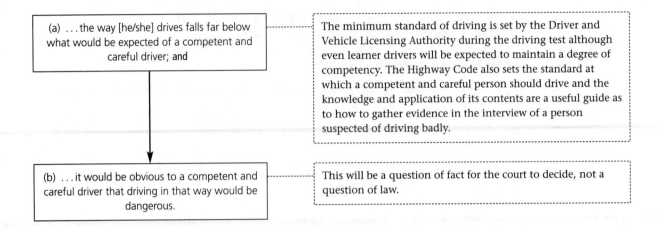

(a) . . . the way [he/she] drives falls far below what would be expected of a competent and careful driver; and	The minimum standard of driving is set by the Driver and Vehicle Licensing Authority during the driving test although even learner drivers will be expected to maintain a degree of competency. The Highway Code also sets the standard at which a competent and careful person should drive and the knowledge and application of its contents are a useful guide as to how to gather evidence in the interview of a person suspected of driving badly.
(b) . . . it would be obvious to a competent and careful driver that driving in that way would be dangerous.	This will be a question of fact for the court to decide, not a question of law.

The following are examples of driving activities which may support an allegation of dangerous driving under s 2A(1):

- racing or competitive driving style;
- driving at a speed which is highly inappropriate for the prevailing road or traffic conditions;
- aggressive driving, such as sudden lane changes, cutting into a line of vehicles, or driving much too close to the vehicle in front;
- disregard for traffic lights and other road signs which, on careful analysis, would appear to be deliberate, or disregard for warnings from fellow passengers;
- overtaking in circumstances where it could not have been carried out safely;
- impaired driver ability such as having an arm or leg in plaster, or impaired eyesight;
- driving when too tired to stay awake;
- using a mobile phone for a conversation or to send/receive text messages (*R v Browning* [2001] EWCA Crim 1831; [2002] 1 Cr App R (S) 88).

11.13.1.2 Dangerous state of a vehicle

Section 2A(2) of the Road Traffic Act 1988 states that:

> a person is to be regarded as driving dangerously . . . if it would be obvious to a competent and careful driver that driving the vehicle in its current state would be dangerous.

In determining the state of a vehicle for the purposes of s 2A(2), the weight or height of the vehicle as well as any load carried should be considered in relation to restrictions on the road. It is for the jury or magistrates to decide whether it would be 'obvious' (to a competent and careful driver) that driving the vehicle in such a state would be dangerous. During evidence gathering (such as interviews of witnesses and suspects), use the Highway Code and Construction and Use Regulations 1986 as a benchmark.

The following are examples of driving which may support an allegation of dangerous driving in relation to the state of a vehicle under s 2A(2):

- driving a vehicle with a load which presents a danger to other road users;
- driving wi th actual knowledge of a dangerous defect on a vehicle.

11.13.1.3 Investigating dangerous driving

To summarize, when considering an offence of dangerous driving, it will be your responsibility to investigate whether:

- the suspect's driving fell far below the fixed and objective standard of a competent and careful driver; and
- it would be **obvious** to a competent and careful driver that the suspect's driving at that time would be dangerous.

During the interview it is advisable to consider the wide range of defences that can be used to avoid prosecution for this offence. Care should be taken to collect evidence to contradict all of the defence strategies that might be employed by the defence counsel (see 11.13.3 below).

The offence of dangerous driving is triable either way and the penalty is:

- summarily: six months' imprisonment and/or a fine;
- on indictment: two years' imprisonment and/or a fine.

11.13.2 Careless or Inconsiderate Driving

Legislation concerning careless or inconsiderate driving is provided by s 3 of the Road Traffic Act 1988.

Section 3 states that an offence is committed by a person who:

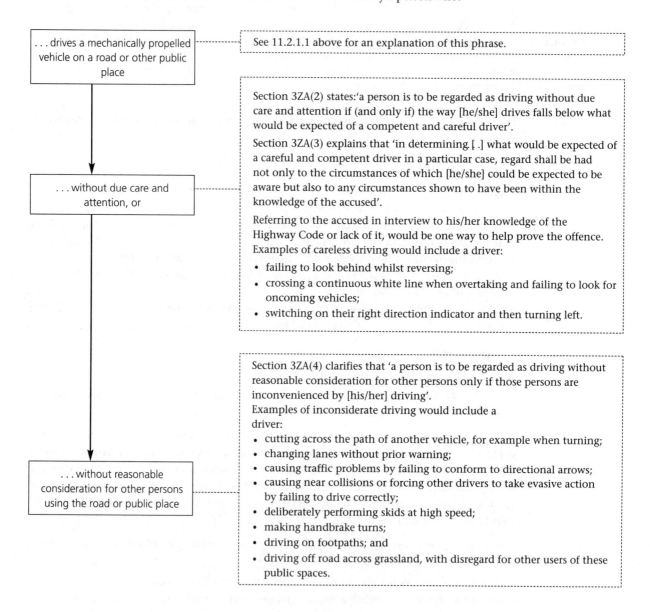

. . . drives a mechanically propelled vehicle on a road or other public place	See 11.2.1.1 above for an explanation of this phrase.
. . . without due care and attention, or	Section 3ZA(2) states: 'a person is to be regarded as driving without due care and attention if (and only if) the way [he/she] drives falls below what would be expected of a competent and careful driver'. Section 3ZA(3) explains that 'in determining . [.] what would be expected of a careful and competent driver in a particular case, regard shall be had not only to the circumstances of which [he/she] could be expected to be aware but also to any circumstances shown to have been within the knowledge of the accused'. Referring to the accused in interview to his/her knowledge of the Highway Code or lack of it, would be one way to help prove the offence. Examples of careless driving would include a driver: • failing to look behind whilst reversing; • crossing a continuous white line when overtaking and failing to look for oncoming vehicles; • switching on their right direction indicator and then turning left.
. . . without reasonable consideration for other persons using the road or public place	Section 3ZA(4) clarifies that 'a person is to be regarded as driving without reasonable consideration for other persons only if those persons are inconvenienced by [his/her] driving'. Examples of inconsiderate driving would include a driver: • cutting across the path of another vehicle, for example when turning; • changing lanes without prior warning; • causing traffic problems by failing to conform to directional arrows; • causing near collisions or forcing other drivers to take evasive action by failing to drive correctly; • deliberately performing skids at high speed; • making handbrake turns; • driving on footpaths; and • driving off road across grassland, with disregard for other users of these public spaces.

However, note the following:

- the offence applies only to driving on roads or public places;
- the offence only applies to drivers of mechanically propelled vehicles;
- careless or inconsiderate driving is a question of fact for the court to decide;
- a driver can only be charged with careless or inconsiderate driving, not both.

This offence is triable summarily and the penalty is a fine. The driver may also be disqualified.

11.13.3 Defences to Dangerous, Careless, or Inconsiderate Driving

There are various defences that may be offered by a suspect in respect of committing the offences of dangerous or careless or inconsiderate driving (see 11.13.1 and 11.13.2 above). These are summarized in the table below:

List of defences

Automatism	Automatism is 'the involuntary movement of a person's body or limbs' (*Watmore v Jenkins* [1961] 2 All ER 868) and it must occur very suddenly with little or no warning. It may include an epileptic fit or a sudden attack by a stinging insect, but will not include situations (established through case law) where a person falls asleep at the wheel or goes into a hypoglycaemic coma (as a result of poorly controlled diabetes).
Unconsciousness or sudden illness	This would include situations where a person suddenly becomes unconscious as a result of circumstances beyond his/her control, such as being hit on the head by a stone that has smashed through the windscreen.
Assisting in the arrest of offenders	Here, the driver may have a defence (even though he/she was driving dangerously) if it can be proved that he/she shunted another car off the road intentionally in order to help the police arrest a suspect (in the shunted car) who had committed an indictable offence (*R v Renouf* [1986] 2 All ER 449).
Duress by threats	In order to claim this defence, the suspect must be able to show that he/she drove dangerously as a result of a threat. However, he/she must neither place him/herself voluntarily under the threat, nor avoid the opportunity to escape from it.
Duress of necessity (of circumstances)	The suspect must be able to show that he/she drove dangerously out of necessity in order: • to avoid death or serious injury to him/herself or anybody else and • that he/she could not reasonably have been expected to act otherwise, as a result of the circumstances in which he/she found her/himself.
Sudden mechanical defect	If this causes the driver to totally lose control, this may be a defence. However, it does not apply if the driver is already aware of the defect or it could have been easily discovered by superficial examination, eg of tyres (*R v Spurge* [1961] 2 All ER 688).
Authorized motoring event	A person will not be guilty under ss 1, 2, or 3 of the Road Traffic Act if he/she drove in accordance with an authorization for a motoring event given by the Secretary of State (s 13(A), Road Traffic Act 1988).

11.13.4 Other Offences Involving Dangerous Driving

There may be occasions when dangerous driving has taken place but you cannot use the Road Traffic Act 1988 as the basis of a prosecution, such as:

• when the driving was not on a road or other public place;
• when the vehicle used was not a mechanically propelled vehicle (for example, it was a bicycle or horse-drawn vehicle);
• when the statutory Notice of Intended Prosecution was not given (see 11.11.4 above).

In these situations there is an alternative offence you might consider: s 35 of the Offences against the Person Act 1861 states that it is an offence for anyone 'having the charge of any carriage or vehicle … [to cause] or cause to be done bodily harm to any person' by:

• **wanton or furious** driving, racing; or
• other wilful misconduct; or
• wilful neglect.

The offence can only be committed if the driver has a degree of subjective recklessness; he/she must appreciate that harm was possible or probable as a result of his/her bad driving (*R v Okosi* [1996] CLR 666).

This offence is triable by indictment only and the penalty is two years' imprisonment. Disqualification is discretionary, although endorsement (three to nine points) is obligatory if the offence is committed in a mechanically propelled vehicle.

11.13.4.1 Riding a cycle carelessly, inconsiderately, or dangerously on a road

It is an offence under the Road Traffic Act 1988 for a person to ride a cycle on a road without due care and attention, reasonable consideration for other persons using the road (s 29), or dangerously (s 28(1)).

These offences are triable summarily and the penalty is a fine.

11.13.5 Causing Death by Driving

The offences of causing death by dangerous driving, careless or inconsiderate driving, or whilst being unlicensed, disqualified, or uninsured are described in the table below, along with the corresponding section number of the Road Traffic Act 1988 for each offence:

Causing death by		
dangerous driving (s 1)	careless or inconsiderate driving (s 2B)	driving whilst unlicensed, disqualified or uninsured (s 3ZB)
An offence is committed by a person who causes the death of another person by driving a		
mechanically propelled vehicle		motor vehicle
dangerously	without due care and attention, or without reasonable consideration for other persons using the road	whilst committing an offence of: • driving otherwise than in accordance with a licence (s 87(1)); • driving while disqualified (s 103(1)(b)); or • no insurance (s 143)
on a road or other public place.		on a road.
Triable by indictment only and the penalty is: • 14 years' imprisonment • obligatory disqualification • obligatory endorsement—licence endorsed between 3 and 11 points.	Triable either way and the penalty is:	
	• summarily: 12 months' imprisonment • on indictment: 5 years' imprisonment • obligatory disqualification • obligatory endorsement—licence endorsed between 3 and 11 points.	• summarily: 12 months' imprisonment • on indictment: 2 years' imprisonment • obligatory disqualification • obligatory endorsement—licence endorsed between 3 and 11 points.

There are two important points to note:

1. Causing death by driving whilst unlicensed, disqualified, or uninsured can only be committed whilst:
   • driving a **motor** vehicle only (see 11.2 above for the definition of 'motor vehicle');
   • on a road (see 11.2.1.3 above for the definition of 'road').
2. For each of the three offences, the death must (of course) be of a person other than the suspect. It is not relevant whether the deceased person was inside or outside the suspect's vehicle at the time of the incident.

11.13.5.1   **Causing the death of another person whilst under the influence of drink or drugs**

Section 3A of the Road Traffic Act 1988 states it is an offence:

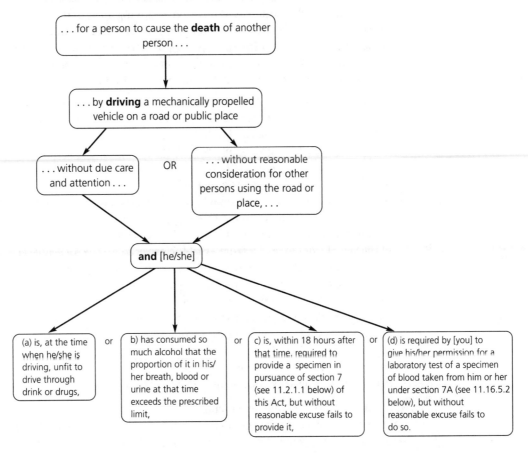

. . . for a person to cause the **death** of another person . . .

. . . by **driving** a mechanically propelled vehicle on a road or public place

. . . without due care and attention . . .

OR

. . . without reasonable consideration for other persons using the road or place, . . .

and [he/she]

(a) is, at the time when he/she is driving, unfit to drive through drink or drugs,

or

b) has consumed so much alcohol that the proportion of it in his/her breath, blood or urine at that time exceeds the prescribed limit,

or

c) is, within 18 hours after that time, required to provide a specimen in pursuance of section 7 (see 11.2.1.1 below) of this Act, but without reasonable excuse fails to provide it,

or

(d) is required by [you] to give his/her permission for a laboratory test of a specimen of blood taken from him or her under section 7A (see 11.16.5.2 below), but without reasonable excuse fails to do so.

This offence is triable by indictment only and the penalty is 14 years' imprisonment and/or a fine.

TASK 13

1. Who would be held to be 'driving' in each of the following scenarios? Use the case suggested as guidance.

   (a) Jerry sits in the driver's seat and lets car freewheel downhill with the steering lock on. See *Burgoyne v Phillips* [1982] RTR 49.

   (b) Maz, a passenger in a car 'driven' by Mel sees a friend walking along the roadside towards the moving car. To frighten the friend, Maz snatches the steering wheel from Mel's grasp towards himself in order to make the car veer in that direction. Would Maz be held to be 'driving'? See *DPP v Hastings* [1993] 158 JP 118.

   (c) Hari is in the driving seat of the car and 'driving' along the road. Pat leans over from the front passenger seat and steers the car while Hari manipulates the other controls. Hari's view forward is partially obscured by Pat. After some distance, the car runs into a ditch while Pat is steering. Pat had been able to reach both the handbrake and the ignition key and knew the consequences of using the various controls, but did not have access to the foot pedals. See *Tyler v Whatmore* [1975] RTR 83. Who was driving?

2. Answer the questions (a) and (b) by selecting the correct option(s) from the list below.

   (a) Where can dangerous driving and causing death by dangerous driving be committed?

   (b) In what location(s) does s 35 of the Offences Against the Persons Act 1861 apply?

      (i) anywhere

      (ii) on a road

      (iii) in a public place other than a road

      (iv) in a public place only

535

11.13.6   Other Offences involving Standards of Driving

Other offences relating to poor standards of driving are described in the Road Vehicles (Construction and Use) Regulations 1986. The term 'driving' has a wide meaning under s 192 of the Road Traffic Act; pulling up by the side of a road with the engine running, for example, could be considered as driving. The offences apply not only to the driver, but also to any person causing or permitting (see 11.3 above) another person to drive inappropriately. The following regulations are relevant to offences involving standards of driving:

- No person shall drive (or cause or permit any other person to drive) a motor vehicle on a road if the driver is in such a position that he/she cannot have **proper control** of the vehicle or have a full view of the road and traffic ahead (reg 104). The penalty is an obligatory endorsement (three points) and a discretionary disqualification

- No person shall open, or cause or permit to be opened, any **door** of a vehicle on a road so as to injure or endanger any person (reg 105).

- No person shall drive a motor vehicle on a road if the driver is in such a position as to be able to see directly, or by reflection, a **TV or similar apparatus** (reg 109). (This does not apply to satellite navigation apparatus or other apparatus used to display information about the state of the vehicle, nor to devices that assist the driver to see the road adjacent to the vehicle.)

- Driving a motor vehicle on a road while using a **hand-held phone** (eg a 'mobile') is an offence, and also applies to similar devices with an 'interactive communication function' (reg 110). (Communication by two-way radio, such as 'CB', is excluded from this offence, although obviously the general need for safe driving still applies.) Apart from applying to drivers, this offence can also be committed by anyone supervising a driver with a provisional licence. Employers providing the employee with a company hand-held phone can be held liable if they fail to prohibit their employee from using it while driving on company business. The penalty is an obligatory endorsement (three points) and a discretionary disqualification.

It is important to note that, as a member of the police service, you, together with members of other emergency services, are granted some exemptions from road traffic regulations. However, as a police officer, you will be expected to drive at least as well as other motorists; you should aim to provide a positive role model for other drivers—look back at 5.5 above where we discuss personal authority. It is very important that your driving meets the standards prescribed by the level of your training and that you are fully aware of your force policies before taking on any emergency response.

11.13.6.1   Refusal by driver or rider to provide name and address

It is an offence under s 168 of the Road Traffic Act 1988 for a person who is driving a mechanically propelled vehicle or riding a cycle either dangerously, carelessly, or inconsiderately to refuse to give his/her name or address (or to give a false name or address) to any person having reasonable ground for making such a request. Examples of such people might include police officers, a pedestrian, or another driver who has been involved in a road traffic collision.

This offence is triable summarily and the penalty is a fine.

> **TASK 14**
>
> 1. What other offences might be considered for a person using a hand-held mobile telephone while driving, apart from the offence following from reg 110?
> 2. Apart from a driver using a phone, suggest some other circumstances or activities that might lead to a fall in standards of driving.

11.13.7 Off-road Driving

The law surrounding off-road driving is covered in s 34 of the Road Traffic Act 1988.

Section 34 states that an offence is committed by a person who:

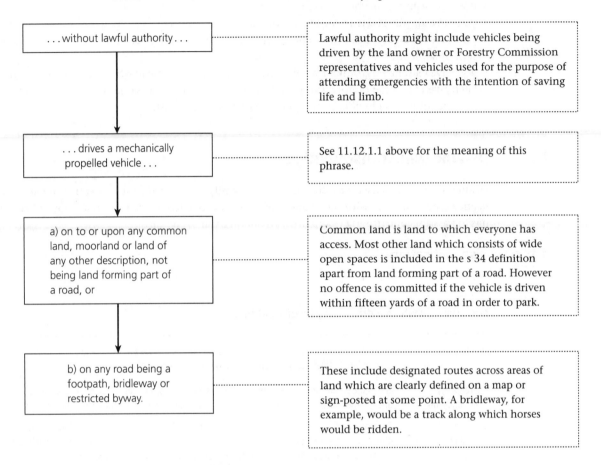

. . . without lawful authority . . .	Lawful authority might include vehicles being driven by the land owner or Forestry Commission representatives and vehicles used for the purpose of attending emergencies with the intention of saving life and limb.
. . . drives a mechanically propelled vehicle . . .	See 11.12.1.1 above for the meaning of this phrase.
a) on to or upon any common land, moorland or land of any other description, not being land forming part of a road, or	Common land is land to which everyone has access. Most other land which consists of wide open spaces is included in the s 34 definition apart from land forming part of a road. However no offence is committed if the vehicle is driven within fifteen yards of a road in order to park.
b) on any road being a footpath, bridleway or restricted byway.	These include designated routes across areas of land which are clearly defined on a map or sign-posted at some point. A bridleway, for example, would be a track along which horses would be ridden.

This offence is triable summarily only and the penalty is a fine.

11.14 Vehicles and Harassment

If you attend an incident involving people racing in their cars and therefore causing concern for other people in the area, what powers are available to you? You may have reasonable grounds for believing that a mechanically propelled vehicle has been driven carelessly or inconsiderately (s 3 Road Traffic Act 1988), unlawfully off-road (s 34 Road Traffic Act 1988), or that a motor vehicle is involved (or is likely to be involved) with other motor vehicles in unlicensed on-street racing. If, as a result of the way the vehicle is being driven, members of the public are caused (or are likely to be caused) alarm, distress, or annoyance, you have the power to seize the vehicle under s 59 of the Police Reform Act 2002. You may take the following actions:

- **stop** the vehicle if it is moving;
- **seize** and **remove** the vehicle, after warning the driver;
- **enter** certain types of premises in order to stop or seize a vehicle;
- **use reasonable force** to carry out the above actions.

The term premises does not include a private dwelling or home, nor does it include any garage or other occupied structure with the dwelling house, nor any land attached to the dwelling house. You must have reasonable grounds for believing the vehicle is on the premises.

Failure to stop is an offence under s 59(6) of the Police Reform Act 2002. It is triable summarily, and the penalty is a fine.

11.14.1 Warning the Driver Before Seizing a Vehicle

You cannot seize a vehicle unless you have issued a warning to the driver that you will seize it if the improper use continues. However, you do not have to warn the driver if:

- it would be impracticable to do so;
- you have already given a warning on that occasion;
- you have reasonable grounds for believing that such a warning has been given on that occasion by someone else; or
- you have reasonable grounds for believing that the person is one to whom such a warning has been given (whether or not by you or another or in respect of the same vehicle or the same or a similar use) on a previous occasion in the previous 12 months.

11.15 Driving whilst Disqualified

Disqualification means that a licence is temporarily suspended, but revocation means the licence is permanently withdrawn and is effectively cancelled. A driver with a revoked licence has to pass a second driving test in order to obtain a full licence again.

11.15.1 Disqualification

Disqualification can occur in a number of different ways, as shown in the table below.

Main ways in which a driver may be disqualified

Endorsement and penalty points	Penalty points are awarded according to the type and seriousness of the offence and are endorsed on the driving licence. When **twelve points** in a **three-year** period have been accumulated ('totted up'), the driver must be disqualified.
Discretionary disqualification	This is the penalty for certain offences, such as 'failing to stop after an accident' (see 11.12.2 above). The court may disqualify for a period of its choosing (but not for an indefinite period).
Obligatory disqualification	The Road Traffic Act 1988 sets out minimum periods of compulsory disqualification for certain offences, such as drink-driving. In some cases, the court can disqualify a person until he/she has retaken and passed the appropriate driving test again. In such a case, a disqualified person will become a provisional-licence holder during the period leading up to the test. A failure to satisfy any of the requirements of a provisional licence means the person will commit the offence of disqualified driving.

A person is guilty of an offence under s 103(1) of the Road Traffic Act 1988 if, whilst disqualified from holding or obtaining a licence, he/she:

(a) obtains a licence (s 103(1)(a)); or
(b) drives a motor vehicle on a road (s 103(1)(b)).

In order to successfully prosecute the disqualified driver at court there must be admissible evidence of the original disqualification (see *Mills v Director of Public Prosecutions* (2008) EWHC 3304 (Admin)). There are several forms of evidence you can use to prove that a driver is disqualified:

- a certificate of conviction under s 73 of the PACE Act 1984;
- the defendant's admission at interview;
- the defendant's admission in court;
- evidence of a person who was in court when the original disqualification was imposed.

These offences are triable summarily. The penalties are as follows:

- for obtaining a licence while disqualified: a fine;
- for driving a motor vehicle on a road: imprisonment for a term not exceeding six months and/or a fine, discretionary disqualification, and obligatory endorsement (six penalty points).

11.15.2 Revocation of Driving Licences

Section 3 of the Road Traffic (New Drivers) Act 1995 provides for the revocation of the driving licence of a new driver who has accumulated six or more penalty points within two years of passing his/her driving test.

A driver's licence may be revoked when:

- a licence holder is convicted of an offence involving obligatory endorsement; or
- a licence and counterpart have been sent to the fixed-penalty clerk, and there are six or more penalty points to be taken into account.

The court (or the fixed-penalty clerk) must send the licence and the counterpart to the Secretary of State who will then revoke the licence. If a driver has had his/her licence revoked within the two-year probationary period, he/she reverts to the status of a learner driver and has to take a driving test again, but is not subject to a further probationary period if he/she passes the test.

A new driver who has had his/her licence revoked commits an offence if he/she drives without a new provisional licence, or without 'L' plates and appropriate supervision (see 11.7 above).

TASK 15

1. How could a disqualified driver or 'new driver' with a revoked licence conceal the fact that he or she is disqualified?
2. What resources are available to you on Independent Patrol, if you need to establish whether a person is disqualified?

11.16 Alcohol, Drugs, and Driving

Before we consider the details of the legislation on driving offences involving alcohol or drugs, you may be asking yourself how you might first become involved in such a case. Some situations will be clear cut, but for others—how can an officer decide when such an offence might have been committed, and when to intervene in the lives of citizens? Of course, you must not administer random breath tests or other preliminary tests; you can only test a person if you have reason to suspect the driver might be under the influence of alcohol, if a moving traffic offence has been committed, or if the vehicle has been involved in an accident.

Scenarios for testing for drink/drug driving offences

General scenario	Example
An accident	A vehicle runs into the back of another vehicle at a junction.
A moving traffic offence	You see a driver cross a red traffic light (a moving traffic offence).
Inappropriate style of driving	You are called to investigate a traffic jam in a quiet part of a town. A dumper truck has stalled at some traffic lights and the driver has failed to restart the engine. His speech is slurred when he attempts to respond to your questions.
Vehicle stopped for another reason, and then you become suspicious	You stop a vehicle under s 163 RTA 1988 (see 11.3), to carry out a test and inspection of the vehicle for roadworthiness. There are beer cans on the seat, the driver has a sleepy grin on his face, and his breath smells of intoxicating liquor.
Other information about drink/drug consumption	A witness observes a group of people consuming alcohol in a pub. They stagger into the adjacent car park and after some shouting all squeeze into a small car, which moves off with a jerk. The witness then contacts the police and supplies the registration number of the car.

The level of alcohol or drugs in a driver's blood is not always easy to judge. If you are suspicious that alcohol or other drugs may be present, a **'preliminary test'** is administered at the roadside in order to confirm your suspicions. The best known of these tests is the so-called 'breath test'. The results of such a test do not form part of the evidence for the prosecution and only provide grounds for suspicion that the proportion of alcohol in the person's breath or blood exceeds the prescribed limit (an offence under s 5 of the Road Traffic Act 1988: see 11.16.3 below).

There are two main driving offences relating to driving while under the influence of alcohol or other drugs, and these are both covered under the Road Traffic Act 1988:

- driving, or attempting to drive, or being in charge of a **mechanically propelled vehicle** while **unfit to drive** through drink or drugs (s 4, Road Traffic Act 1988);
- driving, or attempting to drive, or being in charge of a **motor vehicle** with **alcohol in excess of the prescribed limit** (s 5, Road Traffic Act 1988).

The key difference between these two offences is that, for a s 4 offence, the prosecution has to prove that the suspect's ability to drive was actually impaired, whereas for s 5 offences a high blood, breath, or urine alcohol level is the only evidence required.

We will first consider the definitions of some key terms and concepts in the legislation relating to alcohol, drugs, and driving, and then go on to look at preliminary and evidential tests in more detail.

11.16.1 Definitions of Key Terms from the Relevant Legislation

The legislation relating to offences committed whilst driving under the influence of alcohol or drugs uses many terms employed in other pieces of road policing legislation. You might find it useful at this stage to look back at 11.2 above to refresh your memory, particularly in relation to the definition of mechanically propelled vehicles and motor vehicles.

Sections 4(2) and 5(1)(b) of the Road Traffic Act 1988 refer to a person being **in charge** of a vehicle. (This term only occurs within ss 4 and 5 of the Road Traffic Act 1988, and is not therefore covered in 11.2 above.) In order to decide if a person is in charge of a vehicle the court is likely to consider the following:

- Was the person in question the most recent driver?
- How long ago had he/she been driving the vehicle?
- Where was the person found, in relation to the vehicle?
- Did he/she have the keys?

It may be necessary to negate defences in relation to being 'in charge'. For example the defendant might attempt to prove that there was no likelihood of his/her driving the vehicle in the near future (while still under the influence of alcohol or dugs). A stated intention not to drive is insufficient (see *CPS v Thompson* [2007] EWHC 1841 (Admin)). A suitable defence might include that he/she had booked a hotel room for the night, or that the vehicle had been wheel-clamped (see *Sheldrake v DPP* [2003] 2 All ER 497). The defence might also claim that the driver was so badly injured that he/she was unable to drive the vehicle, or that the vehicle could not be driven due to severe damage, but the court may choose to disregard any injury to the suspect (or damage to the vehicle) when assessing the likelihood of the suspect driving.

11.16.2 Unfit to Drive through Drink or Drugs

These offences are covered under s 4 of the Road Traffic Act 1988. Sub-section 4(1) states that a person commits an offence when:

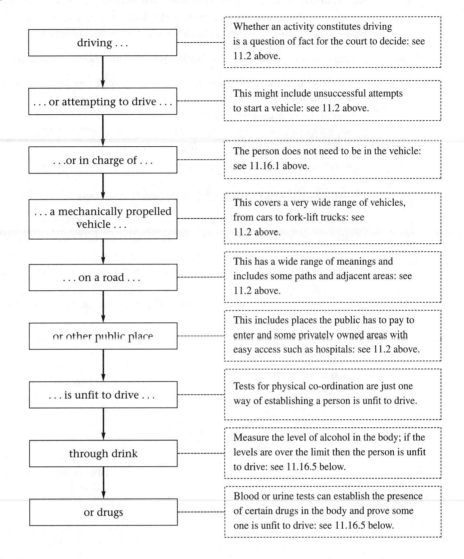

driving . . .	Whether an activity constitutes driving is a question of fact for the court to decide: see 11.2 above.
. . . or attempting to drive . . .	This might include unsuccessful attempts to start a vehicle: see 11.2 above.
. . .or in charge of . . .	The person does not need to be in the vehicle: see 11.16.1 above.
. . . a mechanically propelled vehicle . . .	This covers a very wide range of vehicles, from cars to fork-lift trucks: see 11.2 above.
. . . on a road . . .	This has a wide range of meanings and includes some paths and adjacent areas: see 11.2 above.
or other public place	This includes places the public has to pay to enter and some privately owned areas with easy access such as hospitals: see 11.2 above.
. . . is unfit to drive . . .	Tests for physical co-ordination are just one way of establishing a person is unfit to drive.
through drink	Measure the level of alcohol in the body; if the levels are over the limit then the person is unfit to drive: see 11.16.5 below.
or drugs	Blood or urine tests can establish the presence of certain drugs in the body and prove some one is unfit to drive: see 11.16.5 below.

Remember, there is no need to administer a preliminary test for breath alcohol levels or for drug consumption before arresting a driver for this offence.

The suspect's level of impairment and ability to drive properly is assessed by a police medical practitioner at a police station through an evidential test. Specimens of breath, blood, or urine may also be taken for other evidential tests, particularly to prove the presence of drugs in the body (which would imply impairment). In addition, even though a suspect has been arrested for a s 4 offence he/she may eventually be charged with an offence under s 5, depending on the results of evidential tests measuring the level of alcohol in the body. Section 4 can also be used if the driver is over the limit for alcohol but the vehicle involved is not a motor vehicle.

The evidence presented to a court for a s 4 offence is likely to include:

- the style of driving before the accused was stopped;
- his/her demeanour at time of stop (speech, unsteadiness);
- the report by a medical examiner whilst in custody (particularly if evidential specimens are not obtained to prove the presence of drugs in the body);
- the results of evidential drug tests (using blood or urine samples).

Remember that it may be necessary to present evidence to counter a defence that the driver was not likely to drive whilst under the influence of drugs or alcohol, when investigating an 'in charge' offence (see 11.16.1 above).

There is no power of arrest for a s 4 offence under the Road Traffic Act 1988. Instead, use your s 24 PACE 1984 powers of arrest if the circumstances are appropriate, such as suspicion the offence is being committed and that the arrest is necessary for a prompt and effective investigation of the offence (see 11.11 below). You have a power of entry under s 17(1)(c)(iiia) of the PACE Act 1984 to arrest a person under s 4 of the Road Traffic Act 1988, but only if you have reasonable grounds for believing the suspect is on the premises.

Offences under s 4 of the Road Traffic Act 1988 are triable summarily and the penalties are:

1. for **driving and attempting to drive** whilst unfit due to drink or drugs (s 4(1)):
   • six months' imprisonment and/or a fine;
   • obligatory disqualification.
2. for being **in charge** of a vehicle whilst unfit due to drink or drugs (s 4(2)):
   • three months' imprisonment and/or a fine;
   • discretionary disqualification.

11.16.3 Blood Alcohol in Excess of the Prescribed Limit

For this offence (under s 5 of the Road Traffic Act 1988) the evidence required is a blood, breath, or urine evidential test result showing that the level of alcohol in the driver's body was above the prescribed limit. There is no need to provide evidence that the suspect was unfit to drive in terms of their demeanour or behaviour. The flowchart below shows the wording for a s 5 offence; bold-edged boxes draw your attention to the features that distinguish a s 5 offence from a s 4 offence. Section 5 of the Road Traffic Act 1988 states that it is an offence for a person to:

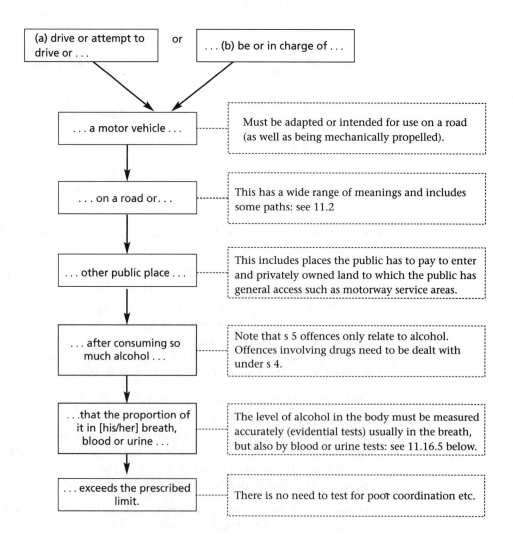

The prescribed limits are shown in the table below. Note the units: microgrammes (µg), milligrammes (mg), and millilitres (ml).

Type of sample	Amount of alcohol per 100 millilitres	
Breath	35 microgrammes	A good way to help memorize these figures is to remember that all the digits in each measurement add up to 8.
Blood	80 milligrammes	
Urine	107 milligrammes	

These offences are triable summarily and the penalties are:

1. for **driving or attempting to drive** above the prescribed limit (s 5(1)(a)):

    *   six months' imprisonment and/or a fine;
    *   obligatory disqualification.

2. for being **in charge** of a vehicle above the prescribed limit (s 5(1)(b)):

    *   three months' imprisonment and/or a fine;
    *   discretionary disqualification.

11.16.4 Preliminary Tests

Preliminary tests are frequently referred to as roadside tests and are covered in ss 6A, 6B, and 6C of the Road Traffic Act 1988. They are only used for drivers of motor vehicles (and not mechanically propelled vehicles). Preliminary tests are used to find out if it is **likely** that a drugs- or alcohol-related driving offence has been committed; they only provide grounds for **suspicion**. More detailed tests (evidential tests) will be required to provide evidence for a subsequent prosecution. The three main types of preliminary test are:

*   a **preliminary breath** test to indicate whether the proportion of alcohol in the breath or blood is likely to exceed the prescribed limit (s 6A, Road Traffic Act 1988);
*   a **preliminary impairment** test of whether a person is unfit to drive (whether due to drink or drugs). This is done by observing the person's performance during a set of tasks or observing his/her physical state. You can only carry out such a test if you are approved for that purpose by the chief officer of the police force to which you belong (s 6B, Road Traffic Act 1988);
*   a **preliminary drug** test to indicate the presence of drugs in a person's body. A specimen of sweat or saliva is obtained and tested with an approved device (s 6C, Road Traffic Act 1988).

If you require a person to take part in a preliminary test, you do not need to be in uniform. However, the police officer actually administering a preliminary test must be in uniform (except after an accident). You will need to complete a Home Office statistical return form after administering a preliminary test.

In some situations it might not be clear who was driving, so you should first clarify who was in the vehicle at the time of the accident; witnesses may be able to help on this matter. However, remember that you only have to 'reasonably believe' that a person was driving a vehicle at the time of the accident, and therefore if no one admits to being the driver you can test more than one person from the same vehicle.

You have a power of entry (s 6E of the Road Traffic Act 1988) in order to administer preliminary tests, but only after an accident in which you reasonably suspect a person has been injured. You may enter any place, using reasonable force if necessary.

The following flowchart summarizes the circumstances for administering preliminary tests:

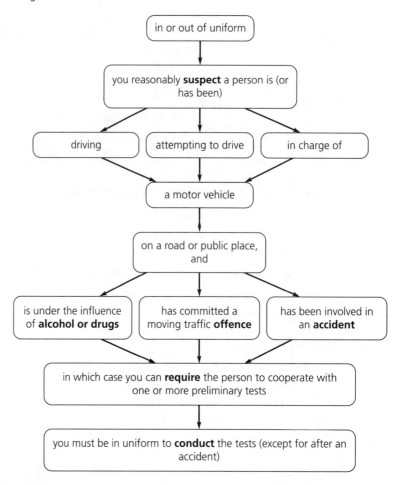

The meaning of the term 'accident' has not been defined by statute and remains a question of fact for the courts to decide. However, in *R v Morris* [1972] RTR 201 'accident' was held to be 'an unintended occurrence which has an adverse physical result' and when such a situation arises out of the presence of a motor vehicle on a road it 'is a fair basis on which a police officer may request the provision of a specimen of breath'.

11.16.4.1   **Preliminary breath tests**

You will be given training in the use of the preliminary breath-test equipment chosen by your own organization. There are currently two styles of preliminary breath-test devices approved by the Secretary of State. Electronic devices include models such as the Lion Alcolmeter, the Alcosensor IV, the Draeger Alert, and the Draeger Alcotest 7410. Others (such as Alcotest 80 and R80A and the Alcolyser) are not electronic and involve the inflation of a bag. All of the devices test air that has come from deep within the lungs. It is most important that you follow the manufacturer's instructions as well as force policy when using these devices.

You must say to the suspect (when you are requesting a specimen of breath)

> I suspect that you are driving a motor vehicle on a road under the influence of alcohol. I require you to provide a specimen of breath for a breath test here. Failure to do so may make you liable to arrest and prosecution.

You must also ask the person when he/she had last drunk alcohol or smoked; if the person has been drinking or smoking recently you must comply with the manufacturer's instructions to wait a period of minutes before administering the test (as recent smoking of a cigarette or cigar can 'mask' the measurement of alcohol content). Failure to ask these questions will not invalidate the test (*DPP v Kay* 1998) and innocent failure to follow the instructions will not make the arrest and subsequent evidential test unlawful, although the results may be considered as less reliable.

To carry out the test you should ask the driver to take a deep breath and to blow into the machine in one continuous breath until requested to stop. Tell the person the result of the test.

A positive result from a preliminary breath test directly justifies arrest; you must tell the suspect that he/she is under arrest (s 6D(1) of the Road Traffic Act 1988) on **suspicion** that the proportion of alcohol in his/her breath or blood exceeds the prescribed limit and caution him or her. The reason for the arrest is **not** that the breath test has produced a positive result. You should then conduct an evidential breath test (see 11.16.5.1 below). A patient in a hospital must never be arrested (s 6D(3).

11.16.4.2 What to do after a preliminary test

If the results of a preliminary breath test are negative but (due to his/her demeanour) you still suspect the driver of being under the influence of drugs:

1. consider administering a preliminary impairment or drugs test if you are qualified and have the apparatus available or
2. consider arresting the driver on suspicion of the s 4 offence of driving whilst unfit, using your s 24 PACE powers of arrest.

If no other offences have been committed, then the driver is free to leave.

The chart below summarizes the actions that should be taken in relation to other outcomes from preliminary tests:

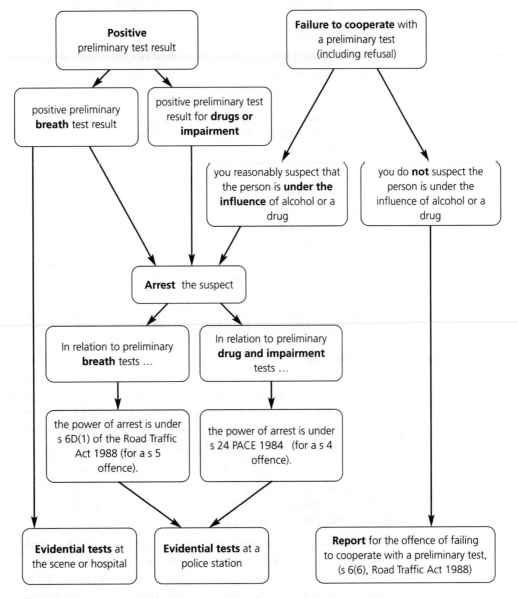

You have the **power of entry** in order to arrest a person who has provided a positive preliminary test and has been involved in an injury accident. This power is given under s 6 of the Road Traffic Act 1988.

11.16.4.3 Failure to cooperate with a preliminary test

The number of opportunities you should provide for completing a preliminary test will be determined by your organization's policy. If, despite further opportunities, a person still fails to complete a preliminary test, the action you should take depends on whether you suspect the influence of alcohol or drugs, as shown in the chart above.

If the driver cannot complete a preliminary test (for example, due to a medical condition) you should arrest him/her and arrange for blood or urine tests, but only if you reasonably suspect that he/she is under the influence of alcohol or a drug. However a patient in a hospital must never be arrested (s 6D(3)).

If you do not suspect alcohol or drugs, you cannot arrest him/her; you should instead report him/her for the offence of failing to cooperate with the provision of a specimen for a preliminary test under s 6(6) of the Road Traffic Act 1988. You will need to ascertain the person's true identity (carry out computer checks with control), obtain identification documentation from the person, and check the address they give is genuine. Complete an interview with him/her under caution (all recorded in your pocket notebook), and finally report him/her for the offence of failing to cooperate with a preliminary test and caution again. This offence is triable summarily and the penalty is obligatory endorsement (four points) and discretionary disqualification.

11.16.5 Evidential Tests

The results of these tests (for drugs, alcohol, and impairment) can be used as evidence in a court. The tests are usually carried out at a police station (or hospital if the suspect is a hospital patient) but some may also be conducted at the roadside.

The requirement for an evidential test (all types) is made at a police station or hospital but the requirement for an evidential breath test can also be made at the roadside. It is usual to arrest a suspect before you make the requirement for an evidential test, though you are not obliged to do this by law. You cannot arrest a suspect if they are a hospital patient (s 6D(3), Road Traffic Act 1988).

At a police station the evidential breath test will always be used in preference to blood or urine tests, unless at least one of the following conditions (s 7(3), Road Traffic Act 1988) applies:

- you have reasonable cause to believe that a medical reason prevents the use of a breath test;.
- the approved device for conducting a breath test is not available;
- you have cause to believe the approved device for a breath test gave an unreliable result;
- a preliminary drug-test result suggests you have reasonable cause to believe that the suspect has a drug in his/her body;
- the medical examiner has advised that the suspect's condition might be due to some drug, and you suspect an offence under s 4.

11.16.5.1 Evidential breath tests

The test can be required and conducted at (or near) a place where a relevant preliminary breath test has been administered, at a police station, or in a hospital (s 7(2), Road Traffic Act 1988). There is no need to have carried out a preliminary breath test if the suspect is being investigated for the offences of causing death by careless driving when under the influence of drink or drugs, or for being unfit to drive (ss 3A and 4, Road Traffic Act 1988 respectively).

Two samples of breath are required for the test. The process and period of time in which the two samples are collected by a breath-analysis device is referred to as a 'cycle'. Only the sample containing the lower proportion of alcohol will be used as evidence and the other will be disregarded (s 8(1), Road Traffic Act 1988).

The samples will be analysed by a device approved by the Secretary of State (currently the Camic Datamaster, the Lion Intoxilyzer 6000, or the Intoximeter EC/IR). The breath-test machine will be operated by someone who has been trained in its operation (often the custody officer) and it will first be tested to check that it is working properly. You must make sure that the MG DD forms are available to record the breath-test procedure as these completed forms will constitute your 'notes made at the time'.

When you require a person to take a breath test, you must warn him/her (s 7(7), Road Traffic Act 1988) that failing to provide a suitable specimen (two samples) may render him/her liable to prosecution. The volume of air provided in each sample must be sufficient for the analysis, and must be provided in such a way that the measurements can be made accurately (s 11(3), Road

Traffic Act 1988). If a sample has been affected by regurgitation of stomach contents this does not matter as it does not affect the accuracy of the measurements (see *Ryan McNeil v Director of Public Prosecutions* (2008) EWHC 1254). The number of opportunities to be made available for a suspect to provide two suitable samples will be determined by your organization's policy.

The prescribed limit for alcohol in the breath is 35 microgrammes of alcohol per 100 ml of breath (see 11.16.3 above). Some forces do not proceed with a s 5 prosecution unless the level is above 40 microgrammes; see your own organizational policy for the limit at which a person will be prosecuted. If the result is between 35 and 50 microgrammes of alcohol in 100 ml of breath the driver can choose to replace it with a blood or urine sample (s 8, Road Traffic Act 1988). This is known as the 'statutory option', and you must inform the driver that it is available. After the test, the MG DD forms are completed and if the result is above the prescribed limit the driver can be charged and bailed to court.

If the driver fails to provide two samples of breath (and refusal is equivalent to failure (s 11(2), Road Traffic Act 1988)) then he/she commits the offence of failing to provide a specimen of breath for an evidential breath test (s 7(6)). Failure includes when not enough breath is provided for the alcohol level to be measured accurately (see *Rweikiza v Director of Public Prosecutions* (2008) EWHC (Admin) 386). The suspect is not obliged to inform you of any medical condition which could prevent him/her from providing a sufficient volume of breath, but if the suspect later claims that a failure to provide a breath specimen was due to a medical condition, the court does not have to accept the excuse (see *Piggott v Director of Public Prosecutions* (2008) WLR (D) 44).

If the testing machine registers an error on the second sample of breath in each of two cycles you are entitled to require further breath samples. If the suspect fails to comply, he/she commits an offence of failing to provide a specimen (see *Asif Hussain v Director of Public Prosecutions* (2008) EWHC 901) even though previous samples were supplied. You must allow the suspect sufficient time to provide the samples in each subsequent cycle; if you do not (and the suspect does not supply adequate samples) a successful prosecution for failing to provide a specimen may not be possible (see *Plackett v DPP* (2008) EWHC 1335 (Admin)).

11.16.5.2 Blood and urine tests

These may either be requested by the suspect (the 'statutory option' see above), or be required under s 7(3) of the Road Traffic Act 1988 (see above). The requirement to provide a specimen of blood or urine can only be made at a police station or hospital.

Before such a blood or urine sample is taken you must tell the driver:

- the reason(s) why breath specimens cannot be taken (from the list under s 7(3) above); and
- that he/she is therefore required to give a sample of blood or urine; and
- that failing to provide the specimen could result in his/her prosecution.

Apart from medical considerations, the driver cannot choose whether the sample will be blood or urine; the choice is yours. Before proceeding with a blood test you should ask the driver if there are any medical reasons for not taking a blood sample. A blood sample must of course be taken by a medical examiner.

After the sample has been obtained the driver can be bailed to return to the police station when the results arrive back from the laboratory. Blood and urine samples are usually sent to the laboratory by post (refer to your own organizational policy).

If the driver refuses (or is unable) to provide blood or urine samples then he/she will have committed the offence of failing to provide samples for an evidential test (s 7(6), Road Traffic Act 1988).

11.16.5.3 Allowing for the delay between the offence and taking samples

As the human body continually breaks down alcohol it is assumed that the level of alcohol in a suspect's breath, blood, or urine at the time of an alleged offence will gradually decrease over time (if no more alcohol is consumed). It is a fact of law that a court will assume the level of intoxicants in the body at the time of the alleged offence were not less than the levels measured in the evidential test (s 15(2), Road Traffic Offenders Act 1988).

However, the accused may claim the 'hip-flask defence', insisting that he/she consumed alcohol or drugs **after** the offence but **before** the evidential sample was taken. If the accused can prove this, the assumption under s 15(2) (see previous paragraph) cannot be made. The accused might claim for example that he/she ran off after a collision and went for a drink before the police arrived, or that having been given a preliminary test, he/she consumed intoxicants from a container in the vehicle, such as the proverbial (and sometimes actual) hip flask, before the evidential specimen was taken. This is formally referred to as 'post-incident drinking'.

If a driver provides an evidential specimen and alleges he/she has consumed further intoxicants since the time of the alleged offence, the Forensic Science Service (FSS) (or a private laboratory) may advise that **back calculations** could be used to establish that the driver was in excess of the legal limit when the offence occurred. These calculations are based on the rate of elimination of alcohol from the driver's body, the time elapsed since the offence, and the subsequent consumption of alcohol.

Evidence for back calculations should be recorded on Form MG DD/D at the police station. However, if this defence is not raised until later, the FSS should be provided with as much information as can be obtained from the case papers and the officer in charge of the case.

The following information is relevant, where available:

- the type and quantity of alcohol consumed **before** the offence and, if possible, the times at which individual units of alcohol were consumed;
- the type and quantity of alcohol allegedly consumed **after** the offence but before the provision of a breath or laboratory specimen;
- the **driver's** characteristics: weight, height, build, age, sex, and any medical conditions;
- details of any **food** consumed from six hours before the offence until the provision of a breath or laboratory specimen;
- details of any **medication** taken regularly or within four hours prior to drinking.

11.16.6 Key Differences between ss 4 and 5 Road Traffic Act 1988 Offences

	s 4 'Unfit to drive'	s 5 'Over the prescribed limit'
Vehicle	Mechanically propelled vehicle; includes motor vehicles (see 11.16.1 above).	Motor vehicle only (see 11.16.1 above)
Offence	Unfit through drink or drugs.	The proportion of alcohol in breath (or blood or urine) exceeds the prescribed limit. Failing/refusing to provide a specimen.
Preliminary tests	Not mandatory. However if a motor vehicle is being used a drugs or impairment test can be carried out (assuming you have the equipment/have been trained).	Preliminary breath test required (unless arrested or being investigated for s3A or s4 offences).
Evidence	Impairment test, and blood or urine test results for drugs or alcohol (if available).	Breath, or blood, or urine test results for alcohol.
Arrest	The power is provided by s 24 of the PACE Act 1984 which requires you to have a reason why it is necessary, such as 'to allow the prompt and effective investigation of the offence'.	After a positive preliminary breath test the power to arrest (on suspicion that the proportion of alcohol in the person's breath or blood exceeds the prescribed limit) is provided by s 6D(1), Road Traffic Act 1988.
Power of entry	Power of entry to arrest. (Section 17(1)(c)(iiia), PACE Act 1984).	Power of entry (s 6E(1), Road Traffic Act 1988) for the purposes of: • making the requirement for a preliminary test • arresting on suspicion that the proportion of alcohol in the person's breath or blood exceeds the prescribed limit but only after an accident involving injury to any person.

> **TASK 16**
>
> 1. Find out what preliminary test equipment is available for you to use and how you use it. This information should be available at your police station or from your force policies documents.
>   - Would you only be authorized to use equipment to test for breath alcohol or could you test for drugs as well?
>   - Would you be able to carry out a preliminary impairment test?
> 2. The commission of a moving traffic offence is relevant to your power to require a driver to be tested for the presence of alcohol in his/her body. Find examples of moving traffic offences under the Public Passenger Vehicles Act 1981, the Road Traffic Regulation Act 1984, and the Road Traffic Offenders Act 1988.

11.17 Drink-driving, Drugs, and Admission to Hospital

Here we consider situations where a driver has been admitted to hospital after an accident (s 9, Road Traffic Act 1988). Before you make any requirement or carry out any test on the person, you must notify the medical practitioner in immediate charge of his/her case of your proposals for tests, explain the procedures, and give him/her the opportunity to object (s 9(1), Road Traffic Act 1988), as the welfare of a patient is of primary importance. A further complicating factor is that the suspect is also a patient and might be given drugs as part of his/her medical treatment, and these may interfere with the accuracy of alcohol and drugs tests carried out as part of a police investigation.

A hospital is defined by the Act to mean an institution which provides medical or surgical treatment for in-patients or out-patients. The term patient is not defined and will be a question of fact for the court to decide, but generally speaking a patient is a person who is currently on hospital grounds receiving medical treatment (or waiting to receive medical treatment).

11.17.1 Obtaining Samples from a Hospital Patient

The regulations governing such procedures are given in s 9(1) of the Road Traffic Act 1988. (A general description of preliminary and evidential tests is given in 11.16.4 and 11.16.5 above.) Before making any requirements you must notify the relevant medical practitioner (see above). The following paragraphs summarize the regulations.

11.17.1.1 Preliminary tests in a hospital

The doctor will object if the process is prejudicial to the care or treatment of the patient. If the doctor does not object, you may proceed to require the **patient** to cooperate with a preliminary test. If the result of the test is negative, you must explain to the patient that no further action will be taken with regard to tests for alcohol.

If the patient does not cooperate and refuses to have the test, you will need to report him/her for an offence under s 6(6) of the Road Traffic Act 1988. Remember, you cannot arrest a person for failing to cooperate with a preliminary test while he/she is a patient in a hospital (s 6D(3)).

11.17.1.2 Evidential Tests in a Hospital

If the result of the preliminary test is positive (or the patient fails to complete the test), you need to proceed to evidential tests. The outline procedure is shown below.

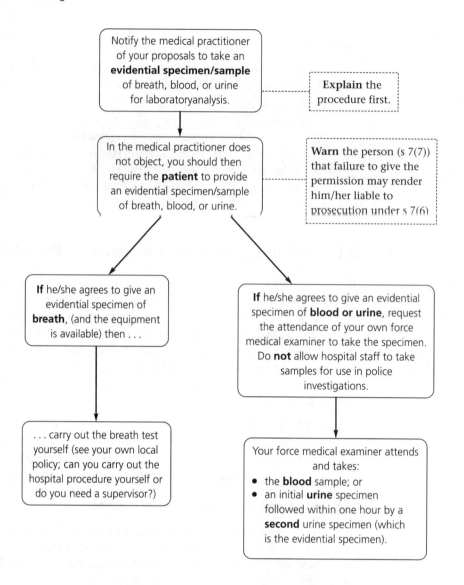

For a blood test, a police medical practitioner must take the specimen of blood. If this is not possible then another medical practitioner may be asked (this is very rare), but he/she should not have a responsibility for the clinical care of the patient.

11.17.2 Unconscious Patients and Tests for Drugs or Alcohol

Clearly an unconscious patient is not able to take part in a breath test and so a blood sample will be required, and once again you will need to notify the relevant medical practitioner (see 11.17.1 above and s 9(1A), Road Traffic Act 1988). It is not possible to seek consent from an unconscious patient but in these circumstances it is lawful for a medical practitioner to obtain a specimen of blood (s 7A(3)). However, this must not be subjected to a laboratory analysis unless the patient later gives permission (s 7A(4)), and if the patient refuses, he/she commits an offence (s 7A(6)).

TASK 17

Whilst on Independent Patrol you are required to attend the accident and emergency department at the local hospital. At the hospital you make a lawful requirement for a sample of breath, blood, or urine from a patient who was the driver of a vehicle at the time of a collision. Unfortunately, whilst waiting for your medical practitioner to arrive, the patient is discharged from hospital and leaves the building.

Does the obligation to provide that sample still stand? Refer to *Webber v DPP* [1998] RTR 111 for your answer.

11.18   Offences Related to Highways

There are a number of offences that relate to vehicles obstructing a highway or conducting other activities on a highway that might cause distress or inconvenience to other road users.

11.18.1   Wilful Obstruction

Wilful obstruction is an offence under s 137 of the Highways Act 1980. It is an offence for a person:

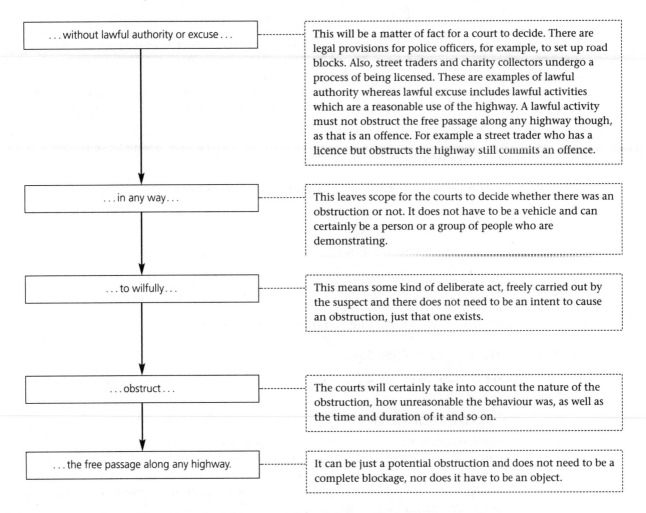

. . . without lawful authority or excuse . . .	This will be a matter of fact for a court to decide. There are legal provisions for police officers, for example, to set up road blocks. Also, street traders and charity collectors undergo a process of being licensed. These are examples of lawful authority whereas lawful excuse includes lawful activities which are a reasonable use of the highway. A lawful activity must not obstruct the free passage along any highway though, as that is an offence. For example a street trader who has a licence but obstructs the highway still commits an offence.
. . . in any way . . .	This leaves scope for the courts to decide whether there was an obstruction or not. It does not have to be a vehicle and can certainly be a person or a group of people who are demonstrating.
. . . to wilfully . . .	This means some kind of deliberate act, freely carried out by the suspect and there does not need to be an intent to cause an obstruction, just that one exists.
. . . obstruct . . .	The courts will certainly take into account the nature of the obstruction, how unreasonable the behaviour was, as well as the time and duration of it and so on.
. . . the free passage along any highway.	It can be just a potential obstruction and does not need to be a complete blockage, nor does it have to be an object.

This offence is triable summarily and the penalty is a fine.

11.18.2   Directing 'Unauthorized Campers' Away from the Roadside

Section 77 of the Criminal Justice and Public Order Act 1994 provides local authorities with the procedure for removing persons residing in vehicles 'on any land forming part of a highway; on any other unoccupied property, or on any occupied land without the consent of the owner'.

11.18.3   Vehicles or Trailers in a Dangerous Position on a Road

Section 22 of the Road Traffic Act 1988 states that it is an offence for a person in charge of a vehicle to cause or permit:

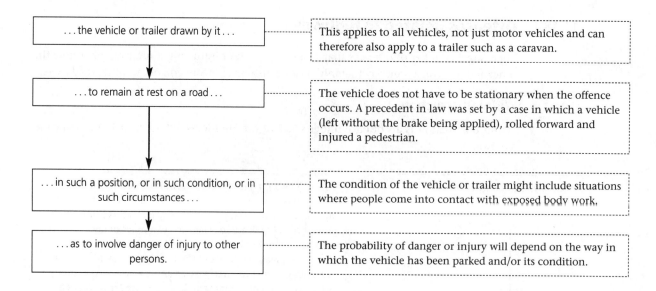

This offence is triable summarily, and the penalty is a fine.

11.18.4 Lighting Fires or Letting off Firearms near a Highway

Section 161 of the Highways Act 1980 prohibits any person (without lawful authority or excuse) from:

- depositing anything on a highway which leads to someone getting injured;
- lighting a fire on or over a carriageway; or
- discharging a firearm (or firework) within 50 feet of the centre of a highway, if it could injure a user of the highway.

This offence is triable summarily, and the penalty is a fine.

11.18.5 Interfering with Road Signs

Road users may be put at risk from other people interfering with road signs, other traffic equipment, or vehicles.

Traffic equipment is defined as:

- anything lawfully placed on or near a road by a highway authority;
- a traffic sign lawfully placed on or near a road by a person other than a highway authority;
- any fence, barrier, or light lawfully placed on or near a road (eg to protect street works), or any item placed by a constable (or other person) acting under the instructions (whether general or specific) of a chief officer of police.

Section 22A of the Road Traffic Act 1988 states that a person is guilty of an offence if intentionally and without lawful authority or reasonable cause they:

- cause anything to be on or over a road;
- interfere with a motor vehicle, trailer, or cycle; or
- interfere (directly or indirectly) with traffic equipment (see below).

This applies only if the activities would be regarded as obviously **dangerous** to a reasonable person or bystander (injury to a person, or damage to property is likely to occur). The reasonable person or bystander does not have to be a motorist (*DPP v D* [2006] EWHC 314) and it is irrelevant that the suspect was unaware of the potential danger. This will be a question of fact for the court to decide given the circumstances.

This offence is triable either way and the penalty is:

- summarily: six months' imprisonment and/or a fine;
- on indictment: seven years' imprisonment and/or a fine.

11.18.6   Repairing Vehicles in the Road

The repairing of vehicles in the street is a relatively common occurrence but may give rise to nuisance to other residents and may even cause environmental damage.

Under s 4 of the Clean Neighbourhoods and Environment Act 2005, a person commits an offence if he/she 'carries out restricted works on a motor vehicle on a road'. In this case **restricted works** means:

- the repair, maintenance, servicing, improvement, or dismantling of a motor vehicle or of any part of or accessory to a motor vehicle;
- the installation, replacement, or renewal of any such part or accessory.

However, no offence is committed if the works:

- were **not** carried out for gain or reward or as part of a business, and gave no reasonable cause for annoyance to persons in the vicinity; or
- arose from an accident or breakdown and repairs were necessary on the spot or carried out within 72 hours.

TASK 18

Several complaints have been made by the residents in the neighbourhood of a club. They say that at closing time they have seen people throwing rubbish bins and other items about the streets, tampering with traffic lights, and deflating vehicle tyres.
What offences might have been committed?

11.19   Answers to Tasks

TASK 1

As you approach and examine the vehicle, consider health and safety implications (see the answer to Task 6 below for more details). You need to consider gathering the following evidence:

1. whether the wheels of the car can rotate freely (at least one wheel appears to have seized)
2. whether the normal vehicular controls are operative (the steering appears locked)
3. whether the brakes are in working order, and
4. if the engine can be started.

In such cases (where proof is required to determine whether or not a motor vehicle is still a motor vehicle for the purposes of the Road Traffic Act 1988), evidence would be more appropriately obtained by a thorough examination by a qualified and authorized vehicle examiner. Your local procedure will explain how this can be arranged.

If the results of the examination reveal that the car can still be classified as a motor vehicle, then the van driver will be 'using' the car in a legal sense.

TASK 2

1. The form you will need is an HORT/1 (Home Office Road Traffic Form 1), known colloquially as a 'Horti'.
2. One major problem associated with the use of this form is that, if the driver has not given you details of his/her true identity, you will probably not be able to find the driver again and he/she will continue to drive, and will avoid prosecution.
3. Make checks of the details you are given:

   - always check the driver and vehicle details with the PNC to establish if they match;
   - use the PNC to check whether the driver has a criminal record;
   - request further proof of identity, for example passports and credit cards;
   - request a voters' register check through the control room;
   - request telephone numbers and ask control room to call the numbers to verify the existence of the person.

There may be no need to use an HORT/1 if the person's verified address is nearby.

TASK 3

You might ask the driver:

- if he is insured to drive the vehicle;
- the name of his insurance company;
- the starting and expiry date of his policy;
- the cost of the policy.

Further questions might include:

- What is the engine size of the vehicle in question?
- Has the vehicle been modified in any way?
- What type of vehicle (including the engine size) is he entitled to drive on his policy?

If you suspect that the engine size of the actual vehicle differs from the engine size described on the PNC, then request the vehicle to be examined by an authorized vehicle examiner.

On completion of your enquiries, contact the insurance company and speak to a police liaison representative of the company to determine exactly what type of vehicle the person is insured to drive.

TASK 4

The date of first registration can be obtained from the Certificate of Registration and/or the PNC.

Possible defences to not having a valid test certificate can be countered by asking the driver what was the starting point and what is the destination of his/her journey? If the answer to either of those questions involves the testing of the vehicle, then further questioning may be necessary to counter the possible defences of vehicles travelling to a **pre-arranged** test and where the vehicle has **failed the test**.

TASK 5

- Use your investigative skills to locate the user or keeper by accessing the PNC or undertaking house-to-house ('H2H') enquiries in the vicinity of the vehicle.
- If you cannot find the driver or keeper, use a DVLA form CLE 2/8 (from your stationery store (or from administration) at your police station). There are a number of other ways of notifying DVLA of a vehicle not displaying a licence including completing and submitting an online form at <http://www.dvla.gov.uk/onlineservices/report_unlicensed.aspx>.

TASK 6

As you approach the vehicle, think of health and safety implications and consider the potential problems associated with the:

- driver attempting to move off in the vehicle;
- traffic passing by the location;
- engine running;
- driver making off;
- location of the ignition keys;
- handbrake not being applied.

You could follow the following sequence:

1. Speak to driver and introduce yourself.
2. Outline your reason for stopping the vehicle.
3. Ask the driver for his/her name, address, and date of birth.
4. Ask the driver for his/her connection with the vehicle (is he/she the owner too?).
5. Ask the driver for details of his/her intended destination and the place where he/she began the journey.

6. Examine the vehicle whilst considering the potential health and safety implications associated with:
   - moving parts inside the engine compartment such as thermostatically controlled cooling fans;
   - high temperatures associated with parts such as brakes, exhaust systems, radiators, and engines;
   - harmful liquids such as hydraulic fluids, battery acid, anti-freeze, and hot engine coolant;
   - sharp objects such as exposed tyre cords or faulty bodywork;
   - movement of the vehicle and anything in, on, or under the vehicle;
   - movement of other vehicles and persons around you;
   - the surface upon which you and the vehicle are positioned and the existence of harmful objects or substances.
7. Note any possible offence(s) detected in the usual way, through gathering evidence using your senses (that is, what you saw, felt, smelt, and so on).
8. Point out the possible offence(s) to the driver.
9. Caution the driver using the 'when questioned' form described in 8.4 above and ensure that you satisfy the PACE Act 1984, Code C 10.2 (for example, explain to the driver that he/she does not have to remain with you).
10. Write down questions and answers about the offences in your PNB, for example when the person last inspected their vehicle, how long ago did he/she begin her or his journey, was he/she already aware of the defect?
11. Offer the PNB entry to the driver to read and sign that the notes are a true record of the interview.
12. Report the driver for the offences.
13. Caution the driver.

TASK 7

How did your list compare?

No vehicle is permitted to use blue flashing lights unless it belongs to a defined list (such as police vehicles); however, the number of types of vehicles so permitted continues to grow. A recent decision was made to allow 'vehicles owned by HM Revenue and Customs and used in pursuit of serious crime to be fitted with blue warning beacons' (Explanatory Memorandum to the Road Vehicles Lighting (Amendment) Regulations 2005 No 2559).

TASK 8

1. **True.** The term 'hours of darkness' refers to a period in time which is half an hour after sunset to a half an hour before sunrise.
2. **False.** It is the Road Vehicles Lighting Regulations 1989 as amended by the Road Vehicles Lighting (Amendment) Regulations 1994.
3. **False.** The correct rate is 60 to 120 pulses per minute.
4. **False.** The lawful circumstances are:

   (a) while stationary to warn other road users of a temporary obstruction
   (b) to summon assistance to the driver, conductor, or inspector of a bus (PSV)
   (c) on a motorway or unrestricted dual carriageway to warn following drivers of the need to slow down due to a temporary obstruction ahead
   (d) in the case of a school bus, while loading or unloading (or about to do so) passengers (under 16 years of age) provided the bus displays the statutory yellow reflective signs indicating the presence of schoolchildren.

5. **True.**
6. **True.**
7. **True.**

TASK 9

1. The order is as follows, with percentages for 2005:

Order	Factor	Percentage of fatal collisions/accidents*
(d)	Driver/rider error or reaction (eg loss of control, failure to look properly)	64%
(c)	Injudicious action (eg exceeding speed limit, going too fast for conditions)	32%
(f)	Behaviour or inexperience (eg careless, reckless, or in a hurry; aggressive driving)	29%
(e)	Impairment or distraction (eg impaired by alcohol, illness, or disability)	19%
(a)	Road environment (eg road layout, slippery road)	12%
(g)	Vision affected (eg by road layout, dazzling sun)	8%
(b)	Vehicle defects (eg defective tyres, defective brakes)	3%

(* Note that the total is over 100% as some collisions/accidents have more than one contributory factor.)

2. Some of the ways in which you might be able to help reduce the number of deaths in subsequent years are to be found in the Roads Policing Strategy agreed between ACPO, DoT and Home Office in 2005 and which can be found at: < www.dft.gov.uk/pgr/roadsafety/drs/roadpolicingcommitment.pdf>

They include investigation of the following offences:

- excessive and inappropriate speeding;
- failure to wear seatbelts;
- drink- and drug-driving; and
- careless, dangerous, and generally threatening driving and riding.

In 2007 ACPO also issued practice advice on roads policing, available at <http://www.acpo.police.uk/asp/policies/Data/Policing-of-Roads.pdf>.

TASK 10

See the Highway Code for answers. The Highway Code is available online at <http://www.direct.gov.uk/en/TravelAndTransport/Highwaycode/DG_070190>.

You can also practise your understanding online via the DSA website at <http://www.theory-tests.co.uk/home/>.

TASK 11

1a Driver is unable to produce driving documents	**1b** Fixed-penalty notice offence	**1c** VDRS offence
Make requirement for each document to be produced **Produced:** examine and record details of any document produced in PNB **Not produced:** • point out offence • caution + 2 • questions and answers • complete + issue HORT/1 • report the suspect • caution ('now' version).	**NON-ENDORSABLE FPN** Driver present: • point out offence • caution + 2 • question and answers • complete and issue NEFPN • report the suspect • caution ('now' version). Driver not present: • complete and affix NEFPN to vehicle. **ENDORSABLE FPN** • point out offence • caution + 2 • questions and answers • offer FPN in lieu of court • report the suspect • caution ('now' version). **Accepted and licence available** • less than 12 points and driving licence surrendered—issue full FPN • 12 points or more—report the suspect. **Accepted and licence unavailable: issue provisional FPN.** **Not accepted:** no further action on the street.	• Point out offence • Caution + 2 • Questions and answers • Offer VDRS (voluntary) • Report the suspect • Caution ('now' version). **Accepted:** issue VDRS **Not Accepted:** no further action on the street.

2. The following are all offences (with section numbers) for which you can issue a non-endorsable fixed-penalty notice

Road Traffic Act 1988

14	No seatbelt—adult, front or rear
15(2)	No seatbelt—child in front of vehicle
15(4)	No seatbelt—child in rear of vehicle
16	No helmet—motorcycles
19	Parking LCV on verge or footway
22	Leaving vehicle in dangerous position
23	Unlawful carrying of passengers on motorcycles
24	More than one person on a pedal cycle
34	Driving a motor vehicle off-road
35	Failure to comply with traffic directions
36	Failure to comply with traffic signs
40A	Using vehicle in dangerous condition, etc
41A	Construction & Use Regulations relating to brakes, steering, and tyres
41B	Construction & Use Regulations relating to weight (goods and passenger vehicles)

42	Other Construction & Use Regulations relating to lighting offences
87(1)	Driving other than in accordance with a driving licence
163	Failing to stop vehicle for constable in uniform
172	Failing to notify the police of driver's identity

Highways Act 1835

| 72 | Cycling on the footway (not Scotland) |

Highways Act 1980

| 137 | Obstruction of highway by a vehicle |

Road Traffic Regulation Act 1984

5(1)	Contravention of Traffic Regulation Order outside London
8(1)	Contravention of Traffic Regulation Order inside London
11	Breach of experimental traffic order
13	Breach of experimental traffic scheme inside London
16(1)	Use of vehicle against temporary prohibition/restriction orders at roadworks
17(4)	Contravention of motorway regulations
18(3)	Contravention of one-way traffic on trunk road
20(5)	Contravention of restriction/prohibition of use of vehicle on a particular road
25(5)	Breach of pedestrian crossing regulations
29(3)	Use of vehicle in street playground
35A(1)	On-road parking restrictions, etc
47(1)	Failure to pay excess charge at parking place
53(5)	Breach of parking place Designation Order, etc
53(6)	Breach of parking place Designation Order, etc
88(7)	Contravention of minimum speed limit
89(1)	Speeding offences

Vehicle Excise and Registration Act 1994

33	Using or keeping vehicle without excise licence
42	Driving or keeping vehicle without registration mark
43	Driving or keeping a vehicle with obscured registration mark
43C	Using incorrectly registered vehicle

Road Vehicles (Display of Registration Marks) Regulations 2001

| | Registration mark not in prescribed format |

Greater London Council (General Powers) Act 1974

| 59 | Parking on footways, verges, etc |

Zebra, Pelican and Puffin Pedestrian Crossing Regulations and General Directions 1997

| Reg 24 | Overtaking a moving or stationary vehicle in controlled area of a crossing |

TASK 12

The legislation that gives you the power to implement such a policy is s 6A of the Road Traffic Act 1988. Whilst in uniform or not, if you reasonably believe that a person:

- is driving;
- has been driving;
- is attempting to drive; or
- is in charge of a motor vehicle

on a road or public place at the time of an accident, you may require the person to cooperate with one or more preliminary tests including a breath test. You must be in uniform to administer the test.

The computer checks that you are likely to carry out on the drivers involved include:

(a) a PNC check to:
- discover if the driver is wanted, or disqualified from driving;
- ascertain if there are any reports regarding the vehicles being stolen;
- establish details of the keepers of the vehicles

(b) local checks to determine whether the drivers' names and addresses are valid and/or if they are locally wanted on warrant.

TASK 13

1. (a) Jerry is driving.
   (b) Maz is not driving
   (c) Both Hari and Pat are driving.
2. (a) (ii) and (iii): It applies on a road or in a public place.
   (b) (i): It applies anywhere.

TASK 14

1. Using a hand-held mobile telephone (mobile) while driving could easily amount to failing to have proper control of the vehicle, or even dangerous driving (see 11.13.1 above).
2. Other 'careless driving' activities may include lighting a cigarette, turning round and shouting at children, searching for a station on the radio, changing CDs, looking for sun glasses, looking in the mirror and applying make-up, or any other similar action that diverts the attention from driving.

TASK 15

1. Knowing that he/she was likely to be disqualified from driving, a person might contact the DVLA to obtain a duplicate licence before the court hearing and then submit one or the other of his/her licences and keep one which he/she could produce to you in the future. Alternatively, the person could obtain a stolen licence and produce it to assume the identity of another person (if it was an old-style licence without a photograph).
2. You should carry out PNC checks, local database checks such as the voters' register, and question the person about his/her identity to match the details given to you with the details held on police computer databases. Your local knowledge will be very important here as you will be able to ask about the description of localities and names of places to help verify the identity of the driver.

TASK 16

1. Currently there are two types of preliminary test that can be administered to trigger further investigations into the possible level of intoxication of people in control of different forms of transport. One of these tests relates to the consumption of alcohol and the other to the use of drugs.
   You will most probably receive training quite early on in the use of an Electronic Breath Screening Device (ESD) which will be a type approved by the Secretary of State. This training will enable you to administer preliminary breath tests for alcohol. The equipment is usually

a hand-held device which will be issued to you during Supervised Patrol. There will be a need to change the mouthpiece into which the suspect will exhale breath each time you carry out a test and you will be trained in the procedure for assembling the equipment and interpreting the tests results.

A preliminary drug test on the other hand is a procedure whereby a specimen of sweat or saliva is obtained and, through the use of a device approved by the Secretary of State, an indication is given as to whether or not the person to whom the test is administered has a drug in his or her body. Currently, each force has different policies relating to which members of staff can carry out this procedure and therefore you might not be trained in the use of such a device straight away.

You can only carry out a preliminary impairment test if you are approved for that purpose by the chief officer of the police force to which you belong.

2. Moving traffic offences include:
   • contravention of traffic regulations, for example speed limits;
   • failing to comply with traffic signs and directions, for example traffic lights.

TASK 17

Yes, in such circumstances, the required sample may then be taken at a police station, regardless of whether an appropriate breath-analysis machine is available. See *Webber v DPP* [1998] RTR 111.

TASK 18

Section 22A of the Road Traffic Act 1988 states that a person is guilty of an offence if he/she intentionally and without lawful authority or reasonable cause:

(a) causes anything to be on or over a road
(b) interferes with a motor vehicle, trailer or cycle, or
(c) interferes (directly or indirectly) with traffic equipment.

12 | Intelligence and Criminal Investigation

12.1 Chapter Briefing

In this chapter we start by examining the forms of intelligence available to the police and set these in the context of the National Intelligence Model. We then look at a number of aspects of criminal investigation, including the use of interviews, the need to 'record, retain, and reveal' certain materials, and preparing and submitting case files. Finally we illustrate some of the issues surrounding giving evidence in court.

12.1.1 Aim of the Chapter

This chapter examines in detail the place of open and closed intelligence and how it is used to support policing objectives. We also aim to provide the background you need to meet the more general requirement to conduct investigations and, if required, to present evidence to a court.

This chapter will enable you to:

- understand the meaning and importance of intelligence in a policing context;
- appreciate the place of the NIM in policing;
- develop your skills in interviewing;
- appreciate how CPIA affects the way you conduct investigations;
- understand when 'bad-character' evidence may be used;
- identify case papers relevant to your investigation;
- develop your ability to give evidence in court;
- develop the underpinning knowledge required for a number of NOS elements, several of the PAC headings, and entries for your Learning Diary Phase 3 and the CARs of your SOLAP.

12.1.2   Police Action Checklist

This chapter will provide you with some of the underlying knowledge and theory to meet the following requirements of the Police Action Checklist.

12.1.2.1   Investigation

- Interview—conduct a witness interview using the PEACE model.
- Interview—conduct a suspect interview using the PEACE model.

12.1.2.2   Finalize investigations

- Adhere to court procedures.
- Give evidence at court.

12.1.3   National Occupational Standards

This chapter will provide you with some of the knowledge required to demonstrate aspects of the following NOS elements:

National Occupational Standards Elements

CI101.1 Conduct priority and volume investigations

CJ101.1 Plan and prepare interviews with victims and witnesses

CJ101.2 Conduct interviews with victims and witnesses

CJ101.3 Evaluate interviews with victims and witnesses and carry out post-interview processes

CJ201.1 Plan and prepare interviews with suspects

CJ201.2 Conduct interviews with suspects

CJ201.3 Evaluate interviews with suspects and carry out post-interview processes

2G4.1   Finalize investigations

12.1.4   IPLDP Phases and Modules

This chapter will provide you with resources to support the following Operational Modules, and Legislation, Policy, and Guidelines of the IPLDP:

OP 2   Obtain, evaluate, and submit information and intelligence to support local priorities

OP 3   Respond to incidents, conduct and evaluate investigations

OP 6   Prepare, conduct, and evaluate interviews

OP 9   Prepare and present case information, present evidence, and finalize investigations

---

The aspects of Legislation, Policy, and Guidelines are:

- Crime (LPG 1.1);
- Investigation and Interview (LPG 1.7).

12.1.5   SOLAP

The contents of this chapter are relevant to the 'knowledge' evidence requirements of CARs CI101, CJ101, CJ201, and 2G4.

12.1.6   Learning Diary Phases

The contents of this chapter may provide you with stimulus material for completion of your Learning Diary (Phase 3) and the following headings in particular:

- Crime;
- Police policies and procedures;
- Investigation and interview.

12.2   **Introduction**

This chapter is concerned with intelligence (both open and closed forms) and the process of criminal investigation, including interviewing and giving evidence in court. We have included intelligence and investigation in the same chapter as they are often linked in practice.

The ability to undertake the successful investigation of volume crimes (see 13.2 below) is considered to be a fundamental skill of a police officer, but is perhaps also one of the more demanding parts of the role. It is perhaps a cliché to say that 'all police officers are also investigators' but it is certainly true to note that the development of investigative skills will feature extensively in your training. Past inadequacies in police investigation of crime are well documented (eg Macpherson, 1999) and recent years have seen determined efforts by the police (previously centred on the work of NCPE under the leadership of Sir David Phillips, now under the stewardship of the NPIA) to improve the levels of knowledge and skills of all investigators.

You may encounter the IPLDP 'Crime Investigation Model' during Phases 3 and 4 of training if your force uses IPLDP nomenclature. The IPLDP Crime Investigation Model consists of seven stages: instigation, initial response, investigative assessment, suspect management, evidence assessment, charge and post-charge activity, and finally court (Home Office, 2004c).

In other chapters we have already examined many aspects of the IPLDP's seven stages and we discuss most of the remaining ones in this chapter. However, during initial training you may also be taught a model of investigation drawn from the NCPE Practice Advice on Core Investigative Doctrine (Home Office, 2005d), which posits five groups of tasks: initial investigation, scene management, further investigation, investigative and evidential evaluation, and finally, suspect and case management. There are a number of activities within these groups of tasks, which we have interpreted below.

The links between Core Investigation Doctrine and NOS Units

Core investigative doctrine activity	Example of activity	Linked NOS units
Initial Report	Control room instruction, incident log, etc	BE2
Police Response	Risk assessment, recording the incident, etc	BE2, CJ101, CK1, CK2, CD1
Scene Attendance	Provide immediate support to victims, etc	CI101, 4G4
Crime Scene Assessment	CPIA 1996, protecting the scene, minimizing contamination, etc	CD1
Witnesses	Identify and question witnesses, CCTV, etc	CI101
Information/Intelligence	Force intelligence reports, CHIS, etc	CI101
Suspect?	Initial lines of enquiry, description, names, etc	CI101
Enquiries to trace offender	PNC, NDNAD	CI101
Arrest	Arrest strategy, PACE Act 1984/SOCPA 2005 powers of arrest, etc	CD5
Searches	Legal authority, seizure of items, proportionality, etc	DA5, DA6
Custody Procedures	Escort to custody, give grounds for detention, etc	CJ101, CJ201
Interview(s)	PEACE, interview strategy, etc	CJ101, CJ201
Charge, Caution, Bail, NFA (No Further Action), etc	CPS charging standards, prepare case files, evaluate investigation, etc	DA5, DA6, 2G4

(Based on Home Office, 2005e)

The Core Investigative Doctrine informed the development of PIP Level 1 (see 3.10 above) which you are also expected to attain before the end of your initial training.

Whichever model of investigation you are asked to apply, remember that you will at the same time be collecting evidence towards the achievement of the NOS, and your involvement in investigations will provide many opportunities for this. For example, when you respond to an incident you will make entries in your pocket notebook and record statements, both of which can be used towards the achievement of a number of units.

An important change in recent years is an attempt to 'recast' the process of investigation as a 'seeking after the truth' rather than the 'building of a case' against a suspect from the outset. (This is not to say that case building does not feature in investigation; it is just that it should not be the focus.) What this means in practice is that you will be expected to pursue just as vigorously those reasonable lines of enquiry which point towards the innocence of the suspect(s) as you do for those that point towards guilt, and you need to be **seen to have done so**. We have reflected this more modern approach to investigation throughout the remainder of this chapter in a number of key ways: our approach to describing intelligence, our case study description of interview and giving evidence at court, and our decision to introduce you to the complex area of 'disclosure'.

Finally, note that the following legislation is relevant to undertaking investigations:

- The Criminal Justice and Public Order Act 1994 (CJPOA);
- The Police and Criminal Evidence Act 1984 (PACE) and Codes of Practice 2004;
- The Criminal Procedure and Investigations Act 1996 (CPIA);
- The Human Rights Act 1998 (HRA);
- The Regulation of Investigatory Powers Act 2000 (RIPA);
- The Serious Organised Crime and Police Act 2005 (SOCPA).

12.3 The National Intelligence Model

Here, we will examine in detail the National Intelligence Model (NIM) and how it relates to the wider needs of the police for useful, accurate, and timely intelligence concerning criminal activity. An understanding of the NIM is an important requirement for student police officers, and it features either explicitly or implicitly within many parts of the IPLDP, including PIP Level 1, the IND modules, and particularly the OP 2 module. The NIM was launched by NCIS in 2000, and police forces throughout England and Wales are expected to adopt the model in their day-to-day work.

We might note, in passing, that for crime at Level 3 the national intelligence agencies link closely with the police. HM Revenue and Customs, for example, has an investigation branch (now part of the Serious Organized Crime Agency) which uses intelligence-led principles to track illegal imports (of any kind: drugs, people, contraband), and the Security Service (MI5) uses intelligence to counter threats to national (internal) security.

12.3.1 The Definition of Intelligence

The NIM has obviously some connection with the concept of 'intelligence'. Intelligence, in the investigative context, may be considered a form of information, but of a special kind—that is, it is information which has taken on meaning.

Simply put, the police deal with three distinguishable forms of incoming data:

- **Information:** normally from a source that needs no confidentiality constraints or protection. It is overt information such as a call from the public advising the police of an occurrence.
- **Intelligence:** is more difficult to define but is generally considered to be information derived from many sources (some confidential) that has been recorded, graded, and evaluated.
- **Evidence:** can be either of the above, and is generally material that is capable of being admitted in a court of law and abides by the 'rules of evidence'—that is to say, it is admissible.

It is essential that a police officer is able to recognize these three forms of data as each requires different types of action.

For example, we may have information concerning an increase in the number of thefts of radios from cars in a particular area. If we link this information to a change in payment policy by a local drug dealer (who is now accepting goods in lieu of money in payment for drugs) we begin to derive intelligence from the information.

In an open society information is freely available, but most criminal intelligence is not. In fact, criminals will usually go to some lengths to prevent knowledge about what they do leaking out. Criminals will often seek to protect key questions about a crime or a criminal, such as:

- Who did it?
- Who is going to do it?
- When?
- Where?
- How?
- Why?

Finding out about criminal intentions before a crime is committed, or using covert (hidden) methods after a crime has been committed, is one aspect of **intelligence-led policing** (ILP).

Perhaps a more detailed practical example will help at this point. In one county a series of crimes were committed in which luxury cars were stolen from garage forecourts, taken to a criminal dealer (often called a fence), and quickly disposed of in Europe. This was a major criminal business and very lucrative, resulting in millions of pounds for the dealers. Conventional policing would usually focus on making it harder to steal the cars and then target the thieves. Intelligence-led policing does not rule out such preventive or investigative methods, but would also bring the disciplines of **assessed intelligence**, **crime analysis**, and a **targeting 'package'** to bear on the crime series, and would focus initially on the dealers rather than the thieves. In the case above, within six weeks the use of intelligence had identified the major dealers, an operation was mounted, and three dealers were arrested and charged. The evidence against them, including some of the tracked stolen cars, was convincing and each received a custodial sentence. In the interim, the conduit for selling-on stolen luxury cars was blocked, and it was a relatively simple matter to clean up the front end of theft; the thieves had lost their usual buyers for the stolen vehicles and made the mistake of trying to sell the cars to undercover police officers.

You will have noticed that a number of words in the case study have been highlighted. This is because these are key concepts in intelligence-led policing which we consider below. However, first we need to look at the central reasoning behind intelligence-led policing, and that is found in the National Intelligence Model, usually referred to as the NIM.

12.3.2 Key features of the NIM

The Home Office describes the NIM as 'a validated model of policing [...] representing best practice in the use of intelligence to fight crime' (Home Office, 2001, p45). All police forces in England and Wales are required to implement the NIM. The NIM is also utilized by the Serious and Organised Crime Agency (SOCA), other agencies such as the UK Border Agency, and the local CDRPs.

The NIM should perhaps be clearly distinguished from Intelligence-led Policing (ILP) although the two are often juxtaposed. (For example, the 2007 ACPO practice advice 'Introduction to Intelligence-led Policing' is almost entirely devoted to the NIM, and the Bichard Inquiry explains that the purpose of the NIM is to 'enhance intelligence-led policing' (Bichard, 2004, p119).) The key difference between the two is that whereas ILP is essentially concerned with using intelligence to counter crime, the NIM is more concerned with using intelligence to determine priorities for policing.

The following is a diagram of the model in relation to decisions on the use and gathering of intelligence:

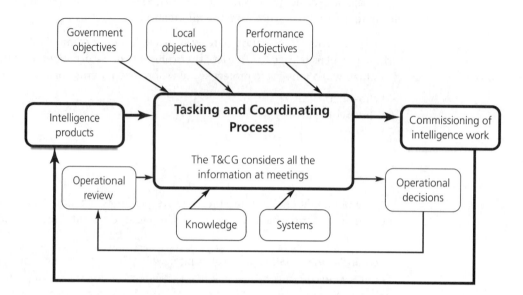

The bold lines indicate the key aspects of the process and emphasize the use of intelligence products to determine what further intelligence work needs to be commissioned. It is a continual cycle of policy development, implementation, and review, and bears some resemblance to Kolb's learning cycle, referred to in Chapter 4.

The key part of the process is in the centre; the **Tasking and Coordinating Process**, overseen by Tasking and Coordination Groups (**T&CG**). The Tasking and Coordinating Process determines the operational responses to crime and disorder, and prioritizes intelligence requirements (such as identifying crime hot spots, or obtaining information about a series of burglaries). The process is conducted at three levels to correspond with the specified levels of incident:

- Level 1 (local BCU level) in relation to local crime capable of being managed by local resources (which may include the most serious crime) and anti-social behaviour;
- Level 2 (force and regional) in relation to force, inter-force, and regional criminal activity, usually requiring additional resources;
- Level 3 (national) in relation to the most serious and organized crime.

The classification of the crime is significant for resources. A single BCU does not have the resources to cope with, say, a group of criminal associates mounting robberies from ATMs (cash machines) across the force area. In such instances, there is a need for a force-level response, which is usually coordinated and directed centrally. Most forces will have a **Strategic-level T&CG** which will deal with serious level 2 crime. Level 3 crime is dealt with by linking with national agencies such as the Serious Organized Crime Agency (SOCA), in cooperation with its international counterparts. Whether on a national, regional, or local scale, the use of assessed intelligence to inform operational decision making follows the same principles as set out in the NIM. Care must be taken not to confine work to these levels in isolation. Issues at the next level must be taken into account to ensure that opportunities are not missed, and that appropriate resources are applied.

At the heart of the business process are the **Strategic Tasking and Coordination Group** (Strategic T&CG) meetings. The purpose of these meetings is to initiate a **Control Strategy** which establishes the intelligence requirement and sets the agenda for prevention, intelligence, and enforcement priorities. The Strategic T&CG do not routinely determine the operational tactics to be deployed but maintain an overview of priorities. So, for example, if the Strategic T&CG required that ATM machine raids are to be made a priority (based on intelligence analysis) then specialist operations (such as surveillance and CHIS recruitment) would be 'tasked' specifically to challenge this criminal network. Strategic issues are considered every six months at force-level Strategic T&CG meetings. Members of a Strategic T&CG include the force-wide senior management team, intelligence specialists, crime analysts, and other senior staff as required.

A second category of T&CG meetings also takes place: the **Tactical Tasking and Coordination Group** meetings. At a BCU level (level 1) the Tactical T&CG meets at least every two weeks and comprises the senior supervisory officers and support staff from the local Area. Their purpose is to apply the planned response to the Control Strategy, review progress, and make changes to plans if judged appropriate. They can call on other agencies to assist in tactical decisions, but there is generally not such a wide range of senior staff present at Tactical T&CG meetings (as at Strategic T&CG meetings).

12.3.3 The Tasking and Coordinating Process

The Strategic T&CG has to take all of the above influences and information into account (including the level of available resources) and then determine the Control Strategy.

12.3.3.1 Inputs to the tasking and coordinating process

The T&CGs are informed by intelligence products which have been researched and written by analysts working with police officers. Both the strategic planning at force level and the local-tasking operational planning at BCU level are guided by these intelligence products and other forms of analysis.

Strategic Assessments are long-term strategy documents, usually produced every six months and **Tactical Assessments** review the progress of current operations and approaches. The T&CGs also commission, and are subsequently informed by, two further types of intelligence product:

* **target/subject profiles** about named offenders, victims, or networks; and
* **problem profiles** about issues of concern (such as a hot spot or increased availability of a particular street drug).

Analysts will use information from police (and other) databases as a source of information (sometimes known as 'systems products') as well as information contributed by officers in the force (see 12.4.5 below for further details).

The decisions taken by the T&CG will be influenced by a number of other factors such as:

* **Government objectives:** for example to raise the profile of thefts from cars, or dealing with public order issues.
* **Local objectives:** including force objectives, such as dealing with problem families, problem estates, local disorder, and so on. These views will have been canvassed both by the police, through community liaison officers, and through local government councillors, local authority officials, and other parts of local government. All will be conveyed to the area or BCU commander (usually a superintendent) through routine meetings and consultations, and will be arranged into local objectives.
* **Performance objectives:** the long-term (yearly) objectives for the BCU will also be taken into account. These may be to develop strategies to reduce all crime locally (and might include reducing burglaries by a specific percentage, for example), or dealing with anti-social behaviour, or arrest rates, or 'brought to justice' data. These determine the BCU Commander's strategic approach.
* **Knowledge:** the professional knowledge required by staff in order to contribute fully to the NIM and other aspects of police work. It includes knowledge of legislation, codes of practice, and force policies.
* **Systems:** the IT systems and associated procedures for the storage, retrieval, analysis, and dissemination of intelligence information.

12.3.3.2 Outputs from the tasking and coordinating process

Implementation of the Control Strategy will include the commissioning of new intelligence work and making operational decisions to improve the management of crime and the local community. Teams may be assembled to tackle particular issues, and budgets set; the overtime budget is frequently of particular significance.

As well as the weekly or fortnightly Tactical T&CG meetings at BCU level there are likely to be daily meetings to monitor and direct daily aspects of police work. The daily meetings (sometimes known as 'Intelligence—Daily Briefing' meetings, or more colloquially in some forces as 'Morning Prayers') are not full T&CG meetings but they are part of the process of ensuring that the T&CG strategy is implemented and kept on track.

12.3.4 Links with the Wider Policing Role

The full picture is considered at T&CG meetings, of which the intelligence on criminal matters is only a part. For example, it would not be appropriate for the T&CG to recommend an operation targeting thefts from cars when local priorities were largely focused on reducing alcohol-related violence. (That said, operational command rests with the BCU Commander, and it may be that disrupting car thefts is judged to be a temporary but urgent priority.) These are the types of issue that are dealt with at a T&CG meeting.

It sounds highly complex (and some aspects of planning strategies against crime present particular challenges) but the NIM is intended to be the engine room that drives the policing machine. Police officers undertake much of their non-reactive work at the direction of the T&CG, in order that policing in their area is coordinated, specific, and focused. The NIM seems to work, at least in parts, and its results are at least measurable.

Underpinning this central process are assumptions of what policing is about, within the overall concept of the NIM. If crime is managed adequately through the T&C process, then the community should be safer, crime should be reduced, criminals will be arrested or have their activities disrupted, hot spots will be managed, and potentially dangerous offenders will be controlled, or their capacities blunted (see John and Maguire (2003) for a recent analysis of the NIM).

12.3.5 The NIM in Practice

To illustrate the way in which the model works, rather than simply describing its components, we will track through a crime from start to finish.

Suppose we receive reports of an 'artifice burglary'. In this context 'artifice' crime is when a criminal uses trickery to gain admission to a person's house. The usual victims are elderly people living alone (in fact, statistically, very elderly), and a clever, plausible artifice burglar could easily commit ten offences in the same locality in a day. Not all artifice crimes are reported, either because the victim is unaware at first that the burglary has occurred (it might be some days before an object is noted as missing), or because the victim is reluctant to be involved with the police. Artifice burglars usually commit 'spree offences' (a series of similar crimes within a short period of time). This is likely to be because the net haul from each residence is relatively small.

The reports of artifice burglary enter the process as information and a key early requirement will be for analysts to assess the criminal's *modus operandi* (MO): the type and location of targeted property, the methods and tricks used to gain entry, the type of items stolen, and so on. The findings may be incorporated into a subject profile (if the offender is known) or a problem profile (if the identity of the offender has not yet been established).

The T&CG may then task police staff responsible for gathering intelligence to find out whether there is access to this type of criminal (perhaps through a regular 'fence'), and whether there is knowledge locally of such individuals. (As distinct from usual burglary, where the burglar's home and the crime scenes are usually just a few kilometres apart, artifice burglars do not tend to 'work their own patch', perhaps because they run the risk of being recognized.)

The T&CG will assign a **priority** to the investigation of the artifice burglary and will commission further work (for example by the R&D units of Intel), which will include checking the force's criminal databases, matching any other likely spree offences elsewhere in the force area, or in neighbouring forces. Analysts may note, for example, that the offences have all taken place within half a mile of a railway station, in which case the force may approach British Transport Police for help, and any CCTV footage may be scrutinized.

Suppose the frequency of artifice burglaries increases, and one of the victims falls ill due to the shock of what happened (quite a common occurrence). This may increase the perceived need to catch the perpetrators. Therefore, at the next T&CG meeting, the priority level of the case will be raised and operational plans will be developed to attempt to tackle the problem further. Possibly at the back of the BCU Commander's mind will be the government's **objectives**, local feelings about the nature of the crime, media pressures, and the chances of catching the culprit.

Now imagine that a CHIS (a police informant, normally paid for information: see 12.4.1 below) gives useful information to his/her handler and a report is submitted. It is assessed by the research and development unit and compared with other intelligence. We now have a name, a preferred location, and a clear idea of the MO. An operation is mounted, two people are arrested, and a case is prepared. The final outcome could well be a prison sentence but equally, a caution (possibly the new conditional caution), a fine, seizure of assets, or community service. Other outcomes might include displacing the activity of artifice burglars elsewhere, the development and implementation of a crime reduction (prevention or disruption) strategy, and probably some useful media coverage.

The NIM process has led to an assessment of the nature of the crime, to tasking the intelligence-gathering parts of the force, and giving the crime a higher priority level in the midst of competing claims for attention. The newly acquired intelligence was assessed and used to develop a package of operational measures through the T&CG, the resulting police action disrupted that type of crime, and it probably reassured the community to some extent.

This is a simple example of the **business-process model of policing**, and the same principles will operate whether the issue is the vandalizing of cars or a more serious crime enquiry, such as the systematic robbing of cash machines (ATMs).

An early evaluation of the NIM was published in 2004 (John and Maguire, 2004) using the results of fieldwork carried out in 2002 but based only on the implementation of the model in three police areas. A total of ten recommendations were made, centred on a lack of understanding of the NIM itself, insufficient systems for sharing intelligence, leadership issues, and the need for greater investment in analysis (John and Maguire, 2004, p6). Some of these problems seem to have persisted. For example, the Bichard Inquiry observed in 2004 that, despite minimum standards for the NIM, there was 'a lack of clear, national guidance for the police about information management' (Bichard, 2004, p119).

There were early concerns too, over the adequacy of the training of analysts and their deployment. HMIC noted in 2000 'a continuing and serious concern relates to the use of analysts. Given the specialist skills needed, it is often the case that analysts are used for non-core tasks or are difficult to retain' (HMIC, 2000, p75). Cope found significant problems remained within crime analysis, particularly in terms of both the products that analysts used and how the work of the analysts was integrated into police working practices (Cope, 2004, p202). Cope *et al* also identified another problem in relation to the NIM: information overload (Cope *et al*, 2005, p. 43). A more general criticism was made by Ratcliffe in 2004 when he noted that the NIM 'was introduced prematurely before a significant proportion of standardised templates had been formulated, leaving forces to design their own versions and leading to [...] inconsistencies across the country' (Ratcliffe, 2004, p184).

More latterly Maguire & John (2006, p69) note that 'the introduction of the NIM has not only had to overcome cultural resistance within local forces, but has had to compete with a number of other major policing initiatives, some of which pull in contrary directions'. These 'major initiatives' include reassurance and neighbourhood policing. However, others argue that the NIM is more than simply a way in which police forces can be directed to employ intelligence-led methods. In essence, its designers intended it to be a business model and the 'business' can be as much about neighbourhood policing or public reassurance as it is about, for example, intelligence from informants and surveillance.

TASK 1

Now it is your turn: using the NIM, describe what would happen if the BCU Commander wanted to deal with:

- a crime hot spot involving alcohol-fuelled violence;
- a spate of break-ins into vehicles;
- a series of attacks on students to steal credit cards?

What factors do you think would influence the prioritizing of the crimes? What would you expect the crime analysts to provide? How would you task the collection of intelligence? What operational considerations would there be?

12.4 Gathering and Managing Intelligence

We turn now to consider some of the components of intelligence gathering: sources, source handling, surveillance, research and development, the intelligence 'target package', and some of the laws and rules around what you can and cannot do with intelligence. Some of the material may not appear immediately relevant to the work of a student police officer but you will discover its importance as you move through your training, and particularly so when you are engaged on Supervised Patrol and undertaking the IPLDP OP 2 module.

Many of the serious and organized crime investigations which result in a successful prosecution have their origins in good intelligence. Very few investigations into level-2 crime (and few of those at level 1) would be effective without intelligence, and certainly much police time would be ill-directed and fruitless. However, intelligence is not the only tool available; this Handbook also describes other complementary approaches, such as forensic investigation.

Recent cases (such as the Rhys Jones murder on Merseyside and recent arrests for suspected terrorist offences) have highlighted both the importance and the difficulty of converting intelligence into evidence. In each case the police had information and intelligence from numerous sources but it proved highly problematic to convert the intelligence into admissible evidence. In the case of Rhys Jones, the police were able to use new legislation under which a key witness gave evidence of fact as a 'protected' witness (under the 'Assisting the Prosecution' programme), and the police also obtained recordings of conversations (using hidden audio devices) and key forensic DNA evidence. Through these means the identity of the offenders was confirmed. However, in the case of the terrorist suspects, these evidential links could not be established in the same way and the suspects were released without charge.

12.4.1 Covert Human Intelligence Sources

The police term for an informant or source is 'CHIS', which stands for Covert Human Intelligence Source. Criminals use many more descriptions (mostly unflattering) such as 'grass', 'snout', and 'nark'. Many intelligence sources are themselves criminals, and we need to look closely at what constitutes a source. Members of the public who volunteer information about criminals or crimes are not generally defined as sources. However, they are regarded as sources if they have access to hidden criminal intentions or plans. As we noted earlier, criminals will go to some lengths to hide what they are doing or planning, and normally the only people with real access to this process are fellow criminals. The exception to this is the **undercover police officer**: see 12.4.2 below.

It is interesting to note, in the Home Office Codes of Practice under the Regulation of Investigatory Powers Act (RIPA) 2000, that many government agencies are permitted to use sources to gain intelligence. Such agencies and departments include HM Revenue and Customs, the Ministry of Defence, the Departments of Health, Trade and Industry, and Work and Pensions, the Environment Agency, the Armed Forces, and the Food Standards Agency. Any agency using a CHIS must have a responsible authorizing officer and observe the other requirements of the RIPA 2000. However a recent announcement by the Government seeks to review the authority granted to local authorities for using such techniques as it suggested that they have been badly managed and have become intrusive.

12.4.1.1 The Definition of a CHIS

The law is clear about what constitutes a source. Under s 26(8) of the RIPA 2000 a person is a source if he/she establishes or maintains a personal or other relationship with a person for the **covert** purpose of:

- obtaining information or providing access to information to another person; or
- disclosing information obtained by the use of such a relationship, or as the consequence of the existence of such a relationship.

This probably needs some explanation. In essence it means that a CHIS is someone who cultivates another person to obtain information, or who provides access to information, or who discloses information. Notice that the words criminal or unlawful are not used here. This is because the information need not necessarily be crime-related, at least to start with. It is the 'covert' part which is important. Thus, people like solicitors or bank officials who pass details of suspicious activity to the police are not sources, because they are working in an open relationship with the police and not acting covertly.

But what does covert actually mean? In general terms it usually means hidden, but the RIPA 2000 provides an exact legal definition (s 26(9)(b)–(c)):

> a purpose is covert in … a relationship if it is conducted in a manner which is calculated to ensure that only one of the parties to the relationship is unaware of the purpose [and]
> [a] relationship is used covertly, and information obtained is used or disclosed in a manner that is calculated to ensure that one of the parties to the relationship is unaware of the use or disclosure in question.

What this means in straightforward terms is that the person being cultivated by the CHIS (or from whom information is obtained because of that relationship) **does not know** that the CHIS is informing the police. This can be confusing, as we are in the realms of 'he knows that she knows that he doesn't know'. As an alternative, consider this as a working (but strictly speaking, 'non-legal') definition: a CHIS is tasked by the police with cultivating or sustaining a relationship with a third person, and that third person does not know about the police involvement.

Under the RIPA 2000, any use or conduct of a CHIS by the police will always require authorization granted by the **force authorizing officer** (a senior police officer, usually a detective superintendent or higher) who is answerable to a surveillance commissioner with a national remit. The authorization (or 'authority') will normally last 12 months.

12.4.1.2 Source handling

Most forces use a qualified and experienced detective constable as a source handler, probably paired with another (perhaps less experienced) handler. It is good practice to have two handlers so that a CHIS (who could be manipulative and might bring his/her own agenda) has less chance of exerting control over the handlers. A further advantage is that two can share the responsibility of handling, welfare issues, and recording of meetings with a CHIS. Sometimes, especially when meetings or intelligence taskings are urgent, there have to be 'singleton' meets between one handler and a source, but most forces recommend that this should never be routine.

The dedicated source-management unit is staffed by a CHIS controller, CHIS handlers, and support staff. The CHIS controller is responsible for the supervision, management, and control of all the staff in the unit. The CHIS handlers are responsible for the day-to-day management and recruitment of CHISs.

Handlers are usually detectives who have undergone an intensive training programme during which they learn (through scenarios and role play) how to:

- handle devious, dishonest, manipulative, and fantasizing sources;
- task informants;

- arrange secure meetings; and
- keep control.

> ### TASK 2
>
> What qualities do you think would make a good source handler? Discuss this with your colleagues and produce a list of attributes, skills, and competencies necessary to handle a covert source with access to criminal information.

A handler submits a report detailing the intelligence obtained from his/her CHIS and writes a separate note to his/her controller detailing the meeting itself. The intelligence is passed in its raw state to the Research and Development (R&D) unit where it is assessed against what is already known, considered in the wider context, and then sanitized (see 12.4.5.1 below).

12.4.1.3   Restrictions on the use of sources

We have already noted that the RIPA 2000 governs the definitions of a source and what is meant by covert, but the Act also determines the legal and practical parameters for handling a CHIS. We do not need to go into all the detail of the Act here, but you should know that there are special safeguards for vulnerable or young people, and a regular audit of authorizations by a surveillance commissioner, appointed nationally under a chief surveillance commissioner.

Attention is also drawn throughout the RIPA 2000 to **proportionality** and to Articles in the Human Rights Act 1998 legislation, particularly with respect to the right to a private life. RIPA 2000 provides the necessary framework for the ethical and legal use of CHISs by properly trained source handlers who are aware of their powers (but will not abuse them), as well as ensuring that the risks are proportionate to the expected gain. To make this a little more concrete, you would not use a source with excellent access to the upper echelons of criminality in order to establish the identity of a local graffitist.

> ### TASK 3
>
> We noted above that a police CHIS is often a criminal, because it is usually through criminals that access can be gained to other criminals. What do you think the problems might be for a police force when recruiting and using an active criminal as a CHIS? Aside from the ethical and moral considerations, what practical difficulties might there be? How might they be met and overcome?

12.4.1.4   Problems when using sources

In Task 3, you might have referred to the difficulty of using an active criminal as a source. If a CHIS takes part in an organized crime, or is involved in criminal planning, these are offences (eg conspiracy) for which the CHIS could be charged and brought before a court. A further difficulty is whether, in order to obtain the intelligence they need, the police have to allow a crime to go ahead, and let their source take part.

When allowing a crime to go ahead, the practical solution to this is to designate the CHIS as a **participating informant** (PI). The first consideration for the police is whether, if the identity of the informant is made known, there will be a serious risk to his/her life (or of serious harm or injury). If this is the case, the identity of the 'informant' will never be revealed, and if the informant provides the main source of evidence the prosecution of a case in open court is likely to be abandoned.

This does not mean that the source will not be charged if he/she is involved in a crime (particularly if he/she has exceeded any pre-arranged limit to his/her involvement in the crime). For example, it might have been pre-arranged that an informant would limit his/her involvement to merely driving a car in a bank robbery (it is very likely that if/she does not fill that role, others will). But if the informant were then to take a more active part in the crime—for example enter the bank and point a weapon—then the decision to prosecute might well be reviewed. The justification for the use of a PI in this case is that a dangerous team of criminals may be captured, thereby preventing their future use of firearms and the subsequent risk to the public. If for some reason the offender is charged, the court may consider an informal process known as a 'text'. The police (with the concurrence of the prosecution) make the sentencing judge aware (in confidence) of the assistance provided by the accused, whether in relation to the present case or more generally.

Even when not active as a PI, an informant may be able to take advantage of the new 'assisting prosecutions' legislation contained within the Serious Organised Crime and Police Act 2005. An investigator (or the legal representative of an offender) may ask a prosecutor to consider making a formal agreement with an offender in order to secure evidence for the prosecution of other offenders, or other information of vital importance to protecting the public interest.

The police and the Crown Prosecution Service usually adopt what they see as a pragmatic approach: if there is a risk to the source, the prosecution is very likely to be withdrawn and charges dropped. The principle here is that it is better not to proceed with a prosecution and retain a source who can be used again, rather than expend a valuable source of criminal intelligence for just one prosecution. No one can pretend that these are easy judgements, but the decision is the judge's alone. You may like to read further on this matter: see Harfield and Harfield (2005) and (2008).

Confidentiality protects the source; a source should be informed of this at the outset. Sources are also told that there is no automatic right to be exempt from criminal charges if they engage in crimes whilst acting as informants; there is no 'get out of jail free' card to be waved in court.

12.4.1.5   Motivation of informants

Why do criminals choose to become covert human intelligence sources? We need to think about the psychology involved. It should be noted at the outset that this is a very under-researched area and hence what follows should be treated with some caution. With this warning we may explore some possible reasons for becoming a CHIS.

TASK 4

Consider for a moment why someone might decide to become a source for the police. Why would you betray your criminal colleagues? How would you keep it up, week after week, month after month? How do you keep the secret of your relationship over a period of time that may extend to many years?

Many sources will suggest that it is for the money. Informants are paid for the intelligence and the better it is, the more he/she will be paid. The payments vary according to a number of factors and may be considerable in some very exceptional cases. However, a CHIS might well make more money from the criminal enterprise he/she is reporting on, therefore we must look a little deeper into what might motivate the source.

Motivation is psychologically complex and will always have a bearing on the value of the intelligence gained and on any selectivity on the part of the CHIS in providing intelligence. There have been occasions when an experienced and 'lifestyle' criminal has informed on other criminals threatening his/her dominance, in order to leave the field clear for his/her own criminal activities. Revenge is often cited in the research as a strong motive, especially when the informant has been 'bested' by another criminal. Other sources may have motivations of greed, vanity, a distaste for the crimes which the target criminal is engaged in (people trafficking, for example), or disgust at a criminal's sexual perversions. In one contemporary case a young woman (with two young children) was motivated to inform on her brother, a prominent local criminal, because she had seen him downloading child pornography on his computer and suspected that he was an active paedophile.

It often seems that there are as many motivations as there are sources, and the handler needs to determine what the potential source's primary motive or motives might be (even before recruitment takes place). It is easy to overlook the human needs of sources: like most people, they want affection, praise, contact, reward, encouragement, and a sense of being valued. Handlers can provide all these things for a source, but there is a danger that a source might become too emotionally dependent upon a handler and be unable to function adequately (in other aspects of his/her life) without the handler's help. (Doctors, psychiatrists, and counsellors also recognize this dependency in some patients and clients, but their professionalism ensures they attempt to keep a distance and remain objective. Handlers have to do the same, but under more difficult clandestine circumstances.) Other ethical dilemmas may also arise; for example, imagine a CHIS who is a drug user and overdoses on drugs purchased with the money paid to him by police. To what extent are the police ethically or morally responsible?

We have established that there are complex reasons why criminals become sources. A handler needs to assess whether the primary motivation at the outset is enough to sustain the source throughout the long period of gathering intelligence.

12.4.2 Undercover Officers and 'Test Purchase' Operations

Before we leave covert human intelligence sources and look at other forms of intelligence gathering, we need briefly to look at the role of undercover police officers and the kinds of intelligence operations with which they are involved.

A highly trained police officer can work to penetrate a group of criminals, for example, posing as a drugs importer or a supplier of documentation (such as passports). The same legal principles surround this use of a police officer as surround other CHISs. The risk must be proportionate to the outcome, and so an undercover officer would only be used in relation to very serious crimes, such as high-profile robberies or conspiracy to murder. The risk assessment must be very detailed and every possible permutation of danger, risk, or accident carefully anticipated. Of course, all operations using an undercover officer require authorization.

Officers cannot sustain undercover roles for long and need to be reintegrated into the police force before they are compromised or exhausted by the continuous strain ('turned or burned' in police parlance). This requires fastidious timing by the handler and supervisors, in order to maximize the benefits.

A specialist undercover role, which police officers can slide into and out of, is a **test purchase** operation. This is when a police officer poses as a potential buyer of some illegally acquired item such as drugs, contraband, or luxury goods. (The problem for many criminals is converting goods or items they have illegally acquired into the most CRAVED item of all—cash (see 5.15 above for an explanation of CRAVED)). The whole transaction is monitored carefully (surveillance teams deployed and uniformed officers on hand) and when the moment is right, the dealer or seller is arrested and charged. The reason that police officers are used extensively on such 'sting' operations is that they only need to appear once in one location. The advantage from the policing point of view is that the criminal is caught in action. This may result in a guilty plea at court and saves time, both for the police and the criminal justice system.

TASK 5

What do you think are the qualities and competences of a good undercover officer? What might be the problems, both logistical and operational? What would you think about when planning a test purchase operation?

12.4.3 Surveillance

The term surveillance is used in an everyday sense and in a legal sense, and the meanings are slightly different. In an everyday sense, surveillance means watching over something, but in a police and legal sense surveillance generally means covert surveillance. The subject of the surveillance is unaware that he/she is being monitored, and the monitoring is planned in advance.

Surveillance is defined (in s 48(2) of the RIPA 2000) as:

monitoring, observing, listening to persons, their movements, their conversations or their other activities or communications ... recording anything monitored, observed or listened to in the course of surveillance [and] ... surveillance by or with the assistance of a surveillance device.

A word of caution: it is appropriate to provide you with only a general description of what is involved in these intelligence-gathering techniques, for obvious reasons. Details will be given to you as a student police officer as and when appropriate.

In addition, there are principles about liberty and freedom here to which the police are expected to subscribe, especially if, in the process of undertaking the surveillance, there is an infringement of the 'right to privacy and family life' (Sch l, Art 8 of the Human Rights Act 1998, deriving from the European Convention on Human Rights: see 5.12 above).

The use of covert surveillance (when the observed person is not aware that he/she is being observed) is tightly controlled by the RIPA 2000. However, other types of monitoring (such as the use of CCTV by local authorities) generally do not involve the planned observation of a particular person (but see 12.4.3.1 below).

12.4.3.1 CCTV

The simplest and most obvious form of surveillance is the ubiquitous CCTV camera, overlooking public and private premises, walkways, town centres, banks, railway stations, airports, and yes, even police stations. The benefit of CCTV is that it gives 24-hour coverage of a location and its images are retrievable within a certain period; the disadvantage is that the location of a CCTV camera is fixed—cameras cannot follow a target round a corner. In addition CCTV cameras are usually easy to spot, so an aware criminal will note the locations of cameras and avoid them, or take care to wear something which disguises his/her features.

CCTV cameras are principally operated by local authorities or shop security officers. If an operator of a CCTV camera spots a person behaving suspiciously and decides to observe him/her using the CCTV for a while, this is not covert surveillance as it is not part of planned operation; the observation is spontaneous as it is in response to immediate circumstances. The police can have access to film from these cameras (as in the Jamie Bulger case, when two young children enticed away and murdered a young child). Furthermore, the new 'Sprint 2' technology enables some police forces to access CCTV coverage of town and city centres remotely and thus directly respond to any incidents unfolding on the screens.

Some local authorities and other organizations (see Sch 1 of the RIPA 2000 for a full list) carry out directed surveillance using CCTV for their own enforcement activities for example to monitor criminal behaviour such as fly tipping. The deployment of CCTV by local authorities for monitoring some anti-social activities is controversial, and policy is being reviewed. Occasionally, local authority CCTV is monitored on behalf of the police, (generally a location rather than specific person(s)) and this is usually subject of local protocols or a Memorandum of Understanding (MOU).

The procedures for seizing CCTV footage are covered in 13.5.13.1 below.

12.4.3.2 Covert surveillance

Surveillance is defined as covert:

if, and only if, it is carried out in a manner that is calculated to ensure that the persons who are subject to surveillance are unaware that it is or may be taking place (s 26(9), RIPA 2000).

Covert surveillance is planned in advance and therefore does not include discreet spontaneous observations of a crime that is unexpectedly taking place.

The Act divides covert surveillance into two types, depending on the level of intrusion:

- directed surveillance, which is carried out on people anywhere other than residential premises or vehicles;
- intrusive surveillance, which is carried out on people in residential premises or vehicles.

The distinctions are important particularly because of the different levels of authorization required (see 12.4.3.4 below).

Directed surveillance is defined in s 26(2) of the RIPA 2000 as follows:

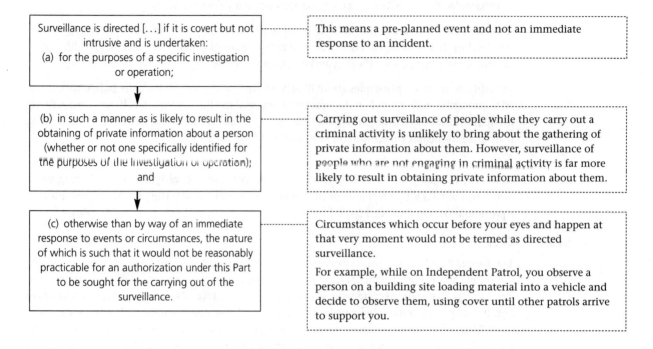

Surveillance is directed [...] if it is covert but not intrusive and is undertaken: (a) for the purposes of a specific investigation or operation;	This means a pre-planned event and not an immediate response to an incident.
(b) in such a manner as is likely to result in the obtaining of private information about a person (whether or not one specifically identified for the purposes of the investigation or operation); and	Carrying out surveillance of people while they carry out a criminal activity is unlikely to bring about the gathering of private information about them. However, surveillance of people who are not engaging in criminal activity is far more likely to result in obtaining private information about them.
(c) otherwise than by way of an immediate response to events or circumstances, the nature of which is such that it would not be reasonably practicable for an authorization under this Part to be sought for the carrying out of the surveillance.	Circumstances which occur before your eyes and happen at that very moment would not be termed as directed surveillance. For example, while on Independent Patrol, you observe a person on a building site loading material into a vehicle and decide to observe them, using cover until other patrols arrive to support you.

The provisions in the RIPA 2000 are intended to ensure that police actions are proportionate and justified. Student police officers should perhaps remember the JAPAN principles in this context: Justification, Authorization, Proportionality, Auditable, and Necessary. An example of directed surveillance might be the installation of a concealed camera in a tree opposite a criminal's residence; the camera would act as a 'trigger' to alert surveillance teams that the subject was moving. The installation must be positioned to ensure that only the subject premises is under surveillance. If the camera is poorly situated and captures the neighbours' house and their activities, this is 'collateral intrusion' and authority may be withheld until such intrusion has been minimized or avoided. If CCTV is to be used for a covert pre-planned investigation, then authority should be sought.

Intrusive Surveillance (s 26(3) of the RIPA 2000) is described as follows:

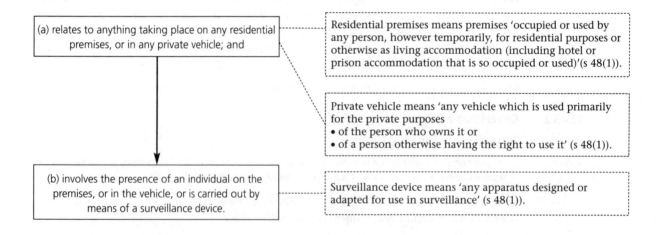

(a) relates to anything taking place on any residential premises, or in any private vehicle; and	Residential premises means premises 'occupied or used by any person, however temporarily, for residential purposes or otherwise as living accommodation (including hotel or prison accommodation that is so occupied or used)'(s 48(1)).
	Private vehicle means 'any vehicle which is used primarily for the private purposes • of the person who owns it or • of a person otherwise having the right to use it' (s 48(1)).
(b) involves the presence of an individual on the premises, or in the vehicle, or is carried out by means of a surveillance device.	Surveillance device means 'any apparatus designed or adapted for use in surveillance' (s 48(1)).

An example of intrusive surveillance would be a covert entry into a property such as a hotel room or an office to instal a listening device, and this would require authority on several levels.

Surveillance will cease to be intrusive without the presence of a person or a device on the relevant premises or vehicle(s), nor is it intrusive if:

- it is carried out by a device designed or adapted principally for the purpose of providing information about the location of a vehicle (a tracking device) (s 28(4)(a));

- it consists of any one-sided consensual interception (of a postal service or telecommunication system) where there is no intercept warrant (s 28(4)(b)); or
- it is carried out by means of a device not on the premises nor in the vehicle, unless that device consistently provides information of the same quality and detail as might be expected to be obtained from a device actually present on the premises, or in the vehicle (s 28(5)).

12.4.3.3 Covert surveillance in practice

Surveillance work involves a variety of approaches, depending on the information required.

Static observations can be carried out from a fixed vantage point, known as an Observation Point or OP, from a park bench or an unmarked parked police vehicle for example. If the OP is on private property special provisions apply: the operation must be carefully planned to avoid compromising the identity and safety of the owner or user of that property. The surveillance could be either directed or intrusive, depending on the location of the subject whilst under observation.

Mobile Conventional surveillance involves officers following the subject (on foot or in a vehicle) away from his/her office, home, hotel room, or other private place. This would be classed as directed surveillance, as long as the only information collected is the position and movements of the subject. The teams who undertake conventional surveillance are highly trained and a great deal of operational planning goes into such operations. Two key factors to consider are:

- the awareness of the subject: and
- the location in which surveillance will take place.

A tightly-knit rural community is an example of a difficult location for a surveillance team, as strangers and unknown cars will 'stand out' (may be very noticeable) in a small village or a quiet residential street. Different, but equally complex, problems present themselves in busy high streets, where the presence of many pedestrians means that keeping the target in sight is fraught with difficulty, especially when there are many shop entrances offering temporary concealment or exit points. Some criminals use sophisticated counter-surveillance techniques to shake off such surveillance, though by doing so, of course, they demonstrate that they probably have something to hide. Shaking off surveillance is not that easy, but compromises sometimes happen, and the operation has to be aborted.

Mobile Technical Surveillance involves attaching tracking devices to vehicles, packages, or other items, and if the device is used to simply identify the position of an object then this is directed surveillance. Tracking by GPS is commonly used by the police and private sector organizations; you may have seen security vans for transporting money with a sign indicating that the vehicle is being tracked.

Audio and visual surveillance employs devices such as binoculars, cameras, or recording equipment. These can be used when:

- following a subject;
- observing and recording a subject from an OP (perhaps while he/she is inside his/her own home);
- recording a subject's speech using microphones and sound-recording equipment, for example when an undercover officer engages in conversation with the subject in order to obtain evidence or intelligence. The American expression frequently used for this is 'wearing a wire'.

The use of such audio-visual equipment for surveillance is of course regulated and approval is given to the specific methods named in a particular authorization.

12.4.3.4 Authorization for covert surveillance

Authorization for covert surveillance must be given in writing and is valid for three months. Authorities are scrutinized (usually monthly in the case of intrusive surveillance) by a surveillance commissioner who can quash or cancel an authorized operation and demand the destruction of any intelligence obtained, if he/she is not satisfied that the grounds were reasonable and the justification proportionate. Spontaneous observations do not require authorization as these are not planned and do not meet the legal definition of covert surveillance.

For directed surveillance, the authorization must be given by a police officer not below the rank of superintendent. In urgent cases, oral authorizations may be given by a superintendent (lasting only for 72 hours from the time the authority was granted). Where a superintendent is absent and the case is urgent, written authority may be given by an officer not below the rank of inspector, which will again last for 72 hours. For both types of urgent authorization, written authority should be sought from the superintendent prior to the expiry of the 72-hour period.

Intrusive surveillance is a highly specialized area of police work and will only be authorized if it involves serious crime. All intrusive surveillance operations must be authorized by a person holding the rank of chief officer (that is, assistant chief constable rank and above) and the authorization must be approved by a surveillance commissioner.

Some operations involve the use of a CHIS, OPs, and mobile surveillance, and therefore multiple applications for authority need to be considered. Why are the procedures so complex and so carefully overseen? The purpose is to ensure that the police (and other agencies) operate in a system which is open to both scrutiny and monitoring, in compliance with the Human Rights Act 1988. Ultimately, the procedures are safeguards against any abuse of the powers granted to law-enforcement agencies by the citizens whom they protect.

12.4.4 Open Sources of Intelligence

We should not think that the only sources of information or intelligence about crimes or criminality are covert or clandestine. There are 'open' (or 'overt') sources.

TASK 6

Can you think of some open sources of intelligence?

The first and most obvious source of 'open' intelligence about crime and criminality is likely to come from the general public. People notice all kinds of things and should be encouraged to report to the police if what they see is odd, suspicious, or out of character.

There is much to be gleaned about the lifestyles of criminals from simple observation or from engaging members of the public in conversation. Criminals live within communities, they have to go shopping, wear clothes, socialize, and enjoy their leisure, and of course they are very likely to have families, hobbies, or interests which have nothing to do with crime. Profiles can be built up of a criminal's daily habits: where he/she buys newspapers, goes for a drink, which supermarket he/she shops in, what cars he/she drives and so on. Think of neighbours, garages, newsagents, dog walkers, joggers, parking attendants, crossing attendants, fitness instructors, and the like; all may have information that could be useful in an investigation.

Other sources of information may be obtained from police interviews (either with the criminal or with others who know the criminal) and, whilst this is covert in a conventional sense, there is a certain advantage in letting colleagues know that you are interested in a particular individual and would welcome any useful information which they might pick up in the course of such interviews. The same applies of course to police patrols, which should spend some part of their duty deployment on open observation and interaction with the public (even though the officers will tell you that the whole shift is spent responding to 999 calls).

Do not ignore information which may be obtained from prisons. Although the gathering of intelligence in prisons is subject to strict protocols and risk assessments, there is likely to be plenty of miscellaneous and open information about criminal targets of interest available from prison visits, interviews, preparations for release, and so on.

You might note the details in your local newspapers as well. Most provincial newspapers are served by a small army of volunteers who send in reports every week on the events in their localities, and whilst there is much that is not relevant, it is sometimes possible to pick up open references to criminal targets.

There are some other sources too which, whilst not 'open' in the sense of being available to anyone to tap into, nonetheless may provide you with useful information about a criminal target. These sources include other police forces. You are probably aware of the Bichard report published in 2004, which concluded that police forces should routinely communicate information which, though itself trivial or incomplete, might have a bearing on the activities of someone in another police force area (Bichard, 2004). However, as we have noted elsewhere, the infrastructure for such information exchange is not yet in place. Nonetheless, you might give thought to routine enquiries with other forces, perhaps including those where your target has worked, was born, got married, or goes on holiday.

Lastly, there is information which is obtained under the provisions of the Proceeds of Crime Act 2002. Part of this Act, designed to seize illegally gained money and assets from criminals, places an obligation on occupational groups such as bank managers and solicitors to report the handling of sums of money for which there is little or no justification. A bank manager, noting the sudden deposit of large sums in cash, can report this fact to the authorities. There could be an innocent explanation such as a win at the races (but proof may be required), or it could be the profits from a drugs deal. The information you obtain from such officials can be privileged, but that does not mean that it cannot be used to build up a picture of, or even a circumstantial case around, your criminal target.

We need to consider a couple of important points about you as a police officer and the collecting of information: there is no justification for gathering information about someone unless there is a criminal justice reason or requirement. You (as a police officer) cannot just gather information about your neighbour just because she is noisy and rude. That would not be an appropriate (or proportionate) use of your time, and could well be construed as abuse of your 'office of constable' (technically misfeasance: see 5.4 above). In other words, there has to be a reason (which will stand up to scrutiny) for gathering information. Even if the target is demonstrably criminal, you still have to remember proportionality and the JAPAN principles. If you do not (and incidentally, if you do not discuss what you are doing with your sergeant or inspector) you could be open to charges of harassment.

12.4.5 Intelligence 'Packages'

Intelligence packages (the term comes from the idea of bundling different items together) may then be constructed. These can be highly accurate pictures of how particular crimes are carried out in a given locality, by whom, with what success, how the acquisitions from the crime are fenced, how money is laundered and by whom, what the likelihood is of repeat victimization, and how the crime series is likely to develop. That perhaps would be an ideal package; many lack such detail and are much more likely to combine hard intelligence with some speculative hypothesis-setting and testing. Any 'guesstimates' should be clearly designated as such—as non-specific and unevidenced supposition.

The intelligence package is fundamental to police operational planning at the T&CG level (and above). Note also that intelligence packages are not just put together as a response to crime, but may also be used to support other policing objectives. An example might be in policing operations for public order: it could be problematic to deploy just 20 police officers to supervise a demonstration involving over 8,000 protestors—amongst which might be hostile and antagonistic groups. Conversely, providing 600 public-order police officers equipped to control a crowd of 15 might not only be wasteful but also be viewed as oppressive. A good intelligence package would assist the police in estimating both the likely size of the demonstration and the possibility of disorder arising. The accuracy of the intelligence-led prediction is vital; an intelligence package should provide the right level of detailed, meaningful information in order that the use of resources and tactics in the subsequent police operation is proportional, economic, and effective.

12.4.5.1 Sanitizing intelligence

Sanitizing removes any features of the intelligence that could identify the source or the circumstances in which the intelligence was obtained. For example, no R&D staff would allow a report to go into circulation which began:

> At 5.30 pm, on Tuesday 15 August, 'Fat Jimmy' saw the well-known criminal Sam 'Toucan' Belmont in the Three Feathers pub in Harpenden, where he told Jimmy the following …

Such obvious indicators could quickly identify the source and compromise his/her access, and at worst, might lead to violence against the source. Sanitizing the report does not dilute the intelligence, but offers some security to those engaged in its acquisition.

12.4.5.2   Intelligence reports

Intelligence is usually reported on forms called '5 x 5 x 5'. The numbers refer to 'qualities' of the intelligence, measured in three categories, using an ordinal scale of 1 to 5. For example, in terms of a CHIS they refer to the reliability of the CHIS, the importance of the intelligence, and the level of security to be implemented.

These 5x5x5 forms are a major part of the intelligence inflow into R&D which ensures that the reports of value are circulated to those who need to know, which in the majority of cases will be the T&CG. Reports dealing with a common theme may be collated from a number of sources, and be circulated as a single composite intelligence item (further protecting each source). Occasionally, reports from 'quality' sources with access to particularly important intelligence will be seen by staff higher in the organization, which makes the sanitizing process all the more important. The more people who know about a piece of intelligence (the 'circle of knowledge'), the more likely there will be a leak, and consequently a danger to the CHIS who originally reported it. There is a 'need to know' principle common to many policing activities and this applies to protecting sources, because the police want the source to continue his/her covert relationship with the target. R&D staff may return to the handler(s) with requests for further work, directions to pursue, and more targets; a productive source will be heavily tasked.

At some point in the distribution chain (this varies from force to force), analysts will examine the intelligence and match it with what is known. It will be another piece in the jigsaw. In some forces, this happens with the raw intelligence, in others with the sanitized version. Either way, the assessed intelligence helps to fill out the picture which the analysts are trying to create. As we noted above, the R&D unit in turn will try to gather enough intelligence to construct a 'targeting package' for the T&CG to consider (see 12.3.3.1 above).

12.5   Investigation and Interviewing

Interviewing witnesses, victims, and suspects will be a core part of your role as a police officer in investigations, and something which you will do nearly every day. Why is it so important? The short answer is that **interviewing is the way in which you obtain important evidence or information in relation to something that has happened** (which may or may not be a crime). Interviews are the best method to obtain accurate and reliable information from suspects, victims, or witnesses in order to discover the truth about events or matters which you are investigating as a police officer.

The modern approach to police interviewing in the UK is to see the interview as a means of seeking to establish the truth. This sounds obvious but it does in fact represent a marked change in emphasis from the past; it is no longer simply a case of 'points to prove'. Instead, interviewing is now much more akin to the 'inquisitorial approach' to justice that we discussed in 5.8.1 above.

Here we will examine in detail what is involved in interviewing people, and the recommended methods for conducting interviews. Under the IPLDP you will undertake extensive study and practice of interviewing procedures and techniques, including the relevant codes and legislation. In your Learning Diary (Phase 3) under the heading 'Investigation and interview' you may find it useful to record some of your reactions to this part of Chapter 12.

12.5.1   Obtaining initial accounts

You need to ask a few preliminary questions to determine whether any persons present could be reasonably suspected to have been involved in a criminal offence, based upon your initial appraisal of the situation. If this initial assessment provides you with reasonable grounds for suspicion that a person has been involved in a criminal offence you should caution him/her at this stage (see 8.4.2 above for further details) before asking any further questions.

Any conversation that takes place before a caution is given to a suspect should be summarized in your pocket notebook, as the court may decide they wish to take it into consideration. The PACE Codes of Practice do not affect your ability to speak to or question a person in the ordinary course of your duties (PACE Code of Practice A Note 1). The PACE Note explains that when trying to discover whether, or by whom, an offence has been committed, you may question any person from whom useful information might be obtained.

The decision to arrest is an individual decision for the officer at the scene and cannot be coloured by observers or even supervisory officers (see 8.7 above for more detail). The individual officer has to form his/her own reasonable suspicion, for example formed as a result of listening to witnesses. Once a decision has been made to arrest a suspect, he/she cannot be interviewed about the offence except at a police station (Code C 11.1) unless the delay would irretrievably hinder the investigation, as outlined in 8.9.9 above.

Identification of the suspects will be a priority, and you should also request a PNC check to find out about any 'warning signals' (for example that the suspect has been violent in the past), or if he/she has a criminal record. You should also let your local designated custody suite know that you are bringing the suspects in.

Another priority is to identify possible witnesses. You need to exercise judgement in establishing who was a **material witness** to the event (who actually saw it) and who was not. You should eliminate from your enquiries any people in the vicinity who were not involved or who did not see what happened, but this is not as easy as it sounds. People can become over-excited when they think they have witnessed a crime and will be keen to give you their (possibly derivative) account.

The most beneficial way of using witness evidence is to ask the witness to explain to you what he/she saw in the presence and hearing of the suspect(s) and record in your pocket notebook exactly what the witness says. You will then be able to use your record as evidence in court, because even though it is evidence of what someone other than the suspect has said (hearsay evidence: see 12.9.4 below), you can still use it in your duty statement and say the words in court, because it was originally said by a witness in the presence and hearing of the accused.

Initial accounts from witnesses may provide the information you need to plan an interview later with the suspects, or to construct a 'handover pack' for other officers to conduct the interviews (see 8.16 above) . In addition, a 'first account' may be compared with the account given under oath verbally at court, and any inconsistencies between the two accounts would require an explanation from the witness.

Remember, too, that you need to think about compliance with the Criminal Procedures and Investigation Act 1996 (CPIA) because there have been occasions when police officers have not recorded 'relevant material', to the detriment of the prosecution or defence of the suspects. You must make sure that you (as will your colleagues) have recorded in your PNB information about **all** the witnesses, and any actions, statements, comments, or other relevant material. It might not be used by the defence, but it could be. The case would be potentially undermined if the defence asked you, in court, about what was said by one material witness, and there was no record of what was said in your PNB. We look at the need to 'record, retain and reveal' in 12.6 later in this chapter. Refer to 8.3 above to refresh your memory about the PNB and its importance.

12.5.2 Key Principles for Interviewing

There are some general principles to be followed, even though every interview is different and every witness, victim, or suspect will behave differently. You have to be prepared for these differences and plan accordingly, and the general principles will help you cope with the wide range of interviews you are likely to encounter.

Home Office circular 2/1992 on investigative interviewing provides the following seven principles:

- The role of investigative interviewing is to obtain accurate and reliable information from suspects, witness and victims in order to discover the truth about matters under police investigation.
- Investigative interviewing should be approached with an open mind.
- Information obtained from the person who is being interviewed should always be tested against what the interviewing officer already knows or what can reasonably be established. When questioning anyone a police officer must act fairly in the circumstances of each individual case.
- The police officer is not bound to accept the first answer given. Questioning is not unfair merely because it is persistent. Even when a suspect exercises the right of silence the police still have a right to put questions.
- When conducting an interview, police officers are free to ask questions in order to establish the truth: except for interviews with child victims of sexual or violent abuse which are to be used in criminal proceedings, they are not constrained by the rules applied to lawyers in court.
- Vulnerable people, whether victims, witnesses, or suspects must be treated with particular consideration at all times. The interviewing of victims, witnesses and suspects is an everyday part of the police role.
- It is the formal means by which vital information and evidence is obtained in relation to incidents. This requires specific skills to obtain this information and evidence in a way that conforms to the laws of the land.

The legislation around police interviewing is complex, and here we cover the basics, sufficient for the student police officer. In addition, it is recommended that you familiarize yourself with the following:

- ss 76 and 78 of the PACE Act 1984, including provisions under Code C, Code E, and Code F;
- Part III and ss 34, 36, and 37 of the Criminal Justice and Public Order Act 1994 (CJPOA), including 'special warnings' (see 12.5.5.9 below);
- criminal law relating to the offence(s) for which suspects are charged (including the Theft Act 1968 and Offences Against the Person Act 1861);
- the Human Rights Act 1998 (see 5.12. above);
- the CPIA 1996;
- the Youth Justice and Criminal Evidence Act 1999 (especially on 'vulnerable', 'intimidated', and child witnesses).

There are other laws with specific provisions which we will refer to later, but those noted above are the principal sources governing the legality of what you do and say during an interview (and the observance of which will give you confidence in presenting your evidence in court).

Of course, simply knowing the law is not enough; applying the law is the key role for a police officer. If you make mistakes through incompetence, poor practice, or acting in 'bad faith' during the interview process, you may render parts of the evidence void or inadmissible. This could mean that a guilty offender may avoid prosecution and be free to offend again, or an innocent person may be wrongly charged and convicted.

Legislation such as the PACE Act 1984 has certainly helped to reassure the public, lawyers, academic commentators, and the police themselves that interviewing is now more tightly controlled, more ethical, and often more effective. However, the crucial question is **whether the evidence obtained from interviewing will stand up to scrutiny in court**, and that question should perhaps be at the forefront of your mind during an interview.

It might help you to have copies of the PACE Act 1984 and the CJPOA 1994 to hand while you work through this part of the chapter. Copies of both are available from <http://www.opsi.gov.uk/legislation/about_legislation> by following the relevant links.

12.5.3 The 'PEACE' approach to Interviewing

To assist you with structuring interviews, police forces have adopted the 'PEACE' approach. PEACE (which more strictly should be PPEEACCCE) is an acronym which stands for:

P	Planning and Preparation
E	Engage and Explain
A	Account, Clarification, and Challenge
C	Closure
E	Evaluation

You will often hear the process referred to in your force as the 'PEACE interview'.

We will look at each of the elements of PEACE in turn, but the detail will depend on whether we are interviewing suspects or cooperative witnesses.

The key points to consider are listed below:

- **your objectives** (focus on what you hope to achieve and how you intend to achieve it. Remember, the emphasis is to establish the truth);
- **the relevant law** (research the law and recent stated cases, eg intention, effect of drink/drugs on intention, recklessness, etc);
- **possible defences** (consider, for example, statutory defences, reasonableness, mistake, coercion, duress, self-defence, etc);
- **possible mitigating and aggravating factors;**
- **pre-interview disclosure** (consider what you should disclose to solicitors or legal representatives: see 12.5.5.4 below).

We devote considerable time to looking at the preliminaries, but it has been found to be beneficial to establish an appropriate tone, mood, and format for an interview from the very start. Remember that most people you interview will not know what is happening; he/she may have never even been in a police station before.

For an evaluation of the use of PEACE by police forces in England and Wales, see Clarke, (2001).

12.5.3.1 PEACE—planning and preparation

Many aspects of an interview appear to be merely practical issues, but on closer inspection many of these factors could also influence the whole outcome of the interview, so you need to plan carefully. For example you might take a different approach to the interview depending on which of your colleagues will also be present. It is worth bearing in mind the seven Home Office principles given in 12.5.2 above before you plan an interview. There is no substitute for careful and detailed planning before you start.

One of the first things you need to decide is what potential offence or offences you are investigating. You should consult the relevant legislation and work out what you need to know. Once you have information such as witness accounts or statements and any other available evidence you will be able to decide what contribution the interview is going to make to your investigation. Remember that, if an offence has actually occurred, you have to prove the existence of:

1. **Criminal intent** (*mens rea*): What was in the suspect's mind at the time? Why did he/she commit the offence?
2. **Criminal action** (*actus reus*): What did he/she actually do? How did he/she do it?

An interview should explore these aspects carefully (see 5.10 above for further details). The suspect may be guilty or, if the course of the interview suggests otherwise, a 'refused charge' may be the outcome (see 8.15.10 above).

You also need to find our more about the person you are going to interview:

- Have you confirmed his/her identity? You could conduct a Livescan and IDENT1 check (see 13.5.10.1 below).
- Do you know his/her age? (Establishing the age of a person is not necessarily a simple process. Some adults will claim to be younger, in an attempt to mislead you and to avoid prosecution.)
- Does he/she have any previous convictions? If so could they be used in interview as evidence of 'bad character'—pointing to propensity to be dishonest or reprehensible behaviour (see 12.8 below).
- Is he/she on the force's intelligence database? Is he/she suspected of other crimes elsewhere or flagged as active or of interest to other police forces or agencies?
- Is he/she already on bail? Is he/she in breach of bail, an ASBO, or a court order, or wanted for a crime elsewhere?

The key questions you ask in the interview should be planned in advance. You should aim to ask **open questions** (which normally cannot be answered with a simple yes or no) as this style of question invites a fuller response. In any interview, the more detail you obtain in the interviewee's own words, the more you can refute a denial of guilt, mitigate or establish innocence. You should avoid using leading questions which might lead a person to overstate or understate the truth. In a suspect interview, in order to prove the *mens rea* the interviewer might ask an open question, for instance starting with the words 'what were you feeling when you ... ?' or 'what were you thinking when you were ...?' For any interview, a great deal of thought should go into planning the focus question as it tends to set the agenda for the rest of the interview and also, to a certain extent, dictates interviewing tactics.

A written plan should be made (with reference to the PACE Codes of Practice for an interview with a suspect). The plan should include the following points:

- the range of topics you want to cover;
- the points needed to prove the possible offence(s) under investigation;
- evidence that the suspect committed the offence(s) and the specific parts of the criminal law under which the suspect may be charged.

The plan will help you keep track of what has been covered and what remains to be explored. It will also help you if the accounts from different interviewees contradict each other or vary significantly from what you currently believe to be the facts. The plan may contain a series of prompts or be used as an *aide mémoire* during the interview itself, however prompts need to be used with care if you are to appear professional and in control of the interview. One common form of written plan used widely in police interviews is known as the SQ3R (see the answer to Task 8 in Chapter 4 above). Remember that whatever sort of plan you choose to use, your interview plan is relevant material (as set out in the CPIA 1996) and must therefore be retained as a document to be revealed (see 12.6.4 below).

Practical aspects to be covered in your plan include:

- Who will you interview first (if there is more than one person to be interviewed)?
- Will you have a colleague in the interview with you?
- When and where will you interview?
- When will you take breaks?
- Do you have a seating plan?
- How many tapes do you need?

For interviews with suspects (see also 12.5.5 below), there are other practical considerations, such as recording the interview and the PACE requirements for rest and review times.

Normally the same interview team would conduct all interviews relating to one incident, but if you 'hand over' the responsibility for an interview to another officer (perhaps from a dedicated unit for prisoner handling) after arrest and detention procedures are complete, you may need to brief the interviewing officer very fully, so he/she can prepare properly for the interview (see 8.16 above on handover procedures).

12.5.3.2   PEACE—engage and explain

You should explain what is going to happen and how things will proceed in order to reassure and relax the person you are interviewing. If you do all this in a friendly and non-threatening manner, you are halfway to a cooperative interview. Remember, encouraging the person to talk is a primary aim of the interview process. In this stage of a PEACE interview, you should:

- **establish a rapport** by including introductions, concerns, considerations, and the use of appropriate humour, thereby creating a compatible atmosphere and establishing common ground;
- **explain the reasons for the interview** (for a suspect, this should include an explanation of the alleged offence, the grounds for arrest, and that the interview provides an opportunity for the suspect to put his/her account of what happened, and for you, the police officer, to seek the truth);
- **describe the routines**—depending on the nature of the interview this might include explaining why certain persons are present, the use of tapes and recording equipment, the need for you to refer to your notes and make further notes, the production of exhibits, etc;
- **set out the route map**—what happens during and after the interview process, and the general (not the specific) line of questioning;
- **state the expectations**—ground rules such as no over-talking or interruptions, politeness, time to think, and the need to seek clarification of questions and answers;
- **explain legal rights** and the role of the solicitor and legal advisers.

Setting the right tone is very important. For each interviewee you should note and take into account any cultural or behavioural factors, such as how you address the person. Asking directly how he/she wishes to be addressed might provide an easy ice-breaker at the beginning of the interview. You could offer the interviewee a cup of tea or other refreshment (however, before making a gesture of this type you should ensure that the facility is available to you—there is a certain loss of face if you then cannot deliver!).

When referring to your plan do not simply read from it as this is likely to convey a general lack of flexibility (and alertness). You might find it beneficial to look back at 6.18 above on communication, and be aware of your non-verbal communication (NVC) as well as taking account of the words you use. The suspect's NVC is not recorded in an interview under PACE, apart from the interviewing officer making references to actions.

12.5.3.3   PEACE—account, clarifications, and challenge

This is the main part of the interview. In the following order you should:

- **Seek a 'free' account**, without any interruption from you if possible.
- **Develop the account** by phasing the incident, and then moving systematically from one phase to another, clarifying or seeking greater detail. You may need to bear in mind *Turnbull* and the ADVOKATE checklist (see 8.6 above).
- **Summarize the account** and then select topics that are relevant, in dispute, and checkable for examination in greater detail. Does the account make chronological sense?
- **Seek new/additional information** and summarize each topic with commitment and agreement if possible.
- **Clarify and challenge** but restrict your challenges to inconsistencies and checkable, provable, and admissible facts. When challenging, do not criticize or accuse—instead ask for explanation, especially where discrepancies emerge.
- **'Special warning'**—consider if one is needed (see 12.5.5.9 below).
- **Bad-character evidence**—if appropriate (see 12.8 below), and if it has been introduced in a way that is relevant to the nature of any likely charges—has it?

> **TASK 7**
>
> What special interview techniques may be used to help the interviewee's recall, particularly for witness interviews?

You will find breaks useful for making arrangements and gathering your thoughts, particularly if the interview has taken an unexpected turn; such developments often happen during the course of an interview. You may even need to revise your plan for the rest of the interview. After a break it is good practice to summarize what has been said and to invite the interviewee to comment on the accuracy of the summary. This demonstrates to him/her that you have been listening carefully and have realized the significance of what has been said, and that he/she is being taken seriously.

12.5.3.4 PEACE—closure

You should check the following points before finishing the interview:

- review the interviewee's account in full;
- allow the interviewee the chance to correct, confirm, deny, alter, or add to his/her account;
- ensure you have covered all the questions you wish to ask;
- check whether the interviewee (or the solicitor, if present) wants to ask any questions;
- explain what will happen in the future.

Once you have addressed the points above you can formally close the interview. As with formally starting the interview, there are a number of requirements to be met, and you will be taught these as part of your training. This stage is likely to include recording the time when the interview finishes. For interviews with suspects, there are additional requirements relating to the tapes used to record the interview (see 12.5.5.7 below).

You should aim to maintain the good rapport you have built up during an interview as you may need to interview the same person again, especially if any new evidence emerges or you receive guidance from the CPS.

12.5.3.5 PEACE—evaluation

After the interview you should referring to your plan and reflect on what went well, what might have gone better, and for next time, which areas you would try to develop or improve. Make sure you consider the following questions:

- Have you discovered other reasonable lines of enquiry (such as an alibi)?
- Have you discovered other forensic opportunities?
- Have you covered all the points to prove from the offence under investigation?
- Have you considered statutory defences, mitigation, or explanation, perhaps pointing to innocence?
- Have you achieved your objectives?
- Does the interview add to your investigation as a whole?
- Have the requirements of the CPIA 1996 been satisfied?

Assessing your personal level of skills and knowledge in relation to interviewing may well provide an opportunity for Learning Diary entries, and this self-critical process is also important in learning to become even more professional in the conduct of interviews.

12.5.4 The Needs of the Interviewee

Many suspects will be anxious and want to know what is going to happen next and in the longer term. If the suspect asks you directly to provide an indication of future procedures you should answer fairly and honestly as to how you think matters may follow. The common questions are 'will I be released?', 'will I get bail?', and 'how long will I be here?' You have to give an honest appreciation of the situation but you cannot determine the decisions of the custody officer or the CPS reviewing lawyer, and you should say so.

12.5.4.1 Meeting the needs of all interviewees

As an interviewer, you (as well as the custody officer) should be alert to the special circumstances involved in interviewing a person with a physical or mental impairment. You should always try to ascertain the nature and extent of the impairment, although the individual may or may not be willing to divulge it. Remember that the PACE Act 1984 'allows you to proceed on an assumption', either because you have been told or because you suspect an impairment. This obviously needs careful and sensitive handling. Do not simply and bluntly say (to a witness, suspect, or victim) 'are you deaf?', but instead ask 'do you have a physical impairment we should be aware of?' or other more neutral language of this kind. Make arrangements for a signer to attend the interview if the individual is profoundly deaf or if there are problems with lip-reading. Do not shout or raise your voice to a deaf person, but ensure that he/she can see your face in order to lip-read, and that you speak one at a time. You might also find it useful to attract his/her attention by lightly touching his/her sleeve. (You may also suggest these things to the legal adviser.)

It may be difficult to arrange Braille texts in order for blind people to make statements, but it would be a good initiative for you (in consultation with your force diversity team) to establish whether Braille texts are available which explain, for example, a suspect's rights, the caution, and the management of tapes after interview. If there are none, you should arrange that some are made, for instance through contacting the local branch of the Royal National Institute for the Blind. (However, you also need to be aware that not all blind people can read Braille).

Other impairments may be more difficult to deal with, such as speech impediments, but you should always be sensitive to the individual's needs and requirements, and do your best to meet them. What should guide your actions and approach is the simple question: 'Have I done all I can to ensure that this person is not disadvantaged in any way because of a disability or impairment?' If your answer to this is 'yes', then you have taken all reasonable steps. No one should be placed at a disadvantage in a police interview because of physical or mental impairment; the criminal justice system is not well served unless this principle is upheld.

12.5.4.2 The use of an 'appropriate adult'

An interviewee (witness, victim, or suspect) may be a 'vulnerable person'. The PACE Act 1984, Code C 1.4 suggests that, if an officer has any suspicions that a person may be 'mentally disordered or otherwise mentally vulnerable', then the person should be treated as a vulnerable person requiring the additional presence of 'an appropriate adult'. This extends, obviously, to children under the age of 17 and, further, to any person who, because of an impairment such as a serious visual handicap, deafness, illiteracy, or who has difficulty in articulation because of a speech impediment, may find an interview problematic. It is usually the custody officer who considers whether an appropriate adult is required, not you as the interviewer.

In such circumstances, you should be prepared for an appropriate adult to be present at your interviews, acting on behalf of the person being interviewed. The legal adviser does not play this role; legal advisers seldom have experience or expertise in dealing with impairment or mental handicap, and his/her role is confined to the legal interests (and to a lesser extent the longer-term welfare) of the person as a client.

The PACE Act 1984 Code C 1.7 sets out the categories of person who can be an appropriate adult, and his/her duties are also described. The appropriate adult for a juvenile is, first, a parent or guardian, or, if the juvenile is in care, a suitable representative from the care authority or voluntary organization. Failing the availability of any of these, a social worker may stand *in loco parentis* (in the place of a parent). As a last resort, any responsible person aged 18 or over who is unconnected with the police in any way, may act as the appropriate adult. The PACE Act 1984 does not define what is meant by responsible, but it will not include the juvenile's friends nor anyone with a criminal record.

For a person who is 'mentally disordered' or has a reduced mental capacity, an appropriate adult is a relative, guardian, or other person responsible for their care and custody, or someone who has experience of dealing with mentally vulnerable people (such as an approved mental health professional (AMHP) as defined by the Mental Health Act 1983, or a specialist social worker). Failing either of these two categories, some other responsible person aged 18 or over may be the appropriate adult. Again, anyone connected with the police is not eligible.

The appropriate adult does not have a passive role, sitting in the interview as a mere observer. The custody officer should read the following statement (from the custody record) to anyone acting as the appropriate adult:

> Where you are present at an interview, you are not expected to act simply as an observer. The purpose of your presence is to advise the person being questioned, to observe whether or not the interview is being conducted properly and fairly and to facilitate communication with the person being interviewed.

The appropriate adult will be invited to sign the custody record to show that he/she understands the responsibilities involved. You would be well advised as interviewer to check that this has been done. If it has not, you should remedy that, and obtain a voluntary signature from the appropriate adult before the interview begins.

A couple of other practical points: you may assume that such interviews may take longer, especially if there is interpretation involved, for example by a signer. The same applies to interviews involving a language interpreter; even simple questions have to be translated from English into the other language, and the reply translated back into English. Allow at least twice as long as normal for this, and do not hurry the process or become impatient. The interviewee of course has more time to consider his/her replies, and you might find the slower pace an advantage as you will have more time to observe and consider the suspect's NVC and demeanour, though of course any interpretations you make must always allow for cultural and linguistic diversity.

12.5.5 Interviews with Suspects

A suspect interview is defined as 'the questioning of a person regarding their involvement or suspected involvement in a criminal offence or offences which must be carried out under caution' (PACE Code of Practice C 11.1A). This definition covers any conversation (no matter how short and wherever it takes place) once a caution has been given, and it is irrelevant whether the suspect has been arrested or not. The usual place for an interview with a suspect is at a police station, and if a person has been arrested the interview **must** take place at a police station (PACE Code of Practice C 11.1).

12.5.5.1 General rights of the suspect

The suspect has the normal rights of being treated with dignity, fairness, and objectivity, and the right to a legal adviser during interview, and for a vulnerable person, an 'appropriate adult' should also be present (see 12.5.4.2 above). The suspect should have his/her rights explained, and this should be reinforced by providing the suspect with a written explanation. The suspect should be assessed as 'fit for interview'; you need to consider whether the suspect is ill, hurt, or suffering from a psychological condition. Normally a doctor or custody nurse will ascertain fitness for interview, but it can be done on the person's own say, supported by the custody officer's independent observations.

A number of laws and associated Codes regulate the process of police interviews, in order to protect the person being interviewed. Unquestionably, there are many instances in the past of the police abusing their powers to question suspects (some of which may have been motivated in part by the so-called 'noble cause corruption' discussed in 5.4 above). This could range from oppressive behaviour used to obtain confessions under duress, to a lack of safety provisions when interviewing someone who was vulnerable (due to a disability or learning difficulty, for example). Many of the unfair practices adopted by the police to secure a 'confession' from a suspect in custody have been identified and made more difficult, if not impossible, by legislation and practice guidelines. The custody officer and the suspect's legal advisor (often a solicitor) both have a responsibility to monitor the suspect's rights and the process of interviewing, and this has greatly reduced the opportunities for foul play.

12.5.5.2 Planning suspect interviews

As well as the general PEACE considerations for planning interviews covered in 12.5.3.1, there are other factors to consider that apply only to suspect interviews, such as:

- the legal framework for interviews with suspects;
- the suspect's right to a free independent legal adviser and for the adviser to be present throughout the interview;
- the arrangements for recording the interview.

These requirements need to be covered in your plan. You also need to consider what defences the suspect might employ and how you might you counter these defences.

12.5.5.3 The role of the defence solicitor

The PACE Act 1984 Codes of Practice Code C, Note 6D states that:

> The solicitor's only role in the police station is to protect and advance the legal rights of his client. On occasions this may require the solicitor to give advice which has the effect of his client avoiding giving evidence which strengthens the prosecution case.

A 'duty solicitor' comes from a retained panel of solicitors available to advise arrested people who do not have a solicitor of their own (or, if they do, that person is not available for the interview). Duty solicitors provide 'free and independent legal advice' (FILA) and are there to advise their clients at any time. They are of course independent of the police and the CPS.

The defence solicitor is obliged to prevent his/her client from further assisting the police by way of self-incrimination, if that is not in the client's interest. It is sometimes difficult for a student police officer to accept that a solicitor's advice can stop a suspect giving details about a crime, or an admission of guilt in committing a crime. Indeed, more experienced police officers may also argue that there is not a 'level playing field' with the accused. However a jury may adversely interpret a suspect's silence in the face of reasonable questioning, where that suspect relies on evidence in court which he/she could have provided earlier (see 12.5.5.9 below).

This does not always mean that the solicitor will advise a client to avoid self-incrimination, because sometimes an admission of guilt is better for the client, especially if there is strong or irrefutable evidence, or strong mitigation (an excuse or reason for what has been done).

A solicitor might also adopt an 'active defence' role (Ede, 2000). The solicitor will seek to find out what the police case is against the suspect in order to ascertain:

- the strength of the evidence and therefore whether to advise the suspect to admit the offence or not. (If the evidence looks weak or merely circumstantial, the solicitor will probably advise the suspect to either remain silent, submit a prepared statement they will compile together, or not to volunteer information. If the evidence is very strong the solicitor may depict the suspect as a victim who has been manipulated by unscrupulous others).
- the intended police line of questioning, in order to attempt to head off any lines of enquiry which will be difficult for the suspect (and possibly to suggest to the police officer in charge of the case that there is insufficient evidence to prove that the suspect committed the offence).

A solicitor employing active defence might try to dominate an interview (an accepted tactic), particularly if the interviewing officer seems to lack experience or is unprofessional when interviewing the suspect. It is unlikely that you will ever encounter a solicitor who behaves so inappropriately that you have to exclude him/her from the interview (though it has happened), but you may encounter a solicitor who becomes so disruptive that you have to deal with him/her or 'lose the interview'. Remember, however, that the whole interview is on tape, and the court will take a negative view of a disruptive solicitor, and this might even prejudice the suspect's chances.

12.5.5.4 Briefing the solicitor before the interview

Before you commence the interview you will need to brief the solicitor so that his/her client may be properly advised. You need to tell the custody officer that you are the point of contact for the defence solicitor (the custody officer will have made contact with the solicitor, following a request from the detained suspect). You must ensure that you do not leave prisoner handover documents or witness statements attached to the custody record.

In a well-planned meeting, the encounter between the police officer and the defence solicitor will take place in a quiet room without interruptions. Sometimes though, the encounter will take place in a corridor with others passing by, with all the noise and disruption you associate with a busy police station, and the solicitor may to attempt to take advantage of this; do not be persuaded to say more than you should. For the same sorts of reason, do not brief the defence solicitor on the phone; tell him/her that you will make yourself available when the solicitor attends at the police station.

You should plan what you are going to disclose. Ask yourself these questions (and make sure that your answers are robust):

- What evidence do I have?
- What evidence shall I disclose immediately?
- What evidence shall I withhold?
- When will I disclose this evidence in the interview process?
- Can I justify withholding this evidence?

You should not disclose evidence derived from intelligence, vital forensic evidence, or details which relate to a particular MO until you have to, and disclosure becomes inevitable (see 12.6.4 below).

At the start of the meeting you should explain exactly how you intend to conduct the encounter, and say that you will answer the solicitor's questions when you have completed the disclosure of your evidence. Brief at a pace which enables the solicitor to take notes and bring him/her up to date with the welfare of the client. In serious cases the solicitor or the interviewing officer will record the pre-interview disclosure on tape.

Outline the case you have against the suspect, including the evidence you have and upon which you intend to base the interview. Then you can invite questions; the solicitor will want to know everything you know about the case, and will encourage you to divulge every piece of evidence, claiming that he/she will not to be able 'properly to advise' his/her client without further information from you. However, you should not be defensive and disclose only in answer to the solicitor's questions as this may increase the likelihood of a 'no comment' interview, and you should try to anticipate any difficult questions from the solicitor, so you can plan your answers accordingly.

There are two major warnings which you must heed in briefing the solicitor: **never overstate or understate your evidence**. You should not allow yourself to be led if the solicitor asks for your views on the likely outcome for his/her client, and you should avoid phrases such as 'the evidence proves your client's guilt' or 'there is not much in the way of evidence as yet'. Either phrase will (quite rightly) provoke the solicitor, and it is likely that he/she will comment as follows:

> **Solicitor:** Your comment on my client's guilt or otherwise is most inappropriate and highly prejudicial to my client. I am making a note about this matter, and I shall be making representations both to the Custody Sergeant and the CPS, and it may be a matter for the court.
>
> or:
>
> **Solicitor:** If, as you have just said, the evidence is thin for the detention of my client and you evidently lack proof that he committed the alleged offence, why are you continuing to detain him? He should be refused charge and released immediately. Any further detention is unlawful. This could be a matter for civil proceedings.

The interviewing officer needs to remain calm and self-possessed in the face of a solicitor's persistent questioning. A solicitor may try all sorts of different tacks, such as switching abruptly from questions about evidence to questions about other aspects of the case. The more you know the case, and the more you know and understand the law, the more confident you will be in dealing with any legal adviser.

12.5.5.5 The start of a suspect interview

Time spent now on relaxing the suspect, engaging with him or her, explaining what is going to happen and following procedure properly, may well prove productive later (as well as not giving the defence solicitor any irregularities to use in the defence of his/her client). If the suspect has chosen not to have a solicitor or legal adviser present then you would ask him/her about this at the outset of the interview.

At the start of the taped interview (or after a break) and **before** any questions about the offence are put, you need to:

- caution the suspect (see Codes C10.8 and C 11.4) and check his/her understanding; and then
- discuss any **significant statement** (see 8.5 above). The suspect must be given the opportunity to confirm, deny, or add to an earlier statement. Sometimes it may be difficult to distinguish between a significant statement and a 'relevant comment' (again see 8.5 above), but if you are in any doubt, still put the statement or comment to the suspect before the interview proper begins.

Can you explain the caution in simple terms? A detailed account of the various cautions and how to use them is given in 8.4 above. You might say to the suspect, for example:

> You have an absolute right to remain silent if you wish, you cannot be compelled to answer my questions. However, if you choose not to tell me something in answer to a question I put to you now but later in court you **do** provide an answer to the same question, then the magistrate or jury are entitled to ask themselves why you did not answer the question earlier, when I asked you. They might then think that the answer you give in court is not truthful, and that it has been concocted and is in fact a lie. I must warn you that a recording of this interview may be played back in court.

(Do not be tempted to ask the solicitor to explain the caution, or to acknowledge that his/her client understands the caution. If you do, the solicitor will invariably remind you that this is the responsibility of the Interviewing Officer.)

12.5.5.6 The solicitor's tactics during the interview

Most defence solicitors, particularly those who are duty solicitors, will have a good understanding and plenty of experience of the PEACE interview model and the approaches which an interviewing officer will adopt. For example, the solicitor will know that you will try to build a rapport with the interviewee, but do not expect the solicitor to help you or assist with the process. You might start with a few informal words about a non-contentious topic (such as whether he/she would like a drink) to encourage the suspect to open up, but unless it relates directly to his/her welfare, the solicitor is likely to challenge its relevance.

The Codes of Practice provide some guidance on what is acceptable behaviour by the solicitor in an interview. A legal adviser may:

- seek clarification of an issue or question;
- advise the client not to answer a question;
- challenge an improper question or the manner in which it is put;
- wish to offer the client further advice.

However, a legal adviser may not:

- answer questions on the client's behalf; nor
- provide the client with written responses to quote.

The solicitor will also closely monitor the interview process itself because however overwhelming the evidence, a flaw in police procedure can mean the dismissal of charges against the suspect or an application to have the evidence ruled inadmissable at trial. A solicitor has no obligation to immediately point out police failings or non-adherence to the appropriate Codes. Indeed he/she may choose to sit back and quietly note the shortcomings, and only mention them at a later stage, when it is of particular advantage to the client, for instance in court. This is one of the reasons why you need to know the law and the associated police procedures very well indeed. If you ask any leading questions or adopt a threatening or bullying manner, or seek to offer the suspect a lighter sentence in exchange for giving more evidence, the solicitor will intervene (and rightly so). If, however, you are acting fairly, proportionately, and properly, the solicitor's grounds for intervention are much reduced.

12.5.5.7 Recording suspect interviews

If the interview takes place other than at a police station, for example at the roadside in relation to a motoring offence, or at a juvenile's home (with an appropriate adult), then an accurate record complying with PACE Code of Practice C 11.7 must be made. Your PNB is the most appropriate place to record such an interview in writing. If you are at the police station and you interview a suspect who is not under arrest, then the interview should be taped.

There are many technical requirements at this stage (in which you will be trained) that adhere to the requirements of the PACE Act 1984 and other legislation and codes. For example, any **audio tapes** used to record the interview will be sealed when you collect them and take them to the interview room, and the sealed tapes must be shown to the suspect so that he/she can see that they are new and have not been tampered with.

You need to record the following information in your PNB or on the paper seals that will be wrapped around the tapes at the end of the interview (see Code C 11.7, PACE Act 1984):

- the time, day, date, location;
- the name, rank, role of the interviewer;
- the name, address, date of birth of the interviewee;
- the persons present;
- a description of the layout of the room and the equipment.

The suspect must be informed that when the tape recorder is first switched on there will be a continuous sound from the machine during which time nothing can be recorded (while the tape is winding on to the recording part of the tape).

Two tapes are recorded simultaneously; at the end of the interview one will be sealed (the master tape) and the other (the working copy) will remain with the case file and will be transcribed, at least in part. A further copy will also be provided for the solicitor on request. The master tape remains in the possession of the designated responsible person in your force. It is sealed and posted into a secure container where it is filed away and will never be opened unless it is needed in exceptional circumstances or to be examined on direction of a judge or a senior member of the CPS. The **continuity of evidence** chain is very important in this respect.

> **TASK 8**
>
> Do you know the procedures for tape recordings for your force? Summarize them now.

At the end of the interview:

- you must record the time when the interview finishes (before switching off the machine);
- the labels for the tapes must be signed by the suspect, the interviewing officer, and the solicitor;
- the master tape must be sealed in presence of the suspect.

If a suspect or the solicitor refuses to sign the labels this has to be recorded. Tell the suspect what will happen to the tapes, reinforcing this by providing a written explanation.

Code F of the PACE Act 1984 Codes of Practice states that there is no statutory requirement to visually record interviews (eg using a video camera). However, if a police force chooses to record an interview visually, the suspect has the right refuse. Code F describes in some detail the process to be followed where a suspect declines to be video-recorded. In such circumstances the interview can continue to be audibly recorded. If the suspect further refuses to have the interview recorded audibly, the interviewing officer must make a written record of the interview. PACE Code F Note 4G states that any decision to continue recording the interview either visually or audibly against the wishes of the suspect may be commented upon in court.

Further details concerning taped interviews may be found in the ACPO Investigation of Volume Crime Manual, Appendix H (ACPO, 2001).

12.5.5.8 Hostile interviewees

This is a common experience for most police interviewers: the interviewee has no intention of being cooperative and is not prepared to volunteer anything except abuse, hostility, and the stonewall tactic of 'no comment'. However, you should persist and remain polite, rational, and relaxed (or at least appear relaxed), and proceed with your questioning as planned.

The common tendency for an interviewing officer is to confront the solicitor or to start rushing the questions. **This must be avoided**. You are very likely to feel uneasy if the interview is not going as well as you had hoped; asking questions without receiving an answer is difficult and challenging, particularly as you cannot follow on from the suspect's responses so easily, but you should **not** be drawn into:

- asking closed questions (requiring a yes or no reply);
- speeding up, allowing little time for answers;
- asking the suspect to justify why he/she is not answering the questions; or
- showing any reciprocal hostility to the suspect or the solicitor.

The simple advice in this situation is to adhere to the PEACE model of interviewing and not be thrown by the suspect's refusal to answer your questions. Skilful and persistent questioning—perfectly properly within the context of the interview—may slip under a hostile suspect's defences and catch him/her unprepared for a sudden change of tack and a new line of questioning. He/she may forget to brazen it out with a repeated 'no comment' and provide you with vital evidence or information.

12.5.5.9 Adverse inference and special warnings

Special warnings are used when a person suspected of an offence fails to, or refuses to answer questions satisfactorily after due warning. If the suspect presents a 'no comment' interview when asked questions, or fails to respond to questions based on special warnings, then at trial a judge may advise the jury that they are entitled to draw an 'adverse inference'.

Adverse inference applies if the suspect presents new significant information in court, and due to its significance the court would expect the defendant to have already divulged it at interview. If the suspect failed to mention at interview matters that he/she later relied on at court (remember the caution?) the jury are entitled to ask themselves 'why did he/she not answer the question at the time of the interview?' and may conclude that the suspect has something to conceal (that might count against him/her), or that the suspect might be lying in court. Therefore during the interview you must ensure that you have asked all the questions necessary to ensure that adverse inference can be drawn in court if appropriate. After all, if you did not ask the crucial question during the interview, then the defence might be able to convince the court that the suspect would have provided the crucial information at interview, if only you had given him/her the opportunity.

Special Warnings may need to be issued to a suspect who has been caught directly in the commission of a crime (*in flagrante* or 'red-handed'), and are covered under ss 36 and 37 of the CJPOA 1994. Section 36 warnings relate to objects, marks or substances, or marks on such objects, if the person refuses or fails to account for the objects, marks, or substances. Section 37 warnings relate to the failure of a person to account for his/her presence at a place at or about the time that the offence for which he was arrested, is alleged to have been committed. The flowcharts below show this in more detail.

Section 36 of the CJPOA 1994 states that if:

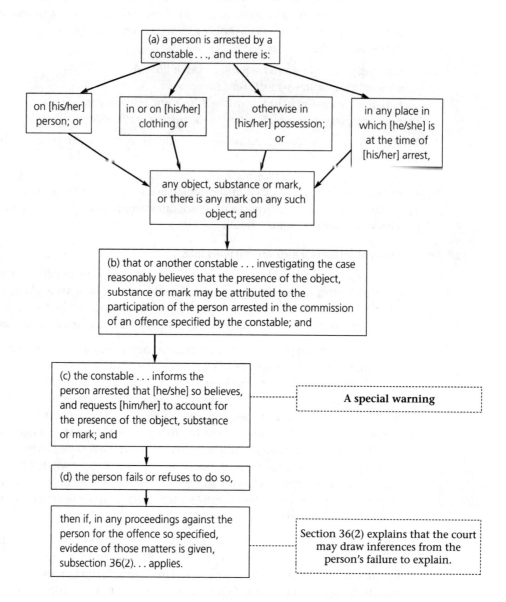

Section 37 of the CJPOA 1994 states that:

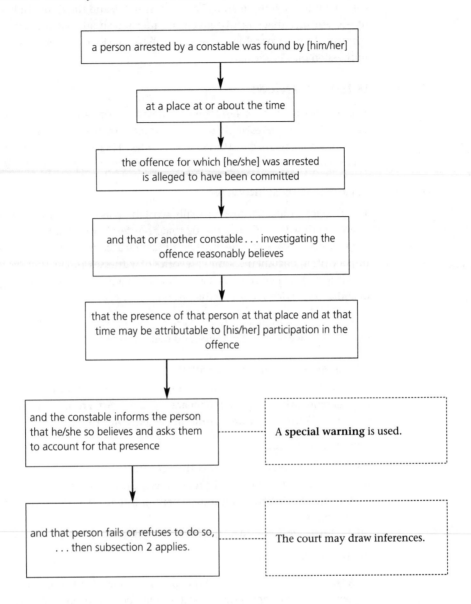

| a person arrested by a constable was found by [him/her] |

| at a place at or about the time |

| the offence for which [he/she] was arrested is alleged to have been committed |

| and that or another constable . . . investigating the offence reasonably believes |

| that the presence of that person at that place and at that time may be attributable to [his/her] participation in the offence |

| and the constable informs the person that he/she so believes and asks them to account for that presence | - - - - - | **A special warning** is used. |

| and that person fails or refuses to do so, . . . then subsection 2 applies. | - - - - - | The court may draw inferences. |

If a suspect has given a reasonable account of the fact in question, do not use a special warning. Inappropriate use of the special warning can be interpreted as oppressive behaviour, and will almost certainly entail an intervention by the suspect's legal adviser.

TASK 9

When do you think the special warning should be used? Before caution? During the 'engagement' phase? At the end of the interview, as things are being brought to a close?

The special warning should include the following five points, put in language which the suspect will understand:

1. the offence being investigated;
2. the particular fact you want the suspect to account for;
3. that you believe that the fact arose because the subject was involved in the offence;
4. that a proper inference may be drawn if the suspect fails to account for that specific fact; and
5. that a record of the interview is being made.

Suggested wording and more guidance on special warnings may be found in Appendix H of the ACPO Investigation of Volume Crime Manual (ACPO, 2001).

The use of a special warning is, in a sense, a further caution to the suspect and to the suspect's legal adviser. Sections 36 and 37 are very specific, and the Codes of Practice outline the nature of the warning that must be given in order for an adverse inference to be drawn later. Any continued silence or refusal to answer will be considered carefully by the court and an adverse impression may be created.

12.5.6 Witness Interviews

The evidence of a witness (and this includes the victim(s)) may be vital in obtaining a conviction. The PEACE procedures apply to witness interviews (see 12.5.3 above) but interviews with witnesses are not governed by the PACE Act Codes of Practice. Different approaches can be adopted, depending on the nature of the interview in prospect, but nearly all witnesses will cooperate.

12.5.6.1 Recording witness interviews

The account from a witness is usually written up as a witness statement (see 8.13.1 above). In a serious crime the SIO may decide that an interview with a key or significant witness should be video-recorded to capture his/her initial oral account of events. This will later be transcribed into a written document. Some categories of witnesses and victims (eg vulnerable or intimidated witnesses) are better interviewed away from a police station, at designated facilities capable of audio- and video-recording the interview.

Under s 9 of the Criminal Justice Act 1967, a witness statement can be read out in court in the place of oral evidence from the witness (and hence is often referred to as a 'section 9 statement').

12.5.6.2 Vulnerable or intimidated witnesses

Vulnerable and intimated witnesses may require 'special measures' at both the interview stage and subsequently in any court appearance. These two groups of witnesses are defined by Part II, s 16 of the Youth Justice and Criminal Evidence Act 1999.

A vulnerable witness is:

(a) A young person or child under the age of 17;

(b) A witness with a 'mental disorder' (this is the phrase used in the Act);

(c) A witness with significant impairment of intelligence and social functioning (eg a learning disability);

(d) A witness with a physical disability or a physical disorder.

An intimidated witness is:

(e) A witness in fear or distress about giving evidence (eg as the result of behaviour towards the witness on the part of the suspect, or members of the family or associates of the suspect);

(f) A complainant in an alleged sexual offence.

Witnesses who are either under 17 years of age or complainants in sexual cases (categories (a) and (f) above) always require these special measures. Witnesses in the other categories may require special measures, but further assessment will be required through the use of an MG 2 form (see 12.7 below) in order to determine whether this is appropriate.

Unless you are trained in interviewing vulnerable and intimidated adults and children (unlikely as a student police officer) you will probably only engage with such witnesses in obtaining an initial account. However, this is an essential part of the process, and what was said and recorded will be scrutinized very carefully later. Interviews that are likely to be more difficult or protracted will be conducted by specialist officers (qualified to at least PIP Level 2) according to ABE (*Achieving Best Evidence*) guidelines.

12.5.6.3 Reluctant witnesses

Reluctant witnesses include witnesses who:

• decline to cooperate at all; or

• make a statement, but then refuse to attend court.

If the police can establish that such a witness has important material evidence to offer, a witness summons can be issued which compels the witness to attend court. This procedure is not infrequent and can lead to the arrest of a witness and their production in court.

12.5.7 Intelligence Interviews

An often-overlooked by-product of a formal police interview is the 'intelligence interview'. An intelligence interview is the process through which the police attempt to gather criminal intelligence on the activities and lifestyle of the interviewee and others. The process must be separate from the criminal investigation. Two things apply here:

- an intelligence interview is a separate process from your interview, and must be undertaken by specialist intelligence officers;
- you have nothing more to do with the intelligence process apart from alerting your intelligence section to the potential of the interviewee.

The intelligence interview and your interview must be kept separate and distinct from each other. The intelligence interview is ring-fenced and, on the need-to-know principle, you should not have any further dealings with the matter.

All police officers should be alert to the potential for an intelligence interview and carefully note those people (known as 'subjects' in this context) who would have access to information about Category B targets, 'nominals' (literally 'names'—normally a police reference to known active and repeat criminals), associates, or offenders whose criminality comes within the force's strategic intelligence requirement. The access which the subject has should be reported to the BCU Intelligence Unit, and then arrangements will be made for the Unit to conduct an interview. In many forces, the intelligence interview is conducted by a field intelligence officer (FIO) from the BCU Intelligence Unit (who may go on to be the principal informant handler), sometimes in conjunction with a colleague (who may become the co-handler).

However, some forces have concluded that the potential exposure of the covert identity of an informant handler in the cells or in interview rooms (where they might be seen by other criminals in transit) is too great a risk. Instead, the exploratory intelligence interview is carried out by a fully trained intelligence analyst or researcher, who does not work 'in the field' and therefore runs less risk of being recognized by other criminals. This is not just a protective measure for the officer; it also has a very real impact on the security of the potential informant. The potential informant may be reassured by such professionalism and thereby more likely to cooperate.

As a student police officer you are unlikely to be involved in the detail of any of this, but you should know that it is going on. Any interview conducted whilst the subject is in custody (and this is often the only opportunity for a secure approach) must be recorded on the custody record, but without specific reference to the purpose. The record will simply record the transfer of custody from one police officer to another. The intelligence interview should not be recorded on tape and no other people should be present, in order to enhance the confidentiality of the process. Any information obtained as a result of the interview will be recorded on a 5x5x5 (see 12.4.5.2 above).

Should you subsequently reinterview someone who has been the subject of an intelligence interview, no reference should be made to that interview in the presence of others or while the interview tapes are running, since this will be potentially disclosable (see 12.6.4 below). Under some circumstances, intelligence officers can offer inducements, such as trading of charges in exchange for intelligence (see 12.4.1.4 above). You should be aware that this goes on and that it is a function of the wider intelligence and investigation picture to which you can contribute positively. However, you are advised by most forces not to speculate about any intelligence interview with others who do not need to know.

12.6 Record, Retain, Reveal, and Disclose

Here we look at the need to 'record, retain, and reveal' information that you gather in the course of your duties as a police officer. The revealed material is considered by the CPS, who then decide which parts of it should be disclosed to the defence. You should be aware that although this process involves 'revealing to the CPS and disclosing to the defence' (two completely separate processes), both are often referred to as 'disclosure'. The legislation around disclosure is complex, as recent research continues to demonstrate.

Some officers regard revelation and disclosure as a process that both confuses the courts and facilitates the work of the defence. However, the prosecution has access to significant professional services and capabilities which are used to produce the bulk of the evidence for the prosecution, whilst the suspect has perhaps only one person, the defence solicitor, employed in his/her defence. Therefore, to create a 'level playing field'—perhaps better phrased as 'the equality of arms'—the police investigator has to actively search out evidence which will not only point to guilt, but also (with equal enthusiasm) any evidence which points to innocence. Put another way, investigations need to be conducted as a search for the truth.

Investigation has a wide meaning in this context and includes:

- investigations into crimes that have been committed;
- investigations to ascertain whether a crime has been committed, with a view to the possible institution of criminal proceedings;
- investigations which begin in the belief that a crime may be about to be committed (for example, an investigation involving surveillance, even if the subject is not yet suspected of a particular offence).

We have made a number of references to evidence that you will gather, such as witness statements, completed MG forms (see 12.7 below), and other information. In many cases these materials will be an important element in the decision to prosecute a person for a crime. They could also be influential in the decision by the accused to plead guilty to a charge (as so-called 'advanced information', which is provided in advance of a 'guilty' or 'not guilty' plea).

In general terms, all police officers have a responsibility to record and retain **relevant material** obtained or generated by themselves or others during the course of the investigation, even if it is not subsequently used by the prosecution ('unused evidence'). If this is not recorded, recorded wrongly, or not retained then it is 'lost' to the defence, and hence has not been properly shared with them through the CPS. This could be a serious loophole that the defence may exploit.

You will need to identify and record all relevant material. These two words have a precise meaning in law and it is important to note that relevant material has a much wider meaning than, for example, the term evidential material. The Disclosure Manual (CPS, 2006a and henceforth referred to as the 'Manual') suggests the following meanings (rephrased in our words):

- **material** refers to information and objects obtained in the course of a criminal investigation, and includes written materials, videotapes, and information given orally;
- these materials are **relevant** when they have a bearing on any offence under investigation or any person being investigated, or on the surrounding circumstances of the case.

Unused material is defined by the Manual as 'material that may be relevant to the investigation that has been retained but does not form part of the case for the prosecution against the accused'.

It may be difficult to recognize whether materials are relevant (whether they do or do not have a bearing on an investigation and any possible subsequent criminal case). However, you will often need to make such a decision very quickly. You should also note that the responsibility to record and retain relevant material does not just relate to prosecution material, but also to material which may assist the defence. It is impossible to second-guess a defence strategy at this time and you must remain aware of the possibility that the defence may wish to call you as a witness or potential witness for them.

What follows is more detailed guidance for you in terms of the relevance, recording, and retaining of material in the course of your initial investigation of a crime or arising from being an officer involved in a response to an incident. We call this the '3 Rs': Record, Retain, and Reveal (this is an approach common in national police training). The information presented here is drawn largely (but not exclusively) from the CPIA 1996 and its associated Code of Practice.

Before we examine the 3 Rs in detail we will first illustrate the importance of this topic with an example.

12.6.1 The Importance of Record and Retain

Consider the following set of circumstances that take place when your tutor takes you to observe a court case in your local magistrates' court. The events (fictitious) illustrate the importance of recording and retaining relevant material.

The prosecution counsel opens the case by outlining the circumstances in which a major public disturbance has taken place outside a nightclub in Maidbury town centre. The incident was witnessed by a number of people. Officers from the nearby police station and surrounding areas attended the scene. A woman was arrested and the arresting officer consequently provided a statement regarding the arrest and, eventually, a number of statements were taken from independent witnesses who provided good evidence of an assault by the defendant. The decision to prosecute is made by the CPS and a case file is built, the suspect is subsequently charged and bailed to court.

The one and only witness first gives evidence for the prosecution, and is then cross-examined by the defence counsel. Next, the arresting officer is asked to take the witness stand and the prosecution asks the officer to outline the evidence of the arrest. After this has been done, the defence counsel rises, and says:

> **Defence:** Officer, I have only two questions for you … we will hear shortly from my client that there were several other police officers at the scene of the alleged assault. Who were these other officers and why are they not giving evidence today?
>
> **AO:** There were approximately ten officers at the scene; I do not know their names as they came from a neighbouring police area.
>
> **Defence:** Officer, the last witness has told this court that, when you arrived at the location, you had a conversation with him about what actually happened. Where are your notes of that conversation?
>
> **AO:** I have no record of the conversation; I remembered the name and address and then a statement was taken later.

The defendant now takes the stand and tells the court the reason for the assault was self-defence and that the arresting officer was completely wrong about how drunk she was. The defence counsel asks his client if there is anybody who can corroborate what she is saying and she replies that, if the other police officers and witnesses had been at court, they would be able to confirm her account, but not the police officer's account.

The focus of the lawyer has now switched from what his client actually did at the scene (which is what you are probably thinking is the most important issue), to examining the efficiency of the police officer in relation to two key issues: recording the verbal transactions with the accused, and ensuring that the lines of enquiry to identify the other police officers had been adequately undertaken.

The defence now apply to stay the proceedings on the basis that their client is being deprived of the right to a fair trial under Sch 1, Art 6 of the Human Rights Act 1998 (see 5.12 above), stating that the prosecution have effectively prevented their access to a number of witnesses who are crucial to the defence of their client.

The magistrates retire to deliberate. At this point you may be thinking that, whether the application is successful or not, a lot of time and effort has been wasted because important information was not recorded, and as a consequence the case may be lost.

12.6.2 Record

It is the responsibility of the officer in charge of the investigation to ensure that the material is **recorded** in a durable or retrievable form, for instance, in writing, on video- or audiotape, or on computer disc.

The following is a list of material which you and colleagues are routinely required to record and retain, as described in paragraph 5.4 of the CPIA Code of Practice:

1. **Crime reports** (including crime report forms, relevant parts of incident report books, and your PNB)
2. **Custody records**
3. Records which are derived from **tapes of telephone messages** (for example, 999 calls) containing descriptions of an alleged offence or offender
4. **Final versions of witness statements** (and draft versions, where their content differs from the final version), including any exhibits mentioned (unless these have been returned to their owner on the understanding that they will be produced in court if required)
5. **Interview records** (written records, or audio- or videotapes, of interviews with actual or potential witnesses or suspects)
6. **Communications between the police and experts** such as forensic scientists, reports of work carried out by experts, and **schedules** of scientific material prepared by the expert for the investigator, for the purposes of criminal proceedings
7. **Records of the first description of a suspect by each potential witness** who purports to identify or describe the suspect, whether or not the description differs from subsequent descriptions by that or other witnesses
8. Any **material casting doubt on the reliability of a witness**

There is a particularly important point concerning potential witnesses, known to exist by the police, but not interviewed. In the case of *R v Heggart and Heggart* (CA, November 2000), it was determined that the courts should assume that any evidence from such witnesses would either undermine the prosecution case or assist the defence case. Therefore, in the example of the court case above, a record should have been made of any witness details and what they observed in relation to the incident at the scene. There is, however, a notion of proportionality here. If an incident happens at a football match with 25,000 spectators then you would not be expected to record details of all 25,000.

12.6.3 Retain

Material relevant to an investigation is required to be **retained** for specified periods. These periods are dependent upon a number of factors such as whether or not the case continues to court and, if so, the suspect is acquitted, or the length of sentence following conviction. This is explained in more detail in paragraph 5.8 of the CPIA Code.

12.6.4 Reveal

Your main responsibilities as a student police officer are to record and retain all relevant information and make it available when required. Responsibility for revealing relevant unused material to the prosecutor is achieved through use of unused material schedules. The type of offence under investigation and your force procedures will determine whether this is a responsibility for yourself or another individual. The designated Disclosure Officer must make every effort to understand and comply with the responsibilities, and fully appreciate the 'disclosure test' application. Disclosure officers (who are members of police staff but not necessarily police officers) will examine the material that is retained for the investigation and reveal unused material to the CPS. However, it does not automatically follow that all this information revealed to the CPS will by necessity be disclosed to the defence.

12.6.5 Disclosure

Disclosure is a term used in policing and legal circles and according to the Manual (drawing on the CJA 2003 amendments) it refers to:

> providing the defence with copies of, or access to, any material which might reasonably be considered capable of undermining the case for the prosecution against the accused, or of assisting the case for the accused, and which has not previously been disclosed.

Hence disclosure occurs, for example, after a not-guilty plea. Pertinent information has already been shared with the defence and now the question settles on the unused material (unused by the prosecution).

The CPS decides what should be disclosed; but you should note that certain materials should not initially be disclosed to the defence, due to their sensitivity. These include materials which are marked confidential and use, for example, Form MG 6D (see 12.7 below). Such material might be documents that provide personal details of a CHIS (see 12.4.1 above) or of a person giving information through the Crimestoppers scheme.

You should learn about disclosure at some point during your training (it is part of the IPLDP module LPG 1.7). You will also learn about the role played by disclosure officers, the CPS, and the legal representatives of the suspect in the process of disclosure. Some of the intricacies of disclosure are both detailed and complex and beyond the scope of this Handbook. The Disclosure Manual is available on the CPS website at <http://www.cps.gov.uk/legal/d_to_g/disclosure_manual/> though the internet version does not contain the chapters that deal with sensitive matters such as the use of a CHIS. The full version of the Manual should be available from your force.

12.6.6 A Further Example

We can further illustrate the principles of the 3 Rs by means of another example. Consider the situation where you have collected CCTV recordings of an incident involving assault outside a nightclub in the centre of a town. In terms of the 3 Rs you would view the tape in terms of whether it contains relevant material with a bearing on:

- the offence under investigation;
- any person being investigated; or
- the circumstances surrounding the alleged offence.

That much is obvious. However, remember that the test of relevance here applies to both the potential defence and the prosecution in a case. The tape is relevant material if it is of potential use to either party involved in any subsequent prosecution. You may have started viewing the tape for evidence on who hit whom, and when, with what force, and at what time and so on, and perhaps there is nothing of relevance in these respects. However, the tape may show one of the individuals under suspicion talking to a bouncer outside the club, and this is potentially relevant as an alibi for the suspect. So the tape is **relevant material**, and hence it must be retained and recorded in a durable and retrievable format. If the tape also becomes **evidential**, it will be exhibited and form part of the prosecution case; if the tape is relevant and **non-evidential**, its contents will be described on Form MG 6C (see 12.7 below). However, if the tape has been considered to be **irrelevant** (at that time), there is no legal requirement to retain it, but a summary of what the tape contained should be made.

This is complicated, but as a police officer acting as an investigator, your obligation, under the statute, code, common law, and any operational instructions, is to record, or record and retain, material if it seems that it might be relevant in any way, even to the smallest extent.

TASK 10

If you were the officer giving evidence in the court case above, what evidence would you have collected?

TASK 11

In order to undertake the following task you may need to consult the Manual of Guidance referred to above or your own force documentation.

1. Reference is made above to material that is relevant but non-evidential and therefore will not be used as evidence. In relation to the disclosure process, what title will this material be given?
2. Who is responsible for examining the records created during the investigation with a view to revealing the material to the prosecutor?
3. How is unused material revealed to the prosecutor, and how must it be described?

12.7 Preparing and Submitting Case Files

The interview record that we discussed in 12.5 above will form only one part of the case file that will be used in any subsequent prosecution. There will be numerous other forms involved, including charge sheets, lists of exhibits (often forensic evidence), and so on. Successful investigations require the preparation and submitting of good quality and accurate case files. We recognize that paperwork is rarely popular, but all officers acknowledge the particular importance of case files. Do not regard case-file preparation as a mere technical exercise—the successful prosecution of a person who is guilty of a serious offence may depend on your ability to work with these files.

Before the introduction of the IPLDP, shortcomings in the training of student officers in the skills of case-file preparation were noted within a number of forces (Cambridgeshire Constabulary, 2005). You are likely to find the subject dealt with extensively during the latter half of your training. There are a number of NOS Units and elements directly concerned with this aspect of your training, notably:

National Occupational Standards Elements

DA6.1 Prepare case files
DA6.2 Submit case files and progress enquiries
2G4.1 Finalize investigations

The PAC under the 'Finalize Investigation' heading also lists 'Complete pre-charge files', 'Complete post-charge files', and 'Complete summons files'.

In addition to any notes and training you may receive from your force, you could also download and read section 1 of the 2004 edition of the *Prosecution Team Manual of Guidance* available from <http://police.homeoffice.gov.uk/news-and-publications/publication/operational-policing/prosecution-manual-intro.pdf>.

You may sometimes hear case files referred to as 'MG files'. This is because you will be using nationally produced forms which have the prefix MG (short for Manual of Guidance). Examples include MG 4, 'Charge Sheet' and MG 11 'Key witness statement(s)'.

You will be given training by your force in case-file preparation and the roles of others who also share responsibility, such as the CPS. Detailed explanations of the processes involved would be inappropriate for a Handbook of this kind. Instead we have produced (using the *Prosecution Team Manual of Guidance* mentioned above) a list of the MG forms that you are likely to require in two different circumstances:

- straightforward cases (that is, without complications such as certain sensitive disclosure issues) where a guilty plea is entered;
- contested ('not guilty' pleas) or Crown Court cases.

Before a charging decision has been made, the required case file is known as a Pre-charge Expedited file. Once the charge has been made, a Post-charge Expedited File is required for the court. If a 'not guilty' plea is entered, or if the case is to be heard in Crown Court, upgrading to a Full File is required. If the case is disposed of at the first court appearance, then upgrading is not required.

The likely case-file forms in each eventuality are summarized below (CPS, 2004). A tick indicates that it is very likely a particular form will be needed and a question mark indicates that the form might be needed.

Form	Description	straightforward		contested		full file
		pre-	post-	pre-	post-	
MG 1	File front sheet		✓		✓	✓
MG 2	Initial witness assessment		?		?	?
MG 3	Report to Crown Prosecutor	✓	?	✓	✓	✓
MG 3A	Further report to Crown Prosecutor		?		?	
MG 4	Charge sheet		✓		✓	✓
MG 4A	Conditional bail form		?		?	
MG 4B	Request to vary police conditional bail		?		?	
MG 4C	Surety/Security		?		?	
MG 5	Case file summary; might include SDN (see below)	✓	✓	✓		✓
MG 6	Case file information	✓	✓	?		✓
MG 6B	Police officer's disciplinary record					?
MG 6C	Schedule of non-sensitive unused material					✓
MG 6D	Schedule of sensitive material					✓
MG 6E	Disclosure officer's report					✓
MG 7	Remand application		?		?	?
MG 8	Breach of bail conditions		?			
MG 9	Witness list					✓
MG 10	Witness non-availability	✓	✓		✓	✓
MG 11	Witness statement(s)		✓	✓	✓	✓
MG 12	Exhibits list			✓	✓	✓
MG 13	Application for order on conviction		?		?	
MG 15	Interview record: this could be a SDN, a ROTI, or a ROVI*	✓		✓	✓	✓
MG 18	Offences taken into consideration		?		?	?
MG 19	Compensation form (plus supporting documents)		?		?	?
SDN	Short Descriptive Note; may be written on MG 15, MG 5, or officer's MG 11		✓			✓
Phoenix print	Computer print-out of the suspect's previous convictions, cautions, etc	✓	✓	✓	✓	✓
Copy of documentary exhibits/photos			✓	✓		✓
Police racist incident form/crime report			?		?	?
Crime report and incident log			✓			
Any unused material which might undermine the case					✓	
Custody record						✓

* ROTI: Recording of a Taped Interview; ROVI: Recording Of a Video-recorded Interview.

12.8   Bad-Character Evidence (BCE)

You will probably look at bad-character evidence (BCE) as part of your training as it features in IPLDP Operational Module 9 'Prepare and present case information, present evidence, and finalise investigations' and under LPG 1.4 'Bad character evidence'. BCE is also relevant to case files, covered in 12.7 above.

Here we provide an overview of bad-character evidence introduced by the Criminal Justice Act 2003 and which is relevant to the student police officer. The NCPE (now part of the NPIA) have produced Practice Advice on Evidence of Bad Character on behalf of ACPO which you may wish to consult via your police force (it is not a publicly available document). If you need the full details, then the CPS website on bad character evidence is a good starting point and is publicly available at <http://www.cps.gov.uk/legal/a_to_c/bad_character_evidence/index.html>.

12.8.1   The Definition of Bad Character

The definition of bad character provided under s 98 of the Criminal Justice Act 2003 (see below) is wide enough to cover behaviour **not** amounting to crimes as well as obvious instances such as previous convictions. The law makes it clear that reprehensible behaviour falling short of a conviction also counts as bad character. For instance, a person may have a propensity to be violent if he/she gets drunk, and this may become relevant in a case of assault against a family member, irrespective of whether the accused has been previously convicted in relation to similar behaviour.

Bad character is defined by s 98 of the Criminal Justice Act 2003 in the following way:

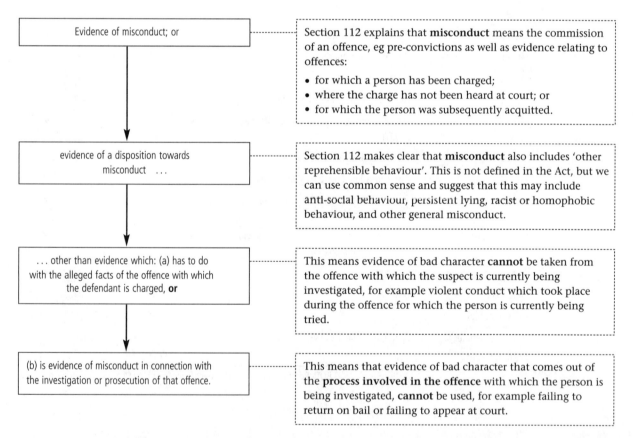

From this you can see that police officers should record matters relating to bad-character evidence contemporaneously, and provide such intelligence to the relevant department, as such information could be crucial to a subsequent criminal investigation. When dealing with criminal cases, officers should always consider whether relevant bad character exists. Form MG 16 (see 12.7 above) will need to be completed in order to notify the CPS of any relevant bad character, and officers should also consider raising relevant bad character with the defendant in interview.

12.8.2 Introducing BCE in Court

For the bad character of a **non-defendant** to be called in evidence in criminal cases, either the defence or the prosecution must make an application for leave to the judge under s 100 of the Criminal Justice Act 2003. The judge must then decide whether that bad character can be brought up in the case. The main principle behind s 100 of the Criminal Justice Act 2003 is to protect witnesses and victims from having their previous history brought up unless it is truly considered relevant to the case. Case law shows that judges are unlikely to allow such evidence to be introduced unless it really is of significant value to the issues in the case (see *R v Bovell* [2005] 2 Cr App R 401).

For a **defendant** s 101(1) of the Criminal Justice Act 2003 lists the seven circumstances where BCE is admissible. This does not require leave of the judge, but does require the prosecution to give notice to the defence regarding the bad-character evidence they propose to call about the defendant. In some cases, the defence can consider making an application to the judge to disallow its use.

Seven circumstances where BCE may be admissible for a defendant

Section 101(1) of the Criminal Justice Act 2003	Comments and explanations
(a) 'all parties to the proceedings agree to the evidence being admissible'	That is, the defence and prosecution agree (perhaps unlikely).
(b) 'the evidence is adduced by the defendant [him/herself] or is given in answer to a question asked by [him/her] in cross-examination and intended to elicit it'	Called a 'waiver by the defendant'. This would include for example, situations where suspects introduce evidence of their own bad character brought up during interview. It can also happen that during cross-examination the defendant chooses to reveal something of bad character; eg 'I couldn't have been there because I was in prison at the time'.
(c) 'it is important explanatory evidence'	So, for example, in the case of disqualified driving, evidence is submitted to the court that the defendant had been previously disqualified from driving.
(d) 'it is relevant to an important matter in issue between the defendant and the prosecution ...'	Defined as 'a matter of substantial importance in the context of the case as a whole'. This part is a major break with previous practice and should be read in conjunction with s 103, that is whether a defendant has a propensity to: • habitually commit crimes of the kind with which they are charged • be untruthful (eg previous convictions for perjury).
(e) 'it has substantial probative value in relation to an important matter in issue between the defendant and a co-defendant'	In this instance, a co-defendant may wish to provide evidence of the defendant's bad character, thus trying to prove that it was less likely that he/she committed the offence, and more likely it was the other defendant.
(f) 'it is evidence to correct a false impression given by the defendant' or	Here the prosecution may wish to introduce evidence which is relevant, in order to correct a false impression that the defendant has given in relation to his/her character, eg saying that he/she is known for his/her honesty, when in fact he/she has previous convictions for deception.
(g) 'the defendant has made an attack on another person's character'	In this instance, the defendant attacks another person's character by accusing him/her of committing an offence or behaving in a reprehensible way (whether true or not). Note that this also applies at the time the defendant was being charged or interviewed under caution—hence include such an attack in the records kept.

Finally, note that guidelines concerning exclusions to bad-character evidence and non-defendant bad-character evidence can be found on the CPS website (see above).

> **TASK 12**
> Find out which MG form is used to place evidence of bad character into the case file of the defendant.

12.9   Forms of Evidence in Court

You will be asked to think about the nature and types of evidence during your training, for example in LPG 1.7 'Investigation and Interviews'. Evidence is information which is presented to a court so that it may decide upon a fact ('did the accused do this act by this means?'). In the sense that we use the word throughout this Handbook, evidence is almost always linked with crime in some way. Evidence is usually regarded as consisting of four kinds:

- **oral** (also called verbal or spoken);
- **real** (an article, object, or thing with material existence, that is, it can be produced in court);
- **documentary** (a document, paper, or record, which can be electronic);
- **hearsay**.

12.9.1   Oral evidence

This is the most common form of evidence presented to a court. A witness will say 'I saw him push the block over the parapet of the bridge', or 'I heard her scream and then felt a hand on my bottom', or 'the drink tasted bitter, which it hadn't before I went to the lavatory'. It is what has been directly experienced by someone on the spot at the time that the alleged offence was committed, and it must relate directly to the individual who is giving testimony. In other words, a witness to an act must have perceived (seen, heard, felt, tasted, or smelled) that act directly, through his/her senses.

12.9.2   Real evidence

This is any article or thing which can be produced for the court, however large or small. Real evidence can range from microscopic bloodstains or particles of explosive, through to objects which the court will have to see *in situ* (such as a large lorry, a crash site, or piece of machinery). Real evidence has to have a material existence independent of anything else. Its link to the accused generally has to have supporting testimony, such as 'this is the iron bar which I saw the accused waving and then tried to take away from him', or 'these bloodstains were recovered from the clothing worn by the accused at the time of his arrest and which match the blood type of the man found lying in the stairwell'. It is common to have to explain in court the significance of a piece of real evidence, especially if the relevant item is not within everyone's common experience, such as an explosive detonator for triggering a bomb, or the motherboard from a computer.

> **TASK 13**
>
> Can you think of potential problems associated with the use of, and production in court, of 'real evidence'?

There must be an auditable trail for the article produced as real evidence, from the moment it was discovered or recovered until it is produced in court. This is referred to as continuity of evidence or the chain of evidence, and it simply means that the prosecution must be able to prove that the article has been held securely and that it has not been tampered with, modified, or changed in any way. It is the responsibility of the reporting or arresting police officer to ensure the secure retention of exhibits and their production to the court. In complex cases, an exhibits officer will be appointed to the case, and in some police forces a designated specialist has the responsibility for safeguarding specialist materials, such as forensic items or CCTV footage. Chapter 13 provides further details on procedures to ensure the continuity of evidence (see particularly 13.3.11 below).

12.9.3   Documentary evidence

This is written material (including electronic records of documents) which is produced in court. The medium through which it is written can vary from a Last Will and Testament on parchment with spidery copperplate writing, to an electronic file recording the use of a credit card on line. A document is of course also 'real evidence', but is separately classed because of its referential nature and because often authorship can be proven (which would be more difficult with a common-pattern kitchen knife, for instance).

The rules about the legal status of documents are complex but the general point is that the document should be produced in court by the person who created it and who can testify to its contents. This is not always possible (people who write wills have a regular habit of dying) but courts can sometimes invoke the services of handwriting experts who can testify that, within limitations, the author of one particular document is likely to be the author of another particular document. This becomes even more complex when it comes to electronic text, and specialists differ over degrees of certainty about the authorship of, for example, web documents, particularly if they are not signed or copyrighted. Some documents will be seized as evidence by the police and will then be submitted to the court—the classic example is a suicide note—and of course the points made above about 'continuity of evidence' also apply to documents.

12.9.4 Hearsay evidence

This is evidence provided by one person about what another person said. Hearsay can also include documents whose existence cannot be proven by the author, or whose contents cannot be similarly proven. It is generally inadmissible in court because of the potential for ambiguity or malice ('she told me that he threw the knife... ' is not evidence).

> **TASK 14**
>
> There are a number of exceptions which allow for hearsay evidence to be used. Can you think of any possible exceptions that might apply?

12.9.4.1 Hearsay evidence and the Criminal Justice Act 2003

In legal terms, s 114 of the Act defines hearsay evidence as 'any statement not made in oral evidence in the proceedings'. However, the same Act also changed the law relating to the admissibility of hearsay evidence in criminal proceedings, and the new hearsay rules applied from April 2005. Essentially, the old law was criticized for being too complicated, too difficult to obtain (because it was in different Acts of Parliament or case law), and too inflexible. In a trial for indecent assault (*R v Sparks* (1967)) the court would not allow a defendant to use as evidence the fact that the alleged victim had described the attacker to her mother in circumstances that showed that it probably was **not** the defendant who committed the crime. The judgment indicated that the hearsay rule was inflexible, and that as a consequence Sparks was not able to plead significant evidence in his defence. He was convicted of the crime.

The new law can be seen as a major shift in attitudes towards hearsay evidence. There are now four 'gateways' to admissibility of hearsay evidence. These are:

1. The Criminal Justice Act 2003 or any other Act indicates it may be used. (This will include, for instance, circumstances in which a witness may have given evidence to police but now cannot attend court for various reasons such as illness, death, or being in fear.)
2. Any of the common law exceptions which have been preserved by the Criminal Justice Act 2003. (This will include confession evidence and many other areas.)
3. All parties to the proceedings agree to the evidence being given.
4. The court concludes that in the interests of justice the hearsay evidence should be admitted.

Gateways 1 and 2 effectively allow for many of the old exceptions to be admissible in proceedings, but there are some significant differences. The new law now allows for **verbal hearsay** to be admissible, whereas previously it was limited to certain circumstances.

Defence and prosecution may also agree upon hearsay evidence being used in a trial. Gateways 3 and 4 both make it clear that, when submitting evidence in the form of statements or cases, officers should also include hearsay evidence so that proper consideration can be given to the issues.

Gateway 4 is particularly welcomed by the prosecution. It is clear that if evidence is hearsay, but does not fit any of the recognized exceptions, then it could **still be admissible** if the court concludes that in the interests of justice it should be admitted. This section is known as the 'safety valve' and permits the use of relevant evidence even if it does not quite fit the other recognized exceptions.

12.9.4.2 Recording hearsay evidence

For student police officers, it is essential that you record what happens contemporaneously, and that you record what witnesses and victims actually **say** to you, noting the exact words used. Some oral evidence is not acceptable as evidence in a criminal court, but it might apply at a tribunal or Coroner's court, where your notes of what was said may be admissible as evidence. Of course, if you have not recorded anything, then the prosecution will not be able to even consider using victim and witness contemporaneous utterances as evidence. You do not need to learn all of the hearsay provisions, but merely record (in your PNB) what is said to you.

12.10 Giving Evidence in Court

Now we have come to the stage where the final phases of the investigative process will be played out: the magistrates' or Crown courts. You may wish to re-read 5.14 above on the CJS at this point.

Remember that a magistrates' court hears all summary and elected hybrid criminal cases (cases that can also be tried in the Crown Court) in its particular area (called the petty sessional area). A large majority of cases do not progress further; the offender is tried and either punished or acquitted. Serious criminal offences may be referred to trial at a Crown Court, but they are always initially presented at magistrates' court (where in some rare cases the court may decide that there is sufficient evidence to support a trial at the higher court). A magistrates' court has either a bench of magistrates (lay persons, unpaid, who are Justices of the Peace) or a stipendiary magistrate who is a legally-qualified and paid practitioner. Some courts have both at different times.

Perhaps describing this as a 'stage' is apt: the course of events in a magistrates' court, and more so in a Crown Court, certainly bear a striking resemblance to scenes in a theatre and the participants perform very particular roles.

The 'actors' in the court

Participants and others	Description of the role
The Magistrate(s)	Concerned local citizens who act 'for the people' in hearing petty offences or the evidence of crimes.
The Stipendiary	The paid professional dealing with local offences.
The Clerk	The paid professional who knows the law and advises the lay magistrates.
The Accused	In the dock and trying to create the best possible impression, whether guilty or not.
Prosecution	The retributive voice of the people; a professional lawyer (Crown Prosecution Service).
Defence	The upholder of justice acting for the client(s); equally a professional lawyer or solicitor.
The Public	The 'theatre audience' (but can be the families of victims, or relatives of the accused, with an interest in the outcome).
The Judge	In a Crown Court, a professional lawyer whose legal experience qualifies him/her to assume the role of objective and dispassionate 'arbiter'. Judges have seen lots of legal tricks and heard plenty of courtroom arguments, but may remain curiously innocent of many of life's common features. It is not uncommon for example, for a judge to ask questions such as 'what is an iPod?'
The Jury	The jury is nominally '12 good persons and true' and are present in Crown Court trials at which the defendant has pleaded 'Not Guilty'. The members of the jury are theoretically drawn from any walk of life. However, until Lord Justice Auld's recommended reforms (2003), most were white people in employment from socio-economic groups C and D.
Witnesses	Some witnesses may be overwhelmed by the big occasion; this type of witness plays the role of a rabbit caught by headlights. Other witnesses are specialists with expert knowledge (for example, pathologists or forensic scientists) who are well used to appearing in court.
The Media	Usually present at big trials claiming to represent the people and apt to dramatize events as much as possible. Court reporters are almost always present at the petty level.

This is the cast of players, with the first likely to appear at the magistrates' court (where the drama is often brief and low-key) and the remainder at the Crown Court, where the drama can be prolonged and at fever pitch. Add to this heady mix the panelled court room, the eighteenth-century costumes and wigs, the rituals, and the ceremonial, and you have a stage set. It may be considered somewhat trivializing or even inappropriate to ask a student police officer to view the enactment of justice as a play and the venue as a stage set. However, in our experience such an analogy helps police officers understand the culture of the courtroom and emphasizes the inherently adversarial nature of the courts in England and Wales. It is also a pretty accurate description of what takes place. Tensions may run high in court, and not all persons present will necessarily behave as they should; see 9.10.1 above on offences relating to harassment and intimidation of witnesses and jurors.

Being 'warned for court' can be a frustratingly long-drawn-out process. Remember too that delay serves the purposes of the defence team as the longer a case is delayed, the fainter are the witnesses' recollections and the less detail people can remember. Most magistrates and judges are wise to this defence tactic and will deal with it brusquely after a reasonable period, but some will not. Be prepared for this and talk to the CPS lawyer about making a protest if the defence appears to be postponing or prolonging matters unnecessarily.

You will need to refer to the information given here again and again until it is embedded in your knowledge, but we must emphasize that there is no substitute for familiarizing yourself directly with court procedure at all levels (magistrates' court and Crown Court) by visiting them and observing the procedures live.

12.10.1 The Adversarial Justice System in Court

In the dramatic setting of the court, the contest is played out between the two adversaries or opponents, the defence and prosecution lawyers. The defendant can choose to conduct his/her own defence, although this is rare in a criminal trial. The adversarial justice system is covered in more detail in 5.8.1 above.

The defence and the prosecution must comply with the rules of evidence. The prosecution has a duty to ensure that all relevant evidence is disclosed; the defence has no such obligation. The defence challenges the prosecution's proofs, and where the proof is very strong (such as in DNA evidence) the defence will instead attempt to fault the process by which his/her client has ended up in court. The defence will challenge (in the following order):

- that the alleged offence did not take place (such as in a rape case);
- that the defendant did not do it;
- that there were justifiable reasons for the defendant having committed the alleged offence, such as self-defence; or
- that something was wrong in the process which brought the defendant to court.

This last point is the final resort and is used if the defendant did commit the crime and there is little to be said in mitigation (excuse).

Indeed it is the role of the defence counsel to expose flaws in the prosecution case if that helps the defendant. Again, this is professional, it is not personal, though some student police officers feel uncomfortable with these aspects of the defence counsel's role, believing such approaches to be morally ambiguous. This misses the point: the defence will do anything it can (within legal and ethical bounds) to help the defendant, including making the evidence or testimony appear shaky, challenging the veracity or integrity of a witness, attacking the legal process, or exploiting loopholes in the law.

A minor example can illustrate this last point quite graphically. A solicitor nicknamed by the media as 'Mr Loophole' specializes in defending the rich against charges of drink-driving or speeding. He has helped film directors, footballers, and others able to afford his £10,000 a day retention fee, to 'get off' the charges they have faced. The solicitor concerned rejects any suggestion that he should feel guilty about this:

> The laws I argue have been put in place by our democratically elected parliament … It is not me who is to blame. If they [the prosecuting authorities] did their jobs properly, nobody would ever get off. All I am doing is protecting people from the police not doing their job properly (Mr Loophole, cited in Jenkins, 2005).

So, in this sense, the police have to get it absolutely right every time, whilst the defence does not. Rightly or wrongly (in a moral sense), the essential fact remains that defence lawyers will naturally seek and exploit every loophole, every aspect of a process which has been blurred or not properly followed, and every shortfall in police procedure. As a student police officer and subsequently as a qualified police officer you may not agree with this approach, but we would argue that morality has very little to do with the day-to-day administration of justice. That is why our emphasis is always upon your getting the procedure right first time, and every time thereafter.

The bench (lay or stipendiary) in a magistrates' court and the jury in a Crown Court will decide on the basis of the evidence that has been given whether the accused is guilty or not. The magistrates' clerk and the judge (in a magistrates' or Crown court respectively) ensure that the rules of evidence are followed. If the accused pleads guilty, there is (of course) no need for a jury and hearings or trials are thereby much shortened.

Evidence is usually presented in court in the form of the testimony of a witness. As we noted above, witnesses give evidence of what they heard, saw, smelled, tasted, or felt. Other forms of evidence are covered in 12.9 above. Sometimes, an expert witness (usually, one with a special kind of knowledge) may be asked to give an opinion, such as a pathologist giving an opinion on the cause of death in a murder case, but ordinary witnesses, including police officers, will seldom be asked for an opinion. Witnesses who attend courts frequently (such as police officers) are known as professional witnesses as distinct from expert witnesses.

12.10.1.1 A court as a public arena

Both Crown courts and magistrates' courts have a public gallery, and any member of the public may attend to watch any trial or hearing in progress. Police officers are very much encouraged to attend, in or out of uniform, to see the procedures applied during a trial.

However, when friends or relatives of the defendant and the accuser attend, it can occasionally result in public order problems, and therefore the ushers and security staff need to be alerted to this possibility. The judge or chairman of the bench may well be alerted to possible problems and warn the public gallery as to consequences (removal, arrest, or incarceration for contempt of court).

Similarly, jury members may be in the full glare of the public gallery and whilst efforts have been made to design out the problem there are occasions when a jury member is intimidated by glares and gestures ('eyeballed') by members of the defendants's circle of associates. In this event you should alert the prosecution (or the defence) team. The judge will be informed and invited to take stringent action against those identified as responsible. In some rare instances the public gallery will be cleared leaving the press bench to represent the public's interest.

It is not just in the courtroom however that the instances arise; in communal corridors, cafes, and smoking areas, people with interests in the defendant and those giving evidence against the defendant have opportunities to meet, and this has to be managed. Separate rooms are available in most courts for witnesses to sit away from other people if required.

Police officers are not immune from threats or intimidation, and should identify and bring to the court's attention any person who challenges, or seeks to threaten or intimidate an officer. However you should avoid direct confrontation if at all possible. Lunch breaks away from the court or at the close of the day (when leaving court) are common times for officers to be confronted or challenged or 'signalled to'. At the end of a trial when sentence is carried out, after conviction, attention can swiftly turn to officers who have given evidence leading to conviction, and officers have to be careful. Vehicles in which they arrived at court may also be targeted.

12.10.2   Giving evidence as a police officer

At the outset you may be 'warned' to attend court; you are notified that you are required to attend court. For a magistrates' court attendance you will receive a simple letter or notice stating the time and date you are expected to attend. For a Crown court, there are two forms of witness warning—a 'conditional' or a 'full' warning.

In the event of a conditional warning the officer is put on notice that a trial or hearing is listed to be heard before a judge, and that although the officer is a potential witness it seems that the evidence to be given is not to be contested by the other 'side'. If nothing more is announced or communicated he/she can stand by and is unlikely to give evidence (unless either side move to have the witness called—perhaps if the trial takes an unexpected turn). Note however that a conditional warning does not mean you are not a witness; the evidence you may be called to give should not be discussed with any third party before or during the trial.

If a full warning is received you will certainly be called to attend court, but may still not be called to give evidence. It is a serious matter not to obey a full warning and can lead to disciplinary and judicial action. Again, your attendance is absolutely required and you should report to the court on time. If at the actual start of the trial it becomes clear that you will not be required to give evidence (a sudden change of plea to guilty is common), you should not leave the court until the matter has been completely resolved. In rare cases police officers may be called to deal with aspects of antecedent history—providing background that aids the judge in sentencing.

You will experience, from an early stage in your training as a student police officer, what it is like to give evidence in court. You will give evidence at both a magistrates' court and a Crown Court. You will be assessed against the NOS in terms of the standards that you reach, most notably Unit DA5. Giving evidence also features as one of the PAC headings, a key aspect of qualifying to undertake Independent Patrol.

Appearance in court in whatever capacity requires you to give as much attention to planning and preparation as you would for conducting a police interview, which we covered in 12.5 above. You certainly cannot just turn up at court on the day and expect to recall the criminal investigation with accuracy, or perform your role as a witness in a professional fashion.

Initially you will probably give evidence in court as the officer in the case. Later in your career, you may attend court as an expert witness (for example, in the forensic recovery of data from a computer hard drive), but at this stage you have no more privileged status than any of the other witnesses. However, you will be more familiar with court procedures than the non-specialist witnesses, and you know more about the case being tried (or you should) than anyone else present.

You will soon become experienced at court, but do not expect your subsequent court appearances to be frequent, though this varies between forces. After qualifying as a police officer you may not attend court again for years; indeed, to some extent the opportunities for you to experience court during your training are specially arranged. As you progress through the ranks, the less likely you are to give evidence in court, unless you are a detective working on volume crime issues on a BCU, or involved in a major police operation which requires your appearance. It is something of an irony that you are more likely to go frequently to court if you remain a constable than if you become a superintendent.

The reasons behind this diminishing frequency of court appearances are complex but we should note that the proportion of 'guilty' pleas at court has increased over the years, probably because of advances in DNA evidence. Also, the Auld Review into criminal justice (2001) cleared away the necessity for a court appearance (particularly at magistrates' courts) for many petty offences, and increased the use of statutory fines or penalties (see 8.15.2 above), so there are now fewer reasons for police officers to go to court. However, court appearances by police officers now tend to relate to more serious offences and involve a substantial criminal trial, so it is all the more important for you to get it right.

If you are what is termed 'the officer in the case' (that is, you made the arrest, the charge, the interview, and prepared the case papers for the CPS, or you were in charge of a team of people for this purpose), you will have to do more than just give evidence. On the contrary, you will have a great deal to do, from liaising with the CPS lawyer(s) on the case to arranging for witnesses to attend. You will also be responsible for ensuring that any exhibits in police possession are made available to the court. In a real sense, the success of the case will depend very much on how well prepared and organized you are.

As a witness you are not normally allowed to speak to the accused, unless you have permission from the CPS lawyer, and you will not be allowed to sit in the courtroom once your case has begun. You will have to wait until summoned, along with the other witnesses in the case. Do not expect your case to be heard quickly: many commentators acknowledge the slowness of the criminal justice system, and it may be for any number of technical or procedural reasons that the case is put back, postponed, rescheduled, or otherwise not heard on that day.

12.10.2.1 Planning for giving evidence

Let us now look at your role, and your planning and preparation before you go to court. You need to:

- review the case, reread the case papers, reread your PNB;
- familiarize yourself with the rules of evidence (particularly on hearsay evidence and opinion);
- check that everything in the case is administratively in order, including labelling the exhibits;
- go and look at the court premises, familiarize yourself with the layout, sit through part of a case;
- speak to the CPS lawyer who will be prosecuting;
- think about what will happen and try and prepare yourself to deal with it;
- reread this part of the Handbook!

Now, let us go into some detail. You are there because this was your investigation into an offence and, as a result of your work, a person has been charged and brought before the courts. Your role in court is the next phase of the investigation in a sense, because it is the calling to account of the case against the accused and a consideration (a weighing) of the evidence. You are there to help the court to reach a decision based on the evidence placed before it. You do this by presenting your part in the process which brought the accused to the dock.

You are not there to secure a conviction: that is the role of the Crown Prosecutor from the CPS. You are not there to decide on guilt or innocence: that is the role of the magistrates or the jury. You are not there to impose punishment: that is the role of the bench or the judge. Your job is to explain what part you played in this story, to tell what you have done, heard, seen, or recorded, as clearly and as concisely as you can. You must do it honestly, without exaggeration, remembering that you are sworn to uphold the law. That said, the facts alone are not enough. Juries and judges are human and are apt to be influenced by impressions almost as much as by the facts.

12.10.3 In the witness box

Your evidence, and that of other witnesses, is given from the witness box (often surprisingly small and modest in reality, unlike those you may have seen on TV or film). You should face towards the judge or to the bench when you give your evidence. When you are asked a question, you should face the questioner, but your answer should always be delivered to the bench or to the judge.

12.10.3.1 The oath

Evidence must be given on oath by any witness or defendant at a statutory legal process (magistrates' court, employment tribunal, judicial enquiry, Crown Court, Parliamentary Select Committee enquiry, and so on). This is enshrined in law (the Perjury Act 1911 and the Oaths Act 1978), which requires that a person must be sworn in the particular form or manner which is binding on his/her conscience. There are prescribed forms for those who profess a religious belief and for those who profess no belief, with which you should be familiar.

The essence of the oath is that you, the witness, will 'tell the truth, the whole truth and nothing but the truth', under the provisions and strictures of your religious belief or through a secular (non-religious) attestation.

Taking the oath

Belief system or religion	Wording of the oath
Most Christians	'I swear by almighty God …'
Hindus	'I swear by the Gita …'
Muslims	'I swear by Allah …'
Sikhs	'I swear by Guru Nanak …'
All non-believers, most Buddhists, some Quakers, Jehovah's Witnesses, and others.	'I do solemnly, sincerely, and truly declare and affirm … '

Those adhering to a religious belief touch or hold (covered or uncovered) their respective Holy Books when giving the oath, but there may be other observances involved such as a ritual washing (cleansing of the hands or mouth for example) or taking the oath in front of a picture (such as that of the Dalai Lama for Buddhists). Whatever the variation invoked by the individual, the taking of an oath obligates the individual to tell the truth, both before his/her religion and before the law. The law is clear: lying on oath is perjury, which is a serious criminal offence.

12.10.3.2 Introducing yourself

You should introduce yourself, giving your rank, police number, name, and the police station where you are based, thus:

> I am Police Constable 10899 Alison Winn of Carlton Road Police Station in Hemel Keynes.

12.10.3.3 Giving your evidence

Evidence can take a number of forms such as oral, real, documentary or hearsay, and these are covered in detail in 12.9 above. In most straightforward cases, you may be asked by the Prosecuting Counsel (CPS) to give your oral evidence directly. That means that you will give a detailed and accurate chronology of events, without any prompting from the prosecution. In more complex cases, and always at a Crown court, you will give your evidence in response to questions from prosecuting counsel. Again, the chronology of events is likely to be followed, but the prosecuting counsel will seek to draw out detail from you.

If you want to refer to your PNB in court, you should ask for permission to do so. The PNB entry may have been disclosed in evidence and the court will follow your reading of it. This may lead the defence to ask you to explain the manner and time of your notes, and whether your notes represent a 'contemporaneous account' (written at the time) or whether you wrote up your PNB afterwards. Provided that the writing up was reasonably soon after the event, this should be acceptable, but if there is a significant time lag (two days or longer), you should expect the defence to question you very closely and probably in a hostile manner.

If your PNB entry has not been submitted in evidence, the court and the prosecution and defence may want to examine your PNB entry physically. This may make you nervous, but do not be: you were there and you recorded the event, not them. (So always make sure that your grammar and spelling are up to scratch and that your handwriting is at least legible!)

You could be tempted to try to learn your evidence by heart and then recite from memory when you give evidence, but this is most inadvisable. For a start it will sound rehearsed and artificial. Secondly, the defence will try to put you off with questions so that you lose your thread and flounder, and finally it suggests that maybe you do not have the confidence to rely on your recall of events. There is nothing wrong with referring to your PNB entries, and if you do so confidently and with permission, you will continue to look and sound professional—after all, the lawyers constantly refer to their notes and so does the judge or stipendiary. However, you should not rely on your PNB exclusively as the court will not gain a good impression of you if you merely read from your notes. How much better it will be if you give your evidence clearly and confidently, referring only now and then to points in your PNB to refresh your memory, or to quote some complex fact.

12.10.3.4 Cross-examination

Once you have concluded your evidence (either directly or in response to the prosecution's questions), the defence may wish to ask you questions. This is called cross-examination; the questioning 'crosses' from one side of the adversarial contest to the other.

By now you should know what the defence's tactics are likely to be in the case, but try to be prepared too, for the unexpected, such as 'Pc Winn, what formal training have you had in interview techniques and did that training, if indeed you had it, cover the use of oppressive interrogation?' Watch the answer here; because the defence has used a common tactic of double questioning, as well as launching straight into querying the police officer's qualifications. This is her calm response:

> [to the judge] I was trained in cognitive interview techniques at the Bramshill Police College in August last year, in addition to the basic and advanced interview courses run by my own force in February and April of the same year.
> [turning back to the defence] Would you repeat the second part of your question, sir?

Note her politeness and refusal to be flustered or stampeded by the defence's approach. In fact, the completeness of her first reply establishes her as a professional and credible witness and the defence may seem merely querulous (questioning for its own sake). If the defence persisted in making an innuendo in this deliberately provocative tone the judge may intervene to ask where this is leading.

Never be hesitant about asking the defence (or anyone else) to repeat a question which you did not hear, did not understand, or which you want clarified. It also gives you an extra moment to think. You also need to take particular care with questions which appear innocent but which are barbed—whatever your answer, you are 'damned if you do and damned if you do not'. Do not try to be too 'clever'—remember the importance of portraying yourself to the jury as a competent professional. Multiple questions should be dealt with one at a time. You might have noticed how Pc Winn 'collects' the question from the lawyer and delivers her answer directly to the judge, before politely asking the defence lawyer for the second part of his question. This shows that she has been attentive, brief, and to the point and is not to be hurried into giving confused (or confusing) answers to compound or complex questions.

The defence would normally approach you with more caution than that shown here, taking you back over the evidence and probing for any weakness which may be favourable to the defendant. There will be occasions when your evidence is favourable to the defendant and, naturally enough, the defence will want to make use of this. You should expect to be questioned about how you conducted the investigation, the evidence you have already given, and any additional facts which you have not already given. Do not be defensive; rather be confident and positive.

There will be times when, at the end of the cross-examination, the prosecutor will come back to ask you further questions. These will be designed to clarify any confusion or to point up a particular fact or issue. New evidence cannot be introduced at this stage.

12.10.3.5 Creating the right impression

The impression which you create in court, as we have noted above, will have an influence on your credibility. There are a number of factors which build an impression in the minds of those observing and listening to you giving your evidence. Imagine the situation:

Prosecutor: Please tell the court what happened next.

Sergeant: Well, John, when I got down to the edge of the, like, disco area, there was your man bigging it up and asking all comers, like, if they wanted a piece of him, and he said 'you're having a laugh', and I turned round to him and said 'you're nicked', and this other bloke says 'Nah', and he said to him 'you're a cocky sod ain't you?' and swung a punch, like, so I stopped the music, sort of thing, and took them all in.

Prosecutor: Then what?

Sergeant: We got down the station and Pete Finch was on custody, no, hang on a minute, it was Debbie Johnson, I think. Just a sec. [He consults his PNB.] I got it down here somewhere.

Judge: Sergeant, have you or have you not a record of this very confusing scene? Whom did you arrest? On what charge?

Sergeant: Sorry, your Worship, I've got it on a bit of paper somewhere, I arrested the bloke in the dock, 'Smasher' Higgins. We know him all right, he's got a record as long as your arm. Put him away twice myself.

This exchange is deliberately exaggerated, of course, but the poor impression which the sergeant gives is not just of himself, but also of his police force and of the police in general. No one listening to this exchange would give the police officer any credibility and he is dangerously close to contempt of court.

You might have noticed too that, unprofessionally, the Sergeant reveals that the accused has a police record and has served a prison term. The defence counsel would almost certainly have intervened at this point and lodged a strong objection to the 'evidence' being given as it is likely to prejudice the case against the accused—it does not fit the 'bad character' rules which we looked at earlier in 12.8. Watch your attitude to both the defendant and your evidence in general, because you must avoid any suggestion of prejudice; an obvious bias against a defendant on the part of the police officer in the witness box will actually aid the defence. More importantly, it will be deeply unhelpful to the prosecution case.

No one would advise you to talk like a legal text book when giving your evidence but you should be careful about using jargon or slang expressions. Not only will some of these not be understood but they can give the impression of being too relaxed, or even complacent. The language of 'street cred' should be used when expressing the flavour of an idiom, such as the language used by the accused.

You need to show that you are confident and at ease. Using the correct terminology will help: calling the Judge 'My Lady' or 'My Lord', and the lawyers on both sides 'Ma'am' or 'Sir', creates the impression of a person who understands the rules of the ceremonial game. ('Your Worship' is for the magistrates' court, but even there, 'Sir' or 'Ma'am' will do.)

You need to look as smart as you sound. It would be easy for us to ignore this aspect through some sense of 'politeness' and respect for individual personal style. However, the court is no place for a police officer witness with unpolished shoes, unkempt hair, a sloppy uniform, or badly creased clothes. A smart uniform, polished shoes, and neat hair can seem petty restrictions, but they help you assert your authority (see 5.5 above). The smartness also aids your confidence when you are in the witness box.

The temptation is always to say too much and to keep on talking. Instead, keep your answers to questions short and to the point:

> **Prosecutor:** Constable Winn, were you shown the effects of the assault which Ms Bent says was perpetrated by the accused?
>
> **Pc Winn:** Yes, I was. This was at first during the initial interview, when Ms Bent showed me an extensive and fresh bruise to her left upper breast area and left collar-bone.
>
> **Prosecutor:** What did you do next?
>
> **Pc Winn:** I arranged for the Force Medical Officer to examine Ms Bent and to give a view on the cause of the bruising.
>
> **Prosecutor:** With what result?
>
> **Pc Winn:** The Force Medical Officer concluded that Ms Bent had been recently assaulted.
>
> **Prosecutor:** My Lord, I refer to the statement taken from Dr Salim Khan, Force Medical Officer, which is in bundle 6, document 44A.

Notice that Pc Winn gives clear answers, but does not elaborate (she knows that the prosecution—or, equally, the defence—will follow up with another question if there is more to be said). Note too that she does not try to give a medical opinion or to paraphrase Dr Khan's evidence or statement. This is because Pc Winn has no medical qualifications and she knows that she cannot speak with any authority, so all she can say is that the FMO's view was that Nina Bent had been assaulted because that is what Dr Khan had told her. The temptation to use someone else's evidence in your answers is strong, especially if you know the case well and have carefully read all the statements and written evidence, but you must resist the temptation.

Another point: do not use long words or over-formal constructions. The lawyers and the judge will probably understand you if you do, but some members of the jury may not. You might look as though you are trying too hard to impress if you say something like this, especially if your grasp of the meaning of words is a little shaky:

> I proceeded in a southerly direction towards the connurbative encompassment of commercial premises which is characterized by the soubriquet of 'shopping mall'. The chronological observation which was then essayed by myself was recorded contemporaneously as 13.45 hours, British Summer Time. It was at that juncture that I espied the trio of adult males engaging in what I deemed to be behaviour which warranted a sufficiency of explanation as to make my legitimated suspicions subside ...

Perhaps all you needed to say was:

> I was on patrol in the Shopping Mall at 1345 when I saw three men behaving suspiciously, so I challenged them.

Even this is fairly formal, but it has the great merit of being brief. Remember the impression you are creating as a concise, well-prepared professional.

We looked at cross-examination in outline earlier. How would you respond if you were the object of this defence argument?

> **Defence:** I put it to you officer, that this whole case is a tissue of invention from beginning to end. You have said that the defendant assaulted Nina Bent with his fists on the evening of May 16, but that is not true is it?
>
> **Pc Winn:** It is true, sir.

Defence: I'll tell you what is true. It is true that you and your colleague decided between you that you didn't have enough evidence against the defendant to put him away this time, didn't you? You have lied in evidence, you have lied about the events, and you have lied about framing the defendant for something he didn't do!

Pc Winn: None of those things is true. I have told the truth.

Defence: You're lying now!

Pc Winn: No, sir, I am not.

Judge: Mr Moyne, I am growing tired of this. Kindly make your point now, or move your questioning to something we all understand.

You will recall (or if not, you will soon experience) abuse from people you have arrested, or when you have intervened in a fight, or when you have tried to sort out a domestic quarrel. You will have been called names, spat at, sworn at, jeered, and belittled. If you kept your temper then, keep it now. The defence is trying to provoke Pc Winn, to probe beneath her calm and to make her lose her temper.

You will experience, at some point in your career, an attack on your integrity. If you lose your temper or reply in kind, your credibility as a police officer on oath in court is in danger of collapse. Police officers can be subject to more personal scrutiny than any other witness likely to appear; your record, your training, your job performance, and even your personal life may be closely investigated by the defence before the trial takes place. Anything which can undermine your credibility or make the jury dubious about how reliable your testimony is, will be fair game to the defence, and a defence lawyer will not hesitate to confront you with it when you are being cross-examined.

TASK 15

What rule must you always follow if your training, your integrity, and your standing as a police officer are so fundamentally challenged?

12.10.3.6   **After you have given evidence**

You should wait in the witness box until the magistrate or judge gives you permission to leave. There are two forms of 'permission to leave' and these are:

- to be **stood down** which usually requires you to be available for possible recall by either side;
- to be **discharged** which usually signals that the court will not expect you to be recalled and your attendance is not required further.

If you are in doubt you must speak to the CPS lawyer prosecuting the case or instructing Counsel at a convenient moment, and remain available within the court building.

Should you wish to remain in court you are entitled to do so. You would normally sit in the public gallery—where witnesses and family for the accused may also be seated, so you might not feel particularly comfortable. You should also avoid making eye contact, muttering, feigning disbelief, or nodding in agreement; this sort of action on your part might encourage the defence to question any influence you may be having on the jury or the magistrates, and could easily lead to criticism of your conduct in open court.

You also need to take care in relation to other witnesses who have not yet given evidence. Imagine you travelled to court with a colleague and that you have given evidence and been discharged. Your colleague on the other hand has to give her evidence first thing in the morning. You travelled together by car and intend to return home the same way; however you need to take care not to talk about the case. You can have a normal conversation about other matters, but be aware that for your colleague there may be opening questions the following morning about how she travelled, who with, and whether the case was discussed. The defence may look for forms of collusion, or inconsistency between her written statement and the evidence she gives orally, and suggest that any differences are an indication that she changed her account to suit others.

12.11   Answers to Tasks

TASK 1

You should consider where the hot spot is. Is it in a town centre? Close to a series of pubs or clubs? When does it happen? Would a police presence act as a deterrent? Who is likely to have brought the incidents to police attention? What would be the feelings and fears of the local community?

Are the vehicle owners reporting the crime? What is taken? Is there a pattern? What is the location? Are particular kinds of cars targeted? What preventive action would help (for example, leafleting car owners, warnings in the media not to leave valuables on view, posters of the 'Watch out! There's a thief about!' variety, and CCTV coverage)?

Are the credit card thefts seasonal (that is, do they happen in the summer, at the start of a new term, at the approach of Christmas)? What is the MO? What do students do about it? Is violence involved? How is the crime reported? Are women students more at risk than men? Are there criminals on the database who specialize in this sort of crime? What preventive action might you recommend? (Hint: think about crime prevention, raising awareness, liaison with college and university authorities to put cash points on campuses, credit card theft prevention schemes, talking to the banks, posters near ATMs (cash machines), security awareness, CCTV, and so on.)

You can see from these suggestions what sorts of questions are involved. A T&CG has to consider all the angles, all the permutations, as well as assess the intelligence, commission more work, and decide what to do operationally. It may be months or even years before you attend a T&CG, but if you understand how the process works, you will understand why you are tasked and how your work will feed into the NIM.

TASK 2

You may have come up with a list like the following (which is not exhaustive!):

integrity
honesty
patience
attention to detail
strong-minded
not easily diverted
experienced
knowledgeable about crime and criminals
ordinary/normal in appearance, so can blend into a crowd
reticent or discreet
firm sense of duty
objective
understands the 'bigger picture' of force needs and intelligence requirements
adaptable (can think on his/her feet)
flexible
professional in the relationship (courteous but not close)
willing to work long or unsocial hours
resilient
stable as a personality
good listener
empathetic ('emotional intelligence').

These qualities, skills, or attributes are not common in such combinations. A good source handler can be trained to a high pitch, but there must be strong character traits already there upon which the training can build. You can see, I hope, that being a source handler is not something you can waltz straight into doing; it takes someone with considerable investigative experience and 'life skills' to do well in the role.

TASK 3

This is discussed in the text immediately after the question. In addition, you might like to look at the work of Dunnighan and Norris in respect of the use of informers (Dunnighan, 1996 and Dunnighan, 1999).

TASK 4

Motivation is notoriously difficult to understand and identify, and particularly so with informants. As we have noted, most informants are themselves criminals and we have several layers to peel back. As Canter and Alison (2000) noted, the motivation that a person may put forward for their actions is not necessarily the most useful for understanding that person's actions and is only one of a number of possible explanations.

TASK 5

You could indicate resilience, self-sufficiency, strong professionalism, the ability to work alone, the ability to pass yourself off as something you are not, the focus and concentration to know what intelligence is needed, a very good relationship and trust with your handler, and a personal inclination towards the clandestine.

Logistical and support problems include a good cover story (both for the criminal target and to explain the officer's absence back in the force), payment, nothing to identify the officer as from the police (in clothing, residence, possessions), career planning, reassuring family members, diverting curious colleagues, and so on. There are a host of problems associated with going undercover long-term and a team of people are used to support the lone officer.

In planning a Test Purchase (TP) operation, you would have to think about the original intelligence and its reliability, the patterns of movement (and MO) of the target criminal, when to insert the TP officer, how to monitor what is happening, how to intervene and disrupt or arrest, and whether you have the authorization to proceed.

TASK 6

Open sources of intelligence have grown rapidly in recent years, largely as a result of the availability of electronic resources such as the internet. Whereas in the past we might need to search manually through paper copies of newspapers and magazines selling used cars for evidence of possible 'ringing' now we can use the search facilities available on most websites. Indeed, the widespread availability of information is causing some concern with the advent of crimes such as identity theft (putting aside the obvious general desire to maintain personal privacy). As an experiment, try to find out as much about yourself as you can by using freely available internet resources. For example, start with <http://www.192.com> and enter your own name. You may be surprised at what you (and others) can find out.

TASK 7

For interviews with cooperative witnesses (remember that some may be friends or associates of the suspect and hence not cooperative) we may be able to employ the 'cognitive interview' (CI) technique. Although CI may be part of your PEACE training it is not often used by police officers investing volume crimes, nor by student police officers whilst undergoing training. CI uses memory-enhancing techniques such as context reinstatement, which involves recreating the other events that were also encoded at the same time (or before or after) the event that we are interested in. You are probably familiar already with this idea—for example, what techniques do you use to locate misplaced keys or your wallet? If you want to know more about the cognitive interview and other interview techniques then *Investigative Interviewing—Psychology and Practice* by Rebecca Milne and Ray Bull is a good start (Milne, 1999).

TASK 8

Copies of the recording are made: one for the case file, one for the suspect, and another for the solicitor. The source (original) tape is sealed and is kept safe by the designated responsible person. You will no doubt be issued with detailed guidance and instructions when you reach this stage of training.

It is not usual to type a full transcript (Record of Taped Interview or ROTI) as this is very costly and takes time, but a shortened version of the interview will be prepared for the reviewing lawyer (a Short Descriptive Note (SDN)).

TASK 9

Many police practitioners argue that the best place to use a special warning is after the suspect has had a full opportunity to account for what happened, but has not done so; in the 'challenge' phase of the PEACE interview (see 12.5.3.3 above).

TASK 10

When you attend an incident, you are a potential witness, not necessarily only for the prosecution, but also for the defence.

- When you arrive at the scene of an alleged disturbance and you do no more than establish that your colleagues dealing with the incident require no further assistance, then record that fact in your PNB.
- If there are groups of people milling around you may decide to stay in the area in case of any further trouble. If that is the case, then make a short note to that effect.
- If you are present and involve yourself in assisting an arresting officer, then make an entry to that effect.
- If you talk to witnesses or potential witnesses, record their details and record what they observed in relation to the incident.

TASK 11

1. Unused material.
2. A disclosure officer is responsible for examining the records created during the investigation (and any criminal proceedings arising from the investigation).
3. It is revealed to the prosecutor on Schedules MG 6C and MG 6D (forms from the Manual of Guidance series of forms). It must be described in sufficient detail and with sufficient information to enable the prosecutor to make an informed decision as to whether or not the item contains anything which might undermine the prosecution case.

TASK 12

You should have discovered that Form MG 16 is used.

TASK 13

You might have referred to the 'continuity of evidence'. You will remember from many examples in this Handbook that this is a mundane but vital part of case preparation.

TASK 14

The exceptions usually agreed to be taken as evidence are declarations on the point of death; and statements made as confessions (if the witness heard the confession him/herself).

TASK 15

Perhaps one rule to follow is 'do not to be provoked'.

Different police officers have different strategies to achieve this. Some mentally count to three before responding to allow themselves time to compose a calm response. If you remain calm and collected, you will impress those watching and listening with your professionalism.

Crime Scenes and Forensic Investigation

13.1   Chapter Briefing

This chapter is primarily concerned with attending crime scenes and the use of forensic investigation, both important elements in many successful investigations of crime. Throughout we link both subject matters to your own training as a student police officer. We also examine attending and dealing with incidents involving loss of life, often sudden deaths although not necessarily of a suspicious nature.

13.1.1   Aims of the Chapter

The aim of this chapter is to assist in the development of your knowledge of attending crime scenes, and to help extend your understanding of forensic investigation, and the role it plays in policing. The chapter also aims to introduce you to police procedures surrounding sudden deaths. This chapter will enable you to:

- understand your responsibilities when attending a crime scene and the ancillary requirements concerning the care of exhibits;
- gain a comprehensive understanding of the basis of forensic investigation, how it supports police investigation, and your role in evidence protection and collection;
- understand the police approach to the process surrounding sudden death;
- develop the underpinning knowledge required for a number of NOS elements, several of the PAC headings, and entries for your Learning Diary Phase 3 and the CARs of your SOLAP.

13.1.2   Police Action Checklist

This chapter will provide you with the underlying knowledge and theory to meet aspects of the following requirements of the Police Action Checklist.

13.1.2.1 Investigation

- Demonstrate crime scene management;
- provide support and advice to victims and witnesses;
- conduct the initial investigation and report of sudden death;
- correctly handle exhibits.

13.1.2.2 Custody officer procedures

- Obtain fingerprints;
- obtain DNA sample.

13.1.3 National Occupational Standards

This chapter will provide you with some of the knowledge required to demonstrate the following NOS elements:

National Occupational Standards Elements
AF1.1   Identify the hazards and evaluate the risks in the workplace
CD1.2   Respond to incidents
CI101.1   Conduct priority and volume investigations

13.1.4 IPLDP Phases and Modules

This chapter will provide you with resources to support Operational Module OP 3 'Respond to incidents, conduct and evaluate investigations' (and particularly OP 3.2 to 3.6 inclusive). It will also provide guidance on the following topic areas of LPG 1:

- Policies and Procedures (LPG 1.4);
- Investigation and Interview (LPG 1.7).

Much of the chapter relates to IPLDP Phase 3 (Supervised Patrol) and Phase 4 (Independent Patrol).

13.1.5 SOLAP

The contents of this chapter are relevant to the 'knowledge' evidence requirements of CARs CD1 and CI101.

13.1.6 Learning Diary Phases

The contents of this chapter may provide you with stimulus material for completion of your Learning Diary (Phase 3) and the following headings in particular:

- Crime;
- Police Policies and Procedures;
- Investigation and Interview.

13.2 Introduction

In this chapter we examine three important aspects of your training as a police officer: attendance at crime scenes (both volume crime and major crime), dealing with incidents involving deaths, and finally forensic investigation and the associated procedures and processes. Volume crimes are frequently occurring crimes such as property crimes and certain forms of interpersonal crime such as assault. Volume crime includes:

- street robbery;
- burglary ('dwelling');
- burglary ('non-dwelling');
- theft (including shoplifting);
- theft of vehicles;

- theft from vehicles;
- criminal damage;
- common assault;
- illegal drugs (often linked with acquisitive crime).

It follows that, statistically at least, you will more often be attending volume-crime scenes than major crime scenes.

Major crimes are generally defined as crimes that include one or more of the following:

- serious violence or the potential for serious violence (such as murder, manslaughter, and stranger rape);
- resources beyond those of a single BCU (such as a major robbery by organized criminals);
- terrorism or the threat of terrorism;
- incidents that are likely to be of grave public concern (such as the abduction of a child).

Major crimes are classified as shown in the table below. The level of resources put into an investigation relates to the category of the crime.

Major crime classifications

Category A	A major crime of grave public concern: for example where the victim is a child or where multiple murders, or the murder of a police officer occurs.
Category B	A 'routine' major crime where the offender is not known.
Category C	A major crime where the identity of the offender is known.

In addition, a senior officer with responsibility for the investigation of major crime (eg a detective superintendent who is head of a Major Crime Unit) may also designate any crime as a major crime, in order that the appropriate resources may be made available for its subsequent investigation.

In a number of key respects, the principles of attending a volume-crime scene are no different to those employed when attending the scene of a major crime: in many cases any differences might simply be those of scale. However, as we noted in 9.28 above, emergencies, major and critical incidents may give rise to crime scenes of significant geographical size and complexity (such as the bombings in London in July 2005) and the events might require multi-agency emergency responses, adding to the demands of crime-scene management.

13.3 Attendance at Crime Scenes

You need to be very familiar with the procedures used at crime scenes; many of these relate to protecting evidence and minimizing the risk of contamination. Later, in 13.5 below, we examine the broader subject of forensic investigation in more detail, including the types of evidence that you may encounter.

The material covered here is relevant to NOS element CI101.1

> **National Occupational Standard Element**
>
> CI101.1 Conduct priority and volume investigations

and in particular the requirements to 'identify and preserve the initial scene(s)' and 'identify and deal with evidence'.

The relevant knowledge and understanding from CI101.1 is:

- the reasons for preserving the scene(s);
- how to apply the investigative mind-set to maximize useful material and minimize loss of potential evidence;

- how to prevent the cross-contamination of material;
- how to identify the types of material which may be present at the scene(s);
- the procedures for retaining and recording material;
- the reasons why the integrity and continuity of evidence must be maintained;
- current developments in forensic science and other areas.

The information presented here will also help you to satisfy the PAC requirement to 'correctly handle exhibits' under the general heading of 'Investigation'.

13.3.1 The Crime Scene

The crime scene is frequently the most important component of any investigation, because it is from here that physical evidence may be located which demonstrates guilt or innocence, which identifies suspects, and which corroborates or refutes statements made by witnesses. Early and effective protection of the crime scene ensures that the greatest amount of potential evidence is available for recovery and, therefore, maximizes its value to the investigation.

The first police officer who attends the scene (possibly as the result of an emergency call) is known variously as the **First Attending Officer** (FAO), the First Officer Attending the Scene (FOAS), or sometimes the Initial Responder. We use FAO in the remainder of this chapter but remember that your force might use a different acronym.

The FAO may be of any rank and position within the organization—indeed, it could be you whilst under supervision or whilst undertaking Independent Patrol.

13.3.1.1 What is a crime scene?

Crime scenes are not purely geographical locations to which we can apply an address, postcode, or map reference. Whilst it is true that homes, open spaces, and town centres have all witnessed much criminal activity, it is unduly restrictive to limit our consideration to just these areas. Treating a person (a victim) as a crime scene may be distressing and potentially offensive to the person and to his/her family or friends, but it is vital that we consider people as sources of evidence and intelligence. This is to ensure that we effectively 'protect and preserve' such people, and recover from them the evidence or intelligence we need.

A crime scene is not just a place: crime scenes are sources of evidence or intelligence. By using this definition, crime scenes can also be seen to include the intangible: computer hard drives, digital storage media, and networked environments.

13.3.2 Preserving the Scene—Safety First

The overriding principle applied to the management of crime scenes is that all attending officers rigorously ensure the safety of the public, their colleagues, and themselves. Any physical location in which an offence has occurred may include emotional, aggressive, or confused people who may represent a danger. In addition, damage to premises, such as by fire, may weaken the structure of a building, resulting in further hazards.

All physical evidence is expendable when balanced against human life. Hence the FAO should not preserve a crime scene to the extent that it causes unnecessary delay which results in aggravating a victim's injuries or leads to increased danger to life and limb.

This is not to say that one can disregard physical evidence during the life-saving process. After all, the FAO can advise the ambulance crew where not to tread and can carefully move furniture away from the victim to facilitate medical aid when necessary. However, if such actions are carried out, it is essential that moved items are left where they are and that all such activity is clearly reported to attending crime-scene investigators (CSIs) early on in the investigation. Movement of furniture, switching on lights, and even opening doors represents contamination (in its loosest sense) and may take the item out of context. All these actions must be reported to the CSI and should be recorded in your pocket notebook (see 8.3 above). All police officers attending crime scenes, including the FAO, should wear protective clothing for their own safety and to prevent the addition of misleading material to the scene.

13.3.3   Cordons

Once any victims have been treated and removed (or confirmed dead), the venue of the offence must be cordoned to prevent access by the public. The first few minutes after a major crime may be confusing and the FAO should control any person in the vicinity, including colleagues, and direct them to carry out urgent tasks since he/she is effectively the 'scene manager' at this time. The FAO should not be afraid of instructing superiors in this respect; if an action urgently needs completing then it must be done without delay and the superior officer should respect this.

The golden rule in cordoning is to make the cordon larger than you think is immediately necessary. The inner cordon (also known as the first cordon) must encompass specific areas:

- the venue of the offence;
- all possible routes into or out of the venue taken by the offender/s and victim/s;
- any location where physical evidence may be found: for example, communal bins, under cars in the street, nearby gardens;
- any location identified as routes, or as significant, by witnesses.

The cordon is erected using police tape and should be attached to fixed objects and made secure. Attaching the tape to potential evidence, for instance a parked car of interest, may erase evidence like bloodstains and fingerprints because of the action of the wind, or people moving the tape. The presence of fixed objects must not determine the cordon size: if necessary, the tape can be affixed further out from the centre until poles are made available. Whilst putting this in place the officer must also control witnesses and keep them out of the freshly cordoned area. This is sometimes difficult.

Once the initial cordon is in place a secondary cordon (the outer cordon) can be installed. The outer cordon is placed to manage the public's access and view and is strictly a matter of control. If the public can see significant evidence then this cordon is too small. It also makes sense to position the cordon so that vehicles can turn around, minimizing local congestion.

The policy of some police forces is to position the cordons so that the area between the inner and outer cordon might contain material of importance to the enquiry. Typically this could be a discarded weapon, clothing, telephone kiosks, or shoe marks which are not within the inner cordon.

Once the inner cordon is in place, nothing—not even a patrol car—may leave it until sanctioned by a CSI, unless it is required to save life—for example, an ambulance or fire appliance. Vehicles moving through the cordoned area may damage vital evidence which has not yet been seen and recovered. Additionally, the offender may have leaned on a vehicle outside the venue of the offence when he made off, so CSIs may wish to examine every vehicle within the cordon or, on occasions, every vehicle in the street.

Nearly all officers carry a mobile phone with extensive features nowadays, including cameras. Officers should avoid the temptation to photograph the crime scene with a mobile phone. Whilst this may occasionally assist an investigation in the early stages, the telephone then becomes a source of evidence and will need to be retained for analysis of the image in its original state. There are some circumstances where this might help (for instance, when a wet shoemark is evaporating) but generally the situation is best avoided.

13.3.4   The 'Golden Hour'

The first period of any incident at a crime scene or a critical incident is often described as 'the golden hour'. It is actually unlikely that you will be on your own for that long, unless the incident is in a really remote and inaccessible place, or there are corollary problems (such as a natural disaster of some kind) and access roads are blocked. You may be relieved by a senior officer quite quickly, but you may not. If you are not, the golden hour is your responsibility (and that of your colleagues, if present).

The golden hour is normally a shorthand reference to the need to preserve a scene quickly so that evidence can be gathered while it is still fresh and undisturbed. For example, bloodstains should be sampled before they are diluted by rain and the body of a deceased person should be examined before rigor mortis sets in.

It is also a real advantage to interview witnesses whilst their recollections are still clear. You should listen carefully to witnesses and evaluate what they say in the light of what you know already. Consider the Soham murders as an example: Ian Huntley, a caretaker at a school in Soham, had murdered two young girls. The first alarm that was raised was the disappearance of the two girls. Imagine that you were the first police officer to respond to the alert. What triggers or signatures would you expect?

Your notes might include questions about what you were told. How long had the girls been missing? Was it normal for them to wander off without telling anyone? Were they going anywhere specific, such as to a shop or to visit a relative or friend? Had there been any difficulty at home, such as a row or a quarrel because one of them had been forbidden to do something? Had anyone seen anything suspicious? Did the girls have a favourite 'bolt hole' to which they would go if they thought they were in trouble? Did either have a special or particular friend? Did they have mobile phones? Where did they like to go for a walk or to 'hang out'? What were they wearing? Are there any recent photographs? Remember that, in instances like this, parents, guardians, or carers might well be distraught with anxiety and worry. It is not unusual for anxiety to turn to anger. Expect anger, but do not be deflected by it; be calm and in control. Remember too that this might not just be a matter of a missing person or persons; it might be a homicide, abduction, or kidnapping.

13.3.5   The Rendezvous Point (RVP)

The rendezvous point (RVP) is vital to the smooth running of the investigations at the scene, and should have been carefully chosen early on in the investigation. It may be required to hold a number of vehicles, rest stations, food vans, major incident vehicles, and even a command tent. RVPs should never be placed in a narrow street with restricted access. They should always be in a roadway or on land with good access, and which is unconnected to the investigation. When attending the scene of a suspicious explosion, care must be taken to search the RVP for secondary devices which have been deliberately placed to cause maximum casualties to the emergency services.

13.3.6   The Common Approach Path (CAP)

This is the route from the cordon's edge into the crime scene proper and should be guarded by a **scene control officer**. This may be you, whilst under supervision.

The CAP should **not** be the route likely to have been taken by victim or offender. Nor should it necessarily be the same route taken by the FAO (who was initially acting without full knowledge of the facts). If the scene is empty (there are no living victims on the crime scene), there will be more time to choose the most suitable route for the CAP.

The route of the CAP should minimize damage to potential evidence, particularly material which is small or almost two-dimensional—such as shoe marks and blood. Wherever possible, the CAP should be laid on solid ground. This will help to prevent accidental concealment of evidence which might occur if personnel walked over a CAP consisting of softer materials such as grass and soil.

Ideally the CAP should be marked with tape but, in the early stages, this may not be possible. Attending personnel should not be tempted to anchor the tape with rocks and other debris in the vicinity, since one of these may have been a weapon.

Some of the problems associated with CAPs are:

- The eagerness to establish a CAP through the rear of the premises: entering the premises via a back door and searching for a key may destroy vital evidence.
- How do you choose the route for a CAP in a flat, featureless field?
- There may be only one entrance to the building.
- There may be no available means to mark the CAP.

One of the early tasks of the CSI is to search the CAP for evidence. It is possible the CSI will want to move the CAP to another location as a result of finding material.

13.3.7 The Log

Perhaps the most important document at the crime scene is the log. This is a booklet or sheet upon which the details of all attending personnel are recorded. It must be copied and disclosed to the defence who will study it and compare it to statements and other scene logs (see 12.6 above). In essence, it records any event that could have led to contamination of evidence. The log should contain details of:

- every person already at the scene when the FAO arrived;
- every person who subsequently attended the scene;
- every person who entered the inner cordon (for whatever reason);
- the time and date of their entry and exit;
- preferably, the reason for their attendance;
- preferably, a description of the CAP.

Failure to maintain the log may render some or all of the evidence removed from the scene unusable within the context of the CJS. It is the responsibility of the scene control officer and every individual to ensure the log is completed correctly. As a student police officer, ensure that you know who the scene control officer is when attending a crime scene under supervision.

13.3.8 Attending Personnel

Ambulance crews carry out an essential role and are to be allowed controlled access in order to save life. Ambulance crews are generally aware of how to behave in a crime scene but may have to be reminded not to touch anything needlessly and to show caution where they walk. Crews should be accompanied by the FAO who should take their names for later elimination (particularly of shoes, clothing, and fingerprints) and point out apparently significant evidence to be avoided. Clearly, ambulance personnel should wear gloves, as should the FAO.

A doctor is not always required to certify death in cases involving fatalities, since some ambulance trusts have devolved this responsibility to their crews. If a doctor attends, he/she should wear protective clothing and carry out the minimum disturbance to the body that is necessary. The use of oral, rectal, or deep-tissue thermometers is not generally permitted. The doctor is also requested not to turn the body nor search through clothing to view hypostasis or injuries (see 13.4 below).

Other police colleagues (such as senior officers) are generally not allowed to enter the inner cordon unless:

- the offender is likely to be within and must be apprehended;
- they are saving life;
- they can assist in urgent and immediate acts to prevent loss of the scene (for example a fire);
- a dog is required to pick up a track from within the cordon.

In the case of deaths, there is no requirement for a senior officer to enter the scene once death has been confirmed, nor to confirm that a death is suspicious. In addition, it is not necessary to confirm observations made by other officers.

The CSI will attend at the RVP (see 13.3.5 above) and, together with the FAO and other personnel, make a judgement as to how exactly to proceed. In general terms, the CSI's initial role is to gather information, start with photography where appropriate, advise detectives and uniformed police on the arrangements for any arrested persons, and call for assistance from colleagues. Once this has been achieved he/she may be in a position to examine the CAP, record and recover vulnerable evidence from it, and occasionally move the CAP to another location. It is common for the CSI to enter the scene with the doctor to certify deaths.

The Crime Scene Manager (CSM) is appointed in a major crime enquiry to manage the crime scene and to deal with scientific resources. In some cases a single CSM may be appointed, who will deal with all parts of the investigation. In a more serious or complex case there may be a number of CSMs and a crime scene coordinator (CSC). Typically, the CSM will be hands-on, but be flexible enough to attend strategy meetings and deal with other issues.

A variety of emergency personnel may attend a scene. Whether they are recorded in the log (see 13.3.7 above) depends on whether they enter the crime scene or assist elsewhere. The first five groups (in bold) in the list below will also keep independent records of attendance for their own personnel:

- **the fire service;**
- **Explosives Ordnance Disposal (EOD) (in the case of explosions or suspected explosive devices);**
- **coastguard and RNLI;**
- **mountain rescue and their dogs;**
- **lowland search organizations;**
- borough or district surveyors;
- structural engineers;
- Transco (for gas leaks);
- scaffolding contractors.

13.3.9   Fast-Track Actions

In every major crime the senior investigating officer (SIO) will consider fast-track actions which might resolve the investigation rapidly. These decisions are taken after careful consideration, and are noted in the policy file (which records the decision-making process of the senior officer). However, in the very early minutes of an investigation, some actions may be necessary to prevent the loss of evidence or facilitate the apprehension of a suspect. These can include the following:

- the use of a dog to track the offender, particularly if the scent is not contaminated—this may necessitate the dog's entry to the inner cordon. (If you are involved with this, you should be guided by the handler.)
- the immediate collection of evidence which is in danger of being lost, such as wadding and cartridge cases blowing down a street;
- switching off a cooker if it might start a fire;
- in poor weather, covering shoe marks and tyre marks with boxes or bin lids taken from an area well away from the crime scene;
- an urgent search of the street (sometimes called a flash search) for evidence which has been discarded, especially when the area is busy;
- controlling large groups of people in confined situations, such as a public house (pub), which might cause the loss (or gain) of fibre evidence.

In these circumstances care must be taken to make the right decision and, where necessary, protective clothing (at the least, clean medical-style gloves) should be worn to prevent contamination of the evidence. Police officers, including supervised student police officers, should be prepared to justify their actions (or lack of them) to the senior investigating officer.

13.3.10   Volume-Crime Scenes

At volume-crime scenes you should bear in mind the points made above, but note that the actions of the CSI and others are likely to be less extensive. Officers will also try to minimize disruption to normal life in the immediate vicinity of the crime. If the CSI is delayed, a police officer (and hence you) may be required to carry out these actions:

- close doors to control children and pets, instead of using cordon tape;
- close windows and consider boarding up in inclement weather;
- cover shoe marks inside with a chair (not a piece of paper which is more likely to be moved or trodden on);
- bring broken glass and property inside, handling it by the edges and wearing gloves, as moisture makes fingerprinting difficult;
- cover shoe and tyre marks outside with bin lids, trays, or boxes, even in sunny weather;
- allow the victims to make drinks and food and facilitate this, unless doing so would damage good evidence or cause a health risk;
- use the blanket or quilt to funnel any material on the beds to a corner of the room;
- if boarding-up is to be arranged, ensure the original window is left rather than being removed by the contractor.

Whilst these actions may help a victim's state of mind, there are other considerations which must be borne in mind, such as the preservation of evidence. The most important consideration is that you should protect any articles that you move by wearing gloves and handling material carefully: **gloves do not prevent fingerprints from being destroyed**. Second, continuity must be considered, as the police officer who moves articles of interest should—technically—exhibit them. You should follow local protocols on this issue.

13.3.11 Exhibits and Exhibiting

According to common law 'it is within the power of, and is the duty of, constables to retain for use in court things which may be evidence of crime' (*R v Lushington ex p Otto* [1984] 1 QB 420). These 'things' can include physical objects, such as knives, and are often referred to as **exhibits** (as they may be exhibited to a court). Under a Code of Practice within the Criminal Procedure and Investigations Act (CPIA) 1996, any police officer investigating alleged crimes 'has a duty to record and retain material which may be relevant to the investigation' (see 12.6 above). Sections 21 and 22 of the PACE Act 1984 describe the powers of police to retain exhibits.

Any police officer or member of the public who produces or finds an article which may be used as evidence should exhibit it—that is, to formally record certain facts about the object. Here, we outline the principles employed; the procedures for packaging exhibits are covered in detail in 13.5.19 below.

Packaging materials often have labels printed on the outer surface which can be used for noting facts; otherwise a simple label can be affixed. The basic information required is:

- name of the person exhibiting;
- an exhibit number: normally the person's initials and a sequential number;
- a description, which should be brief and to the point—to prevent other people shortening the description for convenience (you should include index numbers or serial numbers for clarity);
- the date and time the exhibit was found;
- where the exhibit was found.

It is the mark of a professional to make detailed notes about the exhibit to assist other investigators. If detailed and accurate records are not kept about the contents of a package, another person might be obliged to open it to check the contents. This is a possible source of contamination. In your detailed notes, you should record any identifying marks, the size of clothing, any damage or stains, any logos or identifying features, serial numbers, and describe the precise location of the exhibit and its orientation. (A final search of any clothing should be made **after** the clothing has been placed in the bag, so any debris which falls from it is retained within the bag—see 13.5.17.3 below).

13.3.11.1 When should I sign an exhibit label?

The exhibit label records the **continuity** (or chain of custody) of the exhibit. Ideally, the chain should be unbroken from its seizure until it arrives at court. Every person who takes control of the exhibit should sign the label (and later write a statement) unless local protocols dictate otherwise. For instance, the movement of bulk quantities of exhibits is often recorded on a *pro forma* by the driver, and major-crime exhibits officers do not normally write a statement for every receipt of every exhibit.

If a police officer temporarily passes a packaged exhibit to another officer for comment but it remains in the original officer's custody, the other officer need not sign the label. An example might be where he/she asks for a casual opinion:

- Have you ever seen one of these before?
- Is this a ball-peen hammer?
- Should I call this a herbal substance or dried plant material?

However, if a professional opinion is given, then the other officer should sign the label and write a statement describing his/her actions.

Finally, do not accept an unpackaged exhibit from anyone other than a member of the public. This is a potential cause of contamination.

13.3.11.2 Firearms as exhibits

It is not the purpose here to advise you on firearms safety, but safety must always be considered when dealing with firearms as exhibits. Firearms are excellent sources of evidence. As well as providing ballistic evidence, their smooth surfaces are good sources of fingerprints and DNA can be collected from their rough control surfaces such as the grip, slide, and trigger. We consider this in more detail in 13.5.16 below. We have already looked at the different types of firearm and the associated law in 9.20–9.25 above.

Chiefly, at scenes of crime:

- treat every weapon as if it is loaded;
- never handle or move a firearm;
- never stand in front of a firearm;
- never point a firearm at any person, even when safe;
- never kick, move, or drop an article onto a firearm;
- ensure every person who passes a firearm to you clearly demonstrates that it is safe and vice versa;
- never make a weapon safe whilst pointing it at the floor or wall if it is possible that people may be below you or on the other side of the wall;
- call for expert assistance—it is normal practice for a photographer or CSI to be present during the process of making safe by a firearms officer;
- never convey a loaded firearm to the police station or laboratory unless this is necessary and suitable safety measures are in place;
- never dry-fire a firearm or tamper with any controls apart from those necessary to make it safe;
- never move a firearm by poking a pen, or any other object, into the barrel or trigger guard.

Above all: expect every firearm to be loaded and ready to fire.

In truth, very few guns can fire by being dropped or knocked since the majority of them have in-built safety features, but the consequence of a weapon firing by accident can obviously be extremely serious.

13.3.12 Contamination

Contamination is the transfer of trace evidence by any means other than direct or indirect involvement with the crime. It can be accidental or deliberate. The term is also broadly used to describe damage to an exhibit or altering its state in some way that is not required for its preservation.

Certain forms of forensic evidence are, in all practical senses, incontrovertible (see 13.5 below). Nonetheless, such evidence will be scrutinized by the defence in a criminal case, with the intention of casting doubt on the integrity of an exhibit and to have it disallowed by the judge.

An effective defence team will look for:

- errors in continuity;
- errors in packaging and handling;
- any possible source of contamination.

Consider the contamination issues regarding vehicles, prisoners, and colleagues. Make your concerns clear. For example, if you are tasked to deal with a suspect and you have been to the crime scene you will contaminate him/her with material from the crime scene. This may reduce the value of evidence that links the suspect with the crime scene.

Proper packaging and storage can prevent contamination becoming an issue, and this is examined in detail in 13.5.19 below. However, if you are required to package exhibits then the following general advice applies:

- Always wear gloves and a face mask, as a minimum, when dealing with exhibits or whilst inside a crime scene. (In the absence of a face mask, at the very least, you should avoid coughing or talking over exhibits.)

- Always pack your own exhibits.
- Damp or recently worn items of clothing should be packed in paper bags which allow the exhibit to breathe.
- Wet items should be brought to the attention of the CSI who will control the drying-out process. As a temporary measure, items can be stored in unclosed polythene bags sealed into a paper sack. However, items soaked with blood are best left to the CSI, as any folding of the exhibit may cause transfer of the blood onto other parts of the item.
- Always use new paper and plastic bags, containers, and boxes, and select the best material for the task.
- Never package your search gloves with an exhibit; they are a source of your DNA as they are normally soaked in sweat.
- Store exhibits properly to prevent decay and damage.
- Never deal with exhibits from two facets of the same offence, such as victim and suspect exhibits. Care should be taken when considering dealing with clothing from two people arrested together, for instance in the same vehicle.
- Clothing from one person in an offence should not be dealt with (packaged; taken out of packaging) in a room that has previously been used for sampling another person.
- Do not place a prisoner in a cell until it has been cleaned.
- Never convey two people from the same offence in the same vehicle, even at separate times, until all parties have been forensically examined.
- Clean or wash down police vehicles which contain blood, once any forensic examination has been completed.
- Regularly and fastidiously valet patrol cars.

13.3.13 Attending Major Crime Scenes

We discussed major crimes in the introduction to this chapter. They often attract significant police resources during the subsequent investigation. Let us consider the actions that should be taken by the first officer at the scene of a major crime (the FAO: see 13.3.1), recalling that the objectives are to protect the scene and preserve evidence, and to ensure the safety of police officers and others at the scene. You will notice (no doubt) that many of the actions listed below are common to the procedures to be followed at any crime scene:

- cordon off the scene and prevent unauthorized entry—make the cordon as wide as practicable (it can always be reduced later);
- do not enter the scene yourself, except to preserve life;
- create a CAP for all who come to the crime scene, ensuring that this path does not trample on evidence or compromise the crime scene in any way—you should use this route too;
- begin a 'scene attendance log' in which you record all authorized persons who come to the site;
- if deaths have occurred, do not cover bodies; if in public view, remove the public or screen off the view;
- record witness details and any comments they make: listen carefully to them;
- make a record of anything that is disturbed or moved;
- consider whether you need assistance to preserve the scene;
- continue to be in communication with the force control centre and keep them informed of what you are doing and why. Explain if you think you will need specialist help, or a doctor, or other emergency services;
- remain calm, be positive, and manage the situation until help arrives.

TASK 1

In what ways might the subsequent investigation into a major crime differ from other investigations?

Most police forces have specialist (often centrally based) departments or units which deal with major crime investigations. The investigation is headed usually by a specially trained **senior investigating officer** (SIO), usually of detective inspector or detective chief inspector rank.

Many of the elements involved in investigating major crime have been covered elsewhere in the Handbook and we do not repeat them here.

13.4   Incidents involving Deaths

In Chapter 9 we considered a number of situations in which you may encounter death and injury as the result of major and critical incidents. However, you will also experience attending scenes where there is a dead person who may well have died through natural causes such as illness and old age. The local police station may be called by the neighbour of an elderly person to report that they have not seen their neighbour for some time or that there are other circumstances which give cause for concern. Of course, these situations are not restricted to the elderly; you may have the particularly distressing task of attending a scene of the death of a child or young person.

Any death which occurs outside the hospital environment and is in some way unexpected is referred to in police circles as a 'sudden death'. All sudden deaths will be subject to some form of investigation but of course this does not mean that the death is associated with criminal activity. However, at any scene with fatalities it is essential that student police officers and constables are never afraid to ask questions and, above all, if **you** believe an incident is suspicious it is **your responsibility** to say so. If you do not understand something, you should ask. Senior officers may thank you for it; a senior police colleague recounts the following story to every new group of student police officers he trains:

> After the death of a child in London, the body was returned to a hospital in the county concerned for a post-mortem examination. During the initial stages a new Pc asked: 'do bodies change colour after death?' The answer was: 'yes, in fact they change colour quite a lot due to hypostasis, decay, and even mummification'. Later he asked if dead bodies could heal themselves. The curious pathologist answered that this was not possible and, incidentally, why was he asking? The answer was that the new Pc had seen the deceased in London, where the child appeared Caucasian and had a hole in its forehead, yet here at the post mortem was an apparently Asian child and there was no hole. The hospital had handed the wrong child to the police.

The story may be apocryphal but the moral of the story is certainly not: you must ask questions. In particular, if you are in early attendance at a scene of a fatality, ask yourself:

- Is the event which probably caused death at this scene likely or possible?
- If it is a suicide, were the means available to the victim?
- Was the victim physically capable of the act?
- Is there any sign of a struggle?
- Is anything apparently missing?
- Is there evidence of a forced entry?
- Does the position or state of the body logically fit with the information received?

13.4.1   Attending Incidents with Deaths

The general procedure to follow for sudden deaths will vary from force to force although all subscribe to certain basic principles (and relate to the procedures for attendance at a crime scene: see 13.3 above). You should:

1. Ensure your own safety before approaching, as the scene of a death can be dangerous.
2. Establish and use a CAP (see 13.3.6 above) to preserve the scene.
3. Beware of bodies in contact with live electrical systems, as well as toxic fumes, poisons, firearms, needles, and body fluids.
4. Touch nothing until you have made a visual inspection.
5. Is there a chance the person is still alive; can you administer first aid and is an ambulance required?
6. Consider that any death might be the result of crime if it is in any way suspicious.

Next, begin a PNB entry (see 8.3 above) which records the following information:

- the location and position of body;
- any physical evidence in the immediate area;

- a general description of the body, including any visible injuries;
- the evidence of any witnesses;
- the identity of the deceased, if known.

A death or injury on a railway line is a sudden death, and is very likely to be a major or critical incident. The death may be due to an accident (for example at a railway crossing), or from suicide, or as the result of a crime. You should be aware that bodies on or near railway lines will often be dismembered. Do not approach a body or injured person until the power has been switched off (touching a body still in contact with a live rail, for example, could electrocute you). Sometimes it may be imperative to move a person from contact with the live rail before power can be cut. In such cases, you must take extreme care and use a non-conducting material such as a dry wooden pole to push the casualty clear of the line. It is always better to leave such actions to experts or specialists if you can. The CHALETS principles (see 9.28.1 above) will apply whatever the crash site, and wherever it happens. The surrounding circumstances may, of course, complicate what you have to do, in terms of scale, access, site control, preservation of evidence, and local hazards.

As can be seen from the above, the circumstances in which you may encounter a deceased person vary widely, and the appropriate response must be adapted according. However whatever the cause of death, there are common processes that occur in all bodies after death that you need to be familiar with, and some of these changes are described in 13.4.3 below. All deaths also need to be certified for legal and administrative purposes, and this is covered first, below.

13.4.2 Certifying Death

Where there might be the slightest chance a victim is alive, seek medical assistance. If a victim has been beheaded you may presume death has occurred; however, in other cases a medical professional is required to attend the scene. (This author, on one occasion, reluctantly called a police surgeon to a skeleton.) You will need to call a doctor (or arrange for one to be called) either to provide medical advice or to certify that 'life is extinct'. The procedure to be followed depends on whether the death was expected or unexpected (see below).

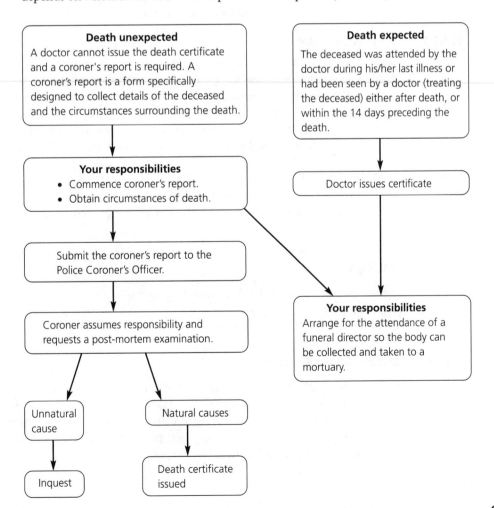

Certainly in the case of 'unnatural causes' a police investigation would ensue, although in most cases of this kind it would already be under way.

13.4.3 Changes to the Body after Death

There are several changes that take place in a body after death, and some of these are externally evident and may contribute to an investigation.

13.4.3.1 Hypostasis

When people die, the blood settles to the lowest parts and enters the skin where it creates a port-wine-coloured stain. This is also known as post-mortem lividity or *livor mortis*. Where a body is upright, blood drains to the lower parts of the limbs, cheeks, and ears.

In addition to this discoloration, wherever pressure is exerted on the skin, blood and tissue fluid cannot enter and are displaced into adjacent areas of tissue. As a result, the deceased's skin may take on an impression of the surface beneath it (for example from a tiled floor). The pattern of the fabric or seams from the victim's clothing may also be very clearly imprinted on the skin.

After some time (around three to four hours), the blood clots (solidifies) and can no longer flow, so if the body is subsequently moved, the signs of hypostasis will no longer be on the lower or underside parts of the body.

13.4.3.2 Rigor mortis

After death, chemical changes in the muscles gradually cause them to stiffen. The process normally begins in the head and works down the body. In very general terms it might start after 4 hours and disappear after 24 hours (when the body begins to break down biologically); however, the process is dependent upon a number of factors, not least of which is the ambient temperature (the process is quicker at higher temperatures). Crucially, immediately after death the body becomes limp and will flop to rest on adjacent structures, and if left for a number of hours, rigor mortis will stiffen it in that position. If subsequently moved, the body will be rigid and will not flop against the surrounding structures.

13.4.3.3 Body temperature

The core temperature of the deceased will equalize with the ambient temperature (so it will usually cool down) after death and then, due to decay and insect activity, the body temperature may increase. The relationship between the lowering of the core temperature and the ambient temperature is well documented but not so reliable that the pathologist can give an estimate of the time of death to within a few minutes—as is commonly seen on television. The ambient temperature, amount of clothing, and general health of the victim may all affect the temperature drop.

13.4.3.4 Suicide by cutting

Where a suicide victim has stabbed him/herself or severed an artery, often in the throat, wrist, or groin, one would normally expect to see tentative cuts—minor cuts carried out prior to the lethal wound.

TASK 2

When attending an incident with a fatality, in what circumstances can you effectively presume death has occurred?

13.4.4 Murder Investigations

Murder investigations involve a huge investment in terms of police time and resources. The majority of murders are committed by close family members, or others known to the victim, and although the circumstances leading to such events are often shocking on a domestic scale, it is the abduction and murder by strangers (particularly when children are victims) which attracts the majority of media attention and police resources.

> **TASK 3**
>
> What is the CATCHEM database and what does it tell us about a particular category of victims and their murderers?

The level of resources put into a murder investigation depend on the classification of the murder. Murders are classified as Category (Cat) A, B, or C within a more general system of categorizing major crime (see 13.2 above). Cat A and Cat B murder investigations will be led by an SIO who will probably be centrally based, while a Cat C murder could be investigated by detectives in a local BCU. However, there are variations on these basic categories, and a Cat C murder can often turn out to be more complicated than first thought, so that a largely local response is not always appropriate.

The **Murder Investigation Manual** ('MIM') (ACPO, 2006) and the **Practice Advice on Core Investigative Doctrine** (ACPO Centrex, 2005) offer an investigative model which most police forces will follow as a template for enquiries into a major violent crime. The model consists of five stages (fast track, theoretical process, planned method of investigation, suspect enquiries, and disposal), but within this Handbook, we have only referred to the first stage (see 13.3.13 above). This stage includes crime-scene and evidence preservation, but it also covers the initial police response to the reporting of the crime and the priority actions which follow.

> **TASK 4**
>
> You are called to a crime scene in a part of town with many multiple occupancy dwellings. The body of a young woman is slumped on the floor of a blood-splattered bed-sitting room. Curious and worried onlookers are present, and the landlord of the property (who discovered the body) is nervously waiting for you just inside the bed sit door. He says that he heard a disturbance and a lot of screaming. He used his master key to open the door and has not touched anything.
>
> What do you do to ensure proper incident management, remembering Stage One of the MIM includes 'crime-scene and evidence preservation'? What are your tasks in priority order?

The priority at the scene of a major violent crime is the preservation of life followed by the preservation of evidence. In the golden hour (see 13.3.4 above) evidence (including forensic evidence) can be gathered while still fresh and witnesses interviewed while their recollections are clear and unhampered. Amongst the people at the scene, there might be a suspicious eagerness on the part of someone to help. For example, Huntley, the murderer in the Soham case (see 9.27.1 above for a fuller account), volunteered to help with the initial search for the two girls. He was conspicuously present around the police search teams for days and was eager to be informed of progress. This can be (though by no means always will be) an indicator of guilt or complicity, and is characteristic of a type of murderer who is excited and stimulated by the purposeful activity which his/her act has caused. This is, however, a very complex area of human psychology and we are not recommending that you adopt some of the more populist approaches on 'reading a signature', although you might want to undertake further reading, perhaps starting with Blackburn (1995). However, in an investigation you should be attentive to these possibilities and keep a proper record in your PNB.

Getting your part right in this process could mean the difference between a guilty person being arrested and convicted, and someone literally getting away with murder because the crime scene has been disturbed and contaminated, or vital information from witnesses overlooked.

13.5 Forensic Investigation

Here we examine those aspects of forensic investigation that are relevant to your initial training. Forensic investigation is used for a number of reasons in policing and criminal investigation and we look at some of these in 13.5.5 below. This means that we will explore not only the subject of forensic investigation itself (and its relationship with forensic science) but also your specific roles in assisting the crime scene investigator, such as 'bagging and tagging' evidence, and collecting evidence from suspects.

13.5.1 Introduction

Unapologetically, we devote considerable length to this part of Chapter 13. Our reasons are simple: an understanding of forensic investigation and how you support that process is vitally important in terms of both convicting the guilty and exonerating the innocent. This importance is reflected in the IPLDP; there are a large number of learning outcomes that relate to forensic investigation in the modules OP 3, LP 1, and LPG 2.

13.5.2 Locard's Principle and Individualization

We take a knife from a drawer and replace it. In so doing, material (for example, sweaty deposits from our fingertips) is transferred from the hand to the knife and may remain there, for a little time at least. Material is also transferred from the knife to our hand—for example, particles of dust or even tiny fragments of the wooden handle. Edmond Locard (1877–1966) is credited with the development of this **Principle of Exchange.** His assertion was that material from the crime scene would be found on the suspect and vice versa. This is commonly expressed as: 'every contact leaves a trace'. As a simple example, this could mean that the offender could leave fingerprints, blood, and shoe marks at the crime scene and might take away glass fragments on his/her clothing.

Locard's Principle has been a mainstay of forensic investigation, but not all of these contacts can actually be proven because the quantities of the physical material transferred may be so minute that they defy the ability of current technology to locate them. The principle is really inductive reasoning by another name and hence cannot be considered a scientific law in the Popperian sense (look back at 4.13). Until relatively recently, however, this did not much concern the courts. The fingerprint, for example, is still assumed to be unique. In practice, Locard's Principle manifests itself in reverse in forensic investigation—it tends to use the transfer as demonstration of contact. First, there are the so-called traces that include debris like glass, paint flakes, hairs, and fibres. Traces can also include saliva, blood, and other DNA-rich material which is often classified separately. Second, there are 'impressions' which include 'prints' made by fingers, shoes, tools, typewriters, and printers. Note also, that Locard's Principle is not restricted to these traditional and tangible examples: it can also be extended to intangible digital data held by electronic media, such as computers, discs, and mobile phones. Trust in the principle requires a leap of faith but, even after assuming we can find the transferred material or impressions, we then need to show that it came from the source we are concerned with. This brings us to the concept of individualization or uniqueness.

13.5.2.1 Individualization

Despite what we may think or believe to be true, no two things can actually be identical, apart from at an atomic or molecular level. Thus everything we are concerned with in forensic investigation should be considered as unique, or a one-off. This represents another leap of faith on the part of the investigator and forensic scientist because this concept, again, is not strictly a scientific law. If you are interested, it cannot be considered to be a scientific law because there is no way it could ever be falsified. However, as with Locard's Principle, the CJS does not consider this a particular problem (and it is doubtful whether it has ever featured in deliberations in the courts).

Many objects which appear to be identical are markedly different, and those that are very similar (perhaps too similar to measure) become visibly or measurably unique during use. This unique quality is brought about by the development of **individual characteristics**. The majority of industrial processes impart very similar characteristics to the same products. In commerce, this is a matter of quality control which ensures the product is fit for purpose and conforms to standards to ensure safety and homogeneity.

Consider a standard 'slot' screwdriver:

- the shaft is typically cylindrical and appears identical in each screwdriver made on the production line;
- the tip is hammered flat and a subsequent sharpening process grinds the blade tip to preset dimensions, creating an edge which is generally very similar in every screwdriver.

The end-products of the manufacturing process are thousands of screwdrivers which—to unaided eyes—are identical in every way. During subsequent use (and misuse) each screwdriver develops unique characteristics, which provide the means for the forensic scientist to tell them apart, or individualize them.

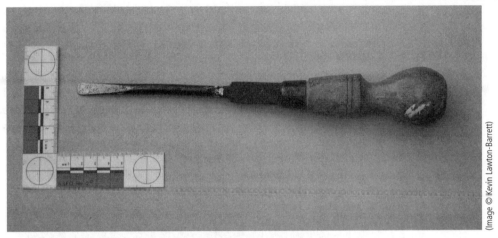

(Image © Kevin Lawton-Barrett)

A used screwdriver has inevitably acquired unique characteristics

Anything which can be associated with its source is said to have individual characteristics: for instance, a fingerprint to a finger, a tool-mark to a tool, and so on. There are different types of characteristic:

- **Class characteristics** are qualities produced by a controlled process, typically a manufacturing process: for instance, the manufacture of a screwdriver, where each one is similar to the naked eye.
- **Sub-class characteristics** are the features on a batch of screwdrivers, particularly those which distinguish them from other batches. These features may be imparted by poor quality control or minute changes in settings, grinders, and so on.
- **Individualization** follows from the premise that two items are derived from a common source, but that damage caused to the screwdriver during use individualizes it. Any marks it makes can be matched with the screwdriver in question.

Locard's Principle holds well for situations such as applying a well-used screwdriver to force a window frame, but it is not a panacea ('instant remedy') for difficulties in criminal investigations. Essentially, there are further issues to be investigated before the principle can be properly employed in the investigative context:

- Who owns the screwdriver?
- Who was holding the screwdriver when it forced the window?
- Indeed, where is it now?

Clearly, owning the screwdriver is not an offence. Using the screwdriver to force the window is an offence, but was the screwdriver borrowed or stolen to commit the crime? Investigators frequently say that they wish to 'put the suspect at the scene'. Whether this is a screwdriver alone or the screwdriver attached to the offender **at the time of the offence** is for you to consider and discuss.

Locard's Principle is primarily used to create physical links between the differing parts of an investigation. This is set out in its simplest form below.

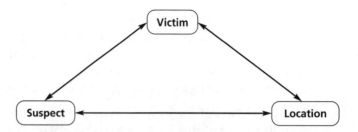

The links are normally created by forensic scientists comparing a 'questioned sample' with a 'control'. For instance, the CSI will recover control samples from the crime scene, perhaps a sample of paint and a tool mark, and will aim to have these compared to the questioned sample, which might be a screwdriver you have taken from a suspect. A control in crime scene investigation terms comes from a known source.

13.5.2.2 Two-way transfer

Clearly, the link may be between two or more people, a suspect and the scene only, or any permutation of these. A chief aim of forensic investigation is to locate and recover the physical material which will allow the links to be made. Although any police officer may be involved in searching a crime scene—whether a place, person, or thing—the majority of scenes are examined by specially trained CSIs. The best links are two-way instead of one-way, and may be referred to sometimes as 'best evidence'.

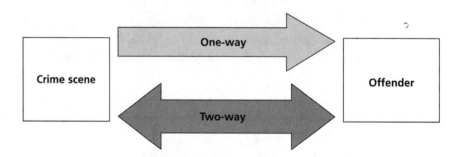

Locard's Principle does not cease to apply after the commission of the offence. All trace material or articles which leave an impression continue to change: fibres on the guilty party are lost, shoes continue to wear out, screwdrivers become blunter, DNA decays. The objective of the police is, therefore, to intervene as quickly after the crime as possible to recover the potential evidence and stop it changing further.

13.5.3 The Role of the Crime-Scene Investigator (CSI)

The CSI serves a number of roles within the police service. (As we have noted elsewhere, some forces continue to use the term Scenes of Crime Officer (SOCO), or even Crime-Scene Examiner (CSE), but CSI is now mostly accepted.) The CSI is typically the first port of call for all enquiries regarding forensic science, such as taking samples from suspects and victims and, principally, the examination of crime scenes. Chief amongst the CSI's crime-based activities are:

* the l ocation, assessment, and recovery of physical evidence (including fingerprints) from crime scenes such as burglary, murder, arson, and theft;
* the photography of crime scenes, articles, or people associated with crime, such as weapons, injuries, victims, and suspects;
* the packaging, storage, and documentation of recovered material;
* attending post-mortem examinations for sudden and suspicious deaths;
* provision of advice to police officers and investigators on matters related to physical evidence, photography, and laboratory submissions;
* gathering intelligence in support of the NIM, whether the spoken word, personal observations, or physical material for use in databases (see 12.3 above).

CSIs also carry out their activities at non-crime-related events such as the investigation, photography, and scene analysis of some sudden deaths, most suicides, and fatal industrial accidents on behalf of HM Coroners and in support of Health and Safety Executive investigations, and may become even more deeply involved in 'accidents' and work-related deaths following the Corporate Manslaughter and Corporate Homicide Act 2007. CSIs may also be involved in the recording of loss through fire (especially at high-value scenes, prior to arson being ruled out).

The majority of CSIs in the UK police are police support staff. They are attached to a force's Scientific Support Department which includes other complementary services such as a photography unit, fingerprint bureau, and a laboratory for the enhancement of fingerprint evidence.

13.5.4 Forensic Science

Forensic science is commonly described as the application of scientific disciplines to the legal system. The fields of science so employed are many and varied: from archaeology through every conceivable speciality to zoology. Any scientific discipline may have a function to play in the investigation of offences and it is the experts in these fields who produce the evidence the investigator requires by **interpreting** the material provided to them.

13.5.5 Employing Forensic Investigation

Forensic investigation is often concerned with two main forms of (largely physical) evidence:

1. **Corroborative evidence:** material that will confirm or refute a hypothesis about the crime, for instance that a powder is, or is not, heroin.
2. **Inceptive evidence,** which identifies an unknown, for example a person.

The investigator may employ forensic investigation and forensic science in a variety of ways when considering these two main forms of evidence. These include:

- **Describing the modus operandi (MO)**: the attending CSI can help form a hypothesis of the method used by the offender to commit the crime. This is an early stage in the forensic investigation. These data can be analysed for patterns to link offences. For example, scientists may analyse a fire scene to establish the MO for an arson or the events which caused a road crash.
- **Answering investigative questions**: in order to progress an enquiry. For instance whose DNA is this? Is there a connection between the weapon used in this crime and this suspect?
- **Establishing that an offence has occurred**: by examining exhibits it may be shown that an offence has been committed, for instance the analysis of a white powder; the classification of a firearm; the calculation of alcohol in urine or blood.
- **Identifying an offender or suspect**: in the right context, DNA and fingerprint evidence can identify the offender; normally they identify suspects.
- **To corroborate or refute witness statements**: this is particularly useful when applied to very specific issues raised during interview.
- **To establish a physical link between suspect, crime scene, and victim**: although the route for this may be circuitous, for instance linking the suspect to a weapon and the weapon to the incident.
- **To identify an individual**: fingerprints and DNA (and some other techniques) can be employed to identify people, including suspects, arrested persons, or found bodies.
- **To further inform an enquiry**: often by clarifying issues or providing some form of descriptive information or intelligence. An example would be a specialist helping to identify the make and model of a vehicle involved in a hit-and-run RTC.

13.5.6 Forensic Science Laboratories and Forensic Scientists

It is the responsibility of the forensic scientist to analyse and test materials supplied by an investigation in order to determine facts about the case. This evidence may point to the guilt or innocence of a suspect, neither of which should be a consideration for the scientist. There are a number of important principles which the scientist is bound by, and chief amongst these is the concept that—although paid by the police in this instance—scientific responsibility is to discover the truth in an unbiased way. Some might say that this is the essence of science itself. It is, as we have seen in Chapter 12, also the essence of a police investigation, and the primary focus of the criminal court.

In order to provide an efficient and effective service to the police, your scientist expects:

- unbroken continuity;
- correct packaging with intact integrity seals;
- utmost care in preventing contamination;
- a clear communication which explains the investigative need and describes the perceived relevance and place of the evidence;
- up-to-date information whenever the investigation changes tack; and
- clear guidance on any deadlines, such as bail dates or court appearances.

The scientist also needs you to understand that **forensic evidence is context-sensitive.** This means that the information or a statement provided by the forensic scientist is based upon the place the evidence occupies within the investigation. It is the investigator's responsibility to communicate this information clearly to the scientist in order to achieve the best—and most relevant—results. Some examples of context are:

- A fingerprint found near the point of entry in the female toilets of a burgled pub was found to belong to the barman. The context of this apparently innocent mark changed when, during interview, he categorically denied ever having been in the toilet.
- Blood on a suspect's clothing was explicable because he had provided first aid to a victim when flagged down in his car. Crucially, the person who stopped him for assistance had disappeared. Upon closer analysis it was apparent that the blood must have spattered onto his clothing during the commission of the offence.

In order to provide the correct information and to explain its importance to the case, the **Forensic Science Service** (FSS) provides a form called the MG FSP which, if followed closely, will guide the investigator through the submissions process. Different police forces have different systems and policies regarding the submission of exhibits to laboratories. It is in your interest to ensure that you follow the procedure laid down by your force; otherwise, you risk problems in any subsequent prosecution.

13.5.7   Establishing the Time and Date of an Event

This is about establishing the precise time at which an event occurred and is sometimes known as 'time- and date-stamping'. Some evidence may occur in a form which shows it was created during the commission of the offence—this is potentially of great value. Examples include:

- The distribution of blood, particularly that found on the suspect, might indicate he/she was present during an assault, and even establish his/her distance and position in relation to **the** victim.
- The presence of unusual stained glass from a broken church window on the suspect's upper clothing may indicate they were present when **the** window was smashed.
- Locating the residue from burnt firearm propellants (firearm discharge residue or FDR) on a suspect may show that he/she was present when **a** firearm was discharged.

Note that in the examples above the words 'the' and 'a' are highlighted. The DNA within the victim's blood and the unusual glass on the suspect may show he/she was present at the specified offences during their commission. Finding firearm discharge residue (FDR) on a suspect does not actually prove that the suspect fired the specific gun during the specific offence in question. Challenging suspects in interviews can, however, be used to reinforce many forms of evidence. CSIs and forensic managers prefer absolute statements from suspects because this can make the context of the evidence stronger. There are two important points here:

1. When a laboratory result is received (either in statement form or by other means) officers must consider their interview strategy, that is, how best to employ the information received. This is an example of forensic science driving the investigation forward.

2. If a suspect or other person makes an early statement, this information should be carefully considered: it may be of value to the scientist and must, at least, describe any admissions made by the suspect.

In a simplified example, where a man is suspected of a shooting, the forensic manager and scientist will weigh the value of the FDR evidence after interview thus:

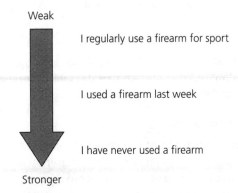

Weak

I regularly use a firearm for sport

I used a firearm last week

I have never used a firearm

Stronger

Clearly, if the man is guilty, it is preferable (from the investigator's point of view) for the suspect to deny the use of firearms on any occasion as this weakens the value of his statement if FDRs are found. If this were the case, consideration must be given to his activity in recent days:

- Has he been in the vicinity of a firearm which has been used?
- Was he arrested by an officer who recently used a firearm, say, for sport?
- Was he conveyed in a vehicle which had contained people who were contaminated with firearms residues?
- Was he arrested by an officer who was environmentally contaminated through using firearms at work?

The forensic scientist would need to know this sort of information so that an informed assessment of contamination can be made. This in turn may impact on the guilt or innocence of a suspect.

13.5.8 Seizing Exhibits

When an exhibit is taken from a crime scene or a person, this is often described as **seizing**. The rights of the police in this respect are described in 13.3.11. Although most exhibits are never examined at a forensic laboratory, police officers must always consider that they **might** be needed for later analysis, so all personnel must take care not to contaminate exhibits, and must package and record them correctly.

When taken, the exhibit must be named and numbered. The exhibit number is typically made up of the officer's initials and a number is allocated using the following method:

- In an enquiry where PC Alison Brown takes an exhibit she would call her first exhibit AB/1, her second exhibit AB/2, and so on.
- In the next enquiry, she would call her first exhibit AB/1 and so on.
- If she returned to the first enquiry, she can restart at AB/3.

However, if she returns to an enquiry and has no idea what number to allocate (although she should refer to her PNB) she might elect to use AB/100 or a similarly high number, because duplicating exhibit numbers in an enquiry can cause great confusion, particularly when statements are received from the laboratory.

TASK 5

How is this problem avoided in your force?

Exhibit names should be brief and to the point, to prevent other people shortening them. Extra, expansive descriptions of the article can be made in your PNB or in special documentation (such as an exhibits book).

It is important to note that recent developments in evidence-tracking databases may mean that your force has elected to change the standard exhibit numbering system, so that the first exhibit seized at the beginning of the year would be AB/1, but the sequence of numbers would continue to rise throughout the year instead of restarting at AB/1 for every enquiry.

13.5.9 Types of Physical Evidence

Physical evidence can be divided into a number of groups, and different authors have varying opinions on the approach that should be adopted. We have chosen a relatively simple method for classifying types of physical evidence.

13.5.9.1 Trace materials

Trace material can be any material transferred from the suspect to the crime scene (or a victim) and vice versa. It ranges from common materials such as glass fragments and paint flakes transferred during property crimes to the more exotic, such as pollens, soils, and even insects or their fragments. Do not allow your imagination to be limited to any specific groups: creativity is a vital element in investigation.

Glass is manufactured in different ways in order that it can be used for different purposes: this provides us with varying degrees of discriminatory power (that is, the ability to distinguish one object made of glass from another). The addition of colourants and physical processes can make this outwardly common material very useful in the right criminal circumstances.

Glass is a mix of silica, sodium carbonate, and calcium compounds which are smelted to form the base material, to which physical processes or chemical additives are applied, imparting a number of properties. Police officers often encounter the following types of glass in an investigation:

- **Plain window glass**: sometimes called 'float glass', this is the most common window glass manufactured today. The molten glass is poured on to a bath of molten tin and when it cools, it forms flat sheets.
- **Container glass**: which includes bottles, drinking vessels, and computer screens.
- **Toughened glass**: which is inherently strong and normally difficult to break—as used in telephone kiosks and the side windows of vehicles. When it breaks it forms thousands of cube-shaped granules. Toughened glass breaks easily if struck with force near the edge, particularly by a sharp object.
- **Laminated glass**: where two sheets sandwich a plastic filling. This prevents the pane shattering and it retains its position in the frame. Windscreens and many low-level windows are constructed in this way.
- **Optical glass**: found in lenses.
- **Mirrors**.

Glass is associated with special health-hazard warnings: obviously the shards may be exceptionally sharp and small, and in some applications are very dangerous. Always wear goggles and gloves when dealing with broken glass. Large, unsupported broken windows are a particular hazard if they are not laminated, and can collapse and kill without warning. Fortunately there are very few non-laminated large panes still in existence because of their inherent dangers and subsequent legislation governing glazing practices.

Glass found on the suspect or other articles can be compared to samples recovered from the broken window frame by a variety of chemical and physical techniques. Where the glass is unusual (perhaps very old or specially coloured) the scientist may provide a forensically important statement.

Glass can be **broken** in a variety of ways and different authors have different views on classification. In a criminal context, glass is typically broken by slow-moving to fast-moving objects, by some form of stress, by heat, or by an explosion. Frequently, the cause is deduced at the scene, but windows and glass objects can be reconstructed in order to demonstrate the cause, point, and direction of the breakage.

One of the most valuable attributes of breaking glass is a process called **backward fragmentation**, where a breaking window throws out fine particles of glass. These may land on the offender in a characteristic way, which can demonstrate he/she was in the vicinity of the window when it broke. Part of this process involves the development of fractures through the glass, either radiating from the point of impact or running concentrically around it. The edges (viewed 'end on') of some of these fractures can assist in determining from which side a window was broken.

Soils are found nearly everywhere, but they can vary significantly over short distances because of a number of important geological and geomorphological ('rock shape') factors, such as the source rock contributing to the soil. The scientist examines the source minerals, amounts of organic material, and grain size of the sample. Of particular note are areas where the soil has been modified by the inclusion of chemicals, waste material, and industrial processes. Soil is sampled during exhumations to demonstrate that any suspected toxins have not leached into the coffin and body of the deceased.

Soil's main general limitation is difficulty in showing that it came from a very specific location (perhaps a few square metres of a field) related to the offence unless that location is, perhaps, inaccessible to anybody innocently passing the site.

Fibres can be natural, man-made, or mixed. They are frequently transferred from clothing, seats, and carpets on to receptive surfaces, especially when the contact has been violent or has occurred over a long period. There is some police reluctance about using fibres as a form of evidence because they are (wrongly) thought of by many to be very similar and common. However, manufacturers use different fibre mixes and dyes for a variety of reasons and these features mean that a garment or other fabric may have an unusual or characteristic mix. Man-made fibres, in particular, can survive conditions which cause decay in natural materials like wool and cotton.

Paint is applied to window and door frames, manufactured objects, and cars as a protective or cosmetic coating. Its chemical components are designed to give the paint specific properties, such as rust-proofing, weather-proofing, fungal resistance, and even an identification measure. These elements and the enormous variety of colour and finish types ensure that any surface which has been chipped or scraped may be examined and compared with paint fragments found on a suspect's clothing, tools, or other objects in his/her possession.

Since paint on houses is applied over time according to individual tastes and changing fashions, the profile of the layers of coatings on, say, a forced window frame, can be unique. The more layers of paint on an object, the more likely its profile will be unique. Unusual colourings or paint types can also be very useful.

Vegetative material can often be used by forensic botanists to identify the species of a plant from small fragments of leaf, stem, seed, flower, or wood. Palynologists can identify the species of plant from the pollen they leave behind. If the knowledge of both scientific specialists is pooled or synthesized, the source species of vegetable material is likely to be accurately identified. In many circumstances, an association between scene and suspect can be made by the mix of vegetative materials, and if this is linked with other forms of evidence such as paint the results can be powerful.

Note should be made of the fact that many plants occur naturally in specific locations owing to climate, soil type, and plants' relationships with animal and insect species, so plant material can also identify a broad location, such as heathland, deciduous forest, proximity to the sea, and so on. Of further note is the fact that plant material, especially wood, is used in thousands of domestic and industrial applications, and some of these require unusual imported species. The treatments carried out on woods for cosmetic or protective purposes may also be valuable to the investigator.

Insects, apart from the common pest species, are sensitive to their food source and climate. As a result, many species are found in limited ranges and, when insects are identified during forensic investigation, they may be helpful in determining the geographic origin of materials such as cannabis resin, or the previous locations of vehicles and people. Forensic entomologists can also use known data on insect life cycles—especially that of blow flies—to identify when a body became available for them to feed upon. It is possible that this information may be of value when attempting to determine the time of death.

13.5.9.2   Impressions

These are the marks left by shoes, tools, fingers, stamping machines, printers, and typewriters. Whilst these can be a direct 'stamped' effect, many are made up of irregular scrapes and smudges and even cutting or drilling marks.

Shoe marks or **footwear marks** are a useful but potentially short-lived form of evidence. Footwear is readily modified by use when people walk over surfaces which scratch and tear the soles or add particles such as glass and stones. The resultant damage to the soles occurs at random and is, therefore, unique to every shoe. When a shoe leaves an impression at a crime scene the mark left is readily comparable to the shoe in question. However, the shoe (and the suspect) must be located and recovered before the relevant damage (to their shoes or footwear) is further eroded.

Marks can be on a flat, two-dimensional surface, or they can be impressed into a soft substrate to form a three-dimensional pattern. Importantly, the surface must be fine enough to receive the mark: soft clay is clearly better than shingle.

Trainers in particular are readily identifiable (either from databases or by an expert in the field) and this data can be used for intelligence purposes in order tentatively to link crime scenes. The addition of MO, times of offence, and target properties can make such databases invaluable.

In theory, marks should be present at almost every crime scene since almost all offenders will walk within the venue. Always be aware of this and take care where you walk. Remember the discussion in 13.3.6 above about the Common Approach Path (CAP) to a crime scene.

A variety of techniques can be used to recover the marks: photography, casting, lifting, or removal of the surface upon which the mark rests.

Tool or **instrument marks** are marks imparted to receptive surfaces by the application of force. Typical examples are those where an offender has forced a window or cashbox. The marks can be made in a variety of ways:

- levering to force open a window, door, or cashbox—one edge of the target surface acts as a fulcrum and both this and the moving part will be marked;
- cutting—the action caused by scissors, wire cutters, and bolt croppers;
- drilling—the waste material from drilling can bear the impression of the cutting edge of the drill bit.

The actions used will impress into the surface (or cut into it) the shape of the tip or cutting edge of the tool which, like a shoe, has been individualized through its previous use.

Stamps, dyes, and **manufacturing marks** are impressions into a surface, similar to tool or instrument marks, and can be made by any item. This includes plastic-label printers, metal-numbering dyes, franking machines, rubber stamps, and other such devices. All are modified by accidental damage and ageing.

Any material which is set in a mould or extruded also takes on an impression of the mould or extrusion head, particularly where debris has built up. Examples include copper pipes, plastic bags, and plastic components. Many of these latter marks are visible as lines and dimples and, if invisible, can be viewed using microscopy or polarized light. The sequence of manufacture of rolls of bags, in particular, can be demonstrated by the scientist and may help to show that an offender used a bin bag (from a particular place), for instance, to carry away goods from a burglary.

Vehicle tyres leave impressions, are found in soft soils, on roads, smooth concrete floors, glass, and paper—particularly at 'ram raids'. Tyres are modified during use by the surfaces over which they pass, and may pick up inclusions such as glass and gravel, and these individual details will show in a subsequent impression. The resulting pattern can be two- or three-dimensional depending upon the solidity of the surface but the surface must be fine enough to receive the impression. In addition, the impression may be of a rotating tyre or it may be of a skidding tyre. The laboratory can assist in identifying the make of tyre from a recovered print which may include or exclude vehicles from the enquiry.

A full circumference of a car tyre is 3.14 times the diameter, so a car tyre that is 50 cm in diameter needs over 150 cm to leave a print of one full rotation. (Finally, that geometry you did at school has proved useful!) As a result, you must never assume that only part of a print needs to be preserved; always preserve as much as possible for your CSI.

Bite marks are valuable sources of evidence. The position, number, layout, orientation, and cutting surfaces of teeth make our dentition highly individual. It is the role of the odontologist to compare marks found on victims and in foodstuffs with the teeth of the suspect. This is carried out by taking a three-dimensional impression and comparing it with photographs or with impressions of the damage or injury.

Whenever bite marks are located always consider that DNA may be present. Older bite marks on skin may be visible under ultraviolet (UV) lighting and can be photographed some time after the incident. The apparent lack of a bite mark is not, therefore, a 'lost cause'.

Typewriters, printers, and **copiers** can also provide useful evidence. The fonts chosen by typewriter manufacturers can be identified when found on letters or other material, even with the demise of the traditional typewriters in favour of computers. A targeted search of premises can be made to locate a particular design of typewriter. When the metal letters, golf ball, or daisy wheel are damaged or aged they take on individual characteristics which are easily compared with characters contained in documents you may be considering as evidence.

Any fault which develops in computer printers may also be compared with suspect documents, especially when 'banding' occurs in large blocks of colour or across text. Currently, research is under way to link printers (without faults) to specific pages of text. Photocopiers superimpose an image of the glass screen, or platen, on the copies they produce. The more damage (or dried correction fluid) on the platen, the better the evidence. Paper feeders and rollers may also impart marks. Modern copiers (and all printers) are digital, which means that the pages which have been printed are digitally stored within the device's limited memory for some time after printing.

13.5.10 Fingerprints

About 5 per cent of the human body is covered in a horny layer of skin bearing ridge detail. This is found on the fingers, palms, soles, and toes. Every finger and toe print on every person is considered by the CJS to be unique. The prints left by any part of the hand or foot are, therefore, capable of identifying an individual with certainty. The ridges form classifiable patterns on the horny layer which are clearly visible to the naked eye. Upon close examination it is apparent that the ridges are not uniform lines: they split (bifurcate), they start and stop, and the lines sometimes cross over. These features are normally referred to as 'minutiae'.

The ridges develop in the womb and remain identical until death—or well past death if the body is preserved sufficiently. The only difference between the patterns on the foetus's fingers and those when fully grown are size and the effects of ageing or injury. The ridges on the fingers and toes are thought to have three main functions:

- to increase friction for gripping;
- to allow sweat to dissipate along the furrows;
- to permit more nerve endings to be present in the corrugated skin.

Humans are still physiologically quite primitive and react in primitive ways: when nervous, our hands and feet sweat more, which is part of the 'fight or flight' response to stimuli. Poor quality marks can sometimes be left by nervous offenders with very wet fingers, but crucially, as the offender moves through a building, the hands dry out sufficiently to leave marks of good quality further inside the scene. Because of this, it is always better to preserve a **whole crime**

scene rather than just the point of entry. Similarly, a suspect in custody may be nervous which can cause difficulties when taking fingerprints for later comparison. You are reminded to thoroughly and repeatedly dry the suspect's fingertips to prevent sweat smudging inked marks.

Fingerprints are found on all the surfaces we touch, but only if the surface texture is fine enough to receive them. The easiest test to determine whether a non-porous surface might yield fingerprints or not is to scratch it gently with a nail: if the nail makes a noise, then the surface might be unsuitable. A completely smooth surface will be silent. (Clearly, this practice should be carried out with caution, and never at serious or major crime scenes.)

CSIs locate marks in one of three ways:

- They can see visible marks, also called **positive** or **patent** marks, which are then photographed—these might be three-dimensional, normally called **plastic** marks.
- They can search for invisible or **latent** marks with a torch and by dusting with powders using a fine brush. This is the commonest process; the fabric of the building can be examined, and bulky items can be left in place. After 'visualizing' the mark, it should be photographed and, where appropriate, lifted with an adhesive material and placed on to an acetate sheet, or other substance as appropriate.
- They presume marks may be present and remove the article of interest for later chemical or physical enhancement. Occasionally, laboratory services are taken out to complex scenes where the fabric of the building is searched using chemicals and light sources.

Laboratory analysis normally involves employing different wavelengths of light which cause the mark to fluoresce, or by the application of chemicals which react with the non-aqueous components of the print. (Sweat is approximately 98.5 per cent water and the remainder is made up of other components such as salts, fats, and amino acids.)

Whilst CSIs routinely 'dust' smooth non-porous surfaces, it should be borne in mind that many other surfaces may yield marks, such as textured plastics, polythene bags, paper, smooth wood, and even wall coatings. The majority of marks at scenes or on exhibits are invisible, or latent, which means they are easily damaged by clumsy actions. Police officers first on the scene should always wear gloves and handle potential exhibits by their edges. Since the majority of fingerprints are invisible, or latent, you should never assume that fingerprints are absent simply because you cannot see them.

13.5.10.1   IDENT1

The IDENT1 database contains the fingerprints and palm prints of arrested persons, and crime-scene marks recovered by CSIs and other personnel. The system covers England, Scotland, and Wales, and includes Home Office forces as well as British Transport Police, SOCA, HM Revenue and Customs, and the Immigration Service. IDENT1 is a truly national database which incorporates Scottish fingerprint and palm-print collections. Prior to this, the old system (NAFIS) was more parochial.

IDENT1 contains 7.8 million individuals' tenprints and 5.9 million palm prints (2009 figures) and identified about 45,500 marks from crime scenes between May and October 2008. The basic functionality of IDENT1 is not especially new; it essentially compares:

- crime-scene marks to crime-scene marks to search for links;
- tenprints and palm prints against crime-scene marks (and vice versa); and
- new tenprints to those already on file to confirm identity or to establish that an arrested person is using a pseudonym.

Once the system identifies a suspect print, experts then verify the result; contrary to television shows, the computer does not form an 'opinion' which is of use to the CJS.

A chief benefit is that IDENT1 is linked to 440 Livescan tenprint scanners (in police stations) which electronically capture suspects' fingerprints. The use of this digital technology means that suspects' identities can be verified in about ten minutes, a so-called Live Identification. One hundred portable devices (called Lantern units) are also linked to the system.

13.5.11   Biological Material Yielding DNA

As with fingerprints, note that the PACE Act 1984, Code D applies when sampling detainees for biological material. Biological material that yields DNA is of major interest to the forensic investigator, and by extension to you, the police officer concerned with the investigation. Examples of such material include blood, saliva, semen, hairs with a root, and many other secretions such as ear wax and mucus. Indeed, nearly every cell and every secretion from the human body has the potential to provide DNA. You should be aware however, that all such biological material can also be very easily contaminated by victims or by police officers through talking, coughing, sneezing over, or mishandling the material.

Every cell in the human body—with a few exceptions—contains a nucleus, and within the nucleus are chromosomes. Chromosomes are made up of genes which instruct the body to manufacture proteins and therefore govern the biological and physical processes within the cell and, consequently, the body. Individual genes are constructed from DNA. Many texts refer to DNA as the 'blueprint' for humans and other living things but you should note that **DNA fingerprinting** is not to be taken literally—you cannot establish fingerprint patterns through DNA analysis.

Every nucleus contains a copy of the DNA for the entire organism, so a cell from the cheek contains exactly the same material as a white cell from the blood. Since it is the blueprint for humankind, a large proportion of DNA is the same in every human, but small differences occur which account for variations, like hair and eye colour, other (invisible) characteristics, and genetically-related illness.

Amongst this important variable material are sections of DNA called Short Tandem Repeats (STRs) which are commonly referred to as 'junk DNA'. The junk DNA is highly variable between individuals and, as a result, can be used to distinguish between people. Clearly, there is no mileage in employing common genetic material in order to identify suspects because it is shared between so many people.

A DNA 'hit' is a calculation concerning a selection of a person's STRs and is supplied by the scientist as a 'match probability'. If the match probability is one in a billion it means that there is a one in a billion chance that another person **selected at random** has the same profile. It does not mean that there is a one in a billion chance that the suspect is innocent, nor does it mean that one in every billion people shares the same profile. These errors are called **fallacies** (see 4.13 above). If the DNA recovered for analysis is degraded through age or lack of proper handling, the match probability applied to the comparison may be reduced, which can cause some concern, but remember that other evidence should be used to support the prosecution case.

DNA is typically found on articles or at scenes yielding blood, semen, saliva, hair with roots, some bodily secretions, and pieces of body tissue. It is important to treat all body fluids as potential health hazards. Not only do people need protecting from the biological material (which might contain pathogens or disease-carrying bacteria): the biological material also needs protecting from us, since our own DNA can easily contaminate it.

At the laboratory the DNA is removed from the swab or material upon which it is found, then copied many times using a process called Polymerase Chain Reaction to ensure enough is available for analysis.

The term **DNA LCN** means that only a very small amount of DNA is available ('low copy number'). If the quantity of DNA recovered is very low (or where it is believed some **may** be present), extra cycles of the PCR copying process are carried out to ensure enough is present for subsequent analysis. This has yielded sufficient DNA for analysis from a number of unexpected sources (according to the FSS) such as tools, clothing grabbed by the suspect, and weapons.

Mitochondrial DNA (Mt DNA) is a different form of DNA which can be extracted from bone, hair, faeces, and teeth. Mitochondrial DNA is doughnut-shaped and is found within all cells in organelles called 'mitochondria' (which break down sugars to release energy for cells). The advantage to investigators is that the doughnut-shape makes the DNA more resilient to external influences so it may last for many years. It does, however, have limitations in that it cannot uniquely identify a person: only the maternal line. This means, for example, that you share your Mt DNA with:

- your brothers and sisters;
- your mother and her siblings;
- your grandmother and her siblings;
- if you are female, with your children.

If you are male, your children do not share any of your Mt DNA.

Mt DNA can be beneficial when applied to the study of old and degraded samples where normal (nuclear) DNA is unavailable. It was famously used by the FSS to identify Tsar Nicholas II and Tsarina Alexandra, whose bodies (along with three children) were found near Yekaterinburg, Russia, in 1991 (the royal family having been killed by the Bolsheviks in 1919).

Y STRs are a variable genetic feature found on the Y chromosome. The male or Y chromosome is found only in men and can be used to determine paternal ancestry by studying a specific set of STRs. Since females have no Y chromosome to pass on to a son, Y chromosomes only pass from father to son. In Western culture (though not in Iceland), this is traditionally paralleled by the transfer of the surname; hence Y chromosome analysis has gained commercial popularity as a genealogical tool and may assist in some investigations. The value of Y STRs is, of course, diminished in males whose paternity is not ascertained.

13.5.11.1 The National DNA Database

The National DNA Database (NDNAD) is a database of the DNA of persons who are arrested, cautioned, convicted, and charged for recordable offences. The NDNAD is the property of the police but is managed by a custodian, currently the Forensic Science Service (FSS). The database stores all DNA recovered from crime scenes (where applicable) and all people who have been sampled subject to legal and operational criteria. The 2006–07 NDNAD Annual Report shows that there are in excess of 4.1 million subject samples retained on the database (over 6 per cent of the UK population) and 47,717 crimes with DNA matches.

The simple elegance of the system is based upon the theory that, although many offenders who commit minor crimes will cease their criminality, others will continue as volume-crime offenders or will step up their activity to more serious offences. Very few armed robbers, for example, when arrested, are found to be free of a criminal record. By taking the DNA sample of relatively new or volume-crime offenders, the police effectively 'bank' this for the future, in the same way that they do with fingerprints. There may also be a deterrent effect. We put to one side however, the concerns over the civil liberty implications surrounding the NDNAD, and the recent (late 2008) European Court of Human Rights' decision that retaining a DNA record of innocent individuals on the NDNAD is a breach of human rights.

Each time a new crime-scene or suspect sample is received it is entered in the database and cross-checking occurs. The results have been noticeable; in 2000 there were some 8,612 DNA detections, rising to 19,800 in 2005. The functionality of the system is similar to IDENT1 (for fingerprints) in that it also identifies linked crimes. Whilst this may not seem to be a vital ability, consider **the case of John Wood**: a man sexually assaulted two young girls in 1988 in Canterbury, Kent, and was not apprehended at the time. Later, in 2001, a John Wood was arrested for shoplifting in Derbyshire (only £10 worth of groceries). The arresting Pc took the suspect's sample in accordance with local instructions and the DNA taken from Wood was matched to DNA found at the crime scene in Canterbury. The Pc was, therefore, directly credited for Wood's arrest and for the detection of the Canterbury offences. Wood admitted the offences and was sentenced to 15 years.

13.5.12 Toxicology

The poison, alcohol, or drug content within a person's body may be crucial to an investigation for a number of reasons:

- to calculate whether he/she is over the drink-drive limit;

- to establish that alcohol or drugs may explain behaviour such as violence or drowsiness; or
- to establish cause of illness and death.

Roadside breath tests and those carried out by an Intoximeter are still the most common forms of toxicological measurement carried out by the police, but these are normally used as screening tests prior to a full laboratory analysis (see 11.16 above). A variety of field-test kits and covert-sampling devices can be employed to screen for drugs but, ultimately, the opinion of an expert toxicologist should be sought to provide evidence suitable for a prosecution. Do bear in mind that some policies exist, particularly for marijuana possession, that if the suspect makes a guilty plea, he/she will merely be cautioned. Elaborate analysis is not therefore required (or at best, not embarked on), since the case will not go to court.

In driving cases, you should use the laboratory submission forms MG/DD A to E. In cases where a back calculation is required (to establish a previous level of alcohol in a suspect: see 11.16.5.3 above), police officers should **always** seek the advice of a CSI based at the BCU (or a Scientific Support Unit adviser) since the forms required for such a calculation can be quite complex. Regardless of this, always try to seize original bottles and glasses marked-up to show what the suspect claims to have drunk, but bear in mind that a 'gulp' or 'swig' is not a scientifically-accepted measurement of alcohol consumption!

Commonly, blood or urine are the substances sent for analysis but other samples from the body tissue and eyes of deceased victims may be used, depending upon the circumstances. Remember: toxicology samples must always be treated as a potential health hazard.

13.5.13 Digital and CCTV Evidence

Digitally stored data is retrievable from hard drives, discs, CDs, DVDs, mobile phones, tele-coms equipment, credit cards and credit card reading devices, video systems, and any other electronic recording or processing device. These sources of data can provide evidence of the commission of a crime. Special protocols exist for the seizure of digital evidence in every force in the UK; make sure you are aware of the procedures used in your force. We provide an overview of the particular issues surrounding the seizure of electronic equipment below in 13.5.20.

The forensic techniques required from recovery to analysis of digitally-based evidence (such as a deleted file recovered from a PC's hard drive, or the address book from a mobile phone SIM card) are a specialist field within investigation. ACPO has published good practice guidelines for the handling of digital evidence and recommends that digital evidence strategies should form part of the wider investigative process (ACPO, 2007a). Typically the responsibility for the recovery and the analysis of digitally-based intelligence and evidence is undertaken by a specialist unit within your force, such as a Digital Forensics Unit. However, police forces may choose to 'outsource' some digital forensic analysis to non-police contractors, but these contractors are also expected to meet the good practice guidelines.

13.5.13.1 CCTV footage

At some crime scenes, CCTV footage might provide vital information. Most CCTV cameras are automatic and many are actually unmonitored, with tapes being renewed on average about every seven days. There is an expectation in CPIA 1996 that any CCTV footage will be retained and revealed if relevant (see 12.6 above). You are not simply trying to establish the sequence of events, or looking for evidence of the crime; you are looking for any relevant material, even if it supports the defence case. This would apply even if the footage did not show the crime itself, and only showed the suspects near to the time the crime was committed.

You should not access the video-recording machine without first establishing the storage format for the footage and the technical requirements for its recovery. Often the images are stored on a disc, and taking the machine away (or its hard drive) in its entirety is not always achievable. (Working copies must be made for viewing purposes.) As a student officer you should ensure that the recording system is safe and secure and then refer the matter to your supervisor; he/she might recommend calling out specialist services.

However, if it is at all possible, you should ensure that you view the CCTV footage as soon as possible, and if it contains relevant material, seize the tape and 'bag' it in accordance with the rules about the preservation of evidence (see 13.5.19 below).

13.5.14 Documents and Forensic Investigation

Under the term 'documents', forensic investigators normally include all letters, paperwork, invoices, cheques, transfers, application forms, handwriting, and any other written material, whether handwritten or printed by typewriter, computer printer, photocopier, or other device.

Document analysis can be carried out in a number of ways: some examples are:

- **'Impressed' writing** can be enhanced using Electrostatic Document Apparatus (ESDA). Typically this situation arises when a pad of paper is used, and an impression of writing on one page may be found on others below it.
- **Handwriting analysis** involves the comparison of material obtained during the investigation with samples provided by a suspect.
- **Printers** and **typewriters**: the suspect printer or typewriter is compared with a specimen document. The presence of printer-head faults, 'banding', or damage to typefaces can be reproduced under laboratory conditions and compared with the suspect document.
- **Physical features** of paper can be compared, such as tear marks, staple holes, and altered text.

Other document features such as watermarks, obliterations, security features, paper types, security inks, concealed marks, and 'reactive fibres' can be analysed in a number of ways using microscopy and a Video-Spectral Comparator to enhance images and features using a variety of wavelengths of light.

13.5.15 Mechanical Fits, 'Jigsaw', or Physical Matches

This is a form of evidence which is of exceptional power in many police enquiries. It is an extended application of the theory that all things are unique and can be individualized (see 13.5.2 above). In its simplest form, if an object breaks into two or more parts, and if those parts are found separately and can be **reconstructed** as 'a fit', then they must all originate from the same source. For example, small fragments of a blade were found in the chin of a deceased male. Later, another male was found in possession of a damaged craft knife. The blade of his craft knife and the metal fragments were reconstructed.

13.5.16 Firearms and Forensics

First, a note on safety. If you are required to attend the scene of a shooting incident you must be sure in your mind that there is no danger from the offender. If you find shotgun cartridges at the scene or nearby you must inform your colleagues, since the offender may have reloaded. Key factors that need to be considered include:

1. Has he/she been taken into custody?
2. Has he/she made off from the scene? (But how reliable is this informant?)
3. Has he/she been incapacitated and disarmed?

If the offender is still at the scene and the incident is running, you should identify the rendezvous point (RV or RVP: see 13.3.5 above) and go there unless instructed otherwise.

Firearms, and the law relating to them, are covered in 9.20–9.25 above. Here we consider firearms in relation to forensic issues.

Since 2008 the importance of firearms as sources of valuable intelligence on a national scale has been recognized: ACPO and the Forensic Science Service set up the National Firearms Forensic Intelligence Database (NFFID) which aims to build an intelligence picture to link crime scenes through recovered bullets and other material, and to link seized weapons to scenes. Your force will have special protocols regarding what should be done with recovered firearms.

For the CSI and scientist the potential evidence from bulleted cartridge components (see 9.20.1 above) is described in the following table.

Potential evidence available from the bulleted cartridge components

Bulleted cartridge component	Available evidence
Cartridge case	The actions of loading, firing, and ejecting the cartridge will scratch the polished brass casing and leave comparable marks upon it. These marks are caused by the magazine (if used), the ejector, extractor, breech face, and firing pin. Since bullet, cartridge design, and extractors vary, it may be possible to identify the type of weapon from which the cartridge was ejected. Manufacturer's details, calibre, and type of round are normally engraved on the head stamp (base) of cartridges.
Bullet	This will normally identify the calibre of the weapon used, and since there is huge variation in bullet design, specialist rounds and sometimes the type of weapon can be identified. Most important though, is the scratched impression on the bullet of the rifling grooves within the gun barrel. Variations in the twist (left or right) and the number of grooves may assist in the identification of the make and model of the gun used, and can be compared to a suspect weapon. Even badly deformed bullets are useful to the scientist.
Powder	During burning, the powder gives off quantities of smoke and particulates which are emitted from the muzzle. Minute particles of the bullet, unburnt powder, and other debris are ejected in several directions. Some also contain small particles of lead, barium, and antimony which form small granules. These firearms discharge residues (FDR) can be found on the clothing, face, and hands of the offender and other people and items in the vicinity. Swabbing kits are available to retrieve this material. Suspects should be swabbed as soon as possible because the residues fall off easily.

For bulleted cartridges, the cartridge and bullet design vary for a number of reasons, such as:

- type of weapon (rifle, revolver, etc);
- type of loading system;
- type of firing mechanism (pin-fire, needle fire, rim-fire, centre-fire);
- manufacturer;
- function of the bullet (anti-personnel, tracer, armour-piercing).

Shotgun cartridges vary both in their overall design and the number and size of lead shot they contain (see 9.22 above). For the CSI and scientist the potential evidence from shotgun cartridges is summarized in the following table.

Potential evidence available from the shot cartridge components

Shot cartridge component	Available evidence
Cartridge case	This is normally retained in the weapon until reloading; however it may be ejected by automatic or self-loading weapons. It can be used to establish the bore of the weapon and the manufacturer and type of cartridge. Scratches on the brass base and the impression of the firing pin and breech face can be compared to suspect weapons. In automatic weapons marks from the extractor, ejector, and magazine may be found.
The shot	The size of the shot may eliminate some types of cartridge. The spread of the shot is useful in establishing the range of the weapon (when the possible use of a 'choke' is taken into consideration).
Powder	FDRs are available.

Shot cartridge component	Available evidence
Wadding	The presence of wadding indicates that a shotgun has been discharged. It can frequently give an indication as to the bore of weapon used, and a hint as to the cartridge manufacturer. Plastic wadding fired from a sawn-off weapon can sometimes be compared to the finish at the sawn-off muzzle end: if the finish is poor the wadding may bear scratches which can be reproduced during controlled tests. Wadding is normally badly deformed during discharge, so irregular lumps of plastic, felt, or cork at the scene should be collected and preserved.

13.5.16.1 Laboratory examinations of firearms evidence

The most frequently asked questions at the laboratory are:

- Is this a firearm as defined by the Act(s)? (See 9.20–9.25 above).
- Is this an imitation firearm? (See 9.25 above).
- What weapon fired this bullet (or cartridge case)?
- Did **this** weapon fire **this** bullet (or cartridge case)?
- How far was the weapon from the victim?
- Can this weapon fire accidentally?
- Do these swabs/items of clothing bear firearm discharge residues?
- Which is the entry wound/exit wound on this victim?

(Adapted from a number of unpublished Forensic Science Service publications.)

13.5.17 Taking Samples from People

Note at the outset that when taking forensic samples from suspects you must follow the procedures set out in the PACE Act 1984, Code D. This is covered in detail in 8.12 above.

As noted earlier, people are sources both of **evidence** (potentially to be used in court) and **intelligence** (for example, to provide leads in an investigation). Hence there are a number of reasons for taking samples from people:

- to prove or disprove their involvement in the offence;
- to corroborate or refute statements;
- to show a link between them and another person, or them and the scene or an exhibit;
- to establish drug, toxin, or alcohol levels in the body;
- to further inform the enquiry;
- to provide a reference sample (DNA, fingerprints, or footwear impressions) for direct comparison, for elimination, or for a database.

When taking samples from people always use brand new, unused packaging equipment as using old equipment usually causes contamination. Specific kits are available, for example, for the sampling of hair or urine. Make sure that you use the appropriate kit.

Material found upon samples can include debris and DNA-rich material in or on any part of the body, including:

- foreign blood, saliva, and semen, which are sources of DNA;
- firearm and explosive residues;
- trace material such as glass, paint flakes, fibres, grease, or soil;
- bite marks, weapon marks, and bruises;
- chemicals, such as alcohol, toxins, and drugs within the blood and urine, or chemical traces upon the skin;
- DNA and fingerprints;
- handwriting characteristics.

Although the sampling of suspects (whether arrested or not) must be carried out under the PACE Act 1984, Code D, there is no PACE requirement for those people (usually, but not exclusively, victims) who provide samples to support investigations. This means it is not always necessary for a police surgeon or other medical practitioner to take certain types of sample. Police officers do, however, have to behave towards victims and volunteers in accordance with the Human Rights Act 1998 (see 5.12 above). This is an important consideration when arriving at a scene or dealing with a victim who attends the police station where no CSI or medical assistance is immediately available.

TASK 6

Consider what you might do if:

- A woman attends the police station and claims to have been 'date-raped'. GHB and Rohypnol (examples of so-called 'date-rape' drugs) are rapidly excreted from the human body. Would you find a 'urine module' and request an immediate urine sample? How might this affect potential DNA evidence?
- You attend a robbery and a man says he bit the offender. He can still taste blood in his mouth. Would you ask him to spit into a sterile bottle?
- A victim claims a man sexually assaulted her and ejaculated over her hand. Would you glove or bag her hand, or even take a swab from it (if trained)?

13.5.17.1 What samples should be taken?

The types of sample taken from victims and suspects will depend on the nature of the criminal offence. The following table describes the minimum samples for consideration (represented by a tick in the table). Note that the PACE Act 1984, Code D and the Human Rights Act 1988 must be complied with, and you should note your reasons for taking a particular sample in each case.

Minimum samples

	Cheque or other fraud. Hate mail	Burglary or other property crime	Sexual assault or rape (a special kit may be used)	Theft from motor vehicle with damage caused	ABH and other assaults	Homicide (the sexual offences kit is often used for victim and suspects)
Blood and/or urine for toxicology			✓		✓	✓
Clothing (inner)			✓		✓	✓
Clothing (outer)		✓	✓	✓	✓	✓
DNA	✓	✓	✓	✓	✓	✓
Fingerprints	✓	✓	✓	✓	✓	✓
Hair (combing)		✓	✓	✓	✓	✓
Hair (pulled/cut)		✓	✓	✓	✓	✓
Handwriting sample	✓					
Photographs of injuries	When relevant	When relevant	When relevant	When relevant	When relevant	Effectively mandatory
Sexual offence kit			Mandatory			
Shoes		✓	✓	✓	✓	✓

13.5.17.2   The sampling procedure for taking evidence from people

Whenever you take a sample from a person, you must comply fully with the PACE Act 1984 and Human Rights Act 1988. The PACE Act 1984, Code D applies to taking samples from suspects and is covered in detail in 8.12 above. Victims (who normally volunteer samples) are not covered by Code D. Typically, if you require a sample from one person or place you should ensure a corresponding sample is recovered from elsewhere for comparison. Inform your CSI when samples have been taken, so that correct storage and subsequent preservation can be arranged.

Always wear gloves as a **minimum** form of protection. For serious offences, or where health warnings exist, officers should wear protective clothing to protect them and the evidence from contamination. It is essential that brand new, clean packaging equipment is used. There are two main types of sample.

1. An **intimate sample** is defined by the PACE Act 1984, Code D as:

   a dental impression or sample of blood, semen or any other tissue fluid, urine, or pubic hair, or a swab taken from any part of a person's genitals or from a person's body orifice other than the mouth.

The mouth is not included chiefly because swabs from the inside surface of the cheeks are used for DNA analysis. An orifice includes the ears and nose as well as the genitals and anus.

2. A **non-intimate sample** is defined by the PACE Act 1984, Code D as:

   a sample of hair, other than pubic hair, which includes hair plucked with the root, a sample taken from a nail or from under a nail, a swab taken from any part of a person's body other than a part from which a swab taken would be an intimate sample, saliva, a skin impression which means any record taken in any form and produced by any method, of the skin pattern and other physical characteristics or features of the whole, or any part of, a person's foot or of any other part of their body.

Swabs from the body include skin swabs from hands and face as well as elsewhere. Skin impressions include ear-prints, lip-prints, and prints of the skin. Non-intimate samples may be taken at a police station from a detainee using reasonable force, subject to proper documentation.

13.5.17.3   Clothing and footwear samples

Clothing and footwear can be used as a source for samples, for the following purposes:

- for the recovery of fibres, hair, and particulate material and traces, wet or dry blood, and chemicals;
- for comparison use as a control of the fibre mix and to recreate impressions left by clothing or shoes on vehicles following RTCs and at scenes;
- damage to clothing may assist in describing weapons used on a victim;
- damage to fibres may indicate proximity to fire or explosion.

When taking clothing from suspects and victims, it is essential that the subject stands on a clean paper sheet which catches any debris which may fall. Material recovered from the floor of custody areas or medical facilities is not suitable for laboratory examination since it has no provenance, and the majority of force quality-control systems will prevent the submission of such articles.

Ensure any samples from the skin, hands, head, and mouth are taken first in order to prevent material from those areas contaminating the clothing or vice versa—for example, pulling a sweater covered in glass over the head which does not contain glass is contamination, so deal with the head hair first.

Remove the clothing in a logical manner and exhibit and package each piece separately in front of the subject. A final search of pockets may be carried out within the bag to prevent the unnecessary loss of material.

There is almost certainly a shoe-mark intelligence system operating within your force, which may be linked to the National Footwear Reference Collection; you should follow the accepted procedure. It is inadvisable to scan or copy shoes which may be needed for the analysis of trace materials and DNA, since the action of using the scanner may contaminate the shoes or cause the loss of material.

Finally, ask the person to brush off his/her bare feet onto the paper sheet before stepping off, since material on the sheet will adhere to sweaty feet. The paper sheet on the floor is now an exhibit, so treat it with necessary care before it is despatched for analysis.

Without fail, make notes about the condition of clothing: its size, the presence of blood, colour, logos, and any damage. This prevents the need for another person to open the packaging in order to screen or describe the contents.

13.5.17.4 Head hair samples

Head hair samples can be used for the following purposes:

- for the recovery of fibres, hair, and particulate material and traces, wet or dry blood, and chemicals;
- for comparison use as a control of the subject's hair (structure, length, colour, and treatments) when found at scenes or on other people;
- for DNA from a hair root.

Head hair may contain glass, plant material, foreign hairs, and so on. Deal with the head hair before the clothing in order to limit contamination by or from other samples (this is especially important in offences where windows have been smashed). Hair samples must be taken over a sheet of pre-folded paper which catches debris. The technique in many police forces is as follows:

- Holding a piece of pre-folded paper, at least A4 size, comb the person's hair from front to back all over the head so that debris falls onto the paper. Continue until no more debris is found. Clearly, this is not easy when the person is not compliant. Exhibit the paper containing the debris and the comb.
- For matted hair, or dreadlocks, wear a glove and gently brush the hair with your hands and even a new small hairbrush if possible (with care). Exhibit the paper containing the debris, the glove, and the brush.
- Hats (where worn) should be exhibited first.
- Where religious head coverings are worn, such as turbans, ask permission from the person first and, time permitting, make arrangements for alternative head coverings prior to removal.
- Blood or other matted material in the hair should be cut out over a sheet of pre-folded paper. Exhibit the cut section, paper, and the scissors.
- When you have finished, a 'control' of head hair is required and ideally this is pulled out so it contains the root material. Take at least twenty-five hairs including all colours and length variations.

13.5.17.5 Skin swabs

Swabs from the skin can be used as a source for samples, and may show the presence of blood, saliva, or chemical residues such as explosives traces. Generally, this is best left to a CSI (particularly explosive and firearm traces and the photography of blood) or a medical examiner, but do not permit unnecessary delays to occur. Refer to your CSI training officers or CSI on area for the latest protocols on recovering blood and other fluids from non-intimate areas on suspects' skin.

13.5.17.6 Samples for DNA analysis

DNA will be present in some of the types of sample described above. However, you will also be trained to take samples that will subsequently only be used for DNA analysis. In general terms, the subject should not eat, drink, or smoke for at least 20 minutes before the test. This allows the mouth to regenerate dead or damaged cells. Open the pack—which contains a buccal swab kit and a hair sampling kit—and check its contents. Always wear the gloves provided. If you cough or sneeze over the pack once it is opened, or drop any part of it, you should discard it in its entirety. Never use a swab picked up from the floor.

Carry out the sampling process first and complete the associated paperwork last. This might save you time, because if you fill in the paperwork first and then drop a swab, you will have to fill in a new form for the next swab. Finally, seal everything into the 'tamper-evident' bag so that the forms can be read through the bag. Follow your force's protocols for subsequent handling and storage.

Under the PACE Act 1984, the subject may refuse a buccal swab, in which case he/she may elect a hair sample which is pulled to include the root. The hair sampling site can be chosen by the subject on condition that it is not in an intimate area.

Samples from people must be correctly **stored and transported.** Blood, semen, and saliva contain DNA and should be frozen immediately. Where DNA is not required, for instance for the comparison of paints and oils, it is best practice to air-dry the samples securely or to freeze them if this is not possible.

13.5.17.7 Prints and impressions from people

Fingerprints are a useful and non-invasive form of evidence. You will be specially trained so that you can fingerprint suspects and victims. Your force will use one of these methods at police stations:

- Livescan—a digital finger and palm scanning device which is found in all main police stations.
- Ink—the traditional copper plate and printers' ink system which is now mainly used to take elimination fingerprints from, for example, victims of crime but, additionally, there are simpler, portable systems such as an ink pad or peel-apart pre-inked strips.

Tooth impressions or bite marks may contain DNA found in the saliva which is normally present; you must consider how this DNA evidence is going to be preserved. A registered dentist is required under the PACE Act 1984 to take impressions of a suspect's teeth. Contact your CSI or Scientific Support Unit for advice.

Other body impressions may also be required at times. Consult your CSI for other impressions of the body.

13.5.17.8 Handwriting samples

These are used most effectively when a variety of material is submitted for comparison. This can include:

- samples produced in front of a police officer;
- material sourced from the suspect's home address, work, or other places—such as diaries, letters, general paperwork—which is identifiably written by the suspect (this is referred to as 'course of business' handwriting);
- material as above which is assumed to have been written by the suspect (but of poor value).

When taking a handwriting sample, the suspect must be given a well-used ballpoint pen and must write the sample material in the same format as the document under consideration as possible evidence: if the document is in capitals, then the sample piece must be in capitals, and so on. If the offence was committed on a specific form, ask the supplier to give you a bundle and use these too. Dummy cheques are available from your CSI or Fraud Unit (which may be combined with your Computer Crime Unit) if necessary.

Ask the suspect to write out the contents of the document a minimum of five times (unless this would be unreasonable). For cheques, at least 15 samples are needed. Each time the suspect completes a sample, remove it so that he cannot see the style in which he has previously written. Never allow the suspect to see the original document in question: always dictate. The suspect should sign and date every page.

Under no circumstances ask the suspect to write 'The quick brown fox jumped over the lazy dogs.' This sentence is of no use, since a person's writing style is partly determined by the letters before and after every other letter.

When a suspect is identified, the investigator should exploit any fingerprints on paper or probable DNA on envelope flaps and stamps.

13.5.18 Sampling from Crime Scenes

Your CSI trainer may teach you to take the following samples and provide you with packaging guidance; please ensure you use this book as a guide and refer to your CSI for up-to-date information on your force's protocols. Different forces employ a variety of Crime Scene Investigation staff whose chief role is the recovery of physical material from crime scenes, but there are many occasions where a police officer may seize exhibits in the course of duty. Such instances include:

- where the officer is part of a search team;
- where there is no apparent evidence save for one or two items which can be safely recovered without a CSI (such as documents, cheques, or a single moveable shoe mark)—note that local policies must be followed;
- where the CSI is unable to attend;
- where evidence may be lost if not recovered immediately (such as a shotgun cartridge on a windy day).

13.5.18.1 Recovering 'controls'

A control is for comparing with other samples, for instance samples retrieved from a suspect or an item involved in a crime. Where a simple control of material is needed, including from a single building, site, or vehicle window, or a single set of paint controls from a car involved in a RTC, a police officer may gather the control samples. For anything else, consult a CSI.

Glass controls should be taken as follows:

- Glass must always be taken from the frame which supports it because glass on the ground has no provenance. Where no glass remains you must satisfy yourself, the **scientist**, and a potential **jury** that the glass did, indeed, originally come from the frame.
- Take a minimum of six pieces of glass and mark the inside or outside of each with a pen or 'chinagraph' pencil. Sample from all around the break. Wear thick gloves and goggles as a Health and Safety minimum.
- Where a toughened glass window has broken, merely remove the cube-shaped debris from around the hole.
- If a large laminate window has broken, the slabs can be extremely dangerous. You must sample the complete thickness, not only the dusty ground glass on the surface. Consider that shoe marks may be present on the glass.
- Place the fragments into a suitable sturdy box with **every** edge sealed with tape. Fragments must not puncture or escape through the box. An outer polythene bag is essential.
- Apart from in vehicle windows, always measure the window void and its exact position above the ground and provide this as a plan drawing.

Paint controls should be taken as follows:

- Never use adhesive tapes to recover paint samples.
- If there is a tool mark present, you should consider calling a CSI.
- On window and door frames, slice out a section (at least 20 mm) of the paint (and preferably include some base material) with a sharp knife. Use a new knife. Do this from several areas around the damage.
- Place the fragments into a paper fold and then put into a polythene bag.
- Remember, if you are considering paint samples there may be tool marks—you may need a CSI anyway.
- On vehicles, cut out a 10p-sized section of paint, all the way to base metal (include filler where present) from several places near to, and remote from, the damage in question. Repeat the process where foreign paint is found.
- On vehicles with damaged panels the paint sometimes falls away in rectangular slabs. If so, take them from the car, not the ground beneath it.
- Because paint is brittle it may lend itself to a mechanical fit. In this case the entire object and all the chipped paint are required.

13.5.19   Packaging Techniques

Using the correct packaging prevents damage and contamination and is, effectively, a demonstration of the care and skill that accompanied the seizure of the exhibits. Always follow local force protocols, which are based on those laid down by forensic science laboratories. Specifically, guidance can be found in the FSS publication *The Scenes of Crime Handbook* (not publicly available, although your force should have copies).

13.5.19.1   Types of packaging and how to use them

The following table summarizes the types of packaging available and common techniques used when employing them. Note that some of the terms used in the table are explained later.

Types of packaging

Packaging	Procedure
Paper bags	• Place the article within and fold the top down twice, approximately 25 mm (one inch) per fold. • Seal over the joint with a signature seal (an adhesive label) bearing your signature, name, and number. • Completely seal the entire join between folds and bag and attach an exhibit label if required.
Polythene bags	• Attempt to locate and use a tamper-evident bag. • If a tamper-evident bag is unavailable, use a plain bag. • Place the article within. • Tent a signature seal over the top. • Tent a line of tape over the top along the entire open edge and attach an exhibit label if required. • Pinch the ends of the tape and cut off, about 10 mm from the bag. • Be cautious of packaging documents in plain bags: they should be packed in stout card folders or boxes to prevent people leaning on the documents or writing over them.
Nylon bags	• Place the article in a nylon bag, 'swan neck', tie the top, and seal. ('Swan neck' is a secure closure for a bag. The method is to twist the neck of the bag until it resembles a rope, loop this over itself in to an inverted U shape, then secure with tape or a cable tie.) Note the cable tie should not have 'teeth' which may puncture the bag. Place this bag into a polythene bag, swan neck, and seal. Use a nylon bag for hydrocarbons (such as petrol) and a nylon bag within a polythene bag for non-hydrocarbons (such as methylated spirits, alcohol, and acetone). • If you are unclear as to whether you are packaging a hydrocarbon or not, use a nylon bag within a polythene bag. • Place the entire package into a rigid container, seal, and label. • These articles should not be stored in proximity to other samples.
Boxes	• Signature-seal and seal with tape around all edges. Special perforated inserts are available for securing the item with string or cable ties. If you do not have these, simply puncture the box, but sign and seal over the holes.
'Paper folds'	• These are required for the safe collection and storage of dry materials such as powders, paint fragments, and hair combings. They are not adequate for storing glass. Always pre-fold the paper before use and work the debris down into the greyed section before refolding. Seal into a suitable polythene bag. (See diagram below).

The following is a common technique used to construct a 'paper-fold' container.

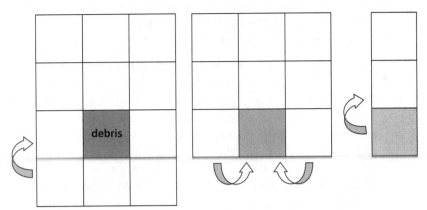

1. Work the material into the grey area and fold the base up

2. Fold in the left and right sides

3. Fold the base upwards and tuck the last fold in

(Image © Kevin Lawton-Barrett)

A Nylon bag 'swan necked' prior to securing with a cable tie

13.5.19.2   How to package items of forensic importance

Bedding and recently worn clothes or shoes must be sealed into paper bags which allow them to breathe. Sealing articles which are even slightly damp into plastic encourages the growth of mould and bacteria. You should also:

- affix a health hazard warning where any biological material may be present or where it is known or believed that articles have come from a possibly contaminated source (eg a known drug addict);
- if needed, affix an exhibit label. If bags are not pre-printed, it is advisable to write the exhibit details on the bag as a fail-safe measure.

Articles that are **slightly wet or soaked with liquids** (including blood) need to be dried. Contact a CSI without delay for advice and assistance with drying. You should also:

- avoid the temptation to fold clothes bearing wet blood as this causes the blood to transfer to other parts of the article;
- in an emergency, consider sealing into a polythene sack for transport but make contact with a CSI as a matter of priority. The sack should be sealed into a robust paper sack for protection.

Articles which may bear **flammable substances** should not be stored in paper bags because flammable chemicals (accelerants) will evaporate through paper sacks and be lost, as well as contaminating other material in storage and transit. Where biological material is also believed present, consult your CSI since DNA may be destroyed by flammable substances. It is likely that the CSI will recommend immediate transport to a laboratory.

Sharps, bladed weapons, screwdrivers, and **other pointed objects** represent a very serious health hazard. Hypodermic needles are rarely dispatched to laboratories. You should:

• Always use a sharps storage pack for needles. Consider disposing of the needle in a sharps bin prior to packaging the syringe if specialist syringe and needle storage boxes are not available. However, do not do this in major-crime cases; you must seek further advice.

• Always use a knife tube for blades, but if unavailable, consider a clean, unused, sturdy box.

• Screw-thread knife tubes are also inherently dangerous: never hold your palms over the ends since the screwing action 'jacks' the knife through the end of the tube if too much pressure is exerted.

• It is best practice to signature-seal and tape the joints between the two halves of knife tubes and sharps packs prior to packaging in a polythene bag.

• If wet blood or water is present, the articles should be air-dried first or frozen, but consult your local force policy. If a syringe contains liquid local policy may require it to be decanted into a bottle. In this case consult a CSI.

Firearms represent a serious and immediate high-risk hazard. Student police officers must never handle nor package a firearm without training: previous military expertise is not sufficient. It is best practice to call for the assistance of a Firearms Officer and CSI to properly record the making-safe process. Firearms are first made safe and then sealed into boxes (unless they are of no forensic interest, for instance when the owner of a firearm is considered to be unfit to continue possessing a firearm, and the weapon is being removed to the police station for safety).

Bottles and **glasses** may have sharp edges; think health and safety, and follow these procedures:

• to protect fingerprints or DNA, bottles and glasses must be immobilized in a sturdy box;

• signature-seal and seal with tape around all edges. Special perforated inserts are available for securing the item with string or cable ties. If you do not have these, simply puncture the box, but sign and seal over the holes;

• when providing bottles and glasses for back-calculation alcohol analysis (see 11.16.5.3 above) ensure they are marked up to show the levels the suspect claims to have drunk and package securely in a box to prevent breakage.

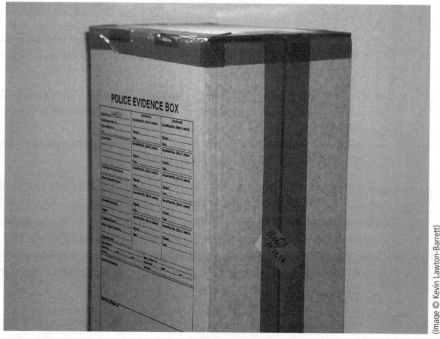

(Image © Kevin Lawton-Barrett)

Police evidence box

Urine samples may be required in a crime investigation or be taken from drivers under the Road Traffic Act 1988 (see 11.16.5.2 above). Custody officers have access to 'RTA-type' urine kits which contain a special preservative—use this kit unless local policies dictate otherwise. In other crime, the subject is asked to urinate into a plastic pot which is then decanted into a suitable bottle containing a preservative. Ensure the bottle is properly secured and place in a rigid outer container. Some urine collection pots bear a temperature gauge to ensure that the sample came from a living person, rather than from, say, a supply secreted for the purpose (those of you who have seen the film *Withnail and I* will understand why).

TASK 7

Discuss the following questions with a BCU CSI or your trainers:

1. At a major crime scene, what are the usual problems with the common approach path and cordons?
2. What is the best form of evidence? A fingerprint or DNA? (They are very likely to all have different views, based almost entirely upon the context of the evidence they have found in the past.)
3. What is worse, genuine contamination of an exhibit, or the suspicion of contamination?

13.5.20 Attending a Venue Containing Digital Media

To an extent digital evidence includes nearly any electronic device of any description, since so many contain clocks and programmers. Digital equipment includes computers, palmtops (a type of PDA), mobile phones, PDAs, electronic organizers, satellite navigation equipment ('GPS' devices), credit card skimmers, and an array of domestic devices that include timers and programmers (such as modern washing machines). Storage media includes floppy discs, CD-ROMs, DVDs, memory sticks, flash cards, and portable hard drives. There are also likely to be games consoles (eg the Sony Playstation 3, the XBox360) in many homes—remember that most of these consoles are also capable of storing digital media (pictures, sound, and video) and also able to access the internet.

You may be involved in the seizure of such equipment, which we discuss below. However, remember also that other items of a 'traditional' (non-digital) nature may also be present and important at venues where digital media are also seized. For example, there may be printed emails and handwritten notes with passwords or other instructions relating to the storage of digital media. In cases of suspected downloading and distribution of child pornography there may be printed images close to the digital equipment.

Police officers should only turn off digital equipment at a crime scene or other site if they have been trained to use the appropriate procedures. The most common message given to people who are experiencing problems with electronic equipment (apart from the traditional 'give it a bang') is to turn the device off. Whilst this may work well enough for your own domestic equipment, if you are seizing a computer as part of an investigation, you should never turn it off by going through the routine that you may be familiar with at home or work (by first closing down Windows and so on).

To seize a computer for forensic purposes, your police force will train you instead to remove the power cables from the back of the PC while it is still on. This is a precaution in case the computer has an Uninterruptible Police Supply (UPS), and also prevents automated routines from being activated (these might destroy vital evidence on the hard drive). Just as important is that you should never turn on a digital device if it is an off state. We look at the seizure of computers in more detail in 13.5.20.1 below. More information may be found in Bryant (2008).

13.5.20.1 Computers

Analysis of computer and associated storage media can provide evidence about:

- deleted files and images;
- emails;
- images and text, whether downloaded or created locally;
- address books and contact details;

- times and dates of activity;
- hidden files and data.

However, even reasonably unsophisticated criminals may have sufficient ability to booby-trap their computers so that the machines can execute certain procedures when interfered with—be particularly aware of wireless networks. Whilst data can sometimes be recovered even after deletion, causing deletion to happen is a form of contamination and must be avoided if at all possible.

Where a seizure is **planned**, the Digital Forensics Unit (or Computer Crime Unit) should be contacted in advance for advice and, where necessary, attendance at the scene. Digital Forensics personnel are specially trained to recover data and present it in a form acceptable to the CJS.

Where a seizure is **unplanned**, contact should be made with the Digital Forensics Unit (or Computer Crime Unit) for advice. In the meantime:

- do not turn on or off any device;
- do not touch any key or the mouse;
- do not interrupt the power supply (unless you have been trained in the seizure of computers and have been instructed in how to do so)—an exception to this rule occurs in the circumstances when the computer may be executing instructions to format the logical drives or other 'destructive' activity; this will be explained to you during your initial training;
- do not interfere with any other device on a network;
- do not use the telephone system in any scene;
- do not take the advice of the owner or user.

You should however take the following actions:

- take advice from the Digital Forensics Unit if possible;
- secure the scene and move people away from the equipment and any power supplies;
- photograph the screen, if it is displaying;
- allow a printer to complete its run;
- if the computer is on, and the Digital Forensics Unit advise you accordingly, interrupt the power supply in the way that you have been trained to do (normally by removing the power lead from the back of the PC base unit);
- photograph or sketch the device and any associated cabling where practicable.

Laptops can be a particular problem in unplanned seizures because removing the power lead will not close them down. You may be trained by the Digital Forensics Unit to remove the battery from a laptop as well as the power cable in the circumstances of a laptop being on, but as in all matters concerning the seizure of digital equipment, be guided by local force policy. If you have removed the battery, remember to also seize this.

If you are required to 'bag and tag' computer equipment, be guided by force policy. Most forces will expect you to:

- use one bag for every PC base unit;
- not to use paper bags for the PC base unit, but see-through plastic ones instead (but see 13.5.20.4 below);
- as always, to seal the bag properly;
- to use a cardboard exhibit label.

13.5.20.2 Small portable devices

These include items such as USB pens, digital cameras, PDAs, and organizers. If these are unconnected to other devices the Digital Forensics Unit may suggest a simple seizure, but seek advice and check policy. Remember that some of these devices can still communicate with other systems through Bluetooth and Infrared, and wireless receivers and transmitters. Do not view call lists, pictures, or any other files on portables.

In terms of seizure, be guided by local policy. However, you will probably be expected to:

- package different media separately (eg USB pens separately from CDs);
- note the exact number of items in each bag (eg 'a large quantity of CDs' is not likely to be an adequate description);

- where applicable, keep media in their cases (remember to check inside cases);
- not to put any labels on discs;
- seize cradles/power packs for PDAs and similar equipment.

13.5.20.3 Mobile phones

Mobile phones are seized from nearly every major crime scene and prisoner, and your force will have specific policies relating to their seizure and packaging. This may include storage in special packaging to prevent them communicating with the network. Mobile phones and the network supplier's databases contain an enormous amount of information relating to calls, texts, and even their movement through the cellular network—so-called Cell Site Analysis. Do not view call lists, pictures, or any other files on mobiles.

13.5.20.4 Transport and storage of computers and other large items

You must follow your local policy during all seizures and storage, particularly relating to packaging.

When carrying computer equipment it is difficult to transport such equipment without touching the surfaces. The outer skin of most computers is mildly textured and commonly will not yield marks (in volume crime) but the screen and areas which are not normally seen, such as the inside, under the support foot and at the rear, are often very smooth. However, remember that polythene bags will obliterate fingerprints if they touch the smooth surfaces.

In serious or major crimes great care must be taken: remember that the whole device may be required for DNA and fingerprint analysis.

TASK 8

Answer the following questions and instructions to gauge your recall and learning of the forensic investigation topics covered in 13.5 above. Some of the questions simply require you to locate the information, but others are more demanding. You may also find that an informal meeting with your local CSI is of benefit when you are on Supervised Patrol at your BCU, or whilst on a course.

1. Who is credited with the development of the Principle of Exchange?
2. List three types of trace evidence or material which might be found at a burglary.
3. List three types of impression.
4. List three sources of DNA.
5. List three things an investigator might employ forensic science for.
6. What is inceptive evidence?
7. In an emergency, can you lawfully ask a victim to provide a urine sample if he/she tells you he/she was the victim of a drug-induced rape?
8. You are tasked to attend a crime scene and take a control sample of glass. How many pieces should you take? From where? What should you mark on them?
9. You are taking a DNA sample from an arrested person. You drop the swab on the floor. What action do you now carry out?
10. Which PACE Act 1984 Code applies to fingerprinting suspects?
11. What does Mitochondrial DNA establish: male or female lines?
12. Imagine you have a quantity of fine debris you wish to store. Taking a sheet of A4 paper, make a paper fold to retain it.
13. Clothing thought to be contaminated with hydrocarbons (like petrol) is packed into what sort of bag?
14. What does FSS stand for?

13.6 Answers to Tasks

TASK 1

You may have noted that major-crime investigations are often long-term and complex, especially when dealing with 'stranger murders' or 'stranger rapes'.

You could note too that crimes of violence attract considerable **media** interest and widespread publicity which, whilst helpful in publicizing the crime, have the potential to adversely affect an investigation if not handled properly.

TASK 2

When a person is decapitated.

TASK 3

Although it is beyond the scope of this Handbook (and not something that you are likely to encounter unless you become an SIO) you might like to research the CATCHEM (Central Analytical Homicide and Expertise Management) database. Research conducted on child murder with a sexual motive revealed complex mathematical relationships between places of abduction, and aspects of the offender. This is described in Aitken *et al* (1995). One inferential model the authors describe suggests that, in the case of a boy victim, aged 0–10 who had been abducted, there are high probabilities that the offender lives within five miles of the contact point (75 per cent chance) and is aged 21+ (77 per cent).

The pioneering work of Aitken *et al* continues to be developed and extended by, amongst others, the Serious Crime Analysis Section of NCOF.

The research used has now been applied to the more general crime of homicide (Francis *et al*, 2004). For example, if the victim is aged 18–24, male, ethnically of Asian background, unemployed, and 'stabbed in a rage' then the model predicts that the offender is over 21 (68 per cent likelihood), also Asian (55 per cent), and an acquaintance of the victim (60 per cent).

TASK 4

You would probably note that the first priority is not to let anyone else over the threshold of the crime scene, and that might well extend to the area outside the bed sit, to include stairs, stairwell, communal areas, and adjoining corridors or passages. You would clear people away, including the landlord, and close off the scene as swiftly as possible. You would enter the room yourself, principally to ascertain if the presumed victim is still alive. If she were still alive you would follow the Airways, Breathing, Circulation (ABC) procedures; your duty is to support her until the paramedics arrive. You would ensure that nothing else was touched.

You would be in urgent communication with your force control centre, describing what you can see, the location and any other relevant requirements, such as the attendance of paramedics, an ambulance, and a doctor. You would request the attendance of CSIs and probably the duty SIO or duty detective officer, since it is evident that a violent crime has been committed. It might or might not be murder, but that will determined by the subsequent investigation.

Then what? If you have a colleague with you, you could share the note taking, including the names and addresses of all those present, whether they have volunteered as witnesses or not. (Bear in mind the need to 'record, retain, and reveal' that we discussed in 12.6 above.) You would find out from the landlord (whose details you have also recorded) information about the victim and any information about visitors to her that day, including of course any information about the other person or persons present at the apparent altercation which the landlord heard. You would log your actions, and begin arranging the CAP to the crime scene. You would note anything which you observed (such as a murder weapon, scattered possessions, blood splashes, and so on).

TASK 5

The majority of investigative bodies in the UK use the simple format described here, namely AB/1. Your force might operate a different system, particularly in the light of the development of exhibit-tracking databases. The reason many people sanction a large jump in exhibit numbers when they return to an inquiry is to prevent confusion. You can never understand how serious this confusion might be until it happens to you!

When exhibiting drugs, in particular, this issue becomes even more difficult. If you search premises and find a box containing ten wraps of drugs, bear in mind that the wraps may be 'sub-exhibited' at a later stage—even on your behalf and without your knowledge. Thus the box may be AB/1, the wraps AB/1A to AB/1J and the contents of the wraps could become AB/1A/1 or similar. Imagine the confusion later. One system to prevent this is to exhibit the box as AB/1, then the wraps as AB/2 and so on. This at least reduces the future problem. Seek advice and follow your local force policy in this respect.

TASK 6

In all these instances you could **lawfully** have taken the evidence. If you elected not to do so the evidence would quite possibly be lost.

It is acceptable, in an emergency and when a CSI or medical assistance is not available, for anyone to take a sample from a victim in a case such as this. Clearly, the dignity and psychological well-being of the victim must be uppermost in your mind, but there are occasions when decisive action will benefit the investigation. Crucially, you would have to have access to the appropriate sterile equipment for the task and you would preferably have received previous training.

Many police forces have evidence kits at the front counter for just these unlikely situations. Out on Supervised or Independent Patrol these kits may not be available and you may have to 'make do', but remember: immediate actions like these can be required at any time.

TASK 7

1. Common Approach Paths sound simple but raise many problems, not least of which is where to put them. Essentially, they should be on a hard surface and should not be the likely route that the offender or victim took to, or from, the crime scene. The next issue is: how can you mark them out on a windy day without anything to secure the tape? You cannot really do this until assistance arrives. Ask your CSI what happened at their last few incidents. They will probably be able to explain that, with hindsight, the FAO could have employed better tactics.
2. Fingerprints are assumed to be unique, but there is disagreement over this issue since it is difficult to actually **prove** this point in a scientific sense. Our DNA is unique, too, but many people feel more comfortable with DNA because it has been the subject of much recent research. The best evidence, ultimately, only occurs where the context for it is right; thus on one occasion DNA can be of no use, whilst the next day it is very powerful.
   If speed is the best measurement, then fingerprints win since the turnaround for a fingerprint in an emergency can be a few hours, at most, from any point in the UK by using Livescan or digital transmission techniques. The best that DNA can manage is around 12 hours. To improve this, DNA can now be analysed at the crime scene in a special vehicle and the results can be communicated to the FSS by BT communications systems.
3. If your CSI **knows** contamination has occurred he/she can warn the scientist and, occasionally, there may be a way to overcome the problem. If there is a **suspicion** or **accusation** that it has occurred then there may be no resolution, particularly if the Crown is 'ambushed' in court. By ensuring rigorous standards at the scene (or elsewhere) and by admitting we have made a mistake the prosecution might be able to rebut these accusations. The most important point is that we 'never' allow contamination to occur, but if it does we inform the CSI or scientist immediately.

TASK 8

Answers are as follows.

1. Edmond Locard.
2. Fibres, glass, paint, soil, pollen, fibres, etc.
3. Tool marks, shoe marks, impressions from stamps and dyes, extrusion marks, finger marks, clothing, gloves, etc.

4. Blood, semen, ear wax, mucus, saliva, etc.
5. A possible list:

   - describing the *modus operandi* (MO);
   - answering investigative questions;
   - to establish that an offence has occurred;
   - to identify an offender or suspect;
   - to corroborate or refute witness statements;
   - to establish a physical link between suspect, crime scene, and victim;
   - to identify an individual;
   - to further inform an enquiry.

6. That which identifies an unknown, eg a person.
7. Yes. There is nothing to stop you asking for a sample in an emergency (and assisting in its collection). However, you should respect the human rights of the individual concerned, and remember to act with common decency.
8. Six pieces from the frame (around the hole) and mark the inside or outside of each.
9. Destroy the entire kit.
10. Code D.
11. Mitochondrial DNA comes from the female line, ie from the mother.
12. Compare the result to the diagram in 13.5.19.1 above.
13. Nylon. Nylon bags are crinkly: remember 'Nylon is Noisy'.
14. Forensic Science Service or the Forensic Science Society (sometimes FSSoc): see the glossary in Chapter 1.

Developing as a Police Officer

14.1　Chapter Briefing

You will naturally be concerned at the outset of training with the successful completion of your two-year probationary period. However, towards the end of your training (or in some forces, in the second year of training) you may be asked to consider the possibility of undertaking a specialist role within your force. Even if this is not the case, you may well be thinking about prospects for promotion. This chapter will be of value to you when you begin to consider your career development within the police service.

14.1.1　Aim of the Chapter

The aim of this chapter is to assist you in your future development within the police service.

This chapter will enable you to:

- understand the variety of policing roles open to you after confirmation;
- appreciate the need to maintain and, where appropriate, further develop your skills;
- understand the process of promotion within the police and the new roles and responsibilities you will be asked to adopt if you are promoted;
- develop the underpinning knowledge required for an NOS Unit and a CAR of your SOLAP and future entries in your PDP.

14.1.2　National Occupational Standards

This chapter will provide you with the knowledge required to demonstrate aspects of the NOS Unit AE1 'Maintain and develop your own knowledge, skills, and competence'.

14.1.3   IPLDP Phases and Modules

This chapter will provide you with resources to support some aspects of the Induction Modules IND 3 'Develop one's own knowledge and practice' and IND 4 'Develop effective relationships with colleagues'.

The relevant IPLDP Phase is Phase 4 (Independent Patrol).

14.1.4   The SOLAP and the PDP

The contents of this chapter are relevant to the 'knowledge' evidence requirements of CAR AE1. After you are confirmed your SOLAP is likely to be succeeded by a PDP as part of the PDR process. If this is the case, then you might find some of the material in this chapter useful in terms of personal development planning for the future.

14.2   Introduction

This chapter is about you: your aptitudes, preferences, and where you want to go in the police. There is no point in our being prescriptive because we cannot determine what you want to do, or whether you will achieve your ambitions. You may want to be a chief constable/commissioner of the Metropolitan Police Service, be a computer-crime specialist, work with police dogs for the rest of your career, or command a BCU; only you can decide. You know that you will need certain skills and competencies for each role, and you may also need some luck, to be in the right place at the right time and to be able to take advantage of the opportunity offered.

TASK 1

As a first step towards considering the rest of your time in the police service, write down where you want to be in three, five, and ten years' time.

These timings are deliberate. Within three years of completing your probation, you could be a sergeant or you could be a specialist constable. Within a further two years, you could be an inspector or overseeing the work of a specialist unit. After ten years, you could be a superintendent, a highly specialized officer such as a source handler, or a tactical adviser to a firearms incident commander; or you could be in another career entirely, having left policing. As we will see later in this chapter, the possibilities are numerous: there are at least 25 separate roles you could perform as a constable, at least 9 as a sergeant, and at least 10 as an inspector. The options narrow as you move up the promotion ladder, but at the same time you increase your breadth of knowledge and experience of command, determining tactics, and managing the staff who work for you.

It may be that whatever initially drew you into policing is not what you end up doing at all because, as you study and learn more about the police, you find that there are other roles which attract you and about which you knew very little when you joined. A survey in 2004 of newly-joined probationers in an English police force suggested that most male recruits wanted to be responsible for patrol cars and most female recruits wanted to undertake foot patrol in town centres. They were surveyed again after six to eight months by which time the gender difference had become blurred, and most officers (irrespective of gender) wanted to work in crime investigation or uniformed patrol, and only a few wanted to join 'Traffic' for roads policing. Many were attracted by community policing and some had already decided that they wanted to be involved with public-order policing. And such choices are not irrevocable; there are many opportunities to change work streams as you progress, and we shall look at some of them later on.

Of course, your choices are often guided by your tutors and more experienced officers; you are likely to be able to observe aspects of their work, and you will see what a specialist or generalist choice entails, and you may be influenced by their enthusiasm for what they do. Equally, a cynical, disengaged, or uninterested instructor can put you off a particular job for a long time, if not for ever.

However, decisions about your posting are taken with the needs of the whole force in mind, and your preferences may come second. You are now a Crown servant, a sworn officer, and the force to which you belong may determine (at least in the immediate term) the broad parameters of what you do. If your police force is short of foot-patrol officers, or there is an urgent need for people to staff a crime desk, you may find yourself being nudged (sometimes none too gently) in a particular direction. However, if you have a strong desire, say, to become a detective, it will probably not be long before opportunities arise and, in time, the force will be likely to accede to your wishes once its own needs have been met. Facilitating your career moves is the shared role of your supervisor and the force's HR team, but the major part is yours to play. (You should bear in mind, however, that you will not be very popular if you change your mind too frequently or do not make a proper attempt at a job which you find uncongenial at first.)

Let us suppose that you work for a well-resourced, forward-thinking, and lively police force and you have enjoyed every task set for you during your training as a student police officer; you have done well, have obtained good assessments, and your personal development portfolio is bulging with development opportunities and positive experiences. Your probation is over; you are 'confirmed', there are no foreseeable staffing crises, and you have been told that you can choose where you go next. What do you do now?

14.3 Generalist or Specialist?

One of the first decisions will be whether to specialize or generalize. You should refer to the Integrated Competency Framework (see 3.5 above) for the constable role at this point, and remind yourself what is involved in reaching the required standard for the generic role.

You will already have the 'core responsibilities' competencies; you are able to complete the administration procedures associated with the role, maintain the standards of professional practice, work as part of a team, provide first aid when required, and comply with health and safety legislation. You will also make the best use of technology (both in IT and telephony) and you promote equality, diversity, and human rights in all your working practices, as well as being part of an organizational response which recognizes the needs of all communities. You employ an effective problem-solving approach to all community issues in which you become involved and you make good use of intelligence to support the policing objectives of your force.

In addition, you will have attained the **behavioural competencies** (see 3.7 above) as follows:

Generic behavioural competency	Level for a Constable
Respect for race and diversity	A
Team working	C
Community and customer focus	C
Effective communication	B
Problem solving	C
Personal responsibility	B
Resilience	A

You will remember that these grades represent **levels of difficulty** or sophistication in your achievement of the necessary competence. The grades listed above are the minimum grades required for a patrol constable; higher grades may be required for other roles as a constable. Indeed, for particular competencies, the requirements may be higher for some constable roles than they are for sergeants or inspectors (in those same competencies).

Thus equipped, you should be ready to take on any general task as a constable, and to serve anywhere in the force that you are needed. For some people that is enough and they are perfectly happy refining these competencies and behaviours, building experience, and interacting with the public on a daily basis; some officers will never want to move away from this generic role for their entire careers. That said, we doubt if any force will let an officer remain in this position without encouraging him/her (at the very least) to pass on the knowledge he/she has accumulated to new recruits as a tutor constable (or assessor constable in some forces), or to work in a local Professional Development Unit (PDU).

In some police forces, it is assumed that the generic role of constable means that the post-holder can go anywhere and do anything. Whilst it is clearly an advantage for a constable to be able to take on a wide range of tasks and responsibilities, it is perhaps wasteful to assume that any one individual can meet *any* challenge, no matter how specialist or demanding. An example may be in posting a constable to perform a role in Finance or in Human Resource Management, a practice not unknown in the past.

TASK 2

Can you say what the pitfalls and problems might be in such a practice?

TASK 3

Can you think of other competencies which 'non-specialists' can acquire where performance does not have to be at a high level to be effective?

Neither the generalist nor the specialist has the monopoly on effectiveness. One simple rule of thumb is that specialist knowledge can be acquired by the generalist, but the process often turns the generalist into a specialist. Alternatively, where highly specialized knowledge is required, and the post is not a sworn one (in other words, it does not have to be filled only by a police officer), the best solution often is to employ a member of the support staff who possesses that particular specialist skill.

14.4   Specialization

Suppose that you wish to specialize whilst a constable.

TASK 4

Write down the range of jobs and roles which you think may be on offer. Try to be as specific as you can. You should be able to think of at least ten different roles.

You will have been exposed to the work of three major divisions of policing during your initial training: investigation, patrol policing, and community policing. We now examine each of the three areas in turn.

14.4.1   Investigation

A decision to follow the **investigative route** does not mean that you are closing off the other avenues for ever. It is quite common to move in and out of roles and across the streams of central police work, but as a rule you will stay within the detective branch or department if you specialize in investigation. In many forces, the route to becoming a skilled investigator is through service on an investigation team based locally in a BCU. In some forces, this is called a 'tactical criminal investigation department' or TAC CID.

Level 1 PIP is linked with the IPLDP and the NOS units for initial policing and so you automatically achieve Level 1 if you successfully complete your initial training. You will learn interviewing techniques, investigation methods and models, law, case files, major and serious crime procedures, and put your skills into practice in the investigation of crimes of all types, ranging from petty theft to 'Cat C' murders.

14.4.1.1 ICIDP

The NPIA Initial Crime Investigators' Development Programme (ICIDP, or sometimes referred to as the National ICIDP (NICIDP)) is a programme designed for trainee Detective Constables (TDCs) and provides the basis for the investigation of more serious and complex criminal cases. ICIDP is linked with PIP Level 2, which is in turn linked with the NOS units relevant to investigation: CI102, CJ102, and CJ202 ('Conduct serious and complex investigations', 'Interview victims and witnesses in relation to serious and complex investigations', and 'Interview suspects in relation to serious and complex investigations' respectively).

The ICIDP consists of three phases and details are available online (NPIA, 2008a). We provide a summary of each phase below:

Phase 1 (for the trainee investigator) is a period of self study using printed materials, and takes a minimum of 14 weeks (NPIA, 2008a, p1). The content is law-based and covers property offences, assaults, drugs, firearms, sexual offences, offences against children and other vulnerable persons, and evidence.

Phase 2 of the ICIDP is typically a six-week taught course, and concludes with sitting the National Investigators Examination (NIE) which tests knowledge of the four sub-areas of property offences: assaults, drugs, firearms & defences; sexual offences; and evidence (NPIA, 2008a, p3). There is some flexibility in how forces structure the course (some, for example, base it on a case study and might also incorporate a Hydra simulation) although all courses are likely to be linked to the NOS Units and elements, to subscribe to the NPIA specified aims and objectives, and will at least cross-reference the ACPO Core Investigative Doctrine. In many forces, before commencing Phase 2 there is also a requirement to complete a 'tier 2' (after initial training) investigating interview course.

Practice varies between forces in terms of a formal assessment of the knowledge and understanding gained during Phase 2 (eg whether a formal written examination is set or not).

Phase 3 of ICIDP will always involve demonstration and assessment of competence in the work place against the three NOS units given above. This involves supervision by a tutor (normally an Accredited Detective Constable (Level 2) or an Investigative Adviser) and collecting evidence in a Professional Development Portfolio (PDP). Experienced investigators (who will have been in position before the advent of the ICIDP) are able to access Phase 3 through APL procedures. On successful completion of Phase 3, investigators are 'registered' at the BCU level as qualified at PIP Level 2.

14.4.1.2 Further investigator training

Should you stay with this kind of work, you may move to internal force departments such as a central unit investigating level 2 serious crime, or you may join a specialist homicide team, investigating 'Cat A' and 'Cat B' murders, manslaughter, or GBH. This will probably involve taking the **Initial Management of Serious Crime** (IMSC) course, which is designed primarily for Detective Sergeants and is, in effect, a bridging course between the ICIDP and the more advanced programmes for SIOs. (Note, however, that the course is currently under review by NPIA.)

The **Senior Investigating Officer Development Programme** (SIODP) is designed for investigators already qualified to at least PIP Level 2 (eg through the ICIDP) or its equivalent, and who are likely to become responsible for investigating serious crime (such as homicide and rape by stranger). Students of the SIODP are typically of Detective Inspector rank or above. As with IPLDP and ICIDP, the SIODP is linked with the NOS, in this case the single unit CI103, to 'Manage major investigations' (with a total of five elements). The course typically lasts 15 days, although a one-week 'Hydra' simulation course (based on the investigation of a serious crime) is also often recommended as a follow-up, and is in some cases a compulsory element. The SIODP is usually delivered on a regional rather than local-force basis in order to provide good access to specialist inputs, and for reasons of economy of scale (the numbers involved are significantly lower than for the ICIDP). The course usually covers the ACPO Core Investigative Doctrine (particularly in terms of initial response, gathering information, and the use of forensic investigation), inter-agency working, family liaison, resource management, the use of intelligence, record keeping (particularly in terms of policy logging and disclosure), self-evaluation and the evaluation of others, and handling the media. The course also involves the collection of evidence to claim competence against the NOS Unit, presented as a PDP, leading to the achievement of PIP Level 3.

14.4.2 Patrol Policing

If you decide that **Patrol** is your preferred interest, there are plenty of roles to take, from Traffic to Tactical Operations, from Firearms to Public Order. In this type of work you will be at the forefront of visible uniformed policing; yours is the face and figure most seen by the public. As we have seen with investigation, you will still have much training in prospect and a systematic development route to specialize within Patrol. Currently there are few training programmes which deliver advanced qualifications in Patrol, although a number of police forces are researching and designing possible ways to do this, some in conjunction with Skills for Justice and the NPIA. One of the things you should consider, before opting to go into the Patrol stream, is what opportunities there are for you to obtain further qualifications, and to find out whether there is a partnership programme with academic institutions. If Patrol is a 'default option' in your force, in which there is little evident development and no deliberate or systematic learning processes, you might want to think twice before committing yourself. If, on the other hand, your force is pursuing such partnerships, links, and development opportunities, you will find that Patrol is far from a backwater and may be the most vibrant and innovative part of your force. It very much depends on your local circumstances.

There is no doubt that Patrol can be an immensely satisfying part of policing: you will often be the first officer attending a crime scene (with all the responsibilities we outlined in Chapter 13, in terms of the 'golden hour' and your vital role in the preservation of life and of evidence), and you will have a major part to play in policing demonstrations, large gatherings, public events, and disorder. Your contact with the public will be an integral part of the reassurance agenda and you will be foremost in the policing of volume crime and public disorder. That said, it is also the most physically demanding of all police roles, and you will also be in the forefront of dealing with violence, collisions, tragedies, and human disaster. The dynamic risk assessments for many of the roles in Patrol will be crucial to the safety of you, your colleagues, and the public, and you should not underestimate the strains and stresses of front-line police work, particularly in the role of firearms officer.

14.4.3 Community (eg Neighbourhood) Policing

Community policing is different again. Here, you will work with smaller teams, and often bridge the space between Patrol and Investigation. You will learn new skills and your development will probably be geared to specializing in one of a number of roles. For example, you may opt to work as a **Community Liaison Officer** (CLO), in which case you will begin to know the leaders and members of groups within your local community and you will help to develop sophisticated partnership-working arrangements to meet community needs. Diversity skills will be vital, as will the accumulation of intelligence on crime in the community. You will often be the first port of call from your detective colleagues when investigating crime within your area, and your advice will be needed, and usually respected and acted upon, especially when there are local sensitivities, such as minority ethnic communities or the investigation of a homophobic crime.

You may become part of a **Neighbourhood Policing Team** (NPT) alongside members of the wider policing family such as PCSOs and Special Constables. This will involve both responding to local issues and needs surrounding crime and disorder (often in collaboration with other agencies, such as local authorities), and taking proactive action in reassuring the public. You will be a named contact for members of the local community so they may access policing services in their area, and you will also be responsible for providing feedback on actions taken and the consequences.

A **Family Liaison Officer** role is also specialist and of key importance within community policing. You will be trained in negotiation, mediation, and some group-management techniques so that your work with families (usually the victims or witnesses of crime) is as productive, reassuring, and positive as possible. You will be the focus for the family in the wake of a crime, especially a crime of violence, and will help them through the difficulties of the search for the offender, arrest, and charge, and you will support the family through the subsequent court proceedings. In a very real sense, you will be the 'face of policing' to that family, and often it will be you who helps them provide vital evidence. An FLO played a leading part, for example, in obtaining evidence in the Lyn and Megan Russell murders in Kent in 1996. This was a particularly disturbing crime, in which Mrs Russell and her daughter Megan were attacked with a hammer or similar instrument and beaten to death. Another daughter, Josie, was attacked and badly injured, but not killed. In the investigation which followed, the skills of the FLO in gaining Josie's trust and confidence were integral to the successful prosecution of Michael Stone for the murders.

Working closely with neighbourhoods and their varied communities is, for many officers, what policing is really about, and offers its greatest rewards. This is not to say that the work is easy; to gain the community's trust and respect means working long hours, having highly developed personal skills, and understanding how community dynamics and partnerships work. The development of NPTs based on BCUs, in which there may be a mix of police officers, PCSOs, Special Constables, and members of other agencies, is a pointer to the importance of local and citizen-focused engagement. Should you opt for a community-policing role, you may well find yourself in time supervising the work of others, and/or managing a neighbourhood-policing team. Many officers find this a deeply satisfying activity and are reluctant to leave it. Other work, such as crime reduction, schools' liaison, and working with crime-reduction partnerships also provide considerable rewards in return for persistence, professionalism, and receptivity, but the results in terms of crime reduction are often long-term rather than immediate. Communities appear to dislike frequent changes of police personnel, as it takes time to build relationships. If you opt for community policing, you need to be aware that it is often for the long haul.

14.5 Maintaining and Developing Your Skills

It is important that, in whichever of the 'strands' of policing you choose to follow, you continue the practices you learned during your time as a student police officer. This principally means that you sustain your competencies and add to them through the accumulation of experience, and that you continue to update your **professional development portfolio** (PDP, also known as 'personal development programme' and a variety of other names). The PDP is not only considered by some to be good practice (it encourages you to reflect on what you are doing and to think about what you have learned) but you will also need your PDP to give evidence of your competencies and experience when you seek promotion. If your ambition is to become a sergeant in the shortest permissible time, two years from the end of your confirmation, you will need to evidence your exceptional capabilities to perform at the next rank. Part of that evidence will be in your PDP and part in the tasks you have undertaken and excelled at. Whenever possible you should talk to those already holding the substantive rank and find out what they do and why. You will also need to look at the competencies and role requirements of the generic sergeant role and any specialist functions which a supervisor performs. If you can, you should seek opportunities to 'act up' in the rank, perhaps by supervising a patrol of constables for a limited time, or by seeking temporary promotion whenever it is offered. It is helpful here to understand a difference here in terminology: **acting rank** means that you do it for a short time, probably on a casual basis; **temporary rank** means that you perform the role of that rank for a period of at least three months, and you receive the pay of that rank.

It is not a requirement in the police service, as it is in the armed forces, to spend some time in the acting rank before being eligible for consideration for promotion. However, the opportunity for people to act in the rank above is often a good opportunity for them to show that they can do the next job; it accrues experience in the role and gives the opportunity for assessors to make judgements on a person's actual performance rather than simply on potential.

Whether you seek promotion early or not, you have an obligation to sustain your **continuous professional development** (CPD). The nature of this CPD varies from force to force; in some it means gaining the necessary experience and qualification through training (such as in Firearms Teams to gain authorization as a Firearms Officer, or the ICIDP programme—see, 14.4.1.1 above). In other forces it can mean pursuing further study which links your professional development with an academic partner, resulting in a further academic award such as a two-year occupation-based Foundation Degree, vocational qualifications such as an NVQ or SNVQ, or a higher award such as a BSc (Hons) in Policing or a Master's degree. Some forces allow all these forms of CPD, and this breadth is strongly encouraged by Skills for Justice which seeks to develop the skills and capabilities you will need as you progress in policing (laterally or vertically). Your force is likely to have a number of academic partners through whom further professional study may be pursued, but, if not, plenty of institutions advertise their courses or programmes in publications such as *Police Review*, or through the NPIA's periodic bulletins.

Note that you will probably need permission to engage in further study, since the force has to balance your CPD with the demands of your current job and it will tend to look with disfavour on something which might add up to 25 hours to your working week, unless this can be justified in both organizational terms (it helps the police through your increased professionalism) and individual aspiration. Also, of course, if your agreed further study is directly related to your policing function, your force might pay the fees and allow you some duty time to study, but always check first.

14.6 Promotion

As a student police officer your priority will naturally be to achieve full confirmation at the end of two years' training. However, if not now, then probably at some time in the future, you may begin to think about promotion to a higher rank. As described in 6.3 above, promotion for police officers is from the rank of constable to sergeant, followed by sergeant to inspector, and then to the higher ranks of chief inspector and above.

TASK 5

Do you know the formal qualification for being a sergeant or inspector? What is the current examination and assessment system, and what is involved?

14.6.1 Promotion from Constable to Sergeant

The statutory basis for promotion of constables to sergeant in England and Wales is to be found in the Police (Promotion) Regulations 1996, incorporating the Police (Promotion) (Amendment) Regulations 2005.

In most police forces in England and Wales the current system for promotion from constable to sergeant requires the applicant to:

- be a 'substantive' constable (that is, have successfully completed the probationary period of initial training and hence be confirmed);
- have passed the Objective Structured Performance-Related Police Promotion Exam (OSPRE®) parts I and II (see below);
- have gained the support of their immediate line manager, eg an inspector;
- have no adverse disciplinary or attendance records;
- have evidence of potential or actual leadership ability (eg through the PDR); and then
- successfully pass an interview process (a 'Promotion Panel').

Passing the OSPRE® examinations alone is therefore no guarantee of promotion from constable to sergeant because actual (permanent) promotion will depend upon the availability of vacant posts and meeting other criteria as outlined above.

14.6.1.1 Sergeants' OSPRE®

Part I of the Sergeants' OSPRE® takes the form of a multiple-choice examination paper. The time allowed is three hours and there are 150 questions. The syllabus may vary from year to year; in

2009 the syllabus is divided into four categories: crime; evidence and procedure; road policing; and general police duties (NPIA, 2008f). Each of the four subject categories is then further divided into greater detail (for example, 'handling stolen goods') and related to legislation where applicable.

Part II is an Assessment Centre based on the behavioural competencies in the Integrated Competency Framework, each assessed at different levels according to rank.

Generic behavioural competency	Level for a Sergeant
Community and customer focus	B
Effective communication	B
Maximizing potential	B
Planning and organizing	C
Problem solving	B
Resilience	A
Respect for race and diversity	A

The Assessment Centre consists of a series of seven practical exercises, each lasting approximately 90 minutes (NPIA, 2008d). Part II must be passed within 12 months of passing Part I (NPIA, 2008c, p 10).

Until 2004, the pass requirement was a norm-referenced figure. This meant that a pre-set proportion of the candidates taking the examination would automatically pass. It was then changed to an absolute standard (or criteria-referenced) system, which means that all candidates reaching a certain pass-mark (regardless of the number passing) are deemed to have passed, rather than simply a proportion of them. The pass-marks are currently 55 per cent for Part I and 45 per cent for Part II of the Sergeants' OSPRE®.

14.6.2 Promotion from Sergeant to Inspector

In England and Wales the current system for promotion from sergeant to inspector normally requires the applicant to:

- be of sergeant rank;
- have passed the inspectors' Objective Structured Performance Related Police Promotion Exam (OSPRE®) parts I and II (see below);
- have no adverse disciplinary or attendance records;
- have evidence of potential or actual leadership ability (eg through a number of recent PDRs); and then
- successfully pass an interview process (a 'Promotion Panel').

As for promotion to sergeant, passing the relevant OSPRE® examinations does not guarantee permanent promotion, as outlined above.

14.6.2.1 Inspectors' OSPRE®

Part I of the inspectors' OSPRE® takes the form of a multiple-choice examination paper. As with the sergeants' examination, it is a three-hour exam with 150 questions and the syllabus may vary from year to year. In 2009 the inspectors' OSPRE® syllabus is divided into four categories: crime; evidence and procedure; road policing; and general police duties (NPIA, 2008g). As should be expected, the knowledge tested is more complex and demanding than the sergeants' examination—for example, understanding evidence of bad character. The pass-marks for the inspectors OSPRE® are currently 65 per cent for Part 1 and 45 per cent for Part II.

Part II is an Assessment Centre based on the behavioural competencies in the Integrated Competency Framework, each assessed at different levels according to rank.

Generic behavioural competency	Level for an Inspector
Community and customer focus	B
Effective communication	B
Maximizing potential	B
Personal responsibility	A
Planning and organizing	B
Problem solving	B
Respect for race and diversity	A
Strategic perspective	C

The Assessment Centre consists of a series of seven practical exercises, each lasting approximately 90 minutes (NPIA, 2008d, p 7). Part II must be passed within 12 months of passing Part I (NPIA, 2008c, p 10).

14.6.3 The National Police Promotion Framework

The NPIA National Police Promotion Framework (NPFF) is a new system for promotion to sergeant and inspector ranks which is expected to replace the current arrangements (NPIA, 2008c). Seven police forces have been trialling this new 'Stepwise' approach to the process of promotion. It consists of four steps:

- Step 1 considers the suitability of a candidate by assessing his or her competence in his or her current rank through the PDR;
- Step 2 is the Part 1 OSPRE® examination process described above;
- Step 3 involves an assessment against role-specific competencies and matching these to the existing vacancies. This might involve structured interviews, psychometric testing, and so on;
- Step 4 is temporary promotion and work-based assessment (WBA) for a period of least 12 months when the individual will be required to demonstrate competence in the role, against the National Occupational Standards.

This all underlines the need for you to sustain the process you began in your initial training:

- recording experiences and learning;
- reflecting on the learning;
- evidencing your competencies;
- keeping detailed notes on the variety of policing experiences which you encounter;
- showing how your skills have developed;
- ensuring that entries are continually made in your PDP.

It will serve you well when you come to be considered for the next rank. You can read the preparation notes, commentaries, and tests which are published regularly for all the OSPRE®-type examinations in *Police Review*.

14.6.4 The High Potential Development Scheme

Structures exist to 'fast-track' officers with the potential for early promotion and there are nationally accepted learning programmes which are designed to develop officers for upward movement.

The High Potential Development Scheme (HPDS) is a programme for 'talented individuals to become the police leaders of the future' (NPIA, 2009b), and has recently been reformed. Successful 'graduates' of the HPDS are expected to reach at least the rank of superintendent during their careers (NPIA, 2008b p vii). The HPDS is deliberately targeted at only constables (including student police officers) or sergeants. Content of the HPDS includes 'Leadership and Public Value, Managing People and Change, Operations and Performance Management, Partnership Working, Stakeholder Management and Community Engagement, Policy Making and Strategy, and Managing and Using Resources' (NPIA, 2009c). It is not yet clear if the assessment of students undertaking the HPDS is articulated with the National Occupational Standards, although it is designed either to relate to (or to be based in) the workplace (*ibid*). Before the recent reform, HPDS utilized the ICF for 'performance assessment in the workplace' (Skills for Justice, 2006, p 3).

Unusually, the HPDS has now become a four-year programme (most police learning programmes are much shorter). Academic accreditation is provided in the form of a Postgraduate Diploma in Police Leadership which may then lead to a Masters degree from Warwick University Business School. However, applicants do not have to be graduates to join the HPDS (NPIA, 2008c) but are instead selected using a three-stage process to assess their suitability (the final stage is based on the Senior PNAC—see 14.8.6 below).

> **TASK 6**
>
> List or find out about some other nationally accepted learning programmes for police officers.

The list of development opportunities is being added to all the time, and the best advice we can give to the aspirant to early command is to familiarize yourself with what is on offer, either through your own force resource centres or through the Bramshill Police Staff College in Hampshire. Be warned though: standards are very high on these flagship programmes, and you will need to be able to demonstrate exceptional potential to be considered.

14.6.5 Success and Failure

If you pass the OSPRE® tests, if your portfolio of evidence is comprehensive and well presented, and if you perform well at the interview process, you still might not get through to secure that promotion. (If you do, of course, congratulate yourself and move on.) If you have failed to get through on this occasion, always think of it as a temporary setback. Nearly all promotion panels will feedback to you on your performance, so this should be seen as an opportunity to get it right next time. For example, the panel might say that you lack experience or exposure to crime-prevention techniques, or you have not had an operational role on a BCU since probation, or that you need some more work on demonstrating leadership skills. Take these points on board and do something about them, and as soon as possible. The reason to hurry is that you need to act before the opportunity to improve goes out of your head or is replaced by the day-to-day business of your job. Also, in larger forces, the promotion boards may sit as often as twice a year, which gives you about four months to remedy your shortfalls before you are applying for the next board. Time may be of the essence. Also of course, you will be showing how positively you respond to constructive criticism and how effectively you have moved to put remedies in place. These will be plus points on the next round.

When you receive your feedback, remember to ask questions, such as:

- What other areas for improvement should I think about?
- What did I not evidence well?
- What should I have done to make you select me for promotion to sergeant?

Some forces operate a mentoring scheme. If you can secure the services of a **mentor** (usually a senior officer), you can run your interview performance past him/her and ask for some objective advice. Mentors will **not** coach you, but will indicate courses of action which you are free to accept or reject.

As you move up the promotion ladder in your own force (or if you move, on promotion, to another force), it might be worth seeking a mentor elsewhere. That is, try to obtain a mentor within the police service, but not in any force you have served in or are serving in. Sometimes an internal mentor is not always able to work outside his/her own force priorities in advising or counselling you.

If your performance shortfall can be remedied by some **training** (for example, to bring your knowledge of first aid up to speed, or to refresh your knowledge of procedures in a custody suite), make sure that you consult your local training officer or talk to your force training team(s). They may be able to point you in the direction of good self-tutoring packages, e-learning, or information resource. There may even be a training programme which you could sit in on and refresh your skills. (If this means time away from your primary tasks, make sure you have agreement to absent yourself.)

Begin preparation for the next promotion board process as soon as you can. Get a friend or colleague to look through your portfolio for you, picking out examples of how you meet the competencies for the next rank. They may spot things you missed. Consult existing holders of the rank and find out what kinds of experience are persuasive for the promotion board. Submit your new application in good time, with refreshed text and evidence, concentrating especially on those areas where the promotion board had seen a shortfall last time. Remember 'the Five Ps': **previous preparation prevents poor performance** (or vulgar variants on this advice) and the better you are prepared, the more confident and assured your performance at the next board will be. Do not give up. Sooner or later you will make it to the next rank; if not in this force, then in that one, always assuming you have the skills and behaviours required for the job.

14.7   Interviews for Promotion

It would be appropriate here to think briefly about the recurrent feature of nearly all selection processes in the promotion stakes: the **interview**. Whilst there are plenty of critics of the interview system, especially of its subjectivity and the often ritualized formality of the process, nothing more substantial or satisfactory has yet been devised which can reproduce the impression which an individual can give when questioned. There are species of commercially available psychometric tests, which seek to assess you and your responses to a number of more or less complex case studies; there are verbal and numerical reasoning **tests** which try to establish how good (or not) you are at understanding words and figures; and there are batteries of tests of both Intelligence Quotient and Emotional Intelligence (IQ and EI respectively) which are claimed to measure your capacity for reason or your capacity for empathy. It may be traditionalist, elitist, and even discriminatory, but the interview process is more popular—and more trusted—within the police force (after initial selection) than most of these alternative tests of ability.

> **TASK 7**
>
> Your turn: what constitutes a good interview performance by the candidate for promotion?

You may have referred to the importance of creating a good first impression; being smart, well turned-out, formal without being 'stand-offish', attentive and eager without being unctuous. You may have gone on to talk about being well prepared, anticipating some of the obvious questions which a panel will ask, carefully marshalling the evidence of your competencies and your track record, and thinking about how you will convey how utterly suitable you are to move up to the next rank. You might have listed listening skills, brief but cogent answers, and the need to impress the panel with your competence. You may have warned against seeming to be arrogant when you want to convey confidence, seeming to be disorganized when you want to appear calm, and seeming to be thrown by a question for which you had not prepared an answer. Indeed, nearly every self-help book on interview techniques seems to concentrate on what you should **not** do rather than on what you should.

However, there are some tips, based on experience, which can make the difference between success and failure at an interview.

14.7.1   What Does the Interview Panel Want to Know?

The interview panel often wants to know:

- Can you do the job or a substantial percentage of it?
- Are you willing to put in the effort to make the job or role a success?
- Are you manageable?

You need to be able to assure the members of the panel that you meet most of the competencies required. You can do this by demonstrating:

- detailed examples of past performance (ensure they are relevant);
- how you solved a problem and what steps you took to do so;
- evidence of how you meet the competencies for the next rank (and showing that you know and understand those competencies well);
- that you have the potential to go beyond the formal requirements;
- that you are eager to learn (no one expects you to be perfect);
- that you have good related qualifications, professional knowledge, or training.

14.7.2 'Body Language' and the Interview

The first impression you give as you walk in the door could be the most lasting. Perhaps we should not be influenced by a person's body language, but undoubtedly many people are. We should also perhaps be aware of cultural differences that may lead to a misunderstanding of body language. This is a complex subject, and here we offer some simple advice concerning the unintentional 'negatives' and the intended 'positives' of body language.

14.7.2.1 Unintentional negatives

- Frowning, grimacing, sniffing, biting or chewing your lips: these can all be read by others as symptoms of unease, discomfiture, or puzzlement (the opposite of the impression you want to give);
- folded arms (seen by some as a defensive posture);
- tapping your fingers or drumming with a pen (viewed by some people as a sign of nervousness or impatience);
- nodding too much (perhaps impatience and an over-eagerness to speak);
- putting hands behind your head (suggests to some arrogance or over-assuredness).

14.7.2.2 Intended positives

- Firm handshake (pump twice or three times, no more);
- eye contact (do not stare unblinkingly but be aware of cultural differences);
- smile frequently, but not 'mechanically';
- take a moment for thought, but try not to break eye-contact with at least one of the panel;
- tilt your head slightly to one side when you respond to questions (this suggests to some that you are thinking and listening);
- adopt an upright, alert posture (but not stiff, otherwise you suggest rigor mortis);
- mirror all positive body language across the table (in other words, watch the body language of the panel members and **subtly** reflect it back to them).

You should be aware of your body language and a tendency to 'leak' information which you would rather conceal, such as nervousness or apprehension. An interview is often a nerve-racking process but if you are aware of your leakage, you can control some of it most of the time. As an exercise, try a short mock interview with a friend or colleague, getting the second person to note your body language and feed the results of the observation back to you. You will be surprised how much escaped your consciousness.

14.7.3 Answering Questions in Interviews

Always listen carefully to the question and then answer it. This sounds obvious, but many candidates fail promotion interviews by giving the answer which they have prepared rather than answering the question which has been asked. **Your answers should be brief, thorough, and to the point.** Do not waffle or start on long, pointless anecdotes. Try to keep your thread. Limit yourself to about two or three points in each answer. The panel will ask follow-up questions if they are interested in what you have to say, so do not try to say everything at once.

Further, consider illustrating your points with examples (members of an interview panel are likely to find concrete examples easier to follow than abstract descriptions). Beware of using too much specialist jargon. Most of the panel will understand you, but you cannot guarantee that. The police service is peculiarly prone to the use of acronyms but they are not all shared or understood. If you begin your reply with 'I saw the IP during the cas evac and rep'd on the PR what the FME had said, before asking the FCC for an ARV ... ', you could lose your audience, or worse, look as though you are trying too hard to impress.

Whatever the line of questioning, you must get three basic points across to the promotion panel. These are:

- that you can work unsupervised;
- you can be trusted;
- you are, nonetheless, a team player.

Use your examples and case studies of your achievements to emphasize these points. Through out your interview, avoid politics and name-dropping: doing either will alienate the panel and make them think that you are perhaps a pretentious and manipulative person.

14.7.3.1 Difficult questions

Every promotion interview panel will pose tough questions to probe your claims of experience, knowledge, or qualifications, and a good interview candidate anticipates as much as possible what these questions will be, and prepares answers for them. Your questioners are looking for drive, initiative, motivation, leadership and communication skills, determination, reliability, and pride in the work. Your answers must demonstrate how you have these attributes. Let us look at some sample questions at police promotion interviews:

- What have you done that shows initiative?
- Have you ever had to deal with an awkward colleague?
- Tell me something you have done that you are not very proud of.
- What part of being a sergeant do you think is most crucial?
- What would you do if your patrol encountered a fight outside a pub and one of your officers was injured?
- How do you react to criticism?
- What orders would you give if one of your patrol crews reports a multiple vehicle traffic accident?
- How would you respond to a complaint about one of your constables?
- What would you do if you heard one of your officers make a sexist comment?

After listening carefully to the question, you can help yourself by reflecting back to the questioner some of the question structure (it also helps you to focus your answer), such as:

> I respond to criticism by treating it as a learning experience, and so I make sure that I take what is said on board and use it to modify my actions.

Another tack is to put a positive spin on the question (especially if it asks you to be self-critical), perhaps by saying:

> We all do things sometimes which we're not proud of. The important thing is to understand why you reacted that way and treat it as an experience which will guide you in the future. I remember one occasion when I did not intervene to challenge a colleague who said women were not physically up to front-line policing. What I should have said was...

Another form of questioning is what is called quick fire. The panel members ask you questions in a short, brisk fashion. Your answers should reflect the tempo and practical nature of the question. An exchange might run like this:

> Q. How long does it take you to do an appraisal?
> A. In short, about three hours, depending on the difficulty I'm dealing with.
> Q. One of your officers is always ringing in sick. What do you do about it?
> A. Visit the person, find out what's wrong, and use the positive attendance management process. I'm not medically qualified, so I'd rely on expert opinion.
> Q. What three things must you think about at a crime scene?
> A. Communicate, preserve life, preserve evidence.

Q. You're just finishing a long shift and a report comes in about a suspected rape. You could go to the scene, but it's going-home time. Do you leave it to the incoming sergeant?

A. No, my duty says I must attend, but having done all I can to secure the scene and set up the support mechanisms for the victim, I'll choose the right moment to go off duty.

Hammered at you relentlessly over 15 or 20 minutes, this kind of questioning can be a nervous and exhausting experience for you. The interviewers are testing your response to stress and decision making, but they are also probing for signs of weakness. Had you agreed that you would just go home when your shift finished, the chances are that you would have not been promoted this time around, especially since you are expected to show enthusiasm and professionalism in the next rank. Although the questions are short and your answers equally brief, you should expect a battery of follow-up questions: 'Why do you say that? How would you do this? What if the relief sergeant didn't show up? What if the sick officer tells you that her illness is chronic and comes under the auspices of the Disability Discrimination Act? What would you do next? What if your appraisal is challenged? How would you react to one of your officers taking out a grievance against you?'

14.8 Roles and Responsibilities of Ranks Above Constable

Here we describe the roles and requirements for the ranks above constable. This is not to prescribe your route to promotion, but rather to suggest to you that each step up in the police service brings new challenges and new opportunities. You should be aware of what they are before you start your bid for promotion.

14.8.1 A Sergeant's Role

The sergeant rank is the first management rank in the police, though it is often described as supervisory rather than management. Formally, a sergeant is expected to supervise the work of those in his/her team, to deal with any people-management issues, and to appraise performance.

The core responsibilities of the generic rank of sergeant are listed below.

Personal responsibilities—as a sergeant you will be expected to:

- complete administration procedures;
- maintain standards of professional practice;
- make best use of technology;
- promote equality, diversity, and human rights in working practices;
- work as part of a team.

Managing and developing people—as a sergeant you will be expected to:

- carry out performance reviews;
- delegate work to others;
- develop individuals and teams to enhance performance;
- supervise the work of teams and individuals;
- address disciplinary and unsatisfactory performance procedures;
- deal with grievances;
- manage the welfare needs of individuals;
- supervise health and safety;
- provide first aid.

Intelligence—as a sergeant you you will need to:

- conduct 'intelligence-driven' briefing, tasking, and debriefing; and
- use intelligence to support policing objectives.

The **behavioural competencies** we have looked at already in our consideration of the OSPRE® examinations, but you might usefully look back at those now to refresh your memory.

TASK 8

Looking at the core responsibilities for a sergeant, can you say what has fundamentally changed from that of the constable? Assuming that a sergeant now has supervisory responsibility for the team of which he/she was recently a part, is there anything in the new role which you consider might create difficulties?

Much of what others do makes up the sergeant's supervisory portfolio, and this can be especially difficult as the sergeant moves from being part of a team to becoming its leader. The nature of friendships can change, and camaraderie can be lost if the one time team player and friend is suddenly the boss. It is actually considered good practice in many police forces to move a newly promoted sergeant to another section (or even to another BCU) to ensure that such difficulties are avoided. The sergeant is expected to be objective and rigorous in assessment, which is easier to do with a team of people with whom you have not socialized in the recent past.

Most forces have a programme of training and learning for the newly promoted sergeant, to cover matters such as enhancing team performance, tasking, briefing and debriefing, administration and supervision, as well as an introduction to management. Sometimes, these learning programmes are integrated with the duties and responsibilities of the custody officer (since this is often the first uniformed role which promoted sergeants take on; not unrelated to the fact that custody is currently unpopular as a sergeant's role).

It is worth looking at one or two of the core responsibilities and spelling out what is involved in a little more detail. The two areas we shall examine are delegation and the development of others.

First though, try the following task.

TASK 9

What do you think is involved in the delegation of work? Can you itemize some problems and some benefits from this activity?
What do you think is involved in developing others? How should sergeants (and other managers) go about developing their staff and what sorts of problems and benefits might there be in such a process?

A detective sergeant has responsibility for ensuring that investigations are effective and professional and that all work in support of a criminal investigation is properly carried out. There may be some overlaps with other sergeants' roles, particularly in managing police operations (though within the investigative stream, operations are more likely to be covert). Other roles (delegating work, managing staff, and dealing with the problems and rewards of human resource management) are common to all sergeants, but are given a particular spin by the detective role.

Unlike a uniformed sergeant, whose teams generally work specific shifts, time at work is more loosely defined in investigation. One important and implicit role of the DS is to manage the workload of the detective teams, especially on a major enquiry where the desire to do a good job can result in significant overtime payments.

TASK 10

Write down some job-specific activities which a DS would have and which would not necessarily be common to, say, a patrol sergeant or a sergeant in a custody officer role.

We have dipped into parts of the police sergeant's role and commented on various aspects of the job. It is important to emphasize that these are well-known elements of a range of managerial or command roles, and are just as important for an inspector, chief inspector, superintendent, or chief officer (and their support-staff counterparts) as they are for sergeants. This brings us to consider an inspector's role.

14.8.2 An Inspector's Role

We noted above the change which results from promotion from constable to sergeant.

> **TASK 11**
>
> What do you think will be the changes involved in promotion from sergeant to inspector? Try to be specific.

Inspector is the first command rank and the first role to carry the designation 'senior officer'. It is the rank for which payment of overtime ceases, and it is assumed that you maintain this role out of professional pride as well as for the financial reward—a rather scant comfort when your sergeants and constables can earn more than you do while putting in the same or fewer hours. Police pay and the differences in salary are outside the scope of this Handbook, even though they will, of course, matter to you.

As an inspector, whether as a detective or as an operations officer in uniform, it is assumed that you have the capability to have a tactical overview of policing operations, that you can handle the responsibility of a wide range of police work—anything from writing tactical appreciations to handling a major series of investigations. Let us begin by looking at the generic role requirements and post profiles for an inspector.

Some aspects of overseeing and supervision are extensions of the sorts of work which sergeants do. New generic 'core responsibilities' include the ability to implement plans for change, participate in meetings, supervise the work of teams and individuals, and monitor and evaluate PDRs. For the first time, there is a responsibility for operating budgets (and thereby a financial accountability for public funds) and there are two new behaviours—'strategic perspective', where the individual inspector will be expected to attain a 'C' grading, and 'personal responsibility', where an 'A' grading is expected. A level of public and personal accountability, both for team and for individual performance, now goes with the rank of inspector. There is a higher public profile through attending meetings, and a greater measure of managerial responsibility through the overseeing of the PDR work of the inspector's sergeants. As we noted earlier, while the focus and variety of work decreases with rank, the responsibilities increase and the remit to deliver widens. If we take all this as implicit in the role of inspector, what sorts of jobs do you think an inspector might do?

If you looked at the Integrated Competency Framework roles, you will have noted that inspectors could expect to serve as:

- bronze or ORC commander (see 9.28.2 above) for firearms incidents and other crises;
- community inspector;
- detective inspector;
- detective inspector (Special Branch);
- operations inspector;
- patrol inspector;
- senior investigating officer;
- unit executive officer;
- negotiator (though this is often work additional to the 'day job' and is usually unpaid);
- area intelligence officer.

There are a number of variations on these within different police forces but, in general terms, these are the kinds of activity that you could expect to be doing if you were promoted to inspector.

As you can see, the remit for the role has widened considerably; inspectors are expected to have responsibility for, and deliver a core part of, the policing business. For example, a detective inspector might head a high-profile investigation, or a series of investigations within a BCU. A senior investigating officer (SIO) might be involved with major investigations such as a Cat A or Cat B homicide or series of rapes. In Patrol, an inspector might be responsible for a whole geographical area of the BCU, or for the effective deployment of traffic patrol vehicles on the strategic road network within a force area. In Special Branch, an inspector might be tasked with the threat assessment of, and consequent security measures to protect, some important person living in the force area, such as a politician or member of the Royal Family. An operations inspector could deal with the deployment of resources to contain a public order situation, or might be responsible for coordinating the actions of officers to police inner-city unrest.

The variety is wide, and the responsibility which falls on the inspector is considerable. Although no longer operating day-to-day on the 'front line', the safety of quite large numbers of police officers (not to mention the safety of the public at large) is now the inspector's responsibility; in place of that practical hands-on element comes public accountability. The inspector role is sometimes called 'up, down, and sideways' because of the number of people to whom and for whom an inspector is responsible.

TASK 12

What sort of crimes might a SIO investigate?

The SIO is the pivotal figure in the investigation of major and serious violent crimes, managing everything from family liaison to progress reviews, from house-to-house enquiries to the following-up of all leads, as well as the interviewing of witnesses, victims, and suspects. This is not a job that every detective could do, even with the requisite training and experience, because there are certain personal qualities such as resilience, detachment, objectivity, and persistence which make a good SIO. Some of these must be to some extent inherent within the individual, rather than acquired.

In small forces, SIOs are often detective inspectors; in larger or metropolitan forces, the SIOs are usually detective chief inspectors and, rarely, detective superintendents. (This will become even rarer since the National Centre for Policing Excellence—now part of NPIA—now 'owns' SIO training and licensing on behalf of the police service. An SIO 'licence' will be given only to those officers who habitually or usually investigate major crime as part of their remit.)

TASK 13

Whatever the rank, what do you think the salient qualities should be for a SIO?

The SIO role includes:

- managing family liaison;
- managing the initial responses to a major investigation;
- managing the ongoing investigation;
- facilitating closure of the investigation;
- maintaining effective relationships with the media;
- obtaining and managing the use of finance and resources;
- representing the police at partnership meetings and meetings with other agencies;
- adopting a problem-solving approach to community issues.

These are the core elements of being an SIO, though there are other competencies with which you are familiar, as they stem from the generic role. You will see that the competencies for the SIO are tightly organized around the management and progress of an investigation. Forces invest a good deal (of time and money, selection, and training) in producing and sustaining their SIOs, and they do not do it lightly.

TASK 14

What reasons are there for a force to make such a substantial investment in SIOs?

14.8.3 The Role of Chief Inspector

The range of responsibility widens significantly at the chief inspector (CI) rank. A CI is more likely to take charge of a major incident, a major event, a major public order event, and a major crime investigation. As we noted, large forces 'default' to CIs as their SIOs, and this is very often the rank you find at the top end of specialist crime knowledge or specialist squads. Typically, CIs will have served more than 15 years in the police, some as many as 25 years. It is a fairly rare person who becomes CI within seven or eight years, but it is not unknown.

The same core responsibilities that we found with inspectors are defined, though there is now a higher level of expectation about attainment. So, too, expectations around behaviours are higher, even though the behaviours themselves are given somewhat low scores; this is mostly to do with the greater range of duties which operate at CI rank. You should be aware that there is no national examination for CI (or superintendent and chief superintendent), though the government has been consulting about the creation of a qualification for superintendents, especially for those who will command a BCU. Nothing is yet decided, but any outcome is likely to incorporate parts of the Leadership programme for senior officers. Currently, most forces rely on a complex interview and portfolio process in which candidates for promotion must evidence their fitness to perform at the next rank. That said, there is no consistency across England and Wales when it comes to the promotion of inspectors to CIs, or beyond, and it is very much left to individual forces to decide whom they want in key senior roles. The framework for such national standards is implicit in the National Occupational Standards and in the Integrated Competency Framework, but at the time of writing, no progress has been made in creating a core national assessment standard for CIs. Let us glance at the core responsibilities briefly and then at the behaviours.

A chief inspector should be able to chair meetings, manage organizational change, maintain standards of professional practice, delegate work to others, and manage the performance of teams and individuals. In addition, CIs are expected to monitor and evaluate PDRs, promote equality, diversity, human rights, and health and safety, as well as manage the welfare needs of others, and deal with grievances, discipline issues, or unsatisfactory performance. Exploitation of intelligence opportunities and the best use of technology and problem-solving approaches are seen as part of the CI's battery of skills, whilst some skills in the management of finance and budgets are measured.

As far as behaviours are concerned, there is such a wide range of required behaviours across such a wide spectrum of activities, that while the levels for leadership, working with others, and achieving results are either 'As' or 'Bs', it is not as easy to reach the standards for behaviours as might be supposed. In addition, the behaviours have developed towards working in partnership, inter-agency liaison, and a results-driven performance regime. It is clear that the bar has been raised. More is expected of CIs than inspectors, and the criteria for measurement have expanded in parallel with the expectations of the role.

These are the specific roles which a chief inspector will undertake, as opposed to the generic areas we have already examined and itemized:

- Criminal Justice Unit CI;
- DCI (Detective CI);
- DCI (Special Branch);
- Operations CI;
- Silver Commander.

You can see from this list that many specialisms have dropped away. For example, a detective chief inspector may have expertise in fraud investigations, but the average DCI will oversee many other kinds of criminal investigation of which fraud may only be a part. Essential core detective skills, the capability to manage a team, responsibility for a large tranche of policing business, and the delivery of required outcomes are what define (but do not limit) a CI's range. This is the case whether it entails a complex investigation for a DCI or the command of an emerging situation on the ground as Silver Commander of an incident. You might at this point refresh your memory of the roles of Silver and Gold Commander which we looked at in 9.28

above. An operations chief inspector based on a BCU, for example, may be responsible for all uniformed operations which take place on a day-to-day basis within the BCU's geographical area, whereas a DCI might bear parallel responsibility for all detective-led investigations for the same BCU. Alternatively, the DCI and CI posts may be within specialist groups, based centrally or at Headquarters. It is not unusual for a large force to have 'Heads of Specialist Training' at DCI and CI rank, whilst, as we have seen, SIOs in large forces are almost always at DCI rank. Another role which has emerged in recent years is that of **critical incident CI** (or inspector, in some forces), where a cadre of trained senior officers respond to critical incidents, ranging from searches for missing persons through to the immediate scene management in the aftermath of terrorist incidents.

Promotion beyond Inspector to Chief Inspector normally uses the Integrated Competency Framework (ICF) for benchmarking, an interview (supported by a detailed case for promotion), and other forms of assessment against evidence produced by the applicant (for example, from the PDRs). In addition, some forces use an Assessment Centre in order to attempt a robust and objective measure of attainment against the levels of behavioural competence required for the particular role profile in the ICF. The details of practice in promotions to chief inspector vary from force to force, but most will also require a good attendance record and no major disciplinary or integrity issues.

14.8.4 Lateral Development

Although we have looked so far at the ways in which a police officer may move upwards, through the ranks, you must not lose sight of the need for lateral development (through the increase in a range of skills or the accretion of valuable experience, allied to qualifications and professional recognition) of police officers within a particular skills set. It is as true of the police service as it is of the other emergency and armed services that recognition tends to come through promotion, but it is equally the case that recognition can come through the acquisition of fundamental skills even though the rank may be lowly. We are acquainted, for example, with a number of detective constables who have PhDs in criminology and law, or Masters' degrees in investigative science. They would be listened to with as great a respect for their chosen expertise as someone who had mere rank.

It is time now to turn our attention to command rank, and look at the ranks which carry autonomous responsibilities for the delivery of very large, strategic parts of policing, in ascending order: superintendent, chief superintendent, and chief officer. This is to provide an insight into the experience and qualifications of those who are in command.

14.8.5 The Role of Superintendent

At one time, there was little distinction between the ranks of superintendent and chief superintendent, even though the roles performed by each rank were carefully distinguished. From 1994 until around 2004, in the wake of reforms to police ranks suggested by Sir William Sheehy, there was no distinction *in rank* between inspector and chief inspector, and between superintendent and chief superintendent. The latter pair was distinguished by the terms 'Range 1' superintendent and 'Range 2' superintendent, but gradually the old rank distinctions returned, as did the distinct rank of deputy chief constable. We shall assume that, even if your force persists with the designations 'Range 1' and 'Range 2' superintendent, there is in essence a difference between the functions of a superintendent and those of a chief superintendent. As a student police officer you are still likely to come across more experienced police officers who lived through the 'Sheehy era'.

As we noted for chief inspectors, appointments to the rank of superintendent and chief superintendent are by examination. Most forces will have a 'gateway' interview process followed by a panel interview (which is likely to include the chief constable), eligibility for which is probably predicated on a portfolio of evidence, itself based on the competencies for the rank. Note that when discussing chief inspector selection, the government is considering the notion of some kind of formal qualification for the superintendent rank.

TASK 15

In more general terms, what do you think are the essential differences between a chief inspector and a superintendent?

For superintendents, there are changes in core responsibilities as well as in function which we might note, as well as increases in the behavioural scores. So, noting the generic core responsibilities for a chief inspector which we considered above, add the following for a generic superintendent:

- develop and maintain quality assurance systems;
- evaluate and improve organizational performance;
- develop management teams;
- enable the organization to retain personnel from all communities;
- select required personnel.

And in terms of behaviours:

Behaviour	Minimum level required
Strategic perspective	B
Openness to change	B
Community and customer focus	B
Problem solving	B
Planning and organizing	B

Clearly the role of superintendent has developed a wider spectrum of responsibility and there is autonomy of (and therefore individual accountability for) command. A superintendent will run a distinct part of police business, within which he/she will be responsible for the management of senior teams and for meeting targets. When the superintendent is the uniformed commander of a small BCU, the entire performance and efficiency of the BCU is his/her responsibility. Although the tendency amongst larger, amalgamated forces is for a chief superintendent to be the commander of a larger BCU, superintendents are often responsible for a geographically distinct part of that BCU under the chief superintendent's overall command.

For the first time, the role of superintendent entails responsibility for the selection of staff. This does not necessarily imply that a BCU commander or head of squad can cherry-pick his/her staff, but rather that there will be consultation and some degree of negotiation over who is wanted and who can be given up in exchange. This means that the ability to choose appropriate staff in any given set of circumstances is important. Also, a superintendent is expected to innovate, and to implement changes which improve the organization. Most superintendents and chief superintendents are very experienced and nearing the end of their service, so they will know the force well and the individuals within in it very well indeed. Obviously, this can be a harder process for someone who has fast-tracked through the ranks.

A superintendent will have a strategic perspective on the force as a whole, and will be intensely aware of the pressures to deliver results. For the first time, the superintendent will be fully cognizant of the external political and social pressures which impact on policing, and will be in a position to gather a team in which he/she is confident in the context of those pressures. One of the privileges of command (as well as its fundamental pressure) is that the buck stops with the person who makes the decision. Other core responsibilities concerning people management include performance appraisal, grievances, development, and discipline, as well as the retention of staff. It is not enough to get people into the force; the command structure must ensure that people are retained, developed, and progressed within the profession.

A word or two about the chief superintendent role before we consider chief officers. Just as the superintendent rank is about command, it might be fair to say that the chief superintendent rank is about coordination of commands. Indeed, in some police forces, the rank of chief superintendent is designated as coordinator. Sitting directly below chief officers, the chief superintendents in a police force will be the expert practitioners, with enormous experience in a variety of roles, and with a profound understanding of the strengths and limitations of the force. Chief officers in a large force will delegate to chief superintendents, involving them in discussions about the management of police work. Unlike their police-staff counterparts, most chief superintendents will still do duty at nights and at weekends, usually as duty Gold commander, responsible for the deployment of staff to an incident, and for its effective containment, sometimes in coordination with other emergency and civil agencies.

14.8.6 The Role of Chief Officer

There are three chief officer ranks in most forces. In ascending order, they are:

- assistant chief constable (ACC);
- deputy chief constable (DCC);
- chief constable.

(These ranks differ in the MPS: see 6.3 above.)

Potential chief officers are selected from among the ranks of existing superintendents and chief superintendents, and are invited to take part in a national two-day selection and aptitude process at the **Senior Police National Assessment Centre** (Senior PNAC). Successful candidates are then enrolled on the **Strategic Command Course** (SCC) at the Bramshill Police Staff College in Hampshire, for a minimum of six months, during which potential chief officers work in teams to consider the society in which they live and work, strategic leadership, politics, criminology, and a variety of other subjects and themes.

Graduation from the SCC does not guarantee success at the next rank. Most candidates for ACC posts will go through three or four interviews before obtaining a position within a police force. The interviews are held by the local police authority (which includes lay members) rather than the police service, and candidates may not necessarily find that their training has prepared them for a buffet lunch while being quizzed on everything from fly-tipping to stab-proof vests!

Chief officers belong to the **Association of Chief Police Officers** (ACPO), which itself acts as the voice of the strategic end of the police service. Each chief officer will be expected to take some form of national portfolio, through which that chief officer will contribute to the development of police thinking across a host of issues. Current portfolios range from roads policing to counter-terrorist strategies. The range encompasses all aspects of policing but also includes society's attitude to crime, studies of criminality, law, criminal justice, and social order.

A chief officer leading on one of these topics for ACPO is expected to bring together people from different parts of society—not just police officers—to ensure that the fullest possible picture is available. For drugs rehabilitation issues, doctors and other workers in the medical professions, social workers, housing advisers, the probation service, other agencies, and academics playing a prominent role in counter-drugs strategies may be consulted. ACPO members are also expected to speak with authority to the media on your portfolio.

Chief officers also have a force-centred portfolio. Most forces of substance have between four and six ACCs, who rotate between the commands of local policing, operations, support services, and investigations. The titles accorded to these divisions of the policing task vary from force to force, but will generally require the post-holder to undertake (in consultation with his/her senior staff) strategic planning and delivery of major parts of the police business.

You should be aware that both ACPO as a body and the chief officer structure generally in police forces in England and Wales have been subject to criticism over the last few years: for example, the selection process for chief officers is considered by some to be too conservative, and there have been accusations that ACPO is too open to political influence. You might want to read Reiner's *The Politics of the Police*, now in its third edition, as a general introduction to this whole subject. His book on chief constables (Reiner, 1991) is also of interest.

Finally, a word about job security at the chief-officer level. It is most unusual for chief constables to be appointed for a single term exceeding five years. Additionally, the Home Secretary has taken powers to dismiss chief constables who fail to meet the standards expected of them. It is not usually possible to make it to the top within the same force. The HMIC and the Home Office encourage chief officers to move forces at the DCC level or, if DCC rank is reached in one force, the rank of chief constable must be sought in another force.

This chapter has been about developing as a police officer, whether by increased lateral specialization in a role or by a programme of promotion. However, there are one or two further areas to consider before we move on.

TASK 16

Try to answer this question: am I prepared to serve in the police for the next 30 to 35 years?

If you replied 'yes', you may well be in a minority. Many studies of attitudes to, and expectations of, work, suggest that people no longer expect or want a long career within one kind of organization. The single major exception is medicine, but all other professions report that young people work with them for periods of five to ten years and then move on to something new. So what this means for the police service is that individuals may be content with up to ten years' service and no more and will leave variously at the rank of constable, sergeant, or up to superintendent (if fast-tracked), with a number of marketable skills. What then happens to the longer-term posts at the top end of the organization, and to those specialist posts such as computer crime? The government appears to be arguing that such posts could be filled from outside the police service, an argument which is supported by the longitudinal studies of work preferences. We may begin to see people entering the police service at the rank of chief inspector or above. For example, in the matter of leadership, you might find that someone who has served in the armed forces meets the general competency requirement, and requires only some on-the-job training to meet the police specific competencies. Alternatively, someone who has held a financial shares portfolio in the city, or who has held a post as a senior teacher, might equally possess the general competencies.

There is, though, a second element which modifies all this: the matter of demography. This is the study of population profiles with special reference to age. The whole of Europe is ageing (and the trend appears to be worldwide) because generally people are living longer and are having fewer children. This may have a particular impact on the police service. Most constables and sergeants generally retire after 30 years' service, or aged 55, whichever comes first, while inspectors and higher ranks usually have to retire by the age of 60. If the population as a whole works longer, this may mean that the current 30-year rule (35 for those joining after 5 April 2006) will disappear, and officers may be able to work until 65 or 70.

Might there simply not be enough people in the future to resource the police service? We might have to turn to initiatives centred on the roles of community support officers and wardens to make up the shortfall in police officers. Where does that leave the trained police officer and what effect will this have on the Criminal Justice System?

All we can be certain of is that the future of policing is not certain. There are complicated demographic issues, affecting types of crime as well as types of policing. The recruitment and management of police officers will have to be more imaginative and innovative than it is at present. The police service will be fishing in an increasingly diminishing pool of talent, and will have to offer something out of the ordinary to attract even the minimum number of young people into policing. There is an argument that policing itself must become a profession, but there is as yet no consensus on how this change may be brought about, though Skills for Justice has taken the initiative.

14.9 Answers to Tasks

TASK 1

No doubt you wrote down your own aspirations. However, were they rank-specific ('I want to be a sergeant') or were they role-specific ('I want to be a detective')?

TASK 2

You may have noted that many jobs in Finance or in HR are actually highly complex and require specialist skills and training. Without an accounting qualification, for example, an individual may make damaging errors in budget setting, or in any of the other complex processes involved in properly audited financial transactions. Similarly, whilst it is possible for a non-specialist to try drawing up contracts or establish grievance procedures, the legal consequences could be serious if he/she gets it wrong. At worst, a well-meaning but nonetheless amateur interpretation of employment law could cost the force a significant sum if it subsequently loses an employment tribunal.

TASK 3

Your list might include driving skills (though these can always be improved and extended), or the ability to research through the internet, liaison skills in partnership working, or the use of technical equipment such as CCTV or handheld filming (for example, at demonstrations), or diversity awareness (another core competency), or keyboard skills, or team working, and so on.

TASK 4

The list which follows is not exhaustive (some forces have roles which other forces do not), but it gives you an idea of the spread of roles available to you:

- authorized firearms officer;
- community constable;
- crime reduction/architectural liaison;
- dog handler;
- intelligence (research and development);
- intelligence: source handler;
- roads policing;
- schools involvement;
- search specialist;
- family liaison officer (FLO);
- community liaison officer (CLO);
- crime desk;
- detective (fraud, computer crime, serious crime, major crime, tactical CID, Special Branch);
- leading a neighbourhood team;
- tactical adviser (firearms, public order, etc);
- tutor constable;
- youth-offending team;
- air operations;
- trainer/teaching staff;
- tactical operations and public order;
- patrol;
- wildlife and the environment.

TASK 5

You should have been able to find the relevant information from a variety of internet sites. Bear in mind however that many internet sites may be out of date and still be describing the system in use prior to changes made in mid-2009.

We provide a detailed answer immediately after the task.

TASK 6

Development programmes are run by NPIA for the police in which leadership is emphasized. The NPIA's Core Leadership Development Programme (CLDP) is designed to develop the leadership skills of all police ranks up to inspector and is accredited by the Chartered Management Institute. Forces may deliver the programme locally, if suitably 'licensed' by the NPIA.

Other courses include the Senior Leadership Development Programmes (SLDP1 and SLDP2) for those in chief inspector roles or above (including ACPO ranks in the case of SLDP2). However, a number of local police forces have also developed their own complementary leadership programmes, some in collaboration with universities or professional bodies. For example, Kent Police has its Kent Core Leadership Development Programme (KCLDP) accredited at CMS, DMS, and MBA levels (Kent Police, 2008).

Note that, as with OSPRE®, the leadership programmes offered by the NPIA are subject to change and you should consult their website for the latest information.

TASK 7

Some suggestions are provided immediately after the task. There are also numerous books and websites with both general advice about interviews, and particular advice concerning police promotion.

TASK 8

You might have noted the fact that the sergeant has responsibility for team performance as a whole as well as for the individuals within that team. The sergeant will be held responsible for any shortcomings in performance, and accountable for the team's collective and individual achievements or mistakes. Additionally, the sergeant now assesses individual performance and reports on it (Appraisal or Performance Development Review, PDR), and is expected to develop the staff who make up the team, deal with grievances, and sort out unsatisfactory performance.

TASK 9

Delegation is an activity which some find painful. It means passing some of your work downwards to let others complete it for you. Some people cannot delegate at all (and as a consequence, can sometimes make poor leaders). There are several emotional activities taking place at the same time, and it is worth unpicking some of them.

The first component of delegation is **trust**: you have to trust your staff (under supervision) to deliver what you want. By pushing some of your work tasks downwards, you spread the load and give members of the team a chance to deliver against performance. At the same time, you are signalling to the team that you trust them, indeed, rely on them, to deliver.

However, the second component is that you have to assign some measure of **responsibility** to the individual or small team, to whom you have delegated. Perhaps one of the worst things you can do is delegate and then not give autonomy in how the work is delivered. This can be compounded by over-intrusive supervision. No one likes to feel that they have been entrusted with a job or part of a job, only to have you breathing down their necks at every opportunity. Remember that delegation entails trust, and that may involve letting people make mistakes and you then having to step in to help remedy what went wrong. Treat each error as an opportunity for learning rather than blame. This is not just management-speak: people learn from doing, and will learn the more willingly if they are not given criticism every time they get a small or trivial part wrong. You should be aware that many employees in the police service believe that large parts of the service are still rooted in a 'blame culture', which means that people learn negatively rather than positively. It is rather like saying 'this is what I **don't** want you to do' rather than saying 'this is what I want you to do'.

That is not to say that you should condone serious mistakes when you are a supervisor, or excuse people who make mistakes through inadvertence or ineptitude. Ensure that your initial explanation is clear and your instructions precise. Make it plain to the team or individual that you are trusting them to deliver on the task, because you think they are ready to take on the responsibility and you are confident that they will deliver. Watch what happens but only interfere if it really is going badly wrong.

The logical extension of **staff development** is that you will lose the staff. Accept this at the outset, and give yourself a timetable by which the development can be achieved, and then you will not be surprised when the individual outgrows what you can give him/her. Remember how it happened to you? Did your tutor constable or your trainer let you grow in the role of a police officer, encouraging and giving you opportunities? Or did your supervisor criticize your efforts and predict that you would never come to anything? The first is an empowering, positive developer of staff; the second is somebody who is unable to accept that people change and develop.

In 2004, a Home Office report suggested that the majority of police officers who left policing did so citing poor management as the reason. You can read a media report here: <http://news.bbc.co.uk/1/hi/uk/3691821.stm>.

TASK 10

You would obviously concentrate on supervising investigation and detection. A DS would have to have the competencies of the generic sergeant role, but would additionally:

- allocate investigative work to a detective team or individual;
- manage scene preservation;
- monitor and evaluate the quality of investigations;
- plan and manage searches;
- recruit covert human intelligence sources (CHIS, see Chapter 12);
- monitor and evaluate interview processes;
- plan, manage, and evaluate police operations.

TASK 11

We discuss this fully in the paragraphs that follow; it is likely that your response included at least some details about the inspector role and how it compares with the work of a sergeant, such as attending more strategic meetings and having more responsibility, including for budgets.

You will probably be taken by surprise by the comment about pay. On 1 September 2009, a sergeant on point 4 (the highest point) would be paid £40,020 per annum. An inspector on promotion was paid £45,624. (Both figures are for outside London). However, sergeants are paid additional sums at 'time plus a third' for overtime which can easily close the gap.

TASK 12

In practice, for SIOs it is really the major crimes such as homicide (including manslaughter) and series rape, though they might be involved in investigations into some 'serious and organized' crime. We discuss this more fully in the paragraphs that follow the task.

TASK 13

In 2000, Smith and Flanagan published a report which analysed the qualities of the SIO and identified three particularly important areas:

- investigative ability: this includes the skills associated with the assimilation and assessment of information coming in to an enquiry and the process by which lines of enquiry are generated and prioritized;
- knowledge levels: this relates to the different types of underpinning knowledge an SIO should possess;
- management skills: this refers to the different types of management skill an SIO should possess. They encompass a broad range of skill types that were further subdivided into people management, general management, and investigative management.

(Smith and Flanagan, 2000)

TASK 14

Your answer probably focused on what an SIO is for. Forces are judged as effective, efficient, and professional on the basis of how quickly and competently a murderer or rapist is caught and brought to justice. Nothing is as certain to undermine a force's reputation as a poorly executed investigation into a crime which scares the public.

How much does it cost to train an SIO? This is actually a more interesting question than it seems. We do not know very clearly how much it costs to train a student police officer. One estimate put the cost of training a pre-IPLDP student police officer at about £27,000 up to Independent Patrol (evidence submitted to the Morris Inquiry, 2004), less than half-way through training.

TASK 15

You would almost certainly point to the range of responsibilities and the autonomy of command as being the essential distinction between the two ranks, but there is often a blurring between the roles of a highly specialist DCI and a generic detective superintendent.

All this discussion concerning the demands of progressing through the ranks may have begun to depress you by now, so it is time for a digression into history. A little-known experiment in policing in the USA in the 1970s, which became known as 'team policing', involved the elimination of the existing rank distinctions between patrol and detectives altogether. It also involved all police officers working out of uniforms:

> The new, non-traditional uniform consisted of a forest green sport coat blazer worn over black slacks, a white shirt, and a black tie (Johnson, 2005).

The experiments were considered a failure and were abandoned after two to three years. However, team policing possibly laid the foundations for what is now almost the orthodox policing model in the USA, that is Community Policing

TASK 16

Of course there is no right or wrong answer to this question! Surprisingly, the precise current average length of service in the police is not known. In a reply to a Parliamentary question in the House of Commons in September 2005 Hazel Blears responded:

> Information on length of service on leaving is collected in groups of years. This means average length of service of a police officer on leaving is not available. (Blears, 2005).

Bibliography and References

ACPO (1999), *National SIO Development Programme Murder Investigation Manual* (London: Stationery Office Ltd).

——(2001), *ACPO Investigation of Volume Crime Manual* (London: Stationery Office Ltd).

——(2005), *Guidance on the Management, Recording and Investigation of Missing Persons* (London: Stationery Office Ltd).

——(2006), *Murder investigation manual* (3rd edn.) (Wyboston: National Centre for Policing Excellence).

——(2007a), *Good Practice Guide for Computer-based Electronic Evidence* [online] available at <http://www.acpo.police.uk/asp/policies/Data/ACPO Guidelines v18.pdf> (accessed 23 July 2009).

——(2007b), *Practice Advice on Critical Incident Management* [online] available at <http://www.acpo.police.uk/policies.asp> (accessed 23 July 2009).

ACPO Centrex (2005), *Practice Advice on Core Investigative Doctrine,* (Camborne: National Centre for Policing Excellence).

Aitken, C, Connolly, T, Gammerman, A, Zhang, G, and Oldfield, R (1995), *Predicting an Offender's Characteristics: An evaluation of statistical modelling. Police Research Group Special Interest Series* 4 (London: Home Office).

Alderson, J (1998), *Principled Policing: Protecting the public with integrity* (Winchester: Waterside Press).

Alegre, S and Leaf, M (2003), *European Arrest Warrant: A solution ahead of its time?* (London: Justice).

Anderson, DM and Killingray, D (eds) (1991), *Policing the Empire* (Manchester: Manchester University Press).

Audit Commission (1993), *Helping with Enquiries: Tackling Crime Effectively* (London: Audit Commission).

Auld, Lord Justice (2001), *A Review of the Criminal Courts of England and Wales* (London: Stationery Office Ltd).

Banton, M (1964), *The Policeman in the Community* (London: Tavistock).

Bayley, DH (1994), *Police for the Future* (Oxford: Oxford University Press).

BBC (2002), *Doctors and Nurses 'Most Respected'* available at: <http://news.bbc.co.uk/1/hi/uk/2014128.stm> (accessed July 23 2009).

Beattie, JM (2001), *Policing and Punishment in London, 1660–1750: Urban crime and the limits of terror* (Oxford: Oxford University Press).

Benner, P (1984), *From Novice to Expert* (Menlo Park, CA: Addison-Wesley).

Berne, E (1968), *Games People Play: The psychology of human relationships* (Harmondsworth, Middlesex: Penguin Books Ltd).

Bichard, Sir M (2004), *Return to an Address of the Honourable the House of Commons dated 22nd June 2004 for the Bichard Inquiry* (Report HC 653, London: The Stationery Office).

Billingsley, R, Nemitz, T, and Bean, P (2001), *Informers: Policing, policy, practice* (Cullompton: Willan).

Blackburn, R (1995), *The Psychology of Criminal Conduct: Theory, research and practice* (Chichester: Wiley & Sons).

Blears, H (2005), *House of Commons Hansard Written Answers for 12 September 2005* (pt 93) available at <http://www.parliament.the-stationery-office.co.uk/pa/cm200506/cmhansrd/cm050912/text/50912w93.htm> (accessed July 23 2009).

Bloom, BS (1964), *Taxonomy of Educational Objectives: Handbook 1/Cognitive domain* (London: Longman).

BNP (2005), *Rebuilding British Democracy* (British National Party General Election Manifesto, 2005) [online] available at: <news.bbc.co.uk/1/shared/bsp/hi/pdfs/BNP_uk_manifesto.pdf> (accessed on July 23 2009).

Bowers, KJ, Hirschfield, A, and Johnson, S (1998), 'Victimisation revisited: A case study of non-residential repeat burglary in Merseyside', *British Journal of Criminology* 38 (3), 429–52.

——Johnson, SD and Pease, K (2004), 'Prospective hot-spotting: The future of crime mapping?', *British Journal of Criminology* 44(5), 641–58.

Bowling, B and Foster, J (2002), 'Policing and the police', in M Maguire *et al* (eds), *Oxford Handbook of Criminology* (3rd edn., Oxford: Oxford University Press).

British Crime Survey 2006/07 Home Office Statistical Bulletin 11/07 [online] available at <http://www.crimereduction.homeoffice.gov.uk/statistics/statistics066.htm> (accessed 23 July 2009).

Brogden, M and Shearing, C (1993), *Policing for a New South Africa* (London: Routledge).

Bryant, R (2008), *Investigating Digital Crime* (Chichester: John Wiley & Sons).

Button, M (2002), *Private Policing* (Cullompton: Willan).

Caless, B, (2007), '"Numties in yellow jackets": The nature of hostility towards the police community support officer in neighbourhood policing teams', *Oxford Journal of Policing* Vol 1, 187–195.

‍

Caless, B, (2008a), 'Corruption in the police: The reality of the "dark side"', *The Police Journal* 80(1), 3–84.

Caless, B, (2008b), 'Persistent dark matter: Police corruption in the last ten years', in P Villiers (ed.), *Ethics in Policing*, Vol 1, No 2.

Cambridgeshire Constabulary (2005), *Local Performance Plan 2003—2004* [online] available at <http://www.cambs-pa.gov.uk/policies.cfm> (accessed 20 May 2008).

Cambridgeshire Constabulary (2007), *Cambridgeshire Policing Plan 2006–2007* [online] available at <http://www.cambs-pa.gov.uk/policies.cfm> (accessed 20 May 2008).

Canter, D and Alison, L (2000), *Precursors to Investigative Psychology: Criminal detection and the psychology of crime* (Aldershot: Ashgate).

Caulfield, P (2007), *Home Office accused of not investigating credit card fraud* [online] available at <http://www.24dash.com/billpayments/22639.htm> (accessed 23 July 2009).

Center for Problem-Oriented Policing (2009), *Community Safety, Crime & Drugs Audit, 2004* [online] available at <http://www.popcenter.org/problems/residential_car_theft/PDFs/BrightonHove.pdf> (accessed 23 July 2009).

Centrex (2005), Level 1 Investigator Professional Development Portfolio.

Chan, JBL (2003), *Fair Cop: Learning the art of policing* (Toronto: University of Toronto Press).

Chenery, S, Henshaw C, and Pease, K (1999), *Illegal Parking in Disabled Bays: A means of offender targeting*, Police and Reducing Crime Briefing Note 1/99 (Home Office, London).

City & Guilds (2005), *For the Attention of the Police/Community Justice NVQ Co-ordinator* (NVQs in Policing).

Clarke, C and Milne, R (2001), *A National Evaluation of the PEACE Investigative Interviewing Course* (Home Office Report PRAS/149).

Clarke, RV (1999), *Hot Products: Understanding, anticipating and reducing demand for stolen goods*, Police Research Series Paper 112 (London: Home Office).

Coleman, R, (2004) *Reclaiming the Streets: Surveillance, social control and the city* (Cullompton: Willan).

Conan-Doyle, Sir A (1887), *A Study in Scarlet*.

——(1894), *The Adventure of Silver Blaze* available at <http://etext.virginia.edu/toc/modeng/public/DoyBlaz.html> (accessed 23 July 2009).

Cope, N. (2004), 'Intelligence-Led Policing or Policing-Led Intelligence?' *British Journal of Criminology*, 44(2), 188–203.

Cope, N, Fielding, N, and Innes, M (2005), 'The Appliance of Science? The Theory and Practice of Crime Intelligence Analysis' *British Journal of Criminology*, 45(1), 39–55.

Copi, IM (1982), *Introduction to Logic* (London: Macmillan).

Cottrell, S (2003), *The Study Skills Handbook* (Basingstoke: Palgrave Macmillan).

Cozens, C and Tryhorn, C (2005), 'Police data sold to newspapers', *The Guardian*, 16 April 2005.

CPS (2004), *Prosecution Team Manual of Guidance 2004 Edition* [online] available at <http://police.homeoffice.gov.uk/operational-policing/prosecution-manual-guidance> (accessed 23 July 2009).

——(2006a), *Disclosure Manual* [online] available at <http://www.cps.gov.uk/legal/d_to_g/disclosure_manual/> (accessed 23 July 2009).

——(2006b), *Offences Against the Person, Incorporating Charging Standard* [online] available at <http://www.cps.gov.uk/legal/l_to_o/offences_against_the_person/> (accessed 23 July 2009).

——(2008), *CPS issues public policy on sexual transmission of infection* [online] available at <http://www.cps.gov.uk/news/pressreleases/119_08/index.html> (accessed 23 July 2009).

Crawford, A, (2003), 'The pattern of policing in the UK: Policing beyond the police' in T Newburn (ed.), *Handbook of Policing*.

Crawshaw, R, Devlin, B, and Williamson, T (1998), *Human Rights and Policing: Standards for good behaviour and a strategy for change* (The Hague: Kluwer Law International).

Critchley, TA (1978), *A History of Police in England and Wales* (London: Constable).

Daly, M (2003), 'My life as a secret policeman' available at <http://news.bbc.co.uk/1/hi/magazine/3210614.stm> (accessed 23 July 2009).

Davis, M (1996), 'Police, discretion, and the professions', in J Kleinig, *Handled with Discretion: Ethical Issues in Police Decision Making* (Lanham, MD: Rowman & Littlefield Publishers).

Delattre, EJ (2002), *Character and Cops: Ethics in policing* (4th edn., Washington, DC: AEI Press).

Department of Transport (2007), *Road Casualties in Great Britain* [online] available at < http://www.dft.gov.uk/pgr/statistics/datatablespublications/accidents/casualtiesmr/rcgbmainresults2008 > (accessed 23 July 2009).

——(2008), *Traffic Speeds and Congestion* [online] available at <http://www.dft.gov.uk/pgr/statistics/datatablespublications/roadstraffic/speedscongestion/> (accessed 23 July 2009).

Dobash, RE, Dobash, RP, Cavanagh, K, and Lewis, R (2000), *Changing Violent Men* (London: Sage).

Duncan, G (2005), 'All around the world, the future is grey', *The Times*, 24 October 2005, 37.

Dunnighan, C and Norris, C (1996), 'A risky business: Exchange, bargaining and risk in the recruitment and running of informers by English police officers', *Journal of Police Studies*, 19(2), 1–25.

——(1999), 'The detective, the snout, and the Audit Commission: The real costs in using informants', *The Howard Journal* 38(1), 67–86.

Ede, R and Shepherd, E (2000), *Active Defence: Lawyer's guide to police and defence investigation and prosecution and defence disclosure in criminal cases* (London: Law Society Publishing).

Edexcel (2005), *NVQs in Policing Guidance for Centres*.

Edwards, S (1989), *Policing Domestic Violence* (London: Sage).

Ekblom, P (2001), 'The conjunction of criminal opportunity: A framework for crime reduction toolkits', Home Office Policing and Reducing Crime Unit, Research Development and Statistics Directorate available at <http://www.crimereduction.gov.uk/learningzone/cco.htm> (accessed 23 July 2009).

Elliott, J, Kusher, S, Alexandrou, A, Dwyfor Davies, J, Wilkinson, S, and Zamorski, B (2003), *Review of the Learning Requirement for Police Probationer Training in England & Wales* (University of East Anglia and University of the West of England).

Emsley, C (2003), 'Policing since 1945', in T Newburn (ed.), *Handbook of Policing*.

——(1996), *The English Police: A political and social history* (2nd edn., London: Longman).

——(2003), 'The birth and development of the police', in T Newburn (ed.), *Handbook of Policing*.

Everson, S and Pease, K (2001), 'Crime Against the Same Person and Place: Detection Opportunity and Offender Targeting', in G Farrell and K Pease, (eds), *Crime Prevention Studies* Vol 12 (Monsey, NY: CRC Press).

Facione, PA (1998), *Critical Thinking: What it is and why it counts* (Santa Clara University) available at <http://www.calpress.com/pdf_files/what&why.pdf> (Accessed 20 May 2008).

Farrall, S and Gadd, D (2004) 'Evaluating crime fears: A research note on a pilot study to improve the measurement of the 'Fear of Crime' as a performance indicator', *Evaluation*, 10(4), 493–502.

Feldberg, M (1985), 'Gratuities, corruption and the democratic ethos of policing: The case of the free cup of coffee', in FA Elliston and M Feldberg (eds), *Moral Issues in Police Work* (New Jersey: Rowman & Allanheld Publishers) 267–76.

Felson, M (2002), *Crime and Everyday Life* (London: Sage).

Flanagan, Sir R (2004), *A Report on the Investigation by Cambridgeshire Constabulary into the Murders of Jessica Chapman and Holly Wells at Soham on 4 August 2002* (HMIC).

Francis, B, Barry, J, Bowater, R, Miller, N, Soothill, K, and Ackerley, E (2004), 'Using homicide data to assist murder investigation', Home Office Online Report 26/04 (London: Home Office).

Garb, M, Erzen, B, and Jelusic, L (2004), 'Police in peace operations: The case of missions in south-east Europe and the case of Slovenian peace-keepers', in G Mesko *et al* (eds), *Dilemmas in Contemporary Criminal Justice*.

Gelles, R and Cornell, C (1990), *Intimate Violence in Families* (London: Sage).

GMC (2008), *Licensing and revalidation* [online] available at <http://www.gmc-uk.org/ doctors/licensing/index.asp > (accessed 23 July 2009).

Grace, S (1995), *Policing Domestic Violence in the 1990s*, Home Office Research Study 139 (London: HMSO).

Haigh, J (2006), 'Forensic science and the legal process' available at <http://www.maths.sussex.ac.uk/ Staff/JH/Fslp/FSLPnotes.pdf> (accessed 23 July 2009).

Hanmer J, Griffiths S, and Jerwood, D (1999), *Arresting Evidence: Domestic violence and repeat victimisation*, Police Research Series Paper 104 (London: HMSO).

Hanvey, P (1995), *Identifying, Recruiting and Handling Informants*, Home Office Police Research Group Special Interest Series Paper 5 (London: Home Office).

Harfield, C and Harfield, K (2005) *Covert Investigation* (Oxford: Blackstone/OUP).

Harfield, C and Harfield, K (2008) *Intelligence: Investigation, Community, and Partnership* (Oxford: Blackstone/OUP).

Hay, D and Snyder, F (eds) (1989), *Policing and Prosecution in Britain, 1750–1850* (Oxford: Oxford University Press).

Health and Safety Executive (2006), Publications available at <http://www.hse.gov.uk/pubns/> (accessed 23 July 2009).

Heaton, R (2000), 'The prospects for intelligence-led policing: Some historical and quantitative considerations', *Policing & Society* 9, 337–55.

Hebenton, B and Thomas, T (1995), *Policing Europe: Co-operation, conflict and control* (London: Macmillan).

Highway Code (2004) available at < http://www.direct.gov.uk/en/TravelAndTransport/Highwaycode/DG_070190> (accessed 20 July 2009).

HMIC (1999), *Police Integrity, England, Wales and Northern Ireland: Securing and maintaining public confidence* (London: HMSO).

——(2000), *Calling Time on Crime: A Thematic Inspection on Crime and Disorder conducted by Her Majesty's Inspectorate of Constabulary,* (London: HMSO).

——(2002), *Training Matters* (London: HMSO).

——(2005a), *Inspection of Kingston upon Hull BCU Humberside Police July 2005,* available at <http://inspectorates.homeoffice.gov.uk/hmic/inspections/bcu/humberside/bcu05-hull-humberside.pdf?view=Binary> (accessed 23 July 2009).

——(2005b), *Police National Computer Data Quality and Timeliness Second Report on the Inspection by HM Inspectorate of Constabulary* (London: HMSO).

——(2006), *PNC Compliance Report: City of London (Aug 2005)* (London: HMSO).

Home Office (1989), *Criminal and Custodial Careers of those Born in 1953, 1958 and 1963* Home Office Statistical Bulletin 32/89 (London: Home Office).

——(1997), *Police Health and Safety, Volume 2: A guide for police managers,* Police Policy Directorate (London: Home Office).

——(2000a), *Domestic Violence: Break the chain. Multi-agency guidance for addressing domestic violence* (London: HMSO).

——(2000b), *Domestic Violence: Revised circular to the police,* Circular No 19/2000 (London: HMSO).

——(2001), *Policing a New Century: A Blueprint for Reform,* Cm5326 (London: Home Office).

——(2003), *Safety and Justice: Domestic violence consultation paper* (London: HMSO).

——(2004a), *Building Communities, Beating Crime: A better police service for the 21st century* (London: HMSO).

——(2004b), *Campaign to Warn of Net Paedophiles* (London: HMSO).

——(2004c), *Initial Police Learning and Development Programme (IPLDP) Version 1* (London: Home Office).

——(2004d), *Initial Police Learning and Development Programme Force Learning and Assessment Manual* (London: Home Office).

——(2004e), *Violent Crime Unit, Domestic Violence Strategies: A guide for partnerships* (London: HMSO).

——(2005a), *Initial Police Learning and Development Programme (IPLDP),* Letter to Chief Police Officers 7 November 2005 (London: Home Office).

——(2005b), *IPLDP Central Authority, Practitioner Guidance, Community Engagement & Professional Development Units* (London: Home Office).

——(2005c), *IPLDP Guidance for Chief Officers and Police Authorities Version 2* (London: Home Office).

——(2005d), *PIP Guidance for Completion of the Professional Development Portfolio Investigators and Assessors* (London: Home Office).

——(2005e), *Rationale for Changing the Overall Module Structure of the IPLDP,* IPLDP Central Authority Executive Services (London: Home Office).

——(2005f), *The National Community Safety Plan 2006–2009,* Annex A: 'The National Policing Plan' (London: HMSO) 28–9, para 12.

——(2006), 'Making a victim personal statement' available at <http://www.cjsonline.gov.uk/downloads/application/pdf/victimstate.pdf> (accessed 23 July 2009).

——(2008a), *Home Office Counting Rules For Recorded Crime* [online] available at <http://www.homeoffice.gov.uk/rds/pdfs06/countrecstan06.pdf> (accessed 23 July 2009).

——(2008b), *Home Secretary's Strategic Policing Priorities 2009–10* available at <http://police.homeoffice.gov.uk/publications/national-policing-plan/strategic-policing-priorities> (accessed 23 July 2009).

——(2008c), *National Community Safety Plan 2008–2011* (London: HMSO).

——(2008d), *The Policing Pledge* [online] available at <http://www.homeoffice.gov.uk/documents/policing-pledge?view=Binary> (accessed 23 July 2009).

——(2009), *Crime in England and Wales 2007/08 A summary of the main findings* [online] available at <http://www.homeoffice.gov.uk/rds/crimeew0708.html> (accessed 23 July 2009).

Hoyle, C (1998), *Negotiating Domestic Violence* (Oxford: Clarendon Studies in Criminology).

Ingleton, R (2002), *Policing Kent 1800–2000* (Chichester: Phillimore & Co Ltd).

Innes, M (2004) 'Crime as a signal, crime as a memory', *Journal for Crime, Conflict and the Media* 1(2), 15–22.

——(2005) 'What's your problem? Signal crimes and citizen-focused problem solving', *Criminology & Public Policy* 4(2), 187–200.

Jenkins, R (2005), 'How Mr Loophole overtakes the law', *The Times,* 10 December, 41.

Jewkes, Y (2003), 'Policing cybercrime' in T Newburn (ed.), *Handbook of Policing.*

——(2003) (ed.), *Dot Cons: Crime, deviance and identity on the internet* (Cullompton: Willan).

John, T and Maguire, M (2003), 'Rolling out the National Intelligence Model: Key challenges', in K Bullock and N Tilley (eds), *Crime Reduction and Problem-Oriented Policing* (Cullompton: Willan).

John, T and Maguire, M (2004), *The National Intelligence Model: Early Implementation Experience in Three Police Force Areas* (Cardiff: Cardiff University).

Johnson, R (2005), 'The psychological influence of the police uniform' available at <http://www.policeone.com/police-products/apparel/uniforms/articles/99417/> accessed 23 July 2009).

Johnston, D and Hutton, G (2005), *Blackstone's Police Manual, Volume 2: Evidence and Procedure* (Oxford: Oxford University Press).

Jones, T and Newburn, T (1998), *Private Security and Public Policing* (Oxford: Clarendon Press).

Junger, M, West, R, and Timman, R (2001), 'Crime and risk behaviour in traffic', *Journal of Research in Crime & Delinquency* 38(4), 439–59.

Kelly, L (1999), *Domestic Violence Matters: An evaluation of a development project,* Home Office Research Study 193 (London: HMSO).

Kent, JR (1986), *The English Village Constable 1580–1642: A social and administrative study* (Oxford: Clarendon Press).

Kershaw, C, Nicholas, S, and Walker, A (eds) (2008), *Crime in England and Wales 2007/08 Findings from the British Crime Survey and police recorded crime* Home Office Statistical Bulletin 07/08 (London: Home Office).

Kleinig, J (ed.) (1996), *Handled with Discretion* (Lanham, MD: Rowman & Littlefield).

Klitgaard, R (1988), *Controlling Corruption* (Berkeley, CA: University of California Press).

Knutsson, J (2004), 'Police use of firearms a constant? The Swedish and Norwegian experience', in G Mesko *et al* (eds), *Dilemmas in Contemporary Criminal Justice*.

Kolb, D (1984), *Experiential Learning: Experience as the source of learning and development* (New Jersey: Prentice Hall).

Lee, M and South, N (2003), 'Drugs policing', in T Newburn (ed.), *Handbook of Policing*.

Leishman, F and Mason, P (2003), *Policing and the Media: Facts, fictions and factions* (Cullompton: Willan).

Levi, M (1997), 'Violent crime', in M Maguire, R Morgan, and R Reiner (eds), *The Oxford Handbook of Criminology* (2nd edn., Oxford: Oxford University Press).

Loader, I and Mulcahy, A (2003), *Policing and the Condition of England: Memory, Politics and Culture* (Oxford: Oxford University Press).

Luft, J (1970), *Group Processes: An introduction to group dynamics* (Palo Alto, CA: National Press Books).

Macpherson, Sir W (1999), *The Stephen Lawrence Inquiry: Report of an inquiry by Sir William Macpherson of Cluny*, Cm 4262 (London: HMSO).

Maguire, M and John, T (2006), 'Intelligence-Led Policing, Managerialism and Community Engagement: Competing Priorities and the Role of the National Intelligence Model in the UK', *Policing and Society*, 1(1), 67–85.

Matassa, M and Newburn, T (2003), 'Policing and terrorism', in T Newburn (ed.), *Handbook of Policing*.

Mawby, RI (1999), 'Police services for crime victims', in RI Mawby (ed.), *Policing Across the World: Issues for the twenty-first century* (London: UCL Press).

——(2003), 'Models of policing', in T Newburn (ed.), *Handbook of Policing*.

McNee, D (1983), *McNee's Law* (London: Collins).

Mesko, G, Pagon, M, and Dobovšek, B (2004) (eds), *Dilemmas in Contemporary Criminal Justice, Policing in Central and Eastern Europe* (Slovenia: The University of Maribor Press).

Metropolitan Police (2006), *The History of the Metropolitan Police* available at <http://www.met.police.uk/history/> (accessed 23 July 2009).

Miles, A (2005), 'One rule for them, 1,000 new ones for us', available at <http://www.timesonline.co.uk/tol/news/politics/article586778.ece> (accessed 23 July 2009).

Miller, J (2003), *Police Corruption in England and Wales: An assessment of current evidence*, Home Office Online Report 11/03 available at <www.homeoffice.gov.uk/rds/pdfs2/rdsolr1103.pdf> (accessed 23 July 2009).

Milne, R and Bull, R (1999), *Investigative Interviewing: Psychology and practice* (Chichester and New York: John Wiley & Sons).

Morgan, R and Newburn, T (1997), *The Future of Policing* (Oxford: Clarendon Press/Oxford University Press).

Morris, W, Burden, A, and Weekes, A (2004), *The Case for Change: People in the Metropolitan Police Service* (Morris Inquiry) available at <http://www.morrisinquiry.gov.uk/report/> (accessed 23 July 2009).

Morton, J (1993), *Bent Coppers: A survey of police corruption* (London: Little, Brown and Co).

Moses, D (1997), *The Watford Rail Incident Inter-Agency De-briefing Report* available at <www.herts.police.uk/FOI/Significant_Information/r_Watford rail_ crash-REDACTED.pdf> (accessed 23 July 2009).

Munro, T (2004), 'OSPRE needs to adapt or die', *Police Federation Magazine*, March, 11–13.

Murphy, R (2005), *Investigative Interviewing for Patrol Officers Level 1* (unpublished).

National Police Training (1995), *Police Probationer Training Foundation Course Notes* (Police Central Planning & Training Unit, a division of National Police Training).

Newburn, T (1999), *Understanding and Preventing Police Corruption: Lessons from the literature*, Police Research Series Paper 110 (Home Office: London).

——(2003) (ed.), *Handbook of Policing* (Cullompton: Willan).

——(2005), 'A Force for Change', *Police Federation Magazine*, August, 12–13.

——and Neyroud, P (2008) *Dictionary of Policing* (Cullompton: Willan).

Neyroud, P and Beckley, A (2001), *Policing, Ethics and Human Rights* (Cullompton: Willan).

Neyroud, PW (2003), 'Policing and ethics', in T Newburn (ed.), *Handbook of Policing*.

Nicholas, S, Povey, D, Walker, A, and Kershaw, C (2005), *Crime in England and Wales 2004/2005* (Home Office Statistical Bulletin 11/05).

Nolan, Lord (1995), *First Report of the Committee on Standards in Public Life*, Cm 2850–I (London: HM Stationery Office).

Norfolk Constabulary (2006) *Training and Development*, available at <http://www.norfolk.police.uk/-article.cfm?catID=818&artID=7419&> (accessed 23 July 2009).

Nozick, R (1974), *Anarchy, State and Utopia* (Oxford: Blackwell (2003 print)).

Office of Public Services Reform (2004), available at <archive.cabinetoffice.gov.uk/opsr/documents/pdf/sem_choice_summ.pdf> (accessed 23 July 2009).

NPIA (2008a), Guide to the National Investigators' Examination Version 14—2009 exams [online] available at <http://www.npia.police.uk/en/docs/Guide_to_the_National_Investigators_Examination_2009_.pdf> (accessed 23 July 2009).

——(2008b), *The High Performance Development Scheme Manual of Guidance* (November 2008, NPIA).

——(2008c), National Police Promotion Framework, 60-second briefing (NPIA).

——(2008d), *Rules & syllabus qualifying for promotion to the ranks of sergeant and inspector 2009* [online] available at <http://www.npia.police.uk/en/docs/Rules_Syllabus_2009__Final_Version_2.pdf> (accessed 23 July 2009).

——(2008e), *SIO Register* [online] available at <http://www.npia.police.uk/en/10175.htm> (accessed 23 July 2009).

——(2008f), *Subject Areas Assessed in the Sergeants' 2008 OSPRE® Part I* [online] available at <http://www.npia.police.uk/en/docs/Subject_Areas Assessed_in_the_Sergeant_2008_Examination.pdf> (accessed 23 March 2009).

——(2008g), *Subject Area Breakdown—OSPRE® Part I Inspectors' Examination 2008 OSPRE® Part I* [online] available at <http://www.npia.police.uk/en/11795.htm > (accessed 23 July 2009).

——(2009a), Guidance to Forces: IPLDP Learning Development Review (LDR) (February 2009, NPIA).

——(2009b), *High Potential Development Scheme* [online] available at <http://www.npia.police.uk/en/8563.htm <http://www.npia.police.uk/en/8563.htm> (accessed 23 July 2009).

——(2009c), *HPDS Programme Details* [online] available at <http://www.npia.police.uk/en/10634.htm> (accessed 23 July 2009).

——(2009d), Senior Police National Assessment Centre [online] available at <http://www.npia.police.uk/en/7012.htm> (accessed 23 July 2009).

Osterburg, J and Ward, R (2004), *Criminal Investigation*, (4th edn., Cincinnati: Anderson).

Patten Commission (1999), *A New Beginning: Policing in Northern Ireland,* Report of the Independent Commission on Policing for Northern Ireland.

PCeU (2009), *Computer Crime Team* [online] available at <http://www.met.police.uk/pceu/computer_crime_team.html> (accessed 23 July 2009).

Pease, K (1997), 'Crime prevention', in M Maguire, R Morgan, and R Reiner (eds), *The Oxford Handbook of Criminology* (2nd edn., Oxford: Oxford University Press).

——(2002), 'Crime reduction', in M Maguire, R Morgan, and R Reiner (eds), *The Oxford Handbook of Criminology* (3rd edn., Oxford: Oxford University Press), 947–79.

Peters, R (1973), *Authority, Responsibility and Education* (London: Allen and Unwin).

Phillips, C (2002), 'From voluntary to statutory status: Reflecting on the experience of three partnerships established under the Crime and Disorder Act 1998', in G Hughes, E McGlaughlin, and J Muncie (eds), *Crime Prevention and Community Safety: New directions* (London: Sage).

Plotnikoff, J and Woolfson, R (1998), *Policing Domestic Violence: Effective organisational structures,* Police Research Series Paper 100 (London: HMSO).

Popper, K (1990), *Conjectures and Refutations: The growth of scientific knowledge* (London: Routledge).

Ratcliffe, J (ed.) (2004), *Strategic Thinking in Criminal Intelligence* (Sydney: Federation Press).

Rawlings, PJ (2002), *Policing: A short history* (Cullompton: Willan).

Reid, J (2007) Common values for the police service of England and Wales: A message from the Home Secretary. Letter sent to all police services on March 6th 2007 (London: Home Office). Available at <http://police.homeoffice.gov.uk/publications/police-reform/policing-values-letter> (accessed 23 July 2009).

Reiner, R (1991), *Chief Constables* (Oxford: Oxford University Press).

——(1997), 'Policing and the police', in M Maguire, R Morgan, and R Reiner (eds) (2002), *The Oxford Handbook of Criminology* (2nd edn., Oxford: Oxford University Press).

——(2000), *The Politics of the Police* (3rd edn., Oxford: Oxford University Press).

Reynolds, EA (1998), *Before the Bobbies: The night watch and police reform in Metropolitan London, 1720–1830* (London: Macmillan).

Robinson, D and Campbell, R (2006), *Contributory Factors to Road Accidents,* Transport Statistics: Road Safety (Department for Transport).

Rogers, A (1996), *Teaching Adults* (2nd edn, Buckingham: Open University Press).

Rose, G (2000), 'The criminal histories of serious traffic offenders', HORS 206 (London: Home Office).

Rothschild, J (1993), *Return to Diversity: A political history of east Central Europe since World War II* (Oxford: Oxford University Press).

Rowe, M (2002), 'Policing diversity: Themes and concerns from the recent British experience', in *Police Quarterly*, 5(4), 424–46.

Safer London Committee (2005), *Transcript of Item 5—Scrutiny on Planned Civil Defence and Recovery in Response to a Catastrophic Event in London,* available at <http://www.london.gov.uk/assembly/past_ctees/safe_lon/2005/mar0905/minutes/safelonmar09trans.pdf> (accessed 23 July 2009).

Scarman, Lord (1981), *Report into the Brixton Disorders,* Cmnd, 8427 (London: HMSO).

Shearing, C and Stenning, P (1981), 'Modern private security: Its growth and implications', in M Tonry and N Morris (eds), *Crime and Justice: An annual review of research Vol 3* (Chicago: University of Chicago Press).

Shepherd, E (2001), *SE3R A Resource Book* (East Hendred: Forensic Solutions Ltd).

Sherman, LW (1985), 'Becoming bent: Moral careers of corrupt policemen', in FA Elliston and M Feldberg (eds), *Moral Issues in Police Work* (Totowa, NJ: Rowan and Allanheld).

Shorter Oxford English Dictionary (2002) (5th edn., Oxford: Oxford University Press).

Simmons, AJ (2001), *Justification and Legitimacy: Essays on rights and obligations* (Cambridge: Cambridge University Press).

Skills for Justice (2003), *Integrated Competency Framework*.

——(2004), *Skills Foresight 2004: Identifying the current and future skills needs of the police sector*.

——(2005), *Policing as a Profession: Managing the professional workforce*.

——(2006), *National Occupational Standards,* available at <http://www.skillsforjustice.net/template01.asp?pageid=37> (accessed 23 July 2009).

——(2007a), *Police Assessment Support Project*, End of Project Report May 2007.

——(2007b), *Unit 2C1*, available at <http://www.skillsforjustice.com/websitefiles/NOS_POLICE06_2C1.doc> (accessed 23 July 2009).

——(2007c), *Unit AA1*, available at <http://www.skillsforjustice.com/websitefiles/NOS_POLICE06_AA1.doc> (accessed 23 July 2009) .

——(2007d), *Unit AB1*, available at <http://www.skillsforjustice.com/websitefiles/NOS_POLICE06_AB1.doc> (accessed 23 July 2009).

——(2008), *Unit CD 1*, available at <www.ukstandards.org.uk/File_Download.aspx?FileId=40715&SuiteNosID=21573&FormMode=DownloadFile> (accessed 23 July 2009).

Smith, MJ and Tilley, N (2005), *Crime Science: New approaches to preventing and detecting crime* (Cullompton: Willan Press).

Smith, N and Flanagan, C (2000), *The Effective Detective: Identifying the skills of an effective SIO*, Police Research Series Paper 12 (Home Office).

South Yorkshire Police (2007), *Statement Of Agreed Policy 7/2007 Title: Critical incident management* [online] available at <http://www.southyorks.police.uk/foi/information_classes/our_policies/viewer.php?id=234> (Accessed 30 May 2008).

Stockdale, J and Gresham, P (1995), *The Presentation of Police Evidence to Court*, Police Research Series Paper 15 (Home Office).

Sussex Police (2006), 'Freedom of Information Act Previous Requests', available at <http://www.sussex.police.uk/foi/request_faq_lists.asp?id=Professional%20Standards> (accessed 23 July 2009).

Svensson, R (2002), 'Strategic offences in the criminal career context', *British Journal of Criminology* 42, 359–411.

Taylor, D (1999), 'Cannabis cautioning notice pilot programme training module—Bunbury and Mirrabooka', 5–6 (Alcohol and Drug Coordination Unit).

Taylor, M (1986), 'Learning for self-direction in the classroom: The pattern of a transition process', *Studies in Higher Education* 11(1), 55–72.

Thames Valley Police (2005), *Join Us: Training to be a police officer,* available at < http://www.thamesvalley.police.uk/joinus.htm> (accessed 23 July 2009).

Tilley, N and Laycock, G (2002), *Working Out What to Do: Evidence-based crime reduction*, Crime Reduction Research Series Paper 11 (Home Office: London).

Townsend, M (2006), 'Row over second jobs for police deepens', *The Observer,* 5 February.

Vrij, A (2000), *Detecting Lies and Deceit: The psychology of lying and implications for professional practice* (Chichester: John Wiley and Sons).

Waddington, PAJ (1999), 'Domestic violence and the social divide', *Police Review*, 26 March.

——(1999a), *Policing Citizens* (London: UCL Press).

——, Stenson, K, and David, D (2004), 'In proportion: Race, and police stop and search', *British Journal of Criminology* 44, 889–914.

Wadham, J (2004), 'Conference on data protection and information sharing', 15 July 2004 (London).

Walker, A, Kershaw, C, and Nicholas, S (2006), *Crime in England and Wales 2005/06* Home Office Statistical Bulletin.

Wall, D (ed.) (2001), *Crime and the Internet* (London: Routledge).

West Yorkshire Police, (2009), IPLDP Programme [online] available at <http://www.bishopgarth.com/programme.html> (accessed 23 July 2009).

Wilson, JQ (1996), 'On deterrence', in J Muncie, E McLaughlin, and M Langan (eds), *Criminological Perspectives: A reader* (London: Sage).

Wolfenden Report (1957), *Report of the Committee on Homosexual Offences and Prostitution,* Cmnd 247 (London: HMSO).

Woolcock, N (2006), 'Forces fail the equality test as women and blacks quit', *The Times*, 16 January.

Wright, A (2002), *Policing: An introduction to concepts and practice* (Cullompton: Willan).

Young, T (2007), *High-tech crime units lack central support,* [online] available at <http://www.computing.co.uk/computing/analysis/2173353/tech-crime-units-lack-central> (accessed on 23 July 2009).

Zedner, L (2002), 'Victims', in M Maguire, R Morgan, and R Reiner (eds), *The Oxford Handbook of Criminology* (3rd edn., Oxford: Oxford University Press).

Index

Index